Important disclaimer

This publication is sold on the understanding that the information provided within it is for guidance only, and that the publisher is not in business to provide legal or accounting advice or other professional services. Readers entering into transactions on the basis of, or otherwise relying on, such information should seek the services of a competent professional adviser.

Whilst every care has been taken to ensure the accuracy of the contents, the editors and the publishers cannot accept responsibility for any loss occasioned to any person acting or refraining to act as a result of any statement in it.

Indicator FL Memo

ISBN: 978-1-910784-00-6
TIPS & ADVICE VAT - ISBN: 978-1-910784-01-3

Indicator - FL Memo Ltd
Calgarth House
39-41 Bank Street
Ashford, Kent TN23 IDQ

Telephone: (020) 7803 4666
Fax: (020) 7803 4699
Email: flm@flmemo.co.uk
Website: www.flmemo.co.uk

Registered in England Company Registration No. 3599719. VAT GB 726 598 394

British Library Cataloguing in Publication Data.
A catalogue record for this book is available from the British Library.

VAT

2015-2016

Abbreviations

The following abbreviations are used in *VAT Memo*:

ABTA	Association of British Travel Agents
Aka	Also Known As
Art	Article
BHA	British Horseracing Authority
C & E	Customs and Excise
CH	HMRC Compliance Handbook
CEMA	Customs & Excise Management Act 1979
CJEU	Court of Justice of the European Union (formerly ECJ)
CLA	Country Landowners' Association
CRCA	Commissioners for Revenue and Customs Act 2005
CSE	Cost Sharing Exemption Manual
DEFRA	Department for Environment, Food and Rural Affairs
DMBM	HMRC Debt Management and Banking Manual
DVLA	Driver and Vehicle Licensing Authority
EC	European Community
ECJ	European Court of Justice (now CJEU)
EDR	Effective date of registration
EEA	European Economic Area
ESC	Extra-Statutory Concession
EU	European Union
FA	Finance Act
FRS	VAT Flat Rate Scheme Manual
FSMA	Financial Services and Markets Act 2000
GAAP	Generally Accepted Accounting Principles
HMRC	Her Majesty's Revenue and Customs
ICTA 1988	Income and Corporation Taxes Act 1988
IPT	Insurance Premium Tax
Ltd	Limited
NATO	North Atlantic Treaty Organisation
NBCG	Non-Statutory Business Clearance Guidance
NCA	National Crime Agency
NFU	National Farmers Union
NIC	National Insurance Contributions
Oao	On the Application Of
Para	Paragraph
PAYE	Pay As You Earn
PE	Partial Exemption Manual
PLR	Potential lost revenue
POCA	Proceeds of Crime Act 2002
PR	Press Release
RCPO	HMRC Criminal Prosecutions Office
Reg	Regulation
S	Section
Sch	Schedule
SDLT	Stamp Duty Land Tax
SE	Societas Europea
SFP	Single Farm Payment
SI	Statutory Instrument
SMMT	Society of Motor Manufacturers and Traders
SP	Statement of Practice
t/a	Trading As
TOGC	Transfer of a Going Concern
TOMS	Tour Operators' Margin Scheme
VAEC	VAT Assessments and Error Correction Manual
VAT	Value Added Tax
VATA 1994	Value Added Tax Act 1994
VATAAS	VAT Annual Accounting Scheme Manual
VATAFRS	VAT Agricultural Flat Rate Scheme Manual
VATCEP	VAT Civil Evasion Penalties Manual
VATDREG	VAT Deregistration Manual
VATFIN	VAT Finance Manual
VATGPB	VAT Government and Public Bodies Manual
VATREG	VAT Registration Manual
VATSC	VAT Supply and Consideration Manual
VATTOS	VAT Time of Supply Manual
VBANDG	VAT Betting and Gaming Manual
VBDR	VAT Bad Debt Relief Manual
VBNB	VAT Business/Non-Business Manual

VBOOKS	VAT Relief for Books Manual
VBURC	VAT Burial and Cremations Manual
VCAS	VAT Cash Accounting Scheme Manual
VCP	VAT Civil Penalties Manual
VCULTURE	VAT on Cultural Services Manual
VDIM	VAT Default Interest Manual
VDS	VAT: businesses supplying digital services to private consumers
VFOOD	VAT Manual: Food
VGROUPS	VAT Groups Manual
VIT	VAT Input Tax Manual
VPOA	VAT Payments on Account Manual
VPOST	VAT Postal Services Manual
VR	VAT Refunds Manual
VRS	VAT Retail Schemes Manual
VSME	VAT Small and Medium Enterprises Assurance Manual
VTAXPER	VAT Taxable Persons Manual
VTD	VAT Tribunal Decision
VTOGC	VAT Transfer of a Going Concern Manual
VTRANS	VAT Transport Manual

Contents

Part 8: Business situations

Part 9: Cross-border transactions

General information

Preface

VAT Memo is now in its ninth edition, giving you comprehensive coverage of this subject in the distinctive FL Memo style.

VAT is an important business issue for most traders and evolves almost on a daily basis via legislation, case law, HMRC Briefs and other official material.

VAT Memo 2015-2016 has been fully updated to reflect changes in law and practice up to and including the date of the 2015 Budget (18 March 2015) and, as with all our Memo publications, we will keep you **updated with the changes** as they happen throughout the year via our fortnightly **online updates**, posted on our website (www.flmemo.co.uk) and sent to subscribers via email.

VAT Memo 2015-2016 is unique in its style, with the full complexities of VAT explained in a language you can understand, reliably written by our experienced in-house tax professionals. The **precise text** is founded on statute, case law and official publications, with legislative and other references given throughout. The book is also packed with **worked examples** and practical tips to enhance the expert commentary.

VAT Memo 2015-2016 is **easy to navigate**, progressing from section plan through chapter outline to specific paragraph, which means you can easily find the answer to your particular query. Each section is devoted to a separate area of VAT, comprehensively indexed and fully cross-referenced to related topics. The appendix contains essential numerical and factual data, with a full presentation of the governing EC Directive and a useful table of the cases cited in the text.

Indicator - FL Memo Ltd
April 2015

PART 1

Scope of VAT

Scope of VAT
Summary

The numbers cross-refer to paragraphs.

CHAPTER 1

Basic principles

OUTLINE ¶¶

This section aims to give a **broad overview** of the main principles behind the operation of the VAT regime. It provides an outline of the rationale and workings of the VAT system, together with the compliance and reporting requirements. 10

Full details are contained in the respective relevant parts of *VAT Memo*.

A. What is VAT?

VAT is a tax on **the supply of goods and services and imports**, which is charged at each stage in a supply chain as goods or services flow from one trader to another. It is not a tax on profits. 15 EC Directive 2006/112

The VAT system is designed to allow every taxable person (¶30) in the supply chain to **recover** any VAT that is incurred by the taxable person on costs. In this way it is the end consumer who bears the tax burden.

VAT is charged on:
- the supply of goods and services in the UK;
- the acquisition of goods and receipt of services in the UK from another EU member state; and
- the importation of goods and services from outside the EU.

Scope

The current VAT system forms the basis of the measurement of the contributions by each member state towards the budget of the European Union (EU). It is designed to establish a **common basis of indirect taxation** and provide a means of harmonising the fiscal treatment of transactions within the EU. 20

The principles of the system are contained in EU Directive 2006/112 (¶9997). Many, although not all, of the provisions of this Directive are binding on member states. This means that national law in the EU member states must **implement** the provisions in the Directive, although member states often have a choice as to the methods they use to achieve that. However, if a member state fails to implement a provision, or does so incorrectly, those subject to the tax are entitled to rely on the **direct effect** of the provision.

All member states are obliged to introduce and operate VAT to the exclusion of any other turnover tax. In addition, many other non-EU countries have introduced VAT in some form or another. It is often called Goods and Services Tax (GST), if not VAT.

B. How does VAT operate?

25 VAT is a transaction-based tax; the charge is levied on any transaction that is:
- a supply of goods or services (¶240+);
- made within the UK (see below);
- by a **taxable person** (¶30);
- in the course or furtherance of a **business** (¶100+);
- in return for consideration (¶247+); and
- neither exempted from (¶350+), nor specifically outside the scope of (¶252+), VAT.

MEMO POINTS 1. In general the **UK** includes:
- England, Scotland, Wales, Northern Ireland and the Isle of Man, but not the Channel Islands or Gibraltar; and
- the territorial waters surrounding them.

In certain circumstances the Isle of Man is excluded from the definition.
2. Special rules apply to treat certain **cross-border transactions** as being made in the UK (¶9000+).

Taxable person

30 Broadly, under UK legislation a taxable person is an individual, partnership, company or other trading entity which is either **registered** for VAT, or is **required** to be so registered (¶2600+).

In the UK a person is required to be registered if it makes taxable supplies above certain value limits. Traders that make supplies below these limits can choose to be registered voluntarily.

MEMO POINTS 1. Any person who makes **wholly exempt supplies** is unable to register for VAT. There is an extensive list of exempt supplies, contained in statute, including health and welfare services, education, etc (¶350+).
2. **Person** takes its legal meaning and therefore includes individuals, partnerships, companies and charities.
3. The EU uses a wider definition of a taxable person, as a person who independently carries out any **economic activity**, irrespective of the purpose or results of that activity.

Place of supply

31 For a supply of goods or services to fall within the scope of UK VAT, it must be **made in the UK**. It is therefore necessary to determine the place of supply. The rules differ depending upon whether the supply is one of goods or services (¶275+). Particular rules apply for cross-border transactions to determine whether they are within the scope of VAT (¶9000+).

32 To be treated as supplied in the UK, goods must either be:
- located and supplied in the UK (¶278); or
- installed or assembled in the UK (¶9154+).

Goods that are installed or assembled by, or on behalf of, the supplier are supplied where the installation or assembly takes place. This may result in a UK trader being required to register overseas, or an overseas trader being required to register in the UK (¶9154+).

MEMO POINTS 1. If the contract between the parties is for two supplies (one for the supply of goods, the other for installation), they will usually be treated as a single composite supply (¶310+).
2. If the installation or assembly is subcontracted to a third party, the place of supply for the manufacturer remains the place of installation or assembly.

1. Mechanics

35 At a very simple level, each VAT-registered business in a supply chain will pay VAT on the supplies of goods and services it buys and charge VAT on the supplies it makes by selling goods and services. The VAT charged by a business on supplies made (sales) is known as

output tax (¶750+), whereas the VAT paid by a business on supplies received (purchases) is known as input tax (¶1800+).

Output tax

Output tax **must be charged** on all taxable supplies at the appropriate VAT rate, depending upon whether they are standard-rated (¶1095), reduced-rated (¶1110+) or zero-rated (¶1180+) supplies. The tax must be accounted for according to the time at which the supply is made (¶750+). 40

Where the value of a supply is quoted as exclusive of VAT, the VAT is simply the appropriate percentage of that value. However, where a supply is quoted at a VAT-inclusive value, the amount of VAT is calculated by applying a VAT fraction to the value, as follows:

Supply	VAT rate	VAT fraction
Standard-rated	20%	1/6
Reduced-rated	5%	1/21
Zero-rated	0%	0

EXAMPLE Ms A makes a standard-rated supply to Mr B valued at £3,000.
If this was the VAT-exclusive amount, the VAT due is £600. (20% x £3,000)
If £3,000 was the VAT-inclusive amount, the VAT due is £500. (1/6 x £3,000)

MEMO POINTS Special methods of computing output tax are available for:
- retailers (¶6300+); and
- sales of second-hand goods (¶6620+).

Input tax

Input tax is incurred on all taxable purchases made by a trader for the purposes of its business. This tax is **recovered** by offsetting it against any output tax charged by the trader. The net figure after this offset is either paid to or repaid by HMRC, as appropriate. 45

VAT is therefore a real cost when charged to an **end consumer** (any person who is not a VAT-registered trader), because a non-registered person cannot offset or reclaim VAT incurred. VAT can also be a real cost to a trader which makes exempt supplies (see ¶2075+).

EXAMPLE C Ltd (a VAT-registered trader) incurred the following standard-rated purchases and made the following standard-rated supplies in the course of its business:

Transaction	Value	VAT
	£	£
Purchases (inputs)	16,000	3,200
Supplies (outputs)	40,000	8,000

The net payment due to HMRC is £4,800. (£8,000 - £3,200)

MEMO POINTS 1. A trader's input tax and output tax are **accounted for** on a quarterly basis to HMRC (or sometimes monthly, if the trader requests) on the VAT return (¶65).
2. Any person that makes **wholly exempt supplies** (¶350+) is unable to register for VAT and is therefore treated as an end consumer (so that any VAT paid on inputs is a real cost).
3. The extent to which a trader can recover input tax depends upon whether it makes wholly taxable supplies, or a **mixture of taxable and exempt** supplies (¶2070+).

2. Exceptions

There are two exceptional circumstances where the basic principles of VAT are not followed - that is, in the case of: 46
- abuse; or
- fraud.

Where there is **abuse**, the VAT effect of the transactions actually undertaken is ignored. Instead a non-abusive alternative series of transactions is deemed to have occurred. These transactions will have as closely as possible the same end result in commercial terms as the abusive transactions and the VAT effect of these deemed transactions will be attributed to the trader concerned.

In case of **fraud**, a trader may not be entitled to recover input tax claimed (see ¶1998). Alternatively, it may be inherent in the fraud that no actual supplies have taken place (see ¶1952). However, where actual transactions have been carried out, a fraudulent motive will not prevent those transactions from being part of an economic activity (and thus being within the scope of VAT). *Optigen Ltd and others v CCE* [2006]

Identification of abuse

48 If the apparent VAT effect of an actual series of transactions is potentially to be replaced with the (different) VAT effect of a deemed series of transactions, it is obviously important to know when that substitution might take place.

The CJEU has stated that abuse will occur where:
- the transactions concerned, although apparently in compliance with VAT legislation, result in the accrual of a tax advantage contrary to the purpose of that legislation; and
- the essential aim of the transactions concerned is to obtain a tax advantage.

The CJEU added that abusive transactions "must be redefined so as to re-establish the situation that would have prevailed in [their] absence". *Halifax and others v HMRC* [2006]

Identification of a **tax advantage** is relatively straightforward (generally, paying less or claiming more than otherwise) but whilst it is helpful to know that the test is whether the effect of the transactions is **contrary to the purpose of the legislation**, knowing what that purpose is, or is not, in a given set of circumstances will not always be easy. The Courts have certainly not found it plain sailing so far (although this is a relatively new area of the law and settled principles are at least starting to emerge). Here are some examples for illustration.

Abusive	Not abusive
A German company obtained refunds of MST (German VAT) on goods exported to Switzerland. The German authorities discovered that the goods had been shipped back to Germany, so they cancelled the refunds. The company appealed. The CJEU held that the company's practice was abusive, stating that "abuse presupposes an intention to obtain an advantage from the Community rules by creating artificially the conditions for obtaining it". *Emsland-Stärke GmbH v Hauptzollamt Jonas* [2001]	A German company (with a UK VAT registration) which leased cars to UK customers, but accounted for no output tax in Germany or the UK, nevertheless sought to deduct input tax on the purchase of the cars. Due to the interaction of UK and German VAT law, the company enjoyed an unintended VAT advantage, but the CJEU said it was for Germany and the UK to align their legislation to prevent that advantage, not for the company to account for VAT as if the legislation were consistent. Legislation which sought to implement the Principal Directive was being taken at face value, so there was no abuse. *HMRC v RBS Deutschland Holdings GmbH* [2010]
An Italian company made taxable supplies of leasing cars. It arranged for an associated company to provide exempt insurance services to its leasing customers, at a price which maximised the value of the exempt supplies and therefore minimised the value of the taxable supplies. The CJEU held that "there can be a finding of an abusive practice when the accrual of a tax advantage constitutes the principal aim of the transaction or transactions at issue". The Italian courts subsequently re-heard the case and held that the transactions were abusive. *Ministero dell'Economia e delle Finanze v Part Service Srl* [2008]	Two associated companies supplied purchasers of holiday homes with separate supplies of land (standard-rated) and construction services (zero-rated). This arrangement was held to be abusive by the First-tier Tribunal, because it aimed to create a VAT advantage. However, that decision was overturned by the Upper Tribunal, which observed that "a supply of land by a landowner and a supply of construction services by an independent trader are separate supplies to be taxed as such". It held that there were genuine commercial reasons for the companies to treat their supplies as separate. *Lower Mill Estate Ltd* [2010]

Abusive	**Not abusive**
A company bought goods for leasing to two other members of a corporate group (not a VAT group), for use in their exempt insurance business. The assets were leased to them through another unconnected company (S Ltd). By accounting for VAT on lease rentals, instead of incurring irrecoverable VAT on fixed assets for use in exempt transactions, the scheme delayed the payment of irrecoverable VAT by the group. It was conceded that this was one of the purposes of the arrangements. HMRC argued that because the purpose of the scheme was to gain a tax advantage, this was enough for it to be viewed as an abuse of the VAT system. It was held in the High Court, however, that even though the series of transactions was artificial and not a commercial operation, this was insufficient to make it contrary to the purpose of EU or UK VAT law. On referral, the CJEU agreed that it was not abusive to lease rather than buy assets, provided that the full amount of VAT is paid eventually. The introduction of S Ltd, however, was abusive, since it was only done in order to sidestep UK law which allowed transactions between connected companies to be treated as being at market value. The transactions must be redefined so that VAT was paid as if the lease rentals had been at market value. *HMRC v Weald Leasing Ltd* [2010]	A UK supplier of exempt loan broking services moved part of its operations to Jersey, in order to recover input VAT incurred on advertising costs. The First-tier Tribunal held that the arrangements were genuine and had real substance, and that the Jersey part of the operation was not a mere cosmetic insertion. It also held that the purposes of the legislation had not been contravened, since it was open to any trader to arrange its operations in order to achieve a genuine VAT result. The Upper Tribunal referred questions to the CJEU, which confirmed that the VAT treatment of a transaction does not have to follow the contractual position, if the contractual position does not reflect the actual substance of the transaction. Since, as noted above, the First-tier Tribunal has ruled that the arrangements were genuine, the CJEU's decision should not permit the Upper Tribunal to reverse the First-tier Tribunal's decision. However, it is still open to the Upper Tribunal (if it considers the transactions abusive) to conclude that there was no rational basis for the First-tier Tribunal's findings. *HMRC v Newey t/a Ocean Finance* [2013]
The owners of a golf course transferred the golf club business to two companies, which purported to make exempt supplies to customers and pay exempt rent to the owners. The arrangements were not abusive in themselves but there was nonetheless abuse, because the owners charged artificially high rent to the companies. As the First-tier Tribunal put it: "… there are (at least) two types of abuse: adoption of a structure which of itself gives rise to an abusive tax advantage, or adoption of tax-efficient structure on terms which are not commercial and which give rise to an abusive tax advantage". *Massey (J&B) t/a Hilden Park Partnership* [2013] (TC02787)	A car dealer entered into arrangements with third-party finance companies for the sale of "demonstrator" cars. The issue was whether demonstrator cars came within the second-hand margin scheme; hence whether VAT was due only on the profit, or on the full selling price. HMRC argued that the structure which enabled the cars to qualify for the margin scheme was abusive. The First-tier Tribunal concluded that the essential aim of the transactions was to obtain finance, not to obtain a tax advantage. In addition, as the Principal VAT Directive provides that second-hand goods should be sold under a margin scheme, the arrangements were not abusive, because the purpose of the legislation had been met, not undermined. The Upper Tribunal overturned the First-tier Tribunal's decision, holding that the arrangements were indeed abusive. The Court of Appeal reinstated the First-tier Tribunal's decision. It held that the Upper Tribunal had identified no error of law in the First-tier Tribunal's decision. The Upper Tribunal was not, in those circumstances, permitted to come to its own decision. *Pendragon plc and others v HMRC* [2013]

Abusive	Not abusive
The university sold and leased back a building on which it had incurred substantial input tax. This had the effect of postponing the university's non-recovery of input tax to be suffered in small doses as each lease rental was paid, rather than up front. Following *Weald Leasing* (see above), it was held that this was not contrary to the purposes of the VAT Directive. However, HMRC argued that the university had acted abusively in two ways: – it had sold the building to a specific type of trust in order to get round the anti-avoidance rules which prevent an option to tax having effect between certain connected persons; and – it intended to collapse the lease (and had in fact in the meantime done so). The First-tier Tribunal held that neither type of behaviour was abusive, because: – the legislation specifically stated which persons would be connected and the university was entitled to sell the building to a person which was not connected under those rules and so preserve the option to tax; and – the time to allege abuse would have been when the lease was collapsed, not when a mere allegation could be made that the university intended to collapse it. The Upper Tribunal overturned the First-tier Tribunal's decision, holding that the arrangements were abusive as a whole and from the start. There was no reason to wait until the lease was collapsed to make a finding of abuse: the university's intention to make an absolute VAT saving by collapsing the lease at some time in the future was sufficient to make the entire scheme abusive. The Upper Tribunal did, however, suggest (without formally deciding) that it is not abusive to find a loophole in anti-avoidance legislation. The legislation in this case set clear limits as to what was a connected party for the relevant purposes. The abuse principle (probably) did not extend to apply that anti-avoidance legislation to arrangements which did not come within those limits but which might conceivably be viewed as nonetheless within the spirit of the anti-avoidance legislation. *HMRC v University of Huddersfield Higher Education Corporation* [2014]	Odeon sells cinema tickets: a standard-rated supply. If Odeon made a charge for card processing, that would also be standard-rated, since there would be a single supply, to which the card-processing supply would be incidental. Odeon therefore set up a separate company to process card transactions, which might then be exempt supplies of transactions concerning payments. HMRC alleged that setting up a separate company was abusive, since it was done solely for tax-avoidance purposes. However, the First-tier Tribunal rejected this argument. There are two requirements for abuse: a transaction contrary to the purpose of the legislation; and which is carried out for tax-avoidance purposes. HMRC was effectively ignoring the first requirement. The Tribunal held that the arrangements were genuine, not artificial, and that they were not contrary to the purpose of the legislation. *Bookit Ltd* [2014] (TC03972)

3. Cross-border transactions

Within the EU

50 As the VAT regime is intended to facilitate a European free market, the following special rules apply for intra-EU supplies:

– **between registered** traders: such supplies are zero-rated by the supplier and the recipient accounts for "acquisition VAT" on goods (¶9010+), or the reverse charge for services (¶9700+), which essentially applies tax at the local rate which would have applied at the time of acquisition, if the goods or services had been supplied in the member state in which they were acquired; and

– **to a non-registered** person: VAT on such supplies of goods is generally charged and accounted for by the supplier, unless the value of such supplies breaches certain registration thresholds, in which case the recipient will need to register and account for VAT in the customer's country. In addition, special rules apply in relation to purchases of new means of transport, goods subject to excise duty, and mail order and other distance sales to non-VAT-registered persons. VAT on supplies of services is also generally accounted for by the supplier.

Outside the EU

Exports and imports of goods from outside the EU are generally taxable supplies, although various exemptions and reliefs apply (¶9400+), ostensibly to reflect the fact that VAT is a European, rather than an international, tax. 55

C. Procedure

The VAT compliance regime is self-administered by VAT-registered businesses. In particular, traders are responsible for: 60
- **registering** for VAT when required (¶2600+);
- maintaining appropriate **records** of all transactions (¶2790+);
- **calculating and reporting** the net output or input tax for each period (¶2980+); and
- **paying** the appropriate amount to HMRC (¶3160+).

Normal compliance

VAT **returns** (¶2985+) are generally made for a 3-month period, known as a **VAT period** or **accounting period**. When registering for VAT, each person is allocated a VAT period. To spread the VAT cycle, different persons will have return periods ending in different months. This is known as having a different **stagger**. 65

EXAMPLE D Ltd has a VAT period of 3 months, with the first return being due for the period to 31 January. Subsequent returns are made for the quarters to 30 April, 31 July and 31 October.
Mr E also has a VAT period of 3 months but prepares his returns to 28 February, 31 May, 31 August and 30 November.

MEMO POINTS 1. A person may apply to HMRC to **change its stagger**, so that the VAT cycle (or a return period) coincides with its accounting year end.
2. HMRC may authorise a person to complete **monthly returns** (¶2990). This is generally reserved for businesses that are due to receive regular refunds of VAT and provides a cash flow advantage.
3. Where smaller businesses operate the **annual accounting scheme** (¶4745+), they are required to submit only one VAT return per year.
4. HMRC has the power to require all **associated businesses** to account for VAT on the same cycle where there is little commercial rationale for different cycles to apply.

Special schemes

VAT compliance responsibilities are extensive and can be onerous. To recognise this, special schemes (the flat rate scheme, cash accounting and the annual accounting scheme) aim to simplify matters for **smaller businesses** (¶4600+). 70

In addition, certain **trade sectors** enjoy special VAT regimes due to the specific nature of their business, including:
- farmers (¶5900+);
- racehorse owners (¶6100+);
- retailers (¶6300+); and
- tour operators (¶7460+).

Enforcement

75 All compliance obligations are subject to **supervision** by HMRC. To this end HMRC has extensive powers (¶3400+), ranging from authority to request documentation to the physical search of premises.

These powers can generally only be exercised by an **authorised officer**, defined as any person acting under the authority of the Commissioners of HMRC.

In addition, the National Crime Agency (NCA) (¶3602+), working in conjunction with HMRC, has specific authority in relation to the enforcement of VAT in order to prevent and detect serious organised crime, including tax fraud.

CHAPTER 2

Business activity

OUTLINE ¶¶

Under the Principal Directive, VAT applies to any person who independently carries out any **economic activity**, whatever the purpose or results of that activity. Economic activities for this purpose comprise: **100** EC Directive 2006/112 art 9
- all activities of producers, traders and persons supplying services;
- activities of the professions; and
- the exploitation of tangible or intangible property for the purpose of obtaining income on a continuing basis.

CJEU case law has established that the concept of economic activity has a wide scope; the activity must be looked at objectively, without considering its purpose or results.

MEMO POINTS 1. The use of the word **independently** means that employees and persons bound to an employer by contracts of employment, or other legal ties, are not considered to be carrying on an economic activity.
2. The CJEU decided in 2009 that **external advertising activities** carried out by a publicly funded political party were not an economic activity. The case involved publicity expenses incurred on behalf of local district party groups by the provincial arm of an Austrian political party. The party recouped a proportion of the costs from the local groups but the CJEU has held that this did not constitute an economic activity for VAT purposes. The party was not in competition with commercial advertising agencies. *SPÖ Landesorganisation Kärnten v Finanzamt Klagenfurt* [2009]
3. On the other hand, in 2013 the CJEU ruled that the placing of **solar panels** on a domestic roof and consequent **intended** supply of electricity to the grid is **capable** of being an economic activity. This will presumably allow suppliers of such electricity to register for VAT and reclaim input tax on purchase of the panels. It will also require such suppliers who are already registered for VAT to account for output tax on sales of electricity to the grid. *Finanzamt Freistadt Rohrbach Urfahr v Unabhängiger Finanzsenat Außenstelle Linz* [2013]

The provisions of UK legislation relating VAT to "business" activities are derived from the Principal Directive. They provide that VAT is chargeable on supplies of goods and services made by taxable persons in the **course or furtherance of a business**. Business includes any trade, profession or vocation but is not defined any further. **102** ss 4(1), 94 VATA 1984

Certain specific types of transaction are defined by UK law to constitute business activities (¶134) but most of the UK practice on business activities is derived from case law (¶105+).

MEMO POINTS If a trader undertakes a **number of activities**, the business activity test must be applied to each activity in isolation.

SECTION 1

Case law

A. General principles

105 VBNB21000, 22000 A significant body of UK case law has developed to assist with the definition of "a business". The **key cases** from which the UK definition has evolved are *C & E v Lord Fisher* [1981] and *C & E v Morrisons Academy Boarding Houses Association* [1978].

These cases form the basis of the following **six tests**, which are used by HMRC to assess whether an activity is a business activity. The tests do not constitute a checklist; an activity can still be a business activity even if it does not display all of the features indicated.

Test	Comment	¶¶
Is the activity predominantly concerned with the making of supplies for consideration?	Over time this has come to be seen as the most important test	¶245+
Is the activity a "serious undertaking earnestly pursued"?	This excludes activities which are merely hobbies, etc	¶107
Is the activity carried on with reasonable continuity?		¶110
Does the activity have a certain measure of substance?	As measured by the quarterly or annual value of taxable supplies made	¶115
Is the activity conducted on sound and recognised business principles?	This test does not necessarily require the making of a profit	¶117
Are the supplies of a kind commonly made by those who seek to profit by them?	The profit motive is not decisive	¶120

Serious undertaking or occupation

107 This will usually exclude **hobbies** or other pastime activities carried out by traders. As a general rule, hobbies which involve a registered trader making minimal supplies are unlikely to be seen as business activities, whereas hobbies which involve making substantial supplies may grow to become business activities.

When judging whether a hobby should be seen as business, HMRC may look to see if the activity is treated as trading for direct tax purposes.

EXAMPLE The use of premises by a local authority as a cooking centre for the provision of school meals amounted to a serious activity earnestly pursued - one that would not normally be carried on for pleasure or social enjoyment. *Rael-Brook Ltd v Minister of Housing and Local Government* [1967]

Reasonable continuity

110 This test examines the regularity and frequency with which supplies are made and will generally **exclude** one-off supplies or a series of infrequent, unconnected supplies. However, it is also important to consider the underlying nature of the activity.

EXAMPLE

1. A jeweller whose hobby was collecting specialist cars was held to be carrying on a business activity, on the basis that he had owned at least 100 cars over an 18-year period. *Adams* [1975] (VTD 175)

2. In contrast, an engineer collecting old machinery as a hobby and regularly selling on pieces (at a profit) as and when he needed to raise funds, was held not to be carrying on a business activity. *Atkinson v C & E* [1994]

3. A **one-off activity** can also occasionally amount to an economic activity and therefore attract VAT, as illustrated by this case. The appellant helped the owner of a valuable house find a buyer for it and shared in the commission with three other parties, earning in excess of £100,000. The appellant claimed to have been paid the fee as a gift but the First-tier Tribunal found on the facts that the appellant and the owner had agreed in advance that if the appellant were to find a buyer, the owner would be prepared to pay him a commission. The Tribunal said: "The basis on which we decide that the appellant was acting in the course of a business is that, as we must give a wide meaning to the notion of "business", and that essentially there should be a liability to VAT where any supplies are made in "an economic activity", then those tests must be satisfied even if the business encompasses only the one activity, where the activity has been conducted in an entirely business-like manner... the appellant's role in this case was one where he and others expected from the start to earn fees for the provision of a service, a role that was entirely commercial and commonly conducted as a business, and we conclude that the appellant was therefore acting in the course of a business." *Alexander Spencer-Churchill* [2014] (TC03763)

Substance

It is necessary to look at the **value of taxable supplies** that are intended to be made. For example, an activity that is expected to bring in only £5 a week is less likely to be considered a business than one that is expected to make £10,000 a week. **115**

EXAMPLE An individual had owned racehorses for many years and subsequently decided to begin breeding them. He kept his horses at stud farms (not owned by him) in England and France but he made consistent net losses.
It was held that, despite the losses, the breeding activity showed all the traits of a business activity and initial losses were to be expected, as horse breeding, by its very nature, is a long-term activity. *DD Prenn* [1979] (VTD 793)

Other cases have looked at the substance of the **overall activity** to determine whether it can be said to constitute a trading activity.

EXAMPLE A company was registered for VAT for its pig farming business. It reclaimed input tax on the purchase of a yacht, which was used by directors of the company and their families and was also let on hire.
It was held that the chartering of the boat was a non-business activity because of the small number of charters, the limited nature of advertising and the company's selectivity in accepting hirers (all of which were associated with the company). *Rainheath Ltd* [1982] (VTD 1249)

Sound and recognised business principles

Although this is one of the indicative tests, it is not in itself conclusive. The business does not have to be operating at a profit in order to meet this test, not least because VAT is a tax on turnover, not on profits. **117**

EXAMPLE A couple set up a business in 1980 with the aim of breeding horses and teaching riding. The appeal concerned the initial period of trading up to December 1982. Although the business was run on sound and recognised business principles, it did not constitute a business activity, because there was no regular making of taxable supplies (there was no income from riding lessons or dressage activities during the period, with the only income coming from the sale of an unsuitable horse). Although a start-up business can be given a period of time before supplies are expected to be made, it must be anticipated that such supplies will be made in the reasonably foreseeable future. *K & K Thorogood Ltd* [1984] (VTD 1595)

Similarly, the mere fact that commercial operations are being conducted in an inefficient manner does not necessarily lead to the conclusion that the activities are not business activities.

EXAMPLE It was the practice of the RSPCA not to enforce payment of fees charged following any treatment which it gave to sick animals. This did not prevent its activities from constituting business activities. *RSPCA* [1991] (VTD 6218)

Similarity to common trading activities

120 If the activity is **similar in nature** to businesses commonly carried on by other persons on a commercial basis, the activity is more likely to be regarded as a business activity.

This test may be easy to establish in the majority of cases - where, for example, a person's stated intention is to provide goods and/or services of a type normally provided in a commercial manner in the course of everyday life. However, in a small number of cases this test may not be so clear - examples are professional sportspeople, statutory bodies and those who make their living from domestic hospitality. Although the dividing line may be difficult to draw, it is a real distinction and all the facts of a particular case must be considered to establish whether an activity is one carried on for purely social or recreational enjoyment, or that of a professional.

EXAMPLE

1. The execution of statutory repair works by a local authority was held not to constitute a business activity, as the service was being carried out by the authority in its capacity as a public body. Although the repair works could be said to be similar to supplies made by other persons carrying on a business activity, the facts of the case were that no such actual services could be carried out by any other person or body. *Glasgow City Council* [1998] (VTD 15491)

2. A charity provided care and support to sufferers from epilepsy. It requested a ruling from HMRC on whether the cost of construction of a new national centre would qualify for zero-rating as a building intended solely for charitable use. The ruling issued was that the construction costs would not be zero-rated, because the appellant was providing services in the course of a business, demonstrated by the fact that it raised invoices to and received payment from health bodies for those services. The appellant had a defined customer base (primarily the NHS) and although its objects were charitable, it had chosen to make supplies in the course of a business to meet those objectives; that there was no competition for the services was irrelevant. The appellant argued that consideration was not indicative of an economic activity, since its predominant concern was providing care; it was not financially independent and there was no link between the costs of care provision and the invoices raised to the NHS. Quite often the health bodies would propose a lower figure, which the appellant would have to accept. The tribunal noted that the supplies were uncommon, rarely (if at all) made for profit and there was no general market for the services. These were strong indicators that no business was being carried on. The tribunal held that as the appellant was not, in any real sense, carrying on a commercial activity, the construction costs of the new facility would qualify for zero-rating. *Quarriers* [2008] (VTD 20660)

124 Whether the activity is **pursued for profit** or some other private purpose is not determinative one way or the other in deciding whether the activity is a business, but naturally it is seen as a powerful indicator.

EXAMPLE

1. Charges made by the RSPCA for treating animals were held to be similar to the activities of ordinary commercial veterinary practices. The fact that most of the RSPCA's income was from donations was relevant only in determining the dividing line between business and non-business activities. *RSPCA* [1991] (VTD 6218)

2. In contrast, the lease of premises at a less-than-market rate to a charity (for the purposes of running a children's playgroup) was held not to be a business activity, as neither the landlord nor the tenant was carrying out activities for profitable purposes. *C & E v Yarburgh Children's Trust* [2002]

In the past HMRC has said that in its view the *Yarburgh* decision does not necessarily apply to all playgroups and each case will have to be considered on its own merits. For further details of charities see ¶8000+.

B. Special situations

Mixed business and private activities

126 VBNB26000 When a person undertakes a number of activities, it is important to apply the business activities test to each activity in isolation. An activity might form part of the overall organisational objectives but be non-business for VAT purposes - for example, a service provided for free.

EXAMPLE A sole trader, registered for VAT as an accountant, also owned three houses which he let to tenants. It was held that the letting activity had to be considered separately from the accountancy business; however, the degree of control and management of the houses exercised by the sole trader was sufficient for the letting to be regarded as a business rather than an investment activity. *David Allan Walker* [1976] (VTD 240)

Disposal of private assets

The disposal of private assets **through a trader's own business** may occasionally be treated as a business activity. When deciding this HMRC will consider: **128** VBNB28000
- whether the goods are of a type normally sold through the business;
- whether the sale was dependent upon the contacts and reputation of the business; and
- how the receipts were dealt with and accounted for.

EXAMPLE The sale by a jeweller of his wife's own jewellery through the business was held to be a business activity, because the goods were sold from the retail premises and the proceeds were paid into the business bank account. *Jodh Singh Mittu* [1983] (VTD 1275)

The **independent disposal** of private assets merely to raise funds for a business is non-business and outside the scope of VAT.

EXAMPLE A house (which formed part of a large estate) was leased to a rifle club. Throughout the term of the lease several paintings were kept locked in a storeroom, although some were kept on display in the rooms used by the club. When the lease expired, the paintings and a valuable stamp collection were sold separately from the house, with the proceeds being paid into the owner's business as capital. This was held not to be a sale in the course of a business activity, on the basis that the items had been sold in a purely personal capacity. *RWK Stirling* [1985] (VTD 1963)

Boats and aircraft

The **leasing** of a boat or aircraft (a "craft") may constitute a business activity of the owner, where it is leased directly to: **130** VBNB46000

a. the public (although the business activities test (¶105) will need to be applied); or

b. a hire company if:
- there is large-scale leasing to such hire companies (taken to be at least three craft leased to a hire company);
- the owner also lets the craft to members of the public for part of the year;
- the owner is actively involved in the business of the hire company; or
- the owner has other business activities, of which the leasing of craft to hire companies forms part.

(If these conditions are not satisfied the activity will usually nonetheless be considered to be a business activity of the hire company.)

EXAMPLE

1. An individual bought a luxury yacht from a company. Under the agreement the company undertook to manage the yacht and attempt to lease it to customers for a minimum period of 12 months. The individual who owned the yacht attempted to register for VAT (and reclaim input tax) on the basis that he was carrying on a business of yacht chartering.
However, it was held that he was not carrying on any business, because the letting of the yacht to the company was a one-off transaction which "was not part of a sequence of transactions amounting to economic activity". *M & C Berwick* [2002] (VTD 17686)

2. A partnership bought a boat from a company with a view to making it available for hire. Under the terms of the purchase agreement the company retained possession of the boat for use in its boat hire business, and maintained, insured and provided fuel and stores for the boat. Bookings could be taken by either the company or the partnership. The partnership received 45% of the hire charges where the booking was made by the company and 50% where the partnership made the booking.
It was held, on appeal, that the partnership was carrying on a business activity on the basis of:
- the fact that the partnership received more consideration if it obtained the bookings itself; and

– the actual efforts that the partnership made to attract customers (advertising in the local press, printing business cards, etc). *Longbow* [1977] (VTD 551)

132 If the owner of a craft enters into an agreement with a hire company but the **owner retains control** of the craft, the hire company is likely to be acting as agent of the owner (¶7090+).

Comment Boats and aircraft may be purchased for business entertainment purposes. If the provision is to third parties (e.g. a boat is chartered for corporate events), this constitutes a business activity and the related input tax will be deductible. Contrast this with the position of goods purchased for the purpose of providing business entertainment in-house, where input tax is generally not deductible (¶1926+).

EXAMPLE A Ltd purchases a boat for the purpose of leasing it out for use in corporate hospitality events. This is a business activity and the input tax on the purchase of the boat is deductible.
If, however, A Ltd had purchased the boat for the purposes of its own corporate hospitality events, this would not constitute a business activity and the input tax deduction would be blocked.

SECTION 2

Statutory definition

Summary

134 s 94 VATA 1994 The UK statutory definition of "business" covers the following **specific situations or transactions** which, if carried out in the course of a trade, profession or vocation, will constitute a business activity:

Activity	Comment	¶¶
The admission to premises for consideration	Must be a compulsory admission fee (voluntary payments will not suffice)	¶140
Services provided by an office-holder (as opposed to an employee)	For example, a trustee or executor	¶145
The provision of facilities by a club, association or organisation	For example, use of a golf course, monthly newsletters, etc	¶8145+
Supplies in connection with the termination (or intended termination) of a business		¶8600+
Supplies in connection with a transfer of a going concern and/or disposal of business assets or liabilities to third parties		¶8646+

Admission charges

140 s 94(2)(b) VATA 1994 Charging for admission to premises is always a business activity, and will include charging for one-off events and admission by programme.

This provision may encourage organisations that would not normally charge for admission to levy a charge in order to recover input tax on related purchases. However, note also that certain admission charges are exempt (¶386).

MEMO POINTS 1. Any **voluntary donations** for admission to premises will not constitute income from business activities, even if they are in addition to a minimum stated charge (¶8054). Moreover, flags and tokens given in recognition of a voluntary donation are not subject to VAT.
2. If charging is **by programme**, HMRC will, in most cases, treat the supply as a single supply of admission, with the programme being only ancillary. However, if the admission charge includes

a charge for written material, a reasonable apportionment can be made between standard-rated admission and zero-rated written material (¶314).

EXAMPLE Admission to a testimonial football match was held to constitute a business activity, because each ticket sale actually granted a right of admission. This was despite the fact that the real motive of the people who bought tickets was to show their appreciation of Mr Taylor. *Eric Taylor Deceased Testimonial Match Committee* [1975] (VTD 139)

Office-holders

Services of office-holders (as opposed to employees) are treated as being made in the course of a business. This provision essentially only **applies to professionals** (solicitors, accountants, etc) who are already in practice, where: **145** s 94(4) VATA 1994; VBNB41000
- the appointment is due to that person's professional expertise, as already exercised in the practice; and
- that professional expertise is used in the course of the person's duties as an officer.

These provisions **do not apply** to professionals who:
- are not in practice when they accept the appointment;
- are appointed for reasons other than their professional expertise;
- accept their appointments in a purely private capacity (notwithstanding that they are partners in professional firms);
- have the status of employee of the bodies in which they hold the offices; or
- do not otherwise provide professional services.

MEMO POINTS 1. An office-holder includes, **for example**:
- an accountant holding an appointment as auditor of a company;
- a solicitor holding an appointment as registrar of a company; and
- a trustee or executor.

2. **Payment** is usually in the form of fees, expenses or an annual retainer, although even where payments are referred to as "salary" it will not affect the status of the office-holder if the facts support a business activity.

If a **partnership** is involved, the payments should be made directly to, and retained by, the individual partner if VAT is to be avoided under these rules. HMRC will normally take this as evidence that the appointment was in a private capacity and that VAT is not due. If the fees accrue to the partnership, that would be taken to indicate that the office was accepted in the course of a profession and VAT would normally be chargeable by the partnership. **147**

EXAMPLE A firm of solicitors, practising as a partnership, actively encouraged its partners to accept appointments as office-holders (essentially to raise the profile of the partnership). The partners had to obtain the managing partner's approval before accepting any such appointments and had to account to the firm for any fees received. The firm would only be liable to account for VAT on the fees received if (a) there was a connection with the firm's business and (b) the appointment was accepted both (i) in the course or furtherance of the solicitor's profession and (ii) in the course or furtherance of the partnership business.

On the facts of this particular case, only one such appointment (the appointment of a solicitor to the board of a building society purely on the basis of his conveyancing expertise) was held to be sufficiently linked. The firm was therefore liable to account for VAT on these fees but all the other appointments were held to have been awarded to the solicitors in a purely personal capacity. *Birketts (a firm)* [2002] (VTD 17515)

CHAPTER 3

What is a supply?

OUTLINE ¶¶

VAT is chargeable on a supply of goods or services made in the course of a business (¶100+) in return for consideration. Such a supply is said to be "within the scope" of UK VAT. **240**

A supply which does not meet these conditions, or is otherwise designated as being "outside the scope", is not subject to VAT.

If a supply is within the scope of VAT, it is then necessary to determine:
- whether it is a supply of goods or of services (¶275+); and
- whether it is a single or a multiple supply (¶310+).

SECTION 1

Meaning of supply

The UK **statutory definition** is not particularly helpful, merely stating that it "includes all forms of supply, but not anything done otherwise than for a consideration". **245** s 5 VATA 1994; EC Directive 2006/112 art 14, 24

The **Principal Directive** (¶9997) is of more assistance, stating that a supply of goods means "the transfer of the right to dispose of tangible property" and that a supply of services means "any transaction that does not constitute a supply of goods".

In practice, a supply can be identified as being within the scope of VAT by applying the following criteria:
a. Is it made in return for consideration (¶247+)?
b. If not, is it of a type which is deemed to be a supply (¶251)?
c. In either case, is it of a type which is specifically outside the scope of VAT (¶252+)?

Artificial and abusive transactions

246 HMRC has argued that a transaction which is **wholly artificial** or otherwise **abusive** of the VAT system should not constitute a supply. The CJEU ruled, however, that a transaction carried out for the purposes of obtaining a tax advantage will still be a supply, although abusive transactions cannot give rise to a VAT advantage. *Halifax and others v HMRC* [2006]

Similarly, the UK courts have held that a transaction can be artificial, and even abusive, whilst still being a supply for VAT purposes: *HMRC v RBS Deutschland Holdings GmbH* [2010]. Abuse will only prevent a VAT advantage if the result does not achieve the purpose of the Principal Directive or domestic legislation.

Further information on the abuse principle is given at ¶46+.

Consideration

247 VBNB22000 Consideration is not defined in either European or UK legislation. It was **previously defined** (in the EC 2nd VAT Directive, Annex A, para 13) as meaning "everything received in return for the supply of goods or the provision of services, including incidental expenses (packing, transport, insurance, etc) that is to say not only the cash amounts charged, but also, for example, the value of goods received in exchange ..." Though that Directive no longer applies, this definition is still sometimes quoted.

248 Consideration is taken to include not only any **monetary** (¶930+) amounts received but also the value of any **non-monetary** consideration (¶936+).

Conversely, some payments are not consideration, including:
- dividends; and
- compensation payments (¶264).

MEMO POINTS Other common examples of **payments that are not consideration** for a supply include:
- **gratuities**, tips and service charges freely given;
- **grants and donations** freely given with no expectation of anything in return (¶8040); contrast this with sponsorship, which normally involves the sponsor receiving clearly identifiable benefits in return;
- **disbursements** (¶7190+); and
- fines and **penalty** charges; here a distinction must be drawn between genuine fines and those that are additional charges for a supply; in one case, a fine for the late return of a video was held to be a payment for an extended hire period and therefore consideration for a supply. *JG Leigh (t/a Moor Lane Video)* [1990] (VTD 5098)

HMRC Brief 57/08 HMRC's guidance in relation to fines at car parks distinguishes privately owned from local authority owned car parks. Treatment depends on the **contract terms**:
- where these allow for an extension to the parking, with an additional fee payable, the payment will be consideration; and
- where the terms do not permit an extension, it is considered a penalty and, as such, outside the scope of VAT; such payments would include those for failure to display a valid ticket, parking outside a marked bay, or failure to return within a specified time.

The Court of Appeal has confirmed that the treatment of car park owners laid down in this HMRC guidance also applied, based on the specific contractual position, to a **third party** who contracted with the car park owner to provide parking control services. *Vehicle Control Services Ltd v HMRC* [2013]

249 To be consideration "for" a supply, there must be a **direct link** between the payment and the supply. To identify this link it is necessary to look at any agreement between the parties, written or otherwise. In most cases the link will be fairly obvious, but difficulties may arise where the payment is for services, as by their very nature these supplies will be less tangible than a supply of goods. For example, it may not be easy to distinguish whether a payment is a payment for a supply of services or merely compensatory (which is outside the scope of VAT).

However, if the supplier is not carrying on a business (¶100+), identifying a link between a payment and a supply will not make that payment into consideration or the supply taxable. *Quarriers (No 2)* [2008] (VTD 20670)

Consideration is a complex area of the law, best illustrated by outlining a number of cases which have specifically dealt with that issue. 250

Consideration	No consideration
Individuals paid a subscription to a society formed to oppose legislation against field sports. The society pursued its aims by carrying out campaigning activities on behalf of its members. These activities were held to be for the protection of the rights of its members, which constituted a direct link between the consideration paid for the subscription and the supplies made. *C & E v British Field Sports Society* [1998]	Mandatory charges imposed by a statutory body on registered growers did not constitute consideration. The statutory body could not therefore deduct input tax on its expenses. It was held that there was no direct link between the consideration and the supply. Indeed, the benefits provided by the statutory body accrued to the whole industry and it was possible that some individual growers received no benefits at all. *Apple and Pear Development Council v C & E* [1988]
A UK tour operator (which had an overseas parent company) ran coach tours. The UK company received a set percentage of the brochure price from the parent company as consideration for this supply. It was held that the operator was the person that the customers contracted with, as there was a direct link between the consideration paid by the customer and the supply by the tour operator. The fact that the operator did not receive the full consideration was because it permitted the parent company to deduct sums by way of commission. As a result, the tour operator should account for VAT on the full consideration paid for the service, before deduction of any commission to the parent company. *Trafalgar Tours Ltd v C & E* [1990]	A charity ran a school for children with emotional difficulties. The school provided educational and related care services, including accommodation for the pupils. HMRC argued that the charity was acting in the course of a business, as fees were paid by local authorities on a per-child basis: there was therefore a direct link between the supply and the consideration received. The charity also received a central government grant which partly covered capital outlays and the charity subsidised the school from its other activities. HMRC argued that the provision of accommodation and care was a business activity and that the school was not unique in its function. The tribunal rejected this approach, holding that the predominant concern of the charity was a social need, not an economic function. The key concern in establishing whether the charity was in business or not was the function it performed, not whether there was a direct link between payment by the local authorities and the provision of care to the children. The fact that the charity had no profit motive supported the fact that its key concern was a social need, not an economic function. *Quarriers (No 2)* [2008] (VTD 20670)

Deemed taxable supplies

There are certain transactions which the legislation specifically treats as **deemed taxable supplies** and for which it specifies the value of the supply. The most common examples are: 251
- gifts of business goods (¶1465+);
- self-supplies of certain goods or services (¶1490+);
- private use of goods or services originally acquired for a business (¶1520+); and
- retention of business assets on deregistration (¶8610+).

SECTION 2

Outside the scope of VAT

Certain transactions will be outside the scope of VAT, either because they: 252
a. do not meet the criteria detailed at ¶25; or
b. fall within one of the following categories:
- supplies that are specifically defined in the legislation as supplies of neither goods nor services (¶258);

– compensation or damages (¶264);
– supplies of inherently illegal products (¶266);
– the loss or destruction of an asset (¶268+);
– the issue of new shares by a company (¶2420+);
– a business gift costing not more than £50 (¶1465+);
– the provision of a sample for no consideration (¶272); or
– the transfer, by a property developer, of a privately owned road, a footpath, communal parking, a sewer or ancillary works.

Notice 742 paras 8.1, 8.2

MEMO POINTS A transfer by a property developer, as referred to above, is not a supply if it is made:
– for no (or nominal) consideration, to a local authority or sewerage undertaker; or
– for no consideration, to a management company for ongoing maintenance.

Consequences

254 No VAT can be **charged** on supplies that are outside the scope of VAT.

Notice 742 para 8.2; Business Brief 12/05

Input VAT incurred on the costs of making supplies which are outside the scope is usually irrecoverable, except for the following cases:
– the issue of new shares (¶2420+);
– in connection with a transfer of a business as a going concern (¶2260+);
– transfers by property developers (when the related input tax incurred on the building costs is attributable to supplies of the land and buildings of the development itself); and
– certain overseas supplies affected by the reverse charge provisions (¶9700+).

A. Neither goods nor services

258 The following supplies are treated as supplies of neither goods nor services:

Area	Type of supply	Reference	¶¶
Transfers within same entity	The transfer of a business as a going concern	SI 1995/1268 reg 5	¶8646+
	Transfers between companies in a group where a group registration is in force	s 43 VATA 1994	¶8832+
	Transfers between different VAT-registered divisions of the same company	s 46 VATA 1994	¶2750
Margin scheme	Removal of goods to the UK from the EU, where the goods were supplied under the margin scheme	SI 1995/1268 reg 8	¶6780
	Services in connection with the supply of margin scheme goods provided by agents or auctioneers acting in their own name, where the consideration for the services is included in the price obtained	SI 1995/1268 regs 9, 10	¶6750+
Repossessed or pawned goods	The disposal of goods by a person who has repossessed them under the terms of a finance agreement, or in settlement of an insurance claim. The goods sold must: – be in the same condition as when repossessed; – have been charged to VAT if imported into the UK; and – be non-taxable if a supply of the goods was made by the person from whom the goods were repossessed	SI 1995/1268 reg 4 SI 1992/3122 reg 4	
	Return of goods by a pawnbroker to the person who originally pawned them, provided that the transaction occurs not more than 3 months after the acquisition by the pawnbroker	SI 1986/896 reg 3	

Area	Type of supply	Reference	¶¶
Hire purchase/ conditional sale	The assignment of rights under a hire purchase or conditional sale agreement by the owner, to a bank or other financial institution	SI 1995/1268 reg 5(4)	
Cars[1]	The disposal of a car for no consideration (for example, by scrapping) where, on a previous supply, input tax on the car concerned has been blocked	SI 1992/3122 reg 4	¶1890+
	The letting or hire of a car for no consideration (or less than full consideration)	SI 1992/3122 reg 4	
	Making a car available for private use (for example, to an employee)	SI 1992/3122 reg 4	
Temporary importations	The sale of goods which have been temporarily imported and remain subject to the temporary importation arrangements, provided that the sale is to a person outside the EU	SI 1992/3130 reg 2	¶9509+
	The sale by auction of second-hand goods or works of art which have been temporarily imported and remain subject to the temporary importation arrangements; the provision of any services relating to such a transfer are also outside the scope	SI 1995/958 reg 3	¶9509+
Fiscal warehousing	The supply of imported goods whilst warehoused in bond, if the goods are supplied before payment of the duty	ss 18 - 18F VATA 1994	¶9242+

Note
1. For the provision of a car to an employee in exchange for a salary sacrifice see ¶941.

B. Settlement of disputes

The treatment of a payment made under a settlement (whether out of court or under a court order) depends upon the nature of the settlement, so that where it: **262** VATSC36000
- represents compensation or damages, it will be outside the scope of VAT;
- is for a future supply of goods or services, it will be subject to VAT in the normal manner; or
- represents extra consideration for an earlier or later taxable supply, it will be in return for a supply for VAT purposes.

If the customer invoices the supplier in respect of poor workmanship, etc, this is also outside the scope. *Galaxy Equipment (Europe) Ltd* [1993] (VTD 11415)

A just and reasonable apportionment will be made where the settlement consists of more than one of the above components.

EXAMPLE The payment of an out-of-court compromise settlement was held not to be in return for a supply for VAT purposes, on the basis that the settlement was not in respect of an outstanding invoice or supply. Instead, the point at issue between the parties was whether a supply had been made at all. As judgment had never been obtained on that point, the settlement could not be held to represent extra consideration for an earlier taxable supply. *L Reich* [1992] (VTD 9548)

Compensation

Compensation is generally outside the scope of VAT. **264**

The following table details the VAT treatment of particular kinds of compensation.

Compensation for	Detail	VAT treatment	Reference
Damage or loss whilst assets out of owner's possession e.g. during haulage	Payments received for repair/replacement	Outside the scope	VATSC 61800
Breach of contract	Effectively cancels contract and damages result	Outside the scope	*Financial & General Print Ltd* [1995] (VTD 13795)
Early termination of contract	Where there is a contractual right to terminate in lieu of liquidated damages (loss of earnings)	Outside the scope	*Holiday Inns (UK) Ltd* [1993] (VTD 10609) *F Penny (t/a FMS Management Services)* [1993] (VTD 10398)
	Where no right to terminate exists e.g. a variation to a lease to allow the tenant to vacate	Consideration for VATable supply	*Lloyds Bank plc* [1996] (VTD 14181)

C. Illegally supplied goods or services

266 VATSC99000

A supply of illegal goods or services (for example, the sale of a stolen car) may still be within the scope of VAT. The mere fact that supplies are made illegally does not exempt them from the VAT regime.

The CJEU has ruled that "a line must be drawn between, on the one hand, transactions that lie so clearly outside the sphere of legitimate economic activity that, instead of being taxed, they can only be the subject of criminal prosecution, and, on the other hand, transactions which though unlawful must nonetheless be taxed, if only for ensuring, in the name of fiscal neutrality, that the criminal is not treated more favourably than the legitimate trader". *Witzemann v Hauptzollamt München-Mitte* [1989]

This means that goods or services which are inherently illegal in all member states (for example, trafficking in illegal drugs or counterfeit money) are outside the scope of VAT.

EXAMPLE

1. An escort agency provided escorts for the purposes of prostitution. A distinction was made between lawful activities within the scope of VAT (the provision of escort services) that were, in fact, operated unlawfully and "straightforwardly criminal" activities which were not within the scope of VAT. In this case, it was held that although the provision of prostitutes is an illegal activity, the particular supply of the escorts was within the scope of VAT because if the supply was made lawfully (i.e. a legal supply of escorts for purely social purposes), it would be within the scope of VAT. To rule otherwise would breach the principle of fiscal neutrality between lawful and unlawful traders. *C & E v Polok and another* [2002]

2. Contrast this with a case involving the illegal sale of drugs such as amphetamines or hashish. This was held not to be an economic activity and thus not a supply for VAT purposes. The supply of narcotic drugs was outside the scope of the fiscal neutrality principle, because by their very nature they are totally prohibited from being put into circulation in all EU member states. *Vereniging Happy Family Rustenburgerstraat v Inspecteur der Omzetbelasting* [1988]

D. Lost or destroyed assets

268 Notice 700 para 8.10

If assets have been lost or destroyed prior to disposal, this will **generally** not be treated as a supply.

However, if a trader **cannot prove** that the assets have been lost or destroyed, HMRC may require the trader to account for VAT on such goods in the normal manner.

EXAMPLE Quantities of cigarettes were stolen from a warehouse. The Belgian tax authorities attempted to charge VAT on the company that owned the warehouse. The CJEU held that the theft of goods did not constitute a supply of goods and as such could not be subject to VAT. The CJEU also stated that there is no legal basis under which national legislation can impose VAT in such circumstances. *British American Tobacco International Ltd v Belgian State* [2005]

This can be contrasted with the **theft of cash takings**. Because "takings" are the result of a sale, a supply for VAT has already been made and consideration received, even though the consideration is subsequently stolen. Consequently, output VAT must be accounted for in the normal manner. *Gerald Benton* [1975] (VTD 185) **270**

VAT must also be accounted for where the supplier has provided credit and the purchaser subsequently fails to pay (although bad debt relief may be available (¶840+)).

EXAMPLE A manageress of a hotel did not record all takings for room reservations in the hotel books (instead taking the cash for herself).
It was held that the supply had occurred at the time that the bookings were made and consequently VAT was due from the owners in respect of the stolen proceeds in the usual manner. *CJ Huntley & RJ Brooks t/a Brimar Guest House* [1991] (VTD 5847)

E. Samples

The provision of a sample of goods for no consideration is **not a taxable supply**. This includes the case where samples are provided through an intermediary (for example, supplied by a manufacturer to a retailer to pass on to its customers), provided that the following conditions are satisfied: **272** Sch 4 para 5(2)(b) VATA 1994

- neither the supplier nor the intermediary charges for the sample;
- the sample is supplied for genuine business purposes as an example of a product;
- the sample remains the property of the supplier until it is given to the final customer; and
- all unused samples are either returned to the supplier or destroyed.

For the difference between samples and business gifts or inducements see ¶1470.

MEMO POINTS Before 19 July 2011, if a number of identical samples (or samples not differing in any material respect) were given to the same person, only one of them was considered to be outside the scope of VAT. The law was **changed** following the CJEU decision in *EMI Group plc v HMRC* [2010].

SECTION 3

Supply of goods or services?

The distinction between a supply of goods (¶277+) and a supply of services (¶300+) is important because of differences in the law relating to: **275**

- place of supply (see below);
- time of supply (¶750+);
- rate of VAT (¶1090+); and
- recovery of pre-registration input tax (¶8560+).

MEMO POINTS 1. For a transaction to fall within the scope of UK VAT it must be made in the UK. It is therefore necessary to determine the place of supply. The rules differ depending on whether the supply is one of goods (¶278) or of services (¶9682+).
2. Particular rules apply for cross-border transactions to determine whether they are within the scope of UK VAT (¶9000+).

A. Goods

277 The following are defined to be supplies of goods:

Supply	Reference	¶¶
Any transfer of the whole property in goods	Sch 4 para 1 VATA 1994	¶280+
The transfer of possession of goods in some circumstances	Sch 4 para 1 VATA 1994	¶290
Returned goods in some circumstances	SI 1995/1268 reg 4	¶292
Sales in satisfaction of a debt	Sch 4 para 7 VATA 1994	¶294
A transfer or disposal of business assets	Sch 4 para 5 VATA 1994	¶296+
A gift of business assets	Sch 4 para 5(2) VATA 1994	¶1465+
Permanent private use of business assets	Sch 4 para 5(1) VATA 1994	¶1524
Self-supply	s 5(5) VATA 1994	¶1490+
Deemed supplies on retention of business assets on deregistration	Sch 4 para 8 VATA 1994	¶8610+
The transfer of own goods between EU member states	Sch 4 para 6 VATA 1994	¶9286+
The grant, assignment or surrender of a major interest in land	Sch 4 para 4 VATA 1994	¶5249+
The supply of any form of power, heat, refrigeration or ventilation[1]	Sch 4 para 3 VATA 1994	¶1116+
The supply of water	SI 1989/1114	

Note:
1. Supplies of electricity and gas are specifically defined as being supplies of goods.

Place of supply

278
s 7 VATA 1994

Goods will be liable to UK VAT if they are located in the UK (¶25) and they **do not leave or enter the UK** in the course of the supply. To be treated as supplied in the UK, goods must either be:
- located and supplied in the UK; or
- installed or assembled in the UK.

There are **special rules** for:
- goods installed or assembled in the UK (¶9154+);
- supplies made on board ships or aircraft (¶9302+);
- goods in a fiscal warehouse (¶9242+);
- supplies of electricity and gas, and heating and cooling (¶9300); and
- certain cross-border transactions, including a transaction involving three parties based in different EU member states (known as triangulation (¶9214+)).

MEMO POINTS Goods are still treated as supplied in the UK if, during the course of the supply, they **temporarily leave and re-enter the UK** (for example, a transfer of goods from Northern Ireland to England where the goods pass through the Irish Republic).

Transfer of the whole property in goods

280
Sch 4 para 1 VATA 1994; VATSC70400

This means the transfer of **title** and **all rights of ownership** of the goods (without retaining any reversionary interest), including, for example, outright sales, credit card sales and gifts. In practice it will be fairly easy to establish whether title has been transferred but if the situation is unclear, it is necessary to look at the conduct of the parties and the wording of any written contract or agreement between them.

EXAMPLE A company carried on the business of training racehorses. The principal shareholder (R) provided the feed and labour for all the horses in the yard (including his own). There was no physical differentiation between the feed and labour provided to the principal shareholder's own horses and that provided to the others. However, the company was only invoiced for the feed and labour that was supplied to horses that did not belong to R.
It was held that title to the goods provided by R for his own horses had not passed to the company. Only title to the balance had passed to the company. *Spigot Lodge Ltd v C & E* [1985]

MEMO POINTS If a transaction is for a sale of **specific or ascertained goods**, the title will pass when it is intended to pass, as determined by contract law. However, if the goods are unascertainable at the time of the transaction, title will only pass when they are ascertained.
Note that it is important not to confuse this with **forward contracts** (i.e. contracts where it is agreed that there will be a supply of goods at a specified date in the future). In such a case the goods have to be manufactured/acquired by the vendor before the supply can be made but the important point is that they will ultimately be allocated or delivered to the purchaser. The supply is a supply of goods. It is not a supply of services when the contract is made, followed by a supply of goods when title in them passes.

Shared title Where title to an asset (for example, a racehorse) is commonly shared between several individuals, a sale **by all the owners together** will constitute an agreement for the sale of goods and is therefore treated as a supply of goods. *Sir John Astor* [1981] (VTD 1030) 284

MEMO POINTS 1. Contrast this to the sale of any number of **individual shares** (less than the whole), in which case the sale is treated as a supply of services (¶300+).
2. For details of the **bloodstock industry** see ¶6100+.

Transfer of possession of goods

If possession is transferred **followed by a later transfer of title**, the transfer of possession will be treated as a supply of goods if the transfer is under an agreement: 290 Sch 4 para 1 VATA 1994; VATSC71800
- for the sale of the goods; or
- which expressly contemplates that title to the goods will pass at some future time.

The time at which title passes must be determined by the agreement and must be no later than the time at which the goods are fully paid for.

The simple transfer of possession of goods (with **no later transfer of title**) is a supply of services (¶300+).

MEMO POINTS **1. Hire purchase contracts** involve a later transfer of title, as do other credit agreements (for example, option payment or balloon payment contracts). Where such agreements include a **charge for credit** (as is usual), provided that the charge for the credit is separately identified in the agreement, it will be treated as a separate exempt supply of services (¶362+). Where the amount is not so identified, all payments made under the agreement will be payments for a supply of goods. VATSC73600
2. It is HMRC's view that a supply will still be treated as a supply of goods even if the contract specifies that **title will not pass for some period after the final payment** for the goods (for example, 7 or 14 days). VATSC72800
3. Transfer of possession means the transfer of control of the goods, in that the recipient is able to use and enjoy the goods before title is passed. If there is any uncertainty over whether possession has been transferred, it is necessary to look at the intentions of the parties, who actually has control of the goods, and the wording of any written contract or agreement between them.

Returned goods

Legally, returned goods are treated as repossessed goods for VAT purposes. In practice this has the following effects. 292 SI 1995/1268 reg 4; VATSC70600
a. If goods are returned because they are **not in accordance with the sales contract** (for example, because they are faulty), the transfer of title is cancelled and neither the original sale nor the return is treated as a supply. If the faulty goods are **replaced**, in practice the original VAT invoice will stand (although strictly speaking the replacement goods constitute a new supply). If the faulty goods are **repaired or improved** in order to satisfy the original

contract, the work is treated as part of the original supply and there is therefore only one supply.

EXAMPLE

1. The return of a child car seat after 4 years for a full refund was held to form part of the original transaction, such that the credit note cancelled out the original supply. *Kwik Fit Ltd* [1992] (VTD 9383)

2. In contrast, a supplier agreed to buy back, for a guaranteed minimum amount, television sets which he had previously sold. The buy-back was held to constitute a separate transaction unconnected with the original supply. *WH Trace & Son Ltd* [1987] (VTD 2306)

b. If goods are returned **after title has passed** (and not because they are faulty), they will pass back to the supplier and a second supply is considered to have been made.

c. If goods are repossessed or returned voluntarily **before title has passed** (for example, under a hire purchase contract (¶364)), this does not affect the nature of the original contract (i.e. it is treated as a supply of goods from the outset) and VAT must be accounted for accordingly. The goods simply return to the original owner and are outside the scope of VAT. Similarly any subsequent sale is also outside the scope of VAT. If, however, as a result of the return, the price actually paid by the customer is reduced, the value of the consideration (¶925+) for VAT purposes is correspondingly reduced.

EXAMPLE Cars were sold to the public on finance terms, allowing the purchaser to make monthly payments throughout the term of the lease and a balloon payment at the end in order to purchase the car outright. Provided that all the monthly payments had been made, customers had the option of not paying this final payment and instead returning the car.
It was held that where a car was returned voluntarily (or was the subject of a default repossession) and the price actually required to be paid by the customer was reduced, there would be a consequent reduction in the amount of VAT accounted for on the sale, as the consideration had been reduced. *C & E v General Motors Acceptance Corporation (UK) plc* [2004] Note that this treatment does not apply to simple credit sales.

Sales in satisfaction of a debt

294 Sch 4 para 7 VATA 1994

Where a **creditor sells goods** belonging to its debtor in satisfaction of a debt owed to it, the sale is treated as a **supply of goods by the debtor** and output tax is due in the usual manner. This is because the creditor simply has the "power to sell" the goods and the title to them has remained with the debtor until the sale.

This provision will not apply where the creditor has **illegally repossessed** the goods but only where it has a power in law to sell them.

Transfer or disposal of business assets

296 Sch 4 para 5 VATA 1994; VATSC77400

The disposal of goods which are business assets will be treated as a supply of goods and output tax must be accounted for in the usual manner. (This includes assets which are used wholly or partly for exempt activities.)

This provision **applies to** the following types of transaction:
- assets taken into private use;
- assets given away; and
- the sale of fixed assets.

Exceptions to this rule are industrial samples (¶272) and gifts where the cost to the supplier is less than £50 per recipient per year (¶1465).

298 Sch 4 para 9 VATA 1994

If the business assets include **land**, the grant or assignment of the following will be treated as a supply of goods:
- a major interest in the land (¶5249+); or
- any interest in, right over, or licence to occupy the land where it is granted for no consideration.

Otherwise, a supply of land is treated as a supply of services.

B. Services

Supplies of services are **defined** by exclusion - that is, as being anything done for consideration that is not treated specifically as a supply of goods (¶277+). 300 s 5 VATA 1994

MEMO POINTS 1. It may be difficult to **link consideration** to the particular services supplied; each case must be considered on its own facts.
2. Services are more difficult to classify than goods, since they tend to be defined by description rather than being available for inspection. VAT attaches to the "true substance" of a transaction.

EXAMPLE
1. Company A was established by a number of cash and carry companies (member companies) to negotiate lower prices from suppliers. Some suppliers made periodic "overrider" payments to Company A, based on purchases of promoted products by Company A. The "overrider" payments were passed on by Company A to the member companies in proportion to their purchases. Company A did not account for VAT on the "overrider" payments. It was, however, held that these payments were consideration for a supply of services (the introduction of the member companies to the suppliers) by Company A. *Landmark Cash and Carry Group Ltd* [1980] (VTD 883)

2. The Council agreed with a vendor that the latter could park his van in a certain part of a specific council car park at defined times. The vendor would be permitted to sell ice creams at those times. This, potentially, was a supply of a licence to occupy land (exempt), or a supply of the right to park a vehicle (standard-rated), or a supply of the right to sell ice creams (standard-rated). The Tribunal said its job was to identify the **true substance** of the transaction and thereby the supply made by the Council. This was not a supply of a licence to occupy land, since the vendor did not have the right to exclude any other vehicle from the designated parking space (albeit that it was marked "Reserved ice cream van"). Nor was it a supply of parking, because the true substance of the transaction was a supply of the right to sell ice creams. *Fareham Borough Council* [2014] (TC04129)

In addition, the following **specific transactions** are stated as being supplies of services: 305 Notice 700 para 8.6

Supply	Reference	¶¶
The transfer of any undivided share of title in goods	Sch 4 para 1 VATA 1994	¶284
The transfer of the possession only of goods	Sch 4 para 1 VATA 1994	¶290
Exchange of reconditioned articles [1]	SI 1995/1268 reg 6	
Work on another person's goods [2]	s 30 VATA 1994	
The granting, assignment or surrender of an interest in land which is not a major interest	Sch 4 para 4 VATA 1994	¶5540+
Temporary private use of business assets	Sch 4 para 5 VATA 1994	¶1525+
Private use of business services	SI 1993/1507 reg 3	¶1544+

Note:
1. If a person **in the normal course of a trade** supplies reconditioned goods in exchange for unserviceable goods of a similar type, this is a supply of services. If a supply of this kind is made by a person **other than as part of the normal course of a trade**, the supply will be treated as a part exchange (¶1028+).
2. Work done on another person's goods is a supply of services whether or not the work **changes the character** of the goods or **results in new or different** goods. Ordinarily the standard rate of VAT applies to processing services but if work carried out on goods results in the production of **zero-rated goods** (e.g. children's clothes, food, etc) the supply of services can be zero-rated as well.

SECTION 4

How many supplies?

Where a transaction is made up of a mixture of elements, such as the supply of two or more goods or services, or a combination of goods or services, it is necessary to **distinguish between**: 310 VATSC80600

a. a single composite supply, where there is a single supply made up of a number of constituent elements which are ancillary, integral or incidental to the main supply; and
b. a mixed supply, where multiple supplies are made (although in many cases there is only one payment) and the components of the supply are not ancillary, integral or incidental to each other.

With one exception, neither UK nor EU legislation explains how to distinguish between the two. The principles in this section therefore derive from case law and HMRC guidance.

MEMO POINTS 1. The **exception** relates to printed matter supplied in connection with other goods or services (¶1255).
2. A service will be regarded as **ancillary** if, for customers, it does not constitute an aim in itself, but a means of better enjoying the principal service. *Card Protection Plan* [1999]
3. A service is regarded as **integral** if it is intrinsically part of the whole thing which is being supplied. It can therefore include both essential and non-essential elements, although a necessary element will almost certainly be an integral part of the main supply.
4. An **incidental** element of a supply is something which naturally accompanies the main supply.
5. The **CJEU** adopted the description of ancillary supplies to determine whether a supply was, or was not, a composite supply. **UK cases** have used the terms integral and incidental, although the three terms address the same concept.

A. Possible options

Composite supplies

312 This is the easiest situation as regards VAT liability, as there is only one supply.

Mixed supplies

314 In this case, each part of the supply is treated as a separate principal supply in its own right and, where relevant, different **rates of VAT** (and possibly time and place of supply rules) are applied to each element. Where a mixture of VAT rates is applied, the value of the supply of each different element must be established; for these purposes any apportionment of the total price must be done on a fair and reasonable basis (unless the tour operators' margin scheme applies (¶7592+)).

Two-part tariff

315 Sometimes distinguished from a composite supply, this occurs where there are two or more payments at different times but for a single supply. The original example was the purchase of a student railcard and later of a ticket associated with it, which were held to constitute two parts of the same supply: see *British Railways Board (No 2)* [1977] (¶325).

B. Deciding on the correct treatment

316 Whether a supply is a composite or mixed supply is a difficult area and there have been numerous cases on this matter. The leading CJEU case of *Card Protection Plan* [1999] provides guidance on the tests to be applied (although it must be stressed that the guidance is only of general application - the decision stated that it was not possible to give definitive guidance on such matters due to the commercial diversity of all transactions).

HMRC's guidance

In light of the *Card Protection Plan* case, HMRC guidance was issued to clarify the official approach on this matter, which essentially reiterated the CJEU's approach. The guidance states that when determining whether a single composite or mixed supply has been made: **318** VATSC82400
- consideration must be given to all the **circumstances** of the transaction and all the tests explained in the *Card Protection Plan* case;
- every supply must be treated as distinct and independent, without **artificially splitting** single supplies;
- a supply will be treated as a single composite supply if any **constituent elements** are only ancillary to the principal service; and
- the charging of a single **price** may not be decisive one way or the other. A service provided to customers which consists of several elements for a single price may suggest there is a single service. If the circumstances of the transaction indicate that customers intended to purchase two distinct services to which two different tax liabilities apply, the single price would need to be apportioned.

MEMO POINTS 1. In the past, HMRC indicated that if a **distinct service element represents 50% or more of the price** of a bundle of goods and services, it would consider that to be a strong indicator that the service is not ancillary to a principal supply of any other goods or services in that bundle. The consideration may need to be apportioned accordingly. Obviously, if HMRC believes there is a tax avoidance motive, any apportionment may be challenged.
2. For details of **subscriptions**, which may be either a composite or mixed supply, see ¶8180+.

In **practice**, HMRC considers the following factors to be indicative of either a single composite or mixed supply: **320** VATSC82800, 87400

Single composite supply	Mixed supply
One single price paid irrespective of how much of the package the customer receives or uses	There is separate pricing or invoicing
Elements are advertised as a package and the components are not available separately	Where the constituent components are available separately
Where it would not normally make sense to supply the elements separately (for example, a new fridge and its delivery from a warehouse)	There is more than one supplier
Customer perceives that there is a single supply	There is a time differential between various parts of the supply
The different elements are integral to one overall supply such that, if one or more is removed, the nature or quality of the supply would be affected	The components are not interdependent or connected
Goods are physically packaged together (e.g. plastic toys enclosed with cereal)	
Separation of items on an invoice is artificial or simply provides the customer with a cost breakdown	

This list is obviously by no means exhaustive and each case will be judged on its own merits.

Case law

The following **examples** illustrate supplies that were treated as either single composite or mixed supplies. Cases which pre-date the *Card Protection Plan* case should be viewed in the light of HMRC's policy following that decision (¶318). **325**

It should be noted that legislation was introduced in Finance Act 2011 (¶1255) which overturns the *Telewest* case described below. In any case, the CJEU ruled in *Part Service Srl* [2008] that it was potentially abusive (and would, if so, be ineffective for VAT purposes) for different but connected persons to make distinct parts of what would otherwise be a single supply (¶48).

Single composite supply	Mixed supply
The supply of food packs and associated counselling services supplied as part of a weight loss programme constituted a single indivisible standard-rated supply. The important factors were the **economic indivisibility** of the elements of the supply and the perspective of the consumer. The support services offered were integral to the achievement of weight loss for the customer and therefore could not be separated from the food supplies. *David Baxendale Ltd v HMRC* [2009] This decision is consistent with the judgment in the similar case of *Weight Watchers (UK) Ltd* [2008], in which it was decided that the provision of weekly classes and printed matter constituted a single standard-rated supply.	A TV guide was a separate supply from the subscription service. The reasons for this decision were that: – the guide was sourced from a separate subsidiary in the group; – existing customers were notified they would receive guides from the publications company; and – the contract for new customers stated that the two supplies would be received from different companies. *Telewest Communications plc and another v C & E* [2005]
Airport parking, where a bus is provided to take motorists to the airport, was a single supply of standard-rated parking services with no separate supply of zero-rated bus transport from the car park to the airport. The tribunal distinguished airport parking from town centre "park and ride" schemes where the secure parking element would not be as significant. The CJEU later confirmed this decision. *Purple Parking Ltd v HMRC* [2012]	The supply of a soft drink, packet of crisps and sandwiches was held to constitute separate supplies (sandwich plus the crisps and drink) on the basis again that each element of the supply was complementary to the other; it was not possible to argue that one was ancillary to the other. *De Montfort University Students Union* [2003] (VTD 18434)
Distance learning where students were provided with specially prepared written material for them to study on their own. This was a single supply of education, to which the printed material was ancillary. *College of Estate Management v C & E* [2005]	On-board food provided on a river boat trip, as the trip and the catering aspect of the cruise were complementary to one another and neither dominated. Therefore it was not possible to argue that one was ancillary to the other. *Durham River Trips Ltd* [2001] (VTD 17329)
Free motor insurance provided with a motor car was a single supply of a motor car. *Peugeot Motor Company plc and another v C & E* [2003] In a contrasting case, the vendor made a charge for the insurance, which was therefore held to be a separate supply. *Lindsay Cars Ltd* [2005] (VTD 18970)	The supply of promotional services to clients for an annual fee and additional services, including the supply of brochures, which were paid for separately were held to be separate supplies. The brochures were invoiced and itemised separately from the promotional services. As a matter of commercial reality, the brochures were not ancillary to the promotional services. *Appleby Bowers (a firm) v C & E* [2001]
A TV guide provided to subscribers was a single supply of broadcasting services despite the fact that the TV guide was also available separately to buy. The key factor in this decision was that the broadcasting agreement expressly stated that a TV guide would be included as part of the broadcasting service. *British Sky Broadcasting Group plc* [2001]	In the provision of day excursions and charters on the Orient Express train which included the provision of meals, the catering element was sufficiently significant to constitute an aim in itself. It was not merely a way of better enjoying the travel and constituted a distinct supply in its own right. *Sea Containers Services Ltd v C & E* [2000]
Provision of first-class air travel plus limousine transport to the airport, as: – the place where the transport supply began or ended was the passenger's home; and – the single price charged for the package of the limousine service and flight indicated a single supply. *Virgin Atlantic Airways Ltd* [1995]	A supply of transport by hoteliers to their customers to enable the latter to get to the hotel and subsequently on sightseeing tours, as: – the supply of transport went beyond that reasonably expected of hoteliers; and – the transport services were not ancillary to the supply of accommodation (they were not a means of better enjoying the accommodation, but formed a principal service in their own right). *TP Madgett & RM Baldwin (t/a Howden Court Hotel) v C & E* [1998]

Single composite supply	Mixed supply
Provision of in-flight catering as: – the provision of catering was linked to the quality of flight supplied; – the meal was provided regardless of whether the customer wanted it; – the airline was not contractually bound to provide the meal; and – customers were not entitled to a refund if they did not take the meal. *British Airways plc v C & E* [1990]	Insurance provided with the hire of a television set was a separate supply. The sets were let on hire by one subsidiary company; another subsidiary provided the insurance. *Thorn EMI plc* [1993] (VTD 9782)
Two payments were made for a student railcard and ticket. The first payment was for the card itself (which enabled the student to buy cut-price rail tickets), the second was made when the actual ticket was purchased. Both payments were for a single supply of travel, with the payment for the card being viewed as a part payment in advance for the supply of future transport. The related payments were not optional extras or subject to availability; both payments had to be made to the same legal entity. *British Railways Board (No 2)* [1977]	A subscription to the AA covered multiple supplies, involving a handbook, a magazine, maps, breakdown services and repairs. *The Automobile Association v C & E* [1974]
A business made zero-rated sales of caravans but was assessed for VAT on the removable contents as HMRC insisted these elements were standard-rated. The CJEU agreed, even though a single supply was being made, that the UK was entitled to limit the zero-rating to the caravan itself. *Talacre Beach Caravan Sales Ltd v C & E* [2006]	

C. Special cases

Packaging

In **general**, normal and necessary packaging (including ordinary tins, jars, etc) is treated as part of the goods contained within it, where the packaged goods are sold for a single price. **327** Notice 700 para 8.2

However, the general rule is **modified** if:

– the packaging goes beyond what is normal and necessary (for example, the container is a reusable storage container, or could be sold separately), in which case the packaging is treated as a supply in its own right; or

– a separate charge is made for a container to ensure its safe return. Unless this charge is refunded on the safe return of the container, it will be treated as a separate supply charged to cover the loan, hire or use of the container.

EXAMPLE

1. A tin containing biscuits was held to constitute "normal and necessary" packaging. The fact that the tins *could* be used after the biscuits had been consumed was not material. *C & E v United Biscuits Ltd* [1992]

2. In a contrasting case, a butter dish was held to constitute more than normal and necessary packaging, as the container *would* subsequently be used in its own right. *MD Foods plc* [2001] (VTD 17080)

Linked items

329 Notice 700/7 para 6.1 By **concession**, where a minor article (such as a promotional item) is linked with a main supply (of either goods or services) and sold with it for a single price (for example, an empty plastic storage jar sold with a packet of cereal), the supply can be treated as a single supply of the main item. For this "linked article concession" to apply, the minor article must:
- not be charged for separately to the customer;
- not cost more than 20% of the total cost of the combined supply (excluding VAT); and
- cost a maximum of £1 for a retail sale, or £5 otherwise.

Mixtures of food items

331 Notice 701/14 para 6 Where mixtures and assortments of standard-rated and zero-rated food items are sold together, they can be treated as a single zero-rated supply if they consist of:
a. a main zero-rated item and a minor standard-rated item which falls within the terms of the linked item concession (¶329);
b. an **assortment of biscuits**, where the weight of standard-rated chocolate biscuits does not exceed 15% of the net weight of the whole;
c. fruit and nut mixes, including Bombay and other savoury mixes, where the weight of standard-rated items does not exceed 25% of the net weight of the whole; or
d. an **assortment of petits fours** containing either:
- sweets (but not chocolate biscuits), where the weight of standard-rated sweets does not exceed 25% of the net weight of the whole; or
- chocolate biscuits, where the weight of standard-rated chocolate biscuits (and sweets if any) does not exceed 15% of the net weight of the whole.

Packages of printed matter

333 Notice 701/10 para 6.5 Where a supply of a **package** consisting entirely of paper or card is made, the trader can choose to treat the supply as either:
- a mixed supply, apportioned between standard-rated and zero-rated items; or
- a single supply, taxed at the rate applicable to the principal supply.

MEMO POINTS 1. A **package** is a collection consisting entirely of printed items, usually enclosed in some sort of wrapper. The items must have a common link, in that they are intended to be used together (for example, packages sent to shareholders which include company reports, circulars, proxy voting forms and a pre-paid envelope).
2. **Digitised publications** (for example, CD ROMs, e-journals, etc) when supplied with traditional paper publications can, depending on the facts of the supply, be treated as either:
- a single supply (of paper publications or digitised publications as appropriate); or
- a mixed supply of both.

Based on former HMRC pronouncements, the subscription to an e-journal with a paper journal being supplied at no extra cost is likely to be treated as a single composite (standard-rated) supply, with the paper journal being ancillary to the e-journal. In contrast, a combined digitised and paper package (with the paper publication being offered at a discount on purchasing the digitised publication) will probably be treated as a mixed supply, with the consideration apportioned accordingly. See also ¶6938.

CHAPTER 4

Exempt supplies

OUTLINE ¶¶

VAT is not chargeable on exempt supplies. A person making only exempt supplies cannot register for VAT. But if a person makes both exempt and taxable supplies in the course of business: **350**
– income from the exempt supplies does not count towards the value of taxable supplies for registration threshold purposes (¶9960); and
– input tax incurred in the course of making the exempt supplies is irrecoverable, subject to certain de minimis limits (¶2075+).

Comment Contrast this position with **zero-rated supplies**, which do count towards a person's turnover for registration purposes. Moreover, any input tax incurred in the course of making zero-rated supplies is recoverable.

Summary

The list of exempt supplies is contained in statute, with the **most common ones** being as follows: **352** Sch 9 VATA 1994

Supply	Comment	¶¶
Land	Complex exceptions apply	¶5100+
Finance	Includes dealing with money, credit facilities and consequent administrative requirements	¶356+
Cultural services	– includes admission to museums, galleries, etc, and theatrical/musical performances – supplied by public bodies and non-profit-making bodies	¶384+

Supply	Comment	¶¶
Charity fundraising events	Includes admission charges, and related goods and services	¶392+
Education	Includes: – education, research and vocational training supplied by and to "eligible bodies" – private tuition – examination services	¶398+
Sports competitions and physical education	Includes the grant of rights to enter sports competitions and the supply by eligible bodies of sporting services	¶418+
Health and welfare	Supplies made by doctors, dentists, opticians, etc	¶425+
Insurance	Services provided in connection with the supply of insurance	¶442+

The following supplies are also exempt:

Supply	Comment	¶¶
Antiques, works of art, etc, from historic homes		¶460
Betting, gaming and lotteries	Whether lawful or not	¶462+
Burial and cremation	Including making of preparatory arrangements	¶468+
Investment gold	Supplies of such gold, including the grant, assignment or surrender of a right to acquire gold	¶6830+
Postal services supplied by the Royal Mail	Excludes, for example, payments made by stamp collectors for valuable stamps and postal services not subject to price control	¶474
Subscriptions to trade unions, professional and other public interest bodies	Excludes supplies made that do not automatically form part of the subscription	¶476+
Onward supplies of goods on which input tax cannot be recovered		¶1885+

Cost-sharing groups

354 Sch 9 Group 16 VATA 1994; Information Sheet 7/12; CSE1000+

In 2012 a **new** exemption was added to the categories listed above. It applies where two or more organisations (whether businesses or not) join together to form a separate cost-sharing group (CSG). Organisations which make exempt supplies and those which make supplies outside the scope of VAT - in other words, which cannot recover all their input tax - are able to form special groups for this purpose. It should be noted that the exemption **applies only** to supplies of services (any goods supplied will only be covered by the exemption if they are ancillary to a single supply of services, under normal principles (¶310+)).

Even before this exemption was introduced, there was nothing to prevent businesses from getting together to share costs and thereby enjoy economies of scale. However, if one entity incurred the costs and then made recharges to the others, it had to charge VAT, which would be largely (or wholly) irrecoverable by them. Such recharges are now exempt from VAT. **Certain restrictions** are placed on the exemption; unless all of the following conditions are satisfied, the exemption will not apply:

– there must be a group of persons (a CSG) which supplies services to persons which are its members;

– the CSG must be independent of any control, ownership or influence outside its membership;

– members of a CSG must make exempt and/or non-taxable supplies;

– supplies by the CSG to its members must be at cost (specifically, the CSG must claim from its members "exact reimbursement of their share of the joint expenses");
– to be qualifying supplies, the services supplied by the CSG to its members must be "directly necessary" for the members' exempt and/or non-taxable supplies; and
– cost sharing, using the exemption, must not cause a distortion of competition.

As it is itself a single taxable person, it is the **CSG**, not its members, which **is responsible for administering its own VAT affairs**. Note though that the availability or denial of the exemption depends on the use to which the recipient member(s) put the services which are received from the CSG.

EXAMPLE West of Scotland Colleges Partnership was a CSG which asked for equal contributions from its members and made no attempt to assess any member's actual share of expenses. The First-tier Tribunal ruled that the Partnership had not qualified for the exemption, because it had not claimed from its members "**exact reimbursement** of their share of the joint expenses". Whilst "exact" did not have to be interpreted with "unwarranted" stringency, nonetheless the word "exact" was clear in its meaning and: "at least some effort or attempt has to be made to differentiate the interests of and benefits accruing to each of the members in assessing their shares of the joint expenses". *West of Scotland Colleges Partnership* [2014] (TC03746)

SECTION 1

Common exemptions

A. Finance

Most services provided in connection with finance are exempt and can broadly be divided into the following categories: **356** Sch 9 Group 5 VATA 1994

a. dealing in money, or securities for money (¶358+);
b. loans and credit facilities (¶362+);
c. intermediary services (¶370+); and
d. management of collective investment undertakings (¶376+).

MEMO POINTS When a business provides financial services, it will usually be the main activity of the organisation, leading to a severe restriction on the recovery of input tax. Certain trade bodies have therefore reached **administrative agreements with HMRC** to simplify the recovery process. Notice 700/57

1. Money

The supplies which are included and those which are specifically excluded from this exemption are as follows: **358** Notice 701/49 paras 2, 3; Business Brief 21/05

Included	Excluded	
	Supply	Treatment
Issue, transfer, receipt of or any dealings with: – money [1]; – securities for money [2, 3]; or – a note or order for the payment of money [4]	Issues of shares and securities for the purposes of the business [5]	Not a supply for VAT purposes
	Preparatory services [6]	Dependent upon the nature of the supply
	Issue of banknotes by the Bank of England, or by Scottish and Northern Irish banks	Zero-rated
Operation of any bank or building society account	Supply of banknotes, coins, etc, as collectors' items or investment articles [7]	Standard-rated

Note:
1. This covers all dealings with money (in sterling or foreign currencies) and includes financial transactions which are normally carried out by a bank or similar institution, for example:
- acceptance of money on account;
- money transfer services; and
- exchange of legal tender.

2. This includes, for example:
- certificates of deposit, government bills, etc; and
- bills of exchange, promissory notes and postal orders.

This excludes, however, vouchers which entitle the bearer to receive services.

3. The following ancillary services are also exempt:
- valuation, research and advisory services when they form an ancillary part of an otherwise exempt supply (otherwise they are standard-rated);
- dealing systems and electronic data services; and
- clearing and settlement services.

4. Includes, for example, postal orders, giros and cheques. Any charges made on the issue or subsequent "cashing in" of the orders are exempt (for example, a charge made by a building society to a customer for withdrawing funds).

5. HMRC had in the past taken the view that an issue of shares was exempt. However, following a CJEU decision (*Kretztechnik AG v Finanzamt Linz* [2005]), HMRC's current view is that any input tax attributable to the costs of issue is recoverable in the usual manner, to the extent that the company's outputs are taxable transactions (¶2420+).

6. This includes payroll services and the counting and transport of specie. May be exempt if carried out by an intermediary (¶370+).

7. Sales of some gold coins are exempt as investment gold (¶6830+). Sales of other items may be eligible for a second-hand scheme (¶6620+).

MEMO POINTS HMRC has proposed the following treatment for Bitcoin-related transactions, which will also apply in relation to similar crypto-currencies.
1. Income received from Bitcoin mining activities will generally be outside the scope of VAT on the basis that the activity does not constitute an economic activity for VAT purposes because there is an insufficient link between any services provided and any consideration received.
2. Income received by miners for other activities, such as for the provision of services in connection with the verification of specific transactions for which specific charges are made, will be exempt from VAT under Article 135(1)(d) of the EU VAT Directive as falling within the definition of "transactions, including negotiation, concerning deposit and current accounts, payments, transfers, debts, cheques and other negotiable instruments".
3. When Bitcoin is exchanged for sterling or for foreign currencies, such as euros or dollars, no VAT will be due on the value of the Bitcoins themselves.
4. Charges (in whatever form) made over and above the value of the Bitcoin for arranging or carrying out any transactions in Bitcoin will be exempt from VAT under Article 135(1)(d) as outlined at 2., above.
5. However, in all instances, VAT will be due in the normal way from suppliers of any goods or services sold in exchange for Bitcoin or other similar crypto-currency. The value of the supply of goods or services on which VAT is due will be the sterling value of the crypto-currency at the point the transaction takes place
HMRC notes in addition that it is pre-empting an EU-wide decision on how to apply VAT to Bitcoins. If the EU consensus which finally emerges is different from this proposed treatment HMRC will not seek to backdate the consensus treatment (although traders will, presumably, be free to do so).

360 The following table provides **examples of common transactions** associated with the issue of money and the corresponding VAT treatment.

Transaction	Comment
Payment services for household bills	Any charge made for this service is exempt
Foreign exchange transactions	Either as principal or intermediary are exempt
Automated teller machines (cashpoints)	Provision of ATM equipment and software is standard-rated. Replenishment services are standard-rated but any charges levied - for example, for the withdrawal of cash, etc - are exempt. The provision of a site for a cashpoint is a licence to occupy land and is exempt (subject to the option to tax (¶5602+)).

Transaction	Comment
Electronic banking	May be part of a package of services: see ¶310+. If separate charges are made: – for information, they are exempt if related to the customer's accounts at the bank (and are otherwise standard-rated); – for the hire or use of equipment, they are standard-rated; and – for services generally, the tax status depends on the nature of the services supplied and the surrounding circumstances.
Compensation payments for dishonoured cheques	Exempt if paid by a bank; outside the scope of VAT if paid by a supplier.
Deductions from pay	Any charges made by an employer to deduct items such as insurance premiums, or union subscriptions, are exempt. Any charges made to deduct pay under an attachment of earnings order (for example) are seen as expenses incurred in carrying out a statutory duty and are outside the scope of VAT.

2. Loans and credit facilities

Charges (usually in the form of interest) for the making of any advance or the supply of credit are exempt from VAT, **provided that** the separate charge is disclosed to the customer. 362 Notice 701/49 para 4

Scope

This exemption specifically includes the following transactions. 364

a. Free-standing loans or credit advances (including mortgages and overdrafts), where a separate charge is made for the credit.

b. The **management of credit** by the person granting the credit (e.g. credit checking, valuation of assets, monitoring payment records, etc).

c. Hire purchase, conditional sale or credit sale agreements where repayments are required to be made in instalments. If a finance company provides the credit, it must separately disclose the charge to the customer for the credit element to be exempt. If goods are sold on **interest-free credit**, there is no charge for the credit so there is no exempt supply (but VAT is levied on the goods in the normal manner). Any **administration charges** are also exempt, unless the contract explicitly states that the charge relates, wholly or partially, to the supply of goods. Fees relating to the goods are only exempt if they do not exceed £10.

d. Charges made to retailers by card companies in connection with particular credit or debit cards. This includes items such as interest charges and joining fees charged to merchants.

e. Pawnbroking.

f. Deferred payments (e.g. where an annual subscription is payable in instalments over 12 months, any charge for this facility is an exempt supply).

The following are **not exempt supplies**:
- penalties for late payment (these are outside the scope of VAT); and
- discounts for prompt payment (see ¶1000).

Debt assignment

The unencumbered sale of a debt for a consideration is also an exempt supply, with the **value** being the gross amount that the assignee pays for the debt. This may be less than 100% of the debt but this has no effect on the amount of VAT payable on the original supply. 366 Notice 701/49 para 5
CISS Ltd [2004] (VTD 18839)

The VAT treatment of debt assignment transactions depends upon the **method used to assign the debt**.

Factoring, including invoice discounting (see below), is a kind of debt collection service and is taxable. The assignment or transfer of a debt to a factor is not a supply for VAT.

Factors and invoice discounters may provide a number of services to their clients. These might include the prepayment of part of the value of the debt. Any consideration attributable to the latter is regarded as payment for an exempt supply of credit.

The factor's charges to the client may be consideration for a number of standard-rated administrative, clerical and accounting services. The balance, less an agreed retention, is available for the client to draw upon. Where the client draws on the balance, the factor debits a further charge, often described as "discount". This is consideration for the exempt supply of credit by the factor to the client.

In a **recourse** agreement, the responsibility for bearing any loss will be on the client. If the debtor defaults, the factor will reassign the debt to the client. In a **non-recourse** agreement the factor accepts the risk of default and any charge made for doing this is standard-rated. The assignment of a debt under a non-recourse agreement is exempt, whereas the assignment or reassignment of a debt under a recourse agreement is disregarded for VAT purposes.

Service	VAT implications
Discount or interest charge	Exempt supply by the factor
Administration or service charge	Standard-rated supply by the factor
Guarantee of payment	Standard-rated supply by the factor
Fee for advance of funds to client prior to assignment of debt (if charged for separately)	Exempt supply by the factor to the client

Invoice discounting is simply a form of factoring where fewer taxable support services are provided to the client.

VATFIN3225 **Block discounting** is a method of raising finance on goods which are subject to a hire agreement. The supplier assigns an interest in the goods, and the hire purchase income, to a finance company in return for an advance of less than 100% of the total income stream. The difference represents a finance charge.

If title in the goods is transferred to the finance company, there is a supply of goods and the VAT liability depends upon the liability of the goods. The finance house becomes the lessor and accounts for output tax on the rental payments.

If title is not transferred, but the agreement is essentially one of hire purchase or conditional sale, there is no supply of goods for VAT purposes. The assignment of the right to receive income is exempt.

367 **Debt negotiation** services are exempt if the provider of the service brings together the credit provider with the debtor and acts between them to try to bring about a change to the payment terms. On the other hand, **debt collection** services are taxable (see also ¶374). If the debtor's primary aim is to recover the debt rather than to renegotiate the debt, the supply of the service will be taxable. *HBOS plc* [2008]

An **individual voluntary arrangement** (IVA) allows a debtor to pay creditors a (usually) reduced amount according to a structured plan, without undergoing bankruptcy. It requires the services of a nominee (who proposes the terms of the IVA to the creditors) and a supervisor (who ensures that the terms of the IVA are adhered to). Although normally carried out by professionals, these services fall within the exemption for debt negotiation. It is part of the supervisor's duties to collect payments but this is not standard-rated debt collection because the supervisor acts for the debtor, not the creditors. *Paymex Ltd v HMRC* [2011]

HMRC Brief 03/12 HMRC's guidance indicates that the VAT exemption arising from the *Paymex* ruling applies to:

- individual voluntary arrangements;
- company voluntary arrangements;

– partnership voluntary arrangements; and
– protected trust deeds (applicable in Scotland).

HMRC's guidance also states that, despite the views of the tribunal in *Paymex*, only the **nominee** stage of the IVA process is exempt from VAT and the **supervisory** stage will therefore only be exempt when supplied together with the nominee stage. Accordingly, it is HMRC's view that: HMRC Brief 17/13
– if the nominee and supervisor are in the same firm, their services to the debtor would comprise a single exempt supply;
– where a supervisor from a different firm is appointed, either at the creditors' meeting or subsequently as a successor insolvency practitioner, the supervisor's fees will be standard-rated;
– where a new firm acquires a portfolio of cases and a new supervisor is appointed, the supervisor's fees will be standard-rated;
– where a new firm acquires a portfolio of cases but the supervisor moves across with the cases and so remains in office, the supervisor's fees will nonetheless be standard-rated; and
– the only exception would be if an insolvency practitioner could demonstrate that the core part of the service as supervisor is debt negotiation, in which case HMRC says it would "consider exemption". However, HMRC sees this as "unlikely to arise in practice".

HMRC also takes the view that the situation is the same for **company voluntary arrangements**, in that the supervisory stage is likely to give rise to standard-rated supplies.

Insolvency practitioner services in all other insolvency processes remain liable for VAT at the standard rate.

3. Intermediary services

The services of a financial intermediary are exempt, provided that the intermediary is one who: **370** Notice 701/49 paras 6, 9
– brings together a person seeking financial services with a person who provides exempt financial services;
– stands between the parties to a contract and takes an active part in assisting them to reach an agreement; and
– undertakes specialised work preparatory to the completion of a contract for providing financial services, whether or not it is completed.

Such services will **include**, for example:
– the negotiation of a trade in securities between a buyer and a seller;
– underwriting services in connection with dealings in money, etc, only (this therefore excludes underwriting services in connection with loans and credit facilities, which will be standard-rated); and
– services provided by organisations in the securities markets (e.g. assisting with completion of forms, matching parties to share deals and identifying payments for transactions).

Exclusions

The exemption does not cover the following services, which are usually therefore standard-rated: **372**
– credit management (unless it is provided by the person supplying the credit);
– investment advice, analysis, etc (this includes the services of an independent financial adviser);
– financial investigations;
– initial stages of a corporate finance arrangement;
– market research, product design, advertising, etc;
– safe custody services; and
– share registrar services (e.g. registration of grants of probate, or operation of a company share register).

HMRC Brief 11/13 In *Deutsche Bank* C-44/11 the taxpayer was making supplies of both portfolio management and effecting share purchases and sales; the former is standard-rated, the latter exempt. Although the fee for the latter was separately stated, the taxpayer was making a single supply of services for a regular, flat fee. Neither individual service was predominant and the single service could not be described as effecting share purchases and sales; accordingly, the single service could not be exempt from VAT. HMRC has since addressed the practical implications of this decision. If a portfolio manager charges regular fees and carries out both portfolio management and share transactions, that will be a single, standard-rated supply, even if the share transaction fee is separately identified. Share transaction fees will **only be exempt** if they are charged specifically per transaction. Until 1 December 2013 HMRC allowed exemption of share transaction fees if separately identified, even if charged on a periodic basis.
Finanzamt Frankfurt am Main V-Höchst v Deutsche Bank AG [2012]

Notice 701/49 para 1.8 MEMO POINTS 1. It is HMRC's view that **outsourced financial services** are not exempt from VAT simply because the customer is making exempt supplies. The VAT liability of the outsourced service provider depends on the nature of the services actually performed.
2. There is a practice known as **soft commissioning**, whereby intermediaries will, in recognition of the amount of business a client has put through them, use some of the commission received to fund further services for the client (for example, for every £1.20 received in commission, the intermediary will use £1 to fund further services on behalf of the client). Such supplies are outside the scope of VAT.

Card processing

374 Business Brief 18/06 HMRC treats charges made to process debit and credit cards as VAT-exempt supplies of card-handling services, provided that:
- the **charge is levied by** an agent acting for the supplier; and
- the **service supplied by** the agent includes transmitting the card information, security information and the card issuer's authorisation codes to its own bank.

It therefore follows that in HMRC's view charges for card-handling services are not exempt (and the VAT treatment matches the liability of the goods or services supplied) if they are levied:
- for any other type of card-handling service (e.g. the collection of card information from the customer, the transmission of that information to the card issuer and receiving authorisation codes from the card issuer); or
- by the supplier. If a supplier requires a customer to pay an additional charge, for payment by credit or debit card, that charge is treated as further consideration for the purchase of the goods or services.

However, the First-tier Tribunal has held that the supply may be exempt notwithstanding that:
- the charge does not approximate to the cost suffered by the supplier for the service in question (in this case NEC charged considerably more than it had to pay for the service); and
- the supplier did not act directly with the card issuer to effect payment but instead was part of the chain of suppliers which effected payment.

National Exhibition Centre Ltd [2013] (TC02695)

Comment Since this decision contradicts points of detail in Business Brief 18/06, HMRC will be keenly awaiting the result of a referral to the CJEU in *Bookit Ltd* [2014] (TC03972), which may provide helpful guidance, or may merely remind member states that it is up to them to interpret the law, not the CJEU.

EXAMPLE

1. A company that took bookings for Odeon cinemas through call centres and the Internet charged a fee of 50p for dealing with credit/debit cards (in addition to the normal cost of a cinema ticket). It was held that the taking of card details from the customer, obtaining security codes from the card issuers and then transmitting this data to its bank was an essential element of taking the payment, and fell within the exemption for financial services. *Bookit Ltd v C & E* [2006]

2. Contrast the case above with the situation where a company owned premises which were leased for public exhibitions and events. The company charged a booking fee on sales of tickets by credit card. In this particular case, it was held that the booking fees charged did not fall within the exemption for financial services on the basis that:
– the booking fee greatly exceeded the credit charge levied on the transaction; and
– the box office and telephone service provided was extensive (for example, staff regularly gave information about future events, parking and restaurant facilities). These services enabled the better promotion of the company exhibition premises as a good venue for future promoters, etc. *Scottish Exhibition Centre v C & E* [2006]

3. A payment processing fee charged by a telecommunications provider for certain methods of payment was part of the overall supply of telecommunications and did not represent an exempt financial service in its own right. The CJEU has confirmed this decision. *Everything Everywhere Ltd (formerly T-Mobile (UK) Ltd)* [2010]

4. A company in Axa's group ran a dental insurance scheme. It collected premiums from members and used them to pay reinsurance premiums and its own commission. The remainder was paid to the dentists who provided services under the scheme to the members. The VAT Tribunal identified transactions carried out by the company which constituted exempt payment processing similar to the services in *Bookit* (2006 decision). However, the CJEU held that in this context the company was acting as a debt collector (although the members were not behind with their payments), not a payment processor and as such was not making any exempt supplies. *HMRC v Axa UK plc* [2010]

4. Management of special investment funds

In general, the **management** of any investment fund is taxable. However, the management of the following types of investment fund is exempt: **376** Notice 701/49 para 7
– authorised unit trust schemes;
– authorised contractual schemes;
– open-ended collective investment undertakings (CIUs);
– closed-ended CIUs;
– investment trust companies (ITCs); and
– venture capital trusts (VCTs).

Definitions and conditions

A **CIU** is an entity in the business of collective investment. It raises capital from the public and invests it in return for a fee (or "management charge"). This management charge is exempt from VAT, provided that the applicable conditions are satisfied. **377** VATFIN5260, 5280

Open-ended CIUs have variable capital. The number of shares in issue continually changes, as new shares are issued to new investors and shares are cancelled when investors decide to cash them in. They include recognised overseas schemes, which are established and authorised in one of the following places and have notified the FSA of their intention to market to UK investors:
– another EU member state;
– Jersey, Guernsey, Bermuda or the Isle of Man; or
– anywhere else which is regulated similarly to UK collective investments.

An open-ended CIU must also satisfy a **de minimis condition**. A scheme which has been marketed to UK retail investors, but is no longer so marketed, is not covered by the VAT exemption if less than 5% of its shares or units are held by UK retail investors (but not institutional investors) at the time that active marketing ceases. After that, if the level of investment by UK retail investors falls below 5%, the exemption ceases to apply. Schemes which have never been marketed in the UK do not fall within the exemption.

Closed-ended CIUs have fixed capital. Shares are traded on a stock exchange rather than redeemed and issued. The conditions for the management fees to be exempted are that:
– the sole object is to raise capital from the public and invest it wholly or mainly in securities;
– the assets must be managed on the principle of spreading risk; and

– all of the ordinary shares are included on the UK official list and are admitted to trading on a regulated market in the UK.

Many larger CIUs are structured as an **umbrella fund with sub-funds**. The exemption only applies to those sub-funds which are actively marketed to UK investors. The de minimis condition above also applies.

MEMO POINTS 1. Prior to 1 October 2008 exemption did not extend to open- and closed-ended CIUs which were not companies. It was extended to them following the decision in *JP Morgan Fleming Claverhouse Trust plc* [2007].

Sch 9 Group 5 notes 6, 6A VATA 1994; SI 2008/1982

2. An **authorised unit trust** is defined as a unit trust authorised under FSMA 2000.
3. The CJEU has held that a **defined benefit** pension scheme is **not** a special investment fund, management of which is an exempt supply. This is because "the members of the scheme do not bear the risk arising from the management of the fund and the contributions which the employer pays into the scheme are a means by which he complies with his legal obligations towards his employees". *Wheels Common Investment Fund Trustees Ltd and others v HMRC* [2013] C-424/11
4. On the other hand, the CJEU has also held that a **defined contribution** pension scheme **can be** a special investment fund, because it is the members of the scheme which bear the investment risk. *ATP PensionService A/S v Skatteministeriet* [2014] C-464/12

Meaning of "management"

378 Exempt fund management covers the following **key activities**:
– assessment of financial and investment risk;
– making decisions regarding investments, including purchase and disposal; and
– involvement in the property held by the fund.

Business Brief 7/06

Other **peripheral activities** which qualify for exemption include the following (provided that they are subsumed into a single composite supply (¶310+) of fund management services):
– legal and fund management accounting services;
– dealing with customer queries;
– value and pricing (including tax returns);
– regulatory compliance monitoring;
– management of the unit-holder register;
– distribution of income;
– unit issues and redemptions;
– contract settlements (including certificate despatch); and
– record-keeping.

However, fund management **excludes** the services of trustees or depositories.

Third party involvement

380 Business Brief 7/06

The **administration** of a CIU may be delegated to a third party. In this case, the third party need not perform all of the regulatory administrative functions required by the Financial Services Authority. However, it would be usual for a bundle of services to be supplied, incorporating some of the various activities listed above. An isolated service (for example, legal drafting of documents, or an external audit of fund accounts) does not automatically become exempt because it relates to an investment fund. If a third party is delegated to carry out a package of administrative services which overall has the distinct characteristic of a single supply of fund management services, this too will be exempt.

EXAMPLE

1. A company acted as the authorised corporate director of an OEIC. However, the management of the fund was subcontracted to eight different fund managers, who undertook the following functions:
– computing the amount of income;
– calculating the price of units or shares;
– valuation of assets;
– accounting;
– preparation of statements for the distribution of income;
– preparation of information and documentation for periodic accounts;
– income forecasts;

- tax returns;
- data processing;
- record-keeping; and
- dealing with customers.

HMRC challenged the exemption of the company's services, proposing that the company was making a taxable supply.

The CJEU held that "fund management" could be interpreted as meaning that a third party could administratively manage a fund, provided that the services supplied formed a distinct whole, being specific to, and essential for, the fund's management. In this case, all of the activities undertaken combined to effect fund management. *Abbey National plc v HMRC (No 2)* [2006]

2. The CJEU has held that **advisory** services concerning investment in transferable securities, provided by a third party to an investment management company which is the manager of a special investment fund, are themselves exempt management of special investment funds. *GfBk Gesellschaft für Börsenkommunikation mbH v Finanzamt Bayreuth* [2013] C-275/11

B. Cultural services

Cultural services include the supply by a public body, or a non-profit-making organisation, of **admission** to: 384 Sch 9 Group 13 VATA 1994
- a museum, gallery, art exhibition or zoo; or
- a theatrical, musical or choreographic performance of a cultural nature.

Exempt admission charges

The following admission charges are exempt: 386 Notice 701/47; Business Brief 28/03

Admission to	Charged by	Conditions
- museums[1]; - galleries/art exhibitions; - zoos; and - theatrical, musical or choreographic performances	Local authorities, government departments or non-departmental public bodies	Unless exemption is likely to distort competition and put a commercial organisation at a disadvantage
	Non-profit-making organisations	The performance must be provided by one or more of the bodies of the type in column 2

Note:
1. There is **no definition** of a museum or gallery; each case is taken on its own merits.

MEMO POINTS Charging for admission to premises is a business activity (¶247+); if the charge is not exempt any related input tax can be recovered.

Non-profit-making organisations

A non-profit-making organisation is one which: 388 Sch 9 Group 13 note 2 VATA 1994; VCULTURE2100 - 2400
- is prohibited from distributing its **profits**;
- **reinvests** any profits from its cultural activities to the continuance or improvement of cultural facilities; and
- is **managed and administered** on an essentially (i.e. not exclusively) voluntary basis by persons who have no direct or indirect financial interest in its activities.

MEMO POINTS 1. If **person(s) managing the organisation** at the highest level are remunerated, the body will not qualify for exemption, even if those individuals waive their rights to receive the remuneration. If the only persons remunerated are those simply implementing the policy decisions, the organisation will qualify for exemption.
2. In HMRC's view **direct or indirect financial interest** will only affect entitlement to exemption if the interest is actual, not potential. The following are HMRC's examples of **actual** interest. HMRC Brief 27/07

Element	Actual financial interest	No actual financial interest
Amount and basis of payments	If the payments are: – above the market rate; – paid as routine overheads; or – profit-related (whether below, at, or above market rates)	If the payments are: – allowed by the constitution; or – not above market rates and/or are not linked to profits
Level of participation in decision-making	If there is a link between the payments and the individual's participation in the direction of the activities of the cultural body	If the recipient of a contract award is excluded from any decision-making regarding the award of that contract
Ability to profit from entity		If the only potential is for a financial loss (for example, where a risk is underwritten or guaranteed, so that the guarantor only stands to lose money and not gain money as a result)

390 Where admission is granted in return only for **buying a programme** (which is zero-rated anyway), HMRC will accept that this constitutes a single supply of admission, with the programme being only ancillary to the admission charge.

C. Charity fundraising events

392
Sch 9 Group 12 VATA 1994; Notice 701/1 para 5.9; HMRC Brief 36/08; VAT Manual V1-9 para 9.3

The supply of goods and services in connection with a charitable event is exempt if:
a. the **supply is made by** either a charity or non-profit-making organisation;
b. the **event is organised for** charitable purposes, or the purposes of the non-profit-making organisation; and
c. the **primary purpose** of the event is to raise money.

This exemption **also covers**:
– all admission charges;
– the sale of commemorative brochures;
– the sale of advertising space in those brochures;
– any other items sold by the charity, etc, at the event (for example, T-shirts, non-donated auctioned goods), unless the items would normally be zero-rated (¶1180+); and
– sponsorship payments directly connected with the qualifying event.

HMRC's views in this area are set out in a **helpsheet** entitled *Fund-raising events: Exemption for charities and other qualifying bodies*, available online at flmemo.co.uk/vm392.

MEMO POINTS 1. For the definition of a **charity** see ¶8005. See ¶8000+ for further details of charities generally.
2. A **non-profit-making body** falls within this exemption only if it is:
– a trade union, professional association or other public interest body (¶476);
– an eligible sporting body (¶418+); or
– an eligible cultural organisation (¶388+).
3. Supplies are only exempt if made **by** the charity or non-profit-making body. Supplies made **to** the charity or body retain their normal VAT status even if made in connection with a charitable event.

Exceptions

394
Sch 9 Group 12 notes 4, 9, 11 VATA 1994

The exemption **does not cover**:
– multiple events at the same location throughout the year (where a charity, etc, organises more than 15 events of the same kind in the same location in any one financial year, none of the events is exempt; an event is ignored for this purpose if its gross takings in any week are less than £1,000);

– commemorative goods sold after a fundraising event (including, for example, audio or video recordings);
– events where accommodation is also provided for more than two nights (for example, holiday fundraising events); and
– activities where the exemption would be likely to distort competition with VAT-registered commercial providers.

Where an event includes a **package of travel and accommodation**, bought-in accommodation, or more than two nights' accommodation from the charity's own resources, the charity will be making a taxable supply. The value of the taxable supply depends on whether the charity is **acting as principal or undisclosed agent**, or as a disclosed agent for a third-party organiser. **396** Sch 9 Group 12 notes 8, 9 VATA 1994

If the charity is acting as principal, it must use the tour operators' margin scheme, TOMS (¶7490+), to calculate the value of the supply. If the charity is acting as a **disclosed agent**, it is taxable on the commission received from the company organising the event. In **all other cases**, the charity will be deemed to be acting as principal and must use TOMS.

MEMO POINTS 1. If **payment is made before** the participant is allowed to take part, there will be a taxable supply for VAT purposes. It does not matter how the payment is calculated. For example, the payment may be a registration fee, deposit, or prepayment of part of the fundraising target. Notice 701/1 para 5.9
2. HMRC's guidance states that the charity will be a **disclosed agent** if there is an agreement between the charity and the company organising the event that the charity can act as the company's agent, or the organising company is disclosed to the participant. For example, a company's name may be on the tickets or marketing literature and the charity is not taking any commercial risk regarding the organisation of the event. Notice 701/1 para 10.2
3. The guidance applies equally to **trading subsidiaries** which charities might use for fundraising.

D. Education and sporting services

1. Education

Educational supplies will be exempt if they are of a specified type and are provided by an **eligible body**. Both of these requirements are detailed in the table below. **398** Sch 9 Group 6 VATA 1994;

The supply must also be made **in the course of a business**. If it is not (for example, if the education is free, or funded by national or local government), it will be outside the scope of VAT. If a charge is made but does not cover the full cost of the education and the balance is (for example) funded by government grants, the activities will be partly business and partly non-business. An apportionment must then be made. Notice 701/30

The exemption extends to the provision of:
– educational services, including vocational training (¶402+);
– research (¶408); and
– **closely related** goods and services (¶410).

Type of supply	¶¶	Provided by
Education, research or vocational training	¶402+	Schools, universities [1], sixth form colleges, tertiary or further education colleges or other centrally funded higher or further education institutions Public bodies [2] Charities and other non-profit-making organisations which carry out essentially public natured educational services Commercial providers of tuition of English as a foreign language (EFL) [3]
Private tuition	¶412	
Examination services	¶414	
Youth club facilities	¶416	

Note:
1. HMRC takes the view that **subsidiary companies set up by universities**, etc, will not qualify as eligible bodies where these companies do not have educational services as their principal purpose (e.g. a subsidiary company set up to operate the students' union). *University of Leicester Students' Union v C & E* [2001]

Information Sheet 3/10 However, a university-owned or university-controlled company with close academic links to its parent university, which is delivering university-level education leading to a qualification, is likely, in HMRC's view, to be acting as a college or an institution of the university and therefore to be an eligible body. Absence of formal recognition as an eligible body, or the fact that the company may trade with a view to profit, does not exclude it from classification as such.

2. For HMRC's view of what constitutes a public body see ¶7832+.

3. The exemption granted to **commercial providers of EFL tuition** is a specific exemption. Other commercial operators (e.g. secretarial colleges) are not within the exemption.

EC Directive 2006/112 art 132.1(i); Sch 9 Group 6 VATA 1994

EXAMPLE The Principal VAT Directive exempts education supplied "by bodies governed by public law having such as their aim or by other organisations recognised by the Member State concerned as having similar objects". The UK implementing legislation exempts education supplied by an "eligible body", which Note 1 to Sch 9, Group 6, VAT Act 1994 defines to include "a United Kingdom university, and any college, institution, school or hall of such a university". London College of Computing (LCC) sought exemption on the basis that it was a "college ... of" Middlesex University. The First-tier Tribunal (FTT) dismissed LCC's appeal, partly on the basis that students did not "typically progress" to a university degree at MU after taking a course at LCC. The Upper Tribunal agreed with LCC that there was no such test that for an institution to be a college of a university, students of that institution must typically progress to a degree. However, LCC was nonetheless not a college of MU and the FTT had been right so to hold. **A college of a university** must at least be recognised as such in some way by the university, in practice if not in those exact terms (LCC was not so recognised by MU). Moreover, the FTT should have considered (and did so, in fact) whether the objects of LCC were "substantially the provision of university education" (thus similar to the aim of MU) and whether LCC was "adequately enmeshed with" MU. LCC's appeal was dismissed. *London College of Computing Ltd v HMRC* [2013]

399 Certain transactions involving educational supplies must be **reported** to HMRC (¶3064+).

a. Mainstream education and training

Educational services

402 Notice 701/30 These are not defined by the legislation, and must therefore be given their ordinary everyday meaning of instruction and assessment (as opposed to mere supervision, etc) and will **include**:
- lectures, seminars, conferences;
- holiday, sporting and recreational courses; and
- distance teaching and associated materials (provided that the student is subject to assessment by the teaching institution).

The **key factor** to consider is the primary function of the eligible body. If that function is educational, the body should qualify for exemption, even if it also has a small recreational element. *Allied Dancing Association* [1993] (VTD 10777)

Bodies which carry out predominantly recreational activities are unlikely to qualify for exemption.

EXAMPLE Charges for admission to a zoo were held not to be in return for supplies made for educational purposes, as the primary function of the zoo was not educational but recreational. *North of England Zoological Society v C & E* [1999]

MEMO POINTS Note that *Allied Dancing Association* was decided on legislation which was replaced in 1994. Such a case might not now be decided in favour of exemption.

404 **Vocational training** Supplies made in the course of vocational training will be exempt from VAT if they are:
- made by an eligible body (¶398); or
- subcontracted to a non-eligible body which is funded by a government-approved vocational training scheme.

MEMO POINTS **Government-approved vocational training schemes** are: Notice 701/30 para 13.1
a. schemes approved by:
– the Department for Education;
– the Department for Work and Pensions (through Job Centre Plus); or
– devolved administrations in Wales, Scotland and Northern Ireland;
b. schemes administered and funded by:
– the Education Funding Agency (EFA) (previously the Young People's Learning Association (YPLA));
– the Skills Funding Agency (SFA);
– local authorities in England (working together with the EFA);
– the Welsh Assembly;
– Skills Development Scotland; and
– the Training and Employment Agency in Northern Ireland;
c. approved schemes which are paid for using funds derived from the European Social Fund;
d. further education colleges, funded by any of the bodies in **a**. and **b**.;
e. training workplace assessors in connection with National Vocational Qualifications; and
f. training in additional skills for use in the workplace (for example, to Health and Safety and First Aid Officers).

Vocational training **consists of** training, retraining or work experience (including goods and services provided direct to trainees) for any paid employment or voluntary work in areas beneficial to the community (e.g. health, safety, or charity work). **406** Notice 701/30 para 5.3

Supplies which are not directly related to vocational training are **excluded** from exemption - for example:
– funding which is received by the training provider to pass directly on to the trainees e.g. travel costs, living expenses, etc (outside the scope of VAT);
– any charge made by a training provider (including statutory living allowances payable to unemployed trainees) to a business which is providing work experience to a trainee (standard-rated); and
– counselling, advice, careers guidance, etc (standard-rated).

Research

With effect from 1 August 2013, the exemption for business supplies of research services between eligible bodies has been withdrawn. This followed notification from the European Commission that the exemption did not comply with European legislation. However, a significant proportion of such research is in any case outside the scope of VAT. This is because whilst such research appears to be supplied by one eligible body to another, there is in fact no supply because the research is carried out by both bodies on a collaborative basis. HMRC has issued detailed guidance on the manifold situations in which there will be no supply of services within the scope of VAT. **408** Notice 701/30 para 5.6; HMRC Brief 10/13

Transitional measures were put in place to ease the withdrawal of the exemption. HMRC Brief 21/13; Information Sheet 11/13

Research **other than** that provided between eligible bodies qualifies for exemption if it **consists of** original investigation with the intention of expanding knowledge or understanding in a particular area (including devising software for use in a research project). Here the **key factor** is the intention at the start of the process. If the intention is there but in fact there was no expansion of existing knowledge, the activities should still qualify for exemption.

EXAMPLE Support and maintenance of a database coupled with the production of useful applied information from the database was held to be research for the purposes of the exemption. *Joseph Rowntree Foundation* [1996] (VTD 14534)

Closely related goods and services

To be exempt the supply must be made by an **eligible body** (¶398). Supplies made otherwise will not qualify for this exemption, even if made to an eligible body. **410** Notice 701/30 para 8

Supplies related to education are treated as follows:

Provided to	Type of supply	Treatment
– pupils/students; – another educational institution; or – a non-educational eligible body (¶398), provided that the recipient intends to use the supplies for a qualifying educational purpose	– supplies necessary for the direct use of the pupils/ students or the delivery of the education; – accommodation; – catering; – transport; or – school trips/field trips	Exempt
	Ancillary to the supply of education, e.g.: – sales of surplus goods; – admission charges (other than for taking part in sporting activities); and – administration and management charges	Non-exempt
Others, such as staff or non-eligible bodies		Non-exempt

MEMO POINTS 1. It is not sufficient for an educational institution to **interpose a subsidiary company** in the supply chain between itself and the recipient of educational or vocational training services in order to make the institution's supplies subject to VAT. The taxpayer (an eligible body) assigned its contract with the Secretary of State to a subsidiary company and entered into an agreement with the subsidiary to provide services to allow the subsidiary to carry out the educational supplies. In reality the institution remained in control of staff, provision of courses and awarding of qualifications. There was no material change from the position before the contract was assigned. Therefore the eligible body's supply remained exempt, although it was now supplied to its subsidiary rather than to the Secretary of State. *HMRC v Board of Governors of Robert Gordon University* [2008]

2. The Upper Tribunal has confirmed that supplies closely related to education **do not have to be made to the student** in order to be exempt. In this case the college organised restaurant meals and theatrical entertainments, for which tickets were sold to students' friends and family. The supplies were held to be exempt, albeit that supplies of catering and entertainment were made to friends and family, not to the students themselves. Exemption was afforded to these supplies because the events concerned were put on solely in order to educate the students (who themselves did the cooking or performed the entertainments). The supplies were thus closely related to the students' education (in catering or entertainment). *HMRC v Brockenhurst College* [2014]

b. Private tuition

412 Notice 701/30 para 6

Private tuition will be exempt if it is:
– **provided by** a sole proprietor or member of a partnership (as opposed to by an employee or person connected with the business); and
– in a **subject** that is regularly taught in a number of schools or universities.

Where one or more other teachers are employed **to assist the tutor**, the services of the employees will be standard-rated, so it is necessary either to:
– apportion supplies between exempt and standard-rated; or
– treat all supplies as taxable.

It is immaterial whether the **recipients** of the tuition are individuals or organisations and it can be provided on a one-to-one or group basis.

Note that **goods and services** provided by a tutor are not exempt, even if closely related to the educational activity.

MEMO POINTS 1. Cases in this area tend to turn on whether the subject matter of the lessons is of a type "usually" taught in schools; reported cases have usually been decided against the teacher. For example, driving lessons (*MC Smith (t/a Qualified School of Motoring)* [2006] (VTD 20275)), tran-

scendental meditation (*C Beckley (t/a The College of Meditation)* [2005] (VTD 19860)) and yoga (*Stuart Tranter t/a Dynamic Yoga* [2014] (TC04071)) have been held not to be of such a type.
2. A subject will not be school or university education if it is "purely recreational". However, even if it is more educational than recreational, it will nonetheless not qualify for exemption if it is only provided at an insignificant number of institutions. Thus supplies of tuition in pilates were not exempt. *Christine Joy Hocking* [2014] (TC04130)

c. Examination services

Examination services will be exempt if they are either **provided**: 414 Notice 701/30 para 7
a. by or to an eligible body (¶398); or
b. to an individual receiving education or vocational training which is either exempt or outside the scope of VAT (because the activity is not pursued as part of a business activity).
Examination services **include**:
– setting and marking examinations (e.g. GCSEs, AS levels);
– setting educational training standards;
– making assessments; and
– services provided with a view to ensuring educational and training standards are maintained (e.g. inspections, registering candidates, etc).

d. Youth clubs

Facilities provided by a qualifying youth club (or an association of youth clubs) to its members will be exempt if: 416 Notice 701/35
– they are provided to members **in return for** subscriptions (or an additional payment); and
– the facilities are **directly related** to the club's ordinary activities.

MEMO POINTS 1. A **qualifying youth club** will:
– have members that are mainly under 21 years of age;
– have its own constitution and produce its own accounts; and
– not distribute any of its profits (instead reinvesting any profits made in providing services to its members).
2. **Single activity clubs** (e.g. swimming clubs) and **youth sections** of larger organisations are not youth clubs for the purpose of this exemption, unless they are separately constituted.

2. Sporting and physical education services

Supplies by an **eligible body** of the following are exempt: 418 Sch 9 Group 10 VATA 1994
– entry to certain sporting activity and physical recreation **competitions**; and
– sporting or physical education services.

Eligible bodies

An eligible body is one established for sporting or recreational purposes and which is: 419 Notice 701/45 paras 4, 5
– non-profit-making;
– bound by its constitution to limit any distribution of surpluses to another non-profit-making body, or to its members on dissolution; and
– free from commercial influence.

MEMO POINTS 1. HMRC publishes a list of activities which it regards as falling within the **definition of sporting activity** in Notice 701/45. This list is not exhaustive and applications from other sporting bodies will be considered.
2. **Commercial influence** means that the body either:
– is part of a wider commercial undertaking;
– receives from a commercial body a grant of land (other than for sports purposes), a supply of services, or any other supply for more than market price; or
– pays emoluments which are related to its level of income or profits.
A sports club for company employees may receive supplies from the company without falling foul of these rules.

Competition entry fees

420 Notice 701/45 para 6

The grant of a right to enter a competition in a sporting activity or physical recreation is exempt from VAT where:
- the consideration to enter is in money and the **total amount** of the entry fees is put towards a prize for that competition; or
- the right to enter is granted by an eligible body.

If the entry fee includes the body's normal fee for admission to its grounds or facilities, that part is not exempt. If the fee is a composite supply (¶310+), it may still all be exempt but otherwise an apportionment is required.

MEMO POINTS HMRC guidance states that **physical recreation** includes such activities as greyhound or pigeon racing, clay pigeon shooting and darts, but excludes non-physical activities such as chess, card games, dominoes, spot the ball competitions, etc.

Services related to sport

422 Sch 9 Group 10 item 3 VATA 1994 Notice 701/45 para 3

The provision of sporting or physical education services will be exempt if they are **provided by an eligible body** and are:
- closely related to sporting activities;
- essential to the sport in question; and
- provided to an individual who is taking part in the activity.

This will therefore **include** such activities as umpiring, coaching, use of changing rooms and playing equipment.

Exemption **does not extend to** supplies of residential accommodation, catering or transport.

Where there is no subscription involved, supplies by non-profit-making organisations of services relating to sport or physical education to **persons taking part** in such activities are exempt. The CJEU has considered the scope of the term "persons" and held that the services must be both closely linked to sport or physical education and supplied to the person taking part, but that the exemption could apply to activities carried out on an individual basis and also to sports carried on **in groups or through clubs**. *Canterbury Hockey Club and Canterbury Ladies Hockey Club* [2008]

MEMO POINTS 1. The First-tier Tribunal held in 2011 that UK law was wrong to exclude exemption in relation to supplies of sporting services to non-members. The decision limited exemption to cases where the club budgeted year on year for income from non-members and that income was used to meet the club's ordinary running expenses. More generally, exemption of supplies to non-members was later confirmed by the CJEU. *HMRC v Bridport and West Dorset Golf Club Ltd* [2013] The UK legislation was amended from 1 January 2015 to remove the distinction between supplies to members and those to non-members.
2. Sports **coaching by professionals** is not within the exemption, as it is not provided by a non-profit-making body, although it may qualify for exemption as a vocational educational service.
3. **Membership subscriptions** are usually exempt where they entitle the member to take part in the sporting activity. If there are any significant non-playing benefits as a result of the subscription, an apportionment may need to be made. Purely social or non-playing membership subscriptions are standard-rated. A payment for a right to be on a waiting list does not normally qualify for exemption unless it forms part of the first subscription or entrance fee, or is refundable if the person does not eventually become a member. A joining fee may entitle a member to benefits additional to those provided by the subscription and, if so, its VAT status depends on the nature of those benefits.
4. Services cannot be exempt if they are linked to the **operation of the sports club** rather than the sporting activities. An example of such a service would be marketing and sponsorship advice. In addition, services cannot be exempt if their basic purpose is to obtain additional income for the supplier in direct competition with commercial enterprises which are liable to VAT.

HMRC Brief 25/14

Comment HMRC has accepted the CJEU's ruling in the *Bridport* case that supplies of sporting services by non-profit-making bodies are exempt from VAT whether supplied to members or non-members. HMRC is now ready to deal with claims and has issued preliminary guidance. The four-year time limit on claims will be enforced strictly. Moreover, HMRC is saying that it expects claimants to reimburse their customers as a condition of HMRC making a repayment (HMRC is relying on the unjust enrichment defence); since claimants will also have to make an input tax adjustment to reflect the reduction in taxable supplies in their partial exemption calculation for the affected periods, claimants will be worse off overall if they **do make a claim** under these conditions. The next step, therefore, is for a claimant to **challenge** HMRC's reliance on the unjust enrichment defence. Such a claimant would have to show that the price charged to non-members was such that the claimant can be shown to have absorbed the VAT charge. The claimant might also show that the price it charged to non-members took into account the input tax it could claim on the basis that the supply was standard-rated.

E. Health and welfare

1. Health services

Most services (including related goods and services) provided in the health sector will be exempt, provided that: **425** Sch 9 Group 7 VATA 1994
- the supply is for medical (as opposed to, for example, cosmetic) purposes; and
- its **primary intention** is to protect, maintain or restore the health of an individual.

Medical care

The supply of services consisting of the **provision of medical care** by a person or persons who are enrolled or registered on various medical and dental registers is exempt. This includes: **426** Notice 701/31; Notice 701/57
a. persons registered as:
- medical practitioners;
- ophthalmic or dispensing opticians (although any spectacles provided are standard-rated);
- osteopaths;
- chiropractors;
- health visitors, midwives or nurses;
- health professionals registered under the Health Professions Order 2001 (this will include podiatrists, dieticians, occupational therapists, etc);
- dentists, dental surgeons, dental hygienists or dental technicians;
- pharmacists (although drugs supplied are zero-rated (¶1332+));
- dispensers of hearing aids (and those employing dispensers of hearing aids); and
- practitioner psychologists.

The exemption also applies to services of persons who are not registered or enrolled as above, on condition that the services are either:
- **wholly performed** by a registered or enrolled person (for example, where the service is provided by a company through an employee who is such a person); or
- **directly supervised by** such a person.

MEMO POINTS 1. The requirement to be registered or enrolled excludes **alternative therapists** such as acupuncturists, hypnotherapists and homeopaths.
2. The requirement that the primary purpose of the services must be to **protect, maintain or restore the health of an individual** does not impact on primary health care and core NHS services, which remain free from VAT. However, for some supplies, the VAT liability will be dependent on the purpose for which the supply is made (the "purpose test"). HMRC Brief 06/07; Notice 701/57 para 2.5
HMRC details the following **examples** of supplies which will usually be standard-rated:
- paternity testing;
- writing of articles and reports;
- services directly supervised by a pharmacist; and
- general administrative services, such as countersigning passport applications and providing character references.
3. **Direct supervision** is interpreted by HMRC to require a strict set of conditions. The service must be supervised by a registered health professional (as listed above) who: Notice 701/57 para 5.3
- has a direct relationship with the staff performing the service;

– is contractually responsible for providing supervision and can demonstrate having monitored the work done; and
– has a say in the level of care to be provided to the client (usually by seeing the client prior to the commencement of the service).
A supervising professional must be available for the whole time that the care service is provided; no one professional may supervise more than 2,000 hours per week of staff time.
4. When **drugs are administered by a doctor**, they will form part of an exempt supply but where a **doctor supplies drugs** to a patient because, for example, the patient is unable to get to a pharmacist, the doctor is treated as a pharmacist for VAT purposes and the supply will be zero-rated (NHS prescription supplies) or standard-rated (private prescription supplies). *Dr Beynon and partners v C & E* [2004]
5. Services of **psychologists excluded from VAT exemption**, which therefore remain taxable, include:
– services of psychologists who work only in academic research and experimental psychology and do not offer services to the general public; and
– services that are not primarily for the benefit of the patient - for example, assessing patients' mental condition for legal reasons at the request of a third party.
6. **Group therapy services** supplied to persons who wish to overcome nicotine addiction can be exempt from VAT under the exemption for medical care when provided under the direct supervision of a qualified doctor. The care suppliers do not have to be medically qualified; they merely have to be supervised by someone who is so qualified. *Allen Carr's Easyway (International) Ltd* [2009] (TC00136)

Supplies of staff

427 Sch 9 Group 7 item 5 VATA 1994; Notice 701/57 para 6; HMRC Brief 12/10

Most supplies of health professional staff are taxable for VAT purposes. This includes:
– the supply of most types of health professionals to a hospital or medical practice; and
– the supply through an agency of the services of a **self-employed locum GP**, even though that GP is a registered person.

The fact that the agency or other body supplying the staff is state-regulated does not change this position.

However, the following supplies of staff are exempt:
– the services of a deputising doctor, as provided by the doctor in person;
– **subcontracted health care**, in which a state-regulated body provides welfare services to the final consumer which are contracted and paid for by a local authority or other third party; and
– subject to conditions, the supply by a state-regulated agency of nurses (including midwives, nursing auxiliaries and care assistants).

MEMO POINTS 1. The exemption for **nurses** is non-statutory and is known as the "nurses' concession". To qualify, the nurse must be registered (or supervised by a registered person) and must supply the patient with some direct form of medical care (as opposed to personal care such as washing or catering, or general work in a care home).
2. The First-tier Tribunal has confirmed that the supply of a **deputising doctor** by an **agency** is standard-rated.
Sch 9, Group 7, item 5, VAT Act 1994 provides that "the provision of a deputy for a person registered in the register of medical practitioners" is exempt. This suggests that the supply of a deputy by an agency is exempt, as well as the supply of medical care by the deputy in person. The Tribunal decided that this literal interpretation cannot be right, in view of the Principal VAT Directive's limitation of the exemption to "the provision of medical care in the exercise of the medical and paramedical professions". The Tribunal therefore decided that item 5 should be read as saying "the provision of [medical care services provided by] a deputy for a person registered in the register of medical practitioners", with the words in brackets to be implied. Supplies of **locum** staff by agencies are therefore standard-rated. *Rapid Sequence Ltd* [2013] (TC02826)

2. Related goods and services

428 The following related goods and services are also exempt from VAT:
– the supply of **minor goods** (¶430) required at the time of supply of medical services;
– **care** (including medical and surgical treatment) provided in hospitals and state-regulated institutions (¶432);

– **welfare** services (¶434+);
– the supply of **human blood** (including products derived from human blood), organs or tissue (¶438);
– **transport** for sick or injured people (e.g. ambulances), although this does not include the transport of human organs for transplant operations; and
– **making goods available for hire** if they are let in connection with the supply of health services.

In HMRC's view the supply of laboratory pathology services that directly relate to the provision of healthcare for individual patients is exempt from VAT. This applies to all businesses that are **state-regulated** and supply laboratory pathology testing services, whether they supply the services to the NHS or to independent hospitals. On the other hand, exemption does not apply when the services are not: HMRC Brief 16/13
– concerned with the protection, maintenance or restoration of the health of specific patients - for example, the analysis of samples for general research purposes or for autopsies; or
– performed primarily for the protection, maintenance or restoration of the health of the person concerned but are done solely to provide a third party with information necessary for taking a decision on a non-medical matter, such as an insurance claim, or for legal purposes.

Minor goods

Where minor goods are provided at the time of the care they will fall within the scope of the exemption if they are inseparable from the treatment. This will **include**, for example, bandages, dressings, prostheses and the administration of drugs. Items which are separable from the treatment (for example, privately dispensed drugs supplied for self-medication during overseas travel) will not be exempt. **430** Notice 701/57 para 3

MEMO POINTS Although by this rule contraceptives are not exempt, they may be reduced-rated (¶1110+).

Care given in certain premises

Goods and services are exempt if they are for care, medical or surgical treatment **provided in** institutions that are approved, licensed or registered as: **432** Sch 9 Group 7 item 4 VATA 1994; Notice 701/31 para 2
– hospitals, hospices, nursing homes;
– children's homes, residential homes for needy people;
– nurseries, crèches, playgroups; or
– after-school clubs (or similar providers of non-residential care for children).

Specifically included within the scope of this exemption are:
– **hospital accommodation** and food provided to patients (including food provided to a parent of a child patient); and
– care provided by an **outside contractor** (provided that the services are performed in the relevant institution).

MEMO POINTS 1. To be exempt goods provided in this way must form **part of a package** of care or treatment.
2. A company providing **cosmetic medical services**, including hair removal, facial implants, massage therapy and skin peeling, in clinics which were state-regulated institutions was not required to exempt its supplies merely because the services were supplied in a hospital or licensed institution. *Ultralase Medical Aesthetics Ltd* [2009] (TC00142)

Welfare services

Welfare services are exempt **if they are provided by** a: **434** Sch 9 Group 7 item 9 VATA 1994
– charity;
– government department;
– local authority;
– public body (which performs functions similar to a local authority or government department); or
– state-regulated or private welfare institution/agency.

Notice 701/1 para 5.18.2

MEMO POINTS 1. Services **provided by a charity directly to distressed individuals** at significantly below cost (i.e. subsidised by at least 15%) are outside the scope of VAT.
2. Services **commissioned by a local authority** will be exempt if they are directly connected with the provision of welfare services. *Age Concern Leicestershire & Rutland* [2008] (VTD 20762)
3. For taxable supplies of welfare advice see ¶1160.

436 Sch 9 Group 7 note 6 VATA 1994; HMRC Brief 12/10

Specifically included within the exemption are services which involve:
a. the provision of care, education, etc, to promote the physical or mental welfare of elderly, sick, distressed or disabled people (for example, the provision of home help services: *Watford and District Old People's Housing Association* [1998] (VTD 15660));
b. protection of children and young persons; and
c. spiritual welfare provided by a religious institution if it is provided:
– on a not-for-profit basis; or
– in return for a subscription or some other consideration paid as a condition of membership.
This last category also includes the supply of goods, including accommodation and catering, where it is ancillary to the spiritual welfare provided.

Human blood and organs

438 Sch 9 Group 7 items 6, 7, 8 VATA 1994

Supplies of human blood and **products derived** from human blood (which are to be used for therapeutic purposes) are exempt.

Similarly, supplies of human (including foetal) **organs and tissue** for diagnostic or therapeutic purposes or for medical research are also exempt.

F. Insurance

442 Sch 9 Group 2 VATA 1994; Notice 701/36

The provision of insurance (and/or reinsurance) is exempt from VAT, provided that it is supplied in the UK (¶25+). The value of the insurance supplied is the total amount due under contract, with no deduction for broker or agent commissions.

Scope

444 The term "insurance" is not defined in the legislation, so it is given its **common everyday meaning** (and will include, for example, life assurance, endowment policies, etc, as well as the more usual insurance products). To be a valid contract of insurance, a contractual relationship must exist between the insurance provider and the insured person.

Practice in this area depends considerably on HMRC interpretation.

EXAMPLE An insurance company ran the business of another insurance company but did not conclude contracts or assume any related risks.
This was not a supply of insurance, as there was no contractual relationship between the insurance provider and the insured party. *Forsakringsaktiebolaget Skandia* [2001]

446 MEMO POINTS 1. Input tax attributable to insurance of items which are for **export** from the EU to a place outside the EU is recoverable, provided that the insurance covers the risks of the person who owns the goods, or is directly responsible for their export (e.g. a freight forwarder). An apportionment is made on a fair and reasonable basis where the insurance also covers some other forms of risk.

EXAMPLE Insurance provided to cover the risk of a UK warehouse burning down would not fall within this relief simply because the warehouse was used for storage of goods prior to their export from the UK.
Insurance provided to persons who belong (¶9688+) in the UK for the export of their goods from Germany to China would be exempt because the place of supply is the UK.

2. In general, the treatment of **marine, aviation and/or transport** insurance contracts does not differ from the normal rule. However, where there are multiple parties, it may not be possible to identify the place of belonging of each of the parties. To simplify matters in this situation, a system of coding has been developed to help input tax recovery, which generally allows for the address shown on the broker's slip or equivalent document to be taken as the place of belonging of all the parties.
3. **Medical and welfare funds** set up to provide specified, non-discretionary benefits in the event of, for example, illness are exempt, provided that the subscriber has a legal right to the benefits. If there is no such legal right, any subscriptions will be outside the scope of VAT, as they do not represent payment for any particular supply.
4. A **funeral plan**, if written under a contract of insurance (so that on death the insurance policy pays the cost of the funeral), is exempt. If the funeral plan instead represents a pre-payment for the funeral, this will not be an exempt supply of insurance but may be eligible for exemption as the provision of burial services (¶468+).
5. **Pension fund management and administration** carried out by permitted insurers is exempt.
6. **Warranties/guarantees** provided by a trader will not fall within the exemption where they are financed or backed by an insurance policy undertaken by the trader. In this case the exempt provision of insurance is from the insurance company to the trader.
7. A sale of a **part-paid endowment** policy is not an insurance transaction but is instead exempt as a supply of finance (¶356+).

Block policies

Insurance cover provided under a block arrangement (i.e. when one person procures insurance cover for several third parties) is also exempt, provided that there is a contractual relationship between the policyholder and the third parties. 448

EXAMPLE Mr A employs five people and arranges annual travel insurance for them all with an insurance company. The provision of the insurance will be exempt, provided that each employee is granted a separate policy.

Related services

Related services provided by a broker or agent **in an intermediary capacity** are also exempt, even if no insurance contract ever materialises. 450 Sch 9 Group 2 item 4 VATA 1994

To be acting in an intermediary capacity, the person must be involved somewhere in the chain of supply of insurance. (A service which involves no contact (direct or indirect) with the insured party will not be exempt.)

Exclusions The following are specifically excluded from this exemption when related to a supply of insurance: 452 Sch 9 Group 2 notes 7 - 10 VATA 1994
a. incidental services (e.g. secretarial, general computer services);
b. supply of (or collection of information for) **market research**, product design, advertising, promotional or similar services, **unless**:
– the intermediary is paid per successful take-up of an insurance policy and is targeting its own customer base; or
– the product is endorsed by the intermediary;
c. valuation and inspection services (unless they are ancillary (¶310) to the exempt supply of insurance, in which case they will be exempted);
d. services of **loss adjusters**, motor assessors, etc, unless the services are performed as part of an insurance claim; and
e. services (as opposed to payment) which are **provided** following an insurance claim (e.g. repair of goods).

EXAMPLE The sale of health insurance over the telephone on behalf of an insurance company was held not to constitute a promotional service, as the customers were put "on risk" at the point of the call. The supply was therefore within the scope of the exemption. *Teletech* [2003] (VTD 18080)

MEMO POINTS 1. The VAT status of **Internet insurance services** has been clarified by the High Court and the Court of Appeal in two cases where the tribunals gave contradictory rulings. Both HMRC Brief 31/10

taxpayers provided online introductory services between people seeking insurance and a panel of insurers. The court considered:
- whether a taxpayer who merely introduced parties to each other could be regarded as an insurance agent/broker; and
- whether the services provided by the taxpayers were the exempt services of an insurance broker or agent acting as an insurance intermediary.

The High Court ruled that "introducers" of those seeking and those providing insurance services on insurance comparison websites (such as "click-through" services) should benefit from VAT exemption, whereas VAT applies only to those who are mere advertisers. The Court of Appeal upheld that decision, stating that it was sufficient for exemption if an intermediary was one of a chain of persons bringing together an insurer and an insured, provided that the intermediary carried out the functions of an insurance agent or broker. The intermediary did not need to have a direct legal relationship with either or both of those parties. HMRC has accepted the verdict of the Court of Appeal and has issued guidance on what it considers to be exempt insurance intermediary services provided via the Internet. HMRC states that the supplier must be "doing much more than acting as a 'mere conduit' through which a potential customer is passed to a provider" (although the Court of Appeal merely noted that the taxpayers in fact did much more than acting as conduits and did not set "doing much more" as a test of exemption).

InsuranceWide.com Services Ltd [2010]; *Trader Media Group Ltd v HMRC* [2010]

2. Where a person takes out **fidelity insurance** (a form of insurance to protect the insured person against dishonesty by, for example, an employee), the contracts often provide for the insurer to carry out reference checks to establish the level of risk. It appears that HMRC will apply the principles established in *Card Protection Plan* (¶316+) in deciding whether the checks are ancillary to, or separate from, the supply of insurance.

SECTION 2

Other exemptions

458 Exemption also applies to the following less common types of supply:
- antiques from historic houses (¶460);
- betting, gaming and lotteries (¶462+);
- burial and cremation (¶468+);
- postal services (¶474); and
- subscriptions to public interest bodies (¶476+).

A. Supplies of antiques, etc, from historic houses

460 Sch 9 Group 11 VATA 1994; Notice 701/12

A disposal of an asset from an historic house which is open to the public and charges admission (i.e. it is run as a business activity (¶100+)) is exempt from VAT.

To qualify for exemption:

a. the **asset** must be of heritage property (i.e. of national, scientific, historic or architectural interest - for example, a work of art, or an antique); and

b. the **disposal** must be either:
- a privately arranged sale to a specified public body (e.g. a UK national museum or gallery) which is exempt from inheritance tax and capital gains tax; or
- to HMRC in lieu of inheritance tax.

MEMO POINTS 1. Sales of assets from **historic houses that are not open to the public**, i.e. used as private residences, are outside the scope of VAT.

2. On the acquisition of an asset which will be used wholly or partly for the business activities of the historic house, it is possible to make an **election to treat the asset as a private asset**. Consequently, no input tax on the purchase can be recovered and on sale it would be outside the scope of VAT.

3. To encourage owners to care for heritage property, it is possible to make an **application to postpone inheritance tax** on a transfer of such property (either a lifetime transfer or one made on death). Where inheritance tax is deferred in this manner, no charge to capital gains tax will arise either. See *Tax Memo* for details.

B. The betting and gaming industry

Provision of facilities

Facilities for betting or gaming, or the playing of dutiable games, are an exempt supply. **462** Sch 9 Group 4 VATA 1994; Notice 700/57 para 15

Specifically **included** within this exemption are:
- participation fees for playing bingo and other games of chance;
- small-scale gaming at clubs and institutions for fundraising purposes; and
- payments made by players entering competitions in card rooms, provided that the competitions are run in accordance with the agreement which HMRC has entered into with the Gaming Board for Great Britain (now the Gambling Commission).

No deduction is made for any **betting duty** payable.

MEMO POINTS 1. **Facilities** include the services of pools agents, bookmakers, etc.
2. To be exempt the **games** must be games of chance played for prizes. Free plays are not prizes for this purpose, neither are sports (because they lack the explicit element of chance).

The following are specifically **excluded** from exemption and are chargeable at the standard rate: **464** VBANDG 03000
- the supply of machines (e.g. roulette wheels) to persons running a casino, etc;
- the takings, hire charges, etc, of gaming and amusement machines (e.g. jackpot machines);
- admission charges to betting and gaming premises; and
- facilities provided on payment of a club subscription.

MEMO POINTS 1. **Illegal gambling** falls within the exemption: see ¶266.
2. The High Court decided in favour of the taxpayer in a case concerning the VAT treatment of **participation fees for mechanised cash bingo** and **slot machine takings**. The Court confirmed that there had been a breach of fiscal neutrality, because some fees and takings had been taxed, whereas others had been treated as exempt. The ruling means that fees and takings should have been exempt from VAT. HMRC therefore invited businesses to submit claims for repayment of any output tax wrongly accounted for in relation to bingo fees. *HMRC v Rank Group plc* [2009] HMRC Brief 105/09
3. HMRC also stated in 2009 that it intended to await a final decision of the courts before deciding its position on slot machine takings. The Court of Appeal finally decided that issue in HMRC's favour, so it is assumed that HMRC will not accept claims in relation to slot machine takings. *HMRC v Rank Group plc* [2013]
4. The Treasury issued a consultation paper on the taxation of gaming machines in 2009. The consultation sought views on moving from the then current regime involving Amusement Machine Licence Duty (AMLD) and VAT to a gross profits tax. Machine Games Duty (MGD) replaced AMLD on 1 February 2013 and where MGD applies, no VAT is payable. This means that some businesses may have become fully or partly exempt as a result of the introduction of MGD.

Lotteries

Granting the right to take part in a lottery is an exempt supply. This **includes** selling lottery tickets to the public but **excludes** the playing of gaming/amusement machines. **466**

Where the **lottery is free**, VAT may be due on prizes which are not cash, as these will equate to gifts (¶1465+).

MEMO POINTS 1. The supply of **lottery management services** to a promoter is taxable at the standard rate. This may include activities such as the printing of tickets, publicity events, etc.

2. An electronic lottery ticket vending machine, whilst a gaming machine (which would normally, therefore, make taxable supplies), was held to grant the right to participate in a lottery, which is an exempt supply. *Oasis Technologies (UK) Ltd* [2010] (TC00581)

C. Burial and cremation

468 Sch 9 Group 8 VATA 1994; Notice 701/32

The following services are exempt from VAT:
- disposal of the remains of the dead; and
- the making of arrangements for the disposal of the dead.

The **commemoration** of the dead, however, is not within the exemption.

Disposal of the remains of the dead

470 This **covers** burial (including burial at sea) and cremation of human remains but **excludes** the burial or cremation of animals and exhumation services.

Making of arrangements

472 The following table summarises the VAT treatment of various activities which relate to the making of arrangements for the disposal of the dead:

Type of supply	VAT treatment
Use of a chapel of rest	Exempt
Digging, preparation and refilling of graves (including the cleaning, removal or refixing of headstones to allow further burial, but excluding the brick lining of graves)	Exempt
Supply of commemorative headstones, plaques, etc (including maintenance and adding inscriptions to existing ones)	Standard-rated
Supply of the coffin, casket or urn (including any covers, shrouds, robes and fittings) and transport of the corpse[1] and mourners to the burial or cremation grounds	Exempt
Selling coffins, urns, etc, unconnected with any funeral	Standard-rated
Transport of the corpse to a mortuary or research institution, etc, for medical research	Standard-rated
Embalming	Exempt
Provision of bearers	Exempt
Providing flowers, wreaths, etc	Standard-rated
Bell tolling and music at the service	Exempt
Fees paid to the Registrar, or to a church for the services of a minister	Outside the scope
Hire of a hearse with driver, or of a limousine with driver for transporting mourners as part of a funeral, to another undertaker	Exempt
Hire of a vehicle without a driver, or to someone other than another undertaker	Standard-rated
Newspaper announcements	Standard-rated
Catering, etc, after the funeral	Standard-rated

Note:
1. **Transport** of a body to and from the UK is treated as a supply of goods. Consequently transporting a body:
a. from the UK to another EU state will be:
- outside the scope of UK VAT if the customer is registered for VAT in an EU state other than the UK (¶25+); and
- standard-rated otherwise;

b. from another EU state to the UK will be:
- standard-rated if the customer is UK VAT-registered; and
- outside the scope otherwise, although there may be a requirement to register in the other member state (¶9040+); and

c. between the UK and a non-EU state will be zero-rated to the extent that the supply takes place in the UK. There is no requirement to account for VAT on any part of the supply.

D. Postal services

Certain delivery services (and any related services) supplied by the Royal Mail are exempt from VAT. By **concession**, this exemption also applies to any wholly owned subsidiary of the Royal Mail. **474** Sch 9 Group 3 VATA 1994; Notice 48 para 3.33; VPOST4150, 6000

The exemption for postal services is now restricted to supplies of public postal services (and incidental goods) by the Royal Mail. Postal services supplied on terms which are individually negotiated, and services not subject to price or regulatory control, are standard-rated.

MEMO POINTS 1. **Stamps** do not attract VAT, unless they are sold above face value.
2. **Additional charges** (surcharges) for postage of goods either:
– follow the liability of the goods where there is a single supply of delivered goods; or
– are standard-rated where there is a separate charge for delivery.

EXAMPLE A delivery charge paid by a customer to a supplier was taxable as consideration for a supply of goods and a delivery service. The taxpayer was unsuccessful in arguing that there should be no charge to VAT on the delivery charge, as the supplier was merely acting as agent for the Post Office (and simply passing on a charge it incurred). *C & E v Plantiflor Ltd* [2002]

Note:
For details of disbursements see ¶7190+.

E. Subscriptions to public interest bodies

Supplies made in return for a subscription will be exempt if the body making the supply is a non-profit-making organisation falling within any of the following categories: **476** Sch 9 Group 9 VATA 1994; Notice 701/5 paras 11, 12

Organisation	Definition
Trade union[1]	A body whose main objective is to undertake negotiations on the pay or conditions of service of its members
Professional association	An association which restricts its membership wholly or mainly (at least 75%) to those holding, or seeking to hold, a recognised qualification from it Membership must be at least customary for those pursuing a career in the profession There is no legal definition of profession, so occupations that are generally understood to be professions will fall within this exemption
Learned society	A body whose primary purpose is the advancement of knowledge or the fostering of professional expertise Its membership must be restricted wholly or mainly (at least 75%) to those whose employment is, or was, directly connected with its aims
Representational trade association	A body whose primary purpose is to make representations to the UK government on matters which affect the business or professional interests of its members Its membership must be restricted wholly or mainly (at least 75%) to persons whose business or professional interests are directly connected with the association's aims
Other public interest body	Bodies which have aims of a religious, political, patriotic, philosophical, philanthropic or civic nature to benefit the community

Note:
1. Charges made by employers to deduct trade union subscriptions from employees' pay are also exempt.

478 Notice 701/5 para 13 Specifically **excluded** from the scope of this exemption are:

– supplies made to non-members;

– meals, accommodation, etc, provided for no additional charge (unless the hospitality is directly connected with the organisation's aims - for example, an annual conference);

– supplies which are not referable to the scope of the organisation (as detailed in its rules, articles of association, etc);

– admission charges (payments for admission in addition to a subscription are always standard-rated but if admission to an event is subsidised by subscriptions, an element of the subscription will be standard-rated and a reasonable apportionment will need to be made); and

– supplies that are not provided automatically as part of the subscription package.

Registration fees payable by members of certain professions before they can go into practice are:

– outside the scope of VAT if payable to a statutory body;

– exempt, provided that the fee is paid as part of a subscription and the service of registration is referable to the aims of the body to which it is paid; and

– standard-rated otherwise.

PART 2

Output tax

Output tax
Summary

The numbers cross-refer to paragraphs.

CHAPTER 1 Time of supply

CHAPTER 2 Value of supply

CHAPTER 3 Rate of VAT

CHAPTER 4 Deemed supplies

CHAPTER 1

Time of supply

OUTLINE ¶¶

VAT becomes due on a supply at the time it is made. There are general rules which fix the time at which a supply is considered to take place (often referred to by the non-statutory term **tax point**), which differ depending upon the type of supply made. **750**

The general rules are modified:
- for certain types of trader (¶796);
- for certain supplies of goods or services (¶798);
- if the trader has requested a different tax point (known as an "accommodation tax point" (¶814)); or
- if the VAT rate has changed (¶762).

SECTION 1

Tax point

The tax point is relevant for: **755**
- determining the applicable rate of VAT (because the exact nature of a supply is determined at the tax point);
- VAT accounting (because VAT must be accounted for on the return covering the period in which the tax point falls, unless the trader is using cash accounting (¶4880+));

- the calculation of turnover for VAT registration purposes (¶2600);
- allocating supplies to the correct period for partial exemption purposes (¶2075); and
- establishing when input tax can be deducted (¶2012).

A. General rules

760 s 6 VATA 1994

In general, the **basic** tax point is the default position that will apply if the **actual** tax point is not used, as summarised below:

Type of supply	Basic tax point	Actual tax point
Goods	Date that the goods are removed by, or made available to, the recipient	Either the date of: **a.** issue of a **VAT invoice**, if it is either: – before the basic tax point; or – up to 14 days[1] after the basic tax point; or **b. payment**, if it is before the basic tax point
Services	Date that the services are performed	

Note:
1. A trader can opt out of this 14-day rule or, with the approval of HMRC, extend the period (¶768).

762 s 88 VATA 1994; Notice 700 paras 14.5, 30

When either the VAT **rate changes** or items are **moved between the VAT bands** (for example, if items that were zero-rated become standard-rated), and the basic tax point is on one side of the change and an actual tax point on the other, the supplier may elect for the rate to be determined in accordance with the basic tax point provisions. This is the case even if the basic tax point would not usually apply to the supply.

It is **not possible to make this election** where goods are sold in satisfaction of a debt, or where a self-billing invoice (¶2904) has been issued.

However, for VAT **accounting purposes**, the actual tax point will continue to apply and this will determine, for example, in which VAT return the supply is included.

1. Basic tax point

764 s 6(2), (3) VATA 1994

In practice, most supplies are subject to an actual tax point. However, it is still necessary to go through the process of determining the basic tax point, as it is only by reference to this date that the actual tax point can be determined.

The basic tax point for **goods** is the date that the goods are removed by, or made available to, the recipient.

For **services** the basic tax point is the date on which the services are performed.

MEMO POINTS 1. Goods are treated as **removed** when physical possession is transferred. If they are removed before it is known that a supply will take place, the tax point is the earlier of:
- the time it becomes certain that a supply has been made; or
- 12 months after the removal.

2. Goods are **made available** if they are provided in situ. This test is not restricted to goods that are incapable of ever being removed.

VATTOS4320, 4330 3. Services are treated as **performed** when all the work except invoicing is complete. Where there is no particular point in time at which the services can be said to be performed, there is no basic tax point and the rules for continuous supplies may apply (¶808). If there is any dispute between the supplier and customer as to whether the contract for the supply of services has been performed, the determining factor is the view of the supplier. If work under a contract ceases as a result of a dispute, any services previously performed are treated as being performed at the time that the work ceased.

2. Actual tax point - invoice

The issue of a valid VAT invoice (¶2840) **overrides the basic tax point** if it is: 766 s 6(4), (5) VATA 1994
a. for a positive-rated supply (i.e. not a zero-rated or exempt supply); and
b. physically issued or delivered to the recipient before, or up to 14 days after, the basic tax point (the **14-day rule**).

To be valid (¶2860) the invoice must show the time of supply and the date of issue.

If there is an unexpected delay in issuing or delivering already prepared invoices, the tax point will be the date that the invoice was issued, not the date it was prepared.

EXAMPLE Invoices created (but not issued) prior to the date of an increase in the rate of VAT did not amount to the issue of an invoice for the purposes of creating a tax point. They had simply been drawn up, agreed and shown to the customer. *Woolfold Motor Co Ltd* [1983]

MEMO POINTS 1. Invoices issued under a **self-billing arrangement** (¶2904) will not create a tax point unless they are issued after the basic tax point and fall within the 14-day rule.
2. Invoices sent via **electronic data interchange** will be deemed to be issued when the data is transmitted (provided that the recipient is able to receive it).
3. The time of supply rules do not apply to the issue of **credit notes** (¶2925). The issue of a credit note has no effect on the tax point of an invoice if it is issued once the original tax point has been established. All a credit note does is permit the supplier to adjust any VAT previously accounted for.

The 14-day rule

The 14-day rule **can be varied** by: 768
- opting out completely (¶770);
- electing for an extension to the 14-day limit (¶772); or
- the trader invoicing on a monthly basis (¶776).

Opt out Suppliers can notify HMRC in writing that they wish to opt out of the 14-day rule. 770 VATTOS5235
Any opt-out will generally **apply to** all supplies but can apply selectively if the supplier has a genuine commercial need to do so (for example, where supplies are made by separate companies within a group registration, or to permit supplies made under a self-billing arrangement to be treated differently from conventional supplies).

Extension It is also possible to apply in writing for an extension to the 14-day limit, provided 772 s 6(6) VATA 1994; VATTOS5240
that the supplier can demonstrate a genuine commercial need to do so (for example, because the price of the supply cannot be fixed until the supplier has been invoiced for materials). To create a valid tax point, the invoice must then be issued within the time allowed.

The **length** of any extension granted by HMRC will depend upon the individual circumstances but in general is unlikely to exceed 3 months.

For commercial ease, a number of organisations have **negotiated centrally agreed** 774 VATTOS5245
extensions to the 14-day rule, as summarised below:

Suppliers	Goods/services subject to extension	Length of extension[1]
Solicitors	All supplies	3 months[2]
All traders supplying government departments[3]	All supplies subject to an agreed/provisional price where the supplier's invoicing is delayed due to government procedures	4 months
Traders that supply government departments and are members of: - The British Electrical and Allied Manufacturers Association; - The Scientific Instruments Manufacturers Association; - The Electronic Engineering Association; and - Members of the Society of British Aerospace Companies (SBAC)		1 year[2]

Suppliers	Goods/services subject to extension	Length of extension [1]
Members of SBAC [4]	Non-government contracts	6 months [2]
Local authorities	All taxable supplies made in the course of a business activity	2 months
Patent agents	All supplies	3 months [2]
Scrap metal dealers	All supplies	3 months [2]

Note:
1. It is possible for traders to request longer extensions than those centrally agreed but these will need to be negotiated on a case-by-case basis with HMRC.
2. If consideration is not ascertainable at the date of the basic tax point.
3. Includes the Post Office and quangos. If this extension is insufficient for suppliers to the Ministry of Defence, HMRC will agree a tax point as the earlier of:
– the date that a VAT invoice is issued or payment is received; or
– 6 years after the goods are removed or the service is performed.
4. The Society of British Aerospace Companies. Similar extensions may be made to traders in the aerospace industry which are not members of SBAC.

776 VATTOS6200 **Monthly invoicing** Where traders invoice on a monthly basis (and provided that this represents the trader's normal accounting practice), HMRC will agree an **application** by a trader for the time of supply to be either:
- the last day of the period covered by the invoice; or
- the date of issue of the invoice.

3. Actual tax point - payment

778 s 6(4) VATA 1994 Any payment made **before the basic tax point** moves the tax point to the date of payment, provided that the payment is received by the supplier of the goods or services.

When is payment received?

780 VATTOS5115 Payment will be treated as being received when the customer has done everything it can contractually do in order to make payment (that is, when the supplier no longer has the right to sue for payment).

This applies even if payments are made under **arrangements which restrict the recipient's use** of the money. This means that a tax point cannot be artificially avoided by simply transferring payment to, for example, a separate bank account, trust account or suspense account in the accounting records.

EXAMPLE A contract price was required to be paid by a customer to the supplier, which was then immediately lent back to the customer. The loans were then repaid as the work was carried out. It was held that the initial price paid created an actual tax point, as it was a genuine transaction, meaning the supplier could no longer sue for the funds. *C & E v Faith Construction Ltd* [1990]

782 VATTOS5145 - 5160 The **time at which a payment can be said to be received** depends on the method used, as follows:

Type of payment	Time of receipt
Cheque	When cheque has cleared into the recipient's account (normally 5 working days) [1]
Credit card/charge card, etc	When sums are paid over to the supplier by the card company [2]
Bank transfer	When payment is actually transferred to the recipient's account
Book entry ("set-off")	When entries are made in the accounting records (provided that the debt is also settled when making these entries)

Note:
1. If it is common for the trader to use the **date the cheque is received** as the tax point, HMRC will accept this date, provided that the cheque is subsequently presented without undue delay.
2. As for cheques, if it is common for the trader to use the **date of acceptance** of the card as the tax point, HMRC will accept this date, provided that there is no unreasonable delay in processing the transaction.

Partial payments

A partial payment (for example, a **deposit or stage payment**) creates an actual tax point but only for the amount of that partial payment. This rule applies even if, under the contract, a deposit is refundable in certain circumstances, or is conditional on some outside event. **784** VATTOS5120

EXAMPLE

1. Customers were required to pay a deposit when booking holiday accommodation. In the event of a cancellation, the deposit would be refunded unless the accommodation could not be re-let. It was held that the initial deposits did form part of the total price payable and therefore did create a tax point. If the supply subsequently did not take place, any VAT accounted for could be adjusted for accordingly. *C & E v Moonraker's Guest House Ltd* [1992]

2. Deposits were received for the sale of licences to occupy time-share holiday lodges, which were yet to be completed. Purchasers were entitled to a refund of their deposits if the lodges were not completed on time. It was held that these deposits did create a tax point, even though they were conditional on some outside event. *Clowance Owners Club Ltd* [2004] (VTD 18787)

3. A club was set up for the benefit of former pupils of a school, the subscription for which was collected during the pupil's time at the school. If, on leaving the school, the pupil chose not to join the club, or was not elected as a member, the amounts paid would be refunded. The initial payments did not create a tax point, because no supply was made unless and until the ex-pupil expressed a wish to be a member and was in fact so elected. *Old Chigwellians Club* [1987] (VTD 2332)

A tax point will only be created under these rules if it is the parties' intention that the **payment is for a particular supply**. This will usually be fairly obvious from the facts but the following situations are cited by HMRC as examples of payments that are **not for a particular supply**: **786** Notice 700 para 14.2.3; VATTOS5135

- payments made to a third party acting as a stakeholder for (as opposed to an agent of) the vendor in a supply of **land** (a tax point will only be created when the money is released to the vendor);
- payments taken as **security** (for example, to ensure the safe return of hired goods) - in this situation, an actual tax point can be created if, for example, hire charges are later offset against the refund of the deposit but only if this occurs before the basic tax point (i.e. before completion of the hire period); and
- payments made in respect of services to be performed on the happening of some **future** event (which had not occurred at the time of payment).

Difficulties may occasionally arise for certain arrangements where **payment is made before** a firm order is placed, or any supply has been made. **788**

EXAMPLE

1. A Ferrari dealership took deposits from potential customers before they could be admitted to a waiting list to buy a Ferrari. This deposit did not guarantee the customer a Ferrari and indeed it was only once a car became available that the customer was required to complete an order form and pay a further deposit. It was held that the initial deposit did not create a tax point, as it was not a payment under contract but merely an agreement to make an agreement. *Nigel Mansell Sports Cars Ltd* [1981] (VTD 6116)

2. It was BT's usual practice to retain any customer overpayments against future bills (unless the customer specifically requested a repayment). Any such accidental overpayments by customers did not create a tax point, because they did not represent payment for a contractual supply. *C & E v British Telecommunications plc* [1996]

Retention clauses

Certain contracts will include a retention clause, allowing part of a contract price to be held back pending confirmation that the supplier has satisfactorily completed the contract. This is common for building contracts and contracts for the supply and installation of plant and machinery. **790** SI 1995/2518 regs 89, 93

The tax point for such payments is the **earlier** of:
- the date of issue of the VAT invoice; or
- the date when payment is made.

As the **retained amount** is paid over at a later date, these special provisions are necessary because without them the tax point would default to the basic tax point (as no invoice would have been issued or payment made to create an actual tax point).

MEMO POINTS A similar rule applies to **stage payments** in the construction industry (¶5208).

B. Special rules

794 Special provisions apply to determine the time of supply for certain goods and services. These provisions are necessitated by the fact that the general time of supply rules (¶760) do not sit well with the commercial reality of these situations.

To prevent any mismatch, special rules apply:
– generically to certain **types of trader** as a whole (¶796);
– to **specific supplies** of goods and services (¶798); and
– where HMRC has agreed a different tax point for certain commercial transactions because compliance with the ordinary rules would cause excessive difficulty (these are referred to as **accommodation tax points** (¶814)).

1. Certain types of trader

796 Specific rules apply for certain types of trader, which are discussed elsewhere in *VAT Memo*:

Type of trade	Ref	¶¶
Certain travel agents	SI 1987/1806 reg 4	¶7568
Barristers and advocates	SI 1995/2518 reg 92	¶7746
Retailers	SI 1995/2518 reg 67	¶6368
Agents	s 47 VATA 1994	¶7150 and ¶7154
Bloodstock breeders	VATTOS9650	¶6124
Land and property traders	SI 1995/2518 regs 84, 85	¶5245
Construction trade	SI 1995/2518 reg 93	¶5202

2. Supplies of specific goods and services

Summary

798 The time of supply for certain supplies of goods and services is specified by law, as follows:

Type of transaction	Time of supply	Reference	¶¶
Goods on sale or return, or approval	Earlier of date of adoption or 12 months after removal This is **overridden** if a VAT invoice is issued either: – before the above dates; or – within 14 days[1] after the above dates	s 6(2)(c), (4) VATA 1994	¶800
Supplies through coin-operated machines	Date that machine is used (although for "accounting convenience" the supplier may wait until takings are removed from the machine to account for the VAT)	Notice 48 para 3.6	¶803

Type of transaction	Time of supply	Reference	¶¶
Royalties, licences and similar payments	For periodic payments: earlier of receipt of payment or issue of a VAT invoice	SI 1995/2518 reg 91	¶804
Continuous supplies of services	In **general** the earlier of receipt of payment, or issue of a VAT invoice However, **special rules** apply for: – advance invoices (¶810); and – supplies between connected parties (¶812)	SI 1995/2518 reg 90	¶808
Water, gas, electricity and other forms of power, heat, refrigeration and ventilation[2]	Earlier of receipt of payment, or issue of a VAT invoice[3] However, **special rules** apply for: – advance invoices (¶810); and – supplies between connected parties (¶812)	SI 1995/2518 reg 86	
Disposal of business assets	Date of transfer or disposal	s 6(12) VATA 1994	¶296
Temporary non-business use of business services	Last day of each accounting period during which the supplies occur	SI 1995/2518 reg 81	¶1544
Temporary non-business use of business goods	Either: – the time the goods are appropriated for non-business use; or – if the non-business use is of a continuing nature, the last day of each period during which the goods are appropriated	s 6(13) VATA 1994 SI 1995/2518 reg 81	¶1525
Suppliers' goods in the possession of the buyer	Earliest of the date: – of appropriation[4] by the buyer; – of payment; or – a VAT invoice is issued	SI 1995/2518 reg 88	
Gold	Only the basic tax point and the sale or return provisions apply to the sale of gold	s 55 VATA 1994	¶6830+
Warehoused goods	Earlier of: – date goods are removed from the warehouse; or – the "duty point" (the date when there is a requirement to pay any duty due)	s 18 VATA 1994	¶9242+
Fiscally warehoused goods	When the goods are removed from the fiscal warehousing regime (unless there is a subsequent supply while they are still within it)	s 18B VATA 1994	¶9242+
Goods either: – removed to another EU member state; or – acquired in the UK from another EU member state	If supplied to a: **a.** non-VAT-registered person, the general time of supply rules apply (¶760); **b.** VAT-registered recipient, the time of supply is the earlier of: – the 15th day of the month following that in which they are sent to or collected by the customer; and – the date of issue of the VAT invoice	s 6(7) VATA 1994	¶9010+

Type of transaction	Time of supply	Reference	¶¶
Services supplied outside the UK, where the recipient is required to account for VAT under the reverse charge procedure	For single supplies: the earlier of the time the service is completed and the date it is paid for For continuous supplies: at the end of each billing or payment period. In the absence of a billing or payment period the taxpoint will occur on 31 December each year unless an earlier payment is made	s 8 VATA 1994	¶9702

Note:
1. The 14-day period can be extended at the request of the trader.
2. Such supplies are deemed to be supplies of goods. Similar supplies, such as of coal or bottled gas, do not fall within this regulation and are therefore within the general rules.
3. Where a supply of water, gas, electricity, etc is made to a taxable person in another EU member state, the time of supply is always the date of the invoice: SI 1995/2518 reg 87.
4. If a VAT invoice is issued (by the supplier or customer as a self-billed invoice) within 14 days of the date of appropriation, that date is the tax point, unless the supplier has notified HMRC that the 14-day rule is not to apply. Invoices must be physically delivered or issued. If there is an unexpected delay in issuing already prepared invoices, the tax point will be the date that the invoice was issued, not the date it was prepared (see ¶766).

Goods on sale or return, approval or other similar terms

800 s 6(2c), (4) VATA 1994; VATTOS9550

The time of supply for such goods is **generally** the earlier of:
- the date of adoption; and
- 12 months after removal of the goods.

This is **overridden** by the date of the VAT invoice, if it is issued either:
- before the above dates; or
- within 14 days after the above dates.

Any **payment received in advance of the basic tax point** (¶764) will not create an actual tax point unless it indicates that adoption has taken place. For instance, in some commercial arrangements, it is common for the recipient to pay an amount to the supplier to receive the goods (for example, car dealers often pay car manufacturers to receive cars for their showrooms). Provided that such payments do not restrict the recipient's right to return the goods, a basic tax point will not be created.

MEMO POINTS 1. Goods are said to be **adopted** when they are provided to the recipient and either the recipient indicates a wish to keep them or they are subsequently:
- permanently modified or adapted by the recipient;
- allocated, hired out, etc to the recipient's customer; or
- used by the recipient for some purpose other than display or demonstration.

If the supplier's terms set a sale or return time limit of less than 12 months, allowing that limit to expire also indicates adoption of the goods.

2. The tax point for any **interest charged** is the date the interest is paid. Where this may cause problems see ¶816.

802 These special provisions apply to goods that are supplied to a recipient on a sale or return agreement (or something similar) that gives the recipient the **unequivocal right to return the goods** at any time until they are adopted (in other words, where ownership remains with the supplier until the recipient indicates in some form or other a wish to adopt the goods).

VATSC73920 Sale or return agreements are generally between commercial entities where the goods are intended for onward resale and are, for example, provided to the recipient for display purposes. They **do not apply** to agreements where the customer does not have the option to return the goods, even if the title remains with the supplier until the goods are paid for (as in a Romalpa clause).

The real **practical difference** is whether a contract can be said to be a contract of sale which the customer has a right to rescind, or whether no contract can be said to have been made until the recipient decides to adopt the goods. For a discussion of this point in relation to Internet selling see ¶6930+.

MEMO POINTS Any VAT planning which includes an extended approval period would need to be disclosed to HMRC (¶3058).

EXAMPLE

1. A company supplied goods by mail order. The mail order catalogue stated that goods could be returned within 14 days of delivery for a refund or replacement if the customer wished, provided that they were in a "new" condition.
It was held that these transactions did not amount to a sale or return transaction, but a contract that the customer had a right to rescind. This decision was largely made on the basis that payment was due from the customer before the end of the 14-day period. *Littlewoods Organisation plc* [1997] (VTD 14977)

2. For demonstration purposes, a company delivered tools for grinding machines to agents of grinding wheel manufacturers.
It was held that this was a sale or return contract, because the tools remained the company's property and when a tool was delivered, it was not the expectation of either party that it would be sold to a customer. Instead, it was expected that a customer would see how the tool worked and then order one that met the customer's requirements. Ownership of a demonstration tool would not pass unless the agent, by some separate act, indicated a wish to purchase it. *Diaform Ltd* [1993] (VTD 11069)

Coin-operated machines

The time of supply for such machines is the date the machine is used but, as an **accounting convenience**, operators are permitted to delay accounting for VAT until the takings are removed from the machine. **803** Notice 48 para 3.6

The normal time of supply rules apply for **all other purposes**. Therefore in the event of a theft of takings from such machines, VAT must be accounted for in full on supplies made from the machine. This also means that if there is a **change of VAT rate** (¶762), operators must apply the normal tax point rules to calculate the VAT on takings before and after the rate change.

Royalties, licences and similar payments

The granting, assignment or surrender of any right is a supply of services. Such a supply can be in the form of a licence (for example, a licence that permits a trader to exploit the copyright of a painting by printing and selling postcards of the image). Alternatively a supply may be a permanent assignment of rights (for example, by an actor performing on a TV show). The tax point rules for licences are as follows: **804** VATTOS9500

- where a licence is supplied in return for a **single payment**, it is treated as a single supply of services and is subject to the normal rules, with the basic tax point being when the licence is granted; and
- where a licence is supplied in return for **periodic payments**, it is treated as a continuous supply of services (¶808).

A **permanent assignment** of rights is treated as a single supply of services subject to the normal rules, with the basic tax point being when the rights are assigned. Usually such contracts will also allow the assignor future royalty income based on, for example, the level of repeat showings. The tax point for such supplies is the earlier of the receipt of payment and the issue of a VAT invoice, although the VAT rate remains the rate which applied at the time the rights were assigned. SI 1995/2518 reg 91

Continuous supply of services

A continuous supply of services is essentially a single supply that is performed over an extended period of time (as opposed to a series of separate supplies). **808** SI 1995/2518 reg 90; VATTOS9150

In **general**, the time of supply for such services is the earlier of receipt of payment, or issue of a VAT invoice. There is no basic tax point.

Special rules apply for:
- advance invoices (¶810);

– supplies between connected parties (¶812); and
– supplies of cross-border services received by businesses in the UK (¶9702).

VATTOS8110, 9160 MEMO POINTS 1. The important elements **determining a continuous supply** are the existence of a contract to that effect and the ongoing nature of the supply. HMRC provides the following **examples** of continuous supplies:
– accountants providing ongoing advice to their clients (e.g. maintaining their accounting records, tax work, etc) - in contrast, a specific one-off management project (e.g. receivership, liquidation, etc) will be treated as a single supply of services;
– ongoing regular work of a trustee;
– regular maintenance work;
– club membership;
– management services; and
– hire, lease or rental of equipment (for details in relation to the letting of land see ¶5100).
2. The rules for advance invoicing (¶810) and supplies between connected parties (¶812) also apply to supplies of water, gas, electricity, etc, even though these are supplies of goods.
3. See ¶8582 for details of payments received for **supplies made before registration**.

810 VAT Notice 700 para 14.3

Advance invoices A supplier can issue an advance invoice for a continuous supply of services (other than one demanding royalty or other similar payments). Provided that such an invoice covers a period of not more than 1 year in advance, the services are treated as separately and successively supplied at the earlier of the time payment becomes due or is received.

MEMO POINTS This type of invoice **must show**:
– the dates on which any parts of the consideration become due for payment;
– the amount payable (excluding VAT) on each invoice; and
– the rate of VAT in force at the time of the issue of the VAT invoice and the amount of VAT chargeable on each payment.

811 VATTOS9165

Requests for payment Providers of continuous supplies may issue requests for payment, or other kinds of bill, that **do not amount to a VAT invoice**. This is usually done by clearly marking the document "This is not a VAT invoice". The actual VAT invoice is only issued after payment has been received. The supplier therefore avoids having to account for VAT before payment is received from the customer.

812 SI 1995/2518 reg 94B; VATTOS9170+

Connected parties A supplier must conform with certain **anti-avoidance** provisions when all of the following conditions apply:
– continuous supplies of positive-rated (not exempt or zero-rated) services are made;
– the supplier and recipient are connected (¶962), or are members of a group undertaking other than a VAT group; and
– the supplier is unable to show that the recipient is entitled to a full input tax deduction.

Such supplies are normally given an **annual tax point**. The first such tax point falls 12 months from the date on which the supply commenced and subsequent tax points occur on a 12-month cycle thereafter. The supplier can, however, agree a different 12-month cycle with HMRC.

The **value** of the supply is determined by comparing:
– the value of the services which the customer has received up to the annual tax point date; and
– the amount which has been invoiced or paid for at that date.

The annual tax point date is then the time of supply for any amount of services which have not then been invoiced or paid for.

However, if the supplier issues a VAT invoice or receives a payment within **6 months following** the annual tax point, that replaces the annual tax point as the time of supply for the amount concerned. The supplier can agree with HMRC to:
– vary the 6-month limit; or
– disapply this rule altogether and simply use the annual tax point.

MEMO POINTS If the supply commenced before 1 October 2003 the first annual tax point is 1 October 2004 and subsequent tax points fall every 12 months thereafter.

EXAMPLE A Ltd makes a supply of electricity to B Ltd (a connected company), which is partly exempt. The supply is never invoiced by A Ltd, nor is payment made by B Ltd. The supply commenced on 1 September 2014.
The tax point in 2015 will be 1 September 2015, except to the extent that an invoice is raised or payment made by 1 March 2016.

3. Accommodation tax point

HMRC will, in certain situations, agree a general tax point for some transactions. These agreed tax points are known as accommodation tax points. They essentially **alter the time of supply** for some or all of a trader's supplies where following the normal rules would prove excessively difficult. 814 s 6(10) VATA 1994; VATTOS6100

HMRC will agree applications for an accommodation tax point in the following situations:

Type of trader	¶¶
Traders invoicing on a monthly basis	¶776
Traders charging interest for supplies of credit	¶816
Traders using corporate purchasing cards	¶818
Assigned debts	¶820
Wine merchants	¶822
MoD contracts	¶774
Members of the Institute of London Underwriters	¶824

Applications in **other circumstances** are not encouraged and will only be considered if the trader can demonstrate that complying with the usual rules would cause genuine difficulty. VATTOS6900

Supplies of credit

It is common practice for **interest to be charged** for goods purchased on credit or on loans advanced for any purpose. In practice it may be difficult for the supplier to identify the proportion of any repayment that represents interest (as opposed to capital repayment). This may cause problems, as the usual tax point for credit charges is the date of receipt of each instalment. Therefore the **supplier can nominate** a single accommodation tax point for the credit charge, provided that the nominated date is before the date that would occur under the normal rules. 816 VATTOS6310 - 6320

Applications should be made in writing and must contain the following information:
- the identity of the supplier;
- sufficient details to identify the supplies to be covered by the nomination; and
- the nominated date.

The officially approved wording for an application can be found online at flmemo.co.uk/vm816, although alternative applications are acceptable, provided that all the necessary information is included.

MEMO POINTS The supply of **goods** will be dealt with under the normal rules for a sale where title to the goods passes at the outset. In most cases there will be only one supply of goods, although there may be two where the goods pass from a supplier to a financier (lessor) and then on from the financier to the customer.

Corporate purchasing cards

Corporate purchasing cards are operated either by a card company or a bank; their **aim** is to eliminate much of the paperwork traditionally surrounding the purchasing process. One of the main features of purchasing cards is that, under normal circumstances, suppliers are not required to issue invoices to their customers. 818 Notice 701/48; VATTOS6410 - 6420

Typically a **customer** (usually an employee of a company) will use such a card when purchasing high levels of low-value items (for example, stationery, spare parts, books, etc) from a supplier. The **card company** (usually a bank) will pay the **supplier** but will not issue a VAT invoice to the customer until the agreed statement date. Consequently, suppliers are **permitted to use** an accommodation tax point of the date that the details are transmitted to the card company by the supplier (usually the date the card is used by the customer).

In practice, card companies operating corporate purchasing cards will insist that suppliers apply for an accommodation tax point and, with this in mind, HMRC has agreed that **applications** can be included as part of the supplier's application to join the purchasing card scheme. Alternatively, the officially approved wording for an application can be found online at flmemo.co.uk/vm818.

MEMO POINTS This accommodation tax point was introduced because, **under the normal rules**, it is very often the issue of an invoice which creates the tax point for a supply. In the case of purchasing cards, the supplier will be unaware of the date on which the card company actually issues the invoice (on behalf of the supplier) to the purchaser. It is common practice for invoice reports to be issued to card users on a monthly basis. Therefore if the normal rules were applied, a supplier could potentially be faced with a mixture of tax points, depending on whether or not the invoice report was issued within 14 days of the basic tax point (¶764).

Assigned debts

820 VATTOS6600 Where an unpaid debt is assigned to a third party (¶366), any **repayment** of that debt to the third party is treated as being made to the original supplier, with the tax point arising in accordance with the normal rules.

In practice this may cause difficulties, as the supplier may not be aware when a payment has been made. Consequently, a written application can be made for an accommodation tax point occurring on the date of assignment. The officially approved wording for an application can be found online at flmemo.co.uk/vm820.

MEMO POINTS A trader who wishes to claim **bad debt relief** (¶840) on an assigned debt (which has been subsequently assigned back) must take into account any payments received by the original assignee.

Wine merchants

822 VATTOS8600 Some UK wine merchants deal in what is known as "en primeur" wine - that is, wine sold while it is still lying abroad in the producer's cellars for delivery to the UK at a later date.

The customer normally pays the VAT-exclusive price of the wine on placing an order, with the VAT being paid at the time of delivery into the UK. This may cause problems when applying the normal tax point rules, as at the time that the net price is paid, it is not certain that the wine will ever be delivered to the UK and even if it is, it may be sold by the customer before taking delivery (and while it is still subject to a warehousing regime (¶9242)). Consequently it **has been agreed with HMRC** that if VAT does become due, the tax point is the time the customer is invoiced for the VAT (where this takes place immediately prior to delivery in the UK).

Members of the Institute of London Underwriters

824 VATTOS9450 All claims on members of the Institute of London Underwriters (ILU) are processed centrally by the ILU. When a claim has been finalised, the ILU issues a "claim closing slip" to underwriters, advising each of them of their share of the liability. This will include details of **services received from abroad** which have already been paid for on the underwriters' behalf.

If the supplies take place in the UK under the reverse charge procedure (¶9700), and are connected with the provision of marine and aviation insurance, the tax point is the end of the day on which the claim closing advice is issued by the ILU.

SECTION 2

Bad debt relief

As debts can remain unpaid and may eventually have to be written off as irrecoverable, **suppliers** can claim a refund of any VAT accounted for, provided that the debt is still outstanding 6 months after it was due and certain other administrative conditions are met. 840 s 36 VATA 1994; SI 1995/2518 regs 165-172B; Notice 700/18

Any corresponding input tax recovered by VAT-registered **customers** must be repaid to HMRC (¶868).

The amounts claimed or repaid relate to the amounts **originally** accounted for or recovered. Thus a **change of VAT rate** subsequent to those events has no effect on bad debt relief (albeit that the rate change may come before the relief is claimed or repayment has to be made).

Special rules apply for:
- supplies of goods to which the **second-hand margin scheme** applies (¶6642); and
- suppliers using the **tour operators' margin scheme** (¶7582).

MEMO POINTS Bad debt relief does not apply to suppliers using the **cash accounting** scheme (¶4880) or one of the **retail schemes** (¶6300), as VAT is only accounted for when payment is actually received.

A. Supplier

1. Conditions for a claim

The **conditions** under which a claim for VAT bad debt relief can be made are summarised in the following table: 845

Category	Conditions
Time limits	The debt remains unpaid 6 months after the relevant date[1]
	The claim is made no later than 4 years and 6 months from the relevant date[1, 2]
Treatment of the debt	Output VAT on the supply has been accounted for and paid to HMRC
	The value of the supply does not exceed its open market value
	The debt has not been sold or factored (¶850)
Administrative requirements	The debt is written off in the supplier's normal VAT account
	The debt is transferred to a separate "refunds for bad debt relief" account (¶864)

Note:
1. The relevant date is the later of:
- the time payment was due and payable (¶872); and
- the date of the supply.
2. HMRC applies these time limits strictly.

The claim will be made by the supplier, except where the business is **transferred as a going concern** and the transferee has taken on the transferor's VAT registration (¶8678). 847

In a **VAT group registration** (¶8800), the representative member (¶8845) will claim any refund on behalf of each member of the VAT group.

A company which **leaves a VAT group** may claim relief on debts incurred while it was in the group. This is because even though the VAT was originally accounted for and paid by the representative member, it is the individual company that funded the VAT and suffered the economic loss.

850 A claim cannot be made where a debt has been **sold, factored or assigned**. If the assignment is only temporary, bad debt relief is not allowed until the debt reverts back to the original supplier.

Business Brief 20/04

MEMO POINTS By concession, if a **gas or electricity customer** switches suppliers and any outstanding debts are also transferred, the new supplier is entitled to treat the transferred debt as a bad debt if it is not subsequently paid within 6 months after the transfer.

2. Amount of the claim

852 The basis of a claim is the VAT attributable to the outstanding debt after deduction of any payments towards the debt.

A **payment will include** not only cash but also:
- the value of an enforceable security;
- non-monetary payments (goods or services);
- third-party payments (for example, from a customer or guarantor of the debtor);
- set-off of mutual debts; and
- the proceeds of sale from repossessed goods where no VAT is chargeable (¶858).

A **payment does not include** an insurance payout from a policy taken out by a company to protect against customer default.

MEMO POINTS The amount of bad debt relief is normally the **VAT fraction** of the outstanding amount. However, in 2011 the Upper Tribunal held that in very limited circumstances relief may be given for the entire unpaid sum. The appellant was a firm of solicitors. It supplied services in connection with insurance claims. In compliance with an agreement between HMRC and the insurance industry, it issued VAT-only invoices to VAT-registered insured parties (the main charge being invoiced to the insurer). The Upper Tribunal decided that any amount of such VAT-only invoices which remained unpaid after 6 months was available in full for bad debt relief. In 2013 the Court of Session overturned the Upper Tribunal's decision, holding that in these circumstances the amount of bad debt relief was indeed only the VAT fraction of the outstanding debt. *HMRC v Simpson & Marwick* [2013]

EXAMPLE It was held that a company (A) which agreed to write off debts of another company (B) during the management buy-out of company B, in return for a 4-year exclusivity contract, had received consideration for the outstanding debts (in the form of the exclusivity deal) and was not entitled to bad debt relief. *Berck Ltd* [2007] (VTD 20051)

853 Payments received are **allocated to supplies** as follows:

SI 1995/2518 reg 170

Payment	Allocation
Not allocated to any specific supply	Allocated to earliest supply first
Specifically allocated to a supply by the customer and the payment settles the allocated debt in full	Allocated to the supply specified
Relates to two or more supplies which were made on the same day	Pro rated equally across all those supplies[1]
Relates to goods provided on credit (e.g. a hire purchase or credit sale agreement)	Pro rated between the taxable goods and the exempt credit charge (¶854)

Note:
1. Using the formula:

$$\text{Total payment made} \times \frac{\text{Debt}}{\text{Total debt}}$$

EXAMPLE
1. Mr A made the following supplies to Mr B:

Date	Gross £	VAT £
5 January	360.00	60.00
12 March	840.00	140.00
14 April	1,200.00	200.00
14 April	480.00	80.00

The following payments were received for these supplies:
£840.00 (specified to be for the 12 March supplies)
£400.00
£310.00
These payments are allocated as follows:

Date	**Debt**	**Payments made**	**Outstanding debt**	**Bad debt relief claim**	
	£	**£**	**£**	**£**	
5 January	360.00	360.00	nil	nil	
12 March	840.00	840.00	nil	nil	
14 April[1]	1,200.00	250.00[2]	950.00	158.33	(1/6 × £950.00)
14 April[1]	480.00	100.00[3]	380.00	63.33	(1/6 × £380.00)

Note:
1. The payment made for these supplies in total is £350.00 (payments of £400 + £310, less £360 allocated to the January debt). As these supplies were made on the same day, the payment made is allocated equally between them using the formula:
Total payment made × debt/total debt
2. £350.00 × 1,200/(1,200 + 480)
3. £350.00 × 480/(1,200 + 480)

2. Mr A wishes to claim bad debt relief in respect of an invoice for £10,000 plus VAT, issued to B Ltd 12 months ago. Mr A owes B Ltd £750 (including VAT), which he has refused to pay until the bad debt is cleared. The bad debt relief is calculated as follows:

		£
Debt due from B Ltd	10,000 + VAT	12,000
Set-off of debt due from A		(750)
		11,250
Bad debt relief due	VAT @ 1/6 of £11,250	1,875

Goods supplied on credit

A trader who supplies goods on credit makes **a taxable supply of goods** and an **exempt supply of credit**. 854

If a customer makes some of the **periodic payments** before defaulting, these payments will cover both the goods and interest. In order to work out the amount of bad debt relief claimable on the goods, the supplier will need to look back at the payments the customer made before **defaulting** and allocate them between the goods and interest. The supplier will then be able to calculate how much remains unpaid for the goods and how much bad debt relief can be claimed.

MEMO POINTS Any amounts on which **interest is not charged** (for example a deposit payment) are excluded. Such payments are fully allocated to the goods.

The bad debt **relief is calculated** using the following formula: 855 SI 1995/2518 reg 170A

$$\text{Total debt outstanding} \times \frac{\text{Total charge for the goods}}{\text{Total charge for the goods + interest}}$$

The **interest** figure in this formula means the total interest as set out in the agreement, less any rebates and interest attributable to unpaid instalments (in other words the interest figure should reflect the commercial basis of apportionment adopted by suppliers).

EXAMPLE

1. Mr B sold a table and chair set for £20,000 on credit (£15,000 for the goods and £5,000 for the credit). The customer only paid £12,000 of this debt.
The outstanding £8,000 is allocated between the taxable goods and the exempt credit, with bad debt relief being available on the amount attributable to the goods, as follows:

$$£8{,}000 \times \frac{15{,}000}{15{,}000 + 5{,}000} = £6{,}000$$

Therefore bad debt relief available is £1,000. (1/6 × £6,000)

2. Mr C buys a car for £10,000 (which includes interest to be charged for credit). He pays a deposit of £1,000, with the £9,000 balance on credit (£6,000 for the goods and £3,000 interest). He then pays another £2,000 under the credit agreement before defaulting.
The outstanding £7,000 is allocated between the taxable goods and the exempt credit, with bad debt relief being available on the amount attributable to the goods, as follows:

$$£7{,}000 \times \frac{6{,}000}{6{,}000 + 3{,}000} = £4{,}666.67$$

Therefore bad debt relief available is £777.78. (1/6 × £4,666.67)

Margin schemes

856 SI 1995/2518 reg 172A Where the supply is made under a margin scheme, the bad debt relief available is the VAT element of the outstanding **profit element** of the supply. See ¶6642 for details.

Repossessed goods

858 Where repossessed goods are re-sold in the **same condition** as when repossessed, the transaction is generally outside the scope of VAT. This means that, in practice, anything other than cleaning or adding instruction manuals may make the sale VATable. If VAT is charged, the proceeds do not constitute payment for bad debt relief (i.e. the proceeds cannot be treated as payment towards the previous bad debt).

For **cars**, VAT is chargeable on a resale if the VAT charged on the original sale of the car was fully recoverable by the purchaser of the car (i.e. it was not blocked (¶1885)).

3. Payment subsequently received

860 SI 1995/2518 reg 171 If, after making a bad debt relief claim, the supplier receives payment (**in full or in part**) of the debt, it must repay the relief previously given that is covered by the subsequent repayment, using the following formula:

$$\text{Original relief claimed} \times \frac{\text{Payment subsequently received}}{\text{Debt outstanding when claim was made}}$$

EXAMPLE Continuing the example **1**. at ¶853, if Mr A received a subsequent repayment of another £600, he would be required to repay £100, calculated using the following method:
Original relief claimed was £158.33 + £63.33 = £221.66. The outstanding debt at that time was £950 + £380 = £1,330.
Original relief claimed × payment subsequently received/outstanding debt: £221.66 x (600/1,330) = £100.00.

The **adjustment** is generally **recorded** on the VAT return (in box 1), for the period in which the payment is received. Suppliers who have ceased to be VAT-registered should notify HMRC in writing of the payment.

MEMO POINTS 1. If the supplier is **insured** against non-payment of debts, any recovery under the insurance policy is ignored for bad debt relief purposes.
2. Where a debt is **assigned** to a connected party (¶962) after a bad debt claim has been made and the customer then pays, VAT must be repaid by the original claimant.

4. Administration

862 SI 1995/2518 reg 166 A **claim is made** on the VAT return for the accounting period in which entitlement to relief arises. The amount being claimed should be included as part of the overall claim for input tax (currently box 4 of the return).

Where suppliers use the **annual accounting scheme** (¶4745), output tax on the supply can be accounted for and bad debt relief claimed on the same return (assuming that all the other conditions are met).

Record keeping

The following **records** need to be retained in respect of a claim for bad debt relief: **864** VBDR1500; SI 1995/2518 regs 167-169
- a copy of the VAT invoice;
- evidence of the period in respect of which the output tax was accounted for and paid to HMRC;
- details of the amount claimed (including any payments received); and
- evidence that the qualifying conditions have been met (¶845).

The qualifying conditions require the trader to keep a separate **refunds for bad debt relief account** (which may be maintained separately from its normal accounting systems), containing the following information:
- the outstanding amount to which the claim relates;
- the period in which the output tax was accounted for and paid to HMRC;
- the amount of relief claimed;
- the period in which the claim was made;
- the VAT chargeable on each supply;
- the payments (if any) received for each supply; and
- the date and number of each invoice issued.

In a **VAT group**, each member company must keep its own separate bad debt records for debts written off.

MEMO POINTS If no invoice has been issued the records must show the date, the name of the purchaser and the nature of the supply.

If a trader identifies bad debts **after deregistration** it is still possible to make a claim, provided that it is **made within** 4 years and 6 months of the date the debt became due and payable, or the time of supply. **865**

The claim should be made on form VAT427, which can be found online at flmemo.co.uk/vm865 and sent to HMRC with the original invoices.

MEMO POINTS 1. The address for the VAT427 team is:
HMRC
Accounting & Adjustments
V427 Team
Regional Post Room
St John's House
Merton Road
Liverpool
L75 1BB
2. It is important to note that the claim must be made within the normal time limits. The **deadline is not** 4 years from the date of deregistration.

B. VAT-registered customer

A customer who has recovered input tax on a supply must repay the recovered input tax to HMRC if it has not paid the supplier's invoice within 6 months of the later of: **868** s 26A VATA 1994; SI 1995/2518 regs 172F-172J; Notice 700/18 para 4 Notice 48 para 3.20; VBDR5700
- the date of supply; or
- the date payment became due and payable.

MEMO POINTS Repayment of input tax is not required where a supply was made **prior** to the commencement of **insolvency proceedings**. A trader who recovers input tax **during** a period of insolvency is required to repay the input tax recovered if the supplier has not been paid within 6 months. Insolvent businesses are required to repay any bad debt relief claimed, should their debtors make subsequent repayments.

Date of supply The date of supply is **generally** the tax point, as determined in accordance with the rules detailed above (¶750+). This means that it will not necessarily be the same **870** VBDR5300 date as the invoice. However, for **administrative convenience**, the date of the invoice can be treated as the date of supply.

This relaxation of the rules **will not apply** in the (albeit uncommon) situation where an invoice is issued at least 14 days after the date of supply but before the due date for payment. In this case the input tax will become repayable 6 months after the date of supply or (if later) the date when payment was due.

EXAMPLE Mr A supplies goods to Mr B on 1 June. It is agreed that payment is also due on 1 June but an invoice for the supply is not issued until 1 July. The invoice is not settled.
Mr B would usually calculate the date for repaying the input tax from the date of the invoice, which would mean that he must repay it on 1 January. However, because he has agreed a payment date prior to the invoice date, he must calculate from the later of:
- the date of supply (1 June); and
- the due date of payment (1 June).
Hence he must repay the input tax on 1 December.

872 VBDR5400-5500 **Date payment is due and payable** Where businesses allow customers a period of time from the invoice date to settle (for example 30 days or 60 days), the due date for payment is this extended date.

EXAMPLE Mr A supplies goods to Mr B on 1 August. An invoice is raised on 1 September but it is agreed that Mr B has until 1 October before payment is due. Mr B will need to repay any input tax reclaimed if the invoice remains outstanding 6 months after 1 October.

874 Similarly, if goods are paid for in **instalments** (for example, under a **hire purchase** or **conditional sale contract**), the due date for payment is the date of each instalment. If the customer defaults, any later payments will usually be deemed to be due at the date of the default. This date therefore becomes the due date of payment for repayment of input tax.

Where a supplier simply gives the customer **longer to pay** (in order to ensure payment is eventually made), this does not alter the time at which input tax is required to be repaid by the customer, as this is seen as a form of debt management by the supplier, not a change in the original due date.

Where both the supplier and the customer are **in dispute about a particular invoice**, both parties may agree to delay settlement. Provided that there is evidence to support the fact that both parties have agreed to a delay, the revised payment date will be seen as the due date for payment for these provisions.

1. Amount of repayment

876 SI 1995/2518 reg 172H The amount of input tax to be repaid is calculated using the following formula:

$$\frac{\text{Input tax originally deducted} \times \text{Gross unpaid consideration at the end of the accounting period}}{\text{Total consideration for the supply}}$$

EXAMPLE Mr A received goods from Mr B and was invoiced £1,000 plus £200 VAT (which was fully recoverable by Mr A). Payment was due by 1 March but by 1 September he had only paid £500 of this invoice. This left £700 unpaid. He must therefore repay input tax of $\frac{(200 \times 700)}{1,200}$ = £116.67.

2. Payment subsequently made

878 SI 1995/2518 reg 172I If the customer subsequently settles the debt (**in whole or in part**) after a repayment of input tax has been made, the allowable input tax is calculated using the following formula:

$$\frac{\text{Amount settled by the customer} \times \text{Input tax repaid}}{\text{Outstanding amount at the date when input tax repaid}}$$

EXAMPLE Continuing the example at ¶876, if Mr A paid a further £200 to Mr B by 1 December, he could claim an input tax deduction of $\frac{(200 \times 116.67)}{700}$ = £33.33.

3. Administration

Input tax is repaid to HMRC by reducing the value of the input tax claim (currently in box 4 on the VAT return) for the accounting period in which the 6-month date falls. If the input tax to be repaid is greater than the input tax being reclaimed in the relevant period, the box 4 figure will be negative. **880** VBDR5600

CHAPTER 2

Value of supply

OUTLINE ¶¶

Consideration is that which is given in exchange for a supply. It can be monetary or non-monetary. Non-monetary consideration must be valued, in order to establish how much VAT must be accounted for, since the value of the supply is the value of the consideration given for it. **925**

SECTION 1

General valuation rules

A. Monetary consideration

If a supply is made for monetary consideration, the amount of **VAT chargeable** is calculated by applying the appropriate rate to the VAT-exclusive value of the goods or services. If the price charged is a VAT-inclusive price, the appropriate VAT fraction (¶1090) is applied to determine the amount of VAT chargeable. **930** s 19 VATA 1994

The total **value** of the consideration is the VAT-exclusive amount plus the VAT chargeable.

EXAMPLE

1. Mr A purchased standard-rated goods from Mr B for a VAT-inclusive price of £100 in cash:
- the VAT element is £16.67 (1/6 × £100);
- the value for VAT purposes is £83.33; and
- the total consideration is £100.

2. Mr A purchased standard-rated goods from Mr B for a VAT-exclusive price of £100 in cash:
- the VAT element is £20 (20% × £100);
- the value for VAT purposes is £100; and
- the total consideration is £120.

s 96 VATA 1994; SP 11/91

MEMO POINTS 1. The amount on which VAT is due expressly excludes VAT, stamp duty and stamp duty land tax, but includes all other **taxes, duties and levies**.
Consequently, any other taxes, etc, levied on a supply form part of the purchase price and VAT is due accordingly (for example, VAT is due on any duty charged on alcohol).
2. **Non-sterling** currencies are included within the definition of money. See ¶9032 for the rules regarding conversion into sterling.
3. If a monetary payment is **artificially low**, HMRC can only increase the value for VAT purposes if:
- the transaction is between connected persons (¶962); or
- it relates to supplies of goods made to non-taxable persons for retail sale (¶990).
4. Any VAT planning that diverts the customer's payment away from standard-rated goods to zero-rated or exempt add-ons will need to be **disclosed** to HMRC (¶3056).

Multiple supplies

932 Notice 700 para 32 Where a single payment is for two or more supplies of **different liabilities** (a mixed supply (¶310+)), the consideration given must be apportioned between the supplies.

No particular **method of apportionment** is stipulated in the legislation. The usual methods are to apportion the consideration in proportion to either:
- the costs of the goods or services supplied; or
- their customary selling price (if sold separately).

It is for the supplier to suggest a method of apportionment. HMRC will usually accept any method, provided that it produces (in HMRC's view) a fair and reasonable result.

For certain small items linked with a major item which is liable to VAT at a different rate, the linked articles concession may apply (¶329).

B. Non-monetary consideration

936 This denotes a situation in which **goods or services are provided** as consideration in addition to, or instead of, money.

Services provided could include the giving up of a right, refraining from doing something, or agreeing to suffer some loss, etc, in return for the supply.

Value

938 s 19(3) VATA 1994 If a supply is made wholly or partly for non-monetary consideration, the value of the non-monetary consideration must be established, to determine how much VAT is due.

EXAMPLE Mr A purchased standard-rated goods from Mr B. These goods were not paid for in cash; instead, Mr A provides services to Mr B. These services are valued at £100.
- the VAT element is £16.67 (1/6 × £100);
- the value for VAT purposes is £83.33; and
- the total consideration is £100.

Put simply, the value of non-monetary consideration is the amount that the particular recipient would otherwise have paid the supplier, if the payment had been in money.

When identifying and valuing non-monetary consideration it is important to note that:
- both **goods and services** can form non-monetary consideration; and
- if the non-monetary consideration is a **service**, it must be capable of being evaluated and expressed in monetary terms.

940 There are essentially **two methods** that apply when valuing non-monetary consideration, derived from the cases of *Naturally Yours Cosmetics* and *Empire Stores Ltd* (see examples below).

– The "Naturally Yours" approach is used when there is a **clearly identifiable monetary equivalent** that would have otherwise been paid. For example, A provides goods with a retail price of £100 to B in return for services. The non-monetary consideration (the services) will be valued at £100 and VAT accounted for accordingly, as there is a clearly identifiable monetary equivalent.
– The "Empire Stores" approach is used when there is **not a clearly identifiable monetary equivalent** that would have otherwise been paid. For example, A provides goods which are not available for sale to the general public to B in return for services. The non-monetary consideration (the services) will be valued at the cost price to A of supplying the goods and VAT accounted for accordingly.

The **guidance** formerly provided by HMRC advocated the approach in *Naturally Yours Cosmetics* as the default position, with the *Empire Stores* approach being used when there is no clearly identifiable monetary consideration that would have otherwise been paid.

EXAMPLE

1. Naturally Yours was a wholesaler of cosmetics. It sold goods to beauty consultants who then resold them, at retail prices recommended by the company, at parties which the consultants had encouraged hostesses to arrange. As a reward, a consultant gave the hostess a pot of cream (which had been purchased from the company) for £1.50 instead of the usual wholesale price of £10.14.
It was held that VAT was due on £10.14. The consultants were providing the company with a service (arranging for the hostess to hold the party) in addition to the cash paid. The value of the service was £10.14 less the £1.50 payment. The fact that the price was reduced only if the party actually took place showed that the parties subjectively assigned a value to the service. *Naturally Yours Cosmetics v C & E* [1988]

2. Empire Stores was a mail-order company that sold goods via catalogues. Two schemes were introduced to attract new customers: a "self-introduction scheme" and an "introduce-a-friend scheme". Under the first scheme, a person was entitled to select an item from a list for no extra charge once she had supplied her personal details, been approved as a customer and placed an order for goods from the catalogue. Under the second scheme, an established customer could also select an item if she recommended a friend as a potential customer and the friend had then been approved and made a first payment on an order for goods. It was held that the value of the non-monetary consideration for the introduction service was the cost of the goods to Empire, on the basis that this was the value which Empire had (as recipient) attributed to the service. Consequently VAT was due on the cost price of the goods. *Empire Stores Ltd v C & E* [1994]

Salary sacrifice arrangements

Following the CJEU decision in *Astra Zeneca* (see below), HMRC announced that from 1 January 2012 a salary sacrifice will be regarded as **consideration** for the supply by the employer of whatever is provided in return. **941** HMRC Brief 28/11; HMRC Brief 36/11

The value of the supply is normally equal to the amount of salary forgone. If this is **less than the true value** of the benefit (for example, if the employer supplies the benefit at less than cost), the value will be the cost to the employer.

MEMO POINTS 1. A **salary sacrifice arrangement** is one under which the employee opts to receive benefits from the employer, forgoing some element of salary in return. The employee enters into a new employment contract, or the existing contract is amended to reflect the new arrangement. HMRC formerly took the view that the reduction in salary did not constitute consideration, so that no output tax was due. Amounts deducted from salary in return for benefits were, however, regarded as consideration.
2. In limited circumstances, this treatment **does not apply** to arrangements which:
– were in place before 28 July 2011; and
– extend beyond 31 December 2011.
In such cases the salary forgone in return for taxable benefits will continue to be free of VAT until the earliest of:
– the date that a fixed-term agreement expires, or a fixed number of salary sacrifice payments specified within the agreement have been made;
– the date of the employee's next annual salary or benefits review; and
– the date of any other review or renegotiation that leads to a change in the provision of benefits under a salary sacrifice agreement, or to a change in the employment contract.
3. In HMRC's view, if a fixed-term salary sacrifice agreement **expired** before 1 January 2012, any agreement subsequently entered into gives rise to a taxable supply.

EXAMPLE A company issued face value vouchers (¶1016) to employees as part of a remuneration package. The company argued that it was not required to charge output tax on the supply of the voucher to the employee, as there was no consideration. The CJEU ruled that the supply of a voucher by an employer to an employee is a supply of services in the course of an economic activity. Where the voucher is supplied in return for a salary sacrifice by the employee, that sacrifice is consideration given by the employee in return for the supply of services by the employer. Accordingly, the employer must account for VAT on the supply of the voucher. *AstraZeneca UK Ltd* [2010]

942 HMRC's view of the treatment of specific benefits provided under salary sacrifice arrangements is as follows:

a. Cycle to Work Scheme An employer who purchases bicycles and safety equipment, and provides them to employees under a salary sacrifice arrangement, must account for output tax based on the salary forgone by the employee. The employer can recover VAT on the purchase of the equipment but must account for VAT when disposing of a bicycle. The bicycle may be valued for this purpose by using the same table as for income tax purposes (see *Tax Memo* for details).

b. Face value vouchers The employer must account for output tax on the salary sacrifice (as in *Astra Zeneca*), but can recover input tax on the purchase of the vouchers.

c. Child care vouchers The vouchers themselves are exempt from VAT. This means that input tax incurred on associated administrative costs is subject to the rules for partial exemption (¶2075+) and may not be fully recoverable.

d. Food and catering The employer must account for output tax on the value of the supplies unless they are zero-rated, but can recover the input tax on related purchases.

C. No consideration

944 Sch 6 para 6 VATA 1994

Where a **deemed** supply of **goods** is provided for no consideration, the **value of the supply** is the amount that would be payable if the person making the supply were to purchase goods identical to those supplied (or, where this cannot be determined, goods similar to those supplied) at the time of the disposal.

If it is not possible to establish this figure, the fall-back value is the cost of producing the goods if they were produced at the time of disposal.

In addition, the legislation specifically treats certain transactions as **deemed taxable supplies**, despite the absence of consideration, and specifies the value of such supplies (¶248).

SECTION 2

Special valuation rules

955 Sch 6 VATA 1994

There are special valuation rules for certain types of transactions or consideration, as follows:

Group	Type	¶¶
Specific transactions	Connected parties	¶960
	Long-term accommodation	¶984
	Retail sales	¶990
	Gaming machine takings	¶992
Specific types of consideration	Discounts	¶998
	Vouchers and coupons	¶1004
	Part exchange	¶1028
	Barter transactions	¶1032
	Loyalty schemes	¶1040

In addition, special rules apply when valuing consideration for the following **overseas** transactions:
- acquisitions from the EU (¶9030);
- imported goods (¶9421);
- reverse charge services (¶9704); and
- warehoused goods (¶9242).

A. Specific transactions

1. Connected parties

a. Valuation

HMRC has power to issue a **direction** (called a "Notice") requiring transactions made **at less than open market value** between connected persons to be valued at their open market value if: **960** s 19(5), Sch 6 para 1 VATA 1994
- the supply is a taxable supply;
- the consideration is wholly monetary (¶930); and
- the recipient of the supply is not entitled to deduct all of the VAT (in practice this means that a direction will only be made if the recipient is not VAT-registered or is wholly or partly exempt from VAT).

Open market value means the consideration in money which would be payable for that supply by a person having no relationship (with anyone) of a kind which would affect the amount of consideration.

This rule **does not apply** for a supply of accommodation or catering provided by an employer to an employee (¶1549).

MEMO POINTS It appears that non-monetary consideration (¶936) is excluded. For this reason, if the consideration is **partially non-monetary**, HMRC may insist on an apportionment (¶938).

Any direction under these provisions must be **given within** 3 years from the time of supply and can specify that VAT on future supplies made under identical conditions must be accounted for on the open market value. It is possible to **appeal** against a notice; the notice itself may be varied or withdrawn by a further notice. **961**

MEMO POINTS If the parties can demonstrate that the transaction was priced at less than market value for a legitimate commercial reason, not connected with tax avoidance, HMRC has **discretion not to revalue** the transaction at open market value.

b. Who is connected?

There are different rules for determining whether individuals, trustees or companies are connected. **962** s 993 ITA 2007

Individuals

The following are connected with an individual: **964**
- spouse;
- relative (brother, sister, ancestor or lineal descendant);
- spouse of a relative;
- business partner of the individual;
- spouse of a business partner; and
- relative of a business partner.

MEMO POINTS 1. The term spouse includes registered **civil partner**.
2. **Spouses** will remain connected despite the issue of a **decree nisi**, until such time as a decree absolute is issued.
3. If the only connection is by reason of **partnership**, bona fide commercial transactions for acquisitions or disposals of partnership assets will not be treated as being carried out by connected persons.

Trustees

965 The following are connected with a trustee:
- any individual settlor of the trust;
- any individual connected with that settlor (see ¶964); and
- any company which is connected with that settlement.

The trustees of a **subfund settlement** are connected with the trustees of the principal settlement and with the trustees of other subfunds of that principal settlement.

Companies

966 A company may be connected with either a person or another company **depending on** who has control of the company.

ss 1122 - 1124 CTA 2010

MEMO POINTS 1. **Control** is defined as the ownership of (or entitlement to acquire) more than 50% of either:
- share capital;
- voting power;
- distributable profits; or
- net assets on a winding-up.

SI 1995/2518 regs 84, 93, 94

2. When considering control in relation to:
- continuous supplies of services (¶812);
- construction services (¶5210); and
- land and buildings (¶5652);

a company is **not connected** with another company merely because both are under the control of:
- the Crown;
- a Minister of the Crown;
- a government department; or
- a Northern Ireland department.

968 The following table illustrates the types of connection that can occur, with examples.

Type of connection	Example
A company is connected with any **person** who has control of that company	Mr A owns 100% of A Ltd. A Ltd is therefore connected with Mr A, as he has control of the company.
A company is connected with a person if that person, **acting alone or with persons** connected with them, has control of it	Mr A owns 40% of A Ltd and his three children, B, C and D, each own 20%. Mr A is connected with his children; the company is therefore controlled by Mr A and persons connected with him. The company is therefore connected with Mr A and with each of his children.
A company is connected with another company if the **same person controls both** companies	Mr A owns 100% of the shares in both A Ltd and B Ltd. As the same person controls both companies, A Ltd and B Ltd are connected.
A company is connected with another company if one is controlled by a person and the other is controlled by **persons connected** with that person	Mr A owns 100% of the shares in A Ltd. His son, B, owns 100% of the shares in B Ltd. As Mr A and B are connected, the companies are also connected with each other.
A company is connected with another company if one is controlled by a person who, **together with persons connected with them**, controls the other	Mr A owns 100% of the shares in A Ltd and 40% of B Ltd. The remaining shares in B Ltd are owned by his three children. As Mr A is connected with his children, he, together with persons connected with him, controls both companies and therefore A Ltd and B Ltd are connected.

Type of connection	Example
A company is connected with another company if the **same group of persons** controls both	Four friends, Mr A, Mr B, Mr C and Mr D, each own 25% of the shares in both X Ltd and Y Ltd. Both companies are controlled by the same group of persons and therefore X Ltd and Y Ltd are connected.
A company is connected with another company if each company is controlled by a separate group of persons but **each group could be the same** if the actual members were replaced by connected persons	Mr A, Mr B, Mr C and Mr D each own 25% of the shares in X Ltd. Mrs A, Mr B's sister, Mr C's son and Mr D's father each own 25% of Y Ltd. Substituting a connected person for each of the shareholders in Y Ltd produces the same group as the holders of X Ltd. X Ltd and Y Ltd are therefore connected.

2. Long-term accommodation

Many people for a variety of reasons "live" in hotels or similar establishments for long periods. As the exemption from VAT for supplies of residential accommodation (¶5490) does not extend to the accommodation provided by hotels, such people would be at a disadvantage if they were treated as being in receipt of taxable hotel accommodation when what they are receiving is, arguably, residential in nature. **984** Sch 6 para 9 VATA 1994; Notice 709/3 para 3; Business Brief 15/06

For greater consistency of treatment, a special valuation rule applies where accommodation in a hotel, inn, boarding house or similar establishment is:

a. provided for a **continuous period of more than 28 days** either:
- directly to an individual for occupation (alone or with others) by them; or
- to a third party who allows individuals to occupy the accommodation; and

b. not holiday accommodation (¶5502).

MEMO POINTS 1. A guest's stay **must be continuous** to qualify for the reduced value rule. For example, if a guest stays for 3 weeks in every month, VAT must be charged in full. If another guest stays for 5 weeks, leaves for a week, then returns to stay for 5 more weeks, the reduced value rule applies only to the fifth week of each separate stay. Since 1 April 2015 hotels, etc must treat all breaks in a guest's stay as starting a new period, unless guests can return at any time and continue their occupancy in the same, or similar room, as if they had never vacated it.
Prior to that date, departure did not interrupt a continuous stay, provided that the guest:
- was a long-term resident and left for an occasional weekend or holiday;
- was a student who left during the vacation but returned to the same accommodation for the following term; or
- paid a retaining fee.

In these cases the time away was ignored and VAT was only charged in full for the first 28 days of the overall stay. It did not matter whether or not the guest returned to the same room.
2. Where accommodation is **let to a third party**, the occupier must be the same individual for more than 28 days. This means that where, for example, a hotel contracts with the local authority or some other organisation for the provision of accommodation (typically for homeless people or asylum seekers), this special valuation rule can still apply. The rule does not apply to long-term bookings by third parties if the accommodation is used by a succession of short-term occupants, where each individual stay is less than 28 days.

Calculation

From the 29th day of the stay VAT is only charged on that part of the payment which is not for accommodation (that is, the amount paid for meals, drinks and other services or facilities). **986**

In HMRC's view an inclusive charge for bed and board must be apportioned (¶938), with VAT being charged on the full amount relating to meals, drinks and other services. The remainder is the amount which relates to the accommodation; at least 20% of this must also be subject to VAT (representing "other services"). **988** Notice 709/3 para 3.2

HMRC gives the following example in its guidance.

EXAMPLE Weekly terms for accommodation, facilities and meals are £120 (£100 plus £20 VAT), which includes a VAT-inclusive charge of £48 for meals. The VAT charge is as follows:
a. for the first 4 weeks - the full £20 per week; and
b. from day 29 onwards - £10.40 per week (as the long-term accommodation concession means that, from this date, VAT is only due on the non-accommodation element of the consideration).

Calculation of reduced VAT charge:
The reduced VAT charge is calculated slightly differently, depending upon whether the initial charges are expressed in VAT-exclusive terms or not, as follows:

1. Charges expressed in **VAT-exclusive** terms:

	£	£
Total VAT-exclusive charge	100.00	
Less VAT-exclusive charge for meals	(40.00)	8.00
	60.00	
VAT-exclusive taxable value of facilities (20% of £60.00)	12.00	2.40
VAT due		10.40

2. Charges expressed in **VAT-inclusive** terms:

	£	£
Total VAT-inclusive charge	120.00	
Less VAT-inclusive charge for meals	(48.00)	8.00
Balance for facilities and accommodation	72.00	
VAT included (1/6 x £72.00)	(12.00)	
Balance (exclusive of VAT)	60.00	
VAT-exclusive taxable value of facilities (20% of £60.00)	12.00	2.40
Total VAT due		10.40

Comment HMRC's view is open to question, as the legislation states that "not less than 20%" should be treated as relating to the provision of facilities other than the right to occupy the accommodation. No distinction is drawn in the legislation between provision of meals and provision of other services.

3. Retail sales

990 Sch 6 para 2 VATA 1994 Where a taxable person sells goods to **non-taxable persons** for the latter to sell on by way of retail, HMRC may direct that the consideration for such a supply be the price paid by the final consumer. An appeal may be made against such a direction. For further details see ¶7292+.

4. Gaming machine takings

Machine games duty

992 ss 23, 23A VATA 1994; Sch 9 Group 4 VATA 1994; Notice 701/29 The former amusement machine licence duty was replaced by machine games duty (MGD) on 1 February 2013. Gaming machine takings are now subject to either MGD or VAT but not both.

Takings from a gaming machine that are subject to MGD are exempt from VAT (¶462+).

Takings from other gaming machines are taxable on the net takings basis.

If it is not reasonably practicable to attribute or apportion payments and winnings between machines, some of which are and some of which are not subject to MGD, they must be attributed or apportioned on a just and reasonable basis

VAT is charged on the **net takings** from a gaming machine: that is, the money put in, after adjusting for the float, less any winnings paid out. The take is regarded as VAT-inclusive, so the VAT fraction (¶1090) must be applied to it. There is no deduction for any rental or other costs of running the machine.

MEMO POINTS 1. Special rules apply for valuing **tokens** depending upon whether they are replayable or non-replayable: Notice 701/29 para 11.3
a. replayable tokens are treated as a cash receipt equal to the amount that would be paid in cash to play the game (for example, the value of a replayable token issued by a machine which costs £1 per game is £1); and
b. non-replayable tokens are valued differently, depending upon whether they have:
– a recognised cash value (i.e. they are exchangeable for goods sold by the business), in which case they are valued as for replayable tokens; or
– no recognised cash value (i.e. they are only exchangeable for goods not sold by the business), in which case they are ignored for the purposes of establishing the consideration paid.
2. Electronic **lottery** terminals are exempt lottery ticket dispensers. Notice 701/29 para 7

B. Specific types of consideration

1. Discounts

Where goods or services are provided with a discount, the valuation rules **depend upon** whether the discount is unconditional or contingent. **998** Sch 6 para 4 VATA 1994; Notice 700 para 7.3.2

MEMO POINTS The legislation only refers to discounts for prompt payment. Other discounts are subject to HMRC practice.

If goods or services are sold with a **discount for prompt payment**, the value of the consideration is the amount actually paid. When issuing invoices offering this sort of discount **HMRC advises** that the full price and full VAT should be shown. The supplier and customer should both then record the full amounts in their records initially. The invoice should state that a credit note will be issued if the discount offer is taken up, both parties amending their records at that time for the note. **1000** HMRC Brief 49/14

If **no credit note** is to be issued HMRC suggest the following wording to be used on the invoice:

"A discount of X% of the full price applies if payment is made within Y days of the invoice date. No credit note will be issued. Following payment you must ensure you have only recovered the VAT actually paid."

The supplier must then amend its records on receipt of payment where the discount is taken up. The customer should also amend their records accordingly and it is advised both parties retain bank statements to show the correct position.

If the supplier offers some other type of **unconditional discount**, the taxable value is taken to be the discounted amount if that is the amount the customer actually pays.

MEMO POINTS Prior to 1 May 2014 for supplies of telecommunication and broadcasting services to consumers, and 1 April 2015 for all other supplies, the value of the consideration was the discounted price, whether or not the discount was taken up.

EXAMPLE A Ltd supplies telecommunication services to B for £850 plus VAT prior to 1 May 2014.
If B pays within 7 days, a 5% discount is offered, falling to 1% if B pays within 30 days.
The value of the supply is 95% of £850, i.e. £808; the related VAT is £161. (£808 x 20%)
B Ltd pays for the goods after 14 days and is therefore entitled to a 1% discount. A Ltd will actually receive a payment of £1,009, i.e. £841 (99% of £850) plus VAT of £168.

If goods or services are sold with a discount that is **contingent** on some event after the time of supply (for example, 10% discount for an order if another order is made within 1 month), the value of the consideration is the amount actually paid. If the discount is subsequently taken up, a credit note must be issued and the appropriate adjustments made to the VAT account. **1002**

EXAMPLE Mr A makes a standard-rated supply to Mr B for £12,000 including VAT. If Mr B's purchases exceed £50,000 over a 3-month period, a 2.5% discount is offered on all those supplies.
At the time of the original supply, the value of the supply is £10,000 and the VAT £2,000.
If Mr B meets the discount criteria, the value of the supply will be reduced to £9,750, plus VAT of £1,950.

2. Vouchers and coupons

1004 Vouchers and coupons come in various forms; the VAT position depends upon the conditions attached to their issue and redemption. For this purpose there are two types of voucher:
- a money-off voucher; or
- a face value voucher.

a. Money-off vouchers

1006 Notice 700/7 para 7 Money-off vouchers (referred to as "coupons" by HMRC) are offered to the public with the promise of a price reduction on the purchase of specified items. They include mailshots, electronic vouchers, cut-out coupons and so on. It does not matter whether or not the voucher is attached to any particular product.

Issue of vouchers

1008 Where the voucher is issued **free**, no consideration is attributed to it and there is no taxable supply. This applies even if its issue is dependent upon the purchase of other goods, provided that those other goods are sold at their normal selling price.

1010 Where such vouchers are **sold for consideration**, the VAT consequences depend upon how and where the coupons can be used:
a. if they are sold **by a retailer entitling the purchaser to discounts from the retailer itself**, the payment received must be excluded from the retailer's daily gross takings (¶6368); and
b. if they **entitle the purchaser to discounts from several traders**, the consideration is treated as being for a standard-rated supply of services.

For details of how to include the consideration when using a retail scheme see ¶6532+.

Redemption of vouchers

1012 If a business **uses a retail scheme**, the treatment depends on who issued the voucher:
a. If the voucher was issued by the retailer itself, its value should be included in the retailer's daily takings (¶6368).
b. If the voucher was issued by a third party, its value must not be included in the retailer's daily takings (when the voucher is redeemed by the third party, that payment is included in the retailer's takings).

In either case, any additional payments received from the customer must also be included in the retailer's daily takings.

1014 If a business does **not use a retail scheme**, VAT is due (at the time of supply) on the consideration due from the customer on any further payment due (for example, from the manufacturer of the goods involved). Any such payment from a third party forms part of the consideration from the customer; a VAT invoice must not be issued to the third party.

Where vouchers can be redeemed for goods or services without further payment, they are treated as supplied for no consideration. "Reward goods" are therefore treated as gifts and accounted for accordingly (¶944). Note that these provisions do not apply to face value vouchers (¶1016+).

EXAMPLE A company ran a promotion scheme under which customers were offered vouchers with purchases of fuel. Whether or not customers accepted the vouchers, the price of fuel was the

same. The vouchers could be redeemed for goods ("reward goods") or occasionally services without further payment.
The CJEU held that the amounts paid by customers were entirely attributable to their original purchases and no part of the payments could be attributed to the supply of reward goods. The reward goods should therefore be treated as gifts and taxed accordingly. *Kuwait Petroleum (GB) Ltd v C & E* [1999]

MEMO POINTS Any **handling charges** made to manufacturers by retailers are exempt from VAT. However, any charge made by the retailer for handling, promoting or advertising the vouchers represents consideration for a supply of the retailer's services and is taxable.

b. Face value vouchers

These are vouchers (either physical or electronic) which represent a right to receive goods or services up to a specified value that is stated on the face of the voucher. Common **examples** are gift vouchers, postage stamps and electronic top-up cards. **1016** Sch 10A VATA 1994; Notice 700/7 para 8

EXAMPLE A company sold a single pass allowing entry to a number of attractions. There was no monetary limit on this but the pass had a time limit. Such a pass was held not to be a face value voucher, as it had no face value. *Leisure Pass Group* [2008]

The legislation splits face value vouchers into five categories, as follows:
a. in the case of a **credit voucher** the issuer does not redeem the voucher for goods or services but instead undertakes to give complete or partial reimbursement to the person who does redeem the voucher (this category includes, for example, gift vouchers issued by trade bodies or associations that can be redeemed at a number of different retailers);
b. a **retailer voucher** is issued and redeemed for goods or services by the same person and if the voucher can be redeemed elsewhere, the issuer undertakes to fully or partially reimburse the redeemer (this category includes, for example, gift vouchers issued and redeemed by a high street retailer);
c. a **single purpose voucher** represents a right to receive goods or services of one type which are subject to a single rate of VAT (this category includes, for example, pre-paid telephone cards, electronic download vouchers and vouchers for a specific service (but not book tokens, which might be redeemed for a zero-rated book or a standard-rated e-book));
d. **postage stamps**; and
e. **other kinds** of vouchers (those which do not fall within the above categories) - this encompasses all vouchers that are supplied by an intermediate supplier and includes, for example, vouchers that a high street retailer has sold to an intermediate supplier (by definition, such vouchers are no longer retailer vouchers when subsequently supplied by the intermediate supplier).

MEMO POINTS The category of **single purpose vouchers** was introduced with effect from 10 May 2012. Businesses were not required to account for VAT under this provision until 17 July 2012. Note that not every voucher for a single type of good or service will be a single purpose voucher.

EXAMPLE A UK company sold phone cards to distributors resident in other EU member states. The distributors resold the phone cards to consumers. The UK company did not account for VAT on its sales of phone cards, on the basis that the place of supply was the member state where the distributor was established.
The CJEU held that the sale, by an operator to a distributor, of phone cards which display all the information necessary for making international telephone calls using the infrastructure provided by that operator, and which are resold by the distributor, makes a supply of telecommunications services for consideration to the distributor. However, the operator does not make a supply of services for consideration to the end-user when that user exercises the right to make telephone calls using the card. *Lebara Ltd* [2012]

As explained below, VAT may need to be **accounted** for on the issue and/or redemption of face value vouchers, with the **exception of postage stamps**. Postage stamps are redeemed for an exempt supply of postal services and therefore pass from the issuer through any intermediate suppliers and on to the final customer without VAT being charged. **1017**

MEMO POINTS Certain cross-border transactions in face value vouchers need to be **disclosed** to HMRC (see ¶3072 and ¶3106).

Issue of vouchers

1018 Sch 10A para 7 VATA 1994; Notice 700/7 para 8

Where the voucher is issued **free** no consideration is attributed to it.

This applies even if:

– its issue is dependent upon the purchase of other goods (provided that the other goods are sold at their normal selling price); or

– it is supplied as part of a package with other goods or services (provided that the total consideration for the goods or services is not significantly different from what it would be if the vouchers were not provided).

Input tax on related costs (for example, the purchase of the voucher from the issuing party) can be reclaimed subject to the normal rules, but output tax must then be accounted for on the issue of the vouchers, to the extent of the input tax claimed.

EXAMPLE Selected couples who purchased wristbands on entering an amusement park were offered a voucher which entitled them to a free wristband for use at another amusement park. It was held that there was no consideration for the issue of the voucher, as the purchase price of the wristband was the same irrespective of whether they took the voucher or not. *Blackpool Pleasure Beach (Holdings) Ltd* [2005] (VTD 19014)

1020 Sch 10A paras 4-6 VATA 1994

Where a voucher is issued for **consideration** it is a supply of services and the amount upon which VAT is accounted for depends upon which type of voucher has been issued, as follows:

Voucher type	Consideration value
Credit vouchers Retailer vouchers	Any consideration is disregarded unless: – the consideration exceeds the face value of the voucher[1]; or – the redeemer of the voucher (¶1024) fails to account for the VAT[2]
Single purpose vouchers	The consideration on each sale of the voucher is taxable[3], whether the voucher is being sold by the issuer or by a subsequent distributor
Postage stamps	Any consideration is disregarded unless the consideration exceeds the face value of the stamp[1]
Other kinds of vouchers	Any consideration on the sale of a voucher is taxable[3, 4]

Note:
1. VAT is due on the excess.
2. This allows VAT to be collected from the original issuer. In practice this is only used where there has been a deliberate attempt to avoid VAT. In cases of simple error or insolvency, VAT will be recovered from the redeemer.
3. At the standard rate, unless the voucher can only be redeemed against non-standard-rated items, in which case the appropriate rate will apply.
4. For example, if a high street retailer sells gift vouchers to an intermediate supplier, the onward sale of the vouchers by the intermediate supplier is taxable.

MEMO POINTS 1. **Issuers** of retailer vouchers must issue a full VAT invoice if the vouchers are sold to a VAT-registered intermediate supplier. As the issuer does not need to account for VAT until the voucher is redeemed, HMRC suggests that the invoice states "the issuer of the voucher will account for output tax under the face value voucher provisions in Schedule 10A VAT Act 1994".

2. Any seller of a **single purpose voucher** must account for VAT on the sale of the voucher at the time it is sold and must issue a full VAT invoice to a VAT-registered purchaser.

3. **Intermediate suppliers** of face value vouchers (other than credit vouchers and retailer vouchers) must account for VAT on the sale of the vouchers at the time the vouchers are sold. They will need to issue a full VAT invoice to any further intermediate supplier in the supply chain. They will be entitled to reclaim input tax on the purchase of the vouchers, subject to normal requirements.

4. Such intermediate suppliers may include sales of face value vouchers in their **retail schemes** (¶6300+).

Redemption of vouchers

Where the vouchers were **issued free** and redeemed for goods or services for: **1024** Notice 700/7 para 8
- no consideration, the value of the supply is as detailed in ¶944; or
- consideration (monetary or non-monetary), the value of the supply is the total amount received.

The redemption of a **single purpose voucher** is not subject to VAT. HMRC Brief 12/12

Otherwise, where the vouchers were **issued for consideration** and redeemed for goods or services for:
- no further consideration, the value of the consideration is the face value of the voucher; or
- further consideration, the value of the consideration is the face value of the voucher plus any actual payment made by the customer.

Where the voucher was **issued at a discount** (i.e. less than face value), the discounted consideration received may be substituted for the face value on redemption, provided that the business can identify the voucher and the amount for which it is purchased. *Argos Distributors Ltd v C & E* [1996]

MEMO POINTS VAT must be **accounted for** at the standard rate on the redemption of a non-single-purpose voucher. Information Sheet 12/03 para 10
However, where it is known that the voucher has been **redeemed for zero-rated, reduced-rated or exempt goods or services, or those outside the scope of VAT**, a subsequent adjustment may be made by an intermediate supplier to reflect the liability of those goods or services. Both input tax and output tax would need to be adjusted to reflect the liability of the final supply.
An intermediate supplier who knows in advance that the voucher can be redeemed for zero-rated, reduced-rated, or exempt goods or services, or those outside the scope of VAT, may use a percentage split from the outset and avoid the need to make later adjustments. Information regarding any split in liability can only be provided by the issuer who redeems the voucher.
In order to avoid the need to **track individual vouchers**, redeemers can base adjustment figures on retail scheme percentages or other overarching calculations, provided that the result is just and reasonable. If the redeemer chooses to make this information available to intermediate suppliers, they may include the percentage split on any VAT invoice they issue to an intermediate supplier. This split should be quoted on any further VAT invoices issued by intermediate suppliers in the supply chain.

3. Part exchange

A part exchange transaction is one in which goods are supplied in return for both money and other goods. **1028**

In **general**, goods taken in part exchange are valued at the amount by which the monetary consideration has been reduced to take account of those goods. The value of the supply is therefore equal to the tax-exclusive amount of monetary consideration that would otherwise have been payable. This is in accordance with the rules for non-monetary consideration (¶936+).

EXAMPLE

1. A sells goods to the majority of its customers for a retail price of £100. To customers in the same line of business, A offers the same goods at £95.
B is a "normal customer" who brings in a part exchange item, which A values at £10.
C is a "trade customer" who also brings in a part exchange item, which A values at £10.
The total value of the supply to B is £100 (monetary consideration of £90 plus non-monetary consideration of £10 - i.e. the amount by which the goods have been reduced for B).
Similarly, the total value of the supply to C is £95 (monetary consideration of £85 plus non-monetary consideration of £10).

2. A company (P) sold golf clubs, some of which did not comply with the Rules of Golf and so could not be used for golf competitions. P offered to supply a new club for £22 to anyone surrendering one of the "illegal" clubs in part exchange. The new clubs had a normal wholesale price of £49.99 and a normal retail price of £72.

HMRC argued that the "illegal" clubs had a part exchange value of £27.99, so that P had to account for VAT on the normal wholesale price of £49.99. However, it was held that the "illegal" clubs had no value, so that output tax was only due on the consideration of £22 which P actually received. The scrap value of the old clubs could be ignored and the value of the non-monetary consideration involved was nil. *C & E v Ping (Europe) Ltd* [2002]

1030 Notice 700/7 paras 10.8, 13.7

The **general rule is modified** in the following situations.

a. Where a **fixed allowance** (irrespective of age, condition, etc) is offered for traded-in goods as part of a sales promotion offer, the allowance is treated as a discount. The value of the supply is therefore the amount of consideration actually received.

b. Where a car dealer accepts a **second-hand car in part exchange**, treating the part exchange value as the deposit required by the finance company, because the finance company normally requires a minimum deposit, it is common practice to inflate the part exchange value and the sales price of the replacement car by a similar amount, so that the minimum deposit can be met without resort to a cash payment from the customer (a practice known as "bumping"). In such cases the value of the supply is the inflated price of the car. *North Anderson Cars Ltd v C & E* [1999]

c. Where a manufacturer **reimburses a retailer** for a money-off coupon, the value of the manufacturer's taxable supplies is reduced by the amount of the reimbursement.

Cash-back transactions

1031 Notice 700/7

The term "cash back" refers to the situation in which a manufacturer (directly or via a recovery agency) makes a **payment to the customer** of a wholesaler or retailer. The basic rule is that the value of the supply is reduced by the amount of the cash given back. *Elida Gibbs Ltd v C & E* [1996]

In HMRC's view the **correct VAT treatment for a cash-back** transaction is therefore as follows:

- manufacturers should reduce the output tax on their sales in respect of the cash given back, provided that they charged and accounted for VAT on their original supply (and the supply is not one involving a change of VAT rate); and
- customers who are VAT-registered should reduce their input tax claim proportionately and are responsible for checking the correct position with the manufacturer.

However, **no adjustments** are required in the following situations:

- cross-border transactions;
- cash backs provided by an intermediary for telecommunications service (for example, when an intermediary provides line rental reimbursement): as the intermediary is not providing the phone service, the cash back cannot be treated as reducing the consideration payable by the customer for that service;
- by wholesalers who do not get involved in the cash-back transaction; or
- where goods were supplied to the customer free of VAT.

Where the **VAT liability** of the goods **changes in the supply chain** (e.g. where a charity buys certain goods zero-rated from the wholesaler which were standard-rated for VAT when supplied by the manufacturer), manufacturers cannot reduce their output tax in relation to the cash paid back to the charity.

MEMO POINTS 1. If the **customer is supplying something in return** for the price reduction, such as advertising space, the customer is making a supply to the manufacturer and an invoice should be raised by the customer for the value of the reduction.

SI 1995/2518 reg 38ZA; VAT Information Sheet 03/14

2. **Manufacturers and "first suppliers"** should still make the VAT adjustment even if they do not provide the goods or services directly to the consumer.

EXAMPLE

1. A company sold mobile phones. It received commission from service providers in addition to consideration from the purchasers of phones. Under a promotional scheme, it offered customers a cash-back payment, exceeding the price of the phone, if they remained with the relevant service provider for a specified length of time. It treated these cash-back payments as deductible from the consideration which it received.

It was held that a payment cannot be treated as a cash-back award (and consequently cannot reduce the value of a supply) if the payment of the cash back was not solely linked to the supply of the goods; and there were conditions attached to the payment that were dependent upon other external factors. *JAG Communications (Plymouth) Ltd* [2007] (VTD 20002)
Although the case concerned only cash-back offers, the **impact of the decision** could be extended to cover other customer offers, such as the provision of free goods, etc (see ¶6524).

2. Everest sold double-glazing, etc, and offered a cash-back payment to some customers who entered into a finance agreement to buy Everest's products. It was a condition of the cash-back payment that the customer serviced the finance agreement without default for 180 days, thus entitling Everest to commission from the finance company. Nonetheless, it was held that the cash back related solely to the supply of the goods. *Everest Ltd* [2010] (TC 00863)

4. Barter transactions

A barter transaction **is one in which** no monetary payment is made. It may involve goods or services (or a mixture of both) being supplied in return for a supply of goods or services (or a mixture of both) from the other party. **1032** Notice 700 para 8.7

Each trader's supply constitutes the consideration that trader is providing in return for the supply from the other party.

An **example** of a common barter transaction is where a publisher runs a competition in which prizes have been "donated" but the publisher is contractually bound to provide advertising to the donor of the prize in return. Notice 700/7 para 12.3

EXAMPLE Mr A wishes to buy a plot of land from Mr B in order to provide access to Mr A's property. Mr B is willing to sell the land for £10,000 but instead agrees to take a field which adjoins his property from Mr A (who is short of cash). Mr A had previously obtained planning permission and the field is valued at £40,000. Mr A was obviously prepared to pay the equivalent of £40,000 to purchase the land and therefore the consideration for the supply of his field is £40,000. The value of the supply made by Mr B is only £10,000.

MEMO POINTS One or both of the supplies may lack a clear value (for example, when a newspaper prints "vouchers" or "tokens" which a purchaser can collect in order to obtain free or discounted goods or services from a trader, both the newspaper and the trader hope to gain increased sales, but neither is providing those sales to the other). HMRC considers the VAT position to be as follows: Notice 700/7 para 12.4
- a reward consisting of goods should be treated as a business gift of goods (¶1465);
- a reward consisting of services should be treated as a business gift of services (¶1465), which will usually mean that no VAT is due; and
- if the coupons offer some sort of discount, they are money-off vouchers (¶1006).

5. Loyalty schemes

In a loyalty scheme, customers (known for this purpose as "collectors") accumulate points on qualifying purchases of goods or services and later redeem the points in exchange for rewards. **1040** Notice 700/7 para 10

The rewards can consist of either goods or services and may be obtained in several ways, as shown in the following table:

Method	VAT treatment
Rewards given directly in return for points	Reward is treated as a business gift (¶1465)
Rewards given for a combination of cash and points	VAT must be accounted for, based on the total consideration received
Vouchers are exchanged for points, which are in turn exchanged for rewards	The vouchers are treated as face value vouchers (¶1016)

A points scheme may also allow customers to donate points to schools or other institutions. The institution then redeems the points for goods or services. The redemption is treated as a business gift of the appropriate type (¶1465).

In HMRC's view, payments made by a sponsoring business to a **third-party reward supplier** generally represent consideration for supplies made by the reward supplier to collectors. On this view, any VAT charged by the reward supplier cannot be reclaimed as input tax by the paying business, because the supply is made to the collector. The reward supplier must account for VAT on goods and services supplied to the collector in the usual way. The consideration will typically be the total of any payment received from the collector, plus any consideration received from the sponsoring business.

MEMO POINTS 1. HMRC's view is considered too simplistic by the **Supreme Court**, as the following case demonstrates.
A company operated the Nectar card promotion scheme, which gave points to customers who made purchases from certain retailers. It was agreed that the purchase price paid by the customers did not include any consideration for the points.
The points could then be used to acquire further goods or services from suppliers within the scheme. These goods were paid for by the company; the company claimed input tax on these supplies. HMRC challenged the reclaim on the basis that the supply was made to the customer, not the company.
The CJEU held that the payment to the supplier for the reward goods was both third-party consideration for the supply of goods to the customer and consideration for a supply of services to the company. The Supreme Court, however, decided that the company was entitled to a full input tax deduction for payments made to suppliers for providing reward goods and services under the scheme. The Supreme Court considered that the wrong questions had been referred to the CJEU, so its judgment did not need to be applied slavishly.
HMRC's analysis was that there had been a supply of reward goods or services by the supplier to the customer and that the company had paid for that supply - a clear case of third-party consideration with no right on the company's part to an input tax deduction, since the supply had been made to the customer, not the company. The Supreme Court explained that whilst there had indeed been a supply of reward goods or services to the customer, there had been a separate supply of services by the supplier to the company, for which the company's payment was consideration, thus entitling the company to an input tax deduction. Thus the gift (or sale) of reward goods or services to the customer could be a supply both to the customer and separately to the company - it did not have to be one or the other. *HMRC v Aimia Coalition Loyalty UK Ltd (formerly Loyalty Management UK Ltd)* [2013]
2. For more about **loyalty store cards** see ¶6540.

CHAPTER 3

Rate of VAT

OUTLINE ¶¶

All registered persons making taxable supplies are required to account for output tax on those supplies at the appropriate VAT rate. 1090

When the value of a supply is quoted as exclusive of VAT, the output tax is simply the appropriate percentage of that value. When a supply is quoted as a VAT-inclusive value, the amount of VAT is calculated by applying a **VAT fraction** to the value, as follows:

Supply	VAT rate	VAT fraction
Standard-rated	20%	1/6
Reduced-rated	5%	1/21
Zero-rated	0%	n/a

EXAMPLE Mr A makes a standard-rated supply to Mr B valued at £2,000.
If this is the VAT-exclusive amount, the VAT due is £400. (20% × £2,000)
If this is the VAT-inclusive amount, the VAT due is £333.33. (1/6 × £2,000)

SECTION 1

Standard-rated supplies

1095 The standard rate is the default rate which applies if the supply is not:
- exempt (¶350);
- reduced-rated (¶1110);
- zero-rated (¶1180); or
- outside the scope of VAT (¶252).

SECTION 2

Reduced-rated supplies

Summary

1110 s 29A VATA 1994 The following supplies are taxable at the reduced rate:

Supply	Reference	¶¶
Fuel and power	Sch 7A Group 1 VATA 1994	¶1116
Energy-saving materials	Sch 7A Group 2 VATA 1994	¶1136
Grant-funded: – supply and installation of heating supplies; – connection of a mains gas supply; or – security systems	Sch 7A Group 3 VATA 1994	¶1144
Woman's sanitary protection products [1]	Sch 7A Group 4 VATA 1994	
Children's car seats (including seat bases)	Sch 7A Group 5 VATA 1994 Notice 701/23	¶1156
Certain residential conversions, renovations and alterations of dwellings	Sch 7A Groups 6,7 VATA 1994	¶5404
Contraceptive products [2]	Sch 7A Group 8 VATA 1994	
Welfare advice or information	Sch 7A Group 9 VATA 1994	¶1160
Installation of mobility aids for the elderly	Sch 7A Group 10 VATA 1994	¶1166
Smoking cessation products	Sch 7A Group 11 VATA 1994	¶1162
Imported works of art, antiques and collectors' items	s 21(4) VATA 1994	¶1164
Static holiday caravans	Sch 7A Group 12 VATA 1994	¶1170
Carriage of passengers on small, cable-suspended transport systems	Sch 7A Group 13 VATA 1994	¶1174

Note:
1. Only applies to products specifically designed for use during menstruation or following childbirth. Items designed for use as an incontinence product are not eligible for the reduced rate but in most circumstances will be zero-rated anyway. Complementary goods, such as clothing or feminine wipes, are not eligible for the reduced rate. See Notice 701/18.
2. This does not include:
- any product designed for the purpose of monitoring fertility;
- any exempt supplies of goods in any hospital, etc, in connection with medical or surgical treatment (¶428); or
- contraceptives obtained on the prescription of a medical practitioner, which are zero-rated (¶1334).

1112 Reduced-rating also applies where the above supplies are **imported** or acquired from **overseas**.

A. Fuel and power

To qualify for reduced-rating, supplies must meet all of the following conditions: 1116
Sch 7A Group 1 VATA 1994; Notice 701/19
1. The supply must be made from the actual supplier directly to the **consumer** or a landlord (¶1120).
2. The fuel or power must be used for a **qualifying use**, defined as:
- for domestic use (¶1120); or
- by a charity for non-business purposes.

Note, however, that supplies falling within certain **de minimis limits** (¶1122) are always deemed to be for domestic use, even when supplied to a business.
3. The supply must **consist of**:
- coal, coke or other solid substances held out for sale solely as fuel;
- fuel gases (¶1124);
- fuel oil, gas oil or kerosene which is relieved from excise duty (or charged at a reduced rate) and not supplied for road fuel; or
- electricity (¶1128), heat or air-conditioning (¶1129).

MEMO POINTS **Other solid fuels eligible** for reduced-rating include peat, charcoal and firewood.

Any **fixed or standing charge** that is inseparable from a supply of fuel is also subject to VAT at the reduced rate, provided that the supply of the fuel is for a qualifying use. 1118

However, where standing charges are made by a **third party** (for example, a local authority) rather than the fuel supplier, they do not form part of the supply of gas and are standard-rated, regardless of the customer.

There are numerous charges that can be made by power and fuel suppliers but the following table provides **examples** of the most common charges that may occur and the VAT treatment: 1119

Charge	VAT treatment
Any services supplied for a qualifying use but by a contractor other than the supplier of fuel or power	Standard-rated
Rental charges for meters, generators or fuel tanks	Standard-rated
Services in connection with tests carried out, for example, at the request of estate agents or prospective purchasers of premises	Standard-rated
Servicing contracts	Standard-rated
Repairs, maintenance and replacement of pipes not belonging to the fuel or power supplier (normally those on the consumer's side of the meter)	Standard-rated
Replacement by the gas or electricity supplier of dangerous, obsolete or inefficient appliances or parts, after the meter, under statutory contractual obligation	Outside the scope of VAT

Domestic use

A supply is for domestic use if it is provided for use in: 1120
- a building (or part of a building) which is used for a relevant residential purpose;
- a dwelling;
- self-catering accommodation;
- a caravan; or
- a houseboat.

Fuel and power used in **outbuildings** and **detached garages** also qualify for reduced-rating, provided that the building forms part of qualifying premises.

The reduced rate applies not only to supplies made to households but also to supplies made to **institutional landlords** for eventual domestic use by their tenants (for example, schools providing student accommodation, or residential care homes). This is because such tenants are unlikely to receive individual fuel bills, as the supply is to an institution.

MEMO POINTS 1. A building used for a **relevant residential purpose** means:
- a home or other institution providing residential accommodation for children, or persons in need of personal care by reason of old age, disablement, past or present dependence on alcohol or drugs, or past or present mental disorder;
- a hospice;
- residential accommodation for students or for members of any of the armed forces;
- a monastery, nunnery or similar establishment; or
- an institution which is the sole or main residence of at least 90% of its residents.

Hospitals, prisons and hotels are not qualifying premises.
2. Fuel supplied to one customer for a number of **different premises** is treated as being supplied separately at each location.

1122 Supplies within the following **de minimis limits** are always deemed to be for domestic use, even where supplied to a business.

Supply	Conditions
Wood, peat or charcoal	Any amount, provided that it is not intended for sale by the recipient
Piped gas	Supply rate does not exceed 150 therms or 4,397 kilowatt hours a month
Electricity	Supply rate does not exceed 1,000 kilowatt hours a month[1]
Petroleum gas in a liquid state (LPG) in cylinders	Cylinders weigh less than 50 kgs and either: - less than 20 cylinders are supplied; or - if more than 20 are supplied, they are not intended for sale by the recipient
LPG to installed tanks	Tank has a capacity of no more than 2 tonnes
Coke or coal	No more than 1 tonne[1] for sale as domestic fuel
Fuel oil, gas oil or kerosene	No more than 2,300 litres[1]

Note:
1. These limits are applied on a daily basis per customer; therefore, for example, two 600 kg deliveries of coal in one day would amount to one 1.2 tonne delivery and would not fall within this automatic provision. Instead the end use of the supply would need to be determined to establish if the reduced rate applied.

Connection to the mains

1123 HMRC Brief 43/11 One-off charges for a first-time connection to mains gas or electricity are standard-rated, **except** as shown in the following table:

Circumstance	VAT treatment
First-time connection of a new dwelling or relevant residential or relevant charitable building (¶5105+)	Zero-rated if the connection is made as part of the construction of the building
Connection is supplied by the same person (or a member of the same VAT group) as the fuel	Follows the treatment of the fuel (normally reduced-rated)
Connection is supplied by a person other than the supplier of the fuel[1]	Standard-rated
Provided in connection with a residential conversion, renovation or alteration (¶5404)	Reduced-rated if performed on the immediate site of the building
Grant funded	Reduced-rated (subject to conditions (¶1144))

Note:
1. Also applies if the supplier of fuel has not been determined at the date of connection.

Fuel gases

1124 These **consist of**:
- coal gas, water gas, producer gas or similar gases; and
- petroleum gases or other gaseous hydrocarbons (gas or liquid state).

Specifically **excluded** from reduced-rating are supplies of gases for use as road fuel, which are standard-rated.

The following rules apply to **supplies made in cylinders or cartridges**: 1126

Initial supply	Treatment
Refillable cylinder	The value of the supply must be apportioned between the value of the cylinder itself (which is standard-rated) and the gas (which is reduced-rated). Any subsequent supply is reduced-rated even if the empty cylinder is taken in exchange for a full one.
Disposable cartridge (supplied at an inclusive price)	The supply is standard-rated throughout the supply chain until the point of final sale to the consumer, when it is taxable at the reduced rate.
Rented cylinder	VAT must be accounted for at the standard rate on the hire charge When an empty cylinder is exchanged for a full one of the same size, any refill charge (including any nominal charge for inspection or maintenance) can be taxed at the reduced rate (subject to qualifying use of the gas). Any charge made for a lost or damaged cylinder (such as the loss of a deposit) is outside the scope of VAT. But if a separate charge is made for the retention of a cylinder this is standard-rated.
Bulk storage tanks (installed on the customer's premises)	Tanks remain the property of the supplier. Charges for gas consumed are at the reduced rate (subject to qualifying use) but any charge specifically for repair or maintenance, etc, of equipment is standard-rated.

Electricity

The following rules apply to supplies in connection with the provision of electricity: 1128

Supply	Treatment
Standing charges	Reduced-rated if included in the overall price for the supply.
Mobile generator	Reduced-rated if the generator is operated by the supplier. The standard rate applies to the hire of a generator for operation by the customer and to the installation of stand-by equipment.
Batteries	Standard-rated, irrespective of the operation involved (new batteries, replacements, recharging, etc).

Hot water, refrigeration and air-conditioning

Steam and heated water are reduced-rated if they are provided for a qualifying use and have been deliberately heated by geothermal, solar or other natural heat or energy source. This is not a zero-rated supply of water (¶1246). 1129

Reduced-rating **does not apply** to water that:
- has been heated as part of a treatment process but is supplied at the temperature at which it was before it was heated - that is, after it has cooled down; or
- is hot because it is drawn from a hot spring.

The reduced rate also applies to supplies for a qualifying use of:
- air-conditioning, refrigeration or quick-freezing; and
- ventilation, air-conditioning or refrigeration from a central plant.

There is **no de minimis** amount for any of these supplies.

Responsibility for charging the correct rate of VAT rests with the supplier, who must therefore be satisfied as to the extent of the customer's qualifying use. To assist suppliers in this matter, customers can give suppliers a certificate to evidence qualifying use. It is the supplier's responsibility to check the validity of a certificate, but HMRC says that if the supplier is subsequently found to have charged the **incorrect rate of VAT in good faith**, HMRC will not attempt to recover the VAT due from the supplier. 1130 Notice 48 para 3.11

Mixed use

1132 If at least 60% of a supply is for a qualifying purpose, the whole supply will be reduced-rated. In all other cases a reasonable apportionment must be made. There is no prescribed method of apportionment, so any fair and reasonable method should be accepted by HMRC.

B. Energy-saving materials

1136 The **supply and installation** of energy-saving materials are reduced-rated if they are provided together for use in residential accommodation (¶1120).

Sch 7A Group 2 VATA 1994; Notice 708/6

MEMO POINTS Since 1 August 2013, reduced-rating **no longer applies** to the installation of energy-saving materials in buildings intended solely for charitable use.

What are energy-saving materials?

1138 Energy-saving materials include the following:
- insulation to walls, floors, ceilings, roofs, water tanks, pipes and plumbing fittings;
- draught stripping for doors and windows;
- controls for central heating and hot water systems;
- solar panels;
- wind turbines;
- water turbines;
- ground source heat pumps;
- air source heat pumps;
- micro-combined heat and power units; and
- boilers designed to be fuelled solely by wood, straw or similar vegetal matter.

MEMO POINTS The installation of **double glazing** or **energy-efficient home appliances** is not eligible for the reduced rate.

EXAMPLE Polycarbonate panels and reflective strips supplied for conservatory roofs were held by the First-tier Tribunal to be reduced-rated energy-saving materials. The products achieved "a demonstrable reduction in heat loss", and reduced-rating was not restricted to "panels to be attached to existing roofs", but included "all types of roofing insulation including those designed for use as a roof or as component parts of a roof". *Pinevale Ltd* [2012] (TC02283) However, on appeal the Upper Tribunal overturned this decision, stating that a roof panel is part of a roof and as such could not be considered to be insulation for a roof. *HMRC v Pinevale Ltd* [2014]

Installation

1140 To be reduced-rated, the energy-saving materials must be installed at the time of supply. The supply of goods for DIY purposes does not qualify for reduced-rating. Materials supplied as part of the construction of a new dwelling (¶5105+) are zero-rated.

Reduced-rating also extends to any **ancillary work** performed as part of the installation process. This includes, for example:
- minor building work (e.g. planing doors or windows, enlarging loft hatches and painting/plastering to make good); and
- the installation of any permanently fixed walkways, walkboards and ladders as part of the installation of roof insulation.

If the installation of energy-saving materials is **incidental to another supply**, or if goods and services are provided as an ensemble with no single dominant supply, reduced-rating may not apply. For example, suppose a contractor installs a central heating system. Although some components of the system might be reduced-rated if supplied on their own, here they form part of a wider supply of a central heating system. An entire central heating system is not included in the list of materials eligible for the reduced rate, so the whole supply is standard-rated. This approach has been confirmed by the First-tier Tribunal. *AN Checker Heating & Service Engineers* [2013] (TC02895)

C. Grant-funded supplies

Certain heating and security supplies are reduced-rated if: 1144 Sch 7A Group 3 VATA 1994; Notice 708/6 para 3.9
a. the payment for the supply is grant funded (either as a payment direct to the householder, or to the installer) from an **organisation with a stated objective** to fund the installation of heating for "less well-off people"; and
b. the **supply is made to** the sole or main residence of a person who is either over the age of 60 or in receipt of one or more specified benefits.

Note that supplies paid for, or contributions made, **by householders** out of their own pockets are not covered by the reduced rate under this heading, although they may qualify as supplies of energy-saving materials (¶1136).

MEMO POINTS 1. The **specified benefits** are:
- council tax benefit;
- working tax credit;
- any element of the child tax credit (other than the family element);
- disability living allowance;
- housing benefit;
- income-based jobseeker's allowance;
- income support;
- disablement/war disablement pension;
- personal and armed forces independence payments; and
- universal credit.

2. If **two or more people live in a dwelling**, and one person is a qualifying person and the others are not, the reduced rate will only apply if the supply is made to the qualifying person In practice, the supply will be at the reduced rate if the qualifying person is responsible for ordering the work to be done.
3. Where funding covers only **part of a qualifying supply** a reasonable apportionment (¶1152) must be made.
4. HMRC guidance formerly stated that reduced-rating **also applied to** the following where they were supplied as part of a single grant-funded package of heating or security supplies:
- compact fluorescent light bulbs, provided that they are not given to recipients for DIY installation; and
- energy efficiency advice.

However, items such as "cold alarms" and "carbon monoxide detectors" were not covered by the reduced rate. This guidance has been withdrawn, but there is no information about any change in HMRC's practices.

Heating supplies

The following grant-funded heating supplies are reduced-rated: 1146

Supply	Detail
Supply and installation of heating appliances	This only applies to: - gas-fired room heaters that are fitted with thermostatic controls; - electric storage heaters; - closed solid fuel fire cassettes; - electric dual immersion water heaters with factory-insulated hot water tanks; - gas- or oil-fired boilers; and - radiators
Supplies of goods or services for the installation, repair or maintenance of central heating systems	This also includes: - renewable source heating systems; and - micro-combined heat and power systems which are heating systems that also generate electricity. The electricity generated can then be used by the householder or "sold" by the householder to the National Grid

Supply	Detail
Supplies of goods or services for the connection or reconnection of a mains gas supply	

1148 Where a supply consists of the **leasing of goods** that form the whole or part of the installation of a central heating system the supply will also be reduced-rated, provided that the payment is grant funded and made to a relevant person (¶1144). Under this type of arrangement, the installer fits the central heating system as usual but then sells the equipment to a leasing company (standard-rated), which makes an annual "lease" charge to the householder, which is paid for by grant funding (reduced-rated).

Security goods

1150 In principle, the grant-funded **supply and installation** of the following security goods are reduced-rated:
- window and door locks or bolts;
- security chains;
- spy holes; and
- smoke alarms.

Notice 708/6 para 3.5

HMRC's guidance remarks, however, that there is currently no such grant-funded scheme available.

Apportionment

1152 Where a grant funds not only a reduced-rated supply but also some other supply, the value attributable to the reduced-rated supply is calculated as follows:

$$\frac{\text{Value of supply which is partly funded by the grant} \times \text{Amount of funding}}{\text{Total cost of supply}}$$

EXAMPLE A grant covers the following costs:

Supply	£
Cost of installing new heating system	6,000
Cost of installing new shower/bath	2,000
Total cost	8,000
Total grant	3,000

The value of the grant that can be treated as attributable to the cost of the central heating system (and therefore subject to 5% VAT) is £2,250. $\frac{(6{,}000 \times 3{,}000)}{8{,}000}$

D. Children's car seats

1156 Children's car seats, seat bases, booster seats, and cushions and carrycots with restraint straps are reduced rated. Child seats supplied as an integral part of a vehicle are **excluded** from reduced-rating.

Sch 7A Group 5 VATA 1994; Notice 701/23 para 5

Currently there are two types of **travel systems for babies** on the market that enable the car seat to be incorporated into the pushchair for ease of transport. The tax treatment is as follows:

Type of travel system	Treatment
A safety seat and a pram or pushchair that can be fitted together, although each element can be used independently of the other.	– safety seat is reduced-rated; – pram or pushchair is standard-rated
A safety seat, a related wheeled framework and a pram/pushchair seat. Any combination of the three elements may be supplied together but either the safety seat or the pram or pushchair seat can be attached to the framework for use as a pram. The framework is only of use when one of the other two elements is attached.	– when all three elements are supplied separately only the safety seat is reduced-rated (the other two are standard-rated); – when all three elements are supplied together, the safety seat and the wheeled framework are reduced-rated (the pram seat is standard-rated); – when just the safety seat and the wheeled framework are supplied the whole supply is reduced-rated; and – when just the pram and the wheeled framework are supplied the whole supply is standard-rated

E. Welfare advice or information

Supplies of welfare advice and information are reduced-rated if they are **provided by** a charity or state-regulated private welfare institution or agency and **relate to**: 1160 Sch 7A Group 9 VATA 1994
- the physical or mental welfare of elderly, sick, distressed or disabled persons; or
- the care and protection of children and young persons.

Specifically **excluded** from reduced-rating are supplies:
- that would be exempt as education (¶398);
- of goods, unless they are wholly for the purpose of conveying the advice or information; and
- that are tailored solely to a specific recipient's needs.

F. Smoking cessation products

Supplies of **over-the-counter** smoking cessation products are reduced-rated. This rate will apply to all products held out for sale as intended to help people stop smoking (for example, nicotine gum or patches). 1162 Sch 7A Group 11 VATA 1994

MEMO POINTS Smoking cessation products dispensed on **prescription** are zero-rated.

G. Imported works of art, antiques and collectors' items

There is an **effective reduced rate** of VAT applicable to imported works of art, antiques and any collection or collector's piece. Such goods are valued at 25% of their true value for the purposes of VAT. This results in an effective 5% VAT rate for these goods. 1164 s 21(4) VATA 1994; Notice 48 para 3.36

This **rate does not apply** if:

a. the whole of any **import VAT is relieved by** virtue of any HMRC direction; or

b. the **goods were exported from** the UK at any time in the 12 months preceding the date of the importation with the aim of artificially obtaining this effective reduced rate.

Reduced-rating will apply if the antiques, etc, have been exported and re-imported under any of the **following reliefs**:
- temporary importation relief (¶9509);
- returned goods relief (¶9447); or
- reimported goods relief (¶9443).

MEMO POINTS Traders may opt to use the **margin scheme** (¶6785) for imported works of art and other items in this category.

H. Installation of mobility aids for the elderly

1166 Sch 7A Group 10 VATA 1994

The **installation and supply** of the following mobility aids for the elderly are reduced-rated, if they are for use in domestic accommodation:
- grab rails;
- ramps;
- stair or bath lifts;
- built-in shower seats or showers containing built-in seats; and
- walk-in baths with sealable doors.

A person is **elderly** if he or she is aged over 60 at the time of the supply.

MEMO POINTS For this purpose **domestic accommodation** is defined as a dwelling, or part of a building containing a dwelling or a number of dwellings.

I. Static holiday caravans

1170 Sch 7A Group 12 VATA 1994; Notice 701/20; Information Sheet 04/13

Supplies of static holiday caravans are taxable at the reduced rate. The former zero-rating (¶1322+) applied up to 5 April 2013. Reduced-rating also applies to:
- the transfer of any undivided share in;
- the lease or hire of; or
- the private or non-business use of

such a caravan.

A **static holiday caravan** is defined as a static caravan (¶1323) which is not manufactured to BS 3632:2005. This is the current standard for residential caravans and confirms that a caravan is designed and manufactured for continuous year-round occupation. A caravan manufactured to a previous version of standard BS 3632 and which was occupied before 6 April 2013 may still be zero-rated (¶1322+).

Reduced-rating does not apply to any **removable contents**, other than those of a kind ordinarily incorporated by builders as fixtures in a new dwelling (such as sinks, baths or WCs). If necessary the purchase price must be apportioned between the caravan and its contents. For the treatment of other goods and services associated with caravans see ¶1328.

J. Cable transport

1174 Sch 7A Group 13 VATA 1994

The reduced rate applies to services involving the carriage of passengers by small, cable-suspended transport systems.

This **includes** any form of chair, bar, gondola or similar vehicle, provided that it is designed or adapted to carry not more than nine passengers. Transport in larger vehicles is zero-rated (¶1282).

Standard-rating applies to cable transport which is provided to, from or within a place of:
- entertainment, recreation or amusement; or
- cultural, scientific, historical or similar interest,

by the person who supplies a right of admission to, or a right to use facilities at, such a place, or by any person connected (¶966) with that person.

SECTION 3

Zero-rated supplies

Although no VAT needs to be accounted for on zero-rated supplies, it is important to identify such supplies correctly because they are **taxable supplies** (albeit taxed at 0%). As such: **1180** ss 26, 30, Sch 1 paras 1, 9, 14 VATA 1994
- **input tax** can be recovered on costs relating to the zero-rated supplies; and
- the supplies are taken into account when determining whether a business is liable to **register for VAT**.

MEMO POINTS 1. A business which **only** makes zero-rated supplies can apply to be exempt from registration (¶2650).
2. If a business makes a **combination of taxable and exempt supplies**, it will be partly exempt (¶2075) and only able to recover a proportion of the input tax it has incurred.

Summary

There is an extensive **statutory list** of zero-rated supplies. The table below summarises the groups of supplies where zero-rating applies. There are conditions attached to zero-rating and as such not all supplies in a category will necessarily qualify. **1182**

Supply	Sch 8 VATA 1994	¶¶
Food	Group 1	¶1136
Sewerage services and water	Group 2	¶1246
Books, etc	Group 3	¶1252
Talking books for the blind	Group 4	¶1366
Buildings and engineering works	Groups 5 and 6	¶5100+
International services	Group 7	¶9788+
Transport	Group 8	¶1280
Caravans and houseboats	Group 9	¶1322
Non-investment gold[1]	Group 10	¶6830
Bank notes[2]	Group 11	
Drugs, medicines, aids for the handicapped, etc	Group 12	¶1332
Imports and exports	Group 13	¶9418, ¶9581
Supplies to charities	Group 15	¶1362
Clothing and footwear	Group 16	¶1394
Supplies made to a European Research Infrastructure Consortium (ERIC), sited in a member state, for the ERIC's official use	Group 18	

Note:
1. Supplied to or by a central bank or a member of the London gold market.
2. Charges made by one bank to another for the use of automated cash machines by customers are not consideration for a zero-rated supply of bank notes but are consideration for the facility to obtain money. Consequently the supply is exempt (¶358).

MEMO POINTS Zero-rating also applies to certain **transactions in commodities**, the detail of which is outside the scope of *VAT Memo*. s 50 VATA 1994; SI 1973/173

A. Food

1186 Only food which falls within one of the following categories can be zero-rated:

Food item	Group 1	¶¶
Food (which includes drink) of a kind used for human consumption	item 1	¶1188
Animal feeding stuffs (including those for birds, fish, crustacean and molluscs)	item 2	¶1192
Seeds etc supplied to grow plants for human or animal consumption	item 3	¶1196
The supply of live animals (including birds, fish, crustaceans and molluscs) if they are of a kind generally used as, or to supply, food for human consumption	item 4	¶1204

However, food and drink, even of the above types, which is supplied in the course of **catering** (¶1220) is standard-rated.

There are several items which are **specifically excluded** from zero-rating and are therefore standard-rated. Most of the items excluded are deemed to be non-essential, or luxury items: see ¶1205+.

In addition, special rules apply where there is a **mixed supply** of standard-rated and zero-rated items (¶1240), or a third party provides a service of **processing food products** to produce a new food product (¶1242).

1. Food or drink for human consumption

1188 Sch 8 Group 1 item 1 VATA 1994; Notice 701/14; Notice 701/38

"Food" and "drink" should be interpreted according to their ordinary, everyday meaning and therefore **include**:

a. basic foodstuffs such as meat, cereals, fruit and vegetables, provided that they are intended for human consumption;

b. products sold for use as **ingredients in home cooking or baking**, such as flours and sugars (including artificial sweeteners), provided that they will form an integral part of a food substance, have some form of nutritional value and are used solely or predominantly in the manufacture of food other than excluded items (so, for example, ice-cream mixes are standard-rated because ice-cream is an excluded item);

c. processed foods such as canned or frozen food, or ready meals, generally follow the liability of the underlying ingredients, but any food designed to be **eaten while frozen** (¶1208) is standard-rated;

d. most traditional **bakery products**, such as bread, biscuits and cakes, are zero-rated, but not items classed as confectionery (¶1210);

e. some specialised **sports foods**, invalid foods, diabetic and hypoallergenic foods, slimmers' products, religious foods and health foods;

f. products used in **commercial food manufacture**, provided that they are used solely or predominantly for their nutritional value or are essential to the production of a particular foodstuff (such as stabilisers, artificial sweeteners and flavourings); and

g. items that are marketed as **medicinal** (e.g. herbal teas), if they are of a type ordinarily consumed by humans as **food** (supplies to practitioners of the individual ingredients will vary depending upon whether they are of a type ordinarily used for human consumption - the list of plants accepted as culinary is extensive and can be found in Notice 701/38).

MEMO POINTS 1. Zero-rating has been agreed for the following food products which have exclusive **sacramental use**:
- communion wafers used in the celebration of the Christian Communion, Mass or Eucharist;
- unfermented communion wine (fermented wine is standard-rated); and

– unfermented grape juice for use at the Jewish Seder or Kaddish, provided that it is marked prominently in English "for sacramental use only".
Otherwise, where religious laws require certain foods to be prepared in particular ways (for example, kosher, halal), the VAT liability of the final product is not altered.
2. Most **commercial additives**, including preservatives, flavour enhancers and flour improvers, are not classed as food and are therefore standard-rated.

Food disposed of because it has reached its **sell-by date** remains zero-rated, provided that it is still fit for human consumption. **1189**

EXAMPLE A supplier withdrew his haddock and mackerel from sale for human consumption and sold it to fishermen as bait for commercial reasons. This supply was zero-rated, because the fish was still fit for human consumption when sold. *North Isles Shellfish Ltd* [1995] (VTD 13083)

Zero-rating **does not apply** where nutrition is not the main purpose of ingestion. **1190**

Where a product has a purely medicinal effect (such as indigestion remedies) the test is whether the main purpose of eating the food is nutritional (zero-rated) or therapeutic (standard-rated). If medicated foods are administered to a person (for example, in hospital), they will be classed as foods, as the aim is to meet a patient's nutritional requirements as well as administer medicine. Medicated foods include liquid products designed to promote weight gain and formulated liquids administered intravenously.

Most **vitamin, mineral and herbal substances** are standard-rated, whether supplied in pill, capsule or powder form, although powdered food supplements can be zero-rated if they have a high nutritional content and/or provide a significant dietary requirement, and are taken in a manner normally associated with food (for example, mixed with other food and eaten).

Waste or contaminated food will be standard-rated (because it is not fit for human consumption), unless it is used as animal feeding stuff.

2. Animal feeding stuffs

This covers all products fed to animals (including birds, fish, crustaceans and molluscs) for the purposes of nourishment. It is very wide-ranging and **includes** grass, manufactured feeds and ingredients for animal feeds (including nutritional supplements and organic products, even if in pill or capsule form). **1192** Sch 8 Group 1 item 2 VATA 1994; Notice 701/15

Zero-rating **does not apply** to animal feed that:
– is held out for sale as **pet food**, or food for wild birds (¶1218), or for some non-food purpose (for example, hay sold as bedding);
– incorporates medicines to the extent that they alter the essential nature of the product as food; or
– has little or no nutritional value, even if supplied as ingredients for animal feeding stuffs, e.g. flavourings, appetisers, binders and colouring agents.

MEMO POINTS 1. **Grazing rights** (the right to graze animals on someone else's land) are zero-rated. The keeping of animals where the service incorporates an element of care for the animals, such as mucking out, is standard-rated; feed cannot be zero-rated separately.
2. **Stabling** is:
– normally an exempt supply of a right over land, in which case feed can be zero-rated if the service includes no element of caring for the animal;
– a standard-rated supply if the owner has exercised the option to tax (¶5602), in which case feed forms part of the standard-rated package; or
– standard-rated if the stable provides special-purpose services, such as training.

Often, animal feed products have **dual purposes**. For example, oil-bearing seeds may be used as ingredients in poultry food or in the manufacture of oils for industrial use. **In most cases** it will not be difficult to identify whether a supply is for animal food or not, as strict guidelines have to be adhered to on the composition and purpose of such products. If there is **any doubt**, the VAT treatment will depend upon how the product is being held out for sale. **1194**

3. Seeds, etc, to grow plants for human or animal consumption

1196 Sch 8 Group 1 item 3 VATA 1994; Notice 701/38

Seeds, seedlings, crowns, spores, tubers and bulbs of edible fruit and vegetables that are specifically grown to produce food of a kind for human or animal consumption are zero-rated. Any **treatment or process** is similarly zero-rated.

Zero-rating **does not apply** to:
- rootstocks (other than cucumber or tomato);
- pre-germinated grass seed (including turf); or
- plant-growing kits (unless the non-seed element of the kit accounts for less than 10% of the total cost, or the kit provided is no more than a method of simplifying the planting process, for example, peat cubes of less than 125cc impregnated with seeds, or thin layers of tissue incorporating seeds).

If a **mushroom growing kit** is provided, the whole supply can be zero-rated if it is provided in a cardboard box or other non-reusable container. If it is provided in a reusable container, VAT must be accounted for on the container, with the remainder being zero-rated.

Fruit-producing plants

1198 Notice 701/38 para 3.5

The following fruit-producing plants can be zero-rated:

Almond (not "flowering almond")
Apple
Apricot
Blackberry
Blackcurrant
Blueberry
Boysenberry
Bullace
Cherry (not "flowering cherry")
Citrus trees (not ornamental varieties)
Cobnut
Common quince (not chaenomeles)
Cowberry
Crab (only fruiting varieties)
Cranberry
Damson
Fig
Filbert
Gages
Gooseberry
Grapevines
Hazel
Huckleberry
Loganberry
Medlar
Mulberry
Nectarine
Peach
Pear
Raspberry plum (not "flowering plum")
Redcurrant
Strawberry
Sweet chestnut
Tayberry
Walnut
Whitecurrant
Wineberry
Worcesterberry

Herbs

1200 Notice 701/38 para 4.2

The following herbs can be zero-rated irrespective of how they are held out for sale:

Angelica
Anise
Anise hyssop
Basil
Borage
Caraway
Cardamom
Cardoon
Celery wild
Celery wild alpine
Chervil
Chicory
Chives
Coriander
Cumin
Curry leaf
Dandelion
Dill
Fennel
Fenugreek
Garlic
Ginger
Good King Henry
Horseradish
Lemon grass
Liquorice
Lovage
Marjoram
Mint
Onion
Orache
Oregano
Parsley
Pennyroyal
Rocket
Rosemary
Saffron
Sage
Salad burnet
Savory
Skirret
Sorrel
Tarragon
Thyme
Watercress

1201 Notice 701/38 para 4.3

In addition, some herbs with recognised culinary uses that satisfy all of the following conditions can be zero-rated:
- they have been raised according to the Food and Environment Protection Act 1985;
- they have been held out for sale as culinary herbs;
- they are supplied in individual pots (not bedding strips) of a size less than 2 litres; or

– in the case of bay plants, they do not exceed 50cm in height and have not been clipped shaped or subject to topiary in such a way as to specialise them as ornamentals.

Herbs supplied for **medical use** rather than culinary use are not eligible for zero-rating as "food" and are standard-rated, even if they have been raised under the same conditions as culinary herbs. This includes plants used in the preparation of food supplements (for example, evening primrose and ginseng). Notice 701/38 para 4.4

Seeds producing edible flowers

The following seeds can be zero-rated where they are held out for sale as food of a kind used for human consumption: **1202** Notice 701/38 para 5.2

Bergamot	Lavender	Pelargonium	Poppy	Sunflower
Clove pink	Nasturtium	Pink	Pot Marigold	Violets

4. Live animals

The supply of live animals (including birds, fish, crustaceans and molluscs) is zero-rated if their meat is of a kind generally consumed by humans, or they produce food for human consumption (such as milk or honey). Such animals are zero-rated even if they are not specifically intended to be eaten (such as sheep kept for their wool). **1204** Sch 8 Group 1 item 4 VATA 1994; Notice 701/15

HMRC's view is that "generally" in this definition means "generally in the UK".

Zero-rating **does not apply** to racing pigeons, or a right to fish. If a separate charge is made to take away any fish caught, this can be zero-rated if the fish is of a type consumed by humans.

The following are **examples** of zero-rated and standard-rated supplies:

Zero-rated	Standard-rated
Show animals that generally produce food or are used as food for human consumption will still be zero-rated (for example, prize bulls)	Animals removed from the human food chain because they are no longer fit for human consumption (for example, because of disease)
Embryos of species which are normally used for human food if they are to be used for breeding	Anything below the embryo stage, **except** eggs and fish roes that are normally used, and fit, for human consumption
Chicken, game birds and ostriches	Ornamental breeds of birds
The following breeds of ducks, geese and turkeys, and their derivatives or crossbreeds: – ducks: Aylesbury, Campbell (Khaki Campbell), Indian Runner, Muscovy and Pekin; – geese: Brecon Buff, Chinese Commercial, Embdem, Roman and Toulouse; and – turkey: Beltsville White, British White, Broadbreasted White, Bronze (Broadbreasted Bronze) and Norfolk Black	
Rabbits (other than ornamental breeds), even if kept as pets	Kangaroos and other animals of a kind not generally reared for food in the UK
Freshwater fish, shellfish, etc, ordinarily recognised as food for human consumption	Bream, perch, pike, carp and tench; ornamental fish; fish for aquariums; bait (unless fit for human consumption)
Honey bees	Bumble bees

5. Items specifically excluded from zero-rating

Certain items are excluded from zero-rating because either they fall within the statutory exclusions (¶1206), or they are made in the course of catering (¶1220). **1205**

a. Statutory exclusions

The following items are generally excluded from zero-rating as they are not deemed to be "essential" to life: **1206** Notice 701/14; Notice 701/15

- ice cream and similar products (¶1208);
- confectionery (¶1210);
- certain savoury snacks (¶1212);
- certain beverages (¶1214);
- home brew (¶1216); and
- pet food (¶1218).

Ice cream and similar products

1208 Notice 701/14 para 3.5

The **key factor** when determining if a food item falls within this category is whether the product is designed to be eaten frozen. The following **examples** are standard-rated:
- all types of ice cream, ice lollies, sorbets, and sauces, toppings, cones or wafers provided with the ice cream;
- frozen yoghurts, gateaux and cakes that contain ice cream and which are **designed to be eaten frozen**; and
- mixes and powders for the preparation of ice creams, etc.

MEMO POINTS 1. If **cones or wafers** are sold separately they are zero-rated, unless they are covered in chocolate, in which case they are standard-rated.
2. When **cakes are sold frozen** and/or stored in a freezer they can be zero-rated if it is intended that they are completely defrosted or cooked before consumption.
3. Frozen, in relation to **yoghurt**, has been held to mean something reduced to below the freezing point of water. *Meschia's Frozen Foods v C & E* [2001] However, yoghurt unsuitable for immediate consumption when frozen is zero-rated.

Confectionery

1210 Notice 701/14 paras 3.4, 3.6

Confectionery and chocolate biscuits are standard-rated, whereas cakes are zero-rated. The following **factors will be considered** when deciding whether or not a product is a cake, biscuit or other type of confectionery:
- appearance, size, ingredients, taste and texture;
- manufacturing process;
- time and place of eating;
- marketing and packaging; and
- the view of the ordinary man on the street.

MEMO POINTS 1. Confectionery **disposed of** because it has reached its **sell-by date** remains standard-rated, unless it is not fit for human consumption and is disposed of as animal feed, in which case it will be zero-rated.
2. **Cake decorations** are standard-rated if they either resemble confectionery or are inedible. However, if such decorations are supplied with a cake, they do not give rise to a mixed supply (¶1240) if they meet the conditions for a linked supply (¶329).

1211 The currently accepted definition and **examples** of standard and zero-rated confectionery and biscuits are as follows:

Product	Standard-rated	Zero-rated
Confectionery	Any item of **sweetened** prepared food which is normally eaten with the fingers, or on a stick, for example: - chocolate; - cereal bars (provided that they are sweetened)[1]; - chewing/bubble gum; - marshmallows/florentines; - jelly confectionery; - dry fruit confectionery[2]; - glacé and crystallised fruits (with the exception of glacé cherries, as they are predominantly used in cooking)	- toffee apples; - chocolate used in manufacturing or cooking (e.g. cake decorations, baking ingredients, chocolate spread); - cakes[3]; - jaffa cakes; - flapjacks; - dry fruit for home baking[2], drained cherries, preserved ginger and candied peel; - chocolate crispcakes; - chocolate cups; - caramel shortbread; - marshmallow teacakes; - traditional ethnic delicacies

Product	Standard-rated	Zero-rated
Biscuits	All biscuits that are wholly or partly covered on the outside in chocolate or some other product similar in taste and appearance	– plain biscuits (e.g. choc chip); – Bourbon biscuits (i.e. chocolate on the inside only); – gingerbread men with chocolate eyes; – biscuits covered in icing or caramel (not chocolate)

Note:

1. At one time it was believed that a cereal bar would be zero-rated unless it was sweetened artificially. However, it has been held that a bar containing only cereal and fruit, but sweetened with syrup, was nevertheless sweetened even though the syrup was also used to bind the dry products together. *Bells of Lazonby Ltd* [2007] (VTD 20490)
2. Sweetened dried fruit held out for sale both as confectionery and for home baking can be zero-rated. If it is just held out as confectionery it will be standard-rated. Dried fruit that is naturally sweet and has had no sweetening matter added to it remains zero-rated.
3. The definition of a cake has been the subject of many cases. The test to be applied is whether the ordinary man in the street would view the product as a cake. Where a product can be a cake or a biscuit, it should be placed in the category to which it is most akin. One test often used to distinguish between the two is that when stale a cake becomes hard whereas a biscuit becomes damp or soft.

Savoury snacks

Savoury snacks are zero-rated unless they are specifically excluded. The table below details the conditions for exclusion from zero-rating and provides examples of some products which have been deemed to be standard-rated or zero-rated: **1212** Notice 701/14 para 3.8

Product	Conditions for exclusion from zero-rating	Examples	
		Standard-rated	Zero-rated
Potato based products [1]	– **sold in** a retail pack for eating out of the packet without any further need for preparation by the customer; and – **wholly or substantially** made from potato, potato flour or potato starch	– prawn crackers [2]; – potato crisps; – savoury flavoured rice cakes [3]; – peanuts; – cashew nuts; – "Hula Hoops" sold with a BBQ sauce sachet – "Pringles"	– breadsticks; – tortilla chips; – bagel chips; – "Twiglets"; – "Doritos"
Cereal based products [1]	– **sold in** a retail pack for eating out of the packet without any further need for preparation by the customer; and – **obtained by** the swelling of cereals or cereal products (e.g. savoury popcorn)		
Roasted or salted nuts [1]	**Not sold in** their shells		

Note:

1. Products that are sold for use in cooking continue to be zero-rated.
2. Prawn crackers made from tapioca are zero-rated.
3. Sweetened rice cakes will fall within ¶1210. Unflavoured rice cakes are zero-rated.

Beverages

There is no statutory definition of a beverage, but it has been **defined** by case law as being any liquid that is consumed to increase bodily liquid levels, slake thirst, fortify or give pleasure. *Bioconcepts Ltd* [1993] (VTD 11287) **1214** Notice 701/14 paras 3.7, 4.6

Standard-rating **applies to** all beverages including syrups, concentrates and essences for the preparation of beverages, with the **exception** of the following, which are zero-rated by statute:

– tea, maté, herbal teas and similar products, and preparations and extracts thereof;

– cocoa, coffee and chicory and other roasted coffee substitutes, and preparations and extracts thereof;

- milk and preparations and extracts thereof; and
- preparations and extracts of meat, yeast or egg.

The following table summarises the current approach taken by HMRC in relation to **some common products**:

Standard-rated products	Zero-rated products
All fruit juices	Lemon/lime juice sold for cooking purposes
Bottled water sold for drinking[1]	Bottled water not sold for drinking[2]
Ice cubes made from substances other than plain tap water	Ice cubes made from plain tap water
Flavoured soya or rice milk	Milk or milk based drinks including flavoured milk (from sheep or goats)[3, 4, 5, 6]
Syrups designed to prepare a beverage (e.g. with the addition of water)	Plain soya or rice milk, unsweetened and unflavoured
Sports nutrition drinks (¶1215)	Coconut milk
All drinks containing alcohol	Leaf tea, tea bags, instant tea, herbal teas (but not soft drinks containing tea - e.g. iced tea)
Alcohol-free beer and wine	Fruit preserved in alcohol; rum babas
All hot beverages	Slimming drinks and bodybuilding drinks (i.e. complete meal replacements)[7]
All carbonated drinks and fruit cordials	Coffee beans, instant coffee, cocoa

Note:
1. Includes all types - flavoured, still, sparkling, etc.
2. For example, water sold to refill a car battery.
3. Substitutes for dairy milk are also zero-rated, as they are for people who are allergic to dairy products.
4. Also edible products made from milk are relieved (e.g. coffee whiteners, baby milk, lactose).
5. Drinks that consist of a mixture of milk extracts and other ingredients (e.g. smoothies) will be zero-rated if the milk product is the predominant ingredient.
6. Products designed to flavour milkshakes are standard-rated unless they are made from cocoa or coffee.
7. If these are not designed to be complete meal replacements they will be standard-rated, unless they are preparations based on milk.

Comment There have been several cases on the VAT liability of **fruit and vegetable "drinks"**. In the case of *Unilever Bestfoods UK Ltd* [2007] (VTD 20016) it was held that a product comprising **liquidised** fruit and vegetables was zero-rated, as it was not sold or consumed to replace bodily fluids, or slake the thirst and was not consumed for pleasure (and hence not a beverage). Similarly in the case of *Ocean Grown UK Ltd* [2008] (VTD 20562) a health drink made of wheatgrass was not considered to be a beverage (because of its unpleasant taste) and was zero-rated. These decisions should be compared with *Kalron Foods Ltd* [2007], where it was held that **pulped** fruit and vegetables which were not offensive in taste or colour could be consumed as a beverage and were therefore standard-rated. More recently in *Innocent Ltd* [2010] (TC00771) a "smoothie" made of liquidised fruit was held not to be zero-rated because it was not simply liquidised fruit salad: fruit juice was added to the pulped fruit to make what the Tribunal considered to be a beverage.

A cautious approach should therefore be taken when considering whether a fruit or vegetable drink is standard-rated or zero-rated.

Sports nutrition drinks

1215 Information Sheet 15/12

Standard-rating applies to sports nutrition drinks, **defined** as drinks that are advertised or marketed as products designed to enhance physical performance, accelerate recovery after exercise or build bulk. This includes:
- drinks supplied in liquid form;
- syrups, concentrates, essences, powders, crystals or other products that can be made up into a liquid by the consumer; and
- any drinks similar to the defined items.

Sports energy gels are normally zero-rated.

MEMO POINTS 1. HMRC say that they will assess the **advertising or marketing** of drinks on the basis of factors including:
- the target market and design of the product;
- packaging and advertising; and
- retailing (for example, a product sold in a sports shop is likely to be standard-rated).

2. Prior to 1 October 2012 the scope of standard-rating was slightly different. Full details can be found in previous editions of *VAT Memo*, but the main differences are that from that date the following are **no longer zero-rated**:
- milk-based sports drinks (although milk itself remains zero-rated); and
- sports drinks intended primarily for rehydration.

3. Lucozade Sport is marketed as an **isotonic drink** but because its attraction to customers was its association with high-performance sport, rather than its isotonicity (it was mainly purchased by "armchair enthusiasts"), it was held to be standard-rated. *Glaxosmithkline Services Unlimited* [2010] (TC00688)

Home brew

The **following products** are standard-rated: **1216** Notice 701/14 para 3.7.4

a. home brew kits;
b. retail packs of products specific to home brewing or wine making (for example, grape concentrates, hopped malt extract, malted barley, roasted barley, hops, brewer's yeast); and
c. retail packs of foods not necessarily specific to home brewing or wine making but held out for sale for home brewing or wine making (for example, dried or tinned fruit, barley, glucose, plain malt extract).

Any sales of brewing or wine making materials to **commercial enterprises** are zero-rated.

Pet foods

The **following products** are standard-rated: **1218** Notice 701/15 paras 6-8

a. canned, prepared or packaged food (other than biscuits and meal) for pets, that is held out for sale as pet food (therefore if food is held out for sale exclusively for non-pets such as working dogs or farmed fish, it will be zero-rated (¶1192));
b. biscuits and meal for all cats and dogs (irrespective of whether they are for pets, working animals, or sold packaged or not);
c. packaged food held out for sale for wild birds, other than poultry or game, but not including:
- food which is sold loose and simply put into bags at the point of retail sale;
- food for game birds;
- pigeon food (unless containing ingredients similar to food for pet birds); and
- pigeon grit;

d. commodities that have, and are held out for sale for, a non-feed purpose (such as hay that is also marketed as bedding); and
e. foods with minimal nutritional value (such as medicines, flavourings and appetisers).

MEMO POINTS 1. There is no **definition of a pet**, but an accepted definition is an animal (tamed if it was originally wild) which is kept primarily as an object of affection, including an animal kept primarily for ornament. *Popes Lane Pet Food Supplies* [1986] (VTD 2186) HMRC lists the following as pets:
- cage birds;
- cats;
- dogs (except working dogs);
- ferrets;
- goldfish, aquarium fish and pond fish; and
- guinea pigs, hamsters, gerbils, rats and mice (except laboratory animals).

2. It is the **intention of** the seller (not the customer) that determines whether a product is being sold as pet food or not. Food is zero-rated, provided that it is not held out for sale as pet food and is:
- intended for animals of non-pet species but which may be kept as pets such as reptiles, chickens, horses, ponies or rabbits (this includes food in the form of dead animals such as mice or chicks); or
- fresh, frozen or chilled meat and fish products, for dogs or dogs and cats, which has not undergone any preparation other than mincing or dicing and even if it is packaged.

3. Food is treated as **prepared** if it undergoes a process, for example:
– cooking of meat or meat products;
– addition of colouring, flavouring, preservative or gelling agents;
– mixing or blending of ingredients to meet specific nutritional requirements of a pet species; or
– dicing or mincing.
Simply sterilising the meat or cutting it from the bone is not preparation.
4. Food is treated as **packaged** if it is pre-packed for retail sale in any can, sealed bag, carton or other container of 12.5kg or less.
5. **Biscuit or meal** is any dry product that is either:
– coarsely ground basic commodities; or
– baked products consisting predominantly of cereal and fat and not providing all the nutrients required by the animal.

---

b. Supplies in the course of catering, etc

1220 Notice 709/1 Any supply of food and drink in the course of catering, or for consumption on the premises where it is supplied, is standard-rated.

Hot food is standard-rated regardless of where it is consumed.

Special rules apply to catering supplies made by hospitals and educational institutions (¶1234), from vending machines (¶1238), or on board a means of transport (¶1239).

In the course of catering

1222 Notice 709/1 para 2 Catering is not **defined** in law so the ordinary, everyday meaning is used. HMRC views catering as the supply of prepared food and drink involving a significant element of service. Examples include:
– supplies made in restaurants, cafes, canteens and similar establishments (except for cold take-away food);
– catering for events and functions, such as wedding receptions, parties or conferences;
– cooking and/or preparation of food at the customer's home (for example, for a dinner party); and
– delivery of cooked ready-to-eat food or meals (with or without crockery or cutlery).

Food **sold at an event** is not necessarily supplied in the course of catering, as there must be an intention for it to be consumed in the course of the activity concerned. For example, a bag of doughnuts sold at an exhibition may be zero-rated, although sales of individual doughnuts in the same circumstances might not be.

Supplies made under an ongoing **catering contract**, for example, the sale of sandwiches in an office, are not necessarily in the course of catering, if the supplier has no right to be on the premises and is reliant on the goodwill of the reception staff, etc, to permit access *Zeldaline Ltd* [1989] (VTD 4388).

VFOOD4140 HMRC will apply a list of **catering indicators** if it is not obvious whether a supply has been made in the course of catering, including:
– whether the food is ready to eat without further preparation;
– the existence of a menu; and
– any element of service to the customer.

These indicators are not exhaustive and even where the answer to one or more of these indicators is no, it may be that, based on the facts, the supply is nonetheless one of catering.

1223 Foods that require any form of **customer preparation** after purchase are not a supply of catering and may be zero-rated. For this purpose, preparation includes thawing, cooking or reheating food and arranging food on plates.

VFOOD5220 **Wholesale supplies** made to caterers for onward sale are not supplies in the course of catering and follow the normal rules for food (¶1186+).

MEMO POINTS 1. **Grocery items sold by a caterer**, for example, cartons of milk, or jars of coffee, are not supplies in the course of catering, provided that they are cold, in the same form as when sold by a grocer or supermarket, and are clearly not intended for on-premises consumption.

2. **Packed lunches** provided for an event or a function (e.g. a coach party or a race meeting) are treated as being supplied in the course of catering and standard-rated. However, where a hotel or similar establishment supplies a packed lunch for which a separate charge is made, then provided that the supply is for consumption off the premises, the supply can be zero-rated, apart from any food items which are always standard-rated.
3. Where the supply by a hotel consists of **accommodation and meals at an inclusive price**, for example, full board, half board, or bed and breakfast, this should be treated as a single standard-rated supply, even if any of the meals are taken as packed lunches. For food provided during conferences see ¶5498.
4. In HMRC's view the CJEU decision in *Finanzamt Burgdorf v Manfred Bog* [2011] does not allow UK **supplies of hot snacks** to be treated as supplies of goods in the UK (and hence avoid being standard-rated as supplies made in the course of catering). UK law specifies that zero-rating does not apply to any supplies (whether of goods or services) made in the course of catering. Supplies of hot food are supplies made in the course of catering, whether those supplies are deemed to be of goods or of services. VFOOD4120
5. A **service charge** is always standard-rated, whereas tips are outside the scope of VAT.

Consumption on the premises

Any food supplied for consumption **on the premises** where it is supplied is standard-rated, irrespective of whether the supplies were made in the course of catering. Any supply of cold food for consumption away from the premises is zero-rated, provided that it meets the conditions in ¶1188; but see also ¶1228+. **1224** Notice 709/1 para 3; VFOOD4500+

"Premises" for this purpose are **defined** to include any area that is:
– occupied or controlled by the food retailer; or
– set aside for the consumption of food by the retailer's customers, whether or not the area may also be used by the customers of other suppliers.

HMRC's opinions on the extent of various premises are shown in the following table:

Premises	Includes
A restaurant	The whole restaurant area, plus any chairs or tables on the pavement, concourse or similar adjacent[1] area
A retail outlet in a shopping centre	The outlet itself, plus any chairs or tables in designated areas belonging to the outlet or provided for its exclusive use
A retail outlet in a food court	The outlet, plus the chairs and tables within the food court, if either: – the retailer contributes to the upkeep, provision and cleaning of the facilities; or – the facilities are in an area clearly delineated for the use of customers to consume their food purchases.
A stall in a sports stadium, amusement park, exhibition, gallery or similar pay-entry venue	The stall itself, plus any facilities provided adjacent[1] to it for the use of customers
A retail outlet within an office building	The outlet, plus any area provided for consumption adjacent[1] to it, such as a seating area or dining room

Note
1. Premises also include any areas which are not immediately adjacent to the outlet, but are within its vicinity and are designated for the use of its customers. It does not include areas with chairs and tables for genuinely communal use and which are not the responsibility of the retailer.

MEMO POINTS HMRC's view is that the leading case remains that of *HMRC v Compass Contract Services UK Ltd* [2006] (see below), in which a food court area was held to be "premises". More recent cases, such as *Made to Order Ltd* [2009] (VTD 20959), have applied a more restricted definition of "premises", but HMRC considers that these cases were decided on their particular facts and do not create a precedent.

EXAMPLE
1. Compass was contracted to provide catering services in six outlets within BBC Television Centre. The Court of Appeal held that supplies by Compass of cold take-away food (sandwiches, etc) were zero-rated on the basis that the food was not intended to be eaten on "the premises".

Crucially, it was held that "the premises" only extended to the outlets controlled by Compass, not the entire Television Centre. *HMRC v Compass Contract Services UK Ltd* [2006]

2. A company ran retail food kiosks and buffet bars at railway stations. It was held that premises did not extend to the station area around the kiosk, as the packaging of the cold food sold from the kiosks was designed to keep the contents fresh for several hours and it was not the company's purpose that its food should be consumed on the station premises. *Travellers Fare Ltd* [1995] (VTD 13482)

3. In contrast to the above, a trader had an agreement with a football club to sell food and drink from a number of kiosks within the club's ground.
It was held that the premises comprised the whole ground, because the food was intended to be eaten there. *Bristol City Football Supporters Club* [1975] (VTD 164)

4. A trader ran a food stall in an amusement park. There was no entrance fee to the park and no restriction on public access. It was held that the supplies were not linked to a particular event (and were therefore not supplies in the course of catering) and the stall and the park together could not be regarded as a single set of premises. *Fresh Sea Foods (Barry) Ltd* [1991] (VTD 6658)

5. A trader sold sandwiches from a counter in the common room of a hospital postgraduate centre. It was held that the premises were restricted to the common room only and did not extend to the adjacent roof terrace (even though seating was provided on the roof terrace), on the basis that access to the roof terrace was open and unrestricted. *Carpenter & Hayles (t/a Carpenter Catering)* [2003] (VTD 18148)

6. A company sold seafood from a kiosk in a shopping centre. The kiosk was one of several surrounding a food court with tables and chairs for almost 400 people. It was held that the premises comprised the kiosks and the courtyard together. The kiosk supplies were therefore standard-rated. *Crownlion (Seafood) Ltd* [1985] (VTD 1924)

7. A company sold snacks from vending machines. The tribunal rejected the company's claim to zero-rate its supplies, holding that the snacks were intended "for consumption on the premises on which they were supplied". *West Country Vending Service Ltd* [2010]

Hot take-away food

1228 Notice 709/1 para 4

All sales of hot food (except for sales of freshly baked bread) are standard-rated.

In order for food to be considered hot it must be above ambient air temperature at the time it is provided to the customer and must satisfy any one of a series of additional criteria (¶1230).

MEMO POINTS 1. It is not necessary for the **whole item** to be hot. For example, a bacon sandwich is standard-rated, even if the bread is not heated.
2. **Provided to the customer** means at the time the item is handed over. For example, a hot chicken sold by a supermarket is standard-rated, even if it has cooled down by the time the customer reaches the checkout.
3. **Prior to 1 October 2012** a supply of hot food was excluded from zero-rating if it, or any part of it:
– had been heated for the purpose of consuming it at a temperature above the ambient air temperature; and
– was above that temperature at the time it was provided to the customer.
The key factor was the trader's intention at the time of supplying the food. For factors taken as indicative of the trader's intention see previous editions of *VAT Memo*. This test is retained as the first of the additional criteria (¶1230) but the trader's intention is not relevant from 1 October 2012.

1230 To be standard-rated, the hot food must also satisfy any one or more of the criteria shown in the following table:

Criterion	Examples
Food has been heated[1] for the purposes of enabling it to be consumed hot	Fish and chips, take-away meals (for example, Chinese, Indian, pizzas, kebabs, etc), baked potatoes, hot dogs, hamburgers, soup, hot drinks
Food has been heated[1] to the customer's order	Toasted sandwiches, garlic bread, pizza, hamburgers, kebabs

Criterion	Examples
Food has been kept hot after being heated[1, 2]	Warm pastries (such as croissants or pretzels), hot deli chickens, pies kept in ovens
Food is provided to a customer in specialised packaging[3]	Foil-lined bags, foil trays, pizza boxes, heat-retentive grease-proof bags for chickens
Food is advertised or marketed in a way which indicates that it is supplied hot[4]	Rotisserie chickens, roasted chestnuts, hot soup

Note
1. "Heated" and similar expressions also include cooking or reheating.
2. This includes being kept in heated cabinets, hot water, ovens, etc, or on spits or hot trays, or under hot lamps.
3. That is, packaging which retains heat (whether or not it was primarily designed for that purpose), or s specifically designed for hot food.
4. Not including food that is advertised or marketed as "freshly baked".

EXAMPLE

1. Mr F sells joints of beef that are kept hot in a cabinet after roasting. The sale of these joints is standard-rated. At the end of the day, he removes any unsold joints from the heated cabinet and either sells them cold next day or uses them to make cold take-away sandwiches. As they are not hot at the time that they are provided to the customer, these items are zero-rated.

2. Mrs G sells Cornish pasties that are baked and then left to cool naturally. She sells a pasty that is still hot when it is provided to the customer. However, Mrs G does not intend the pasty to be eaten hot by the customer; it has not been cooked to order; it has not been kept hot after being cooked; it is provided to the customer in an ordinary paper bag; and it is advertised as "freshly baked". This satisfies none of the five creiteria, so the sale of the pasty is zero-rated.

3. If Mrs G keeps her pasties under hot lamps to slow down the cooling process, the pasties are being kept hot after they are cooked and will be standard-rated. Similarly if Mrs G advertises her pasties as "hot" rather than "freshly baked", they will be standard-rated.

Where a **single supply is made of both hot and cold food**, the treatment varies depending upon the nature of the supply: 1232
- where it is a hot supply with only a single cold ingredient (for example, a hot dog in a bun), the whole supply is a single standard-rated supply; but
- where it is a supply of several hot and cold items (each of which can be purchased separately from a menu, for example, burgers, chips and a milkshake), the supply is treated as a mixed supply and VAT is apportioned accordingly (¶1240).

Any minor items for which **no charge is made** (for example, salt, pepper, vinegar or mustard) can be ignored.

Institutional catering

Hospitals and other institutions registered by statute Supplies of catering by these institutions **to their patients** in the course of their care is exempt from VAT. The exemption **does not extend to** supplies to staff or visitors. 1234 Notice 709/1 para 2.7

Educational institutions Where the education supplied from such institutions is: 1236 Notice 709/1 paras 2.6, 5.5
- exempt (¶398), supplies in the course of catering will also be exempt; or
- non-business, as in the case of a local authority school, the supply of catering will also be non-business, provided that it is made at, or below, cost.

These rules do not apply to supplies to staff or visitors (except visiting students). However, the Upper Tribunal has recently confirmed an **exception** to this rule. In this case the college organised restaurant meals, for which tickets were sold to students' friends and family. The supplies were held to be exempt, albeit that supplies of catering were made to friends and family, not to the students themselves. Exemption was afforded to these supplies because the meals were put on solely in order to educate the students (who themselves did the cooking or served the customers). The supplies were thus closely related to the students' education in the field of catering. *HMRC v Brockenhurst College* [2014]

Where a **student union** supplies catering or hot take-away food to students on behalf, and with the agreement, of the parent institution, it can treat its supplies in the same way as if the parent institution were making the supply. This means that a student union can treat its supplies as:
– exempt when made at a university or other institution supplying exempt education; or
– outside the scope of VAT when supplied at a local authority further education or sixth form college.

This **concession does not cover** food and drink sold from campus shops, bars, tuck shops, vending machines or similar outlets, because such sales are not considered to be supplies made in the course of catering.

Vending machines

1238 Notice 709/1 para 2.4 Supplies from a vending machine follow the same general principles as other supplies of food and drink. In particular:
– all standard-rated items (for example, beverages or confectionery) remain standard-rated:
– supplies from vending machines in canteens and restaurant areas are standard-rated as supplies to be consumed on the premises; and
– supplies from machines in thoroughfares and areas not designated for the consumption of food follow the liability of the product sold.

If the machine is in a **canteen or similar area**, an apportionment will only be allowed if the food seller can demonstrate that a proportion of the items of cold food (that would be eligible for zero-rating) are taken away from the premises.

If there is an **ongoing catering contract** to provide food and drink for a particular group of people from the vending machine, the supplies are standard-rated on general principles, whether hot or cold and wherever the food is consumed.

On board catering

1239 Notice 709/1 para 2.5 A separate supply of catering on board an aircraft, ship, train or other means of transport is standard-rated, unless it is provided for consumption during a journey from the UK to another EU member state or on a journey to a country outside the EU.

6. Mixed supplies

1240 A supply of standard- and zero-rated food items, or zero-rated food items and standard-rated non-food items, together for a single price, may be a composite supply or a mixed supply (¶310).

In **general**, the consideration should be allocated between the supplies and VAT accounted for accordingly.

Areas of particular concern in relation to food items include:
– packaging (¶327);
– minor linked items (¶329); and
– mixtures and assortments (¶331)

7. Processing

1242 Notice 701/40 A supply of processing services which results in the **production of** a new zero-rated food product will also be zero-rated. Processing which does not result in the production of a new food product, or which results in the production of a standard-rated food product, is standard-rated.

A **new food product** comes into being if the process has altered the essential characteristics of the original goods. This may include size, shape, appearance, composition, use, and readiness to use or eat.

The following are **examples** of zero-rated and standard-rated processes:

Zero-rated processes	Standard-rated processes
Smoking salmon (as the salmon is immediately edible following the process)	Smoking herring (a kipper is still not immediately edible, so the essential characteristics of the fish have not changed)
Butchering carcasses, including boning, jointing or curing meat	Slaughtering animals without further processing
Processing meat into sausages	Skinning fish; shelling shrimps, prawns or other shellfish
Drying, cleaning and coating seeds or grain to make them marketable as seed for sowing	Cleaning and conditioning grain
Cooking, canning or otherwise preserving fruit and vegetables	Roasting or salting peanuts or other nuts
Processing of liquid milk into dried milk	Blending tea
Kneading blocks of frozen butter, adding salt and water and packing	Pasteurisation or sterilisation
Roasting and grinding coffee beans	Maturing, sorting, grading or packaging

B. Sewerage services and water

The **general rule** is that supplies in connection with sewerage services and water supplies are zero-rated. **1246** Sch 8 Group 2 VATA 1994; Notice 701/16

However, the rule **is modified** in several situations:

Type of supply	General rule	Exceptions
Water (including ice)	Zero-rated if provided to domestic and non-industrial customers	Standard-rated if water: – is provided for a relevant industrial activity[1]; – is distilled water, de-ionised water, or water of similar purity; – falls within any of the excepted food items as a beverage, etc (¶1214); or – is heated water[2] Reduced-rated if: – heated water is supplied for domestic or charitable non-business purposes (¶1129)
Sewerage services	Zero-rated if service relates to: – reception, disposal or treatment of foul water or sewage in bulk; or – emptying of cesspools, septic tanks or similar receptacles	Standard-rated for: – cleaning and maintenance of sewers and drains; or – emptying of cesspools, septic tanks, etc, if supplied to an industrial user[1]

Note:
1. A **relevant industrial activity** is one which falls within the following activities:
– energy and water supply industries;
– extraction of minerals and ores other than fuels;
– manufacture of metals, mineral products and chemicals;
– metal goods, engineering and vehicle industries;
– other manufacturing industries; or
– construction.

If the water is used **both for relevant industrial activities and other purposes**, the liability of the supply depends upon the predominant activity of the customer. Any supply is therefore taxed according to the predominant activity, as there is no apportionment. The only exception to this is if a supply is made to an industrial customer who has two or more business activities (one of which is both non-industrial and exempt). The supply relating to the exempt activity can remain zero-rated, provided that the supply can be separately identified and a separate invoice is raised.

2. Water which has been heated up but **allowed to cool** (i.e. sterilised by boiling) is not heated water for this purpose.

Connection charges

1247 HMRC Brief 40/12 The treatment of connection charges depends on whether the service is a first-time connection or a replacement connection:

Occasion of supply	Circumstances	Treatment of connection charge
First time	Connection is made by the same taxable person as provides the water supply	Zero-rated[1]
	Connection is made by another party, or the water supplier has not been identified at the time of connection	Standard-rated
	Connection made as part of the construction of the building	Zero-rated if the building is a dwelling (¶5152), a relevant residential property (¶5158), or a relevant charitable building (¶5170)
	Connection made as part of civil engineering work in the development of a permanent park for residential caravans	Zero-rated: see ¶5192
Replacement	In most circumstances	Standard-rated
	Following demolition of a previous building and replacement by new property	Zero-rated[1]
	Following division of a property into multiple units	Zero-rated[1], unless the units continue to share a single connection
	As part of conversion of the building by a housing association to residential use	See ¶5430

Note:
1. Unless the customer is carrying on a relevant industrial activity (¶1246), in which case the connection charge is standard-rated.

Although these treatments were only announced by HMRC in December 2012, they are considered always to have applied. Suppliers may **claim** repayment of VAT incorrectly accounted for, subject to the usual 4-year time limit (¶3018).

1248 Notice 48 para 3.11 **Responsibility for charging the correct rate of VAT** rests with the supplier, who must therefore be satisfied as to the extent of the customer's qualifying use. To assist suppliers in this matter, customers can give suppliers a certificate to evidence qualifying use. It is the supplier's responsibility to check the validity of a certificate, but HMRC says that if the supplier is subsequently found to have charged the **incorrect rate of VAT in good faith**, HMRC will not attempt to recover the VAT due from the supplier.

C. Books and written material

1252 Sch 8 Group 3 VATA 1994; Notice 701/10 The following supplies of written material are zero-rated:
- books, booklets, brochures, pamphlets and leaflets (including amendments to ring-bound books and self-contained instalments of books (¶1256));
- newspapers, journals and periodicals (¶1264);
- children's picture books and painting books (¶1270);
- music (¶1272);

- maps, charts and topographical plans (¶1274); and
- covers, cases and other articles supplied with the above items (¶1276).

MEMO POINTS 1. The **lending or hiring** of an article which is zero-rated under these rules is also zero-rated. Libraries which charge for the loan of books will therefore be making zero-rated supplies. This will also apply to reference libraries which charge for the use of their books on their own premises.
2. **Talking books** for the disabled may be zero-rated in certain circumstances (¶1366).
3. The CJEU has confirmed that e-books that are supplied as downloads from the Internet are treated as a supply of services and are standard-rated. *EC v France and Luxembourg* 2015

Some **services directly relating to the production** of zero-rated items are also zero-rated, because the service supplied is the production of zero-rated goods. However, original, or specialist, services (such as writing or translation) will always be standard-rated, as the (potentially zero-rated) item produced will be incidental to the (standard-rated) supply of services. HMRC provides the following examples in its guidance: **1254** Notice 701/10 para 7

Service	Zero-rated	Standard-rated
Preparatory or post-production work	Any preparatory or post-production services (other than alterations) performed in conjunction with a contract to supply zero-rated items, whether or not the supplier itemises the various processes on its tax invoice and charges for them separately and even if the supplier has employed subcontractors	Post-production alterations
Subcontract work	Production of new zero-rated goods - for example, binding pages together to make a book with cover	Typesetting (even if the final product is zero-rated by the main contractor)
Work on other people's goods	If the supplier applies a treatment or process to someone else's goods, which produces new goods, the liability of the supplier's service follows that of the goods produced - for example, binding loose papers into a book	Any other service is standard-rated, including post-production alterations - for example, re-covering or otherwise repairing an old volume

Zero-rating does not apply to a supply of printed materials that is **connected with a supply of services** made by a different supplier. The supplies of printed matter and of services are connected if, had they both been made by the same supplier, they would have been treated as a single standard-rated, reduced-rated or exempt supply of services. **1255**

1. Books, booklets, brochures, pamphlets and leaflets

Excluded from zero-rating and therefore standard-rated are: **1256** Notice 701/10 para 3
a. items that do not convey information by text, for example:
- books of plans or drawings for industrial, architectural, engineering, commercial or similar purposes;
- picture card and stamp albums, unless they contain a substantial amount of reading matter which is complete in itself and no more than 25% of the album is set aside for the mounting of cards and stamps;
- completed stamp albums; and
- products that are essentially stationery items, for example, diaries and address books;

b. items (other than school books: ¶1258) whose main significance lies in the fact that they need to be filled in, such as:
- diaries;
- account books; and
- exercise books;

c. posters; and
d. letters, unless bound into a book.

Books and booklets

1258 Notice 701/10 paras 3.1, 5.2; VBOOKS3110; Notice 48 para 3.15

Books and booklets normally consist of text or illustrations and are **bound** in a cover stiffer than their pages. They may be printed in any language or characters (including Braille or shorthand), photocopied, typed or hand-written, provided that they are found in book or booklet form.

Zero-rating is allowed not only for the usual forms of books but also for:
a. loose-leaf books, manuals or instructions, whether complete with their binder or not;
b. binders supplied on their own, if they are designed to contain a loose-leaf book, provided that the exact title of that book is printed on the outside (a company name alone is not enough for zero-rating);
c. a **binder supplied with loose-leaf pages** to make a book (the binder is treated as part of the zero-rated supply whether titled or not), although all other binders or files for general or office use are standard-rated (this includes binders for part works, journals or periodicals, whether specifically titled or not);
d. card-based **boxed publications**, even though not bound or held together other than in or by their container, provided that they have all the other characteristics of a book.

EXAMPLE A binder was supplied after the first issue of a magazine series with the intention of holding all the issues as a set. It was held that the binder was standard-rated, because it was not an essential part of a book (although the magazines were zero-rated as periodicals). *Marshall Cavendish Ltd* [1973] (VTD 16)
Note: This is an old case and might well now be treated differently by HMRC, in accordance with the principles listed above.

MEMO POINTS **School workbooks**, exam papers and educational texts generally that take the form of questions and answers are usually zero-rated, as the spaces for the insertion of the answers are incidental to the publication.

1259 HMRC Brief 4/12

HMRC has issued guidance on when **photobooks** can be zero-rated. HMRC draws a distinction between books which are the purpose of the supply (which may be zero-rated) and those which are an incidental result of a supply of **services** (which are always standard-rated). An example of the former is a book which is printed by the supplier after the customer designs the book from photographs chosen by the customer and uploaded to a website template provided by the supplier. An example of the latter is a book of wedding photographs as an end product, where the main supply is of organising, taking and processing the photographs.

If the **supply is one of goods** (that is, services are not the predominant purpose of the supply), the following are necessary characteristics of a book (which, if met, will enable zero-rating):
- a significant number of leaves;
- those leaves being usually of paper;
- held together by front and back covers;
- those covers being usually more substantial than the leaves.

The book **must also be designed** to be read or looked at. However, HMRC does not accept a photobook as falling within the zero rate if either:
- the photobook's pages have the appearance and quality of individual photographic prints; or
- the photobook is capable of being dismantled, with individual pages that are removable, or where individual pages can be easily removed without damaging the binding, for example, spiral binding.

Brochures and pamphlets

Brochures usually consist of several sheets of reading matter fastened or folded together, which are not necessarily bound in covers and are designed to be held in the hand for reading. They usually contain advertising material in the form of text or illustrations. Pamphlets are similar but are usually comprised of material of a political, social or intellectual nature. **1260** Notice 701/10 paras 3.2, 3.4; VBOOKS3200

EXAMPLE A company published glossy cards, which it described as "tax cards", containing various items of information relating to tax. The cards were scored in such a way that they could be folded into three, enabling them to be kept in a jacket pocket. These were held to be standard-rated, as they consisted of a single sheet and were not leaflets, since they were printed on stiff card, whereas a leaflet must be limp. However, HMRC now accepts that a single-sheet brochure may be zero-rated. *Tax Briefs Ltd* [1991] (VTD 9258)

MEMO POINTS Brochures, pamphlets or leaflets **primarily intended for completion or detachment** cannot be zero-rated. In practice, if more than 25% of their total area is for completion or detachment they will not be zero-rated. Note that whatever the area for completion, a publication which is designed to be returned whole after completion is always standard-rated.

Single-sheet brochures and "wallet"-type brochures designed with a flap may be zero-rated, provided that they: **1261**
- convey information and contain a substantial amount of text, with some indication of contents or of the issuing organisation;
- are not primarily designed to hold other items; and
- are supplied complete.

Leaflets

Leaflets **include** items which have the following characteristics: **1262** Notice 701/10 para 3.3; VBOOKS3300
- convey information;
- limp or flimsy;
- designed to be held in the hand for reading by individuals;
- generally no more than A4 size (or if larger, scored so as to fold down to a size of no more than A4);
- complete information sources in themselves not forming part of larger works; and
- either of an ephemeral nature (designed to be read a few times and then thrown away) or designed to accompany some other product or service, for example, an instruction leaflet.

Items printed on **stiff paper and card** are not automatically excluded from being leaflets but HMRC regards the use of stiff paper and card as an indicator that the items have a function which would exclude them from this category. On that basis examples of items that are not leaflets are:
- calendars;
- event tickets;
- cricket scorecards;
- discount cards;
- reference materials; and
- items for completion or return.

HMRC considers that items printed on **laminated paper** are designed to be kept and are therefore not leaflets. On the other hand, orders of service may be zero-rated, because they are not normally designed to be kept.

2. Newspapers, journals and periodicals

Factors common to all these publications are that they: **1264** VBOOKS3400, 3500
- **consist of** several sheets of paper, folded or bound together; and
- are **published** at some regular, predetermined interval, for example, weekly or monthly.

The publication date must be fixed in advance and not dependent upon some external event. This excludes publications such as theatre or sporting programmes, which are only published to support a specific event. Even if the event takes place regularly, it is the event which dictates the frequency of the publication programme. This does not, however, exclude special or souvenir editions of zero-rated newspapers or magazines.

The following publications have been held **not to fall within** the zero-rating provisions:
- monthly property guides supplied to an estate agent for free distribution to clients rather than for sale to the general public *Snushall Dalby & Robinson* [1982]; and
- a betting guide published on every day on which an afternoon greyhound meeting was held. *Greyform Publications* [1988] (VTD 3158)

Delivery charges are zero-rated but occasionally a publisher will pay for a free magazine to be inserted in a newspaper. The publisher will pay the newspaper proprietor, which will in turn pay its newsagents. These payments are **handling charges** and are standard-rated.

Newspapers

1266 Notice 701/10 para 3.5 For a publication to qualify as a newspaper, its **content** must consist predominantly of news. This may exclude some free newspapers which, although published in a newspaper format, consist largely of advertisements. They may, however, still qualify as periodicals (¶1268).

Journals and periodicals

1268 Notice 701/10 para 3.6 To be a journal or periodical, a publication's **primary purpose** must be to convey information (as opposed to being a vehicle for self-promotion) and it must be designed for reading.

Poster magazines that consist entirely of pictures are not zero-rated, but where a magazine which is published regularly has text on one side of the page and a picture designed to be used as a poster on the other, it will qualify for zero-rating.

3. Children's picture books and painting books

1270 Notice 701/10 paras 3.7, 3.8; VBOOKS3600 To qualify for zero-rating, both picture and painting books must:
- have several pages;
- be bound, fastened, or folded concertina-style; and
- be printed on paper, card, plastic or fabric, for example, a children's rag book.

Children's **picture** books are zero-rated, unless the article is essentially a toy.

Examples of standard-rated **toys** are:
- pop-out or cut-out books, if the pop-out or cut-out part is the main part of the book (although HMRC accepts that books with at least 25% text (other than assembly instructions) related to the material for cutting out can be zero-rated); and
- items where the pages are boards for games.

Examples of zero-rated children's **painting** books are:
- children's painting and drawing books with sample pictures for copying, or outlines of pictures for colouring, painting or drawing;
- similar books with "invisible" outlines to colour which can be made visible by rubbing with a pencil or applying water with a paint brush;
- painting books in which the small amounts of water colour required for colouring are contained in the book, for example, in the form of a palette; and
- activity books which combine pages of colouring with pages of puzzles, quizzes and suchlike.

4. Music

1272 Notice 701/10 para 3.9; VBOOKS3700 Zero-rating applies to any complete printed, duplicated or manuscript **music** which is **presented on paper**. It can be instrumental or vocal, printed or hand-written, bound or on loose sheets, illustrated, or in any system of notation, including numerical symbols or Braille.

However, educational aids, such as flash cards or pictures of guitar fingerings, music rolls, blank music manuscript and pieces of music commissioned from a composer are all **standard-rated**.

5. Maps, charts and topographical plans

Zero-rating applies to all two-dimensional printed maps and charts designed to **represent** the natural or artificial **features** of countries, towns, seas, the heavens, etc. They can be printed on paper or other material (such as cloth) and in the form of single or folded sheets, or a collection of such sheets bound together in book form (for example, an atlas). There is no requirement for the information to be **complete** or **to scale**. **1274** Notice 701/10 para 3.10; VBOOKS3800

HMRC specifically lists the following as **standard-rated**:
– plans or drawings for industrial, architectural, engineering, commercial or similar purposes, in any format;
– framed maps whose primary purpose is decorative;
– posters;
– pictorial wall charts;
– aerial photographs;
– globes, three-dimensional models, mugs and similar articles; and
– decorative maps printed or woven into textile articles such as scarves, handkerchiefs, tea-towels, tapestries, rugs, etc.

6. Covers, cases and other articles supplied with the above items

Zero-rating **applies to** covers, cases and other articles supplied with any one of the above items (¶1256 to ¶1274) for which a separate charge to the customer has not been made. Examples would include dust covers, clasps, book marks or presentation cases. **1276** Notice 701/10 paras 5, 6.2; VBOOKS3900

In **addition**, zero-rating is extended to the provision of plastic dust-jackets, ticket pockets, etc, to public libraries, even though separate invoicing is usually made for such items.

Covers which are used as a means of packaging several distinct items together, and folders for storing printed matter, are standard-rated.

A **package of printed items** should follow the liability of the significant or dominant item. Where no single item dominates, an apportionment may be carried out, or a simplified package test should be applied, whereby the liability of the whole package follows that of the larger number of items. Notice 701/10 para 6.5

MEMO POINTS Where a package of printed matter is **supplied to a charity**, some items connected with collecting monetary donations can be treated as zero-rated, provided that they meet the qualifying conditions (¶1380). Notice 701/10 para 4.6

D. Transport

The provisions on zero-rating for non-freight transport can be split broadly into supplies for: **1280**
a. all types of transport; and
b. qualifying ships or aircraft.

As zero-rating only applies to those services which take place in the UK, for details on the place of supply for transport see ¶9726.

Type of supply		Reference	¶¶
All types of transport	Passenger transport	Notice 744A Sch 8 Group 8 item 4 VATA 1994	¶1282
	Pilotage, salvage or towage services	Sch 8 Group 8 items 7, 8 VATA 1994	¶1294
	Services provided to overseas businesses	Sch 8 Group 8 item 11 VATA 1994	¶1296

Type of supply		Reference	¶¶
Qualifying ships or aircraft	Supply and repair of ships and aircraft	Notice 744C Sch 8 Group 8 items 1, 2 VATA 1994	¶1302
	Supply of certain parts and equipment for ships and aircraft	Notice 744C Sch 8 Group 8 items 2A, 2B VATA 1994	¶1308
	Survey and classification services	Sch 8 Group 8 item 9 VATA 1994	¶1314
	Air navigation services	Notice 744C Sch 8 Group 8 item 6A VATA 1994	¶1316
	Handling services	Notice 744C Sch 8 Group 8 item 6 VATA 1994	¶1318
Other services	Lifeboats[1]	Sch 8 Group 8 item 3 VATA 1994	¶1368
	Making of arrangements[2]	Sch 8 Group 8 item 10 VATA 1994	
	Travel services outside the EU	Sch 8 Group 8 item 12 VATA 1994	¶7460+
	Freight services to Madeira or the Azores	Sch 8 Group 8 item 13 VATA 1994	¶9790

Note
1. Lifeboats and associated equipment are zero-rated if supplied to a charity.
2. Includes arrangements for the supply of, or of space in, any ship or aircraft, or for services or goods listed above this item in the table, other than transport services provided to overseas businesses.

Sch 8 Group 8 item 5 VATA 1994

MEMO POINTS 1. **Freight transport** supplies that take place entirely in the UK are generally standard-rated. If the supply taking place in the UK is part of the international transportation of the goods see ¶9772.
2. For on-board catering services see ¶1239.
3. The sailaway scheme for yachts is dealt with at ¶9616.

1. All types of transport

Passenger transport

1282
Notice 744A

Passenger transport can be defined as the supply of a vehicle, ship or aircraft, **together with** a driver, or pilot, which involves taking passengers from one place to another.

EXAMPLE
1. A ride on a big dipper was held not to be a transport of passengers, because the movement was effectively confined to one spot and did not amount to the deliberate removal of a passenger from one spot to another. *C&E v Blackpool Pleasure Beach Co* [1974] Similar principles have been applied to exclude other rides and guided tours.

2. Individuals paid to sail a boat as a sail training and experience holiday. It was held that they were still passengers for the purposes of zero-rating, because although they were encouraged to crew the boat, they had no actual responsibility/compulsion to do so. *The Cirdan Sailing Trust* [2004] (VTD 18865) Note that the supply was nevertheless held to be standard-rated because the yacht was only designed to accommodate seven passengers.

3. The transport of individuals by chair lift and tows for the purpose of skiing was held not to be in a vehicle, as the chair lifts were not capable of independent movement. *Lecht Ski Company Ltd* [2003] (VTD 18163)

MEMO POINTS 1. Where **no driver** is provided, this will amount to a supply of a means of transport, which is generally standard-rated. Similarly the services of a driver alone are standard-rated. See ¶9112 for cross-border supplies of new means of transport within the EU.

2. Where a **driver is supplied** together with transport, the supplier must keep appropriate details (name, address, driving licence information, references, identity card, job description, etc) and evidence to demonstrate that the supplier exerts some control over the driver.

To **qualify for zero-rating** the transport must either be provided: **1284** Notice 48 para 3.33
– in a vehicle designed to carry ten or more persons, or which would have been so designed but for the fact that it has been designed or adapted for wheelchair users;
– by the post office;
– on any scheduled flight; or
– from a place within to outside the UK (or vice versa).

Zero-rating **also extends to** any:
– services of intermediaries making arrangements for passenger transport (¶7126); and
– handling and storage services for ships or aircraft, provided that they meet the direct needs of the ship, aircraft or cargo, for example, port and harbour dues, or aircraft landing fees. Long-term storage is excluded from this, as it does not meet a direct need, as is the storage of luggage landside which is of direct benefit to the passenger. *HMRC v EB Central Services Ltd* [2008]

Specifically **excluded** from zero-rating are:
– pleasure flights;
– transport in connection with airport car parking provided by the person who provides the car parking or anyone connected (¶962) with that person; and
– transport provided to, from or within places of entertainment provided by the person who supplies the right of admission or anyone connected with that person.

Special rules apply to incidental services supplied with the transport (¶1286), ferry transport (¶1288) and pleasure cruises (¶1290).

MEMO POINTS 1. When passenger transport is supplied by a **tour operator** from an establishment in the UK and bought in and resupplied without material alteration or further processing, the tour operators' **margin scheme** must be used (¶7490).
2. It should be noted that when considering whether the vehicle is **designed to carry ten passengers** or more, **the seat count includes** the seats for pilot or driver, co-pilot (if any) and any seats required for the crew. Thus a minibus with nine passenger seats and a driver's seat would meet the test for zero-rating. However, a suitably-designed vehicle is not excluded simply because it is not legally permitted to carry ten persons. VTRANS020500

Incidental and ancillary services Special rules apply where services that are incidental or ancillary to the provision of passenger transport are provided, as follows: **1286** Notice 744A para 9

Type of supply	Liability	Examples
Incidental services[1]	Where an additional charge is made it is treated as a supplement to the fare and will follow the main supply (so if the main supply is zero-rated, this will be too)	Seat reservations, sleeping berths, duplicate season tickets
Ancillary services[2, 3]	Normally standard-rated, unless they can be zero-rated under some other provision	Cycle storage facilities, lost property facilities, transport of unaccompanied luggage

Note:
1. These are treated as a supply of services provided as part of the main supply. Often no separate charge is made.
2. These are not part of the single supply of passenger transport services but are treated as being supplied separately.
3. By concession, when certain conditions are met the following **perks offered by airlines** to passengers may be treated as a single zero-rated supply of passenger transport:
– limousine transport to and/or from the airport;
– up to two days' car hire for a one-way ticket (four days for a return ticket);
– car parking at the airport; and
– hotel or similar accommodation, provided that it is for no more than one night's stay with breakfast and there is a direct connection with the zero-rated travel, for example, where it is necessary to catch a connecting flight, or it is required for the night prior to take off, or on the night after landing.
To be within the scope of this concession, the following **conditions must be met**:
– the perks must be an integral part of the transportation, included in the ticket price for the class of travel concerned, with no discount if the perk is not taken up;
– they must not be gifts of goods (except where currently permitted, for example, in-flight catering, or toiletries); and
– they must be restricted to one per customer, although the customer may be offered a choice of options.

1288 Notice 744A paras 2.3, 2.4

Ferrying of vehicles on ships, trains etc The following supplies are treated as supplies of **passenger transport**:
– the carriage of a bus, coach or taxi with passengers (whether or not charged under the private car rate by the ferry company);
– the carriage of any other vehicle (with driver or passengers) that is charged under the private car rate; and
– the carriage of a small commercial vehicle, charged under the private car rate whether carrying passengers or freight.

The transport of unaccompanied vehicles is treated as a supply of **freight transport**.

1290 Notice 744A para 10; Notice 709/5 para 7.3; VTRANS021400

Pleasure cruises and excursions Sea and river cruises provided independently by a business are **generally treated as** a single zero-rated supply, if:
– the essential nature of the supply is passenger transport and the normal conditions are met (¶1284);
– all elements of the cruise are integral and it would be neither practical nor reasonable to separate them; and
– the cruise is sold at a specific price, with no discounts for particular services not taken.

MEMO POINTS 1. A cruise is **treated as being provided independently** if the business:
– uses its own ship;
– charters a vessel from the owner for 2 years or more, whether only with deck/engine crew or with deck/engine crew and domestic/catering crew (the vessel need not necessarily be in service continuously throughout the period but the owner must not have the right to use the vessel to make supplies to other customers during the period); or
– takes a vessel including deck/engine crew but employs or engages its own domestic/catering staff.
2. Sea and river cruises **bought from a third party and resold** are accounted for under the tour operators' margin scheme (¶7490+).
3. HMRC accepts that some excursions on historic railway **trains** can be zero-rated if the catering or entertainment element is incidental (such as Santa Specials). Dining-car trips are likely to be standard-rated.

1292 VTRANS021340

However, **in certain situations** cruises will be standard-rated, or treated as part of a multiple supply:

Single standard-rated supply	Multiple supply[1]
Where the cruise contains only a minor transport element which is purely incidental to another standard-rated supply (such as a wedding reception)	Where: – it is practicable, reasonable and realistic to separate the elements of the cruise; and – separate and identifiable charges are raised or negotiable

Note:
1. Where a single charge is made for a multiple supply, a reasonable apportionment of consideration can be made when accounting for VAT.

Pilotage, salvage or towage services

1294 Notice 744C paras 9.3, 9.4; VTRANS160200

Zero-rating **applies** to all such services supplied to any shipping (not just qualifying shipping (¶1298)). In the case of non-pilotage services it also extends to any floating object, such as an inland waterways vessel, and to dock gates, piers, bridges and buoys.

Zero-rating does extend to any **salvage** of a ship's cargo, even if the ship itself is not salvaged.

MEMO POINTS A **pilot** in this context is any person (whether or not qualified as a ship's pilot) who has the conduct of a ship, not being the ship's master. It has nothing to do with aviation. Any subsequent repair work following salvage or towage is not zero-rated under this provision, although if the ship is qualifying, repairs may be zero-rated (¶1302).

Services provided to overseas businesses

1296 Sch 8 Group 8 item 11 VATA 1994

Zero-rating applies when:
a. the service consists of the **handling or storage of goods** at, or their **transport to or from**, a place to which they are to be exported or at which they have been imported from outside the EU; or

b. the service consists of:
- **air navigation** services (¶1316);
- **ship or aircraft handling** (¶1318) performed in a port or Customs and Excise airport;
- **ship or aircraft surveys** (¶1314); or
- the making of arrangements for the **supply of, or of space in**, any ship or aircraft; and

the **customer belongs outside the UK** and receives the supply for the purposes of a business carried on by that person.

MEMO POINTS 1. A **port** is defined as any port so appointed by HMRC and specifically includes all UK seaports. ss 19, 21 CEMA 1979
2. A **Customs and Excise airport** is defined as an airport designated for landing or departure of aircraft for the purpose of the Customs and Excise Acts (essentially this is all UK airports).

2. Qualifying ships and aircraft

A **qualifying ship** is one which has a gross tonnage of at least 15 tonnes and is neither designed nor adapted for recreation and/or pleasure. This will **include** submarines, hovercraft, mobile floating docks and offshore oil or gas installations which are designed to be moved from place to place. Permanently-moored vessels and fixed installations do not qualify. **1298** Notice 744C paras 2, 3

MEMO POINTS 1. **Cruise ships** are treated as qualifying ships, provided that they fall within the above definition, are unsuitable for private use and are used for recreation or pleasure for fee-paying passengers.
2. Following the High Court case of *Lieutenant-Commander Stone* [2008], HMRC revised its policy on barges and similar vessels which are designed for, and used as, permanent residential accommodation. HMRC now accepts that such **residential vessels** can constitute qualifying ships for zero-rating purposes. As a result, the supply of such vessels, and some supplies of goods and services to the owners of such vessels, may be zero-rated by suppliers. Note that such vessels are distinguished from houseboats (¶1326) by having a means of propulsion. HMRC may carry out a wider review of this policy and propose legislation in future.

A **qualifying aircraft** is one which is: **1300**
- used by an airline operating for reward chiefly on international routes; or
- supplied to a State institution, has a maximum authorised take-off weight of at least 8,000kg, and is not designed or adapted for recreation or pleasure.

MEMO POINTS There is no statutory definition of aircraft. HMRC accepts that **drones, helicopters and airships** are aircraft for this purpose, but considers that **space craft and satellites** are not. VTRANS110610

Supply and repair

Supply A supply is zero-rated insofar as it **consists** of: **1302** Notice 744C para 4
- the sale, leasing, hiring and chartering of a qualifying ship or aircraft; or
- normal fixed and loose equipment and finishings necessary for the operation, navigation and safety of a vessel (where provided under the same contract as the supply of a vessel).

Specifically **excluded** are supplies that consist of:
- a partially completed ship or aircraft;
- transport of passengers (although this may qualify for zero-rating as passenger transport) or freight;
- accommodation;
- entertainment; and
- education.

Subcontracted services are standard-rated, because the subcontractor is not making the supply of a qualifying ship or aircraft.

Repair and maintenance The repair or maintenance of a qualifying ship or aircraft is zero-rated. This **also includes** the repair or maintenance of parts and equipment, provided that at least one of the following conditions is met: **1304** Notice 744C para 6

Ships	Aircraft
The repair is carried out on board	The repair is carried out on board
The part or equipment is removed for repair and replaced in the same ship afterwards	The part or equipment is removed for repair and replaced in the same aircraft afterwards
	Following the repair, etc, the part or equipment is returned to be held in stock for future use as a spare in a qualifying aircraft
	If they are unserviceable parts, etc, they are exchanged for identical parts which have themselves been reconditioned, repaired or maintained

1305 Any **parts, components or materials** provided by the supplier for the repair or maintenance are also zero-rated. Maintenance includes testing, cleaning, fumigation and ship's laundry (provided that the articles are not personal to the crew or passengers).

Subcontracted services can similarly be zero-rated. The subcontractor is advised to obtain evidence to substantiate zero-rating from the main contractor.

Information Sheet 15/07

MEMO POINTS HMRC has published guidance confirming that supplies to qualifying ships and aircraft **under construction** will qualify for zero-rating, provided that the vessel becomes **seaworthy**, or the aircraft becomes **airworthy**, at a later date. This provision extends to a vessel or aircraft which temporarily loses its seaworthy or airworthy status.

1306 **Modification or conversion** The modification or conversion of a qualifying vessel is zero-rated, provided that the ship or aircraft is qualifying both before and after.

This also includes **design work** for a conversion or modification where it is **integral to** the overall works and only where a supplier specifically contracts with a customer to design and supply, modify or convert a qualifying ship or aircraft. In all other circumstances a supply of design services is standard-rated.

Subcontracted services can similarly be zero-rated. The subcontractor is advised to obtain evidence to substantiate zero-rating from the main contractor.

MEMO POINTS Services in relation to preparing a vessel for a new lease, when it is known that the lease will be of a qualifying vessel, can be zero-rated even though strictly speaking the vessel is at the time non-qualifying.

Supply of certain parts and equipment

1308
Notice 744C para 7

Zero-rating **applies to** the following parts and equipment supplied or hired out for the purpose of installation or incorporation in a qualifying ship or aircraft:
- parts and equipment of a kind ordinarily installed or incorporated in the propulsion, navigation or communications systems, or the general structure of a vessel; or
- part-assembled structures, such as a hull or fuselage; or
- life jackets, life rafts, smoke hoods and similar safety equipment for use in a ship or aircraft.

The **making of arrangements** for the above supplies is also zero-rated.

If the customer is a **government department or charity**, in order to qualify for zero-rating the supply must be:
- in the course of a business carried on by the customer; or
- for a qualifying ship or aircraft used for providing rescue or assistance at sea (¶1368).

EXAMPLE

1. A supplies B with eligible parts and equipment to be incorporated only into a qualifying military aircraft. B supplies those same parts and equipment to the Ministry of Defence (MoD) but not in the course of the MoD's business, or for rescue or assistance at sea.
A's supply to B is zero-rated. B's supply to the MoD is standard-rated.

2. C supplies eligible parts to the MoD for use on a qualifying helicopter which is occasionally used for sea rescue, but is normally used for military purposes.
C's supply is standard-rated.

3. D supplies the MoD with eligible parts and equipment for incorporation into a qualifying ship, which is being repaired at an MoD dockyard dedicated to business.
D's supply is zero-rated.

The following table provides **examples** of items that are included or excluded from this provision: 1310

May be zero-rated	Standard-rated
Anchors	Aircraft ground equipment
Industrial catering/laundering equipment	Domestic catering equipment
Winches	Unfixed furniture
Fixed equipment to control, operate or launch weapons	Tooling and equipment used for manufacturing parts or equipment
Propellers and rudders	Underwater cameras

Responsibility for charging the correct rate of VAT rests with the supplier, who must therefore be satisfied as to the extent of the customer's qualifying use. To assist suppliers in this matter, customers can give suppliers a certificate to evidence qualifying use. It is the supplier's responsibility to check the validity of a certificate, but HMRC says that if the supplier is subsequently found to have charged the **incorrect rate of VAT in good faith**, HMRC will not attempt to recover the VAT due from the supplier. 1312 Notice 48 para 3.11

Surveys and classification services

Zero-rating **applies to** survey and classification services, provided that they: 1314 Notice 744C para 9; VTRANS160200
- are on qualifying ships or aircraft; and
- involve an actual physical inspection and essentially constitute a snapshot view (thus continuous surveys over a period of time are unlikely to be zero-rated).

Specifically **excluded** from zero-rating are:
- tonnage measurements or surveys of ships for registration or other purposes required by statute carried out by Department of Transport surveyors (this also covers other surveyors directly appointed by that Department to do the work under statutory authority); and
- services for the arranging for the registering or reregistering of ships for the Merchant Shipping Acts.

MEMO POINTS 1. Qualifying supplies are also zero-rated where they are **provided for any ship or aircraft** and supplied to a person who belongs outside the UK and receives the supply for the purposes of a business carried on by that person.
2. HMRC has confirmed that **loss-adjusting services** supplied in connection with marine and aviation insurance claims are not zero-rated. Because HMRC admitted that its guidance may have been misleading in cases where a physical inspection was necessary, this ruling was applied from 1 September 2013 only in such cases. Traders who have zero-rated supplies of loss-adjusting services in cases where no inspection was necessary will be treated as having accounted for VAT in error, unless they can demonstrate to HMRC that they have been misled by HMRC's guidance. HMRC Brief 13/13; Notice 744C para 9.5

Air navigation services

Air navigation services provided to qualifying aircraft **include** information, directions and other facilities supplied in connection with the navigation or movement of aircraft, plus the control of movement of vehicles in any part of an aerodrome used for the movement of aircraft. 1316 Notice 744C para 9.1

MEMO POINTS Such supplies are also zero-rated where they are **provided for any aircraft** and supplied to a person who belongs outside the UK and receives the supply for the purposes of a business carried on by that person.

Handling services

Any services provided for the handling of qualifying ships or aircraft in a port or Customs and Excise airport (¶1296) are zero-rated. 1318 Notice 744C para 8

To **qualify for zero-rating** handling services must meet the direct needs of the ship, aircraft or cargo - for example, port and harbour dues, aircraft landing fees. Specifically **excluded** are:
– long-term storage (it does not meet a direct need);
– letting or hire of any goods, even if it takes place in a port or airport; and
– the storage of luggage "landside" which is of direct benefit to the passenger. *HMRC v EB Central Services Ltd* [2008]

MEMO POINTS Such supplies are also zero-rated where they are **provided for any ship or aircraft** and supplied to a person who belongs outside the UK and receives the supply for the purposes of a business carried on by that person.

E. Caravans and houseboats

1322 Sch 8 Group 9 VATA 1994

Zero-rating **applies to** supplies of certain non-touring caravans and houseboats that are:
– sold;
– leased (for more than 1 year);
– loaned; or
– adopted by the owner for non-business purposes.

Special rules also apply to **other related supplies** made in connection with the supply of a caravan or houseboat (¶1328).

Caravans

1323 Notice 701/20; Information Sheet 11/12; Information Sheet 4/13

Definitions There is no statutory definition of a caravan. HMRC's guidance defines a caravan as a structure which:
– is designed or adapted for human habitation;
– when assembled, is physically capable of being moved from one place to another (either by towing, or by transporting on a suitable motor vehicle); and
– is not more than 20 metres long (excluding its drawbar), 6.8 metres wide or 3.05 metres high (measured internally).

To be **designed or adapted for human habitation** means that it consists of self-contained living accommodation, including facilities for preparing food and for washing. This includes mobile homes and static caravans, but note that HMRC does not accept that motor homes are caravans.

A **static caravan** is one which cannot legally be towed on the public highway by a family car. At present this means that it exceeds 7 metres in length or 2.55 metres in width, excluding towing bars and similar apparatus used solely for the purpose of attaching it to a vehicle.

EXAMPLE Supplies of portable units with no cooking facilities were held not to be caravans, as they did not constitute self-contained living accommodation. *University of Kent* [2004] (VTD 18625)

1324

Zero-rating applies only to supplies of **static residential caravans** which are either:
– new; or
– second-hand and were occupied before 6 April 2013.

Other types of caravan are taxed as follows:
– other static or similarly-sized touring caravans: at the reduced rate (¶1170); and
– small touring caravans, not exceeding 7 metres in length and 2.55 metres in width: at the standard rate.

A **static residential caravan** is a static caravan (¶1323) which is manufactured to standard BS 3632:2005 (or, in the case of a second-hand caravan, a previous version of that standard). BS 3632:2005 is the current standard for residential caravans and confirms that a caravan is designed and manufactured for **continuous year-round occupation**.

MEMO POINTS **Prior to 6 April 2013** any caravan which exceeded 7 metres in length or 2.55 metres in width was zero-rated.

Houseboats

Houseboats are **defined** as boats or other floating, decked structures designed or adapted for use solely as places of permanent habitation, with no means of self-propulsion (and which cannot be readily adapted for self-propulsion). **1326** Notice 701/20 para 7.1

Other related supplies

The following rules are applied by HMRC to other supplies made in conjunction with a supply of a caravan or houseboat: **1328** Notice 701/20

Supply in respect of	Type of supply	Treatment
Caravans only	Receipt of commission on sales of second-hand sited caravans	Will follow the liability of the pitch fee (¶5510); any extra charge to the seller in connection with the sale will be standard-rated, as is any commission received from a third party (such as a caravan manufacturer or dealer)
	Brick skirting	Will follow the liability of the caravan supplied
	Garaging and parking spaces	Exempt if supplied in connection with the supply of a zero-rated caravan, provided that the supplier retains ownership of the land on which the garage or parking space is sited and it is reasonably close to the caravan
	Recharged business rates	Will follow the VAT liability of the pitch fee (¶5510)
Houseboats only	Mooring rights	Exempt
	Garaging and parking spaces	Exempt if supplied in connection with the supply of the houseboat, provided that it is supplied by the person who is supplying the mooring and it is reasonably close to the mooring
Caravans and houseboats	Fixtures, fittings and removable contents	Only those supplies that are of a kind ordinarily incorporated by builders as fixtures in a new dwelling are zero-rated (e.g. sinks, baths, WCs); furnishings are standard-rated
	Charge for connection to mains services	Will follow the VAT liability of the pitch fee (¶5510), unless the service is metered to the individual customer at the pitch, in which case the charge will follow the liability of the utility (reduced-rated for electricity and gas, zero-rated for water and sewerage)
	Ongoing utility charges for gas and electricity	Reduced-rated if metered, otherwise will follow the liability of the main supply
	Recharged water and sewerage costs	Will follow the VAT liability of the pitch fee (¶5510), unless metered to the individual customer at the pitch, in which case they are zero-rated
	Charge for delivery, unloading and positioning	Any reasonable charge to the owner for delivery, etc, will follow the liability of the main supply; however, the provision of a delivery service will be standard-rated if it is not connected with the supply of the caravan or houseboat
	Holiday accommodation	Standard-rated if it is on a park that is advertised as holiday accommodation; off-season letting may be exempt if the property is let as residential accommodation for more than 28 days (¶5508)
	Residential accommodation	Exempt where it is on a site designated by the local authority for permanent residential use

F. Drugs, medicines, aids for the handicapped

1332 Sch 8 Group 12 VATA 1994; Notice 701/7

Group 12 bundles together two categories related under the broad heading "medical":
- dispensing of qualifying goods by a pharmacist; and
- supplies of goods and services (as detailed at ¶1342) to a handicapped person, or to a charity for the use of handicapped persons.

Such supplies are, subject to various conditions described below, zero-rated, **unless** they are provided by a hospital, care home or other similar institution (in which case they will usually be exempt).

MEMO POINTS **Handicapped** means chronically sick or disabled. HMRC uses the word disabled in its guidance instead of handicapped, because the latter is potentially offensive. This commentary will hereafter do the same. Thus a disabled person has a long-term, chronic condition, or is terminally ill. This therefore excludes supplies to individuals that are simply frail, or are only temporarily disabled with, for example, a broken limb.

1. Qualifying conditions

1334 Notice 48 para 3.24

Qualifying goods are any goods designed or adapted for use in connection with any medical or surgical treatment, except hearing aids, dentures, spectacles and contact lenses.

Supplies of goods can only be zero-rated if they are either:

a. dispensed to individuals for their personal use, by a registered pharmacist on the prescription of a doctor, dentist, physiotherapist or podiatrist; or

b. provided to:
- disabled persons (or their parents or guardians) for their own personal or domestic use; or
- a charity or eligible body that makes the goods available to disabled persons for their own personal or domestic use.

MEMO POINTS 1. The dispensing of goods on **private prescription** by a doctor is always standard-rated.

2. Supplies are for an individual's **personal or domestic use** if they are for the specific use of an individual. Communal supplies (for example, a stair lift in a communal area) do not qualify.
Specifically excluded from being treated as for personal or domestic use are supplies made when a person is receiving care or treatment at a **hospital or nursing home**. However, by **concession**, this restriction does not apply if:
- the equipment is designed solely for use by a visually disabled person and is supplied by a charity at or below cost;
- the recipient is a resident in, or is attending the premises of, an approved institution; and
- the charity is not actively engaged in supplying such goods solely to disabled persons who are resident in, or attending the premises of, approved institutions operated, managed or controlled by the charity.

3. **Eligible bodies** include certain healthcare bodies and hospitals with charitable funds.

4. Eligible goods that are **acquired from overseas** by a disabled person or charity are zero-rated on importation. Such goods will be standard-rated on importation by a supplier. The disabled person or charity (as the case may be) must make a declaration in the appropriate form and lodge it with the import entry declaration made to HMRC at the port, airport or postal depot of importation.

1336 Notice 701/7 para 3.7 - 3.9

In practice, HMRC advises that suppliers should obtain a **written declaration** from each customer (or parent or guardian where appropriate) claiming entitlement to VAT relief. Such a declaration should contain sufficient information to demonstrate that a customer fulfils all the criteria for eligibility. The declaration should be separate, or clearly distinguishable, from any order form or invoice against which the goods or services are supplied. A customer signing an order should not automatically be signing a declaration of eligibility for VAT relief.

Where **electronic declarations** are made (for example, when making an online purchase) the declaration need not be signed, provided that sufficient proof is retained to identify the customer.

The **supplier** must take all reasonable steps to check that supplies should be zero-rated. Where, however, zero-rated supplies are made incorrectly but in good faith, HMRC says it will not seek to recover the VAT due from the supplier. Notice 48 para 3.11

2. Scope of zero-rating

The following supplies are **excluded** from zero-rating: 1340

Supply	Liability
Drugs supplied by hospitals and nursing homes to in-patients and residents [1, 2]	Exempt healthcare services
Eligible goods (¶1342) supplied by all institutions to in-patients and residents [1, 2]	
Most hearing aids, dentures, spectacles and contact lenses (but see ¶1342)	Standard-rated
Medical and surgical appliances (including parts and accessories), incontinence products and wound dressings provided by independent suppliers to in-patients and residents	
Supplies of eligible goods arranged or paid for, directly or indirectly, by any hospital or similar institution or NHS body	
Drugs dispensed direct to hospitals or other care institutions [3]	
Supplies of incontinence products to NHS patients in their own homes, or in-patients/residents of institutions	

Note:
1. Wheelchairs, invalid carriages and relevant parts and accessories remain zero-rated.
2. Such supplies will be zero-rated if they are unrelated to the care being received as an in-patient.
3. A pharmacist who is satisfied that the goods will not be used while the patient is in the institution may zero-rate the supply.

Supplies **eligible** for zero-rating are as follows: 1342 Notice 701/7

Supply	Details
Adaptation of goods	Adaptations of general purpose goods (for use by a disabled person) are zero-rated when provided to a disabled individual or a charity; as zero-rating only applies to the service of adaptation (not the goods themselves), a reasonable apportionment of the consideration must be made when accounting for VAT
Adjustable beds, chair lifts, stair lifts, hoists and sanitary devices	A bed must clearly stand out as being something specialised for the use of disabled people; chair lifts and stair lifts must be designed for use in connection with wheelchairs
Alarm systems	An emergency alarm call system provided to a disabled individual or a charity that is designed to be capable of operation by a disabled person is zero-rated, as is any service performed by a control centre in receiving and responding to calls received; zero-rating does not apply to the supply of ordinary telephones, internal communication systems, intruder alarms or the service of installing ordinary telephone lines
Boats [1]	Which are designed (or, prior to supply, substantially and permanently adapted) for use by disabled persons or to carry disabled persons; a boat should include all or most of the following features: – a ramp for wheelchairs; – lifts and level surfaces to accommodate wheelchair movements; – specialised washing and lavatory facilities accessible to disabled people; – specially equipped galley, sleeping areas and steering facilities designed for use by disabled people; – handrails; and – wheelchair clamps

Supply	Details
Dispensing of goods, drugs, etc	The dispensing of any goods designed or adapted for use in connection with any medical or surgical treatment; this includes the letting of goods on hire
Building works	See ¶1344
Installation of goods	Provided that the goods qualify for zero-rating
Medical and surgical appliances	Which are designed solely for the relief of severe abnormalities or injuries
Auditory training aids	Hearing aids designed for auditory training of children with a small amount of residual hearing
Low-vision aids	Only specialised low-vision aids custom-made to an optician's prescription and identified as a low-vision aid, or designed exclusively for visually impaired people
Motor vehicles	See ¶1346
Equipment and appliances designed solely for use by disabled people	See ¶1352
Parts and accessories	Provided that they are designed solely for use in or with goods[1] which themselves qualify for VAT relief; zero-rating does not extend to general use items even if purchased to be used in a zero-rated product (e.g. standard batteries)
Repair and maintenance of goods	Provided that the goods qualify for zero-rating

Note
1. Zero-rating does not apply to the separate supply of parts and accessories designed solely for use in, or with, boats that are designed or adapted for use by disabled persons. Parts and accessories supplied with the boat, or in connection with the repair or maintenance of such a boat, are still zero-rated.

Building works

1344 Notice 701/7 para 6

The following building works are zero-rated:

a. construction of **ramps**, and widening of existing **doorways and passages**, provided that if the supply is to:
– an individual, the work must be carried out on the individual's private residence; or
– a charity, the work can be for any building;

b. extension or adaptation of **bathrooms**, **washrooms and lavatories**, provided that the supply is necessary because of the disabled person's condition and if it is provided to:
– an individual, the work must be carried out on the individual's private residence; or
– a charity, the work must be carried out on residential accommodation, or a day centre where at least 20% of the individuals using the centre are disabled persons (if the work is just in relation to a washroom or lavatory, the supply can still be zero-rated if the work is carried out in a building used principally for charitable purposes);

c. installation, maintenance or repair of **lifts** for the purpose of facilitating movement between floors, provided that if the supply is to:
– an individual, the work must be carried out on the individual's private residence; or
– a charity, the lift must be installed in a day centre or a building in which the charity provides either temporary or permanent residence for disabled people;

d. any related **preparatory work**, restoration and making good; and

e. supplies of goods for all of the above.

MEMO POINTS It has been held that the services of an architect involved in the installation of a lift at a residential care home will also be zero-rated, as this is not specifically excluded by the legislation. *Friends of the Elderly* [2008] (VTD 20597)

Motor vehicles

The following supplies are zero-rated: **1346** Information Sheet 1615; Information Sheet 1616

Supply	Recipient	Qualifying conditions
Purchase, hire or lease of vehicles (including motability vehicles) that have been adapted[1, 2] (¶1348) for disabled persons	Disabled person who normally uses a wheelchair or stretcher	The vehicle must be provided for domestic or personal use
	Charity	Provided that the charity is making the vehicles available (whether by sale or otherwise) to individual disabled people for their domestic or personal use
	Eligible body[3] (other than charity)	Eligible bodies which are not charities must use wholly charitable funds or wholly voluntary contributions for the purchase of the eligible vehicle in order to obtain VAT relief
Costs of adaptation of the vehicle to suit the disabled person's condition	Disabled person, charity or eligible body[2]	
Unadapted vehicles	Charity or eligible body[3]	See ¶1350

Note:
1. The **repair and maintenance** of an adapted motor vehicle is also eligible for zero-rating insofar as the work relates to a vehicle, or an adaptation to a vehicle, that was eligible for zero-rating when it was supplied.
2. The vehicle must have been adapted **before** being supplied to the disabled user.
3. For the **definition** of eligible body see ¶1374.

MEMO POINTS 1. The sale of a **second-hand adapted vehicle** can be zero-rated if the conditions in ¶1348 are met. Although second-hand cars are usually sold under the second-hand margin scheme (¶6620), an eligible vehicle can be sold outside that scheme and invoiced normally. The dealer simply closes the relevant entry in the margin scheme stock book.
2. A **sale of a leased motor vehicle** from the Motability scheme is also zero-rated, provided that the sale is the first supply after the period of letting. In practice the vehicles are sold back to the car dealer and any subsequent sale on by the dealer is within the second-hand margin scheme (¶6660).

An **adapted vehicle** is any vehicle which is designed or substantially and permanently adapted for use by a disabled person, wheelchair or stretcher user (but not a mobility scooter user), and: **1348** Notice 701/59 para 3
- seats no more than twelve persons;
- is provided to a disabled person who normally uses a wheelchair or stretcher to be mobile;
- is adapted to enable the disabled wheelchair, or stretcher, user to enter, drive or otherwise travel in the vehicle; and
- is for the domestic or personal use of the disabled person.

In certain situations supplies of **unadapted vehicles** to charities or eligible bodies can be zero-rated where the vehicle: **1350** Notice 701/6 para 4.7
- has between seven and 50 seats and is purchased or hired for use by an eligible body or charity for the transportation of blind, deaf, mentally handicapped or terminally ill people; or
- has been permanently adapted to carry at least one disabled person in a wheelchair. The minimum number of seats that need to be adapted to make the vehicle eligible for zero-rating increases on a sliding scale as follows:

Number of seats in vehicle	Minimum number of adapted seats
1-16	1
17-26	2
27-36	3
37-46	4
47-50	5

Where vehicles have been so adapted there also must be either:
- an electrically powered or hydraulically operated lift for wheelchair access; or
- for vehicles with less than 17 seats, a ramp for wheelchair access.

Equipment designed solely for use by disabled people

1352 Notice 701/7 para 4.5

Equipment that is manufactured or designed solely for meeting the needs of disabled persons will be zero-rated. This means that equipment which has been designed to be useful to able-bodied and disabled persons alike will not be zero-rated.

In addition, **special rules** apply for incontinence pads (¶1356) and certain computer equipment (¶1358).

MEMO POINTS The **manufacturer or designer** must retain evidence to demonstrate that the equipment has been designed for the sole purpose of meeting the needs of disabled persons. This may include, for example:
- details of the disability that needs to be addressed;
- test results demonstrating that the product meets the design intention; and
- a patent or patent application.

1354 The following **examples** illustrate when zero-rating can be applied:

Zero-rated	Standard-rated
Braille embossers	Contact lenses and spectacles
Whistling cups and white canes for the blind	
Tinnitus maskers	General hearing aids
Induction loop equipment	
Wheelchairs [1]	Dentures [2]
TENS machines [3] where the conditions at ¶1352 are met	TENS machines provided to sufferers of short-term pain (e.g. labour pains)
Long-handled pick-up sticks	Items for use in cosmetic surgery

Note:
1. Certain mobility scooters also qualify for zero-rating.
2. Exempt if supplied by a dentist, dental auxiliary or dental chemist.
3. Transcutaneous electrical nerve stimulators.

1356 **Incontinence pads** Retail, online and mail-order sales of incontinence pads are zero-rated, provided that the sale is to an individual. Sales to **institutions** are standard-rated.

However, suppliers will need a signed declaration that sales are to an individual, not an institution such as a nursing home, where **customers buy more** than:
- 200 disposable pads;
- 50 washable pads;
- 5 collecting devices; or
- 10 pairs of waterproof or leak-proof underwear.

1358 Notice 701/7 paras 4.5, 9

Computer hardware or software The following concessions can be applied to supplies of computer hardware or software when provided to a disabled person for personal or domestic use as a tool to help that person **overcome communication problems**:
- the provision of a central processor can be zero-rated when it is sold as part of a computer system which has software installed on it to enable disabled persons to use the computer effectively when they would otherwise not be able to; and
- the supply of a computer package can be treated as a single composite supply where it contains significant specialist items designed solely for the use of disabled persons. The rate of VAT charged on the supply will be based on supplies of such systems made by that supplier over a recent representative period. This concession also includes the value of any central processor and any costs charged to the customer for the installation of, and training on, the equipment.

MEMO POINTS These concessions **only apply to** the supply of complete new packages and do not extend to the supply of replacement units or upgrades.

EXAMPLE A Ltd makes several supplies of computer systems, which are made up of zero-rated and standard-rated items. To take advantage of the concession (and ensure that the correct amount of VAT is declared), A Ltd will need to calculate a composite rate for its supplies by looking at all qualifying "package" supplies made over a 3-month period, as follows:

Supply	Zero-rated	Standard-rated	Net value £	Total net value £	VAT £
A	Central processor		1,500		0
		Printer	500		100
				2,000	
B	Speech synthesizer		750		0
		Keyboard	300		60
				1,050	
C	Braille embosser		1,200		0
		VDU	400		80
				1,600	
				4,650	240

The composite rate of VAT is 5.2%. ($\frac{240}{4,650} \times 100\%$)

A Ltd would then be entitled to apply a composite rate of 5.2% to all sales of qualifying packages, to ensure that the correct amount of VAT was declared.

In order to ensure that the rate reflects changing trade patterns, the business would have to recalculate the overall composite rate every 12 months.

G. Supplies to charities, etc

Zero-rating also applies to certain other supplies made to charities (for supplies made by charities see ¶8000+). 1362

A body is considered to be a charity if it has charitable status. Charitable status is usually **evidenced by** the entity's registration with a charity regulator. However, not all charities are required to be registered, for example, those which are too small, or exempted by statute (usually because they are supervised by another type of regulator).

On application, unregistered charities may be recognised as having charitable status by HMRC.

MEMO POINTS The various **regulators for each region** of the UK are:
- England and Wales, Charity Commission (flmemo.co.uk/vm1362a);
- Scotland, Office of the Scottish Charity Regulator (flmemo.co.uk/vm1362b); and
- Northern Ireland, Charity Commission for Northern Ireland (flmemo.co.uk/vm1362c).

Summary

The supplies that can be zero-rated are detailed in this table. Not all of the reliefs are available to all charities. For some classes of expenditure there are **further conditions** which must be satisfied for zero-rating to apply: 1364

Type of supply	Reference	¶¶
Talking books, wireless receiving sets, cassette players and associated apparatus	Sch 8 Group 4 item 1 VATA 1994	¶1366
Lifeboats and associated equipment	Sch 8 Group 8 items 3, 10 VATA 1994	¶1368
Aids for the handicapped	Sch 8 Group 12 VATA 1994	¶1340
Sale of donated goods	Sch 8 Group 15 items 1, 1A, 2 VATA 1994	¶1372
Specified goods purchased from voluntary contributions	Sch 8 Group 15 items 4 - 7 VATA 1994	¶1374

Type of supply	Reference	¶¶
Media advertising	Sch 8 Group 15 items 8 - 8C VATA 1994	¶1378
Medicinal products and substances used in medical research	Sch 8 Group 15 item 9, 10 VATA 1994	¶1390
The grant of a major interest in a building, provided that it is intended solely for a relevant charitable purpose	Sch 8 Group 5 item 1 VATA 1994	¶5247
Services in the course of constructing a new building intended solely for charitable use	Sch 8 Group 5 item 2, 4 VATA 1994	¶5132

Sch 8 Group 4 item 3 VATA 1994; Notice 48 para 3.11

In addition, **imports** by a charity of certain goods can be free of VAT (¶8090).

It is the responsibility of the supplier to ensure that all the conditions for zero-rating are met. HMRC recommends obtaining a **written statement of eligibility** from the recipient. If, however, an error is made in good faith and the supplier can demonstrate having taken all reasonable steps to check the validity of a supply, HMRC says it will not seek to recover the tax from the supplier.

MEMO POINTS A supply to a charity means any supply made to it by any person, including its **separately registered trading subsidiary**.

Talking books

1366 Sch 8 Group 4 item 1 VATA 1994; Notice 701/1 para 6.1.6

This **includes** sound recording and reproduction equipment, or parts and accessories for such equipment, when it is:
– supplied or hired to a charity or voluntary body which cares for the blind and visually impaired, for example, the Royal National Institute for the Blind, National Listening Library; and
– specifically adapted to meet the needs of the blind and visually impaired.

In particular, the **following supplies** fall within this provision:
a. magnetic tape for recording and reproducing speech;
b. recorded magnetic tape;
c. cassette players;
d. wireless receiving sets;
e. apparatus for:
– transferring recorded speech from one magnetic tape to another;
– transferring recordings to magnetic tape;
– rewinding magnetic tape;
– reproducing speech from recorded magnetic tape; and
– making sound recordings on magnetic tape; and
f. repair and maintenance of the above.

The zero-rating provisions **do not extend to** supplies of reproduction equipment available for use by anyone, or to cassette tapes.

MEMO POINTS 1. Although **radios and cassette recorders** may be used by anyone, if a charity purchases them for free loan to blind or visually impaired people, the sale to the charity can be zero-rated.
2. **The legislation** specifically refers to magnetic tape and **does not cover** more modern forms of technology. However, it is likely that most forms of modern recording equipment would be zero-rated under the concession for computer hardware and software (¶1358).

Lifeboats and associated equipment

1368 Sch 8 Group 8 items 3, 10 VATA 1994

The following supplies to a charity providing **rescue or assistance at sea** are zero-rated:
– any lifeboat;
– carriage equipment and tractors designed solely for the launching and recovery of lifeboats;

- winches and hauling equipment for the sole use of the recovery of lifeboats;
- the construction, modification, repair or maintenance of slipways used solely for the launching and recovery of lifeboats;
- the supply of spare parts or accessories for all the above items;
- the supply of equipment that is to be installed, incorporated or used in a lifeboat (and is of a kind ordinarily installed, incorporated or used in a lifeboat);
- repair and maintenance of all of the above items; and
- fuel for use in a lifeboat.

Sale of donated goods

The sale (or letting on hire) by a charity of goods donated to it for sale is zero-rated, provided that the goods are **not altered** in any way, or used by the charity, prior to sale. **Cleaning or repairing** goods for sale is not an alteration. **1372** Sch 8 Group 15 items 1, 1A, 2 VATA 1994; Notice 701/1 para 5.5

If the sale is by a **trading subsidiary** of a charity (¶8010), the subsidiary must distribute its profits to the charity for zero-rating to apply.

Some charities **restrict sales of their goods** to certain people. In this case zero-rating can apply, provided that the goods are sold to disabled people, or people receiving benefits.

By concession, where the donated goods are of such poor quality that they are **not fit to be sold to the general public**, they can be sold to, for example, a scrap metal merchant at the zero rate. Notice 48 para 3.21

MEMO POINTS 1. **Goods**, in this context, are given their everyday meaning and zero-rating does not apply to items that are essentially services but are deemed to be goods (¶277). **Land** is therefore excluded from zero-rating under this provision.
2. Charities that save abandoned animals, or are given them by local authority dog wardens, the police or members of the public (other than the animals' owners), can zero-rate the onward sale, or "adoption", of the animals. *Gables Farm Dogs and Cats Home* [2008] (VTD 20519) HMRC Brief 14/08

Specified goods purchased from voluntary contributions

Certain qualifying goods are zero-rated when they are: **1374** Sch 8 Group 15 items 4-7 VATA 1994; Notice 701/6
a. purchased (or hired) from voluntary contributions or charitable donations; and
b. supplied directly to an eligible body, or to a person who proposes to donate the goods to an eligible body.
In addition, the eligible body must **not contribute funds** that were raised from voluntary contributions, or donations, to purchase (or hire) the goods. However, this **requirement is waived** if the eligible body is a charity.

MEMO POINTS 1. The **eligible health bodies** are:
- a Health Authority in England, Scotland, Northern Ireland or Wales;
- a hospital or research institution whose activities are not carried on for profit;
- a Primary Care Trust;
- a National Health Service Trust; and
- the Common Services Agency for the Scottish Health Service, the Northern Ireland Central Services Agency for Health and Social Services, or the Isle of Man Health Services Board.
2. The **eligible charitable bodies** are:
a. charitable day centres that provide care, or medical or surgical treatment for disabled people, insofar as the goods are for use within the day centre;
b. any other charitable establishment that provides institutional care or medical or surgical treatment for disabled people;
c. a charitable domiciliary care provider that provides medical, personal or nursing care to disabled people in their homes, insofar as the goods are used in the course of the domiciliary care; and
d. any charity that:
- provides rescue or first aid for humans or animals;
- provides transport mainly to disabled people; or
- has the provision of care for disabled people as its sole purpose and function.

1376 Notice 701/6 para 4

The **qualifying goods** that can be zero-rated are:

Goods	Detail
Medical, scientific, computer, video, sterilising, laboratory or refrigeration equipment for use in medical or veterinary research, training, diagnosis or treatment	Includes parts or accessories for use in or with these goods Excludes bulk materials, clothing and materials
Ambulances	
– Medical and surgical appliances – Adjustable beds, chair lifts, hoists and sanitary devices – Motor vehicles – Equipment and appliances designed solely for use by disabled people – Parts and accessories – Boats	See ¶1342+
Telecommunication, aural, visual, light-enhancing or heat-detecting equipment used solely for the purpose of rescue or first aid services by a charity	Must not be equipment ordinarily supplied for private or recreational use (e.g. mobile phones, binoculars, pagers)
Repair and maintenance of any of the above goods	Provided that the goods are owned by the eligible body

Media advertising

1378 Sch 8 Group 15 items 8 - 8C VATA 1994; Notice 701/58; HMRC Brief 25/10

Any advertising undertaken by a charity is zero-rated, provided that the advertisement:
– **complies with** the charity's objects; and
– **communicates with** the public at large, i.e. it is not an advert to selected groups of people (this therefore excludes advertising and marketing through telesales, direct mail or e-mail); and
– **is a supply of** someone else's advertising time or space (therefore supplies to a charity to enable it to produce its own advert on, for example, its own website or its own greeting cards will not be zero-rated under this provision).

MEMO POINTS 1. When a charity uses an **advertising agency** instead of having a contract direct with the supplier of advertising material or printing, the VAT liability depends on whether the agency is acting as a principal or an agent (see ¶7090+).
2. **Abortive advertising costs** will remain zero-rated if they would have been zero-rated had the advertisement been placed. Supplies cannot be zero-rated if they were not originally intended for advertising purposes, even if they were subsequently so used.
3. A reasonable allocation of costs should be made if only **part of the supply qualifies** for zero-rating.
4. HMRC has confirmed that where a charity pays a search engine for each click through to the charity's website from a link on the search engine's website (known as **pay-per-click** advertising), this is zero-rated advertising and not a simple, standard-rated means of access to the charity's website.

1380 Zero-rating **also extends to**:
– related design or production costs of the advertisement;
– certain printed stationery used for appeals, for example, letters appealing for donations, printed envelopes, money collecting envelopes;
– collection boxes and receptacles; and
– lapel stickers and similar tokens.

1382 **Design and production costs** This includes supplies of goods closely related to the design and production, including:
– a finished article such as a film;
– an element to be incorporated in the advertisement as a photograph, picture or a sound-track; or
– all alternative versions of an advertisement produced, to see which works best, even if it is the intention that only one version will be used.

1384 Notice 48 para 3.3

Printed stationery Supplies of the following goods can be zero-rated:
– collecting envelopes which ask for donations of money;
– pre-printed appeal letters primarily aimed at seeking money for the charity (to qualify it must be a letter, not just a form to fill in and return with a donation); and

– envelopes used to send out appeal letters and envelopes for forwarding donations to the charity, provided that each type is over-printed with an appeal request related to that contained in the letter, or is distinguishable from the charity's usual stationery.

Collection boxes and receptacles All types of boxes and receptacles used for **collecting** money can be zero-rated, provided that they are: **1386** Notice 48 para 3.3; Notice 701/58 para 7
– secure;
– clearly identified as charity collecting boxes for a named charity; and
– either bear the name of the charity, or allow for the charity's name to be added later.

Also included are bucket lids designed to provide a secure seal for use solely in connection with collecting money for charity.

Specifically **excluded** from this concession are receptacles that have:
– another purpose and a coin slot is simply added, for example, wishing wells or fonts, although a simple collecting box fixed to any of these items would still qualify; or
– some sort of mechanical part with the aim of providing entertainment, for example, gaming or quiz machines, although where there is only a simple balancing mechanism which moves the money from one level to another or the weight of a coin causes it to roll into the collecting area, the receptacle should still qualify.

Lapel stickers and similar tokens Only lapel stickers, emblems and badges which meet the **following conditions** can be zero-rated: **1388** Notice 48 para 3.3; Notice 701/58 para 8
– they are given free as an acknowledgement to donors of money (if they are offered for a fixed price, even if this is £1 or less, they cannot be zero-rated);
– they have no intrinsic value and are low cost to the charity, i.e. stickers given in return for any non-specified donation or a suggested donation of up to £1; and
– they are designed to be worn on clothing (larger versions for decorating buildings, cars, etc, cannot be zero-rated under this provision).

Zero-rating **also extends to** constituent parts bought by a charity for assembly in-house, although equipment used for manufacturing cannot be zero-rated.

Medicinal products

The supply of any medicinal product is zero-rated if the supply is made to a charity providing **care, medical or surgical treatment** for humans or animals; or a charity undertaking **medical or veterinary research**. **1390** Sch 8 Group 15 item 9, 10 VATA 1994

A **medicinal product** is defined as any product that is to be administered to humans or animals for medicinal purposes, or any ingredient in such a product.

MEMO POINTS HMRC has confirmed that a supply of condoms distributed by a **sexual health charity** will qualify for zero-rating. However, supplies of condoms to customers other than charities that provide care, medical or surgical treatment will continue to be reduced-rated (¶1110). Business Brief 16/06

H. Clothing and footwear

Zero-rating applies to: **1394**
– **children's** clothing and footwear (¶1396); and
– **protective** clothing (¶1400).

Children's clothing and footwear

The sale, hire or making (but not alteration or repair) of clothes and footwear is zero-rated if they are both **designed** and **only suitable** for children. A child in this context means a person less than 14 years old. **1396** Sch 8 Group 16 Item 1 VATA 1994; Notice 714

Clothes and footwear are treated as designed for a child on the basis of the item's physical measurements (for example chest size or shoe size), full details of which can be found in VAT Notice 714.

These **size restrictions do not apply** to clothing that would in practice only be available to children under 14, such as Brownie uniforms, or school uniforms where the school only takes children under the age of 14. Garments of any size can be zero-rated, provided that they are designed exclusively for, and clearly identifiable as, the uniform of the organisation concerned.

Suitability is normally determined by the goods being held out for sale as suitable only for young children and therefore unsuitable for older people. Goods labelled with sizes or measurements which exceed those specified in VAT Notice 714 will not qualify for zero-rating.

Specifically **excluded** from zero-rating are articles:
a. suitable also for persons aged 14 or over, for example, one size fits all stretch garments; and
b. made wholly or partly from real (not artificial) fur skin, with the **exception of**:
- headgear;
- footgear;
- gloves;
- buttons, belts and buckles; and
- garments merely trimmed with fur skin (unless the trimming covers more than 20% of the area of the outside material or, in the case of a new garment, exceeds the cost to the manufacturer of the other components).

MEMO POINTS **Fur skin** means skin with fur attached, other than from rabbits, sheep, lambs, bovines, equines, chamois, gazelles, deer or dogs, or most breeds of goats and pigs.

1398 The following **examples** illustrate which items can be zero-rated:

Zero-rated	Standard-rated
Hats (including caps and other items of headgear) suitable by design only for young children, for example, babies' bonnets, school hats, or hats clearly held out for sale as for young children	Alice bands, hair ribbons, scrunchies, etc (as they do not cover the whole head, so cannot be equated to a hat)
All belts, braces, neckties, gloves, garters, scarves, ruffs, collars and shirt frills, provided that they are held out for sale as for under-14s	Safety accessories, including reflective armbands or buoyancy aids, badges, collars, cuffs, patches and other sew-on or iron-on items
Boots, shoes, sandals and slippers, even if they are designed for special purposes (such as ballet shoes or studded football boots)	Shoe accessories, for example: – blades or rollers sold on their own, or platform type roller skates for attaching to normal shoes; and – shoelaces, insoles, heel protectors and stick-on soles sold as separate items
Package kits for making children's clothing if: – the material is already cut to the pattern, or the pattern is indelibly printed on the material; and – it is clear from the labelling or other promotional material that the made-up garment is only suitable for young children	Alteration, repair, embroidery, etc, to children's goods, as such services do not usually create a new item. However, if a new item is created from the work, the service can be zero-rated, for example, where a jacket is made into a waistcoat.
Most items of babywear, including: – bibs, including plastic bibs with a curved tray at the base; – nappies (and nappy liners), both disposable and reusable, provided that they are held out for sale appropriately; and – towelling bathrobes designed with a hood or sleeves enabling the baby to be wrapped in them as a garment	Non-clothing items, such as: – pram and pushchair covers (unless designed to serve as a rain cape outside the pram or chair); – disposable nappy material sold in a continuous roll; or – sleeping bags not designed with neck and arm holes, or sleeves and/or legs Shawls intended to wrap around both mother and child

Protective wear

Protective **boots and helmets** for industrial use, and motor or pedal **cycle helmets**, are zero-rated. **1400** Sch 8 Group 16 Items 2, 3 VATA 1994; Notice 701/23

To qualify for zero-rating such **items must**:

- be manufactured to the appropriate European or British standard (or an approved alternative specification);
- bear a mark indicating conformity with that standard; and
- be for industrial use (if applicable).

This provision also includes **accessories** that are fitted as an integral part (for example, visors or ear protectors). However, accessories supplied on their own are standard-rated.

Excluded from zero-rating are:

- protective shoes;
- motor-cycle boots; and
- supplies to employers, for use by their employees, of boots and helmets for industrial use.

CHAPTER 4

Deemed supplies

OUTLINE ¶¶

Even in the **absence of consideration**, the following transactions are treated as supplies and are therefore within the scope of the VAT regime (with attendant provisions to value the supply): 1460
- gifts of business goods and services (¶1465);
- self-supplies of certain goods and services (¶1490);
- private use of goods or services originally acquired for business purposes (¶1520); and
- retention of business assets on deregistration (¶8607).

SECTION 1

Gifts

Gifts of **business goods** are supplies that are subject to VAT; output tax should be accounted for by the donor. 1465

Sch 4 paras 5, 9 VATA 1994; Notice 700/7 paras 2, 3

However, gifts of goods made in the course or furtherance of a business are **not supplies if** the cost of acquiring or producing all gifts made to the same person in any 12-month period is less than £50.

Gifts of **services** are generally **not treated as supplies**, unless they have been bought in from a third party, in which case VAT must be accounted for. If a taxable person simply pays a third party to provide services to someone else as a gift, any VAT charged by the third party is not recoverable, as the supply is not to the person who has paid the VAT.

There are special rules for goods and services **supplied free to employees** (¶1468).

MEMO POINTS 1. Goods given as a gift are only subject to VAT **if input VAT has been recovered** (in whole or part) on the cost of those goods.
2. **Gifts to a charity** are zero-rated supplies, provided that the goods are donated for sale or export by the charity (¶1372).

3. No VAT is due on **gifts from outside the EU** (other than tobacco products or alcoholic beverages) where they are:
– to members of visiting forces and certain conditions are met (¶9455); or
– sent on an occasional basis as a gift of friendship or goodwill between bodies, public authorities or groups carrying on an activity in the public interest. The goods must not be of a commercial character.
4. Special rules apply when accounting for VAT on gifts made by traders using the **retail schemes** (see ¶6300+ for details).
5. The CJEU has considered the £50 limit on gifts and concluded that it is lawful. However, the limit is to be applied not to each employer but to each of their employees separately. *EMI Group Ltd v HMRC* [2010]

What is a gift?

1467 Notice 700 para 8.9; Notice 700/7 para 2.1

A gift is **defined** by HMRC as the voluntary transfer of property for no consideration. **Examples** are:
- brochures, posters and advertising matter;
- long-service awards and retirement gifts;
- goods supplied to employees under attendance or safety at work schemes;
- items distributed to trade customers;
- prizes dispensed from amusement and gaming machines; and
- prizes of goods in betting, gaming and free lotteries.

EXAMPLE

1. A company sold jewellery. It occasionally rewarded regular customers by giving them an additional item of jewellery. It was held that these additional items were gifts, as they were freely given for no consideration. *Boodle & Dunthorne Ltd* [2002] (VTD 18429)

2. A company which operated motorway service stations provided free meals to coach drivers in return for bringing passengers to the service stations. To claim a free meal, a driver had to be carrying at least 20 passengers, and was also required to sign a book and produce his PSV licence. Drivers were also given gift stamps which could be exchanged for goods.
It was held that the free meals and gift stamps were not gifts. They were consideration given by the company to the drivers in exchange for the service of bringing potential customers to the service stations. *Granada Group plc* [1991] (VTD 5565)

3. Under a sales promotion scheme, a company gave free hamburgers to readers of a newspaper, on production of a completed voucher from the paper.
It was held that this was not a gift. It was a supply for consideration (the production of the completed voucher being the consideration). *McDonald's Restaurants Ltd* [1988] (VTD 3884)

Free supplies to employees

1468 Notice 700/7 para 3.3

The general rules apply to **gifts by an employer to its employees**. Services supplied by the employees to the employer are not treated as consideration for the free gifts (¶936). If the gift also includes non-employees (for example, spouses), input tax incurred on the cost of the goods may be blocked (¶1885).

There are special rules for the provision of certain benefits to employees:

Type of supply	VAT treatment
Fuel for private motoring	Deemed supply: see ¶1536
Catering	Free[1] food and drink: no output tax due Restaurant meals as rewards: supply is direct by the restaurant to the employee, so input tax not deductible Free food and drink to non-employees: no taxable supply, but input tax not deductible
Accommodation	Free accommodation for employees at own business premises (hotel or similar): no output tax due Cost of an employee's stay in a hotel: supply is direct by the hotel to the employee, so input tax not deductible

Note
1. **Free** means that there is no charge, either in cash or by deduction from salary.

Supplies which are not gifts

A gift should not be confused with a discount, sample or inducement. **1470**
- If a **discount** is given, VAT need only be accounted for on the discounted value (¶998). Notice 700 para 8.9; Notice 700/7 para 4
- Where a trader gives a **free sample** to a customer there is no supply (¶272).
- Gifts given in the expectation of some valuable return are **inducements**. These are treated as supplies; output tax must be accounted for, regardless of the value of the inducement.

EXAMPLE Gifts were offered by a trader to induce customers to attend a sales pitch. These gifts were not "freely given business gifts" but were assets supplied in the course of the business for non-monetary consideration. *Mitrolone Ltd* [1989] (VTD 4301)

Competition prizes are usually business gifts. When a car is provided as a prize, the donor can reclaim any input tax incurred on the car, provided that it is not made available for private use before it is given away.

Accounting for VAT

The **donor** must account for output tax on the value of the gift at the date it is given. This should be **based on** the cost the donor would have to incur to buy an identical product at that date, or, if such a product is not available, one similar in age and condition. Failing this, the **cost price** of the gift provided, at the date of the gift, should be used. **1472** Notice 700/7 para 2.3

Where a business gift is **used by the recipient** for its business, it can treat this VAT as input tax and recover it in accordance with the normal rules, based on a tax certificate (¶1474) issued by the donor.

Administration

The donor cannot issue a tax invoice (as there is no consideration) but can instead issue a **tax certificate**. This can be the donor's normal invoicing documentation overwritten with the following statement: **1474**

"Tax Certificate - No payment is necessary for these goods. Output tax of £(insert amount) has been accounted for on the supply."

Full details of the goods must be shown on the documentation; the amount of VAT shown must be the amount of output tax accounted for to HMRC, based on the cost of the goods to the donor.

SECTION 2

Self-supplies

A self-supply takes place where eligible supplies (¶1494) are taken possession of, or produced, by a person in the course of business and they are then **consumed by that person** for business purposes. In other words, the supplies are neither provided to another person, nor incorporated into goods produced in the course or furtherance of the producer's business. **1490** ss 5(5) - (7) VATA 1994

1. Implications

Where there is a self-supply, the **goods or services are treated** as being supplied both by and to the trader. Accordingly, the trader: **1492**
- must account for output tax on the goods or services; and
- is treated as having incurred input tax on the same supply, which the trader may be able to recover.

If the **business is fully taxable**, there is no net effect on its VAT position, as the input VAT on the self-supply will be fully recoverable. If a **business is partly exempt**, the input VAT is only recoverable according to the partial exemption method in place. The self-supply is ignored when calculating taxable turnover for the standard method of partial exemption (¶2126).

A self-supply may require a **non-registered trader** to register for VAT (¶2605).

MEMO POINTS The self-supply **rules are designed** to ensure that partly exempt traders cannot gain a VAT advantage by producing goods or self-supplying services for use in their business which would otherwise have carried irrecoverable input VAT.

EXAMPLE Mr A, a partly exempt trader, uses his own employees to carry out alterations on his own premises. In the absence of the self-supply rules, he could avoid suffering any VAT on this supply. However, the self-supply rules treat this as a supply both to and by Mr A and he therefore:
- has to account for output VAT on the supply; and
- can recover input tax on the value of the supply in accordance with his existing partial exemption method (which probably means he will not be able to recover it in full).

2. Eligible supplies

1494 The self-supply rules only **apply to** a few limited supplies, as summarised below:

Type of supply	Detail	Time of supply	Value of supply
Property services	Builders constructing own buildings (¶5330)	¶5334	¶5334
	Change from residential or charitable use (¶5297)	¶5302 and ¶5312	¶5304 and ¶5314
Motor cars	¶1496	¶1498	¶1500
Transfer of a going concern	¶1502	¶1504	¶1504
Assets on hand on withdrawal from flat rate scheme	¶4726	¶4726	¶4726

Motor cars

1496 SI 1992/3122; Notice 700/64 para 3.10

There is a deemed self-supply when a trader uses a car for a purpose on which input tax would be blocked. Generally this occurs where the vehicle is available for private use and either:
- input tax was originally recovered on the purchase or import of the car (¶1902); or
- the car was manufactured by the trader.

MEMO POINTS There is no self-supply if private use is made of a car by a dealer or manufacturer who **intends to sell it as stock** within 12 months. Instead the supply is treated as a temporary private use of a business asset and output tax is charged on the element of private use (¶1528).

1498 s 6(11) VATA 1994

Time of supply The time of supply is the date the vehicle is appropriated for the use which triggers the self-supply.

1500 Notice 700/57 para 14

Value of the supply The value of the supply depends on whether the car is new or used.

If the car is **new**, the value of the supply by a:
- **UK manufacturer** is the full cost of manufacturing the vehicle, including related production overheads (for volume manufacturers, this can be taken to be 2/3rds of the current retail list price; non-volume manufacturers may also use this approximation with the agreement of HMRC); and
- **non-manufacturing trader** is the purchase price plus any cost of incorporated parts of UK manufacture and delivery charge (discounts received after the time of supply should be

disregarded, unless contractually agreed before that time; where delivery charges cannot be determined, a fixed charge of £50 per vehicle may be used).

If the car is **used**, the value of the self-supply is its "replacement value", being the current purchase price of an identical vehicle (or, failing that, a similar one) at the time of the disposal. If it is not possible to establish this figure, the fall-back value is the cost of manufacture as at the time of disposal. If this cannot be determined, a value of 2/3rds of the current list price for a new car is acceptable.

MEMO POINTS Where a commercial vehicle **is converted into a car**, the value of the supply is the current value of the vehicle at the time of the conversion, including the cost of conversion. Notice 700/64 para 2.4

EXAMPLE

1. A trader purchased a Citroen van and reclaimed input tax. Subsequently they modified the van by fitting windows behind the driver's seat. It was held that this amounted to a conversion of a vehicle into a motor car, which was a self-supply. *Browsers Bookshop* [1988] (VTD 2837)

2. A company purchased a number of Peugeot 205 and 305 vans. It modified the vehicles, for safety reasons, by adding a window on each side, behind the driver's seat. Although this case appears to be similar to *Browsers Bookshop*, it seems that the case turned on the type of van, as it was held that this was not a conversion of a commercial vehicle into a motor car, because the "accommodation available behind the driver's seat in the modified vehicles could not realistically be described as reasonably suitable for the carriage of passengers". *John Beharrell Ltd* [1991] (VTD 6530)

Transfer of a going concern

There is a deemed self-supply by the representative member of a VAT group when **any member** of that VAT group acquires a business by means of a transfer of a going concern (TOGC (¶8646)), if the **VAT group** is partly exempt, or becomes partly exempt during the year. 1502 s 44 VATA 1994

This deemed supply **is not triggered** in relation to:
– assets which were the property of the transferor for more than 3 years prior to the date of the transfer;
– goodwill;
– zero-rated or exempt assets; or
– assets which fall within the capital goods scheme (¶2280).

MEMO POINTS Where HMRC believes that transactions have been devised to **manipulate the 3-year time limit** (e.g. where assets that have been held for 3 years and 1 day are transferred), it has powers to direct that the self-supply provisions apply notwithstanding the strict rules. Sch 9A VATA 1994

The self-supply charge will be **accounted** for by the representative member (¶8832) and will apply to all chargeable assets that were transferred as part of the TOGC. In other words, it will account for output VAT on the value of the chargeable assets transferred and recover input tax in accordance with its current partial exemption method. 1504

Chargeable assets are essentially all assets that would constitute a positively taxable supply - that is, not an exempt or zero-rated supply.

The **value of the self-supply** is the open-market value of the chargeable assets at the date of the transfer. If VAT is not due on some of the assets transferred, the consideration must be apportioned between the taxable and non-taxable assets on a reasonable basis.

MEMO POINTS 1. **The time of supply** is the date when the assets are transferred.
2. The self-supply **charge can be reduced** if:
– the seller's partial exemption recovery rate during the tax year in which the assets were purchased is equal to or less than the buyer's recovery rate during the year in which the buyer purchased the assets; any VAT charged will be reduced to nil, although no tax will be refunded; or
– the buyer can show that the previous owner did not recover all the input tax incurred on the original purchase because, for example, the input tax was blocked (¶1885).
3. This anti-avoidance provision was **introduced** to stop partly exempt VAT groups using stand-alone, fully taxable, VAT-registered subsidiaries to gain a tax advantage by acquiring goods (therefore recovering VAT) before transferring the goods as part of a TOGC, at a later date, to the partly exempt VAT group.

SECTION 3

Private use of business goods or services

1. Goods

1520 Sch 4 paras 5, 5A, 6, 8 VATA 1994 If an asset of a business is withdrawn from the business, or made available for non-business purposes, there will be a taxable supply of goods for private use, **unless**:
- no consideration is received for the asset or use of the asset; and
- no input tax was previously claimed on it by the person carrying on the business.

The **time of supply** is the time at which the asset is withdrawn from the business, or made available for private use.

The **value of the supply** is the amount of any consideration received. If no consideration is received, the value of the supply will depend on the circumstances.

MEMO POINTS 1. There is also a deemed supply if input tax was claimed by any **predecessor** as owner of the business, defined to mean anyone from whom the present owner acquired it by way of a transfer as a going concern (¶8646), or a chain of such transfers.

Sch 6 para 1 VATA 1994 2. If the consideration received is below **market value**, HMRC has power to direct that market value be used if the transfer is between connected parties (¶960), or involves a demonstrator car (¶1528).

1522 The output tax treatment of business goods used for private purposes is summarised in the following table:

Duration of use	Type of asset	Treatment
Permanent (assets cease to be business assets)	Cars	See ¶1528
	Motor fuel	See ¶1536
	Other	Supply of goods
Temporary (assets put to or made available for non-business use)	Land and buildings[1]	Supply of goods
	Ship, boat or aircraft	Supply of goods
	Other	Deemed supply of services

Note
1. Only if it constitutes a major interest (¶5249) or there is no consideration. Includes an interest in land; a building or part of a building; civil engineering works; and goods incorporated or to be incorporated in any of the preceding.

Private use as a supply of goods

1524 Sch 6 para 6 VATA 1994 The **value of the supply** is the "replacement value".

Replacement value is the amount that would be payable if the person making the supply were to purchase goods identical to those supplied (or, where this cannot be determined, goods similar to those supplied) at the time of the disposal.

If it is **not possible to establish this figure**, the fall-back value is the cost of producing the goods on the assumption that they were produced at the time of disposal.

EXAMPLE An old computer is given away free to an employee for permanent use at home. The accumulated depreciation and maintenance costs of the computer are £1,750. The replacement cost is £900. The value of the deemed supply of goods is therefore £900 and VAT of £180 must be accounted for (£900 x 20%).

Private use as a deemed supply of services

1525 Sch 6 para 7 VATA 1994; SI 1995/2518 reg 116A; HMRC Brief 02/10 If goods are temporarily taken out of a business, there is a **supply of services**. HMRC has published extensive guidance on the method of accounting for output tax in this situation.

The method is called the **Lennartz method** following the CJEU case of the same name (¶1842). The Lennartz method is no longer available in relation to land, property, ships and aircraft. Full input tax recovery is therefore not available on the purchase; instead recovery is restricted to the business use proportion.

Moreover, the Lennartz method is **no longer available** where an asset is purchased and will be used wholly for business purposes, but the purchaser carries out not only economic activities but also business activities which are outside the scope of VAT. HMRC has made it clear that Lennartz is only available where the purchaser intends to use the asset both for business and non-business purposes. Where arrangements are already in force to apply Lennartz, HMRC expects businesses to honour those arrangements and account for VAT in accordance with the method agreed.

For the deemed **time of supply** see ¶798.

Lennartz calculation The Lennartz method works by apportioning the cost of providing the asset between business and private use. **1526** SI 1995/2518 reg 116C - 116F; Information Sheet 14/07; HMRC Brief 02/10

For assets acquired at any time since 31 October 2007 (excluding land, property, ships or aircraft acquired after 31 December 2010), the following **formula** applies:

$$\frac{A}{B} \times (C \times U\%)$$

where:
- A is the number of months in the relevant VAT period which fall within the economic life of the assets concerned;
- B is the total number of months of the economic life;
- C is the full cost of the assets; and
- U% is the extent, expressed as a percentage, to which the assets are put to any private use as compared with the total use of the goods during the VAT period.

The **full cost** should be determined by reference to the taxable VAT-bearing costs of the asset, excluding VAT itself. Any exempt or zero-rated costs of purchase, acquisition or construction are excluded.

Where there is either **no use or no private use** during a VAT period, no deemed charge arises. However, the number of months taken into account in a subsequent VAT period where there is private use will need to include any previous periods of non-use since the last deemed charge arose.

If the asset is **sold**, the economic life is ended.

EXAMPLE

1. Mrs X, a taxable person, buys a painting for £1 million (the full cost) plus £200,000 VAT. As she intends to use the painting for both business and private purposes, she decides to apply the Lennartz method.
The painting is actually used for private purposes for 50% of the time in the first VAT quarter.
It has an economic life (for this purpose) of 60 months.
Applying the formula gives a taxable value of £25,000. (3/60 × 1,000,000 × 50%)
So the output tax charge for this quarter is £5,000. (25,000 @ 20%)

2. Continuing the first example, in the second period, no private use of the painting occurs. In the third period, private use is again 50%.
So in this calculation, "A" is 6 months (i.e. 2 VAT quarters).
Applying the formula gives a taxable value of £50,000. (6/60 × 1,000,000 × 50%)
So the output tax charge for this quarter is £10,000. (50,000 @ 20%)

MEMO POINTS 1. The **economic life** of goods for the purposes of the Lennartz method from 1 November 2007 is 10 years for **land and buildings** and 5 years for **all other goods**. Before that date the economic life of land and buildings was deemed to be 20 years.
2. **Transitional provisions** provide for the economic life of goods to be treated as commencing from 1 November 2007 (rather than upon the first use of the goods), but adjusted to take account of (and give credit for) any deemed supplies arising from private use up to that date.
3. The economic life **commences on** the day of first use (for any purpose) after the supply of the goods or property to a person (or any predecessors of that person, where a business has been transferred).

4. Where a trader is **partly exempt**, the calculation may be more complex and further reference to HMRC material may be required. Traders' partial exemption methods should be reviewed in light of the Lennartz rules to ensure they still give a fair and reasonable rate of VAT recovery.

1527 HMRC states that the **transitional provisions** should have **no effect on** any asset which is not land or buildings and where, before 1 November 2007, the taxable person was already using a 5-year basis for calculating the output tax charge.

Where assets have been **used before 1 November 2007**:
- only for business purposes, the duration of the part of their economic life after that date will be the remainder of the period of 10 or 5 years (as appropriate) which commenced on the first use of the goods; or
- for private purposes, the economic life commences on 1 November 2007, with allowance made for the output tax already paid under the old system i.e. if a 20-year period had previously applied and 2 years have already been accounted for, the taxable person would only need to account for a further 9 years of deemed supply under the new rules, recognising that 10% of the life has already elapsed. For this purpose, the following **formula** applies:

$$D \times ((E - F)/ E)$$

where:
- D is the "normal" economic life of the goods concerned (i.e. 5 or 10 years as appropriate);
- E is the full cost of the goods; and
- F is: (G × 100)/(X% × 100)

where:
  - G is the total value of the relevant goods on which VAT will be accounted for on pre-1 November 2007 non-business use; and
  - X% is the extent to which the goods have been used for non-business purposes (as compared to business use) in the pre-1 November 2007 period.

EXAMPLE A taxable person constructed a commercial property at a cost of £1 million plus VAT of £175,000. It was first used on 1 November 2005. The taxable person originally chose an economic life of 240 months, in line with HMRC's stated policy at the time. Private use of the building was constant at 65% (X% in the formula above).

Value already charged under old rules
Until 1 November 2007, the taxable value for each quarter was £8,125 (3/240 × £1,000,000 × 65%).
As 8 quarters occurred between the date of first use and 1 November 2007, the cumulative deemed supply (G) was £65,000. (8 × £8,125)
So F is £100,000. (£65,000 × 100/(0.65 × 100))
This means that £100,000 of the full cost of the property has already been charged.

Length of calculation from 1 November 2007
The calculation is carried out for another 9 years or 108 months. (120 × (1,000,000 - 100,000)/ 1,000,000)

Deemed supply for quarters from 1 November 2007
Applying the usual formula gives a taxable value of £16,250. (3/120 × £1,000,000 × 65%)
So the output tax charge for this quarter is £3,250. (£16,250 x 20%)
Note that the economic life is now 120 months and not 108 months.

Motor cars

1528 Sch 6 paras 1A, 7 VATA 1994 It is common for a motor manufacturer, dealer or those running car-related trades to permit employees, and occasionally their families, to have **temporary** private use of motor cars (¶1892) which are intended to be sold as stock within 12 months. These cars are often referred to as **demonstrator cars**. This temporary private use is treated as a supply of services.

SI 1992/3222 reg 2 MEMO POINTS 1. A **motor manufacturer** is someone who constructs cars, either from scratch, or by conversion.
2. A **motor dealer** is someone who buys in cars for the purpose of resale, either new or second hand, and sells them on with a view to making an overall profit. Fleet purchasers, who buy cars in bulk to use for a short period and then sell on for profit, are not motor dealers for this purpose.
3. See ¶1496 for details of a similar charge when **non-demonstrator cars** are used for private purposes.

Value of the supply If there is **no consideration**, output tax must be accounted for on the full cost to the manufacturer or dealer. 1530 Sch 6 paras 7, 8 VATA 1994

If there is **consideration**, output tax must be accounted for on the amount of the consideration.

MEMO POINTS As an anti-avoidance measure, HMRC may direct that where only **nominal consideration is charged**, the value of such a supply is to be its open-market value. Sch 6 para 1A VATA 1994
Any direction under these provisions must be given within 3 years from the time of supply and can specify that future supplies made under identical conditions are to be made at open-market value. It is possible to appeal against a notice and the notice itself may be varied or withdrawn by a further notice.

EXAMPLE One motor dealer argued that a £10 charge for 10 years' use of a car fixed the consideration at £10. The charge was made in 2004, before the open-market value direction legislation came into force on 1 January 2005. The First-tier Tribunal held that the dealer made a supply of a car in each accounting period, so HMRC's open-market value direction, made to take effect from 1 April 2005, was effective for each accounting period thereafter. *Lookers Motor Group Ltd* [2009] (TC00165)

Alternatively, manufacturers or dealers may **opt to use a simplified method**, which they must then adopt for all their cars used occasionally for private use. This effectively allows output tax to be accounted for on the basis of a charge akin to the fuel scale charge (¶1538), provided that the car is made available to the employee free of charge. Different agreements apply for manufacturers and dealers, as shown in the table below: 1532 Notice 700/57 paras 24, 25; Information Sheet 8/11

List price incl VAT	Average list price incl VAT	VAT due on annual return		VAT due on quarterly return		VAT due on monthly return	
		Manu-facturer	Dealer	Manu-facturer	Dealer	Manu-facturer	Dealer
£	£	£	£	£	£	£	£
0-8,999.99	7,470	70.86	78.64	17.71	19.66	5.90	6.55
9,000-11,999.99	10,320	93.12	103.87	23.28	25.97	7.76	8.63
12,000-16,999.99	14,620	126.72	141.95	31.68	35.49	10.56	11.83
17,000-22,999.99	20,470	172.42	193.74	43.11	48.44	14.37	16.15
23,000-30,999.99	27,590	228.05	256.79	57.01	64.20	19.00	21.40
31,000-39,999.99	35,600	290.62	327.71	72.66	81.93	24.22	27.31
40,000-49,999.99	44,500	360.16	406.51	90.04	101.63	30.01	33.88
50,000-64,999.99	58,500	469.53	530.47	117.38	132.62	39.13	44.21
65,000-79,999.99	72,000	513.60	650.00	143.75	162.50	47.92	54.17
80,000 upwards	Individual calculation based on actual cost prices						

A similar simplified agreement applies to cars that are used for **self-drive hire cars** (¶1906) as follows (the figures have been updated from those shown in the Notice to take account of changes in the standard rate of VAT): 1534 Notice 700/57 para 26; Information Sheet 8/11

List price incl VAT	Average price incl VAT	VAT due on annual return	VAT due on quarterly return	VAT due on monthly return
£	£	£	£	£
0-8,999.99	7,470	46.89	11.72	3.91
9,000-11,999.99	10,320	60.01	15.00	5.00
12,000-16,999.99	14,620	79.81	19.95	6.65
17,000-22,999.99	20,470	106.75	26.69	8.90
23,000-30,999.99	27,590	139.53	34.88	11.63
31,000-39,999.99	35,600	176.41	44.10	14.70
40,000-49,999.99	44,500	217.39	54.35	18.12
50,000-64,999.99	58,500	281.84	70.46	23.49
65,000-79,999.99	72,000	344.00	86.00	28.67
80,000 upwards	Individual calculation based on actual cost prices			

Fuel

1536 s 56 VATA 1994

There is a **deemed supply** when fuel is provided at or below cost by a taxable business to its proprietors or staff if:
- the fuel is provided for such individuals' motor cars (motorcycles, vans, pool cars and the like do not fall within these provisions); and
- there is any element of private use of the fuel.

However, the input tax incurred on the fuel is then deductible, despite the element of private use.

1538 s 57, Sch 6 para A1 VATA 1994

Value of the supply The business may account for VAT on either:
- the open-market value of the fuel supplied; or
- a scale charge (¶1539), based on the CO_2 emissions of the car.

The chosen option must be applied to all private fuel provided by the business.

1539 The table below sets out the scale charges which apply to VAT periods beginning on or after 1 May 2014. This is now known as the "flat rate basis of charge". HMRC is obliged to update the table at 12-monthly intervals using a specified formula.

CO_2 band	Annual return		Quarterly return		Monthly return	
	Charge (gross) £	VAT included £	Charge (gross) £	VAT included £	Charge (gross) £	VAT included £
120 or less	627.00	104.50	156.00	26.00	52.00	8.67
125	939.00	156.50	234.00	39.00	78.00	13.00
130	1,004.00	167.33	251.00	41.83	83.00	13.83
135	1,064.00	177.33	266.00	44.33	88.00	14.67
140	1,129.00	188.17	282.00	47.00	94.00	15.67
145	1,190.00	198.33	297.00	49.50	99.00	16.50
150	1,255.00	209.17	313.00	52.17	104.00	17.33
155	1,315.00	219.17	328.00	54.67	109.00	18.17
160	1,381.00	230.17	345.00	57.50	115.00	19.17
165	1,441.00	240.17	360.00	60.00	120.00	20.00
170	1,506.00	251.00	376.00	62.67	125.00	20.83
175	1,567.00	261.17	391.00	65.17	130.00	21.67
180	1,632.00	272.00	408.00	68.00	136.00	22.67
185	1,692.00	282.00	423.00	70.50	141.00	23.50
190	1,757.00	292.83	439.00	73.17	146.00	24.33
195	1,818.00	303.00	454.00	75.67	151.00	25.17
200	1,883.00	313.83	470.00	78.33	156.00	26.00
205	1,943.00	323.83	485.00	80.83	161.00	26.83
210	2,008.00	334.67	502.00	83.67	167.00	27.83
215	2,069.00	344.83	517.00	86.17	172.00	28.67
220	2,134.00	355.67	533.00	88.83	177.00	29.50
225 or more	2,194.00	365.67	548.00	91.33	182.00	30.33

Where the CO_2 emissions figure of a vehicle is not a multiple of 5, the figure is rounded down to the previous multiple of 5 to determine the charge.

For a bi-fuel vehicle with two CO_2 emissions figures, the lower figure should be used.

For cars which are too old to have a CO_2 emissions figure, identify the CO_2 band based on engine size, as follows:
- cylinder capacity 1,400cc or less, use band 140;

- cylinder capacity exceeds 1,400cc but does not exceed 2,000cc, use band 175; and
- cylinder capacity exceeds 2,000cc, use band 225 or above.

See ¶9968 for historic fuel scale charge rates.

MEMO POINTS 1. There is no provision allowing the scale charge to be reduced where a car is **available for only part of a period**.
2. Where a person has **two cars during a period**, the scale charge will apply to only one of the vehicles, if:
- the cars are available for different periods, i.e. not concurrently; and
- at the end of the period, one of the cars is no longer available.

If the cars fall within the same category (i.e. fuel and engine capacity), the fuel scale charge for that category applies. If the cars are not in the same category, the fuel scale charges for both relevant categories must be apportioned accordingly. Alternatively, the scale charge for the higher category can be used.
3. The VAT charge should be included in box 1 of the **VAT return**, whilst the net amount producing the VAT charge should be entered in box 6.
4. An extra-statutory concession, under which **partly exempt** traders were permitted to account for reduced fuel scale charges based on their recovery rate, was withdrawn on 1 January 2014 and replaced with a proposed new "fuel sector formula".
Partly exempt traders who reclaim input tax on fuel only recover their partial exemption percentage of that input tax, under normal rules. HMRC accepts that it is unfair if such traders nonetheless have to account for the full fuel scale charge. HMRC has therefore proposed an alternative means of recovering input tax, which, HMRC suggests, will remove any potential unfairness. Partly exempt traders are free to propose an amendment to their current partial exemption method if that can be shown to be more fair and reasonable.
HMRC proposes the following formula: VAT on fuel scale charges + ((VAT charged on fuel purchased in the period - VAT on fuel scale charges) x partial exemption recovery rate).
For example:
- VAT on scale charge due: £300.00;
- VAT incurred on road fuel: £630.00;
- PE recovery rate: 40%.

Calculation: 300 + ((630 - 300) × 40%) = 300 + (330 × 40%) = 300 + (132.00) = £432.00 input tax recovery.

EXAMPLE 1541

1. For the VAT quarter beginning 1 August 2014, Mr C drives a car with a CO_2 emissions figure of 188g/km.
The CO_2 emissions will be rounded down to 185g/km and Mr C will declare VAT of £70.50 in his quarterly VAT return (with the gross charge being £423).

2. During the return period to 30 November 2014, A Ltd provides two cars for Mr B to use, with the following CO_2 emissions:

Car	Emissions	Availability
Car 1	183g/km	1 September to 30 September
Car 2	203g/km	1 October to 30 November

The fuel scale charge for Mr B's cars is calculated as follows:

Car	Gross		VAT	
	£	£	£	£
Car 1: scale charge	408.00		68.00	
Available for 1 month: taking 1/3		136.00		22.67
Car 2: scale charge	470.00		78.33	
Available for 2 months: taking 2/3		313.33		52.22
Total		449.33		74.89

If A Ltd is partly exempt and able to recover, say, 76% of its residual input tax, the gross fuel scale charge for Mr B's car would be 76% × £449.33, i.e. £341.49.

A business may **avoid** the fuel scale charge in the following ways: 1542
Notice 48 para 3.1; Notice 700/64 para 8
a. by agreeing not to claim a deduction for any input tax suffered on the acquisition of any road fuel, whether for business or private use (this option is concessionary and must be agreed in advance with HMRC). Depending on the amount of the potential input tax reclaim,

this option may be cheaper, and administratively easier, for the business than applying the scale charges; or

b. by analysing the fuel costs, separating out the amount relating to business journeys and only claiming input tax on that amount. This option requires the following additional records to be kept, which results in an administrative burden and as a consequence is used less often by businesses:
- mileage travelled;
- whether the journey is business or private;
- rate of mileage allowance; and
- amount of input tax claimed.

EXAMPLE Mr A drives 8,000 miles, of which 5,000 are business miles. The cost of the fuel is £875.
The fuel cost relating to the business miles is £546.88. (5,000/8,000 × £875)
The related input tax reclaim for business mileage only is £91.15. (£546.88 × 1/6)

2. Services

1544 Similar rules apply to non-business use of services, although this **rarely occurs in practice**, as it is easier for traders to apportion between business and non-business use and only recover the portion of input tax that relates to business use.

1546 There is a **deemed supply** of services if:

Sch 6 paras 7, 8A, 10 VATA 1994; SI 1993/1507; Business Brief 17/94

- a trader uses, or allows another person to use, for a private purpose services that were initially provided for the business;
- the trader has claimed (or will claim) all or part of the input tax for the services concerned; and
- the user makes no payment for the private use of the services.

These provisions **do not apply** if:
- the services consist of the provision of catering or accommodation to employees (¶1549);
- 50% of the input tax has already been blocked, for example on leased cars (¶1885); or
- there has already been an apportionment of input tax based on mixed business and private use (¶1838).

For the appropriate **time of supply** rules see ¶798.

MEMO POINTS **Minor or occasional private or non-business use** will be ignored and will not give rise to a VAT liability.

1548 **Value of the supply** The value of the supply is the amount that would reasonably represent the cost of providing the service (with the proviso that the total VAT liability accounted for cannot exceed the input tax claimed when the services were obtained). Typically, where the service supplied consists of the private use of a business asset, this is done using the depreciation on the asset. The trader should stop accounting for output tax when the depreciation value reaches nil, or (if earlier) the total output tax accounted for equals the amount of the input tax attributable to non-business use.

There are no set rules about the **calculation**, provided that the result is fair and reasonable, although HMRC mentions the following possible method, based on the depreciation of comparable business assets:

$$\frac{\text{Cost of services} \times \text{Projected period of non-business use}}{\text{Total depreciation period of comparable assets}}$$

For the valuation of intra-group supplies from overseas see ¶8898.

EXAMPLE Ms B is an accountant who, in Year 1, had an extension built onto her house, to use as her business premises. The cost of the extension was £40,000.
In Year 11, Ms B changes the use to private, because her business moves to a separate office building. The life of a comparable asset is 20 years, so there is a projected period of private use of 10 years.

Applying the formula gives £20,000 as the value on which output tax is due. ($\frac{40{,}000 \times 10}{20} = 20{,}000$)

This is then spread over the next 10 years (equivalent to 40 quarters), to give a quarterly amount of £500. ($\frac{20{,}000}{40} = 500$)

The quarterly output tax charge is therefore £100.00. (£500 x 20%)

Where an employer makes a supply of goods or services to its employees of: **1549**

- food or drink in the course of **catering**; or
- **accommodation** in a hotel, inn, boarding house, etc,

the value of the supply is equal to the consideration (if any) actually paid by the employee. Where consideration is paid for such a supply, it is treated as a VAT-inclusive payment.

PART 3

Input tax

Input tax
Summary

The numbers cross-refer to paragraphs.

CHAPTER 1 **Deductible input tax**

CHAPTER 2 **Recoverable input tax**

CHAPTER 3 **Special situations**

CHAPTER 1

Deductible input tax

OUTLINE ¶¶

As VAT is a tax on consumption, registered businesses which are intermediaries in the supply chain should not suffer VAT on their expenditure. The basic idea is that a trader who charges output tax (¶40) can recover any input tax suffered. **1800**

However, as VAT is not chargeable on exempt supplies, the related input tax cannot be recovered; there are special rules for traders who make both taxable and exempt supplies (¶2070).

In this Part of *VAT Memo* we refer to input tax incurred for business purposes, which is not blocked, as deductible input tax (dealt with in this chapter). Once the various eligibility conditions are satisfied (¶1950+) deductible input tax becomes eligible input tax. If the input tax relates wholly to taxable supplies made by the business it is recoverable input tax

(¶2070+), as is the portion of input tax which does relate to taxable supplies in a partial exemption calculation (¶2075+).

SECTION 1

General principles

1805 A **VAT-registered business** can deduct VAT incurred by it on expenditure on goods and services.

There are **restrictions** where:
- the expenditure is not wholly for business purposes;
- a deduction is specifically prohibited (blocked);
- one or more of the eligibility conditions is not met; or
- a claim is not properly made.

In addition, users of the **flat rate schemes** (¶4635 and ¶5970) cannot recover input tax.

VAT is a self-assessed tax, so the onus is on the business to ensure that input tax is correctly calculated and claimed.

What is input tax?

1807 Input tax is the VAT incurred by a VAT-registered business in respect of supplies made to it and which it uses, or intends to use, for the purposes of its business. It follows that any VAT suffered on acquisitions for non-business purposes, or by a non-VAT-registered business, is generally not input tax.

> EXAMPLE A VAT-registered computer shop purchases 100 computers from its supplier for £50,000. The supplier charges output tax of £10,000 on its invoice, which the shop can treat as input tax. The shop then sells the computers to customers and charges VAT on each sale.
> Unless the customer is VAT-registered, the VAT charged to the customer is not input tax.

1810 The following diagram summarises these principles.

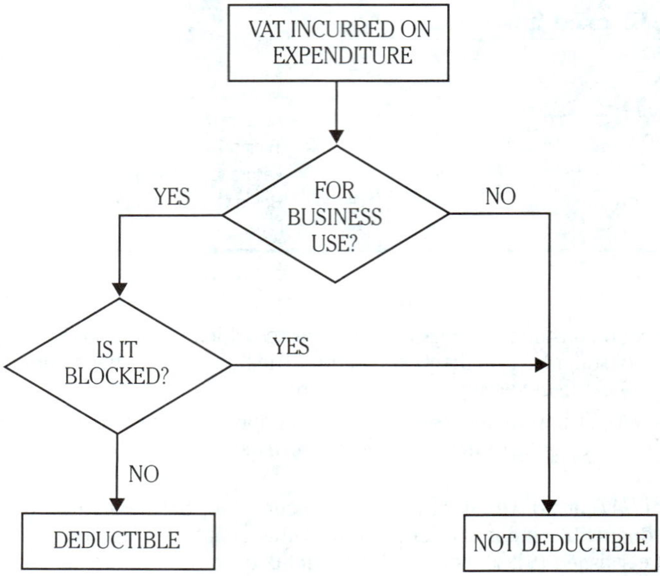

Supplies where input tax levied

Input tax is incurred on goods and services purchased from another VAT-registered business in the UK. Unlike direct tax, there is no distinction between **capital and revenue** items of expenditure, the only important issue being how the goods and services are used or to be used. The exception to this is the capital goods scheme (¶2280), under which recovery of input tax is adjusted according to use over an extended period. **1812** s 24(1) VATA 1994

In an **international context**, input tax is also suffered on the following: **1814** s 26 VATA 1994
- acquisitions from the EU (¶9017);
- most services received from the EU (¶9682);
- goods imported, and services received, from outside the EU (¶9400 and ¶9680); and
- goods removed from a fiscal warehouse (¶9258).

MEMO POINTS In relation to **EU acquisitions and services from outside the UK**, the recipient of the supply charges itself VAT. In this way, the administration of VAT across borders is simplified because the person accounts for input tax and output tax at the same time. This is known as the reverse charge mechanism (¶9700).

Onward use of the supplies

Input tax is deductible where such supplies are **used** in making the trader's own taxable supplies. A person who is **intending** to make taxable supplies can register for VAT and deduct input tax on supplies **to be used** in making taxable supplies. A recently registered trader can deduct input tax on certain goods and services received before becoming VAT-registered (¶8560). **1816**

MEMO POINTS In a case which originated in Bulgaria the CJEU held that it was lawful for the tax authority to **restrict** the deductibility of input tax in relation to goods which the trader could not sell because they had been **stolen**. *PIGI* [2012] C-550/11

Accounting for irrecoverable VAT

Any VAT which cannot be recovered from HMRC should be included in the **financial statements** with the expenditure heading to which it relates. This is particularly important for assets which are capitalised in the accounts, as balance sheet values will be increased. **1818** SSAP 5

SECTION 2

Business purpose

For input tax to be deductible, the related goods or services must be acquired for the **purposes** of any business carried on, or to be carried on, by the taxable person. Whether a business is carried on is a question of fact. If a person is repeatedly making sales and receiving consideration, this will normally be taken to be carrying on a business. An individual may undertake different activities, some or all of which may constitute a business. **Each activity** must be examined separately and matched to related expenditure. Particular difficulty applies to investment businesses and holding companies, which often incur costs while passively retaining assets. However, assuming that a VAT-registered person is carrying on a business, the question remains whether VAT has been incurred for the purposes of that business, one possible alternative being that the VAT was incurred for the owner's private purposes. **1825** EC Directive 2006/112 art 168; s 24(1) VATA 1994

EXAMPLE A company called ADIL was formed to act as vehicle for the takeover of the airport operator BAA by Spanish company Ferrovial. ADIL was charged VAT on professional fees connected with the takeover. Subsequent to the takeover ADIL joined the BAA VAT group and sought to deduct the takeover VAT as incurred in relation to a cost component of BAA's ongoing business. The First-tier Tribunal permitted the deduction, the Upper Tribunal allowed HMRC's appeal, denying that there was a direct and immediate link between the takeover and BAA's ongoing business, and the Court of Appeal then dismissed BAA's appeal on the ground that ADIL was not carrying on an economic activity.

The crucial fact was that at the time of the takeover ADIL had no intention to make any taxable supplies. It was in existence only to facilitate the takeover. Thus, **when it incurred the VAT** in question it was not carrying on an economic activity and therefore had no right to deduct that VAT. *BAA Ltd v HMRC* [2013]

Where income is received which is **outside the scope** of VAT, or **exempt**, related input tax may still potentially have been incurred for business purposes. For example, certain grants may support the main business activity, or shares in subsidiaries may have been sold to raise finance for the business activities of the group in general (¶2422).

For a detailed examination of whether an activity constitutes a business see ¶100+.

s 94 VATA 1994; SI 2001/2879

MEMO POINTS 1. The following are **deemed** to be businesses for VAT purposes:
- a club or other organisation offering benefits in return for **membership** subscriptions;
- **admission** to premises for consideration (museums and galleries which do not charge for admission are entitled to recover their input tax under a special regime);
- performance of duties by **office holders** in the course of a trade, profession or vocation (¶145);
- **termination** or intended termination of a business, including the disposal of related assets and liabilities (¶8600); and
- disposal of a business as a **going concern** (¶8646).

Notice 48 para 3.34; Business Brief 19/05

2. Input tax is deductible in relation to fundraising in support of a **charity's** taxable business activities, such as the work involved in obtaining legacies or donations. Gifts to donors may be a deemed supply of a business asset, if there is a link to the charity's business activities (e.g. a newsletter advert). For details about charities and VAT see ¶8000+.

A. Intention

1827 There is no statutory **definition** of incurred for a business purpose, so the meaning must be divined from case law. It is something more than just being beneficial to a business. In fact there must be a clear **connection** between the supplies made by the business (generally its core activity) and the expenditure. The CJEU has stated that there must be a **direct and immediate link** between the two.

For example, if a business owner is prosecuted for an offence committed as an individual, any related legal fees would not be sufficiently close to the business purpose, even though the business would not survive if the owner were imprisoned. For an exception see ¶1860.

In cases where the **connection is not obvious**, the following procedure is applied:
- the motive behind the expenditure is examined; then
- the strength of the link between the intention and the business activity (i.e. what the business does to earn profits) is considered.

EXAMPLE A company claimed an input tax deduction in relation to the cost of maintaining an alarm system at the **business address**. This property was **also** occupied by the controlling director as a **private residence**. The claim was rejected by HMRC, its view being that the costs were not for business purposes. However, the First-tier Tribunal agreed with the company that the expenditure was incurred for business purposes, because the insurance company had made installation and maintenance of the system a **prerequisite** of its policy. *Darragh House Ltd* [2012] (TC02105)

Comment The trader's intention is also decisive for other VAT topics, including:
- commencing a business;
- ceasing a business; and
- the initial use of purchases for taxable and exempt supplies.

When?

1830 The **key factor** is the trader's intention at the time that the expense is incurred. If the business intention is not borne out in practice, and the idea was actually a bad one, this does not preclude a deduction. This would include business failures. An inventor can therefore register for VAT and reclaim input tax, whether or not it is subsequently possible to patent the product and whether or not the business is commercially successful.

Intention, by its very nature, is subjective, so subsequent events are irrelevant unless they illustrate the trader's motive. However, the **onus of proof** is on the trader to demonstrate the business purpose at the time of the expenditure. Contemporaneous records, such as board minutes and business plans, should therefore be retained. If a trader appeals the denial by HMRC of an input tax deduction in relation to a luxury, amusement or entertainment, it will be necessary to show that HMRC acted unreasonably (¶1834), or the appeal cannot succeed.

EXAMPLE

1. A racehorse was used to promote a manufacturing company at races. Even though the company made plastic mouldings and storage tanks, the court held that the associated input tax could be deducted, as it was the trader's intention to use the horse for business purposes. It was of no relevance that this intention was unlikely to be achieved and that the idea was probably a poor way of satisfying the commercial objective. *Ian Flockton Developments Ltd v C & E* [1987]

2. In contrast, a company which supplied non-ferrous metals sought to deduct input tax on the purchase and training of a racehorse, which had been bought for promotional purposes.
The tribunal was unable to see any connection between the name of the horse, "Metalco", the company and the nature of its business, so the related input tax was not deductible. *MSS (North West) Ltd v C & E* [1980]

3. A restaurant ceased to trade but was still committed to making lease payments (and incurring related costs) for a further 5 years. The Danish authorities challenged the deductibility of the associated input tax on the basis that no taxable activities were being carried on and no output tax was being declared. The CJEU held that there was a direct link between the lease payments and the previous economic activity, so input tax could be deducted. *I/S Fini H v Skatteministeriet* [2005]

Luxury goods and activities

The business purpose of luxury items, such as racehorses, yachts and aircraft, is often challenged by HMRC. In addition, sponsorship of sports events, such as polo tournaments, may be challenged on the basis that there is a private benefit. Though such costs may be validly incurred for the purposes of advertising, any private benefit can be detrimental to input tax deduction. In addition, input tax incurred in relation to business entertainment is normally blocked (¶1926), except as regards **overseas clients**. **1832**

Traders should retain **evidence** in support of the business intention, for example, orders resulting from the advertising. Where business promotion is genuine, the business name and logo would normally be expected to appear where possible in connection with the luxury goods or activity. In particular, HMRC will examine the **personal involvement** of any individuals (including family members) to see whether the business is actually subsidising that person's hobby or lifestyle.

HMRC has issued specific guidance in relation to private use of **yachts and pleasure craft** owned by individuals and via companies. It should also be noted that, since 1 January 2011, immovable property, ships and aircraft have been excluded from Lennartz accounting; higher-value items are within the capital goods scheme (¶2280). HMRC Brief 53/10

Where an **individual** has legal ownership of a craft and:
- it is used for private (non-business) purposes by that individual, there is no entitlement to register for VAT and therefore any associated input tax is non-deductible; or
- **charters the craft** to others with sufficient frequency to be considered as an economic activity (although using it personally as well), it will be considered as used partly for business and partly for private purposes. In such a case the individual can register for VAT and can choose to apportion the VAT incurred on the craft at the outset and deduct the proportion which relates to business use. Prior to 1 January 2011 it was also possible to use the Lennartz approach (¶1842), in which case the VAT incurred was treated as input tax and was deductible in full, subject to any partial exemption restriction.

Where individuals arrange for **ownership via a company or other structure**, such as a limited liability partnership, HMRC will closely examine details and arrangements and will apply economic activity tests to see:

- if there is an entitlement to registration; and
- whether personal use of the craft affects the amount of VAT recovery.

EXAMPLE The taxpayers carried on business in partnership as a firm of monumental masons. The input tax claimed on the purchase of a racing car was disallowed. The car was used for advertising purposes, as one of the partners competed in races which were publicised in the local press and on radio. The car was also exhibited.
During the period of racing the business had ceased to use forms of advertising other than the racing, yet sales had increased by more than 50%. It was accepted that this increase was probably due to the publicity obtained from the car and it was held that:
- the car was purchased for the sole purpose of advertising the business;
- this was a decision an ordinary businessman in the same position would have made; and
- any personal enjoyment of the racing was insignificant and was not part of the intention or purpose behind acquiring the car. *Myatt & Leason* [1995] (VTD 13780)

1834
s 84(4) VATA 1994

Appeals If a business does not agree with HMRC on the business use of a supply which falls within the ambit of luxury, amusement or entertainment, an appeal may be made to the tribunal.

If the item in question was indeed a luxury, amusement or entertainment, the **tribunal can only allow the appeal** if HMRC acted unreasonably in disallowing the input tax. This includes situations where new evidence is brought before the tribunal which was not available to HMRC at the time.

However, the UK rules may contravene the EU position.

EXAMPLE In *Myatt & Leason* (¶1832), it was held that insofar as the UK legislation implied that HMRC's decision was conclusive (as to whether expenditure was in the nature of a luxury, amusement or entertainment) the legislation was incompatible with EU law. Incidentally, the tribunal also decided that the UK legislation did not provide that HMRC's decision is final as to that question.

B. Private and business expenditure

1838
s 24(5) VATA 1994

Expenditure should be attributed as far as possible to business and non-business activities, therefore sometimes leaving an unattributed amount, which must then be dealt with.

Some expenditure is automatically assumed to have non-business use, which outweighs the business use to such an extent that the input tax is blocked (¶1885).

For other unattributed expenditure, where **non-business use is insignificant**, HMRC has discretion to allow the business to deduct input tax in full, for as long as the use remains insignificant.

Where **non-business use is significant**, the trader can either:
a. apportion the VAT, so that the input tax will be the amount relating to the business use; or
b. deduct the whole amount of input tax incurred and account for output tax on any private use (commonly known as the Lennartz method (¶1842)). Since 1 January 2011 the Lennartz method has been unavailable in respect of purchases of immovable property, ships and aircraft. Full input tax recovery is not available on the purchase; input tax is instead restricted to the business use proportion.

There is no requirement to agree a method with HMRC beforehand, although in cases of doubt a particular apportionment method can be approved.

Once a method has been chosen, it is not possible to change to the other method.

VIT25400

MEMO POINTS 1. Whether non-business use is **significant** is not defined and it is a matter of judgement. HMRC's practice is to decide whether it is worth requiring the trader to apportion the expenditure, based on time and cost considerations. Any concession will only apply for as long as the existing proportion of non-business use continues.
2. The treatment of the initial input tax will have consequences for **subsequent supplies**, such as the sale of the asset, or the deemed supply on deregistration (¶8600).
3. For **ships, aircraft, computers and immovable property**, the interaction of the apportionment with the capital goods scheme should be considered (¶2280+).

In relation to **immovable property**, the Lennartz method was available **until 31 December 2010** for: 1841 Information Sheet 14/07
- the construction of a new building or civil engineering works, which was treated as a separate asset from the land on which it was built;
- the construction of an extension or annex to an existing building (i.e. built on new land adjoining the existing building and increasing the footprint by at least 10%); and
- the fundamental reconstruction of an existing building (which effectively created a new asset from that which existed before).

Lennartz treatment is not available now but businesses which had made use of this treatment prior to 1 January 2011 must continue to account for output tax on non-business use for as long as the asset continues to be used by the business (¶1844).

MEMO POINTS 1. Where any construction was **zero-rated**, only that portion of the building's value which related to the VAT incurred was included within the Lennartz calculation.
2. **Construction costs exclude** the costs of:
- feasibility studies;
- demolition of pre-existing buildings on site;
- clearance and cleansing of land;
- financial advice (including costing of the project);
- obtaining planning permission; and
- consulting an architect or surveyor before a final decision to embark on the construction project.
3. The change of use of a building which required **refurbishment work** was held to be covered by Lennartz, as the taxpayer would be using "goods forming part of the assets of the business" for non-business use. There was no basis to confine Lennartz to a building before construction work was carried out. *Whitechapel Art Gallery* [2008] (VTD 20720)

1. Lennartz method

This method is named after the following European case. 1842

EXAMPLE A German taxpayer tried to make a belated claim for input tax on the purchase of a car (Germany then had no input tax restriction covering cars) which, at the time of purchase, was used almost wholly for private purposes. The claim was made following a significant increase in the level of business use of the car. The German authorities refused the claim on the grounds that the business use of the car was considered to be de minimis at the time the car was originally purchased.
In 1991 the CJEU issued a judgment that taxable persons were entitled to a full and immediate input tax deduction on goods (not services) which are to be used partly for business and partly for private use, saying:
- the right to deduct depends on the taxable person's intention at the time of purchase;
- a taxable person is entitled to a full deduction of input tax at the time that the purchase is made in respect of goods which are purchased for business and private use;
- the entitlement to deduct input tax is not affected by the extent of private use of the goods, provided that there is some genuine business use; and
- the private use of goods forming part of the assets of a business is to be treated as a taxable supply of services made by the business. *H Lennartz v Finanzamt Munchen III* [1991]

In practice, this method has the following **consequences**: 1844
- output tax must be accounted for on all private use (¶1520+) in every VAT period (¶2987+); and
- records must be maintained to show how the asset has been used.

Since 1 January 2011, the Lennartz method is no longer available in respect of purchases of immovable property, ships and aircraft. Full input tax recovery is not available on the purchase; input tax is instead restricted to the business use proportion.

Comment For assets **purchased or constructed between 1 December 2008 and 31 December 2009**, VAT will have been recovered at 15% and, **between 1 January 2010 and 3 January 2011**, at 17.5%. From 4 January 2011 VAT has been due in respect of non-business use at 20%.

2. Apportionment

1846 It is important to identify a fair and reasonable basis of business use apportionment. Several methods may achieve this.

Costs incurred subsequent to purchase, such as an asset's maintenance costs, must be apportioned based on use in that VAT period. At the end of the VAT year the apportionment should be recalculated based on the annual figures.

The CJEU has held that where a taxable person sells property, part of which has been reserved for private use, the private part must be excluded from any VAT calculations. In this case a hotelier used part of the hotel for the domestic purposes of his own family. *Finanzamt Uelzen v Armbrecht* [1995]

Methods

1848 VBNB33000 There is no **specified** method of apportionment; the following are examples of methods which will be acceptable in the appropriate circumstances. The crucial test is whether the method is based on reliable indicators of business activity.

Basis of method	Calculation	When appropriate
Fixed percentage	Trader adopts a percentage based on experience	Balance of activities does not fluctuate Simplest method
Income	Business income / Total income	Often used where there is timely access to information on income Most common method (can be adapted to ignore distorting income)
Time	Time of staff on business use / Total time	If detailed time records kept and staff time is indicative of the business use made of goods and services
Expenditure	Business expenditure / Total expenditure	Only if a good proportion of the expenditure can be attributed to the business activity Least reliable method
Transaction (such as admissions, or items sold)	Number of business transactions / All transactions	Only if transactions are recorded for non-business activities

EXAMPLE Ms A incurred VAT of £5,000 on overheads in the last quarter. She undertakes both business and non-business activities, each taking up the same amount of time on average. She believes that a fixed percentage of 70% is a fair estimate of the business-related input tax. Her total income was £30,000, with business activities accounting for £20,000 of that. The associated total expenditure was £20,000, £16,000 of that relating to business activities.

Taking the first four apportionment methods in turn:

Method	Calculation	Input tax relating to business use £
Fixed percentage	£5,000 x 70%	3,500
Time basis	£5,000 x 50%	2,500
Income basis	£5,000 × 20,000/30,000	3,333
Expenditure basis	£5,000 × 16,000/20,000	4,000

Ms A's potential deductible input tax ranges from £2,500 to £4,000, although HMRC would be likely to challenge her use of the expenditure-based method. The fixed percentage would be the simplest method, provided that Ms A regularly reviews her business use.

Changes to the method

1850 VBNB35000 The trader should keep its business use under review and notify HMRC if any change occurs which is not reflected in the method currently being used.

Retrospective changes to methods will often be resisted, as the objective of any particular method can only be to give an estimate, therefore a change to a method does not mean that earlier calculations were wrong.

Comment However, any actual **error** in applying a method should be rectified (¶3014).

EXAMPLE The trustees of a museum discovered a new apportionment method would increase input tax recovery. The trustees sought to apply it retrospectively. This was denied because the old apportionment method was adequate and its prior application did not constitute an intrinsic error. *Victoria and Albert Museum Trustees v C & E* [1996]

HMRC says it will normally approve a retrospective change to a previously agreed method of apportionment if the business can demonstrate that:
- the former method did **not** produce a fair and reasonable result; and
- the proposed method does achieve this objective;

3. Subsequent changes in use

Subsequent private use

Where a trader starts to use a business asset or **goods** (in respect of which a full input tax deduction has previously been made) for private purposes, there is a deemed supply (¶1520). **1852**
For **services** see ¶1544.

Subsequent business use

Where a supply is acquired for **100% private use**, any subsequent business use is ignored, so no input tax can be deducted. **1854**

4. Frequent areas of dual use

Summary

The following items commonly involve mixed use. **1856**

Item	¶¶
Luxury goods	¶1832
Accountancy fees	¶1858
Legal fees	¶1860
Mobile phones provided to employees	¶1862
Working at home	¶1864
Clothing	¶1874
Road fuel	¶1876
Staff welfare	¶1878
Acquisition and leasing of motor cars	¶1890
Entertainment	¶1926

Accountancy fees

Although HMRC takes a pragmatic approach, if the accountant makes a separate charge for any personal work undertaken for a **sole trader** or **partner**, input tax on this is likely to be disallowed. **1858** VIT13700

Similarly, for **companies**, input tax is only likely to need to be disallowed where fees relate exclusively to a non-business item, such as inheritance tax advice to a company director.

Legal fees

1860 VIT13600 VAT deductibility for legal fees which relate wholly to the trade presents no problem.

Legal proceedings concerning the **ownership of a business** are not carried on as part of the trade itself. Similarly, fees relating to the financing of the business by the owners are also not incurred for business purposes.

A **distinction** must be drawn between fees relating to a person, be it a director or a sole trader as an individual, and those relating to the business itself. Fees relating to cases involving **employees** where there is potential vicarious liability for the employer are usually incurred for business purposes.

EXAMPLE

1. Mr Rosner was the proprietor of a foreign language school. He was subject to prosecution for the charge of involvement in illegal immigration. The business paid Mr Rosner's legal fees and it was held that these were not incurred for business purposes, because there was an insufficient connection between the business activity (i.e. teaching students) and the immigration charge. Even though the business clearly benefited from relieving Mr Rosner from a possible criminal conviction, this benefit was not sufficient to constitute a business purpose. *C&E v Rosner* [1994]

2. Legal fees relating to the defence of employees against a charge of manslaughter were held to have a business purpose, even though they also benefited the employees. If any of the employees had been found guilty, the company could have faced charges of corporate manslaughter, which would have had an obvious adverse impact on its business. *P & O European Ferries (Dover) Ltd* [1992] (VTD 7846)

Mobile phones provided to employees

1862 Business Brief 14/99; VIT43940 HMRC has published the following **guidance** on deductible input tax relating to the provision of mobile phones to employees by an employer.

Cost	Treatment of private use by employer	Input tax deduction
Initial purchase of phone, including connection	n/a	100% if some business use
Call costs which are evidenced as business	Must be prohibited (HMRC will ignore incidental private use)	100%
All call costs	Charged to employees	100%, but output tax must be accounted for on the charges
	Free	Business proportion only

Working at home

1864 VIT41600 If a trader uses **specific rooms** at home for business purposes, input tax relating to a proportion of the running costs, such as for heat and light, can be deducted. In addition, input tax relating to the furnishing and decorating of the rooms is also deductible. There are special rules for directors (¶1870).

Where the trader undertakes **property repairs** at home, or incurs home-improvement expenditure, the apportionment may be influenced by factors such as the functionality of the expenditure in relation to the whole house (such as a repair to a leaking roof, or a general improvement such as double glazing).

1866 HMRC Brief 85/09 **Computers** An employer which provides its employee with a computer for home working can only deduct all of the related input tax where the provision of a computer is **necessary for** the employee to carry out the **duties** of the employment. This means that any private use must be insignificant when compared with the business need for providing the computer in the first place.

Otherwise, where a business **cannot demonstrate such a necessity**, only a portion of the input tax incurred will be recoverable. For this purpose HMRC will accept any method of apportionment, provided that the result fairly and reasonably reflects the extent of business use.

Farmhouses In relation to farmhouses **occupied by** a taxable farmer (other than a director), there is an agreement between the NFU and HMRC which categorises expenditure into repairs and improvements, in a similar way to the direct tax distinction between revenue and capital items. **1868** Business Brief 18/96; VIT41800

Up to 70% of the related input tax can be deducted on:
- repairs, with a lower amount (unlikely to exceed 30%) applying to occupants who only work part time; and.
- improvements, where the expenditure is undertaken for a predominantly business purpose.

MEMO POINTS 1. **Repairs** include maintenance and renovations with the intention of restoring the building to its original state.
2. **Improvements** are where the building work results in an alteration, e.g. building an extension.

EXAMPLE A company carried on a farming business. It deducted the full input tax relating to improvements to a bungalow, which were made so that the directors' son, who worked for the company, could move in after his marriage. The son's rent-free occupancy of the bungalow was regarded as part of his remuneration as an employee of the company. There was therefore a mixed purpose to the improvements.
It was found that both the personal and business purposes of the improvements to the bungalow were significant; on that basis the company was entitled to deduct 50% of the input tax. *FJ Meaden Ltd* [1995] (VTD 13215)

Provision of accommodation to a company director Input tax incurred on any goods or services used to provide any domestic accommodation to a director, or anyone connected with the director (¶962+), is not deductible. Such **goods or services** would include repairs, refurbishment, professional fees and furnishings. **1870** VIT13100

Other expenses incurred, such as for telephone calls, are dealt with under the normal rules. There is no requirement for the company to own the property and it is irrelevant whether the director pays any consideration in return for using the accommodation.

Comment All accommodation is affected, except hotel accommodation provided during business trips.

MEMO POINTS 1. A **director** is defined as:
- a member of the board of directors which manages the company;
- a single director who manages the company; or
- a member of the company where the company is managed by its members.

2. There is no relaxation of the rules for **overseas directors**.
3. Where a director who **runs a hotel** also **lives in that hotel**, input tax is deductible and no output tax charge is required. Sch 6 para 10 VATA 1994

As an **exception**, where a director uses private accommodation for business purposes, input tax can be recovered on the business proportion of the expenses, commonly repairs. Apportionment should be undertaken using an objective method, such as a time-used basis. **1872** s 24(5) VATA 1994

EXAMPLE A company was a consultant to the oil industry. It purchased two one-week time-shares of a holiday lodge in Scotland. The business purpose was for the company's directors to use the lodge as a business base, because client meetings could be held there and the directors could work in private on confidential matters. Only the directors stayed at the lodge.
It was accepted that the time-shares were purchased by the company for the purpose of the directors' business visits. However, to the extent that the accommodation was used by the directors for domestic purposes, it could not be treated as used for the company's business.
An apportionment of the input tax was therefore necessary; this was to be based on the 8-hour working day of the time-share periods. $\frac{8 \times 5}{24 \times 7}$
Approximately one quarter of the input tax was therefore deductible. *Suregrove Ltd* [1993] (VTD 10740)

Clothing

1874 VIT43800 It is important to realise that **direct tax** principles (in particular the findings of *Mallalieu v Drummond* [1983]) are irrelevant for VAT purposes.

Input tax can be deductible on **uniforms** or protective clothing but not ordinary attire.

Specific items required for business, such as stage costumes and wigs, can also result in an input tax deduction. *J M Collie* [1991] (VTD 6144)

However, a claim that a **high standard of dress** is required for business reasons does not justify an input tax deduction. *Ms JK Hill and Mr SJ Mansell* [1982] (VTD 2379)

For **barristers** see ¶7766.

Road fuel

1876 VIT55400 Where a **business purchases** road fuel, it has three options with regard to VAT:
- reclaim all input tax and pay a scale charge via the VAT return (¶1536) for any private mileage;
- keep a mileage log and only reclaim input tax on the business miles; or
- make no claim for input tax on any road fuel (especially if total mileage is low).

SI 1991/2306; s 56 VATA 1994 If the cost of fuel is **reimbursed** or a **mileage allowance** is paid, this is treated as expenditure incurred for business purposes, even where some private mileage has been undertaken. Again, scale charges would be relevant for any fuel provided for private use.

Information Sheet 8/05 Since March 2005 input tax can only be **claimed** where the employer holds a valid VAT receipt (this can be a full or less detailed invoice, depending on the amount of fuel purchased (¶2856)). **Receipts** may cover business fuel provided in more than one VAT period (particularly where fuel is purchased towards the end of the period). HMRC states that a claim **cannot be supported** by a receipt which is dated after the date of an expense claim. HMRC advises that employees should retain all fuel invoices, so that the value of their claims is always covered by a receipt.

MEMO POINTS The need for the employer to hold a receipt arose due to a decision against the Netherlands regarding supplies to employees (¶1962)

EXAMPLE Mr B is an employee who drives 1,010 miles on behalf of his employer's business in April. His employer allows employees to claim 45p per mile, with 15p representing petrol costs.
The amount to be reimbursed in respect of petrol is therefore £151.50. (1,010 × 0.15)
The employer reclaims input tax of £25.25. (151.50 × 1/6)
Mr B retains the following invoices for April:

Date	£
4 April	52.40
14 April	16.87
18 April	53.56
25 April	47.22
Total	170.05

As Mr B only needs £151.50 to support his fuel costs, the £16.87 receipt could be lost and there would still be sufficient receipts for the employer to reclaim the full amount of input tax.

Staff welfare

1878 VIT43950 Where an employer makes the following available to all **employees generally**, related input tax can be deducted:
- canteen facilities, including food or drink provided for free;
- a recreational room; and
- sports facilities, such as corporate membership of a private gym.

SECTION 3

Blocked input tax

Input tax is not deductible (and is known as blocked input tax) in respect of the following types of supply, the presumption being that most of these supplies will be put to non-business use. Alternatively, VAT is only calculated on the profit margin. **1885** s 25(7) VATA 1994

The **onward sale** of these items, where input tax has been blocked on acquisition, is exempt.

Summary

1887

Supply	Reference	¶¶
Motor cars - acquisition and leasing	SI 1992/3222 reg 7	¶1890
Business entertainment	SI 1992/3222 reg 5	¶1926
Provision of accommodation to a director		¶1870
Certain goods installed in dwellings	SI 1992/3222 reg 6	¶5275
Private imports	s 27 VATA 1994	¶9429
Services and goods acquired by tour operators	SI 1987/1806 reg 12	¶7490
Goods and services acquired under a margin scheme	SI 1992/3222 reg 4(2)	¶6620

A. Motor cars - acquisition and leasing

Subject to the exceptions listed at ¶1902, input tax deduction on the acquisition or leasing of cars is very restricted. It is of course vital to know whether a particular vehicle is a car, as input tax can be fully deducted on other types of vehicle. **1890**

HMRC produces a guide (see flmemo.co.uk/vm1890), which includes links to lists of specific vehicles, with HMRC's ruling on which side of the line each falls.

What is a car?

For these purposes, a motor car is **defined** as a vehicle which: **1892** SI 1992/3122 reg 2
- is normally used on public roads and has three or more wheels;
- is constructed or adapted mainly to carry passengers; and
- has roofed accommodation behind the driver's seat which is fitted, or could be fitted, with side windows.

However, the following vehicles are **excluded** from being a car:
- ambulances, caravans, prison vans and other vehicles (such as hearses) constructed for a specific purpose which does not include the carriage of people;
- those with space for only the driver;
- vehicles with capacity for twelve or more passengers;
- those weighing at least 3 tonnes when unladen; and
- vehicles which can carry a payload of at least 1 tonne.

MEMO POINTS 1. In addition, vehicles which would otherwise pass the 12-passenger test but which have been **adapted for wheelchair users** will not fail the test solely because of that adaptation.

2. For **double cab pick-ups**, which are not cars if the payload is at least 1 tonne, the addition of a hard top will decrease the required payload by 45kg. SMMT agreement on double cab pick-ups; VIT56600

1894 Business Brief 16/04; VIT50600

Car-derived vans These vehicles have the functionality of a van, because the rear seats and seat belts are removed, the foot well is covered over and the side windows are made opaque.

Where such vehicles are not designed to carry passengers, it is possible to treat them like vans for VAT purposes, if they satisfy all of the following criteria:

Vehicle property	Criteria
Load area	Highly unsuitable for passengers Functionality of a commercial van
Seat belt mountings	Completely removed or disabled and bolt holes welded up or bonded shear bolts fitted
Seat mountings	
Rear foot well	Permanent fixed cover welded or fixed on top
Windows	Made completely and permanently opaque Mechanism for lowering and raising disabled or removed

1896 Business Brief 16/04; VIT50900

Combination vans These are vans which have seats (permanent or folding) behind the driver's seat and are **usually classed** as a motor car, **except** when:
- the seat belts and seat mounting have been completely removed or disabled;
- the load area is of such a size that the carriage of goods is the predominant use of the vehicle; or
- the payload capacity (which will be reduced by any seating) is still in excess of 1 tonne.

1898 VIT51200

Motor caravans Motor caravans are not cars, provided that the following **characteristics** are present:
- permanently installed sink and cooker;
- at least one bed of a length of 1.82m or more;
- permanently installed fresh water tank with a minimum capacity of 10 litres; and
- seating around a meal table.

1900

Conversions The purchase of a car to convert it into another vehicle gives rise to deductible input tax if **conversion was intended** from the start. Conversion following a change of intention does not give rise to any retrospective right to input tax deduction.

SI 1992/3122 reg 5; VIT51800

Where a commercial vehicle is **converted** into **a car**, there is a self-supply (¶1496) by the owner, which means output tax must be charged, to balance the input tax already recovered.

1. Cars where input tax is deductible

1902 SI 1992/3222 reg 7(2)

Input tax is **not blocked** on the following types of qualifying car:
- stock for resale;
- cars acquired for the purpose of a car-related trade; and
- cars acquired wholly for business use and not intended to be made available for private use.

SI 1992/3222 reg 7(2A)

A **qualifying car** is one which has never entered final consumption. In practice, this means that:
- the car has never been purchased by a non-taxable person; or
- no input tax has ever been blocked on a purchase by a taxable person.

Whilst new cars obviously fit these criteria, cars **sold by leasing companies** are also likely to be qualifying.

Stock for resale

1904 VIT52400

When a stock-in-trade car of a motor manufacturer or motor dealer is intended to be **sold within 12 months** of production or acquisition, the related input tax is available for deduction. The private use of such a car has no effect on the amount of deductible input tax.

A stock-in-trade car could be second-hand, provided that it is a qualifying car (¶1902).

MEMO POINTS 1. A **motor manufacturer** is someone who constructs cars, either from scratch or by conversion. SI 1992/3222 reg 2
2. A **motor dealer** is someone who buys in cars for the purpose of resale, either new or second-hand, and sells them on with a view to making an overall profit. Fleet purchasers, who buy cars in bulk to use for a short period and then sell them on for profit, are not motor dealers for this purpose.

Car-related trades

A car acquired, whether purchased outright or leased, for the following purposes will not result in blocked input tax: **1906** SI 1992/3222 reg 7(2F); VIT53300
- **hiring** it out as a taxi to carry passengers;
- **leasing** to disabled persons, or to a business which undertakes such leasing;
- **short-term self-drive** hire, where the hirer (or an employee of the hirer) will drive the car; or
- driving instruction given by a **driving school**.

MEMO POINTS 1. Use as a **taxi** encompasses chauffeuring services and minicab.
2. The period of **self-drive hire** must normally be less than both:
- 30 consecutive days; and
- a cumulative total of 90 days per annum.

In practice, therefore, HMRC only refuses a deduction for input tax where the period of hire regularly exceeds 30 days.

Wholly for business use

This test is very difficult to satisfy, because the trader must not **intend** to make the car available for private use, including letting it to another person at an undervalue. In practice, this means trying to prove a negative. Even where a car is not insured for private use, this does not necessarily prohibit private use, as another insurance policy could be taken out. In addition, where a car could be used privately in an emergency only, this is enough to fail the wholly business use condition. *DW Bevan and AD Bevan* [2000] (VTD 16830) **1908** VIT54800

Cases involving business use of cars often appear at tribunal, although almost always the subjective question of intention is so difficult to reconcile with the objective facts that the taxpayer loses. Board resolutions and employment contract terms (for companies) precluding private use by employees have, however, been instrumental in the tribunal's finding that cars were used wholly for business purposes.

EXAMPLE
1. A sole trader acquired a Lamborghini car for use in his business, which involved visiting night clubs and apparently necessitated a car such as this. He conducted his business 7 days a week, from 8am to midnight or later and he never made personal use of the car. However, as he was unable to obtain insurance excluding private use, it was held that the car was made available to him for personal use, so input tax recovery was blocked. The trader was taken to have intended the results of his actions, in the absence of evidence to the contrary. *C & E v Upton t/a Fagomatic* [2002]

2. A company acquired a car which was stated to be used wholly for the business, even though the car was driven by the company's sole employee, the director. The car's insurance cover permitted private use, but this was only because the broker had stated that it was impossible to insure a car for business use only. A Board minute noted that the company intended to limit the use of the vehicle to business only, so if the car had been used for private use, this would have constituted a breach of the employee's contract of employment. Therefore the input tax was deductible. *Elm Milk Ltd v C & E* [2006]

3. As the directors of a company all had their own private cars, a company Range Rover and Jaguar were held to be wholly business vehicles, as any private use was forbidden. Office equipment was kept in the Range Rover, which was used for overnight emergencies at work sites. The Jaguar was only used to chauffeur customers around. *Squibb & Davies (Demolition) Ltd* [2002] (VTD 17829)

HMRC will usually only accept the following **other situations** as putting a car to wholly business use: **1910**
- car leasing business;
- vehicles unsuitable for private use, such as marked emergency cars; and
- valid pool cars.

Notice 700/64 para 3.7

MEMO POINTS 1. A **valid pool car** is one which is:
- normally kept at the principal place of business;
- not allocated to an individual; and
- not kept at an employee's home.

2. Cars used for **research and development** can be taken home at night, where this is necessary for testing, such as driving in rush hour traffic.

1912 SI 1992/3222 reg 7(2G)

Car leasing business A car purchased in order to be hired out is used exclusively for business purposes, **unless** it is:
- let on uncommercial terms not at arm's length; or
- made available for private use and not let on hire.

Otherwise, **lessors** can reclaim input tax, it being irrelevant whether there is any private use of the car by the lessee.

2. Blocked cars

1914 SI 1992/3222 reg 7

Input tax incurred on the **acquisition** cost of all other motor cars is blocked. For these purposes hire purchase is treated as an outright acquisition.

Input tax deduction by the hirer of a **leased** car is restricted to 50%.

Acquisition cost

1916 The cost of the car includes delivery charges and optional accessories fitted by the supplier **before the car is delivered**, even if invoiced separately. It is therefore advisable to acquire the car first, then fit the accessories.

Optional accessories fitted by a different supplier under a separate contract are not part of the cost of the car. **Personalised number plates** are usually treated as private expenditure, unless there is a strong business case for the acquisition, such as a defined promotional objective which is reflected in the choice of plate, or it is intended to sell the plate as a trading venture (in which case the trader will have to account for output tax on sale).

EXAMPLE

1. A fleet customer often collected cars it had just purchased from a dealer (to avoid the hefty delivery charge). The customer tried to claim that the delivery costs it did actually incur could be separated from the cost of the cars and input tax should therefore be deductible.
It was held that delivery was incidental to the main supply of the car. Therefore it should be treated as part of the supply of the car and hence no input tax could be claimed. *C & E v British Telecommunications plc* [1999]

2. Mr Hooper ran a restaurant which was known locally as "Hoopers".
He purchased the number plate "HO 02 PER" at a cost of £256, in order to publicise the business, which was located in a small village.
It was held that this was business expenditure. *Colin Hooper* [2005] (VTD 19276)

Subsequent expenditure

1918 Input tax relating to subsequent expenditure, such as servicing, repairs and modifications, is potentially available for deduction even where there is **private use** of the vehicle (but only to the extent that there is business use).

EXAMPLE A management consultancy partnership reclaimed input tax on an engine upgrade for an Aston Martin, which had only travelled about 6,000 miles. The upgrade would allow the car to travel at 175mph.
The tribunal denied the claim, holding that, whilst the car was driven for business purposes, there was no clear association between the upgrade and the business. The upgrade had been carried out simply to empower the vehicle to achieve a speed grossly in excess of the permitted speed limit. *Trade Development Associates* [1994] (VTD 12700)

Leased cars

For **short hires** which do not exceed 10 days (such as where the car is needed for a specific business trip), there is no restriction on the input tax recovery. 1920 Notice 700/64 para 4.4; VIT53300

Otherwise, there is a 50% reduction in the amount of input tax which can be claimed on a qualifying car if there is any private use, unless the lessee is a **taxi driver**, **car hire firm**, or **driving instructor**, in which case full recovery may be made. The lessor must notify the lessee that the car is a qualifying car (¶1902).

MEMO POINTS 1. For these purposes a **lease** does not include any arrangement under which the lessee eventually obtains ownership of the vehicle and so excludes hire purchase.
2. Where a car is bought, immediately sold, then leased back (**sale and leaseback**), the related input tax can be recovered insofar as there is no private use.

EXAMPLE C Ltd leases two cars under a contract hire agreement. The Mercedes costs £500 per month, has a related VAT charge of £100 and is used 80% for private purposes. The Ford costs £300 plus VAT of £60 per month, with a maintenance charge of £40 plus VAT of £8, and is privately used for only 30% of the time.
The monthly amount of input tax that C Ltd can obtain a deduction for is calculated as follows:

Car		Input tax £
Mercedes	100 @ 50%	50
Ford	60 @ 50%	30
Maintenance	8 @ 100%	8
		88

Where a lease is **terminated early**, the lessor may either charge an additional payment, or give back a rebate (depending on whether the payment required to terminate the lease exceeds the rebate given in respect of the value of the car at the time of termination). In either case, the lessor may choose whether to treat the event as a taxable supply, or a supply outside the scope of VAT. 1922

If VAT is charged on an additional payment, the lessee may recover 100% of the input tax. If a rebate is received, the lessee should account for 50% of the related VAT as output tax, if 50% of the original input tax was deducted.

EXAMPLE Mr D leases a car and decides to terminate the lease. The lessor treats the termination as a taxable supply.
If a termination payment of £150 is charged, the related input tax of £30 can be deducted by Mr D. (£150 x 20%)
If the termination charge is set off against the lease payments already made, resulting in a rebate of £100 due, Mr D only needs to account for £10 of output tax. (£100 x 20% x 50%)

B. Business entertainment

In most cases no input tax can be recovered on goods and services used to provide business entertaining, **except** certain **staff entertaining**, where there is an obligation to provide entertainment under a **reciprocal arrangement**, or where the recipient of the entertainment is an overseas customer. 1926 SI 1992/3222 reg 5; HMRC Brief 44/10; VIT43200 - 43600

As regards **overseas customers**, input tax is deductible in relation to business entertainment of a kind and scale which is reasonable, having regard to all the circumstances. SI 2011/1071

It is very hard to delineate where normal subsistence ends and entertaining begins. In general, the intention of the business and the wording on the invoice are often key areas which are reviewed by HMRC.

Scope

1928 Entertainment is usually provided for free or virtually free. However, where a **realistic charge is made**, the expenditure is not business entertainment for this purpose.

Otherwise, business entertainment **includes** hospitality in any guise, such as:
- food and drink;
- accommodation and travel;
- leisure activities, such as tickets to the theatre or a sports event;
- entry to clubs and night clubs; and
- an asset, such as a yacht or aircraft, being made available.

Even where entertainment is an **incidental** objective, such as a snack lunch during a training day, no related input tax can be recovered. *C & E v Shaklee International and another* [1981]

Exclusions

1930 The **following situations** are excluded from the block on input tax:
- free drinks given with meals in restaurants, where this is a usual business practice;
- sampling of alcohol by trade customers and journalists;
- entertainment to attract members of the public off the street;
- where club members are entertained in return for subscription monies;
- catering and accommodation provided for delayed airline passengers, where any refreshment is part of the normal service (¶1960);
- free meals provided to coach drivers at service stations; and
- entertainment provided by local authorities at public functions.

Dual purpose

1932 Where expenditure is only partly incurred for business entertainment purposes, there should be an apportionment to calculate the deductible input tax. *Thorn EMI plc v C & E* [1995]

In practice, the costs of a particular event may include an element of entertainment, but this is often bound up with other tangible business objectives. Where an invoice does not state any amount for entertainment in such circumstances, a fair and reasonable apportionment should be made, such as in the following examples:
- an event held to entertain staff as well as non-employees;
- hire of a hospitality suite where part is used as an office; or
- sponsorship of an event where there is an intention to advertise to a wider audience than just current customers.

Comment To avoid any doubt, the supplier should be asked to detail the **separate services** on its invoice.

Supplier receives hospitality

1934 Suppliers are often accommodated at their customers' expense whilst performing a service, for example an audit team working at the client's premises. The VAT treatment depends on **who incurs the cost** of accommodation and travel as follows:
- if a customer pays the hotelier, etc, direct, this is treated as business entertainment and the input tax is blocked; whereas
- if the supplier incurs the cost, then charges it on to the customer, the related input tax included on the supplier's invoice will be deductible, as the accommodation is part of the supplier's overall service.

Staff entertaining

1936 Notice 700/65 **Who?** The notion of staff strictly excludes anyone who is not an employee, such as family members, pensioners, shareholders (unless employed as well), potential recruits, agents or subcontractors. However, the following persons are **deemed** to be employees:
- directors;

- anyone engaged in the management of a company; and
- people hired casually or temporarily to work at a sporting event or similar occasion.

Where a **recognised sporting body** provides accommodation and meals to sports persons and officials, this is also treated as staff entertaining. Notice 48 para 3.10

Employees Where staff are entertained for a **business purpose**, such as to reward good performance and boost morale, input tax is deductible. *Ernst & Young* [1997] (VTD 15100) 1938

Where it is necessary for staff to lunch outside the office on occasion in order to have **private discussions**, this can be for business purposes, provided that the participants are not the business' owners or directors.

If staff entertainment is an **incidental purpose** of an event, all of the related costs are treated as business entertainment. However, if, as part of a travelling arrangement, an employee takes a client out to lunch, the employee's own meal is staff entertainment, whereas that of the client is business entertaining. By contrast, if an employee leaves the normal place of work for a lunch appointment, this is all business entertaining.

MEMO POINTS 1. Where a **group company** provides entertainment to group staff who are not its employees, any related input tax is blocked, unless a VAT group registration (¶8800) is in place.
2. Where **hotel staff** are able to enjoy meals and accommodation in-house, the related input tax can be recovered.
3. If an employer agrees to pay for an **extended stay at a hotel** where the employee has been accommodated for work purposes, HMRC will allow all of the related input tax to be deducted, provided that the employer pays the bill.

Directors and business owners For directors or business owners, input tax can be deducted on **subsistence** during business trips, or where other staff are also being entertained. Lunching outside the office in order to have private discussions will always be treated as business entertainment. 1939

Events involving directors and business owners only are not staff entertaining, because HMRC does not accept that there is any business need to reward or motivate these individuals.

Guests Where staff can bring guests for **free**, the input tax attributable to the guests is blocked and a fair apportionment should be made. *KPMG (No 2)* [1997] (VTD 14962) 1940

If a **charge** is made for guests, the related input tax is deductible but output tax must be levied on the charge. The charge does not have to represent cost, but should be sufficient that the entertainment is not effectively provided for free. *Ernst & Young* [1997] (VTD 15100)

EXAMPLE E Ltd throws a Christmas staff party to which employees can bring a partner. In the event, 100 employees attend, with 50 partners. The cost of the party is £3,000 (with £600 of input tax incurred).
If no charge is made for any attendee, 1/3rd of the input tax is blocked. (50/150)
If E Ltd charges £10 for anyone who is not an employee, the full £600 of input tax can be recovered, but output tax of £83.33 (£500 × 1/6) must be accounted for in respect of the £500 received. Full input tax recovery is made, even though the full cost was not charged on to the guests. Overall, E Ltd receives a net VAT refund of £516.67. (£600 - £83.33)

Reciprocal arrangements

In certain business sectors it is common for a taxable person to be obliged to entertain others under a reciprocal agreement. In such cases input tax is not blocked because a supply is made. 1942

EXAMPLE

1. A visiting football team was treated to hospitality by a UK club on the understanding that it would reciprocate for the return fixture. Under the UEFA rules, each club was obliged to pay for its visiting opponents' board and lodgings as well as for the travelling and accommodation expenses of the match officials.

As the visiting teams had reciprocal obligations to meet the club's accommodation expenses when the club played its away matches, the entertainment was not free to the visiting teams, so the club was entitled to deduct input tax. *Celtic Football & Athletic Co Ltd v C & E* [1983]

2. A chat show provided its audience with a buffet meal, which was promised along with travel expenses, so that those appearing on the show would not incur any costs.
It was held that the meal was consideration in return for the participants appearing on the show. The meal was therefore not entertainment, because it was not provided for free. *C & E v The Kilroy Television Co Ltd* [1997]

3. In contrast to **2.** above, in a case involving hospitality laid on for celebrities at the premiere of a film, it was held that the guests did not provide any consideration just by attending. Hence they were entertained. *The Entertainment Group of Companies Ltd* [2000] (VTD 16639)

SECTION 4

Eligible input tax

1950 Input tax is deductible where all of the following criteria are satisfied:

Criteria	¶¶
Incurred for business purposes	¶1825
A supply has been made	¶1952
The supply was made to the claimant	¶1956
Input tax has been correctly charged	¶1966
There is evidence to support the claim	¶1972

A. A supply has been made

1952 s 24(1) VATA 1994 Usually it is obvious whether a supply has actually been made. However, on some occasions the **normal pattern** of ordering, receiving, invoicing and payment is **disrupted**, which therefore causes input tax deduction to be put in jeopardy. For example, an aborted supply will not result in deductible input tax, even where the customer pays for a supply which is never received, including paying an amount which relates to VAT on the supply.

In one case, a no-show charge in relation to cancelled hotel accommodation was held to be taxable. *C & E v Bass plc* [1993] More recently, a forfeited deposit relating to an unoccupied hotel room was held to be compensation and therefore outside the scope of VAT. *Société Thermale d'Eugénie-les-Bains v Ministère de l'Économie, des Finances et de l'Industrie* [2007]

EXAMPLE In the context of a fraud involving smuggled gold, a taxpayer claimed input tax credit on the basis of sham invoices and then issued false invoices showing onward sales. He accounted for the output tax shown on those invoices.
It was agreed that the taxpayer had not made any supplies for VAT purposes and there were no statutory provisions which deemed a sham supply to be a taxable supply. Hence no input tax could be claimed. *Sandell* [1992] (VTD 9665)

1954 If the supply never actually occurs and input tax has **already been claimed**, it must be repaid to HMRC. It will be in the supplier's interest to issue a credit note, in order to cancel the output tax on the original invoice, but the credit note must be issued to the customer, who must account for the VAT thereon (as negative input tax).

The **customer cannot claim** bad debt relief in this situation, even if the supplier does not make a refund, because that relief is only available to suppliers.

B. Supply made to the claimant

It is normally impossible **under EU law** to deduct input tax on an invoice made out to someone else, even where a taxable person has paid for it, because the supply is not made to the person making the claim. **1956** EC Directive 2006/112 art 178(a); Notice 700 para 12.1

In the **UK**, however, input tax may be deducted in relation to certain expenses incurred for the employer's business purposes by an employee.

MEMO POINTS New rules applying to independent financial advisers discourage the charging of commission and promote the charging of consultancy fees. Essentially, **commissions** are exempt from VAT, since they are charges for acting as an intermediary in setting up a pension or insurance contract, whereas **consultancy** fees are subject to VAT, being charges for supplying advice. Charges for advice given by a consultant to an employer on the setting up of a pension scheme are therefore likely to attract VAT. Provided that the supply of advice is made to the employer in the course or furtherance of the employer's business (which it usually will be), the employer will be able to deduct that VAT (subject to the usual partial exemption restrictions). Some confusion may arise because of the way that payment is collected by the consultant. In keeping with the old, commission-based system, it is possible that payment may appear to originate from the pension provider because the funds concerned are deducted from contributions to the pension scheme and channelled back to the consultant. Provided that the consultant issues a VAT invoice **to the employer**, the employer will be able to deduct the VAT as input tax. HMRC Brief 09/13

Case law

Where a person contracts and pays for a supply, but **someone else benefits**, input tax may be deductible. **1958**

EXAMPLE

1. HMRC sought to disallow input tax on estate agent fees which were incurred by a builder. In order to incentivise prospective housebuyers, the builder agreed to pay the fees relating to the sale of the buyer's old house. The argument centred on whether the estate agent's services were supplied to the builder as well as to the housebuyer.
The House of Lords held that the builder had a valid claim to input tax on the agency fees because it received a supply of services, as it:
- selected and instructed the estate agent;
- agreed the selling price of the housebuyer's old home based on the agent's valuation; and
- made sure the agent was trying to sell the house as quickly as possible.

The builder therefore had control over the sale of the housebuyer's old house. In addition, the housebuyer was invited to enter into an agreement with the agent so that no other agent could be instructed. *C & E v Redrow Group plc* [1999]

Note: Business Brief 27/99
HMRC issued **guidance** in light of the *Redrow* case, which states that input tax will only be deductible in situations where the facts are very similar. In particular, the supplier must have contracted for the service and the service must be used for the supplier's taxable business.

2. A football club reclaimed input tax on amounts paid to footballers' agents. The invoices were made out to the club and not to the footballers.
However, HMRC argued that the agents made supplies to the football players, not to the club itself.
Although this was upheld at tribunal (which also stated that the club did not receive a supply similar to that in the *Redrow* case), the High Court subsequently held that the tribunal had misdirected itself. The case was remitted back to the tribunal for further findings of fact, which gave the football club an opportunity to give additional evidence to support its case. *Newcastle United plc v HMRC* [2007]

3. A company in financial difficulties needed to restructure its finances. In these circumstances banks and other creditors require the provision of financial information before deciding to lend. The appellant's accountants set up an arrangement whereby the appellant was a party to the engage-

ment with the banks. The accountants liaised with the relevant banks and other creditors and carried out a strategic review. Their bills were made out to and paid by the appellant. HMRC took the view that the appellant was not entitled to recover VAT on the accountants' fees. Whilst they accepted that the appellant had benefited from the services, they considered that only the banks, as engaging institutions, were the recipients of the supplies. The tribunal disagreed with HMRC and allowed the appeal. This was on the basis that the appellant:
- requested the review and received a copy of the report;
- authorised the adviser to do the work and undertook to pay;
- used the services for the purpose of the business; and
- was involved in deciding who was appointed.

The Upper Tribunal reversed this decision, allowing HMRC's appeal and holding that the accountancy services, etc, were supplied to the lending institutions and that the company merely contracted to pay for the services, not to receive them. The company was therefore not entitled to any input tax recovery in respect of the payments it made. *HMRC v Airtours Holiday Transport Ltd* [2010]

4. The Supreme Court has strongly backed the *Redrow* decision in a case concerning the Nectar loyalty programme run by a promoter unconnected with the various retailers involved with the scheme.
Certain retailers contracted with the promoter that customers who bought goods and services from those retailers would be issued with points. Certain other retailers contracted with the promoter that if they gave or sold goods or services to the customers either free or at a reduced price, the promoter would reimburse those retailers (and deduct an appropriate number of points from the customer's account, in accordance with the promoter's agreement with the first set of retailers).
The crucial issue (in this context) was the Court's analysis of the payment by the promoter to the retailer who had given (or sold) free (or reduced price) goods or services to a customer redeeming Nectar points. HMRC's analysis was that there had been a supply of goods or services by the retailer to the customer and that the promoter had paid for that supply, a clear case of third-party consideration with no right on the promoter's part to an input tax deduction, since the supply had been made to the customer, not the promoter. The Supreme Court clarified *Redrow* considerably by explaining that whilst there had indeed been a supply of goods or services to the customer, there had been a separate supply of services by the retailer to the promoter, for which the promoter's payment was consideration, thus entitling the promoter to an input tax deduction. Thus the gift (or sale) of goods or services to the customer could be a supply both to the customer and separately to the promoter. It did not have to be one or the other.
This decision of the Supreme Court may go some considerable way to undermining the third-party consideration explanation by HMRC as to why a person who has made a payment is not entitled to a deduction. This is because a person will rarely make a payment which is not in return for something and that something is likely to be a supply to it (albeit that it may also be a supply to someone else). *HMRC v Aimia Coalition Loyalty UK Ltd (formerly Loyalty Management UK Ltd)* [2013]

5. An insurance business was seeking input tax recovery in respect of car repair charges. It sought to structure its contracts so that the repairs were supplied to a group company, WHA, and WHA in turn made supplies to another group company which were supposed to give WHA the right to deduct. A similar interpretation of *Redrow* to that in *Aimia* would have emerged if the Supreme Court had decided that the car repairer supplied both repairs to the car owner and some other contractual service to WHA in return for WHA's payment. However, in this case the Court decided that the repairs were simply supplied to the car owner and WHA contributed third-party consideration with no attendant right to deduct input tax.
This was not in contradiction to *Aimia* or *Redrow*, though, since the true substance of the transaction was that the car owner had the car repaired and WHA agreed to indemnify the car owner for the cost. The repairs were supplied to the car owner, not WHA, and the car repairer made no supply to WHA. Although WHA made a payment to the repairer, it was not in return for anything, it was just a short-cut way of indemnifying the car owner (as opposed to the car owner paying the repairer and WHA making a separate payment to the car owner), with the added benefit for WHA of controlling to some extent the cost of the repair. However, that added benefit did not amount to the car repairer making a supply to WHA for the payment made to it. *WHA Ltd and another v HMRC* [2013]

1960 Another case involved delayed flight passengers, when food and drink were provided by an airline.

EXAMPLE A company set up a flight voucher scheme with certain airside restaurants so that food and drink would be provided to its passengers on the production of a voucher or a boarding card for a delayed flight. Passengers were entitled to a maximum value of refreshment depending on the length of the delay; if this value was not fully used no change would be given.

It was held that the right to have goods or services supplied to its passengers was a supply of services to the company for the purposes of its business. The company exercised control of the supplies under the scheme, because it decided which restaurants participated and could withhold payment if the scheme terms were ignored. The company therefore obtained the right to have its passengers fed at its expense and thus the right to an input tax deduction. *British Airways plc* [2000] (VTD 16446)

Comment In light of a recent EU directive which obliges airlines to offer refreshment and compensation to delayed passengers, the deductibility of input tax should no longer be in doubt.

Employee expenses

This is an exception to the normal rule that the invoice or receipt must be made out to the taxable person. The employer can deduct input tax on invoices made out in the employee's name, where a **specific reimbursement** is made (commonly travel and subsistence expenses). This includes car fuel which is bought by the employee for business journeys, then reimbursed by the employer (including through the mechanism of a mileage allowance (¶1876)). 1962 Notice 700 para 12

If an employee incurs expenses in the course of the employment duties, this does not always mean that supplies are made to the employer. This is particularly the case where the employee has complete autonomy on the choice of supplier and on what is bought and has no authority from the employer to make the purchase. However, if the employee uses the employer's credit card, supplies are always treated as made to the employer. SI 2005/3290; s 24(4) VATA 1994

MEMO POINTS 1. **Round sum** allowances and **flat rate expenses** do not give rise to any input tax deduction, even if the VAT incurred is subsequently evidenced by the employee.

2. In relation to **relocation expenses**, the employer can recover input tax relating to the following, even where the invoices are made out to the employee: VIT43920
- fees from solicitors and estate agents;
- storage and removal of household and personal effects; and
- services such as the plumbing in of washing machines or altering curtains.

3. An important case was decided in the CJEU in 2001 concerning a similar rule in the Netherlands, which went against the Dutch practice, because it was argued successfully that the employee bought fuel as a private individual, then sold it on to the employer. As the employee was not a taxable person, the supply to the employer could not be one where input tax was deductible. *EC Commission v Kingdom of the Netherlands* [2001]

In March 2005 the CJEU held that the **UK rules also infringed** EU law on this point. *EC Commission v UK (No 4)* [2005] See ¶1876 for the UK's response.

C. VAT correctly charged

VAT must be charged correctly for a valid input tax deduction to be made. 1966

When VAT is **wrongly** charged, the purchaser cannot make the normal input tax deduction. This issue can arise in two situations:
a. where input tax should never have been charged, because the supply was zero-rated, exempt, or outside the scope of VAT (an error in applying the law); or
b. where the wrong amount of VAT has been charged (an arithmetical error).

It is also possible for an **unregistered trader** (who ought to be registered) to charge VAT, leading to a valid input tax deduction (¶1984).

Error in applying the law

This type of error means that **any VAT charged** is not true input tax, so the taxpayer's only remedy is to request a credit note (¶2925) from the supplier. 1968 s 4(1) VATA 1994

Common situations where this problem may occur are on the transfer of a business as a going concern, which is outside the scope of VAT but only where certain conditions are met (¶8646) and in relation to interests in land.

Comment Any **major contracts** will usually include a term which indemnifies the purchaser from incurring extra VAT. When undertaking an unusual type of transaction which is unfamiliar, the purchaser will usually seek to obtain evidence of HMRC's approval for any VAT charge before accepting the supplier's invoice.

Arithmetical error

1970 Where **insufficient VAT** has been charged, the taxpayer must request an additional invoice from the supplier.

Where the **VAT charge is too large**, the taxpayer will only be able to deduct the correct amount of input tax and should request a credit note for the excess VAT charged.

The taxpayer should never change the supplier's invoice.

D. Evidence

1972 Evidence is vital to any input tax claim.

For traders who supply mobile phones, computer chips and similar electronic goods, there are anti-evasion rules which require burdensome checks to be made and the VAT accounting can be more complicated.

1. Common situations

1974 s 24(6) VATA 1994; SI 1995/2518 reg 29(2)

Normally, no input tax can be deducted without the required evidence, which usually comprises a valid VAT invoice. In certain situations, however, this requirement is relaxed.

On **control visits** HMRC always checks whether a business has the appropriate evidence to back up input tax deductions.

Notice 700/63

MEMO POINTS 1. Invoices may be sent **electronically** (¶2848+) or via fax. A trader who does not wish to receive electronic invoices should discuss this with the supplier. The most important control that a trader should consider is the avoidance of duplicate invoices, which will lead to a problematic over-recovery of input tax.

SI 1995/2518 reg 13B

2. If a customer receives an invoice in a **foreign language**, HMRC can issue a notice requiring a translation within 30 days.

Low value supplies

1976 Notice 700 para 19.7.5

There is no invoice requirement, or other specific evidence requirement, for the following supplies valued at **below £25** (including VAT):
- coin-operated machines;
- car parking (excluding charges from on-street meters which are not subject to VAT);
- toll charges; and
- telephone calls.

For all supplies **below £250**, a less detailed invoice is allowed (¶2868), which means the VAT may not be identified. To calculate the input tax on:
- a standard-rated supply, the price should be multiplied by 1/6; and
- a reduced-rate supply, the price should be multiplied by 1/21.

EXAMPLE Mr F receives an invoice showing a price of £210.
The invoice states that the rate of VAT is 20%, so he calculates the VAT to be £35. (£210 × 1/6)

MEMO POINTS For the relevant fractions for earlier periods see ¶1090.

Other forms of evidence

Other forms of evidence **would include** authenticated receipts for supplies in the construction industry (¶5216), self-billing invoices (¶2904) and cash and carry receipts (¶2876). **1978**

In particular, **pro-forma** invoices are not adequate evidence; the taxpayer must wait until a proper invoice has been received from the supplier before claiming the related input tax.

For **non-UK supplies** the following types of evidence are expected: **1980**
- for EU acquisitions, the required documentation of the EU state, including a description of the goods, VAT numbers of the supplier and customer, and the VAT-exclusive price (¶9017);
- for services, an invoice from the overseas supplier; and
- for imported goods, certificate C79 (¶9426).

Missing evidence

Evidence may be missing because either the trader: **1982** HMRC Brief 36/07; SP "VAT Strategy: Input Tax deduction without a valid VAT Invoice" March 2007
- **has never held** the proper evidence; or
- held the proper evidence when the claim was made but has subsequently **lost or destroyed** it.

In the first instance, a trader should ask the supplier for a revised invoice which properly complies with the VAT rules. If this is not possible, provided that the trader carried out normal commercial checks to review the legitimacy of the supplier, an input tax deduction may be allowed at the discretion of HMRC. In addition, the trader should collect and retain such other supporting evidence as is available. It is possible to check a supplier's VAT registration details (for example, to verify that a false name is not being used) by contacting HMRC.

MEMO POINTS **Other supporting evidence** that HMRC would take into account includes:
- alternative documentary evidence held (for example, the supplier's statement of account);
- evidence of receipt of a taxable supply;
- evidence of payment;
- evidence of how the supply has either been consumed by the trader, or incorporated into its own supplies; and
- an explanation of how the trader came to be aware of the supplier and what knowledge the trader possesses about the supplier's business.

EXAMPLE A farmer appealed against an assessment disallowing input tax because the related invoices were not available at the time of a control visit. He stated that the invoices had been lost during a move. Although he obtained copy invoices covering about one third of the tax claimed, he was assessed on the balance of £11,615. The farmer gave evidence as to:
- the work done and the goods and services with which he had been supplied; and
- the obtaining of invoices and receipts which he passed to his book-keeper, who corroborated the farmer's evidence.

In addition, the VAT records showed the names of suppliers, the VAT-exclusive amount and VAT, which were noted down from the invoices.

It was held that the claimed input tax related largely to genuine supplies and that the invoices had been held and lost. The appeal therefore largely succeeded. *MS Vaughan* [1996] (VTD 14050)

For traders receiving **supplies involving** the following types of goods, a higher level of proof is required to support the contention that a valid supply has occurred (¶2002):
- **computers** and **telephones**;
- **alcohol** which is subject to excise duty;
- all **oils** that are held out for sale as road fuel.

Unregistered supplier

If a registered customer has been charged VAT by an unregistered supplier and deducted it as input tax in **good faith**, by concession HMRC will usually waive recovery proceedings and pursue the supplier for the missing VAT. **1984** VAEC9640

If HMRC is **not satisfied** that the deduction was made in good faith, or otherwise decides to take action against the customer, an assessment will be raised for the incorrectly deducted tax, with interest and possibly penalties becoming due (¶3955).

Where there is evidence that the supplier and customer have **colluded**, recovery action may be taken against either party or both. The action taken depends on which option is most cost-effective and likely to be successful.

Input tax can sometimes be deducted on a taxable supply from an unregistered person who is **liable to be registered**, i.e. someone who has exceeded the registration thresholds. The input tax is calculated as 1/6 of the price paid. HMRC will consider the evidence which shows that the supplier was required to be registered at the time of the supply and whether the purchaser was complicit in any way, such as having a close working knowledge of the supplier's business. However, it is irrelevant whether the output tax has been, or is likely to be, recovered from the supplier by HMRC.

EXAMPLE

1. Input tax was disallowed on the construction of four industrial units because the invoice number and trader details were false. There was evidence that work had been done to the extent invoiced and cash withdrawals by the trader exactly matched the payments which were supposedly made to the supplier.
The tribunal was satisfied that the trader had acted in good faith and had received and paid for supplies as invoiced. It was also satisfied that those supplies were made by a person who was required to be registered, so the trader had validly incurred input tax. *Ellen Garage Ltd* [1994] (VTD 12407)

2. It has since been confirmed that there is no automatic right for the customer to deduct input tax where an unregistered supplier who is liable to be registered purports to charge VAT. HMRC has a discretion whether to accept the claim and, provided that HMRC acts reasonably in considering the evidence, its decision is final. *Masood Ahmed t/a New Touch* [2009] (VTD 20119)

1985 Notice 48 para 3.9

Where an amount of VAT is shown on an invoice issued by a person who is neither registered nor liable to be registered, HMRC has a right to collect that amount as if it were VAT. By concession, HMRC will make an allowance for VAT suffered by that person in connection with the transaction.

2. Missing trader fraud

1987 For many years, HMRC has been very concerned about the substantial loss of revenue resulting from fraud involving **mobile phones, computer chips** and other high-value, easily-transportable goods.

As a result, the reverse charge mechanism is in place for certain transactions (which means suppliers do not charge VAT because it is the customer who becomes liable to account for the output tax instead), and suppliers in a chain of transactions are also jointly and severally liable for any lost VAT (¶2002).

Overview

1988 This type of fraud **can occur** where goods are sold from one EU member state to another. For example, if goods are brought into the UK from elsewhere in the EU, the purchaser in the UK (P) will not be charged VAT by its non-UK EU supplier. P will charge VAT to its customer in the UK but P may disappear without paying that VAT to HMRC. The goods are typically bought and sold several times in the UK (in order to seek to disassociate the important parties to the fraud) before being sold outside the UK, at which point the vendor (V) does not charge VAT but does reclaim input tax from HMRC. HMRC loses out if it pays V's input tax claim but does not recover output tax from P, the missing person who purchased the goods in the UK from an EU supplier. HMRC has sought means over the years to deny V its claim, because that is a more practical solution than trying to find the missing trader, P. This type of fraud is broadly known as MTIC (missing trader intra-Community) fraud and if the same goods are sent round in a circle several times, with the original UK purchaser disappearing each time, it is known as carousel fraud.

HMRC sought at first to demonstrate that transactions involving fraud were not economic activities and therefore not liable to VAT (with the consequence that no trader would have a right to deduct input tax, because it would have been wrongly charged). The CJEU stated in response that the right of a taxable person to deduct VAT cannot be affected by the fact that another transaction in the chain is fraudulent, where that person has no knowledge of the fraud and indeed no means of acquiring that knowledge. In a supply chain, each transaction must be regarded on its own merits; its character cannot be altered by earlier or subsequent events.

HMRC was therefore forced to make substantial repayments in respect of denied input tax recovery claims for periods between 2003 and 2006.

However, the CJEU later confirmed that a trader who knew or should have known that its transactions were connected with fraud did not have a right to deduct input tax. *Kittel v Belgium* [2006] As a result of this case, HMRC is now enjoying more success in denying input tax to traders caught up in fraudulent chains of transactions.

a. Investigations

Where HMRC suspects a trader is knowingly involved in MTIC fraud, the trader will be invited to a **meeting**, at which HMRC will state: **1989** CC/FS 20
- the reasons for those suspicions and in what way the dishonest conduct is believed to have occurred; and
- that the investigation is not being conducted with a view to prosecution.

The trader will have an opportunity to **disclose** any indirect tax irregularities at the meeting, including matters which are not related to the investigation, although immunity from prosecution will not extend to the latter.

HMRC will invite the trader to make **payments** on account towards any tax arrears, both at the initial meeting and throughout the investigation, so reducing any interest charges.

A **civil penalty** (¶3955+) will be imposed where HMRC believes that the tax irregularities are due to conduct involving the trader's dishonesty. However, the level of penalty will be mitigated where the trader has co-operated during the investigation.

After the **investigation is concluded**, HMRC will write to the trader, stating the amount of tax, interest and any penalty due. The trader should sign and return a copy of the letter, unless further information needs to be supplied in order for HMRC to review the case. The trader can also request a review and/or appeal direct to the tribunal (¶4220+).

On receipt of the signed letter HMRC will issue a formal **assessment** and request payment of outstanding amounts. If the trader has difficulty in paying, it may be possible to arrange payments by instalments.

HMRC also offers a **Contractual Disclosure Facility** (¶4150), under which those suspected of fraud are able to avoid criminal investigation in return for agreeing to enter into a contract to disclose details of the fraud.

b. Reverse charge regime

Scope

For the reverse charge (¶9700) to apply, the affected goods or services must be **sold to** a taxable person (¶2620) for a business purpose. **1990** s 55A VATA 1994; HMRC Brief 24/07; Information Sheet 8/07

However, the reverse charge will **not apply**:
- where the seller chooses to use a second-hand margin scheme; or
- where goods are supplied for free as gifts or samples.

MEMO POINTS 1. **Payments on account** (POA) (¶3182) depend on the trader's annual VAT liability, which includes reverse charges. However, affected businesses can apply to HMRC to exclude the output tax due under the reverse charge when:
- deciding whether a business is required to make POA; and
- calculating the size of monthly payments.

2. Any reverse charge transaction is, for the customer, excluded from the **cash accounting** (¶4880+) and **flat rate** (¶4635+) schemes.

Affected goods or services

1991 HMRC Brief 23/14 The affected goods are mobile phones, computer chips and emissions allowances. Since 1 July 2014 wholesale supplies of gas and electricity are also included.

Mobile phones include BlackBerrys and Pay As You Go phones, but **exclude**:
- phones which are supplied with an airtime contract (also replacement phones and upgrades supplied under the terms of an airtime contract);
- walkie-talkies;
- 3G data cards; and
- WiFi cards.

Any **accessories** which are supplied within a single package (e.g. a charger, battery, cover or hands-free kit) are also treated as part of the phone supply and therefore subject to the reverse charge. Accessories supplied separately from a phone are not subject to the reverse charge.

The reverse charge applies to **computer chips** when they are in a state prior to integration into end-user products, or sold separately and not as part of an assembled item. All chips covered by the reverse charge fall within the tariff commodity code 8542 3190 00, which includes:
- all integrated circuits (i.e. central processing units or CPUs);
- discrete integrated circuit devices, that is, microprocessors or microprocessor units (MPUs) and microcontrollers or microcontroller units (MCUs); and
- chipsets which are the dedicated cluster of integrated circuits which support MPUs.

The reverse charge also applies to **emissions allowances**, which until 1 November 2010 were zero-rated.

If there is **any doubt** whether the reverse charge should apply, a written ruling should be obtained from HMRC.

De minimis limit

1993 Where an invoice is for £5,000 or less the reverse charge will not apply. The de minimis limit **relates to** the total value of goods which are supplied together and detailed on a single invoice. So where separate low-value orders are combined into one invoice, this limit may easily be exceeded. Similarly, where a bulk order is fulfilled in separate consignments, no reverse charge may arise due to the de minimis limit. However, if both parties agree, smaller invoices which combine to fulfil an order in excess of £5,000 can all be subject to the reverse charge, ignoring the limit altogether.

If an **invoice** includes both affected goods and other supplies, only the affected goods are subject to the reverse charge.

For the purpose of the de minimis limit, unconditional discounts can reduce the value of the goods. So, for example, the reverse charge will not apply to an invoice value of £5,400 where there is a prompt payment discount of 10% (and that discount is actually taken up).

Effect on the supplier

1994 **Checking the customer's status** The **supplier** should undertake **reasonable checks** on the VAT and business status of the customer, as follows:
- normal commercial checks on creditworthiness and customer status which are good commercial practice for the trade sector;

– consider whether the VAT registration number is genuine and belongs to the person who is quoting it;
– consider whether there is any indication in the pattern of orders that the customer is attempting to manipulate the £5,000 de minimis limit; and
– consider whether there are any grounds to doubt the bona fides of the customer.

A trader who takes no such action could be liable for any VAT unpaid by the customer.

A seller who has any **doubts as to the veracity of information supplied by the customer** must consider whether the transaction should go ahead; if deciding to proceed the supplier may wish to ask the customer for a refundable deposit equivalent to the output tax for which the supplier will become liable if the reverse charge is applied in error. This may be especially helpful if the customer has applied for, but not yet received, a VAT registration number.

If a **retailer** (including an online supplier) is unable to ascertain the business status of its customer, VAT should be charged in the normal way. However, the usual checks which are put in place to prevent fraud and money laundering should be used to prevent manipulation of the de minimis limit.

Invoicing Suppliers must show all the information normally required to be shown on a VAT invoice (¶2858). In addition, the invoice should **clearly indicate** that the reverse charge applies and that the customer is required to account for the VAT. The amount of reverse charge VAT due must be identified on the invoice but should not be included in the amount shown as total VAT charged. HMRC states that any of the following are acceptable: **1997**
a. "customer to pay output tax of £x to HMRC";
b. "UK customer to pay output tax of £x to HMRC"; or
c. the amount of tax is shown elsewhere on the invoice and one of the following is indicated:
– "VAT Act 1994 Section 55A applies";
– "s 55A VATA 94 applies";
– "customer to account for the VAT to HMRC";
– "reverse charge supply - customer to pay the VAT to HMRC";
– "customer to pay VAT to HMRC"; or
– "UK customer to pay VAT to HMRC".

MEMO POINTS 1. Where **electronic invoicing** is used, HMRC is prepared to allow coded representation of the above instead of actual text.
2. A purchaser who is using **self-billing** (¶2904) will issue the invoice and also account for VAT on the reverse charge. The supplier must still complete a Reverse Charge Sales List (¶1998). In relation to the invoice, HMRC states that any of the following are acceptable:
a. "we will account for and pay output tax of £x to HMRC";
b. "as the UK customer we will pay output tax of £x to HMRC"; or
c. the amount of tax is shown elsewhere on the invoice and one of the following is indicated:
– "VAT Act 1994 Section 55A applies";
– "s 55A VATA 94 applies";
– "we will account for the VAT to HMRC";
– "reverse charge supply - we will pay the VAT to HMRC";
– "as the customer we will pay VAT to HMRC"; or
– "as the UK customer we will pay VAT to HMRC".

Reporting by suppliers Reverse Charge Sales Lists (RCSLs) follow the submission dates of the trader's normal VAT return (¶2985+). **Traders must notify** HMRC within 30 days of making the first supply to which the reverse charge applies; also when they cease to make such supplies (and subsequent recommencement). Lists must always be submitted, even where no reverse charge transactions have been made. The list must contain the VAT registration number and the total value of reverse charge supplies made each calendar month to each affected customer (including nil months). Traders selling goods under the reverse charge procedure will therefore need to obtain the VAT registration numbers of affected customers. **1998**

When **completing the VAT return**, a supplier excludes any reverse charge output tax from box 1, although the value of such sales must be entered in box 6.

Effect on taxable customers

1999 Customers must account for the **VAT due** on the supply as indicated on the invoice, applying the normal time of supply rules. Failure to comply will result in an assessment for the amount of output tax as reduced by any likely input tax claim. Further, where the customer fails to tell the supplier that the reverse charge should apply and output tax is charged by the supplier, HMRC will take this to indicate fraud and any input tax claimed by the customer will be subject to stringent verification.

When **completing a VAT return** a customer must enter the reverse charge output tax in box 1 but must exclude the value of the purchases from box 6. The input tax is reclaimed in box 4 in the normal manner (subject to any partial exemption restriction) and the value of the purchases is included in box 7.

MEMO POINTS 1. Where customers will be using goods for **both business and non-business purposes** (e.g. charities and local authorities), the reverse charge still applies. The customer should therefore account for output tax under the reverse charge procedure and apply the appropriate restriction to the deduction of the resulting input VAT.
2. The reverse charge will apply to **onward sales** of affected goods which are sold to another VAT-registered business in the UK if the invoice value is £5,000 or more.
3. **Unregistered customers** will need to take into account the purchase of affected goods when monitoring the registration thresholds (¶2668), although the first £1,000 of such purchases per month is disregarded.

Price adjustments

2000 Where the price of a transaction is subsequently adjusted, HMRC states that the **easiest solution** is for both parties to agree not to amend their VAT records (which takes advantage of an existing concession). However, the supplier will still need to amend the RCSL.

Otherwise, the following guidance applies:

Reverse charge originally applied?	Situation	Action by supplier	Action by customer
Yes	Return not yet submitted	Adjust the records of the sale and make sure the corrected figure feeds through to the VAT account	Adjust the records of the purchase and make sure the corrected figure feeds through to the VAT account
	Return already submitted and reverse charge still applies	None	Adjust any reverse charge output tax and any input tax to reflect the new values
	Return already submitted and adjustment takes the supply out of the reverse charge	Output tax needs to be accounted for and collected from the customer	Must reverse the output tax already entered into the records and correct the input tax entry to reflect the amended value
No	Adjustment brings the supply into the reverse charge	Credit the output tax accounted for and give back any VAT collected from the customer	Adjust the input tax to reflect the new value and bring the reverse charge output tax to account in the same VAT period

c. Joint and several liability

2002
s 77A VATA 1994 This power enables HMRC to collect VAT from any traders caught up in a fraudulent supply chain, where one of the traders in the chain has disappeared without accounting for VAT.

However, the following **situations are excluded**, where: Notice 726 para 4.9
- VAT is unpaid because of a genuine bad debt or business failure; or
- the business purchases the goods for its own use and not for resale.

Otherwise, where a trader receives a supply of the relevant goods and either **knew** or had reasonable grounds to **suspect** that some or all of the VAT payable in respect of that supply (or an earlier or subsequent supply of those goods) would go unpaid, HMRC can serve notice on the trader. This must state the amount of unpaid VAT and that the trader is jointly and severally liable with the supplier. Unpaid VAT will be subject to recovery proceedings (¶3730).

There is a presumption that the trader had knowledge or grounds for suspicion where the **price** paid was less than: Notice 726 para 2.6
- the lowest open-market price; or
- the price payable on any previous supply of those goods.

The only **protection** that a trader can invoke is to have completed due diligence procedures, or that there is a legitimate reason for the low price, unconnected with fraud. Most traders buying affected goods will require professional assistance to comply with these rules. Notice 726 para 3

The CJEU has confirmed that the joint and several liability rules accord with EU principles, although a demand for security (¶3570) is unlawful where there is no joint and several liability. *C & E and another v Federation of Technological Industries* [2006]

MEMO POINTS 1. The **relevant goods** are: **2003**
- telephones and any other equipment, including parts and accessories, made or adapted for use in connection with telephones or telecommunication;
- computers and any other equipment, including parts, accessories and software, made or adapted for use in connection with computers or computer systems, including satellite navigation systems; and
- electronic goods used for leisure, amusement or entertainment.

2. The **amount of VAT** payable is the lower of: Notice 726 para 2.2
- the VAT chargeable on the supply; and
- the amount of VAT due from the supplier taking into account any input tax deduction and repayments due from HMRC.

3. Before the notice of liability is served, a **notification letter** is sent giving the trader 21 days to explain why the price paid for the goods is legitimately low. Notice 726 para 4.2

4. The trader can ask for reconsideration and lodge an **appeal** against a notice.

Due diligence

The due diligence **requires the trader** to: **2004** Notice 726 para 6.1

a. undertake reasonable commercial checks to consider the **legitimacy of customers or suppliers**, for example:
- what is the supplier's history in the trade;
- are normal commercial arrangements in place for the financing of the goods;
- are the goods adequately insured; and
- what recourse is there if the goods are not as described;

b. undertaking reasonable checks to ensure the **commercial viability** of the transaction, for example:
- is there a market for this type of goods, such as superseded or outdated mobile phone models;
- is it commercially viable for the price of the goods to increase within the short duration of the supply chain;
- have normal commercial practices been adopted in negotiating prices; and
- is there a commercial reason for any third party payments;

c. undertake reasonable checks to ensure the **goods will be as described** by the supplier, for example:
- do the goods exist;
- have they been previously supplied to the trader; and
- are they in good condition and not damaged;

d. check the validity of the supplier, for example:
– obtaining copies of its certificate of incorporation and VAT registration certificate;
– verifying VAT registration details with HMRC;
– obtaining letters of introduction on headed paper;
– obtaining some form of trade reference, either written or verbal;
– obtaining credit checks or other background checks from an independent third party;
– insisting on personal contact with a senior officer of the prospective supplier, making an initial visit to its premises whenever possible;
– obtaining the prospective supplier's bank details, to check whether payments would be made to a third party, and whether the bank is located in the same country as the supplier; and
– checking details provided against other sources, e.g. website, letterheads, telephone land-line records; and
e. retain additional paperwork, such as purchase orders, delivery notes, airway bills and inspection reports.

SECTION 5

Making a claim

2005 s 25 VATA 1994 This section deals with taxable UK traders incurring UK VAT only.

There are special provisions relating to UK input tax incurred by overseas traders (¶9875 and ¶9908) and EU VAT incurred by UK traders (¶9845).

For traders making any exempt supplies see also ¶2070+.

Method

2007 Input tax is claimed **on a VAT return**, by putting an entry in box 4. The amount of input tax deductible in any VAT period is the sum of the recoverable input tax shown on all purchase invoices with a relevant tax point (¶750+).

Amount

2010 s 19(2) VATA 1994 Without any other indication, the **price** charged on an invoice is deemed to include VAT, so input tax will be 1/6 of the price. However, the supplier normally makes sure that the net and VAT amounts are clearly marked.

SI 1995/2518 reg 29(3) HMRC may allow a person to **estimate** a part of the deductible input tax for any period where it is not possible to identify the exact amount available for relief. The estimate should then be corrected as soon as possible.

For the position where the amount is expressed in **foreign currency** see ¶9032.

Timing

2012 s 25(2) VATA 1994 Input tax should **usually** be claimed in the VAT period in which the tax point of the invoice falls, or, if later, the VAT period when the invoice was received. However, there are **exceptions** for cash accounting (¶4880+) and authenticated receipts relating to construction services, in which case input tax is claimed when payment is made.

If the trader is using any **apportionment calculations** in relation to non-business use or partial exemption, it is particularly important to claim input tax in the correct period.

MEMO POINTS 1. For **foreign supplies** the important dates are:
– for EU acquisitions, the date of acquisition;
– for imported goods, the date of the import declaration; and
– for goods removed from a customs and/or excise warehouse, the date of removal.

2. **Earlier payment** of input tax (i.e. before the end of the trader's normal VAT period) may be authorised where serious delay has occurred as a result of HMRC's actions, for example, a delay in processing an application for registration.
3. For details of the **cash accounting** scheme see ¶4880+.
4. For details of **authenticated receipts** see ¶5216.

EXAMPLE Ms G has a calendar year VAT cycle and is preparing her VAT return for the quarter to 31 March. She receives some invoices with tax point dates of 1 and 2 April before she submits her return at the end of April.
She cannot claim the related input tax on these invoices in the quarter ending 31 March. She must wait until the quarter ending 30 June.

A claim for input tax cannot be made until the **evidence** (¶1972) which is required to substantiate that claim is held. **2014** s 80(4) VATA 1994; SI 1995/2518 reg 29(1A)

In any event, an input tax claim must be made **within** 4 years of the first VAT period when that evidence was held.

The **method** of the claim may be by return, or by voluntary disclosure (¶3020). There are particular rules where a late claim is made by a partly exempt trader (¶2254).

If a supplier has used the **wrong VAT rate**, or been subject to **compulsory backdated registration**, a customer may then receive a belated VAT invoice. By concession the customer may recover the input tax within 3 years of receiving the invoice. HMRC must be satisfied that the supplier has paid the output tax and the customer has paid the supplier's invoice.

MEMO POINTS 1. No **transitional period** was given when the previous 3-year **cap** was introduced; the CJEU held that this was a breach of EU law. *Marks & Spencer plc v C & E* [2002] Following further case law, the law was changed so that it was possible to make a claim up **until 31 March 2009** for input tax relating to the period from 1 April 1973 to 1 May 1997. *Fleming (t/a Bodycraft) v HMRC* [2008]; *Conde Nast Publications Ltd v HMRC* [2008] s 121 FA 2008
2. The status of **post-May 1997 claims** was clarified in 2009, when the Inner House of the Court of Session ruled that the 3-year cap was only invalid in respect of claims that arose before it was enacted. Therefore HMRC invited taxpayers with claims which extended beyond the *Fleming* 1996/1997 time limits to withdraw those claims or proceed to appeal before the First-tier Tribunal. *HMRC v Scottish Equitable plc* [2009]
3. Where a taxpayer has made a **claim** for input tax, which is later discovered to have been **erroneous**, an assessment can be raised by the later of:
– 2 years after the end of the prescribed accounting period; or
– 1 year after HMRC is in possession of sufficient evidence to make the assessment, which must also be within 4 years from the end of the prescribed accounting period.
The prescribed accounting period, for these purposes only, is the VAT accounting period of the taxpayer in which the repayment is made by HMRC.
4. In a case where a company incurred and was invoiced for substantial amounts of input VAT in April 1997 which it did not deduct on its VAT return for the period to 30 June 1997, the Tribunal ruled that no *Fleming* claim could be made on 1 May 1997 because the **right to deduct did not arise until it became exercisable** at the end of the accounting period. It was therefore out of time and the late claim was denied. *Cable and Wireless plc* [2009] (TC00004)
5. HMRC issued guidance to its staff in 2009 on the handling of historic VAT claims by traders following the *Fleming* and *Conde Nast* cases. The guidance also includes information on how HMRC will deal with claims by assignees and transferees after the Court of Appeal decision in *Midlands Co-operative Society Ltd v HMRC* [2008], which held that the right to claim for overpaid VAT can be assigned, transferred or sold. In addition it covers HMRC's policy on verifying claims, set-off, and their views on claims for compound interest.
The guidance can be found at flmemo.co.uk/vm2014.

Failure to pay supplier

If a customer does not pay its supplier **within** 6 months, the related input tax already claimed by the customer must be repaid to HMRC (¶868+). In practice, if the invoice is paid within the VAT period when the 6 months expire, no repayment is necessary. **2018** s 26A VATA 1994

If the invoice is **subsequently paid**, the input tax can be claimed again.

MEMO POINTS 1. If no input tax was recovered because it related to **exempt supplies**, none needs to be repaid.

2. If the input tax related to **mixed supplies** (i.e. taxable and exempt) and only a proportion was recovered, the amount to be repaid will only take into account that proportion.
3. In some industries it is common for there to be a **delay in payment** but the 6-month rule still applies, whether or not there is a bad debt in reality.

EXAMPLE Mr H receives a purchase invoice on 10 January. His VAT periods end on 28 February, 31 May, etc. He therefore claims input tax on the return for the period ending 28 February.
The 6-month deadline expires on 10 July. However, provided that Mr H pays the purchase invoice by 31 August, no repayment of input tax is necessary.

Refund

2020 At its simplest, the net amount of VAT payable to or recoverable from HMRC is:

Output tax - Input tax

If **input tax exceeds output tax** in a VAT period, a refund will usually be paid to the trader (¶3230), unless the trader has other VAT debts.

Input tax is not recoverable until it is claimed on a VAT return (¶2985), or by error correction (¶3020).

CHAPTER 2

Recoverable input tax

OUTLINE ¶¶

Once deductible (¶1800+) input tax has been identified and verified as eligible (¶1950+), recoverable input tax can be calculated. For a trader who is **making only taxable supplies**, all eligible input tax will be recoverable, subject to the special rules for traders who are newly registered or who are deregistering (¶8550+). 2070

In **any other case**, partial exemption and the capital goods scheme must be considered.

The following table indicates when these subjects are relevant:

Situation	**Partial exemption** (¶2075+)	**Capital goods scheme** (¶2280+)
Incurred VAT on a supply involving immovable property costing at least £250,000 (excluding VAT)	✓	✓
Acquired computer hardware, a ship or an aircraft costing at least £50,000 (excluding VAT)	✓	✓
Making other exempt and taxable supplies	✓	

SECTION 1

Partial exemption

A. What is the issue?

2075 Notice 706 Subject to certain de minimis limits (¶2194), input tax which relates to exempt supplies cannot be recovered. Traders who make only **exempt supplies** cannot be registered and cannot recover any input tax they incur.

A business has **the right to recover VAT** incurred in making:
a. taxable supplies (at any rate, including the zero rate);
b. supplies outside the UK that would be taxable if made in the UK; and
c. certain other supplies outside the UK and certain supplies which would be exempt if made in the UK, in respect of which input tax is recoverable because a specific right to deduct has been granted by Treasury Order (¶2098).

A trader making a **mixture** of taxable and exempt supplies can usually only recover input tax on expenditure attributable to taxable supplies. Such traders are referred to as partly exempt.

These principles are summarised in the following diagram.

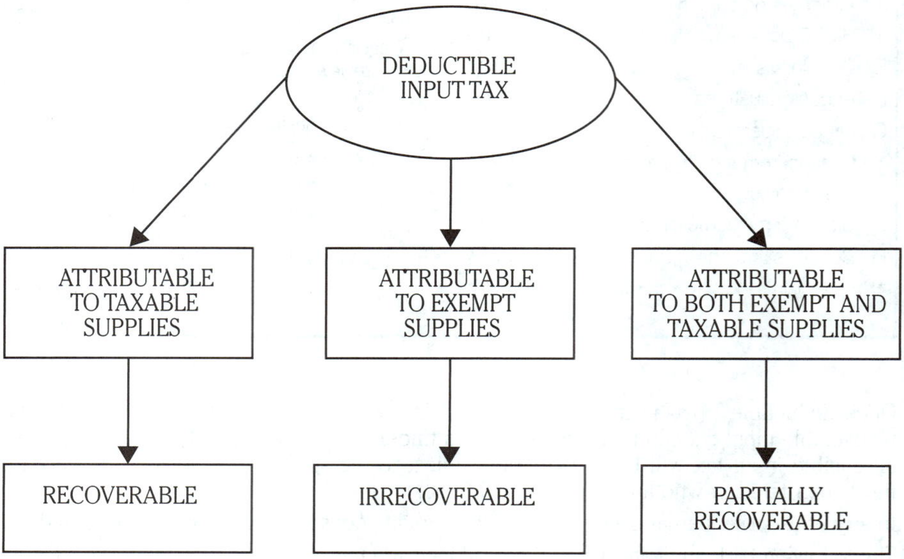

2077 SI 1995/2518 reg 99 Any input tax which is irrecoverable because it is incurred on the receipt of goods or services which are used wholly or partly to make exempt supplies is known as **exempt input tax**. This includes any VAT incurred on overheads, not just VAT that is directly attributable to exempt onward supplies.

SI 1999/3121 **Use** of goods and services includes the trader's intended use when the input tax is first incurred, as there may be a delay between purchase and actual use. For the consequences of a **subsequent change** in intention see ¶2224.

MEMO POINTS 1. For this purpose, **exempt supplies include** those with a place of supply (¶31) outside the UK which would be exempt if made in the UK, except for certain intermediary supplies of insurance and financial services in relation to supplies made outside the EU.

2. The **exempt onward supplies** are those made by the trader who incurred the input tax, unless a transfer of a going concern has occurred, in which case the subsequent owner can make the relevant exempt supplies.

EXAMPLE

1. A private school makes wholly exempt supplies. It incurs input tax of £8,000 on its equipment. None of this VAT can be recovered, which means that the VAT is a real cost to the school.

2. A hairdresser incurs input tax of £4,000, whilst charging output tax of £6,000 to his customers. As this is a fully taxable business, all of the input tax can be recovered and a net payment of £2,000 will be made to HMRC. (6,000 - 4,000)

3. A funeral director makes a mix of taxable and exempt supplies, so she is partly exempt. She incurs input tax of £5,000 on her overheads; only a fair proportion of this will be recovered.

Becoming partly exempt

There are several ways in which a trader may become partly exempt. **2080**

1. A trader may **diversify**, commencing a new venture in addition to the existing business, which has a different VAT liability from the supplies already being made.
2. A **taxable trader** may become partly exempt through undertaking certain types of business transaction, such as letting a commercial property.
3. An **exempt trader** who starts making taxable supplies may be required to register for VAT. Often this occurs where the trader has to charge itself VAT in relation to:
- the self-supply of construction services (¶5330);
- the reverse charge on international services (¶9700); or
- acquiring goods from the EU (¶9017).

MEMO POINTS 1. In addition, the **onward supply** of goods on which **input tax was not recoverable** (that is, because either they were used for wholly exempt supplies, or the input tax was blocked, for example, in relation to a car) is exempt. *EC Commission v Italian Republic* [1997]
2. Traders should check that their **insurance policies** will cover any irrecoverable input tax in the event of a claim, especially previously taxable persons who start to make exempt supplies.

Period of application

It is important to identify the **date** when a trader becomes partly exempt, which will usually be the beginning of the VAT period (¶2987) in which exempt input tax is first incurred. Partial exemption status is only lost when a whole VAT year (¶2990) has elapsed without any exempt input tax being incurred. **2082** SI 1995/2518 reg 99(4)

EXAMPLE Mr A has been trading for 20 years, making only taxable supplies. He is VAT-registered and submits returns for the quarters ending on 30 April, 31 July, etc. He decides to let surplus premises, which will be an exempt supply. The first let commences on 10 June but Mr A has already received an invoice for repairs dated 15 March.
Mr A will be partly exempt from 1 February, which is the beginning of the VAT period in which exempt input tax was first incurred.

Where a VAT business is: **2084** SI 1995/2518 reg 99(5)

a. newly registered, the trader becomes partly exempt from the later of the date of registration and the date exempt input tax was first incurred; or
b. registered late, the trader will be partly exempt from the date on which exempt input tax is first incurred.

Where a trader becomes partly exempt in the **registration period** (i.e. the period between the date of registration and the end of the first VAT year) and the registration period exceeds 6 months, it will be broken down into shorter periods of 3 months.

EXAMPLE

1. Ms B is newly registered from 1 November. Her registration period ends on the following 31 March. Ms B sells books but is also planning to teach maths privately, which will be an exempt supply. She buys some teaching materials, incurring the cost on 28 February. As this date falls within the registration period, Ms B is partly exempt from 28 February.

2. Mr C is newly registered from 13 August; his registration period ends on the following 31 May. Mr C's VAT periods will be:
- 13 August to 30 November;
- 1 December to 28 February; and
- 1 March to 31 May.

Mr C first incurs exempt input tax on 31 October, so he is partly exempt from that date.

Calculation of recoverable input tax

2086 A business making taxable and exempt supplies must go through the **steps** listed below in order to calculate recoverable input tax, **unless** the trader's exempt supplies are less than 50% of total supplies, in which case one of the simpler de minimis tests may be satisfied (¶2196).

The **first step** is to attribute input tax directly to taxable supplies and exempt supplies. The more input tax that can be properly attributed to taxable supplies the better, as this will increase the recovery rate. If input tax **attributable to exempt supplies** (including a proportion of input tax incurred on overheads) is below the de minimis limits (¶2194), all of the input tax can be recovered.

	Type of supply input tax relates to:			
	Total	**Taxable**	**Exempt**	**Mixed**
Deductible VAT	X			
1 Isolate VAT on specified supplies (¶2098) and attribute based on use	(X)	X	X	
	X			
2 Allocate input tax between taxable and exempt supplies as far as possible	(X)	X	X	X
3 Apportion remaining residual input tax		X	X	(X)
		X	X	-

This procedure is undertaken for each VAT period and then reviewed again at the end of each VAT year (unless annual accounting (¶4745) applies), via the annual adjustment (¶2202), which is designed to accommodate fluctuations in the amounts of exempt input tax incurred during the year.

Information Sheet 14/07

MEMO POINTS Where an **asset** (other than immovable property, a ship or an aircraft) is used for both non-business and business purposes, the owner may use the **Lennartz method** of accounting (¶1842), which has the effect of making all input tax deductible (but not necessarily recoverable), irrespective of any private use. The input tax will then be subject to the trader's usual partial exemption method to ascertain how much of it is recoverable. The output tax due, as calculated by Lennartz (¶1525+), is entirely independent of the partial exemption method.

B. Direct attribution

2095 SI 1995/2518 reg 101

In many cases a business can easily attribute its input tax to either taxable or exempt supplies, leaving a residual amount relating to both, which is then subject to apportionment (¶2112). The **essential test** is whether there is a direct and immediate link (¶2102) between the cost incurred and a supply.

It is up to the business to make the attribution, provided that the **result** is both fair and reasonable. If it does not agree with the attribution, HMRC may raise an assessment (¶3625).

The **principle of use** is a concept which derives from EU legislation and CJEU case law. The question of whether input tax on expenditure has been used in making a particular supply is common in VAT cases.

Comment The related supplies may **pre-date** the purchase, be concurrent, or be intended for future use. Any knowledge about how the expenditure will be used should be taken into account when making the attribution.
It is important to be thorough at this stage, as it is likely that this will improve input tax recovery.

1. Input tax on specified supplies

Input tax incurred on the following **types of supply**, which are outside the scope of UK VAT, is to be attributed to those supplies in accordance with the **use made** of the related purchases: 2098 SI 1995/2518 reg 103(1)
- supplies made outside the UK that would be taxable if they were made within the UK; and
- finance and insurance supplies made by a UK business to a customer belonging outside the EU.

The **annual adjustment** (¶2202) is also calculated on the basis of use.

There are special rules for **investment gold** (¶6843).

It is up to the business to make the use-based attribution, provided that the **result** is both fair and reasonable. Otherwise HMRC can raise an assessment (¶3625) to rectify the position. HMRC can also agree a **formal method** of calculating use as part of a special method (¶2148) only.

The input tax relating to these supplies, and the value of the supplies themselves, are normally ignored for the remaining parts of the partial exemption calculation. This means that any input tax not attributed to taxable use which relates to these supplies is treated as exempt input tax.

2. Other input tax

All other input tax must be attributed to the trader's taxable or exempt supplies as appropriate based on the **actual or intended use** of the goods and services when they are received. The goods and services **cannot be artificially split**, so each supply must be attributed as a whole to either taxable or exempt use. Where this is not possible, the related input tax will be treated as residual input tax (¶2110). 2100

MEMO POINTS 1. For **land-related** transactions, the trader should consider whether the intention is to make a taxable supply and whether an option to tax will be made (¶5602).
2. Where the **intended use changes** within 6 years, or actual use does not reflect the intended use, special rules apply (¶2224).
3. For **VAT groups** (¶8800), any supplies between the group members themselves should be ignored.
4. When using **cash accounting** (¶4880+) businesses must base partial exemption calculations on amounts received and paid in a VAT period.

EXAMPLE

1. A company sold mobile phone packages including accessories and a free 3-month insurance deal. The company acted as an intermediary for the insurance services, which were provided by another company. The customer could choose to extend the insurance after the initial free period and the phone company would then receive commission. The company incurred input tax on advertising costs and argued that this was all directly attributable to the mobile phone service.
It was held that the advertising had a dual purpose. It was irrelevant that the sale of insurance cover was less important than the phone supplies made by the company. The related input tax was therefore residual. *Dial-a-Phone Ltd v C & E* [2004]

2. Ms D purchases a roll of carpet on which she incurs input tax. She uses 45% of the carpet for the purposes of taxable supplies and 55% for the purposes of exempt supplies.

As the carpet was bought in a single purchase, she cannot just claim 45% of the input tax. She must treat the input tax as residual and apply an apportionment method in order to calculate the recoverable input tax.

3. E Ltd provides education and training services for a secretarial college (taxable) and also an exam marking service for the local university (exempt).

E Ltd incurs the following expenses in the quarter ended 31 March.

Expense		**Net**	**VAT**
		£	**£**
Salaries		15,000	-
Secretarial college:	Repairs	3,000	600
	Light & heat	400	80
	Rent	10,000	2,000
	Telephone	1,000	200
Stationery for whole business		4,000	800
Audit fee		600	120
Training for markers		400	80
Computers for marking service		14,000	2,800
Total			6,680

E Ltd attributes the input tax as follows:

Expense		**Total**	**Taxable supplies**	**Exempt supplies**	**Residual**
		£	**£**	**£**	**£**
Secretarial college:	Repairs	600	600	-	-
	Light & heat	80	80	-	-
	Rent	2,000	2,000	-	-
	Telephone	200	200	-	-
Stationery for whole business		800	-	-	800
Audit fee		120	-	-	120
Training for markers		80	-	80	-
Computers for marking service		2,800	-	2,800	-
Total		6,680	2,880	2,880	920

Direct and immediate link

2102 In a typical business the direct costs relating to turnover will be shown in cost of sales. Other income, such as bank interest received and rental income, would normally be identified separately. Overheads will then be deducted from the gross profit, because these relate to the whole business. In this scenario, it is relatively simple to identify the cost components of each type of income.

General overheads of a business have no direct and immediate link with any specific supplies made by that business. Thus the input tax incurred on them will always be residual and must be apportioned.

2104 In deciding whether a purchase has been used to make a specific taxable supply, it is necessary to establish a direct and immediate link between the cost and the supply. Input tax cannot be recovered on expenditure which is used partly in making exempt supplies (or in carrying on any activity other than the making of taxable supplies).

Where input tax is attributed under a partial exemption method, the tax must be linked directly to a taxable or exempt output. This has been interpreted in the CJEU to mean that the **ultimate aim** of a transaction, which might be linked to a taxable supply, must be ignored if the input tax can be more **closely linked** to an intervening exempt supply. *BLP Group plc* [1995]

Comment Some doubt has been cast on this by another decision of the CJEU. A parent company sold shares in two subsidiaries and sought to deduct input tax incurred in association with those sales. The CJEU held that the input tax was not to be disallowed as being wholly attributable to the exempt share sales. Instead, insofar as there was a direct and immediate link with the parent company's overall economic activities, the input tax was allowable. *Skatteverket v AB SKF* [2009]

EXAMPLE

1. A company purchased some land (incurring VAT on the price) which was then sold to a housing association, with which the company subsequently entered into a development contract to build on the land. The company considered that the input tax paid on the purchase of the land was recoverable, because it was directly linked to the building work.
However, it was held that there was no direct and immediate link with the contract, so the input tax on the cost of the land was not a cost of the contract. Although the development contract would not have been made but for the associated land purchase and sale, this was not sufficient to be a direct and immediate link; there was nothing about the development contract that made the land transactions essential. *C & E v Southern Primary Housing Association Ltd* [2003]

2. In another case the point at issue was whether the VAT incurred on legal costs defending a claim alleging negligent misrepresentation was wholly attributable to the zero-rated supplies previously made by the claimant, or whether it should be apportioned as being attributable to the taxable and exempt supplies made by the bank as a whole.
The CJEU ruled that, because the input tax on the legal costs was not used for the purpose of carrying out the zero-rated supplies, but incurred as a consequence of having made the zero-rated supplies, the expenditure involved was not a cost component of the taxable output transaction. It was therefore not directly attributable to those taxable supplies and was residual. *Midland Bank plc v C & E* [2000]

Particular situations

2106

Industry	Rules	Reference
Advertising costs	An estate agent incurred advertising costs in making taxable supplies of estate agency services. Exempt mortgage services were also offered by a company in the same VAT group. It was held that the VAT incurred when advertising houses for sale related only to the taxable supplies of estate agency services, provided that the advert did not mention that the advertiser also offered mortgage services. However, input tax could not be wholly attributed to standard-rated supplies where the mortgage services were specifically referred to in advertising; in that case the input tax could only be recovered according to the partial exemption method.	*Skipton Building Society v HMRC* [2009] (TC00146)
	A supplier of sofas sought to recover VAT on advertising costs. It made taxable supplies of the sofas, in addition to certain exempt supplies of anti-stain or payment protection insurance (although none of the supplier's advertisements made reference to any form of insurance). It was held that the advertising costs had a direct and immediate link to the taxable sales of furniture and no such link to the exempt insurance. The related input tax was therefore recoverable in full. This was because the exempt insurance intermediation services took place after, and were less commercially important than, the primary sales activity. Whilst there was a link between the advertising costs and the exempt activity, it was not sufficiently close to be a direct and immediate link.	*DFS Furniture Company Ltd* [2009] (TC00157)

Industry	Rules	Reference
Theatres	HMRC now accepts that theatrical production costs can be residual but only if they relate to specific taxable supplies as well as exempt admission charges. HMRC's examples of when production costs relate to taxable supplies include cases where a theatre has contracted to, or intends to: – secure sponsorship, in which case the sponsorship must relate to an event or a clearly defined run of events over a clearly defined time and putting on the shows must be a condition of the sponsorship; – take the production on tour; or – record the show for later sale on CD or other media. HMRC maintains that securing general corporate sponsorship does not make production costs residual, even if the sponsorship package includes the provision of seats at performances.	HMRC Brief 65/09; *Garsington Opera* [2009] (TC00045)
Hire purchase	Traders who make supplies under hire-purchase (HP) agreements with consumers are usually making exempt supplies. HMRC has stated that overhead costs incurred by such traders are cost components of the exempt supply of credit. However, where overheads are used to make both HP transactions and other supplies on which VAT is charged (such as taxable purchase option fees or sales of repossessed goods), it is arguable that some VAT on overhead costs is recoverable, so the partial exemption method should reflect the extent to which the overhead costs are a cost component of each particular supply.	HMRC Brief 82/09
GPs	GPs commonly buy drugs in separate supplies that are then periodically invoiced together. Where this is the case, the input tax on individual supplies received can be directly attributed if they are for use exclusively for taxable or exempt onward supplies. HMRC accepts that the amounts shown on the NHS statements can be used as the values of zero-rated and exempt supplies for the partial exemption standard recovery method for the period in which the statement is dated. Further, to determine the value of exempt supplies from the Dispensing Drugs Statement, HMRC considers that the net value calculated from the VAT allowance shown on the statement can be used as a proxy value for the exempt supplies of drugs, that is practices can take their VAT allowance figure, divide it by 20 and multiply it by 100.	Information Sheet 12/06

3. Residual input tax

2110 Any remaining input tax **after direct attribution** is known as residual input tax or non-attributable input tax. Input tax incurred on goods and services which are used for both exempt and taxable supplies is residual. It is typically incurred on overheads such as audit fees and stationery, which cannot be exclusively allocated either to taxable or exempt supplies.

Apportionment methods

2112 There are two methods of apportioning residual input tax:
– the **standard method** (¶2124), which is the default option, has fixed rules and is relatively straightforward; or
– a **special method** (¶2148), which requires specific permission from HMRC.

All apportionments must be based on the known facts at the time that the input tax is incurred.

Comment When first deciding on a method a business should review the various available options (perhaps trying out some sample calculations), in order to maximise its input tax recoverability, always bearing in mind that the result must be fair and reasonable.

C. The standard method

The standard method is commonly used by smaller businesses, as it is relatively **simple to apply** and is usually appropriate to their needs. It can also easily be used to check whether input tax is within the de minimis limits (¶2194). 2124 SI 1995/2518 reg 101; Information Sheet 4/09

Most businesses can use the standard method without the prior **approval** of HMRC. The **exception** is a business that is already using a special method.

If **changes** are needed to the standard method to meet the requirements of the business, a special method must be agreed.

Overview

The standard method apportions residual input tax to taxable supplies by applying the **ratio** of the value of taxable outputs to total outputs of the business in the period concerned. It deals with all input tax on all supplies (including supplies made outside the UK), with the **exception** of input tax: 2126

- incurred on investment gold (¶6843);
- related to supplies of financial instruments (e.g. shares and bonds), which is attributed on the basis of the use made of the costs; and
- related to supplies made from overseas establishments, which is similarly attributed on the basis of use.

Supplies on which input tax is specifically recoverable should be dealt with first (¶2098).

For **larger businesses** incurring large amounts of residual input tax, a standard method override adjustment may be required at the end of the VAT year (¶2240).

Newly partly exempt businesses

A newly partly exempt business **can opt** to recover input tax on the basis of **use** rather than the values of taxable and exempt supplies. 2127 Information Sheet 4/09

This means that input tax is attributed in accordance with the use, or intended use, of VATable costs in making taxable supplies. HMRC states that a business plan, prepared in accordance with cost accounting principles, will form an ideal basis for a fair recovery of input tax in this case.

The use-based calculation can be **applied during** the **period** when exempt input tax was first incurred, which will be either:

- the registration period (i.e. the period running from the date of registration to the day before the start of the first VAT year);
- the first VAT year (normally the first period of 12 months commencing on 1 April, 1 May or 1 June following the end of the registration period); or
- any VAT year, provided that no exempt input tax was incurred in the previous VAT year.

Once the **relevant period has expired**, the business must revert to the normal values-based calculation.

Where a business calculates its recovery of input tax on the basis of use, it is also required to calculate its **annual adjustment** (¶2202) on the basis of use to ensure consistency. A newly partly exempt business may choose to apply the normal calculation during each VAT period (i.e. using the values of taxable and exempt supplies) but then calculate a use-based annual adjustment. In any event, there is no need to notify HMRC.

Normal calculation

2128 For traders who have **not performed an annual adjustment previously**, the following formula must be used in each VAT period to calculate the percentage of residual input tax which is attributable to taxable supplies:

SI 1995/2518 reg 101(2)(d)

$$\frac{\text{Total value of taxable supplies in the period (excluding VAT)}}{\text{Total value of all supplies in the period (excluding VAT)}} \times 100 = \text{Taxable \%}$$

SI 1995/2518 reg 101(4) The resulting percentage is **rounded up** to the nearest whole number (e.g. 28.1% becomes 29%), **except for very large businesses** with residual input tax per quarter exceeding £1.2 million (on average), in which case the percentage must be stated to two decimal places. This percentage is then applied to the residual VAT to give the amount that can be recovered, in addition to the input tax attributed to taxable supplies.

Information Sheet 4/09 A trader who has **already completed an annual adjustment** (that is, who has been partly exempt for a while) has the option to use the previous year's recovery percentage (ignoring both the de minimis rules (¶2194) and any override calculation (¶2240)) to calculate the provisional amount of residual input tax recoverable in each VAT period. The annual adjustment (¶2202) will then calculate the amount of recoverable input tax for the whole year using actual figures for taxable and exempt supplies.

MEMO POINTS When applying the **prior year's recovery rate** there is no need to notify HMRC, although the chosen method (i.e. either using the past year's rate or calculating the rate afresh for each VAT period) must be applied consistently during the VAT year.

Value of supplies

2130 SI 1995/2518 reg 101(3) The value of the following supplies must be **excluded** from the outputs used in the standard method values-based calculation:
- any sums receivable for the sale of capital goods (¶2132);
- supplies of land if they are incidental (¶2136);
- financial transactions if they are incidental (¶2136);
- sales of goods, such as cars, on which input tax has previously been disallowed;
- self-supplies (¶2144);
- reverse charge services (¶9700);
- the value of any goods and services which are neither a taxable nor an exempt supply, such as the transfer of a business as a going concern (¶8646);
- supplies of financial instruments (e.g. shares and bonds); and
- supplies which are made from overseas establishments.

2132 **Sales of capital goods** A capital item for this purpose has substantial durability and value compared to other items used in the day-to-day business, and is not limited to items included in the capital goods scheme (¶2280). *C & E v JDL Ltd* [2002]

The **principle** behind excluding such supplies is to avoid the distortion caused by unique transactions, for example, the sale of redundant machinery or surplus property, as this could unfairly increase the value of taxable supplies and consequent input tax recovery.

2136 **Incidental supplies of land and finance** The **meaning** of incidental depends on the facts of each particular case. It is usually taken to indicate an activity which is unusual for the business and which does not normally recur. In addition, an incidental activity should not exceed the extent of the normal activity, which is not necessarily just measured in financial terms. It has been held that an incidental activity is one which is subordinate to another, or merely fortuitous. *C & E v Beazer (CH) Holdings plc* [1989]

The CJEU has stated that even where the **income associated with the activity** in question is greater than that generated by the main activity, the activity in question can still be incidental. *Empresa de Desenvolvimento Mineiro* [2004]

The sale of shares to persons located outside the EU is subject to special rules (¶2426).

EXAMPLE

1. A partly exempt holding company sold a minority shareholding in another company. For the purposes of apportioning input tax, the proceeds from the sale were excluded.
It was held that as the company was an active industrial holding company and not in reality an investment company, the sale was incidental to the company's business activities. The proceeds were rightly excluded from the calculation. *C & E v Beazer (CH) Holdings plc* [1989]

2. A property management company received sums in advance from co-owners and lessees which it invested itself, retaining the bank interest. This investment activity was intertwined with the whole business, being a necessary extension of the taxable activity. It was not an incidental activity.
The CJEU held that the bank interest received must be included in total supplies. *Regie Dauphinoise-Cabinet A Forest Sarl v Ministre du Budget* [1996]

3. A corporate group consisted of many holding companies and their subsidiaries. The holding companies supplied administrative and accounting services, and loan finance, in return for which they received dividends and interest on the loans. The companies claimed the right to deduct all of the input tax suffered by them. The issue was whether the dividend and interest income should be included in total supplies when calculating recoverable input tax under the standard method.
It was held that entitlement to dividends was merely a function of holding shares, so there was no direct link between a dividend and a supply of services. Dividend income was to be excluded from total supplies.
Loan transactions were subject to VAT only if they constituted either an economic activity or the direct, permanent and necessary extension of a taxable activity. Loans were an economic activity where there was a purpose of maximising returns on capital investment. It was a question of fact whether loans to subsidiaries were linked to management services. In this case, it was held that the interest could be excluded from total supplies. *Floridienne SA and another v Belgian State* [2000]

In practice such transactions are likely to be either unique, or regular but immaterial (such as bank interest income). HMRC tends to identify all the activities of the business and consider whether the transaction is incidental to any of them. It is possible for a transaction to be distorting but not necessarily incidental; in this case a special method should be agreed, because the standard method will not give a fair and reasonable allocation of input tax. 2138

Self-supplies The main self-supply charges are in-house construction services in excess of £100,000 and the self-supply arising on change of use of a residential building. See ¶1494+ for full details. 2144

Typical calculation The following example indicates a number of the issues involved: 2146

EXAMPLE Ms F is completing her quarterly VAT return. From her VAT records, she has extracted the following information:

	£	£
Total VAT suffered	11,950	
Relating to non-business use	1,400	
Input tax on business entertainment	150	
Input tax wholly attributable to taxable supplies	3,700	
Input tax wholly attributable to exempt supplies	1,600	
Value of taxable supplies (excluding VAT)		71,000
Value of exempt supplies		30,000
Value of plant sold to French purchaser (excluding VAT)		1,500
Reverse charge on German accountancy fee		1,000

1. The residual input tax is calculated as follows:

	£	£
Total VAT suffered		11,950
Less: Non-business VAT	1,400	
VAT on business entertainment (blocked)	150	
		(1,550)
		10,400
Attributable to taxable supplies	3,700	
Attributable to exempt supplies	1,600	
		(5,300)
		5,100

2. The percentage of recoverable input tax is then calculated:
Value of taxable supplies is £68,500. (71,000 - 1,500 - 1,000)
Value of all supplies is £98,500. (68,500 + 30,000)
Putting these figures into the formula:

$$\frac{68,500}{98,500} \times 100 = 69.54\%, \text{ rounded up to } 70\%$$

3. The recoverable input tax is therefore:

	£
Proportion of residual input tax relating to taxable supplies i.e. 5,100 x 70%	3,570
Input tax already attributable to taxable supplies	3,700
Total recoverable	7,270

For the application of the de minimis limits see ¶2194.

D. Special methods

1. Scope

2148 The prerequisite for using a special method is that it must give not only a fair and reasonable result but also a fairer and more reasonable result than the standard method, through accurately reflecting the use of expenditure made by the business.

HMRC will agree a combined special method which covers both **UK and foreign** supplies, where this gives a fair and reasonable result.

A business may also use a single special method which takes account not only of exempt and taxable use, but also elements of **non-business use**.

Examples of circumstances where a special method would be **appropriate** include:
– a delay in using purchases; and
– a business which undertakes two or more activities, one labour-intensive (not using any input tax), the other using most of the bought-in purchases.

SI 1995/2518 reg 103 MEMO POINTS 1. A combined special method can include all **overseas supplies** which a business makes that would be taxable if made in the UK (e.g. advertising services), provided that this is clearly stated in the proposal (¶2172).
2. However, a **combined method** will still **exclude** input tax relating to:
– supplies of investment gold; and
– financial instruments.

Basis

2150 SI 1995/2518 reg 102 In general, a special method will dictate how the:
a. direct attribution is undertaken; and
b. apportionment is then achieved.

In large businesses a third stage may be inserted in between **a**. and **b**. above, where a **business can allocate** its non-attributable input tax across cost centres or departments. The input tax so allocated can then be recovered at separate recovery rates applying to each cost centre or department, depending on the level of taxable activity in that sector. The basis of allocation must be stated in the method and could, for example, include staff numbers or floor areas. The recovery rates for each centre might also be calculated by using different criteria. For example, one department might use output values and another use transaction counts.

VAT groups may wish to utilise a method based on the separate legal entities, or on cost centres which may be spread across the different companies involved. Renegotiation of a special method may be required on reorganisation. Intra-group supplies must be ignored under any special method.

EXAMPLE A garage has the following separate departments:
- new and used car sales involving taxable sales of cars and exempt financial services;
- servicing and parts; and
- a forecourt shop.

Residual input tax could be allocated using the number of staff working in each department, before being apportioned at a recovery rate set for each department based on output values

Fair and reasonable

The resulting apportionment must be fair and reasonable (and indeed the business must make a declaration to this effect (¶2170)), which **means** that: **2152** Notice 706 para 3.9
- the method reflects all of the business activities;
- it is possible to apply and easy to check; and
- the apportionment reflects the actual use made of the supplies.

Deciding on what is fair and reasonable is subjective and is not an absolute concept, as it depends on the available alternatives. *Merchant Navy Officers Pension Fund Trustees Ltd and Merchant Navy Ratings Pension Fund Ltd* [1996] (VTD 14262)

In a tribunal case, the overall outcome of the partial exemption method, and particularly whether the parties involved liked the result, said little about its fairness. *The University Court of the University of Glasgow* [2005] (VTD 19052)

The **onus** is therefore on the business to show why its chosen method does exhibit these characteristics. In addition, certain trade bodies have agreed methods with HMRC, although every business is free to choose its own calculation. For example, in May 2013 HMRC agreed with the British Universities Finance Directors' Group and the Higher Education Funding Council for England the latest version of its guidance on partial exemption special methods for higher education institutions (flmemo.co.uk/vm2154a). An equivalent for housing associations was originally agreed in November 2013 although it is a rolling document (flmemo.co.uk/vm2154b). **2154**

HMRC will also expect the method not to be inordinately **complex**, as this would create a disproportionate amount of work for both the business and HMRC, and could increase the risk of error. Ideally, a method will be closely aligned with the business, so it can be demonstrated to give a fair reflection of its transactions on an ongoing basis.

MEMO POINTS Other **industry sectors** which have agreed aspects of apportionment include: Notice 700/57
- banks and building societies;
- brewers;
- finance houses;
- insurance;
- Lloyd's underwriters; and
- investment and unit trusts.

Where there is **unfairness**, the chosen method may be subject to an override and another method may need to be applied in future. HMRC has the power to change any method where VAT avoidance is occurring, or where it believes that a method does not produce a fair result. However, the rules do not allow any temporary or provisional method to be imposed by either the business or HMRC. **2156** Notice 706 para 3.10

2. Types of methods

As each method is bespoke, its details will depend on the nature of the agreement reached with HMRC. It is very important that the reliability of the method is reviewed frequently, to ensure that the results are still fair (¶2170). **2158**

The input allocation should be based on the actual use made of the various costs.

Calculation

2160 Notice 706 para 6.7 Whatever the basis for the special method, the **percentage recovery rate** must be expressed to at least two decimal places. *Royal Bank of Scotland Group plc v HMRC (No 6)* [2008]

A special method cannot be structured so that none of the residual tax is recoverable. *Ampleforth Abbey Trust* [1998] (VTD 15763)

Apportionment

2162 HMRC will **not accept** any method which involves sampling or fixed percentages, as neither of these bases is reactive to business changes.

The actual apportionment **could**, however, **use** any of the following:

Notice 706 para 6.6
- numbers of transactions;
- time of staff involved in each activity (¶2164);
- headcount;
- outputs;
- input tax or purchases;
- cost centre allocations (¶2166);
- floor area, with certain caveats (¶2168); or
- information contained in management accounts.

MEMO POINTS 1. The use of an **input tax basis** may require that the residual input tax itself is included in the formula.

PE45500 2. If records are missing to support **historical claims**, HMRC will accept an estimated recovery method, perhaps based on the entries in the financial statements.

EXAMPLE G Ltd makes the following supplies:

	Turnover £	No of transactions
Taxable supplies	1m	3
Exempt supplies	4m	7
	5m	10

The total input tax incurred is £365,000, attributed as follows:

	Input tax £
Attributable to taxable supplies	100,000
Attributable to exempt supplies	180,000
Residual	85,000
	365,000

G Ltd proposes the following methods to HMRC:
1. Taxable input tax/total input tax; or
2. Transaction

If no special method is agreed, the standard method will apply.

Method	Calculation	Apportioned to taxable supplies £
1. Input tax	$85,000 \times \frac{100,000}{365,000}$	23,288
2. Transaction	85,000 x 3/10	25,500
3. Standard	85,000 x 1m/5m	17,000

If either of the first two methods gives a fair and reasonable result, the input tax recovery will be greater than using the standard method.

2164 **Staff** For staff time, it is obviously imperative that staff do in fact record their time accurately. This method is often appropriate where time sheets are used for the overall business purpose (e.g. in accountancy or the legal profession), rather than imposed just for operating the special method.

Where information on staff time is not available, **headcount** may be used instead, particularly where staff are employed in exclusively taxable or exclusively exempt areas.

Cost centres Cost centres are used by bigger companies which have the resource of an in-house accounts department. **Expenditure is allocated** to different departments and VAT is apportioned in the same way. Costs allocated to departments which support the main activities of the business are then reallocated to the income-producing departments. 2166

EXAMPLE

1. HMRC disputed a bank's existing special method because it believed that the recovery of VAT on overheads did not relate to the actual use of such costs. To review the bank's allocation of costs to different areas of the business when the bank was not considering VAT, HMRC issued a formal notice demanding to see management accounts.
It was held that HMRC was under a duty to ensure the special method was giving a fair and reasonable result; thus the bank should produce the management accounts. *Lloyds TSB Group plc* [2005] (VTD 19330)

2. H Ltd has identified four departments and allocated input tax as follows on the basis of cost.

Department	Input tax allocated	Relating to Dept A	Relating to Dept B	Reapportion input tax from admin	Reapportion input tax from overheads	Total input tax
	£			£	£	£
A	10,000	100%	0%	5,000	14,000	29,000
B	30,000	0%	100%	5,000	6,000	41,000
Admin	10,000	50%	50%	(10,000)	-	-
Overheads	20,000	70%	30%	-	(20,000)	-
Total	70,000			Nil	Nil	70,000

Now that the input tax has been reallocated to the two main departments, the input tax can be attributed to taxable and exempt supplies.
Dept A makes wholly taxable supplies; Dept B makes both types of supplies; input tax is to be apportioned based on the level of supplies made. In the last quarter, taxable supplies were 40% of the total supplies.

Department		Attributable to taxable supplies		Attributable to exempt supplies
		£		£
A		29,000		-
B	(£41,000 x 40%)	16,400	(£41,000 x 60%)	24,600
Total		45,400		24,600

H Ltd can therefore recover input tax of £45,400 for this quarter.

Floor space Floor area can be used as a basis where most of the: 2168 Business Brief 34/04
- VATable costs relate to premises; and
- floor area is used either for wholly taxable or wholly exempt activities, with only minor areas relating to both.

HMRC has stated that floor area will seldom be appropriate for **retailers** because:
- there are often substantial mixed use areas (for both taxable and exempt supplies), and any allocation of floor area is purely notional and therefore unsubstantiated;
- zoning (where certain areas are given relative weight based on their notional rental values (¶2182)) should be ignored; and
- taxable and exempt supplies (such as insurance offered with products) are often advertised and sold in many areas of the same premises.

HMRC will refuse any floor-based method which has any features of the above.

EXAMPLE An existing floor-based method was cancelled because:
- the method allowed each group company to calculate the recovery percentage based on a representative sample, including new companies which joined the group after the sample had been calculated;
- this was a floor-based method, but only a minority of floor space was included in the calculation;
- the attribution of floor space to taxable and exempt supplies was not fair;
- the method used zoning, which also did not give a fair result; and
- although a large proportion of sales were exempt, the input tax attributed to exempt supplies was a very small proportion of the total input tax. *Banbury Visionplus Ltd v HMRC* [2006]

Obtaining approval

2170 SI 1995/2518 reg 102(9)-(16); PE42500

HMRC will not approve an application unless the business makes a declaration that to the best of its knowledge and belief the method will produce a fair and reasonable recovery of input tax.

MEMO POINTS 1. A **declaration** is required every time a new method is approved, or an existing one is amended. The declaration must confirm that the whole method produces a fair result (both from the effective date of its application and for the foreseeable future) based on knowledge that the person making the declaration could reasonably be expected to know at the time. That person must have sufficient authority and also an adequate understanding of the business and the way its costs are used. Whilst a third party could prepare the declaration, the business remains responsible for its contents.
2. HMRC has issued guidance on the meaning of **reasonably be expected to know at the time** and would consider all available facts and the steps taken by the person before signing the declaration. These steps might include some of the following (the extent of work undertaken by the signatory will depend on the situation and is a matter of professional judgement; although no evidence of action taken is required, it would prove useful in any appeal, etc):
- referring to published guidance on partial exemption;
- communicating with senior managers about planned events which might affect cost allocation;
- taking account of remarks made by auditors, advisors and HMRC during visits to the business, and also any correspondence concerning partial exemption;
- enquiring about new types of income or any changes in expenditure patterns;
- where relevant, maintaining a list of cost drivers (e.g. floor space, departments, etc);
- ensuring that business structure changes (such as mergers, acquisitions and disposals) are reflected within the method; and
- communicating with HMRC if there are any doubts about how partial exemption applies in a particular situation and also notifying it of any risks or issues.
3. If HMRC considers that the **declaration is incorrect** (i.e. the method is not fair, leading to an over-recovery of input tax, and the signatory could reasonably have known this at the time), it can serve an override notice (¶2188) to require the business to operate partial exemption on the basis of use, which would also affect any capital goods scheme adjustments. Under these circumstances, this notice can have effect from the method's inception (subject to the usual 4-year limit). The business may appeal against such a notice; also against any related assessments. Interest and penalties may become due.
4. If the **business discovers** that the **declaration is incorrect**, it should voluntarily disclose this and HMRC will serve a notice as in **3**. above, although HMRC may agree to a new proposed special method instead.

2171 **Informal stage** If the trader is airing a **draft special method** before making a firm proposal, no declaration should be made until the special method has been finalised.

Indeed, it is always advisable to discuss initial ideas with HMRC on an informal basis.

2172 Notice 706 para 6.2

Application A business must write to the local VAT office with details of the **proposed method**, stating:
- the business activities, including the frequency of transactions;
- the supplies to be made and how the costs incurred relate to those supplies;
- an outline of the method, with a worked example taking figures from the actual business where possible; and
- the date when the method will first be implemented.

If HMRC considers that a proposed method:
– can be **approved**, HMRC will write giving details of the agreed method. Usually the business must give an undertaking to keep HMRC informed of any changes in circumstances which will affect input tax recovery; or
– **cannot be approved**, it will discuss this with the business and invite a new proposal and declaration.

The special method will be **rendered invalid** where the business withholds relevant information, or where HMRC subsequently shows that the business made a declaration knowing it to be untrue. In the latter case, HMRC can require a recalculation of recoverable input tax from when the method first took effect, which could go back 4 years.

It is important that the **business is clear** on the details of the approved method, as any areas of doubt could lead to difficulties in recovering certain amounts of input tax. It is not possible for changes to a method to be applied retrospectively, although see ¶2176. **2174** PE47000

In addition, HMRC will approve a new method, even though the old method already gave a fair and reasonable result.

EXAMPLE

1. The approved special method stated that the university's published accounts could be used. As these were consolidated accounts, they did not reflect supplies made by the university to its subsidiaries. HMRC argued that the agreed special method did not allow the use of consolidated accounts.
It was held that HMRC knew or ought to have known that the university was using consolidated accounts and that the method agreed and operated for several years assumed the use of those accounts. The tribunal concluded that the university had correctly applied the agreed special method. *University of Bristol* [2001] (VTD 17316)

2. A bank had been permitted to adopt a special method. It assigned a number of doubtful debts; if these transactions were included in the apportionment calculation, the recoverable input tax would be substantially increased.
HMRC conceded that it had no power to alter the special method retrospectively, but contended that its terms could exclude the assignments. In particular, the preamble to the special method agreement stated that the bank could adopt the method subject to certain conditions, which would have excluded the assigned debts had they been sufficiently defined.
It was held that the conditions in the preamble were preliminary to the adoption of the special method. The main body of the agreement clearly stated that the supplies to be excluded were those set out in an annex, which did not include the assignment of debts. Hence the debts were correctly part of the calculation. *Barclays Bank plc* [1991] (VTD 5616)

3. After method agreed

Change of circumstances

Where a business is **already using** a special method, HMRC must be notified where there is a change in the business circumstances, such as a new branch opening up. For a VAT group, this would include any change in the membership of the group that affects input tax recovery. **2176** Notice 706 para 6.8

The existing method may still be appropriate. If not, an amendment will be required which has the effect of imposing a new method. An override notice or direction may be issued by HMRC.

MEMO POINTS 1. If an **under-recovery** of input tax results from the existing method, the business can apply for a new method to have effect from the start of the current VAT year. Exceptionally, a new method can be backdated 3 years where extraordinary events occur (e.g. a foot and mouth outbreak).
2. If the method needs to change as a result of **new case law** or a change in statute, no override notice (¶2188) will be issued, although action may be taken subsequently where the business does not respond to the change appropriately.

EXAMPLE The university's special partial exemption method did not take account of a recurrent grant, which was the subject of debate with HMRC. The special method was officially withdrawn with effect from 31 July 1997, although that method was to continue to be used in the meantime, until superseded by a new method, which would then be backdated in its application to 1 August 1997. In November 1997 HMRC stated that a recovery rate of 10% would be used with effect from 1 August 1997. However, 10% was actually too low as a percentage, so the university submitted fresh claims in October 2001 for the previous 3 years. HMRC argued that the special method had been replaced by the 10% method, so the university had no further entitlement.
It was held that a 10% rate was not a new special method; a particular method could not be withdrawn if the result was to force a taxpayer to use a less satisfactory one. As HMRC stated that it would only agree a new method which included the grant income, this was held to be unreasonable and unfair, so that the current special method remained in operation. *University of Exeter* [2003] (VTD 18117)

2178 PE22000 Where a business is **using sectors** and a change occurs, such that a new sector is created, the special method may fail to specify how input tax allocated to the new sector is to be apportioned. This can be anticipated by including a provision in the special method agreement which requires that any such input tax is apportioned on the basis of use. Otherwise, the standard method will apply to that input tax only. If this is unsatisfactory, the business should propose a new special method, including the new sector, as soon as possible.

EXAMPLE Input tax recovery under a special method was agreed as follows:

Type of income	Related input tax treatment
Taxable income from sales in charity shops	Recoverable
Exempt income from care homes	Direct attribution and then apportioned on basis of whether: – headquarters' VAT; or – homes' repair VAT
Small amount of taxable income from care homes (e.g. payphone income)	
Non-business income such as donations	Excluded

The company argued that there was a gap in the special method, because some input tax incurred at the care homes was not homes' repair input tax, so the standard method therefore applied to this input tax.
It was held that the phrase "homes' repair input tax" was a term which covered all home-related input tax not already dealt with under the special method. The input tax in question should therefore be treated as covered by the special method. *Sue Ryder Care* [2004] (VTD 18826)

4. HMRC powers

2180 Special methods are usually the subject of negotiation between HMRC and the taxpayer. Unfortunately this procedure can break down where the proposed method is unsatisfactory, or where the current method is perceived to result in the loss of VAT. In such cases HMRC has a number of powers.

Refusal to approve

2182 PE42500 HMRC may refuse a special method where:
- it does not reflect the use of the input tax bearing costs;
- it does not guarantee a more accurate result than the standard method;
- the method cannot be checked by HMRC; or
- it is not comprehensive, so that not all of the incurred input tax is included.

EXAMPLE It was agreed that the standard partial exemption method was fair and reasonable for all of an optician's inputs, except certain property costs. The optician proposed that the input tax relating to property costs should be apportioned on the basis of zoning, which attached more importance to the front retail area part of the shop (because the notional rental value of that area was higher than the notional rental value of the back of the shop). As the front area was used

mainly to make taxable supplies, the input tax recovery would be greater than if floor area alone had been used as the basis. This method was rejected.
It was held that zoning was not a valid basis for apportioning input tax. It was irrelevant that the standard method did not give a fair and reasonable result, and that any method proposed would therefore potentially be an improvement. The important issue was whether there was any direct connection between input tax recovery and the purpose of the purchases; the proposed method did not achieve this result. HMRC had therefore acted reasonably in rejecting the method. *Optika* [2003] (VTD 18627)

Directed method

HMRC has the power to direct a business to use a particular method, or to stop a method being used, although **not in respect of** supplies where input tax is specifically recoverable (¶2098). Directions must be clear. **2183** SI 1995/2518 reg 102(4); Notice 706 para 6.9

Such directions will be **issued only** where a change cannot be negotiated, or where HMRC perceives that the VAT system is being abused. Often they only come into force at a future date, unless there is a significant amount of VAT at risk.

Directions are subject to appeal (¶4260) and there is no penal intention in their use.

In order to issue a direction and ensure the stipulated method is a fair and reasonable one, HMRC will need to have sufficient **information** about the business. **2184**

It is not possible for HMRC to direct a business to stop using a special method where the result is even less appropriate.

Where HMRC directs that a **special method is no longer to be used**:
- the standard method will apply unless a new special method is agreed; and
- if the standard method is less appropriate, the special method still applies.

Merchant Navy Officers Pension Fund Trustees Ltd and Merchant Navy Ratings Pension Fund Ltd [1996] (VTD 14262)

EXAMPLE HMRC was held to have acted reasonably in directing a special method to be used where it had:
- considered all the proposals made by the company and explained why they were inappropriate;
- discussed the proposals with the company;
- invited further proposals; and
- indicated its intention to make a direction with sufficient notice.

BMW (GB) Ltd [1997] (VTD 14823)

A directed method may be **replaced** by another special method proposed by the trader. This will normally be appropriate, as a business tends to change with time. **2185**

Override notices

Special method override notices are very rare. They may be served by HMRC, or submitted for approval by the business. **2188** Business Brief 27/03; Notice 706 para 8

The **purpose** of the notice is to make a correction because the existing special method no longer gives a fair and reasonable result. As a replacement method usually takes time to prepare and approve, the notice facilitates the rectification of the position in the meantime. As such, the notice is designed to be a temporary measure only. Indeed it is intended to motivate both parties into the negotiation of a new permanent method.

HMRC will **only serve** a notice where it:
- has clear evidence that the current special method does not fairly and reasonably reflect the principle of use;
- is satisfied that the time needed for the preparation of a replacement method would result in either the business or itself losing out; and
- has decided that direction of a special method is not appropriate.

MEMO POINTS 1. A notice will **expire** once another method has been agreed, which could include the use of the standard method. Notice 706 para 8.6

Notice 706 para 8.4

2. A notice must **state**:
- that it is a special method override notice;
- the date from which it is to take effect; and
- the reasons why the special method already in use is no longer appropriate.

In addition, any notice served by HMRC must state its effect.

2189 Notice 706 para 8.5

On **receipt** of a notice the business must continue to use its special method, but make a subsequent adjustment. This adjustment is based on the actual use of the expenditure on which the input tax is incurred for any VAT periods beginning on or after the date stated on the notice. The override also applies to the part of an annual adjustment (¶2202) that falls after the date stated on the notice. Where a notice of correction is not made by the business, HMRC may issue a VAT assessment to give effect to the correction.

2190

Appeals can be made to a tribunal (¶4262) against:
- the serving of a notice by HMRC;
- the decision not to approve a notice; or
- any VAT assessments made under the notice.

E. De minimis limits

2194 SI 1995/2518 regs 106, 106A; Notice 706 para 11

These limits are applied when calculating the recoverable input tax on every VAT return and also for the annual adjustment. They are useful for small businesses which incur only minimal amounts of VAT in making exempt supplies.

If **total exempt input tax** (including the exempt proportion of residual input tax and any exempt input tax relating to reverse charges on imported services) is below the de minimis limits (broadly £7,500 p.a.), it is treated as taxable input tax and therefore provisionally recoverable in full. This is an all or nothing test. Whatever the results during the year, the annual adjustment calculation must still be made and the results checked against the limits (¶2202).

Any **capital goods scheme adjustments** are ignored for this purpose.

Thresholds

2195

If the business has exempt supplies which are less than 50% of total supplies, an optional simplification is available.

MEMO POINTS 1. For the purposes of all the de minimis tests, **input tax** excludes any VAT incurred for non-business purposes and blocked input tax.
2. When calculating the **annual adjustment**, the average input tax is measured over the year.
3. For **VAT groups** the limits apply to the group as a whole.
Notice 706 para 15.3
4. A **divisional registration** (¶2744) will not be approved where the entity's exempt input tax exceeds the de minimis limits. Where an entity which is registered in divisions exceeds these limits, it likely that the registration will be cancelled.

2196 SI 1995/2518 reg 105A; Information Sheet 4/10

Exempt supplies less than 50% of total supplies Businesses for which exempt supplies are less than 50% of total supplies have the option to apply either of the following two de minimis tests, both on a VAT period and on an annual basis.

Either:
- **total input tax** must be less than £625 per month on average; or
- **total input tax less input tax directly attributable to taxable supplies** must be less than £625 per month on average.

SI 1995/2518 reg 106ZA

Passing the tests on an **annual basis** permits provisional recovery of all input tax for the whole of the next year (provided that input tax is not expected to exceed £1 million), again subject to review on an annual basis at the end of the year. Of course, if the annual adjustment for the next year shows that the business is not in fact within the de minimis limits, a payment would then be due to HMRC.

If **both of the new tests are failed** at any time, the normal tests can be carried out (¶2197) and if they are passed, full recovery of input tax can proceed.

All businesses To be recoverable, the limits which **exempt input tax** must not exceed under the **normal tests** are: 2197 SI 1995/2518 reg 106
- £625 per month on average (£7,500 per annum), measured over the VAT period; and
- 50% of all input tax in the VAT period.

EXAMPLE Taking the figures from the example at ¶2146, the de minimis limits are applied to Ms F's exempt input tax:

	£
Residual input tax relating to exempt supplies (£5,100 - £3,570)	1,530
Input tax already attributable to exempt supplies	1,600
	3,130
Monthly average (£3,130/3)	1,043
One half of total input tax for period (£10,400/2)	5,200

Even though the total exempt input tax does not exceed half of the total input tax, the monthly average limit of £625 is exceeded, so none of it can be recovered.

Application in practice

Traders cannot choose to recognise invoices late in their accounting records in order to **manipulate** the limits. 2198

EXAMPLE A partnership incurred refurbishment costs on properties which were to be let (an exempt supply). The related input tax for the year was £7,464.82, which is just below the de minimis limit of £7,500.
When the VAT officer visited, however, he found input tax of £412.68 had not been included in the amount above. The partnership stated that:
- at the year end, it was not certain that one of the properties would be let again (an exempt supply); and
- the extra amount was put on a credit card before the year end but only paid and reimbursed to a partner after the year end.
HMRC argued that the partner had been acting on behalf of the partnership when the costs were incurred. In addition, the cost was incurred before the year end as it was the credit card voucher date which was important. The partnership then tried to argue that the amount was so close to the de minimis limit that, in any event, the exempt input tax should be recovered.
It was held that the exempt input tax was above the de minimis limit, so none was recoverable. It is an all or nothing test which must be strictly applied. *The Little Bradley Farm Partnership* [2003] (VTD 18420)

F. Annual adjustment

Recovery of input tax under partial exemption methods in each VAT period is provisional and is subject to review, usually at the end of the VAT year. A partly exempt trader must therefore make an adjustment at the end of the VAT year (which will end in March, April or May, depending on the VAT return stagger (¶2990)) and enter this adjustment on the VAT return immediately following the end of the VAT year. 2202 SI 1995/2518 reg 107; Notice 706 para 12

This means that any fluctuations in the levels of taxable and exempt supplies are smoothed out. It also gives traders the opportunity to review their use of supplies in light of further experience. For example, a trader may initially intend to use goods for taxable supplies but, some months later, the goods are actually used for exempt supplies.

MEMO POINTS 1. It may be easier for the trader to align the VAT year with the **accounting year end**.
2. A trader who submits **monthly returns** will have a VAT year ending on 31 March.
3. Annual adjustments are not the **correction of errors**. Where input tax has been incorrectly treated in previous VAT periods, these should be corrected using the normal procedures (¶3014) and not via the annual adjustment. *Greenpeace Ltd* [2000] (VTD 16681)
4. Traders who are using the **annual accounting scheme** (¶4745+) will not need to make a separate annual adjustment.

Using the standard method

2204 The same calculation as has already been completed for each VAT period (¶2128) is performed on an annual basis, using the same formula but incorporating the **values** of outputs for the whole VAT year. The adjustment is the difference between the cumulative amount of input tax recovered in each VAT period and the amount calculated as recoverable based on the VAT year or longer period.

The business should also compare the annual exempt input tax with the **de minimis limits** (¶2194) to check whether it can all be treated as recoverable input tax.

Traders using the standard method have the **option** to bring forward the annual adjustment calculation and declare it on the last **VAT return** of the VAT year.

EXAMPLE Mr A has the following input tax information for the VAT year ended 31 March. Input tax attributable to exempt supplies is £10,000, so the de minimis limit is exceeded.

Quarter ended	**Recovered residual input tax**	**Unrecovered residual input tax**	**Total residual input tax**
	£	£	£
30 June	4,675	1,575	6,250
30 Sept	4,000	900	4,900
31 Dec	5,000	1,025	6,025
31 Mar	5,000	-	5,000
Total	18,675	3,500	22,175

Mr A makes the following supplies during the year:

	£
Taxable supplies	517,000
Exempt supplies	150,000
Total	667,000

The recoverable input tax for the year is calculated using the following percentage:
517,000/667,000 = 78% (rounded up)
£22,175 x 78% = £17,297
Total input tax already recovered is £18,675 (from the table above).
So Mr A owes £1,378 to HMRC. (18,675 - 17,297)

EXAMPLE B Ltd has the following input tax information for the VAT year ended 30 April.

Quarter ended	**Recovered residual input tax**	**Unrecovered residual input tax**	**Total residual input tax**	**Exempt input tax**	**Taxable input tax**
	£	£	£	£	£
31 July	3,675	-	3,675	525	7,000
31 Oct	3,000	-	3,000	1,040	10,000
31 Jan	4,000	2,025	6,025	2,000	13,000
30 April	3,000	-	3,000	430	14,000
Total	13,675	2,025	15,700	3,995	44,000

B Ltd makes the following supplies during the year:

	£
Taxable supplies	617,000
Exempt supplies	150,000
Total	767,000

The recoverable residual input tax for the year is calculated using the following percentage:
617,000/767,000 = 81% (rounded up)
£15,700 x 81% = £12,717
This leaves £2,983 which is apportioned to exempt input tax. (15,700 - 12,717)
The total exempt input tax is therefore £6,978 (3,995 + 2,983), which is below the annual de minimis limit of £7,500.

Therefore B Ltd can recover all input tax incurred.
During the VAT year B Ltd has recovered £57,675. (13,675 + 44,000)
The total recoverable is £63,695. (15,700 + 3,995 + 44,000)
The annual adjustment is therefore £6,020 repayable by HMRC. (63,695 - 57,675)

If HMRC agrees a **change in VAT year** with the taxpayer, this will affect the timing of the annual adjustment. Taxpayers in this situation should follow the specific advice of HMRC. 2210

EXAMPLE A college used the standard method but omitted to make the annual adjustments required. The longer period by reference to which the annual adjustments should have been made was the VAT year ending on 30 April.
The mistake was discovered during a control visit. An assessment was made on the basis of a VAT year ending on 31 July, coinciding with the college's financial year. The college appealed on the basis that the annual adjustments were made for the wrong accounting periods. It also argued that any change could not operate retrospectively. HMRC contended that the college had agreed to the VAT officer's suggestion that the VAT year be altered, even though there was no written record.
It was held that HMRC had the power to approve a retrospective change of VAT year where no annual adjustment had been made. A change could therefore be agreed and approved informally; an oral agreement in the course of discussions during a control visit was sufficient. *Puskin College* [2000] (VTD 16726)

Using a special method

The same procedure applies to the special method as for the standard method, unless the **approval letter** for a special method states otherwise. Where a special method is changed, this may occur during the VAT year if the method is not applied retrospectively. A mid-year adjustment will then be required. Where relevant, details of how this is to be dealt with should be included in an amendment to the special method agreement. 2212

Adjustment periods

In some circumstances the annual adjustment will occur at a **shorter or longer interval than a year**. In this situation the de minimis limits will be pro rated. 2214 SI 1995/2518 reg 99; Notice 706 paras 12.7 - 12.9; PE37200

Newly partly exempt traders should also see ¶2127.

Circumstance of trader		Length of review period	Adjustment required
Continuing trader	Becomes partly exempt in the VAT year	Begins on the first day of the VAT period when the exempt input tax[1] was first incurred and runs to the last day of the VAT year	Yes, unless became partly exempt in last VAT period of VAT year, in which case no adjustment is made
Newly registered on time	Incurs exempt input tax immediately	Begins on effective date of registration and runs to the day before the start of the first VAT year	Yes
	Incurs exempt input tax later on	Begins on the first day exempt input tax[1] incurred and runs to the day before the start of the first VAT year	Yes
Newly registered but late	First return covers a period in excess of a year	Break period down into: – period before VAT year starts; and – subsequent VAT years; then follow rules for newly registered on time	Yes
Deregisters		Begins day after the end of the final elapsed VAT year and runs until the date of deregistration	Yes - on final VAT return

Note:
1. The reference to **exempt input tax** includes any that is within the de minimis limits.

EXAMPLE

1. C Ltd incurs exempt input tax for the first time on 20 October 2013. It has a VAT year which ends on 31 May.
The first quarter for which apportionment needs to be completed ends on 30 November 2013; the annual adjustment will take into account the period from 1 September 2013 to 31 May 2014.

2. D Ltd registers on time on 1 December 2013 and is allocated a VAT year ending on 30 April by HMRC.
If D Ltd incurs exempt input tax immediately, the first annual adjustment will be for the period from 1 December 2013 to 30 April 2014.
If D Ltd does not incur exempt input tax until 1 January 2014, the annual adjustment period will run from 1 January 2014 to 30 April 2014.

3. E Ltd was required to register with effect from 1 October 2012 but did not actually register until 25 January 2014. HMRC therefore backdates the registration and allocate the business a VAT year ending on 31 March.
The first VAT return will cover the period from 1 October 2012 to 31 March 2014. This period is split into the registration period (1 October 2012 to 31 March 2013) and the first VAT year (1 April 2013 to 31 March 2014).
If E Ltd first incurs exempt input tax on 20 January 2013, no annual adjustment is required, as this is the last VAT period in the registration period.

4. F Ltd, whose last VAT year ended on 31 March, deregisters on the following 27 August.
The period of the final annual adjustment will run from 1 April to 27 August.

Reporting

2218 Any adjustment (whether positive or negative) may be **adjusted for** in box 4 on the first VAT return of the new VAT year, although traders using the standard method may choose to include it on the last VAT return of the current VAT year (without prior notification to HMRC).

MEMO POINTS 1. HMRC will agree to the annual adjustment being made on a **later return** where the business has difficulty in completing the calculation earlier and has made an application in writing.
2. For **details** of VAT returns in general see ¶2985.

G. Other adjustments

2222 The recovery of input tax is based on the **intended use** of the goods or services at the time when they are received. If that intention changes, or the actual use does not reflect the initial intention, an adjustment may be required. For certain capital items, further adjustments under the capital goods scheme are required for the next 5 or 10 years (¶2280).

The issue or receipt of **credit notes** can also create the need for an adjustment. Occasionally, HMRC can issue an override notice to a business using the standard method, where the usual calculation is not resulting in a fair recovery.

Where the VAT **liability of a supply changes** because the law is altered, no retrospective adjustment is required.

1. Change from the original intended use

2224 SI 1995/2518 regs 108, 109; Notice 706 para 13

It may be the case that an asset intended for one use at the time of purchase is never used in the originally intended way but is used in a different way. Where this happens **within** 6 years, an adjustment must be made. For example, an asset may have been intended for wholly taxable supplies, although never actually used until year 4, when the asset is utilised for making a combination of taxable and exempt supplies. This has particular relevance for land and buildings (¶5614+).

However, a **change in actual use** does not require any adjustment (unless the asset involved is being accounted for under the capital goods scheme (¶2280)). For example, a machine is used for taxable supplies for the first 3 years and is then used for exempt supplies. No adjustment would be required in this case, because the machine has been in actual use throughout.

MEMO POINTS 1. The 6-year **period starts** from the beginning of the VAT period when the original intention was formed i.e. the VAT period when the related input tax was first recognised.
2. The same **method** as would have been used in the original attribution/apportionment must be used.

EXAMPLE
1. A flat was refurbished with the intention of letting it as taxable holiday accommodation. After a fortnight of letting, the flat was sold to a director of the company.
As there had been a supply of taxable holiday letting, all of the input tax was still recoverable. This was a change of use, not a change of intention. *Pembridge Estates* [1992] (VTD 9606)

2. A company incurred input tax in relation to vacant properties. The properties remained empty for a while until they were eventually leased. After 5 years had passed, the company opted to tax the property and tried to reclaim input tax for the previous 5-year period, on the basis that there had been a change in the intended use of the properties.
It was held that this input tax was not recoverable, because it had already been consumed before the option to tax was effective. At the outset the company had not decided whether it would make taxable or exempt supplies. It was not possible to link input tax incurred during an exempt supply to a subsequent period when taxable supplies were being made. *Royal and Sun Alliance Insurance Group plc v C & E* [2003]

3. A charity purchased a building, originally intending to use the building 50% for non-business activities, 50% for exempt business purposes. No VAT was recovered on the purchase. Approximately 3 years later the charity changed its intention before bringing the building into use, deciding to use it 100% for business purposes. As the charity had changed its intention within 6 years of incurring the input VAT, it made a claim to recover 100% of the VAT originally incurred.
The claim was rejected in part, as the 50% relating to the intended non-business use was not recoverable. *Wellcome Trust* [2008] (VTD 20731)

Temporary change

A temporary change in use must also be taken into account, although this will often **result** in the input tax being apportioned, perhaps on a time basis. 2226

For complications arising when **letting** immovable property see ¶5256.

EXAMPLE
1. A company renovated a listed office building, intending to grant a long lease of 25 years (which would have been zero-rated at the time). However, a tenant could only initially be found for an exempt 4-year lease.
It was held that the input tax should be apportioned so that only 4/29ths of the input tax was exempt input tax, because the company still intended to grant a long lease in excess of 21 years. *C & E v Briararch Ltd* [1992]

2. A company had intended to make a taxable supply in the form of a sale of a building. However, when work on the building was completed, it was impossible to find a purchaser, so the company granted an exempt lease, whilst maintaining its intention eventually to make a taxable supply.
The supplies, in respect of which the input tax had been incurred, were not wholly used in making the exempt supplies, since the constant intention to make the taxable supplies still existed. In such a case, the input tax should be apportioned. *C & E v Curtis Henderson Ltd* [1992]

Aborted supplies

Input tax recovery relating to an aborted **taxable** supply will not need to be adjusted where no supply is made at all and the entire project is frustrated. However, where an **exempt** supply is made instead, this is treated as a change of use, so an adjustment must be made. 2228

Where **advance payment** is made for a supply which is never made, no input tax can be recovered (¶1952).

Comment Aborted supplies typically occur during **property development** projects, which are dependent on various factors outside the control of the developer (¶5616).

EXAMPLE A company incurred input tax when arranging for a coal terminal to be built, which was then compulsorily purchased by the authorities before it could be put to taxable use. The costs were therefore wasted. The tax authorities demanded repayment of the input tax, because the goods and services in question had never been used to make taxable supplies.
It was held that a taxable person was entitled to deduct input tax that had been incurred for the purpose of making taxable supplies. The test was applied when the input tax was incurred. Where unforeseen circumstances prevented the use of the goods or services in relation to taxable transactions, the right to deduct was not lost. *Belgium v Ghent Coal Terminal NV* [1998]

Action

2230 Where intended use changes, the clawback and payback provisions apply as shown in the following table.

Original intention	Revised intention/actual use	Provision applying
Wholly taxable supplies	Wholly exempt supplies	Clawback
	Combination	
Wholly exempt supplies	Wholly taxable supplies	Payback
	Combination	
Combination	Wholly taxable supplies	Payback
	Wholly exempt supplies	Clawback

2232 **Clawback** When a clawback provision applies, too much input tax has been recovered. The **revised** amount of input tax recoverable must be recalculated, based on the change of use but still using the same apportionment method. The amount overclaimed is entered on the VAT return for the period in which the change occurs.

EXAMPLE A construction company builds a residential property with the intention of making a taxable supply, incurring input tax of £20,000. As this is directly attributable to an intended taxable supply all of the input tax is recovered. However, because of poor market conditions, the property is let for 20 years instead, which is an exempt supply.
Because of the change from the intended use, input tax of £20,000 must be repaid under the clawback provisions.

2234 **Payback** When a payback provision applies, there has been an under-recovery of input tax. In this instance the **business must** write to HMRC with details of the amount repayable, calculated using the same apportionment method, but taking into account the change of use. Once this has been approved, the business can then make a corresponding entry on the next VAT return, or use form VAT652 (¶3024).

2. Credit notes

Received

2236 SI 1995/2518 reg 38; PE62750

If a credit note is received:

a. in the **same VAT period** as the original supply, the partial exemption calculation should be made using the adjusted input tax amount, taking both the original invoice and the credit note into account;

b. in a **subsequent VAT period**, but **within the same VAT year**, no adjustment is made when the note is received. However, the annual adjustment will take account of the reduced input tax; or

c. in a **different VAT year**, the annual adjustment originally made must be recalculated to take account of the credit note, comparing with the de minimis limits (¶2194) where appropriate. Any necessary amendment should be included on the VAT return for the period in which the credit note is received. This amendment must be recorded separately from the VAT period's normal partial exemption calculation.

Issued

If a credit note is issued: **2238**
a. in the **same VAT period** as the original supply, the partial exemption calculation should be completed with the amended value of supplies;
b. in a **subsequent VAT period**, but **within the same VAT year**, no adjustment is made when the note is issued, although the annual adjustment will take account of the amended supply value; or
c. in a **different VAT year**, the annual adjustment originally made must be recalculated to take account of the credit note, amending the value of supplies. Any necessary amendment should be included on the VAT return for the period in which the credit note is issued. This amendment must be recorded separately from the VAT period's normal partial exemption calculation.

3. Standard method override

Scope

The override, which is a one-off adjustment, is an anti-avoidance measure and only **affects** businesses with **residual input tax** of at least £50,000 per year (£25,000 for group companies outside a VAT group). It is intended to stop VAT being recovered under the standard method where this does not properly reflect the taxable use of the costs. However, in some cases the override can be beneficial. **2240** SI 1995/2518 reg 107A; Information Sheet 4/02; Notice 706 para 5

HMRC states that its application to businesses other than those abusing the system will be very rare. However, examples of innocent situations which can be caught would include:
- a small number of high-value transactions being incurred which do not consume much input tax; or
- where the trading pattern of a business changes.

MEMO POINTS 1. For **periods shorter than a year** the residual input tax limits are pro rated.
2. **Group company** means a company which must be included in consolidated accounts, or would be but for an accounting exemption. See *Accountancy and Financial Reporting Memo* for further details.

Calculation

An override adjustment must be made if the input tax deducted is substantially different from the amount which would have been deducted **based on** use, or intended use, in making taxable supplies during the year. A difference is **substantial** if it is at least £25,000 and exceeds the lower of: **2242**
- £50,000; and
- 50% of the residual input tax incurred.

The override is usually only relevant once the annual adjustment has been carried out.

Comment Situations where such a difference could occur **include** a timing delay between the acquisition of the goods or services and their actual use in the business, or an unusual business transaction. Of course, for some businesses, the use made of purchases bears no relation to the value of sales.

MEMO POINTS 1. When a business is **transferred as a going concern** (¶8646), use by any successor must also be taken into account.
2. Even where an override adjustment is made, the standard **method** must still be used unless another method is agreed with HMRC.

3. However, where a business is **applying the override regularly**, a special method should be considered which could cater to its own particular circumstances and therefore avoid the distortions occurring through the use of the standard method.

Measuring use

2246 Information Sheet 4/02 appendix 1

The measurement of use should be fair and reasonable.

Where there is a **timing delay** between acquisition and use, forecasts and budgets may be relevant.

EXAMPLE G Ltd incurs £250,000 of residual input tax on purchases which are to be used in the next VAT year.

The following details relate to the current VAT year:

	£	£
Relating wholly to taxable supplies	125,000	
Relating wholly to exempt supplies	75,000	
Residual input tax	600,000	
Total input tax		800,000
Value of taxable supplies	5,000,000	
Value of exempt supplies	4,000,000	
Value of total supplies		9,000,000

1. The standard method is applied.

Using the standard method, the proportion of residual input tax relating to taxable supplies is 56%: $\frac{5,000,000}{9,000,000}$ = 55.56% rounded up to 56%

So the recoverable residual input tax is £140,000 £250,000 x 56% = £140,000

2. In order to assess how much of the residual input tax should be recovered based on use, G Ltd needs to look at its forecast figures for the next year, which are:

	£	£
Value of taxable supplies	7,000,000	
Value of exempt supplies	1,000,000	
Value of total supplies		8,000,000

Using these figures, the proportion of residual input tax relating to taxable supplies is 88%: $\frac{7,000,000}{8,000,000}$ = 87.5% rounded up to 88%

The residual input tax relating to purchases to be used in the next VAT year is £250,000 and the recoverable amount is £220,000. £250,000 x 88% = £220,000

The difference between the recoverable input tax based on use (£220,000) and that calculated using the standard method (£140,000) is £80,000. As this is more than £50,000, the difference is substantial.

So G Ltd can claim an extra £80,000 as recoverable input tax.

2248 Information Sheet 4/02 appendix 2

Any **distorting transaction** should also be excluded.

EXAMPLE H Ltd makes £1,000,000 of taxable supplies which consume hardly any purchases (being very labour-intensive).

The other relevant details are:

	£	£
Input tax relating wholly to taxable supplies	125,000	
Input tax relating wholly to exempt supplies	75,000	
Residual input tax	150,000	
Total input tax		350,000
Value of taxable supplies	1,350,000	
Value of exempt supplies	550,000	
Value of total supplies		1,900,000
Value of machine used in the business and sold	200,000	

1. The standard method is applied as normal

The proportion of residual input tax relating to taxable supplies is rounded up to 68%:	$\frac{1{,}350{,}000 - 200{,}000}{1{,}900{,}000 - 200{,}000} = 67.65\%$
So the recoverable residual input tax is £102,000	£150,000 x 68% = £102,000

2. In order to assess how much of the residual input tax should be recovered based on use, H Ltd must exclude the non-consuming taxable supplies from the calculation:

The revised proportion of residual input tax relating to taxable supplies is rounded up to 22%:	$\frac{1{,}350{,}000 - 200{,}000 - 1{,}000{,}000}{1{,}900{,}000 - 200{,}000 - 1{,}000{,}000} = 21.43\%$
The total recoverable residual input tax is £33,000.	£150,000 x 22% = £33,000

The difference between the recoverable residual input tax based on use (£33,000) and that calculated using the standard method (£102,000) is £69,000. As this is more than £50,000, the difference is substantial.
So H Ltd must pay VAT of £69,000 to HMRC.

Reporting

The difference between the recoverable input tax calculated under the standard method and that based on use must be **entered on** the VAT return immediately after the end of the VAT year (at the same time as the annual adjustment). 2250

If the business was previously below the **de minimis limits** (¶2194) but the override has caused those limits to be exceeded, input tax will be repayable to HMRC. Conversely, if the exempt input tax is below the limits after applying the override (although this will be extremely rare), all input tax can be recovered.

Records of the calculation must be retained.

MEMO POINTS 1. Exceptionally, where **no annual adjustment is undertaken** because the person has:
– just become partly exempt, the override will be completed for the next VAT return; or
– deregistered, the override will be accounted for on the final VAT return.
2. Where an override adjustment is **not made in time**, the affected VAT return must be corrected (¶3020). HMRC also has the power to raise an assessment in cases where reporting is not undertaken by the business.
3. Where a business **cancels its VAT registration**, the difference must be entered on the last VAT return.

H. Special situations

1. Late claims

Where a late claim is made **within 4 years**, the amount of input tax recoverable must be based on the circumstances and rules applying in the VAT period(s) when it was incurred. A late claim may also affect the annual adjustment and the input tax recovery for other VAT periods, where a special partial exemption method based on input tax values is in operation. In addition, the effect of the de minimis limits must be reviewed. 2254 PE63256

As a general rule, where a claim is **outside the 4-year time limit**, the position cannot be rectified. In relation to partial exemption, if the VAT period when the input tax was first incurred is more than 4 years ago, no correction can be made, even if the return for the annual adjustment is within the 4-year limit. In this case, however, the annual adjustment can be amended, by using the corrected figures for the VAT period. 2256

If the claim is in relation to the **annual adjustment only** and input tax has been correctly claimed for all the VAT periods in that year, the input tax can be corrected, provided that the annual adjustment return itself was not more than 4 years ago.

The annual adjustment can also take account of a change of use in an earlier capped VAT period.

> EXAMPLE A Ltd is reviewing its input tax recovery in the last few years. In a particular year, none of the exempt input tax for each of the VAT quarters was below the de minimis limits. Each of these quarters is capped. However, A Ltd finds that exempt input tax resulting from the annual adjustment was below the de minimis limits, so input tax was under-claimed. The annual adjustment return was due less than 4 years ago and is therefore not capped.
> In this case A Ltd can recover the input tax relating to the application of the de minimis limits to the annual exempt input tax, because it is the annual adjustment which is wrong.

2. Transfer of a business as a going concern

2258 Notice 706 para 15.5 The recovery of input tax relating to the transfer of a going concern is different for the seller and the purchaser. In addition, where an asset is subject to the capital goods scheme, the rules in ¶2350 apply.

There are special rules for partly exempt groups which acquire a going concern (¶8912).

Any input tax incurred on expenses relating to any **other form of acquisition**, such as the acquisition of shares in a business, is residual input tax.

Seller

2260 Notice 706 para 15.6 For a seller, the transfer of assets is not a supply for VAT purposes. Input tax which is directly related to the transfer is **treated as** input tax incurred on the overheads of the business being transferred. So where the business or part of a business is making exclusively taxable or exclusively exempt supplies, the input tax will be wholly recoverable or exempt input tax, respectively. Otherwise it will be residual input tax.

> EXAMPLE A company sold its rights to a taxable lease and tried to recover the whole of the input tax incurred on professional services relating to the sale (the transfer of a lease in these circumstances was a transfer of a going concern).
> It was held that the professional fees were part of the economic activity of the whole business before the transfer and constituted overheads of that part of the business. As all the transactions relating to that part of the business were taxable, all of the input tax incurred was recoverable.
> *Abbey National plc v C & E* [2001]

Purchaser

2262 Notice 706 para 15.7 For the purchaser of a going concern who is acquiring assets for a business, the recoverability of the related input tax will **depend on the use** to be made of those assets. So where the assets are used to make wholly taxable or wholly exempt supplies, the input tax will be exclusively recoverable or exempt input tax, respectively. Otherwise it will be residual input tax.

> EXAMPLE A bank acquired some leasing companies in separate transactions. The companies became dormant subsidiaries of the bank and their leasing businesses were then carried on by the bank itself. The bank tried to recover the whole of the input tax incurred on the related professional fees, on the basis that it was wholly attributable to taxable supplies of leasing.
> The court agreed with this approach, saying that it was a finding of fact that there was a direct link between the acquisitions and the making of the taxable supplies. *C & E v UBAF Bank Ltd* [1996]

3. Groups

2264 PE 62000; Notice 706 para 15.1 Groups of companies may consider a group registration (¶8800) as a way of improving input tax recovery. Otherwise, **inter-company charges** (such as recharged salary costs) create unnecessary input tax, which cannot be recovered by any wholly or partly exempt recipient.

A VAT group is **treated as** a single entity trading through its representative member, so only one partial exemption method can apply for the whole group. Subject to a direction from HMRC to the contrary, supplies between group members are disregarded for VAT purposes. A group company which makes exempt supplies to other group members should therefore be included within the VAT group, so that these exempt supplies are disregarded.

When deciding whether a property or land transaction is **incidental**, the activities of the whole group need to be considered separately.

EXAMPLE B Ltd has a surplus property which it lets to C Ltd, a subsidiary company which is in the same VAT group. B Ltd incurs input tax on maintenance and other running costs.
The treatment of the input tax will depend on whether C Ltd makes:
- wholly taxable supplies, in which case all of the input tax is recoverable by B Ltd;
- wholly exempt supplies, in which case none of the input tax is recoverable; and
- a mixture of taxable and exempt supplies, in which case the input tax will be residual and subject to apportionment based on the method used by the group.

Holding companies

A major problem for holding companies is the lack of business activity, as holding (and disposing of) investments, receiving dividends and defending against takeovers do not constitute business activities. *Polysar Investments Netherlands BV v Inspecteur der Invoerrechten en Accijnzen* [1991] **2266** VIT40100; VIT40500

Often a holding company charges its subsidiaries for **management services** (for example, the remuneration of directors is often routed through such a company). Provided that these charges are genuine commercial transactions, a holding company can become VAT-registered and therefore has the ability to join a group registration.

Where a holding company incurs input tax on costs that do not relate wholly to taxable or exempt supplies, the input tax will be treated as residual.

MEMO POINTS For more on **business activity** see ¶1825.

SECTION 2

Capital goods scheme

This scheme is mandatory but **only applies to** traders who: **2280**
- incur input tax on computers, ships and aircraft, and land-related property interests, where the assets are of a prescribed minimum value;
- buy the assets for business purposes; and
- are involved in the making of both taxable and exempt supplies at any time in the subsequent 5 or 10 years (the period depends on the type of asset).

If **no VAT is incurred** on the acquisition of the asset, the asset will not be within the scheme. Similarly, a trader who is not registered for VAT will be outside the scope of the scheme (although if the trader registers after acquiring the asset see ¶2300).

MEMO POINTS The **EU rules** allow a period of up to 20 years for immovable property. EC Directive 2006/112 art 187

Overview

The **aim** is to ensure that input tax is recovered only in proportion to the taxable use made of the asset over the longer time and recognises that the asset is not consumed by the business immediately. In addition, for assets first used on or after 1 January 2011, an adjustment will also need to be made to reflect changes in the proportions of business/non-business use of the asset. **2282**

Therefore this scheme is really an extension of the fair and reasonable principle that underpins the entirety of the partial exemption rules. Indeed, the adjustments required can be beneficial to a business where the levels of taxable use (and/or business use) increase subsequent to the asset's purchase.

Comment Where taxable use and business use are consistent, the effect of the scheme on input tax recovery will be minimal.

EXAMPLE A Ltd makes wholly taxable supplies. It buys a property for £500,000, incurring input tax of £100,000. This input tax is all recovered in the VAT period of purchase.
For the first 4 years the property is used exclusively for the business purpose of making taxable supplies.
At the end of Year 4 A Ltd moves its taxable business to another location and starts to sell insurance from the property, which is an exempt supply.
To reflect this change of use, a certain amount of the input tax initially recovered will need to be paid back to HMRC until 10 years have elapsed since the property purchase. If the property accommodates the insurance business for 6 years, 60% of the input tax relates to exempt supplies, so the end result will be that A Ltd only retains £40,000 of the recovered input tax. (100,000 x 40%)

A. General principles

2286 For items within the scheme, an input tax **adjustment** is required for subsequent VAT years, not just the year when the asset is acquired. Usually, input tax is recovered on the basis of initial use, subject to the provisions relating to a change of intended use (and, from 1 January 2011, on the initial proportion of business as against non-business use). However, because capital items are bought for the enduring benefit of the business and have a useful life in excess of a single VAT year, the input tax recovered must be adjusted where the exempt use (and/or level of business use) changes in subsequent periods.

Comment Where the scheme applies, the value of the asset for **capital allowances** purposes (which includes any irrecoverable VAT) will be affected by any adjustments (¶2344).

Taxable businesses

2288 Taxable businesses will only be concerned with the capital goods scheme if the level of business use of an asset changes, or if they start to make exempt supplies and become partly exempt (which includes an exempt sale of an asset).

When **becoming partly exempt**, the business must look back over the previous 10 years and check if any assets have been acquired which are within the scheme.

A common situation is where an **interest in land is sold** within 10 years of acquisition, which is likely to be an exempt supply and will result in some input tax being repayable to HMRC, unless the supply is:
- made taxable by opting (¶5602); or
- a commercial building sold within the first 3 years (¶5110, ¶5277).

EXAMPLE An accountant purchases a new office, entirely for business use, incurring input tax. After 5 years, due to growth of the firm, new premises are found and the office is sold.
The sale is exempt, which means some of the input tax recovered initially must be repaid to HMRC.

1. Affected assets

2290 SI 1995/2518 reg 113 Assets which are covered by the scheme are new and second-hand:
- **computer hardware** costing at least £50,000 (excluding VAT);
- **immovable property** with a value of at least £250,000 (excluding VAT), where VAT is actually incurred, so exempt and zero-rated acquisitions are excluded; and
- **ships and aircraft** costing £50,000 or more (excluding VAT).

Cost also includes any amount allocated purely to non-business purposes (from 1 January 2011). HMRC Brief 53/10

Where the business purchases such assets as **stock for resale**, the scheme will not apply, unless the asset is actually used by the trader before being sold. If the trader's original intention was to resell the asset, but this subsequently changes, the asset will be subject to the scheme from the date of acquisition. However, adjustments are only required from the time that the asset was not actually held for resale. PE67200

MEMO POINTS 1. The definition of a **capital asset** (¶2674) follows the usual accounting rules, so assets appearing on the balance sheet are usually capital assets and items posted to the profit and loss account are not. HMRC states that common sense should be applied, so the accounting treatment will be acceptable, unless the accounting policies are unusual, or there is clear anti-avoidance activity. Notice 706/2 para 4.1; PE67050

2. **Sale** includes assignment.

3. In relation to a **leased building**, the owner may intend to dispose of it as a going concern. In this case HMRC will still expect the scheme to be applied, because the costs are capital and incurred for the enduring benefit of the trade.

4. In relation to **property developers**, whose intentions are often speculative, see ¶5614+ and ¶5262.

Computer equipment

The scheme will only apply where a **single piece** of equipment has a value of £50,000 or more (excluding VAT): typically mainframe computers and file servers. Equipment which is manufactured by the trader itself is outside the scheme, as are software, networked personal computers and computerised equipment (such as a telephone system or lift). **2292**

The **value** includes:
- delivery and installation costs, unless invoiced separately; and
- import duty.

Comment Computerised equipment may be treated as part of a **building** for the purposes of the scheme.

Ships and aircraft

The capital goods scheme applies to ships (which includes boats and other vessels) and aircraft, where the **cost** is at least £50,000 (excluding VAT). **2293** Notice 706/2 para 3.1

The **value** includes amounts spent on:
- acquisition and construction (including manufacture);
- refurbishment and fitting out; and
- alteration and, where relevant, extension.

Immovable property

Included within this heading are: **2294**
- land;
- a building or part of a building; and
- civil engineering works (or a part of such works).

Buildings which are **used solely for residential or charitable purposes** are outside the scope of the scheme. However, where there is a change of use from either of these purposes, the scheme may apply.

For **further detail** on the property criteria see ¶5750+.

Measurement of value

Where an asset is used for both **business and non-business purposes**, with effect from 1 January 2011, adjustments made under the scheme must reflect changes in the proportions of business and non-business use of an asset, as well as the proportions of taxable and exempt use. This change will mainly affect charities. **2296** Notice 706/2 para 4.2

Estimates may be required in relation to certain projects (usually involving construction), where invoicing and the work done occurs over a longer period, or where a retention clause appears in the contract.

EXAMPLE

1. A Ltd acquires for £400,000 a property, only half of which is to be used for business purposes. If this property had been acquired before 1 January 2011, it would have been outside the capital goods scheme, as the value for the purposes of the scheme was only £200,000. (400,000 x 50%). However, if the property has been acquired in 2011 or later, it will be within the capital goods scheme, as it is the total value which is relevant, not just the business portion.

2. B Ltd buys a yacht in 2014, which is used privately for 20% of the time. The yacht cost £150,000, plus VAT of £30,000.
The input tax relating to business use is £24,000. (30,000 x 80%)
The value of the yacht for the purposes of the scheme is £150,000.

2. Review period

2298 Notice 706/2 para 6.2 The period over which adjustments are required depends on the type of asset:

<table>
<tr><th>Type of asset</th><th>Review period</th><th>Number of intervals [1]</th><th>% of input tax incurred subject to adjustment in each interval</th><th>Number of adjustments</th></tr>
<tr><td>Computer equipment</td><td rowspan="3">5 years</td><td rowspan="3">5</td><td rowspan="3">20</td><td rowspan="3">4</td></tr>
<tr><td>Ships and aircraft</td></tr>
<tr><td>Leasehold interest with less than 10 years to run when scheme starts</td></tr>
<tr><td>Other immovable property</td><td>10 years</td><td>10</td><td>10</td><td>9</td></tr>
<tr><td colspan="5">Note:
1. Interval generally means the VAT year of the trader.</td></tr>
</table>

The **effect** of the capital goods scheme does not actually **start** until the second interval, so there are actually four or nine adjustments, depending on the type of asset.

Notice 706/2 para 6.5 MEMO POINTS 1. Where the **length of the first two intervals together is less than 12 months** and there is no change of use, the whole period is amalgamated and treated as the first interval. This has little relevance for most commercial transactions.
2. Where there is a **transfer of a going concern** involving a scheme asset, or the trader joins or leaves a **VAT group**, the length of an interval will be changed (¶2350+).
3. Where the owner's **interest in the asset will expire** before the full number of adjustments can occur, the number of adjustments will be reduced to compensate for this.

When does the scheme start?

2300 Notice 706/2 para 6.4; SI 1995/2518 reg 114(4) The scheme starts with the owner's first use of the asset. In practice, the start date is **usually** the date of purchase, importation, or acquisition.

The VAT **year of acquisition** will end on 31 March, 30 April or 31 May depending on the trader's VAT stagger.

MEMO POINTS 1. **Use** means being available for use in the business and, in the case of immovable property, usually involves the granting of a lease or physical occupation.
PE67200 2. **First use** takes its natural meaning for assets other than immovable property, in regard to which it means the time when a constructed, fitted out, altered, extended, or refurbished property is used, even if it is just a part of the property involved (where the project is still incomplete). First use **cannot precede** the time when input tax is first incurred.
3. If the owner has a **limited interest** (in the sense that ownership is time-limited) the number of intervals is reduced to one more than the remaining whole years of ownership (subject to a minimum of three, below which the asset would not be treated as a capital item and would therefore be outside the scope of the scheme).

4. If the asset is **first used prior to the owner's VAT registration**, the number of intervals is reduced by one for each whole year between first use and registration.

EXAMPLE

1. D Ltd purchases a 7-year interest in a building costing £1 million.
The number of intervals in D Ltd's adjustment period will be 8. (7 + 1)

2. E Ltd acquired a building which cost £250,000 plus VAT. The building was first used on 1 October 2010 but the company only became VAT registered on 1 January 2012, with its first VAT period ending on 31 March 2012. Thus the company owned the building for more than a year before registration. The building is used for wholly taxable purposes.
The first interval runs from 1 October 2010 to 31 March 2012. There are nine scheme intervals, as one interval is deducted because the business owned the asset for a complete year before it became VAT-registered.

End of the period

When the adjustment period has ended, it is of no consequence if the use of the asset subsequently changes. The **input tax recovered** during the review period is final. **2302** Notice 706/2 para 6.9

B. Calculation

The **trader must** first calculate: **2306**
- the input tax which relates to the asset;
- the recoverable amount in the first interval; and
- the resulting baseline recovery rate.

Only then can the recoverable input tax be adjusted in subsequent intervals.

1. First interval

Initial input tax recovery

The initial input tax recovery is usually calculated using the trader's normal partial exemption **method**, taking into account: **2308** Notice 706/2 para 7.1; SI 1995/2518 reg 116(1)
- the use of the asset made in each VAT period (which, in the case of assets first used after 31 December 2010, must include the proportion of business use as well as taxable/exempt use);
- the annual adjustment at the end of each VAT year; and
- the de minimis limits, if relevant.

Sometimes an asset is used for exclusively taxable or exclusively exempt supplies. Otherwise, the related input tax will be residual and only a proportion will be recovered in the VAT year of acquisition, unless the de minimis limits (¶2194) are not exceeded.

MEMO POINTS 1. For this purpose **input tax** includes that charged on purchase, plus import VAT, input tax charged on EU acquisitions and under the reverse charge (¶9700).
2. For possible complications relating to **immovable property** see ¶5780.

EXAMPLE

1. Mr F is a newsagent who leases premises for £300,000 plus VAT of £60,000.
He makes wholly taxable supplies, so 100% of the VAT is initially recovered.

2. G Ltd sells insurance and buys a computer which costs £60,000 plus VAT of £12,000.
None of this VAT is initially recovered, as G Ltd makes exempt supplies.

3. H Ltd is a toy manufacturer which lets a surplus part of its business property but does not opt to tax. The property itself cost £500,000 plus VAT of £100,000.

As the property is being used for both taxable and exempt supplies, this input tax must be apportioned. The recovery percentage for the VAT period is 60%. When the annual adjustment is completed, the recovery percentage is amended to 65%, so the overall initial recovery is £65,000. (100,000 x 65%)

4. If H Ltd, in the example above, only uses the property 75% for business purposes, only £75,000 of the VAT incurred is input tax. If the recovery percentage is 65%, the initial recovery is £48,750. (75,000 x 65%)

2310 SI 1995/2518 reg 116(2); PE67200 Alternatively, where the trader and HMRC agree that the pre-existing partial exemption method will **not give a fair reflection** of how the asset will be used, a separate method can be adopted. The terms of the agreement must be set out in writing. Any such agreement is completely separate from any pre-existing partial exemption method.

In addition, businesses can agree a **single** special input tax **recovery method** to take account not only of taxable/exempt use but also business/non-business use of an asset (¶2312). Where an asset was previously subject to Lennartz accounting (¶1842), transitional rules ensure that double taxation does not occur as a result of adjustments based on business/non-business use.

Very rarely, **in cases of avoidance**, HMRC can direct that a particular method is used.

Some non-business use

2312 With effect from 1 January 2011, where an asset is used for both business and non-business purposes, an adjustment will be necessary to reflect the proportions of business and non-business use.

Baseline recovery rate

2314 PE67150 Once the rate of initial recovery has been calculated, this is then the baseline rate, **against which** subsequent use is measured.

If there is an **error** in the baseline rate, this can only be corrected by amending it, and only if the correction is made within 4 years. Subsequent adjustments then always refer to the corrected baseline rate.

MEMO POINTS Where a partial exemption **special method** is used involving sectors (¶2178), the baseline rate will be the percentage input tax recovered in the sector in which the asset is used. If the asset is used in more than one sector, the baseline rate should reflect the relative use in each sector.

EXAMPLE A Ltd buys a property and initially recovers 70% of the input tax.
An error, discovered almost 5 years later, shows that the correct baseline rate should have been 40%, but it is too late to correct it.
However, in intervals 5 to 10, the baseline rate will be treated as 40%, so that if the recovery rate in interval 6 is 60%, an adjustment of 20% in favour of the business will be made.

Comment HMRC says this rule can lead to adjustments being made which common sense says should not be. However, notwithstanding this rule, the trader cannot in any circumstances recover more than 100% or less than 0% of the input tax in issue.

2. Subsequent intervals where the asset is retained

2316 No adjustments will be required when the taxable use and the business use of the asset **do not change** during the review period. Where an asset is continually used for exclusively taxable or exclusively exempt supplies throughout the period, with the same proportion of business use, the initial input tax recovery will therefore be a fair result. The **only instances where an adjustment is required** are where:
– the asset is used for both taxable and exempt supplies at the same time, and the input tax is therefore residual; or
– the taxable use and/or the business use of the asset change(s).

Measuring the adjustment

Depending on the type of asset (¶2298), either 10% or 20% of the initial input tax recovered will be reviewed in each interval. 2318

In every subsequent interval, the **proportion of business use** is reassessed and the **taxable use** of the asset is compared to the baseline. In most cases, taxable use is measured using the same method as for the baseline, unless HMRC has agreed to a different method.

MEMO POINTS 1. If the asset is **not used** during some of the adjustment period, for example because of repair, the asset is deemed to still be used for the same purpose as before becoming unoperational.
2. If **expenditure is incurred on an asset both before and after 1 January 2011** this will be a split capital item, so that:
- input tax incurred up to 31 December 2010 must be reviewed in light of any change in the mix of taxable and exempt supplies made; and
- VAT incurred on or after 1 January 2011 must be reviewed separately in light of both changes in business use and also in the mix of taxable and exempt supplies made.

For assets first used on or after 1 January 2011, the **formula** which is used to calculate the adjustment for each interval is: 2320

$$\frac{\text{Total VAT incurred on the asset}}{\text{Number of intervals}} \times \text{(Current business and taxable use - Baseline rate)\%}$$

The result of this calculation is then adjusted to take account of any non-business use of the asset.

MEMO POINTS 1. **Current business and taxable use** describes the proportion of business and also taxable use made of the asset within the interval.
2. For **assets first used prior to 1 January 2011**, the formula which is used to calculate the adjustment for each interval is:

$$\frac{\text{Total input tax incurred on the asset}}{\text{Number of intervals}} \times \text{(Current taxable use - Baseline rate)\%}$$

3. **Total input tax incurred** is detailed at ¶2308.

EXAMPLE On 3 June B Ltd purchases a file server which costs £300,000, incurring input tax of £60,000. The computer is used exclusively for business purposes, but for both taxable and exempt supplies. B Ltd has a VAT year which ends on 31 March.
In the first interval B Ltd recovers 60% of its residual input tax, which gives an initial recovery of £36,000. (£60,000 x 60%)
The level of taxable use in the subsequent intervals is as follows:

Interval	Taxable use
2	70%
3	80%
4	50%
5	30%

So the following adjustments will be required:

Interval	Calculation	Adjustment £	Overall position £
1			36,000
2	$\frac{60,000}{5} \times (70 - 60)\%$	1,200	1,200
			37,200
3	$\frac{60,000}{5} \times (80 - 60)\%$	2,400	2,400
			39,600
4	$\frac{60,000}{5} \times (50 - 60)\%$	(1,200)	(1,200)
			38,400
5	$\frac{60,000}{5} \times (30 - 60)\%$	(3,600)	(3,600)
	Total input tax recovery		34,800

To ensure that this is correct, a quick check can be completed as follows:

Average recovery rate: $\frac{60 + 70 + 80 + 50 + 30}{5} = 58\%$

Applying this rate to the input tax incurred gives £34,800, which agrees to the overall position calculated above. (£60,000 x 58%)

2324 **Deregistration** A final adjustment must be made if the trader deregisters whilst still owning the asset. The calculation is the same as for the additional adjustment on disposal (¶2336).

Output tax may be charged on the deemed supply (¶8610), in which case this is treated as indicating taxable use for the remaining intervals. Otherwise, the use is deemed to be exempt.

Reporting

2326 Any adjustment (whether positive or negative) is normally entered in box 4 on the second **quarterly** VAT return after the end of the VAT year (which always includes September). For example, if the VAT year ends on 30 April, the adjustment will be put on the return for the quarter ended 31 October. For a **monthly** return trader, the adjustment will always be included on the May return.

However, HMRC may allow **another return** to be used for this purpose, provided that the adjustment is reported within 4 years of the end of the VAT period in which it would normally be made.

Comment This avoids the need for the partial exemption annual adjustment and the capital goods scheme adjustment to be made on the same return.

Records

2328 Traders must keep **separate** records of:
- the description of the asset;
- value;
- amount of input tax recovered;
- the start and end dates of each interval;
- when adjustments in respect of taxable and business use are due; and
- the date and value of any disposal within the adjustment period.

It is strongly recommended that these records are kept for the longer of 6 years and the length of the adjustment period.

3. Ceasing to own the asset within the review period

2330 A trader may cease to own an asset (or part of an asset) because of a sale or loss (including destruction).

Comment Prior to 1 January 2011, part disposals of an asset were ignored under the capital goods scheme. To ensure scheme adjustments remain fair and reasonable, part disposals are now recognised.

a. Sale

2332 If an asset (or part) is sold:
- **without ever being used**, it is outside the scope of the scheme and no adjustment is required; or
- as part of a **transfer of a going concern**, special rules apply (¶2350).

Otherwise, the following provisions should be followed.

Method

In the interval when the sale occurs, **two adjustments** are required: **2334**
a. a normal adjustment, as if the asset (or part) had been used for the whole interval; and
b. an additional adjustment, to take into account the remaining intervals after sale.
The sales adjustments are entered on the second VAT return after the end of the VAT year in which the sale occurs.
If ceasing to trade see also ¶8600+.

Additional adjustment

The additional adjustment deems the use of the asset (or part) in the remaining intervals to take the **status of the sale**. So where the sale is: **2336** SI 1995/2518 reg 115(3)
– taxable, the use of the asset during the remaining intervals is deemed to be 100% taxable; or
– exempt, the use of the asset during the remaining intervals is deemed to be 100% exempt.

The VAT attributable to a **part disposal** should be calculated on a fair basis e.g. based on the market value of the part retained compared to the part disposed of, or floor area. HMRC states that if the proportion of VAT attributable to the part disposal is fair, it will not mount a challenge. Notice 706/2 para 10.2

Strictly, the total amount of **input tax deducted may not exceed** the output tax chargeable on its disposal. However, HMRC has announced that no adjustment will be applied to computer equipment, and immovable property will only be affected where the anti-avoidance disposal test (¶5790) is found to apply. Notice 706/2 para 11

So the following adjustments will be required: **2338**

EXAMPLE On 3 June C Ltd purchases computer equipment costing £300,000, incurring input tax of £60,000. The equipment is used exclusively for business purposes, but for both taxable and exempt supplies. C Ltd has a VAT year which ends on 31 March.
In the first interval C Ltd recovers 60% of its residual input tax, which gives an initial recovery of £36,000. (60,000 x 60%) In interval 3 he sells the equipment for £40,000 plus VAT of £8,000.
In interval 2 the taxable use was 70% allowing C Ltd to recover a further £1,200. (60,000/5 x (70% - 60%))
In relation to interval 3 itself, there is no change to the calculation, because the computer is deemed to be owned for the whole period. This means that as taxable use in the period was considered to be 80% a further £2,400 could be reclaimed. (60,000/5 x (80% - 60%))
As this is a taxable sale, the use for intervals 4 and 5 is deemed to be 100% taxable.

Interval	Calculation	Adjustment £	Overall position £
	Brought forward after interval 3		39,600
4	$\frac{60,000}{5} \times (100 - 60)\%$	4,800	
5	$\frac{60,000}{5} \times (100 - 60)\%$	4,800	
Total			9,600
	Total input tax recovery		49,200

b. Loss or destruction

In the event of loss, **only** the normal adjustment is made, treating the asset as if it had been owned for the whole interval and used in the same manner as before it was lost. No other adjustments are then completed. **2340**

Loss for this purpose **includes**:
– destruction;
– theft (of which the trader should keep evidence, such as insurance records); and

– the expiry of a short-term lease (¶5540), being one with a term of no more than 21 years (less than 20 years in Scotland).

Demolition in readiness for a refurbishment would constitute destruction; this is particularly relevant to rolling refurbishment programmes (¶5770).

C. Other consequences

Interaction with direct taxes

2344 The adjustments to input tax affect some areas of direct tax such as capital allowances and capital gains tax computations.

Where a capital goods scheme adjustment requires VAT to be paid to HMRC, this means that the cost of the asset is increased for the purposes of **capital allowances**. Conversely, where an amount of VAT is due from HMRC, this reduces the asset's cost. The timing of the increase/decrease to the cost of the asset occurs in the accounting period when the VAT adjustment is actually made (i.e. the last day of the VAT period of the return which includes the adjustment).

Where **capital gains tax** rollover relief has been claimed and the cost of the new asset changes because of a capital goods scheme adjustment, HMRC will not require the relief to be disturbed.

MEMO POINTS 1. **Capital allowances** are the tax equivalent of depreciation.
2. **Rollover relief** is available for certain trading assets. When an asset is sold the resulting capital gain can be rolled over into the base cost of another asset.
3. For **details of all these topics** see the current editions of *Tax Memo* and *Corporation Tax Memo*.

EXAMPLE D Ltd prepares accounts to 30 June but has a VAT year of 31 March. The company acquires a computer on 1 August 2012 at a cost of £200,000 plus VAT of £40,000. D Ltd makes wholly taxable supplies in interval 1 (ending 31 March 2013), but becomes partly exempt in interval 2 (ending 31 March 2014), able to recover only 80% of its input tax.
Assume D Ltd can claim capital allowances of 18% on a reducing balance basis each year, having used up its annual investment allowance on other assets.
The initial input tax recovered will be £40,000; the cost of the asset for capital allowances purposes is £200,000.
In interval 2, the adjustment will be £1,600 due to HMRC (20% x 40,000/5); this will be disclosed on the return for the VAT period ended 30 September 2014. This increase in cost is treated as occurring on 30 September 2014 for capital allowances purposes.
The capital allowances computation up to 30 June 2015 will be as follows:

Year ended		£
30 June 2013	Acquisition	200,000
	Allowance @ 18%	(36,000)
	Value carried forward	164,000
30 June 2014	Value brought forward	164,000
	Allowance @ 18%	29,520
	Value carried forward	134,480
30 June 2015	Value brought forward	134,480
	Addition (VAT due to HMRC)	1,600
		136,080
	Allowance @ 18%	(24,494)
	Value carried forward	111,586

Standard method override and capital goods

2346 Information Sheet 4/02 appendix 4 The standard method override **applies to** partly exempt businesses incurring large amounts of residual input tax (¶2240).

The override requires a further adjustment to be made to input tax recovered on capital goods. This is made at the same time as the annual adjustment.

If an asset, subject to the capital goods scheme, is **acquired** in a VAT year when an override applies, the input tax relating to the asset is included in the override calculation. The baseline rate will be affected by the override calculation.

EXAMPLE A taxable business purchases a building at a cost of £1 million plus VAT of £200,000, 1 month before the end of its VAT year. It occupies one floor and intends to let the other four floors in the next VAT year. There will be no non-business use. It treats the VAT as residual input tax but, as it is a fully taxable business, all of the residual input tax can be recovered. The business is subject to the override.
In the VAT period of acquisition, the VAT records show:

	£	£
Value of taxable supplies		500,000
Input tax relating to exclusively taxable supplies	50,000	
Residual input tax	200,000	
Total recovered input tax	250,000	

This result is not fair because the business will be making exempt supplies of 80% of the building in the next VAT year.
So the override must be applied.
Based on floor space, the residual input tax relating to taxable use is actually £40,000. (200,000 × 20%)
The total recoverable input tax based on use is therefore £90,000. (40,000 + 50,000)
The difference in the input tax recovery is £160,000. (250,000 - 90,000)
This substantial difference must be adjusted for.
For the purposes of the capital goods scheme, the baseline rate is 20% (i.e. one floor out of five).

For **subsequent intervals**, any adjustments under the capital goods scheme are ignored when deciding whether the override applies. However, the adjustments themselves may be affected. **2348** Information Sheet 4/02 appendix 5

EXAMPLE A Ltd is partly exempt. It acquires a building at a cost of £1 million, plus VAT of £200,000. The baseline rate is 40%.
In a subsequent interval, the business lets out 60% of the building and opts to tax, so that it is making a taxable supply. The standard method percentage recovery rate is 50%, but when the override is calculated, the percentage is amended to 70%.
The adjustment percentage for the capital goods scheme in this interval is 30% in A Ltd's favour. (40 - 70)

Transfer of a going concern

When a trader transfers a business as a going concern (¶8646) and a qualifying asset (¶2290) is transferred as part of the arrangement, the **responsibility for making adjustments** under the scheme passes to the new owner. The provisions relating to a sale do not apply. **2350** SI 1995/2518 reg 114(7); Notice 706/2 para 9.2

So the overall cost of the asset to the purchaser will depend on the subsequent adjustments which must be made.

EXAMPLE A fully taxable company constructs a new building at a cost of £1 million plus VAT of £200,000. The building is used 100% for taxable business purposes by the company for the first 2 years. It is then let under an exempt lease.
After a further 2 years the building is sold. This is treated as a transfer of a going concern because of the sitting tenant. The purchaser does not opt to tax and uses the building for wholly exempt supplies.
The purchaser will need to repay £20,000 of input tax to HMRC in each remaining interval in the review period. (200,000/10)

2352 SI 1995/2518 reg 116(A2) The **adjustment intervals** (¶2298) will depend on whether the VAT registration number is transferred as follows:

VAT reg'n transferred	Seller	Purchaser
Yes	No adjustment made in last interval of ownership	Intervals continue, with the first since the transfer ending on the last day of the purchaser's tax year
No	Interval ends on transfer date Normal adjustment (¶2334) made[1]	Intervals end on anniversary of transfer date Needs to agree a new method[2] of calculating the scheme adjustments with HMRC

Note:
1. The last adjustment for the seller must still **be made** on the return for the second VAT period falling after the VAT year in which the transfer occurs.
2. The **new method** for the purchaser may be based on an average of the recovery rates of the two VAT years which the interval straddles. As both rates may not be available when the adjustment is usually required, HMRC may allow a delay for the entry on the return.

EXAMPLE On 1 September 2014 B Ltd sells its business to C Ltd as a going concern, including a computer subject to the capital goods scheme. B Ltd's VAT year ends on 31 March, whereas C Ltd has a year end of 31 May.
B Ltd does not transfer its registration, so an interval ends on 1 September 2014 (within the VAT year ending 31 March 2015). The adjustment will be entered on the return for the VAT period ending 30 September 2015.
For C Ltd, subsequent intervals will also end on 1 September and the method of calculating the scheme adjustment must be agreed with HMRC.
If B Ltd had transferred its registration, it would have made no adjustment for the VAT year ending 31 March 2015. C Ltd would have made its first adjustment for the VAT year ending 31 May 2015.

Groups

2354 Notice 706/2 para 12 A capital asset may be used for different purposes after the company which owns it joins or leaves a VAT group (¶8800). For example, a company may have been using a property wholly for taxable purposes before joining a VAT group, but may subsequently lease the property to another group company which makes exempt supplies.

Where a company **joins** a VAT group and has already been making adjustments under the capital goods scheme, the current interval will end on the day before joining. Subsequent intervals end annually thereafter and it is the responsibility of the group representative member to make the adjustments.

Where a company **leaves** a VAT group, the current interval will end on the day the company exits. The adjustment will need to be entered on the return for the second VAT period falling after the end of the VAT year in which the exit occurred. Again subsequent intervals end annually thereafter.

In both cases, where the intervals do not correspond with the company's VAT year, the new owner of the asset will need to agree a method of calculating the adjustments due under the scheme with HMRC.

EXAMPLE D Ltd was fully taxable. It acquired a property at a cost of £1 million, plus VAT of £150,000, on 1 September 2010. D Ltd's VAT year ends on 31 March.
D Ltd joins a VAT group on 6 May 2014.
The intervals will be:

Interval	Dates
1	1 September 2010 to 31 March 2011
2	Year ended 31 March 2012
3	Year ended 31 March 2013
4	Year ended 31 March 2014
5	1 April 2013 to 5 May 2014
6 - 10	Year ended 5 May

CHAPTER 3

Special situations

OUTLINE ¶¶

There are special rules which apply to input tax deduction for non-taxable UK persons and transactions involving shares and financial supplies. **2410**

In addition, various sundry items are dealt with at ¶2435+.

A. Non-taxable UK persons

Input tax can **usually** only be deducted by someone who is VAT-registered at the time when the relevant supplies were received. **2415**

As an exception, however, **special rules** allow input tax to be deducted in certain circumstances when supplies are received:
- before registration (¶8560);
- before incorporation (¶8566);
- after deregistration (¶8618); and
- by DIY housebuilders (¶5316).

B. Shares and incidental financial supplies

The treatment of input tax incurred in relation to shares or securities (for these purposes called shares) depends on whether the transaction is an issue of shares or a sale of shares. **2420** Business Brief 21/05

An **issue** of shares that is carried out for the purposes of the business are not supplies for VAT purposes. This means the related input tax is residual (¶2110). The purpose behind the issue could be to raise capital, or effect a takeover or restructuring arrangement (such as a merger or demerger).

The **sale** of existing shares for consideration is an exempt supply.

MEMO POINTS 1. **Shares include** ordinary shares, preference shares, rights issues, bonus issues, scrip dividends, bonds, debentures, loan notes and units in collective investment funds.

Business Brief 30/03 2. Where a company obtains a **stock exchange listing** (including AIM), whether shares are issued or not, this is not a supply for VAT purposes. Any related input tax will be treated as residual.

Attribution when shares are sold

2422 Depending on the facts of the case, input tax relating to a share sale may be attributed to the trader's **wider business purpose**. However, supplies of professional fees should not be artificially split.

EXAMPLE

1. A parent company acquired the issued share capital of a subsidiary, funded by the issue of its own shares. After the acquisition the parent company supplied management services to its new subsidiary.
The parent company deducted the input tax on the related services received from accountants, solicitors and stockbrokers. The relevant invoices from the accountants and stockbrokers were very general and referred only to the offer to acquire the shares, which the court held related to an exempt supply.
However, the solicitor's invoice included the following details:
- advising on the financing of the transaction;
- preparing directors' service contracts;
- preparing a due diligence report;
- investigating title to properties; and
- preparing papers for the AGM following the acquisition.

This detail meant that the related input tax was residual. *RAP Group plc v C & E* [2000]

2. A holding company disposed of some shares in its subsidiary company, in order to raise funds so that the group could continue to trade. It sought to deduct the input tax relating to professional services supplied by merchant bankers, solicitors and accountants in connection with the disposal. It was held that the ultimate aim of the taxable person was irrelevant. As the professional services were incurred for the exempt sale of shares, none of the input tax was deductible. *BLP Group plc v C & E* [1995]

3. Some doubt has been cast on this by another decision of the CJEU in 2009. A parent company sold shares in two subsidiaries and claimed to deduct input tax incurred in association with those sales. The CJEU held that the input tax was not to be disallowed as being wholly attributable to the exempt share sales. Instead, insofar as there was a direct and immediate link with the parent company's overall economic activities, the input tax was allowable. *Skatteverket v AB SKF* [2009]

2424 HMRC has issued general guidance on the recovery of input tax incurred in relation to **mergers and management buy-outs**. HMRC accepts that activities such as due diligence, drafting contracts and regulatory compliance do have a direct and immediate link to a business activity. The related input tax is therefore residual.

EXAMPLE

1. A company incurred input tax on the professional services listed below. These related to the acquisition of a company which was funded by the issue of the acquiring company's own shares. Following the acquisition the acquiring company made taxable supplies of management services. It was held that the input tax incurred could be broken down as follows:

Type of cost	Type of input tax
The introduction of the target company	Residual
The services of a merchant bank in advising on the acquisition, making the formal offer and advising on compliance with regulatory requirements	Residual
Commercial property valuations for inclusion in the offer document	Residual
Solicitors' services in investigating title to the properties, assisting with preparation of the offer document, drafting minutes and preparing contracts for the acquisition and service contracts for the directors	Residual
Printing of the offer document and accompanying papers	Exempt
Accountancy services in connection with the acquisition, including assisting with a due diligence review of the target company	Residual
The services of a public relations firm appointed to handle representation of the acquisition	Exempt

Southampton Leisure Holdings plc [2002] (VTD 17716)

2. A company was invoiced by a public relations (PR) company and a firm of solicitors, in connection with the flotation of the company. The proceeds of the flotation were used to finance the internal growth of the company.
The PR company originally issued a general invoice to cover all of its work. HMRC indicated that none of the input tax would be recoverable, because it was entirely related to an exempt (as it was then) share issue. The PR company therefore issued a credit note and then two new invoices. However, it was held that the original invoice had expressed accurately what the PR company had done.
The solicitor provided only one invoice, indicating that it related to the issue of shares. However, there was a separate schedule of charges with details of the work done, which demonstrated that about 5% of the work did not relate to the flotation. The tribunal ordered the parties to agree figures for the small amount of input tax that might be recoverable, on the basis that the solicitor's fees had been used for both exempt and taxable supplies. *Actinic* [2003] (VTD 18044)

Shares supplied overseas

The VAT treatment of shares **issued** to persons within the EU is no different from the UK situation and therefore any related input tax is residual. **2426** Business Brief 21/05

An **intermediary** arranging an issue of shares to non-EU recipients is making an exempt supply. However, the related input tax is still fully recoverable where:
- the share issue is arranged on behalf of a non-EU issuer; or
- the intermediary's own customer is located outside the EU.

However, the VAT treatment of **sales of existing shares** depends on the location of the purchaser, as follows: **2428**
- a sale of shares to a private person elsewhere in the EU generally comprises an exempt supply;
- shares sold to a business elsewhere in the EU are outside the scope, without any recovery of input tax; and
- shares sold to a business outside the EU are outside the scope, although the input tax is recoverable in full.

The related input tax must be **apportioned** on the **basis of use**. HMRC suggests the following formula:

$$\frac{\text{Number of subscribers outside the UK}}{\text{Total number of subscribers}}$$

A trader who receives goods or services in these circumstances will need to **classify the input tax** by reference to:
- taxable UK supplies;
- exempt UK supplies;
- financial supplies in the EU (not recoverable); and
- supplies outside the EU (recoverable).

EXAMPLE A Ltd sells 500,000 shares in its subsidiary. The purchasers are all businesses and are located in the UK, France and Japan, as follows:

	Number of shares	Number of purchasers
UK	300,000	20
France	150,000	10
Japan	50,000	1
Total	500,000	31

The amount of input tax incurred on professional fees related to the issue is £100,000.
Only the shares sold to Japanese purchasers give any input tax recovery:
An apportionment based:

- on share numbers gives input tax recovery of £10,000. $\frac{50,000}{500,000} \times £100,000$
- on purchaser numbers gives input tax recovery of £3,226. $1/31 \times £100,000$

A Ltd must decide which figure is the more fair and reasonable reflection of use, given the circumstances.
If the figure of £10,000 is chosen, the remaining £90,000 will be exempt input tax.

C. Sundry items

Summary

2435

Item	¶¶
Insolvency	¶2437
Employers	¶2440
Reverse charge	¶2448
Research and development	¶2450
Churches and cathedrals	¶2452
Memorials	¶2454

Insolvency

2437 An insolvent **business** will usually incur input tax on the fees charged by an insolvency practitioner, which will be treated as residual for partial exemption purposes. Any costs incurred from third parties must be treated separately. Input tax recovery will depend on the use made of these costs.

Insolvency **practitioners** that make taxable supplies can reclaim input tax on either form VAT426 or VAT427 (¶8722).

With regard to the practitioner's own costs:

a. where the **business continues to trade**, making taxable and exempt supplies, the input tax will be recovered using the partial exemption method in place; or

b. if the business **ceases to trade**, recovery of the input tax will depend on the supplies made by the business when it was trading. If mixed supplies were made, the same partial exemption method is to apply as when trading was carried on.

Following the change in circumstances, it may be beneficial to change the partial exemption method where the recovery would otherwise no longer be fair and reasonable.

MEMO POINTS For the list of situations in which an insolvency practitioner makes **exempt supplies** see ¶367.

Employers

2440 VATSC23000 **Catering and gifts** Whenever an employer provides food or beverages to its employees, the input tax will always be fully recoverable. It is irrelevant whether any consideration is given by the employees.

If an employer makes other gifts to its employees, the normal business gift rules should be applied (see ¶1465+) and input tax will be recoverable where appropriate.

2442 PE63500 **Private fuel** If fuel is provided for private mileage, the business normally includes a scale charge on each VAT return (¶1536+).

For input tax purposes, employee fuel expenses **must be split** between private and business mileage. Whilst input tax relating to private mileage is fully recoverable (because it is set against the scale charge), input tax attributable to business mileage is only recoverable to the extent that the fuel is used for taxable supplies. If it is **impossible to split** out the fuel expenses between private and business, an enhanced input tax recovery is now available to partly exempt traders (see ¶1539).

2444 VIT44600; VIT44700 **Pension funds** An employer company may provide an occupational pension scheme for its staff, through the mechanism of a trust.

The employer can recover input tax on the **setting up and running costs** (excluding certain investment advice) of the trust, provided that the input tax is otherwise eligible (for example, the invoices are made out to the employer).

For further details see ¶8290+.

Share incentive schemes These schemes enable employees to acquire shares in their employer, via the mechanism of a trust which holds the shares on behalf of the employees for a minimum period. **2446** VIT43900

The employer can deduct input tax on any costs incurred in **running the trust** (such as printing and professional fees). The net amount can then be recharged to the trust.

If **shares are sold** on behalf of the employee, it is the employee who must suffer any input tax incurred on the selling expenses.

Reverse charge

A **partly exempt** business which receives international services (¶9700) must account for output tax and input tax as if a self-supply has been made. As with self-supplies generally, the input tax is not treated as relating to the international service itself. **2448**

The recovery of the input tax will **depend on** the use to which the service is put. Where the assets are used to make exclusively taxable or exclusively exempt supplies, the input tax will therefore, respectively, be wholly recoverable or wholly exempt. Otherwise the input tax will be residual.

The value of the international service must be excluded from the apportionment calculation if the standard method, or a special method relying on turnover, is used.

Research and development

Input tax incurred on research and development expenditure (R&D) will not normally relate to any specific supply. The provisional recovery of input tax is **determined by** the activities of the business for which the R&D is undertaken, so if the activities are: **2450** PE63750

- taxable, the input tax can be recovered;
- exempt, no recovery is possible; or
- mixed, the input tax is residual.

Input tax will only be clawed back where the first directly related supplies are exempt.

Churches and cathedrals

Churches and cathedrals obviously do not exist primarily in order to carry on a business. **2452** VIT45600; VIT45700

However, **substantial income can be derived** from tourists, for example, through the running of a shop or café. In such circumstances the cathedral (or, exceptionally, church) would be carrying on a business. Input tax which is directly attributable to the business activities can be recovered. Other input tax which is not directly linked to non-business activities (such as repairs and maintenance) can be recovered at a fixed rate according to the building's category, as follows.

Category	Circumstances	Input tax recovery
A	Significant admission charges to all main areas	90%
B	No admission charge to the cathedral itself, but significant other income (such as entrance fees to the crypt, or lettings for concerts) derived from a high number of visitors	65%
C	Reasonable number of visitors generating income from other sources	45%
D	Little taxable income	25%

Input tax incurred on **domestic accommodation** does not fall within the above rules; the normal business purpose test (¶1825) should be applied.

MEMO POINTS Grants are available to **listed places of worship** until at least 31 March 2016, to cover up to 100% of the input tax incurred on repairs. Applications can only be made once the cost has been incurred and the VAT actually paid.
Specifically, the scheme applies to:
- repairs, maintenance and approved alterations to listed buildings which are used principally as places of worship; and
- places of worship owned by, or vested in, a number of specified organisations which look after redundant churches.

From October 2013 works to **pipe organs, turret clocks, bells and bell ropes** also became eligible for grants. This additional also included professional fees relating to the repair. Claims can only be accepted where the supporting invoices are not more than one year old.
For this purpose, all listed places of worship of all religions throughout the UK, which are included on the public registers of listed buildings kept for England, Scotland, Wales and Northern Ireland, are eligible.
See flmemo.co.uk/vm2452 for more details.

Memorials

2454 Under a government scheme (which will run until at least April 2015) VAT incurred on the **construction, renovation** and **maintenance** of memorials is refunded. From 1 October 2013 this includes VAT incurred on professional fees, such as those of surveyors and architects. Qualifying costs are those suffered in respect of a memorial which meets all of the following **criteria**:
- people, events or animals are commemorated;
- a commemorative inscription appears somewhere on the memorial; and
- the public are permitted access (even if an entrance charge is payable, or if a key needs to be obtained from a key-holder) for a minimum of 30 hours a week.

VAT is refunded at the full **rate** of 20%. For example, if the construction costs are £210,000 (including VAT), the refund will be £35,000. (£210,000 × 1/6) However, if total claims exceed the scheme's budget of approximately £500,000 per year, refunds will be reduced on a pro rata basis.

Further details on how to claim are available from flmemo.co.uk/vm2454.

PART 4

Compliance

Compliance Summary

The numbers cross-refer to paragraphs.

CHAPTER 1 Registration

CHAPTER 2 Records

CHAPTER 3 Reporting

CHAPTER 4 Payment

CHAPTER 1

Registration

OUTLINE ¶¶

There are various requirements to register, and different forms of registration. However, the implications of registration (¶2610) tend to be the same. **2600**

Anyone who makes wholly exempt supplies (¶350+) is unable to register for VAT.

SECTION 1

Overview

Summary of situations requiring registration

2605 **Situations dealt with in this chapter**

Situation	Detail	Type of registration		¶¶
		Compulsory	Voluntary	
In business and making taxable UK supplies	Intending to make supplies in business		UK	¶2690+
	Supplies of any level up to threshold (¶9960)		UK	¶2688
	Supplies in last 12 months over a certain threshold (¶9960)	UK		¶2676+
	Supplies in next 30 days over a certain threshold (¶9960)	UK		¶2680
	Any supplies in next 30 days, if no UK establishment (¶9688+)	UK		¶2667
Making no UK taxable supplies	Must be in business and special rules apply		UK	¶2700

Situations dealt with in Parts 7 and 9

Situation	Detail	Type of registration		¶¶
		Compulsory	Voluntary	
EU trader selling goods to **non-taxable UK** persons	Intending to sell		Distance selling	¶9177
	Supplies of any level up to £70,000 in calendar year		Distance selling	¶9177
	Supplying dutiable goods of any amount	Distance selling		¶9182
	Exercised EU option re place of supply	Distance selling		¶9184
	Supplies of other goods in calendar year over £70,000	Distance selling		¶9188
UK persons **acquiring goods from the EU**	Intending to acquire goods		EU acquisition	¶9062
	Acquisitions of any level up to threshold (¶9962)		EU acquisition	¶9041
	Acquisitions in calendar year over threshold (¶9962)	EU acquisition		¶9042+
Person previously reclaimed UK input tax under a **directive claim**	Starts making UK taxable supplies	Overseas trader		¶9890
Non-EU person making **electronically supplied services**	To EU unregistered customers	Special EU registration scheme		¶7000

Comparison of the main registrations

2607

	UK supplies	Cross-border distance sales	EU acquisitions
¶¶	¶2640	¶9177	¶9040
Exemption available?	Yes	No	Yes
Registration depends on	Goods and services sold	Goods sold	Goods acquired
Tests for registration	Value of taxable supplies in either: **a.** previous 12 months; or **b.** next 30 days	If any of the following met: **a.** any supply of excise goods made; **b.** trader has exercised an EU option re place of supply; or **c.** value of supplies of non-excise goods in calendar year	Value of acquisitions in previous 12 months
Threshold applies	Yes [1]	Only for test **c.** above	Yes
Voluntary registration	Yes	Yes	Yes
Retrospective registration if request on application	Yes	Yes	Yes
Forms required	VAT1	VAT1A	VAT1B
Legislation	Sch 1 VATA 1994	Sch 2 VATA 1994	Sch 3 VATA 1994

Note
1. Threshold does not apply if the business does not have a UK establishment (¶9688+).

Consequences

Whichever rules the person becomes registered under, **once registered**, VAT is due on all of the following: 2610
- taxable supplies made in the UK;
- goods acquired from another EU member state (¶9017+);
- reverse charge services received from outside the UK (¶9700+); and
- supplies to non-registered persons in other EU member states (¶9100+ and ¶9682+).

In many instances, VAT may also be reclaimed on expenditure incurred.

There are potentially severe consequences for **failing to register** (¶2684).

MEMO POINTS 1. If the trader is registered under the **wrong schedule**, HMRC will review the person's entitlement or requirement to register afresh. VATREG32000+
2. If the registration is **invalid**, the trader will be deregistered (¶2720+), unless the business is liable or entitled to be registered under other rules.
3. Traders whose supplies are **below the UK registration threshold** but who make digital supplies to non-business customers in other EU member states are permitted a special type of VAT registration. These traders may register and account for VAT under the **mini one stop shop** system (¶7000+), but only on their EU supplies, and not on UK supplies.

The register

HMRC maintains an electronic **VAT register** in which the following are recorded: 2612 VATREG02050
- the trader's name and address;
- application form details;
- relevant letters accompanying the application; and
- notifications of subsequent changes.

SECTION 2

Taxable persons

A. Who is a taxable person?

2620 s 3 VATA 1994; EC Directive 2006/112 art 9

The VAT Directive defines a taxable person as someone who undertakes an economic activity - which is itself a requirement for the making of taxable supplies. Thus a taxable person is one who makes taxable supplies. This is a wider definition than that used in the UK, where a taxable person is **defined** as a person who is:
– registered for VAT; or
– required to be so registered.

Registration, in turn, requires a person to be making taxable supplies; but unless a trader chooses to be registered voluntarily, there is no requirement to be registered until turnover exceeds a specified limit. *Finanzamt Groß-Gerau v MKG-Kraftfahrzeuge-Factoring GmbH* [2003]

Registration is a requirement imposed on a person rather than on a business. If a person carries on more than one business, all those business activities must be covered by a single registration, even if one or more of the activities would be below the registration limit if it were carried on alone. *CCE v Glassborow and another* [1974]

A "person" is usually one of the following:
– an individual (a sole trader);
– a partnership;
– a company or other body corporate, including a limited liability partnership; or
– a club or association (¶8140+).

2622 MEMO POINTS 1. For the meaning of **in business** see ¶100+. If a person is making supplies as part of a hobby, there is no liability to register. However, if the hobby becomes serious enough to be classed as a business, registration may be required.
2. **Less common** types of taxable person include:
– charities (¶8000+);
– pension funds (¶8280+);
– local authorities and public bodies (¶7830+);
– the Crown;
– European Economic Interest Groupings;
– Societas Europaea;
– incorporated further education bodies;
– credit unions;
– building societies;
– industrial and provident societies; and
– terminal (commodity) markets.
3. For **VAT groups** see ¶8800+.
4. For **racehorse** owners see ¶6160+.
5. For the **agricultural** flat rate scheme see ¶5970+.

Other persons acting as a taxable person

2624 s 46 VATA 1994

A person acting in a **representative capacity**, such as a personal representative or administrator, is treated as the taxable person after any of the following events:
– death;
– bankruptcy or incapacity;
– liquidation or receivership of a company; or
– where an administration order is placed on a company.

The effect is to allow the existing VAT registration to continue.

SI 1995/2518 reg 30 A person controlling a business in a representative capacity is only liable for VAT relating to that business.

Traders with **no UK establishment** who are liable to register (¶2667) can choose to appoint an agent or a VAT representative, who will deal with their VAT affairs on their behalf (¶7210+).

MEMO POINTS 1. The administrator must **inform** HMRC of the event date within 21 days of commencing to act. Insolvency practitioners must use form VAT769.
2. **Receivership** does not include the appointment of a receiver in respect of specific properties.
3. For further **details of insolvency, incapacity and death** see ¶8700+.

Employees

A person who works for an employer in return for pay makes no taxable supplies. Any **consideration** which that person receives is outside the scope of VAT. **2626**

An employee may **also have a business** and be self-employed, but all monies relating to the employment still remain outside the scope of VAT.

Suspension of activity

If a person **suspends** making taxable supplies, any existing registration will be allowed to continue unless and until it becomes clear that the business will not be resumed. **2628** VATDREG07000

B. Business splitting

Meaning of business splitting

HMRC has powers to intervene if it believes that a **single business has been split** into two or more legally independent parts to avoid one or both being liable to register for VAT. **2629** Sch 1 paras 1A and 2 VATA 1994 VATDSAG 01050+

HMRC may issue **assessments backdated** to the date when the business was split, if:
- the supplies exceed the registration threshold and are actually being made by only one of the businesses; or
- the actual supplies made by one or more of the businesses exceed the registration threshold.

This has a retrospective effect (¶2684) and late registration assessments can go back as far as 20 years (¶3635).

HMRC may issue a notice **making a direction** (¶2636) to treat the separate parts as a single entity for VAT purposes. This cannot be backdated, and may only be issued when the split is "artificial" (in practice, when HMRC reasonably believes the split to be "artificial").

Before making a direction naming any person, HMRC must be satisfied that: **2630**
- that person has made or is making taxable supplies;
- the activities performed by the person, and which give rise to the taxable supplies, form part of a larger business function with other activities being carried on by another person or persons; and
- if all the taxable supplies of that business function were taken into account, a person carrying on that business would be liable to be registered

EXAMPLE Mrs B owns stables from which she provides full livery services. Her annual turnover is £100,000 and she would therefore be required to register for VAT.
However, if the business was structured such that Mrs B only provided the stabling (with an annual turnover of £55,000) and Mr B provided the feed, bedding and other facilities (with an annual turnover of £45,000), the two businesses would, in the absence of a direction, not need to be registered for VAT.
In these particular circumstances, it is likely that HMRC would issue a direction to treat the two entities as one for VAT purposes.

Although there are **no definitive tests** to establish whether a business has been artificially split or not, HMRC is required by statute to consider the financial, economic and organisational links between the persons, including, for example: **2632**
- the existence or otherwise of normal, commercial, arm's-length relationships;
- the apportionment of overhead costs;
- addressing of invoices;

– means of advertising;
– segregation or otherwise of takings; and
– the existence or otherwise of separate bank accounts, accounting records and financial statements.

EXAMPLE
1. A fish and chip shop and two launderette businesses were allegedly run as three separate businesses, with two run by the husband and the other by his wife.
However, they were held to be one business for VAT purposes with the husband as the sole proprietor, largely on the basis that the various trading premises were in his name alone, as was the bank account. All the invoices for supplies to the businesses were addressed to him. The tribunal was satisfied that at all times the "controlling mind" of the business was that of the husband. *RS Sahota* [1997] (VTD 14986)

2. It was claimed that a kebab and pizza take-away outlet was run as two separate businesses, with an arrangement that the pizza outlet traded for one half of the week, and the kebab outlet for the other. Each business employed its own staff (apart from one shared employee). However, on the facts of this particular case, and in the absence of a written agreement between the parties, the activities were held to constitute one business, as the parties did not adequately demonstrate that there was a normal commercial relationship between them. For example:
– there was no separate charge from the freeholder to each business for overheads;
– both parties were covered by one public liability notice;
– all purchases of goods were made by one party; and
– the business was presented to the public as one, both parties using the same trading name and menus. *L & A Eleftheriou (t/a Picnic Kebab House)* [2000] (VTD 16659)

3. In relation to holiday accommodation, see also ¶5954.

2633 MEMO POINTS 1. **Public perception** and the treatment of the business for **direct tax purposes** are unlikely to be of significance for HMRC (although they may be factors which, when considered with others, are indicative one way or the other).
2. Generally, where an **existing business is extended**, the new activity will be regarded as being part of the existing business if the new activities are related to experience or qualifications used in the existing business.

EXAMPLE A barrister, specialising in patent and other intellectual property law, lectured on weekend courses on an ad hoc basis (every 2-3 years). It was held that this was an activity "in the course or furtherance of" his existing business (as a barrister). As his existing business was already registered for VAT, he should have accounted for VAT on the fees received for the weekend lecturing, as the activity amounted to an extension of his existing business. *BC Reid* [1993] (VTD 11625)

Note:
For details of the VAT rules relating to barristers see ¶7700+.

2635 Where **self-employed** individuals are used by a business to provide services to its customers, the key question which HMRC will be concerned with is whether the self-employed individual supplies services directly to:
– the customers (in which case the supply will be made by the self-employed person, and it may be that the trade is below the registration limit); or
– the main business, which in turn supplies services directly to the end customer (in which case it may be that the main business is registered for VAT, and consequently VAT will be due on the supplies).

For full details of the VAT rules relating to agents see ¶7090+.

HMRC directions

2636 Sch 1 para 2 VATA 1994
A direction issued by HMRC must:
– give a description of the business;
– name all the persons who are to be treated as carrying on the single business;
– be served on each of the persons named in it;
– give broad details of the reasons for issuing a notice of direction; and
– specify the date from which registration as a single taxable entity is to take place (which cannot be earlier than the date of the direction itself).

Consequences

The consequences of a direction on the new taxable entity and the individual members are as follows: **2638**
- the **persons** named in the direction must register as a single taxable entity (effectively a partnership which is governed by partnership law) from the date specified in the direction; and
- **existing VAT registration numbers** of any of the persons in the direction must be cancelled.

Supplementary directions

Supplementary directions can be issued to **add more persons** to the direction as appropriate. **2639** Sch 1 para 2(4) VATA 1994
Such directions must:
- make reference to the original direction; and
- be served on the person being added to the direction.

The consequences of a direction apply equally to supplementary directions.

MEMO POINTS When it becomes apparent that a person is no longer involved in the business, HMRC should give notice to that effect, specifying the date from which that person is to be regarded as **removed from the direction**. From this date the person concerned will cease to be:
- liable for any VAT issues of the business; and
- a member of the partnership.

SECTION 3

Persons making UK supplies

A person making taxable UK supplies may be required to register, depending on the value of those supplies. **2640**

A business may register voluntarily if it is making taxable UK supplies, or if there is an intention to make future taxable UK supplies.

Non-UK persons who satisfy particular rules can also register (¶2700).

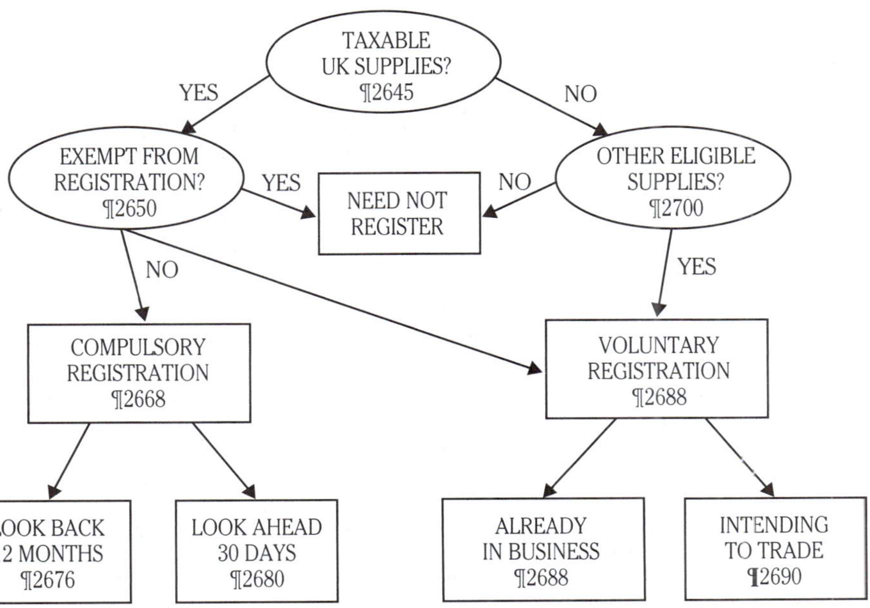

A. Who can register?

2645 A person who makes taxable supplies is eligible to register for VAT, but may be exempt from registration if certain conditions are met.

1. Taxable supplies

2647 s 4, Sch 1 para 1(7) VATA 1994 A taxable supply is **defined** as a UK supply of goods or services (¶245) which is neither exempt (¶350+) nor outside the scope of VAT (¶252+). Disposals of capital assets (¶2674) are generally disregarded for this purpose.

Taxable supplies **include**:
– UK supplies taxable at any rate (whether standard, reduced or zero);
– self-supplies, most commonly of property services (¶1490+); and
– reverse charges which arise when receiving international supplies (¶9700+).

2. Exemption from registration

2650 There are **two instances** where a trader can be exempt from the requirement to register:
– the trader is making predominately zero-rated supplies; or
– turnover is falling, so that taxable supplies will not exceed the deregistration threshold (¶9964).

A person taking advantage of an exemption will not be able to recover any input tax suffered, but will benefit from reduced compliance requirements.

MEMO POINTS 1. HMRC will **notify** exemption by sending a form VAT8.
2. If a **request** for exemption is **not accepted** by HMRC, registration will occur from the day that the trader first became liable to be registered. This means that output tax must be accounted for on any taxable supplies from this date (¶2712).
3. There is **no right to retrospective registration** where exemption has previously been granted.
4. HMRC uses the term "exception" to denote the case where turnover falls below the deregistration threshold.

Zero-rated supplies

2652 Sch 1 para 14 VATA 1994 A trader who makes only zero-rated supplies (¶1180+) can request exemption from registration (although the usual application process (¶2704+) is still required and an appropriate accompanying letter must be included). Both unregistered and registered traders can request exemption.

Traders making zero-rated sales can benefit from registering for VAT, as they can then recover input tax on their expenses. However, registration brings with it an administrative and compliance burden.

2654 Where **not all of the trader's supplies** are zero-rated, HMRC has discretion to allow exemption from registration only if a very small proportion of supplies are standard-rated, and the input tax would normally exceed output tax.

If granted, the exemption will **apply until** either the request is withdrawn by the trader, or a new request would no longer be granted. If HMRC refuses the exemption and still registers the trader, there is a right of appeal (¶4260+).

VATREG20200 MEMO POINTS 1. Where there is a **material change in the nature of supplies**, the trader must notify HMRC within 30 days of the date of the event (or of the end of the relevant calendar quarter, if there is no specific date). A material change would include the situation where, if the trader had been registered, the output tax would have exceeded the input tax in the last 12 months. Failing to notify will result in a penalty (¶4010+). Where appropriate, registration will be effective from the date of the event.

2. Similarly, any change in the **zero-rated proportion** of taxable supplies must be notified to HMRC within 30 days of the end of that calendar quarter (31 March, 30 June, etc).
3. If a trader wishes to **voluntarily register** (¶2688+) after having been granted exemption, the effective date of registration cannot predate the date on which the registration request is received by HMRC.
4. HMRC has no power to grant retrospective exemption for zero-rating.

Falling turnover

A person who would **usually be required to register** because the value of taxable supplies in the previous 12 months exceeds the registration threshold (¶9960), will be exempt if HMRC is satisfied that the value of the next 12 months' taxable supplies will be below the deregistration threshold (¶9964). **2656** Sch 1 para 4 VATA 1994

If the trader is **ceasing to trade** altogether (¶8600+) or **suspends** making taxable supplies for a period of at least 30 days, this exemption does not apply.

Comment Note that this exemption is not available for traders who are liable to be registered because of **future taxable supplies** (¶2680).

EXAMPLE A builder had been trading for many years with no liability to register. He then took on a mortgage for a joint investment in a property, and hired subcontractors so that he could pay off the mortgage. He became liable to register but had already decided to sell the property. His turnover subsequently fell. It was held that when considering the evidence available at the time, the builder was not required to register. Independent evidence was not required to support the builder's stated intentions. *Michael John Clements* [2004] (VTD 19216)

HMRC should be **notified** within 30 days of the trader first becoming liable to register, but no application for registration (form VAT1) is required. **2658** VATREG19250

If HMRC's **approval** to the exemption is **not sought**, the trader remains liable to register for VAT.

MEMO POINTS When considering the trader's entitlement to exemption, the following **factors** are important:
- nature of the business and seasonal fluctuations;
- taxable turnover in prior years;
- any recent increase in turnover; and
- orders and contracts which have been agreed at the time of notification.

Where the exemption is applied, the trader must still **continually monitor** taxable supplies. If the volume of supplies exceeds the threshold, the trader must either register or convince HMRC afresh that future turnover will fall. **2660**

As a concession, where the **same circumstances** give rise to a liability to register as when the exemption was first granted, there is no need to apply for a new exemption, provided that: VATREG19200
- the turnover in any subsequent month is less than 1/12th of the deregistration threshold (¶9964); and
- the trader has no reason to believe that supplies will exceed the deregistration threshold in the following 12 months.

Retrospective exemption is also available where taxable supplies have previously exceeded the threshold, but at the date of notification, future taxable supplies will be below it. However, the trader must satisfy HMRC that at the time when the requirement to register first arose, the only reasonable conclusion would have been that turnover would fall. "At the time" means on the basis of information then available: in particular, hindsight cannot be used. *Nash and Nash* [1997] (VTD 14944) **2662**

EXAMPLE In February 1997 HMRC issued a notice of registration to a trader who had become liable to register from September 1996. The trader appealed on the basis that some of his turnover had now been diverted to a company, so that the current and future turnover attributed to him as a sole trader would be below the deregistration threshold.
It was held that HMRC acted reasonably in not being satisfied that the turnover would fall below the threshold. The relevant date was September 1996 and HMRC had to consider whether it would

have known, based on the available evidence at that time, that turnover would fall. *JG Gray (t/a William Gray & Son) v C & E* [2000]

3. How many registrations are required?

2664 The **obligation or entitlement** to register remains with the person and not the business carried on (¶2620+).

The **same individual** can only be registered once in the same capacity, but may be part of different registrations (for example, as a sole trader, and also as a partner in a partnership (¶2734+)).

On **incorporation** or other **change of entity** (such as from sole trader to partnership), the individual taxable person must either deregister or transfer the registration to the new entity. For further details see ¶8640+.

MEMO POINTS 1. Where a **partnership** carries on more than one business, all the businesses must be included in the same VAT registration (¶2736).
2. A **company** may be allowed different registrations for each of its divisions (¶2744+).
3. A **club** can include all its activities in a single VAT registration, even where not all members partake (¶8225+).

B. Compulsory registration

2666 A person making (or intending to make) taxable supplies in the UK is required to register if:
- that person is not established in the UK (¶2667); or
- the value of taxable supplies exceeds a specified threshold (¶2668).

Non-established taxable persons

2667 Sch 1A VATA 1994 Notice 700/1 para 9 A non-established taxable person (NETP) is **defined**, with effect from 1 December 2012, as a person who makes taxable supplies in the UK (or intends to do so within the next 30 days) and who:
- is not normally resident in the UK;
- is not incorporated in the UK, if a company; and
- does not have a UK establishment (¶9688+).

HMRC gives as examples of an NETP a non-UK trader at farmers' markets, or an Irish service supplier working across the land border.

An NETP is required to register for UK VAT when it either:
- makes its first taxable supply in the UK; or
- first intends to make any taxable supplies in the UK in the following 30 days.

The obligation to register is **regardless of the value of the supply**. In particular, the thresholds (¶2668+) do not apply to an NETP, including for the purpose of intra-EU acquisitions (¶9040+).

The NETP has 30 days from making its first supply, or forming the intention to make supplies, to notify HMRC that it is required to register. If the NETP is not established in an EU country, a VAT representative (¶7210+) must normally be appointed to handle its VAT affairs.

Other taxable persons

2668 Sch 1 para 1(1) VATA 1994 Unless meeting the criteria for exemption (¶2650+), there are **two situations** where a trader may be required to register because the value of taxable supplies in a given period exceeds the threshold. They are distinguished by the period under consideration, which is either:
a. the previous 12 months; or
b. the next 30 days.

The threshold for registration is updated each year (¶9960) and registration is compulsory if the cumulative taxable supplies made by the trader in the period exceed the threshold.

For the registration requirements when a person **buys a business** see ¶8640+.

What is compared to the threshold?

For the purpose of deciding whether registration is required, the following must be ascertained: **2670**
- the **time** of supply (¶750+), which is usually (but not always) the invoice date
- the **place** of supply (¶31+), as only UK supplies are taken into account; and
- the **value** of supplies (¶925), which is taken to be the sales price.

MEMO POINTS 1. For persons who may be **agents** (¶7090+), it is particularly important to determine whether the whole value of the main supply, or just the commission, should be included.
2. An **unregistered person** can make taxable supplies, but no VAT is charged.

There are **particular rules** regarding the following: **2672**

Topic	Amount compared to threshold	Taxable amount once registered	¶¶
Capital assets	Mostly ignored	Mostly ignored	¶2674
Margin scheme for supplies of second-hand goods	Full sales price	Net selling price	¶6620+
Long-term hotel accommodation (supplied to an individual for longer than 4 weeks)	Value of meals, drinks and service charges Excludes charge for accommodation itself	Value of meals, drinks and service charges Excludes charge for accommodation itself	¶984+
Tour operators supplying travel packages	Margin	Margin	¶7490+
Fiscal warehousing	Taxable acquisition or supply on removal from warehouse ignored	Amount which would have been due if goods had not entered warehouse plus value of supply on removal from warehouse	¶9242+

Capital assets Sales of capital assets used in the business, **other than** of a standard-rated interest in land (¶5100+), are excluded when determining liability to register or deregister. **2674** Sch 1 para 4 VATA 1994

Capital assets are tangible or intangible goods of a durable nature, held and used for the enduring benefit of the trade, and which are usually written off over a period of more than one year. *Verbond van Nederlandse Ondernemingen v Inspecteur der Invoerrechten en Accijnzen* [1977]
Other criteria which must be considered include:
- the value of the asset;
- whether the asset is sold or retained by the business; and
- whether the sale is unusual in relation to the turnover and size of the business.

Common examples would be premises, machinery, computers, cars, patent rights and goodwill.

MEMO POINTS 1. Supplies of **property** which the trader has **opted to tax** (¶5602+) are included in taxable supplies. Notice 700/1 para 2.8
2. For **overseas traders** supplying capital assets in respect of which they have recovered UK input tax, see ¶9890+.

EXAMPLE In a contrived avoidance scheme, a company leased cars to third parties for approximately 6 months, before reselling them back to the car dealer. The issue was whether the resale of the cars could be ignored for the purposes of the registration threshold.

It was held that the cars were not capital assets because they did not fit any of the following criteria which would indicate a capital asset:
- durability (in the context of the business);
- length of time asset is held; and
- an unusual transaction which creates a spike in sales.

The sales should therefore be taken into account. *Harbig Leasing Two Ltd* [2000] (VTD 16843)

Looking back

2676 The trader must **continually review**, on a rolling basis, the level of taxable supplies made in the previous 12 months.

Sch 1 para 5 VATA 1994 If, at the **end of any calendar month**, the previous 12 months' taxable supplies exceed the threshold applying at that time, the trader must notify (¶2704+) HMRC within the next 30 days, and registration will take effect from the end of the month following that in which the threshold was exceeded. However, HMRC regards the **effective date of registration** (EDR) as being the 1st of the month after that (see example 1).

MEMO POINTS 1. If HMRC has **exempted** the trader from registration (¶2650+), the liability to notify continues for any following months when the threshold has been exceeded.
2. If **trading for less than 12 months**, the threshold applies to the period since beginning to trade. It is not pro-rated.

EXAMPLE

1. On 21 July Mr A finds that his taxable supplies since the previous 1 August exceed the threshold. He becomes liable to register on 31 July and must notify HMRC by 30 August.
He will be registered from 1 September, so any supplies that Mr A makes in August escape output tax.

2. Ms B has made the following taxable supplies since commencing to trade:

Month	Month's supplies £	Supplies in last 12 months £	Month	Month's supplies £	Supplies in last 12 months £
Mar 2013	3,500	3,500	Mar 2014[1]	8,500	61,000
April 2013	3,500	7,000	April 2014[2]	10,500	68,000
May 2013	3,500	10,500	May 2014	10,000	74,500
June 2013	3,750	14,250	June 2014	11,000	81,750
July 2013	3,750	18,000	July 2014	6,500	84,500
Aug 2013	4,000	22,000	Aug 2014	9,000	89,500
Sept 2013	4,500	26,500			
Oct 2013	4,500	31,000			
Nov 2013	5,000	36,000			
Dec 2013	6,500	42,500			
Jan 2014	6,500	49,000			
Feb 2014	7,000	56,000			

The threshold was £79,000 until 31 March 2014 and then became £81,000.
Therefore Ms B is liable to register once her taxable supplies reach £81,750 in June 2014. She will therefore be registered from 1 August 2014.

Note:
1. The previous 12 months' supplies are calculated by adding on March 2014 to the previous cumulative total and deducting March 2013.
2. The previous 12 months' supplies are calculated by adding on April 2014 to the previous cumulative total and deducting April 2013 (and so on).

2678 Sch 1 para 1(4) VATA 1994 **Previous registration** For the purpose of any **subsequent need to register**, if a trader has previously been registered and **full information** was given to HMRC at the time of cancellation, the taxable supplies made under that previous registration are ignored. If the **previous registration lasted for less than 12 months**, the taxable supplies made prior to the commencement of that registration must still be taken into account (note that the threshold is not pro-rated for this purpose).

However, supplies will not be ignored where the previous registration was **void** because HMRC agreed that the person was not liable to register at the date of registration (under any of the rules). In this case, the person should never have been registered, and no VAT was ever accounted for.

MEMO POINTS 1. To monitor this situation, any previous **VAT numbers** allocated to a person must be disclosed in any registration application.
2. HMRC may require some form of **security or guarantee** (¶3546+) in certain circumstances, such as for a trader with a history of VAT arrears.

EXAMPLE Mr C was previously registered for 8 months from 1 March to 31 October 2014. He gave full information when deregistering.
When reviewing the value of his taxable supplies from November 2014 onwards, he must take into account the supplies made before March 2014, until the 12-month period no longer stretches back that far.

Month end	Months of taxable supplies taken into account
Nov 2014	Dec 2013 to Feb 2014, Nov 2014
Dec 2014	Jan 2014 to Feb 2014, Nov 2014 to Dec 2014
Jan 2015	Feb 2014, Nov 2014 to Jan 2015
Feb 2015	Nov 2014 to Feb 2015

Looking forward

A trader is required to be registered **at any time** if there are reasonable grounds for believing that the value of taxable supplies in the next 30 days alone will exceed the threshold. HMRC must be notified within the following 30 days, but the **effective date of registration** (EDR) will be the first day of that 30-day period. 2680

MEMO POINTS 1. **Reasonable grounds** for belief are a question of fact. The test is whether on balance, taking all relevant factors into account, it was more likely than not - and therefore reasonable to believe - that the threshold would be exceeded. A common circumstance would be a change in the business, such as a successful contract bid which creates a need to register.
2. In relation to a **one-off event**, the organiser will probably be able to anticipate the level of turnover, based on ticket sales and also perhaps previous experience of holding the event. If the organiser genuinely believed that the threshold would not be exceeded, but in actual fact it is, there would be no liability to register, as HMRC waives the requirement in this case. VATREG16200

EXAMPLE On 13 October Mrs D expects her taxable supplies to exceed the registration threshold because of a large order.
She must notify HMRC by 12 November and will be registered from 13 October.

Both tests could apply

Where the trader becomes liable under both tests **at the same time**, registration will take effect from the earliest possible date. 2682

MEMO POINTS A trader who has just **acquired a going concern** may be liable to register based on the previous taxable supplies made by the business before the change of ownership (¶8557+, ¶8640+). In that case, the going concern rules or 30-day rule take precedence over the look-back test.

EXAMPLE Mr E's taxable supplies in the last 12 months exceed the threshold by 20 June. However, on 25 June he takes an order which itself exceeds the threshold.
Applying the look-back test first, Mr E's registration would take effect from 1 August.
Under the look-forward test, Mr E's registration takes effect from 25 June. This is the effective date of registration.

Failing to register

There are **two consequences** of failing to register either on time or at all: 2684
a. registration will be backdated to the date on which it should have become effective (this has particular relevance for artificial business splitting (¶2629+)); and
b. penalties will be due (¶4010+).

The **backdating** of registration has very serious consequences for the trader's profitability, because VAT is chargeable on all taxable supplies made since the date of registration. There is no limit on the period of time which the backdating covers.

The **output tax** is calculated as a fraction of the consideration received from the customer, as shown in the following table:

Supplies		Fraction
Reduced-rated		1/21
Standard-rated	From 4 January 2011	1/6
	1 January 2010 to 3 January 2011	7/47
	1 December 2008 to 31 December 2009	3/23
	Earlier	7/47

Once registered, the trader could, in principle, charge additional VAT to customers by creating a second invoice, and treating the price already charged as the net value. However, this may not be commercially possible, and the trader must then suffer the output tax.

In this case only, the usual 4-year time limit for **input tax** recovery (¶2014) does not apply, so that there is no restriction on the scope of a claim.

EXAMPLE In January 2015 Mr F discovers that he should have registered 12 months ago. His taxable income arising from standard-rated supplies during that period was £90,000.
The output tax due for the backdated period is £15,000. (£90,000 × 1/6)
This must be paid on the due date of Mr F's first VAT return.
Mr F subsequently invoices his customers for VAT, an amount of £18,000. (£90,000 x 20%)
He must account for the additional output tax (£3,000) on the return for the VAT period in which the invoices are issued.

C. Voluntary registration

2688 Sch 1 para 9 VATA 1994 A person who carries on a business, and either makes or intends to make taxable supplies, can choose to register for VAT.

A person who makes supplies outside the UK, which would be taxable if made in the UK, may also choose to register (¶2700).

The **reasons** for choosing to register are usually:
- wanting to reclaim input tax as an intending trader (¶2690+); or
- because the supplies are zero-rated (when the trader receives VAT repayments only); or
- to avoid inadvertently breaching the thresholds for compulsory registration, possibly incurring penalties; or
- to enhance the image of the business and mask its small size.

Intending taxable trader

2690 VATREG22000 A person who intends to make taxable supplies at some time in the future will often want to register as soon as possible in order to **reclaim input tax** on preparatory expenses (¶8560+).

To register as an intending trader, a person must:
- be carrying on a business;
- not yet be making taxable supplies; and
- intend to make taxable supplies in the future.

VATREG22300+ HMRC treats any input tax **refund** as provisional, and repayable if no taxable supplies are ever actually made. In particular, where:
- only exempt supplies are made, all input tax refunded is repayable to HMRC;

- exempt supplies are made but there is still an intention to make taxable supplies, a proportion of input tax will be repayable; or
- trading is abandoned, no input tax is repayable to HMRC.

MEMO POINTS 1. **Preparation to trade** would include the acquisition of assets and the means to use them for profit, but not the issue of shares. *Rompelman-van Deelen v Minister van Financiën* [1985] VATREG22000
2. The trader is not required to estimate either the **first date** of trading or the **value** of taxable supplies.

Before allowing registration, HMRC will review the application carefully, to ensure that the trader has a firm intention to make taxable supplies. **2692** VATREG22100

In particular, the trader must provide evidence of any of the following which may be available to support the contention that the business will be making taxable supplies:
- business plans;
- history of activities;
- efforts to raise finance;
- contracts for work (or bids or tenders);
- contracts for stock, goods or services receivable;
- advertising campaigns;
- invoices for expenditure already incurred; and
- property details (such as planning permission).

MEMO POINTS There are further requirements in relation to **property developers**, who must supply the following information:
- details of the intended supplies;
- notification of the option to tax election (¶5670+) if relevant; and
- evidence of preparations made such as feasibility studies, planning applications, property deeds, and related professional services.

It is not necessary for the option to tax to be made before registration is to take effect. *Beaverbank Properties Ltd* [2003] (VTD 18099)

If HMRC **refuses** an intending trader registration, usually because it is unconvinced by meagre evidence, the trader can either appeal, or reapply when it is obvious that the business is getting off the ground. As input tax on goods can still be recovered in respect of the 4 years prior to registration (¶8562), the trader is unlikely to lose out in the long term (although the recovery period for services is only 6 months), except to the extent that the input tax refund will be delayed. **2694**

Effective date

The effective date of registration will **usually** be the date of the request, **unless**: **2696** VATREG18350
- the trader is giving advance notification of an intention to register, in which case the effective date must be within the next 3 months, and not usually before the date of the first taxable supply; or
- an earlier date is mutually agreed by the trader and HMRC.

A **company** cannot be registered before the date of incorporation. It may, however, be possible for the directors or other representatives to be registered where this is considered necessary (¶8566+). VATREG25450

The registration will be **valid until** the trader ceases either to make, or have the intention to make, taxable supplies.

Retrospective registration

HMRC can agree that registration will be effective from a past date, provided that the trader requests this when making the initial application. **2698** Sch 1 para 9 VATA1994; VATREG25400

At the **date of the request**, for retrospection to be negotiable the trader must be neither registered nor required to register. If previously registered and then deregistered, the date of any subsequent registration cannot precede the original date of registration.

The **limit** on retrospection is 4 years. Notice 700/1 para 5.2

As input tax on goods can be recovered for the 4 years prior to the date of registering in any event (¶8562), retrospective registration may not be beneficial, particularly if the trader does not want to declare output tax on the supplies already made.

Trader not making taxable UK supplies

2700 Sch 1 para 10 VATA1994; VATREG23150+

In special circumstances input tax is recoverable even where no UK supplies are made, in which case a person can voluntarily register provided that all of the following **criteria** are satisfied. The trader must:
- make supplies where the related input tax is specifically recoverable;
- have a business establishment in the UK or a usual place of residence in the UK (¶9688+); and
- have no intention of making taxable supplies in the UK (and not already have done so).

Registration will be valid until the trader requests deregistration, or forms the intention to make taxable supplies in the UK, in which case HMRC must be informed.

MEMO POINTS 1. Supplies where input tax is **specifically recoverable** include:
- those made outside the UK which would be taxable if they were made within the UK;
- warehoused goods (¶9242+);
- finance and insurance supplies specified by the Treasury and made by a UK business to a customer who belongs outside the EU; and
- supplies of investment gold (¶6835+).

2. Where the trader has **no UK business establishment**, and is neither making nor intending to make UK taxable supplies, no registration is available, and input tax can only be recovered by a special directive claim (¶9875+ and ¶9908+).

D. How to register

2704 SI 1995/2518 reg 5 VATREG03000+

A trader will **apply** to register using either the paper form VAT1, which includes a signed declaration that all of the required information is complete and correct, or through the VAT Online service via the Internet.

The form must be **signed by** the person who is liable or entitled to register. This is commonly one of the following:
- sole trader;
- partner;
- director;
- company secretary; or
- trustee.

MEMO POINTS 1. When using **VAT Online**, either the trader or an authorised representative may apply, and an electronic acknowledgement will be received once the application has been successfully made. A VAT number will still be notified in writing.
The advantages of the VAT Online service are said by HMRC to be that:
- it is free and secure;
- it avoids postal delays;
- the application can be completed by an agent on the trader's behalf;
- there is onscreen help and online checks; and
- an immediate acknowledgement is available once HMRC has received the application.

2. If **trading under a different name**, all other names must be disclosed, as the business is subject to section 4 of the Business Names Act 1995.
3. HMRC may require some form of **security or guarantee** (¶3546+) before allowing registration to occur.

Details of the form

2706 To avoid unnecessary delay it is extremely important that the form is completed correctly. The trader should **keep** a copy of the form, in case of loss, and retain evidence of the date of posting. A contact phone number should be entered on the form in case HMRC has an issue to discuss.

The **effective date of registration** (EDR) must be stated (whether this is when the trader became liable to register, or a future date).

The **registered address** should be the principal place of business, which is where orders are normally taken and processed. A private address or the premises of the accountant are unlikely to be the registered address. A PO Box number will not be accepted. VATREG03550

The business can request that its **VAT periods** (¶2987+) coincide with its financial year, in which case financial accounts or other appropriate evidence should be submitted with the form. The business can indicate on the application whether it wants to submit returns on a quarterly or monthly basis. It can also apply for annual accounting, or to submit returns using non-standard VAT return periods.

MEMO POINTS 1. For a **company**, the form cannot be submitted until incorporation is complete, and the relevant details have been received from Companies House.
2. In addition to the form, a **VAT pack** is issued to a trader which includes: VATREG05100
- Notice 700/1: "Should I be registered for VAT? ";
- form VAT2 for partnerships (if appropriate);
- VAT charter document;
- VAT enquiries guide;
- information about simplification for the smaller business (¶4600), including cash accounting; and
- information about late registration penalties (¶4010).

Certificate of registration

Once the application has been processed, a certificate of registration (VAT4) will be sent to the trader, indicating: 2708
- the effective date of registration;
- the trader's VAT registration number;
- the date when the first VAT period ends; and
- the length of future VAT periods.

Although most matters involving registration can be appealed, the details of VAT periods cannot.

MEMO POINTS 1. A trader who **receives no communication** from HMRC within 15 working days should contact HMRC. As a consequence of fraud (¶1988+), HMRC is extending the verification checks it makes with regard to certain registration applications, which is resulting in significant delays. Notice 700/1 para 4.5
2. It is possible for HMRC to issue VAT returns for **periods which fall before** the effective date of registration indicated on the certificate, usually in the case of late registration, if that certificate was issued in error. *Maidstone Sailing Club* [1997] (VTD 511)
3. The **first VAT period** can span a number of years. *Bjellica (t/a Eddy's Domestic Appliances) v C & E* [1995]
4. If the certificate shows a **wrong date**, a corrected replacement will be provided.

VAT number

The trader's VAT number is a unique 9-digit code, which must be quoted on all of the trader's VAT invoices and correspondence. 2710

It used to be possible for a trader to request advance notice of the number but HMRC no longer offers this option.

Standard practice now is that the trader must wait for the application to be processed. HMRC may ask for further information (e.g. in connection with possible missing trader fraud), and if any doubt remains about the veracity of the trader, it will carry out a compliance check (¶3414+) before the first VAT return is due. It may be the case, therefore, that a delay can arise before a VAT number is issued.

Immediate consequences

The business must **charge** output tax on all taxable supplies and maintain the appropriate **records** (¶2790+) from the date on which it became liable to be registered. 2712 Notice 700/1 para 5

Where the trader is already liable to be registered **before the certificate** of registration has been issued, it may be necessary to charge output tax. In this case the price must be inclusive without any separate identification of the VAT element. The business will need to tell VAT-registered customers that a VAT invoice will be issued within 30 days of the certificate being received, so that they can claim the relevant input tax. The output tax will then be declared on the trader's first VAT return.

If the business has **voluntarily registered**, it must charge output tax from the registration date requested on the application form.

Changes in circumstances

2714 Notice 700 para 26.3 The **general rule** for any change in circumstances (such as a change of name, address, legal status) is that HMRC must be notified in writing within 30 days. The trader should state address, VAT number and details of the change, and the registered person must sign the letter. Some changes can be notified online: for details, see flmemo.co.uk/vm2714.

As a result of the change, deregistration may be required (¶2720+).

Penalties (¶4050+) apply when the trader fails to notify HMRC appropriately, although these are not normally levied, except in cases of tax loss.

2716 The following table indicates the **most common** notifiable changes.

Changed circumstances	Details	Electronic notification available
Name of the proprietor(s)		✓
Name of the business or incorporated company		✓
Name or status of an unincorporated company		x
Address of the principal place of business or registered office		✓
Main business activity		✓
Bank account details		✓
Limited company becomes unlimited or the reverse		✓
Limited company becomes a plc or the reverse		✓
Partners in the partnership	If at least one partner remains the same	✓
	Complete change	x
Sale or disposal of the business	¶8640+	x
Death, insolvency or incapacity	¶8700+	x
Incorporation, disincorporation and striking off	¶8566+, ¶8640+, ¶8738	x
Creation/dissolution of a partnership	¶8648+, ¶8678+	x
Ceasing to make taxable supplies	¶2724+	x
Transfer of business between companies	¶8640+	x
Name or address of VAT representative for overseas principal	¶7210+	✓

E. Ceasing to be registered

2720 Sch 1 para 13 VATA 1994; Notice 700/11 A registered business can only **cancel** its registration (also known as deregistering) if it is not required to be registered under any of the rules (UK supplies, distance sales or EU acquisitions).

Certain **circumstances** always require deregistration, whereas in others the trader has a choice.

If deregistration occurs **in error** (when the person is still required to be registered), VAT will be due from the date of re-registration. In cases of incorrect deregistration, an inaccuracy penalty may be levied (¶4000+).

Deregistration can be done online, or by submitting a form VAT7.

MEMO POINTS 1. It is not possible to deregister **retrospectively**.
2. Ceasing to be registered means no further returns are required, which has **consequences** for:
- the final VAT return (¶3010+);
- VAT invoices (¶2840+);
- recovery of input tax (¶8618+);
- output tax on assets held on deregistration (usually stock, but could include an opted building (¶8610+));
- bad debts on invoices issued before deregistration (¶860); and
- the retention of records (¶2797+).

3. To **avoid loss of input tax recovery**, it may be preferable to delay deregistration until the trader's affairs have been sorted out.
4. A trader can voluntarily **re-register** at any time, assuming the relevant criteria are satisfied. See ¶2678 for further details of the treatment of a cancelled registration where re-registration occurs.
5. If the reduced turnover is a result of a **single business splitting into two or more entities** (¶2629+), HMRC will consider the circumstances carefully.

Summary

2722

Circumstances	Details	Deregistration		Effective date
		Compulsory	Voluntary	
Ceasing to make, or having the intention to make, taxable supplies		✓		Date of cessation
Claiming exemption	¶2650+		✓	Date of request
Change in legal status (**unless** continuation of registration requested)	Sole trader becomes a partnership	✓		Date of change
	Dissolution of partnership to a sole tradership	✓		
	Incorporation	✓		
	Corporate winding up followed by a sole tradership or partnership	✓		
	Disbanding of a VAT group	✓		
Sale or disposal of the business	New owner does not take on VAT number	✓		Date of disposal
Taxable turnover in next 12 months below deregistration threshold			✓	Date of request
Partial business closure	Remaining business trading below deregistration threshold		✓	Date of request
Joining a VAT group	¶8800+	✓		Date of joining
Joining the agricultural flat rate scheme	¶5970+	✓		Date of joining
Ceasing to make overseas supplies which would be taxable if made in UK		✓		Date of cessation
Non-EU supplier intending to register under special scheme for electronically supplied services	¶7004+	✓		Date of request

Circumstances of deregistration

2724 **Compulsory cancellation** A registered trader must deregister if the business has ceased to make taxable supplies, or is not otherwise entitled to register under the distance selling or EU acquisition rules. HMRC must be notified within 30 days.

If a person is going to **subsequently** register under the scheme for **electronically supplied services** (¶7004+) either in the UK or elsewhere in the EU, any existing UK registration will be cancelled.

2726 VATDREG02050 **Voluntary cancellation** The trader may request deregistration where the VAT-exclusive **value of future taxable supplies** in the next 12 months will not exceed the relevant threshold (¶9964). However, this voluntary deregistration is only available if the trader is not ceasing or suspending business, because compulsory deregistration has priority (although the only practical consequence is to delay the effective date of deregistration).

The trader must write to HMRC, explaining the **reasons** for the fall in turnover, which may include:
- a reduction in opening hours;
- contracts which have been lost; or
- a change in business practices.

Notice 700/11 para 3.2 This will also have implications for **pricing**, particularly for retailers who charge a VAT-inclusive amount to their customers. HMRC would expect prices to fall post-deregistration in this case, in lieu of the VAT element which is no longer chargeable.

EXAMPLE Ms G plans to make only exempt supplies from 1 April. She currently makes taxable supplies in excess of the threshold. As she knows at 1 January that her taxable supplies in the next 12 months will be below the deregistration threshold, she requests deregistration from 1 January.
HMRC does not allow the deregistration from this date because Ms G is ceasing to make taxable supplies.
Ms G must therefore notify HMRC by 30 April that she has ceased to make taxable supplies, and she will then be deregistered from 1 April.

When deregistration becomes effective

2728 Notice 700/11 para 3.5 Until the operative date is confirmed by HMRC, the trader must continue with VAT accounting as normal.

Where deregistration is **compulsory**, it will take effect from the date of the event causing the cancellation (¶2722).

For **voluntary** deregistration, the date requested by the trader is normally granted, unless a later date is mutually agreed.

If the trader was **not liable to be registered** from an earlier date, that date can be used as the date of deregistration. Otherwise, HMRC never agrees to retrospective deregistration (that is, to an effective date before the date of the application).

If the trader was **never liable to be registered**, then rather than deregistering, HMRC will cancel the registration so that it is deemed never to have had effect. In this case, any input tax already refunded is repayable to HMRC. *Tourick (RM) & Co* [1992] (VTD 7712) Output tax will be repayable to the trader, subject to the usual restrictions (¶3244+).

Voluntary deregistration can be **deferred** on request in order to assist input tax recovery on commercial purchases. Of course output tax will be payable whilst the registration continues, so it may be preferable to utilise the special input tax system for recovery after deregistration instead (¶8618+).

Details of the deregistration are normally notified to the trader online.

F. Special situations

The special situations covered here are partnerships, company divisions and joint property ownership. For group registrations see ¶8800+. 2732

1. Partnerships

A partnership is defined in general law as "the relationship that subsists between persons carrying on a business in common with a view to profit". There is, however, no statutory definition of partnership for tax purposes. 2734 s 1 Partnership Act 1890

A partnership does not include a company or incorporated association.

Unlike a company, a partnership is not a separate legal entity (except in Scotland), and partners are therefore liable for their own actions and those of their partners.

Except for Scottish partnerships (¶2738), all businesses carried on by the partnership will be covered by the same registration. *CCE v Glassborow and another* [1974]

MEMO POINTS 1. The **understanding** may be implicit from the actions and intentions of the parties. There is no need for a contract, and any "no partnership clause" is ignored. *Weiner v Harris* [1910] VATREG08450+

2. HMRC will consider many factors in order to decide whether a partnership exists. The presence or absence of a particular factor will not be conclusive (although it may be persuasive) evidence. The main factors that indicate the existence of a partnership are:
- a partnership agreement;
- the partners sharing losses as well as profits;
- all of the partners having the power to bind the firm in transactions and authorise payments;
- the business being registered as a partnership for VAT;
- the presence of partners' names on letter headings.

3. **Carrying on a business** takes its normal meaning, and includes every trade, occupation or profession.

4. **View to a profit** would include the sharing of income net of expenses (whether this be a profit or loss), but not the sharing of gross income. Entities sharing gross income which are not partnerships include share farmers, joint ventures and consortia.

Who is the taxable person?

Although partnerships have no separate **legal identity** in England, Wales and Northern Ireland, for VAT purposes the partnership has a deemed identity which is separate from the partners. Only if all the partners change is the partnership's registration affected, subject to the actual sale of the business. Penalties, where incurred, will be levied against the whole partnership, irrespective of which partner is at fault. 2736 s 45 VATA 1994

Any notice of **assessment** (¶3625+) will be raised on the partners individually, and may even be directed against a single partner. That partner would then need to recover any amounts due from the other partners.

A partnership cannot be a **partner** in another partnership (except in Scotland), so if the ABC partnership joins with the DEF partnership, a wholly new partnership is created, which will have a separate registration. The original partnerships may also continue to exist, so it is possible that three registrations would be required. VATREG08600

MEMO POINTS 1. The change from a **sole trader to a partnership** or vice versa will usually require deregistration of the former entity and registration of the new entity, unless the registration is being transferred (¶8678+).

2. As a limited partner is unable to take part in the management and running of the partnership business, they cannot be making taxable supplies in the course and furtherance of that business. Consequently for **limited partnerships**, registration is in the name of the general partners only. In the case of multiple limited partnerships, where the limited partner and general partner are not the same, separate registrations will be possible. VATREG09300

3. **Salaried partners** may be employees or full partners, depending on the exact circumstances. If their name appears on the registration application, HMRC will treat them as full partners.

VATREG09100 4. A **trust** may be registered as an association (¶8225+) or a partnership. A copy of the trust deed should be provided with the application for registration.

EXAMPLE
1. The CAD partnership takes on a new partner, B.
The CAD partnership still continues for VAT purposes, and the registration is not affected.

2. If the CAD partnership sells its business to the partnership CEG, this is a change which could require CAD to deregister and CEG to register.

3. L & M, LM & N and LMN & O are all separately registered partnerships.
If N leaves or dies, the LM & N (as was) partnership must deregister because L & M already exists.
The LMN & O partnership registration continues, but with N being removed from the registration.

4. WX is a limited partnership where H is the general partner and J is a limited partner.
The same people are involved in the YZ partnership, but this time J is the general partner and H is a limited partner.
WX can have a separate registration from YZ.

Scottish partnerships

2738 s 4 Partnership Act 1890; VATREG09050

In Scotland, a partnership is a distinct legal person, and if separate partnership agreements exist for **each business**, the same partnership may have a different registration for each business.

Partners are only **personally liable** for the debts of the partnership if it becomes insolvent.

EXAMPLE Mr A and Ms B own five launderettes in Scotland, each covered by a separate partnership agreement.
They may have five different registrations. However, HMRC may wish to consider whether this is "artificial" business splitting (see ¶2629+).

Applying for registration

2740 The normal registration forms must be accompanied by form VAT2, which states the name, address and signature of each full partner. The main application form VAT1 is only signed by one partner.

The firm's **name** should be entered on the forms. If the firm has no name, the full names of all partners should be entered instead.

Notification of changes

2742 The usual time limits apply to changes of circumstances (¶2714+). The most important change for a partnership is the identity of the partners, which can be notified verbally. *Hussein and Asim t/a Pressing Dry Cleaners* [2003] (VTD 18341)

Non-Scottish partners are treated as jointly and severally **liable** for the partnership's VAT debts until HMRC is informed that the partner has left. An ex-partner is still liable for any VAT which arose whilst they were a partner.

2. Divisional registration

2744 Some companies operate on the basis of separate departments or divisions, which each have their own accounting records. This can make the accumulation of information necessary to complete the company's VAT returns very difficult.

s 46 VATA 1994 HMRC may **approve** divisional registration, which means that each division has its own VAT registration number, and submits its own returns. However, the company itself remains liable for the VAT debts of all the divisions, as it is still the taxable person.

Divisional registration cannot apply whilst the company is part of a VAT group (¶8800).

Eligibility

The following **conditions** must all be satisfied: 2746 Notice 700/2 para 8.5

a. the company finds it difficult to submit a VAT return for all the divisions within the normal time scale of 30 days;
b. the company is (or is treated as) fully taxable, so any minor exempt supplies fall below the de minimis limits as applied to the company as a whole (¶2194+);
c. all divisions must be registered, irrespective of activity and scale;
d. all VAT returns will need to be submitted for the same periods (¶2987+); and
e. the divisions must be independent units with their own accounting systems, and distinguished by:
- geographical location;
- items sold; or
- function (e.g. manufacturing, retail etc).

MEMO POINTS 1. Although a company is the most common entity to find divisional registration useful, **other bodies corporate** (such as limited liability partnerships and industrial and provident societies) are also eligible.
2. In relation to **d.** above, the company may request **VAT periods** which are non-regular (not 3-monthly). The option to make monthly returns will be available if the company receives VAT repayments overall.
3. **Overseas** companies are eligible to apply, provided that there are at least two UK divisions. If any overseas parts of a company make taxable UK supplies, one (only) of the UK divisions must be chosen to account for VAT on those supplies as if it had made them itself. Notice 700/2 para 8.9

EXAMPLE A garage company has the following departments:
- forecourt sales;
- used cars; and
- new cars.

Each department has its own accounting function and makes taxable supplies.
The garage could choose to operate divisional registration.

Commencing

The company needs to apply for divisional registration by completing form VAT1 for each division. The application must be accompanied by proof of incorporation, and a letter setting out the reasons why divisional registration is required. 2748 Notice 700/2 para 8.6

If approved, the **effective date** from which divisional registration begins will be notified by HMRC. It is possible for retrospective registration to be requested in exceptional circumstances.

Continuing

Supplies between the divisions are not supplies for VAT purposes, and are therefore ignored for VAT accounting. 2750

It is possible to **change the number** of divisions in the company as follows:
- to add a new division, the full application procedure must be followed for that division; and
- if a division is sold or closed down, HMRC must be notified in writing, so that the division is removed from HMRC's records.

Ceasing

If a division's taxable **supplies fall below** the deregistration threshold, it can only be deregistered if the supplies will be accounted for by another division, because the company as a whole is still the taxable person. 2752 Notice 700/2 para 8.12

If a division **no longer satisfies** the conditions for divisional registration, HMRC must be informed within 30 days. The division's registration will then be cancelled. However, all of the taxable business supplies of the company as a whole must be covered by a registration (either by another division's registration, or the company must revert back to having a single registration).

3. Joint owners of land

2754 Notice 742 para 7.2; VATREG09100

If more than one person (up to a maximum of four) owns a piece of land, a trust is deemed to exist under land law, and a VAT registration must be in joint names.

HMRC's view is that such a situation should be **treated as a partnership** even where no legal partnership exists. The owners must register if they make taxable supplies in excess of the threshold, and can register voluntarily if they do not.

If the joint owners are already covered by an **existing partnership registration**, the land transaction will be covered by that registration. This includes the situation where only four partners are owners, but there are further partners in the partnership.

CHAPTER 2

Records

OUTLINE ¶¶

Records must be retained in order to: **2790**
– satisfy HMRC that the trader is operating VAT correctly; and
– protect the trader from assessments which could otherwise be issued in the absence of supporting evidence e.g. for input tax claims or to prove the volume of sales.

The most important records are the VAT account and VAT invoices.

SECTION 1

General requirements

Records must always be retained for future verification. **2795**

Particular circumstances, or the use of certain VAT schemes, may impose additional requirements.

1. Retention of records

Period

The **minimum time** for which records should be retained is 6 years, unless HMRC agrees in writing to a shorter period (usually because the business has storage problems or would **2797** Sch 11 para 6 VATA 1994 otherwise be subjected to undue expense). In relation to land and buildings, longer periods apply to properties covered by the capital goods scheme (¶5750+), or over which an option to tax has been exercised (¶5602+).

The requirements are the same for electronic records and for paper.

Failure to meet these requirements may result in a penalty (¶4058+).

In practice, the 6-year limit applies as follows:

VATREC3020+

Type of records	Example	Limit applies from
Records of individual events	VAT invoice	Date of issue
Records of a series of events	Day books	Date of last entry
Summary documents	Balance sheet	Date of preparation

Technically there is nothing to stop a trader **destroying parts** of a record as each part becomes out of date. However, HMRC will view such actions as suspicious.

2800 MEMO POINTS 1. The 6-year rule applies even **after deregistration**, unless the business is sold and the buyer takes over the seller's VAT registration (¶8682).

VATREC3030+ 2. When agreeing to a **shorter period**, HMRC considers the following:
- the difficulties imposed on the trader if the 6-year limit is maintained;
- the control risk;
- the past compliance record and reliability of the trader; and
- any review carried out by an independent auditor.

3. If the 6-year requirement is waived by HMRC, there are **recommended minimum periods** depending on the type of document (although the VAT account must always be retained for 6 years). The periods are as follows. For:
- order copies, stock records, job cards, production records: 1 year;
- day books, cash books and documents relating to overseas trade: 3 years;
- invoices, credit notes, and retail scheme paperwork: 4 years; and
- bank statements and annual accounts: 5 years.

Companies must also comply with other statutory requirements, which are detailed in *Company Law Memo*.

CH15800 4. When a company is **liquidated**, the liquidator is only required to preserve the records of insolvent companies for the year following the date of dissolution. HMRC would need to take charge of the records if they were required for longer.

5. For a business which changes ownership by way of **transfer as a going concern**, see ¶8648.

Format

2802 There is no requirement to maintain the records in their **original** format, although HMRC should approve a change to alternative media (e.g. paper to computer records). No prior approval is required for records which are produced on a computer, but then stored on paper.

HMRC has a right to **access** records, irrespective of format and location, and also to request assistance to gain access (e.g. to operate a computer system).

MEMO POINTS 1. If records are kept at an **accountant's premises**, HMRC will agree to check the records there. If any records are removed during an official visit, the accountant must ask for a receipt.

Notice 700 para 19.2.5; VATREC3033 2. If the business uses a **computer bureau**, HMRC expects the records to be made available at the trader's principal place of business.

3. On **approving** a storage system, HMRC will review whether it:
- gives a satisfactory audit trail;
- allows legible information to be extracted;
- can easily be accessed and checked; and
- complies with the minimum retention period.

Notice 700 para 19.2.4 4. A trader who wishes to use **microfilm or microfiche** must obtain prior written clearance from HMRC.

2. All traders

Every trader must **retain** all of the following: **2804** SI 1995/2518 reg 31; VATREC2020; Notice 700/21 para 5.2

Record	Details
Business and accounting records	These should reflect the size and complexity of the business They include the annual accounts, a list of all branches, orders, delivery notes, cash and other accounting books, purchase and sales books, records of daily takings, business correspondence, bank statements, and paying-in books Evidence of the volume of trade outside the accounting records is also extremely useful It is important that they are kept up to date, and are sufficiently detailed, so that the trader can calculate accurate amounts to enter on VAT returns which can then be easily checked by HMRC
VAT account	¶2820+
Copies of all VAT invoices issued	These may be on paper, computer or other media There are special rules for retailers and cash and carry wholesalers (¶2868+)
All VAT invoices received from suppliers	¶1972+
Documentation relating to cross-border trade	The following documents are required: – certificates issued under the rules for fiscal and customs warehouses; – documents received relating to EU acquisitions; – copy documentation for EU despatches and transfers; and – documents relating to imports and exports
Credit notes, debit notes and other documents which change the consideration for a particular supply, with copies retained if originals have been issued	¶2925+
Documents and information relating to self-billing agreements	¶2904+

Failure to comply may result in a penalty (¶4058+), although HMRC often warns a trader before issuing a direction to keep records (¶3485+). s 69 VATA 1994

MEMO POINTS **Non-taxable persons** are only required to keep records of goods acquired from another EU member state which are either subject to excise duty (¶9136+) or are a new means of transport (¶9112+). SI 1995/2518 reg 31(3)

Outputs

Records must be kept of all supplies made, including all taxable and exempt supplies. **2808** Notice 700 para 19.5

If VAT invoices are issued (and copies retained), a trader may keep a **summary** of outputs showing the following, which can then be used to prepare the VAT account (¶2820+):

– output tax;
– VAT-exclusive sales;
– exempt sales;
– VAT due on certain imports (all services, and all posted goods except where they are worth less than £2,000 and datapost is used); and
– credits given to customers (¶2925+).

Tax points for goods sold on approval, or similar terms, should be recorded.

Otherwise, all information which is required to be shown on a full VAT invoice (¶2860+) must be kept.

All output tax must be carried forward to the VAT account (¶2820+).

2810 Notice 700 para 19.5.2 In addition, records of gifts or loans of goods, taxable self-supplies and goods put to private use must be maintained.

MEMO POINTS 1. For **gifts** and goods put to **private use** only the following need be recorded:
- date of gift or change of use;
- description and quantity;
- VAT-exclusive cost; and
- rate and amount of VAT chargeable.

Notice 700 para 19.5.3 2. For taxable **self-supplies** (¶1490+), which generally only involve builders and car dealers, details of the following must be retained:
- tax point;
- taxable value; and
- rate and amount of VAT.

Inputs

2812 Notice 700 para 19.8.1 An ordered **list** of all purchase invoices (including zero-rated supplies) is acceptable, provided that the original invoices can be produced easily if required, and provided that the list shows the following:
- input tax;
- VAT-exclusive purchases;
- VAT due on certain imports (all services, and all posted goods except where they are worth less than £2,000 and datapost is used); and
- credits received from suppliers.

The list should follow the order of the filed invoices.

For details of the **evidence** and therefore records required to substantiate an input tax reclaim, see ¶1972+.

The input tax totals from the list are then carried forward to the VAT account (¶2820+).

MEMO POINTS 1. Invoices **received from one supplier**, or **incidental invoices** may be recorded in a batch, with a summary list attached.
2. Records relating to **blocked** input tax (¶1885+) must also be retained.
3. If using the **cash accounting** scheme (¶4880+), a column can be added to the cash book to record the related input tax.

3. Special situations

2814 **Particular** record-keeping **requirements** apply in respect of the following:

Situation	¶¶
Bad debt relief claims	¶864
Self-billing arrangements	¶2904+
Road fuel scale charges	¶1536+
Capital goods scheme adjustments	¶2328
Flat rate scheme	¶4704
Cash accounting scheme	¶4936+
Construction industry	¶5200+
Agricultural flat rate scheme	¶6016
Retail schemes	¶6412, ¶6454, ¶6488
Second-hand goods	¶6644+
Global accounting	¶6718+
Auctioneers' scheme	¶6766+
Registered non-EU traders supplying electronically provided services	¶7030
VAT representatives for overseas traders	¶7218
Tour operators' margin scheme	¶7644
Barristers	¶7784
Reclaiming pre-registration input tax	¶8578

SECTION 2

The VAT account

Every trader must keep a VAT account, which is a summary of the total output tax and input tax for each VAT period (¶2987+). Usually VAT is added up at convenient intervals, such as at the end of each month. 2820 SI 1995/2518 reg 32

The account may be kept in any **form**, although HMRC gives a very simple pro-forma as a guide. Notice 700 paras 19.12, 19.14

Any VAT **adjustment notified** by HMRC should be excluded from the VAT account, unless the trader is specifically told to include it.

The amounts calculated in the VAT account are then transferred to the VAT return (¶2985+).

Pro-forma

VAT period ended March 2822

Deductible VAT - Input tax	**£**	**Payable VAT - Output tax**	**£**
VAT on purchases		VAT on sales	
January	X	January	X
February	X	February	X
March	X	March	X
	X		X
Deductible VAT on EU acquisitions	X	VAT due on EU acquisitions	X
Net overclaim of input tax on prior returns	(X)	Net under-declaration of output tax on prior returns	X
Bad debt relief	X	Adjustments from special schemes	X
Adjustments from special schemes	X		
	X		X
VAT on credits received from suppliers	(X)	VAT on credit notes issued to customers	(X)
Total deductible VAT	**X**	**Total VAT payable**	**X**
		Less: Total deductible VAT	(X)
		Net due to HMRC	**X**

Deductible VAT

The following deductible items must be **separately identified** and totalled: 2824
- input tax on UK supplies received;
- input tax on EU acquisitions;
- relief claimed on bad debts;
- over-declarations of VAT relating to prior periods, excluding those notified in writing to HMRC; and
- any other adjustments required by the VAT rules.

From the total of the above, any **credits** received from suppliers are then subtracted.

MEMO POINTS Examples of **other adjustments** would include:
- unpaid VAT on goods imported by post (excluding datapost) and international services received;
- input tax on imported goods and those removed from a warehouse, whether the tax has been paid or deferred (¶9405+);
- VAT due on self-supplies;
- partial exemption adjustments; and
- those arising from the use of special schemes (such as capital goods scheme, retailers, tour operators and so on).

Payable VAT

2826 The following items must be **separately identified** and totalled:
- output tax on UK sales;
- output tax on EU acquisitions;
- fuel scale charges;
- under-declarations of VAT relating to prior periods, excluding those notified in writing to HMRC; and
- any other adjustments required by the VAT rules.

From the total of the above, any **credits** issued are then subtracted.

MEMO POINTS Examples of **other adjustments** would include:
- unpaid VAT on goods imported by post (excluding datapost) and international services received;
- VAT due on self-supplies;
- partial exemption adjustments; and
- those arising from the use of special schemes (such as capital goods scheme, retailers, tour operators and so on).

Net VAT due

2828 The net VAT is **calculated** by subtracting the total deductible VAT from the total payable VAT.

SECTION 3

VAT invoices

2840 A VAT invoice is a document which provides evidence of a supply which has occurred. Without an invoice, a customer is usually unable to recover the related input tax.

Where the invoicing rules are not complied with (for example, invoices are not issued, content is not complete, time limits are not met), HMRC will write to the trader pointing out the inadequacies. Continuing failure may result in the restriction of the supplier's own input tax recovery, because the business is not making verifiable taxable supplies.

Whilst it is usual for the supplier to prepare the invoice, sometimes it is more convenient if the customer performs this task. This is known as **self-billing** (¶2904+).

A. Supplier prepares the invoice

1. General principles

Requirement to prepare

2844 SI 1995/2518 reg 13(1) A taxable person must prepare a VAT invoice in any of the following **circumstances**:
- a taxable supply is made to another UK taxable person, excluding most zero-rated supplies;
- an exempt supply is made, and either the customer requests an invoice, or the supply is made to a person in another EU member state which requires invoices to be issued for exempt supplies;
- a supply is made to a person in another EU member state for the purpose of that person's business; or
- a payment on account is received, relating to a supply made (or intended to be made), from a person in another EU member state.

However, no VAT invoices may be issued after the date of deregistration.

There are **specific exclusions**, due to the nature of VAT accounting in the following situations:
- supplies to customers operating a self-billing system (¶2904+);
- business gifts (¶1465+), unless the recipient is both willing and able to claim the related input tax;
- supplies under a margin scheme for second-hand goods (¶6620+);
- supplies by retailers (¶6307), unless the customer requests an invoice; and
- supplies by tour operators under TOMS (¶7584).

MEMO POINTS 1. A trader who is unsure of the **recipient's VAT status** should always issue a VAT invoice.
2. A **zero-rated** supply does not require a VAT invoice unless it is an intra-EU supply.
3. Where **copy** invoices are supplied, or the customer has lost the original, the supplier should ensure that the duplicate is clearly marked as such.
4. Entities within **groups** (¶8800+) cannot charge VAT to each other, so VAT invoices must not be prepared. The same rule applies to **divisions** (¶2744+) covered by separate divisional registrations.
5. For invoicing in relation to disclosed **agents**, see ¶7138.
6. The issue of a VAT invoice by an **unregistered supplier** is illegal; any amounts of VAT shown on such a document are recoverable from the supplier. In relation to input tax recovery by a customer who receives such an invoice, see ¶1984+. Sch 11 para 5 VATA 1994

Time limits

An invoice should usually be **issued within** 30 days of the tax point (¶755+). **2846** Notice 700 para 16.2.3

This time limit is **extended** automatically where:
- the supplier is also waiting for a purchase invoice from another supplier;
- a newly registered person has not yet been notified of the appropriate VAT number (¶2858), in which case the invoice must be issued within 30 days of the notification; or
- HMRC has given specific approval.

Method of delivery

The traditional role of paper invoices is now being overtaken by paperless methods of processing, transmitting and storing transaction data. However, the delivery method is still most likely to be determined by commercial considerations, particularly the customer's ability to cope with newer technologies. **2848**

Even where **paper** invoices are still prepared, they may be transmitted by email or, less commonly, fax. Notice 700 para 17.8

Otherwise, invoices which are transmitted **electronically** are usually stored electronically. Separate permission is required for the storage to be paper-based in this case. Notice 700/63 para 5.3

A business may wish to run a **dual system**, consisting of some paper invoices and some electronic documentation, which will only be valid provided that a controlled trial of electronic invoicing takes place. Exceptionally, approval may be given to continue with a dual system. Notice 700/63 para 2.4

MEMO POINTS 1. To **email** invoices, no special permission is required, unless the invoice is prepared under self-billing arrangements (¶2904+). If corruption occurs, HMRC expects the customer to request a fresh transmission.
2. When an invoice is **faxed** to a machine with thermal imaging, the customer should be warned that the information may not be permanent due to deterioration. If the invoice being faxed is an advance copy, this should be clearly stated, to avoid a duplicate claim for input tax by the customer. VATREC6071

Electronic invoices When a trader **commences** electronic invoicing there is no requirement to notify HMRC. **2850** Notice 700/63 paras 2.5, 6.1

Traders who choose to issue, or receive, electronic invoices must retain them in a readable form, or be able to produce them in a readable form without delay. HMRC can request **access** to:

a. the operations of any computer systems which produce or receive VAT invoices or disagreement documents, and to the data stored on them;
b. any supporting documentation including:
– file structures etc;
– audit trail;
– controls;
– safe keeping; and
– information on how the accounting system is organised; and
c. advice on interrogation facilities which are available on the system.

HMRC also has the right to take copies of information from the system, if required (¶3522+).

Notice 700/63 para 9.1 If the relevant conditions for transmission and storage **cannot be satisfied**, the business must revert to paper invoices.

2852 SI 1995/2518 reg 13A; Notice 700/63 para 4

For electronic **transmission**, the following conditions must be satisfied:
a. the use of an electronic invoice is accepted by the customer;;
b. the following protections are built into the system controls:
– completeness and accuracy;
– prevention of corruption;
– timely processing;
– the ability to demonstrate that there is a recovery plan in case of a system failure or loss of data;
– the maintenance of an audit trail between the electronic invoicing system(s) and the internal application system(s) which are used to process the electronic invoices;
– prevention of duplicated processing by the customer; and
– restriction of input tax recovery by the customer so that it applies only to valid invoices;
Notice 700/63 para 3.2 **c.** the invoice contents comply with the rules described at ¶2860+ (if invoices are sent in batches, the common details need only be stated once per batch); and
d. the environment for the data and transmission are secured using industry recognised technologies (such as https, SSL, S-MIME or FTP).

Notice 700/63 para 4.5 MEMO POINTS 1. A trader who is in any **doubt about the suitability of the system** (and particularly its compliance with the published requirements), should contact HMRC for advice, providing:
– an indication of the standard under which the invoice message has been drafted;
– a formatted "dump" of an example invoice; and
– an overview of the main system concepts, including control over authenticity and integrity of data.

Notice 700/63 para 8.2 2. If **outsourcing** the invoicing procedures, responsibility for the system's compliance remains with the trader.
3. For **self-billing** customers see ¶2904+.
Notice 700/63 para 4 4. An **approved method** is usually one of the following:

Method	Valid for transactions in	Details
Advanced electronic signature	UK and EU	An electronic signature which is unique to each business, and under its sole control Any subsequent alteration or corruption in the data would be traced
Electronic data interchange	UK and EU	Allows automatic data processing Used for high volumes of data Agreed standards (e.g. UN, EDIFACT, ODETTE and TRADACOMS) apply
Using the Internet	UK[1]	Can use electronic data interchange (EDI) over the Internet, perhaps attaching EDI files to emails Any other method may be acceptable (e.g. free format, XML-based, comma-delimited ASCII, PDF or structured text messages sent by Internet emails)

Method	Valid for transactions in	Details
Intermediary service providers	UK[1]	Providers are capable of receiving messages in a wide variety of electronic standards that are most convenient to suppliers They then translate these into a different format which is convenient for the customer System is secured by encryption, use of passwords, electronic signatures, etc
Hosted website	UK[1]	Supplier posts invoices to a hosted website and customer then downloads the relevant documentation

Note:
1. EU member states may accept one of these methods, but they are not automatically approved.

For electronic **storage**, the following criteria apply (to both suppliers and customers): **2854** Notice 700/63 para 5
- the authenticity and integrity of the data must be guaranteed during storage, even where it is compressed;
- the data must be in a readable format, and a recreated invoice must be available if required (containing all the information as originally transmitted);
- files are maintained to be able to locate any past invoice quickly, when required by HMRC; and
- records can be retained for 6 years (although see ¶2800 if there are difficulties with this).

If stored **outside the UK**, data protection must be assured, and invoices must be accessible within a reasonable period of time. Notice 700/63 para 5.5

What type of invoice?

2856

Source	Details	Reference	¶¶
Full invoice	Default requirement	SI 1995/2518 reg 14(1)	¶2860+
Simplified invoice[1]	For supplies not exceeding £250 and not made to a person in another EU state	SI 1995/2518 reg 16A	¶2868+
Less detailed invoice	For retail supplies either: – not exceeding £250; or – of road fuel.	SI 1995/2518 reg 16	¶2872
Cash and carry invoice	Provided by wholesaler	Notice 700 para 17.2	¶2876
Pro-forma invoice	Used to offer goods or supplies to a potential customer; supply will not occur unless payment is received	VATREC9010+	¶2878
Corporate purchasing card	Allow the invoicing to be carried out by the customer's card company or bank	Notice 701/48 para 4	¶2880
Gift - tax certificate	A business gift on which output tax applies is used for the recipient's own business; certificate allows recovery of the input tax	Notice 700/7 para 2.4	¶1474
Self-billing invoice	Customer raises invoice on behalf of supplier	SI 1995/2518 reg 13 Notice 700/62	¶2904+
Authenticated receipts	For construction industry only	SI 1995/2518 reg 13(4)	¶5216
Auctioneer/bailiff sale	Goods sold by auctioneer to satisfy another person's debt; VAT on the sale must be evidenced	SI 1995/2518 reg 13(2)	

Note
1. With effect from 1 January 2013.

2. Contents

VAT number

2858 All VAT invoices must show the VAT registration number (¶2710) of the supplier. A UK VAT number consists of nine digits grouped 3, 4, and 2. The last two numbers are check digits.

Any registered person can verify a VAT number from any member state by using the VAT Information Exchange System (VIES) website at flmemo.co.uk/vm2858

EU governments no longer publish details of the algorithms which they use to generate VAT numbers. Use of the former (and unofficial) numerical procedure for checking the validity of a UK VAT number is no longer recommended.

Full invoice

2860 SI 1995/2518 reg 14(1); VATREC5010

UK supply Subject to special rules for tour operators (¶7520), flat rate farmers (¶6014) and second-hand goods (¶6654), every invoice **must show** the following, unless HMRC agrees to any change:

Element	Details
Identifying number	Must be from a series that is unique and sequential (with evidence retained for any break in the series) It can contain both numbers and letters New businesses do not need to start at 1 It is possible to operate several sequences at the same time
Tax point date	If only one date appears on the invoice, this will be the tax point and it does not need to be identified as such
Date of issue	
Name, address and VAT number of the supplier	
Name and address of the customer	
Description of the supply	Including quantity of goods or extent of services, the applicable rate of VAT, and VAT-exclusive amount The description may be a code, as is often used by cash and carry wholesalers In respect of services, general terms such as "professional services rendered" are acceptable
Unit price	This can be omitted if it is not usually provided in the industry sector, and the customer does not request it The countable element for goods is obvious, but less so for services, when the unit may be an hourly rate or, more artificially, the price for standard services
Use of a margin scheme	Required if the supply is made under a second-hand margin scheme or travel agents' margin scheme: see memo point 2 below
Total amount payable excluding VAT	The amount for every supply and the total invoice value (excluding VAT) may be stated in any currency
Rate of any cash discount	
Total amount of VAT chargeable	Always in sterling To convert into sterling, the trader must use an approved rate of exchange (¶9032)

2862 Notice 700 para 16.5

MEMO POINTS 1. If **zero-rated** or **exempt** supplies are included on an invoice with taxable supplies, separate totals must be shown for each rate, and the invoice should clearly show that no VAT is chargeable on those supplies.

SI 1995/2518 reg 14(1)(n)

2. If a **margin scheme** (¶6620+) is used, the invoice must include the appropriate mandatory reference, as follows:
– "margin scheme: second hand goods";

– "margin scheme: works of art"; or
– "margin scheme: collectors' items and antiques".
If the supply is made by a **travel agent** under TOMS (¶7490+), the invoice must include the words "margin scheme: tour operators".
3. The invoice can be in any **language**, although HMRC can issue a notice to require a translation into English within 30 days.
4. If the customer **pays cash**, the supplier must mark the invoice as paid if so requested, and show the date of receipt.
5. **Solicitors** may issue a two-part document to maintain client confidentiality, which has an upper bill section with full details of the services supplied, and a lower tear-off VAT invoice which is retained as the VAT record and refers to professional services only. The bill section must not show the supplier's registration number, and would ideally state "This is not a VAT invoice". For disbursements, see ¶7190+. VATREC16061
6. Where a trade **leases motor cars**, the invoice must state whether the car is a qualifying car (¶1902+).

2864

EXAMPLE

Issued by:	A Ltd Lexden Rd, Colchester	**VAT Reg No:** 492 6104 45	
Invoice number:	587		
To:	B Ltd 1 High St, Crewe		
Tax point	1 October 2014	**Date of issue**	7 October 2014

Quantity	Description and price	Amount (excl VAT) £	VAT rate %
1	Filing cabinet @ 79.99	79.99	20
4	Hanging files @ 9.99	39.96	20
	Delivery - free	-	
		119.95	
	VAT @ 20%	23.99	
		143.94	

No discount available

EU supply The invoice should show all of the information in ¶2860, with the following **modifications**: 2866 SI 1995/2518 reg 14(2)
– the supplier should prefix the VAT number with "GB";
– the customer's registration number (if relevant) must contain the alphabetical code of the EU member state (¶9082);
– the description of each supply should state the VAT-exclusive amount in sterling, unless no UK VAT is chargeable (e.g. for zero-rated supplies); and
– if the supply is a new means of transport (¶9112+), the invoice should clearly identify it as such.

MEMO POINTS 1. If an **exempt supply** is made, and the customer requests an invoice, HMRC makes the following suggestions as to what should be indicated on the invoice: SI 1995/2518 reg 14(1)(o); VATREC5020
– "Exempt supply";
– "Exempt supply for VAT purposes"; or
– "This supply is exempt from VAT".
2. If a **reverse charge** supply is being made (where the customer accounts for VAT (¶9700+)), one of the following should be indicated on the invoice:
– "Reverse charge supply";
– "This supply is subject to the reverse charge";
– "Subject to reverse charge in the country of receipt"; or
– "Subject to reverse charge in another member state".
The words "reverse charge" must always be used.
3. For **zero-rated transactions**, the invoice must include a reference to the relevant EU or UK legislation, or one of the following can be indicated:
– "Zero-rated intra-EU supply";

– "This invoice is an intra-Community supply"; or
– "Intra-Community supply subject to VAT in the country of acquisition".

EXAMPLE

Issued by:	A Ltd Lexden Rd, Colchester		**VAT Reg No:** GB492 6104 45	
Invoice number:	542			
To:	F SA 1 Rue de Paris, Calais		**VAT Reg No:** FR12345678901	
Tax point	1 September 2014		**Date of issue**	10 September 2014
Quantity		**Description and price**	**Amount (excl VAT)** £	**VAT rate** %
2		Filing cabinet @ 79.99	159.98	0
4		Chairs @ 24.99	99.96	0
		Delivery	20.00	0
			279.94	
Zero-rated intra-EU supply		VAT @ 0% [1]	-	
			279.94	

No discount available

Note:
1. There is no VAT charge because the goods are despatched to a VAT-registered EU business; this is a zero-rated supply, provided that certain conditions are satisfied (¶9077+).

Simplified invoices

2868 SI 1995/2518 reg 16A

An invoice containing reduced information can be issued for any **supply not exceeding £250**, provided that the recipient is not located in another EU member state.

The required contents for a simplified invoice are:
- the name, address and registration number of the supplier;
- the tax point;
- identification of the goods or services supplied;
- the total amount payable, inclusive of VAT; and
- for each rate of VAT charged, the gross amount payable including VAT, and the VAT rate.

Credit card vouchers can be adapted to include all of the required contents for a simplified invoice.

MEMO POINTS Prior to 1 January 2013, only retailers were allowed to issue such invoices.

2872 Notice 700 para 16.6.2

Modified full invoice for retail sales If the supply **exceeds £250** and the customer asks for a VAT invoice, a full invoice can be **modified** by the retailer to show the VAT-inclusive amounts of taxable supplies, provided that the following totals appear at the end:
- VAT-inclusive value of taxable supplies;
- VAT-exclusive value of taxable supplies;
- VAT payable, expressed in sterling;
- value of zero-rated supplies; and
- value of exempt supplies.

Otherwise, all the information stated in ¶2860 must be included.

2874 Notice 700 para 17.1

Petrol and derv For retail sales **valued at**:
- more than £250, the customer's name and address may be replaced with the vehicle's registration number (the type of supply and volume of fuel sold is not required but otherwise the requirements of ¶2860 apply); or
- less then £250, a simplified invoice (¶2868) may be prepared.

Cash and carry wholesalers

Cash and carry wholesalers **generally sell to** VAT-registered customers. Hence there is a requirement for the document to enable the customer to reclaim VAT. 2876 Notice 700 para 17.2 VATREC16020+

HMRC allows wholesalers to use the till roll as an invoice, provided that the following **conditions** are all satisfied:
- the trader uses a product coding system which clearly identifies the different classes of goods sold;
- an updated product coding list is provided to all VAT-registered customers;
- the supply is not of services; and
- the till roll shows all of the information required for a full invoice (¶2860).

The **customer** must retain the till roll and coding lists for a minimum period of 6 years, unless agreed otherwise with HMRC, or there will not be sufficient evidence to support an input tax claim.

MEMO POINTS 1. The **customer's name** and address may be identified by a reference number which is allocated by the wholesaler. The trader must keep a separate record, and separately advise customers of their numbers.
2. The **product code** identifies each class of goods, and is generally at least two digits. A class of goods should include only items of a similar type and profit mark-up.
3. The **rate of VAT** may be indicated on the till roll by a code, e.g. "+" for zero-rated supplies.
4. Any **credits** on the till roll must be clearly identified, and the correct rate of VAT must be taken into account. The total VAT-exclusive amount and VAT totals may show the sales net of any credits.

Pro-forma invoices

Although called an invoice, this type of document does not show a debt owed by the customer and is ineffective for VAT accounting purposes. Instead, it is **used** to offer a supply, on the understanding that payment must be received before a VAT invoice will be issued. Once payment is made, and the goods or services are supplied, a VAT invoice is then provided to the customer. 2878 VATREC9010

To avoid any **confusion** for the customer, pro-forma invoices should be endorsed "This is not a VAT invoice", to make it clear that the invoice cannot be used as evidence for an input tax claim.

Corporate purchasing cards

These cards allow the invoicing to be carried out by the customer's card company or bank, using transaction information which has been transmitted through the purchasing card system. 2880 Notice 701/48 para 4

There are two types of invoice available under this system.

a. Line item **detail** invoices provide itemised information on a line-by-line basis. The date of issue is irrelevant and is not shown on the invoice. The transmission dates are shown for the purposes of the customer's input tax recovery only.

b. Simplified VAT invoices provide a **summary** only, showing the following information:
- value of the supply;
- VAT amount charged;
- VAT rate;
- time of supply;
- description of the goods;
- supplier's name, address and VAT number; and
- customer's name and address.

Where the value of a single use of the card exceeds £5,000, the supplier must still provide sales invoices to account for output tax. Otherwise the transmission of the summary invoice is sufficient unless the customer specifically requests an invoice, which should be endorsed with the words "Paid by purchasing card - Supplementary VAT invoice".

Specific **tax point** rules apply to suppliers who use these cards (¶818).

3. Adjustments

Rounding

2882 Notice 700 paras 17.5, 17.6
As a concession, the **total VAT payable** on an invoice may be rounded down to the nearest whole penny, provided that the VAT paid by the customer equals the VAT paid to HMRC. However, retailers who are not using a retail scheme must not round down.

Where an invoice includes **more than one supply**, the VAT on each line must either be rounded:
- down to the nearest 0.1p; or
- up or down to the nearest 1p or 0.5p.

The method used must be consistent for all transactions.

> EXAMPLE Ms C issues an invoice showing two lines of goods. The actual VAT values are: 97.76p and 196.64p.
> Ms C can either round:
> - down to the nearest 0.1p, which gives amounts of 97.7p and 196.6p; or
> - to the nearest 1p for 97.76p to give 98p, and to the nearest 0.5p for 196.64p to give 196.50p.

2884 Notice 700 para 17.5.2
VAT on **price lists**, where the product is shown per unit, should be calculated:
- by stating it to four decimal places, then rounding down to three places; or
- to the nearest 1p or 0.5p, with a minimum of 0.5p (never nil).

Change in supplier's VAT number

2886 VATREC10000+
The supplier's VAT number can be amended for any number of **reasons**, including:
- a change in the ownership of the business;
- a sole trader becoming a partnership;
- a transfer of a going concern where the new owner does not notify a liability to be registered, and continues using the same VAT number; or
- joining or leaving a VAT group.

Where **invoices** have been **issued** using the superseded VAT number, or the supplier wishes to use up an existing stock of pre-printed invoices, the invoices remain effective if the supplier gives the following written undertaking:

"I/We undertake to account for VAT on any VAT invoices bearing VAT registration number [old number] which have been issued by me/us since [date], as if those invoices had been issued under VAT registration number [new number]."

Change in VAT rate

2888
The UK Government can (sometimes at short notice):
- amend the VAT rating applying to a **particular type of supply** (e.g. a standard-rated supply is made exempt);
- **globally change the percentage** which applies to the standard rate or reduced rate; or
- **add a new rate** (in which case HMRC will issue specific guidance).

Notice 700 para 30.8
On the occasion of a change in VAT rate, the trader can **elect** to account for VAT at the old rate on supplies made before the date of change, ignoring the usual tax points (¶755+) relating to payment and invoicing.

If the VAT rate or liability:
- **increases**, the trader can issue an invoice showing the old rate; or

SI 1995/2518 reg 15
- **decreases**, and the invoice has already been issued, a credit note (¶2925+) must be issued. This should be headed "Credit note - Change of VAT rate".

Replacing goods

2890 Notice 700 para 18.3
If the customer **returns** goods for any reason and the supplier sends a replacement, the invoicing position depends on the exact circumstances. It is important that the supplier's

terms of sale provide for returns by customers, otherwise it could be argued that the supplier is purchasing the goods back and making a second sale of the replacement.

Replacement goods	VAT position	Invoicing
Supplied at same price	Let existing VAT charge stand	No need for additional paperwork, or to account for VAT, provided that no additional charge is made to customer
	Cancel existing VAT charge	Must issue credit note to cancel existing invoice and charge VAT on new invoice
Supplied at lower price	Reduced VAT charge	May issue credit note to reduce value of issued VAT invoice
Supplied at higher price	Increased VAT charge	Must issue additional invoice and account for additional VAT

Errors

Errors usually relate to an arithmetical mistake or the wrong amount of VAT being charged. Only errors which have **occurred** in the preceding 4 years can be corrected. **2892** VAEC 7420

Input tax which arose more than 4 years ago is barred from recovery (¶2014).

The supplier must never destroy a VAT invoice and issue another one with the same number, as this leaves the VAT record incomplete. Instead, there are three ways of making a **correction**. **2894** Notice 700 para 19.10

Comment It is obviously important that both the supplier and customer are aware of how the correction is to be managed, and that reciprocal adjustments are made in their respective VAT accounts.

Method 1 The **most common** solution is for both supplier and customer to adjust their accounts, in which case there are three options: **2896**

a. original invoice is cancelled by issue of a credit note, and the supplier sends a replacement;

b. credit note or supplementary invoice issued by supplier; or

c. debit note issued by customer.

The adjustment is made in the VAT period in which the error is corrected.

Method 2 A supplier who wants to **avoid the customer's involvement** can make a unilateral adjustment based on the VAT due on the gross amount charged. The adjustment goes into the VAT payable section of the VAT account. **2898**

EXAMPLE Mr D issues an invoice as follows:

	£
Net	1,000
VAT	170
Gross	1,170

The correct VAT charge is £200. (£1,000 x 20%)
Mr D has undercharged VAT by £30. (£200 - £170)
Mr D therefore makes the following adjustment in his records:

		£
Gross × VAT fraction 1/6	1,170 x1/6	195
Less: VAT already charged		(170)
VAT adjustment		25

2900 **Method 3 Otherwise**, the actions of the supplier and customer depend on whether the VAT shown on the invoice is:
- excessive, when the supplier accounts for the invoiced amount and the customer only includes the correct amount; or
- insufficient, when the supplier accounts for the correct amount, and the customer accounts for the invoiced amount.

B. Customer prepares the invoice

2904 Notice 700/62 In certain situations the customer is able to ascertain the value of a supply more easily than the supplier. Under an arrangement known as **self-billing**, a customer may prepare the supplier's invoice and forward a copy to the supplier with the payment.

No prior approval from HMRC is required, but various conditions must be satisfied. Self-billing has no geographical restrictions and may be used in respect of UK, EU and rest of the world transactions (¶2918).

Comment The customer may save costs, and staff can work with uniform purchase invoices. Industries where this mechanism is commonly used include construction, agencies, road hauliers, and also scrap metal and waste paper merchants. In addition, it is very useful when invoicing for royalties.

Eligibility

2906 SI 1995/2518 reg 13(3A); Notice 700/62 paras 3, 4 All of the following **conditions** must be satisfied:
- the invoice is provided under the terms of a prior self-billing agreement between a particular customer and a particular supplier, relating to goods or services specified in the agreement;
- the supplier must be a taxable person;
- all transactions between that customer and that supplier must be invoiced using self-billing for the duration of the agreement; and
- the customer must keep an up-to-date record of all suppliers who have agreed to self-billing, to include their names, addresses and VAT registration numbers.

Each **self-billed invoice** must:
  - comply with all the requirements for a full VAT invoice, either for the UK (¶2860) or the EU (¶2866);
  - be clearly marked with the words "Self-billing"; and
  - clearly state "The VAT shown is your output tax due to HMRC".

If any conditions are **not met**, the invoice is ineffective, which means the customer cannot reclaim the VAT as input tax, and the supplier must prepare a separate invoice. The customer may also receive an assessment for incorrect input tax claims. *M J Gleeson Group plc* [1995] (VTD 13332)

Notice 700/62 para 2.2 MEMO POINTS 1. The **method of invoice delivery** can be in paper form or via electronic means (¶2850+). Where a large volume of self-billed invoices are prepared electronically, the customer should ensure that the accounting system can cope, and in particular that input tax is claimed correctly.

Notice 700/62 para 4.4 2. It is possible for a **third party** to prepare the invoices on the customer's behalf, but the compliance responsibilities remain with the customer.

3. The **former 12-month minimum** length for a self-billing agreement was abolished with effect from 1 January 2013.

The agreement

2908 SI 1995/2518 reg 13(3B); Notice 700/62 para 3 The **format** of this document should either be on paper or in electronic form, so that it has binding effect. It must be produced to HMRC on request.

The agreement should include the following **terms**:
- the supplier agrees to receive self-billed invoices in respect of supplies to the customer;

– the supplier will not raise any invoices for those supplies;
– a start date;
– an expiry date, which may be linked to the end of any contract between the parties; and
– the supplier agrees to notify the customer if the business ceases to be VAT-registered, is transferred, or changes its VAT number.

The supplier would probably also want to know if a third party is going to prepare the invoices on the customer's behalf.

MEMO POINTS 1. A customer who wishes to continue with self-billing at the end of the agreement period must **review the agreement**, and obtain evidence that the supplier has agreed to continue with self-billing for a further specified period. It is in any case advisable to carry out a review every 12 months, to confirm that the supplier is still VAT-registered and is willing to continue with the self-billing arrangement. Notice 700/62 para 3.3

2. If the original supplier **transfers the business** as a going concern, and the new owner wants to continue the self-billing arrangement, a new agreement needs to be entered into. Notice 700/62 para 4.3

HMRC suggests the following **pro-forma**: **2910** Notice 700/62 para 8

EXAMPLE **Self-Billing Agreement**

This is an agreement to a self-billing procedure between:

Customer name **VAT number**

and

Supplier name **VAT number**

The self-biller (the customer) agrees:
1. to issue self-billed invoices for all supplies made to them by the self-billee (the supplier) until [date][1];
2. to complete self-billed invoices showing the supplier's name, address and VAT registration number, together with all the other details which constitute a full VAT invoice;
3. to make a new self-billing agreement in the event that their VAT registration number changes;
4. to inform the supplier if the issue of self-billed invoices will be outsourced to a third party.

The self-billee (the supplier) agrees:
1. to accept invoices raised by the self-biller on their behalf until [date][1];
2. not to raise sales invoices for the transactions covered by the agreement;
3. to notify the customer immediately if they:
– change their VAT registration number;
– cease to be VAT-registered; or
– sell their business, or part of their business.

Signed by	**Signed by**
On behalf of	**On behalf of**
Date	**Date**

Note:
1. Insert either an end date for the agreement, or the date on which the contract ends.

Accounting for VAT

The **tax point** of supplies covered by self-billed invoices follows the normal rules (¶755+), except that a self-billed invoice is only effective to create a tax point when issued (¶766+) within 14 days of the basic tax point. The time of supply is therefore normally determined by the date of despatch of goods or performance of services (the basic tax point), unless this is overridden by the date of payment. **2912** Notice 700/62 para 5.1

In any event, the customer must show the tax point on the invoice.

The customer can reclaim the **input tax** in the VAT period in which the tax point falls. If payment is made at the same time as the issue of the invoice, input tax can be reclaimed on the day following the date of issue. **2914** Notice 700/62 para 5.2

Notice 700/62 para 6.5 The supplier accounts for **output tax** in the VAT period in which the tax point falls. It is possible for the tax point to fall before the supplier receives either the invoice or payment.

2916 MEMO POINTS 1. If the **supplier sends an invoice** despite the self-billing arrangement, the customer can only reclaim input tax on the self-billed invoice.

s 29 VATA 1994; VATREC15000+ 2. If the **VAT** on a self-billed invoice is **understated**, HMRC may recover this from the customer instead of the supplier, by issuing a notice to both the customer and the supplier. This is to serve as a deterrent, and is only used in practice when the customer is unable to reclaim the VAT which has been undercharged.

3. To **adjust the value** of a supply, the customer must issue a debit note (¶2925+) to the supplier, as the value of any subsequent self-billed invoice cannot be amended by the customer.

4. For self-billing in the **construction industry** see ¶5214.

Cross-border transactions

2918 Notice 700/62 para 7 For **services** in particular, both parties should be aware of the relevant place of supply rules (¶9682+), and they must agree the place of supply at the outset.

If the **supplier is located outside the UK**, the invoice contents must accord with the local rules of the supplier's country. If using electronic delivery, the customer must check that the chosen method is permissible locally. For an EU supplier supplying goods to the UK, the time of the customer's acquisition (¶9028) may be determined by the invoice date.

Where a **non-UK customer** prepares the invoice for a UK supplier, zero-rating in respect of goods will only apply where all of the relevant conditions are satisfied, whether as an EU despatch (¶9075+) or export (¶9581+). The invoice must meet the usual UK requirements (¶2860).

SECTION 4

Credit and debit notes

2925 Credit and debit notes are documents which amend the details of a supply for which a VAT invoice has already been issued. They must not be used to cancel output tax when the customer has not paid, as bad debt relief is available instead (¶840+).

If the document is issued by the supplier, it is known as a credit note. A debit note is a document prepared by the customer requesting a credit from the supplier. Unless stated otherwise, the following paragraphs apply equally to credit notes and debit notes.

1. Requirements

UK supplies

2927 Notice 700 para 18.2; VATREC13040 To be valid, a credit note which is to **alter the VAT** chargeable must fulfil all of the following **criteria**:

a. be issued to correct a genuine mistake or overcharge, to cancel an invoice or to provide an agreed reduction in consideration;

b. give value to the customer (either set-off of the stated amount against future invoices, or a repayment from the supplier);

c. be issued within a month of when the need to credit arises, which must itself be within 3 years of the end of the accounting period in which the original supply took place;

d. be clearly headed as a credit note or debit note; and

e. show the following information:

– an identifying number and date of issue;

– the reason why it has been issued;

– name, address and VAT number of supplier;

- name and address of customer;
- a description to identify the supply which is being credited, along with quantity and amount;
- total amount credited, excluding VAT;
- rate and amount of VAT credited; and
- a cross-reference to the original VAT invoice, such as its identifying number and tax point

MEMO POINTS 1. Sufficient **evidence** of the need for correction should be retained by the supplier, which could include a letter of complaint or returns documentation.
2. If **zero-rated** or **exempt** supplies are included, there must be separate totals for both, and the credit note should clearly show that no VAT is credited.
3. The **rate of VAT** should be the same as that which applied on the original invoice.
4. Credit notes which **correct errors** on invoices should clearly show both the correct amount of VAT and the error.

Credit notes which are issued **without creating a VAT adjustment** (the supplier and customer agree not to amend their VAT because there is no monetary loss to either party) should be clearly marked as such (for example, with the words "This is not a credit note for VAT"). The outputs (¶2808) of the supplier, and inputs (¶2812) of the customer, will, however, still need to be adjusted in their respective records. **2930**

EU supplies

A credit note issued in respect of an EU supply must show the same details as the respective invoices (¶2866). **2932**

2. Accounting

Credit notes issued

The supplier must adjust the sales figure and the output tax total (assuming that the credit note contains a VAT adjustment) in the VAT period in which the credit note is issued. **2934** SI 1995/2518 reg 38; Notice 700 paras 18.2.4 - 6

MEMO POINTS 1. The tax point for credit notes issued by or on behalf of **insolvent** traders is the date of the original supply.
2. If the **registration has been cancelled** and credit notes are subsequently issued or received, the tax point is the date of the original supply. If the final return (¶3010+) has already been submitted, a separate notification will be required.

Credit notes received

When a credit note is received, the inputs and input tax must be adjusted and clearly recorded in the accounting records, including the VAT account itself. **2936** Notice 700 para 19.9

A trader who has **already sent a debit note** to a supplier, requesting a credit, must ensure that the adjustment is not made twice by mistake.

CHAPTER 3

Reporting

OUTLINE ¶¶

VAT is a self-assessed tax, and the onus is on the business to report taxable amounts to HMRC by making returns. **2980**

In recent years a requirement to disclose the use of VAT-saving schemes has been added to the reporting obligations of some taxable persons, enabling HMRC to monitor such activity (¶3030+).

SECTION 1

Returns

With very few exceptions (see ¶3003), a registered person must submit VAT returns online for every VAT period, and make payment (¶3160+) of any VAT owed at the same time. **2985** SI 1995/2518 reg 25(1)

A professional agent (such as a VAT adviser) can prepare and submit the return, and correspond with HMRC on the trader's behalf.

MEMO POINTS 1. The **professional agent** must be **authorised** by the trader, using an amended form 64-8 for this purpose.
2. For **EU sales lists** see ¶9330+.
3. For **Intrastat** returns see ¶9345+.
4. In cases of **incapacity or death** and the liability to complete VAT returns see ¶8700+.

Senior accounting officers

2986 Finance Act 2009 Sch 46; SAOG12200, 12300

The senior accounting officer of a **large company** is defined as "the director or officer of the company who in the company's reasonable opinion has overall responsibility for the company's financial accounting arrangements". The company must advise HMRC in writing of the identity of the senior accounting officer for the company.

The senior accounting officer is required to:
– take reasonable steps to ensure that the company establishes and maintains accounting arrangements which enable the company's VAT liabilities to be calculated accurately in all material respects; and
– certify annually that the systems are adequate, or specify the nature of the inadequacies and confirm that these have been notified to the company's auditors.

Where a company is the **representative member of a VAT group**, it is for the SAO of that company to be satisfied that the company is receiving accurate information from the other group companies to enable it to complete its VAT returns accurately.

Penalties of £5,000 can be levied on the senior accounting officer for each of the following:
– failure to maintain and monitor that the company has appropriate tax accounting arrangements;
– failure to provide a certificate, or providing a certificate which contains a careless or deliberate inaccuracy;
– failure to provide the company's auditor with an explanation of deficiencies in the tax accounting arrangements before the auditor's report on the company accounts is finalised.

For full details of these requirements see *Corporation Tax Memo*.

MEMO POINTS 1. For these purposes a **large company** is one with turnover in excess of £200 million or a balance sheet total in excess of £2 billion. If the company is part of a group it is the group that will be tested against these thresholds.
2. Prior to **5 August 2013**, the duties of the SAO for the representative company of a VAT group were not explicitly addressed by HMRC's guidance. HMRC says it will not charge penalties where SAOs have not acted in accordance with the new guidance for any period up to the first period commencing after that date.

1. VAT periods

2987 Notice 700 para 20.5

The VAT period (also known as prescribed accounting period, or tax period) **determines** which invoices (both sales and purchases) are included on the particular return, by reference to the tax point (or for users of the cash accounting scheme, by reference to the date of payment (¶4880+)).

The trader is **notified** of the applicable VAT periods after registering, and the relevant details appear on the certificate of registration (¶2708).

Timing

2990 SI 1995/2518 reg 25(1); Notice 700 para 20.5

Unless a specific request is made, VAT periods are 3 months long, and relate to a VAT year ending on 31 March (i.e. calendar quarters), 30 April or 31 May, depending on the allocation by HMRC. This is also known as the VAT stagger or VAT cycle.

The trader can, however, **request** a specific VAT year end, which perhaps coincides with the financial year end for the business. In addition, HMRC may approve the use of monthly VAT periods, annual VAT returns, or non-standard VAT return periods. However, specific requests may be denied for protection of the revenue.

HMRC can **vary the length** of the trader's VAT period (including the current one) at any time, against which there is no right of appeal. For example, if the trader registered late, the first VAT period may span a number of months or even years (¶2684 and ¶2708).

MEMO POINTS 1. If using the **annual accounting** scheme, only one return per annum is required (¶4745+).
2. **Monthly** VAT periods are good for traders who are in a VAT repayment position, but see ¶2993. Traders who voluntarily register cannot have monthly VAT periods. Those who move from

a repayment position to regularly being in a payment position would normally be best advised to move to quarterly returns, for both cash flow reasons and administrative simplicity.
3. If the **registration has been transferred** (¶8678+), the new business owner can request that the existing VAT periods are retained.

A VAT period will be **brought to an end** by any of the following: **2992**
- ceasing either to be registered or liable to be registered;
- using cash accounting (¶4880+) and either ceasing to trade or becoming insolvent;
- ceasing to be eligible for the annual accounting scheme (¶4745+);
- sale of the business where the registration is not transferred; or
- the taking over of the registration by a deemed taxable person, such as a liquidator or administrative receiver (¶2624).

Anti-avoidance

If VAT periods are aligned in such a way between businesses so that an **unjustified and unintended cash flow benefit** is obtained at the expense of the public revenue, HMRC can either withdraw existing permission for monthly periods or issue a direction to vary the VAT periods. **2993** SI 1995/2518 reg 25; VATAC5100+

A **typical example** is where a subsidiary is set up, but remains outside a group registration (¶8800+), and the group's exports (zero-rated) are routed through it. The subsidiary therefore makes zero-rated supplies, and has monthly VAT periods to obtain its VAT repayments. However, the output tax due on the group's standard-rated supplies to the subsidiary is only accounted for once a quarter.

There is no right of **appeal** against this power, although it is subject to judicial review (¶4338+).

2. During registration

First return

The **length** of the first return period may be irregular (not a whole number of months). Output tax must be charged on all taxable supplies from the date of registration. **2994**

MEMO POINTS For the recovery of input tax suffered prior to registration see ¶8560+.

Completing the return

The **declaration** at the bottom of the online return form, which states that full and correct information has been given, is made by clicking the "submit" button. **2996** SI 1995/2518 reg 25

Inaccurate returns may be liable to an inaccuracy penalty (¶4000+).

MEMO POINTS 1. For paper returns, a **minus number** should be entered in brackets. For electronic returns, a minus sign should be entered before the figure.
2. For completion of the return when using the **flat rate scheme** see ¶4702.
3. For the calculation of output tax by **retailers** see ¶6325+. The type of retail scheme used should also be indicated on the return.
4. For completion of the return if using a **margin scheme** see ¶6658.
5. When using the **Tour Operators' Margin Scheme** see ¶7640.

Summary of the form

The VAT return is a document which must cope with a wide range of trading situations. The top half relates to the **VAT position** of the business, whilst the bottom half gives **statistical data** about sales and purchases. **2998** SI 1995/2518 regs 39, 40; Notice 700/12

For traders who have **no EU trade**, only boxes 1, 3, 4, 5, 6 and 7 are relevant.

Box	Summary	Including	¶¶
VAT calculation			
1	Output tax due on supplies and deemed supplies	VAT on sales and other business income, including taxable commission	¶750+
		VAT on scale charges for private fuel	¶1536+
		VAT on gifts costing more than £50	¶1465+
		VAT on private use of business supplies	¶1520+
		VAT on supplies to staff	¶1520+
		A deduction for VAT on credit notes issued in VAT period	¶2925+
		VAT on sale of capital assets unless business is transferred	¶296+
		More **unusual items** would be:	
		– errors from previous periods capable of being amended in the current return;	¶3014+
		– VAT on the full value of goods where a part-exchange has occurred;	¶1028+
		– VAT on self-billed invoices;	¶2904+
		– VAT due on postal imports;	¶9427
		– VAT due on supplies to non-registered EU persons (distance sales); and	¶9177+
		– VAT on the reverse charge relating to services from outside the EU	¶9700+
2	VAT due on acquisitions from other EU member states (if there is an entry in box 9, there should be an entry here)	VAT on all EU acquisitions with a tax point in the period, which is taken as the earlier of: – the supplier's invoice date; and – the 15th day in the month following the date when the goods were received	¶9017+
		Errors from previous periods capable of being amended in the current return	¶3014+
3	Total VAT due (total of boxes 1 and 2)		
4	Input tax reclaimed on purchases	VAT on business purchases and expenses[1]	¶1800+
		VAT on credit notes received from suppliers	¶2925+
		VAT on bad debts less any amounts previously written off which have now been received	¶840+
		More **unusual items** would be:	
		– VAT on imported goods (only if the import VAT certificate has been received);	¶9429
		– errors from previous periods capable of being amended in the current return;	¶3014+
		– VAT on EU acquisitions;	¶9017+
		– VAT on goods removed from a customs warehouse or free zone; and	¶9483+ and ¶9495+
		– VAT on the reverse charge relating to services from outside the EU	¶9700+
5	Net VAT payable or repayable (difference between boxes 3 and 4)		

Box	Summary	Including	¶¶
Statistical data (all entries **exclude VAT**)			
6	Total value of all sales and other outputs[2] including fuel scale charges (¶1536+)	All taxable and exempt supplies (including exports), adding back any cash discounts and deducting credits given to customers	
		Other business income	
		Deposits where invoice raised	¶784+
		Amount in box 8	
		Supplies which are outside the scope of UK VAT due to place of supply	¶252+
		Reverse charge transactions	¶9700+
7	Total value of all purchases and other inputs[2]	Business purchases and expenses, adding back any cash discounts received and deducting credits allowed by suppliers	
		Imports	¶9405+
		EU acquisitions	¶9010+
		Reverse charge transactions	¶9700+
		Amount in box 9	
Trade with EU			
8	Total value of all goods[3] supplied to other EU member states	Goods despatched from the UK to anywhere in the EU: [4] – even if no sale takes place; or – which are installed or assembled in the EU	¶252+ ¶9154+
		Goods despatched to EU recipients on any basis (consignment, sale or return, approval)	¶9075+
		Supply of a new means of transport to unregistered persons in the EU	¶9112+
		Transfer of own goods to the EU	¶9286+
		Process work carried out in the UK for EU persons (temporary transfer of goods)	¶9276+
9	Total value of all acquisitions of goods[3] from other EU member states	Goods acquired from elsewhere in the EU including those removed to the UK without being purchased, or those invoiced to non-EU persons	¶9010+
		Goods installed or assembled in the UK if despatched from the EU	¶9154+
		Process work carried out in the EU for UK persons (temporary transfer of goods)	¶9276+

Note:
1. For box 4, **exclude** VAT on:
- business entertaining;
- private expenses;
- most purchases of cars;
- second-hand goods acquired under a relevant scheme (¶6625+);
- self-billed invoices (¶2904+) received (this is entered in box 1); and
- self-billed invoices issued to suppliers who are not VAT-registered.

2. For boxes 6 and 7, **exclude**:
- wages and salaries, and related taxes;
- drawings;
- loans and gifts of money;
- insurance claims;
- council tax; and
- non-supplies.

3. For boxes 8 and 9, **related services** such as freight and insurance costs should be included in the value, but not legal or financial services.

4. For box 8, **exclude non-excise goods** supplied to private EU customers where the distance selling threshold has not been exceeded in that member state (¶9204+).

3000 Notice 700 para 20.3.3

MEMO POINTS 1. **Nil returns** must still be submitted, and if using a:
- paper return, all boxes should have NONE entered; or
- electronic return, all boxes should be completed "0.00" unless already pre-filled with zeros, and the trader should confirm that a nil return is intended.

2. **Basic checks** should include:
- reviewing figures taken from accounting records and schedules;
- ensuring that the figures have been put in the correct box;
- ensuring the return is arithmetically correct (the online return calculates Total VAT due and Net VAT payable);
- where possible, reconciling sales in the management accounts with the figure in box 1; and
- evaluating whether the VAT payment position is what was expected, given the trading in that VAT period, and also compared to previous returns.

Notice 700/12 para 6.5

3. If an **assessment** (¶3625+) has already been issued, the return for the affected VAT period should still be completed normally, and any VAT owed to HMRC must be paid. Any VAT overpaid will be refunded. If an error has been made, which has been corrected by the issue of an assessment, the correction should not be entered on the next VAT return.

Notice 700/12 para 6.3

4. If the **paper return has been lost**, the trader must either make an electronic submission, or request a new paper one as soon as possible. According to HMRC guidance, the use of photocopies of old returns, or returns for other VAT periods or registrations, is not allowed. However, the tribunal has decided that the use of photocopied returns with the periods amended on them is sufficient. *Warren Bradley Estates* [2008] (VTD 20672) Now that online returns are completed by almost all traders, this issue is virtually redundant.

Submission

3002 Notice 700/12 para 1.2; Notice 700 para 21.3.1

The **due date** for each return is given by the VAT Online service, and is usually a calendar month after the end of the VAT period. For the concurrent payment of VAT, see ¶3160+.

For online filing (which requires **electronic** payment), the deadline is extended by an extra 7 days, unless payments on account (¶3182+) are being made. The annual accounting scheme (¶4772+) has its own rules.

Notice 700/12 para 5.2

For the very few traders who submit a **paper** return in the post, the form must arrive by the due date. The only item which may **accompany** a return is a cheque payment (not stapled to the return). In particular, no letters should accompany the return.

MEMO POINTS 1. To use **VAT Online**, a trader must be authorised to use the service, and payment of VAT must also be made electronically (¶3174). Once a return is submitted, the trader will receive an electronic acknowledgement, and a copy of this should be retained to prove that submission was successful. Alternatively, the trader's professional agent can submit electronic returns on behalf of the trader, provided the agent is fully authorised. See HMRC's website for further details.

2. Paper returns should be **posted to** the VAT Central Unit in the prepaid envelope.

3. Should the return go **astray** in the post, evidence of posting is important to prove a defence (¶4090+) against the imposition of a penalty. Such evidence is normally a Post Office certificate of posting, or a note of the date, time and location of posting.

3003 **Compulsory online filing** applies from 1 April 2012 for all traders except:
- traders subject to an insolvency procedure; and
- those whose religious beliefs prevent them from using computers.

In addition, from 1 July 2014, businesses may obtain exemption from the above requirement where they can satisfy HMRC that it is not reasonably practicable for them to file online because of age (and associated computer illiteracy), disability, or remoteness of location. Such businesses may file on paper.

MEMO POINTS This relaxation was introduced after the First-tier Tribunal held that compulsory electronic filing of VAT returns was **discriminatory** against the elderly, the disabled and those who live in remote locations. HMRC argued that there was no discrimination, because telephone filing was available as an alternative to electronic filing in such cases. However, HMRC was unable to rely on that alternative treatment as a justification, because the existence of telephone filing was kept secret. *LH Bishop Electric Co Ltd and others* [2013]

3004 **Late returns** mean the trader may become liable to a default surcharge (¶4082+).

Failing to submit a return will result in an assessment (¶3625+) for the amount of VAT estimated as due by HMRC. This assessment cannot be appealed until the return itself has been submitted. However, in practice, the assessment will be cancelled if the return is submitted and the related VAT paid.

Comment Payment of an assessment does not fulfil the taxpayer's VAT obligations. Only the submission of a return and payment of the correct amount of VAT (as shown on the return) will do so. Any surcharge will be based on the VAT due as shown on the return

Estimates

The figures on the return may be estimated **only when** previously approved by HMRC, who must be satisfied that the trader cannot accurately calculate the output tax or input tax (and perhaps the related sale or purchase figure), and either: **3006** SI 1995/2518 regs 28, 29(3)
- the estimate will be corrected in the following VAT period; or
- if this is impossible, the correction will be made in the next but one period.

An estimated return submitted under these conditions is not liable to a **penalty**, assuming both return and payment are on time. If approval is requested after the due date of the return, however, the trader will have defaulted (¶4082+), as approval cannot be retrospective

MEMO POINTS 1. **Approval** must be requested in writing and will be subject to whether HMRC accepts that: VATAC2000+
- the reason given for making an estimate is genuine;
- the method of calculating the estimate will not understate the overall VAT liability; and
- the trader will not be advantaged compared to those who comply with the VAT rules without using estimates.

2. Most estimates will be a **temporary** requirement, but if estimates are to be used for the **long term**, a compliance check (¶3414+) may be justified. Long-term use is generally only approved where the business structure is more complex.

3. There is **no appeal** against a decision not to give approval, but the decision is open to judicial review (¶4338+).

Disputed treatment of a transaction

The **default position** is that any VAT return should be completed in line with official guidance, even if the matter is the subject of dispute, irrespective of whether an appeal has been lodged. **3008** Notice 700/45 para 8

An issue may be of such significance, however, that another trader has already begun litigation (¶3252).

If a business **ignores official practice**, HMRC usually issues an assessment for any VAT due, and this will become payable if the ongoing litigation is settled in its favour. In addition, penalties may be due.

The **safest option** is to complete the VAT return in line with HMRC's guidance, but to lodge a protective claim in respect of any ongoing litigation so that the business is not at a disadvantage should another trader's appeal be won.

Clearance procedure

A non-statutory clearance procedure is available for both pre- and post-transaction rulings, in cases where there is **material uncertainty**. **3009** NBCG

In order for an application to be accepted, material uncertainty in the result must be shown. If the uncertainty relates to the rating of a supply, the supplier should make the application. If the uncertainty relates to the recovery of input tax it should be the recipient of the supply.

In the case of **pre-transaction applications**, the business must be able to show that the transaction is being genuinely contemplated.

In order for an **application to be accepted**, full details of the taxpayer, including commercial background, and full details of the transaction must be provided. This should also be accompanied by the taxpayer's understanding of the legislation.

Once HMRC has received the application it will respond in writing, typically within 28 days, in one of five ways:
- accepting the application for clearance, and accepting the taxpayer's interpretation;
- accepting the application but rejecting the taxpayer's interpretation;

– accepting the application but requesting further information;
– rejecting the application and referring the taxpayer to the relevant public guidance; or
– rejecting the application and stating clearly why non-statutory clearance cannot be given.

Applications will **not be accepted** where:
– comments are sought on tax planning advice;
– a previous application has been refused and it is resubmitted with a minor variation (this will not be the case where the facts of the transaction have changed);
– the matter is already covered by published guidance;
– HMRC considers that the motivation behind the transaction is to gain a tax advantage as opposed to being commercially motivated; or
– an audit or enquiry has already been opened.

MEMO POINTS 1. A clearance is binding on HMRC provided that the facts were fully disclosed in the application, and do not change in such a way as to materially alter the transaction. However, the clearance can only be relied upon by the applicant. **Advisers** cannot rely on clearances given for other clients, regardless of how similar the transactions are.
2. HMRC is bound by **incorrect guidance**, provided that it was clear, unequivocal and explicit, the trader relied on it, and the correction of it would cause loss to the trader. Once the trader is notified of the correction, the correct treatment must be used subsequently.
3. If a **court changes the interpretation** of the legislation in question, HMRC will only be bound by an existing ruling if the transaction has already taken place, or there is an opportunity to amend the return on which the transaction is reported. If the change is made by statute, the ruling will not apply once the law has come into force. If the change is retrospective, HMRC will not be bound by any ruling given.
4. Clearance applications should be **sent to** the taxpayer's Customer Relationship Manager (for large businesses) or to HMRC Clearance Team, Alexander House, 21 Victoria Avenue, Southend-on-Sea, SS99 1BD. Further information can be found at flmemo.co.uk/vm3009
5. Between 1 June 2013 and 31 December 2014, EU member states tested a clearance procedure for **cross-border transactions**.

3. Ceasing to be registered

3010 Notice 700/11 para 8.2 A final VAT return (form VAT 193) is required **unless** the VAT registration number is being transferred (¶8678+). This form may be submitted online.

3012 The final return requires the following **information**:
– output tax due on the assets of the business (¶8610+);
– output tax on invoices raised since the previous return as usual; and
– input tax on invoices with a tax point before the deregistration date.

For post-deregistration input tax recovery see ¶8618+.

4. Correcting errors

What is an error?

3014 Notice 700/45 Some adjustments **result from** the intricate VAT rules rather than mistakes.

Common mistakes include:
– claiming input tax which is ineligible (such as on business entertaining);
– charging the wrong VAT on sales (either by applying the wrong VAT rate, or making an arithmetical error);
– omitted sales; and
– transposition errors.

Notice 700/45 para 4.10 MEMO POINTS Examples of such **adjustments** which are **not errors** include:
– credit and debit notes (¶2925+);
– late invoices received from suppliers (¶2012+);
– adjustments for wrong entries on VAT invoices (¶2892+);
– bad debt relief (¶840+);
– pre-registration (¶8560+) and post-deregistration (¶8618+) expenses;

– using an estimate which has been approved (¶3006);
– partial exemption payback and clawback adjustments (¶2230+);
– annual adjustments for partly exempt traders (¶2202+), retailers (¶6300+), and tour operators (¶7602+);
– those arising from the capital goods scheme (¶2298+); and
– adjustments arising from a lack of evidence of export (¶9591).
Such adjustments should be shown separately in the VAT account (¶2820+).

Current return

If an error has been made on a submitted online return, it cannot be recalled or overwritten. **3016**
The error must instead be corrected in accordance with the procedures detailed below.

Previous returns

Generally errors must be corrected **within** 4 years of the end of the VAT period in which the incorrect return was made. For late input tax claims see ¶2014. **3018** SI 1995/2518 reg 34; VAEC 7420

For **tax point mistakes** (where VAT has been entered on a return preceding or following the correct return), the time limits relate to when the entry ought to have been made.

In cases of **fraud**, HMRC may correct the position within 20 years.

Correcting errors after the return is submitted

There are two possible methods of correcting an error after the VAT return for the period has been submitted. These are known as Method 1 and Method 2. Which method a business can use depends on the **net value of the errors**, which is defined as the difference between: **3020** Notice 700/45 para 4.2
– the total amount of VAT undeclared in error; and
– the total amount of VAT over-declared in error.

If the **net error** is either greater than £50,000, or **deliberate**, or **greater than both**: **3021**
– £10,000; and
– 1% of turnover for the period in which the error is discovered,

Method 2 must be used. Otherwise the business may choose Method 1, which is simpler and usually to be preferred.

EXAMPLE Miss A submits calendar quarter returns. She has made the following errors:

Quarter ended	Error	£
30 Sept	Overstated output tax	4,000
31 Dec	Under-declared input tax	8,000
31 Mar	Understated output tax	(10,000)
Net value of errors		2,000

The net effect of the errors is under-declared input tax of £2,000, so this can be corrected by Method 1.

MEMO POINTS 1. In calculating the 1% of turnover limit, the net turnover shown in box 6 of the return in which the amendment is made is used.
2. An important factor in the choice of method is that no interest is charged on VAT underpaid if the error is notified using Method 1. If the business decides to notify HMRC using Method 2, interest will be charged.

Method 1: amending the VAT return

In Method 1, the business simply adjusts its VAT account for the period in which the error occurred, and includes the value of the adjustment on the next VAT return. If the error was careless, a **penalty** (¶4000+) may be imposed (¶3026). **3022** Notice 700/45 para 4.3

Method 2: separate notification

Under Method 2, the business must notify HMRC separately. Form VAT652 should be used for this purpose. However, if the form is not used, the following information should be provided to the address given below: **3024** Notice 700/45 para 4.4, 4.11

- how each error has arisen;
- the VAT period affected;
- whether input tax or output tax was wrongly declared;
- the amount of the error;
- how the error was calculated;
- whether VAT has been overpaid; and
- the total adjustment.

The address is: VAT Error Correction Team, HMRC, 3rd Floor Regian House, James Street, Liverpool L74 4AA (telephone: 03000 527 557).

3026 Notice 700/45 para 4.1

If HMRC considers that an error has arisen through carelessness (or if it is deliberate), an **inaccuracy penalty** (¶4000+) may be imposed. If HMRC discovers the error before the business brings it to HMRC's attention, the penalty is likely to be higher, and an assessment raised (which only has to be calculated to the VAT officer's best judgment (¶3644+)). Errors should therefore be corrected as soon as possible.

It is good practice to **record** all errors as soon as they occur, showing:
- the date the error was discovered;
- the VAT period affected;
- whether input tax or output tax was wrongly declared; and
- where the related documentation is kept.

HMRC guidance states that, as well as carrying out the above steps, the business should notify HMRC of any error which is careless or deliberate, regardless of its size or value so that it may reduce any penalty levied. Note that simply adjusting the VAT account (¶3022) will not be regarded as a disclosure for the purpose of mitigating the penalty (¶3970+): for this, a separate, formal disclosure is required.

3028 Notice 700/45 para 7

Once notification of the error is received by HMRC, a Value Added Tax Notice of Error Correction should be issued to the trader within 21 days, with a Statement of Account showing the amounts owing and details of how to make payment.

It is important to obtain proof of posting of the error notification, in case HMRC does not receive it. This is to ensure that any VAT repayable is not capped by the 4-year rule (¶3250), and that any penalties levied are based on the date of the original notification.

SECTION 2

Disclosure of VAT schemes

3030 To reduce the effectiveness of VAT avoidance, traders with annual turnover (¶3040+) exceeding £600,000 (or their advisers) are obliged to notify HMRC of VAT-saving schemes which are in use. Disclosure is an information-gathering exercise for HMRC, so that it becomes aware of how widespread the use of known schemes is, and also serves as an early warning system for new schemes. Failing to disclose may result in a penalty.

Notification does not undermine the legality of the scheme itself, provided that it is in accordance with UK and EU law. On the other hand, disclosure may provoke future regulation to control or prevent the use of the disclosed scheme.

A. What is a scheme?

3035 Notice 700/8 para 7.3

A scheme is widely **defined** as including any arrangement, transaction or series of transactions, including those which commenced before the rules were introduced (1 August 2004).

Any of the elements involved may lead to a VAT saving or tax advantage (¶3088). However, the following are **excluded** for this purpose: Notice 700/8 para 11
- merely claiming recoverable input tax (perhaps by engaging a VAT specialist to undertake a review);
- using a published concession;
- using the grouping provisions (¶8800+) and making changes to the group members; and
- agreeing a new partial exemption special method (¶2148+) with HMRC.

Scope

In order to focus on avoidance, only the following **types** of scheme are to be disclosed: 3037 Sch 11A paras 3, 4 VATA 1994
- **designated** schemes (¶3048+), which are specifically identified devices already known by HMRC; and
- **hallmarked** schemes (¶3084+), which use certain features (termed hallmarks) that are regularly associated with avoidance.

A scheme may be designated or hallmarked, even where HMRC believes it is either legally ineffective, or unlikely that a tax advantage will be obtained.

Where the business **treats a scheme** as having a feature which is specified by HMRC, the scheme will be notifiable, even if legally (or for another reason) the feature is not actually present. It is the trader's view of the transaction which is important when deciding whether disclosure is required. SI 2004/1933 reg 2; Notice 700/8 para 6.1.1

Turnover limits

There are different **criteria** for disclosing each type of scheme, the most important of which is the size of the business using the scheme, as determined by turnover. 3040 Sch 11A para 7 VATA 1994; Notice 700/8 paras 4.3, 7.6

Annual turnover	Rules which apply	¶¶
Under £600,000	No disclosure required	
£600,000 to £10 million	Only designated schemes	¶3048+
Over £10 million	Both: – designated schemes; and – hallmarks	 ¶3048+ ¶3084+

MEMO POINTS 1. Turnover is **defined** as the trader's total taxable and exempt supplies, measured over both: 3042
- the year ending immediately prior to the VAT return affected by use of a scheme; and
- the VAT return period immediately prior to the affected return (with the limits being appropriately apportioned).

Income which is outside the scope of VAT, such as grants and donations, is ignored for this purpose.
2. For a **quarterly** VAT period, the limits are divided by four.
3. For a **monthly** VAT period, the limits are divided by twelve.

EXAMPLE Mr A has been using a designated scheme which first affects his return for the quarter ending 30 September.
In order to avoid disclosing the scheme, he must check that both his turnover in the:
- year to 30 June is less than £600,000; and
- quarter to 30 June is less than £150,000.

If a business has been **artificially split**, HMRC can direct that the resulting entities should be treated as one for the purposes of these rules (¶2629+). 3044 Notice 700/8 paras 4.3.2, 7.6.2

The turnover limits apply to a whole **group** of companies. 3046 Notice 700/8 paras 4.3, 7.6

MEMO POINTS 1. For this purpose, a group is **defined** as all companies included in the consolidated accounts plus other UK subsidiaries. Company A will therefore be in a group with another company (B) if either:
- company A is the parent of B;
- company A is a subsidiary of B; or
- both companies are subsidiaries of another company.

s 1162 CA 2006 2. A company (A) is a **parent** of another company (B) if either:
a. company A holds the majority of B's voting rights exercisable at general meetings outright, or by agreement with other members;
b. company A can remove or appoint directors of B with a majority of votes;
c. company A has the right to direct the financial and operating policies of B, either by contract or under B's constitution; or
d. company A holds an interest in B for the long term with a view to exercising control (usually at least 20% interest), and:
– actually exercises dominant influence; or
– A and B are managed on a unified basis.

B. Designated schemes

3048 Notice 700/8 para 4

Businesses with an annual turnover of at least £600,000 must disclose use of these schemes when a return or claim is affected and HMRC has not already been notified.

1. Returns or claims affected

3050 Notice 700/8 para 4.2

The requirement to notify HMRC arises when the operation of the scheme results in any of the following **beneficial changes**:
– a VAT return shows a higher or lower net amount of VAT;
– an increased claim is made for the repayment of output tax over-declared or input tax credit under-claimed; or
– a smaller amount of non-deductible VAT is incurred.

It should be noted that there is no motive test under these rules, so the VAT benefit may not have been intended.

Notice 700/8 paras 3.3.3, 3.3.4

MEMO POINTS 1. When a return or claim is affected by **more than one designated scheme**, all schemes must be notified.
2. When **more than one entity** is affected by a scheme, all entities must disclose if they fall within the criteria. A joint notification can be made.

Notice 700/8 para 4.4

3. If the use of a scheme has **already been notified**, and subsequent returns are affected because it is an ongoing arrangement (such as an extended approval period), no further notification is required. However, where the arrangements change but the same scheme is used, fresh notification is required.
4. If a designated scheme was **previously notified as a hallmarked scheme** (because the scheme has since been reclassified as designated), there is no need to make a fresh notification.

2. Notifiable schemes

Summary

3052 SI 2004/1933 Sch 1; Notice 700/8 para 3.4

Scheme number	Title	Affecting	¶¶
1	First grant of a major interest in a building	Property	¶3060
2	Payment handling service charged by retailers	Retailers	¶3054
3	Value shifting between different supplies by retailers	Retailers	¶3056
4	Leasing goods to a connected person	Leasing	¶3068
5	Extended approval period offered by retailers	Retailers	¶3058
6	Partly exempt groups and suppliers	Groups	¶3070
7	Exempt education or training and non-profit-making bodies	Education	¶3064

Scheme number	Title	Affecting	¶¶
8	Taxable education or training by profitable body	Education	¶3066
9	Cross-border face value vouchers for telecommunications, broadcasting and electronically supplied services	Vouchers	¶3072
10	Surrender and subsequent re-grant of a lease	Property	¶3062

a. Retailers

Payment handling service

Some retailers charge for the use of **debit or credit cards** by their customers, even though the price for the goods remains the same as when cash is paid. The scheme relies on the payment handling charge being an exempt supply, thereby reducing the amount of output tax payable by the retailer. 3054 Notice 700/8 para 6.3

This scheme has been shown not to work by a court case involving a major retailer (see below) and subsequent legislative change confirmed this.

Nonetheless, notification of its use is still required.

MEMO POINTS 1. The **commercial rationale** behind this scheme was that the retailers usually suffer an exempt charge from the card issuer every time a customer pays by card, so the scheme was only reflecting the true monetary situation of the retailer.
2. The **finance charge** is an exempt supply levied by an associate of the retailer. The idea was that the retailer reduced the price for the goods by the amount of the charge, and hence the output tax due, whilst still receiving the same amount of takings overall.

EXAMPLE A retailer used a scheme whereby it accounted for output tax on 97.5% of the amount paid by customers when paying by debit or credit card. The remaining 2.5% was paid to a wholly-owned subsidiary, which levied a card handling charge on the customer. This charge was notified by in-store signs and also a written notice on the till receipt. However, customers had to pay the same price irrespective of the payment method. HMRC challenged this treatment by assessing for output tax on 100% of the price paid.
The Court of Appeal held that there was a single contract between the retailer and the customer, and only the retailer was making a supply. Therefore the full consideration given by the customer was in relation to the retail supply only. *C & E v Debenhams Retail plc* [2005]

Value shifting

This is similar to the scheme above, in that part of the **customer's payment** is diverted away from standard-rated goods to add-ons which are either zero-rated or exempt (for example, insurance). The customer enters into a separate agreement for the add-on when making payment. However, the price charged is the same whether the customer agrees to receive the add-on or not. 3056 Notice 700/8 para 6.4

Notification is not required for:
- linked supplies (¶6524) for which no charge is made (because none of the price paid is diverted away from the main supply of goods); or
- normal business promotion schemes (¶6526), where the linked supply is not reliant on a separate agreement with the customer (for example, a promotion in which a purchase of several items entitles the customer to a discount, which is then reflected across all of the items when accounting for VAT).

Extended approval period

This scheme delays the **tax point** until the end of an approval period, even though payment is received up front and delivery has already taken place. The retailer therefore enjoys a cash flow advantage resulting from the delay in accounting for output tax. This device is commonly used by those selling on the Internet or by mail order. 3058 Notice 700/8 para 6.6

The **delay** may be imposed through specific terms or guarantees which treat the sale as one on approval, or which give the customer an extended right to return.

EXAMPLE Ms B is an Internet retailer. She takes payment from the customer's credit card when an order is placed. The goods are delivered as quickly as possible.
However, Ms B's terms of sale state that the customer has a 7-day cooling-off period (which starts from the date of receipt), during which time the customer can return the goods.
Ms B therefore only accounts for output tax once this period has expired.

b. Property

First grant of a major interest

3060 Notice 700/8 para 6.2

This scheme reduces the VAT cost of refurbishment or service charges. It works by transferring certain types of building to a connected person, and thereby accesses recoverable input tax on what becomes a zero-rated transaction.

However, the zero-rated disposals of either a converted building (¶5384+), or substantially reconstructed protected building (¶5392+), are excluded from this scheme.

Notice 700/8 para 6.1.2

MEMO POINTS 1. Persons are **connected** if they are either:
- members of the same group (¶3046), including partnerships and unincorporated associations carrying on a trade; or
- connected to the same trust (as a settlor, beneficiary or trustee), or hold shares in a company under the terms of the trust. A connected person would also be someone on whose behalf such shares are held.

2. The **types of building** concerned are dwellings and buildings which are for solely relevant residential or charitable purposes (¶5148). Common examples are:
- houses;
- student halls of residence;
- children's homes; and
- property used by a charity for non-business purposes.

3. For this purpose **refurbishment** includes extension, enlargement or repair.

EXAMPLE

1. C Ltd builds a children's home and leases it to D Ltd. The initial premium is zero-rated and C Ltd invoices for future repairs for the next 2 years, even though when those repairs are completed, C Ltd will be making exempt supplies of letting.
In this case, the advance invoicing of repairs is linked to the initial zero-rated premium, so this creates an unfair input tax recovery on what is properly an exempt supply.

2. E Ltd, a landlord, wants to refurbish some dwellings which it previously constructed a few years ago. E Ltd sells the property to a subsidiary so that the input tax incurred on the refurbishment is recoverable, because it relates to a zero-rated disposal.
The subsidiary then leases the property back to E Ltd, so that E Ltd can continue to let the dwellings out to a third party.
This means that, commercially, nothing has changed, but input tax has been recovered.

Surrender and re-grant of a lease

3062 Notice 700/8 para 6.11

This scheme involves **tenants who suffer VAT** on their rent because their premises are opted (¶5602+) and they are not making wholly taxable supplies. The **premises** must also be subject to the capital goods scheme or have been subject to it but are now outside the adjustment period (¶5750+).

The occupier of a leasehold building surrenders the opted lease, but remains in the building due to the grant of a new lease. The new lease terms include the right to occupy at least 80% of the original area. However, the new lease is not subject to an option to tax, so the occupier no longer suffers VAT on rental payments. Disclosure must be made where the re-grant reduces the amount of VAT payable by at least 50%.

MEMO POINTS 1. **Surrender** includes termination where a prior agreement or understanding regarding the termination has already been entered into with the lessor.

2. The **lessor** must be the occupier or a person connected with the occupier (¶3060). A landlord can also occupy a building, or part of a building, as a sublessee.
3. **Leasehold** includes any lease, tenancy or licence to occupy.

EXAMPLE

1. F Ltd occupies a building as a tenant and is currently paying VAT on the rent. It surrenders the lease early but continues to occupy the building. The landlord (F Ltd's parent company) grants a new lease, under which the rent is exempt, because of the disapplication rules relating to the option to tax (¶5652+).

2. G Ltd occupies a building as a tenant and is currently paying VAT on the rent. It surrenders the lease early but continues to occupy the building. The landlord (G Ltd's parent company) sells the building to G Ltd, which is an exempt supply because of the disapplication rules relating to the option to tax (¶5652+).

c. Education and training

Provided by non-profit-making body

The aim of this scheme is to avoid charging output tax on educational services, which are usually being **provided to** students who are not registered for VAT. **3064** Notice 700/8 para 6.8

Such services are exempt when provided by eligible bodies. Under the scheme, a normal company which provides education sets up a non-profit-making entity, which qualifies as an eligible body, and is also connected (¶3060) to the company. The education is then provided through this new entity, so that the supply becomes exempt.

The **entity is charged for** certain "key supplies" by the company, so diverting the profits from the education business to the company. In this way, the company still enjoys the profits but at a much lower VAT cost.

Such a scheme is notifiable if, in any one VAT return period, the value of the key supplies comprises **20% or more** of the costs of the education business.

MEMO POINTS 1. For the **scope** of educational services and training see ¶398+.
2. **Eligible bodies** include non-profit-making bodies, where any surplus is reinvested in education.
3. The **key supplies** are:
- supplying (including leasing) capital items, such as premises or equipment, but not including stock;
- providing staff;
- management services;
- administration services; and
- accountancy services.

EXAMPLE A secretarial college is currently making taxable supplies. The college decides to set up H Ltd, whose constitution prohibits any distribution of profits. H Ltd then supplies the secretarial tuition, which is now an exempt supply.
The college levies rent, management charges, and accountancy recharges on H Ltd. The rent is related to H Ltd's gross profit.
The college is therefore receiving the benefit of H Ltd's profit, but not in the form of a distribution.

Provided by a profitable body

The aim of this scheme is to increase the input tax recovery for an eligible body (¶3064), which is **supplying education to** bodies which can recover VAT (such as taxable businesses, NHS trusts, and local authorities). **3066** Notice 700/8 para 6.9

The eligible body sets up another connected (¶3060) entity which is fully taxable and can distribute its profits. The new entity now provides the education which becomes a taxable supply, so input tax can be recovered. The eligible body makes supplies of key services (¶3064) to the entity, and the entity gifts or distributes its profits back to the eligible body.

Such a scheme is notifiable if, in any one VAT return period, the value of the key supplies comprises **20% or more** of the costs of the education business.

EXAMPLE A university has been granted a contract to educate staff who are employed by an NHS trust. In order to carry out the tuition, new premises and equipment are required. As the university is an eligible body, it would be making exempt supplies, and would be unable to recover the input tax incurred on the necessary costs.
The university therefore sets up a subsidiary which can distribute its profits, and which is not an eligible body. The subsidiary can recover all of the input tax on the costs because it is making taxable supplies. However, finance and resources must be provided by the university, as the subsidiary has no independent means of support. In return, the subsidiary gifts its profits back to the university.

d. Other situations

Leasing back goods

3068 Notice 700/8 para 6.5 This scheme **excludes** land transactions, and any transactions between unconnected parties (for the definition of connected persons see ¶3060).

It assists the **input tax recovery** of partly exempt businesses, by enabling them to access a full input tax refund up front and repay the VAT over a period of time. In all affected cases, 90% of the acquisition cost of the goods is financed by the partly exempt business.

The scheme comes in **two guises**, where either:
a. a taxable person acquires the goods and then leases them to a connected partly exempt firm, which uses the goods in the course of its business; or
b. a partly exempt firm sells or leases goods to a taxable connected party, which then leases them back to the firm.

EXAMPLE A banking group needs to purchase a new computer system. As the bank makes exempt supplies, the related input tax would normally be irrecoverable.
However, if the bank's taxable subsidiary acquires the system, it can fully recover the input tax. It then leases the system to the exempt entities in the banking group, charging output tax on every lease payment. The exempt entities suffer a small input tax charge and it may take many years for the full VAT charge to be passed on to them.

Partly exempt groups and third party suppliers

3070 Notice 700/8 para 6.7 In order to minimise the input tax cost of supplies, a group may wish to bring a supplier within the VAT group, as VAT does not apply between members of such a group. Clearly this requires the supplier to be majority owned by a group member.

The scheme is notifiable if the **supplier** is either:
– run for the benefit of a third party (meaning that over 50% of the benefits of ownership accrue to a third party outside the group); or
– not consolidated within the group accounts of the person controlling the VAT group under generally accepted accounting practice.

MEMO POINTS 1. The **third party** usually manages the provision of the service by the supplier.
2. For the rules relating to **consolidated accounts**, see *Accountancy Memo*.
3. Groups with **turnover in excess of £10 million** are subject to additional anti-avoidance rules which may require the degrouping of the supplier (¶8875+).

EXAMPLE A Ltd is partly exempt, but has outsourced its back office functions to B Ltd. A Ltd and B Ltd set up W Ltd, which will provide the functions to A Ltd.
W Ltd is owned 51% by A Ltd, so W Ltd can join A Ltd's VAT group.
However, B Ltd's shares in W Ltd entitle it to 95% of the dividend income and 95% of assets on a winding up. B Ltd also receives a substantial management charge from W Ltd.
Although A Ltd therefore technically controls W Ltd, B Ltd enjoys virtually all the monetary benefits of ownership.

Cross-border face value vouchers

This scheme is complicated, and only relates to vouchers which are used to purchase **relevant services**, meaning telecommunications, radio and broadcasting, or electronically supplied services. It exploits the different treatment of face value vouchers between the various EU member states. 3072 Notice 700/8 para 6.10

A UK business makes a supply of relevant services to a connected (¶3060) EU trader, which then makes an onward retail supply of those same services to an unregistered UK customer. The UK consumer pays for the services using a face value voucher issued from outside the UK (but within the EU).

The EU trader does not account for VAT on the supply anywhere in the EU or in the UK, because of the special place of supply rules which apply to relevant services.

HMRC states that only taxable UK persons who are knowingly involved in this scheme are required to notify.

Since the introduction in 2012 of taxation on each sale of a face value voucher (¶1020), this scheme is probably ineffective, but notification is still required.

MEMO POINTS 1. For details of the place of supply of **telecommunications**, and **radio and broadcasting** see ¶9764+.
2. For details of **electronically supplied** services and the applicable place of supply rules see ¶6990+ and ¶9768.

EXAMPLE

1. An Irish company supplied phone cards to UK customers. The Irish authorities did not collect VAT on the supply, because under Irish law the place of supply was the UK. Business Brief 7/06
Initially, the High Court had held that the cards were supplied in Ireland, where the supplier was located. Even though Irish VAT had not been levied, the UK therefore had no right to any UK VAT on either the supply of the phone cards, or the telecommunications service.
However, the Court of Appeal disagreed, and stated that phone cards supplied to UK distributors by an issuer in another member state are liable to UK VAT on their onward sale by the distributors *HMRC v R (oao IDT Card Services Ireland Ltd)* [2006]

2. A UK company sold phone cards to distributors resident in other EU member states. The distributors sold the phone cards to consumers. The company did not account for VAT on sales of phone cards, on the grounds that the place of supply was the member state where the distributor was established. HMRC argued that the supply was one of telecommunications services to the end user when the phone card was used.
The CJEU held that the sale of a phone card constitutes a taxable supply of telecommunications services at each stage of the supply chain. Thus there is a supply of such services when the card issuer sells the card to a distributor, and a separate supply when the distributor sells to a wholesaler or retailer. Similarly, there is a supply when the retailer sells the card to the end user. There is, however, no supply of telecommunications services by the card issuer to the end user; that supply is made by the retailer who sells the card to the end user.
This ruling prevents cross-border mismatches in the treatment of supplies of phone cards, provided that all member states treat such supplies as taxable at each stage of the supply chain. Legislation introduced in 2012 extended this to face value vouchers generally (¶1020). *Lebara Ltd v HMRC* [2012]

3. How to disclose

Time

Notification must be made **within** 30 days of the: 3074 SI 2004/1929 reg 2; Notice 700/8 para 5.1
- due date of the affected return;
- due date of the return relating to a VAT period where input tax suffered has been reduced;
- date of the affected claim; or
- due date of the first VAT return following a direction (¶3044) received from HMRC.

EXAMPLE

1. C Ltd starts to use a designated scheme on 5 August. The company's VAT periods end on 30 April, 31 July, etc.
The first return to be affected is therefore that for the period ending 31 October, which has a due date of 30 November.
Notification must be made by 30 December.

2. D Ltd makes a claim, affected by a designated scheme, in respect of the VAT period ending 30 September. The claim is made on the following 16 May.
Notification must be made by 15 June.

Failure to notify

3076 Notice 700/8 para 12.1

If a person fails to notify the use of a notifiable VAT scheme in time, a penalty will be levied. If the failure relates to a hallmarked scheme (¶3084+) the penalty is £5,000. If the failure relates to a designated scheme (¶3048+) the penalty is 15% of the VAT saving achieved on every affected return or claim.

Penalties will **not be due** where:
- there is a reasonable excuse (¶4014+) for failing to notify;
- using the scheme has led to a conviction for a VAT offence; or
- a penalty for dishonest evasion has been levied (¶3955, but note that this penalty is now expected to be a very rare occurrence).

Notice 700/8 para 12.5

Penalties may be mitigated in certain circumstances (¶4044+). In cases of reasonable excuse and mitigation, the business should write to HMRC within 30 days of receiving notice of a penalty, requesting reconsideration of the position.

Notice 700/8 para 13

Penalties can be **appealed** to the tribunal (¶4260+) if the business does not agree that it is liable, or if the amount levied is felt to be incorrect.

Notice 700/8 para 12.2

MEMO POINTS 1. The **VAT saving** is quantified as the beneficial change in the amount of VAT payable or repayable due to the use of the scheme.

Notice 700/8 paras 12.6, 12.7

2. The penalty **assessment** is treated as an unpaid VAT liability. It can be issued within 2 years of when HMRC had sufficient facts about the situation, and will state the:
- amount of the penalty and the method of its calculation;
- reasons for the assessment; and
- amount of any mitigation.

3. Even if the scheme is **no longer in use**, a penalty assessment can still be issued.

Method

3078 Notice 700/8 paras 5.2 - 5.5

Disclosure must be in a set format, either in writing or via email.

The disclosure must be **headed** "Disclosure of use of listed scheme - Notification under paragraph 6(2) of Schedule 11A to the VAT Act 1994".

The following **information** must be included in the notification:
- the business name and address;
- VAT number; and
- scheme number (¶3052).

MEMO POINTS 1. The **postal address** to which notifications must be sent is:
Anti Avoidance Group (Intelligence)
VAT Avoidance Disclosures Unit
HM Revenue & Customs
CTIAA Intelligence S0528
PO Box 194
Bootle
L69 9AA
Notifications **sent elsewhere** are invalid.

2. Notifications can be **emailed** to: vat.avoidance.disclosures.bst@hmrc.gsi.gov.uk

3. If using **multiple arrangements** which use the **same sort** of scheme, the number of such schemes must be disclosed.

Subsequent official action

HMRC will acknowledge receipt of the notification. 3080 Notice 700/8 para 5.6

Further action may be taken as appropriate; HMRC will contact the business where necessary.

Existing investigations into any use of schemes are not affected by notification.

C. Hallmarked schemes

Businesses with an annual turnover (¶3040+) in excess of £10 million must disclose use of schemes which include certain hallmarks, when all of the following **criteria** are fulfilled: 3084 Notice 700/8 para 7.1
- the main purpose, or one of the main purposes, of the scheme is to obtain a tax advantage;
- a return or claim is affected; and
- HMRC has not already been notified, either by the business itself or the scheme promoter (who would provide a reference number to the business).

The **scheme promoter** is anyone who designs or sells avoidance schemes in the course of a profession, trade or business of providing taxation services. The promoter may voluntarily register a scheme (¶3118), so that the businesses using the scheme are relieved from any requirement to notify. SI 2004/1933 Sch 2 para 2(2)

1. Motive test

The hallmarked schemes have a **motive test** which depends on the meaning of both main purpose and tax advantage. Note that it is possible to gain a tax advantage without needing to disclose, unless the advantage is a main purpose of the scheme. 3086 Notice 700/8 para 7.3

Tax advantage

Tax advantage is **defined** as any situation where any of the following apply: 3088 Sch 11A para 2 VATA 1994; Notice 700/8 para 7.4.1

a. the net VAT due (output tax less input tax) in any VAT period is less than if the scheme was not in place;

b. a VAT repayment is obtained which:
- would not be available if the scheme was not in use;
- is larger; or
- is received earlier;

c. the amount of a taxable person's irrecoverable input tax is reduced by the scheme;

d. a business recovers the input tax on a supply before the supplier accounts for output tax and this timing advantage is increased because of the scheme; or

e. a non-taxable person suffers less VAT on supplies, EU acquisitions or imports because of the scheme. Any VAT which is refundable because of specific provisions (for example, those applying to local authorities) is ignored for this purpose.

Main purpose

HMRC states that there is **no single factor** which determines whether obtaining a tax advantage is a main purpose of a scheme. 3090 Notice 700/8 para 7.4.4

In general, where the arrangements would not have been implemented at all, or would have been carried out differently, if the tax advantage did not exist, it is likely that a main purpose is to obtain a tax advantage. However, where there are multiple ways of achieving a genuine commercial objective and the choice was made for reasons other than the VAT saving (but a tax advantage is still obtained), it is unlikely that the main purpose test is met.

The following **circumstances** should also be considered:
– the overall objectives of the arrangements, including those of the wider corporate group or owners of the parties to the scheme where relevant; and
– whether certain steps in the arrangements (which might be costly or complex) would have taken place were it not for the tax advantage obtained.

2. Returns or claims affected

3092 Notice 700/8 para 7.5 The requirement to notify HMRC arises when the operation of the scheme results in any of the following beneficial **changes**:
– a VAT return shows a higher or lower net amount of VAT;
– an increased claim is made for the repayment of output tax over-declared or input tax credit under-claimed; or
– a smaller amount of non-deductible VAT is incurred.

Notice 700/8 para 7.7 If the use of a scheme has **already been notified by the business**, and a new scheme is used which is structured in the same way (that is, the workings of the scheme are the same and the tax advantage arises from the same legal provision), no further notification is required.

However, where the structure is different, a fresh notification is required.

Notice 700/8 para 7.8 If the scheme has **already been registered** by the scheme promoter (¶3118), and the scheme reference number has been passed to the business, notification is not required.

MEMO POINTS 1. When affected by **more than one hallmark**, all relevant schemes must be notified.

Notice 700/8 para 3.3 2. When **more than one entity** is a party to the same scheme, all entities must disclose if they fall within the criteria. A joint notification can be made.

3. Notifiable hallmarks

Summary

3094 SI 2004/1933 Sch 2; Notice 700/8 para 3.6

Hallmark	Affecting	Reference	¶¶
Confidentiality condition	Promoters	SI 2004/1933 Sch 2 para 1	¶3096
Promoter's fee contingent on tax advantage	Promoters	SI 2004/1933 Sch 2 para 3	¶3098
Prepayments between connected parties	Connected parties	SI 2004/1933 Sch 2 para 4	¶3100
Supply funded by shares, loans or subscriptions	Connected parties	SI 2004/1933 Sch 2 para 5	¶3102
Grant of property interest between connected persons	Connected parties	SI 2004/1933 Sch 2 para 7	¶3104
Issue of face value vouchers with long redemption period	Connected parties	SI 2004/1933 Sch 2 para 8	¶3106
Agreement to share a tax advantage	Promoters and/or other entities involved in the scheme	SI 2004/1933 Sch 2 para 2	¶3108
Offshore loops	Certain services which are resupplied	SI 2004/1933 Sch 2 para 6	¶3110

a. Promoters

Confidentiality condition

Confidentiality terms will appear in an agreement which a **potential user** of a scheme must sign before the promoter communicates any details. The terms may prohibit or limit disclosure, to protect the competitive advantage of a particular promoter over other promoters. **3096** SI 2004/1933 Sch 2 para 1; Notice 700/8 para 10.2

However, **general** confidentiality conditions relating to all advice given by a practitioner are not a hallmark, **subject to** the HMRC guidance below, which gives the types of conditions which HMRC considers to be **notifiable**:

- a specific or general condition prohibits or limits a person from revealing details of how a particular scheme gives rise to a tax advantage;
- a client is required to agree, either in writing or verbally, not to reveal details of how a particular scheme gives rise to a tax advantage; or
- an adviser specifically draws a client's attention to a pre-existing general confidentiality condition when introducing a scheme to the client, so that the client is prohibited from revealing details of how that particular scheme gives rise to a tax advantage.

Contingent fee agreements

There is a notifiable hallmark if the price paid **in return for** the promoter's initial idea and implementation of the scheme depends on the amount of tax advantage (¶3088) obtained. **3098** SI 2004/1933 Sch 2 para 3; Notice 700/8 paras 10.4, 11.4

Note that employing an outsider to **review previous input tax claims**, where the fee is contingent on the amount of input tax refunded, is not obtaining a tax advantage, merely accessing input tax recovery to which the business is entitled.

b. Connected parties

Prepayments between connected persons

There is a notifiable hallmark if a payment is made to a connected party (¶3060) either: **3100** SI 2004/1933 Sch 2 para 4; Notice 700/8 para 10.5

- before the basic tax point; or
- in relation to a continuous supply before the goods or services are received.

The **amount** and **timing** of the prepayment are irrelevant.

MEMO POINTS 1. The **basic tax point** for goods is the date of despatch or removal (except for those which are subject to customer approval), and, for services, is the date of performance of the services. See ¶760+ for further details.

2. For this purpose, **continuous supplies** are:
- any type of service paid for periodically;
- leases exceeding 21 years;
- supplies of water and power;
- royalties and similar payments; and
- construction supplies.

See ¶808+ for further details.

Supply funded by shares, loans or subscriptions

There is a notifiable hallmark if a supply of goods or services between connected persons (¶3060) is paid for wholly or in part by: **3102** SI 2004/1933 Sch 2 para 5; Notice 700/8 para 10.6

- a loan between connected persons;
- one person subscribing for shares in a connected company; or
- one person subscribing in securities issued by a connected company.

Property transactions

3104 SI 2004/1933 Sch 2 para 7; Notice 700/8 para 10.8

There is a notifiable hallmark if a **partly exempt** business, which makes both taxable and exempt supplies, grants an interest in property to a connected person (¶3060), and any work of construction, alteration, demolition, repair, maintenance or civil engineering has been (or is to be) carried out on the property.

However, the first grant of an interest in the following types of property is **excluded**:
- dwelling (¶5152+);
- building used for relevant residential purposes (¶5158+);
- building used for relevant charitable purposes (¶5170+); or
- reconstructed protected buildings (¶5392+).

MEMO POINTS 1. **Grant** includes assignment, surrender and the supply made by a recipient when an interest is reverse surrendered (¶5570).
2. An **interest in property** includes any right over land and a licence to occupy land (¶5374).

Face value vouchers

3106 SI 2004/1933 Sch 2 para 8; Notice 700/8 para 10.9

There is a notifiable hallmark if such a voucher is issued for consideration, **except** where:
a. the issuer reasonably expects that at least 75% of the face value will be redeemed within 3 years of the issue date; or
b. the vouchers are issued either to:
- an unconnected person; or
- a member of the issuer's VAT group (¶8800+) and that member will not then supply the voucher to a connected person (¶3060) outside the VAT group.

Since the introduction in 2012 of taxation on each sale of a face value voucher (¶1020) schemes using such vouchers are probably ineffective, but notification is still required.

Sch 10A para 1(1) VATA 1994; Notice 700/8 para 10.9.1

MEMO POINTS 1. Face value vouchers are **defined** as any token, stamp or voucher which gives the holder a right to receive goods or services to the value stated on it.
2. HMRC illustrates the **expected redemption rates** as follows:
a. vouchers worth £1 million are issued and the issuer expects £900,000 of these to be redeemed: this is a 90% expected redemption rate, irrespective of the actual amount redeemed; and
b. vouchers which can be partly redeemed are issued: the business expects 100% of the vouchers to be redeemed but only 30% of the value (in this case, the expected redemption rate is 30%).

---

c. Other situations

Agreement to share a tax advantage

3108 SI 2004/1933 Sch 2 para 2; Notice 700/8 para 10.3

There is a notifiable hallmark if there is an agreement to share the tax advantage (¶3088) **with** any other party to the scheme, or with the scheme promoter. The extent of the sharing is irrelevant.

Offshore loops

3110 SI 2004/1933 Sch 2 para 6; Notice 700/8 para 10.7

There is a notifiable hallmark if:
- certain exported services (see memo point) are supplied which allow the exporter to recover related input tax; and
- the services are used by the recipient to make a **subsequent supply** to a UK person and treated as imported services not subject to VAT.

Further **stages** can be inserted in the supply chain, but if the effect is still the same (VAT is avoided in the UK), the scheme must be notified.

HMRC has stated that only suppliers who are complicit in the arrangements are required to disclose.

EXAMPLE A UK lawyer makes a supply to a French business and as the place of supply is France, no UK VAT is chargeable.

The French business then uses this supply to make a zero-rated supply back to a partly exempt UK business.
Although a UK business has effectively made a supply to a UK recipient, no UK VAT is paid by any party to the transaction. This matters because the partly exempt UK business would normally suffer some irrecoverable input tax.

MEMO POINTS The **affected services** are those:
a. where input tax is specifically recoverable (¶2197); and
b. taking place where the recipient belongs (¶9682+).

4. How to disclose

By scheme user

The **date** of notification must occur within 30 days of the due date of the affected return or claim (¶3092). **3112** SI 2004/1929 reg 2

If notification is **not made in time**, a penalty of £5,000 will be levied (¶3076).

For subsequent official action see ¶3080.

The **method** of disclosure may either be in writing or via email. **3114**

The disclosure must be **headed** "Disclosure of use of hallmarked scheme - Notification under paragraph 6(3) of Schedule 11A to the VAT Act 1994". Notice 700/8 para 8.2

The following **information** must be included in the notification: Notice 700/8 para 8.3
- the business name and address;
- VAT number;
- details of how the scheme works;
- a statement of which hallmarks (¶3094) are relevant (this may be included within the scheme details); and
- the law which is relied upon to obtain the tax advantage.

There is no requirement to state the **amount** of the tax advantage.

MEMO POINTS 1. The business must give sufficient information about **how the scheme works**, so that HMRC understands how the tax advantage is obtained, in particular: **3116** Notice 700/8 para 8.4
- how the involvement of any party assists the obtaining of the tax advantage (parties do not need to be identified and may be described as Company A etc);
- a description of each transaction, arrangement or series of transactions;
- the sequence, if any, of the various transactions, all clearly identified;
- the timing of transactions, especially where the scheme relies on either concurrence or a long period between each step; and
- the goods or services involved.

Copies of contracts and documentation are not required. It is recommended that a summary of the scheme is provided, perhaps with diagrams where this facilitates understanding.

2. The **law** relied upon may be UK law, EU law where its effect is more beneficial than the enacted UK law, or overseas law where the other country has a different VAT treatment of the transaction. For example: Notice 700/8 para 8.6
- the EU member state has been granted a derogation not to apply a specific provision;
- the conditions imposed by the EU member state differ from those in the UK; or
- the EU member state has interpreted an EU directive differently from the UK.

3. HMRC will request any **missing information**, and the business is liable to a penalty where this is not provided within the time limit for the notification. Notice 700/8 para 8.9

4. For the postal and email **addresses** to which notifications must be sent, see ¶3078. Notice 700/8 paras 8.7, 8.8

Voluntary registration scheme

To ease the administration burden on users of schemes (the clients), anyone (including advisers, promoters and trade bodies) may **voluntarily register** the scheme with HMRC. **3118** Notice 700/8 para 9

The scheme reference number (a number prefixed with VRS) should then be supplied to clients, removing any obligation to notify on their part. If HMRC decides not to issue a reference number (because the scheme description is unclear, or more than one scheme is covered), the client must make a separate notification.

The person making the notification must write to, or email, HMRC, and provide all the information set out in ¶3114+. The communication must clearly state that it is a voluntary notification.

The notification will be **acknowledged** within 10 working days of receipt, and a scheme reference number will usually be forwarded to the person who has made the notification.

CHAPTER 4

Payment

OUTLINE ¶¶

It is important for a trader to identify the means and due date of a VAT payment in order to **3160**
avoid penalties and interest.

On the other hand, when a repayment is due, the trader has various rights to prevent a disadvantage arising through any action by HMRC, although a claim must usually be made within strict time limits.

Payment of VAT on imports is covered at ¶9426+.

SECTION 1

Payment regime

The payment regime **depends on** the size of the trader's annual VAT liability. For most **3165**
businesses, payment is usually made concurrently with the submission of the return.

However, if the annual VAT liability exceeds **the very large business threshold** (currently £2.3 million), the rules for very large businesses (¶3182+) apply and payments on account are required.

A. Ordinary businesses

Method of payment

3167 The permitted methods of payment depend to some extent on whether the business submits its returns on paper or online (from 1 April 2012 virtually all businesses must submit returns and make payment online - see ¶3003).

Notice 700 para 21.3

HMRC's recommended method is the **Faster Payments Service**. In the correct circumstances (taxpayers should always check with their own bank to ensure that the right arrangements are in place) this allows payments to be made and received on the same day. Full details are at flmemo.co.uk/vm3167.

Payment method	Paper returns	Online returns
Cheque or postal order	Y	N
Bank Giro transfer (takes about 3 days)	Y	Y
BACS (takes about 3 days)	Y	Y
CHAPS (same day transfer, but more expensive)	Y	Y
UK-issued credit card [1]	Y	Y
Direct debit [2]	N	Y

Note
1. If a credit card is used to pay **online**, a fee of 1.4% of the tax due is charged.
2. Payment is not claimed by HMRC until 3 days after the return is due.

A business can **change its method of payment** without previously notifying HMRC of its intention.

3170 MEMO POINTS 1. If a business makes a **duplicate payment**, this will always be repaid, provided that the **refund** is claimed within 4 years of the date of the overpayment (¶3244+).
2. **Incomplete** payments are allocated to the oldest VAT debt first.
3. The **destination bank account** for electronic payments is:
Citi
Citigroup Centre
Canada Square
Canary Wharf
London
E14 5LB
Sort Code: 08 32 00
Account No: 11963155
If paying by BACS or CHAPS, the trader's bank must quote the VAT registration number as its reference number.

Notice 920 paras 3.3 - 3.8

4. It is possible to make payment in **euros**, although the return must still be completed in sterling, and not all banks offer this facility for every payment method. The sterling amount received in HMRC's bank account will be calculated using the exchange rate ruling at the date of clearance. Hence there will almost inevitably be a difference in the amount due and paid on every occasion. However, HMRC does not pass on any costs of conversion to the trader.

Due date for return payments

3172 The standard due date for paying a VAT **liability shown on a return** is the same as the due date for submitting the return - that is, the end of the month following the last day of the VAT period (although now that electronic payment is all but compulsory, most businesses will be allowed a further 7 days - see ¶3174).

SI 1995/2518 reg 40(2)

If payment is made **late**, default interest (¶3880+) will be charged and the trader may also be liable to a surcharge (¶4082+).

A trader who is **unable** to pay all of the VAT due should contact HMRC immediately to explain the reason why. HMRC has discretion to agree a period in which payment can be made. Payment by cheque will be treated as received when funds are cleared into HMRC's bank account, so cheques post-dated to after the due date will automatically lead to a default.

MEMO POINTS 1. **Amounts under £1** are not payable and are not carried forward to the next return. Notice 700 para 21.5
2. On **deregistration**, the due date for payment is a calendar month after the effective date on which the registration is cancelled. SI 1995/2518 reg 40(2B)
3. If a trader **dies or becomes incapacitated**, the representative (¶2624) must make payment by the end of the next calendar month following the event. VAT is payable by the representative only if the trader's assets are sufficient to fund the VAT payment. SI 1995/2518 reg 30

If **paying electronically** (that is, by any method other than cheque or postal order), the due date for return payments is automatically extended by an extra 7 calendar days, **unless** the trader is: **3174** Notice 700 para 21.3
- using the annual accounting scheme (¶4745+); or
- very large (¶3182+), and submits quarterly (rather than monthly) returns.

This extension only applies to payments which relate to returns.

However, there are certain other **restrictions and caveats** which apply to this seemingly generous provision:
- some electronic payment methods are comparatively expensive;
- the payment must actually reach HMRC's bank account by the 7th calendar day (if this falls on a weekend, payment must arrive by the previous Friday; for bank holidays, payment must arrive by the last preceding working day); and
- banks vary on how long they take to process transactions, so the trader should take steps to find out the length of time the transaction will take for a particular bank.

EXAMPLE

1. A company requested its bank to make payment by credit transfer on 7 May, which was a bank holiday. As a result, the payment was actually made on 8 May. However, the company wrote to HMRC on 27 April, saying that payment would be made on 7 May.
On allowing the company's appeal, it was held that the company had made a genuine error, and because of the letter, there was a reasonable excuse for late payment. HMRC should have noticed the error as communicated in the letter, and forewarned the company of the problem. *Avonwave Ltd (t/a Gatewood Joinery)* [2001] (VTD 17509)

2. A company asked its bank to make payment by credit transfer so that it would arrive by the deadline. The payment was still late, because of the bank's error.
It was held that the company had a reasonable excuse. It was noted that there was no official guidance as to the action the taxpayer should take in these circumstances. *H Griffiths Engineering Ltd* [2005] (VTD 19098)

Failing to comply

If the trader is experiencing **payment difficulties**, the return should still be submitted by the due date. The trader must contact HMRC separately to discuss possible options. Sometimes HMRC will agree to the debt being paid in instalments. Note that penalties may still be levied for late payment or non-payment, and security or a guarantee may be requested (¶3524+). **3176** Notice 700/12 para 6.1

If a trader **fails to submit returns**, choosing instead to pay the VAT showing on assessments (¶3654+), HMRC will increase the amount assessed over time. Notice 700 para 21.2.1; Notice 930

On **refusal** by the trader to make payment, HMRC can assert various powers (¶3730+) to recover the debt, including a distress warrant, or even applying for a winding-up order.

Paying assessments

Assessments must be paid **within** 30 days of the date on which HMRC issues the notice. Otherwise, interest will be charged. **3178**

Even if the trader believes that a **repayment** is currently due, payment must still be made, because HMRC will not have sufficient information to verify the position in the absence of a return.

B. Very large businesses

3182 SI 1993/2001 For businesses with an annual VAT liability in excess of the threshold (currently £2.3 million), VAT must usually be paid in advance, in estimated monthly instalments which are notified to the business by HMRC.

Notice 700/60 para 4 However, instead of paying estimates, there are two **alternative** monthly payment methods which may be available (¶3212+).

SI 1993/2001 reg 16 MEMO POINTS 1. For **divisional registration** (¶2744+), each division is regarded as a separate business for the purposes of payments on account, and is separately responsible for making the payments.
2. **Correspondence** on any matter should be addressed to:
Payments on Account Team
4th Floor Regian House
James Street
Liverpool
L75 1AD

1. Overview

Entering the regime

3184 VAT **arising from the following** is taken into account:
- returns;
- assessments;
- voluntary disclosures;
- imports; and
- goods transferred from a fiscal or customs warehouse.

MEMO POINTS The annual VAT liability would normally include **reverse charges** (¶9700+). However, businesses affected by the missing trader reverse charge regime (¶1988+) can apply to HMRC to exclude the output tax due under the reverse charge when:
- deciding whether a business is required to make payments on account; and
- calculating the size of monthly payments.

3186 SI 1993/2001 regs 5, 6 The VAT liability is measured over the **basis period**. Two tests determine whether a business is very large; either measuring during:
a. any year ending at any quarter end, which is relevant when determining when payments on account should commence or cease; and
b. the **reference year** (¶3203), which is used for calculating the payments during each VAT cycle on a continuing basis.

EXAMPLE A Ltd, which submits returns for quarters ending 30 April, 31 July etc, had a VAT liability for the year ended 31 October 2014 of £1.8 million. The VAT liability for the year to 30 April 2015 is £2.4 million, which makes A Ltd a very large business.

Payment method

3188 Notice 700/60 para 2.5 Large businesses must make payment as shown in the following table. Note that only electronic means may be used.

Payments must **clear by** the due date. There is a 7-day extension only for traders who submit monthly returns (¶3212).

The VAT registration number should be used as a reference for all payments.

Method	Details	Destination bank details
CHAPS	Same day transfer	Citi No: 11963155 Sort code: 08-32-00 Account name: HMRC VAT
BACS	Takes at least 3 days	
Internet or telephone banking	Takes at least 3 days	
Standing order	Ensure leaves account early enough to arrive on time	
Bank giro credit	Obtain giro slips Takes at least 3 days	Obtain slips by calling 01702 366376 or 01702 366314, or email electronicpaymentteam@hmrc.gov.uk

Failure to pay on time may result in surcharges (¶4082+). An appeal against a surcharge **3190** SI 1995/2518 reg 47
must be made to the Large Payers Unit. HMRC will take immediate action to recover the debt, and may move the business to monthly returns.

Interaction with returns

Quarterly return **entries** are not affected by payments on account. **3192** Notice 700/60 para 2.6

If the return **shows a VAT repayment**, this will be repaid along with payments on account already made in respect of that return, unless another liability exists against which the repayment will be set off instead (¶3232).

2. Payment schedule

HMRC will notify the business of the amounts, calculations and due dates of payment. **3194** Notice 700/60 para 2.2

Timing

For **standard quarterly VAT periods**, payments on account are normally made in the 2nd **3196** SI 1993/2001 reg 8; Notice 700/60 para 2.4
and 3rd months of the quarter, with a balancing payment being made on the normal due date of the quarterly return.

In practice, this means that the business is making monthly payments throughout the year.

The exact **due date** for:
- a payment on account is always the last working day of the 2nd and 3rd months of every VAT period, irrespective of the actual period end dates; and
- the balancing payment is the last working day of the relevant month.

For **non-standard VAT periods**, the payments on account depend on the length of the period **3198** SI 1993/2001 reg 9
and the number of whole calendar months included.

VAT period covers	Example	Payments on account fall on
Only one complete calendar month	7 March to 7 May	1. Last day of calendar month: 30 April 2. End of period: 7 May
Two and a half calendar months	7 March to 31 May	1. Last day of first calendar month: 30 April 2. Last day of second calendar month: 31 May
3 months beginning mid month	7 March to 7 June	1. Last day of first calendar month: 30 April 2. Last day of second calendar month: 31 May
Longer than 3 months	7 March to 7 July	1. Last day of second calendar month: 31 May 2. Last day of third calendar month: 30 June

The **balancing payment** must clear by the usual due date. If the due date is not a working day, the immediately previous working day becomes the deadline for payment.

Commencing the scheme When the business **becomes very large**, payments on account **3200** Notice 700/60 para 2.2
start from the quarter immediately following that in which the business exceeds the thresh-

old. In the first quarter, only one payment is required; this must occur at the end of the 3rd month. A balancing payment is made with the return submission, then payments on account occur as normal.

EXAMPLE Continuing the example at ¶3186, A Ltd must commence making payments on account in the quarter starting on 1 May 2015.

Amount

3202 Notice 700/60 para 2.3 The payments on account are **calculated by** HMRC as 1/24th of the annual VAT liability. For this purpose, the VAT liability excludes VAT on imports and warehoused goods.

Comment Contrast this with the calculation for the annual VAT liability when entering the regime (¶3184).

3203 SI 1993/2001 regs 11, 12 When the business **becomes very large**, the annual VAT liability will be measured in the basis period (¶3186). The payments then remain the same until that particular VAT cycle ends.

For **subsequent VAT cycles**, the liability in the previous reference year is used to calculate the payments on account.

SI 1993/2001 regs 5, 6; Notice 700/60 para 2.3.2 The **reference year** is determined by the dates of the trader's VAT returns (stagger) as follows:

Quarter end date	VAT cycle begins	Reference year ending
31 Mar/30 June/30 Sept/31 Dec	1 April	Previous 30 Sept
30 April/31 July/31 Oct/31 Jan	1 May	Previous 31 Oct
31 May/31 Aug/30 Nov/28 Feb	1 June	Previous 30 Nov

MEMO POINTS 1. If **in business for less than 12 months**, the payments are calculated on a proportionate basis.

SI 1993/2001 reg 17 2. A **VAT group** is a single taxable person, and therefore all the members' liabilities are totalled to calculate the payments on account required. All group members are jointly and severally liable for each payment.

EXAMPLE

1. B Ltd is a very large business and making payments on account. It had a VAT liability of £2.4 million for the year ended 30 September 2014. This liability will be used to calculate the payments on account for the VAT cycle beginning on 1 April 2015.

2. C Ltd is a very large business because its VAT liability for the year ended 31 October 2014 was £2.5 million (including import VAT of £100,000). C Ltd's VAT cycle begins on 1 May. The payments for the cycle beginning on 1 May 2015 are determined by the VAT liability for the year ended 31 October 2014.
The annual VAT liability (excluding import VAT) is £2.4 million. (£2,500,000 - £100,000)
Each payment on account is £100,000. (£2,400,000 × 1/24)
If C Ltd's return for the quarter ended 31 July 2015 shows a VAT liability of £680,000, the balancing payment is £480,000, payable by 31 August 2015. (£680,000 - £100,000 - £100,000)

3. D Ltd submits calendar quarter returns. It has only been trading for 9 months when it becomes very large because of a cumulative VAT liability of £2.43 million by 30 June 2014.
Payments on account start in the following quarter (beginning on 1 July 2014) and are calculated as £135,000. (£2,430,000 × 1/24 × 12/9)
Payments will remain at this level until the start of the new VAT cycle (1 April 2015), when the payments will be based on the VAT liability for the year ended 30 September 2014 (the reference year).

3204 SI 1993/2001 regs 13, 14 **Change in circumstances** If the VAT **liability** in the last 12 months (measured to any quarter end) **varies** by at least 20% from that of the basis period (¶3186), the payments will be adjusted. However, the business must wait to be notified by HMRC before making any changes to the amounts paid.

In summary:

VPOA3100

Change in annual VAT liability	Action	¶¶
In reference year, falls below the very large business threshold[1]	Will be taken out of payments on account from beginning of next VAT cycle	¶3210
Falls below the very large business exit limit[2] at any time	Request to be taken out of payments on account immediately	¶3210
Decreases by at least 20% compared to basis period	Request to decrease payments on account	¶3206
Increases by at least 20% compared to basis period	HMRC increases payments on account	¶3208

Note
1. The threshold is currently £2.3 million.
2. The exit limit is currently £1.8 million.

If the VAT liability **decreases** (or is likely to decrease) by at least 20%, the trader may apply in writing for the payments on account to be reduced immediately. See also ¶3210. **3206** Notice 700/60 para 3.2

The **request** must be accompanied by detailed forecasts showing the changes in VAT liability. HMRC will give written notice of its approval, and there must be no decrease in payments until it does so.

EXAMPLE E Ltd's VAT liability for the previous reference year (year to 30 September) was £2.7 million.
For the year ending 31 March, the liability has fallen to £2.1 million.
The change of £600,000 is more than 20% of £2.7 million, so E Ltd can apply for the payments on account to be reduced.

If the VAT liability **increases** by at least 20%, HMRC may increase the payments to be made. They will be calculated as 1/24th of the increased VAT liability. **3208** Notice 700/60 para 3.3;

However, it is possible to apply for a subsequent decrease where the trader's VAT liability reduces again by more than 20% (¶3206). SI 1993/2001 reg 15

Ceasing

If the VAT liability falls below £2.3 million in a **reference year**, the business will continue to make payments on account until the end of the current VAT cycle (a delay of 6 months). **3210** Notice 700/60 para 3.4

If a **sudden loss of trade** is experienced, so that the liability in the year to the latest quarter end falls below £1.8 million, the business can request to cease making payments on account. These will then stop from the date on which approval is given by HMRC. SI 1993/2001 reg 7

On **deregistration**, payments on account should continue until the date deregistration is confirmed, unless the business elects to pay the actual liability. Notice 700/11 para 7.12

EXAMPLE F Ltd submits returns on a calendar quarter basis.
If F Ltd's annual VAT liability for the year ended 30 September 2014 was £1.85 million, HMRC would have removed the company from the payments on account regime from 1 April 2015 onwards.
The last payment on account would have been in March 2015.

3. Alternative bases for payment

Monthly returns

The business can opt to submit returns and pay VAT on a monthly basis. The business must apply to HMRC before adopting this basis, either online (¶2714) or by using form VAT 484 (which must be sent to the address shown on the form). **3212** Notice 700/60 para 4.1

A change to a monthly basis must be **sustained for** at least 12 months.

For this situation only, the 7-day extension for paying electronically will apply as for smaller businesses (¶3174). If the business reverts to quarterly returns, the payment extension no longer applies.

Paying the actual liability

3214 SI 1993/2001 reg 12A; Notice 700/60 para 4.2

Under this regime the business elects to pay the liability of the preceding month, as shown in its own records, but is not required to submit returns for each month, as a quarterly VAT period is still retained. A change to this basis must be **sustained for** at least 12 months.

This arrangement may suit businesses with a seasonal trade, but usually results in a cash flow disadvantage, as normal payments on account are only 1/24th of the VAT liability.

MEMO POINTS 1. The **election** must be in writing, giving 30 days' notice of the date when it is to be applied. If an election has been previously made, which has since ceased to have effect, no fresh election can be made until 12 months have elapsed. The notice must be addressed to:
Payments on Account Team
Banking Liverpool
3rd Floor South East
Queens Dock
Liverpool L74 4AA

Notice 700/60 para 4.3

2. Where HMRC is not satisfied that the business is **accurately** calculating the actual VAT liability, it has the power to require a business to submit monthly returns. The business has the right to appeal and request reconsideration (¶4220+) but must do this within 30 days of the date of HMRC's initial decision.

EXAMPLE G Ltd submits returns on a quarterly basis for the periods ending 30 April, 31 July etc, but has elected to pay VAT on a monthly basis.
G Ltd's records show a VAT liability of £260,000 for March.
This liability must be paid by 30 April.

3216 If a **VAT repayment** is due for any particular month:
- the refund will be delayed until that quarter's VAT return has been processed; and
- it must be ignored when calculating the VAT liability for the next month (it is **not carried forward** and set off against the next month's payment).

Businesses which are suffering **cash flow difficulties** due to these rules should consider changing to making monthly returns.

SECTION 2

Repayments

3230 Repayments may arise due to:
- the net VAT position shown on the return (¶3238+);
- an increase in a VAT repayment already due (¶3238+);
- a refund request after VAT has been paid in error (¶3244+); or
- a claim for relief under any of a range of provisions (¶3258).

Repayment supplement (¶3264+) will also be due to the trader in certain circumstances, and statutory interest (¶3270+) is payable in cases of official error.

A. General principles

Right to set off

3232 s 81 VATA 1994

As is normal commercial **practice**, VAT owed by HMRC will be set off first against any other VAT debt, except in the case of insolvent traders. For this purpose, any interest due from HMRC (¶3262+) on the repayment can also be set off.

Similarly, the trader may set off an amount owed from HMRC when making payment of the return liability, provided that HMRC has confirmed in writing that the refund is due (otherwise debt recovery proceedings may commence). VR8200

There is a **general set-off provision** for England, Wales and Northern Ireland. This gives HMRC the statutory power to use a VAT repayment to set against another outstanding debt such as corporation tax. ss 130 - 133 FA 2008

MEMO POINTS 1. **VAT debt** includes other VAT balances, penalties, surcharges and interest.
2. VAT repaid to a trader in order for **customers to be reimbursed** cannot be set off.
3. **Insolvent traders** have a right to a VAT repayment even where a pre-insolvency VAT debt exists, to assist these traders back to business recovery. The repayment must arise after insolvency proceedings have commenced. See ¶8706+ for further details. s 81(4A) - (4D) VATA 1994
4. An **anomaly** allows HMRC to set off the repayment against amounts which would be due if a hypothetical assessment was raised, but that assessment would now be invalid because it is out of time (¶3632+). For example, if a trader has charged VAT on exempt supplies by mistake, HMRC will reduce the VAT repayment to take account of the exempt input tax previously recovered which is now irrecoverable, and this is not restricted by the usual 4-year cap. VR8200

Repayment method

HMRC makes payment by BACS, **unless** the trader's bank account details are unknown, in which case a cheque is issued instead. **3234** Notice 700 para 21.4

B. Repayment returns

If a return is showing a VAT credit (that is, input tax exceeding output tax), a repayment will be made **subject to** whether: **3238** s 25(3) VATA 1994; Sch 11 para 4 VATA 1994; Notice 700 para 21
- the trader owes any other VAT debt, in which case the repayment will be set off;
- there are outstanding previous returns, in which case repayment can be withheld;
- the trader agrees to give security (¶3524+) when requested as a condition of receiving the repayment;
- HMRC needs to investigate the claim for protection of the revenue;
- the repayment results from previously charging too much output tax to customers (¶3254+);
- the time limit for any claim has expired; and
- the balance due is less than £1, in which case no refund is made.

To speed up a **large refund**, the trader should contact the written enquiries team before submitting the return to the VAT Central Unit.

MEMO POINTS The address for the **written enquiries team** is:
HMRC
National Advice Service
Written Enquiries Section
Alexander House
Victoria Avenue
Southend
Essex
SS99 1BD

Investigation by HMRC

If HMRC **suspects** that an amount is not due, even if the return is showing a repayment, it is allowed a reasonable time to investigate the circumstances. **3240** Notice 700/58

In this case, the trader must satisfy HMRC that a repayment is actually due (usually involving an input tax deduction), as repayments must not be made to taxable persons who have or show no such entitlement. *R (oao UK Tradecorp Ltd) v C & E* [2004]

If HMRC decides that the repayment is not wholly or partly due, it has a choice of the following **actions**, depending on whether the amount of VAT:

– has already been repaid, when an assessment can be issued to recover it;
– is greater than the amount HMRC believes to be due, in which case the repayment may be restricted (although the trader can appeal to a tribunal to seek the balance); or
– is actually due from the trader, in which case an assessment will be issued for the net payment due.

MEMO POINTS 1. **Plausible reasons** why a VAT repayment is due include:
– unusual asset purchases;
– stock build-up;
– bad debt relief (¶840+);
– supplies made at a loss; or
– predominantly making exports.
2. For traders in phones and computers, HMRC may impose the **joint and several liability** rules (¶2002+).

C. Other refund situations

1. Overpayments resulting from errors

3244 s 80 VATA 1994; VR2000

VAT may be repaid when a claim is made in respect of:
a. output tax wrongly brought into account on a past return or assessment; or
b. VAT overpaid (for example, through duplicate payments of VAT), but not as a result of failing to claim input tax or declaring output tax in error.

Overpaid **output tax** (**a**. above) is subject to the rules of set-off (¶3232+); repayment is also restricted where HMRC believes that the trader will be unjustly enriched at the expense of the customers (¶3254+).

3246 It is important to note that an error could **result** in an increased repayment being due, or the refund of a previous VAT payment.

EXAMPLE 1. Miss A entered the following on her return:

	£
Output tax	60,000
Input tax	(10,000)
VAT due, and paid	50,000

If there was an error on this return which resulted in a repayment, this would be a refund of VAT already paid.
2. Mr B entered the following on his return:

	£
Output tax	40,000
Input tax	(70,000)
VAT repayment due	(30,000)

If there was an error on this return which resulted in a repayment, this would be a further repayment in addition to that already made.

Claim

3248 SI 1995/2518 reg 37; VR2220

Unless an error is below the level at which it can be corrected through a future VAT return (¶3020), the claim must be **made**:
– in writing;
– with the relevant error and the amount of the claim clearly stated; and
– including an explanation of how that amount is calculated.

The claim should be made by the person who initially paid the VAT to HMRC (so, for example, a trader's customer cannot make the claim), and the trader should retain evidence to back it up.

The usual **time limit** is 4 years after the relevant date, which depends on the circumstances of the claim, as shown in the following table. The relevant date cannot be before 1 April 2006. **3250** s 80(4) VATA 1994

For this purpose, a claim is usually treated as **made on** the date stated in the letter. However, where there is a postal delay, it will be treated as made on the postmark date.

s 80(4ZA), (4ZB) VATA 1994

Type of claim	Relevant date - end of VAT period [1]
Output tax overstated on return	Of return
Output tax overstated in a voluntary disclosure [2]	In which disclosure made
Output tax overstated in assessment which was issued in response to voluntary disclosure [2]	In which disclosure made
Assessment issued in any other circumstance	In which assessment made
Pure overpayment	In which payment made

Note:
1. If **no longer registered**, the term VAT period should be interpreted as if the person was still registered. For details of VAT periods see ¶2987+.
2. In these circumstances the trader has **disclosed** an amount of output tax which was not due and which related to an earlier VAT period.

MEMO POINTS 1. Where a current VAT practice is **subject to ongoing litigation**, or the trader is commencing proceedings (e.g. by appearing at a tribunal), a claim can be made on the basis of a certain outcome, so that the claim will not be out of time once the case is resolved. This is known as a **protective claim**. If the case resolves in a way which validates the claim, the date of its submission becomes the relevant date. The claim must be made as normal; a mere statement that a claim will be made is not sufficient. However, HMRC may also issue a protective assessment (¶3641). **3252**

2. If VAT is **paid in error** the time limit will still apply. HMRC will by concession repay it, provided that the payment does not relate to a duplication of output tax (e.g. including the same invoice twice). *R (oao British Telecommunications plc) v HMRC* [2005]

The CJEU has held that a time limit on claims must not "totally deprive" the taxpayer of the right to a repayment of tax. HMRC's view is that it is not the 4-year time limit which potentially deprives a taxpayer of the right to a repayment, but the taxpayer's own choice to charge VAT wrongly more than 4 years ago (even if following HMRC's guidance). *Banca Antoniana Popolare Veneta* [2011] HMRC Brief 13/12

Unjust enrichment

The idea of unjust enrichment is to prevent a business from being enriched at the expense of others who have in fact borne the economic burden of the wrongly paid VAT. **3254** s 80(3A) VATA 1994; VR3400

If HMRC can prove that a VAT repayment would leave the trader better off than would otherwise have been the case (because the burden of the VAT paid has been borne by the customers), the repayment will be denied, or made only with stringent conditions attached. It is important to note that the onus is on HMRC to prove that, on the balance of probabilities, there would be unjust enrichment.

In response to such a **challenge**, the trader should provide evidence of the direct loss. In the real commercial environment, a trader may have absorbed the VAT by accepting a smaller profit rather than passing all of a VAT charge on to the customers.

MEMO POINTS 1. HMRC takes the following **factors** into account in deciding whether VAT has been passed on to the consumer: VR4340
- the availability of substitute products, particularly where these are zero-rated;
- how price-sensitive the products are, based on such factors as addictiveness or necessity;
- the market strength of the trader;
- the usual price and profit margin;
- the period over which output tax was overcharged;
- whether the overall profits of the trader have fallen; and
- the VAT registration status of the customers.

2. The trader's **customers** may also have a claim against the trader in relation to output tax wrongly charged. The trader could then be in the unfortunate position of owing VAT to customers which HMRC refuses to refund. A trader might therefore include a suitable provision in any sales contracts which limits the liability to repay customers in this case.

EXAMPLE

1. A shop which hires out clothes charges output tax on children's clothing in error (this is a zero-rated supply).
HMRC may review the prices charged in respect of all adult and children's clothing. If the children's are considerably cheaper, they may accept that the shop has absorbed the VAT and agree to repay it.

2. After a previous case decided that debt management services were exempt, another company claimed a VAT repayment in relation to the wrongly charged VAT (less the input tax it would have recovered). The company had charged its customers 15% plus VAT (an effective rate of 17.625 %), and continued to charge this amount after the fees were treated as exempt. HMRC refused to make a full repayment because of unjust enrichment.
It was held that a taxpayer who has paid tax which was not due has a primary right to be repaid the amount of that tax. As HMRC had not satisfactorily proved unjust enrichment (as it could not state what other price the company would have charged had VAT not been added in error), full repayment should be made. In particular, just because a price was described as £x plus VAT, this did not mean that if VAT had not been charged, the price would have only been £x. *Baines & Ernst Ltd v HMRC* [2006]

3. A theatre company initially charged VAT on its ticket sales. However, after a judgment by the ECJ in another case, a repayment claim was submitted on the basis that the tickets should have been exempt. HMRC stated that the theatre would be unjustly enriched and refused the claim.
It was held that the company did not have VAT in mind when the ticket prices were fixed, but merely the amounts that the public would be prepared to pay. If a show was likely to be popular, a higher price could therefore be charged and vice versa. Thus the theatre should be repaid and would not be unjustly enriched. *Newcastle Theatre Royal Trust Ltd* [2005] (VTD 18952)

3256 SI 1995/2518 regs 43A - 43H; Notice 700/45 para 10

HMRC will recognise overcharged output tax in cases where the trader **agrees to reimburse** the customers by observing certain conditions. In this case any statutory interest (¶3270+) paid by HMRC should also be reimbursed to customers as commercial restitution.

Under these arrangements the trader signs an undertaking to comply with certain conditions.

s 80B VATA 1994 Where the business **fails to comply** with the undertaking, HMRC can issue an assessment to recover the relevant VAT from the trader.

MEMO POINTS 1. The **conditions** are as follows:
a. the trader can identify the names and addresses of those customers affected;
b. the customers will be reimbursed within 90 days of the repayment of overcharged VAT by HMRC (an extension is available where customers are not easy to locate);
c. the trader will not levy any kind of administration fee to the customers;
d. reimbursement will be in the form of cash or a cheque;
e. any residual amount not reimbursed will be notified and repaid to HMRC within 14 days after the 90-day period has expired; and
f. full records will be retained of the following, which will be produced to HMRC on receipt of a written notice:
- customers' names and addresses;
- amounts reimbursed, including the amount of interest included; and
- dates of reimbursement.

2. If a **partial** reimbursement is made, these conditions apply to that part.

EXAMPLE C Ltd has overpaid VAT of £60,000. HMRC accepts that £20,000 can be retained by the company; the remainder must be reimbursed to customers.
Only £40,000 is therefore subject to the reimbursement conditions.

HMRC Brief 15/13 3. The Court of Appeal has confirmed that it is possible for a final consumer to make a **claim** for overpaid VAT **directly against HMRC** in certain circumstances (essentially where it is not possible to make a claim against the supplier). However, such a **claim is limited** to the tax which was charged to the final consumer, as reduced by any amount of input tax which has already been reclaimed by the supplier. *Investment Trust Companies v HMRC* [2015]

2. Other claims which result in a repayment

The following table **summarises** the other claims which can be made to obtain a VAT repayment. These claims are not subject to the unjust enrichment rules in ¶3254+. **3258**

Situation	Time limit	Reference	¶¶
Late input tax claim	4 years	SI 1995/2518 reg 29	¶2005+
Pre-registration expenses	4 years	SI 1995/2518 reg 111	¶8560+
Pre-registration expenses where registration compulsorily backdated (also customers can claim the input tax they are charged on supplies received from a trader who is registered retrospectively)	None	VATA Schedule 1 para 2	¶2684
Post-deregistration expenses	4 years	SI 1995/2518 reg 111	¶8618+
Issue of credit or debit note which affects the consideration for a supply	See note	SI 1995/2518 reg 38	¶2925+
Bad debt relief	4 years and 6 months	SI 1995/2518 reg 165A	¶840+
Capital goods scheme adjustments	4 years	SI 1995/2518 reg 115	¶2280+
Adjustments which cancel out (e.g. reverse charge)	None		¶9700+
Tax point errors	4 years		¶3018
Correction of errors	4 years	SI 1995/2518 reg 34	¶3018
DIY housebuilders	3 months	SI 1995/2518 reg 201	¶5316+
Penalties which have been paid but were not due	None		¶3950+
Notes 1. The note should be issued within 1 month of the need arising, which must itself be within 3 years of the end of the accounting period in which the original supply took place.			

D. Interest

Interest may become payable by HMRC to a trader in three situations: **3262**
a. repayment supplement (¶3264+) where there is official delay, and which is in effect a penalty on HMRC;
b. statutory interest (¶3270+) in cases of official error; and
c. interest awarded by a tribunal.

1. Repayment supplement

Supplement applies to most refunds showing on a VAT return and claims, **except** for the following: **3264** s 79 VATA 1994; Notice 700 para 21.6
- EU trader refunds (¶9876+);
- DIY housebuilder refunds (¶5316+);
- post-deregistration services (¶8618+); and
- amounts that HMRC notifies as over-declared (perhaps in response to a voluntary disclosure).

However, in these cases statutory interest (¶3270+) may be due instead.

If any **returns** for earlier VAT periods are still **outstanding**, no supplement will be paid.

MEMO POINTS 1. Supplement also applies to the amounts refunded to **local authorities** and **museums** under the special VAT recovery rules. See ¶7830+ for further details.
2. Supplement is not payable on **statutory interest** itself.

Conditions

3266 s 79 VATA 1994; SI 1995/2518 regs 198, 199

Supplement is only payable if the following conditions are all satisfied:
a. the return or claim is received in time by the due date;
b. the trader has not overstated the VAT position shown on the return by the higher of 5% of the true position and £250; and
c. HMRC has not authorised repayment within 30 days of receiving the return or claim, which cannot predate the VAT period end.

MEMO POINTS 1. HMRC has **authorised** a repayment once a cheque has been issued or payment instruction has been transmitted to its bank. If the taxpayer never receives payment, a tribunal is therefore likely to conclude that it was never authorised. *AA Aston* [1991] (VTD 5955).
Notice 700/58 para 3.2
2. The **30-day period** in relation to **c**. above can in reality be much longer, because HMRC may **exclude** the following periods from the count:
- the date from which HMRC notices an obvious error, until it is corrected;
- the date from which HMRC decides to make a reasonable enquiry into the claim, until the query is answered or the decision is taken not to pursue it;
- any period when returns are outstanding in respect of VAT periods falling before the period of the refund; and
- the date from which HMRC gives written notice of requiring documentation or security, until the request is satisfied.

EXAMPLE D Ltd is due a VAT repayment as shown on its return for the quarter ended 31 March, and satisfies all of the conditions for repayment supplement. The return was submitted on 25 April. The following then takes place:

Date	Action	Supplement clock	Cumulative days which are counted
26 April	Return received by Central Unit	Starts	1
28 April	Information keyed into system		3
29 April	Small error corrected	Stops	3
1 May	Automated credibility test	Starts	4
8 May	Manual checks		11
12 May	Query sent to local VAT office		15
16 May	Query sent to D Ltd	Stops	19
20 May	D Ltd responds		19
24 May	Further scrutiny		19
30 May	Re-input of information	Starts	20
17 June	Authorisation of payment	Stops	38

The clock stops for the correction of the error and the query raised with D Ltd.
This still leaves 38 days when HMRC delayed authorising the repayment, so repayment supplement is due.

Amount due

3268 Notice 700/58 para 3.4

The supplement is strictly **measured** as the greater of £50 and 5% of the net repayment due. It is automatically calculated and paid at the same time as the repayment (unless set-off applies).

However, in cases of exceptional delay, or where the supplement does not match the interest which the trader could otherwise have earned, a further ex gratia payment may be made.

It has been held that **in addition** to supplement, an order for interest may be made by a tribunal as compensation. *Offshore Hydrocarbon Mapping plc* [2006] (VTD 19438) See also ¶3272+.

Notice 700/58 para 3.5

MEMO POINTS 1. Where supplement is **not paid**, an aggrieved trader can write to request an explanation from HMRC. If still unsatisfied, a formal request for reconsideration should be made, followed by an appeal to the First-tier Tribunal (¶4262+).
2. Supplement which is **not in fact due** (perhaps because of a later adjustment, or HMRC's arithmetical error) can be collected as unpaid VAT. The normal recovery proceedings apply (¶3730+).

3. An **ex gratia payment** may also be made in cases of maladministration, on the recommendation of the Parliamentary Ombudsman, or where the level of service is below that advertised. A trader who has incurred fruitless expense should make a written claim, supported by invoices where appropriate, detailing the work undertaken, hourly rate, and who did it.

EXAMPLE E Ltd submits a return showing a repayment due of £5,000. There is an arithmetical error of £200, so that the correct repayment is £4,800.
HMRC fails to authorise the repayment until 40 days have elapsed.
As the error is only 4% of the original repayment claim, E Ltd is due repayment supplement of £240. (£4,800 x 5%)

2. Statutory interest

Statutory interest is intended to give commercial restitution to the trader, who would otherwise have had use of the money mistakenly paid to HMRC. **3270** s 78 VATA 1994

It is only payable when both of the following apply:

a. **repayment supplement** is not due; and

b. an **error by HMRC** (even one made in good faith) has caused a trader to:

- account for output tax which was not due;
- fail to claim eligible input tax;
- pay any other VAT due (e.g. import VAT); or
- suffer delay in receiving a repayment.

This would usually cover the situation where the trader has sought advice from HMRC and been given wrong information (otherwise known as misdirection (¶3687)). However, the withdrawal of an assessment made to HMRC's best judgment is not an error.

Interest will not be paid in respect of **penalties** which have been levied in error, although compensation will be paid, calculated on the same basis as statutory interest.

Calculation

Interest is calculated on a simple daily **basis**, on the amount of net repayment which HMRC is required to make, taking into account any time limit restrictions (¶3276). **3272**

Where the **trader also makes an error**, HMRC reworks all of the affected periods to determine the VAT that the trader would have accounted for had the errors not been made. Any remaining overpayment is deemed to relate to official error for the purposes of calculating interest.

MEMO POINTS 1. **Net repayment** means that any input tax claimed as a result of the error will reduce the amount of repayment.
2. For current and historic **rates** of interest see ¶9973.
3. Following the direct tax case of *Sempra Metals Ltd v HMRC* [2007], some doubt was cast on whether it is open to HMRC to pay only simple interest on amounts owed by It. The Upper Tribunal ruled that HMRC is not obliged to pay compound interest, even though under EU law taxpayers may have a right to it (see the judgment in *FJ Chalke Ltd and Another v HMRC* [2010], where the taxpayers pursued a civil action in the High Court for restitution). *John Wilkins (Motor Engineers) Ltd v HMRC* [2009] The matter was referred to the CJEU, which ruled that "It is for national law to determine... whether the principal sum must bear 'simple interest', 'compound interest' or another type of interest" What was essential, in the eyes of the CJEU, was that the taxpayer should receive "adequate indemnity" for their loss. *Littlewoods Retail Ltd and others v HMRC* [2012] Following the judgment of the CJEU, the High Court subsequently found that Littlewoods were entitled to compound interest, given the exceptional circumstances of the case, but HMRC has received permission to take the matter to the Court of Appeal. *Littlewoods Retail Ltd and others v HMRC* [2014] HMRC Brief 20/14

EXAMPLE
1. F Ltd makes a number of mistakes:
- under-declares £100 output tax;
- over-declares £100 output tax due to official error; and
- over-declares £100 output tax due to its own error.

Overall, F Ltd has overpaid £100 of VAT.
The under-declaration and F Ltd's own error cancel each other out.
Statutory interest will be payable on the £100 overpayment.

2. G Ltd also makes similar errors:
- under-declares £50 output tax;
- over-declares £100 output tax due to official error; and
- over-declares £100 output tax due to its own error.

Overall G Ltd has overpaid £150 of VAT.
Statutory interest is only payable on £100 of the overpayment, because the remaining £50 is attributable to G Ltd's own error.

3274 s 78(4)-(7) VATA 1994

Interest runs during the applicable **period**, which for a:
- **repayment return** usually **starts** from the date on which HMRC authorises the repayment or set-off; and
- **payment return** usually **starts** from the date on which payment was made by the trader.

In **both cases** the period **ends** when HMRC authorises repayment or set-off.

In the case of a delay in receiving the repayment, the period begins when HMRC might have been reasonably expected to authorise repayment (or set-off).

s 78(8)-(9) VATA 1994

However, any periods when the **trader's conduct** delays the authorisation of interest are left out of the calculation. For example:
- unreasonable delay in making a claim for repayment and the related interest;
- failing to provide HMRC with all the information required to determine the amount of repayment and interest, including failing to respond to a specific request; and
- submitting a claim where the business is not wholly entitled to it, in an effort to obtain more interest.

MEMO POINTS 1. The date on which HMRC **became aware** of the error is irrelevant to the interest calculation.
2. **Unreasonable delay** is normally interpreted as exceeding 2 months in most cases, except when the claim is complicated, in which case a period of 6 months should be sufficient. HMRC is likely to take the view that whether a claim is complicated depends on the circumstances e.g. a small amateur operatic society might find any claim complicated because of the book-keeper's unfamiliarity with VAT.

3276 s 78(10), (11) VATA 1994

Claim Interest will only be paid when a written claim is made within 4 years following the end of the applicable period (¶3250).

MEMO POINTS 1. A **denied** claim may be appealed.

s 78A VATA 1994

2. A claim for interest which is settled, but is **subsequently found to be invalid**, will be subject to an assessment to recover any amounts overpaid (¶3625+).

EXAMPLE HMRC makes an error which causes H Ltd to overpay VAT for the quarter ending 31 March 2014. Repayment is made on 31 December 2014.
H Ltd has until 31 December 2018 to make a claim for statutory interest.

E. Refunds made in error

3281

Erroneous refunds may arise where:
- a repayment is made by mistake (¶3282); or
- a trader has made an overpayment, which is then repaid (¶3284), but then it transpires that this refund was wrong.

Mistaken repayment

3282 s 73(6) VATA 1994; VAEC1141

If the trader received a repayment in error (because of a repayment return, or stand-alone voluntary disclosure), an **assessment** can normally only be **raised within** the year following the date on which the error was discovered. However, HMRC can issue an assessment within 2 years of the end of the VAT period in which the repayment/refund was made or credited.

EXAMPLE Mr A entered the following on his return for the VAT period ending 31 May 2014:

		£
Return as prepared	Output tax	40,000
	Input tax	(70,000)
	VAT repayment due	(30,000)
		£
Corrected return	Output tax	35,000
	Input tax	(70,000)
	VAT repayment due	(35,000)

The extra VAT repayment of £5,000 was then claimed in July 2014 and paid by HMRC in February 2015.
However, in March 2015, HMRC discovered that the correct input tax figure should have been £66,000, meaning that Mr A owes HMRC £4,000. HMRC must issue an assessment to recover the VAT by 31 May 2016 (being the later of 2 years after the period in respect of which the repayment was made and 12 months after the matter coming to HMRC's attention).

Refunds of previous overpayments

Where HMRC erroneously refunds an overpayment of VAT (the trader initially paid VAT or it was set off) or interest, an **assessment** can be raised to recover it **within** 2 years of discovering the error, or from the end of the period in which it was repaid/credited, if later. It is irrelevant whether the overpayment arose from over-declared output tax or under-declared input tax. **3284** ss 78A, 80(4A) VATA 1994; VAEC1141

EXAMPLE Ms B entered the following on her return for the VAT period ending 31 March 2014:

		£
Return as prepared	Output tax	60,000
	Input tax	(10,000)
	VAT due, and paid	50,000
		£
Corrected return	Output tax	60,000
	Input tax	(20,000)
	VAT due	40,000

A refund of £10,000 was then claimed in October 2014 and repaid by HMRC in December 2014. However, in March 2015 HMRC discovered that the correct input tax figure should have been £15,000, meaning that Ms B now owes HMRC £5,000. HMRC must issue an assessment to recover the VAT by March 2017 (2 years after discovery).

Collection of VAT

Both types of **assessment** cover the VAT and statutory interest (¶3270+) where relevant. **3286**

HMRC may also decide to levy **default interest** (¶3880+), where this represents commercial restitution, and the trader fails to pay the assessment within 30 days. Interest runs from the date on which the assessment was notified to the trader through to the date of payment.

MEMO POINTS 1. It is possible for both types of assessment to be **raised at the same time**, depending on the complexity of the errors (or where a payment return became a repayment return).
2. Where a repayment has been made during **ongoing litigation**, which is ultimately decided in HMRC's favour, there is some doubt over the time limits which apply for HMRC to raise an assessment to recover it. HMRC may therefore issue multiple assessments under any applicable rules, including protective assessments before the litigation has ended. In addition, a repayment may only be made if the trader signs an undertaking to reimburse HMRC should the case be decided in HMRC's favour.
3. For **unjust enrichment** see ¶3254+.
4. For the **detailed rules** relating to assessments see ¶3625+.

PART 5

Enforcement

Enforcement
Summary

The numbers cross-refer to paragraphs.

CHAPTER 1 Powers

CHAPTER 2 Default interest

CHAPTER 3 Penalties

CHAPTER 4 Reviews and appeals

CHAPTER 1

Powers

OUTLINE ¶¶

3400 As VAT is a self-assessed tax, every stage of the administration process - from registration to the payment of liabilities - is subject to enforcement measures to ensure compliance and deter negligence or evasion. The enforcement measures fall into two main categories:

a. a wide range of **powers** given to HMRC and other agencies, to enable them to:
- supervise and control the VAT system;
- assess under-declared VAT; and
- recover unpaid VAT; and

b. an **interest and penalty regime** for failure to comply with the legislation.

An **appeals system** is available for taxpayers to appeal to a tribunal and the courts against decisions made by HMRC in the exercise of its powers.

SECTION 1

Supervision and control of the VAT system

3405 HMRC has **general powers** of collection and management of VAT.
Sch 11 VATA 1994; Sch 36 FA 2008

It also has **specific powers** which it can exercise in particular circumstances, or in relation to particular types of business. Certain specific powers can only be exercised if a court grants an order or warrant in favour of HMRC.

Powers	Details		Court order required	¶¶
General powers	To inspect business premises		n	¶3416+
	To request information and documents		n	¶3458+
Specific powers	In relation to businesses which hold or deal in goods	To direct that specified records are kept	n	¶3485+
		To search premises in cases of serious fraud	y	¶3500+
		To take samples	n	¶3512
	In relation to business records	To gain access to information where an offence is suspected	y	¶3514+
		To inspect computer equipment	n	¶3522
	In relation to security and production of evidence	In relation to a VAT credit or repayment	n	¶3526+
		To require monthly VAT returns	n	¶3542+
		To require security	n	¶3546+
	In relation to particular types of business	Overseas traders	n	¶3588+
		Businesses which operate gaming machines	n	¶3594
	In relation to criminal offences	Arrest and prosecution	n	¶3596+

Exercise of powers

3408 HMRC will normally **enforce compliance informally** and with the co-operation of businesses. Formal action will generally not be taken where:
- there is minimal tax at risk;
- trading is known to have ceased; or
- the issue of a penalty assessment is likely to add to an irrecoverable debt.

A **decision by HMRC to take formal action** using its legal powers will be based on the likelihood of its success as a compliance tool.

Reviews and appeals

Within **30 days** of the date of notification of a decision by HMRC, a taxpayer can ask for a review, or appeal against the decision to a tribunal. 3410

The **general rules** in relation to reviews and appeals can be found at ¶4210+.

Specific details of reviews and appeals in relation to the exercise of particular powers by HMRC can be found in the sections dealing with those powers.

MEMO POINTS If a taxpayer **requests a review** of a decision from HMRC, this does not preclude the taxpayer from appealing to a tribunal if they do not agree with the decision following the review. Any appeal to the tribunal should be made within 30 days of the date of notification of the result of the review.

A. Compliance checks

HMRC has general powers under which it can visit any VAT-registered business and request information in relation to VAT matters from traders and other persons. These are now standard across all taxes. 3414

1. Inspection of business premises

HMRC has powers to enter premises and inspect them, along with any business assets or documents which are on the premises, provided that the inspection is reasonably required to check a person's tax position. This is usually referred to as a **control visit**. 3416 Sch 36 paras 10 - 11 FA 2008

This has the effect not only of checking the records for accuracy but also deterring negligence and evasion, as traders are aware that such inspections may occur.

The power is **not limited** to the main business premises, but is extended to cover any premises used in connection with:
- the making of taxable supplies where the goods are on site; or
- the acquisition of goods from other member states whereby the goods are on the premises.

This does not, however, extend to any part of the premises that is used solely as a dwelling.

MEMO POINTS 1. **Business premises** are defined as any premises which an officer has reason to believe are used in connection with the carrying on of a business.
2. Premises used as a **fiscal warehouse** (¶9242+) are also included within the premises that can be entered and searched.

a. Pre-visit

Which businesses

All private sector businesses and local authorities are subject to control visits. 3420

When

Frequency HMRC will carry out a visit when it considers it appropriate for the business in question. 3422

HMRC will aim to visit a **new business** within 3 years from the start of trading.

Intervals between visits will depend on the size and complexity of the business, and past compliance. Where there is a good compliance record and little risk to tax revenues, businesses may only be visited every few years. Large or complex businesses, and businesses with a poor compliance record, will be visited more frequently.

3424 Sch 36 para 12 FA 2008 **Time of visit** HMRC will usually seek to agree a time to carry out a visit. However, strictly it **does not require the permission** of the taxpayer to visit in the following situations:
- where the occupier of the premises has been **given 7 days' notice** of the visit (this notice does not have to be given in writing); or
- where the inspection is **carried out by, or approved by**, an authorised officer, in which case no notice is required.

MEMO POINTS The powers which are given to HMRC can generally only be exercised by an **authorised officer** (defined as one who is, or is a member of a class of officers who are, authorised by the Commissioners for the purpose), or a person acting with the agreement of such an officer.

3426 **Notice and objection** Where notice is given, this should indicate the records and assets that HMRC may wish to examine during the course of the visit. However, the inspection is **not limited** to these items.

The notice will **usually also contain**:
- the name and contact number for the officer performing the visit;
- names of the individuals the officer will wish to see; and
- the likely length of the visit.

The **taxpayer** does not have to agree to the notice to visit and can advise HMRC of this. If there is a disagreement about the carrying out of a visit, HMRC can apply to the First-tier Tribunal to approve it. This can also be done before the notice is served. Where approval is obtained before notice is given, the notice must state this to be the case. **Approval will only be given** where:
- the application is made by, or with the agreement of, an authorised officer; and
- the tribunal is satisfied that the circumstances give rise to the need to carry out a visit.

HMRC is entitled to receive some measure of co-operation in order to permit an inspection to take place. Refusal to give any co-operation amounts to deliberate obstruction. *V8680 Ltd* [2014] (TC04047)

3427 **Unannounced visits** It is envisaged that an unannounced visit will **only be required** when HMRC does not feel there is another suitable method of obtaining the information required.

Unannounced visits are likely to be **considered necessary** where:
- previous appointments have not been kept;
- contact could not be made with the taxpayer; or
- HMRC has concerns which an announced visit would not address correctly.

It is **possible to refuse** an unannounced visit. However, if the visit has been approved by the tribunal, a penalty of £300 will be levied for any such refusal or obstruction during the visit where no reasonable excuse is provided.

Where

3428 HMRC normally visits traders at their **main place of business** in order to:
- get a better picture of the business;
- answer any queries which the trader may have; and
- inspect records with minimum disruption to the business.

If it is not possible or appropriate to carry out a visit at the main place of business, this may occasionally be done elsewhere - for example, at an accountant's office. HMRC will normally still wish to see the business premises and discuss matters with the trader.

See ¶4078 for examples of cases where penalties have been charged for failure to make records available at the main place of business.

3430 Sch 36 para 10 (2) FA 2008 HMRC is not empowered to enter any part of premises which is used solely as a **dwelling**. However, HMRC may enter and inspect areas which it has reason to believe are used for carrying on a business.

Who

Visits are generally carried out by one HMRC officer. An additional officer may attend for management, training or safety purposes, or where there is a need to carry out substantial transactional testing. Two or more officers may be necessary for large or complex cases. 3432

Officers will **identify** themselves by name on arrival, and show an identity card.

How long

A visit **may last** for a few hours for a small business, or up to two or more days for a large or complex business. 3434

Advisers

A trader's professional adviser may **attend a visit**, which may be appropriate if there is a need to explain business accounts or a particular issue. 3436

---

b. During a visit

Where the visit is **unannounced**, the officer must, at the time of the visit, provide to the occupier (if they are present) a notice containing details of the consequences of obstructing an inspection. If the **occupier is not present**, the notice may be given to someone who appears to be in charge. Failing this, the notice should be left somewhere prominent on the premises. 3437

This notice may be given with the authority of the First-tier Tribunal and, if it is, the notice must state this to be the case, as this affects the penalty situation (¶3427).

The visiting officer will not attempt to check everything, but will instead concentrate on areas with the greatest perceived tax risk. 3438

The following table outlines the **main aspects** of a visit:

Aspect	¶¶
Verification of registration details	¶3440
Review of business activities	¶3442
Inspection of records	¶3444+
Inspection of premises	¶3448
Monitoring the use of special schemes and methods	¶3450
Property ownership	¶3452
Provision of guidance to traders	¶3454

Verification of registration details

HMRC will check some or all of the details which the trader provided when registering for VAT, to ensure that its own records and the trader's VAT registration details are correct: 3440

Particulars	Details which may be checked
Name and address, website and email addresses	Identity of registered person at date of VAT registration and at time of visit
	Certificate of incorporation (for companies)
Business activity	Trade classification
	Activities carried on
	Any private activity or hobby
Principal place of business	
VAT registration date	History of the business
	Correctness of date of registration
	Turnover prior to registration

Particulars	Details which may be checked
Annual turnover	Taxable and exempt turnover
Repayment trader status	Proportion of VAT returns showing a liability
Associated businesses	Supplies between the businesses
Bank accounts	Name and address of account holder
	Account number and sort code
	All business transactions recorded
	Procedures for deposits, withdrawals and transfers
	Sample transactions from bank statements to records
Name and address of accountant	Accountant's details, to enable checks to be made on other clients of the same accountant, where common risks are identified
Business transferred as a going concern (¶8646+)	All conditions met
	Input tax has been correctly recovered

Review of business activities

3442 Matters which may be checked **include**:
- the structure and organisation of the business;
- whether there has been any change in the activities carried on;
- whether the trader carries on any subsidiary activities;
- whether VAT is being properly accounted for if separate businesses are being carried on, or if there has been a separation of business activities (¶2629+); and
- whether a trader has non-business activities or other sources of income.

Inspection of records

3444 The inspection of records **can cover**:
- the nature and adequacy of the books and records;
- completion of VAT returns;
- principal outputs and inputs;
- numerical sequence of sales invoices;
- regular or large transactions between associated businesses;
- examination of credit notes for large amounts, or to an associated business;
- correct application of tax points;
- zero-rating;
- correct treatment of discounts;
- bad debts;
- expenses incurred by employees;
- application of the fuel scale charge;
- private use and gifts of goods or services;
- disallowance of input tax in relation to items such as cars and non-business activities; and
- sample checks of transactions and stock.

3446 **Accounts** The trader's **annual accounts** and **VAT account** may be examined to:
- compare sales and purchases values with those shown on VAT returns;
- test the credibility of the mark-up on goods sold;
- consider the profitability and viability of the business;
- identify additions and disposals of capital assets; and
- consider any accountants' qualifications or notes with regard to the accuracy of accounts, such as the use of estimates or reliance on directors' statements.

Comment If a trader is using the **cash accounting scheme**, it may not be possible to reconcile the VAT account and the annual accounts (¶4880+).

Inspection of premises

HMRC may inspect a trader's **premises**, **equipment** and **stock** during a control visit, in order to ascertain the nature and extent of activities carried on. 3448

This assists HMRC in **identifying** any matters such as:
- additional business activities being carried on;
- apparent discrepancies between the level of activities and recorded sales; or
- a trader's lifestyle apparently not in keeping with the level of declared income.

Monitoring use of special schemes and methods

The visiting officer will check the operation of any special schemes or calculation methods. 3450

Where appropriate, the officer may also suggest that the trader may consider adopting a certain scheme or method which is not already being used.

Schemes/methods which may be in use	¶¶	Details which can be checked
Retail schemes	¶6325+	– continued eligibility to use the scheme/ method; – compliance with scheme/method conditions; – calculations, including any applicable annual adjustment; – the correct inclusion or exclusion of items; and – the correct recording of standard-rated purchases, where the output tax calculation is affected by apportionment
Annual accounting scheme	¶4745+	
Cash accounting scheme	¶4880+	
Flat rate scheme	¶4635+	
Partial exemption	¶2075+	
Capital goods scheme	¶5750+	
Margin schemes	¶6625+	
Tour operators' margin scheme	¶7490+	
Retail export scheme	¶9603+	
Self-billing	¶2904+	
Estimation	¶3006	

Property ownership

If a business has any property interests, HMRC **will check**: 3452
- details of properties held, current usage and whether opted to tax (¶5602+);
- whether all income from opted properties has been standard-rated, including rent and proceeds from a sale, lease assignment, or surrender;
- new options to tax, disposals and changes of use;
- whether any property falls within the capital goods scheme (¶5750+) and, if so, whether appropriate input tax recovery adjustments have been made; and
- whether the qualifying conditions were met for properties acquired or disposed of as part of a transfer of a going concern (¶8646+).

Provision of guidance to traders

To assist traders and encourage future compliance, HMRC officers are instructed to: 3454

a. offer education and advice, which includes:
- checking whether the trader has all relevant notices and leaflets;
- informing the trader of the VAT notes issued with VAT returns, and the available telephone and Internet assistance; and
- issuing the trader with appropriate HMRC fact sheets;

b. clearly **explain** any misdeclarations; and

c. promote schemes which could reduce compliance costs.

c. Outcome of a visit

The HMRC officer will **record** all aspects of the visit in an Assurance Notebook, which will 3456 VSME2510
be preserved for 6 years.

At the end of the visit, the officer will:
- review their work with the trader;
- discuss any areas of concern;
- explain the nature and reason for any tax adjustment and, where possible, agree this and describe how it will be made;
- advise the trader of any underpayment or overpayment; and
- inform the trader how to appeal against any decision with which the trader does not agree.

After the visit HMRC will, on request or if it considers it necessary, provide the trader with a summary of the visit and any rulings, agreements or recommendations.

MEMO POINTS 1. **Traders are not obliged** to give an immediate answer to questions, and they are entitled to request that a question is put in writing where, for example, the information requested is detailed or not readily available.
2. Traders **cannot assume** that an inspection leading to no further queries implies that there are no errors in their VAT accounting. By necessity a visit will not examine all records and transactions.

2. Power to request information and documents

3458 Sch 36 FA 2008 HMRC has power to issue **information notices** to require information or documents to be provided for the purpose of checking a person's tax position. It will, however, normally use informal procedures and will only use its statutory powers as a last resort.

Persons required to provide

3460 Sch 36 paras 1, 2 FA 2008 With the harmonisation of the powers that HMRC has in relation to the various taxes it administers there was a change in the way information could be requested. HMRC may request information from someone in order to ascertain their VAT position, or request information from a third party.

Information

3462 Sch 36 para 1 FA 2008 **What** HMRC can **request** such information as it may reasonably require.

It **can** require the information to be supplied in written form.

It **cannot** compel anyone to answer oral questions, or make themselves available to be questioned. *C & E v Harz & Power* [1967]

3464 **When** The information requested by HMRC must be provided within such time as it may reasonably require.

In practice, if the information is not provided following an informal request, HMRC will warn the person of its statutory power and then, in the **continued absence** of the information, issue an information notice. If the information is **still not supplied**, a civil penalty (¶4072+) may then be levied. In certain circumstances, HMRC can then **apply** for a court order granting it access to the information (¶3514+).

3466 Sch 36 paras 2, 3, 5 FA 2008 **Information held by third parties** HMRC can issue a third-party notice in relation to a person whose **identity is known**, where it has either the permission of the taxpayer concerned, or of the First-tier Tribunal. The notice must identify the taxpayer to which it relates, unless the First-tier Tribunal disapplies this requirement when approving the issue of the notice.

The **tribunal** can only grant permission where:
- the application is made by, or with the permission of, an authorised officer (¶3424);
- the tribunal believes the notice is justified;
- the third party has been advised of the information or documents requested and has had an opportunity to object, and the tribunal is informed of the objections; and
- the taxpayer has been given the reasons why the notice is being sought.

The last two conditions may be **waived** if the tribunal believes that to impose them would prejudice the collection of VAT.

Where the taxpayer's **identity is not known**, (including where they form part of a class of taxpayers), HMRC may still issue a third-party notice but must first have the approval of the First-tier Tribunal. Before approving such a notice, the Tribunal must be satisfied that:
– the notice will allow the checking of the tax position of unknown taxpayers;
– there are reasonable grounds to believe that there has been a compliance failure by a taxpayer included in the notice, and that this has likely led (or will lead) to serious prejudice to the collection of tax; and;
– the information requested is not readily available from other sources.

Generally speaking, the following **guidelines** apply:

Persons who hold the information	Position
Members of the public who are not taxable persons	HMRC does not request information as a matter of routine, and special consideration is given before making any enquiries.
Banks	In exceptional circumstances, a trader's bank may be asked to provide information or verify taxable supplies. An approach is only made as a last resort, where a formal demand to the trader is impractical or impossible.
Other HMRC officers	HMRC VAT officers can exchange information with officers dealing with income tax or corporation tax matters, and vice versa.
Data users	Under the Data Protection Act 1998, HMRC can require information from a data user who has not included HMRC on its register entry for the purposes of: – the prevention or detection of crime; – the apprehension of offenders; and – the assessment or collection of any tax or duty.

MEMO POINTS 1. A notice can also be served on someone **without approval** where the notice only refers to information contained in the statutory records, and relates to: Sch 36 para 34 FA 2008
– the supply of goods or services;
– the acquisition of goods from another member state; or
– the importation of goods from a place outside the member states in the course of a business.
There is no right of appeal against such a notice.
2. HMRC can also issue a notice to a third-party requesting only the name, address, and date of birth (if an individual) where the identity of the taxpayer is **not known but can be ascertained** from information held by them where: Sch 36 para 5A FA 2008
– the information requested is reasonably required to check the taxpayer's position;
– the identity of the taxpayer can be ascertained by the third-party based on the information HMRC holds, and the knowledge of any details relating to the taxpayer came to the third-party whilst carrying on a business; and
– the taxpayer's identity cannot readily be ascertained by HMRC from other information already held.
This legislation, introduced on 17 July 2012, is intended to bridge a gap which HMRC perceived to exist where there was no serious prejudice to the collection of tax. The notice can be issued by an authorised officer without Tribunal approval, and a right of appeal exists for the third-party involved.
3. There is a general **right of appeal** against a third-party notice on the basis that compliance with it would be unduly onerous, but this is not available where: Sch 36 paras 30, 31 FA 2008
– the information is contained in the third party's statutory records; or
– the notice was approved by the Tribunal.

Documents

What HMRC may: **3468** CH23200+
a. request the production of such documents as it may reasonably require;
b. take copies of, or **make extracts** from, any document produced; or
c. remove any document produced, at a reasonable time and for a reasonable period.

MEMO POINTS 1. Documents **include**:
- written books of account, whether bound or loose-leaf or in any other form;
- profit and loss accounts and balance sheets;
- bank statements and paying-in slips;
- any map, plan, graph, drawing or photograph;
- any disc, tape, sound track or other audio or data record; and
- any film negative, tape or other visual record, including microfilm.

2. For **groups of companies**, if profit and loss accounts and balance sheets are not produced for all group members, HMRC is entitled to request consolidation schedules, or extracts therefrom, supported by an auditor's declaration.

3470 **When** The position is the same as for the provision of information (¶3464).

3472 **Where** The documents must be produced at the principal place of business, or such other place as HMRC may reasonably require.

If a trader is **unwilling** to produce the records at the principal place of business, but offers an alternative address, HMRC will normally agree to this if it appears reasonable.

MEMO POINTS If documents are required from an **overseas trader**, HMRC may exceptionally visit overseas premises, if production of records at the principal place of business in the UK would cause logistical or cost problems. Any visit by HMRC to overseas premises will be at the trader's expense.

3474 HMRC will not normally **remove** records merely for the convenience of examining them in its offices, and will normally request permission. Removal is considered reasonable where a complicated assessment is to be calculated, or there is a safety hazard due to the physical conditions of the trader's premises.

HMRC **must**:
- provide a receipt for any document if requested;
- provide, free of charge, a copy of any document required by the trader for the proper conduct of the trader's business; and
- compensate the trader for any expenses reasonably incurred in replacing any lost or damaged documents.

3476 CH23600+ **Documents held by a third party** Depending on the circumstances, HMRC may either request the person holding the documents to release them, or ask permission for a visit.

A person may not have to release documents which are subject to **legal professional privilege** or **confidentiality**. The following table sets out the position in these and certain other circumstances:

Person holding documents	Nature of documents	Position
Any third party	Documents held under a **lien**, for example, by an accountant or solicitor as security for payment for work done	The duty to produce the documents takes precedence over the lien, but does not prejudice it. The person holding the records will therefore be requested to allow inspection at their premises, or permit HMRC to remove the documents to its offices.
Legal adviser	Documents subject to legal professional privilege (in Scotland, confidentiality)	Certain confidential communications between a legal adviser or patent agent and their client cannot be given in evidence in legal proceedings without the client's permission. HMRC is therefore not normally entitled to request documents from legal advisers in relation to their clients. In one case it was held that the inadvertent removal of some documents which were subject to legal professional privilege did not render the execution of a search warrant unlawful. *R v C & E ex parte Popely and another* [1999]

Person holding documents	Nature of documents	Position
Tax adviser[1]	**Information relating to** goods, services, supplies, acquisitions or importations	HMRC is entitled to request such information.
	Confidential **advice including**: – notes of meetings or telephone conversations; – internal memoranda; – letters and faxes; and – audit working papers and management letters	HMRC will not normally request the trader or their tax adviser to produce a communication relating to confidential opinion or advice. The trader (and adviser) may nevertheless consider releasing information to which HMRC has no statutory power of access, if it would help to resolve a matter quickly. The Supreme Court has confirmed that professional privilege is only available to lawyers providing advice to their clients, and cannot be extended to other professions providing advice, such as accountants. *R (oao Prudential plc) v Special Commissioner of Income Tax* [2013]
	Requested information mixed with confidential advice	HMRC will normally accept extracts relating to goods and services or supplies, acquisitions or importations. The extracts should be supported by a statement from the adviser that, in the adviser's opinion, HMRC does not have the power to see the other parts of the document. The extracts would include information about: – the origin of figures in accounts, returns and other information submitted to HMRC; and – the relationship of those figures with the trader's books and records.
Insolvent business office holder[2]	**Documents relating to** a bankrupt or insolvent trader	An office holder has the legal right to acquire possession of the records of an insolvent business. HMRC must therefore give an office holder any records which it may hold, and inform the trader or any third party who had a lien on the records. HMRC will normally copy all of the records, and must offer to provide copies to the trader or third party.
Computer bureaux and software suppliers	**Documents containing** details of client transactions	For confidentiality reasons, HMRC should only check system packages and not client transactions, unless authorised or requested by the client.

Note:
1. Statement of practice agreed between HMRC and the UK accountancy and taxation bodies in February 1993.
2. An office holder would be an administrator, liquidator, provisional liquidator, official receiver, or trustee in bankruptcy.

B. Specific powers

HMRC has many specific powers which it can exercise in relation to particular types of business or in particular circumstances. These are summarised as follows: 3480

Details		¶¶
Powers in relation to businesses which hold or deal in goods	To direct that specified records are kept	¶3485+
	To search premises	¶3500+
	To take samples	¶3512
Powers in relation to business records	To gain access to information	¶3514+
	To inspect computer equipment	¶3522
Powers in relation to security and production of evidence	In relation to a VAT credit or repayment	¶3526+
	To require monthly VAT returns	¶3542+
	To require security	¶3546+

Details		¶¶
Powers in relation to particular types of business	Overseas traders	¶3588+
	Businesses which operate gaming machines	¶3594
Powers in relation to criminal offences	Arrest	¶3597+
	Prosecution	¶3600

1. Powers in relation to businesses which hold or deal in goods

a. Requiring specified records to be kept

3485 Sch 11 para 6A VATA 1994

HMRC can direct any taxable person to keep certain additional records in relation to certain goods, and to preserve these records for up to 6 years.

The **condition** for making a direction is that HMRC must have reasonable grounds to believe that it would help to identify taxable supplies for which VAT may not have been paid. The taxable supplies may be those made by the person named in the direction, or any other person.

MEMO POINTS This measure is **aimed** mainly at missing trader intra-community fraud ("carousel fraud") (¶1988+), but can apply to any goods.

3487 Sch 11 para 6A VATA 1994

The **direction**:
- must be given by a notice in writing to the person named on it;
- must warn the person of the penalty for failing to comply (¶4141+); and
- remains in force until revoked or replaced by a further direction.

b. Searching premises

3500 s 114 Police and Criminal Evidence Act 1984

Where **serious fraud** is believed to have occurred, HMRC can apply to a justice of the peace (or, in Scotland, a justice) for a warrant to enter and search any premises.

Reasonable grounds

3502

The court must be satisfied that there are reasonable grounds **for believing** that:
- a serious fraud offence (¶4160+) has been committed on the premises; or
- evidence of the commission of such an offence may be found on the premises.

A justice of the peace (or, in Scotland, a justice) **cannot rely on** a mere statement by HMRC that there are reasonable grounds for believing that a serious fraud offence has been committed. Sufficient information must be provided to enable the court to be satisfied that this is the case. *IRC v Rossminster* [1980]

Terms of a search warrant

3504 s 15 Police and Criminal Evidence Act 1984

The requirements are as follows:

Compulsory inclusion	Optional
Name of person who applied for the warrant	Number of occasions on which entry is authorised, if more than one
Date of issue	Number of persons authorised to carry out the search
Enactment under which it was issued	Times of day during which the search may be carried out
Premises to be searched	Uniformed constable to be present
Articles or persons sought, so far as is practicable	

Search procedure

At any **time** within 1 month of the issue of the warrant, HMRC may undertake any of the following **activities**: **3506**
a. enter the premises, by force if necessary;
b. search the premises;
c. seize and remove any documents (or other items) which HMRC has reasonable cause to believe may be required as evidence in proceedings in respect of a serious fraud offence; and
d. search any person found on the premises, where HMRC has reasonable cause to believe that the person may possess any such documents or other items.

MEMO POINTS 1. A **copy** of the warrant, endorsed with the name of the authorised person, must be given to the occupier or other person in charge of the premises, or left at the premises, if unoccupied.
2. A **female** person may only be searched by a female officer.

The search must be **carried out** exactly **in accordance with** the terms of the warrant. Failure to observe any of the terms could result in the search being declared unlawful. **3508**

EXAMPLE
1. HMRC obtained a search warrant for a partnership's business premises, but they also searched a partner's home.
It was held that this was unlawful and ordered that damages be awarded. *R v Thames Magistrates' Court* [2002]

2. HMRC obtained a search warrant which authorised up to four persons to search the premises, but eight officers took part in the search.
It was held that:
– the search had been unlawfully executed;
– the records removed were therefore inadmissible evidence; and
– the trader's subsequent conviction for fraudulent evasion of VAT would be quashed *Singh and another v HM Advocate* [2001]

HMRC must, within a reasonable time, **provide** a record of any items removed. **3510** Sch 11 para 12 VATA 1994
If the person from whom the items were removed requests:
a. access to the items, HMRC must allow supervised access; or
b. a **photograph or copy** of an item, HMRC must:
– allow supervised access to copy the item; or
– photograph or copy the item and supply a copy to the person within a reasonable time from the making of a request.
HMRC **need not grant** such a request if there are reasonable grounds to believe that to do so would prejudice an investigation or criminal proceedings in relation to any offence.

c. Taking samples

If HMRC considers it necessary for the protection of tax revenues, an authorised person (¶3424) may, at any time, take samples of goods in the possession of: **3512** Sch 11 para 8 VATA 1994
a. any person who supplies goods or acquires goods from another EU member state (¶9010+); or
b. a fiscal warehousekeeper (¶9268+).

The **purpose** of taking a sample is to determine how the goods or materials should be treated for VAT purposes.

Compensation must be paid to the trader if a sample is not returned within a reasonable time and in good condition.

2. Powers in relation to records

a. Gaining access to information

3514 Sch 11 para 11 VATA 1994

If HMRC believes that an offence has been (or may be) committed, it can apply to a justice of the peace (or, in Scotland, a justice) for an order granting HMRC access to recorded information, **including** any document of any nature whatsoever.

Comment HMRC will normally only use this specific power where it has been unable to obtain information informally, or by means of an information notice (¶3462+).

Conditions for issue of an order

3516 The court must be satisfied that there are **reasonable grounds** (¶3502) for believing that:
- an offence in connection with VAT has been (or is about to be) committed; and
- any recorded information which may be required as evidence in proceedings in respect of such an offence is in the possession of any person.

Effect of an order

3518 Within 7 days of the date of the order, or at the end of such longer period as may be specified, the **person possessing** the recorded information **must**:
- give an authorised person access to it;
- produce any electronically stored information in a visible and legible form; and
- allow an authorised person to copy, make extracts from, or remove any of the information.

3520 Sch 11 para 12 VATA 1994

HMRC must **provide** a record of any items removed and allow access to the items, as in ¶3510.

b. Checking computer equipment

3522 s 114 FA 2008

An authorised person (¶3424) may, at any reasonable time:
a. access, inspect and check the operation of any computer and associated apparatus used in connection with any document which a person has been required to produce to HMRC;
b. remove or make copies of records or data; and
c. require the person using, or in charge of, the computer to give them such reasonable assistance as they may require.

MEMO POINTS An **electronic till** with a constant memory and processing function is considered to be a computer for these purposes; HMRC may reprogram it if there is no other way to retrieve the data held on the machine.

3. Security required and production of evidence

3524 If HMRC believes that there is a risk to tax revenues, it can impose additional requirements on businesses which owe VAT, or which claim a VAT credit or repayment.

Reason for additional requirement	Possible requirement	¶¶
HMRC has concerns regarding a particular claim to a VAT credit or repayment	Production of evidence of entitlement	¶3526
	Provision of security until claim verified	¶3528+
HMRC has ongoing concerns regarding payment of VAT liabilities	Provision of security as a condition of VAT registration, or of making supplies	¶3546+
	Provision of security from a trader in a supply chain	¶3570+
	Provision of security from an overseas trader	¶3592

a. Powers relating to a VAT credit or repayment

Evidence of entitlement

HMRC may, as a condition of allowing or repaying input tax to any person, require the production of such evidence as it may specify. **3526** Sch 11 para 4(1) VATA 1994

Evidence is **commonly requested when** a business makes an unusual repayment claim, or declares a lower than normal liability. The reason for such variations is often the purchase of a large capital asset, or a property which has been opted (¶5602+). In such cases, HMRC would normally ask the trader to provide the purchase invoice(s) showing the input tax which is claimed.

Security

HMRC can request security before making a VAT repayment. Provision of security **enables** the repayment to be made before it has been verified, so that the trader can receive the benefit of any undisputed element of the repayment. **3528** Sch 11 para 4(1A) VATA 1994

Scope HMRC has the power to require the deposit of security if a trader makes a large or unusual VAT claim which HMRC wishes to verify before making a repayment. **3530**

Security may be **applied** against:
- the amount of any repayment already made, and which is subsequently partly or wholly disallowed; or
- any VAT subject to a notice of joint and several liability (¶2002+) which remains unpaid.

MEMO POINTS Security will normally only be required where a trader makes an unusual repayment claim of **at least £500,000**, which HMRC doubts is eligible and wishes to verify.

If security **is not provided**, the repayment will be withheld until: **3534**
- the repayment claim is verified; or
- any notice of joint and several liability (¶2002+) for unpaid VAT is withdrawn, or the VAT in question is paid.

Amount Security will be required for the element of the claim which needs verification, subject to a **maximum** of the net amount repayable. **3536**

EXAMPLE
1. A Ltd's VAT return for the period ended 31 December shows:

	£
Output tax	50,000
Input tax	(750,000)
Repayment due	700,000

HMRC wishes to verify input tax of £600,000 claimed in respect of purchases from a particular supplier. It may request security of £600,000.

2. B Ltd's VAT return for the period ended 31 December shows:

	£
Output tax	200,000
Input tax	(750,000)
Repayment due	550,000

HMRC wishes to verify input tax of £600,000 claimed in respect of purchases from a particular supplier. It may request security of the net repayable amount of £550,000.

Form of security HMRC will normally accept: **3538**
- a bank or building society peformance bond (guarantee); or
- a cash deposit in a joint bank or building society interest-bearing account.

3540 **Procedure if security enforced** HMRC will issue a **Notice of Requirement** to provide the security.

The trader can, within 30 days of the date of issue, ask HMRC to **reconsider** its decision, or **appeal** against it to a tribunal (¶4262+).

The security will be **returned** to the trader after:
- verification of the repayment claim or payment of VAT; or
- withdrawal of any notice of joint and several liability, or payment of the VAT in question.

---

b. Requiring monthly VAT returns

3542 SI 1995/2518 reg 25(1)(a) HMRC can direct a trader to make monthly VAT returns (¶2990+), which **enable** it to take early action to issue assessments or recover a debt.

MEMO POINTS A direction to submit monthly returns may be considered **if**:
a. there are concerns regarding payment of VAT liabilities;
b. evidence needs to be gathered for a security requirement;
c. any of the conditions for a security requirement are met (¶3550); or
d. a trader takes up this option on being sent a Notice of Requirement for security.

Procedure

3544 HMRC will issue a **Notice of Direction** to make monthly returns.

The notice will **contain**:
- the date of the last quarterly return and the due date for its submission; and
- the periods and payment date of any outstanding VAT.

The trader will be allowed to **revert** to quarterly returns, either at the trader's request or if invited to do so by HMRC, when the trader has become compliant and no longer represents a risk to tax revenues.

---

c. Requiring security as a condition of VAT registration

3546 Sch 11 para 4(2) VATA 1994; HMRC can require security from any trader as a condition of allowing them to become or remain VAT-registered.

A **warning letter** may be issued first, but HMRC may demand security without warning if it believes it has strong grounds for suspecting that there is a risk of VAT not being recovered.

When required

3550 A Notice of Requirement to provide security may be issued if:
a. a **person** has:
- failed to comply with their VAT obligations in their current or previous business; or
- previously been prosecuted or penalised for a VAT offence;

b. other persons concerned in a VAT-registered business are connected with past failures to pay VAT; or
c. a **business** is being run by a disqualified director or an undischarged bankrupt.

Reconsiderations and appeals

3552 ss 83, 84 VATA 1994; If the trader disagrees with a decision to request security, they may, within 30 days of receiving the Notice of Requirement:
a. write to HMRC, asking it to reconsider and providing any further information or pointing out facts which may not have been considered; or
b. appeal against the decision to a tribunal (¶4262+).

Security does not have to be provided before an appeal is heard, and a business can normally continue to make taxable supplies until the outcome of an appeal is known.

It is not the tribunal's function to decide whether it would have issued a demand for security. It can only consider whether HMRC acted reasonably in deciding to make a demand.

The following table gives details of a number of appeals. 3554

Successful appeals	Unsuccessful appeals
Director's involvement with a previous failed company ceased long before it became insolvent. *Exact Electronics Ltd* [1993] (VTD 11391) Partner of partnership which formerly owned the business now only an employee of the company which owned it. *Auldbrook Ltd* [1994] (VTD 11717) Failure of a previous company due to a fire. *Deltaview Ltd* [1985] (VTD 1832) Requirement for security unreasonable due to very low turnover. *RB Cornforth* [1989] (VTD 4532) Directorship of previously failed company not relevant, as current partnership fully VAT-compliant for more than one year. *C Hickson & Others (t/a Flury's)* [1993] (VTD 11455) Previously failed companies not relevant, as 80% of the business's supplies were zero-rated. *Wold Construction Co Ltd* [1993] (VTD 11704) Failure of same business whilst owned by wife was due to employee theft. *S Elliott* [1995] (VTD 13432)	Requirement for security would force company to cease trading and make staff redundant. *Rosebronze Ltd* [1984] (VTD 1668) Events after issue of the demand for security meant that the director was no longer influenced by parents who had controlled previous failed company. The tribunal must consider whether HMRC acted reasonably in demanding security based on the situation when it made the demand, so subsequent events are not relevant to the tribunal's decision. However, the tribunal may suggest that HMRC reviews its demand based on the new evidence. *C & E v Peachtree Enterprises Ltd* [1994] Rules of professional association to which an accountant belonged would ensure that he paid all VAT liabilities. *JL Morrell (t/a Morrell Middleton)* [1996] (VTD 13970)

Amount of security

HMRC **may specify** the amount required, which will be calculated using the most accurate information available to it. 3556 Sch 11 para 4 (4) VATA 1994

The tribunal has accepted that the following levels of security are reasonable (and, indeed, these reflect HMRC's **normal basis of calculation**):

- for traders submitting quarterly VAT returns, security representing an estimate of VAT liability of 2 quarters (6 months); or
- for traders submitting monthly VAT returns, security representing an estimate of VAT liability of 4 months.

An **existing VAT debt** may be added to the amount calculated.

MEMO POINTS An existing VAT debt **includes** VAT, default surcharges, default interest and civil penalties.

Normal basis of calculation The required amount is based on tax declared on VAT returns from the current business. 3558

The most recent two quarterly returns, or six monthly returns, would normally be used. If these returns do not reflect the usual trading pattern, earlier returns may be used. If trading is seasonal, an average may be taken over a longer period.

EXAMPLE

1. HMRC has decided to require security from Mrs C. Her last two quarterly VAT returns showed liabilities of £10,000 and £15,000.
The required security, based on estimated tax for 6 months, will be £25,000.

2. HMRC has decided to require security from D Ltd. The last six monthly VAT returns showed liabilities as follows:

Month	£
1	9,000
2	7,500
3	8,000
4	12,000
5	5,000
6	11,000
	52,500

D Ltd has not paid the liabilities for months 5 and 6.

The required security will be:	£
Estimated tax for 4 months (£52,500 × 4/6)	35,000
Existing VAT debt (£5,000 + £11,000)	16,000
	51,000

3560 **Other bases of calculation** If the required amount cannot be calculated from recent VAT returns, the following alternative bases can be used:
- tax declared on VAT returns from any **previous business** of a similar type and size;
- taxable turnover declared on the **VAT registration application**, taking into account an allowance for estimated input tax for the **trade class** to which the business belongs;
- **estimates** provided by the trader (or the trader's accountant), or information provided by the trader or obtained during a visit to the trader; or
- tax declared on VAT returns from **other businesses** of a similar size in the same trade class, with similar customers.

After establishing a basis amount using one of these methods, the amount of security will be calculated, representing VAT due for 6 or 4 months, under the normal formula.

Form of security

3562 Sch 11 para 4 (4) VATA 1994 HMRC **may specify** the manner in which the security is to be provided, but will normally only accept:
- cash or a banker's draft;
- a guarantee from a bank, building society or other financial institution approved by the Financial Conduct Authority or Prudential Regulation Authority (as appropriate); or
- a cash deposit in a joint bank or building society account.

Comment A trader should pay cash into a joint account, if possible, rather than give it to HMRC as security, as the trader would receive no interest from HMRC.

MEMO POINTS 1. The **minimum duration** of a **guarantee** depends on whether the trader is submitting returns:
- monthly, in which case a 12-month duration is required; or
- quarterly, in which case a 2-year duration is required.

2. Where a **joint account** is opened in the names of HMRC and the trader, the required terms are that:
- no withdrawals can be made from the account without approval from HMRC; and
- the account can only be closed on HMRC's instructions.

The security is deposited in the account and the trader receives the interest earned, less any bank charges.

Procedures if security required

3564 **Request** HMRC will issue a **Notice of Requirement**, which will normally contain an offer to reduce the amount of security if a trader agrees to change from quarterly to monthly VAT return submission.

If **further security** is considered necessary, a new Notice of Requirement must be issued.

3566 **Payment** **Normally**, the security must be provided immediately after receiving a notice of requirement. It is a criminal offence to continue to trade without providing the security, for which a penalty may be charged (¶4197).

MEMO POINTS In **exceptional cases**, HMRC has been prepared to accept payment of security by instalments. HMRC warned that a trader who defaulted on such an agreement would be liable to prosecution for trading without providing security, because the security only became effective with the final instalment.

3568 **Use and return** Security may be used against any VAT owed, and will be returned to the trader when HMRC considers that the collection of VAT is no longer at risk.

HMRC will regularly **review** the requirement to hold the security, within 12 months of it being provided for monthly returns, and 2 years for quarterly returns.

The trader should **provide** any information which may affect the decision to hold security.

d. Requiring security from a trader in a supply chain

HMRC can require security from a trader in a supply chain (¶2002+). **3570** Sch 11 para 4 (2) (b) VATA 1994; Notice 726

This power can be used in relation to any type of trade, but it is **primarily aimed** at combating carousel fraud (¶1988+), where there have been some high-profile cases involving computer and telecommunications goods. Supply chain fraud has also occurred in the fashion and construction industries, and has even involved emissions allowances.

Scope

Security may be **used against** VAT owed by the trader and, if joint and several liability applies (¶2002+), other traders in the supply chain. The CJEU has held that security cannot be required from a person for payment of VAT by another party with whom the person is not jointly and severally liable. *C & E and another v Federation of Technological Industries* [2006] **3574**

Reconsiderations and appeals

If the trader **disagrees** with a decision to request security, they may, within 30 days of receiving the Notice of Requirement: **3576** s 84(4E) VATA 1994

a. write to HMRC, asking it to reconsider, and providing any further information or pointing out facts which may not have been considered; or

b. appeal against the decision to a tribunal (¶4262+).

EXAMPLE A company appealed against a requirement to provide security. It admitted involvement in a supply chain in which there had been an irregularity, but denied that it had caused or permitted the irregularity.
The appeal was dismissed, as it had been established that VAT had been evaded on supplies made to the company, and the requirement to provide security had been reasonable and proportionate. *Balmoral Ltd* [2005] (VTD 19233)

Amount of security

HMRC **may specify** the amount required. This will depend on whether joint and several liability applies. **3577**

Joint and several liability applies The trader can be asked to provide security for VAT owed by others. The amount will be based on an estimate of the VAT that may be unpaid due to evasion of payment by a business or individual in the supply chain. **3578**

The amount will be **in proportion** to the extent of the trader's involvement in current and previous high-risk supply chains, and will be limited to an acceptable amount which the trader should have been able to see would be unpaid.

Any **existing VAT debt** (¶3556) may be added to the amount calculated.

EXAMPLE E Ltd has been involved in three supply chains, where tax losses have been as follows:

Chain		£m
1		1.50
2		1.75
3		2.00
		5.25
Average tax loss	$\frac{1.5 + 1.75 + 2}{3}$	1.75

HMRC might require security of either £1.75m (the average tax loss) or £2m (the most recent loss). HMRC would not seek security for the total tax loss of £5.25m, as this would be disproportionate.

3580 **Joint and several liability does not apply** In this case, the trader cannot be asked to provide security for VAT owed by others. The **amount** will, therefore, be **limited to** an estimate of the VAT that may be unpaid by the trader. *C & E and another v Federation of Technological Industries* [2006]

Form of security

3582 Sch 11 para 4(4) VATA 1994 HMRC may specify the manner in which the security is to be provided. For details of acceptable forms of security see ¶3562.

Procedures

3584 **Payment** The security **must be provided** immediately after receiving a Notice of Requirement. It is a criminal offence to continue to trade without providing the security, for which a penalty may be charged (¶4197).

3586 **Return** The requirement to hold the security will be **reviewed** regularly, and at least within 12 months of it being provided. The trader should put forward to HMRC any information which may affect the decision to hold security.

Security will be **returned** when HMRC considers that the collection of VAT from businesses or individuals in a supply chain is no longer at risk.

4. Powers in relation to particular types of business

Overseas traders

3588 VSME3060 **Control visits** Very exceptionally, HMRC may **carry out** a control visit (¶3416+) at a trader's premises overseas, if it would be difficult or expensive for the trader to produce records in the UK.

This **may apply** where a registered person:
- has no business establishment in the UK;
- has its accounting function in another EU member state; or
- is also registered for VAT in another EU member state.

The **expense** of the visit would have to be met by the trader, and HMRC would **reserve the right** to require production of the records in the UK in future.

3590 HMRC will **check** the following:

Overseas transactions	Details which may be checked
Trade with any other country	Correct recording of overseas transactions in VAT returns
Trade with other EU member states	Evidence of removal of goods from UK where supplies to EU are zero-rated
	Validity of EU customers' VAT registration numbers
	Whether VAT return entries are in accordance with data held on the EU VAT Information and Exchange System
Imports and/or exports of goods and/or services	Whether VAT is properly accounted for on imported goods, goods removed from a bonded warehouse, and associated services not included in the import VAT value
	Percentage of inputs and outputs which are imports and exports
	Evidence of export of goods
Services received from abroad	Place of supply of the service, and whether the reverse charge applies

3592 s 48 (7) VATA 1994 **Requirement to provide security** If an overseas trader **fails to appoint** a UK representative (¶7210+), HMRC may require security as a condition of allowing the trader to make supplies in the UK.

Businesses which operate gaming machines

HMRC may, at any reasonable time, require a person who makes supplies of games of chance on gaming machines, or any person acting on the supplier's behalf, to: 3594 Sch 11 para 9 VATA 1994
- **open** any gaming machine; or
- **carry out** any mechanical procedure which may be necessary to enable HMRC to ascertain the value of supplies made in any period.

Where possible, HMRC will visit premises at a time when the owner would normally empty the machines.

MEMO POINTS A gaming machine is a machine which an individual can use to gamble. An **amusement machine** which offers a game with no gambling element is not a gaming machine.

5. Powers in relation to criminal offences

HMRC has specific powers in relation to criminal offences. In addition, the National Crime Agency (formerly the Serious Organised Crime Agency) has powers relating to VAT matters. 3596

a. HMRC's powers

Arrest

Fraudulent evasion An HMRC officer can arrest anyone whom the officer has reasonable grounds for suspecting to be guilty of any of the **following offences**: 3597 s 114 Police and Criminal Evidence Act 1994
- fraudulent evasion of VAT (¶4160+);
- producing a false document or making a false statement (¶4180+);
- conduct which must have involved the commission of an offence (¶4194+); or
- impersonation, obstruction or assault of an HMRC officer.

Offences in relation to HMRC officers An HMRC officer can **arrest** a person without warrant if the officer reasonably suspects that the person: 3598 s 33 CRCA 2005
- has impersonated, obstructed or assaulted an HMRC officer; or
- is committing or is about to commit such an offence.

Prosecution

The Revenue and Customs Prosecutions Office (RCPO) can, as the Revenue and Customs Division of the Crown Prosecution Service, institute and conduct proceedings in **England and Wales** relating to a criminal investigation by HMRC. 3600 ss 34 - 41 CRCA 2005

b. National Crime Agency

The National Crime Agency (NCA) took over the functions of the Serious Organised Crime Agency (SOCA) in 2013 **with the aim of** preventing and detecting serious organised crime, including tax fraud. The agency exercises the functions of the former National Crime Squad, National Criminal Intelligence Service and Assets Recovery Agency, and some functions of HMRC and the UK Immigration Service. 3602 s 2 SOCPA 2005

Role in relation to VAT

HMRC retains a considerable amount of responsibility for investigating, and RCPO for prosecuting, tax fraud. NCA must consult with HMRC before taking any action in relation to VAT fraud. However, NCA also has extensive powers to investigate, arrest and prosecute offenders, and to recover property from persons who have benefited from criminal conduct. 3604 s 2(7) SOCPA 2005; s 1 POCA 2002

Asset recovery

3608 Criminal conduct **includes** VAT offences which are subject to criminal penalties (¶4150+). HMRC may therefore refer cases involving matters such as the fraudulent evasion of VAT for action by NCA, in order to recover property where VAT has been evaded.

Confiscation orders

3609 ss 6, 7 POCA 2002 NCA can apply to the High Court for an order to confiscate an amount from a person who has benefited from criminal conduct. In some cases the amount to be recovered has been agreed without NCA applying for a court order.

The **amount** will generally equal the benefit received from the criminal conduct, unless the amount available for recovery is lower.

EXAMPLE A person was acquitted of VAT carousel fraud in 2005 but was then investigated by the Assets Recovery Agency. He agreed to hand over £18m, plus a house and four racehorses.

Non-compliance

3611 s 37 POCA 2002 If a person fails to pay the amount ordered they may be imprisoned. The **maximum jail sentence** varies from 7 days, where the confiscated amount was £200, to 10 years, where the amount was over £1 million.

Restraint orders

3612 s 41 POCA 2002 NCA can apply to the High Court for a restraint order in respect of property which may be liable for confiscation following a trial. An order **may be made against** the defendant in a trial, or any other person holding the property.

A restraint order **prevents** the specified person from dealing with the property in any way.

Freezing orders

3614 s 245A POCA 2002 NCA can apply to the High Court for an order to freeze property when recovery action may be taken. An application may be made before or after commencement of recovery proceedings.

Freezing **prevents** the specified person from dealing with the property in any way.

EXAMPLE In July 2006, the Assets Recovery Agency obtained a property freezing order over five properties and seven bank accounts with an estimated value of £1.7m. HMRC contended that the assets had been acquired from the proceeds of VAT fraud involving false invoices.

SECTION 2

Assessment of under-declared VAT

3625 s 73 VATA 1994 HMRC has power to assess VAT which it believes to be due from taxable persons, non-taxable persons and fiscal warehousekeepers.

There are two types of assessment:

a. central assessments, which are automatically generated by the central VAT computer system; and

b. officer assessments, which are raised manually by VAT officers.

Type of assessment	Reason for assessment	¶¶
Central assessments	Required VAT return not submitted	¶3652+
Officer assessments	Central assessment too low	¶3675+
	Incorrect or incomplete VAT return submitted	
	Failure to keep documents or provide facilities necessary to verify returns	

Details of assessments to recover VAT in **special situations** can be found as follows: 3627

Reason for special assessment	¶¶
Notification of error by a trader	¶3020+
Incorrect payment of a refund to a trader	¶3238+
Incorrect payment of statutory interest to a trader	¶3270+
Certain transactions by VAT groups	¶8875+
Unauthorised issue of invoices	¶1984+
VAT incorrectly charged when business sold as a going concern	¶8646+
VAT understated on self-billed documents	¶2916
VAT due on acquisitions of excisable goods by non-taxable persons	¶9429
VAT due from a fiscal warehousekeeper	¶9242+

A. General principles

The following principles apply to both central and officer assessments. 3630

1. Time limits

Normal limit

An assessment must normally be made not later than 2 years after the end of the accounting period to which it relates. 3632 s 73(6), (6A) VATA 1994; VAEC1120+

Where a **VAT refund** has been received or a credit has been made to a trader incorrectly, the accounting period from which the 2-year time limit applies is the one in which the repayment or credit was made.

MEMO POINTS The **date** of an assessment is stated by the legislation to be when it is made; an assessment could, therefore, be notified to a trader some time afterwards. In practice, HMRC takes the date on which the assessment is issued or notified to the trader as the material date for time limit purposes, to avoid challenges to the validity of assessments.

Extended limits

4-year limit An assessment can be made not later than 4 years after the end of the accounting period to which it relates, provided that it is made within 1 year of when HMRC receives **knowledge** of evidence of facts which it considers sufficient to justify making the assessment (¶3638). 3634 ss 73(6), 77(1) VATA 1994

EXAMPLE

1. On 30 March 2015 Mr A received a control visit, in which it was discovered that output tax was under-declared in the accounting period ended on 30 June 2014.
For an assessment to be in time, HMRC must raise it by 30 June 2016 (under the 2-year rule).

2. On 31 August 2015 Ms B receives a control visit, in which it is discovered that output tax was under-declared in the accounting period ended on 31 October 2012.
For an assessment to be in time, HMRC must raise it by 31 August 2016 (under the 1-year rule).

20-year limit In certain **special situations** the time limit is increased to 20 years. 3635

This applies where a person has:
- failed to notify HMRC of their liability to register or account for VAT;
- issued invoices while unauthorised;

– dishonestly evaded VAT (¶4160+), whether or not a dishonest evasion penalty has been charged; *Sirpal Trading Co Ltd* [1995] (VTD 13288) or
– been convicted of fraud, or where **criminal proceedings** are being taken in advance of a conviction for fraud, on the basis that dishonest evasion will have occurred.

3637 s 77(5) VATA 1994 **Deceased persons** The **4-year limit** applies as normal.

The **20-year limit** does not apply. Assessments in the special situations in question are limited to accounting periods ending within the 4 years before the date of death.

A **further restriction** applies so that no assessment can be raised more than 4 years after the date of death.

EXAMPLE Mr C died on 31 January 2014. His executors continued to carry on his business during the period of administration. On 31 August 2014 HMRC discovered that Mr C had dishonestly evaded tax since 1 January 2009, resulting in under-declarations of output tax in each accounting period from 1 January 2009 until 31 January 2014.
The earliest accounting period for which HMRC can raise an assessment is the quarter ended 31 March 2010, which is the earliest accounting period ending within 4 years of the date of death. The time limit for raising an assessment is 31 January 2018.

Evidence of facts

3638 HMRC must make an assessment within a year of receiving knowledge of the facts which relate to the particular assessment in question. This time limit only starts when the **last piece of evidence** which is material and critical for that assessment becomes available. *C & E v The Post Office* [1995]

Knowledge means actual knowledge of the facts, not what HMRC could or should have found out. *CPM Van Boeckel v C & E* [1981]

Additional assessments

3640 s 77(6) VATA 1994 If an assessment is too low, a **supplementary** assessment can be made within the same time limit, where this does not involve new evidence of facts. This will normally apply where an assessment was too low due to a clerical or arithmetical error.

A **replacement** assessment may be made within the same time limit, if the original is withdrawn by HMRC or successfully appealed. This may apply where, for example, HMRC decides to change the method of calculation, or a tribunal decides that an assessment was not made to the best of HMRC's judgment.

If **new evidence of facts** is received, a further assessment may be made within a new 1-year time limit (subject to the overall 4-year time limit).

Protective assessments

3641 VAEC5500+ HMRC may make a protective assessment before the expiry of a time limit where, due to ongoing litigation, it is unclear whether the VAT in question will ultimately be payable.

2. Establishing the amount due

3643 s 73(1) VATA 1994 HMRC must assess the amount of VAT due to the best of its judgment.

For the application of the following principles to:
– **central assessments** see ¶3652+; and
– **other assessments** see ¶3675+.

Best judgment

3644 This **means that** HMRC:
a. must fairly consider all the material before it and, on that material, come to a decision which is reasonable and not arbitrary;

b. must have some material on which it can base its judgment;
c. must perform its function honestly and bona fide; and
d. should not be required to do the work of the taxpayer by carrying out exhaustive investigations. *CPM Van Boeckel v C & E* [1981]

In practice, an assessment is deemed to have been made to the best of HMRC's judgment if it is reasonable. **3646**

A tribunal set out **three tests** of whether an assessment is reasonable:
a. the facts should be objectively gathered and intelligently interpreted;
b. the calculations should be arithmetically sound; and
c. any sampling technique should be representative and free from bias. *CA McCourtie* [1994] (VTD 12239)

A tribunal or court may disagree with **the way in which** HMRC exercised its judgment, but nevertheless decide that the assessment was made to the best of HMRC's judgment. In such cases, the assessment may be increased or decreased instead of being cancelled.

A **failure to exercise best judgment** will only be found where, for example, an assessment: **3647**
– is wholly unreasonable;
– is a spurious estimate or guess, in which all elements of judgment are missing; or
– was made dishonestly, vindictively or capriciously. *Rahman (t/a Khayam Restaurant) v C & E* [1998]

The consequence of a finding of failure to exercise best judgment should not automatically be that the assessment should be set aside. Normally the tribunal should seek to find the correct amount to be assessed, instead of cancelling the assessment altogether. *C & E v Pegasus Birds Ltd* [2004]

3. Administration

Payment and recovery

An amount shown in an assessment is **deemed to be** VAT due from the person concerned and may be recovered accordingly. **3649** s 73(9) VATA 1994; VAEC9600+

Payment of an assessment **is due** within 30 days of the date of issue.

Assessing representatives

If a personal representative, trustee in bankruptcy, trustee, receiver, liquidator, or other person acting in a representative capacity fails to make a return, or submits an incomplete or incorrect return, they may be assessed for the VAT due from the trader. Notification to the representative is treated as notification to the trader. **3650** s 73(5), (10) VATA 1994

B. Central assessments

Central assessments are **automatically** generated by the central VAT computer system, and are also known as "prime" assessments. **3652**

1. General principles

If a VAT-registered person **fails to submit** a required VAT return (¶2985+), HMRC may make an assessment in order to establish a liability for the period in question and create an enforceable debt. **3654** s 73(1) VATA 1994

Only one such assessment can be made for each accounting period, but if this is found to be too low, an officer assessment (¶3675+) can be made.

MEMO POINTS Central assessments are **not issued** to traders who normally receive VAT repayments.

Issue of assessments

3656 Each month, traders who have failed to submit a required VAT return are identified by the central computer system, which computes an amount and generates an assessment. If the amount **does not exceed £100,000**, the assessment is sent direct to the trader.

Where the amount **exceeds £100,000**, the details are sent to the trader's local VAT office to be checked. If the assessment is in order, it will then be forwarded to the trader.

Objecting

3657 s 83(1)(p) VATA 1994 No **appeal** can be made against a central assessment, because appeals against amounts assessed for an accounting period are only permitted where a VAT return has been submitted for that period.

HMRC may exceptionally **withdraw or reduce** a central assessment if:
a. it is fundamentally flawed, for example, where the method of assessment is known to be unsound in a particular case; or
b. the trader notifies HMRC that it is too high, but that they are unable to submit a return for some reason.

2. Calculation of an assessment

3659 Central assessments are normally calculated automatically. Manual calculation may, however, be necessary in certain circumstances.

EXAMPLE HMRC compulsorily registered a trader based on information which it held, and issued an automatically calculated central assessment in the absence of a VAT return for the first period.
It was held that the central assessment was invalid, as it failed to take account of the information known to HMRC at the time it was made, and was not therefore made to the best of HMRC's judgment. *Alan Bennett* [1997] (VTD 14976)

Automatic calculation

3660 The assessable amount is arrived at by a formula containing two elements:
– a previous VAT liability or turnover figure for the trader in question; and
– a factor relating to the trade sector to which the trader belongs.

The resulting calculation meets the requirement that an assessment must be made to the best of HMRC's judgment.

MEMO POINTS The data held by HMRC in respect of all traders is analysed to produce average VAT liabilities and average turnovers for each trade sector.

3662 **Previous period liability formula** This is the **normal** method, and is used when the trader's previous VAT liabilities are known. The liability for any one of the previous three accounting periods is multiplied by a factor relating to the average liability for that trade sector.

3663 **Taxable turnover formula** This method is **only used** if details of previous period liabilities are not available. The trader's taxable turnover is multiplied by a factor relating to the average taxable turnover for that trade sector.

3665 s 73(8) VATA 1994; VAEC2240+ **Inflated assessment regime** The automatically calculated amounts **may be increased** by a certain factor if a trader repeatedly pays central assessments and does not submit VAT returns.

A trader **will enter** the inflated assessment regime if they have paid two or more central assessments in any of the previous four VAT periods.

The trader **will leave** the inflated assessment regime when they have submitted four consecutive VAT returns.

MEMO POINTS 1. Assessments **for less than £10** will be uplifted to £10.
2. An inflated assessment is **not used as** a basis for calculating other assessments.
3. **Default surcharges** (¶4082+) may be higher as a result of inflated assessments.

The following table gives details of the inflation factors: 3666 s 73(8) VATA 1994

Assessment number after entering inflated assessment regime	Inflation factor[1]
1	20%
2	40%
3	60%
4	80%
5 and subsequent	100% [2]

Note:
1. The inflation factor **will revert** to 20% where:
– a trader submits a return after entering the inflated assessment regime; or
– an assessment is based on an amount regarded as a true liability.
2. When an **inflation factor of 100%** is reached, HMRC will visit the business to establish the true liability.

EXAMPLE D Ltd has paid two central assessments in the previous four VAT periods. It pays a further three central assessments in periods 5, 6 and 7, submits a return for period 8, then pays another two central assessments in periods 9 and 10. The central assessments are calculated as follows:

Period	Automatically calculated amount	Inflation factor	Assessment
	£	%	£
5	10,000	20	12,000
6	11,000	40	15,400
7	12,000	60	19,200
8 - return submitted	N/A	N/A	N/A
9	14,000	20	16,800
10	15,000	40	21,000

Manual calculation

Manual calculation **may be required where**: 3668 VAEC2220
– a number of automatic calculations have been issued and VAT returns have still not been submitted; or
– the local VAT office has specific information regarding the VAT liability, enabling a more accurate assessment to be made, meeting the requirement that it be made to the best of HMRC's judgment.

The calculation will be **based on** all the information held by HMRC. Where necessary, the trader will be asked to provide further information.

3. Dealing with an assessment

The trader must **either**: 3670 VAEC2270
a. pay the assessment within 30 days (and notify HMRC within 30 days if the assessment is too low, otherwise the trader may become liable to a penalty); or
b. submit the outstanding VAT return.

If the return shows a:
– **higher** liability, the assessment is simply superseded; or

– **lower** liability, the case will be referred to the local VAT office, where the return will be checked.

3671 A trader who **consistently** pays central assessments and does not submit VAT returns may become liable to a penalty for inaccuracy (¶4000+).

MEMO POINTS The central VAT computer system identifies traders who pay central assessments of **over £3,500** and refers them to the local VAT office, where the position may be reviewed.

C. Officer assessments

3675 HMRC officers can raise assessments at any time in order to recover VAT which appears to have been under-declared for any reason.

1. General principles

Reasons for making an assessment

3677 VAT officers may make assessments where:
s 73 VATA 1994
a. HMRC receives evidence indicating that a **central assessment** (¶3652+) was too low;
b. a **VAT return appears incorrect or incomplete**, which will typically apply following:
– the discovery of under-declarations during a control visit (¶3416+);
– the result of credibility checks carried out on VAT returns;
– a comparison of VAT returns with a trader's annual accounts; or
– the receipt of information by HMRC from other sources; or
c. a trader **fails to keep documents** or provide facilities necessary to **verify returns**.

3678 The following table lists **common errors and omissions**, which give rise to tax under-declarations:

Reason for tax under-declaration	Examples
Accounting errors	Omission of sales invoices or purchase credit notes from VAT records
	Wrong rate of VAT charged
	Failure to account for VAT on sales of business assets
	Tax point errors
	Late entry of sales invoices in VAT records
	Errors in operating cash accounting or retail scheme
	Partial exemption errors
	Arithmetical errors and duplicate input tax claims
	Errors in relation to bad debt relief claims
Under-declaration of cash sales or sales to unregistered persons	Failure to charge VAT
	Failure to charge VAT on sales to private persons in other EU member states
	Suppression (under-recording) of cash takings
Other errors	Failure to account for tax on private use of goods, including fuel scale charges
	Failure to provide purchase invoice as evidence for input tax deduction
	Failure to obtain satisfactory evidence of export or removal of goods from UK
	Input tax claimed on blocked items such as cars and business entertainment

Occasions when assessments not raised

An assessment will **normally** not be made in the following circumstances: 3680

Circumstances	Details	Reference
De minimis level	Amount is less than £100.	VAEC6090
No net loss of tax revenue	For example, where: – acquisition VAT (¶9017+) was omitted from both the output and input tax boxes of the VAT return; or – there is only a reallocation of VAT from one period to another, and one of the periods is more than 3 years old. However, where there may be no net loss of revenue because a **customer might have been able to deduct input tax**, assessments will still normally be made. HMRC will not carry out extensive checks to establish the position, and will assume that tax has been lost. Traders have the option of paying the assessment themselves, or issuing additional or amended sales invoices in order to recover the VAT from customers.	
Misdirection (¶3687)	Where HMRC provides information or advice that is incorrect in law, it will consider itself bound by such advice, provided that it is clear, unequivocal and explicit, and the taxpayer can demonstrate that: – they reasonably relied on the advice where appropriate; – they made full disclosure of all the relevant facts; and – strict application of the statute would result in financial detriment to the taxpayer.	flmemo.co.uk/ vm3680
Input tax claimed in good faith	Where an unauthorised person issued invoices showing an amount as VAT (¶1984+), and a taxable person claimed that amount as input tax, HMRC will not take action to recover it, if it is clear that it was claimed in good faith.	Notice 48 para 3.9
Incorrect declaration made by customer	Where a customer incorrectly declared that a supply was taxable at the reduced (¶1110+) or zero rate (¶1180+), HMRC will not take action to recover the tax due from a supplier who took all reasonable steps to check the validity of the declaration, but failed to identify the inaccuracy and acted in good faith.	Notice 48 para 3.11

Reconsiderations and appeals

A person can ask HMRC to reconsider an officer assessment, or appeal against an officer assessment to a tribunal. 3681

The **general rules** in relation to reconsiderations and appeals can be found at ¶4210+.

Specific details of appeals against particular assessments can be found at ¶3692–.

Periods assessed

If the liabilities for **specific** accounting periods cannot be readily identified, HMRC will attribute the liabilities to accounting periods to the best of its judgment, by whatever method is fair and reasonable. 3683 VAEC6160

An assessment may **normally** be made for the whole of an accounting period, provided that the last day of that period is within the relevant time limit. 3684

EXAMPLE On 20 September 2015 A Ltd receives a control visit, in which it is discovered that output tax was under-declared throughout the accounting periods ended 30 June 2011 and 30 September 2011, in circumstances where the 20-year time limit does not apply.
No assessment can be raised for the period ended 30 June 2011 but an assessment can be raised for the whole of the period ended 30 September 2011, provided that it is made by 30 September 2015.

Applying extra-statutory concessions

3686 When raising an assessment, HMRC should normally apply published non-statutory arrangements or concessions, where the taxpayer has met all required terms and conditions.

MEMO POINTS The **First-tier Tribunal** does not have jurisdiction to decide on questions of the application of discretion by HMRC, such as whether to apply the terms of a concession. Questioning such a decision can only be done by means of an application for judicial review in the Upper Tribunal or High Court. However, see ¶4338+ for a discussion as to whether the taxpayer can rely on the doctrine of legitimate expectation.

EXAMPLE HMRC decided not to apply the terms of an extra-statutory concession, and issued an assessment to recover input tax.
The trader applied for a judicial review and it was held that:
- it would be unfair and unlawful if the concession was not applied;
- the taxpayer was entitled to rely on the concession; and
- the assessment was invalid. *R (oao Greenwich Property Ltd) v C & E* [2001]

Misdirection

3687 HMRC has stated (flmemo.co.uk/vm3687) that where it provides information or advice which is incorrect in law it will consider itself bound by such advice, **provided** that it is clear, unequivocal and explicit and the taxpayer can demonstrate that:
- they reasonably relied on the advice where appropriate;
- they made full disclosure of all the relevant facts; and
- strict application of the statute would result in financial detriment to the taxpayer.

The **First-tier Tribunal** does not have the jurisdiction to rule on the application of this policy, but if a taxpayer considers that it has not been fairly applied, they can make a complaint to the Adjudicator (¶4252+), or make an application for judicial review (¶4338+).

Advice no longer binding

3689 HMRC lists (flmemo.co.uk/vm3689) a number of situations where it will no longer consider itself bound by advice it has given. This may be:
- where advice has been given about a **transaction** but the nature of the transaction has changed;
- where the taxpayer has provided **incomplete** or **incorrect** information when asking for advice;
- where a court decision **changes the previously prevailing interpretation** of the law; or
- where **statutory** change occurs.

Notification

3690 VAEC6010+ HMRC **normally** writes to the trader before making an assessment, to set out the reasons for the assessment and a calculation of the arrears. The trader will normally be allowed 3 weeks in which to reply. The reasons for sending this letter are to provide clarity to businesses and reduce the number of unnecessary tribunal appeals, by:

a. allowing the business:
- time to consider and understand the details of an assessment before it is made;

– to provide further evidence or information which may affect the basis of the assessment; and
– the opportunity to demonstrate reasonable excuse or to request mitigation, if there is the potential liability to a penalty;
b. assisting the business to complete a notice of appeal form, if necessary; and
c. demonstrating that an assessment has been made in a reasonable manner.
A letter **will not be sent** if there is a danger that the time limit for making an assessment will be passed, or the nature of the irregularity is agreed or already clear.

2. Calculation of an assessment

a. Records adequate

Where adequate records are maintained, but tax has been under-declared, assessments will normally be based largely or wholly on the business records. **3692**

Where **some information is missing**, an assessment may be based on an analysis or extrapolation of whatever details are available, if this is done on a reasonable basis.

EXAMPLE Where some of a retail trader's till rolls had been illegible or missing, HMRC arrived at the sales figure for the period in question by using the cumulative grand totals recorded by the till at the start and end of the period.
It was held that HMRC had made the assessment to the best of its judgment. *Majid & Partners* [1993] (VTD 11872)

b. Records inadequate or non-existent

Where records are inadequate or non-existent, other methods of arriving at the assessable amount will be used. There is no single or ideal method of calculating arrears which satisfies the requirement that an assessment is made to the best of HMRC's judgment. **3693**

If there are **no accounting records**, HMRC is entitled to assess an amount at the top end of a wide range of possible figures, and the onus is on the trader to show that the assessment is incorrect. *M Spillane v C & E* [1990]

The **method used** in each case will depend on the nature of the business and the records maintained. Methods used by HMRC include the following: **3695**

Method	¶¶
Mark-up exercise	¶3696+
Observation of the business	¶3699
Invigilation of sales	¶3701
Use of direct tax figures	¶3702
Allowance for input tax	¶3704

Mark-up exercise

HMRC may use estimates of turnover derived from applying an appropriate mark-up to the cost of purchases. **3696** VAEC1490

Whilst a mark-up exercise will be relatively straightforward if a single product is sold, it will be more difficult where sales consist of different volumes of different products with different mark-ups. In such cases **a weighted mark-up** may be calculated.

EXAMPLE

1. A newsagent sells many different products. A weighted mark-up may be calculated as follows:

Band of product	Purchases £	Average mark-up %	Sales based on mark-up £
Tobacco	14,675	9.67	16,094
Newspapers	10,456	22.44	12,802
Confectionery	9,876	13.64	11,223
Soft drinks	5,643	23.89	6,991
Greetings cards	2,345	67.98	3,939
Total	42,995		51,049

The weighted mark-up is 18.73%. $\frac{(51{,}049 - 42{,}995)}{42{,}995} \times 100$

2. An assessment was made in respect of restaurant takings, based on:
- a mark-up of 130% on sales of drinks, being the average mark-up for 13 varieties of drinks; and
- drinks sales being estimated as 12% of total sales.

The trader appealed against the assessment, but it was held that it had been made to the best of HMRC's judgment. *SY Seto v C & E* [1981]

3698 Allowance must be made for **factors** such as wastage, destruction or theft of goods, and sales at a lower price than normal. An assessment based on a mark-up exercise is not made to the best of HMRC's judgment if such factors have not been taken into account.

EXAMPLE An assessment was set aside where HMRC had not taken wastage of materials into account. The tribunal stated that: "It is not enough to go through the motions of a mark-up exercise, however faultless one's arithmetic, merely on the basis of what one is told; one should apply some common sense to the analysis of the situation." *DJ Milliner & RF Burt* [1995] (VTD 13438)

Observation of the business

3699 VAEC1470 HMRC may observe the operation of a business over a period of time, in order to **ascertain** the manner of trading, level of activity and other matters.

The information gathered may be used in making an assessment.

EXAMPLE

1. HMRC observed a food takeaway premises for the whole of the business's trading hours on 4 separate days, made test purchases and analysed till rolls. On the basis of the information and evidence gathered, HMRC concluded that 39.4% of sales were unrecorded, and made assessments accordingly.
It was held that the observation evidence was valid. *Tit Keung Chan* [1997] (VTD 14940)

2. A tribunal reduced the amount of assessments which were based largely on an inadequate observation of numbers of people entering the business premises on one day, and which did not take other factors into account. *Café Da Vinci and Da Vinci Too* [1992] (VTD 7298)

Invigilation of sales

3701 VAEC1480 HMRC may visit a business to check that the trader correctly records sales as they occur over a given period. If the **level of sales** during the invigilation period is higher than previously declared, this may indicate that not all sales have been recorded in the past, and assessments may be made for earlier accounting periods.

MEMO POINTS HMRC's policy is to obtain a trader's **consent** before carrying out an invigilation exercise.

EXAMPLE HMRC checked meter readings on gaming machines at a snooker club on 5 out of 6 consecutive days.

Comparison of the metered figures to previously declared figures indicated an estimated takings under-declaration rate of 29.44%. An assessment, which was upheld, was raised for earlier periods on that basis. *RR Elson* [2001] (VTD 17466)

Use of direct tax figures

In the **absence of other information**, HMRC may base a VAT assessment on figures arrived at for income tax or corporation tax purposes. **3702** VAEC1500

EXAMPLE An income tax assessment was made on a trader following an investigation. HMRC made a VAT assessment based on those figures, which was upheld. *Malcolm Groundwell (t/a Angling and Hiking Centre)* [1994]

Allowance for input tax

An assessment may make allowance for **unclaimed** input tax where, for example, both sales and purchases have been understated. **3704** VAEC3040

Evidence of entitlement to an input tax deduction will normally be required, and an allowance may not be made where sales have been suppressed.

EXAMPLE HMRC made an assessment based on observations which showed that sales had been suppressed. The trader appealed on the ground that the assessment had not been made using best judgment, because no allowance had been made for input tax.
It was held that the assessment was valid, because it was based on suppressed sales which had been calculated in a fair manner. It had been assumed that all allowable input tax would have been claimed, and HMRC was not obliged to examine every invoice. *Nemonthron Restaurants Ltd* [2003] (VTD 18123)

3. Particular situations

Partnerships

Where the members of a partnership have **changed** during a period which is to be assessed, separate assessments must be sent to each group of partners if the partners' names are shown in the VAT-registered name of the business. **3705** s 45 VATA 1994; VAEC6170

Groups

An assessment in respect of a VAT group (¶8800+) may include misdeclarations made by **former group members** during periods when they were part of the group. **3707** VAEC6180+

If the **representative member** of a group **changes**, assessments are always made on the current representative member, irrespective of the period to which the assessment relates. *Thorn plc* [1997] (VTD 15283)

Businesses using retail schemes

If a business uses a retail scheme (¶6325+) for which it is **ineligible**, it will normally be expected to recalculate its liability, using a different scheme if appropriate, and an assessment may be made if any tax has been misdeclared, together with interest and penalties if appropriate. **3708** VAEC3030+

If a trader **changes** a scheme during a scheme year without authority (¶6360+), any necessary assessment will be based on the scheme which the trader should have continued to use.

Dissolved companies

An assessment **cannot be made** where a company has been struck off the register of companies. HMRC will, however, consider reinstating a company in order to make an assessment if: **3710** VAEC3550

- assets are identified which would make this worthwhile; or
- evasion is involved, and tax or a penalty could be recovered from a director.

If a dissolved company was a **sham**, HMRC may be able to establish that the trade was being carried on by one or more individuals, on whom it may be able to make an assessment.

SECTION 3

Recovery of unpaid VAT

3730 VAT which is due from any person is recoverable as a debt due to the Crown.

Sch 11 para 5 VATA 1994; SI 1995/2518 reg 47

MEMO POINTS **Unpaid payments on account**, and any sum shown as VAT on an invoice, even if issued by an unregistered trader, are recoverable as if they were VAT.

A. Informal debt collection procedures

3734 Where appropriate, HMRC will telephone a trader to:
- explain the debt due;
- provide a breakdown of the amount, if required;
- request immediate payment;
- explain the consequences of non-payment; and
- discuss any measures which might help the trader, such as the cash accounting scheme (¶4880+).

Time to pay

3735 If a trader is unable to pay a liability in full by the due date, HMRC may in certain circumstances agree a deferred payment schedule. HMRC will **normally require** payment to be completed before the due date of the liability for the next period. HMRC is unlikely to enter into such agreements on a regular basis.

A **written proposal** should be sent to HMRC, who may require evidence of the trader's inability to pay, including bank and credit card statements, income and expenditure schedules, and evidence of attempts to obtain alternative funding.

Set off against liability

3737 **Amount owed by HMRC** If HMRC owes an amount to a person, it will **normally** set it off against any VAT, penalty, surcharge or interest owed by that person.

s 81(3) VATA 1994

The **exception** to this rule is where an insolvency procedure applies to the person, and:
- the liability to pay HMRC arose, or relates to a period, before the insolvency procedure commenced; and
- the credit from HMRC became due after the insolvency procedure commenced.

MEMO POINTS An **insolvency procedure** is treated as applying to a person when:
- an administration, bankruptcy or winding-up order is made;
- an award of sequestration is made;
- they are put into administrative receivership;
- in the case of a company, a voluntary winding-up resolution is passed;
- an approved voluntary arrangement or registered deed of arrangement takes effect; or
- the person's estate becomes vested in any other person as that person's trustee under a trust deed.

3738 HMRC cannot settle a company's VAT liability by setting off a **repayment due to an associated company** because the legal entities are not the same. Even a VAT repayment due to a VAT group representative member cannot be set off against a debt belonging to another member of that VAT group.

DMBM700060

However, if joint and several liability for VAT applies within a supply chain (¶3570+), a VAT repayment due to any of the entities involved can be set off against the joint and several debt for which all are liable.

3740 **Security** If a trader has provided security (¶3546+), HMRC will call this in and set it against the outstanding liability before taking any further action.

B. Formal debt recovery action

1. General principles

If a debt remains outstanding after informal recovery action, it will be referred to HMRC's Debt Management and Banking unit, and **further action** will be considered where the debt exceeds £10,000, or the trader is considered to be a risk to tax revenues. **3744** DMBM650000+

Guidance has been published in HMRC's Debt Management and Banking Manual (DMBM).

Businesses with annual VAT liabilities of **over £300,000** are dealt with by a separate Large Payers Unit, which will decide on any further debt recovery action.

New measures are likely to be introduced after the general election in 2015 which will give HMRC powers to **recover tax debts directly** from taxpayers' bank and building society accounts. The original proposals were modified in late 2014 to build in a number of safeguards following further consultation. It remains to be seen how the system will operate in practice.

Further action taken depends on the trader's jurisdiction and can include: **3745**

Action	England, Wales and Northern Ireland	¶¶	Scotland	¶¶
Seizing and selling trader's goods	Distress (also known as distraint)	¶3753+		
Enforcing payment from trader's assets or earnings			Diligence	¶3774+
Obtaining a debt recovery judgement	Action in county court or High Court	¶3780+	Action in sheriff court or Court of Session	¶3780+
Compromise agreement with individual trader	Voluntary arrangements	¶3784+, ¶3788	Trust deed	¶3784+, ¶3792
Compromise agreement with company	Company voluntary arrangement	¶3784+, ¶3794	Company voluntary arrangement	¶3784+, ¶3794
Compromise agreement with partnership	Partnership voluntary arrangement	¶3784+, ¶3806	Trust deed	¶3784+, ¶3792
Insolvency proceedings against individual trader	Bankruptcy	¶3810+	Sequestration	¶3815+
Insolvency proceedings against company or LLP	Winding-up petition (High Court)	¶3820+	Winding-up petition (Court of Session)	¶3820+
Insolvency proceedings against partnership	Winding-up petition (High Court) or personal bankruptcy of partners	¶3826+	Sequestration	¶3815+
Recovery in another EU state	Recovery by member jurisdiction	¶3832	Recovery by member jurisdiction	¶3832

Exceptions

Formal debt recovery action will normally not be taken where: **3746** DMBM605420
- this would be undesirable due to the trader's circumstances, including **serious illness, mental illness**, or **extreme old age**, or where there are human rights implications;

– the debt is subject to **dispute or appeal** (though this does not apply to enquiry cases involving avoidance schemes or arrangements);
– there is a **Time to pay** arrangement in place;
– the trader is under **investigation**, or prosecution is being considered;
– the trader is a **trust** or a **registered charity**.

Time limits

3747 DMBM595080 Except in Scotland, the normal limitation period for taking debt recovery action does not apply to the recovery of tax liabilities. HMRC can therefore take recovery action for VAT irrespective of the age of the debt.

The time limit for collection of debts in **Scotland** is 20 years.

Ending formal action

3748 A **taxpayer** can normally bring an end to formal recovery action by paying the outstanding amount in full, or making an acceptable offer with regard to the amount or a payment period.

Particular types of business

3750 DMBM530200 **Unincorporated associations** Although an association is not a legal entity separate from its members, it may be wound up as an unregistered company under Part V of the Insolvency Act 1986 if its constitution and rules provide for it to be so wound up.

3751 **Overseas traders** HMRC will normally only take formal action to recover the UK VAT liability of an overseas trader from a **VAT representative** (¶7210+) after all possible action has been taken against the trader.

No action can be taken against **UK agents** (¶7095+), as they are not liable for debts incurred by the trader.

2. Distress or diligence

a. England, Wales and Northern Ireland

Distress

3753 s 51 FA 1997; SI 1997/1431 The levy of distress (also known as distraint) is the process by which HMRC takes possession of a trader's goods or chattels, sells them, and sets the receipts against the trader's outstanding VAT liability.

A court order is not required, so distraint is often the first type of formal recovery action taken by HMRC, as it is quick and cost-effective. In many cases, the threat of distraint results in traders paying the outstanding VAT to avoid the inconvenience, embarrassment or cost which distraint might cause.

Sch 12 Tribunals, Courts and Enforcement Act 2007 MEMO POINTS Legislation was enacted in 2007 to provide for a **new distress procedure**. However, the legislation is not yet in force.

3754 DMBM 655030, 655710+ **Legal basis** When distress action is taken, **ownership** of the goods which are removed does not pass to HMRC.

If goods **cannot be removed** for any reason, and a walking possession agreement (¶3765) is not signed, the distraint ends, and possession of the goods remains with the owner.

HMRC has a prior right over others to levy distress in satisfaction of a debt. *Attorney-General v Leonard* [1888] Distress does not, however, take precedence over a lien for unpaid rent by a landlord.

When distress can be levied

HMRC has the power to levy distress if a trader does not pay a tax liability after the trader has been sent a written demand for payment. Distress can be levied **after** the end of the time limit for an appeal against the amount demanded. **3756** SI 1997/1431 regs 4, 5

How distress is levied

Authorisation A **warrant** is required, which must: **3757** SI 1997/1431 reg 4
- be signed by an HMRC officer; and
- name the individual authorised to levy distress.

MEMO POINTS Distress can be **levied by**:
- a bailiff alone;
- an HMRC officer alone;
- an HMRC officer accompanied by a bailiff; or
- two HMRC officers.

Action before levying distress A **final request** for payment of the tax will be made, usually by telephone, and if necessary the trader will be allowed to obtain money from a bank, building society or other source. **3759** DMBM655420+

If **payment is not made**, distress will be levied, unless new information of, for example, serious illness, is discovered on arrival.

HMRC recovers **costs** wherever possible. **3760** DMBM655880

If a **Time to pay** arrangement is agreed, one of the conditions is that payments are **allocated** firstly against costs.

In **other cases**, payments are allocated firstly against tax, on the basis that collection of tax is a priority, and costs are a secondary consideration.

Location Distress can be levied anywhere, including on a public highway, provided that the owner of the goods is present. However, distress will **normally be levied** at: **3762** SI 1997/1431 reg 4(3); DMBM655730
- the personal address of a trader;
- the trader's business address; or
- the registered office of a company.

Distress may be levied simultaneously at more than one location if the defaulter has goods in several places (for example, a chain of shops).

Forced entry to premises is not permitted.

Time Distraint can only be **commenced**: **3763** SI 1997/1431 reg 7

a. between 8.00am and 8.00pm; or

b. during business hours, if outside the above hours.

If distraint is commenced within the permitted hours, it can be **continued until** completed.

Walking possession agreements A trader will usually be invited to sign a walking possession agreement as an alternative to removal of their goods and chattels. Under this agreement, the owner of the assets is allowed to retain possession, but the assets must not be removed without the consent of HMRC. **3765** SI 1997/1431 reg 2; DMBM655890

An agreement will normally be **signed by** the proprietor of a business, a partner in a partnership, or a director or company secretary of a company. If some other person signs it, no penalty (¶4130+) can be charged if the agreement is breached.

MEMO POINTS The agreement will **contain** a date on which the goods and chattels will be removed if payment has still not been made. At least 6 days will be allowed; HMRC normally allows 21 days, unless a longer payment period has been agreed.

3766 SI 1997/1431 regs 4, 6 and Sch 1; DMBM655130

Goods and chattels which can be taken Any goods and chattels belonging to the person can be taken, **except** for assets which are subject to a fixed charge, and those listed in the following table:

Location of goods and chattels	Items which cannot be taken
Business premises	Fire fighting equipment for use on the premises
	Medical aids and medical equipment for use on the premises
Dwelling house, where the items are reasonably required for the domestic needs of any resident	Beds and bedding, household linen and furniture used for storing clothing, bedding or household linen
	Chairs, settees and tables
	Lights and light fittings
	Heating appliances
	Curtains and floor coverings
	Food, refrigerators and furniture, equipment and utensils used for cooking, storing or eating food, and furniture used for storing cooking utensils
	Articles used for cleaning the home, or for cleaning, mending or pressing clothes, and furniture used for storing articles used for cleaning the home
	Articles used for safety in the home
	Toys used by any child in the household
	Medical aids and medical equipment

3768 DMBM655110+

It is HMRC's **policy** not to take possession of the following goods and chattels:

Location of goods and chattels	Goods	Details
Business premises	Computers	HMRC will exercise discretion if there are possible issues in relation to copyright or other matters. The owner will also be given the opportunity to remove information or software.
	Machinery, fixtures and fittings	Not taken if permanently fixed to the premises.
	Tools of the trade	Only taken if no other assets available. Those which are taken should be least likely to impair the running of the business.
Any	Perishable items e.g. food	Not taken if they cannot be restored to the owner in the same condition.
	Jewellery	
	Live animals	
	Money	

Post-distress action

3769 DMBM655880

VAT paid before goods sold If the trader pays the VAT liability before any goods or chattels have been sold, they will be restored to the trader, who will need to arrange their return and pay any related costs.

3771 SI 1997/1431 reg 9

Sale of the goods If the VAT liability and costs of distraint have not been paid within 5 days of distress being levied, goods and chattels which are not subject to a walking possession agreement will be sold. The proceeds will be applied in settlement of the VAT liability and distraint costs, and any remaining surplus will be paid to the trader.

Costs The trader is liable for all costs of distraint. 3772 SI 1997/1431 regs 8, 10

Bailiffs can retain their costs from the proceeds of sale, after deducting the VAT liability which is paid to HMRC.

If the **amount** of costs is **disputed**, a county court will assess these and make an appropriate order.

b. Scotland

Diligence

Diligence is the process under which HMRC can enforce payment of VAT from a person's assets, earnings or funds. 3774 SI 1995/2518 reg 213

HMRC must apply to a sheriff for a warrant authorising recovery of the tax due. The application must enclose a **certificate**, which must:

a. set out:
- the amount due; and
- the name of the person who owes the VAT; and

b. state that payment of the sum in question has been demanded but not received.

The **sheriff officer** is then responsible for enforcing payment. If payment is not made after issue of a warrant, the sheriff can order payment by means of:
- an attachment;
- an earnings arrestment; or
- a general arrestment and action of forthcoming.

Attachment The sheriff officer can visit premises and value goods. Normally, only business goods would be subject to this process but any **personal goods** held outside the living area of a home, such as a car, can be included. 3775

The **sheriff officer must report** the list of goods to the court within 14 days, after which 7 days' notice must be given to the owner of the goods before they can be removed. HMRC can arrange for the goods to be sold after 7 days have elapsed after removal, and the proceeds are used to pay the VAT liability.

HMRC may, **in exceptional circumstances**, make a separate application to the court for an Exceptional Attachment Order. This would enable a sheriff officer to enter a home to attach non-essential goods.

Earnings arrestments Under an earnings arrestment, a person's **employer** would be ordered to deduct an amount from each salary payment and pay this direct to HMRC, **until** the: 3777
- liability is fully paid;
- employment ceases; or
- arrestment is abandoned.

Comment As arrestments cannot be made on **self-employed** earnings, VAT would rarely be recovered in this way.

General arrestments Under a general arrestment, a sheriff can order a third party, such as a bank or building society, not to release funds belonging to a trader until payment of the liability has been made. 3778

Payment of VAT can be **effected** by:
- the trader signing a mandate authorising payment to HMRC; or
- the sheriff officer applying to the court for an action of forthcoming, under which the court orders payment of the liability from the funds held by the third party.

3. Court action

HMRC can bring a debt recovery action in a county court or High Court or, in Scotland, a sheriff court or Court of Session. 3780

Enforcement of judgment

3782 ss 13 - 17 Crown Proceedings Act 1947; SI 1998/3132 Schs 1, 2

If the court awards judgment in favour of HMRC, it will order payment of the liability immediately, unless the defendant has applied, and the court has agreed, that the liability may be paid in instalments.

If payment remains outstanding, HMRC can apply for enforcement to be effected by any of the following means:

Means	Details
Warrant of execution [1]	Goods or assets belonging to the taxpayer are seized and sold
Third-party debt order	Amounts owed to the taxpayer by a third party are paid to HMRC instead
Charging order	The amount owed to HMRC is secured against the taxpayer's property [2] or other assets
Attachment of earnings order	If the taxpayer is employed or in receipt of an occupational pension, the employer is instructed to deduct regular amounts from the taxpayer's salary or pension
Bankruptcy, sequestration or winding-up	HMRC can commence separate proceedings for insolvency (¶3808+)
Judgment summons	The taxpayer must explain why they have not paid the outstanding debt; the court may make such order as it considers appropriate, such as payment by instalments

Note:
1. A court bailiff must be instructed if the debt is over £5,000.
2. HMRC will generally not force the sale of a property unless it is empty, a second property, or a piece of land.

4. Compromise agreements

3784 A compromise agreement is one under which a debtor arranges to pay a reduced amount to creditors.

When appropriate

3785 **HMRC** may be prepared to enter into such an arrangement where, for example, the person who owes VAT has a continuing source of income but few or no assets, so that bankruptcy or liquidation would not realise sufficient funds to pay the liability.

A **trader** may be prepared to enter into such an arrangement, rather than risk bankruptcy or winding-up action, because:
- this may allow the business to continue;
- it is less restrictive and costly than bankruptcy or liquidation; and
- it may enable certain assets to be retained.

HMRC's criteria

3787 HMRC considers each case on its own merits. The factors which HMRC will take into account are as follows:

In favour of accepting a proposal	Against accepting a proposal
Full and honest financial disclosure	Evidence of deliberate default or evasion, or past association with a contrived insolvency
Offer to creditors is optimised and achievable	Policy of withholding payment of Crown money
Provision made for payment of all future debts on time	Any proposal which does not provide cash, or which requires a sale of HMRC debt
All creditors within the same class treated equally	Failure to meet obligations under a previous voluntary arrangement

In favour of accepting a proposal	Against accepting a proposal
No exceptional reasons for rejection	Exclusion of creditors entitled to be treated the same as others in the same class
	Person paying some of the debts in consideration for purchase of assets
	Any debt being fully paid when all other unsecured debtors will not be fully paid

Individual voluntary arrangements (England, Wales and Northern Ireland)

An individual voluntary arrangement is an agreement, approved by a court, under which an individual debtor pays a reduced amount to their creditors. The debt is paid immediately or over a period, and the arrangement is supervised by an insolvency practitioner. **3788** ss 1, 252 Insolvency Act 1986; ss 226-237 Insolvency (Northern Ireland) Order 1989

MEMO POINTS 1. The following **conditions** must be satisfied:
- a voluntary arrangement covers amounts owed to all creditors;
- an arrangement cannot be proposed within 12 months of the date of a previous proposal; and
- the proposals must be accepted by over 75% of creditors, by value of the amounts owed, but can be blocked by creditors owed more than 25% of the total debt.

2. The **procedure** is as follows:
a. the **trader** must engage an insolvency practitioner, and apply to the High Court for an interim order preventing creditors from taking further action;
b. the **insolvency practitioner** then sends the court details of the proposal, and states whether a creditors' meeting should be arranged to consider it; and
c. the **creditors** then meet and vote whether to accept the proposal. If accepted, the insolvency practitioner will inform the court and supervise payments to the creditors under the terms of the arrangement.

Trust deeds (Scotland)

A trust deed is a **unilateral offer** by an individual or partnership to pay a reduced amount to creditors, normally over a maximum period of 3 years. Court approval is not required. The arrangement is **supervised** by an insolvency practitioner, who administers the debtor's affairs. **3792** Sch 5 Bankruptcy (Scotland) Act 1985

MEMO POINTS 1. The **procedure** is as follows:
a. the **trader** must engage an insolvency practitioner as a trustee, to whom the trader's estate is conveyed for administration; and
b. the **trustee** then sends the creditors details of the proposal (a creditors' meeting is not mandatory, but may be requested by creditors); and
c. the trustee will supervise **payments** to the creditors under the terms of the arrangement.
2. In order **to obtain protection** for the debtor, the trustee may publish details of the trust deed. Unless more than a third of the creditors by value object within 5 weeks, the trustee may send a copy of the trust deed to the Accountant in Bankruptcy. The Accountant in Bankruptcy may then register the deed, after which all creditors are treated as having agreed to the arrangement.

Company voluntary arrangements

A company voluntary arrangement is an agreement, approved by a court, under which a company pays a reduced amount to its creditors. The debt is paid immediately or over a period, and the arrangement is supervised by an insolvency practitioner. **3794** ss 1-7 Insolvency Act 1986; ss 14 - 20 Insolvency (Northern Ireland) Order 1989

MEMO POINTS 1. The following **conditions** must be satisfied:
- the arrangement covers amounts owed to all creditors; and
- the proposals must be accepted by over 75% of creditors, by value of the amounts owed, but can be blocked by creditors owed more than 25% of the total debt.

2. The **procedure** is as follows:
a. the **directors** of the company must engage an insolvency practitioner, and make a proposal to the company's creditors;
b. the **insolvency practitioner** then sends the court details of the proposal and states whether a creditors' meeting should be arranged to consider it (the directors of an eligible company can

also apply to the court for a moratorium preventing creditors from taking further action whilst the proposal is under consideration); and
c. the **creditors** then meet and vote whether to accept the proposal. If accepted, the insolvency practitioner will inform the court and supervise payments to the creditors under the terms of the arrangement.
3. A company is eligible for a **moratorium** if it qualifies as a small company, **unless**:
a. it carries on certain types of insurance, banking or investment business;
b. it is being wound up, or there is a provisional liquidator, or it is in administration or administrative receivership;
c. a voluntary arrangement is already in force, or ended prematurely following the appointment of an administrator; or
d. a moratorium has been in force, or the company appointed an administrator, in the previous 12 months.
4. A **small company** is one which has:
- a turnover of £6.5 million or less;
- balance sheet assets of £3.26 million or less; and
- 50 or fewer employees.

Partnership voluntary arrangements (England, Wales and Northern Ireland)

3806 SI 1994/2421

Partnership voluntary arrangements are similar to company voluntary arrangements.

In practice they are used infrequently, because partners cannot obtain the benefit of an interim order preventing further action by creditors.

They are **mainly used** by partnerships with a large number of members, who wish to avoid bankruptcy and retain control over personal assets.

---

5. Bankruptcy, sequestration and winding up

3808 s 251 Enterprise Act 2002

HMRC will only take bankruptcy, sequestration or winding-up action in serious cases, and as a last resort.

HMRC's **status as a preferential creditor** ceased on 15 September 2003, except for insolvency actions which commenced before that date. HMRC's status as an unsecured creditor now means that it must consider insolvency action more carefully, as in many cases the funds remaining for unsecured creditors can be minimal.

Bankruptcy (England, Wales and Northern Ireland)

3810 s 267 Insolvency Act 1986; DMBM685500+; ss 238 - 320 Insolvency (Northern Ireland) Order 1989

Bankruptcy **applies to** individuals, and the **minimum debt** for which bankruptcy action can be taken is £750.

If bankruptcy action is considered appropriate, a **final warning letter** will be sent to the trader, giving them 7 days to:
- dispute the debt; or
- pay, or negotiate time to pay, the debt.

In the case of a **VAT group**, a warning letter will be sent to each company in the group.

Bankruptcy proceedings may be **commenced** if there is no satisfactory response.

3811 s 310 Insolvency Act 1986

Payment of the tax Following a bankruptcy order, the trader's assets may be realised and distributed to creditors, including HMRC, who will receive some or all of the outstanding amount, depending upon the availability of funds to pay unsecured creditors. **Future income** may also be used to settle debts.

ss 264, 268, 270, 271, 279, 280, 282 Insolvency Act 1986; SI 1986/1925 rule 7.48

MEMO POINTS 1. HMRC must issue a **statutory demand** to a trader before it can commence bankruptcy proceedings. The statutory demand is a legal document which will normally be delivered by hand, but it may be delivered by post if hand delivery has not been possible. The trader has 21 days to respond to the demand. Within that time the trader may, within 18 days, apply for the demand to be set aside if there are grounds for this.

2. A **petition** can be presented in the High Court at any time after service of the statutory demand. It must normally be presented within 4 months of serving the demand, but an application may be made to the court for an extension if a delay was caused by problems serving the demand.
If the trader intends to **oppose** the petition they must, no later than 7 days before the date of the hearing:
- notify the court of the grounds for objecting to the making of a bankruptcy order; and
- send a copy of the notice to HMRC.
3. If HMRC believes there is a **risk that a trader will remove funds or assets**, it can apply to the court for a freezing order. This would freeze the assets until conclusion of the bankruptcy proceedings.
4. If HMRC considers that a **trader's assets** should be **protected** before a bankruptcy order is granted, it may apply to the court for an interim receiver to be appointed. If the court agrees, the Official Receiver will be appointed and will take possession of the trader's assets. The extent of the Official Receiver's powers will be decided by the court, but in general no other unsecured creditor will be able to take action in priority to HMRC. The Official Receiver's appointment ends when a bankruptcy order is made, or the petition is dismissed.
5. The **court can hear a petition** before the end of the 21-day limit for the trader to respond to the statutory demand, but not sooner than 14 days after service of the demand, unless:
- the trader consents;
- the court is satisfied that an early hearing is appropriate; or
- the trader appears to have absconded.
6. The court can **dismiss a petition** if it is satisfied that the trader:
- can pay all their debts; or
- made a payment offer which was unreasonably refused.
HMRC can appeal to the High Court against the dismissal of a petition.
7. If the court is satisfied that the details in the petition are correct, and that there is no reasonable prospect of the debt being paid, it may make a **bankruptcy order**. The trader can appeal against a bankruptcy order to the High Court or Court of Appeal.
The trader may apply to the court for **annulment** of the order at any time, if they can show that the order should not have been made. Grounds for annulment would include:
- a lack of response by HMRC to a request for time to pay after bankruptcy proceedings had started;
- the existence of an agreed time to pay schedule when the bankruptcy order was made;
- payment of the liability in full before the bankruptcy order was made; or
- an error in instructing the solicitor acting for HMRC.
8. A bankrupt can be **discharged** after:
a. payment of the bankruptcy debts in full;
b. a voluntary arrangement (¶3788) has been agreed with the creditors; or
c. a year has elapsed, whether or not the bankruptcy debts have been paid, unless the bankruptcy is:
- the second in 15 years; or
- based on a criminal bankruptcy order.

Sequestration (Scotland)

Sequestration **applies to** individuals and partnerships. The **minimum debt** for which sequestration action can be taken on the application of a creditor is £3,000. **3815** s 5 Bankruptcy (Scotland) Act 1985; ss 25, 26 Bankruptcy and Diligence etc (Scotland) Act 2007

Action can only be taken by a **creditor** where:
- the debtor is apparently insolvent; and
- the creditor has provided the debtor with a debt advice and information package. This is a bundle of documents including details of advice available locally.

MEMO POINTS . The rules for a **debtor petitioning** for their own sequestration are significantly different.

Payment of the tax Following a sequestration award, the Accountant in Bankruptcy will supervise the administration of the sequestration by a permanent trustee, including the payment of debts. The Accountant in Bankruptcy may also act as the trustee. **3816** s 1A Bankruptcy (Scotland) Act 1985

MEMO POINTS 1. A **petition** must be presented in a sheriff court. If the trader intends to **oppose** the petition they must, within 14 days of being notified by the court, appear before the court to show cause why sequestration should not be awarded. s 12(2), (3A) Bankruptcy (Scotland) Act 1985

2. The court can **dismiss** a petition if the trader:
– shows cause why sequestration cannot competently be awarded;
– pays all the debts forthwith;
– produces written evidence of payment of the debts; or
– shows that there is sufficient security for the payment of the debts.
HMRC can **appeal** to the court against the dismissal of a petition. An appeal must be made within 14 days of the date of the order dismissing the petition.

ss 12(3), 15, 16, 17 Bankruptcy (Scotland) Act 1985

3. If the debtor does not appear before the court, or if the court is satisfied that the details in the petition are correct, it may make a **sequestration award**. The trader can **appeal** to the court against a sequestration award. An appeal must be made within 14 days of the date of the award.

4. A sequestration can be **recalled** if the court is satisfied that:
a. in all the circumstances it is appropriate;
b. the debtor has fully paid all debts or has provided sufficient security for their payment;
c. an alternative sequestration award or equivalent arrangement has been granted; or
d. a majority of the creditors by value reside in a country other than Scotland, and it is more appropriate that affairs be administered in that other country.
A debtor can **petition** the court for a recall within 10 weeks of the date of the award, or at any time where any of **b.** to **d.** above applies.

3817
ss 54, 54A, 54B Bankruptcy (Scotland) Act 1985; s 17 Bankruptcy and Debt Advice (Scotland) Act 2014; SI 2014/261

Discharge For **petitions granted prior to 1 April 2015**, a debtor will be discharged after 1 year from the date of the sequestration, unless the permanent trustee or a creditor applies for a deferment at least 3 months before the date of automatic discharge.

For petitions granted **on or after 1 April 2015**, the rules are significantly different with no automatic discharge. Where the **Accountant in Bankruptcy is the trustee**, they will review the debtor's position after 12 months and can discharge them at any time after this. They will send a report of their decision and give details of the following to the debtor and any known creditors:
– the debtor's assets, liabilities, financial affairs and business affairs;
– the debtor's conduct in relation to the above;
– the sequestration; and
– the debtor's conduct during the sequestration, including compliance with the financial undertakings imposed.

Where the debtor is not discharged the position should be reviewed after a further 12 months.

Where the **Accountant in Bankruptcy is not the trustee**, a slightly different procedure is followed. In this case, the trustee provides a report to the Accountant in Bankruptcy to consider. The debtor and all known creditors are also provided with a copy of the report, and are given the opportunity to make representations prior to the Accountant in Bankruptcy making their decision.

In either case the trustee, the debtor, or any creditor has a **right of appeal** against any decision, and this must be made within 14 days of the date on which notice of the decision is given.

Winding up

3820
ss 117, 120, 123 Insolvency Act 1986; SI 2001/1090 reg 5

Companies and limited liability partnerships HMRC can present a petition for the winding up of a company or a limited liability partnership to the High Court or, in Scotland, the Court of Session.

The **minimum debt** for which bankruptcy or winding-up action can be taken is £750, **unless** it can be proved to the satisfaction of a court that a company is unable to pay its debts as they fall due. A court will normally be satisfied that a **company is unable to pay its debts** if it owes a debt:
– that is due;
– that has been demanded and remains unpaid; and
– which there are no substantial grounds for disputing.

s 143 Insolvency Act 1986

Following a winding-up order, the company's assets will be realised and distributed to creditors, including HMRC, who will receive some or all of the outstanding amount, depending upon the availability of funds to pay unsecured creditors.

MEMO POINTS 1. As a court needs proof that a company is unable to pay its debts, HMRC will issue a **warning letter** to a trader before commencing winding-up proceedings. The letter will set out the amount due and warn that proceedings will be taken if payment is not made. If the trader does not respond within 7 days, HMRC will commence the winding-up action. s 125 Insolvency Act 1986; SI 1986/1925 rules 4.11, 4.25, 7.47; DMBM685500+

2. The winding-up petition must be:
- served on the company at least 14 days before the date of the hearing; and
- advertised in the *London Gazette* or a specified newspaper at least 7 days after service of the petition on the company, and at least 7 days before the date of the hearing, unless the court agrees to dispense with an advertisement (e.g. where it would cause serious damage to the company).

If the company intends to **oppose** the petition it must, no later than 7 days before the date of the hearing:
- notify the court of its grounds for objecting to the making of a winding-up order; and
- send a copy of the notice to HMRC.

The **court can hear a petition** at any time more than 14 days after service of the petition.

3. If HMRC believes there is a **risk that a company will remove funds or assets**, it can apply to the court for a freezing order. This would freeze the assets until conclusion of the winding-up proceedings.

4. If HMRC considers that a **company's assets** should be **protected** before a winding-up order is granted, it may apply to the court for a provisional liquidator to be appointed. If the court agrees, a provisional liquidator will be appointed to carry out such functions as the court directs. The provisional liquidator's appointment ends when a winding-up order is made, or the petition is dismissed.

5. The court can **dismiss** a petition on any grounds. For example, a petition may be dismissed if:

a. it was not advertised as required; or

b. the court is not satisfied that the debt is due or undisputed.

HMRC can appeal to the High Court against the dismissal of a petition.

6. If the court considers it appropriate, it will make a **winding-up order**.

An application can be made to the court for the order to be **rescinded**, within 7 days of the date of the order. The company cannot itself apply, although it can apply jointly with a creditor, shareholder or other person liable to contribute to the company's assets, if it can show that the order should not have been made.

Grounds for cancellation include:
- a lack of response by HMRC to a request for time to pay after winding-up proceedings had started;
- the existence of an agreed time to pay schedule when the winding-up order was made;
- payment of the liability in full before the winding-up order was made; or
- an error in instructing the solicitor acting for HMRC.

7. A company can **appeal** against a winding-up order to the High Court or Court of Appeal within 14 days of the date of the order. The court may postpone advertising the order pending the appeal hearing.

Dissolved companies If HMRC **objects to** an application for a company to be **struck off** the register of companies, it may notify the registrar of companies within 3 months of the date of publication of the striking-off application. **3823** s 1003 Companies Act 2006

Reasons for objecting include:
- ongoing or proposed action to recover money from the company; or
- wrongful trading or commission of a tax fraud or other offence.

MEMO POINTS If HMRC believes that **recovery action** can be taken against a dissolved company it may, within 6 years of the date of dissolution, apply to the court for an order declaring the dissolution to be cancelled and the company restored to the register. ss 1029, 1032 Companies Act 2006; SI 2008/2860

If the company was dissolved before 1 October 2007 under the provisions of the Companies Act 1985 (either on an application by the company or automatically by Companies House), HMRC may apply for a court order for the company's restoration by the earlier of:
- 1 October 2015; or
- 20 years from the date of publication of the company's dissolution.

Partnerships (England, Wales and Northern Ireland) A partnership is not a separate legal entity, but it can be wound up as an unregistered company, which would enable control of the partnership's **business assets** to pass to the Official Receiver. **3826** SI 1994/2421 regs 7, 8

A winding-up or bankruptcy petition may also be presented in relation to one or more of the partners, which would allow access to their **personal assets**.

A **payment** by one or more of the partners discharges the joint liability of other partners. The partners can decide on how payments are to be allocated between them.

3827 HMRC can use **three different methods** to recover VAT from a partnership, as summarised in the following table:

Type of action	Does Official Receiver have access to partner's personal assets?	Winding-up petition must be presented within 3 years of cessation of trading?
Winding up of the partnership	n	y
Winding up of the partnership, and bankruptcy or winding up of one or more partners	y[1]	
Winding up or bankruptcy of one or more partners	y	n

Note:
1. After liquidation of the partnership estate. Partners' personal assets will be frozen from the date of the bankruptcy or winding-up order.

DMBM685500+ MEMO POINTS 1. In all cases HMRC will issue a **warning letter** to a partnership before commencing winding-up proceedings. If the partnership does not respond within 7 days, HMRC will commence the winding-up action.
2. HMRC must issue a **statutory demand** to a partnership and, if applicable, its partners before HMRC can commence winding-up or bankruptcy proceedings. The recipients have 21 days to respond to the demand. Any partner who receives an individual demand may, within 18 days, apply for it to be set aside if there are grounds for this.
3. The rules for **presenting and hearing a petition** for:
- winding up a partnership are as in ¶3820; and
- bankruptcy or winding up of a partner are as in ¶3811.

If petitions are presented both in relation to the partnership and one or more of the partners, the partnership petition is heard first. If a partnership petition is dismissed, any petitions against the partners will also be dismissed.

3830 **Limited partners** The court can dismiss a petition against a limited partner if the partner:
- provides the court with money or security up to the extent of their liability; or
- satisfies the court that they are no longer under any liability in respect of partnership debts.

6. Recovery in another EU member state

3832 EU Directive 1976/308; DMBM560010+ HMRC can ask another EU member state to recover UK VAT on its behalf from a debtor who resides or has assets in that state. The competent authority may take recovery proceedings under the appropriate national legislation.

The following **conditions** must normally all be met:
- the amount owed is at least €1,500 (or the sterling equivalent);
- the debt is as declared on VAT returns or as assessed by HMRC;
- the debt is not subject to review or appeal; and
- recovery action within the UK has been exhausted.

CHAPTER 2

Default interest

OUTLINE ¶¶

Default interest is a compliance measure which is **intended to**: 3880
a. improve the timeliness and accuracy of VAT returns submitted by traders; and
b. provide commercial restitution to HMRC, where tax has been understated.

A trader who **over-declares** VAT does not receive interest on a repayment, but an over-declaration may be set off against an under-declaration in the same VAT period (2987+).

Interest can be charged **in addition to** a civil or criminal penalty.

A. General principles

When chargeable

Default interest can be charged only if HMRC has **made an assessment**, or (in one case only) if it could have made an assessment but the tax concerned has already been repaid. The various possible circumstances are shown in the following table: 3884 s 74 VATA1994; Notice 700/43; VDIM 1030

Situation	Assessed under	Details of the assessment	¶¶
Assessment made for an amount which a taxable person has failed to declare on a VAT return	VATA 1994 s 74(1)(a)(i)	Relates to a period for which a VAT return was submitted	
	VATA 1994 s 74(1)(a)(ii)	Trader has accepted a central assessment which is later found to have been too low	¶3652+
	VATA 1994 s 74(1)(c)	Relates to a period at the start of which the trader was incorrectly exempted from registration on the ground of only making zero-rated supplies	¶2652+
	VATA 1994 s 74(1)(b)	Relates to a period exceeding three months and commencing on the date on which the trader registered or became liable to register	¶2666+

Situation	Assessed under	Details of the assessment	¶¶
Assessment made to recover some other amount	VATA 1994 s 73(2), 80(4A)	Amount incorrectly claimed, and credited or repaid by HMRC	
	FA 2008 Sch 41 para 2	Amount shown as VAT on invoice issued by an unauthorised person	¶4020+
	VATA 1994 s 73(7)	Trader fails to account satisfactorily to HMRC for goods received, acquired or imported in the course of a business	¶3906
	VATA 1994 s 73(7A) - (7B)	Fiscal warehousekeeper fails to account for VAT as required	¶9272
	VATA 1994 s 80B	Trader receives a VAT refund on condition that it be passed on to customers, but fails to do so	¶3256
	VATA 1994 s 78A	Trader receives statutory interest which should not have been paid	¶3270+
	VATA 1994 Sch 9A para 6	Assessment following a direction to change or impose a VAT grouping arrangement	¶8878+
	FA 2012 Sch 38 para 29	Assessment of a penalty on a dishonest tax agent	¶4026
Trader corrects an error above the threshold	VATA 1994 s 74(2)	If HMRC could have made an assessment, but did not need to do so because the tax was repaid voluntarily. Corrections below the threshold do not attract interest.	¶3020+

Exceptions

3886 s 76 VATA 1994; VAT Notice 700/43 para 2.4

The following items are not subject to default interest:
- **late payment of VAT** correctly shown on a VAT return (but see ¶4082+ for the default surcharge);
- **central assessments**, unless accepted and subsequently found to be too low (¶3652+);
- **amendments** made to returns before they have been fully processed;
- **penalties**; or
- **unpaid interest charges**.

Discretion

3888 s 135 FA 2008; VDIM 3020

Except in the case of a disaster of national significance, the legislation makes **no provision** for reasonable excuse or mitigation in relation to default interest. However, HMRC states that it will exercise discretion regarding interest charges where a charge would not amount to commercial restitution.

Appeals

3891 s 83(1)(q) VATA 1994

There is no right of review, and only a limited right of appeal against an interest charge. An appeal cannot be made on the ground that there was a reasonable excuse, and the **matters which can be appealed** are restricted to the following:

Matters which can be appealed	Matters which cannot be appealed
Amount of an interest charge	The imposition of a charge
Issue of an interest assessment outside the normal time limits (¶3896)	The rate at which interest is charged

B. Calculation of interest

The **rate** at which interest is charged is based on a specific formula. The most recent rates can be found at ¶9972. 3895

MEMO POINTS HMRC operates a **harmonised interest regime** for almost all taxes and duties that it administers. The legislation provides for the automatic setting and implementation of interest rate changes. The default interest rate is 2.5 percentage points above the Bank of England base rate.

Period

The **maximum period** for which interest can be charged is three years, ending on the date when the calculation is made. 3896 s 74 VATA 1994; VDIM 2040

Subject to the 3-year time limit, the **start and end dates** for the calculation of interest are shown in the following table:

VDIM 5030-5050

Nature of under-declaration	Start date	End date
Unauthorised issue of tax invoices	Date of invoice	Date on which the tax is assessed or disclosed[1]
Overpaid refund or credit	7th day after the date on which HMRC issued the repayment instructions	
All other under-declarations	Day after the return submission deadline for the period to which the tax relates	

Note:
1. The **end date** is strictly the date of payment of the VAT, but in practice interest is calculated up to the date of assessment or disclosure. Further interest will only be charged if the VAT remains unpaid for more than 30 days thereafter. If a trader can prove beyond reasonable doubt that payment of interest-bearing tax was posted in sufficient time to be received within the 30-day period, no further interest will be charged.

Over-declarations

HMRC does not pay interest on over-declarations. However, when calculating interest on an under-declaration, any separate over-declaration for the same VAT period will be netted off, provided that it has been assessed or disclosed **before interest is charged** on the under-declared amount. *London Borough of Camden* [1993] (VTD 10476) 3898 VDIM 4030

An over-declaration which is assessed or disclosed **after interest has been charged** cannot be set against the under-declaration, and such interest will not be reduced or refunded. *Mackenzie* [1993] (VTD 11597)

EXAMPLE On 1 April 2015 HMRC visited Mr A and discovered the following under-declarations and over-declarations:

Period ended	Liability/ (repayment) shown on return	Under-declarations	Over-declarations	Net under-declaration (over-declaration)
	£	£	£	£
30 June 2014	6,000	3,500	1,000	2,500
30 September 2014	(2,000)[1]		5,000	(5,000)
31 December 2014	7,000	7,000	1,000	6,000

Note:
1. Repayment instructions issued 3 November 2014.

The tax and interest assessment was calculated on 15 April 2015. The assessment was issued on 21 April 2015 and Mr A paid the tax and interest on 1 May 2015.
It was then found during the preparation of accounts for the year ended 31 December 2014 that a purchase invoice dated 20 February 2014 had not been recorded. The invoice showed input tax

of £3,000. On 1 June 2015 Mr A makes a notification of the over-declared tax for the period ended 31 March 2014.

Interest from the start date of 1 August 2014 to the end date of 15 April 2015 is calculated as follows:

Interest period	Number of days	Amount on which interest due	Interest rate[4]	Interest charge[5,6]	Total interest
		£	%	£	£
1 Aug to 9 Nov 2014	99	2,500	3.0	20.34	20.34
10 Nov 2014[1] to 31 Jan 2015	83	(2,500)[2]	-	-	20.34
1 Feb to 15 April 2015	74	3,500[3]	3.0	21.29	41.63

Note:
1. Seven days after repayment instructions issued.
2. £5,000 over-declaration less £2,500 under-declaration brought forward.
3. £6,000 under-declaration less £2,500 over-declaration brought forward.
4. For the default interest rate in force at a specific date see ¶9972
5. The over-declaration of £3,000 on 1 June 2015 does not amend the interest already charged.
6. Interest charged is calculated on a daily basis, e.g. (£2,500 x 3%) x 99/365 = £20.34.

C. Particular circumstances

Insolvency

3902 VDIM 9030, 9040

If the insolvency is:
– **formal** (¶3808+), interest is only charged on under-declarations relating to VAT periods up to the date of insolvency; or
– **informal** (¶3784+), interest may also be charged on under-declarations for periods after the date of insolvency.

Transfer of a going concern

3904 VDIM 9010

Interest may be charged to the new owner of a business in respect of under-declarations by the previous owner, where there was a transfer of a going concern (¶8646+) and the VAT **registration number was transferred** to the new owner (¶8678+).

Comment When a business is transferred as a going concern, it is advisable not to transfer the VAT registration number unless there is a **good commercial reason**.

Supplies overseas

3906 Where a business zero-rates an overseas supply but fails to declare tax after **failing to obtain the required evidence** (¶9086+) of the export or removal of goods from the UK, an interest charge may arise if HMRC issues an assessment for the tax.

If **evidence is subsequently obtained** in a later period, the assessment and interest charge will not be cancelled, as the zero-rating tax adjustment takes place in that period.

CHAPTER 3

Penalties

OUTLINE ¶¶

3950 There are two types of penalty for failing to comply with VAT legislation:
a. civil penalties, which are used to enforce most aspects of VAT compliance; and
b. criminal penalties. Criminal proceedings are normally only taken in cases of serious fraud.

Normally, criminal and civil penalties cannot both apply to the same offence. The only exception to this rule is that the default surcharge (¶4082+) can be levied in addition to a criminal penalty.

MEMO POINTS HMRC has the power to **publish the names** of both corporate and individual taxpayers who:
– are penalised for deliberately understating tax due, or overstating claims or losses, of more than £25,000; or
– deliberately fail to notify HMRC when required to do so, leading to a loss of tax of more than £25,000; or
– are penalised for deliberately committing certain VAT offences leading to a loss of tax of more than £25,000.
Names will **not be published** of those who make a full disclosure, prompted or unprompted, within the required time. Details will be published quarterly within one year of the penalty becoming final and will remain on HMRC's website for 12 months.

SECTION 1

Civil penalties

I. Penalties common to most or all taxes

Introduction of the current system

3955 Sch 24 FA 2007; Sch 41 FA 2008 On 1 April 2009, the system of penalties for dishonest evasion (including evasion by officers of companies), misdeclaration and negligence was **replaced by** a new system of penalties for errors covering all taxes.

Since 1 April 2010, the new regime also applies to a number of other specific failures to comply with the legislation, and the penalty for deliberate inaccuracy is extended to cover acts by third parties.

From a date still to be announced, the default surcharge (¶4082+) will be replaced by a new system of penalties for the late submission of VAT returns and late payment of VAT.

Offences relating to import VAT are penalised as though they relate to customs duty, and are not subject to this regime (¶4104).

SI 2008/568 MEMO POINTS The previous penalty regime is **retained for** any act of dishonest evasion which does not involve inaccuracies in a document or form, or a failure to notify HMRC of an underassessment by them. This is expected to be of very limited application. For details see *VAT Memo 2010-2011*.

Types of penalty

3956 Four types of penalty can be charged under the new regime:
– an **inaccuracy penalty** (¶4000+) for submitting an inaccurate return or other document, or failing to notify HMRC that a VAT assessment is insufficient;
– a **penalty for failure to notify** (¶4010+) HMRC of the trader's position in specified circumstances;
– a penalty in relation to **VAT wrongdoing** (¶4020+) in specified circumstances; and
– penalties for dishonest conduct by tax agents (¶4026).

The four types share a set of general principles.

1. General principles

Commencement dates

The commencement dates in relation to specific offences are as follows: **3960**

Type of penalty	Specific offence	Conditions for new regime to apply
Inaccuracy[1,2,3]	Inaccuracy in a VAT return or other document Failure to notify HMRC of an under-assessment to VAT	Inaccuracy is contained in (or the under-assessment relates to) a VAT return or other document due to be filed on or after 1 April 2009; and the VAT return, document or under-assessment relates to a tax period beginning on or after 1 April 2008
	Inaccuracy in a VAT return or other document relating to a claim for repayment of VAT but which is not related to a tax period	Inaccuracy is contained in a document due to be filed on or after 1 April 2009; and the claim document is dated on or after 1 April 2009
	Inaccuracy in any other case where the person's liability to pay relevant tax arises on or after 1 April 2009	Inaccuracy is contained in (or the under-assessment relates to) a VAT return or other document due to be filed on or after 1 April 2009; and the document is dated on or after 1 April 2009
	Deliberately supplying false information to (or deliberately withholding information from) a person with the intention of making that person's document inaccurate	Inaccuracy is contained in a VAT return or other document due to be filed on or after 1 April 2010; and the return or other document relates to a tax period beginning on or after 1 April 2009
Failure to notify	Any relevant failure (¶4010)	The obligation to notify arose on or after 1 April 2010
VAT wrongdoing	Unauthorised issue of an invoice showing or including VAT	Invoice issued on or after 1 April 2010
Misconduct by tax agents	Dishonesty (¶4026)	1 April 2013

Note:
1. For the submission of forms to reclaim UK input tax incurred by a trader registered in **another EU member state**, the regime came into force on 1 January 2009 for periods commencing after that date.
2. For the submission of forms to reclaim UK input tax incurred by a **trader located outside the EU**, it was 1 July 2008.
3. If a VAT return or other document was due to be **submitted before** 1 April 2009, and it is found that the trader committed dishonest evasion, was negligent, or made a misdeclaration, the previous penalty regime will apply.

Calculation of penalties

Culpability The penalties levied are based on a percentage of the **potential lost tax revenue** (PLR). The PLR is usually the additional amount due or payable once the error has been corrected. This includes amounts of tax incorrectly repaid by a VAT repayment, or amounts that would have been incorrectly repaid. However, if the tax in question is merely **delayed** (for example, where output tax is declared in the wrong VAT accounting period), the PLR is 5% of the delayed tax for each year of delay. If **HMRC discovers an error** before it is corrected (for example, discovery takes place between the period when the output tax ought to have been declared and the following period end, during which the output tax would have been declared), it will calculate the PLR at the 5% rate if correction of the error would have been "automatic". **3965**

Sch 24 paras 3, 8 FA 2007; Sch 41 para 5 FA 2008; CH81110; HMRC Brief 15/11

The **basic percentage applied** depends on the degree of culpability in the taxpayer's behaviour, which is classified as follows:

Degree of culpability	Definition
Innocent	Error made despite taking reasonable care[1]
Careless	Error caused by failure to take reasonable care
Deliberate	Error caused deliberately
Deliberate and concealed	Error caused deliberately and arrangements were made to conceal it

Note
1. In this case no penalty is chargeable.

CH81130 MEMO POINTS Examples offered by HMRC of an innocent error include:
- a **reasonably arguable view** of a situation that is subsequently not upheld;
- an **arithmetical or transposition inaccuracy** which is not so large (either in absolute terms or relative to overall liability) as to produce an obviously incorrect result or be picked up by a quality check;
- following **advice from HMRC** which later proves to be wrong, provided that all the details and circumstances were given when the advice was sought;
- acting on **advice from a competent adviser** which proves to be wrong, despite the fact that the adviser was given a full set of accurate facts; or
- accepting and using **information from another person** where it is not possible to check that the information is accurate and complete.

3966 CH81120 **Reasonable care** HMRC regards the standard of reasonable care as dependent on the trader's **abilities and circumstances**, including (for example) the extent and complexity of the relevant VAT affairs. HMRC considers it reasonable to expect:
- those who encounter transactions or other events with which they are not familiar to take care to find out about the correct VAT treatment, or to seek appropriate advice; and
- those who are still unsure to draw attention to the entry and the uncertainty when submitting the return or other document.

CH81180; CH81190 The **burden of proof** is on HMRC to show that an error was careless or deliberate. The standard of proof is the balance of probabilities.

CH81130 MEMO POINTS 1. In HMRC's view **reasonable care can be demonstrated** if:
- arrangements or systems exist which, if followed, could reasonably be expected to produce an accurate basis for the calculation of VAT due by the trader, or an external agent; and
- despite that, inaccuracies arise in processing which result in a mis-statement of VAT liability; and
- the effect of the inaccuracies is not significant in relation to the trader's overall VAT liability for the relevant tax period.

2. If an error is **not careless or deliberate** and is below the threshold (¶3020+), a taxpayer will be deemed to have taken reasonable steps to inform HMRC by amending a later return. If the error is **careless or deliberate** but below the threshold, separate notification (¶3024+) must be made in order to ensure that disclosure is treated as unprompted.

3968 Sch 24 paras 4–4D, 10 FA 2007; Sch 41 para 6 FA 2008; CH82470 **Standard potential penalties** The standard penalty percentage is set based on the behaviour of the taxpayer that led to the error. This may then be modified based on the behaviour after the error is discovered or reported (¶3970+).

Culpability	Maximum penalty (% of PLR)	Minimum penalty following a disclosure (% of PLR)	
		Prompted disclosure	Unprompted disclosure
Careless[1,2]	30	15	0
Deliberate but not concealed[3]	70	35	20
Deliberate and concealed	100	50	30

Culpability	Maximum penalty (% of PLR)	Minimum penalty following a disclosure (% of PLR)	
		Prompted disclosure	Unprompted disclosure
Understated assessment not notified within 30 days (treated as careless)	30	15	0
Error discovered by taxpayer and no reasonable steps to notify taken (treated as careless)	30	15	0
Error due to the deliberate behaviour of another person	100	50	30

Note:
1. No penalty is charged where an inaccuracy is due to carelessness by an agent, provided that the taxpayer took **reasonable care** to avoid inaccuracy, but the agent could be liable for a penalty.
2. HMRC may suspend all or part of the penalty for a set period, and the suspended penalty may be cancelled if there are no further careless inaccuracies during that period.
3. Where a company becomes liable to a penalty as a result of a deliberate inaccuracy by an officer of the company, HMRC may recover all or part of the penalty from the officer.

Disclosure The trader can obtain a **reduction in the amount** of the penalty by disclosing the error to HMRC. The amount of the reduction will depend on: **3970** Sch 24 para 9 FA 2007; CH82410
- whether the disclosure is unprompted or prompted; and
- the quality of the disclosure.

MEMO POINTS A disclosure will be **unprompted** if the error has not been discovered by HMRC or is not about to be discovered. In all other cases disclosure will be treated as **prompted**. The test is objective and it is unlikely that if disclosure is prompted by a compliance visit, or made during such a visit, it will be treated as unprompted.

The **quality of disclosure** will be judged under three headings, as shown in the following table: **3972** CH82430+

Heading	Maximum % reduction [1]	Includes
Telling	30%	Admitting that the document was inaccurate; disclosing the inaccuracy in full [2]; and explaining how the inaccuracy arose
Helping	40%	Actively helping with quantifying the error and volunteering any relevant information
Allowing access	40%	Access must be freely given to the information when requested, at a convenient location, and additional copies of it provided

Notes
1. The statutory criteria which HMRC must consider in judging the quality of disclosure under these headings include timing, nature and extent.
2. Partial disclosure will not be sufficient to obtain the full 30% reduction.

Calculation of the penalty The actual percentage penalty to be applied is calculated using the following steps: **3980** CH82510
1. Calculate the percentage allowance for quality of disclosure (¶3972).
2. Compute the possible penalty range (in percentage points), according to the degree of culpability and whether the disclosure was unprompted (¶3970).
3. Apply the allowance for quality of disclosure to the possible penalty range. This reduces the penalty from the potential maximum to the final penalty percentage.
4. Apply the final penalty percentage to the PLR (¶3965+), to get the actual monetary penalty.

EXAMPLE Mr A makes an unprompted disclosure of a deliberate error. The PLR is £145,000.
For a deliberate but unconcealed error of which there was an unprompted disclosure, the maximum penalty is 70% and the minimum penalty is 20%. This is a range of 50 percentage points.
HMRC decides that the quality of disclosure merits allowances of 20% for telling, 25% for helping and 20% for allowing access.

	Maximum allowance (%)	Actual allowance (%)
Telling	30	20
Helping	40	25
Access	40	20
		65

The penalty reduction will thus be 65% (the total above) of the possible penalty range (of 50 percentage points). This makes a reduction of 32.5 percentage points (65% x 50) from the maximum penalty of 70%.
The penalty is therefore reduced to 37.5% (70 - 32.5) of £145,000.
The actual penalty charged is £54,375 (37.5% x £145,000).

Special reduction of penalties

3982 Sch 24 para 11 FA 2007; Sch 41 para 14 FA 2008; CH170000+

At the **trader's request**, HMRC can exercise discretion to reduce a penalty because of special circumstances. This reduction can include:
- staying the penalty (stopping or postponing enforcement); or
- agreeing a compromise (effectively forgoing part of the penalty).

HMRC will **only consider** the special reduction of a penalty where exceptional circumstances are identified which cannot be taken into account in arriving at the reduction for disclosure (¶3970+). It is likely that this will be a rare occurrence.

A decision not to allow a special reduction cannot be appealed, although the trader can appeal against the amount of the penalty. The appeal tribunal can apply HMRC's view of the special reduction, or it can apply a different reduction.

Administration of penalties

3985 Sch 24 para 13 FA 2007; Sch 41 para 16 FA 2008

Penalties are charged by issuing an assessment. The penalty is **payable within** 30 days and enforceable as though it were an equivalent amount of tax (¶3730+).

A penalty **assessment must include**:
- the date of the assessment;
- the amount of the penalty;
- the legislation under which the penalty is assessed;
- the tax period or claim to which the penalty relates; and
- the amount (if any) that is suspended.

3986 **Time limits** A penalty assessment may be made up to twelve months after either:
- the end of the period during which the person can appeal against HMRC's correction of an inaccuracy or under-assessment to tax; or
- the time when an appeal against the correction of an inaccuracy is finally decided or withdrawn.

When a **trader puts right the error** before HMRC discovers it (for example, through the error correction procedure (¶3014+)), the penalty assessment must be issued within twelve months of the date the correction was made.

If an **assessment is not needed to correct** the error, the penalty assessment must be issued within twelve months of the date on which the error was put right.

3988 CH83050

Supplementary penalties If, after the issue of a penalty assessment, the **PLR proves** to have been **under-estimated**, a supplementary penalty assessment can be issued for the difference. The time limit is twelve months from the date of the assessment issued to recover the additional PLR.

Agents and principals

A person may be charged a penalty for an error if: **3990** Sch 24 para 18 FA 2007; Sch 41 para 21 FA 2008
- the failure was due to someone acting on the person's behalf; or
- someone acting on the person's behalf knew (or should have known) that action should have been taken, and failed to take reasonable steps to ensure that it was done.

The **behaviour** of the agent is irrelevant: it is the actions of the principal which determine the amount of the penalty. If the principal took reasonable care to avoid the failure (including reasonable care in any dealings with the agent), there will not be a penalty.

An **appeal** can be made by an agent on the principal's behalf.

For dishonest conduct by a tax agent see ¶4026.

Company officers

HMRC can seek to recover all or part of a penalty from a company officer (a "liable officer") if the company is liable to a penalty for a **deliberate error** which can be attributed to the **deliberate action** of the company officer, and either: **3992** Sch 24 para 19 FA 2007; Sch 41 para 22 FA 2008
- there is evidence that the officer gained personally from the error; or
- the company is insolvent, or facing imminent insolvency.

The penalty is always **assessed** on the company, and HMRC cannot recover more than 100% of the penalty from the company and its liable officers together. If the company pays the penalty, proceedings against an officer cannot be taken further. Only the company can lodge an appeal.

The amount of penalty that can be recovered from an officer depends on the culpability of the officer's conduct and the state of the company, as follows: CH84600+
- if the officer acted for personal gain: up to 100% of the penalty;
- if two or more officers acted for personal gain: up to 100% of the penalty, divided between them in proportion to the extent that each gained personally; or
- if the company is insolvent or facing imminent insolvency: up to 100% of the penalty, divided equally between the liable officers, without distinction for varying degrees of disclosure.

MEMO POINTS 1. **A company** means any body corporate or unincorporated association, including an LLP, but not a partnership, a local authority or a local authority association.
2. An **officer** of a company means:
a. for a body corporate, other than a limited liability partnership:
- a director or shadow director;
- a manager; or
- a company secretary;

b. for an LLP, a member of that LLP; or
c. in any other case, the above meanings, but also any other person managing or purporting to manage any of the company's affairs.

VAT groups

In a VAT group, any business carried on by a member of the group is treated as carried on by the representative member. In effect, the representative member company is the one which is **responsible** for any failure for the purposes of the penalty legislation. It is not acting on behalf of (and so is not an agent of) the other group companies. However, if an individual company is required to notify liability to be registered and subsequently moves into a VAT group, the responsibility to notify liability to be registered remains with the individual company. **3994** s 43 VATA 1994

Appeals

A person can appeal against: **3996** Sch 24 paras 15, 16 FA 2007; Sch 41 para 17 FA 2008
- the **imposition** of a penalty;
- the **amount** of a penalty;
- a decision **not to suspend** a penalty; or
- the **conditions set** in relation to the suspension of a penalty.

The appeal follows the normal process of internal review and appeal to the tribunal (¶4220+).

2. Inaccuracy penalties

4000 Sch 24 FA 2007; CH80000 +

Penalties for inaccuracy **apply to**:
- the careless or deliberate submission of an inaccurate document (such as a VAT return);
- failure to notify HMRC, within 30 days of the date of the assessment, that it has under-assessed a VAT liability; and
- an error in a taxpayer's document which has deliberately been caused by a third person.

Note that a failure to notify an under-assessment is penalised for inaccuracy rather than as a failure to notify.

4002 Sch 24 para 1 FA 2007

Meaning of "inaccuracy" A document is **inaccurate** if it amounts to or leads to:
- understatement of a person's liability to tax;
- a false or inflated statement of a loss; or
- a false or inflated claim to repayment of tax.

CH82200

If a document contains **more than one inaccuracy**, a penalty is payable for each inaccuracy. However, HMRC may group inaccuracies together and treat them as liable to a single penalty if:
- they show the same underlying culpability (¶3968);
- they have the same type of disclosure (unprompted or prompted (¶3970+)); and
- any suspension conditions (¶4008) can be aligned.

4003

For a penalty to apply, the inaccuracy must have been caused carelessly or deliberately. However, an innocent error may be treated as careless if the trader discovers the inaccuracy and does not take reasonable steps to inform HMRC. One of the criteria by which reasonableness is tested is how promptly the trader notified HMRC after discovering the error.

MEMO POINTS Examples given by HMRC of what it considers to be reasonable steps include:
- consulting an agent to discuss the position, and asking the agent to inform HMRC;
- telephoning HMRC to discuss the matter;
- emailing, faxing or writing to an HMRC officer with details of the inaccuracy; or
- making an adjustment under the error correction regime (¶3014+) in the return for the period of discovery.

4004 Sch 24 paras 1, 28(h) FA 2007; CH81060

Meaning of "document" For VAT purposes a document means:
- a VAT return; or
- any other return, statement or declaration in connection with a claim. This includes documents submitted under VAT return adjustment or error notification arrangements (¶3014+).

HMRC regards the definition of document as very widely drawn and considers, for example, that it can include the content of a telephone call, or a statement made at a meeting. This appears not to depend on whether a note of the call or meeting has been kept.

4006 Sch 24 para 2 FA 2007; CH81090, 81170

Under-assessment The penalty for not notifying HMRC of an under-assessment applies if:
- the assessment understates the trader's liability to VAT; and
- the trader fails to take reasonable steps to notify HMRC, within the period of 30 days beginning with the date of the assessment, that it is an under-assessment.

In deciding what steps (if any) were reasonable, HMRC must consider:
- whether the trader knew, or should have known, about the under-assessment; and
- what steps it would have been reasonable to take in order to notify HMRC.

4007 Sch 24 para 1A FA 2007; CH81166

Third-party inaccuracy The penalty for an error caused by the action of a third person was introduced to prevent third parties from benefiting from errors which they have caused a taxpayer to make. The penalty applies where the taxpayer has been **provided with a document** which contains **an inaccuracy** and either:
- the third party has deliberately supplied **false information**; or
- the third party has deliberately **withheld information** from the taxpayer.

This could arise, for example, where a VAT return was inadvertently understated by the taxpayer due to the provision of a deliberately inaccurate invoice by a third party.

A third-party penalty can be charged even if the principal trader is not penalised.

MEMO POINTS Special rules apply to large companies and their **senior accounting officers** personally (¶2986).
Penalties for failure to comply are leviable not only on the company but also on the officer concerned.

Suspension of penalties

HMRC has the power to suspend all or part of a penalty for a **careless inaccuracy** for a period of up to two years. There is no power to suspend a penalty for a deliberate inaccuracy. 4008 Sch 24 para 14 FA 2007; CH83100+

Suspension normally depends on the trader meeting certain **conditions**, which will be specified in writing by HMRC in each particular case. Suspension can only be granted if compliance with the conditions would help the trader to avoid further penalties for careless inaccuracies.

If the conditions are fulfilled, the penalty is cancelled at the end of the agreed period. If not, or if the trader incurs a further inaccuracy penalty during the suspension period, the suspended penalty becomes payable.

A **decision not to suspend** a penalty, or to impose particular conditions, can be appealed.

MEMO POINTS HMRC states that the **conditions it imposes** will be: CH83151
- specific to the business or individual being penalised;
- measurable (such that the trader can demonstrate that the conditions have been met);
- achievable and realistic; and
- time-bound (the conditions must be met by a specified date).

3. Penalties for failure to notify

A penalty for failure to notify may be charged if a person does not meet a statutory obligation to notify HMRC of specified circumstances by the appropriate statutory deadline. A penalty **cannot be charged** if the person can demonstrate a reasonable excuse (¶4014+). 4010 Sch 41 FA 2008; CH70000+

By law, each penalty is chargeable in relation to a penalty period, which must be shown on the penalty assessment (¶3985).

The following table shows the VAT obligations which are subject to this type of penalty, and the period for which the penalty applies (¶3985):

Requirement	¶¶	Penalty period starts	Penalty period ends
Notify liability to register for VAT in respect of UK supplies[1]	¶2640+	Date on which the trader should have been registered	Day before the trader notified HMRC of liability to be registered, or (if notice was not given) HMRC otherwise became aware of the liability
Notify liability to be registered in respect of supplies from EU member states	¶9177+		
Notify liability to be registered in respect of acquisitions from EU member states	¶9040+		
Notify liability for registration by overseas traders in respect of disposal of assets for which a VAT repayment claimed	¶9890+		

Requirement	¶¶	Penalty period starts	Penalty period ends
Notify a material change in nature of supplies made by a person previously exempted from registration	¶2656+	Date of the change or alteration concerned	Day before the trader notified HMRC of the relevant change or alteration, or (if notice was not given) HMRC otherwise became aware of it
Notify a material alteration in the proportion of zero-rated supplies made by a person previously exempted from registration	¶2652+		
Notify a change in nature of acquisitions by a person exempt from registration in respect of acquisitions from other EU member states	¶9010+		
Notify relevant change in supplies by an overseas trader exempt from registration in respect of disposal of assets for which a VAT repayment claimed	¶9892		
Notify acquisition of excise duty goods or new means of transport from another EU member state	¶9112+	Start of the period for which VAT is unpaid as a result of the failure	End of the period for which VAT is unpaid as a result of the failure
Notes 1. Relates to all obligations based on past turnover, future turnover, or transfer as a going concern.			

Reasonable excuse

4014 Sch 41 para 20 FA 2008

A penalty cannot be charged for failure to notify if the trader had a reasonable excuse for not notifying HMRC by the appropriate deadline, **provided that** notice was given without unreasonable delay after the excuse had ended.

If **HMRC rejects** an excuse as not being reasonable, the trader can request a review or lodge an appeal (¶4220+).

4015 CH71540+

There is no statutory **definition** of reasonable excuse but the following factors are specifically excluded:

- a lack of funds to pay the tax concerned;
- reliance on someone else to perform a task accurately or without delay.

In addition, **HMRC does not accept** that genuine mistakes, honesty or acting in good faith are sufficient in themselves to amount to a reasonable excuse.

4016

Whether a reasonable excuse exists **depends on** the facts and circumstances in each case.

A **test** set out by a tribunal was whether a reasonable, conscientious businessman (who was aware of and accepted the need to comply with the responsibilities involved in rendering VAT returns) would conclude that a taxpayer, taking the given action in the prevailing circumstances, had acted with due care in the preparation of the return. If so, the taxpayer should be regarded as having a reasonable excuse. *Appropriate Technology Ltd* [1991] (VTD 5696)

In another case, the **factors** to be taken into account in deciding whether a particular taxpayer had acted reasonably included age, experience, health and the incidence of some particular difficulty or misfortune. *The Clean Car Co Ltd* [1991] (VTD 5695)

The principle that **ignorance of the law** is no excuse has been tested in relation to VAT legislation. **In most situations** HMRC will not accept that ignorance is an excuse. There have been several tribunal cases on this point, and in general the defence of ignorance has not been successful. 4017

4. Penalties for VAT wrongdoing

Penalties for VAT and excise wrongdoing apply to a number of actions; the only one relevant to VAT is the **unauthorised issue of an invoice** showing or including VAT. 4020 Sch 41 para 2 FA 2008; CH90000 +

The invoice simply needs either to show an amount of VAT or to include an amount attributable to VAT. It does not otherwise have to qualify as a VAT invoice (¶2840+).

An unauthorised person is anyone **other than** one of the following:
- a person registered for VAT;
- a member of a VAT group of companies;
- a personal representative (¶2624) who is treated as a taxable person (for example, an insolvency practitioner);
- a person who sells goods on behalf of a taxable person in satisfaction of a debt and who is acting as the taxable person for the purposes of the sale (for example, an auctioneer); or
- a person acting on behalf of the Crown.

MEMO POINTS 1. A farmer in the **agricultural flat rate scheme** (¶5970+) is regarded as an unauthorised person if issuing an invoice which does not comply with the requirements of the flat rate scheme, or which is not authorised under the scheme.
2. The same penalties also apply to anyone who misuses a product so that a higher rate of excise duty is payable, or handles goods subject to unpaid excise duty.

The potential lost revenue (¶3965) is the amount shown on the invoice as VAT or the amount to be taken as representing VAT. 4022

A defence of reasonable excuse (¶4014+) is available, and HMRC has powers to make a special reduction in the amount of penalty (¶3982). 4024

5. Dishonest conduct by a tax agent

Since 1 April 2013 HMRC has been able to issue a tax agent with: 4026 Sch 38 FA 2012; CH180000+
- a **conduct notice**, if HMRC makes a determination that the agent has engaged in "dishonest conduct"; usually followed by
- a **file access notice**, which requires production of the working papers of a tax agent found to have engaged in dishonest conduct. Such a notice requires either prior approval by the First-tier Tribunal, or a preceding criminal conviction involving fraud or dishonesty. Where such working papers are no longer in the power or possession of the tax agent, HMRC can require production of them by a third party.

Both types of notice may be appealed.

Tax agent is widely defined, but the conduct involved must be in the course of a business (so, for example, advice from a volunteer or a family member is not caught). **Dishonest conduct** is defined as doing "something dishonest" with a view to bringing about a loss of tax revenue. It does not matter whether a loss is actually brought about.

Once a conduct notice has been issued, it is a **criminal offence** for the agent to conceal or destroy material documents (¶4192). Failure to comply with a file access notice carries a penalty of £300, with daily penalties of up to £60 a day for continuing failure.

There is also a **civil penalty for dishonest conduct** of at least £5,000 and up to £50,000. If full disclosure is not made, HMRC can publish details of the penalised tax agent.

II. Civil penalties specific to VAT

Types of VAT-specific civil penalty

4030 There are two types of VAT-specific civil penalty:
a. penalties for **breach of VAT regulations**, which apply to several types of action; and
b. penalties for **specified VAT offences**.

4032 These penalties may not be charged, or may be appealed, if there was a **reasonable excuse** for the act or omission (¶4014+). However, the reasonable excuse defence **does not apply** to the penalties for failing to comply with a tribunal direction or summons (¶4139).

Penalties may be **reduced** if there are mitigating circumstances (¶4044+).

Where **more than one** VAT-specific civil penalty could apply to the same act, only one penalty can be charged.

Exercise of discretion

4034 VCP10130 The **factors** which HMRC takes into account include the need to:
- maintain equity in the application of civil penalties;
- take full account of the circumstances of each particular case; and
- bear in mind that the fundamental objective of civil penalties is to encourage compliance.

Time limits

4036 ss 73 - 77 VATA 1994 VAT-specific civil penalties **cannot be charged more than** 4 years after the end of the VAT period or the event to which the penalty relates, **except** in the circumstances set out in the following table:

<table>
<tr><th>Penalty</th><th>Time limit</th></tr>
<tr><td>Regulatory penalties requiring a warning letter</td><td>2 years from the date of issue of the letter, if earlier than the 4-year limit</td></tr>
<tr><td>Default surcharge</td><td>2 years from the date when the VAT liability for the period was determined, if earlier than the normal 4-year limit</td></tr>
<tr><td>Penalties charged after a person's death</td><td>4 years after the date of death</td></tr>
<tr><td>Where a person has been convicted of fraud</td><td rowspan="4">Earlier of:
– 2 years from the date the VAT liability for the period was determined; or
– 20 years after the end of the VAT period in question or the event giving rise to the penalty</td></tr>
<tr><td>Penalties for loss of VAT where a person (or a third party acting on the person's behalf) deliberately brings about such a loss</td></tr>
<tr><td>Penalties for knowingly participating in arrangements intended to bring about a loss of VAT</td></tr>
<tr><td>Failure to disclose a VAT scheme</td></tr>
<tr><td>Failure to submit a sales list</td><td rowspan="3">2 years from the date when HMRC became aware of the facts, if earlier than the 4-year limit</td></tr>
<tr><td>Submitting an inaccurate sales list</td></tr>
<tr><td>Failure to keep records in relation to gold</td></tr>
</table>

MEMO POINTS If the end of the accounting period or the importation, acquisition or event giving rise to the penalty occurred on or before 31 March 2010, **transitional rules** provide that the 20-year rule **does not apply** to penalties for:
- causing a loss of VAT by failing to notify a liability to register or account for VAT; or
- failure to comply with an obligation to disclose a VAT scheme where a loss of VAT is attributable to that scheme.

Calculation of tax-related penalties

If unpaid VAT cannot readily be **attributed** to specific periods, HMRC may determine the VAT due for any particular period to the best of its judgment for the purposes of calculating a penalty, surcharge or interest charge based on unpaid VAT for that period. **4038** s 76(4) VATA 1994

Reconsiderations and appeals

A person can: **4040** s 83 VATA 1994
- ask HMRC to review a penalty; or
- appeal against a penalty, or the amount of a penalty, where mitigation is allowed.

The **general rules** in relation to reviews and appeals can be found at ¶4210+.

Specific rules in relation to **particular penalties**, and appeals against particular penalties, can be found at ¶4050+.

Mitigation

Most penalties can be reduced (to nil if appropriate) if there are mitigating circumstances. **4044** s 70 VATA 1994; VCP11710+

Mitigation provides flexibility where there is a degree of reasonableness which falls short of a reasonable excuse. Mitigation can take into account behaviour after an error or offence, whereas reasonable excuse concentrates on behaviour before the event.

The legislation does not define grounds for mitigation, but it **excludes**:
- acting in good faith;
- the fact that little or no tax may have been lost; or
- a lack of funds to pay tax or a penalty.

Exceptions The following penalties cannot be mitigated: **4046**
- default surcharge (¶4082+);
- regulatory penalties (¶4050+);
- penalty for providing an incorrect certificate (¶4100+);
- penalties in relation to sales lists (¶4120+);
- penalty for breach of a walking possession agreement (¶4130+); and
- failure to comply with a VAT tribunal direction or summons (¶4139).

HMRC practice HMRC will normally mitigate a penalty, unless there is a reason not to do so, such as lack of co-operation from a taxpayer. **4047** VCP11740+

Up to 100% of the penalty can be mitigated, although HMRC states that this will only happen in rare cases.

EXAMPLE A penalty of £1,000 might be mitigated as follows:

		%
Full co-operation and quantification of liability		50
Evidence of efforts made to seek advice		10
		60
		£
Total penalty		1,000
Mitigation	£1,000 x 60%	(600)
Penalty due		400

The **general factors** which HMRC takes into account in considering mitigation for penalties are set out in the table below. **4048** VCP11746 - 11748

Specific factors for particular penalties are listed at ¶4050+.

Factor	Maximum total reduction %	Details	Reduction %
How the offence occurred	50	Compassionate grounds such as: – unforeseen illness or death of person responsible for completing VAT returns; or – death of a close relative	20 - 50
		Other unforeseen and relevant events, such as: – computer or software errors; – flood, fire or other damage to premises; – theft or break-in; – pressure of work due to exceptional and significant increase in workload; – staff problems; – clerical errors, particularly in complex circumstances where not identified by management controls	10 - 50
		Complexity of liability in relation to size of business and frequency of transaction	10 - 50
Co-operation	50	Full disclosure, co-operation and quantification of liabilities	Up to 50
		Partial disclosure, co-operation and quantification of liabilities	Up to 25
		Other assistance in quantifying liabilities	Up to 10
Other factors	50	Published guidance unclear or not up to date	Up to 40
		Evidence of efforts made to seek advice	Up to 10
		Evidence of steps taken to correct systems in order to prevent similar failures in future	5 - 25
		Good compliance history over last three years	Up to 25

A. Penalties for breach of regulations

4050 There are general penalties for a failure to comply with **any regulation** relating to VAT.

ss 69, 76 VATA 1994

Any person may become liable to a penalty, as some regulations can apply to persons who are not VAT-registered.

Overview

4052 There are three types of regulatory penalty:
– a fixed amount, for **failure to preserve records** or to **comply with an information notice**;
– the greater of a daily amount or a percentage of unpaid VAT, for **failure to submit** VAT returns or **pay VAT**; and
– a daily amount, for **all other failures**.

Some penalties can only be charged if, within the previous two years, HMRC issued a **warning letter** stating that a penalty would be imposed if the trader did not comply with the relevant regulation:

Offence		Warning letter needed?	¶¶
Failure to preserve records		n	¶4058+
Failure to submit VAT returns or pay VAT		y	¶4062+
Failure to provide information or produce documents required by an information notice (¶3458+)		n	¶4072+
Failure to maintain records when required by a direction (¶3485+)		n	¶4141+
All other failures	Failure to: – maintain the required accounting records (¶2790+); or – notify HMRC of changes in registration particulars (¶2714+)	y	¶4068+
	Failure by a trader to notify HMRC within 30 days of: **a.** cessation of liability or entitlement to be registered (¶2720+); or **b.** circumstances affecting continued registration in respect of: – distance sales (¶9177+); – acquisitions from other EU member states (¶9010+); or – disposals of assets for which a VAT repayment has been claimed (¶9890+).	n	
	Failure by a VAT representative (¶7210+) to notify HMRC of commencement or cessation of appointment	n	
	Failure to comply with any condition imposed by HMRC in relation to fiscal warehousing procedures (¶9242+)	n	
	Failure to comply with any Treasury Order relating to VATA 1994, apart from procedural rules for tribunals	y	
	Failure to comply with any Treasury Order relating to VAT	y	
	Failure to comply with any EU regulation relating to VAT	y	

Continuing or multiple failures A continuing failure is regarded as one failure from the **date** on which it commenced. **4054** s 69(4) VATA 1994

An omission which results in a failure to comply with **more than one regulatory requirement** is regarded as one failure.

A **previous failure** for which there is a reasonable excuse is disregarded.

Multiple penalties In addition to the general rules regarding multiple penalties (¶4054), a **regulatory penalty cannot apply** if any of the following has been imposed for the same failure: **4056** s 69(9) VATA 1994

- the default surcharge (¶4082+);
- an inaccuracy penalty (¶4000+); or
- a criminal conviction (¶4150+).

1. Failure to preserve records

The penalty for failure to preserve records for the required length of time, which is generally six years (¶2797+), is £500. **4058** s 69(2) VATA 1994

Exercise of discretion

On the **first occasion** of a loss or premature destruction of records, HMRC will consider warning a trader that more care should be taken to ensure that records are preserved, and that a penalty may be charged on any future occasion. This will not apply if a trader **wilfully destroys** records despite being aware of the need to preserve them. **4060**

2. Failure to submit VAT returns or pay VAT

4062 s 69(1), (5) VATA 1994

A regulatory penalty applies for failure to submit a VAT return or pay VAT by the due date (¶3172+). **Alternatively**, HMRC may apply the default surcharge (¶4082+), which is more common.

Amount levied

4064 The penalty is £50 or, if greater, a daily tax-related penalty based on the number of failures in the previous two years, as follows:

Number of failures in previous two years	Daily penalty - greater of		Maximum penalty
	Fixed sum £	% of unpaid VAT	
None	5	1/6%	100 days
1	10	1/3%	
2 or more	15	1/2%	

4066 The **daily penalty** is calculated from the date of failure up to the day before the failure is rectified. The **date of failure** for an error made on a VAT return is the day after the due date for submission.

EXAMPLE After several failures to pay VAT on time, HMRC issues a warning letter to A Ltd on 1 April. Details for the remainder of the year are as follows:

Period ended	VAT £	Due date	Date paid	Penalties £	
30 June	80,000	31 July	28 July	n/a	
30 Sept	96,000	31 Oct	11 Dec	6,400	£96,000 × 1/6% × 40 days
31 Dec	75,000	31 Jan	3 Mar	7,500	£75,000 × 1/3% × 30 days

3. Other regulatory failures

4068 s 69 VATA 1994

For all other regulatory breaches (¶4050+), the penalty is £50 or, if greater, a daily penalty based on the number of failures in the previous two years, as follows:

Number of failures in previous two years	Daily penalty £	Maximum penalty £
None	5	500
1	10	1,000
2 or more	15	1,500

4070 A **daily penalty** is calculated from the date of failure to comply with the regulation up to the day before the failure is rectified.

The **date of failure** is defined as the:
- day after the expiry of a time limit specified in the relevant regulation; or
- date of a document, where a trader has made an error in its production.

There is an **exception** to this rule for failure to maintain or produce records, or provide information.

4. Failure to comply with an information notice

Failure to comply

4072 Sch 36 FA 2008

Failure to comply with an HMRC **information notice** (¶3458+) carries an initial penalty of £300. A further daily penalty of up to £60 a day can be imposed for continuing failure.

Failure to comply also includes concealing, destroying or otherwise disposing of a document which is, or is likely to be, the subject of an information notice.

The daily penalty period begins on a date specified in the notice which imposes it, and will **end** on the day before:
- the trader contacts HMRC to arrange production, after which the records are produced as agreed; or
- production of the records without prior arrangement.

Comment In order to **minimise** any penalty, traders should contact HMRC as soon as possible after receiving a demand to produce records and agree a production date.

Exercise of discretion HMRC will **base a decision** whether to charge a penalty on the likelihood of its success as a compliance tool. 4073

A penalty is **unlikely** to be charged where:
- this would probably increase an irrecoverable debt;
- trading is known to have ceased;
- there is minimal tax revenue at risk; or
- in the case of a first failure, the trader contacts HMRC within ten days of issue of the warning letter to agree a date on which to produce the records, and produces the records on that date.

Appeals

Legal grounds for appealing against a penalty may include: 4074
- the demand notice was not received;
- no records of any sort exist;
- records were held by a third party under a lien, or by the police or a government department or judicial body;
- the HMRC officer named in the demand did not attend personally, or at the time and date specified; or
- the records were not produced at the specified place because the premises were no longer owned or occupied by the trader.

Reasonable excuse A penalty will not be charged, or may be cancelled, if there was a reasonable excuse. 4076

Grounds for a reasonable excuse (¶4014+) **may include**:
- fire or flood at premises;
- injury, illness or death of a relative or business official on or about the date for production of records;
- recent burglary or theft of records; or
- genuine transport difficulties on the intended date of production.

The following table gives details of **case law** where the taxpayer appealed against a penalty for not providing information or records, claiming to have had a reasonable excuse: 4078

Offence	Grounds for appeal against penalty	Reasonable excuse?	Outcome
Failure to make books and records available for inspection at principal place of business	Books and records were kept at the registered office, where the inspection could have taken place	No	Not unreasonable for HMRC to demand production of records at principal place of business. *Fabco Ltd* [1992] (VTD 9739)
	Books and records were at accountant's office for several months, for accounts preparation purposes	No	The records could have been returned for one day for inspection. *HEM Construction Ltd* [1995] (VTD 12449)

Offence	Grounds for appeal against penalty	Reasonable excuse?	Outcome
Failure to produce documents	Belief that the demand was invalid, and that the documents in question did not contain relevant information	No	Matters relating to the validity of a demand are not a reasonable excuse for ignoring the demand. *Lloyds TSB Group plc* [2005] (VTD 19330)
	Some documents were subject to legal professional privilege	Yes	The demand to produce the documents was too vague; the penalty notice did not specify which requirements had not been met. *University of Glasgow* [2002] (VTD 17744)
Failure to produce accounts for a period before VAT registration	No obligation to produce information relating to a period prior to VAT registration	No	Requirement to produce information applies to anyone making business supplies. *HH & M Suleyman (t/a Red Rose Dry Cleaners)* [1995] (VTD 13753)

B. Penalties for specific offences

4080 There are specific civil penalties which apply to particular offences. These differ from the general regulatory penalties because the procedure involved, or the method of calculation, is related to the nature of each offence.

These offences broadly fall into two categories, as follows:

Type of offence		Specific penalty	¶¶
Offences in relation to accounting for VAT	Failure to submit VAT returns or pay VAT on time	Default surcharge	¶4082+
	Provision of an incorrect certificate	Provision of an incorrect certificate	¶4100+
Offences in particular situations	Penalties in relation to import VAT	Dishonest evasion	¶4104+
		Breach of rules	¶4112
	Failures in relation to sales lists	Failure to submit a list	¶4121+
		Submission of an inaccurate list	¶4125+
	Breach of a walking possession agreement	Penalty for breach	¶4130+
	Failure to comply with a tribunal direction or summons	Penalty for failure to comply	¶4139
	Failure to notify use of a notifiable scheme	Penalty for failure to notify use	¶4140
	Failure to keep specified records	Failure in relation to certain goods	¶4141+

1. Default surcharge

a. General principles

4082 ss 59, 59A, 59B VATA 1994; Notice 700/50

A default arises for a VAT period if a taxable person **fails** to:
- submit the VAT return by the due date (¶3002+);
- pay part or all of the VAT liability shown in the return by the due date (¶3172+); or

– pay part or all of a required payment on account or balancing payment (¶3194+) by the due date.

MEMO POINTS From a date yet to be confirmed, the following measures will be introduced to discourage late filing of VAT returns and late payment of VAT. They are expected to replace the default surcharge. Special rules will deal with any change from monthly to quarterly returns, or vice versa, and with any exceptional payment obligations which may arise. Schs 55, 56 FA 2009
1. **Late filing** Where returns are supposed to be submitted **quarterly**:
– £100 penalty as soon as a return is late (whether or not the tax has been paid), which starts a 1-year penalty period, extended for each subsequent late submission;
– for each further failure within the penalty period, the fixed penalty increases by £100, to a maximum of £400;
– an additional 5% of the tax on the relevant return if it has not been filed after six and twelve months; and
– a penalty of up to 100% of the tax if, by failing to make the return, the taxpayer is deliberately withholding information to prevent HMRC from correctly assessing the VAT liability.
The penalty for late filing where returns are supposed to be submitted **monthly** is £100 for the first six failures in any penalty period, then £200 for any subsequent failures.
2. **Late payment** Where payment is supposed to be made **quarterly**, penalties will be charged as a percentage of the late-paid tax:
– no penalty for the first late payment, but a 1-year penalty period starts;
– 2% penalty for a second failure within the penalty period, and the penalty period is extended to the first anniversary of the second failure;
– 3% for a third failure within the extended penalty period, and a further penalty period extension;
– 4% for further failures; and in addition
– 5% at 6 and 12 months from the date of the failure.
The penalty for late payment where returns are supposed to be submitted **monthly** is zero for the first failure, 1% for the next three failures in the penalty period, 2% for the next three failures, 3% for the next three failures and 4% thereafter.

Exercise of discretion

HMRC's policy is to issue surcharge assessments automatically unless there is a particular reason for not doing so. HMRC is required to exercise its discretion on this basis. *Dollar Land (Feltham) Ltd v C & E* [1995] **4083** VCP10531

MEMO POINTS **HMRC may agree** that a trader can **delay** submitting a VAT return, or may allow extra time to pay VAT (¶3735). If the trader contacts the Business Payment Support Service before the payment is due and time to pay is agreed, there will be no default provided the return is submitted by the due date. Notice 700/50 para 3.2

Special reasons HMRC states that special reasons for not issuing a surcharge assessment include: **4084** VCP10532
a. national reasons which would affect all traders, for example, industrial action such as a prolonged postal dispute; or
b. specific reasons for a particular trader, including:
– the death of a sole proprietor;
– a misallocated or missing remittance (for example the allocation of a payment to another VAT-registered trader);
– the existence of a duplicate VAT registration, or a registration containing an invalid entry;
– the establishment of a reasonable excuse before a default has been recorded;
– payment of a cash deposit as security; or
– a month's grace for a trader who submits monthly returns, to ensure that a penalty liability notice has been received.

Concessions HMRC does not, in practice, apply the default surcharge rules to traders who are: **4085** VCP10511
– submitting their first VAT return, unless the business was transferred as a going concern (¶8648+);
– classified as repayment traders;
– deregistering;

- insolvent;
- under a missing trader review; or
- local authorities.

4086 Notice 700/50 para 4.2; VCP10544

Small businesses The default surcharge rules are not applied to businesses with a **turnover** of up to £150,000 excluding VAT on the occasion of their **first default** in a 12-month period. Instead, HMRC will send a letter offering help and support.

If there is a **further default** within twelve months, the normal rules will then be applied. This practice will continue for as long as turnover remains within the £150,000 limit.

Appeals

4088 Notice 700/50 para 7.1

A trader may request HMRC to reconsider the surcharge assessment. A **request for reconsideration** (¶4230+) should be made in writing within 30 days of the date of the surcharge notice (¶4094+). Alternatively, a trader can appeal to the First-tier Tribunal (¶4262+) against a surcharge assessment on any of the following **grounds**:
- it can be shown that the return and payment were sent in time to arrive by the due date;
- the trader considers that there was a reasonable excuse for the default;
- no surcharge liability notice was ever received;
- the trader believes that the surcharge is calculated at the wrong rate or on the wrong amount of VAT; or
- there are exceptional circumstances.

Reasonable excuse

4090 ss 59(7), 59A(8) VATA 1994

There will be no **default** if:
- there was a reasonable excuse (¶4014+) for the return or payment not having been despatched on time; or
- the VAT return or payment was despatched in circumstances where it was reasonable to expect that it would have been received by HMRC on time.

If there was a reasonable excuse, any surcharge liability **notice** resulting from the default will be deemed not to have been issued.

MEMO POINTS A company appealed against a default surcharge on the basis that it had a **reasonable excuse** for the late payment of VAT from an **earlier period**. The company was out of time (¶4270+) to appeal against the earlier default, and therefore the surcharge for that period stood. However, the tribunal accepted that had the appeal been in time, then, on the balance of the facts, the VAT tribunal would have found that the company had a reasonable excuse. As such, the tribunal held that the default surcharge for the **later period** should be computed on the basis that the earlier default did not occur. This resulted in the default surcharge being reduced from 15% to 10%.

It should be noted that the tribunal considered the wording of the legislation and found that, on **strict interpretation**, it should not take into account the circumstances of the earlier default when considering the later default. However, the tribunal felt that this was not the **purpose** of the legislation. The tribunal went on to state that the legislation, and HMRC guidance, does not make it clear that if a trader has a reasonable excuse, but does not appeal against an early surcharge which may only have a small (if any) financial penalty, the trader cannot then rely on this reasonable excuse when appealing a larger penalty at a later date. *Aardvark Excavations Ltd* [2007] (VTD 20468)

4091 Notice 700/50 para 6.3; VCP10533

When considering a reasonable excuse, HMRC will **take into account** whether the problem had existed for some time, and whether the trader:

a. could have foreseen the circumstances that led to the delay in submitting the return or paying the VAT, and if so, what steps were taken to make alternative arrangements;
b. contacted HMRC to seek help or advice;
c. gave sufficient priority to completing the return;
d. paid a reasonable estimate of the VAT liability by the due date; or
e. had previously used the same excuse.

HMRC has given **examples** of circumstances in which it accepts that there was a reasonable excuse: **4092** Notice 700/50 para 6.2

Circumstances	Details
Computer breakdown	Where records essential for completion of the VAT return are held on computer and it breaks down, either just before or during the preparation of the return. Reasonable steps must have been taken to correct the fault.
Illness	The person normally responsible for completing the VAT return is ill, and there was no one else capable of completing it. If it is a prolonged illness, reasonable steps must have been taken to allow someone else to complete the return.
Loss of key personnel	The person responsible for completing the VAT return leaves at short notice and there is no one else to complete the return on time for that period.
An unexpected cash crisis	Where funds are unavailable following: – the sudden reduction or withdrawal of overdraft facilities; – sudden non-payment by a normally reliable customer; – insolvency of a large customer; – fraud; – burglary; or – an act of God, such as fire.
Loss of records	Where records are stolen or destroyed. This excuse applies only to the current VAT period.

The following table gives examples of the outcome of **case law** where the taxpayer appealed against a default surcharge on the ground that there was a reasonable excuse: **4093**

Circumstances	Grounds for appeal	Reasonable excuse?	Comments
Compassionate circumstances	Illness or death of a relative	Yes	Overseas visits to ill mother during relevant VAT return periods. *A & A Everett* [1989] (VTD 3669)
		No	Death of mother before start of VAT period. *BA Smyth* [1990] (VTD 5039)
	Illness of book-keeper	Yes	Serious illness of only employee in a small business capable of operating computer. *Servewell Site Services Ltd, Plantasia Ltd* [1989] (VTD 3291)
		No	Company allowed the situation to continue for five successive defaults. *Lees Heginbotham & Sons Ltd* [1989] (VTD 4533)
Computer problems	Malfunctions	Yes	Prolonged breakdown due to installation of unauthorised software. *Television Information Network Ltd* [1989] (VTD 3403)
		No	No back-up copies of data had been kept. *JN Electrical Units* [1989] (VTD 3346)
Loss of key personnel	Sudden resignation or dismissal	Yes	Sudden resignation of finance director. *Gwent Technical Mouldings Ltd* [1992] (VTD 7939)
		No	Redundancy of book-keeper was a decision taken by the firm. *Greenhouse Stirton & Co* [1990] (VTD 5481)
	Absence on business or holiday	Yes	Director and only employee abroad on business. *Loadstone Ltd* [1992] (VTD 7878)
		No	Director should have delegated VAT return completion during his 3-week absence on business abroad. *Ultracolour Ltd* [1989](VTD 3278)

Circumstances	Grounds for appeal	Reasonable excuse?	Comments
Unexpected cash crisis	Late payment by major customer	Yes	The underlying cause of an insufficiency of funds may be a reasonable excuse, if not due to a lack of foresight, diligence or regard. *C & E v JB Steptoe* [1992] It was a reasonable excuse that a connected company was having cash flow problems even though the companies were not in a VAT group. Failure by a major customer was unforeseeable, inescapable and was not a culpable default of any of the VAT-registered businesses; the cash flow problem was not reasonably avoidable. *Stoke Park Ltd* [2008] (VTD 20603)
		No	Problems were relatively short-term, and 20% of business was with other customers. *J McCaig* [1991] (VTD 6362)
Loss or unavailability of records	Records temporarily unavailable	Yes	All VAT records were held by HMRC for inspection. *Windows Direct Ltd* [1990] (VTD 4762)
		No	Some documents were held by HMRC for inspection, but trader had not requested copies. *G & J Spencer Ltd* [1990] (VTD 5428)
	Fire at premises	Yes	Relocation to temporary premises necessary following a fire. *Philip Law Ltd* [1989] (VTD 3466)
		No	10-week period following a fire was long enough for company to deal with its VAT affairs. *John Pargeter & Sons Ltd* [1988] (VTD 3318)
Errors when paying VAT	Words and figures on cheque did not agree	Yes	Bank should have honoured cheque on basis of amount shown in words. *Covercraft Ltd* [1989] (VTD 3558)
	Cheque not signed	Yes	Cheque signed by only one of two signatories, but bank had previously honoured such cheques. *Swanlion Ltd* [1988] (VTD 3399)

b. Charging regime

Surcharge period

4094 s 59 VATA 1994; VCP10545 - 10549

On the occasion of a **first default**, HMRC will issue a surcharge liability notice specifying a **surcharge period**, which begins on the day of the notice and ends twelve months after the end of the VAT period for which the default arose.

If a **further default** occurs before the surcharge period has expired, a surcharge liability notice extension is issued. This extends the surcharge period until twelve months after the end of the VAT period for which the further default arose, and the extended period is regarded as a single surcharge period.

The trader's liability to surcharges expires if all the returns and payments for tax periods ending on or before the end of the surcharge period are submitted on time. In effect, this means that four quarterly returns and payments must be made on time in order to leave the surcharge system.

MEMO POINTS If there is a **change in the legal entity** carrying on a business, or if a **business is transferred as a going concern**, a surcharge period ends and any defaults, surcharge liability notices or surcharge assessments are not transferred to the new owner (unless the old VAT registration is transferred to the new entity or owner (¶8678+)).

Defaults not involving late payment of VAT

Special rules apply if a return is submitted late but: **4095** VCP10543, 10545
- the tax is paid on time;
- there is a nil liability; or
- a VAT repayment is due.

In this case, HMRC will not issue a initial surcharge notice: such a late return does not therefore, by itself, cause a surcharge period to begin.

However, if an **existing surcharge period** is running:
- a default will be recorded and the surcharge period extended; but
- there is no liability to pay a surcharge, and the default does not increase the rate of future surcharges (¶4096+).

Calculation of surcharge

If a default involving late payment of VAT occurs **during a surcharge period**, HMRC may issue a surcharge assessment for £30 or, if greater, a tax-related amount as follows: **4096** s 59 VATA 1994; Notice 700/50 para 4; VCP10542

Defaults during a surcharge period	Surcharge (% of VAT not paid by the due date)
1st	2% [1]
2nd	5% [1]
3rd	10%
4th and subsequent	15%

Note:
1. HMRC has stated that it will not collect a surcharge of **less than £400** calculated at the 2% or 5% rates, but the default is recorded and all other consequences apply as normal.

The following **example** shows how the rules apply: **4097**

EXAMPLE A Ltd has a poor compliance record. The following table summarises its compliance history since it first registered for VAT on 1 April 2013. All VAT payments are made by cheque.

VAT period	Due date	Return submitted	VAT paid	Default?	Action	Surcharge
30/06/13	31/07/13	04/08/13	£4,000 04/08/13	Yes	Issue surcharge liability notice to 30/06/14	n/a
30/09/13	31/10/13	31/10/13	£3,000 31/10/13	No		n/a
31/12/13	31/01/14	31/01/14	£5,000 03/02/14	Yes	Surcharge (2%) Extend surcharge period to 31/12/14	£100 (Not collected - below £400)
31/03/14	30/04/14	05/05/14	£4,500 30/04/14	Yes	Extend surcharge period to 31/03/15	£0 (VAT paid by due date)

30/06/14	31/07/14	30/07/14	£10,000 10/08/14	Yes	Surcharge (5%) Extend surcharge period to 30/06/15	£500
30/09/14	31/10/14	01/11/14	£250 01/11/14	Yes	Surcharge (10%) Extend surcharge period to 30/09/15	£30 (minimum)
31/12/14	31/01/15	30/01/15	£2,500 30/01/15	No		n/a
31/03/15	30/04/15	28/04/15	£5,000 02/05/15	Yes	Surcharge (15%) Extend surcharge period to 31/03/16	£750
30/06/15	31/07/15	08/08/15	£8,000 08/08/15	Yes	Surcharge (15%) Extend surcharge period to 30/06/16	£1,200

4098 s 59A VATA 1994; Notice 700/50 para 4 4; VCP10548

Payments on account regime If a large business is required to make payments on account (¶3182+) and defaults on any payment, the **surcharge liability notice** is issued at the end of the quarterly accounting period.

The surcharge is **calculated on** the total amount of all late payments of VAT in the period, but cannot exceed the VAT due as shown on the return.

If either of the payments is late, but the return itself shows a nil or repayment amount, the treatment is the same as in ¶4095.

EXAMPLE B Ltd is required to make payments on account of £200,000 per month. During a surcharge period, it made two late payments on account in respect of its VAT return for the period ended 30 September. The balancing payment of £120,000 for that period was also paid late. There were no previous defaults in the surcharge period.
The total amount of tax paid late is £520,000. (£200,000 + £200,000 + £120,000)
The surcharge is £10,400. (£520,000 x 2%)

4099 VCP10549

Recalculation of surcharge Where a surcharge is based on a **central assessment** issued by HMRC in the absence of a VAT return (¶3652+) and the return is submitted at a later date, the surcharge will be recalculated using the figures in the return.

A surcharge based on the figures in a **VAT return** will be recalculated if there is a subsequent error notification or assessment showing that tax was over-declared. A surcharge will not be recalculated if tax was under-declared, unless an additional assessment is issued after an assessment in the absence of a return.

2. Provision of an incorrect certificate

4100 s 62 VATA 1994

The **recipient of a supply** may be liable to a penalty for giving a certificate to the supplier which incorrectly states that the supply is:
a. an exempt supply of land, although in practice such certificates are rarely issued (¶5100+);

b. zero-rated, under the rules relating to the construction, renovation or alteration of property, where applicable (¶5100+);
c. at the reduced rate, under the rules relating to:
- supplies of domestic fuel or power (¶1116+);
- the installation of energy-saving materials (¶1136+);
- the grant-funded installation of heating equipment, security goods or a gas supply connection (¶1144+);
- women's sanitary products (¶1110);
- children's car seats (¶1156); or
- residential conversions, renovations or alterations, where applicable (¶5404+); or

d. not subject to VAT, under the rules for warehouses or fiscal warehouses (¶9242+).

Amount of penalty

The penalty is equal to the difference between the VAT due and the amount charged, **unless** the certificate relates to the acquisition of goods from another EU member state (¶9010+), in which case the penalty is equal to the VAT due on acquisition. **4102**

A penalty will **not be charged**, or may be cancelled on appeal, if there was a reasonable excuse (¶4014+), or may be reduced if there were mitigating circumstances (¶4044+).

3. Offences in relation to import VAT

a. Dishonest evasion

A person commits this offence by engaging in any dishonest conduct for the purposes of evading import VAT (¶9010+). **4104** s 25 FA 2003

The evasion of import VAT includes:
a. obtaining, where there was no entitlement:
- a repayment of import VAT;
- relief or exemption from import VAT; or
- a deferral or postponement of a liability to pay import VAT; or

b. evading the cancellation of entitlement to, or the withdrawal of, any such repayment, relief or exemption.

Demands and appeals

The penalty is treated as excise duty rather than VAT. Consequently: **4106**
- HMRC will issue a demand for the penalty, rather than an assessment; and
- an appeal cannot be lodged until HMRC has first conducted a review of the penalty position.

An appeal against a penalty can be made on the **grounds** that:
- the person had not acted dishonestly; or
- there was a fault in the way in which the penalty was charged or notified.

An appeal **cannot be made** on the ground that there was a reasonable excuse.

Amount of penalty

A penalty equal to the amount of import VAT which the person has evaded or sought to evade may be charged. The minimum penalty is £250. The maximum is normally £2,500 but may be increased if HMRC considers that the case is particularly serious. **4108** ss 25(1), 29 FA 2003

HMRC or, on appeal, a tribunal can **reduce** the penalty if there were mitigating circumstances. For the general factors which HMRC will take into account see ¶4048+.

Officers of companies

A director or managing officer may be personally liable to the penalty. For further details see ¶3992. **4110** s 28 FA 2003

b. Breach of rules

4112 s 26 FA 2003 A person commits this offence by engaging in any conduct which contravenes any UK legislation, EU legislation or customs rules, or relevant international rules in relation to import VAT.

ss 26, 29 FA 2003 A penalty of up to £2,500 may be charged. HMRC or, on appeal, a tribunal can **reduce** the penalty if there were mitigating circumstances. For the general factors which HMRC will take into account see ¶4048+.

An **appeal** against a penalty **can be made** on the **ground** that there was a reasonable excuse.

MEMO POINTS **Relevant international rules** are any international agreements which form part of UK law by virtue of any:
- Act or statutory instrument; or
- directly applicable EU legislation.

4. Failures in relation to sales lists

4120 There are two types of sales list that a trader may be required to submit:
a. EC sales lists (¶9330+); and
b. reverse charge sales lists (¶1998).

a. Failure to submit a list

4121 s 66 VATA 1994 If a person fails to submit the required sales list by the relevant due date, HMRC may issue a **notice** stating that a penalty will be charged if the list is not submitted within 14 days of the date of issue of the notice.

The **notice period** lasts for twelve months, beginning on the day after it is issued. A penalty may be charged if:
- the list which gave rise to the notice is not submitted within 14 days; or
- there are any further defaults in the notice period.

If there is a default in a notice period in relation to a list other than the one which gave rise to the notice, the period will be **extended** until twelve months have elapsed without any further default.

MEMO POINTS The relevant **due dates** for submission of the sales lists are as follows.
- **EC sales lists** are generally due 14 days after the end of the month to which they relate (or 21 days if the list is submitted electronically). For further details see ¶9334.
- **Reverse charge sales lists** are due to be submitted on the same date as the VAT return to which they relate (¶1998).

Amount of penalty

4122 s 66(5) VATA 1994 The penalty for each default is £50 or, if greater, a daily penalty from the day after the due date until the date of submission, **based on** the number of penalties incurred in a notice period, as follows:

Number of previous penalties in notice period	Daily penalty £	Maximum penalty £
None	5	500
1	10	1,000
2 or more	15	1,500

EXAMPLE HMRC issues a notice to A Ltd on 1 June, following its failure to submit an EC sales list for the period ended 31 March. Details for the year are as follows:

Month ended	EC sales list Due	Submitted	Late?	Penalty	Action
31 Mar	14 April	10 June	Yes	None - submitted within 14 days of notice	None
30 June	14 July	18 July	Yes	£50 (minimum amount)	Notice period extended until 12 months with no further default
31 Oct	14 Nov	30 Nov	Yes	£160 (£10 x 16)	Notice period extended until 12 months with no further default
31 Jan	14 Feb	16 Mar	Yes	£450 (£15 x 30)	Notice period extended until 12 months with no further default

Reasonable excuse

If there was a reasonable excuse (¶4014+) for failing to submit a list, a penalty will not be charged (or will be cancelled on appeal), and any penalty notice resulting from the default will be deemed not to have been issued. **4124** s 66(7) VATA 1994

HMRC **will accept** that there was a reasonable excuse if:
- the list was despatched in circumstances where it was reasonable to expect that it would have been received by HMRC on time; or
- there was a reasonable excuse for the list not having been despatched on time.

EXAMPLE

1. A penalty was cancelled where the trader had experienced difficulties in obtaining correct VAT numbers from overseas customers, and had sought assistance from HMRC. *The Decal Co Ltd* [1999] (VTD 16274)

2. A trader who had not received a sales list did not have a reasonable excuse for non-submission, because he should have requested a copy from HMRC. *J Proops (t/a JP Antiques)* [1999] (VTD 16409)

b. Submission of an inaccurate list

A person who submits **three or more** sales lists which contain a material inaccuracy may be liable to a fixed penalty of £100. **4125** s 65 VATA 1994

A material inaccuracy is **defined** as the inclusion or omission of any information which is misleading in any material respect.

The **three main types** of inaccuracy for EC sales lists are:
- details which are not valid, such as an incorrect VAT registration number;
- factual inaccuracies, such as showing the value of a supply as £1,000 instead of £1,000,000; and
- missing data.

Comment HMRC's manual does not refer to reverse charge sales lists when giving examples of types of inaccuracy. As the underlying law is the same for EC sales lists and reverse charge sales lists, the above should be used as a guide. VCP11000+

Procedure

4127 HMRC may, **within six months** of the date of discovering the inaccuracy, send a written warning stating that a notice may be issued if any further inaccurate lists are submitted.

If a **further** inaccurate list is submitted within two years of the day after the warning is issued, HMRC may issue a notice within six months of discovering the further inaccuracy. The notice will state that future inaccuracies will incur a penalty.

If **any subsequent** inaccurate lists are submitted within two years of the day after issue of the notice, HMRC may charge a penalty.

Reasonable excuse

4128 s 65(3) VATA 1994; Notice 725 para 17.13

If there was a reasonable excuse (¶4014+) for the inaccuracy, a penalty will not be charged, or will be cancelled on appeal, and any resulting warning or notice will be deemed not to have been issued.

HMRC will not accept that there is a reasonable excuse where a **VAT number** has been quoted for a customer which:
- does not conform to the published format for the EU member state in question; or
- HMRC has stated is not valid.

5. Breach of a walking possession agreement

4130 s 68 VATA 1994; VCP11500 +

A person who is in breach of a walking possession agreement (¶3765+) may be liable to a penalty of half of the VAT liability to which the agreement relates.

This provision does not apply in Scotland, where the law does not provide for walking possession agreements.

The **conditions** which normally need to be fulfilled for a penalty assessment to be raised are that:
- the agreement was signed by a sole proprietor, partner, director or company secretary; and
- an HMRC officer or bailiff has visited the premises and confirmed that the goods in question are not available.

The **amount** of the penalty is 50% of the unpaid amount.

Exercise of discretion

4131 HMRC will not normally charge a penalty if this would only increase the amount to be written off, with **no compliance effect**, where:

a. a company has gone into liquidation, as a penalty is not an enforceable debt against the liquidator;

b. an individual trader (or partner in a partnership) has been, or is likely to be, made bankrupt;

c. a business has ceased and there are no funds or assets; or

d. the trader is missing.

4133 VCP11541

The following table sets out the **factors** which HMRC considers when deciding whether to charge a penalty:

Factors supporting issue of a penalty	Factors opposing issue of a penalty
The tax remains unpaid	The trader pays the outstanding tax, charges and fees
No other goods are available for distraint	Other goods are available for distraint
The estimated forced sale value of the goods removed or sold by the trader is at least 10% of the tax debt	The estimated forced sale value of the goods removed or sold by the trader is less than 10% of the debt
The value of the goods removed exceeds £1,000	The value of the goods removed is less than £1,000

Factors supporting issue of a penalty	Factors opposing issue of a penalty
	An unguaranteed cheque offered in payment was refused without being sent for special clearance
	The trader applies the sale proceeds of goods removed towards settlement of the tax
	The goods are still on the trader's premises but the officer or bailiff cannot gain access
	The trader is normally compliant and has not previously been in breach of an agreement

Reasonable excuse

There is **no power of mitigation** of this penalty. However, a penalty will not be charged, or may be cancelled, if there was a reasonable excuse (¶4014+) for the breach. **4134** VCP11532

The following **circumstances** may represent grounds for a reasonable excuse:
a. the goods were accidentally damaged by fire or in a road traffic accident, where temporary removal was authorised;
b. the goods were stolen by a third party;
c. distraint action was excessive because the value of the goods substantially exceeded the tax debt;
d. the goods were insufficiently detailed in the agreement;
e. the goods were perishable or subject to rapid turnover, such as tobacco, and were sold whilst they still had some value;
f. there was an excessive delay between the date of the distraint action and the removal of the goods, or a lack of regular contact, leading the trader to believe that distraint had been abandoned; or
g. a deferred payment arrangement was agreed, and the trader believed that the walking possession agreement no longer applied.

6. Failure to comply with a tribunal direction or summons

A person who fails to comply with a direction (¶4301) or summons (¶4297) issued by a tribunal may be liable to a penalty of up to £1,000. **4139** Sch 12 para 10 VATA 1994

An appeal against this penalty must be made to the High Court or, in Scotland, the Court of Session.

MEMO POINTS 1. This provision **applies to** HMRC as well as to others.
2. A failure to comply with directions may **result in** an appeal being decided in favour of the other party (¶4308).
3. This provision was **repealed** with the introduction of the First-tier Tribunal on 1 April 2009 but still applies to cases which were before the VAT tribunal before that date (and which remain ongoing).

EXAMPLE HMRC failed to comply with a tribunal direction to serve a statement of case within an extended time limit.
The tribunal awarded a penalty of £200 against HMRC. *Wine Warehouses Ltd* [1993] (VTD 11525)

7. Failure to notify use of a notifiable scheme

If a person fails to notify use of a notifiable VAT scheme (¶3030+) in time, a penalty will be levied. Where the failure is in relation to a scheme that is: **4140** Sch 11A paras 10, 11 VATA 1994
– a **designated scheme**, the penalty is 15% of the VAT saving achieved on every affected return or claim.
– **not a designated scheme**, the amount of the penalty is £5,000.

8. Failure to keep specified records

Specified records in relation to certain goods

4141 s 69B VATA 1994 A person who fails to comply with a direction to keep specified records in relation to certain goods (¶3485+) may be liable to a daily penalty of £200, up to a maximum of 30 days.

In addition, a penalty of £500 may be charged where the records are not preserved for the specified period.

4142 s 69A VATA 1994 MEMO POINTS A person who fails to keep the required records or provide information required in relation to **transactions in gold** (¶6830+) may be liable to a penalty of up to 17.5% of the value of the transactions in question.

A penalty cannot be charged more than two years after HMRC becomes aware of the failure.

The regulatory penalties, including the penalty for a general failure to keep records (¶4058+), cannot be charged in addition to this penalty.

SECTION 2

Criminal penalties

4150 For some offences, HMRC may bring criminal proceedings instead of imposing a civil penalty. HMRC will normally only do so in cases of **serious fraud**.

Proceedings can be brought under specific VAT legislation, or under general criminal law, where VAT legislation does not cover the particular offence.

Conviction may result in a fine, or imprisonment, or both. The amount of a penalty or length of a prison sentence depends on whether the case is brought summarily or on indictment (¶4158).

HMRC offers a **Contractual Disclosure Facility** (CDF), under which those suspected of fraud are able to avoid criminal investigation by taking advantage of the facility. Under the CDF, HMRC will make the first approach, by contacting a taxpayer in writing. HMRC will warn that it suspects the taxpayer of serious tax fraud, and offer the opportunity of entering into a contract to disclose that fraud within 60 days. In return, HMRC agrees **not to begin a criminal investigation**, removing the risk of prosecution by HMRC. The investigation is then carried out using civil powers, with a view to a civil settlement for tax, interest and a financial penalty. Those who do not respond positively to HMRC's offer face a full investigation by HMRC, possibly a criminal investigation with a view to prosecution. Moreover, HMRC says that anyone who signs the contract but does not go on to admit and disclose fraud also faces the possibility of a criminal investigation. In addition, taxpayers who are not under investigation but who want to admit to tax fraud may voluntarily fill out a form to request that HMRC consider their suitability for a CDF arrangement. In these circumstances, HMRC retains discretion to decide which cases are dealt on a civil basis, and which are investigated with a view to criminal prosecution.

Compounding

4152 s 152 CEMA 1979 **As an alternative** to bringing criminal proceedings, HMRC may "compound", or settle out of court, the proceedings by accepting a financial settlement.

However, HMRC will **normally not offer** compounding where the person who committed the offence:
– has obstructed or assaulted an officer;
– is subject to a suspended prison sentence or is on parole;
– is being investigated for other related offences by HMRC, the police or another government department;

- is an undischarged bankrupt or a company in liquidation; or
- is a persistent offender.

The **purpose** of compounding is to save time and money, both for HMRC and taxpayers, by avoiding the need for legal proceedings. **4154** Notice 700 para 27.4

HMRC will only offer a compound settlement where it has sufficient **evidence** for legal proceedings; each case is considered on its own merits.

The following **factors** will be taken into account:
- the seriousness of the alleged offence;
- the penalty which a court might impose;
- the nature and value of any goods involved;
- the amount of tax involved;
- the costs of investigating the offence;
- any aggravating circumstances; and
- the ability of the taxpayer to pay an appropriate penalty.

HMRC will normally prosecute an **offender** who **does not accept** an offer of compounding. An offer to compound cannot be appealed.

MEMO POINTS 1. In **Scotland**, compounding cannot apply to proceedings on indictment.
2. HMRC may **disclose details** of a compounded settlement to:
- the courts, if the offender is prosecuted for a similar offence in the next five years;
- an employer, where the nature of the employment facilitated the offence;
- other government departments whose statutory responsibilities are affected by the offender's actions; or
- the UK Parliament or the media, if it is in the public interest.

Offences subject to criminal penalties

The offences in relation to VAT which are subject to criminal penalties are as follows: **4156**

Type of offence	Details	¶¶
Evading VAT	Fraudulent evasion of VAT	¶4160+
	Being a party to a transaction involving VAT evasion	¶4166
	Cheating the public revenue	¶4168+
	Breach of conditions for VAT relief on goods supplied to visitors to the UK	¶4172+
Relating to documents and statements	Producing a false document or making a false statement	¶4180+
	Making an untrue declaration	¶4183
	Counterfeiting or falsifying documents	¶4184
	Criminal fraud	¶4186
	False accounting	¶4187
	Forgery	¶4189
	Perjury	¶4190
	Concealment	¶4192
Conduct which must have involved the commission of an offence		¶4194+
Trading without providing required security		¶4197
Offences in relation to HMRC officers	Impersonation	¶4198
	Bribery	¶4200
	Obstruction	¶4201
	Assault	¶4204
Failure to make an Intrastat declaration		¶4205

Types of proceedings

4158 s 146A CEMA 1979 Criminal proceedings may be brought in two ways:

Type of proceedings	Details	Time limit for bringing proceedings
Summary	Proceedings brought in a magistrates' court or, in Scotland or Northern Ireland, a court of summary jurisdiction	3 years after offence committed
On indictment	Proceedings brought in a crown court	20 years after offence committed

A. Evading VAT

Fraudulent evasion of VAT

4160 s 72(1), (2) VATA 1994 A person commits this offence by being knowingly concerned in, or in the taking of steps with a view to, the fraudulent evasion of VAT.

Evasion **includes** obtaining payment of a VAT credit or refund.

MEMO POINTS 1. Any **deliberate non-payment** of VAT, whether or not with a permanent intention, is evasion. *R v Dealy* [1995]

2. **Taking of steps** need not mean taking positive steps. *R v McCarthy* [1981]

3. The House of Lords has held that HMRC can also **seek damages** under common law against an entity which is not accountable for VAT, where the VAT cannot otherwise be recovered, as VAT is not an exclusive regime. *HMRC v Total Networks SL* [2008]

4162 Notice 700 para 27.4 **Official policy** The **circumstances** in which HMRC is likely to bring criminal proceedings for the fraudulent evasion of VAT include:

a. registration of one or more businesses whose activities are solely or primarily bogus, or undertaken as a systematic tax fraud;

b. a deliberate attempt to deceive during the course of an investigation into a civil offence;

c. a conspiracy by two or more parties to evade VAT; and

d. evasion:

- perpetrated by professionals, tax officials or government officers;
- also involving other taxes;
- carried out by someone who had previously committed a tax offence;
- by an undischarged bankrupt; or
- whilst trading without having given security requested by HMRC.

4164 **Conviction** The **sentence** may be a fine, imprisonment or both:

Penalty (either or both)	On summary conviction	On conviction on indictment
Fine	The greater of: - £5,000; or - three times the amount of the VAT evaded[1]	An unlimited amount
Imprisonment	Up to six months	Up to seven years

Note:
1. The tax evaded is the aggregate of overstated input tax and understated output tax amounts, or any other amount falsely claimed as a refund or repayment.

Being a party to a transaction involving VAT evasion

4166 s 72(10) VATA 1994 It is an offence to acquire, import or deal with goods, or accept a supply of services, where there is reason to believe that VAT has been or will be evaded.

Summary **conviction** will result in a **fine** of up to the **greater of**:
- £5,000; or
- three times the amount of the VAT evaded.

Cheating the public revenue

The offence of cheating the public revenue is a common law offence. It **includes** any form of fraudulent conduct which results in diverting money from the revenue, whether or not there was a positive act of deception. **4168**

HMRC may **bring proceedings** under these provisions in serious or unusual cases, including those where VAT legislation may not be applicable.

Conviction will result in a fine and/or imprisonment, at the discretion of the court. **4170**

EXAMPLE A director of a company which failed to make VAT returns or account for VAT estimated at over £1.2 million was convicted of cheating the public revenue.
It was held that he had deliberately set out to avoid payment of VAT on a massive scale. He was sentenced to six years' imprisonment and made criminally bankrupt in the sum of £629,000. *R v Mavji* [1986]

Breach of conditions for VAT-free supply of goods to a UK visitor

It is an offence to breach the conditions on which relief from payment of VAT was granted on a supply or importation of goods for persons enjoying certain immunities or privileges (¶9296+). **4172** s 13 Customs and Excise General Duties (Reliefs) Act 1979

A person **commits** an offence by acquiring goods:
- and using them when not permitted to do so, or for a purpose which is not permitted; or
- for use by a person who is not permitted to do so, or for a purpose which is not permitted, or disposes of the goods to such a person.

Summary **conviction** will result in a **fine** of up to £5,000. The goods concerned are liable to forfeiture. **4174**

B. Offences in relation to documents or statements

Producing a false document or making a false statement

It is an offence to: **4180** s 72(3) - (7) VATA 1994
- produce a false document with intent to deceive; or
- knowingly or recklessly make a false statement when providing information for VAT purposes.

This offence **includes**:
- producing, furnishing, sending or otherwise making use of a document which is false in a material particular, including intending to secure that a machine will respond to the document as if it were a true document; or
- causing such a document to be produced, furnished or sent.

Conviction will result in a fine, imprisonment or both: **4181**

Penalty (either or both)	On summary conviction	On conviction on indictment
Fine	The greater of: - £5,000; or - three times the amount of the VAT evaded[1]	An unlimited amount
Imprisonment	Up to six months	Up to seven years

Note:
1. The tax evaded is the aggregate of overstated input tax and understated output tax amounts or any other amount falsely claimed as a refund or repayment.

Making an untrue declaration

4183 s 167 CEMA 1979 It is an offence to make an untrue declaration, or an untrue statement in answer to a question, in respect of any relevant matter.

This offence **includes** making or signing, or causing to be made or signed, or delivering or causing to be delivered, any declaration, notice, certificate or other document to HMRC.

Conviction will result in a fine, imprisonment or both:

Penalty (either or both)	On summary conviction	On conviction on indictment
Fine	£5,000	An unlimited amount
Imprisonment	Up to six months	Up to two years

Counterfeiting or falsifying documents

4184 s 168 CEMA 1979 A person **commits** this offence by:
- counterfeiting or falsifying any relevant document;
- knowingly accepting, receiving or using such a counterfeited or falsified document;
- altering any such document after it is officially issued; or
- counterfeiting any seal, signature, initials, or other mark used by an officer to verify such a document or for any other purpose.

Conviction will result in a fine, imprisonment or both:

Penalty (either or both)	On summary conviction	On conviction on indictment
Fine	£5,000	An unlimited amount
Imprisonment	Up to six months	Up to twelve years

Criminal fraud

4186 s 1 Fraud Act 2006 This is an offence under general criminal law which may in some circumstances apply to VAT matters. It replaces the former offences of obtaining property or a pecuniary advantage by deception.

A person **commits** an offence by conduct with the intention of either making a gain (or providing a gain for another) or causing another person to risk or suffer a loss, through:
- false representation;
- failing to disclose information; or
- abusing a position in which the offender is expected to safeguard, or not to act against, the financial interests of another person.

An officer of a company who is complicit in the company's actions may also be prosecuted.

Conviction will result in a fine, imprisonment or both:

Penalty (either or both)	On summary conviction	On conviction on indictment
Fine	£5,000	An unlimited amount
Imprisonment	Up to twelve months	Up to ten years

False accounting

4187 s 17 Theft Act 1968 This is an offence under general criminal law which may in some circumstances apply to VAT matters. There is no similar statutory offence in **Scotland**.

A person **commits** an offence by acting dishonestly, with a view to making a gain (or with intent to cause loss to another person) through:
- destroying, defacing, concealing or falsifying any account, record or document; or

– producing or using any account, record or document in the knowledge that it is materially misleading, false or deceptive.

Conviction will result in a fine, imprisonment or both:

Penalty (either or both)	On summary conviction	On conviction on indictment
Fine	£5,000	An unlimited amount
Imprisonment	Up to twelve months	Up to ten years

Forgery

This is an offence under general criminal law which may in some circumstances apply to VAT matters. This does not apply in **Scotland**, where the offence is dealt with under common law. **4189** ss 1 - 4 Forgery and Counterfeiting Act 1981

A person **commits** an offence by making, copying, using, or using a copy of, a false instrument with the intention of inducing someone to accept it as genuine.

Conviction will result in a fine, imprisonment or both:

Penalty (either or both)	On summary conviction	On conviction on indictment
Fine	£5,000	(Not applicable)
Imprisonment	Up to six months	Up to ten years

Perjury

This is an offence under general criminal law which may in some circumstances apply to VAT matters. This does not apply in **Scotland**, where the offence is dealt with under common law. **4190** s 1 Perjury Act 1911

A **witness** in any tribunal or court commits an offence by wilfully making a statement in the knowledge that it is false, or in the belief that it is untrue.

The **penalty** for perjury is imprisonment for up to seven years. However, prosecutions for perjury are rare.

Concealment

Once a person has been issued with an information notice (¶3458+) or notified in writing by HMRC that a notice will be issued, it is a criminal offence for that person to conceal or destroy a document which is the subject of the notice, or to arrange for its concealment or destruction. **4192** Sch 36 FA 2008

Once a tax agent has been issued with a notice in connection with dishonest conduct (¶4026), it is a criminal offence for the agent to conceal or destroy a material document, or to arrange for its concealment or destruction.

Conviction will result in a fine or imprisonment:

Penalty	On summary conviction	On conviction on indictment
Fine	£5,000	(Not applicable)
Imprisonment	(Not applicable)	Up to two years

C. Other offences

Conduct which must have involved the commission of an offence

4194 s 72(8) VATA 1994 A person **commits** this offence by conduct during a specified period which must have involved:
- fraudulently evading VAT;
- producing a false document with intent to deceive; or
- knowingly or recklessly making a false statement when providing information for VAT purposes.

This applies whether or not the particulars are known.

4195 **Conviction** will result in a fine, imprisonment or both:

Penalty (either or both)	On summary conviction	On conviction on indictment
Fine	Up to the greater of: – £5,000; or – three times the amount of the VAT evaded[1]	An unlimited amount
Imprisonment	Up to six months	Up to seven years
Note: 1. The tax evaded is the aggregate of overstated input tax and understated output tax amounts, or any other amount falsely claimed as a refund or repayment.		

Trading without providing required security

4197 s 72(11) VATA 1994 It is an offence to supply or receive goods or services without having provided security (¶3546+), following a request to do so by HMRC.

The penalty on summary conviction is a fine of £5,000.

Offences in relation to HMRC officers

4198 s 30 CRCA 2005 **Impersonation** It is an offence to pretend to be a Commissioner or an officer of HMRC with a view to obtaining admission to premises, information or any other benefit.

Summary **conviction** will result in a fine, imprisonment or both:

Penalty (either or both)	On summary conviction
Fine	Up to £5,000
Imprisonment	Up to 51 weeks (six months in Scotland or Northern Ireland)

4200 s 1 Bribery Act 2010 **Bribery** It is an offence to bribe (or attempt to bribe) an HMRC officer. This does not apply in **Scotland**, where the offence is dealt with under common law.

Conviction will result in a fine, imprisonment or both:

Penalty (either or both)	On summary conviction	On conviction on indictment
Fine	Up to £5,000	An unlimited amount
Imprisonment	Up to twelve months (six months in Northern Ireland)	Up to ten years

4201 s 31 CRCA 2005 **Obstruction** It is an **offence** to obstruct an officer of HMRC or a person assisting an officer, in the performance of their duty, without reasonable excuse.

Summary **conviction** will result in a fine, imprisonment or both:

Penalty (either or both)	On summary conviction
Fine	Up to £1,000
Imprisonment	Up to 51 weeks (six months in Scotland or Northern Ireland)

Assault It is an offence to assault an HMRC officer. 4204 s 32 CRCA 2005
Summary **conviction** will result in a fine, imprisonment or both:

Penalty (either or both)	On summary conviction
Fine	Up to £5,000
Imprisonment	Up to 51 weeks (six months in Scotland or Northern Ireland)

Failure to make an Intrastat declaration

It is an offence to fail to: 4205 SI1992/2790
- make a supplementary declaration under the Intrastat system (¶9345+); or
- provide information requested by HMRC in relation to Intrastat declarations.

The penalty on summary conviction is a fine of £2,500.

CHAPTER 4

Reviews and appeals

OUTLINE ¶¶

4210 This chapter deals with the current system of reviews and appeals, **which covers all taxes, including VAT**. This system came into operation on 1 April 2009. Unless otherwise noted, cases referred to in this chapter were decided under the former system of rules and procedures for appeals, but may be persuasive in similar matters under the current system.

MEMO POINTS Prior to 1 April 2009 any person who was affected by a decision made by HMRC could have:
a. asked HMRC to reconsider the decision; or
b. appealed against the decision to a VAT tribunal, provided that the matter was appealable, and that the person had sufficient involvement in the matter.
A request for reconsideration and an appeal could have been made at the same time.
In addition, a trader who was unhappy about the way in which HMRC handled their affairs could make a complaint to the Adjudicator (¶4252+).

SECTION 1

Internal review and appeals: an overview

4220 The current system of appeals to tribunals and courts applies to all appeals made since 1 April 2009.

In an attempt to make dealings with HMRC **more consistent** across all taxes, the following procedures are also available:
- a statutory internal review process (¶4230+); and
- since 2 September 2013, an alternative dispute resolution (ADR) process (¶4240+).

The **procedures in force** for requesting an internal review by HMRC, invoking the ADR system, and appealing to the tribunal are described in sections 2 and 3 of this chapter.

The diagram **Appeal process** opposite illustrates how the system operates and the progress of a matter through the tribunal and court system. The offer of a review is mandatory in VAT cases but does not have to be taken up.

MEMO POINTS 1. Some offences did not come under the **new penalty regime** until 1 April 2010, but any appeals against a decision made by HMRC since 1 April 2009 have to be made under the **new appeals process**. For details of the penalty regime see ¶3950+.
2. Where a decision was issued by HMRC before 1 April 2009, the previous provisions for non-statutory reviews and **reconsiderations** (see *VAT Memo 2008-2009*) continue to apply.
3. **Guidance** on these procedures has been issued by HMRC, and is contained in the Appeals, Reviews and Tribunal Guidance Manual.

Appellant bodies

4225 Tribunals, Courts and Enforcement Act 2007

All appeals against HMRC's decisions are made to one independent body, the Tax Chamber of HM Courts & Tribunals Service. There are two tribunals, known as the First-tier Tribunal and the Upper Tribunal.

The **First-tier Tribunal** hears most appeals in the first instance. The **Upper Tribunal** hears appeals against decisions made in the First-tier Tribunal. The Upper Tribunal also hears some first-instance appeals, depending on the nature and complexity of the matter. It is **still possible** to appeal on a point of law to the Court of Appeal in England and Wales, and Northern Ireland, and to the higher courts (¶4328+), but appeals are no longer made to the High Court. In Scotland appeals are made to the Court of Session (¶4330).

Appeal process

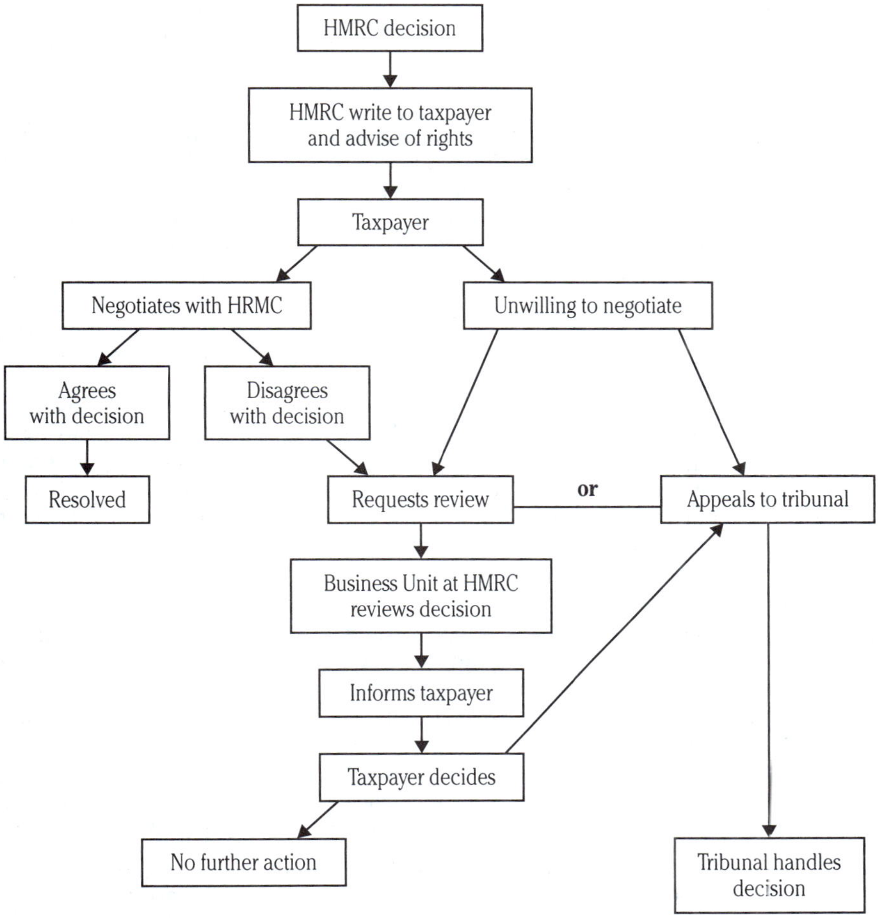

SECTION 2

Internal reviews

A. Statutory reviews

The duty to offer an internal review applies as a statutory first step, but only **if the matter is capable of being appealed**. If the matter can be appealed, HMRC must offer a review. **4230** Notice 700 para 28; s 83A VATA 1994

If the matter **cannot be appealed**, HMRC does not have to offer an internal review, but a person who has an interest in the matter may be able to request a review or apply for ADR (¶4240+).

It may be more appropriate to take up the opportunity of a review than to make an immediate appeal, particularly where a trader can provide further information, or is able to draw HMRC's attention to facts which may not previously have been taken into account.

MEMO POINTS A review will **not be carried** out if appeal proceedings have already begun.

Time limits

4232 ss 83B - 83G VATA 1994 **The trader** has 30 days, from the date on which the decision was first communicated to them, to request a review and, similarly, 30 days in which to accept HMRC's offer of a review.

A person who has an interest in the matter, such as the recipient of a supply in question, has 30 days from the date they become aware of the decision in which to request a review. The offer of a review to a trader takes priority, so if the trader has accepted an offer of a review within the 30-day time limit, HMRC is not required to accept a request from an interested party.

If the offer is not accepted within the 30-day time limit, but the trader or interested party **later decides** that they would like to have a review, **HMRC may accept** the late application for a review, provided that it is satisfied that:
- there was a reasonable excuse for not accepting the offer within the time limit; and
- the request has been made without unreasonable delay after the excuse ceased to apply.

If a trader or interested party requests an HMRC review after the 30-day time limit, and **HMRC refuses the request**, then, with effect from 1 June 2014, there is no right of appeal against this refusal. Given that the request for a review has been made out of time, an application must be made to the tribunal for permission to appeal out of time.

Procedure

4234 s 83F VATA 1994 The review is carried out by a member of HMRC who was previously unconnected with the case. HMRC is normally required to **complete a review** within 45 days of receiving the request, although a longer period may be agreed. The review will consider the trader's representations and all the facts, taking into account any further information provided, and may include taking technical or legal advice if necessary.

MEMO POINTS 1. **Minor discrepancies** may be resolved by discussion with the trader.
2. A **negotiated settlement** may be possible where there is room for compromise, particularly where the amount of tax at stake does not warrant the costs of making or defending an appeal to a tribunal.
3. HMRC has said that it is not the intention of the review procedure to uncover other details about the trader's affairs, but is limited to the matter in question. Nevertheless, traders and their representatives should consider whether the matter can be resolved by a review, or if it may be **disadvantageous** to the outcome they seek. There is no obligation to take up the offer of a review.
4. The HMRC officer dealing with the matter may **communicate** directly with the trader in the course of the review.

4236 If HMRC is satisfied that the **original decision** is technically and legally **valid**, it will notify the trader and provide a full explanation of the reasons for that conclusion.

Alternatively, if HMRC concedes that the **decision was incorrect**, it will be varied or cancelled. In either circumstance a 30-day time limit (¶4270+) for an appeal applies.

If HMRC **does not give a decision** by the end of the review period, the original decision is deemed to be upheld. The trader can then appeal to the tribunal at that point.

MEMO POINTS **Traders who do not receive a decision** from HMRC should be aware that a new 30-day countdown for making an appeal starts as soon as the 30-day review period expires. If there is a delay by HMRC in reviewing a matter and an extension has not been agreed, the trader should be aware that this new time limit has commenced.

Collection of tax

4238 The **tax due must be paid** before a case can be taken to appeal (subject to any application for hardship relief (¶4278)), but payment can be postponed whilst a review is carried out, if HMRC considers this appropriate.

B. Alternative dispute resolution (ADR)

ADR is an informal process for resolving disputes by introducing a member of HMRC who was not involved in the initial issue, and who works with the parties in an attempt to broker an agreement. HMRC refers to this person as a "facilitator", and describes the facilitator as "a neutral and impartial HMRC third party". In some cases an external mediator will also be involved if necessary. HMRC adds that "ADR cannot guarantee resolution of the dispute but by the end of the process, whether or not the dispute is resolved, you will have clarity on the outstanding issues and what happens next." 4240

ADR is mainly intended for **small and medium-sized enterprises**, which in the VAT context means those not classified by HMRC as large or complex cases. HMRC has said that although ADR is open to **large or complex businesses**, it is preferable for such a business to make contact first, with a view to discussing the possible use of ADR, rather than making an immediate application. For further information, see flmemo.co.uk/vm4240

Suitable circumstances for ADR

ADR should generally be considered in any case which is protracted, or which appears to be headed for litigation. For example, it may be appropriate when: 4242
- it is proving difficult to pin down the facts or the essential points of disagreement;
- the working relationship between HMRC and the trader appears to have broken down, or
- an out-of-court settlement is likely to be preferable to a determination by the Tribunal or the courts (for instance, because it is more cost-effective).

MEMO POINTS In HMRC's view, ADR is not appropriate for disputes about:
- payment of tax;
- remission of fixed penalties on the grounds of reasonable excuse;
- default surcharges;
- HMRC delays in using information; or
- cases being dealt with by HMRC's criminal investigators.

The ADR process

Either party to a dispute can suggest ADR as a method of resolving the matter, whether or not an appealable decision or assessment has been made by HMRC. 4244

HMRC states that the application should not be made too early (before all the relevant facts have been established and discussed) or too late (too close to a tribunal hearing, which HMRC generally considers to be at the point where a Statement of Case is due in fewer than 20 days). The best time to apply for ADR is after all the relevant facts have been established and an impasse has been reached.

Application by a trader for ADR should normally be made online at flmemo.co.uk/vm4244.

HMRC aims to respond within 30 days, stating whether or not it will take part in ADR. The trader will be expected to complete a Memorandum of Understanding, to confirm participation in and commitment to ADR. The facilitator will then work with the trader and the HMRC case officer to see if the dispute can be settled, usually through meetings or telephone calls.

If a complete settlement is not reached on an appealable decision, the trader can ask for a statutory review (¶4230+) or lodge an appeal (¶4260+).

C. Complaints to the Adjudicator

Any person who has a complaint about the way in which HMRC has handled their VAT affairs can bring this to the attention of the Adjudicator. 4252

Role of the Adjudicator

4253 The Adjudicator is an independent person who aims to **investigate** and help to **resolve** complaints from individuals and businesses who are unhappy about the way in which their affairs have been handled.

The Adjudicator will:
- **consider** whether HMRC has handled the complaint appropriately and given a reasonable decision; and
- if applicable, **recommend** what HMRC should do to put matters right.

In practice HMRC accept recommendations made by the Adjudicator.

The Adjudicator has a website (flmemo.co.uk/vm4253), from which further information can be obtained.

Scope

4254 The Adjudicator will **consider complaints** about:
- the use of discretion;
- mistakes;
- poor or misleading advice;
- unreasonable delays; and
- inappropriate staff behaviour.

However, the Adjudicator is **excluded** from looking into:
- government or departmental policy;
- matters which can be, or have been, considered on appeal by a tribunal or the courts; and
- complaints which can be, or have been, considered by the Parliamentary Ombudsman.

Further, the Adjudicator cannot ask HMRC to do anything outside its current Codes of Practice or procedural instructions.

Procedure

4256 A complaint can only be made to the Adjudicator **after HMRC's own complaints procedure has been exhausted**, and a final response received.

Full details of the complaint, including what action the complainant alleges HMRC ought to take in putting matters right, should be sent to the Adjudicator's office at:
The Adjudicator's Office
PO Box 10280
Nottingham
NG2 9PF

The Adjudicator will investigate the complaint, but cannot ask HMRC to suspend any action which it may be taking in the meantime. The stated aim is to complete the investigation within six months.

The Adjudicator will normally **inform** the taxpayer of their **findings** in writing, which will include details of any recommendation to be made to HMRC.

Conclusion

4258 If the Adjudicator upholds the complaint, they will either:
a. recommend what HMRC should do to put matters right; this may **include** asking it to:
- apologise;
- meet any additional costs incurred as a result of mistakes or delays; or
- make a payment in recognition of any worry or distress that may have been caused; or

b. mediate between the parties to find a mutually acceptable solution.

A taxpayer who is not satisfied with the Adjudicator's findings can write to their MP or the Parliamentary Ombudsman at:
The Parliamentary and Health Service Ombudsman
Millbank Tower
Millbank
London
SW1P 4QP.
The Ombudsman has a website (flmemo.co.uk/vm4258), from which further information can be obtained.

EXAMPLE In 2006 the Adjudicator received a complaint from a company which arranged hospitality and other events. The company had requested an educational visit from HMRC, who had advised that VAT should not be charged on ticket-only sales. Subsequently, HMRC advised that VAT was in fact due, and requested payment. The company asked HMRC to waive payment under the misdirection concession (¶3687), but HMRC refused to do so.
The Adjudicator found that HMRC had initially provided incorrect advice, and upheld the complaint on the ground that HMRC had made a mistake. The Adjudicator recommended that HMRC take no further recovery action, and reimburse the reasonable costs incurred by the company. HMRC accepted the recommendations.

SECTION 3

Appeals

An appeal against a decision by HMRC must initially be made to the tribunal. After the tribunal's decision, either party may then appeal to the Upper Tribunal and thence to the UK courts (¶4328+), provided that leave to appeal has been granted at each stage. Depending on the issue in point, the tribunal or the courts may refer a case to the CJEU (¶4345+). **4260**

Where there is **no right of appeal** against a decision by HMRC or a tribunal, a person can apply for a judicial review (¶4338+).

A. Appeals to the tribunals

Tribunals are independent of HMRC, and are run by the Tribunals Service of the Ministry of Justice or, in Scotland, the Scottish Executive. They are intended to provide a **less formal** and **less expensive** method of appealing against the decisions of HMRC as compared to that offered by the courts. **4262**

1. Scope

Persons who can appeal

Most appeals are made by VAT-registered persons in relation to the VAT liability of their supplies. **4264**

Appeals can **also** be made by:
– the recipient of a supply, where they have sufficient interest in the matter; or
– a third party with a sufficient interest who is joined to an appeal.

EXAMPLE

1. The recipient of a supply is entitled to appeal against a decision that VAT is chargeable on that supply. *Processed Vegetable Growers Association Ltd* [1973] (VTD 25)

2. A company was joined with HMRC as a party to an appeal, where it had a significant financial interest in the outcome.
It was held that this would allow another informed viewpoint to be heard, and would assist in determining the appeal. *Barclays Bank plc* [1992] (VTD 7911)

Decisions which can be appealed

4265 s 83 VATA 1994

The following matters can be appealed:

Matters covered		¶¶
Penalties common to most or all taxes	Inaccuracy, failure to notify, VAT wrongdoing	¶3955+
Evasion of import VAT		¶4104+
Mitigation of amount	Failure to keep records of gold transactions	¶4142
	Evasion of import VAT	¶4104+
Reasonable excuse (imposition or amount)	Penalties for breach of regulations	¶4050+
	Default surcharge	¶4082+
	Failure to keep specified records	¶4141+
	Provision of incorrect certificates	¶4100+
	Failure to submit sales list	¶4121+
	Submission of inaccurate sales list	¶4125+
	Breach of import VAT rules	¶4112
	Breach of walking possession agreement	¶4130+
All other penalties and related matters	Penalty for failure to notify VAT avoidance scheme	¶3076
	Appeals against liability to, or the amount of, other penalties or surcharges	¶4220+
Assessments	All assessments to VAT	¶3625+
VAT liabilities in general	Decisions regarding registration and deregistration	¶2600+
	Rulings on liability to account for VAT on particular supplies	
	Decisions regarding input tax claims	¶1800+
	Decisions regarding the allowable proportion of input tax	¶2086
	Decisions regarding bad debt relief claims	¶840+
	Directions to treat two or more persons as one entity (business splitting)	¶2629+
	Directions that transactions between connected persons and supplies of goods to non-taxable persons for resale are treated as made at open market value	¶960+
	Directions that acquisitions between connected persons are treated as made at open market value	¶9034
	Requirements in relation to self-billed invoices	¶2904+
	Requirements in relation to electronic production of invoices or other documents	¶2850+
	Direction to notify a VAT saving scheme in cases of business splitting, where a person would otherwise be exempt from a duty to notify	¶3044

Matters covered		¶¶
Payment of VAT and interest	Claims for VAT repayments	¶3230+
	Requirement to provide security as a condition of VAT registration or making a VAT credit	¶3524+
	Notice of joint and several liability	¶2002+
	Recovery of incorrect refunds	¶3281+
	Recovery of refunds or credits under the unjust enrichment rules	¶3254+
	Disputes over payment of statutory interest by HMRC	¶3270+
	Disputes over recovery of statutory interest payments	¶3270+
	Decisions regarding election to base monthly payments on previous month's liability	¶3214+
Use of special schemes	Refusal to allow use of a retail scheme	¶5325+
	Refusal or withdrawal of authorisation to use the cash accounting scheme	¶4887
	Refusal or withdrawal of authorisation to use the flat rate scheme	¶4648+
	Decisions regarding appropriate flat rate scheme percentage	¶4666+
	Decisions regarding refunds to DIY housebuilders	¶5316+
	Refusal, cancellation of membership, or refusal to cancel membership of agricultural flat rate scheme	¶5970+
Groups	Refusal of application for group treatment or membership	¶8845+
	Decision to terminate group membership	¶8865
	Directions in relation to under-declared VAT on transactions by group members or former members	¶8878+
Overseas issues	Rulings on liability to account for VAT on particular imports, and on acquisitions from other EU member states	¶9110+, ¶9405+
	Decisions regarding claims for a refund on supply of new means of transport to another EU member state	¶9112+
	Decisions regarding claims for acquisition VAT on goods acquired in another EU member state	¶9010+
	Decisions regarding import tax claims where goods imported for another person for private purposes	¶9579
	Directions that acquisitions from other EU member states are treated as made at market value	¶9034
	Decisions regarding status of fiscal warehouses and warehousekeepers	¶9242+

Where a **prior decision** relating to the appellant was **not** one of the **appealable** matters listed in ¶4265, an appeal can still be made against a subsequent HMRC decision which is **based on** this prior decision. 4266

A tribunal may uphold such an appeal on the ground that had it been able to consider the initial HMRC decision, it would have decided in the appellant's favour.

Allocation of cases to categories

An appeal must **be sent to** the Tribunals Service for allocation to one of four categories: 4267 SI 2009/273 rule 23
- default paper;
- basic;
- standard; or
- complex.

Allocation to categories is important for the conduct of the case and any possible recovery of costs (¶4279).

Default paper cases will usually be disposed of without a hearing and are likely to include cases which are concerned with a fixed penalty.

Basic cases will usually require a hearing but involve fewer documents, and are likely to include cases which are in connection with mitigation and reasonable excuse appeals.

Standard cases will usually be decided at a hearing, are subject to more detailed case management, and will include all cases not dealt with in any other category.

Complex cases are defined as those which:
- require lengthy and complex evidence;
- require a lengthy hearing;
- deal with a complex or important principle or issue; or
- involve a large financial sum.

Contacting the tribunal

4268 The official forms on which to lodge an appeal can be downloaded from the Tribunals Service website (flmemo.co.uk/vm4268).

Appeals can be submitted by email (using the appropriate downloaded form) or sent on paper to:
First-tier Tribunal - Tax
HM Courts & Tribunals Service
3rd Floor
Temple Court
35 Bull Street
Birmingham
B4 6EQ

Time limits

4270 s 83G VATA 1994 Notice of appeal must be given within 30 days of the date of the document containing the disputed decision. The 30-day period may commence at the conclusion of an internal review (¶4230+). Where a request for an HMRC review is made out of time, then, with effect from 1 June 2014, an application for permission to appeal out of time cannot be made to HMRC, but must instead be made to the tribunal (¶4232).

4272 s 83D VATA 1994 **Extension** An appellant may **apply** for an extension of the limit **to**:
a. HMRC, during the initial 30-day period. HMRC may **notify** the appellant by letter that the time limit will be extended until 30 days after the date of that letter or a subsequent letter; this will normally occur after completion of a review; or
b. the **tribunal**, at any time. The tribunal may extend the time limit without a hearing if:
- either party applies for an extension; or
- the tribunal itself so decides.

MEMO POINTS During a VAT tribunal hearing of an appeal against a default surcharge, HMRC stated that it was its **informal policy** not to object to appeals being made, as long as they were within twelve months of the date the surcharge liability notice was served. *Aardvark Excavations Ltd* [2007] (VTD 20468)
It has not been confirmed whether this informal policy continues under the modernised tribunal system, but the change of legislation which took effect from 1 June 2014 (¶4232) would appear to indicate that HMRC may now be less likely to be supportive.

4273 The tribunal's **discretion** to extend the limit will only be exercised sparingly.

The **factors** which are taken into account in deciding whether an extension is granted are the:
- reason for the delay in appealing;
- length of the delay;
- chances of an appeal succeeding if an extension is granted;

- extent to which the other party would be prejudiced if an extension is granted; and
- hardship to the appellant if an extension is not granted. *WY & YS Wan (t/a Wans Chinese Takeaway)* [1997] (VTD 14829)

The following table gives details of **case law** in cases heard by the former VAT tribunal, stating the grounds for applying for an extension and whether or not the application was successful: 4275

Successful applications	Unsuccessful applications
Illness of one of the partners in a partnership. *WW & JH Hornby* [1974] (VTD 155)	Trader continued to negotiate with HMRC after expiry of time limit. *University of Reading* [1998] (VTD 15387)
Trader believed that his accountants had dealt with the matter. *WR Hallam* [1978] (VTD 683)	Trader claimed to have new evidence, but it was held that there was no real prospect of success. *R Preston* [2002] (VTD 17826)
Trader initially applied for a judicial review instead of appealing. *Conoco Ltd v C & E* [1995]	Trader became aware of possible grounds for appeal after a subsequent tribunal decision in another case. *R Kyffin* [1978] (VTD 617)
Trader entitled to a fair trial in relation to an evasion penalty, under the European Convention on Human Rights. *Mrs A Shatliff* [2001] (VTD 17431)	

The First-tier Tribunal has confirmed that the **principles** it will consider when hearing an application for leave to appeal out of time remain unchanged from those assessed by the VAT Tribunal. However, there is also now an overriding objective to deal with cases fairly and justly which, if anything, permits the tribunal greater leeway in its decision-making. *Wiltshire Council* [2010] (TC00714)

Conditions for hearing an appeal

Before an appeal can be heard by a tribunal, any tax relating to the matter under appeal **must be paid or deposited** with HMRC, unless HMRC agrees or the tribunal decides that the appellant would suffer hardship. 4276

Hardship An appellant who considers that payment of the disputed tax would cause hardship may, within the 30-day limit for appealing, write to HMRC asking it to waive the requirement. The appellant must **demonstrate** their financial position and provide evidence of assets, liabilities, income and expenditure, which may include providing bank statements 4278 s 84(3B) VATA 1994

If HMRC **does not agree** to waive the requirement, the appellant may make a formal hardship application to the tribunal.

If HMRC **opposes** the application, a hearing will be held to decide the matter. The appellant must provide all relevant documents in advance of the hearing, if they have not already done so.

Interest may have to be paid by:
- an appellant who succeeds with the hardship application but loses the appeal; or
- HMRC, if a hardship application does not succeed, but the appellant wins the appeal.

Costs

Tribunals do not charge for dealing with appeals. 4279

Legal aid for **appellants** is not normally available, but may exceptionally be obtained where:
- an appeal is made against a civil dishonest evasion penalty or a criminal penalty; or
- it is in the interests of justice.

In certain circumstances, a tribunal may **award costs** (¶4324) in favour of an appellant, or of HMRC.

The exception to this is the treatment of costs in the **complex category** of the First-tier Tribunal, as the appellant can opt out of the costs rule, and is then only liable for their own costs.

2. Before a hearing

Notice of appeal

4280 SI 2009/273 rule 20 The notice must:

a. state the:
- name and address of the appellant;
- name and address of the appellant's representative (if any);
- address where documents for the appellant should be sent;
- details of the decision appealed against;
- result the appellant is seeking; and
- grounds for the appeal;

b. attach a copy of:
- the document containing the disputed decision; and
- any reasons given for the decision; and

c. if the notice is late, **apply** for permission to appeal out of time with reasons why the notice is late.

The notice of appeal must be **sent to** the Tribunals Service (at the address given at ¶4268). If it admits the appeal, the tribunal will give notice of the appeal to HMRC.

Withdrawal of an appeal

4281 SI 2009/273 rule 17 An appeal (or application) may be **withdrawn** at any time by either party to the appeal, by giving notice of withdrawal to the tribunal.

Striking out an appeal

4283 SI 2009/273 rule 8 The taxpayer's appeal may be struck out in certain circumstances, which means that the appeal can no longer go ahead and the taxpayer will lose. The same sanction **does not apply** to HMRC: in circumstances which would have led to the taxpayer's appeal being struck out, HMRC can only be barred from taking further part in the proceedings, which means it can still win the case, albeit in absentia.

MEMO POINTS 1. If an **appellant fails to comply** with a direction of the tribunal which specifies that failure to comply will lead to the appeal being struck out, the tribunal must strike out the appeal. The tribunal must also strike out the appeal if it does not have jurisdiction to hear it.

2. The tribunal **may strike out** the whole or part of an appeal if:
- the appellant fails to comply with the terms of a direction which specifies that failure to comply may lead to the appeal (or part of it) being struck out;
- the appellant acts in such a way that the tribunal is unable to deal with the appeal fairly or justly; or
- the tribunal considers that the appeal (or part of it) has no reasonable prospect of success.

3. The appellant must be allowed to make representations to the tribunal before an appeal (or part of it) is struck out on the grounds of **lack of jurisdiction**, the **appellant's actions**, or **prospects of success**. The appellant may not make representations where the appeal is struck out for failure to comply with a direction, but instead may apply for the appeal to be reinstated (within 28 days of when the tribunal sent notification of having struck out the appeal).

4. HMRC may be **barred from taking further part** in the proceedings on any of the above grounds, but may apply to be allowed to take further part in the same circumstances as an appellant can apply for reinstatement of an appeal which has been struck out. If HMRC has been barred, the tribunal may still take note of submissions made by it (or take no note, as the tribunal sees fit), or can simply decide the case against HMRC.

Striking out a case has in the past been seen as a severe step, which should not be taken lightly, because a tribunal's main purpose is to adjudicate on the substance of disputes rather than refuse to do so. *Baines & Ernst Ltd* [2004] (VTD 18516)

EXAMPLE

1. A VAT tribunal allowed a trader's appeal against the disallowance of input tax because of failures by HMRC to comply with directions. Witness statements had been served late, exhibits had been omitted, and dates in connection with hearings had not been provided. *UK Tradecorp Ltd* [2004] (VTD 18879)

2. HMRC served a statement of case one day late. The tribunal did not decide the appeal in favour of the taxpayer, as it considered that to do so would substantially prejudice HMRC, whereas the slight delay had only modestly prejudiced the taxpayer. *Baines & Ernst Ltd* [2004] (VTD 18516)

Settling an appeal by agreement

Where possible, HMRC will attempt to resolve a dispute without the need for an appeal hearing. If it appears that agreement may be reached, HMRC will continue to discuss the disputed decision with the appellant. Either party may apply for the appeal hearing to be stood over to allow this process to be concluded. **4284** s 85 VATA 1994

If the appellant:

a. decides not to proceed with an appeal, they may notify HMRC, in which case the decision under appeal will be treated as upheld unless HMRC notifies the appellant within 30 days that it does not wish the appeal to be treated as withdrawn;

b. reaches agreement with HMRC before an appeal is heard, the resulting decision, including any terms in relation to costs, is treated as if it had been made by the tribunal; or

c. wishes to repudiate or withdraw from an agreement, they may notify HMRC within 30 days of the date of the agreement.

Lead cases

Where two or more cases have been started in the tribunal and neither has been concluded, the tribunal may nominate one case as a lead case, where the cases give rise to **common or related issues** of fact or law. Notice must be given to each appellant, who has the right to apply for a direction that the decision does not apply to, nor is binding on, them. The application must be submitted within 28 days of receiving notice of a lead case. **4285** SI 2009/273 rules 5, 18; SI 2008/2698 rule 5

Appeal disposed of by consent If the parties to an appeal (or application) have agreed on the terms of a decision or direction to be given by a tribunal, the decision or direction may, if the tribunal considers it appropriate, be given in accordance with those terms without a hearing. **4286** SI 2009/273 rule 34

Statement of case

In a case allocated to the **basic category**, the case will proceed directly to a hearing and there is no need for HMRC to send or deliver a statement of case to the tribunal. **4287** SI 2009/273 rules 24 - 27

In **all other cases**, after receiving a copy of a notice of appeal, HMRC must deliver a statement of case to the tribunal. The statement of case **must**:
- state the law under which the disputed decision was made; and
- describe HMRC's position in relation to the case.

MEMO POINTS In **default paper** cases, the appellant may send a written reply to the statement of case, which may request that the case be subject to a hearing.

A statement of case must be served within 42 days in a **default paper** case, and within 60 days in a **standard or complex case**. If the statement of case is provided late, it must include an application for an extension of the time limit and an explanation why it was late. **4288** SI2009/273 rule 25

Disclosure, inspection and production of documents

Either party may apply to the tribunal for an order to any person to **produce** such documents in their possession or control as relate to any issue in the appeal. Alternatively, the tribunal may make such an order on its own initiative. A person cannot be ordered to produce any documents which they could not be ordered to produce in other legal proceedings. **4290** SI 2009/273 rule 16

4291 SI 2009/273 rule 27 In a **standard or complex case** each party must, within 42 days of the date of the statement of case, send to the Tribunals Service and each other party a list of the documents on which it intends to rely at the hearing. Each other party is entitled to inspect those documents, unless they are privileged.

Use of third parties

4294 SI 2009/273 rule 16 **Orders** A tribunal may order any person to answer any questions or produce any documents in their possession or control which relate to any issue in the proceedings. A person **may not be compelled** to give any evidence or produce any document which they could not be compelled to give or produce in other legal proceedings.

MEMO POINTS An order **must** state:
- that the person who is subject to it may apply to the tribunal for the order to be varied or set aside; and
- the consequences of failure to comply with the order.

4297 **Summonses** A tribunal may by summons (or, in Scotland, citation) require any person to attend as a witness at a hearing at the time and place specified in the summons or citation. The person will usually be given 14 days' notice, but the tribunal may direct a shorter period. If the **person is not a party** to the appeal, the tribunal may make provision for any necessary expenses incurred by the person in attending the hearing to be paid.

MEMO POINTS A summons or citation **must** state:
- that the person who is subject to it may apply to the tribunal for the summons or citation to be varied or set aside; and
- the consequences of failure to comply with the summons or citation.

Case management and directions

4301 SI 2009/273 rules 2, 5, 6; SI 2008/2698 rule 5 The tribunal is responsible for regulating its own procedures and may issue directions to that end, subject to an overriding objective to deal with cases fairly and justly. This includes dealing with cases proportionately to their importance and the resources of the parties, and avoiding unnecessary delays. A direction may be made **at the request** of either party or at the tribunal's own initiative.

MEMO POINTS A tribunal **may make a direction** to:
- extend or shorten the time for complying with any rule or direction, unless this would conflict with another provision of the law setting down a time limit;
- consolidate or hear together two or more sets of proceedings or parts of proceedings raising common issues, or treat a case as a lead case (¶4285+);
- permit or require a party to amend a document;
- permit or require a party or another person to provide documents, information or submissions to the tribunal or a party;
- deal with an issue in the proceedings as a preliminary issue;
- hold a hearing to consider any matter, including a case management hearing;
- decide the form of any hearing;
- adjourn or postpone a hearing;
- require a party to produce a bundle (sorted file of documents) for a hearing;
- stay (or, in Scotland, sist) proceedings;
- transfer proceedings to another tribunal; or
- suspend the effect of its own decision pending the determination of an application for permission to appeal, a review, or an appeal.

3. At the hearing

4304 SI 2009/273 rules 11, 32 Appeal hearings are in **public**, unless a party to the appeal applies successfully for all or part of the hearing to take place in private.

An **appellant** may conduct their case personally, or appoint any other person as a representative. HMRC may appoint any person to represent it.

Date and time of hearing

The tribunal must **notify** the parties of the date and time of the hearing of an appeal, or a hearing for the purposes of giving directions relating to an appeal, at least 14 days in advance. **4305** SI 2009/273 rule 31

MEMO POINTS 1. Where an **application is made at a hearing** and heard immediately, no notice is required unless a tribunal directs otherwise.
2. An application to **postpone** a hearing should be made to the tribunal as soon as possible after receiving notification of the hearing. The applicant should state the reason for the postponement request, and provide suitable alternative dates.

Failure to appear

If a party to an appeal, or a representative, fails to appear at a hearing, the **tribunal may** decide to proceed with the hearing in any case, provided that the tribunal is satisfied that the missing party has been notified of the hearing (or reasonable steps have been taken to inform the party of the hearing) and it would be in the interests of justice to proceed. The tribunal will **send notice** of its decision to the missing party, who then has 28 days to make a written application to the tribunal to set aside the decision. **4306** SI 2009/273 rules 33, 38

Non-compliance with rules or direction

If a party has failed to comply with a requirement of the tribunal's rules or of a direction of the tribunal, the tribunal may: **4308** SI 2009/273 rule 7
- **waive** the requirement;
- require the failure to be **remedied**;
- **strike out** the case or **restrict** a party's participation in proceedings (¶4283); or
- **refer** the matter to the Upper Tribunal, which has powers to compel compliance.

Order of proceedings

Proceedings before the tribunals are less formal than in a court of law. **4309** SI 2009/273 rule 5

The tribunal can **conduct** a hearing as it thinks fit, and can decide the order of proceedings. The chairman or any tribunal member can question any party to the appeal or any witness called to give evidence.

Evidence

The tribunal has wide powers to **admit or exclude** evidence, and may direct the form in which evidence may be given. **4311** SI 2009/273 rule 15

MEMO POINTS 1. A tribunal **may specify** by direction:
- the issues on which it requires evidence;
- the nature of the evidence it requires;
- whether the parties may or must provide expert evidence, and whether a single expert should provide such evidence;
- a limit on the number of witnesses;
- whether evidence should be given orally or in writing; and
- time limits for evidence to be provided.

2. A tribunal may **admit** evidence which would be **inadmissible** in other court proceedings, or exclude evidence that would otherwise be admissible (if the evidence does not comply with the terms of a direction, or if it would otherwise be unfair to admit the evidence).
3. A tribunal may permit or require evidence to be given on **oath**.

4. Role of the tribunal

A tribunal's overriding objective is to deal with cases **fairly** and **justly**. However, it is recognised that formal proceedings will not always be the best means of approaching the matter, and a tribunal should seek, where appropriate, to bring alternative dispute resolution opportunities to the parties' attention. **4314** SI 2009/273 rules 2, 3

General decisions

4315 Many of the decisions appealed against will have involved **HMRC exercising its discretion**. The tribunal must decide whether HMRC acted reasonably in doing so, and whether it was entitled to make the decision under appeal based on the facts and information available when the decision was made. *C & E v Peachtree Enterprises Ltd* [1994]

In these cases it is **not the tribunal's role** to consider all of the evidence presented at the hearing and make a new decision. *Georgiou and another (t/a Mario's Chippery) v C & E* [1996]

Assessments

4317 s 84(5) VATA 1994

For appeals against assessments, a **two-stage approach** is normally adopted.

The tribunal is likely to consider:
- whether HMRC exercised its best judgment (¶3644+), and if so, was any assessment valid; and
- its own assessment of the amount.

A tribunal may hold that an assessment was made to the best of HMRC's judgment, but may nonetheless reduce or increase the amount of the assessment.

Extra-statutory concessions

4318 A tribunal held in 1993 that it was entitled to consider whether HMRC had correctly applied the terms of an extra-statutory concession. *RW Sheppard* [1993] (VTD 11753)

However, the High Court overruled this decision in 1996, making it clear that the tribunal **does not have jurisdiction** to consider whether or not HMRC ought to have given a taxpayer the benefit of a concession. *C & E v Arnold* [1996]

If a taxpayer wishes to challenge HMRC's decision not to apply a concession, the alternatives are to make a complaint to the Adjudicator (¶4252+), or to apply for judicial review (¶4338+).

EXAMPLE HMRC decided not to allow zero-rating of exported goods because the trader had not provided satisfactory evidence that the goods had been exported.
It was held that the refusal to allow zero-rating by concession was an exercise of discretion which was outside the tribunal's jurisdiction. *G McKenzie & Co Ltd* [1993] (VTD 11992)

Restrictions of powers

4320 s 84 VATA 1994

The powers of tribunals are restricted in the situations set out in the following table:

Subject of appeal	Criteria to be met for appeal to be upheld
Penalty, interest or surcharge	Tribunal can only vary the amount assessed where it is necessary to reduce it to an amount which is appropriate
Amount or proportion of deductible input tax on goods or services of a luxury, amusement or entertainment nature, where HMRC made a determination regarding the: - purpose for which they were to be used; or - extent to which they were to be used in making supplies which were taxable, or which would be taxable if made in the UK	Tribunal considers that the determination: - was unreasonable; or - would have been unreasonable if made with the benefit of further information which is now available to the tribunal
A decision in relation to the flat rate scheme: - refusing or withdrawing use of the scheme; - specifying the percentage to be used; or - on which an assessment is based	Tribunal considers that HMRC could not reasonably have been satisfied that there were grounds for the decision
Refusal of an application for group treatment or membership	Tribunal considers that HMRC could not reasonably have been satisfied that there were grounds for refusing the application [1]

Subject of appeal	Criteria to be met for appeal to be upheld
Issue of a notice terminating membership of a group	Tribunal considers that HMRC could not reasonably have been satisfied that there were grounds for giving the notice[1] Where an appeal relates to the effective date of termination of membership, the tribunal must consider that HMRC could not reasonably have been satisfied that the date was appropriate
Direction to treat two or more persons as one entity	Tribunal considers that HMRC could not reasonably have been satisfied that there were grounds for making the direction

Note:
1. The refusal or notice will **remain effective** until the conclusion of the appeal. If the appeal is upheld, the refusal will be deemed never to have occurred.

However, a tribunal may **recommend** that HMRC should exercise clemency or consider some other action which the tribunal itself has no power to direct. HMRC will then consider whether in the circumstances it would be appropriate to follow the recommendation.

Coming to a decision

Where a tribunal has more than one member, the decision may be taken by a majority of votes, with the chairman having a casting vote. **4322**

The chairman of a tribunal may **announce** the decision or direction at the end of the hearing, or may give it in writing at a later date. A written copy of the decision or direction will be sent to each party within 28 days of the decision finally being made, or as soon as practicable thereafter. SI 2009/273 rule 35

MEMO POINTS The written copy of the decision will contain the findings of fact by the tribunal and the reasons for the decision, unless each party to the appeal agrees that this is unnecessary. However, either party can later call for a detailed statement of facts and reasons if none were given in the decision notice.

If the **amount of a VAT assessment is increased** by a tribunal, the revised assessment becomes effective when the tribunal issues its direction, and the appellant is deemed to have been notified of the amount. s 84(5) VATA 1994

Awarding costs

The First-tier Tribunal may make an order: **4324** SI 2009/273 rule 10

- for **wasted costs** (where costs have been incurred unnecessarily);
- if it considers that either party has **acted unreasonably** in bringing, defending or conducting the case; or
- if the case has been categorised as **complex** and the appellant does not provide written notification for the proceedings to be excluded from the potential liability for costs (which notification means that the appellant cannot have costs paid if they win).

The costs regime in the **Upper Tribunal** is similar to that in the High Court, so that the loser will generally pay the winner's costs. HMRC will not always ask for costs if the case is an appeal from the First-tier Tribunal.

MEMO POINTS 1. Costs **claimed by appellants**, particularly in relation to legal or accountancy advisers, must be reasonable. In deciding what is reasonable, a tribunal will have regard to the:
- complexity, difficulty or novelty of the case;
- skill, specialised knowledge, responsibility and time required;
- number and importance of documents prepared or read;
- place and circumstances in which the business involved is transacted;
- importance of the matter to the client; and
- amount or value of any money or property involved. *VSP Marketing Ltd* [1995] (VTD 13587)

2. **HMRC** advised in the past that it would normally only request costs where:
a. there had been an unsuccessful dishonest evasion appeal;
b. the case was large and complex, involving large sums, and was comparable to a High Court case, unless an important general point of law needed to be clarified; or

c. the taxpayer had misused the system by:
- making a frivolous or vexatious appeal;
- failing to appear for a hearing; or
- introducing new material at a hearing which could have saved public funds if it had been introduced at an earlier stage.

The attitude to the recovery of costs may be more strictly enforced in future, and HMRC may seek to recover its costs in more cases. On 27 March 2009 Stephen Timms, then Chief Secretary to the Treasury, repeated the view of HMRC on recovery of costs: "In considering the exercise of HMRC's discretion, influential factors include the risk of financial hardship to the other party, the involvement of a point of law the clarification of which would be of significant benefit to taxpayers as a whole, and the efficient collection and management of revenue for which HMRC has responsibility. If HMRC is to come to an arrangement of this nature, it would expect to do so in advance of the hearing and following an approach by the taxpayer involved."

3. For appeals brought under the **pre-1 April 2009 rules**, a tribunal can order either party to pay the other party's costs (or, in Scotland, expenses), as it assesses, or a specified amount towards the other party's costs. An order may be made as a result of an application by one of the parties or the tribunal's own decision. Awards of costs are recoverable as a civil debt.

4. In an SDLT case in the First-tier Tribunal, which had been categorised as complex, the appellants had not opted out of the costs regime. HMRC made **alternative** assessments, which had the effect that whilst HMRC won the case and collected the full amount of SDLT, one appeal was successful and one unsuccessful. Costs normally follow the event - that is, costs are awarded to the successful party - so the Tribunal might have awarded HMRC costs of one appeal and the appellant costs of the other. However, costs were awarded to HMRC only. *Vardy Properties and Vardy Properties (Teesside) Ltd* [2013] (TC02514)

5. A taxpayer won in the First-tier Tribunal but HMRC appealed successfully to the Upper Tribunal. HMRC then made an application for its costs. The Upper Tribunal decided **not to award HMRC its costs** (whilst recognising that costs will normally be awarded to the successful party). The Upper Tribunal explained that the taxpayer would not have been at risk of paying HMRC's costs had he lost in the First-tier Tribunal, and could not be blamed for not knowing that he could have made an application in advance of the Upper Tribunal hearing that costs should not be at risk for either party.

In this case, the First-tier Tribunal had made an error which the Upper Tribunal was obliged to correct. It was not fair for the taxpayer to be at risk of paying costs as a result of the First-tier Tribunal's error. In addition the taxpayer had represented himself (presumably to minimise his own costs). The factor which ultimately tipped the balance in the taxpayer's favour was that HMRC had not relied throughout the First-tier Tribunal on the point which it ultimately argued successfully in the Upper Tribunal. *HMRC v Patel* [2014]

Appeal from the First-tier Tribunal to the Upper Tribunal

4325 SI 2009/273 rules 39 - 41

An appeal can be made from the First-tier Tribunal to the Upper Tribunal **on a point of law only**, and only if permission is given by the First-tier Tribunal. If permission is refused, it can be sought from the Upper Tribunal.

On receipt of an application for permission to appeal, the First-tier Tribunal considers whether to **review** (change) its decision. It can review a decision only if there has been an error of law.

If the tribunal decides not to review the decision, it must then consider whether to give permission to appeal.

An application to the First-tier Tribunal for permission to appeal to the Upper Tribunal **must be made within** 56 days of the First-tier Tribunal releasing, or correcting, or refusing to set aside its decision.

B. Appeals to the UK courts

4328 An appeal may normally be made against a tribunal decision to the UK courts.

In addition, where a matter cannot be appealed, it may be possible to apply for judicial review (¶4338+) of a decision by HMRC or a tribunal. The Upper Tribunal also has the right to consider whether the matter should be subject to judicial review.

To the Upper Tribunal/High Court/Court of Session

The Upper Tribunal hears any appeal in the first instance. **4330** s 11 Tribunals and Inquiries Act 1992; SI 2009/273 rule 39

MEMO POINTS 1. For proceedings started prior to 1 April 2009 a party can, on a **point of law** or an **unreasonable finding of fact**:
- appeal against a VAT tribunal decision to the High Court or, in Scotland, the Court of Session; or
- require the VAT tribunal to state a case for the opinion of the High Court.

An appeal must be **made within** 56 days (42 days in Scotland or Northern Ireland) of the tribunal decision.

2. The High Court held that the **56-day limit** for appealing against a tribunal decision ran from the date of the original decision, and was not extended if the tribunal subsequently corrected an aspect of that decision.

In the case in question, the tribunal issued a decision in favour of the appellant on 21 July 2006, which HMRC did not appeal within 56 days. The tribunal then corrected the decision on 13 September 2006 by including an additional paragraph on a particular topic. HMRC argued that this superseded the original decision, but the court ruled that although a new 56-day limit might apply in relation to matters covered by the additional paragraph, the correction did not extend the time limit for a general appeal against the earlier decision. HMRC's appeal was not against the additional paragraph, and therefore it was out of time. *HMRC v Church of Scientology Religious Education College Inc* [2007]

To the Court of Appeal (England, Wales and Northern Ireland)

Appeal from Upper Tribunal An appeal against an Upper Tribunal decision on a **point of law** may be made directly to the Court of Appeal, where either: **4333** SI 2008/2698 rules 44, 45
- the tribunal considers that its decision involves a point of law; or
- there is some other overriding reason for the Court of Appeal to hear the appeal.

An application for **permission to appeal** must be made to the Upper Tribunal within three months of the Upper Tribunal releasing, or correcting, or refusing to set aside its decision. The Upper Tribunal will then consider whether to review (change) its decision and if not, whether to grant permission to appeal. If it refuses permission, the applicant can then apply to the Court of Appeal for permission to appeal.

MEMO POINTS The Upper Tribunal **can only review its decision** if:
- it overlooked legislation or case law which could have had a material effect on the decision; or
- since the decision, a court has made a ruling which could have had a material effect on the decision if it had been made before it.

Appeal from High Court An appeal against a High Court decision may be made to the Court of Appeal. **4335**

Leave to appeal must normally be granted by the High Court.

If **leave is not granted**, the appellant can seek permission from the Court of Appeal. Permission will only be granted if the appeal has a real chance of success, or if there is some other compelling reason why it should be heard.

MEMO POINTS An appeal from the High Court can only be made where proceedings were **started prior** to 1 April 2009, since cases from that date onwards are appealed to the Upper Tribunal and thence to the Court of Appeal.

To the Supreme Court

An appeal against a Court of Appeal or Court of Session decision may be made to the Supreme Court. **4336**

In England, Wales and Northern Ireland, **leave to appeal** must normally be granted by the Court of Appeal. No leave is required from the Court of Session in Scotland.

If **leave is not granted**, the appellant can petition the Supreme Court for leave to appeal. A petition will only be granted if the case involves a point of law of general public importance.

Judicial review

4338 s 31 Senior Courts Act 1981; SI 2008/2698 Part 4

Where there is **no right of appeal**, a person can in certain circumstances apply to the High Court for judicial review of a decision by HMRC or a tribunal. The Upper Tribunal can undertake judicial review proceedings, and in this respect it has a function similar to that of the High Court.

An application for judicial review **may be granted where** HMRC or a tribunal made a decision which:
- it had no power to make, or which exceeded its power;
- was wrong in law;
- it could not possibly have made if it had acted reasonably and with proper regard to the law;
- was not in accordance with the laws of natural justice;
- failed to take account of human rights legislation; or
- prevented the right to a fair hearing, in relation to certain matters.

Questions of **legitimate expectation** (that a public body will retain a long-standing practice or abide by its pledges) can, according to the High Court, be heard and decided by the First-tier Tribunal. *Oxfam v HMRC* [2009] However, the First-tier Tribunal has suggested that it should not take on issues of such a nature. *Magdalene College Cambridge* [2011] (TC01522) Since then, the First-tier Tribunal has explained that there are well-established principles of common law which are within its jurisdiction. These allow it to examine whether, for example, HMRC has acted with conspicuous unfairness, without resorting to issues which would be the subject of judicial review. *Hilltop Syndicate Shoot* [2012] (TC01725)

The Upper Tribunal sought to issue a definitive ruling on this question in 2013. It ruled that:
- the First-tier Tribunal has **no judicial review jurisdiction**, since it is a creature of statute and has been granted no such jurisdiction by statute; and
- the jurisdiction granted to the First-tier Tribunal by statute extends no further than to decide whether or not the taxpayer's tax position accords with what is laid down by the legislation.

The Upper Tribunal declared itself not to be bound by the *Oxfam* decision, and, since the First-tier Tribunal is bound by rulings of the Upper Tribunal, this was clearly intended to put an end to any encroachment by the First-tier Tribunal on extra-statutory issues. *HMRC v Abdul Noor* [2013] However, the First-tier Tribunal has since considered the *Oxfam* and *Noor* cases, and concluded that it does have limited jurisdiction to consider matters which would normally be the subject of a judicial review application. In particular, the Tribunal held that it has jurisdiction to decide whether HMRC has properly applied an extra-statutory concession. *LH Bishop Electric Co Ltd and others* [2013]

4339 The following table gives details of the circumstances in some judicial review cases, and whether or not the application was successful:

Successful applications	Unsuccessful applications
A tribunal had ruled that "premises" meant a whole building, when in fact it should only have been construed as the room occupied by the trader. The tribunal had therefore erred in law. *R v C & E ex parte Sims* [1988]	A tribunal began to hear an appeal against estimated assessments in September 1996 but did not release its decision until May 1998. It was held that the delay was unjustifiable, but that it did not taint the conclusion and findings. *R v C & E ex parte Dangol* [2000]
HMRC had issued an assessment to recover part of a refund which related to a period outside a retrospective 3-year time limit. It was held that HMRC was not entitled to use a retrospective power to override a decision made before the date on which the limit was introduced. *R v C & E ex parte Building Societies Ombudsman Co Ltd* [2000]	HMRC had changed its policy with regard to the way in which certain supplies were treated. It was held that this did not mean that a decision made under the previous policy was unreasonable. *R (oao BSB Group plc) v C & E* [2001]

Successful applications	Unsuccessful applications
HMRC applied for an extension of time to appeal against a tribunal decision. The application was granted on the grounds of the importance of the matter, the strength of HMRC's case and the interests of justice (in particular, that it did not prejudice the company). *C & E v Eastwood Care Homes (Ilkeston) Ltd & Others* [2000]	A company applied for a review of a decision not to require a US-based competitor to account for VAT on its supplies. It was held that HMRC had not acted unreasonably, and that taxpayers were not entitled to request judicial reviews in relation to the tax affairs of others. *R (oao Freeserve.com plc) v C & E* [2003]

Outcome If the court **rules in favour** of the appellant and thus grants a judicial review, it may: **4341**
- quash the decision under review;
- make a specific order; or
- award damages,

as appropriate.

EXAMPLE

1. HMRC obtained a search warrant for a partnership's business premises, but also searched a partner's home. Following a judicial review application, in which the court held that this was unlawful, the court ordered that damages be awarded. *R v Thames Magistrates' Court* [2002]

2. HMRC had obtained a search warrant which authorised up to four persons to search the premises, but eight officers took part in the search.
The court held that:
- the search had been unlawfully executed;
- the records removed were therefore inadmissible evidence; and
- the trader's subsequent conviction for fraudulent evasion of VAT would be quashed. *Singh and another v HM Advocate* [2001]

C. Role of the CJEU

UK VAT law is subject to EU law, and any UK legislation or decisions by UK tribunals or courts must be compatible with EU law. The CJEU (Court of Justice of the European Union - formerly the ECJ, or European Court of Justice) is therefore the ultimate authority with regard to the interpretation of VAT law. **4345**

Comment Although the CJEU is the sovereign court, it can only rule on matters where European law applies. If UK legislation, or a court decision, relates to wholly domestic legislation not governed by European law, no appeal to the CJEU can be made.

Scope

The CJEU does not hear appeals from UK courts, but interprets the law when a matter is referred to it for what is known as a **preliminary ruling**. The UK courts must then decide the case on the basis of the CJEU interpretation. **4347**

The CJEU can **directly** rule on UK tax matters by ruling on the interpretation of the law in a particular UK case. It may also **indirectly** rule on UK tax matters when ruling on a matter in relation to another member state, as UK courts must then decide similar cases on the basis of that interpretation.

The **influence** of the CJEU on UK tax matters is increasing, with changes in practice and legislation becoming necessary following some of its decisions. Important recent judgments have included the following cases: **4348**

Case	CJEU ruling	¶¶
Halifax and others v HMRC [2006]	Transactions could not be disregarded simply because their sole purpose was to avoid VAT, but the abuse of rights principle prevented a tax advantage from being obtained	¶246
Marks & Spencer plc v C & E [2002]	HMRC should have allowed a transitional period to allow uncapped claims to be made before the 3-year cap was introduced	¶2014
Kittel v Belgian State [2006]	A trader in a supply chain was entitled to deduct input tax even though another party in the supply chain had committed a fraud, if the trader had no knowledge or means of knowledge of the fraud However, the CJEU later confirmed that a trader who knew or should have known that its transactions were connected with fraud did not have a right to deduct input tax	¶1988
JP Morgan Fleming Claverhouse Trust plc and The Association of Investment Trust Companies v HMRC [2007]	The UK's definition of a "special investment fund", for the purposes of the exemption from VAT of management services provided to such funds, was too narrowly construed Although member states have discretion under European law to define what a special investment fund is for the purpose of the exemption, their discretion must respect the objective of the Article, "which is to facilitate investment in securities for investors... while guaranteeing the principle of fiscal neutrality"	¶377

Referring a matter to the CJEU

4350 A UK tribunal or court **may** refer a matter to the CJEU for a ruling if clarification of EU law is necessary in order to decide a case.

A UK court **must** refer a matter to the CJEU if clarification of EU law is necessary and there is no right of appeal to a higher court. The Supreme Court must therefore always refer cases which require clarification.

The CJEU may **refuse** to hear a reference where, for example, it considers that:
- the question on which it has been asked to rule is a matter for the internal jurisdiction of the member state; or
- the reference is an abuse of the CJEU process. *Foglia v Novello* [1980]

CJEU procedures

4352 In almost all cases, the **Advocate-General** analyses the issues in a case and presents their submissions, including an opinion. The opinion is not binding, but is intended to assist the court in arriving at its decision.

The court **subsequently** reaches its own judgment, which normally (but not always) follows the Advocate-General's opinion.

PART 6

Simplified accounting schemes

Simplified accounting schemes
Summary

The numbers cross-refer to paragraphs.

CHAPTER 1 Overview

CHAPTER 2 Flat rate scheme and annual accounting scheme

CHAPTER 3 Cash accounting scheme

CHAPTER 1

Overview

OUTLINE ¶¶

A. Comparison of schemes

Special schemes are **available to smaller businesses** to help reduce the time and cost burdens of tax compliance by: **4600** EC Directive 2006/112 art 281
- providing simpler methods for making VAT returns, calculating and paying VAT; and
- deferring payment of VAT.

Comment Although the schemes simplify VAT accounting, they contain many detailed rules, which must be carefully followed to avoid mistakes.

The following table sets out: **4605**
- the main features of each scheme;
- the turnover limits which apply to each scheme; and
- which schemes can be used with which others.

	Flat rate scheme	Annual accounting scheme	Cash accounting scheme
Simpler VAT calculations	✓		
One annual VAT return		✓	
Possible reduction of VAT liabilities	✓		
Deferral of VAT liabilities		✓[1]	✓
Cash flow certainty		✓	
Automatic bad debt relief			✓
Business can join scheme from date of VAT registration	✓	✓	✓
Business can join scheme if annual turnover (excluding VAT) not expected to exceed[2]:	£150,000 (taxable)	£1.35m	£1.35m
Business must leave scheme if annual turnover exceeds:	£230,000	£1.6m[3]	£1.6m[3]
Scheme can be used together with:	annual accounting scheme[4]	– flat rate scheme or cash accounting scheme; – retail or margin schemes[5]	– annual accounting scheme; – retail or margin schemes[5]

Note:
1. There may be a deferral, to the extent of the balancing payment required after the annual accounting period.
2. See ¶4712+.
3. Excluding VAT.
4. Although the flat rate scheme cannot be used at the same time as the cash accounting scheme or a retail scheme, accounting methods with effects similar to those schemes are available to flat rate scheme users.
5. For details of the retail schemes see ¶6325+. For details of the margin schemes see ¶6620+.

B. Choosing a scheme

4610 The following flowchart provides a **guide** to choosing one or more of the schemes:

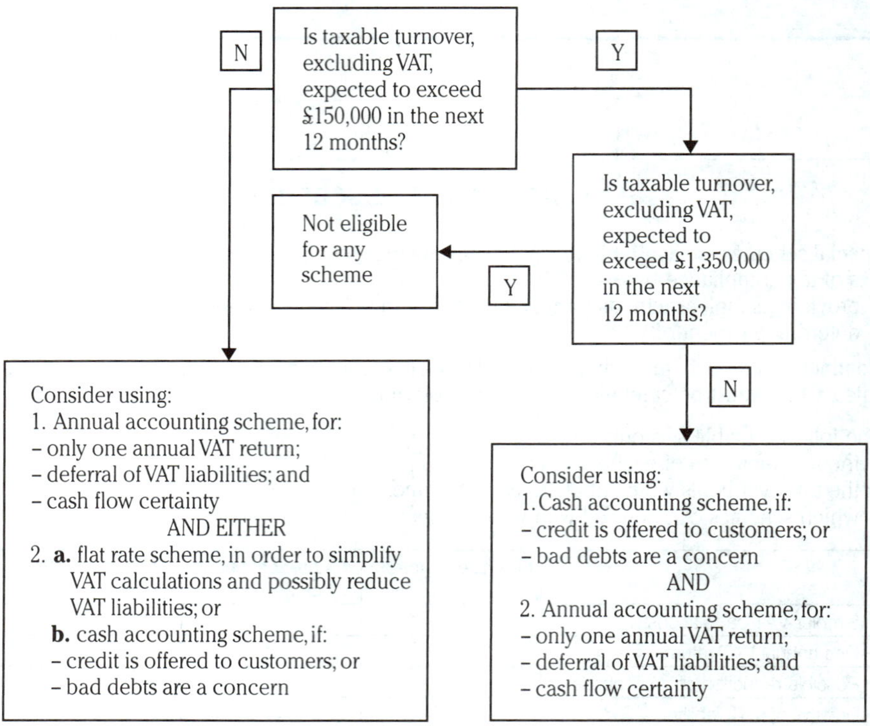

CHAPTER 2

Flat rate scheme and annual accounting scheme

OUTLINE ¶¶

This chapter deals with the flat rate scheme and the annual accounting scheme, and their interaction when both are used at the same time. 4630

SECTION 1

Flat rate scheme

A. General principles

The flat rate scheme is the only simplification scheme which can reduce (or increase) the amount of VAT payable to HMRC by a trader. It is **only available to** small businesses. 4635

MEMO POINTS A separate **agricultural flat rate scheme** is also available (¶5970+).

Purpose of the scheme

4637 s 26B VATA 1994; SI 1995/2518 regs 55A - 55V; Notice 733

The flat rate scheme simplifies VAT accounting for small businesses, but it may also reduce VAT liabilities. The **VAT payable** to HMRC is based on a percentage of turnover.

The scheme **avoids the need to**:
- calculate or record output and input tax, except for a few items not covered by the scheme;
- consider complicated rules regarding input tax deductibility for certain items; or
- carry out partial exemption calculations.

4639 The scheme is **not suitable** for traders who regularly receive VAT repayments, and would **probably not benefit** businesses which:
- make more zero-rated or exempt supplies, or supplies to other EU states, than the average for that trade sector;
- incur more input tax on purchases and expenses than the average for that trade sector; or
- sell a significant amount of second-hand goods.

MEMO POINTS Traders within the scheme will **charge their customers** the normal VAT rate for the supply. It is the amount of the VAT payable to HMRC which is calculated using the flat rate scheme percentage.

Measuring the benefit of the scheme

4640 FRS7300

The **flat rate percentage** depends on the trade sector to which the business belongs. The rate for each sector is designed to produce a VAT liability similar to that which would result under normal VAT accounting, taking into account average input tax claims. If a higher liability would arise under the scheme, a business might nevertheless still choose to use the scheme because of the time and cost savings.

EXAMPLE A Ltd sells a mixture of standard-rated and zero-rated goods. The flat rate for its trade sector is 8.5%. Its latest annual results were as follows:

	VAT	Total
	£	£
Sales	14,500	100,000
Purchases and expenses	6,500	70,000

There were no sales or purchases of items outside the flat rate scheme

The VAT liability for the year, using normal VAT accounting, is £8,000. (14,500 - 6,500)
If A Ltd used the flat rate scheme, the VAT liability would be £8,500. (100,000 × 8.5%)
A Ltd must decide whether the simplified accounting arrangements justify the higher VAT liability.

Eligibility

4644 SI 1995/2518 reg 55L; Notice 733 para 3.1

A VAT-registered person can use the scheme if, on reasonable grounds, they expect that their **taxable supplies** in the next 12 months will not exceed the scheme limit (¶4605). Taxable supplies include standard-, reduced- and zero-rated supplies, but disposals of capital assets are excluded, as is the value of services received under the reverse charge rules (¶9700+).

MEMO POINTS Flat rate traders should **review annual turnover** on each anniversary of joining the scheme, to ensure that they can remain within it.

EXAMPLE Mr B's expected income for the next 12 months is as follows:

	£
Standard-rated normal sales, excluding VAT	140,000
Sale of a capital asset, excluding VAT	20,000
Exempt supplies	30,000

Mr B is eligible to join the flat rate scheme, as taxable supplies are £140,000 (below the scheme threshold). The exempt supplies are not included.

Estimating turnover

4646 Notice 733 paras 3.2, 3.3

Estimates must have a reasonable **basis**, such as accounts or VAT returns for previous periods. A person who has been VAT-registered for less than 12 months may use the estimate given in the VAT registration application. Other acceptable methods include estimates based on business plans, or business information from a previous owner.

MEMO POINTS HMRC has stated that it will not penalise anyone for **incorrectly estimating** that taxable supplies would not exceed £150,000 if there was a **reasonable basis** for the estimate, and that it will normally allow a business to remain in the scheme, if the business has not otherwise become ineligible. If, however, HMRC considers that there was **no reasonable basis** for an estimate, it may immediately exclude a business from the scheme. Records supporting an estimate should therefore be kept in case of any enquiry. Notice 733 para 3.4

Exclusions

The following table summarises the circumstances in which a person will not be eligible to use the scheme: 4648 SI 1995/2518 regs 55A(2), 55B(3), 55L; FRS6100

Reason for exclusion	Details	¶¶
Business circumstances	Using the margin scheme or auctioneers' scheme	¶6625+, ¶6750+
	Intending to use the capital goods scheme	¶2280+
	Eligible for a VAT group registration within the last 24 months	¶8800+
	Part of a VAT divisional registration within the last 24 months	¶2744+
	Associated with another person within the last 24 months	¶4650
	Tour operators	¶7490+
Offences in relation to VAT	Convicted of any offence in connection with VAT in the previous 12 months	
	Made a payment to settle proceedings in relation to a VAT offence in the previous 12 months	
	Been assessed to a penalty for dishonestly evading VAT in the previous 12 months	
Protection of tax revenues	HMRC believes that tax revenues are at risk	
Previous use of scheme	Ceased to use the scheme in the previous 12 months	

A person is regarded as **associated with another person** for these purposes if: 4650 FRS6200
- one is under the dominant influence of the other (for example, where one business has the right to give directions to another business, or where a business generally complies with the instructions of another business); or
- they are closely bound by financial, economic and organisational links.

Persons **are not associated** by reason only of normal business relationships.

EXAMPLE

1. A business is not associated with its customers simply because it supplies goods in the form that they request them.

2. If a husband and wife are, for example, separately VAT-registered as an architect and an antiques dealer respectively, and he rents the upper floor of her shop at a market rate to use as his office, they will not be associated.

B. Joining the scheme

Application

A business can apply to join the flat rate scheme, whether at the time it registers for VAT or subsequently, by **using form** VAT 600FRS. If it is also applying to join the annual accounting scheme (¶4745+), form VAT 600AA/FRS should be used instead. 4654 Notice 733 paras 5.1 - 5.6

In addition to the name, address, and VAT number of the business, the application **must specify** the:
- main business activity; and
- flat rate percentage for the trade sector to which the business belongs (¶9979).

The application **may specify** a chosen start date, which can be the VAT registration date.

If an application is accepted, HMRC will notify the business, normally within 30 days, of the appropriate start date.

Notice 733 para 16.1 If HMRC **refuses an application** the business can ask HMRC to reconsider, and can appeal against a decision to a tribunal (¶4260+).

MEMO POINTS 1. **Postal applications** should be sent to the following address:
National Registration Service
HM Revenue & Customs
Imperial House
77 Victoria Street
Grimsby
Lincolnshire
DN31 1DB
2. **Electronic applications** should be emailed to: frsapplications.vrs@hmrc.gsi.gov.uk

Scheme start date

4656 SI 1995/2518 reg 55B; FRS3100 A business will **normally** start to use the scheme at the beginning of an annual accounting period, or the next VAT return period after HMRC processes the application to join the scheme, **unless** some other date was specified in the application. If the start date is not the beginning of a VAT period, two separate calculations for that period will be required (¶4722).

FRS3200; FRS3300 HMRC may allow a **retrospective start date**. However, HMRC's policy is to refuse retrospection for any period for which the business has already calculated its VAT liability using a different accounting method (unless there are exceptional circumstances).

For further details if also joining the annual accounting scheme see ¶4827.

EXAMPLE

1. A trader was refused permission to join the FRS retrospectively, but argued that he should have been permitted to do so, as he would have saved VAT. In addition, he had not been informed about the scheme in person, despite visits by an HMRC officer.
The tribunal held that although the trader had been made aware of the scheme by way of published leaflets, HMRC had acted unreasonably in not permitting the trader to join the FRS retrospectively, as he had not previously been informed about it in person. The tribunal as such deemed this to be an **exceptional circumstance**. *David Eric Burke* [2008] (VTD 20881)

2. In a similar case the tribunal approved HMRC's policy not to allow retrospective entry to the scheme once VAT for an accounting period has been calculated using another method, since use of the flat rate scheme is not a beneficial simplification if the calculation has already been carried out. The tribunal also considered it rational for HMRC to consider that paying less VAT is not of itself a good reason for retrospective entry. This likely differs from the earlier case as HMRC no longer favours retrospective entry into the scheme as a means of encouraging its use. *Anycom Ltd* [2011] (TC01496)

C. Operating the scheme

1. Accounting for VAT

4660 SI 1995/2518 regs 55D, 55E, 55F Flat rate traders **must still charge** VAT to customers in the normal way, and issue VAT invoices showing VAT at the standard, reduced or zero rate where required (¶2840+).

VAT returns and payments must also be made in the normal way, but the **VAT payable** to HMRC for each VAT period consists of:
- a percentage of turnover; and
- separate output tax and input tax adjustments for transactions which are outside the scheme.

a. Percentage of turnover

The turnover to which the flat rate **percentage is applied** includes and excludes the following: **4662** SI 1995/2518 regs 55C, 55U; Notice 733 paras 6.2, 6.3

Turnover includes	Turnover excludes
VAT	Supplies on which output tax is accounted for separately (¶4684+)
Standard-rated supplies	Recharges of qualifying disbursements (¶7190+)
Reduced-rated supplies	Supplies which are outside the scope of VAT (¶252+)
Zero-rated supplies, including exports	Reverse charges on services received from other countries (¶9700+)
Exempt supplies	Certain supplies of investment gold where the supplier has opted to tax (¶6868+)
Sales of capital assets, if no input tax was claimed when they were acquired	Bank interest *Fanfield Ltd and Thexton Training Ltd* [2011] (TC00919)
The full sale price of any second-hand goods	
The value of goods despatched to EU member states (¶9075+)	
Amounts received where the supply was made under the cash accounting scheme, and the trader has left that scheme and started to use the cash based turnover method of the flat rate scheme (¶4664)	
Excise duty, as this forms part of the consideration received which is subject to VAT whether or not the flat rate scheme is used *G & D Oldershaw (t/a Oldershaw Brewery)* [2004] (VTD 19011)	

EXAMPLE Mr C, a flat rate trader, made the following supplies in a VAT period:

	VAT £	Total £
Standard-rated sales	4,000	24,000
Exempt sales		2,000
Sale of a capital asset on which no input tax had been claimed (including VAT)	200	1,200
Sales of goods to other EU member states		1,000
Supplies outside the scope of VAT		500
Total		28,700
Less: Supplies outside the scope of VAT		(500)
Flat rate turnover		28,200

Methods of calculating turnover

A business must use one of the three methods set out in the following table: **4664** SI 1995/2518 reg 55G; Notice 733 paras 8 - 10

Method	Basis used to calculate turnover	Comments
Basic turnover method	VAT-inclusive value of supplies made, using normal VAT tax point rules (¶760+) If VAT invoices are issued, the tax point is normally the invoice date	Suitable for businesses using invoice-based VAT accounting, or whose customers are mainly VAT-registered
Cash turnover method	VAT-inclusive value of amounts received [1]	Flat rate scheme equivalent of the cash accounting scheme Suitable for businesses which give credit or suffer bad debts If there is a change from the cash turnover method to another method, an adjustment may be required, as in ¶4728

Method	Basis used to calculate turnover	Comments
Retailer's turnover method	VAT-inclusive daily gross takings for both: **a.** retail supplies; [2, 3] and **b.** non-retail supplies, including: – charges for card handling and giving credit; – rent; and – installation or callout charges, if invoiced separately	Flat rate scheme equivalent of a retail scheme

Note:
1. The detailed rules for the following items are as in the cash accounting scheme:
– date of receipt (¶4914);
– amounts received net of deductions, such as commission (¶4928); and
– barter or part-exchange transactions (¶4932).
2. For details of how these are calculated see ¶6368+.
3. For a **florist** who is a member of an organisation such as Interflora (¶6556+), the following rules apply:
– the receipt of payment direct from a customer should be included within daily gross takings by the sending member, but any VAT shown on the agency invoice is not input tax which can be reclaimed; and
– the florist who delivers the flowers must add the order value and the VAT to the flat rate turnover, and this information will be shown on the monthly agency self-billed invoice.

Percentage rate

4666 SI 1995/2518 regs 55H, 55K; FRS7200

The rate to be used **depends on** the trade sector to which the business belongs. For a **list of business types** and the sectors to which HMRC considers they belong see ¶9979.

MEMO POINTS 1. A separate **agricultural** flat rate scheme is also available (¶5970+).
2. **Retail schemes** are available to simplify VAT accounting if a flat rate scheme is not used (¶6325+).
3. HMRC publishes **historic** flat rate percentages in the flat rate scheme manual.

4668 Notice 733 paras 4.1, 4.2

If it is **not clear** which trade sector is appropriate, the sector with the lower flat rate should be chosen, provided that there is a reasonable basis for such a choice. For the avoidance of doubt, a business can ask HMRC to confirm that the chosen rate is acceptable.

4670 Notice 733 para 4.6

If a trader expects to carry on **more than one category** of business, they should use the rate for the category which they expect will have the highest turnover. The chosen rate will apply until each anniversary of the scheme start date.

Comment One of the main opportunities to save tax under the flat rate scheme is where a business with two or more activities has a lower flat rate percentage for its main activity.

EXAMPLE D Ltd provides bookkeeping and secretarial services. In the past 12 months turnover consisted of:

	£
Secretarial services	75,000
Bookkeeping services	25,000

As the majority of turnover derives from secretarial services, the rate for that category of business is applied to the total turnover of £100,000, and the rate for bookkeeping services is not used.

4672 SI 1995/2518 reg 55JB; Notice 733 para 4.5; FRS7100

Reduced rate for newly VAT-registered businesses If a business starts to use the scheme within a year of registering for VAT, the flat rate percentage is **reduced by** 1% until the day before the VAT registration anniversary. The reduced rate normally **applies from** the scheme start date.

EXAMPLE Mr E registers for VAT on 1 January and joins the flat rate scheme on 1 July.
He may use the reduced rate applicable to his business, less a 1% reduction, from 1 July to 31 December, and the normal flat rate subsequently.

If a person **registers for VAT late**, and HMRC allows a retrospective scheme start date, the reduced rate can only be used from the date HMRC was notified or became aware of the requirement to register. If a person registers for VAT more than a year late, they therefore cannot use the reduced rate at all.

Changes of percentage rate

A change in the flat rate percentage **will occur** where: 4674 SI 1995/2518 regs 55H, 55N
- there is a change in the activities carried on by a business; or
- HMRC alters the published rates.

A change of flat rate percentage by a business must be **notified** to HMRC within 30 days of the change taking place.

Change in balance of activities If a trader carries on two or more business **activities which belong to trade sectors with different percentage rates**, the position should be reviewed on each anniversary of joining the scheme. The flat rate should be changed if the balance between them: 4676 SI 1995/2518 reg 55H; Notice 733 para 4.7
- has changed in the year just ended; or
- is expected to change in the year about to commence.

The **new rate** should be applied from the start of the VAT period in which the scheme start date anniversary falls.

EXAMPLE F Ltd, a flat rate trader, sells cars and also repairs vehicles. It makes VAT returns for calendar quarters, and its flat rate scheme start date anniversary is 1 September. In previous years its flat rate was that appropriate to car sales, as the turnover from car sales had been higher than that from car repairs.
However, in the latest year to 31 August, this balance of activities changed (turnover from repairs exceeded turnover from car sales).
A flat rate at the repairing vehicles rate should be applied to all turnover from 1 July (the start of the VAT period in which 1 September falls).

If a trader **fails to review the position**, and applies an incorrect rate following a change in the balance of activities, HMRC can raise assessments for the additional VAT which would have been due if the correct rate had been applied. 4678

EXAMPLE The owners of a pub/restaurant joined the flat rate scheme and accounted for VAT at the rate applicable to pubs. Following a refurbishment of the premises, food sales increased and accounted for the majority of the turnover, but the position was not reviewed, and the previous rate continued to be used.
HMRC raised assessments based on the rate applicable to restaurants, which was higher, and this rate was upheld at tribunal. *Mr & Mrs Morgan (t/a The Harrow Inn)* [2006] (VTD 19671)

Activities starting or ceasing If the trade sector for a business changes due to an activity ending or a new activity starting, the **new rate** must be applied from the date of the change, and HMRC must be notified (using the address in ¶4654) within 30 days of the date of the change. 4680 SI 1995/2518 reg 55H; Notice 733 para 4.8

EXAMPLE Mr G, a flat rate scheme trader who makes VAT returns for calendar quarters, had a monthly turnover of £8,000 from film processing. On 1 June he discontinued film processing and started to sell photographic equipment. Sales of equipment for the month ended 30 June amounted to £9,000.
For the quarter to 30 June, the flat rate for photography should be applied to the turnover of £16,000 for the 2 months ended 31 May, and the rate for retailing (not listed elsewhere) to the turnover of £9,000 in June.

Change by HMRC If the published rate for a trade sector changes, the new rate must be applied from the date specified by HMRC. 4682 Notice 733 para 4.9

MEMO POINTS If using the **cash basis**, supplies made before the change in the VAT rate remain taxable at the rate in force at the time of supply, even if payment is received after the change in rate.

b. Transactions outside the scheme

The flat rate percentage does not apply to certain transactions which are outside the scheme. Output tax and input tax on these transactions must be accounted for separately in the normal way. 4684

Notice 733 para 15.8

MEMO POINTS 1. Output tax is not due on the **private use** of goods or services where no input tax has been claimed on the cost. As a result, flat rate scheme users do not account for the **fuel scale charge**.
2. **Partial exemption** does not apply to flat rate scheme traders, so any allowable input tax is regarded as wholly attributable to the making of taxable supplies.
3. HMRC **will include income** from any source received by the same legal entity (such as rental income received by a sole trader) as being income within the scope of the scheme. This potentially could bring otherwise exempt income within the flat rate scheme. However, income received by a legal entity which is separate from the flat rate scheme business is not aggregated as scheme income.

EXAMPLE Mr H is a sole trader who applies a flat rate of 12%. He receives rental income from a flat, which goes into a separate business bank account. HMRC will consider that the rental income is part of the flat rate scheme income, and will expect Mr H to account for 12% VAT on the rental income he receives.
If Mr H had received the same rental income as income of a partnership of which he is a member, it would not have been aggregated with the flat rate scheme income, provided that he had not artificially split the business (¶2629+).

Pre-registration expenditure

4686 SI 1995/2518 reg 55F

New businesses can **claim input tax** on goods or services supplied before the date of VAT registration in their first VAT period, subject to the normal rules (¶8560+).

Capital assets

4688 FRS6500

Subject to the special rules below, input tax incurred **when acquiring** a capital asset is not deductible.

Sale proceeds are included in the amount on which the flat rate VAT is calculated, even if the sale is exempt, as in the case of a car where input tax recovery was blocked (¶1914+).

Notice 733 para 15.1

MEMO POINTS 1. For this purpose, capital assets are those that would fall within the usual **definition** (¶2674), but also specifically **exclude** any goods covered by the capital goods scheme (¶2280+), and any goods bought to:
- resell;
- incorporate into other goods for onward supply;
- consume (or completely use) within one year; or
- generate business income by being leased, let or hired.

2. For the definitions of **goods and services** see ¶275+.

4690 SI 1995/2518 reg 55E; Notice 733 paras 15.2, 15.3; FRS6500

Input tax If a capital asset with a **value** of over £2,000 (including VAT) is purchased, acquired or imported, input tax can be claimed, no matter whether the asset is used for exempt or non-business purposes.

MEMO POINTS For this purpose, it is a **single purchase** of capital goods which is important when comparing to the value threshold. HMRC gives the following examples of such a single purchase:
- a computer package (computer, printer, camera, scanner, speakers, etc) bought as one transaction; and
- items of kitchen equipment (a pizza oven, a fridge and a dishwasher) bought for a restaurant.

If all the items are from one supplier at one time, they count as one purchase of capital expenditure goods.

EXAMPLE H Ltd, a flat rate trader, made the following purchases of capital assets:

	VAT £	Total £
Computer	360	2,160
Furniture	240	1,440

Input tax of £360 can be claimed, as the VAT-inclusive cost of the computer was more than £2,000.

Output tax If input tax was claimed when a capital asset was acquired, output tax at the standard rate must be separately accounted for on disposal. **4692** SI 1995/2518 reg 55C(4); Notice 733 para 15.9

MEMO POINTS Input tax **may have been claimed** on a capital asset:
- before a business joined the scheme; or
- under the scheme, either as pre-registration expenditure or because the VAT-inclusive value was greater than £2,000.

EXAMPLE A Ltd, a flat rate trader, made the following VAT-inclusive supplies in a VAT period:

	VAT £	Total £
Standard-rated sales	4,000	24,000
Sale of a capital asset on which input tax had been claimed	320	1,920

The flat rate percentage is applied to the turnover of £24,000.
In addition, output tax of £320 is due on the sale of the capital asset.

Acquisitions from other EU member states

Tax on acquisitions **of goods** from other EU member states must be accounted for in the normal way (¶9010+), but the acquisition VAT will not be recoverable as input tax unless the goods are capital assets which meet the conditions in ¶4690. **4694** SI 1995/2518 reg 55C(1)

Bad debt relief

The normal rules for claiming bad debt relief (¶840+) apply, **unless** the cash turnover method is used. **4696** SI 1995/2518 reg 55V; Notice 733 para 14

Under the **cash turnover method**, partial relief at the flat rate percentage is given automatically, as VAT is only accounted for if payment is received. If the normal bad debt relief conditions are met, further relief may be claimed on the difference between VAT:
- at the rate charged to the customer; and
- which would have been paid to HMRC at the flat rate.

EXAMPLE Mr B, whose flat rate percentage is 10% and who uses the cash turnover method, suffers a bad debt of £1,200 including £200 VAT. He may claim bad debt relief as follows:

	£
VAT charged to customer	200
VAT which would have been payable at flat rate (£1,200 × 10%)	(120)
Bad debt relief	80

2. Effect on direct taxes

The **flat rate tax** is deducted from gross sales for income tax and corporation tax purposes. **4700** Notice 733 para 7.8

Non-deductible input tax is included in the cost of the item.

On disposal of a **capital asset**, any VAT which is not accounted for separately (¶4692) is included in the sales proceeds.

EXAMPLE Mr C, whose flat rate percentage is 8.5%, had the following results:

	VAT £	Total £
Sales	20,000	120,000
Purchases and expenses	14,000	84,000
VAT liability under flat rate scheme (£120,000 × 8.5%)		10,200

Mr C's accounts for income tax purposes, compared with those which would result from normal (20%) VAT accounting, are as follows:

	Flat rate scheme £		Normal VAT accounting £	
Sales	109,800	(120,000 - 10,200)	100,000	(120,000 - 20,000)
Purchases and expenses	(84,000)		(70,000)	(84,000 - 14,000)
Net profit	25,800		30,000	

3. Administration

Completing the VAT return

4702 Notice 733 para 7.5 The following comprehensive example illustrates the VAT return (¶2998) entries required under the scheme.

EXAMPLE D Ltd, whose flat rate percentage is 10%, has the following transactions in a VAT period:

	Net £	VAT £	Total £
Standard-rated sales (including VAT @ 20%)	24,000	4,800	28,800
Zero-rated sales	1,500		1,500
Sales of goods to other EU member states	1,000		1,000
Exempt supplies	500		500
Sale of a capital asset on which input tax claimed	2,000	400	2,400
Purchases and expenses including VAT	15,000	3,000	18,000
Purchase of a capital asset	2,400	480	2,880
Purchase of goods from another EU member state	1,400	280	1,680

The VAT return entries are as follows:

Box	Description	Amount £	Calculation
1	VAT on sales and other outputs	3,580	At flat rate: £3,180 ((£28,800 + £1,500 + £1,000 + £500) × 10%) On asset sale: £400
2	VAT on acquisitions from other EU member states	280	
3	Total VAT due	3,860	
4	VAT reclaimed on purchases and other inputs	480	On asset purchase: £480 (No input tax deduction due on acquisition from other EU member state)
5	VAT to be paid to HMRC	3,380	
6	Total value of sales and all other outputs, including VAT	34,200	(£28,800 + £1,500 + £1,000 + £500 + £2,400)
7	Total value of capital purchases over £2,000 and all other inputs from EU states	4,560	(£2,880 + £1,680)
8	Total value of supplies of goods and related services, excluding VAT, supplied to other EU member states	1,000	
9	Total value of acquisitions of goods and related services, excluding VAT, from other EU member states	1,400	

Record-keeping

Businesses **must** keep a record of flat rate calculations for each accounting period, showing the: **4704** Notice 733 para 7.2
- flat rate turnover;
- flat rate percentage used; and
- VAT due.

Businesses **should** also record details of **assets** on which input tax has been claimed, to help check whether output tax should be accounted for when they are sold.

D. Leaving the scheme

1. Leaving by choice

A business can leave the scheme **at any time** by notifying HMRC in writing. HMRC will confirm the leaving date, which will normally be the end of a VAT period. **4708** Notice 733 para 12.1; FRS4100

2. Compulsory termination

A business must leave the scheme if: **4710** SI 1995/2518 regs 55M - 55Q; FRS4400
- turnover exceeds either of the scheme limits;
- it becomes ineligible for another reason; or
- HMRC removes it from the scheme.

Turnover in excess of scheme limits

A business must notify HMRC within 30 days, and leave the scheme, if turnover exceeds either of the scheme limits. **4712** SI 1995/2518 regs 55M, 55Q; Notice 733 para 12.3

For this purpose, turnover **includes** VAT and all business supplies **except** sales of capital assets, and should be calculated in accordance with the trader's usual method of accounting for VAT, i.e. either cash received or invoices paid. Flat rate traders should **normally** review annual turnover on each anniversary of joining the scheme, to ensure that they can remain within it. If a business is **growing rapidly**, it may be advisable to check turnover on a monthly basis.

The following table gives further details: **4714** Notice 733 paras 11.2, 12.2

Condition	Date business must leave	Exceptions
VAT-inclusive turnover for a year ending on an anniversary of joining the scheme has exceeded £230,000	End of VAT period in which anniversary falls [1]	A business can remain in the scheme if the limit was exceeded because of a one-off increase in turnover, and it can show that: - turnover in the coming year will not exceed £191,500; - the increase was due to unexpected business activity which has not previously occurred and is not expected to recur; and - the increase arose from a genuine commercial activity
VAT-inclusive turnover in the next 30 days is expected to exceed £230,000	Start of the 30-day period	

Note:
1. If the annual accounting scheme is also being used see ¶4832.

EXAMPLE Mr E is a flat rate trader who makes VAT returns for calendar quarters, and has a scheme start date anniversary of 1 September. Turnover for the latest year to 31 August is £240,000 including VAT.
He must leave the scheme on 30 September, being the end of the VAT period in which 1 September falls.

Ceasing to be eligible

4716 SI 1995/2518 regs 55M, 55Q; Notice 733 para 12.2

A person **must notify** HMRC within 30 days, and leave the scheme, if they become ineligible for any of the reasons set out in the following table:

Reason	¶¶	Date business must leave
Deciding to use the margin scheme or auctioneers' scheme	¶6625+, ¶6750+	Start of VAT period in which decision made
Intending to use the capital goods scheme	¶2280+	Date on which intention or expectation occurred
Becoming a tour operator	¶7490+	Date on which person became a tour operator
Becoming eligible to join a VAT group, or becoming part of a VAT divisional registration	¶8800+, ¶2744+	Date on which person became eligible to join group, or joined divisional registration
Becoming closely associated with another person	¶4650	Date on which person became associated

Removal from scheme by HMRC

4718 SI 1995/2518 regs 55P, 55Q; Notice 733 para 12.5; VAT FRS4300

HMRC can remove a business from the scheme at any time if:
- it considers removal to be necessary for the protection of tax revenues; or
- a false statement was made in the application to join the scheme.

The **date** on which the business must leave, which can be retrospective, will be specified in a withdrawal notice sent by HMRC. If the business is removed from the scheme because it was never eligible to use it, withdrawal will be backdated to the scheme start date, and normal VAT accounting will have to be used from that date.

A person **can appeal** to a tribunal against a decision to remove them from the scheme (¶4260+). They must not use the scheme until the appeal is resolved.

3. Arrangements on leaving the scheme

4720 Notice 733 para 12.7

If a business leaves the scheme **at the end of a VAT period**, the liability for that period is calculated under the flat rate scheme rules. Normal VAT accounting is used from the first day of the next VAT period.

Notice 733 para 12.4

MEMO POINTS If **deregistering** from VAT, output tax must be accounted for in respect of the following (on the final VAT return):
- sales made up to the last day of registration;
- the value of capital expenditure goods (¶4726) (on which input tax was recovered) which are still owned at deregistration (¶8610+); and
- any pre-registration stock, on which input tax has been recovered at the time of registration, and which is still on hand at the date of deregistration.

4722 Notice 733 para 12.7

If a business leaves the scheme **before the end of a VAT period**, two calculations are required. The liability:
- up to the leaving date is calculated under the flat rate scheme rules; and
- from the leaving date to the end of the VAT period is calculated using normal VAT accounting.

EXAMPLE Mr F, a flat rate trader with a flat rate of 10%, who prepares VAT returns for calendar quarters, was removed from the flat rate scheme by HMRC on 30 November. Details for the quarter ended 31 December were as follows:

		1 Oct - 30 Nov		1 Dec - 31 Dec
		£		£
Standard-rated sales (including VAT)		24,000		12,000
Exempt supplies		2,000		1,000
Input tax on purchases and expenses		(1,800)		(900)
Calculations of VAT liability:				
Output tax	(£26,000 x 10%)	2,600	(£12,000 x 1/6)	2,000
Input tax		-		(900)
Payable to HMRC		2,600		1,100

Total liability: £3,700 (2,600 + 1,100)

Stock adjustment

A person who leaves the scheme when holding stock, but remains VAT-registered, can claim input tax on the **increase in stock values** between the scheme start and end dates. The necessary criteria are that: 4724 SI 1995/2518 reg 55S; Notice 733 paras 12.8, 12.9
– no separate input tax claim has been, or will be, made in relation to that stock; and
– its value is higher than the value of stock at the scheme start date (on which input tax was claimed).

The **claim** is made in the first VAT return after leaving the scheme.

MEMO POINTS A formal **stocktake** is not required but the figures must be reasonable, so businesses should keep a record of how stock was valued in case of any query.

EXAMPLE Mr G, a flat rate trader, held stock valued at £20,000 (excluding VAT) when he left the scheme. The value of stock held at the scheme start date, on which input tax had been claimed, was £10,000 (excluding VAT).
Mr G can claim input tax of £2,000 in his VAT return for the first period after leaving the scheme. ((20,000 - 10,000) x 20%)

Capital assets adjustment

If a flat rate trader **claimed input tax** on a capital asset, but left the scheme before disposing of it whilst remaining VAT-registered, they are deemed to make a self-supply (¶1490+) on the day after leaving the scheme. 4726 SI 1995/2518 reg 55R; FRS6600

Output tax must be accounted for on the value of the asset at the leaving date, but input tax of the same amount will be deductible unless recovery is restricted under the partial exemption rules (¶2075+). The purpose of this rule is to ensure that a partly exempt business does not recover more input tax on an asset than is due, either under the flat rate scheme or under normal VAT accounting.

EXAMPLE H Ltd, a flat rate trader, purchased a capital asset for £3,000 (plus VAT) and claimed the related input tax of £600. When H Ltd left the scheme but remained VAT-registered, the asset was worth £1,000.
H Ltd must account for VAT of £200, but it may also claim input tax of £200 if no partial exemption restriction applies. (1,000 x 20%)

Cash based turnover adjustment

A flat rate trader who leaves the scheme and does not immediately start to use the cash accounting scheme (¶4880+) **must account for** flat rate VAT on all supplies made under the scheme for which they have not received payment, subject to any bad debt relief claim (¶4696+). 4728 Notice 733 para 9.6

The **adjustment** must be **made in** the VAT return for the period in which the trader ceases to use the cash based turnover method.

EXAMPLE A Ltd, a flat rate trader using the cash based turnover method, with a flat rate percentage of 10%, leaves the scheme and starts to use normal VAT accounting at a time when trade debts amount to £2,350 including VAT.
A Ltd must account for VAT of £235. (2,350 × 10%)

Transfer of a business

4730 FRS4500

If a flat rate trader transfers their business as a going concern (¶8646+), and the VAT **registration number is transferred**, the purchaser must operate the flat rate scheme, until such time as the purchaser might choose to leave the scheme. If the VAT number is **not transferred**, the purchaser must use normal VAT accounting unless or until they apply to join the flat rate scheme.

SECTION 2

Annual accounting scheme

4745 SI 1995/2518 regs 49 - 55; Notice 732

The annual accounting scheme is designed to alleviate administrative burdens for small businesses, by simplifying their requirements for reporting and paying VAT liabilities as follows:
- only one VAT return needs to be completed each year;
- fixed interim payments are made towards the eventual VAT liability; and
- an extra month is allowed to complete and submit the VAT return, and pay any balance of tax due.

The scheme would **probably not benefit** a business which normally receives VAT repayments, as the only advantage would be the reduced accounting requirements. In addition, there would be a cash flow disadvantage, because no repayments would be received until after the end of each annual accounting period.

A. General principles

Eligibility

4752 SI 1995/2518 reg 52; Notice 732 paras 2.1 - 2.5

A VAT-registered person can use the scheme if, on reasonable grounds, they expect that their **turnover** in the next 12 months (excluding VAT, exempt supplies and supplies of capital assets previously used in the business) will not exceed £1.35 million.

For further information on **estimating turnover** see ¶4646.

Exclusions

4754 SI 1995/2518 reg 52; Notice 732 para 2.6; VATAAS2100

The following table summarises the circumstances in which a person will not be eligible to use the scheme:

Reason for exclusion	Details
Business circumstances	Member of a VAT group registration (¶8800+)
	Member of a divisional registration (¶2744+)
Protection of tax revenues	HMRC considers tax revenues are at risk, for example as a result of an increasing VAT debt[1] An insolvent person will not therefore be allowed to join
Previous use of scheme	Ceased to use the scheme in the previous year

Note:
1. A decision refusing entry to the scheme cannot be appealed, but a trader can request a reconsideration (¶4230+).

B. Joining the scheme

1. Application

A business can apply to join the scheme **using form** VAT 600AA, or form VAT 600AA/FRS if the business is also applying to join the flat rate scheme (¶4635+). 4758 Notice 732 paras 8.1 - 8.6

In addition to the contact details and VAT registration number of the business, the application **must specify**:

a. the month in which the annual accounting year is to end; and

b. the timing of interim payments, and the preferred credit transfer method (from the following options):

- direct debit;
- standing order;
- bank giro transfer; or
- BACS or CHAPS.

If HMRC **accepts** an application to join the scheme, it will notify the business in writing, and confirm the:

- amount and timing of interim payments;
- method for making interim payments, enclosing a bank mandate form if applicable; and
- due date for submitting the annual return and paying the balance of tax.

MEMO POINTS 1. The form should be sent to the following **address**:
HM Revenue & Customs
Annual Accounting Registration Unit
National Registration Service
Imperial House
77 Victoria Street
Grimsby
North East Lincolnshire
DN31 1DB

2. The application can include a request for interim payments to be made **quarterly** instead of monthly, if this would be more suitable or convenient.

3. If an applicant insists on making interim **payments by cheque or cash**, the business will be refused entry to the scheme.

Choice of year end

The annual accounting year will end on the last day of the chosen month. It may be convenient to choose the financial year end, but any other month can be selected. If the business is **partly exempt**, the accounting year end date must be the same as the year end for partial exemption purposes. 4760 SI 1995/2518 reg 49; Notice 732 paras 3.3, 3.5, 7.3; VATAAS3300

A business may **apply to change** its annual accounting year end after joining the scheme

Comment 1. **Seasonal businesses** may receive a cash flow benefit if there is a considerable gap between the busy season and the annual accounting year end.

2. **Sole traders and partnerships** should aim to avoid the situation where a VAT balancing payment (¶4796) would become due at the same time as income tax self-assessment payments on account.

Start date

If a trader applies to join the scheme when: 4762 Notice 732 paras 3.2, 8.3; VATAAS3100

a. applying to become VAT-registered, the scheme will operate from the date of VAT registration; or

b. already VAT-registered, the scheme start date will be the first day of the VAT period in which the application to join the scheme was processed.

If a return has already been issued, the start date will be the first day of the next period. The application cannot be backdated, even if the return is not yet due.

For further details if also joining the flat rate scheme see ¶4827.

EXAMPLE Mr A has a quarterly VAT return period ending on 30 June and applies to join the annual accounting scheme in May. If HMRC processes the application before the return for the period ending on 30 June has been issued, the annual accounting scheme will start on 1 April.

2. Transition to the scheme

4764 SI 1995/2518 reg 49; VATAAS3200

The **first accounting period** under the scheme, from the start date to the annual accounting date, is known as the transitional accounting period.

EXAMPLE B Ltd makes VAT returns for calendar quarters and applies to join the annual accounting scheme in August, choosing a December year end.
The transitional accounting period will be from 1 July to 31 December.

4766 Annual accounting scheme returns are not issued for a **period shorter than** 3 months. This can result in two periods of less than 12 months, if:
- the year end chosen when joining the scheme would result in a transitional accounting period shorter than 3 months; or
- the year end is changed after joining the scheme.

EXAMPLE Mr C makes VAT returns for calendar quarters and applies to join the annual accounting scheme in July, choosing an August year end.
The transitional accounting period starts on 1 July and will end on 30 September, not 31 August. It will be followed by an 11 month period from 1 October to the following 31 August.

4768 Annual accounting scheme returns are not issued for a **period longer than** 12 months, except for businesses applying to join the scheme from the date of VAT registration, in which case the maximum transitional accounting period is 12 months and 30 days.

C. Operating the scheme

1. Accounting for VAT

VAT returns

4772 SI 1995/2518 regs 50, 51; Notice 732 para 3.6; VATAAS3400

Only one annual VAT return is required, on which the total output tax and input tax for the whole period ending on the annual accounting year end date is entered.

Returns must be **submitted** within 2 months of the end of an annual accounting period, **unless** the period is for less than 4 months, in which case the return must be submitted within 1 month.

The scheme does not affect the nature of the **records** required to calculate output tax and input tax. Care should therefore be taken to keep adequate records throughout the year, despite the fact that they will only be used for VAT return purposes at the end of each annual accounting period, rather than quarterly.

Notice 732 para 7.3

MEMO POINTS 1. **Partly exempt** (¶2075+) businesses only need to make annual, as opposed to quarterly, partial exemption calculations, using the annual accounting scheme figures. No partial exemption annual adjustment will therefore be necessary.

Notice 732 para 6.3

2. Returns can be **submitted electronically**, but no extra submission or payment time is granted, because of the extra month already allowed under the scheme.

2. Paying the VAT

As the VAT liability will not be known until after the end of each annual accounting period, a provisional liability is paid by means of interim payments during the period. A balancing payment is then made after the end of the period when the actual liability is calculated. **4774**

a. Interim payments

General principles

Frequency Interim payments are made monthly, unless a business requests quarterly payments. **4776**
Payments **commence in** the 4th month of each annual accounting scheme period and are **made on** the last working day of each month. SI 1995/2518 regs 49 - 51; Notice 732 para 4; VATAAS4300

MEMO POINTS 1. A **working day** is any day of the week other than a Saturday, Sunday, bank holiday or public holiday.
2. HMRC will normally expect a business to **retain the same payment pattern** for at least a year.

Exceptions Interim payments are not required: **4778**
- in a transitional accounting period (¶4764+) of less than 4 months; or
- if the provisional liability is less than £50.

Liability Where a business has been VAT-registered for **at least 12 months**, the provisional liability is based on the previous year's VAT liability. **4780**

Otherwise, it is based on the estimate of turnover provided in the VAT registration application.

Payments are **rounded** down to the nearest £5.

Method Payments must be made by one of the accepted credit transfer methods (¶4758). Any payments made by cash or cheque will be allocated against any outstanding debts, or held as a non-allocated amount. **4782** Notice 732 paras 5.1 - 5.4; VATAAS4400

If an interim payment is **not made**, HMRC will send a reminder and a request for immediate payment, which must then be made by CHAPS or BACS.

Monthly payments

Each monthly interim payment is equal to 10% of the provisional liability. **4784** SI 1995/2518 reg 49; Notice 732 paras 4.1, 4.5

As payments commence at the end of the 4th month and run until the end of the final month, 9 payments will be made in a **12-month accounting period**, amounting to 90% of the provisional liability.

EXAMPLE D Ltd has an annual accounting year from 1 January to 31 December and a provisional liability of £20,000 based on the previous year's liability.
D Ltd would make 9 monthly interim payments of £2,000 each, commencing at the end of April.

A lower proportion of the provisional liability will be paid in a **shorter accounting period**. **4786**

EXAMPLE Mr E has a transitional accounting period from 1 July to 31 December and a provisional liability of £10,000 based on estimated turnover.
Mr E would make three monthly interim payments of £1,000 each, commencing at the end of October (amounting to 30% of the provisional liability).

Quarterly payments

Each quarterly interim payment is equal to 25% of the provisional liability. **4788** SI 1995/2518 reg 49; Notice 732 paras 4.2, 4.5

As payments commence at the end of the 4th month, three payments will be made in a **12-month accounting period**, amounting to 75% of the provisional liability.

EXAMPLE F Ltd has an annual accounting year ended 31 December and a provisional liability of £20,000 based on the previous year's liability.
F Ltd would make 3 quarterly interim payments of £5,000 each, commencing at the end of April (amounting to 75% of the provisional liability).

4790 A lower percentage of the provisional liability will be paid in a **shorter accounting period**.

EXAMPLE Mr G has a transitional accounting period from 1 July to 31 December and a provisional liability of £10,000 based on estimated turnover.
Mr G would make one quarterly interim payment of £2,500 at the end of October (amounting to 25% of the provisional liability).

Changing interim payments

4792 Notice 732 paras 4.6, 4.7; VATAAS4200

If interim payments appear **too high**, a business may contact HMRC and provide calculations in support of a lower estimate. If appropriate, HMRC will notify the business of the agreed lower interim payments.

A business should also contact HMRC if interim payments appear **too low**. The payments may be increased at the request either of the business or of HMRC.

EXAMPLE A surcharge was imposed on a company, following late payment of a large balancing amount. It was held that HMRC had a duty of care to respond effectively to changes in circumstances notified by the company. This had not been discharged in this case, because realistic revised monthly payments had not been set. The company had been unable to pay the large balancing amount by the due date. Its appeal against the surcharge was allowed. *Lineplan Ltd* [1992] (VTD 9369)

Voluntary payments

4794 Notice 732 para 4.8

An **additional** voluntary payment may be made at any time, by Bank Giro credit, CHAPS or BACS. Payment must be made in multiples of £5.

---

b. Balancing payments

4796 SI 1995/2518 regs 50, 51; Notice 732 para 6.4; VATAAS4600

If the **interim payments** made during an annual accounting period:
a. are less than the actual VAT liability for that period, a balancing payment is required, which should be made within 2 months of the end of the annual accounting period, unless the period is shorter than 4 months, when payment is due within 1 month. The payment method may be by cheque, or any of the accepted credit transfer methods for interim payments (¶4758), with the exception of direct debit; or
b. exceed the actual VAT liability for that period, a repayment will be made by HMRC after the return has been submitted.

A **large balancing payment** may be required if:
- there was a short annual accounting period with few interim payments;
- the estimate of turnover was too low;
- there was a large one-off receipt;
- turnover increased significantly compared with the previous year; or
- interim payments were reduced inappropriately.

EXAMPLE

1. Mr H joined the annual accounting scheme on 1 October, and chose 31 December as the annual accounting year end. His VAT liability for the transitional accounting period from 1 October to 31 December was £8,000.
No interim payments are required, as the period is shorter than 4 months. Mr H must submit the VAT return and pay the full liability of £8,000 by the end of January.

2. A Ltd joined the annual accounting scheme on 1 September, and chose 31 December as the annual accounting year end. Its provisional VAT liability for the transitional accounting period from 1 September to 31 December was £10,000 and the actual liability was £12,000.

A Ltd must make one interim payment of £1,000 at the end of December, and submit the VAT return and make a balancing payment of £11,000 by the end of February.

3. B Ltd uses the annual accounting scheme, with a year end of 31 December. Its provisional VAT liability for the year was £20,000 and the actual liability was £30,000.
B Ltd must make nine interim payments of £2,000 each, in the months April to December, and submit the VAT return and make a balancing payment of £12,000 by the end of the following February.

D. Leaving the scheme

1. Leaving by choice

A business may leave the scheme at any time by notifying HMRC in writing. The leaving date may be chosen by the business. Once the business has left the scheme, it cannot **rejoin** for a period of 12 months. **4800** SI 1995/2518 reg 53(2)(d); Notice 732 para 7.5; VATAAS7200

2. Compulsory termination

A business **must leave** the scheme if: **4802** SI 1995/2518 regs 53 - 55; Notice 732 paras 2.4, 7.6-7.8; VATAAS7300
- turnover exceeds the scheme limit;
- it becomes ineligible for another reason; or
- HMRC removes it from the scheme.

The following table gives further details:

Reason for leaving	Details	Date business must leave
Taxable supplies exceed £1.6 million excluding VAT	Value of taxable supplies in a past transitional or annual accounting period has exceeded the limit	End of the period in which the limit was exceeded
	It is expected that the limit will be exceeded during the current accounting period Notify HMRC within 30 days	End of the period, or any earlier date specified by HMRC
Trading status changes	Ceasing to trade, or to be VAT-registered	Date of event
	Becoming insolvent and ceasing to trade, other than for the purpose of disposing of stocks and assets	
	Dying, or becoming bankrupt or incapacitated	
Removal from scheme by HMRC	If business has a poor VAT compliance record [1], including failure to: - make a return under the scheme; - make interim or balancing payments; or - pay a liability relating to a return or assessment made before joining the scheme	Date on which HMRC withdraws authorisation
	A false statement was made when applying to join the scheme	
	HMRC considers it necessary for the protection of tax revenues	

Note:
1. HMRC will **normally** remove a business from the scheme if it has:
- received four reminder letters in relation to the last six interim payments;
- failed to make interim payments, resulting in a debt greater than 20% of the provisional annual liability; or
- failed to submit two consecutive annual returns and balancing payments.

EXAMPLE C Ltd's taxable supplies for the annual accounting year ending on 31 December reach £1.7 million on 31 October.
C Ltd must notify HMRC by 30 November and leave the scheme on 31 December.

3. Arrangements on leaving the scheme

4806 SI 1995/2518 reg 55(2) If a business leaves the scheme **during** a transitional or annual accounting period, a return and payment of any outstanding tax must be made within 2 months of the leaving date.

If a business leaves the scheme **at the end of** a transitional or annual accounting period, a return and payment of any outstanding tax must be made within 2 months of the end of the period, unless the period is shorter than 4 months in length, in which case the return and payment must be made within 1 month.

A business which **remains VAT-registered** must adopt an alternative method of accounting for VAT from the day after it leaves the annual accounting scheme.

Transfer of a business

4808 If a **purchaser** of a business as a going concern (¶8646+) **wishes to use the scheme**, they must make a new application to HMRC.

SECTION 3

Interaction between the flat rate and annual accounting schemes

4825 Notice 732 para 2.8 A business can use the flat rate and annual accounting schemes at the same time. The year end will be the same for both purposes, and the VAT liability will only need to be calculated annually.

Joining the schemes

4827 Notice 732 para 9 A business can apply to join both schemes by using **form** VAT 600AA/FRS.

If a joint application is made for both schemes, the **commencement date** for the flat rate scheme will normally be the same as for the annual accounting scheme, but a different date can be requested in the application form.

If **different start dates** are chosen, or if a business joins the flat rate scheme when the annual accounting scheme is already being used, two calculations will be necessary:
a. a calculation using normal VAT accounting rules for the period before commencement of the flat rate scheme; and
b. a calculation using the flat rate scheme rules for the period after commencement of that scheme.

Comment To **avoid having to make two calculations**, a business could either wait until the end of an existing annual accounting period before joining the flat rate scheme, or change the annual accounting year end to an earlier date (¶4760), and start a new annual accounting period when both schemes are in use.

Operating the schemes

4830 SI 1995/2518 reg 55H; Notice 732 paras 9.5, 9.6 **Change of flat rate percentage** If a business operates in **more than one trade sector** and:
a. the **balance of turnover changes** during the year, the flat rate percentage in force at the start of the annual accounting year should be used for the remainder of that year, and the new percentage applied at the start of the next year; or

b. the business **ceases** a particular activity, or **commences** a new activity, any new flat rate percentage should be used from the date of the change; two flat rate calculations will therefore be required in the annual accounting period, as in ¶4722.

Leaving the schemes

If a business **becomes ineligible** for one scheme, it may normally remain in the other unless it requests removal. As the two schemes have different conditions, eligibility for both schemes should be checked periodically. **4832** Notice 732 para 9.11; VAT FRS4200

If a business leaves the flat rate scheme:

a. before the end of an annual accounting period, two calculations will be necessary, as in ¶4722; or

b. due to **turnover exceeding scheme limits**, the leaving date will be the earlier of: SI 1995/2518 reg 55Q

– the end of the VAT period in which the flat rate scheme start date anniversary falls; or

– the end of the month following that in which the flat rate scheme start date anniversary falls.

EXAMPLE Mr A uses the flat rate and annual accounting schemes. His annual accounting year ends on 30 April and his flat rate scheme start date anniversary is 1 May. Turnover for the latest year to 30 April was £255,000.
He must leave the flat rate scheme on 30 June.

CHAPTER 3

Cash accounting scheme

OUTLINE ¶¶

The cash accounting scheme enables smaller businesses to defer payment of VAT liabilities by accounting for output tax when payment is received from customers, rather than when supplies are made or invoices issued, which is normally earlier. On the other hand, input tax can only be claimed when payment is made to the supplier. **4880** s 25(1), Sch 11 para 2(7) VATA 1994; SI 1995/2518 regs 56 - 65; Notice 731

This accounting method also ensures that a trader does not have to fund the payment of VAT which has not been received, as **bad debt relief** (¶840+) is automatic.

Comment The scheme should **benefit** businesses which offer extended credit, or suffer significant bad debts. The scheme would probably **not benefit** businesses which:
- have a high proportion of cash sales, such as most retail businesses;
- regularly receive VAT refunds from HMRC (e.g. zero-rated traders);
- make continuous supplies of services (¶808+); or
- are paid in advance by customers but receive credit from suppliers.

SECTION 1

General principles

Eligibility

A VAT-registered trader can use the scheme if, on reasonable grounds, they believe that the **value** of their **taxable supplies** will not exceed £1.35 million in the next 12 months. The value of taxable supplies **excludes** VAT, exempt supplies and any expected sales of capital assets. **4885** SI 1995/2518 reg 58; Notice 731 para 2.1; VCAS2050

VCAS3050 MEMO POINTS A **VAT group** may use the scheme, but:
- the £1.35 million turnover limit applies to the whole group;
- the whole group must leave the scheme if any member causes the £1.35 million limit to be exceeded;
- all members of a cash accounting VAT group must use the scheme; and
- a cash accounting business must leave the scheme if it joins a non-cash-accounting VAT group.

Exclusions

4887 SI 1995/2518 reg 58; Notice 731 para 2.1 The following table summarises the circumstances in which a person will not be eligible to use the scheme:

Reason for exclusion	Details
Poor VAT compliance record	A person is not eligible if they have failed to: - submit all required VAT returns; or - pay all VAT due to HMRC, unless they have agreed to make instalment payments over a specified period
Offences in relation to VAT	A person is not eligible if, in the previous year, they have: - been convicted of any offence in connection with VAT; - made a payment to settle proceedings in relation to a VAT offence (¶4152+); or - been assessed to a penalty in relation to VAT (¶3955+)
Protection of tax revenues	If HMRC considers that tax revenues are at risk, it will notify refusal of permission to operate the scheme in writing, and exclusion will normally be for at least a year[1]
Previous use of scheme	A person is not eligible if they were removed from the scheme by HMRC in the previous 12 months

Note:
1. If HMRC refuses permission to operate the scheme, a trader can ask it to reconsider, within 30 days. This is especially relevant if the trader can provide further information, or believes that some facts may not have been fully considered. The trader may also appeal to a tribunal (¶4260+).

SECTION 2

Joining the scheme

4900 Notice 731 para 3.1 No formal application is required. An eligible business can begin to use the scheme without notifying HMRC, but it is not permissible to apply the scheme retrospectively.

Scheme start date

4902 SI 1995/2518 reg 58 VCAS2100; VCAS2150 A trader can **normally** begin to use the scheme on the date that they become VAT-registered (¶2696), or at the start of any other VAT period.

If a trader **registers for VAT late**, they may not use the scheme until after they have submitted their first VAT return and paid, or agreed to pay, any VAT due.

Comment It may not be beneficial to use the scheme **from the VAT registration date** if input tax on items such as plant, equipment, fixtures and fittings, and initial stocks could be claimed earlier under normal VAT accounting.

Transition to the scheme

4904 Notice 731 para 3.2 **Newly VAT-registered businesses** should take care not to account for output tax on amounts received which relate to pre-registration supplies.

Input tax on qualifying pre-registration goods and services (¶8560+) can be claimed in:
- the first VAT return period, if payment was made before VAT registration; or
- any later VAT return period in which payment was made.

Businesses **changing their VAT accounting method** should take care not to account for VAT on supplies made or received in an earlier VAT period, during which VAT was accounted for under the normal rules.

SECTION 3

Operating the scheme

The scheme must be used for the whole of the business carried on by a taxable trader, apart from certain excluded transactions (¶4916). 4910

1. Accounting for VAT

Output tax is accounted for in the VAT period in which payment is received from a customer. **Input tax** is claimed in the VAT period in which payment is made to a supplier. 4912 SI 1995/2518 regs 57, 65; Notice 731 paras 4.2 - 4.4

MEMO POINTS 1. **Partly exempt** (¶2075+) businesses must base partial exemption calculations on amounts received and paid in a VAT period.
2. The value of any supplies of goods **to other EU member states** in box 8 of the VAT return is the value of supplies made, not payments received. The value of supplies of goods **from other EU member states** in box 9 of the VAT return is the value of supplies received, under the normal rules, as these are excluded transactions (¶4916).

Date on which payment is received or made

The following table sets out the rules for determining the date on which a payment is received or made: 4914 SI 1995/2518 reg 65; Notice 731 paras 4.4, 4.5

Method of receipt/payment	Date of receipt/payment
Cash (coins or notes)	When cash received or paid
Cheque	Later of date on cheque or when cheque received or sent
Giro, standing order or direct debit	When bank account credited or debited
Credit or debit card	When sales voucher created, not when paid by credit provider

Excluded transactions

Certain transactions are excluded from the scheme, with the result that VAT must be **accounted for** when the supply is made or received. 4916 SI 1995/2518 reg 58(2), (3); VCAS2200

The following table gives further details:

Type of exclusion	Details
Sales or purchases of goods under certain types of agreement	Hire purchase or lease purchase agreements, and credit sales or conditional sales
Extended credit terms	Supplies where a VAT invoice is issued, and payment is not due for more than 6 months after the invoice date
Supplies made after invoice date	Supplies where a VAT invoice is issued before a service is performed or goods are delivered or made available, unless there has been partial performance or delivery and the invoice only relates to the goods or service delivered or performed

Type of exclusion	Details
Goods from overseas[1]	Import (¶9405+), or acquisition from another EU member state (¶9010+), or removal from an HMRC warehouse (¶9483+) or free zone (¶9495+)
Sale or purchase of mobile phones and computer chips	The purchaser of mobile phones and computer chips is liable to account for VAT if the value of the goods is over £5,000 (¶1990+)
Note: 1. The scheme may be used for the onward supply of these goods.	

EXAMPLE Mr A uses the cash accounting scheme and had the following VAT-exclusive transactions in a VAT period:

	Amounts invoiced £	Amounts received/paid £
Standard-rated sales	100,000	85,000
Standard-rated sales under hire purchase agreements	10,000	8,000
Standard-rated purchases and expenses	(70,000)	(60,000)

Calculation of VAT liability

Output tax	19,000	(85,000 + 10,000) × 20%
Input tax	(12,000)	60,000 × 20%
Payable to HMRC	7,000	

2. Detailed rules for transactions

Part payments

4918 Notice 731 para 5.7

Receipts or payments which:
- represent part payment of an invoice;
- cover more than one invoice; or
- relate to an invoice for supplies at different tax rates,

must be **allocated** to invoices in the order in which the invoices were issued or received.

If the VAT element of a part payment is not identified, the amount must be treated as VAT-inclusive.

EXAMPLE B Ltd issues an invoice in respect of a standard-rated supply as follows:

	£
Goods	1,000
VAT @ standard rate of 20%	200
Total	1,200

If B Ltd receives a part payment of £780, this represents 65% of £1,200. B Ltd must account for output tax of £130. (200 × 65%)

4920 Notice 731 para 5.7

Part payments which relate to an invoice for supplies at **different tax rates** must be apportioned between the different tax rates.

EXAMPLE C Ltd issues invoices #15 (dated 4 February 2015) and #16 (dated 4 March 2015) for supplies at different tax rates:

	#15 £	#16 £
Standard-rated goods	1,000	2,000
Zero-rated goods	-	1,000
VAT	200	400
Total	1,200	3,400

If the business receives a non-specific part payment of £2,500 in respect of both invoices, this is allocated as follows:

	Gross £	VAT £
Payment	2,500	
1. Against earlier supply (invoice #15):	(1,200)	200.00
	1,300	
2. Against later supply (invoice #16):	(1,300)	
VAT paid: $(\frac{1,300}{3,400} \times £400)$	-	152.94
VAT to be accounted for on the £2,500 part payment:		352.94

Foreign currency If part payments are made or received in a foreign currency, the treatment **depends upon** whether the invoice was only in sterling, or in sterling and another currency. 4922 Notice 731 para 5.11

If the invoice was **only in sterling**, the foreign currency must be converted into sterling at the exchange rate on the date of supply of the goods or services. One of the approved conversion methods (¶9032) must be used consistently. VAT is accounted for by reference to the proportion of the total sterling amount paid. 4924

EXAMPLE Mr D issued an invoice for £1,200 including £200 VAT. He received $1,200 in part payment, representing 62.5% of £1,200 at the exchange rate on the date of supply.
Mr D must account for VAT of £125.00. (200 × 62.5%)

If an invoice is in **sterling and foreign currency**, VAT is accounted for by reference to the proportion of the total foreign currency amount paid. 4926

EXAMPLE Mr E issued an invoice for £1,200 including VAT, which was also expressed as $1,920. He received $960 in part payment, representing 50% of the foreign currency amount due.
Mr E must account for VAT of £100.00. (200 × 50%)

Payments received net of deductions

VAT on payments received net of deductions must be accounted for at the full value before deductions. 4928 Notice 731 para 5.8

MEMO POINTS Such **deductions include**:
- commission deducted by a customer;
- commission or costs deducted by a factor, agent or auctioneer collecting a debt or selling goods on behalf of a business; or
- income tax deducted by an employer or contractor.

Price changes

If the agreed price for a supply changes, the following **actions** should be taken: 4930 Notice 731 para 5.12
- a further invoice or credit note should be issued; and
- further payments or refunds must be recorded in the receipts and payments records as normal.

Rules for special transactions

4932 Notice 731 paras 5.1 - 5.10

Type of transaction	Rules
Deposits	VAT on deposits which represent **advance payment** must be accounted for when the deposits are received or paid. If the deposit is **refunded**, the VAT originally accounted for can be reclaimed. VAT does not apply to deposits **taken as security** to ensure safe return of goods, whether this is refunded upon return of the goods or retained in the event of loss or damage to the goods.

Type of transaction	Rules
Debts collected by an agent	VAT must be accounted for in the VAT period in which **payment** is **received by** the agent, provided that the debt has not been sold to a factoring agent or invoice discounter. VAT is due on the amount paid by the customer to the agent, not on any lower amount received from the agent.
Exports and supplies to other EU member states	If **evidence** of export or supply has not been received by the relevant deadline (¶9585), VAT must be accounted for on any amounts already received. The supply or export may be zero-rated upon receipt of the evidence, and an adjustment made in the VAT return for the period in which the evidence was received.
Factored debts	Output tax must be accounted for in the VAT return period in which the factor **collects payment** from the customer. VAT must be accounted for on the full value of the supply, not on the amount for which the debt is assigned. An adjustment may be made if: – all or part of the debt is reassigned under a recourse clause; and – the debt qualifies for bad debt relief (¶840+). If any invoices cover supplies at **different VAT rates**, payments must be attributed in accordance with the bad debt relief rules in order to calculate how much of the unpaid amount relates to sales at each VAT rate. *RTI Services Ltd* [2002] (VTD 18512)
Payments in kind	VAT on payments such as **barter or part-exchange transactions** must be accounted for on the date of supply of the goods or services given or received instead of money. VAT must be accounted for on the full value of the supply, which is usually the price that would have been charged if payment had been made in money. *A-Z Electrical* [1993] (VTD 10718)
Grants	If part of a supply is **paid** by a **grant from a third party**, VAT is due on the full value, including the grant. *Martin Gibson Ltd* [1990] (VTD 5473)
Client accounts	A **solicitor or accountant** using the cash accounting scheme must account for output tax when money is withdrawn from a client account to pay for services provided. Similarly, a **client** using the cash accounting scheme may claim input tax when money is withdrawn from the client account to pay for services provided.

3. Paying the VAT

4934 SI 1995/2518 reg 65 The scheme does not alter the **method** of paying VAT liabilities, or the due date for payment; the normal rules (¶3165+) apply.

MEMO POINTS If the cash accounting scheme is used, a tribunal is very unlikely to accept that **delays in payment by customers** are a reasonable excuse for late submission of a return or late payment of VAT.

EXAMPLE In a case where a trader was persistently paid late by a major client, the judge commented that if a trader used the cash accounting scheme to account for VAT, he "would have no reasonable excuse for failing to" pay his VAT on time, since the liability would be made up of VAT already collected by the trader. *C&E v JB Steptoe* [1992]

4. Administration

Record-keeping

4936 Notice 731 para 4 Records must **cross-refer** amounts:
- received to the corresponding sales invoices;
- paid to the corresponding purchase invoices; and

– received or paid to the normal commercial evidence, such as bank statements, cheque stubs and paying-in slips.

These requirements will normally **be satisfied by** an analysed cash book, showing amounts received and paid, with separate VAT columns.

A business must identify and separately record any receipts or payments relating to **supplies prior to the scheme start date**, on which VAT was accounted for using the normal rules. VCAS2100

If a **customer pays in notes or coins**, a business must, if asked, provide a receipted and dated VAT invoice, unless an accompanying till receipt or other receipt states "cash sale", or otherwise clearly indicates that cash has been given. **4938** SI 1995/2518 reg 65

If a **supplier is paid in notes or coins**, a business should obtain a receipted and dated VAT invoice.

A business must **retain** receipted invoices from suppliers, and copies of receipted invoices provided to customers, for 6 years.

SECTION 4

Leaving the scheme

A business must leave the scheme if it becomes ineligible, or it may choose to leave. **4950**

1. Leaving by choice

A business can choose to leave the scheme **at the end of** any VAT period if, for example: **4952** SI 1995/2518 reg 60(2); Notice 731 para 6.1; VCAS6050
- the scheme is no longer beneficial; or
- the record-keeping requirements cannot be met.

Such a business would be able to **rejoin** the scheme at the beginning of a later VAT period, provided that the business is then eligible.

2. Compulsory termination

A business must leave the scheme if: **4954** SI 1995/2518 regs 60, 64; Notice 731 para 6.2
- **turnover** exceeds the scheme limit;
- an **offence** has been committed in relation to VAT; or
- **HMRC removes** it from the scheme.

Turnover in excess of scheme limit

A business must leave the scheme at the **end of a VAT period** if turnover is more than £1.6 million in the 12 months then ending. **4956** SI 1995/2518 reg 60; Notice 731 paras 2.6, 6.2; VCAS6100

For this purpose turnover is **defined** as the value of taxable supplies, **excluding** VAT and exempt supplies, but **including** disposals of stocks and capital assets.

If the £1.6 million limit is exceeded due to a **one-off increase in sales** (e.g. the sale of a capital asset), a business may request permission from HMRC to remain in the scheme, if it can show that:
- the one-off increase has not previously occurred and is not expected to recur;
- the sale arose from a genuine commercial activity, and does not give an undue advantage over competitors; and
- there are reasonable grounds for believing that the value of taxable supplies in the next 12 months will be below £1.35 million.

HMRC may request further information, and will consider whether competition might be distorted, or tax revenues endangered, before writing to confirm whether a business can remain in the scheme.

Comment The value of taxable supplies should be reviewed regularly, to allow sufficient time to change the accounting method if a business ceases to be eligible to use the scheme.

EXAMPLE F Ltd uses the cash accounting scheme and makes VAT returns for calendar quarters. Its taxable supplies for the 12 months ended on 30 September amounted to £1.85 million, and are expected to be higher in the following 12 months.
F Ltd must leave the scheme on 30 September and begin normal VAT accounting on 1 October.

VAT offences

4958 SI 1995/2518 reg 64(1)

A trader must leave the scheme at the end of a VAT period in which they have:
- been **convicted** of an offence in connection with VAT;
- made a **payment to settle proceedings** in relation to a VAT offence (¶4152+); or
- been **assessed to a penalty** in relation to VAT (¶3955+).

Removal from scheme by HMRC

4960 SI 1995/2518 reg 64(1)(d); Notice 731 paras 6.2, 6.7 - 6.9; VCAS4300; VCAS6150

HMRC may remove a business from the scheme if it is considered **necessary for the protection of tax revenues**, particularly if a business:
- cannot comply with the record-keeping requirements (¶4936+);
- fails to meet agreed instalment payments;
- consistently incurs penalties (¶3955+) or default surcharges (¶4082+); or
- consistently claims input tax too early.

A business must leave the scheme on the **date** that HMRC withdraws authorisation for its use.

A trader can **appeal** against such a decision (¶4260+), but must not normally use the scheme pending the outcome of the appeal. The scheme can be used whilst other matters are under appeal, unless HMRC considers that the appeal facilitates manipulation of the scheme.

EXAMPLE
1. A company was removed from the scheme because it had incurred five default surcharges. *Vitech Engineering Ltd* [1990] (VTD 5154)

2. A trader appealed against a default surcharge and against a decision to remove him from the scheme as a result of incurring the surcharge. He had incurred four previous surcharges.
It was held that there was a reasonable excuse for the most recent surcharge, so the appeal against removal from the scheme was allowed. *SP Whitehouse* [1991] (VTD 6763)

3. A company was removed from the scheme because it had issued an invoice for £410,592 including VAT of £61,152 to an associated company which did not operate the scheme.
It was held that removal was appropriate, on the ground that there was a risk to tax revenues if the associated company did not pay the invoice. *Marketing Middle East Ltd* [1997] (VTD 15666)

3. Accounting for outstanding VAT

4962 SI 1995/2518 regs 61, 64; Notice 731 para 6.4

A business which leaves the scheme must account for outstanding VAT, unless it immediately starts to use the cash turnover method of the flat rate scheme (¶4664).

The outstanding VAT **consists of**:

	£
Output tax on supplies made up to the date of leaving the scheme, where payment had not been received by that date, subject to any claim for bad debt relief (¶840+)	X
Less: Input tax on supplies received up to the date of leaving the scheme, where payment had not been made by that date	(X)
VAT due	X

The outstanding VAT must be **accounted for at once** when leaving the scheme, **unless** the business is entitled to do so over the next 6 months instead. **4964** SI 1995/2518 regs 61, 64; Notice 731 para 6.5

Entitlement depends on the reason for leaving the scheme, as set out in the following table:

Reason for leaving scheme		Business may account for outstanding VAT over 6 months[1]	Business must settle outstanding VAT when leaving the scheme
Business chooses to leave		✓	
Taxable supplies over £1.6 million in last 12 months	Taxable supplies during the last 3 months did not exceed £1.35 million	✓	
	Taxable supplies during the last 3 months exceeded £1.35 million		✓
Any other compulsory reason			✓

Note:
1. A business does not need to inform HMRC if it chooses this option.

Settling outstanding VAT immediately

The outstanding VAT must be accounted for on the **return** for the period in which the business leaves the scheme, and must be paid on the normal due date for that return. **4966** SI 1995/2518 regs 61, 63, 64; VCAS6200

EXAMPLE G Ltd had to leave the cash accounting scheme on 31 December, as turnover for the year then ended had exceeded the scheme limit. The company did not choose to pay the outstanding VAT over 6 months. At 31 December, customers owed G Ltd £100,000 plus VAT in respect of sales invoiced up to that date. G Ltd owed its suppliers £60,000 plus VAT in respect of purchases invoiced up to that date.

In addition to the normal VAT due under the scheme, G Ltd must account for VAT of £8,000 in its VAT return for the period ended 31 December. ((100,000 - 60,000) x 20%)

Accounting for outstanding VAT over 6 months

The outstanding VAT is accounted for when payment is received or made. These amounts will need to be recorded separately. **4968** SI 1995/2518 reg 61; Notice 731 para 6.6; VCAS6250

If any amounts are **still unpaid** at the end of 6 months, VAT must be accounted for in the return which includes the end of the 6-month period. Bad debt relief may be claimed under the normal rules (¶840+) in respect of any irrecoverable amounts.

EXAMPLE Mr H chose to leave the cash accounting scheme on 30 June and decided to account for outstanding VAT over 6 months.

His transactions included:

Sales			Purchases		
Invoice date	Output tax £	Payment date	Invoice date	Input tax £	Payment date
31 May	4,000	5 July	4 June	200	28 June
15 June	1,000	30 June	27 June	500	26 July
30 June	2,000	31 July	10 July	750	12 August
15 July	500	31 August			

The sales invoice issued on 15 July and the purchase invoice dated 10 July are new supplies. The VAT should be accounted for according to the tax point date.

The invoices with tax points on or before 30 June are accounted for when payment is received or made.

The output tax to be accounted for in July will be £6,500. (4,000 + 2,000 + 500)

The input tax to be accounted for in July will be £1,250. (500 + 750)

4. Specific situations

Ceasing to trade

4970 SI 1995/2518 reg 63 If a trader:
- ceases to trade, or to be VAT-registered;
- becomes insolvent; or
- transfers a business as a going concern (¶8646+), and the purchaser does not take over the VAT registration number,

a final return must be submitted, and any VAT paid, within 2 months of the date of cessation.

Notice 731 para 6.10 MEMO POINTS If a trader ceases to trade, the cash accounting scheme may still be used to account for VAT on disposals of **remaining stocks and assets**, until cancellation of the VAT registration.

4972 SI 1995/2518 reg 63(2), (3) If a business is transferred as a going concern (¶8646+), and the **VAT registration number is transferred** to the purchaser, the seller must inform the purchaser that the cash accounting scheme is in use. The purchaser must operate the scheme for receipts and payments relating to supplies made and received by the seller, and may then leave the scheme if desired, under the normal rules.

Post-insolvency trading

4974 Notice 731 para 6.11; VCAS3150 If **trading continues** after the date of insolvency, the office-holder responsible for the business may continue to use the cash accounting scheme, provided that separate records are kept detailing receipts and payments in respect of transactions already accounted for in pre-insolvency VAT returns.

Rejoining the scheme

4976 SI 1995/2518 reg 58(1)(c)(iv); Notice 731 para 6.3; VCAS6650 A business which leaves the scheme **by choice**, or because **annual turnover** exceeded £1.6 million, is able to rejoin it at the beginning of any subsequent VAT period if annual turnover is then below £1.35 million.

A business which has been **removed** from the scheme by HMRC may rejoin the scheme after a year, if then eligible.

PART 7

Particular activities

Particular activities
Summary

The numbers cross-refer to paragraphs.

CHAPTER 1 Land and property

CHAPTER 2 Farming

CHAPTER 3 Bloodstock

CHAPTER 4 Retailers

CHAPTER 5 Second-hand goods and collectibles

CHAPTER 6 Gold transactions

CHAPTER 7 E-business

CHAPTER 8 Agents

CHAPTER 9 The travel industry

CHAPTER 10 Barristers

CHAPTER 11 Public bodies

CHAPTER 12 Charities

CHAPTER 13 Clubs and associations

CHAPTER 14 Pension funds

CHAPTER 1

Land and property

OUTLINE ¶¶

5100 The property sector has to deal with many VAT issues, each of which depends on the exact nature of the supply being made. For example:
– the transaction may variously constitute construction, work on an existing building, exploitation for economic benefit, or disposal of a property interest; and
– the type of property involved and its use both before, and especially after, the transaction has occurred, or the work has been completed, will affect the VAT treatment.

The **basic position** is that property transactions are exempt from VAT, which means associated input tax cannot be recovered, subject to the partial exemption rules (¶2070).

There are many **exceptions**, which can be summarised as follows.

Property involved	Situation	Details	VAT rate	¶¶
New buildings[1]	Construction costs	Commercial property	Standard rate	¶5150
		Dwellings	Zero rate	¶5152
		Property intended for relevant residential use	Zero rate	¶5158
		Property intended for relevant charitable use	Zero rate	¶5170
		Residential caravan park	Zero rate	¶5188
	Disposal of property interest	Sale of commercial property which is less than 3 years old	Standard rate	¶5277
		Short or long lease of opted commercial property	Standard rate	¶5277
		First sale or long lease of dwelling	Zero rate	¶5247
		First sale or long lease of property intended for relevant residential use	Zero rate	¶5247
		First sale or long lease of property intended for relevant charitable use	Zero rate	¶5247
Land and existing buildings[1]	Building works done	Converting a non-residential property to a dwelling	Reduced rate	¶5404
		Residential conversion for a housing association	Zero rate	¶5430
		Refurbishing empty premises to be used for a residential purpose	Reduced rate	¶5444
		Alterations to protected buildings	Standard rate	¶5452
	Exploitation	Deriving economic benefit without disposing of property interest e.g. parking charges, hotel accommodation, tent pitches	Standard rate	¶5492
	Disposal of property interest	Sale or lease of opted commercial property	Standard rate	¶5602
		First sale or long lease of converted residence	Zero rate	¶5384
		First sale or long lease of substantially reconstructed protected property to be used as a residence	Zero rate	¶5392

Note:
1. Builders and developers making taxable supplies of £150,000 or less per annum may be interested in the **flat rate scheme**, which simplifies VAT accounting (¶4635+).

Place of supply

5102 SI 1992/3121 reg 5 **Services** relating to specific sites or buildings are deemed to be provided where the property is located (¶9714). So where the property is located:
– in the UK, all services are within the scope of UK VAT;

- in another EU member state, the services are outside the scope of UK VAT, but the supplier may need to register in the EU state concerned (goods transferred to the EU state from the UK may also be subject to VAT (¶9100)); or
- outside the EU, all services are outside the scope of VAT.

For this purpose land-related services **include**:
- construction services, such as provided by a plumber, bricklayer or electrician;
- professional services provided by a surveyor, architect or estate agent; and
- accommodation provided in a hotel.

SECTION 1

New buildings

A building is usually a structure of a certain size, which is intended to be enduring for a considerable amount of time. Most buildings are permanent structures. **5105** Notice 742 para 7.9

The supply of fixtures with a building is treated as part of the same supply, the VAT treatment being the same as that for the associated building.

MEMO POINTS A **fixture** is an asset that is installed in, or otherwise fixed in or to, a building or land so as to become part of that building or land in law (¶5138). A chattel is an asset that is tangible and moveable, although it can become a fixture by being attached to a building or land e.g. a radiator.

A. What is a new building?

Identifying a new building, particularly when it is related in some way to an existing building, is crucial to applying the correct VAT treatment. A **commercial building** (¶5150) is treated as new until it is 3 years old. **Other buildings** are only new on completion of construction and until the first supply has been made of the building. **5110**

Broadly, a new building **does not include**: **5112** Sch 8 Group 5 notes 16, 17 VATA 1994
- the conversion, reconstruction or alteration of an existing building (there are special rules which apply for these types of works (¶5400));
- an enlargement of, or extension to, an existing building, unless a new dwelling is created (¶5154); or
- the construction of an annexe, unless it is to be used for a charitable purpose and detailed criteria are satisfied (¶5182).

The planning permission application and consent for the work should identify the nature of the work. The **main test**, however, is the difference between what existed before the construction began and what exists afterwards i.e. what physical characteristics have changed, what effect the work has had on any existing buildings on the site, and the relevant functions of the buildings and any interrelation.

Demolition

If an **existing building** is demolished to ground level and another building is erected, the **replacement building** will be a new building (unless it is a reconstruction of the pre-existing building - see ¶5118). The existing building will be treated as demolished for this purpose if a single façade (double if a corner site) is retained as a result of a condition of statutory planning approval **5114** Sch 8 Group 5 note 18 VATA 1994

If demolition of the existing building occurs after a separate new building has been constructed, the work is not part of the construction of a new building for VAT purposes. Moreover, see the example below.

EXAMPLE A disabled person lived in a bungalow, which he intended to demolish and replace with a more accessible home. During the construction works he needed somewhere to live; due to a

complete lack of alternatives, he had to remain in the existing bungalow. So an extension was built and then the existing bungalow was demolished.
It was held that a new building had not been created, because an extension had been built first, even though the pre-existing building was then immediately demolished. *Graham David Gilder* [2003] (VTD 18143)

5116 Notice 708 para 3.2.1

HMRC has given the following **examples**:

Situation	Construction of a new building?
Making use of the foundations of a previous building which has been demolished to ground level	✓
Building onto an existing wall of another house to form two semi-detached houses; no internal access between the two and planning consent does not prohibit separate use, letting or disposal	✓
Building of a new house within an existing terrace of houses on the site of a demolished house	✓
Construction of a self-contained flat which enlarges an existing building	✓
Construction of a granny annexe which cannot be used separately from the main house	x
Detached enclosed swimming pool	x

5118 The basic test applied in **case law** is whether a reasonable man would say that a building was new, or part of an existing building.

EXAMPLE

1. A company redeveloped a site, which meant some buildings were demolished and a new building was constructed.
It was held that the work constituted the construction of a new building rather than the reconstruction of an existing building, because it was "not a replication or construction anew of what was there before". *Wimpey Group Services Ltd v C & E* [1988]

2. A company, which owned a multi-storey car park, obtained planning permission to build a block of flats on top.
It was held that the flats were a new building, because it was inappropriate to regard the flats as enlarging the existing car park. *Trident Housing Association Ltd* [1993] (VTD 10642)

3. A new residential building was constructed so that it adjoined an existing old people's home. Initially there was no internal access between the two homes. Three weeks after construction an interconnecting door was installed. The proprietor stated that this was due to financial constraints imposed because of the unexpected deaths of five residents.
It was held that the initial intention (decisive to the VAT treatment) had been to construct a new building. *JMB Strowbridge* [1999] (VTD 16521)

4. A new dwelling incorporated a single wall of a previous building, which was not required by planning consent.
It was held that the work related to an existing building. So even though a new building was undoubtedly constructed, the incidental incorporation of a small part of an existing building was fatal to the appellant's case, because the legislation is so specific. *Philip Evans* [2001] (VTD 17264)

5. Usually, retention of any part of a pre-existing building demonstrates that construction work is some sort of alteration to that pre-existing building, whether reconstruction, enlargement or extension. This case shows that in rare circumstances a completely new building can be constructed.
A nursing home was constructed on the site of an old church. The church itself was incorporated in the new nursing home, comprising the reception area. In almost all cases, this would have been viewed as an enlargement of the pre-existing church building. However, the First-tier Tribunal held that a new building had been constructed. The new part of the building had about five times the floor area of the original church and so dwarfed the original building that it was a misdescription to refer to the work as enlargement or extension of that original building.
The Upper Tribunal has now confirmed that the First-tier Tribunal came to the right decision. Retention of part or all of an original building does not preclude a ruling that a new building has been constructed, albeit that the circumstances have to be very unusual for that to be the case. *Astral Construction Ltd* [2015]

B. Work done - construction

In the course of construction

Construction costs of new buildings are standard-rated, unless a specific zero-rating provision applies. Zero-rating is **dependent on** the type of building being constructed (¶5148), the type and source of the cost being incurred (¶5130), and when the work is started and completed. 5120

Before construction can begin, there are usually **preparatory works** required to put the land in a state to be developed. Preparatory works can be zero-rated if they are supplied in the course of construction of a qualifying building. However, if a qualifying building, for whatever reason, is not constructed after the preparatory works have been carried out, the services should be standard-rated.

EXAMPLE

1. A builder acquired some land with a view to constructing bungalows. He cleared the land and made excavations of the foundations. However, before pouring in the concrete, he sold the land. It was held that the builder had sold bare land, not a building in the course of construction, because at the time of the sale there was nothing on the land that was recognisably a building under construction. *Cameron New Homes Ltd* [2001] (VTD 17309)

2. A taxpayer's house was demolished, by order of the council, after an arson attack. Due to a delay in agreeing an insurance pay-out, the landowner was unable to commence building a replacement for several months after demolition.
It was held that as the house was demolished by order, not as part of the construction of a new building, the demolition services were not provided in the course of construction. *Simon Brown* [2006] (VTD 19884)

3. A company carried out the demolition of a building which had been badly damaged by fire. HMRC issued a ruling stating that VAT should have been charged on the demolition, as the services were not in the course of construction of a new building. The company appealed.
It was held that as there was no undue time lag between the demolition and the construction of the new building, the demolition services were, in this case, in the course of construction. *Dart Major Works Ltd* [2004] (VTD 18781)

Completion can also be a problem for projects, as work carried out **after** completion of a qualifying building cannot be zero-rated and must be standard-rated. It has been held that "a building remains in the course of construction until the main structure is completed, the windows glazed and all essential services and fittings, such as plumbing and electricity, have been installed. Thereafter the building ceases to be in the course of construction … and the phase of fitting out and furnishing is ready to begin." *University of Hull* [1975] (VTD 180) 5122 Notice 708 para 3.3.6

HMRC gives the following **indicators** of when construction has been completed:
- when a certificate of completion is issued; Notice 708 para 3.3.2
- the terms of any planning consent;
- when the building is occupied or sold; and
- the intention of the developer.

MEMO POINTS **Retention payments** made under the construction contract are still treated as relating to the new building, even when paid 6 months or more after completion. Special tax points apply (¶5206).

EXAMPLE

1. A builder is constructing a house for sale. The house-buyer wants a conservatory attached to the house, so he pays a deposit to a conservatory specialist to install one prior to him moving in. The conservatory supplier is denied access to the site until after the builder has finished its work and the house has been conveyed to the house-buyer.
The supply by the conservatory specialist is not work "in the course of construction" of the house but work to an existing building. The payment of the deposit is irrelevant, because it is the time of the conservatory's construction which is crucial.

2. A developer constructs and sells flats, which must then be fitted out by the buyer before they can become habitable.
Future work to fit them out is still in the course of construction. Completion would occur when the occupier moves in.

5124 Notice 708 para 3.3.4

HMRC gives the following **examples** of when zero-rating would and would not apply:
- soft landscaping work carried out after the building has been completed, which has been delayed due to seasonal weather conditions, is zero-rated;
- site investigation work carried out prior to the entering into of a building contract is standard-rated; and
- any work delayed until after the building is complete owing to an insufficiency of funds is standard-rated.

5126 Notice 708 para 3.3.3

Snagging or correctional work is usually carried out after the building has been completed. The VAT rating of the work depends on whether it is carried out by:
- the supplier who was involved in the initial building work and the snagging forms part of that contract, in which case it is zero-rated; or
- another supplier as a separate supply (that is, someone who is contracted to correct work performed by another person) and it is performed after the building has been completed, in which case the work is standard-rated.

EXAMPLE Although a certificate of completion had been issued and the building was being occupied, services provided to remedy substandard plastering work could be zero-rated, as the average person would expect plaster work of an acceptable standard in a newly completed building. *Mr & Mrs James* [2007] (VTD 20426)

5128

For zero-rating to apply, it is necessary for there to be a **temporal link** between the initial construction work and any subsequent building which takes place.

EXAMPLE A new secondary school was built in 1979 and opened to pupils in 1981. Two playgrounds were not finished until 1994.
It was held that the playgrounds were a separate project and not part of the original construction work, because the intervening gap of 13 years was too great. *C & E v St Mary's Roman Catholic High School* [1996]

1. Types of costs

5130

Costs incurred when constructing a building will relate to either:
- the services provided by the builder and its subcontractors;
- the materials used in the construction work; and/or
- professional services connected with the development.

Sometimes it is not easy to ascertain whether the supply is one of services or one of goods, or both (¶275). A common example is where doors and windows are made up off-site to the customer's specification and then installed, which may be a supply of services.

If goods are supplied as part of an overall supply of construction services, the VAT liability of the goods follows the VAT liability of the services.

a. Construction services

5132 Sch 8 Group 5 item 4 VATA 1994

All services **supplied by** the main contractor for the construction of a qualifying building (¶5148) are zero-rated.

In the case of **dwellings** (¶5152), services provided by the various subcontractors can also be zero-rated, provided that those services are made in the course of construction.

5133 Notice 708 para 3.4.1

Professional services, including services provided by the following, are standard-rated:
- architects;
- accountants;
- surveyors;

- solicitors;
- consultants;
- project managers; and
- supervisors.

However, if professional services are included within a single **composite supply** (¶312) of construction services for a qualifying building, they will also be zero-rated.

MEMO POINTS 1. Under a **design-and-build** lump sum contract the building client engages a contractor to carry out both the design and construction elements of the project; the VAT liability of the design element will follow that of the building work. Separate supplies of design or other similar professional services are always standard-rated, however.

2. Under a **management contracting** arrangement the client first appoints a professional design team, then engages a management contractor to provide preliminary advice. If the project:
- goes ahead, the management contractor will act as the main contractor for the work and its preliminary advisory services are then treated in the same way as its main construction services; or
- is aborted, the management contractor's preliminary advisory services are standard-rated.

What services can be zero-rated?

The VAT treatment may depend on the scope of the services supplied: **5134**

Notice 708 paras 3.3.4, 3.3.5; Business Brief 7/00; Notice 48 para 3.16

Type of service	Zero-rated	Standard-rated
Demolishing existing buildings and structures	Immediately prior to the commencement of construction work	Any work undertaken prior to the entering into of a building contract [1]
Providing or improving an access point to a building site	To allow deliveries to be made	
Carrying out ground works	Levelling and drainage of land	Any work undertaken prior to the entering into of a building contract [1]
Clearing the site	Providing site clearance so building work can start	Any work undertaken prior to the entering into of a building contract [1] Cleaning of on-site offices
Enabling water and power to be supplied to the building	Can extend to the work required to make the connection to the nearest existing supply	Water and power installed on land which is to be sold as building land [2]
Providing security	Walls, fences and gates	Most electrical appliances
Provision of soft landscaping within the site of a building [3]	The application of topsoil, the laying of grass, the planting of trees and other soft landscaping	Replacement of trees and shrubs that die, or become damaged or diseased Construction of fish ponds, rockeries and other ornamental works The provision of outdoor leisure facilities, such as a tennis court or a swimming pool Screening planted along a roadside verge
The means of providing access to the building within the site	Roads, footpaths, parking areas, drives and patios	
Hire of goods	Labour provided with hired plant e.g. erection and dismantling of scaffolding, crane and operator	If hired on their own e.g. site office portacabin, security fencing, scaffolding

Note:
1. This is HMRC's interpretation. It is possible to **zero-rate** services carried out before a building contract has been entered into, provided that there is an immediate link to the construction (see ¶5120).
2. When the **landowner can demonstrate** that any potential purchaser can only use the building site to construct a residential property, the supply of providing **access to essential services** can be zero-rated. However, if the building land could be used for any other purpose, the supply will continue to be standard-rated. *Douglas Virtue and Sonia Virtue t/a Lammermuir Game Services* [2007] (VTD 20259)
3. HMRC accepts that all **planting** carried out within the plot of a building will qualify for zero-rating where it is detailed on a landscaping scheme approved by a planning authority under the terms of a condition of planning consent.

b. Building materials

5136 The VAT rating of building materials incorporated into a building or its site follows that of the construction services to which they relate.

It is, however, necessary to identify first whether the goods involved are building materials.

The incorporation of **other goods** will be standard-rated. For contractors who then sell the property after construction (i.e. builder-developers), input tax recovery on these items is blocked (¶5275).

Definition

5138 Sch 8 Group 5 note 22 VATA 1994 **Building materials** are goods of a kind which are **ordinarily** incorporated by builders into the type of building being constructed, **during** its construction. Goods fitted once construction is complete cannot be building materials. Most electrical appliances are excluded.

It is obvious that certain goods are building materials - for example, bricks, cement, wiring and cabling, builders' hardware, decorating materials, etc. This is because such goods are ordinarily incorporated in virtually all buildings. However, unusual, or new, materials, or those only incorporated in specialist buildings, may not be viewed as "ordinarily" incorporated.

MEMO POINTS 1. For this purpose **incorporation** means that the article is fixed, so that its removal would either require the use of tools or result in damage to the goods or building (requiring remedial work). So appliances which plug in, carpets and moveable objects (such as sofas, tables and chairs) are not building materials.

2. HMRC views an item as **ordinarily** incorporated when it is commonly used in a building of that generic type - for example, a dwelling, school, etc. Within each type, no further distinction is made, so the same items could be incorporated in a large mansion and a flat, provided that both are classed as dwellings. (This is not necessarily the view of the First-tier Tribunal - see memo point **5**. below.) For certain buildings, the items which are ordinarily incorporated might serve a specific purpose - for example, the use of sound-proofing materials in homes near airports. *British Airports Authority (No 5)* [1977] (VTD 447)

3. The tribunal has concluded that retractable covers and moving floors for **swimming pools** are items ordinarily incorporated in dwellings. The term dwellings covers a wide range of property, including luxury abodes. Hence items ordinarily incorporated in luxury dwellings can be zero-rated. The fact that the covers and floors are powered by electricity does not make them electrical appliances for this purpose. *Rainbow Pools London Ltd* [2008] (VTD 20800)

HMRC Brief 2/11 4. The First-tier Tribunal has decided that **roller blinds** are building materials ordinarily incorporated into a dwelling. *John Price* [2010] (TC00873) However, HMRC has announced that it will ignore this decision rather than appealing against it.

5. The First-tier Tribunal has held also that **fire curtains** (a more flexible alternative to fire doors) are ordinarily installed building materials and so zero-rated. The Tribunal explained that whilst fire curtains are not ordinarily installed in all new houses, that is not the question the legislation poses. It asks whether the materials in question are ordinarily installed in buildings of the type in issue. Fire protection is ordinarily installed in houses which the law requires to be so protected and fire curtains, although not as common as fire doors, are an ordinary type of fire protection. Thus fire curtains are ordinarily installed in that type of building. *Coopers Fire Ltd* [2013] (TC02570)

5139 Notice 708 para 13.9 HMRC gives the following examples of items which are **excluded** from being building materials:
- Aga and similar range cookers (unless they are solid fuel, oil-fired or designed to heat space or water);
- free-standing and integrated appliances such as cookers, fridges, freezers, dishwashers, microwaves and washing machines;
- dryers and coffee machines;
- audio equipment (including remote controls) and built-in speakers;
- intelligent lighting systems;
- telephones;
- satellite and freeview boxes, CCTV;
- garden furniture, ornaments and sheds; and
- electrical components for garage doors and gates (including remote controls).

5140 Notice 708 paras 13.2 - 13.8 HMRC gives the following guidance as to when **goods become** building materials.

Comment This list is not definitive; as attitudes and technology change over time, other items may be treated as building materials.

Type of property	Category	Detail	Building materials?
All dwellings	Furniture	Prefabricated kitchen furniture for fitted kitchen e.g. kitchen sinks, work surfaces and fitted cupboards	✓
		Other fitted furniture	x
	Fixtures	Curtain poles and rails	✓
		Fireplaces and surrounds	✓
		Light fittings, including chandeliers	✓
		Power points (including combination shaver points)	✓
	Storage space	Formed from fabric of building e.g. airing cupboards, under-staircase cupboards	✓
		Provided as a by-product e.g. shelving formed from box work over pipes, or basin supports with cupboard underneath	✓
		Most wardrobes [1]	x
	Heating	Designed to heat water (including dual-use cookers), immersion heaters, boilers, hot and cold water tanks	✓
		Heating systems e.g. radiators and controls, ducted warm-air systems, storage heaters and other wired-in heating appliances, gas fires	✓
		Solid-fuel cookers and oil-fired boilers	✓
	Immovable appliances	Designed to provide ventilation (including cooker hoods), air cooling, air purification or dust extraction (including built-in vacuum cleaners)	✓
		Door entry systems used in a building for multiple occupation	✓
		Waste disposal units or machines for compacting waste used in a building for multiple occupation	✓
		Burglar alarms	✓
		Fire alarms and fire safety equipment	✓
		Devices to summon aid in an emergency - warden call systems (not telephones, electric gates or barriers)	✓
		Lifts or hoists	✓
	Flooring	Carpets, carpet tiles, underlay	x
		Linoleum, ceramic tiles, parquet, wooden floor systems	✓
	Bathroom	Vanity units and bathroom cabinets	x
		Fixed towel rails, toilet roll holders, soap dishes, etc	✓
		Sanitary ware	✓
		Saunas	✓
		Shower units	✓
		Plumbing installations e.g. electric showers and “inline” water softeners	✓
	Exterior	Doors (also internal doors)	✓
		Window frames and glazing	✓
		Fencing permanently erected around the boundary of the dwelling	✓
		Guttering	✓
		Letterboxes	✓
		Solar panels	✓
		Turf, plants and trees (¶5134)	✓
		TV aerials	✓
		Outside lights	✓
	Swimming pool	Inside the house, including water heaters and filters	✓
		Diving boards and specialist equipment	x

Type of property	Category	Detail	Building materials?
Relevant residential	All of the above for dwellings plus	Mirrors	✓
		External lighting systems	✓
		Safes	✓
Relevant charitable	General	Blinds and shutters	✓
		Lighting systems	✓
		Mirrors	✓
		Safes	✓
	Schools	Blackboards/whiteboards fixed to or forming part of the wall	✓
		Gymnasium wall bars	✓
		Notice and display boards	✓
		Mirrors and barres (ballet schools only)	✓
		Laboratory fittings	x
	Churches	Altars	✓
		Church bells	✓
		Fonts	✓
		Lecterns	✓
		Pipe organs	✓
		Pulpits	✓

Note:
1. A **wardrobe** will not qualify as building materials unless it satisfies all of the following criteria:
- encloses a space bordered by walls, ceiling and floor;
- sides and back use three walls, or two walls and a stub wall;
- the building's walls are visible inside the wardrobe, not covered by internal panelling; and
- with only a single shelf, rail for hanging clothes and closing door or doors.

Case law

5142

EXAMPLE

1. A builder installed washbasins supported by basin units instead of pedestals.
It was held that the units were not within the definition of furniture, as their purpose was to support the basins and to hide the piping. So zero-rating applied. *Edmond Homes Ltd* [1993] (VTD 11567)

2. When constructing some exclusive homes, a builder installed electrically operated security gates.
It was held that zero-rating could not apply because the gates were not ordinarily incorporated by builders (in any case, they constituted electrical appliances). *M & G McCarthy (t/a Croft Homes)* [2000] (VTD 16789)

3. A boarding school built some study-bedrooms, installing wardrobes, bed bases, desk tops and shelves. Each shelf constituted a single tier, which was fixed to the wall near enough to allow a pupil access while sitting at the desk top. The desk top itself was basically a large shelf placed at a convenient height for writing on.
It was held that the wardrobes and bed bases were furniture and were therefore excluded from zero-rating. The desk tops and shelves were, however, zero-rated because they were not furniture. *Christ's Hospital* [2005] (VTD 19126)

4. A telephone exchange system was installed in a new university building constructed specifically to house it. The exchange served the entire university and included a test jack frame fixed to one wall with power units, three cabinets and heavy-duty ducting.
It was held that although each component could be removed without much damage to the building, the entire system would break down if any component were missing and this would negate the whole purpose for which the building had been constructed. Accordingly, the exchange components had become part of the building and therefore qualified for zero-rating. *University of Reading* [1989] (VTD 4209)

5. Staff lockers were installed in a nursing home subsequent to its construction.
It was held that the lockers were furniture and, in any case, were installed too late to qualify for zero-rating. *Birmingham Council for Old People* [1998] (VTD 15437)

Interaction with services

The service of **fitting goods** which are not building materials is zero-rated where the relevant conditions are satisfied, even though the goods themselves are standard-rated. 5146

This should be borne in mind when apportioning the overall contract price on a fair and reasonable basis.

2. Types of building

The following summarises the VAT treatment of **qualifying costs** (¶5130) provided in the course of construction of certain types of buildings: 5148

Purpose of new building	Examples	Need a certificate?	VAT rating	¶¶
Dwelling	House, flat	x	Zero-rated	¶5152
Relevant residential use	Children's home, old people's home, hospice, boarding school house	✓	Zero-rated	¶5158
Relevant charitable use	Village hall	✓	Zero-rated	¶5170
Residential caravan park		x	Zero-rated	¶5188
Any other use	Office, shop, multi-storey car park, hospital, hotel, warehouse, factory	x	Standard-rated	¶5150

Non-residential buildings

A non-residential building is **defined** by what it is not - thus it is a building which is not a dwelling and is not intended for relevant residential or charitable use. 5150 Sch 9 Group 1 item 1(a)(i), (ii) VATA 1994

The **construction** of a new non-residential property (including services and building materials) is always standard-rated, unless there is to be some residential use made of the building (termed mixed use (¶5194)).

For the **conversion** of an existing non-residential property to a residence see ¶5400.

a. Dwellings

Both the main contractor and subcontractors can zero-rate their qualifying supplies (¶5130) when constructing a building which is designed as a dwelling or a number of dwellings. 5152 Sch 8 Group 5 item 2(a) VATA 1994

In this instance only, there is no requirement for a tax certificate from the future occupier.

MEMO POINTS The First-tier Tribunal has held that a single dwelling which consists of **more than one building** can be a dwelling for this purpose. *Catchpole* [2012] (TC01995)

What is a dwelling?

The term dwelling is not specifically defined, but should be **interpreted as** "a place where one lives, regarding and treating it as home". Whether food is commonly prepared and consumed at the premises has been held to be of secondary importance. *Uratemps Ventures Ltd v Collins* [2001] 5154 Sch 8 Group 5 note 2 VATA 1994

To be classed as a dwelling for VAT purposes, a building must **satisfy all** of the following **criteria**:

a. self-contained living accommodation;

b. no provision for internal access from the dwelling to any other dwelling (including a part of another dwelling);

c. at the time of planning consent, the building can be separately used, let or sold, free of any restriction imposed by covenant, planning permission, etc; and

d. statutory planning consent has been granted and the building's construction or conversion has been carried out in accordance with that consent.

MEMO POINTS 1. The builder should retain sufficient **evidence** of the nature of the construction in case HMRC should query the VAT treatment of the builder's services. Such evidence would include contracts and instructions agreed with the owner of the site, correspondence with the architect, and photographs of the site before and after the work.

2. The inclusion of a **home office** will not cause a building to fail the dwelling conditions.

3. **Occupation restrictions**, such as age-related, agricultural or forestry requirements, do not affect the separate use or disposal condition in **c.** above.

Business Brief 11/03 4. Where a building consists of **more than one dwelling** (e.g. a block of flats), the construction of **communal areas** (e.g. lounge, laundry and refuse area) will **only qualify** for zero-rating if they are solely used by the residents and guests. If they are used by non-residents, whether or not for a charge, the construction costs of the communal areas will be standard-rated.

HMRC Brief 47/11 5. HMRC has confirmed that the construction and first lease of **extra care accommodation** (i.e. self-contained flats, houses, bungalows, etc, that are sold or let with the option for the occupant to purchase varying degrees of care) is still zero-rated, assuming the usual criteria are otherwise met, even though some local authorities may include these type of buildings in a different planning class.

Case law

5156

EXAMPLE

1. A derelict caravan site was renovated so that prefabricated bungalows could be built on brick foundations. For rating and insurance purposes, they were treated as bungalows. Although removal would theoretically be possible, the cost of doing so would be prohibitive.
It was held that the bungalows were buildings and not caravans or mobile homes, being occupied and used as permanent dwellings. *Mr & Mrs N Smith* [1990] (VTD 5579)

2. An additional floor, containing eight bed-sits with en-suite shower rooms, was added to the top of a care home.
It was held that premises with their own front door, en-suite bathing facilities and the ability to cook with a microwave cooker and a kettle are self-contained living accommodation in the 21st century. *Agudas Israel Housing Association Ltd* [2004] (VTD 18798)

3. An individual obtained planning consent to build a double garage in the grounds of his house. He also built a second storey in which he put a kitchen, living room and a bedroom.
Although the building was self-contained living accommodation, the work did not qualify for zero-rating because it had been carried out contrary to the statutory planning consent. *Al Davison* [2001] (VTD 17130)

4. A new dwelling was constructed next to an existing residential property. There was no internal access between the dwellings, each had its own council tax liability and the properties could be separately sold. The new dwelling contained a small area that had previously been part of the existing building.
It was held that a new dwelling had been created, so the construction work qualified for zero-rating. Any work to incorporate the existing dwelling into the new dwelling should be standard-rated, so apportionment was necessary. *Michael, Gillian and Norman Smith* [2001] (VTD 17035)

5. A single-storey, self-contained building was built in the grounds of an existing house under planning consent for a studio room. A separate sale was not prohibited. It was designed to be large enough to contain facilities for living-in purposes. However, the reason for construction was to provide an artist's studio.
The building consisted of two rooms. The main room had a kitchen sink in a base unit, a worktop and electrical points for cooking appliances. There was central heating provided by electric radiators controlled from a master switch, and hot water connected to the mains and drainage. The small room had a WC and basin, and enough space for a shower.

Even though there was no bath or shower, the studio contained sufficient amenities to allow it to be used as living accommodation.
It was held that the test was whether the building had been "designed as a dwelling". The limited residential use of the building was irrelevant, so zero-rating applied. *Oldrings Development Kirgsclere Ltd* [2002] (VTD 17769)

6. A house was constructed on stilts over a river. A dock for a boat was constructed by attaching the necessary materials to the stilts. This occupied a substantial part of the underside of the house. The house could be entered by a stairway leading up from the dock.
It was held that the construction of the dock was related to the design of the dwelling and was integral to it, so all the works qualified for zero-rating. *Turner Stroud & Burley Construction Ltd* [1998] (VTD 15454)

7. A barn was converted to include residential accommodation, offices and a workshop. As a condition of the planning approval, the residential accommodation could only be occupied in conjunction with the commercial part of the building and could not be sold separately.
It was held that the planning restriction meant that the residential part of the building was not a dwelling for VAT purposes. *Paul Cussins* [2008] (VTD 20541)

Comment The Tribunals are undecided as yet as to whether a planning condition restricting **occupation** of a new house to persons employed in or running a nearby or adjacent **business** is a prohibition on separate "use" of the new house. Tribunal decisions weigh up roughly equally on both sides of this issue. As noted above, a simple occupation condition restricting the type of person who may live in the dwelling is not a restriction on "use". However, a requirement to use the property in connection with a business is such a restriction. These planning conditions appear to straddle both types of requirement, without being one or the other.
The Upper Tribunal has recently held that a planning condition restricting occupation of a new building "to a person solely employed by the equestrian business" at the same address was not merely an occupational restriction; it prevented use of the new building separate from the equestrian business going on at the property. As a result the new building was not a dwelling. *HMRC v Shields* [2014] The Upper Tribunal has still to hear another appeal where the planning condition reads as follows: "The occupation of the dwelling shall be limited to a person solely or mainly employed or last employed in the [fishery business] or a widow or widower of such a person, or any resident dependants." The Upper Tribunal in *Shields* stressed, however, that each case must be decided on the particular terms of the planning condition in question. It is perfectly possible that occupation by a dependant of an ex-employee of the fishery business would be considered permitted separate use of the new building. Thus it is not possible to say that any broad category of planning condition does or does not permit the building to qualify as a dwelling.

b. For relevant residential use

The construction of property which is **intended** solely for relevant residential use is zero-rated, provided that the customer issues a certificate confirming this use. **5158** Sch 8 Group 5 item 2(a) VATA 1994

If there is a **subsequent change of use** within 10 years of completion, the recipient of the zero-rated construction services may have to account for output tax (¶5297).

If there is **mixed use** of a building, the construction costs must be apportioned between zero-rated and standard-rated supplies (¶5196).

MEMO POINTS HMRC has issued guidance for persons involved with the construction and supply of buildings which are both dwellings and to be used for a relevant residential purpose. Zero-rating applies to various supplies in either case but the detailed rules are different. In some circumstances it may be better to proceed as if the building were a dwelling; in other circumstances as if it were to be used for relevant residential purposes. HMRC explains when that choice is available and the restrictions, if any, on switching later to the other category. VAT Information Sheet 02/14

What is relevant residential use?

5160 Sch 8 Group 5 note 4 VATA 1994

The following **uses** are deemed to have a relevant residential purpose:

Type of use	Detail	Institution[1]	Scope of zero-rating
Children's home	Accommodation for children	✓	All areas
Residence providing personal care	For those in need by reasons of old age, disablement, past or present alcohol or drug dependency, or past or present mental disorder	✓	All areas
Hospice	Not hospitals	✓	All areas
School or college	Residential accommodation for pupils and students[2] (e.g. a hall of residence, or boarding school house)	x	Residential accommodation only
Armed forces residence	For a member of any of the armed forces	x	Residential accommodation only
Accommodation for a religious community	Monastery, nunnery, etc	✓	All areas
An institution which is the sole or main residence for at least 90% of the residents	Excluding prisons, hotels, inns, hostels, etc	✓	All areas

Note:
1. Whether a property is classed as an institution affects the scope of other VAT treatments as follows:
– first sale or long lease of the property (¶5254); and
– conversion of non-residential property (¶5426).

One feature of an **institution** is that the residents live there under a system of rules and regulations. However, as the Tribunal has confirmed, the rules need only be appropriate to the level of care needed by those residents. In a 2014 case the Tribunal rejected an argument by HMRC that residents' daily lives should be marked by constant compulsion, so that, for example, the choice whether or not to take part in organised card games should decide the issue. Compulsion would only be a prerequisite for qualification as an institution where compulsion was a feature of residents' care needs. *TGH (Construction) Ltd* [2014] (TC04132)

HMRC Brief 03/14

2. Student accommodation may be used for a relevant residential purpose but HMRC has pointed out that the accommodation is not "student" accommodation if the people living in it are not "students". Where the individual concerned is studying for a recognised qualification, or maintaining a qualification for which accreditation is received, there is no doubt that the individual is a "student" but where the individual is "undertaking a course of study which, whilst not leading to a recognised qualification, has a high level of academic content and is intended to improve the knowledge and understanding of the student in an area of academic interest" this leads to areas of uncertainty. HMRC explains that "The following are examples which are intended to illustrate the kind of educational activity which is included:
– summer schools in which international students and others have the opportunity to undertake a programme of study comparable with the work done by full-time students;
– residential events the purpose of which is to show aspiring university applicants what it is like to study at university - whilst the academic content is high and the participants are school pupils, the purpose of their attendance is not either part of their A-level curriculum nor is it part of a programme which leads to a qualification;
– English as a Foreign Language (EFL) courses;
– academic conferences which offer development and ongoing learning to the academic staff of universities and colleges to ensure that academics are able to share ideas, learn from each other and embed the latest thinking into their own research and teaching."

However, "[p]eople who attend classes, often badged as "summer schools", which may offer a life-enhancing experience and promote greater cultural or spiritual awareness but the subject matter of which falls into the category of hobbies or leisure interests (for example pottery workshops, art or literature appreciation courses, etc) as opposed to receiving educational or vocational training to an academic standard, will not qualify as "students". Whilst persons engaging in theological studies in order to become a minister of faith (such as a priest, rabbi or imam) will qualify as "students", those attending seminaries or religious retreats which do not serve this purpose but are intended primarily to foster or reinforce faith, are not considered to be receiving educational or vocational training to an academic standard and will not qualify as "students"."

5162 Notice 708 para 14.6.3

HMRC takes the following **factors** into account in deciding the **purpose** of a building:
- the use to which the building is actually put;
- whether the building is used in conjunction with other buildings nearby;
- whether there is common ownership, financial control, management or administration;
- how the building is advertised; and
- how the use of the building is licensed by any controlling authority.

MEMO POINTS 1. The meanings of **residence** and **residential accommodation** are taken to imply lodging, sleeping and overnight accommodation. Accordingly, the provision of a communal dining room alone does not qualify. There is no requirement for the residents to stay for a minimum period of time.
2. It is the use of the **constructed building** itself which is important. So a bedroom block constructed in the grounds of an existing registered care home cannot be zero-rated, because it is not, in itself, a home or institution but part of a larger home or institution.
3. HMRC's policy on the VAT treatment of the construction of, and the first grant of a major interest in, **"independent living" units** within the grounds of residential care homes is that such units do not qualify as dwellings because there is usually a stipulation in the planning permission that they cannot be used separately from the care homes. Further, the units do not qualify as relevant residential buildings, because any personal care provided is either arranged privately by the occupants, or is provided by the existing care home or institution. The units themselves do not qualify as institutions. Therefore zero-rating does not apply to their construction or subsequent disposal. HMRC Brief 66/07
4. A **number of buildings** constructed at the same time **on the same site** that are intended to be used together for a relevant residential purpose can all be zero-rated - for example, a dining block and a sleeping block for an old people's complex. Even if the building work progresses in phases, zero-rating should still apply, provided that construction occurs in line with planning permission and is connected (¶5120). If a non-residential part exists on the site, such as a shop, this would be excluded from zero-rating. Sch 8 Group 5 note 5 VATA 1994
5. **Sheltered housing** units, which consist of individual flats with their own facilities, are not relevant residential buildings, although the flats should qualify individually as dwellings.

A building (or part of a building) is not **solely** used for a relevant residential purpose when it is also utilised for other purposes, either at the same time or at a different time. Further, the initial intention must be followed by actual residential use. **5164** Notice 708 para 17.11.1

HMRC interprets "sole" use as meaning for at least 95% of the time.

MEMO POINTS 1. In the case of **student accommodation**, when halls of residence are intended for student use for 10 years from the date of completion but are let out to conference delegates and tourists during vacations, HMRC have allowed zero-rating to apply, even where the construction was outsourced by the university. *R (oao Greenwich Property Ltd) v C & E* [2001] However, from 1 April 2015 vacation use now has to be taken into account in deciding whether the accommodation is used "solely" for a relevant purpose. For transitional purposes, it is possible to ignore vacation use if the building project was started before 1 April 2015 and continues without substantial break thereafter, or a "meaningful" deposit was paid before that date in respect of a sale of the property. Concessionary treatment continues to apply to such buildings so that withdrawal of the concession does not count as a change of use (see ¶5297+) from 1 April 2015 onwards. HMRC Technical Note 31 January 2014 HMRC Brief 14/14
2. Another concession was withdrawn from 1 April 2015, subject to the same transitional rules as noted in the previous memo point. Previously a dining hall was considered to be used "solely" for a relevant purpose if it was used "predominantly" by students. From 1 April 2015 the dining hall must now be used at least 95% by students to qualify.
3. The **transitional rules** have now been clarified so that:
a. certificates of intended relevant residential use which rely on the concession to meet the "solely" test are still valid where:
– for construction services, the first supply was made before 1 April 2015 and relates to a meaningful start to the construction of the building by that date, and the works are expected to progress to completion without interruption (demolition or site clearance works are only accepted where construction started immediately afterwards); or
– for the first grant of a major interest in new student accommodation, either:
1. a meaningful deposit (for example, on exchange of contracts) was paid to the vendor (or the vendor's solicitor) before 1 April 2015 (options to purchase are not accepted - irrespective of intention); or
2. an agreement for lease (or purchase) was signed with the vendor or landlord before 1 April 2015 and a meaningful start to the construction of the building has taken place by that date, and the works are expected to progress to completion without interruption (demolition or site clearance works are only accepted where construction starts immediately afterwards); and
b. for single developments of more than one block of student accommodation constructed in phases, the above rules apply but:
– "meaningful start to the construction of the building" means "meaningful start to the construction of the first building"; and
– "expected to progress to completion without interruption" means "expected to progress to completion of all phases without interruption".

Case law

5166 EXAMPLE

1. A property was used as a rehabilitation home for people who had suffered brain injuries. No medical treatment or diagnosis was provided.
It was held that the home supplied care only and was therefore not a hospital. In any case the average length of stay was 700 days, which far exceeded the usual period spent in a hospital. Accordingly, the construction qualified for zero-rating. *General Healthcare Group Ltd* [2001] (VTD 17129)

2. A new building was constructed to house elderly and mentally infirm residents who could no longer look after themselves. No medical treatment was given, as residents were transferred to a hospital when necessary.
As the residents were elderly and suffering from severe dementia, they needed a secure environment but not medical intervention or treatment. Thus the building was not a hospital and qualified for zero-rating. *Hospital of St John and St Elizabeth* [2005] (VTD 19141)

3. A company agreed with a NHS Trust that it would construct a residential building for people who were mentally ill. The National Health Service Act 1977 defined a hospital as "any institution for the reception and treatment of persons suffering from illness" and the tribunal held that the building fell within this definition. Therefore the costs were not zero-rated. *Wallis Ltd* [2003] (VTD 18012)

4. A building was constructed which was to be used to accommodate women with mental health problems, giving them a home and care. There was no specific treatment and any patient who entered an acute phase in her illness was transferred to hospital.
It was held that the building was not a prison or similar institution, because it did not house anyone convicted of a criminal offence. Neither was it a hospital, because it provided only for the reception and care of the women, not their treatment. Hence the building was constructed for a relevant residential purpose. *C & E v Fenwood Developments Ltd* [2005]

5. Some halls of student residence were constructed along with a building which housed the following:

Area	Qualified for zero-rating
Gym	✓
Music room	✓
Kitchen	✓
Dining room	✓
Conference room	x
Projection room	x
Common room	x
Shop	x
Bar	x

The costs had to be apportioned between the zero-rated areas and standard-rated areas. *University Court of the University of St Andrews (No 2)* [2005] (VTD 19054)

6. An individual tried to claim that a new dwelling built in the grounds of his own home should be classed as relevant residential accommodation, because his children would use it for study and later on his parents might occupy it. The planning permission stated that the building was to be used for the purposes of the individual's household.
It was held that a member of a household moving into the new building to live and study there did not turn the new building into residential accommodation for students or school pupils. The children were occupying the new building as part of the individual's household. *Philip Thompson* [1998] (VTD 15837)

Who can zero-rate construction services?

5168 In connection with a relevant residential use construction project, a supplier can only zero-rate its services (¶5132) if it **receives** a zero-rating certificate (¶5224) from the recipient of those services e.g. a care home. If a supplier is a subcontractor, the supplies should be standard-rated and the main contractor should be able to recover any VAT charged.

Note that the certificate must be received **before** zero-rating can be applied.

c. For relevant charitable use

The construction of any property which is intended for use solely for a relevant charitable purpose is zero-rated, provided that the customer issues a certificate confirming the intended use. If there is mixed use of a building, the construction costs must be apportioned between zero-rated and standard-rated supplies (¶5196). **5170** Sch 8 Group 5 item 2(a) VATA 1994

As with relevant residential use, the **scope of supplies** which can be zero-rated is restricted to those provided by the recipient of the certificate (¶5168).

If there is a **subsequent change of use** within 10 years of completion, output tax may need to be accounted for by the recipient of the zero-rated supply (¶5297).

What is relevant charitable use?

Use by a charity For the zero-rating provisions to apply, the charity must use the building for a non-business **purpose**. **5174** Sch 8 Group 5 note 6 VATA 1994; Notice 708 para 14.7

There is no **definition** of charity in the legislation, so whether an entity is a charity is determined as a matter of general law. *Sport in Desford* [2004] (VTD 18914) A charity which is registered with the Charity Commission will always be a charity for this purpose. See ¶8005 for further details.

Typical qualifying buildings include places of worship and offices which are used for collecting donations. However, where **any charge is made** for the services given, related buildings will be standard-rated e.g. youth club huts where subscriptions are charged, schools where fees are levied, or a charity office which processes entrance fees from fundraising events.

MEMO POINTS 1. For the meaning of **business** in a charity context see ¶8022. It should be noted that business is not just restricted to situations where a profit is made.

2. Following case law, HMRC has stated that it will accept that charities which provide **nursery facilities** for pre-school-age children as part of their charitable objectives, merely making a charge to cover their costs, are not in business (¶8024). The construction of premises for this purpose will, therefore, qualify for zero-rating. Business Brief 2/05

3. HMRC has published guidance which states that a charity cannot claim that it will be using a building for non-business purposes just because its activities fall within the definition of **services provided by bodies governed by public law**. HMRC Brief 27/08

A building is regarded as used **solely** for a relevant charitable purpose if the relevant use is 95% or more. For this purpose any reasonable method may be used to calculate qualifying use. **5176** HMRC Brief 39/09

Local community facilities A **village hall or similar** building providing social or recreational facilities for a local community is **deemed** to be used for charitable purposes. **5178** Notice 708 para 14.7.4

A building must satisfy all of the following **criteria**:
- it is owned, organised and administered by the community;
- the facilities on offer are multi-purpose;
- the building is available to the community in general, rather than just specific groups of people; and
- the facilities are available for use for a variety of public and private purposes.

It is important that the facilities are actually **used by** the community. For example, a building constructed at a hospital to house a medical scanner was held to be used by the hospital, not the charity which paid for the work to be done, even though the scanner would benefit the community. *League of Friends of Kingston Hospital* [1994] (VTD 12764)

The following types of buildings are **usually excluded** and so do not qualify for zero-rating:
- sports centres;
- swimming pools;
- theatres; and
- membership clubs.

Case law

5180

EXAMPLE

1. A church arranged for the construction of a garage next to the church building. The garage was to house cars which were provided by the parish and driven by priests.
It was held that the cars were provided for pastoral use. Any private use was incidental and did not preclude the relevant charitable use. *St Dunstan's Roman Catholic Church Southborough* [1998] (VTD 15472)

2. The construction of a sports pavilion on school land was arranged by a registered charity.
It was held that the pavilion was not providing recreational facilities for a local community, because the people who would use it were a particular section of the community. Further, the pavilion was not operated like a village hall. *Ormiston Charitable Trust* [1995] (VTD 13187)

3. A registered charity arranged for the construction of a leisure centre. Membership was automatically given to the people of ten adjoining parishes.
It was held that irrespective of its size, the centre was used similarly to a village hall in providing social or recreational facilities for a local community. *Bennachie Leisure Centre Association* [1996] (VTD 14276)

4. An amateur dramatic society (which was also a registered charity) arranged for the construction of a theatre in a small town. The society had no full-time employees.
It was held that the theatre was used similarly to a village hall; as 90% of the society's members lived in the town, the facilities were provided for the local people. *Ledbury Amateur Dramatic Society* [2000] (VTD 16745)

Annexes

5182 A new self-contained annexe (or part of it) can only be zero-rated as a new building where it is to be used for a relevant charitable purpose.

Sch 8 Group 5 notes 16, 17 VATA 1994; Notice 708 para 3.2.5 - 3.2.9

5184 **What is an annexe?** The first hurdle to overcome is to satisfy HMRC that the building in question is actually an annexe, as opposed to an extension or enlargement. An annexe should only have minimal physical connection with the existing building, so that it would otherwise be considered to be a separate building.

HMRC considers the level of the annexe's **physical integration** with the existing building. *Bryan Thomas Macnamara* [1999] (VTD 16039) Guidance is given by another case, where it was held that the correct approach is to consider the existing building as it was and then to consider the end result of the construction works. Taking an objective view, does the work done amount to the enlargement of, or an extension to, the existing building, or to the construction of an annexe to it i.e. what is the overall impression? *Colchester Sixth Form College* [1999] (VTD 16252)

5186 **What does the annexe provide?** An annexe should provide extra space for **activities** which are distinct from but associated with those carried out in the existing building. These activities should be carried out without reliance on the existing building (although services such as utilities and water can be shared). Each should form two separate parts of a whole building but operate independently of each other. Also, the main or sole **access** to each part should not be shared.

Sch 8 Group 5 note 17 VATA 1994

Examples would include a day centre added to an existing residential hospice; a church hall added to an existing church; or a nursery added to a school building.

EXAMPLE

1. A new annexe was built to replace a chapel house, which had previously been the caretaker's accommodation and which was contained within the church building. The construction was arranged by the church. The chapel house itself was completely demolished.
The new annexe was built on the same site, and had the same profile, as the chapel house but with the following differences:
- an additional floor in the roof space;
- the building took up a larger land area; and
- an altered internal structure, which housed meeting rooms, childcare facilities, a vicar's study and space for youth activities.

The annexe had its own heating and fire alarm systems, and power was separately metered. It was mainly used at times other than when the church services were held. The roof was lined up with that of the church roof, being held up by steel beams connected to the party wall with the church. The design and style were matched with those of the church and the planning permission was for an extension.

It was held that the dictionary definition of annexe implied a supplementary building; and in this case the annexe was supplementary to the church. It was capable of functioning independently of the existing building and both buildings had their own independent access. So zero-rating applied. *Grace Baptist Church* [1998] (VTD 16093)

2. A church was located in a town centre and had very restricted surroundings. In order to construct a youth centre, a new first floor was created by enlarging the existing roof space and partially reconstructing the roof. A separate entrance was provided by making a new lobby from a room in the existing building, from which a staircase led to the youth centre. The first floor comprised a youth lounge, store room, toilets and shower, and offices for the youth worker and minister. It was held that the work was an extension, not an annexe, as to a passer-by the works had created a two-storey building compared to the previous single storey. In any case, there was no independent access. *Woodley Baptist Church* [2002] (VTD 17833)

3. A school added a new structure to an existing building. Part of the new section was integrated into the existing building and part could function separately.

It was held that the new building did not have to be viewed as a whole. As such, a portion of the new building qualified as an annexe and part did not. *Longparish Church of England Primary School* [2007] (VTD 20464)

d. Residential caravan parks

Zero-rating will apply where necessary **civil engineering work** is carried out to develop a new permanent residential caravan park. **5188**

Permanent park

For these purposes, a residential caravan is one where **occupation** throughout the year is not prevented by any prohibition such as a covenant or planning restriction. So a holiday park or touring caravan park is not a permanent park. **5190** Notice 708 para 20.2

Civil engineering work

The table shows common types of work to caravan parks and whether they qualify as necessary civil engineering works for zero-rating purposes. **5192** Notice 708 para 20.3

If any **existing works** are altered (e.g. an existing road is widened), this is a standard-rated supply.

Work	Zero-rating applies?
Laying new bases or pitches	✓
Laying new roads, drives, paths and parking spaces	✓
Installing power and water	✓
Installing drainage and sewerage	✓
Indoor swimming pools	x
Social centres	x
Shops	x
Fitness clubs	x
Doctors' surgeries	x
Managers' houses	x
Playgrounds	x
Hard landscaping	x

e. Mixed use buildings

5194 A builder may construct a building, part of which will be used as a dwelling, for a relevant residential purpose, or for a charitable purpose, and part of which will be used for non-residential purposes.

Sch 8 Group 5 note 11 VATA 1994; Notice 708 para 16

Common examples include:
- a flat constructed over a shop;
- a communal living area in a block of flats which is used by non-residents; and
- a live-work unit with a discrete work area.

In this case a builder must **apportion** its supplies so as to charge the correct rate of VAT; otherwise all of its charges must be standard-rated.

Costs relating to **structural areas** should be apportioned. Such areas are crucial to all parts of a building and include, for example, the roof, foundations, lifts and wiring/plumbing.

Comment Where the **same part** of a building is used for both qualifying and non-qualifying purposes, the building is not used solely for a qualifying purpose. All of the construction costs must be standard-rated. However, see ¶5176 for a limited exception for relevant charitable buildings.

Apportionment

5196 VAT on costs relating only to the part of the building which qualifies for zero-rating should be charged at 0%. VAT on costs relating only to the part of the building which does not qualify for zero-rating should be charged at the reduced or standard rate, as appropriate.

Any apportionment of the residual costs should give a fair and reasonable result, although no specific **method** is stipulated by HMRC.

Common methods include using cost information from a quantity surveyor, or the floor space occupied for each purpose. Further, the tax certificate (¶5224), if one is required, should indicate which areas of the building qualify for zero-rating.

Where the **customer and builder** are **unconnected** (¶962+), any commercially agreed allocation is likely to be acceptable.

3. Invoicing and administration

5200 The following practices are common in the construction industry:
- retentions;
- stage payments;
- self-billing;
- authenticated tax receipts;
- agreed price variations;
- liquidated damages; and
- tax certificates.

In addition, smaller contractors may be interested in the small business schemes, which aim to simplify VAT administration (¶4600).

Tax point

5202 Construction usually occurs over an extended period of time, as do the payments which are received by the contractor.

If a contractor is supplying services, including a supply of goods and services, the normal tax point rules (¶760) apply for **single payment contracts**. There are, however, **beneficial** provisions when retentions and stage payments are involved.

For supplies of **goods** without services, the usual tax points apply.

5206 **Retentions** A retention is a portion of consideration which is retained by the customer until satisfied that the contract has been fully and satisfactorily performed.

SI 1995/2518 reg 89

Retention payments are taxable at the **earlier** of:
- the date of payment; and
- the date on which an invoice relating to the retention is issued.

The contractor should therefore ensure that it does not issue an **invoice** before it receives payment, as it will have to account for any VAT due based on the invoice date, which will adversely affect cash flow.

Stage payments Supplies of services, with or without goods, made under a construction contract which states that payments will be made **periodically**, are taxable at the earlier of the date: 5208 SI 1995/2518 reg 93
- each payment is received; or
- a VAT invoice (not including a self-billed invoice) is issued.

So no tax point occurs on completion.

MEMO POINTS 1. The term **construction contract** covers the following situations:
- demolition;
- construction;
- repair or maintenance; and
- alteration.

2. **Periodic payments** include a deposit followed by the remaining amount due. A retention payment alone does not qualify as a periodic payment.
3. If the **customer is not VAT-registered**, the supplier is under no obligation to issue a VAT invoice. So the tax point can always be the date that payment is received.

Connected parties To ensure that connected parties (¶962) cannot manipulate input tax recovery there is an **anti-avoidance rule**. 5210 Notice 708 para 24

The anti-avoidance rule **does not apply** when either:
- the occupier can recover at least 80% of the VAT incurred on the construction costs; or
- the supplier (contractor or subcontractor) is unconnected with the occupier and is not funded by it, or anyone connected to the occupier.

Buildings typically affected by the anti-avoidance rule include banks, schools and colleges, private hospitals, and any others where the occupier is not registered for VAT (although any zero-rated work is excluded for this purpose). 5211

Where the supplier is involved in the construction of a building which will be **used by** a mainly partly exempt or non-registered occupier who has helped to **fund** the related costs of that supplier (e.g. by way of a loan), another tax point is created on completion of construction.

On completion, the supplier should account for VAT on the **full value** of the contract, less any amounts on which VAT has already been declared (because a stage payment has been received or invoices have been issued). If the customer is disputing the contract value, the supplier should take into account a reasonable estimate of the amount it will actually receive and keep an appropriate record.

The provision means that if a **subcontractor** is caught, so is the main contractor, although HMRC has stated that its intention is not to penalise a contractor on a technicality.

EXAMPLE A Ltd is a bank which makes exempt supplies and which needs premises for new headquarters. A new building is constructed at a cost of £20m plus VAT.
In order to avoid irrecoverable input tax, A Ltd forms a new subsidiary B Ltd to undertake the construction. A Ltd makes no payments to B Ltd, as the funding for the project is provided by another company, C Ltd, a fellow subsidiary of A Ltd. B Ltd issues no invoice.
As A Ltd will be making exempt supplies once it occupies the building and the funding has been provided by a connected party, a tax point occurs on completion. Hence B Ltd must account for output tax. If B Ltd then invoices A Ltd for the costs plus output tax paid, A Ltd will not be able to recover the VAT.

MEMO POINTS 1. For this purpose the **occupier** of the building may be the supplier, the person providing the funding, or a person connected (¶962) with either. 5212
2. **Providing the funding** excludes the stage payments themselves, but includes:
- loans from banks, etc;

- private funds used by a sole trader;
- share issues for companies;
- arranging for others to provide the finance;
- arranging for someone else to discharge the supplier's debts; and
- providing a guarantee or security for a loan.

SI 1995/2518 reg 93(7) 3. **Related costs** include the costs of goods and services acquired by the supplier in order to make its own construction supply, staff costs and other internal expenses.

Self-billing

5214 VATTOS5225 Self-billing arrangements (¶2904) are often used when subcontractors make supplies to the main contractor.

A self-billed invoice does not create a **tax point** if:
- payments under the contract are made periodically (stage payments - see ¶5208);
- it is issued in advance of the basic tax point (¶764) for a supply under a single payment contract; or
- it is in respect of a retention payment.

However, the issuer (i.e. the contractor) of the self-billed invoice can deduct **input tax** against a notional tax point, which is the day following the date of its issue, provided that a special procedure is followed. This has no effect on the subcontractor's tax point for output tax purposes.

MEMO POINTS The **special procedure** requires the main contractor to:
- retain a copy of the invoice and show on it the day following the date of issue as the notional tax point for its input tax recovery; and
- mark on the subcontractor's copy the date of despatch (although this must not be referred to as the tax point).

The subcontractor must then add the date of receipt, which becomes the tax point for its output tax purposes.

Authenticated tax receipts

5216 SI 1995/2518 reg 13(4) If the supplier and customer both agree (no prior approval is required from HMRC), the **customer** may prepare a receipt when making payment. The supplier then authenticates it when it receives the money and the customer can thereafter use the receipt as **evidence** for an **input tax reclaim**. No other invoice or self-billing documentation should be prepared, as the authenticated receipt records the transaction for VAT purposes. This means that the **supplier** is not required to account for VAT until it receives payment, which therefore protects it from any adverse VAT consequences of bad debts or price disputes.

The receipt must include the normal **contents** of a full VAT invoice (¶2860).

Agreed price variations

5218 If a customer **disputes** the amount to be paid in respect of construction work, the supplier may agree a decrease in price and a credit note will be issued.

However, where an **invoice remains unpaid**, the supplier can only recover the related output tax under the bad debt rules (¶840), which involves significant delay. It is advisable, therefore, for the builder not to issue a VAT invoice until it has received payment.

Liquidated damages

5220 Notice 708 para 22.3 Liquidated damages are paid in the event of a breach of contract.

Damages **received** are not subject to VAT, as they do not represent consideration for a supply.

The **payment** of damages by a builder cannot reduce the value of a supply which has already been made.

Tax certificates

5224 Sch 8 Group 5 note 12 VATA 1994 A certificate of **intended use** is required for the zero-rated construction of relevant residential accommodation and property to be used for charitable purposes.

Such a certificate is issued by the customer i.e. the person who intends to use the building.

HMRC deems a customer to be **using** a building for a relevant purpose if the customer is occupying the building, or part of the building, and carrying out a relevant activity from the building, and/or letting the building from another party on commercial terms. Notice 708 para 17.10

Customer's responsibilities The customer is fully responsible for the **information** included in the certificate. An inaccurate certificate may cause the issuer to be liable to a penalty (¶4100), unless there is a reasonable excuse for the error. **5226** Notice 708 para 17.6

If there is a subsequent **change of use** (¶5297) of the building, the customer will be liable for any VAT which becomes due.

Supplier's responsibilities The supplier must take reasonable steps to establish the **validity** of any certificate received - for example, by retaining correspondence about the detailed use of the building. **5228**

If the supplier makes a mistake in good faith and fails to identify that the **certified use does not qualify** for zero-rating, HMRC states that it will not expect the supplier to account for the VAT which is due. Notice 48 para 3.11

By concession, where a certificate is **issued late** - that is, after the construction work has been invoiced - HMRC will allow the supplier to amend its VAT charge, subject to the usual 4-year time limit for adjustments (¶3018). The customer must be able to prove that, at the time of the construction supply, the intended use of the building was as shown on the certificate. Notice 708 para 17.6

Format HMRC suggests the following format, although the customer may prepare its own, provided that it contains all of the information shown below. **5230** Notice 708 para 18.1

EXAMPLE

Certificate for zero-rated and reduced-rated building work

1. Address of the building

2. Name and address of organisation receiving the building works:
VAT registration number: (if applicable)
Charity registration number: (if applicable)

3. Date of completion (or estimated completion) of the work:
Value (or estimated value) of the supply: £
Name, address and VAT registration number of building contractor:

4. I have read the relevant parts of Notice 708 Buildings and Construction, and certify that this organisation (in conjunction with any other organisation where applicable) will use the building, or the part of the building, for which zero-rating is being sought solely for:

(Tick box)

a. a relevant charitable purpose, namely by a charity in either or both of the following ways:
- otherwise than in the course or furtherance of a business; or ❑
- as a village hall or similarly in providing social or recreational facilities for the local community; or ❑

b. a relevant residential purpose, namely as:
- a home or other institution providing residential accommodation for children; ❑
- a home or other institution providing residential accommodation with personal care for persons in need of personal care by reason of old age, disablement, past or present dependence on alcohol or drugs, or past or present mental disorder; ❑
- a hospice; ❑
- residential accommodation for students or school pupils; ❑
- residential accommodation for members of any armed forces; ❑
- a monastery, nunnery or similar establishment; or ❑
- an institution which is the sole residence of at least 90% of the residents, and will not be used as a hospital, prison or similar institution, or a hotel, inn or similar establishment. ❑

5. I certify that the information given is complete and accurate and acknowledge that if the building, or the part of the building, for which zero-rated supplies have been obtained, within a period of 10 years from the date of its completion:

– ceases to be used solely for a relevant residential purpose and/or a relevant charitable purpose;
– is no longer used to the same extent for a relevant residential purpose and/or a relevant charitable purpose decreases; or
– is disposed of,
a taxable supply will have been made, on which this organisation will have to account for VAT at the standard rate.

Name: (print) Position held:
Signed: Date:

General warning
1. HMRC reserves the right to alter the format of the certificate through the publication of a new notice. You must ensure that the certificate used is current at the time of issue.
Warnings for the issuer
2. You may be liable to a penalty if you issue a false certificate.
3. You are responsible for the information provided on the completed certificate.
Warnings for the contractor
4. You must take all reasonable steps to check the validity of the declaration given to you on this certificate.
5. This certificate does not automatically confer zero-rating or reduced-rating on your supplies. You must check that you meet all the conditions for zero-rating or reduced-rating your supply - see Notice 708 Buildings and Construction.

C. Buying and selling

5245 This section looks at disposals of **a major interest** i.e. the freehold or a long lease. For short leases see ¶5540.

1. Residential and charitable buildings

5247 Sch 8 Group 5 VATA 1994

The **first grant** of a major interest in a building designed to be used as a dwelling, or designed for relevant residential or charitable use, **by a person** having "person constructing" status will be zero-rated.

This also applies to **partly constructed** buildings which are beyond the foundation stage.

Comment The following situations are exempt from VAT, not zero-rated:
– an interest is disposed of by **someone other** than a person constructing;
– it is **not the first** grant of that interest; or
– it is **not a major interest**.
This is an important point because input tax associated with an exempt supply is not recoverable. It is generally not possible to opt to tax supplies for residential or charitable use (see ¶5640).

What is a major interest in land?

5249 Notice 708 para 4.2

A major interest is generally **defined** as a freehold interest or a long lease with a term exceeding 21 years (or not less than 20 years in Scotland).

Notice 742 para 13.6

Location	Major interest
England or Wales	Freehold [1, 2]
	Long lease
Northern Ireland	Freehold [1, 2]
	Long lease
	Includes the estate of a person who holds land under a fee farm grant

Location	Major interest
Scotland	Estate or interest of the proprietor of the dominium utile[1, 2]
	In the case of land not held under feudal tenure: – estate or interest of the owner; or – lessee's interest under a long lease

Note:
1. In respect of a **commonhold** arrangement (¶5265), zero-rating will apply to the:
– first sale of the freehold units in a commonhold to prospective unit-holders; and
– transfer by operation of law of the freehold of the common parts in the commonhold to the commonhold association, on the registration of the commonhold.
2. If a number of freeholds are **converted into** a single commonhold, this will normally be exempt, unless a major interest has not been previously granted in the property (probably because the freeholder was also the person who constructed the building for its own occupation).

Where the major interest is a **long lease**, zero-rating will only apply to the premium payable on the grant. So input tax incurred on further costs (such as repairs) becomes irrecoverable because all other income is exempt. **5251** Notice 708 para 4.3

If **no premium** is payable, zero-rating will apply to the first rental payment due under the lease.

Under a **shared ownership scheme** the occupier only acquires a portion of the freehold, paying rent to a housing association for the part not owned. In this case the initial payment made by the occupier for its portion of the freehold is zero-rated.

EXAMPLE B Ltd develops its land bank by building houses and grants leases to new tenants for a term of 25 years. VAT on professional fees and marketing amounts to £2,500. No premium is payable and the tenants are paying rent of £1,000 per month.
The first month's rent will be zero-rated; all subsequent rental payments are exempt. B Ltd will be able to recover the input tax of £2,500 as the first rent is zero-rated.

When is the first sale?

It is only the first grant of a major interest by **each person** with person constructing status (¶5253) which is zero-rated. So it would be possible for two sales by separate persons, both of whom have person constructing status, to be zero-rated. **5252** Notice 708 para 4.6

It is irrelevant how much **time** has elapsed since the building was completed, provided that the initial intention was to grant a major interest, subject to the provisions described at ¶5262.

MEMO POINTS 1. Where the building has **multiple units**, a block of flats for example, each flat can be the subject of a zero-rated supply. Where the grant of a lease is followed by the sale of the freehold see ¶5262.
2. When the disposal is from one member of a **VAT group** to another, the intra-group transaction will be ignored for the purposes of the zero-rating provisions. Only a disposal to a third party outside the group will be treated as the first sale and zero-rated accordingly.
3. Where a developer has sold the freehold in a new house, which is a zero-rated supply, but then accepts it back in **part exchange** for another house, any subsequent sale by the developer of the original house will be exempt.

Who has person constructing status?

A person will have person constructing status if it is either a: **5253** Notice 708 para 4.5
– developer, which constructed (or arranged for the construction of) the building on land that it owns or has an interest in; or
– contractor or subcontractor, which provided construction services for the building.

MEMO POINTS 1. It is possible for **more than one person** to be acting as either the developer or contractor. Person constructing status cannot be transferred. It is possible for a developer to take over a partly constructed building; provided that each meets the above condition in its own right, both the initial developer/contractor and the second developer can make a zero-rated supply.
2. For **VAT groups** it is the company actually making the disposal which must have person constructing status for the supply to be zero-rated, irrespective of the status of the representative member (¶8832).

3. If there is a **split of legal and beneficial ownership**, it is the beneficial owner which must have person constructing status.

Building types

5254 Zero-rating applies to the disposal of a new:

a. dwelling or number of dwellings (¶5152), **unless** either:

– the interest granted is such that the acquirer is not entitled to reside in the building (or part of a building) throughout the year (this would usually apply to a holiday home); or

– the acquirer is prevented from living there continually, or using it as a principal residence, by the terms of a covenant, statutory planning consent or similar permission (again, this is aimed largely at holiday homes); or

b. building intended for use solely for a **relevant residential** (¶5158) or **charitable** (¶5170) purpose, in which case a tax certificate is acquired. For buildings which are not institutions (¶5160), such as schools, colleges and armed forces buildings, only the residential accommodation is covered by zero-rating.

Notice 708 para 4.8 If the building being disposed of only **partly** qualifies, the vendor must make a fair apportionment of the proceeds (¶5196). Examples would be a site sold which includes new houses along with surrounding infrastructure such as roads and footpaths, or multiple properties sold to a charity when only some of them will be put to qualifying use.

5255 Surrounding **land** sold **with a building** is zero-rated, provided that it is a reasonably sized plot for the type of building. However, the sale of bare land is exempt subject to the option to tax (¶5602).

If a building is **partly constructed** it may still qualify for zero-rating.

Comment The term "partly constructed" is not **defined** in the legislation. There have been several cases on this issue, with the general consensus being that if a member of the public would recognise a building being constructed, the seller will have person constructing status and can zero-rate its sale. Further, depending on the scale of the work carried out below ground, it may be possible to agree with HMRC that a building is under construction even if nothing appears above ground at the date of sale.

Temporary letting of new dwellings

5256 Information Sheet 7/08 Sometimes commercial conditions require a short lease to be granted before a major interest can be granted. In this case the **initial intention** to grant a major interest is paramount and an apportionment of input tax is required, with the element relating to the zero-rated supply being recoverable.

HMRC has published guidance on the **calculations** it expects a business to make in this situation. By deciding to temporarily let the new build on a short lease, the housebuilder or developer is intending to make exempt supplies. As it will already have recovered all of the VAT relating to the property, because the initial intention was to make a zero-rated supply, it may have over-recovered VAT.

MEMO POINTS 1. The guidance states that developers must have **evidence** to support the original intention. Examples of documents which would suffice are board minutes and correspondence or reports from estate agents.

2. Where any **further costs** are incurred while exempt rental income is derived from the property, this will result in exempt input tax which is non-recoverable, subject to the normal partial exemption rules (¶2070).

EXAMPLE A company constructed dwellings with the intention of granting a major interest. Due to market conditions, only short-term leases (exempt) could be granted, but then a major interest (taxable) was granted 4 years later.

It was held that as the company had continued to intend to grant a major interest, the exempt supply only resulted in partial irrecoverable input tax, so there should be an apportionment. In this way, input tax relating to the major interest was linked to the zero-rated supply and could be recovered. *C&E v Briararch Ltd* [1992]

In order to **avoid making an adjustment**, it is possible for a developer to sell the new dwellings to a connected person (¶962), outside its VAT group, before commencing the short lets. This would mean that the developer has made a first grant of a major interest and any VAT incurred relating to the project can be recovered. The entity which acquires the properties will be making exempt supplies by leasing (and eventually selling) the properties and will not be able to recover any associated input tax. **5257** HMRC Brief 54/08

Comment Before undertaking this course of action, the developer should take professional advice, as there may be **other tax implications** of selling the properties on to a connected person - for example, in relation to stamp duty land tax. For further information on other taxes see *Tax Memo*.

If an **adjustment is required**, the action to take will depend on whether the trader is already partly exempt or not. Note that it is necessary to consider the adjustment at the moment when the intention to let arises, not when the property is actually let or rental income commences. **5258**

Comment Going forward, if the developer is receiving exempt rental income, it is possible that it will be in the developer's best interests to agree a special partial exemption method with HMRC (¶2148).

Already partly exempt Where the developer is already partly exempt, the normal partial exemption rules (¶2075) apply and the developer's calculation of the **input tax adjustment** should be based on its partial exemption method in operation at the time when the costs were originally incurred. **5259**

Where the calculation **does not give a fair and reasonable result**, the developer should contact HMRC and request a revised method. This situation is likely to arise if the developer is using the standard method, or a method which does not take account of exempt rental income being received.

Not already partly exempt **Exceptionally**, where a developer has not in the past been partly exempt, HMRC will allow it to adopt a simple check to see if the exempt input tax is below the de minimis thresholds (¶2194) of £625 per month on average and less than half of the input tax incurred. If this is the case, no input tax needs to be repaid. **5260**

To carry out the simple test, a developer must carry out the following **calculation**:

$$\text{Input tax recovered} \times \frac{\text{Length of short lease}}{\text{Economic life of property}}$$

For these purposes, HMRC has stated that the **economic life** of a residential property is deemed to be 10 years.

EXAMPLE A fully taxable developer recovered £20,000 of input tax in Year 1 relating to a house that it intended to sell. After the end of the tax year it decides to defer selling the property as it will not be able to attain the property's expected selling price in the current market. It decides instead to let the house for 2 years, before trying to sell it again.
By letting the property the developer becomes partly exempt, so must carry out the following calculation:
20,000 × 2 years / 10 years = £4,000 of exempt input tax.
As this is below the de minimis threshold for the year of £7,500 (£625 × 12) and is less than half of the input tax incurred, the developer is not required to make an adjustment to the VAT recovered for Year 1.

Comment Developers should be aware that the official guidance states that input tax on **general overheads**, such as office costs, should be included in the simple de minimis calculation.

If, after carrying out the above test, a developer discovers that the exempt input tax it has recovered in each year is **above the de minimis limits**, it may be in a "clawback" position. This means it will have to repay some of the VAT recovered on construction to HMRC. **5261**

The **calculation of the adjustment** is not prescribed but will usually be done using the following method suggested by HMRC, provided that it fairly reflects the use of costs:

$$\frac{\text{Estimated sales value}}{\text{Estimated sales value plus estimated short lease income (premiums and rent)}}$$

Alternatively, the developer may prefer to utilise the partial exemption standard method, or agree a special method with HMRC.

If a developer uses **estimates** for the calculation, HMRC requires that the figures are calculated on a reasonable basis, using reasonable assumptions. Supporting evidence, such as professional estimates of future values, or cash flow statements and funding plans, would make the estimates more credible.

What if a long lease pre-dates the sale of the freehold?

5262 Business Brief 23/06 If a developer grants a long lease in a unit of a building, such as an apartment in a block, and subsequently sells the freehold, the developer may need to repay some of the input tax reclaimed.

The **original grant** of the long lease is a zero-rated grant and the developer is entitled to recover any associated input tax. Any **subsequent sale of the underlying freehold** in the building may be exempt, as a first grant has already been made of a major interest in the building. It is likely that the building will fall within the capital goods scheme (¶5750), so any change in use by the developer (such as making an exempt disposal of the freehold) in the 10 years following the first grant may result in a partial clawback of the original input tax recovered.

EXAMPLE

1. **All flats sold followed by the freehold**
The sale of each individual flat will be zero-rated as a first grant of a major interest. Although the developer will hold a building within the scope of the capital goods scheme when the freehold is sold, HMRC considers that this will only be exempt to the extent that it relates to those areas of the building that were previously leased i.e. the zero-rated grants of individual flats. Most of the sale of the freehold will be zero-rated, because it relates to the common parts that have not been subject to any previous supply. So HMRC states that there is no need for any capital goods scheme adjustments.

2. **Freehold sold before any flats are sold**
The sale of the freehold will be a zero-rated grant and since no leases have been granted, this transaction will not have an effect within the capital goods scheme. Since the freehold is zero-rated, all input tax incurred on the construction costs will be fully deductible.
The purchaser of the freehold will normally make exempt grants of leases to buyers of the flats. Even where the consideration for such sales accrues to the developer, so that VAT law treats the developer as the person supplying the flats, this will not impact on its initial deduction of input tax. However, input tax relating to its selling costs may be restricted under the partial exemption rules (¶2075).

3. **Freehold sold after some of the flats have been sold**
The flats sold before the freehold has been supplied will each be a zero-rated first grant of a major interest. Although the developer will hold a building within the scope of the capital goods scheme when the freehold is sold, HMRC considers that this will only be exempt to the extent that it relates to those areas of the building that were previously leased i.e. the zero-rated grants of individual flats. Most of the supply of the freehold will be zero-rated, as it will relate to the common parts and unsold flats that have not been subject to any previous supply. So no capital goods scheme adjustments are needed.

5263 For **relevant residential property**, provided that the developer makes no exempt supplies other than those arising from the original zero-rated grant, full input tax recovery on the construction costs is available. If the developer subsequently makes a second grant of a major interest (such as selling the freehold), this will be exempt and an adjustment may be required under the capital goods scheme.

Time of supply

The sale of a **freehold property** is a supply of goods, so the basic tax point (¶764) is the date on which it is made available to the customer. This is normally the date of the freehold conveyance (irrespective of when physical occupation by the purchaser occurs); in Scotland it is the settlement date. *Cumbernauld Development Corporation v C & E (No 2)* [2002] **5265** Sch 4 para 4 VATA 1994; SI 1995/2518 reg 84(2)

Care should be taken where a **deposit** is being paid. If the deposit is held by a third party as an agent of the vendor (rather than as a third-party stakeholder), this will create a tax point which could affect the VAT liability of the supply. This is particularly important when considering if a building under construction is being sold (¶5252), or if a building is being transferred as a going concern (¶8664).

When the **total purchase price cannot be determined** at the time when the freehold interest is assigned, the property is deemed to have been supplied in separate transactions, so for the part where the price:

a. was determinable at the time of the grant or assignment, the normal time of supply rules apply (¶760+); or

b. could not be determined, the transaction occurs at the earlier of the time when:
- the remaining part of the consideration was received by the transferor; or
- the transferor issued an invoice in respect of that part.

For all purposes, a commonhold unit is a freehold interest in a property.

MEMO POINTS 1. Where development land is sold to a **relevant social landlord**, it is usual for a deposit to be paid at the time of exchange of contracts. It has become common practice for deposits to be made available to vendors at the point of exchange, when the land is still bare land; this can lead to questions about the VAT treatment of such deposits - in particular, whether they can be treated as part payment for future zero-rated supplies of residential buildings. HMRC's view is that the VAT liability of the deposit is determined by the **anticipated nature of the supply**. Zero-rating will be appropriate if it is clear when the deposit is paid that the eventual supply will be partly completed dwellings, which will have progressed beyond foundation level. It is possible that, at the time of completion, the VAT status of the land will differ from that which was anticipated. Where this is the case, it will be necessary to revisit the VAT treatment of the deposit. HMRC Brief 36/09

2. A **commonhold** agreement confers upon owners of parts of a building, occupied in common freehold interests in their respective parts (units) of the property. The freehold interest in the property's communal areas, and often its structure (the common parts), is owned by a commonhold association, the membership of which comprises the owners of the units. Notice 742 para 13.2

The grant of a **long lease** is deemed to be a supply of goods (¶277). **5267**

Where all or part of the **consideration** for the grant of such a lease or tenancy is **payable periodically**, the goods are deemed to have been supplied separately at the earlier of each time that: SI 1995/2518 reg 85
- a part of the consideration is received by the supplier; or
- the supplier issues a VAT invoice relating to the grant.

The exception to this rule is where, on or around the beginning of any period of up to 12 months, the **supplier issues a VAT invoice** containing the required information. In this case the tax point is the earlier of when a payment becomes due or when a payment is received by the supplier.

MEMO POINTS 1. The **required information** for the invoice is the:
- dates on which any parts of the consideration are to become due for payment in the period;
- amount payable (excluding VAT) on each date; and
- rate of VAT in force at the time of the issue of the VAT invoice and the amount of VAT chargeable on each payment.

2. If there is a **change in the rate of VAT** before any of the payment dates specified by the supplier, a long-term invoice will cease to be treated as a VAT invoice in respect of any supplies for which payments are due after the change and not received before the change.

Compulsory purchase The general rule for compulsory purchase is that the transfer does not take place until a price has been agreed, so that the normal time of supply rules apply (¶760). **5269** SI 1995/2518 reg 84

The **exception** is where the person from whom the land is being purchased does not, at the normal tax point, know the amount of the payment that will finally be received. In this case a supply is deemed to occur each time that a payment is received for the purchase.

When is a tax certificate required?

5271 Notice 708 para 17

A certificate of intended use is required for the zero-rated disposal of property to be used for relevant residential or charitable purposes.

Such a certificate is **issued by** the purchaser - that is, the person who intends to use the building solely for either of these purposes.

For the purchaser's responsibilities in relation to certificates see ¶5226. For the supplier's responsibilities see ¶5228.

5273 Notice 708 para 18.2

HMRC suggests a specific **format**, although the customer may prepare its own, provided that it contains all of the information shown below.

EXAMPLE

Certificate for zero-rated sales and long leases of zero-rated buildings

1. Address of the building

2. Name and address of organisation buying, or entering into a long lease on, the building (or part of the building):
VAT registration number: (if applicable)
Charity registration: (if applicable)

3. Date (or estimated date) of purchase or commencement of the lease:
Value (or estimated value) of the supply: £
Name, address and VAT registration number of developer:

4. I have read the relevant parts of Notice 708 Buildings and Construction, and certify that the building, or the part of the building, for which zero-rating is being sought will be used solely for:
(Tick box)

a. a relevant charitable purpose, namely by a charity in either or both of the following ways:
- otherwise than in the course or furtherance of a business; or ❑
- as a village hall or similarly in providing social or recreational facilities for the local community; or ❑

b. a relevant residential purpose, namely as:
- a home or other institution providing residential accommodation for children; ❑
- a home or other institution providing residential accommodation with personal care for persons in need of personal care by reason of old age, disablement, part or present dependence on alcohol or drugs, or past or present mental disorder; ❑
- a hospice; ❑
- residential accommodation for students or school pupils; ❑
- residential accommodation for members of any armed forces; ❑
- a monastery, nunnery or similar establishment; or ❑
- an institution which is the sole residence of at least 90% of the residents, and ❑
will not be used as a hospital, prison or similar institution, or a hotel, inn or similar establishment.

5. I certify that the information given is complete and accurate and acknowledge that if the building, or the part of the building, for which zero-rated supplies have been obtained, within a period of 10 years from the date of its completion:
- ceases to be used solely for a relevant residential purpose and/or a relevant charitable purpose;
- is no longer used to the same extent for a relevant residential purpose and/or a relevant charitable purpose decreases; or
- is disposed of,
a taxable supply will have been made, on which this organisation will have to account for VAT at the standard rate.

Name: (print) Position held:
Signed: Date:

General warning
1. HMRC reserves the right to alter the format of the certificate through the publication of a new notice. You must ensure that the certificate used is current at the time of issue.
Warnings for the issuer
2. You may be liable to a penalty if you issue a false certificate.
3. You are responsible for the information provided on the completed certificate.
Warnings for the developer
4. You must take all reasonable steps to check the validity of the declaration given to you on this certificate.
5. This certificate does not automatically confer zero-rating on your sale or long lease. You must check that you meet all the conditions for zero-rating your supply - see Notice 708 Buildings and Construction.

Input tax recovery

Normally all input tax incurred on costs relating to a zero-rated supply can be recovered. **5275** Notice 708 para 11

However, for **developers** (¶5253), input tax recovery is blocked on any **goods incorporated** into the building which are not building materials (¶5136). Any onward supply of such goods, where input tax has been blocked, will be exempt. Common examples where this rule applies include carpets and fitted furniture. A developer who sells a show home may be affected by this.

Input tax can be recovered on goods which are **not incorporated** into the building, such as free-standing items. When such goods are sold with the building, a separate supply is deemed to take place and output tax will be due, as appropriate for the item in question.

Comment Anyone who is constructing a new residential or charitable building should ensure that the contractors are charging the **correct rate of VAT** on goods. If a contractor charges VAT on goods that should have been zero-rated as building materials, it is not possible to recover this input tax from HMRC. The correct approach is to request a credit note from the contractor for the VAT incorrectly charged.

2. Non-residential buildings

A non-residential building is **defined** by what it is not i.e. the building is not a dwelling and is not intended for relevant residential or charitable use. **5277**

The grant or assignment of a **freehold interest** in a new non-residential building will be standard-rated, even if the building has not been completed. Sch 9 Group 1 item 1(a) VATA 1994

Any supply relating to a **lease** of a non-residential building is exempt, subject to the option to tax (¶5602).

For the sale of a freehold interest in a non-residential building which is not new see ¶5382.

MEMO POINTS 1. The freehold sale of a partly completed or new **civil engineering** work is standard-rated. **5279** Notice 742 para 3.2
2. A building or civil engineering work is deemed to be **new** if it was completed less than 3 years before the grant, so this can include second-hand buildings.
3. For a building or civil engineering work, the date of **completion** is deemed to be the earlier of:
- the issue of a certificate of practical completion by an architect or engineer; and
- full occupation or use.
4. Supplies of new freehold commercial buildings are standard-rated, even if the **purchase price is determined more than 3 years after completion** of the building. This provision is intended to stop contrived transactions, whereby the bulk of the consideration is paid after 3 years in order to avoid VAT on the cost of purchasing the new building.
5. Freehold includes a **commonhold** interest (¶5265).
6. For the provision of **garages and car parks** in connection with commercial premises see ¶5524.
7. A partly exempt business with **turnover exceeding £10 million**, which grants an interest in commercial property to a connected person, will need to disclose the transaction to HMRC (¶3104).

D. Special situations

5295 The following situations may arise in relation to new buildings:
- a change of use within 10 years of a property which initially qualified for zero-rating;
- construction by a DIY housebuilder; and
- a self-supply charge for a trade builder constructing a building for its own use.

1. Change from residential or charitable use

5297 In order to receive a zero-rated supply of a building intended for relevant residential or relevant charitable use (i.e. for a relevant purpose), a person must give a **tax certificate** (¶5224 and ¶5273) to the contractor or developer.

Output tax must be accounted for by the recipient if **within** the next 10 years there is a change in the recipient's use, or the building is sold or leased to someone who does not use it for a relevant purpose.

These rules **do not apply** to the DIY builders' scheme (¶5316).

a. Without disposal

5300 Sch 10 para 37 VATA 1994 A self-supply will arise if the person subsequently changes the use of all or part of the building within the 10 years from the date of completion, although for this purpose, demolition does not constitute a change of use. The date of completion is the earlier of the issue of an architect's certificate and the date of first use.

As a result, the trader must charge itself output tax and the same amount is potentially claimed as input tax, so a fully taxable business incurs no overall VAT charge. An unregistered person may be required to register (¶2640+) as a result of the self-supply.

5301 Notice 708 para 17.11 A building is regarded as used **solely** for a relevant charitable purpose if the relevant use is 95% or more. For this purpose any reasonable method may be used to calculate qualifying use.

5302 The self-supply **arises** on the first date when the use is not for a relevant purpose.

Amount liable

5304 The self-supply is calculated by **apportioning**, on a time basis, the VAT that would have been charged had the original supply of the building been standard-rated.

Where the deemed value of the self-supply is £250,000 or more and the trader makes exempt supplies in the 10 years following the date of the self-supply, the adjusted input tax recovery will be subject to the capital goods scheme (¶5750).

MEMO POINTS 1. The **rate** of VAT to use in calculating the self-supply is the rate at the time of completion.
2. The **amount liable** to the self-supply charge is not adjusted for any change in the building's market value.
3. For **partial exemption** generally see ¶2075.
4. For the interaction of the **input tax on the self-supply** and partial exemption apportionment methods see ¶2144.

5306 Sch 10 para 37(5) VATA 1994 The following **formula** is used:

$$\text{VAT which would have been charged} \times \frac{(120 - \text{Number of whole months of relevant use})}{120}$$

EXAMPLE C Ltd arranged for a building to be constructed at a cost of £850,000. The building was completed on 1 October 2008 and used by C Ltd from that date as an old people's home.
The construction costs were zero-rated because it was intended that the building would be used for a relevant residential purpose.
C Ltd has decided to use the building as offices from 6 April 2013.
A period of 54 complete months has elapsed since the building was brought into use.
The VAT which would have been charged on the construction costs of a new commercial building in 2008 was £148,750. (£850,000 x 17.5% (the standard rate on 1 October 2008))
The formula is applied as follows:

$$£148,750 \times \frac{(120 - 54)}{120} = £81,812.50$$

C Ltd must charge itself VAT of £81,812.50 and account for it as output VAT on its VAT return for the period including 6 April 2013. As C Ltd makes some exempt supplies, not all of this VAT will be recoverable as input tax and C Ltd must apply its partial exemption method. As the deemed value of the self-supply is more than £250,000, C Ltd must treat the building as a capital goods scheme item and must carry out a capital goods scheme adjustment each year for the 10 years following the date of the self-supply.

Where only **part of the building** is put to a different use, an appropriate proportion of the original cost is entered into the calculation. **5308** Information Sheet 4/11

MEMO POINTS Where there is an **increase in the proportion of non-relevant use** (i.e. a self-supply charge has already occurred), the formula in ¶5306 becomes:

$$\text{VAT which would have been charged} \times \text{Increase in non-relevant use} \times \frac{(120 - \text{Number of whole months of relevant use})}{120}$$

EXAMPLE A charity constructs a new building at a cost of £5m. The construction costs are zero-rated because it is intended that the building will be used for a relevant charitable purpose. The building consists of five floors. During the first 5 years the building is used as intended. After 5 years the charity decides to use the top floor of the building for a business purpose.
A self-supply charge of £100,000 will arise, as 60 months are still to elapse of the 10-year period and one floor out of five is no longer used for a relevant purpose. (£5m x 1/5 x 60/120 x 20%)

b. Disposal

A taxable supply will occur if the person sells or leases all or part of the building within the 10 years after the date of completion and the **new occupier** does not use it for a relevant purpose. The date of completion is the earlier of the issue of an architect's certificate and date of first use. **5310** Sch 10 para 36 VATA 1994

The seller may be able to opt to tax the building, to ensure that the output tax on the self-supply is recovered.

Comment If the vendor sells the building and then leases the building back from the purchaser with the intention of raising funds, but continues to perform a qualifying activity from the building, it may be possible to obtain HMRC's agreement that no self-supply adjustment is required. As this is not a published concession, any trader who wishes to rely on it should obtain HMRC's agreement before the transaction takes place.

Time of charge

The supply **arises** on the date of the sale or commencement of the lease. **5312**

Calculation of VAT

For buildings **completed on or after 1 March 2011** (i.e. the zero-rated supply took place after 28 February 2011), VAT is now accounted for by **apportioning**, on a time basis, the VAT that would have been charged assuming that the original supply of the building had been standard-rated (i.e. the same basis as described at ¶5304+). **5314** HMRC Brief 13/11

For buildings **completed before that date**, VAT is simply accounted for on the disposal proceeds which relate to the part of the building which was initially zero-rated and is now to be subject to a non-relevant use.

EXAMPLE

1. D Ltd arranged for an old people's home to be built at a cost of £850,000, which was completed on 1 October 2008. The construction costs were zero-rated because it was intended that the building would be used for a relevant residential purpose.
D Ltd then grants a lease to E Ltd on 6 April 2015 for a premium of £350,000. E Ltd will not be using the building for a relevant purpose and under the terms of the lease, D Ltd must vacate the building.
If E Ltd uses the whole site for offices, D Ltd must account for VAT of £70,000 as if the supply was taxable in the VAT period including 6 April 2015. (£350,000 x 20%)

2. F Ltd arranged for an old people's home to be built at a cost of £850,000; this was completed on 1 October 2012. The construction costs were zero-rated because it was intended that the building would be used for a relevant residential purpose.
Five years later F Ltd sells the property to G Ltd for £1.5m. G Ltd will not be using the building for a relevant purpose.
F Ltd must account for VAT of £85,000 on the self-supply, as 100% of the property is affected by the change of use and the property will not be used for a relevant purpose for 60 months. (£850,000 x 60/120 x 20%)
In addition, F Ltd must account for VAT on the proceeds arising from the sale of the property.

2. DIY housebuilders

5316 s 35 VATA 1994 HMRC will **refund** any VAT chargeable on the supply, acquisition or importation of any goods used in connection with construction or conversion work and related services where:
a. the work comprises either:
– the construction of a dwelling, or building intended for residential or charitable use (¶5148); or
– a residential conversion, such as a barn converted into a dwelling;
b. the work is carried out lawfully in the UK and is not in the course or furtherance of a business;
c. the goods concerned are building materials (¶5136) which are incorporated into the building or its site during the course of the works; and
d. an appropriate claim is submitted.

The intention is to put DIY developers and converters in the same position as trade builders who are selling a zero-rated property and can therefore recover the input VAT associated with the development. However, refunds are also available where DIY housebuilders do not do any of the work themselves but instead engage others. As services in the course of construction are zero-rated, it is most **important** that any VAT which is to be refunded has been **correctly charged** in the first place.

Property which is **added to** or subsequently completed is within the scheme e.g. buying a "shell" from a developer and fitting it out.

Work done to an **already completed building** is outside the scheme e.g. adding a conservatory, granny annexe, patio, double-glazing, tiling, or a garage.

5318 MEMO POINTS 1. A **residential conversion** is the conversion of a non-residential building (¶5150), or a non-residential part of a building, into:
– a building designed as a dwelling or a number of dwellings;
– a building intended for use solely for a relevant residential purpose; or
– anything which would fall within either of the above if different parts of a building were treated as separate buildings.
2. A building that has **previously been lived in** is excluded from the scheme, unless 10 years have elapsed since it was last occupied, measured from the date that work commences. This means that it is possible to occupy the property while work is being done, provided that this does not pre-date the commencing of the works.

3. A refund will be available where a person carrying out a residential conversion arranges for the work to be done **by a contractor**, provided that:
– the work is carried out lawfully and is not in the course or furtherance of the claimant's business; and
– the contractor is not working as an **architect, surveyor or consultant**, or in a supervisory capacity.
4. For this purpose the **UK** includes the Isle of Man but not the Channel Islands.
5. HMRC accepts that the scheme applies to the construction of new **holiday homes** and to the conversion of non-residential buildings into holiday homes. HMRC Brief 29/10

Scope

If **built at the same time** and covered by the necessary planning permission, a refund can also be claimed for the construction of: **5320**
– a domestic garage;
– a conservatory attached to the dwelling;
– a driveway and main paths on the site, but not ornamental garden features, landscaping or planting; and
– boundary and retaining walls, and boundary fences.

Buildings such as greenhouses, garden sheds and other outbuildings are not included.

A refund will be refused where a single dwelling is created by **converting** both the residential and non-residential parts of a building into a single house. *C&E v Blom-Cooper* [2003]

HMRC accepts that the conversion of a building that contains both a residential part and a non-residential part is within the scope of the refund scheme, provided that the overall number of dwellings is increased. The additional dwelling does not need to derive exclusively from the non-residential part, although any VAT refund will only relate to that part. *C&E v Jacobs* [2005] Business Brief 22/05

Charities Examples of **qualifying buildings** would include: **5322**
– places of worship; and
– offices used by charities for administering non-business activity, such as the collection of donations.

When there is **minor non-qualifying use** (¶5176), a refund will still be forthcoming, subject to making a declaration that the concession is to apply.

Costs incurred

VAT incurred on building materials (¶5136) and eligible services (¶5134) can be **refunded**, whether incurred at the standard or reduced rate. This includes materials acquired from other EU states or imported from outside the EU. **5324**

An input tax **refund will be unavailable** for goods that are not building materials and for the following services (and consumables which are not actually incorporated in the building - for example, tools and equipment or cleaning materials):
– professional and supervisory services, including services of architects and surveyors, and any other services of management, consultancy, design and planning;
– hire of tools and equipment;
– transport and haulage charges, including the purchase of fuel;
– temporary fencing; and
– skip hire.

Making a claim

Refunds must be claimed **within 3 months** of the building work being **completed**. **5326** HMRC Brief 45/09

The following **documents** must be submitted:
– the claim forms;
– supporting calculations, including details of the quantities of goods incorporated into the building;
– supporting VAT invoices and other documents (originals not photocopies);

– plans of the building; and
– evidence that the construction or conversion is completed.

The claim should be **sent to** the HMRC DIY Claims Unit (address below).

5328 MEMO POINTS 1. The following **forms** (including explanatory notes) are available from HMRC, depending on whether the work consists of the:
– **construction of new builds** designed as dwellings or for use solely for certain residential or charitable purposes, in which case form VAT 431NB is needed; or
– **conversion** of a non-residential building, or a non-residential part of a building, into a building designed as a dwelling or for use solely for certain residential purposes, in which case form VAT 431C is required.
2. **Evidence** of completion could include any of the following:
– a certificate or letter of completion from the local authority, for Building Regulations purposes or otherwise;
– a habitation certificate or letter from the local authority (or in Scotland, a temporary certificate of habitation);
– a valuation rating or council tax assessment; or
– a certificate from a bank or building society saying, "This is to certify that the … Bank/Society released on … (date) the last instalment of its loan secured on the building at … because it then regarded that building as complete."
3. The claim should be sent to the following **address**:
Local Compliance
National DIY Team
S0987
PO Box 3900
Glasgow
G70 6AA
4. **Following the submission** of a claim, HMRC should **acknowledge** it within 10 working days and will give an indication of the date when the refund will be received, unless there are any queries. A refund will normally be made within 30 working days from the receipt of the form.

3. Builders constructing own buildings

5330 Notice 708 para 25.1 To put a trader into the same position as if it had purchased building services from a third party, services provided by a trader to itself, which satisfy certain criteria, are deemed to have been both a supply to it in the course of its business and a supply by it (known as a **self-supply**).

The **effect** of this rule is to restrict input tax claims by partly exempt traders, as the output tax accounted for under the self-supply charge may be recovered as input tax only to the extent that the person uses or intends to use the relevant building in making taxable supplies. A self-supply may require a non-registered trader to register for VAT (¶2640).

5332 The services must satisfy the following **criteria**:
– they are taxable but not zero-rated;
– they are made in the course or furtherance of its business;
– they are made other than in return for a consideration; and
– they have an open-market value of at least £100,000 (including any demolition work involved).

5334 MEMO POINTS 1. The **services that fall under this provision** are:
– construction of a building for use in the business which is not a dwelling, nor intended for residential or charitable use (¶5148);
– construction of any civil engineering work;
– carrying out works which increase the floor area by at least 10% of an existing building which is used, or to be used, in the business; and
– carrying out any demolition work at the same time as, or as preparation for, any of the above.
2. The usual **time of supply** rules apply, so that the services are supplied when performed (¶760).
3. The VAT incurred in **purchasing goods and services** for such building works is treated as relating to the taxable self-supply.
4. The **value** of the self-supply is taken to be the open-market value of the services provided. Where the value of the self-supply is £250,000 or more, it is necessary to consider the capital goods scheme (¶5750).

SECTION 2

Land and existing buildings

Land **includes** buildings, civil engineering works, walls, trees, plants and other structures along with natural objects in, under or over it, provided that they remain attached to the land. **5370** Sch 9 Group 1 VATA 1994

The **basic rule** is that supplies of land and existing buildings are exempt, including the **grant of** any of the following:
- an interest in or right over land;
- a licence to occupy land; or
- in Scotland, any personal right to call for or be granted any such interest or right.

It is important to distinguish between a composite supply involving land (such as the supply of **fixtures** with a building or land), in which case the whole supply takes the VAT rating of the land, and a mixed supply, in which case each element has its own VAT treatment (e.g. **fittings**).

For further details of composite and mixed supplies see ¶310.

An **interest** in land may be in the form of legal ownership or a beneficial interest, where the holder has the right to the proceeds arising from the land's exploitation or enjoyment of the land. For VAT purposes, the beneficial owner, rather than the legal owner, is deemed to be the taxable person (¶30). **5372**

What is a licence to occupy?

A licence to occupy land means the licensee has a right over a particular plot of land, or a part of a particular area, for a specified time period without that occupation being upset by the rights of another. **5374** Notice 742 para 2.5; VAT Information Sheets 09/12 and 10/13

Such a licence is authority given so as to avoid a trespass; all of the following **conditions** must be met:

a. it is granted in return for consideration;

b. the rights of occupation must relate to a specified piece of land and must be given to the licensee;

c. the rights of the licensee are not impinged upon by another person's right to enter the land; and

d. the licensee is allowed either to physically enjoy the land, or to economically exploit it for the purposes of a business.

Common examples include the provision of offices and related facilities, space for advertising hoardings and the hiring out of a hall.

Where the element of occupation is missing or incidental, this is a right to enjoy facilities (a **licence for use**) and is treated differently (¶5492). Examples of such a licence would include admission to a swimming pool, theatre or cinema, allowing rubbish tipping, and access to office services without accompanying occupation.

MEMO POINTS 1. **Storage facilities** (i.e. a clearly defined lockable space to which the customer has access for the purpose of storing goods) do not represent a licence to occupy land, as they are specifically standard-rated (with the exception of storage of live animals and supplies between connected parties - for which see below). This affects the following:
- self-storage in purpose-built facilities;
- movable containers;
- garages;
- railway arches;
- lock-ups;
- spare rooms used for self-storage; and
- warehouses and distribution centres.

Anti-forestalling measures apply from 21 March 2012 to seek to prevent continuation of any exemption which may have applied up to 30 September 2012 (after which standard-rating is supposed to apply). Further, to counter possible avoidance, the supply of storage facilities **between connected parties** remains exempt, with no ability to opt to tax.

2. "Self-storage" is no more than a general description of the type of facilities affected by the change in the law in 2012 to confirm certain supplies as standard-rated. In particular, "storage" and "self-storage" are both covered by the new rules and standard-rating is not confined to cases where the customer stores his or her own goods. Suppliers who have misunderstood this and have **not charged VAT** to their customers will need to account for VAT to HMRC notwithstanding. HMRC points out that it is up to the supplier to recover the VAT from the customer if that is contractually possible.

EXAMPLE

1. Two shops were operated by a company at Heathrow; under the terms of an agreement, a percentage of turnover was paid to the airport authority.
It was held that a licence to occupy land (i.e. the shop spaces) had been granted. *British Airports Authority v C & E (No 1)* [1977]

2. Coin-operated telephones were installed at various hospitals. In return, the telephone company paid commission to the hospital owners.
Again it was held that a licence to occupy land had been granted. *British Telecommunications plc* [1999] (VTD 16244)

3. Coin-operated cigarette vending machines were installed in pubs. The CJEU held that this was not a licence to occupy land, because although the owner of the machine still operated and maintained it, he had no real rights of possession, nor any control over the machine while it was located in the pub. He did not have an exclusive right to occupy land. *Sinclair Collis Ltd v C & E* [2003]

4. The owner of two golf courses granted a non-exclusive licence to a club for the occupation of the courses.
It was held that the owner had granted the club a licence to occupy land, not facilities for the playing of any sport or participating in any physical recreation. It was the club which granted such facilities to its members. *Abbotsley Golf & Squash Club Ltd* [1997] (VTD 15042)

Supplies that are not exempt

5378

Type of supply	Condition for exemption not to apply	VAT rate	¶¶
Construction services	In the course of a residential conversion	Reduced or zero	¶5442 and ¶5400
	All other construction services	Standard	
Sale of freehold, or grant of a long lease	The first grant of an interest in a protected building that has been substantially reconstructed from a shell	Zero	¶5392
	The first grant of an interest in a building that has been converted from non-residential to residential use	Zero	¶5384
	Any grant of an interest in a commercial building if the vendor has exercised its option to tax	Standard	¶5602
Rent received	From a commercial building under a short lease when the landlord has exercised its option to tax	Standard	¶5602
Exploitation of land	Specifically identified in the legislation as being standard-rated, for example: – hotel accommodation; – sports facilities; and – parking spaces	Standard	¶5490
Certain transactions between landlord and tenant	Usually if building opted	Standard	¶5546
Storage	Parties to contract are not connected	Standard	¶5374

A. Buying and selling

Disposal of an interest in land includes sale of the freehold and the grant of a long lease. **5380**

For the **time of supply** see ¶5265+.

MEMO POINTS 1. A disposal which is required under a **compulsory purchase order** is exempt, unless an option to tax has been exercised (¶5602). Notice 742 para 7.3

2. The **granting of an option** to purchase a land interest, within a particular time period at a specified price, is a supply for VAT purposes. The VAT treatment follows that of the land interest which is the subject of the option. Notice 742 para 7.4

3. For the VAT treatment of land which is part of a **transfer of a going concern** see ¶8660.

4. If a VAT **registration is cancelled**, a deemed taxable disposal may occur (¶8610).

5. A partly exempt business that grants an interest in property to a connected person must disclose the transaction to HMRC if its turnover **exceeds £10 million** (¶3104).

1. Outright sale

Most sales of existing buildings and land are exempt, unless an option to tax has been exercised in respect of non-residential property (¶5602), or the non-residential property is less than 3 years old. **5382**

The sale of an existing residential building is exempt, except in limited circumstances (¶5262).

There are **exceptions** from exemption for the first disposal of a converted building, or a substantially reconstructed protected building, where a dwelling has resulted from the building works undertaken.

a. Converted buildings

If the vendor has "person converting" status, the first sale of the freehold (or grant of a long lease) in respect of a building which has been converted from non-residential **into** a building either: **5384** Sch 8 Group 5 item 1 VATA 1994

- designed as a dwelling or number of dwellings (¶5152); or
- intended for use solely for a relevant residential purpose (¶5158) (in which case a tax certificate is acquired from the purchaser),

is zero-rated, provided that a holiday home (¶5502) is not created.

Person converting

To have person converting status, a taxable person must be **acting as** one of the following: **5386** Notice 708 para 5.5

- a developer, which owns the building and which either carried out the building work itself or arranged for it to be done by someone else; or
- a contractor or subcontractor, which provided construction services for the building work.

MEMO POINTS 1. It is possible for **more than one person** to be acting as either the developer or contractor. Person converting status cannot be transferred. However, a developer may take over a partly finished project, so the initial developer/contractor and the second developer can both make a zero-rated supply, provided that they independently meet the above criteria.

2. For **VAT groups** it is the company actually making the disposal which must have person converting status for the supply to be zero-rated, irrespective of the status of the representative member (¶8832).

3. If there is a **split of legal and beneficial ownership**, it is the beneficial owner who must have person converting status.

What does non-residential mean?

For this purpose, a non-residential building is one which has either not been used as living accommodation at all, or not put to such use in the 10 years immediately preceding the **5388** Notice 708 para 5.3

date of sale or lease commencement date. It is possible to start work on a building before the full 10 years have elapsed and still zero-rate the disposal (and thereby recover input tax), provided that the disposal actually takes place after the end of the 10-year period.

Previous occupation as living accommodation would include occupation of property which was not necessarily self-contained, or up to modern living standards e.g. a croft or bed-sit. In addition, occasional occupation (e.g. as a second home) still counts as previous occupation. The presence of cooking facilities is generally irrelevant. Illegal occupation by squatters does not make a property residential. Evidence of non-occupation (¶5438) must be retained.

Conversion work

5390 Notice 708 para 5.3

Where **only part of a building is being converted** and the building already contains residential parts, for zero-rating to apply the conversion must:
- be to a building for use for a relevant residential purpose; or
- create an additional dwelling or dwellings.

If only **part of the conversion qualifies** for zero-rating, the vendor must apportion the sales price accordingly (¶5254).

MEMO POINTS 1. Surrounding **land** sold with the building is also zero-rated, provided that it is a reasonably sized plot for the type of building. However, the sale of bare land is exempt (subject to the option to tax (¶5602)). Where two contracts are entered into - one to cover the land and one to cover conversion works - each must be treated separately for VAT purposes.
2. If the project is only **partly finished**, it can be sold at the zero rate, provided that it has progressed beyond merely securing and maintaining the existing structure.
3. A qualifying conversion includes the conversion of a building into a **garage**, which is intended to be occupied with the dwelling, provided that the construction work occurs simultaneously.

b. Reconstructed protected buildings

5392 Sch 8 Group 6 item 1 VATA 1994; VAT Information Sheets 09/12 and 10/12

The first grant of a major interest (¶5249) in, or in any part of, a protected building (¶5452) will be zero-rated when it has been substantially reconstructed and the reconstruction results in a residential or charitable building.

For zero-rating to apply the **vendor** must have "person substantially reconstructing" status.

MEMO POINTS Transitional provisions preserve, **from 1 October 2012**, zero-rating as it applied before that date (for which see previous editions of *VAT Memo*). Projects will continue to benefit from the old rules if listed building consent (or the equivalent approval for listed places of worship) had been applied for before 21 March 2012. The end of the transitional period extends to 30 September 2015.

Person substantially reconstructing

5393 Notice 708 para 10.7

To have person substantially reconstructing status, a taxable person must be **acting as** one of the following:
- a developer, which owns the building and which either carried out the building work itself or arranged for it to be done by someone else; or
- a contractor or subcontractor, which provided construction services for the building work.

MEMO POINTS 1. It is possible for **more than one person** to be acting as either the developer or contractor. Person substantially reconstructing status cannot be transferred. However, a developer may take over a partly finished project, so the initial developer/contractor and the second developer can both make a zero-rated supply, provided that they independently meet the above criteria.
2. For **VAT groups** it is the company actually making the disposal which must have person substantially reconstructing status for the supply to be zero-rated, irrespective of the status of the representative member (¶8832).
3. If there is a **split of legal and beneficial ownership**, it is the beneficial owner who must have person substantially reconstructing status.

Type of building resulting from work

Zero-rating applies to the sale of a building: **5394** Notice 708 para 10.3
a. intended for use solely for a **relevant residential** (¶5158) **or charitable** (¶5170) purpose, where a tax certificate is provided by the purchaser; or
b. designed as a **dwelling** or number of dwellings (¶5152), **unless** either:
– the interest granted is such that the acquirer is not entitled to reside in the building (or part of a building) throughout the year (this would exclude, for example, a holiday home); or
– the acquirer is prevented from living there continually, or using it as its principal private residence, by the terms of a covenant, statutory planning consent or similar permission (again, this is aimed largely at holiday homes).

MEMO POINTS 1. A qualifying reconstruction includes a **garage** intended to be occupied with the dwelling, where the work occurs simultaneously.
2. If only **part of the building or site qualifies** for zero-rating, the vendor must apportion the sales price accordingly.

Substantial reconstruction

For these purposes, a substantial reconstruction occurs where **major** work takes place to the building's fabric and the reconstructed building incorporates **no more** of the original building (that is, as it was before the reconstruction began) than the external walls, together with other external features of architectural or historic interest. **5396** Notice 708 para 10.4

MEMO POINTS The addition of an **extension** does not qualify as substantial reconstruction.

B. Works done

1. Changing a building's function

A **conversion** results in an adaptation of a building's use. **5400**

Conversions of buildings are **usually** taxable at the standard rate.

The **exceptions** are conversions of:
– non-residential premises to a residential use, which can be reduced-rated;
– residential premises for a different residential use, which can also be reduced-rated; and
– non-residential buildings for housing associations only, which are zero-rated.

The reduced rate of VAT is 5%.

In the rare case where both zero-rating and reduced-rating could apply, VAT should be applied at the zero rate.

Comment The **vendor** of a building which is to be the subject of a residential conversion may suffer loss of input tax recovery because the **option to tax** could be disapplied by the purchaser (¶5642), making the sale exempt.

Summary

5402

Work done	VAT rate	¶¶
Residential conversions generally	Reduced rate	¶5404
Residential conversion on behalf of a housing association	Zero rate	¶5430
Refurbishment of empty premises to provide a residence	Reduced rate	¶5444
Other works	Standard rate	

a. Residential conversions

5404 Sch 7A Group 6 VATA 1994

Construction work which **results in** any of the following residential conversions is liable to VAT at the reduced rate:
- changed number of dwellings;
- multiple occupancy dwellings; or
- premises intended for a relevant residential purpose (¶5160).

Notice 708 para 7.6.2

Work undertaken **without** the required statutory planning **consent** or statutory building control will be standard-rated.

Conversion works

5406 Sch 7A Group 6 note 11 VATA 1994

Whether the contractor only, or subcontractors too, are entitled to make supplies at the reduced rate depends on the type of building which is being converted. For conversions **involving**:
- **dwellings**, both the main contractor and subcontractors can make supplies at the reduced rate; but
- properties to be used for a **relevant residential purpose**, only the main contractor can make supplies at the reduced rate and it must receive a tax certificate (¶5224+) stating the occupier's intended use.

Where applicable, reduced-rating applies to the work undertaken on the fabric of the building and also work within the immediate site that is essential for the building to function.

MEMO POINTS The First-tier Tribunal has held that a single dwelling which consists of **more than one building** can be a dwelling for this purpose. *Fox* [2012] (TC01957)

5408 Notice 708 paras 7.6, 7.7

MEMO POINTS 1. **Work to the fabric** includes repairs and maintenance, decoration, and improvements such as an extension or the installation of double glazing. As with other types of construction, the incorporation of goods which are not building materials (¶5136) will be standard-rated.
2. Work within the **immediate site** includes the provision of:
- water and power to the building;
- access to the building;
- the means of drainage or security; and
- the means of waste disposal.

See ¶5134 for further details.
3. The conversion of a non-residential building **into a garage** intended to be occupied with a converted residential premises can also be reduced-rated, provided that the construction work occurs simultaneously. This also includes the construction of a detached garage and work to construct a driveway to serve it.
4. If goods are **acquired from overseas** (either from within or outside the EU), these can be reduced-rated if they would have qualified had they been supplied from the UK.

Summary

5410 Notice 708 para 7.2

	After conversion		
	Single household dwelling	**Multiple occupancy dwelling**	**Relevant residential purpose building**
Before conversion	¶5412	¶5420	¶5426
Single household dwelling	Standard-rated[1]	Reduced-rated	Reduced-rated
Multiple occupancy dwelling	Reduced-rated	Standard-rated	Reduced-rated
Relevant residential purpose building	Reduced-rated	Reduced-rated	Standard-rated
Any other building	Reduced-rated	Reduced-rated	Reduced-rated

Note:
1. If the number of dwellings changes, the supply will be reduced-rated (so the VAT rate will be 5%).

Conversion to single household dwelling(s)

Definition A single household dwelling is a building which: **5412** Sch 7A Group 6 note 4(1) VATA 1994
- is **designed** or has been adapted for occupation of that kind and has not been since adapted for another kind of occupation;
- **consists** of self-contained living accommodation;
- has no provision for internal **access** to another dwelling; and
- can be separately used, **let or sold**, free of any restriction imposed by covenant, planning consent, etc.

Granny flats, or additional rooms at a care home, do not qualify as single household dwellings, so any works carried out to create either would therefore be standard-rated.

If a conversion **results** in a greater or fewer number of dwellings (but not less than one), the reduced rate of VAT will apply. For this purpose discrete parts of a building can be examined, although there is a limit to the minimum size of such a part. **5414**

If the number of dwellings remains the same, standard-rate VAT will apply.

EXAMPLE

1. A block of twelve flats has four flats on each of its three floors. The following work is undertaken:
- three penthouse flats are created from the four flats on the top floor; and
- another flat is put into the ground floor.

Although the number of flats in the block is still twelve overall, each floor should be regarded independently. The conversion work on the ground and top floors can qualify for reduced-rating.

2. Conversion work was undertaken to convert six flats into four. Although most of the work qualified for reduced-rating, the work on the second floor did not, because it remained a single household dwelling before and after the conversion.
It was held that there must be some limitation on the meaning of "part", in that it must have some minimum size, so "any relevant part of the premises must be capable of being identified by reference to physical boundaries, normally walls, floors and ceilings after the conversion; a notional line in the middle of a room would not suffice". *Wellcome Trust* [2003] (VTD 18417)

Converted from HMRC gives the following examples of when the reduced rate of VAT would be available - that is, on the conversion: **5416** Notice 708 para 7.3
- of a property which has never been **used as** living accommodation e.g. an office, shop or barn;
- of **living accommodation** which is not self-contained e.g. a pub with living accommodation on the first floor; or
- of a dwelling which has been **previously adapted** to another use e.g. as offices or a dental practice. In this case the use at the time of the conversion is the only relevant issue.

EXAMPLE

1. A dwelling was converted into an accountant's office some years ago and it is used for this function until the conversion back to a dwelling takes place.
Reduced-rating will apply, because no dwelling existed immediately before the conversion.

2. If the building had two floors and the accountant's office only took up the ground floor, leaving living accommodation upstairs, the conversion of the ground floor would not qualify for reduced-rating, unless it created a separate self-contained dwelling.

3. A property was used as a boarding school from 1950 to 1995. In 1996 it was converted into a large dwelling.
It was held that the former property was non-residential, since pupils would not have considered the school house to be their home. The number of dwellings in the building had to be counted both before and after the conversion, and if there were more on the recount, a qualifying conversion had taken place. On that basis reduced-rating applied to the work. *C & E v Jacobs* [2005]

Other work If other types of work are **undertaken at the same time** as the conversion - for example refurbishment of, or repairs to, an existing dwelling - that work cannot be reduced-rated. **5418** Notice 708 para 7.3.1

EXAMPLE

1. A block of twelve flats has four flats on each of its three floors. The following work is undertaken:
– a lift is installed, which requires every flat to be changed in order to create space for the lift shaft; and
– three penthouse flats are created from the four flats on the top floor.
The overall number of flats therefore decreases to eleven, but only the work on the top floor qualifies as a conversion.

2. As for example **1.**, except that one penthouse flat is converted from two of the existing flats, while the other two are refurbished.
Only the work done to merge the two flats into the one flat qualifies for reduced-rating.

Conversion to multiple occupancy dwelling

5420 Sch 7A Group 6 note 4(2) VATA 1994; Notice 708 para 14.5

Definition A multiple occupancy dwelling is a building which:
– is **designed** or has been adapted for occupation of that kind and has not since been adapted for another kind;
– is not to any extent **used** for a relevant residential purpose (¶5160);
– **consists** of self-contained living accommodation;
– has no provision for internal **access** to another dwelling; and
– can be separately used, **let or sold**, free of any restriction imposed by covenant, planning consent, etc.

5422 Multiple occupancy dwellings are **typically** bed-sits.

The following are **excluded** from this category of property:
– accommodation for au pairs, guests and lodgers which is incorporated into a single household dwelling; and
– establishments such as hotels, inns, etc, which provide accommodation for travellers, tourists and temporary guests.

5424 Notice 708 para 7.4

Converted from Provided that the building, or the part of a building, did not contain any multiple occupancy dwellings before the conversion, reduced-rating should apply. For example, converting the following to bed-sits will be reduced-rated:
– a single household dwelling;
– a property used for a relevant residential purpose; or
– a property never used as living accommodation.

Works carried out to create **additional bedrooms** in a multiple occupancy dwelling are standard-rated.

Conversion to relevant residential purpose

5426 The conversion of:
– one or more buildings;
– one or more parts of a building; or
– any combination of buildings and parts,

into premises intended solely for relevant residential use (¶5160) is reduced-rated.

The customer must issue a **certificate** confirming the intended use and only the recipient of the certificate can reduced-rate its supply (i.e. the main contractor). The customer must be the person putting the building to qualifying use. If the customer **lets** the building to a separate institution, which uses the building for a relevant residential purpose, the reduced rate will not apply to the works.

For **institutions** (¶5160), the new premises must constitute relevant residential buildings in their entirety for reduced-rating to apply. For example, if outbuildings are **converted** into additional bedrooms:
– at an existing care home, reduced-rating does not apply; or
– at the same time as the main building is being converted, thereby resulting in an entire residential premises, reduced-rating would apply.

Converted from Provided that the building(s), or the relevant part(s) of the building(s), were not **last used** to any extent for a relevant residential purpose, the conversion work can be reduced-rated. 5428

For example, conversion to relevant residential use from previous use as any of the following would qualify:
- a single household dwelling;
- a multiple occupancy dwelling; or
- a property never used as living accommodation.

The **remodelling** of an existing relevant residential building would not count as a conversion.

---

b. For housing associations

A conversion, **undertaken on behalf of** a housing association, of a non-residential building into either a dwelling or dwellings (¶5154), or a building intended for use solely for a relevant residential purpose (¶5160), is zero-rated. 5430 Sch 8 Group 5 item 3 VATA 1994

Qualifying customers

The following housing associations qualify for the purposes of zero-rating if **registered in**: 5432 Sch 8 Group 5 note 21 VATA 1994
- Wales, under Part 1 of the Housing Act 1996;
- Scotland, under the Housing (Scotland) Act 2010; or
- Northern Ireland, under Part 2 of the Housing (Northern Ireland) Order 1992.

Private providers of social housing registered under Part 2 of the Housing and Regeneration Act 2008 also qualify.

Qualifying buildings

For this purpose the building to be converted **should not** have been designed or adapted for use as a dwelling or relevant residential building within the 10 years before the conversion work commences and no part of it should have been occupied as a dwelling or residence during that time. 5434 Sch 8 Group 5 note 7A VATA 1994

Common examples of non-residential buildings include offices, warehouses, barns and churches.

MEMO POINTS 1. If only **part of a building** is non-residential, the conversion must either create an additional dwelling or dwellings, or result in a building for a relevant residential purpose for zero-rating to apply. Notice 708 para 6.3.5
2. If the conversion uses a **mixture** of non-residential and residential parts of the same building to produce a new dwelling, none of the work can be zero-rated e.g. a two-storey public house with upstairs living accommodation is converted into a house. This is because no additional dwelling has been created.
3. A conversion of a building into a **garage** intended to be occupied with the dwelling, where the construction work occurs simultaneously, is also zero-rated. Conversion into a stand-alone garage, with no accompanying conversion to a dwelling, would be standard-rated.

For this purpose, **previous occupation** as living accommodation would include occupation of property which was not necessarily self-contained or up to modern living standards e.g. a croft or bed-sits. The lack of modern amenities, such as cooking facilities, is generally irrelevant. If a building has been used as living accommodation within the previous 10 years, the conversion will be standard-rated. 5436 Notice 708 paras 6.3.2, 6.3.4

MEMO POINTS 1. A building which is occupied **occasionally**, such as a second home, is still living accommodation.
2. **Illegal** occupation by squatters does not make the property residential.

EXAMPLE
1. The upper floor of a public house was converted into a private dwelling. Before the conversion the upper floor had only been used to accommodate the publican, partly because the police requi-

red a male staff member to sleep at the premises. The original upper floor had comprised two bedrooms and a bathroom, a sitting room, and an office/storeroom. The toilet in the bathroom had been available to customers of the pub.
It was held that before the conversion the upper floor had been residential, so the conversion did not create an additional dwelling. *G Tobell* [2000] (VTD 16646)

2. A housing association converted twelve bed-sits with shared facilities into five self-contained flats.
It was held that the bed-sits were residential, because they were someone's home. Therefore the conversion did not qualify for zero-rating. *Amicus Group Ltd* [2002] (VTD 17693)

3. A farmhouse, built in the 1700s, was in such a dilapidated state that by 1967 the local council declared the house unfit for habitation and issued a closing order. However, the house continued to be lived in until February 1999, when renovation work commenced. The owners tried to argue that the closing order changed the house into a non-residential building.
It was held that the order did not have this effect, so that the house had always remained a dwelling. Hence the renovation work did not qualify as a conversion. *N & J Hicking* [2000] (VTD 17117)

5438 Notice 708 para 6.3.3 Where relevant, the contractor should obtain **evidence** of non-occupation for the last 10 years. The most useful evidence is information **from** local authority Empty Property Officers (if they are uncertain, an estimate of the date of last occupation should be given); in this case no other supporting material is required.

Otherwise, the following **sources** of information may be helpful:
- electoral roll;
- council tax information; or
- utility company records.

Construction supplies

5440 Only the **main contractor** can zero-rate its work and it must possess a certificate to show that the customer is a qualifying housing association. If converting into a building for a relevant residential purpose, a further certificate of intended use must also be obtained (¶5224+).

Notice 708 para 6.6 The **scope** of supplies which can be zero-rated includes services (¶5134) and building materials (¶5136) supplied by the main contractor in carrying out those services.

If only **part** of the work completed by the contractor **relates to a residential conversion**, it must apportion its costs, otherwise all of its work must be standard-rated. For example:
- it converts a shop into flats, but also refurbishes the existing flats above the shop; or
- the upgrading of a road leading to two properties, one of which is the subject of a conversion, whereas the other is an existing dwelling.

2. Alterations

5442 Refurbishment work and alterations to **existing buildings** are generally standard-rated.

However, if the renovation or alteration is to a **residence** and concerns a building which has been empty for the past 2 years and will be used for a residential purpose (¶5444), the builder's services may be reduced-rated.

In addition, construction work to improve or alter buildings for a **charity** or a **disabled** person may be zero-rated (¶1344).

In the rare case where both zero-rating and reduced-rating could apply, VAT should be applied at the zero rate.

a. Empty premises

5444 Sch 7A Group 7 VATA 1994 The reduced rate of VAT applies to the following **residential buildings**, which must have been empty for the 2 years prior to the renovation work commencing:
a. single household dwelling (¶5412);

b. multiple occupancy dwelling (¶5420); or
c. a building which when last occupied was used for a relevant residential purpose (¶5160) and will be solely used for this purpose after the work is done.

For all types of premises, reduced-rating only applies where any statutory planning **consent** and/or building control for the work has been granted. Sch 7A Group 7 note 4 VATA 1994

MEMO POINTS 1. For **subsequent relevant residential use**, a building which formed one of many buildings on the same relevant residential site will qualify.
2. If goods are **acquired from overseas** (either from within or outside the EU), these can be reduced-rated if they would have qualified had they been supplied from the UK.

Occupation

The requirement for the premises to be empty concerns the **whole premises** which are the subject of the renovation. So for a site which is to be used for a relevant residential purpose, all of the buildings which form part of that site must have been empty for the 2 years prior to the renovation work commencing. Note that not all of the buildings on the site need to be subject to the renovation work. **5446** Sch 7A Group 7 note 3 VATA 1994

MEMO POINTS 1. For the definition of **empty** and the required evidence to prove it see ¶5436+. Notice 708 para 8.3
2. It is possible for the occupier to **move in** during the renovation works. However, any occupation before the works commence would invalidate the reduced-rating.

EXAMPLE
1. An old people's home has been empty for 4 years. It consists of three blocks (A, B and C). Only blocks A and B are renovated, because the owner wants to see how the business goes before committing to further expenditure on block C. The renovation work will be reduced-rated, because the whole site has been empty for at least 2 years.
2. As for example **1**., except that block C has only been empty for 1 year. None of the renovation work will qualify for reduced-rating, because the whole site has not been empty for 2 years.

For **single household** dwellings, an alternative test is available to cover the situation where the dwelling is occupied while the renovation work is carried out. **5448** Sch 7A Group 7 note 3(3) VATA 1994

The following **criteria** must all be met:
- the dwelling was unoccupied for a period of at least 2 years;
- the subsequent occupier (for whom the renovation is done) then acquired the empty property;
- the renovation work is done for the occupier within the first year after acquisition; and
- no works were undertaken during the 2 years before the occupier's acquisition date, other than minor works to keep the dwelling dry and secure.

For this purpose, the occupier must **acquire** a major interest in the land for consideration - that is, broadly, the freehold or a lease in excess of 21 years (¶5249).

EXAMPLE A dwelling has fallen into disrepair and has been empty since June 2010. Consider three alternative scenarios:
1. On 3 October 2014 the dwelling is purchased by Mr A and he immediately moves in while renovation works take place. The work finishes in December 2014. The dwelling has been empty for 2 years and the works are completed within 12 months of purchase, so reduced-rating applies.
2. On 3 September 2014 Ms B purchases it and immediately moves in but the renovation works take place between July 2015 and November 2015. The dwelling was empty for 2 years before occupation but the works are not completed within 12 months of acquisition. Only the works completed before 3 September 2015 can be reduced-rated.
3. On 30 November 2013 the dwelling was purchased by Mr C. Renovation works do not take place until December 2014 and end in March 2015. Mr C occupies the dwelling from July 2014 (i.e. at least 2 years after June 2011). Reduced-rating does not apply, however, because the works do not occur within 12 months of the purchase.

Construction supplies

5450 Sch 7A Group 7 notes 3A, 5 VATA 1994

Supplies **by** the main contractor and subcontractors can be reduced-rated, **except** in the case of a single household dwelling where the owner is occupying it, in which case only the main contractor can apply the reduced rate. If renovating a building for a relevant residential purpose, a certificate of intended use must be obtained (¶5224+).

Where applicable, reduced-rating **applies** not only **to** work on the fabric of the building but also to works undertaken within the immediate site that are essential for the building to function (¶5408).

MEMO POINTS 1. If only **part** of the work completed by the contractor **relates to the renovation** it must apportion its costs, otherwise all of its work must be standard-rated.

Notice 708 para 8.4.1

2. A reduced-rated renovation includes the renovation of a **garage** intended to be occupied with the residential premises when the construction work occurs simultaneously. This also includes the construction or conversion of a garage.

---

b. Protected buildings

5452 Sch 8 Group 6 VATA 1994

A protected building is a listed building or scheduled monument. If a building is both listed and a scheduled monument, it will be treated as a monument under these rules.

5454

Until 30 September 2015 **construction works** in relation to which planning permission was applied for prior to 21 March 2012 are zero-rated when they are in the course of an approved alteration of a protected building, which result in a building:
- designed to remain as, or become, a dwelling or number of dwellings (¶5152);
- intended for use for a relevant residential purpose (¶5158); or
- intended for use for a relevant charitable purpose (¶5170).

Accordingly, alterations to listed buildings in relation to which planning permission was not applied for prior to 21 March 2102 are no longer zero-rated. This obviates the need for any debate over whether works are alterations or mere repairs (see ¶5464+). However, the discussion below remains of relevance while the transitional provisions are in force (that is, until 30 September 2015).

MEMO POINTS 1. Repairs to **listed buildings of worship** qualify for a grant scheme which refunds all of the VAT incurred (¶2452). From 1 October 2012 this scheme also covers approved alterations to listed places of worship.
2. VAT incurred on the construction, renovation and maintenance of **memorials** can also be refunded (¶2454).
3. **From 1 October 2012** anti-forestalling legislation seeks to prevent continuation of zero-rating on or after that date, except under the transitional provisions.

5456 Sch 8 Group 6 note 1(a) VATA 1994; Notice 708 para 9.3

Listed buildings Under the transitional provisions (¶5454) a building qualifies for zero-rating if listed:
- in England and Wales, under the Planning (Listed Buildings and Conservation Areas) Act 1990;
- in Scotland, under the Planning (Scotland) (Listed Buildings and Conservation Areas) Act 1997; or
- in Northern Ireland, under the Planning (Northern Ireland) Order 1991.

Unlisted buildings in **conservation areas** and **local interest** buildings are not listed buildings.

5458 Business Brief 10/04

Any object or structure fixed to the building or within its curtilage (immediate surroundings) is also listed. So **outbuildings** which have formed part of the land since before 1 July 1948 are part of the listed building.

Under the transitional provisions (¶5454) **alterations** to an outbuilding are zero-rated where that building:
- can be shown to be or become a dwelling, or be intended for use for a relevant residential or charitable purpose; or
- is so close to the principal building as to form an integral part of it. *Orme* [1993] (VTD 9975)

It is therefore unlikely that unattached structures, such as boundary walls, qualify.

On the other hand, if the work is not covered by the transitional provisions, it may amount to a residential conversion (see ¶5404+).

The **construction** of a building which is separate from the listed building, but within the curtilage, does not constitute an alteration, even if the work has listed building consent. Sch 8 Group 6 note 10 VATA 1994

EXAMPLE

1. An outbuilding within the curtilage of a listed building was converted from a store and garage into useful living accommodation. This included a lounge, games room, study, bathroom and a swimming pool. The outbuilding had only been lived in for a period of about a year in the 1940s.
It was held that the outbuilding was not altered to remain or become a dwelling. Therefore the work did not qualify for zero-rating. *C & E v Zielinski Baker & Partners Ltd* [2004]

2. Listed building consent was obtained for the rebuilding of a swimming pool enclosure and the construction of a walkway to the protected main house.
It was held that the pool enclosure was a separate building, even though it was physically linked to the house by the walkway. Only the walkway itself qualified for zero-rating. *Collins & Beckett Ltd* [2005] (VTD 19212)

3. In an older case, the owner of a listed farmhouse arranged for the construction of an indoor swimming pool by replacing a barn. He obtained the required planning permission and listed building consent. The new building was connected to the farmhouse by a covered walkway and a brick wall. The local planning officer considered this to be an extension.
It was held that the pool was not a separate building and was therefore part of the protected building. The work was an alteration which qualified for zero-rating. *C & E v M Arbib* [1995]

4. A trader purchased a protected farmhouse and obtained listed building consent to convert the:
- farmhouse into a nursing home; and
- agricultural outbuildings into flats and an office for administration.

The zero-rating of the work relating to the office was challenged.
It was held that relevant residential accommodation may include an ancillary part without which the building could not function. The conversion of the outbuilding into an office meant that all the sleeping accommodation could be housed in the main building, so the work was zero-rated. *Hill Ash Developments* [2000] (VTD 16747)

Under the transitional provisions (¶5454) a **garage** can qualify for zero-rating, provided that **5460** Business Brief 11/05
the particular building is in use as a garage before the alteration takes place and continues to be used as one afterwards. It is not necessary for the garage to have been **constructed as** a garage so that, for example, an alteration which turns a barn, previously used for storing vehicles, into a garage would qualify.

The garage must be **occupied** together with the dwelling and the building should have been constructed or reconstructed at the same **time** as the dwelling.

Monument A monument must be scheduled under either the: **5462** Sch 8 Group 6 note 1(b) VATA 1994
- Ancient Monuments and Archaeological Areas Act 1979; or
- Historic Monuments Act (Northern Ireland) Act 1971.

Approved alteration

Exclusions For the purposes of the transitional provisions (¶5454) an alteration excludes **5464**
repairs, maintenance work and reconstructions. Any physical alteration resulting from repairs is also excluded from zero-rating e.g. tiny changes, or those necessitated by the use of modern building materials.

HMRC defines **repairs** as tasks undertaken to minimise the need for, and mitigate the scale **5466** Notice 708 paras 9.4.1, 9.4.2
and cost of, further attention to the fabric of the building.

Whether the work is a one-off job is irrelevant, as is the amount of the cost.

HMRC gives the following guidance:

Type of work	Detail	Alteration	Repair
General	Extension	✓	
	Opening or closing doorways	✓	
	Damp-proofing		✓
	Redecorating		✓
	Repointing		✓
	Making good - follows treatment of main work	✓	✓
Windows	Upgrading of double glazing		✓
	Installing new window where no window before	✓	
Roofing	Refelt and batten roof		✓
	Replace flat roof with pitched roof	✓	
	Replacement of straw thatch with reed if part of normal replacement programme		✓
	Changes to ridge detail of thatched roof		✓
Wiring and plumbing	Normal rewiring		✓
	Extending wiring and plumbing systems	✓	
	Replacing boilers simultaneously with extending the plumbing system	✓	
	Floodlighting installed on building[1]	✓	

Note:
1. See ¶5474 for the VAT treatment of floodlights installed in the grounds of a building, rather than attached to the building.

5470 Any **reconstruction** work which reinstates, or rebuilds, a protected property will be standard-rated, irrespective of the transitional provisions (¶5454). A reconstruction involves replication or rebuilding of a structure which existed before, in order that the appearance and function is maintained. Note that a "substantial" reconstruction may be zero-rated in its own right (see ¶5392+).

EXAMPLE After a listed building was damaged by fire, a builder replaced the roof and rebuilt part of the exterior wall.
The damage included the total destruction of the roof, first floor and internal timber partitions. Most of the windows had been destroyed and the enclosing stone walls had to be rebuilt, in part as a result of damage to the original timber and loss of structural strength. Listed building consent had been obtained for the reinstatement works (which included a new roof), extensions and structural alterations.
Viewed as a whole, the supply was made in the course of rebuilding or reconstruction; as such it was not alteration and so could not be zero-rated. *C&E v CR Morrish* [1998]

5472 Sch 8 Group 6 note 6 VATA 1994

Criteria to be met Under the transitional provisions (¶5454) an approved alteration **requires**:

a. the work being done to alter the fabric of the building; and

b. permission and consent, where relevant, to be obtained.

Generally, the building should be visibly changed for an alteration to have taken place.

HMRC may give **advance confirmation** whether the works will qualify as an alteration.

5474 Notice 708 para 9.4

HMRC interprets **fabric** as meaning the basic structure, which would include work done to the walls, ceilings, floors, doors, roof, stairs, plumbing, mains wiring and lighting systems.

However, the installation of floodlighting within the grounds of the building is not an alteration to the fabric of the building itself.

Planning **permission** is separate from any additional consents which may be required. **5476**

Sch 8 Group 6 note 6 VATA 1994; Notice 708 para 9.5

Work done under a listed building **enforcement notice** may qualify as an approved alteration. Such a notice is issued by the planning authority where consent was not previously obtained, or the conditions of the consent have not been satisfied.

All scheduled monuments which are altered require scheduled monuments consent, which is obtained from the secretary of state.

The requirements for listed buildings consent are shown in the following table.

In both cases, if consent is given when it is not required, this does not cause the work to become an approved alteration for zero-rating purposes.

Type of building	Relevant law	Consent required?
Ecclesiastical (not dwellings occupied by ministers) [1]	Section 60 Planning (Listed Buildings and Conservation Areas) Act 1990	x
Monument in Northern Ireland	Section 10 Historic Monuments Act (Northern Ireland) Act 1971	✓
Located on Crown [2] or Duchy [3] land		x
Any other case	Authorised under: – Part I Planning (Listed Buildings and Conservation Areas) Act 1990; – Part IV Planning (Scotland) (Listed Buildings and Conservation Areas) Act 1997; – Part V Planning (Northern Ireland) Order 1991; or – Part I Ancient Monuments and Archaeological Areas Act 1979	✓

Note:
1. In **England and Wales** the following denominations do not require consent:
- Church of England;
- Church of Wales;
- Roman Catholic Church;
- Methodist Church;
- Baptist Union of Great Britain and the Baptist Union of Wales; and
- United Reform Church.

In **Scotland and Northern Ireland** all listed ecclesiastical buildings are exempt from consent.

2. **Crown** land is either an interest:
- belonging to Her Majesty in right of the Crown, or a government department; or
- an interest held in trust for Her Majesty for the purposes of a government department, or held in right of the Prince and Steward of Scotland.

3. **Duchy** land is an interest belonging to Her Majesty in right of the Duchy of Lancaster or belonging to the Duchy of Cornwall.

Where relevant, consent must be **obtained before** the work commences, otherwise the owner is committing an offence. The supplier therefore needs to be sure of the required consent for the work it is contracted to do. **5478**

EXAMPLE The planning authorities stated that consent was not required for works to a particular listed building. The builder carried out the alterations and as listed consent had not been obtained, charged standard-rated VAT.
A few months later it became apparent that permission was required, as the planning authority had made an error. Consent was given retrospectively.
It was held that zero-rating could not apply because the retrospective consent related to the retention of alterations which now existed and this was outside the scope of the VAT rules. *Alan Roper & Sons Ltd* [1997] (VTD 15260)

5479 Whether work comprises repairs or an alteration has been the subject of much **case law** (which will, of course, cease to be relevant when the transitional provisions (¶5454) come to an end in 2015).

EXAMPLE

1. The owner of a protected castle obtained listed building consent for alterations which included the installation of new wardrobes along the wall of a bedroom. These wardrobes were hand-built and had been made of materials to blend in with the existing decoration and structures.
It was held that the work substantially affected the fabric of the building and so fell to be zero-rated. *EC Owen* [2004] (VTD 18660)

2. A company re-thatched the roofs of two listed buildings, replacing straw thatching with reeds. It was held that the appearance of the roofs had changed and there had been no need to re-thatch at that time for reasons of repair. Hence the work qualified as an alteration. *Dodson Bros (Thatchers) Ltd* [1995] (VTD 13734)

3. Listed building consent was obtained for the removal of some lead guttering, which was to be replaced by a layer of slates; this caused a change to the roof pitch. Rain would then run off the slates.
It was held that the work was an approved alteration. *D Starr* [2005] (VTD 19176)

4. Permission was obtained to replace the roof of a protected building, because of a water leak and because some of the pitches had collapsed. The original roof comprised stone slates and 14 pitches. The replacement required an alteration in the pitches, timber to be changed and a rebuilding of the roof structure. While undertaking this work, three skylights were removed and a chimney was taken down, although this work was outside the terms of the consent. The new roof was constructed from artificial stone slates, reclaimed natural stone slates and clay tiles.
It was held that the costs should be apportioned, as the replacement of the tiles was a repair and the chimney dismantling was not within the consent. So only the actual structural work which required (and had received) consent qualified as an approved alteration. *CN Foley* [1995] (VTD 13496)

5. Permission was obtained to convert a protected building from three flats into a single dwelling. Further, substantial work was carried out on the roof, including:
- altering the pitch of the roof to allow rainwater to run off;
- re-slating the roof with natural slates in place of the existing mixture of natural slate and asbestos;
- covering the apex of the roof with lead; and
- renewing the lead valleys.

Because written consent had not been received for the roofing works, these did not constitute an approved alteration. *N Brice* [1991] (VTD 6376)

Construction supplies

5480 Notice 708 para 9.6 For **dwellings**, both the main contractor and subcontractors can zero-rate their alteration work under the transitional provisions (¶5454).

In relation to buildings which are to be put to a **relevant residential or charitable purpose**, only the recipient of the tax certificate can zero-rate its supply.

Zero-rated supplies for the **actual physical alteration** include construction services (¶5134) and associated building materials (¶5136).

Notice 708 para 9.6 Under the transitional provisions (¶5454) **other services** which closely relate to the alteration can also be zero-rated - for example, preparation work, or the carrying out of remedial work resulting from an approved alteration.

The services will need to be **apportioned** where:
- repairs are also undertaken;
- only part of the building is protected or will be used for the appropriate purpose i.e. relevant residential or charitable; or
- they are performed on a mixed site development (¶5194).

5482 Any supplier should ensure that it has the necessary **evidence** to support the zero-rating of its supply. In particular, a tax certificate (¶5224+) will be required for buildings intended for use for a relevant residential or relevant charitable purpose.

Other **sources** of evidence may include:
- written confirmation that the building is protected;

- copies of all permissions and consents;
- a copy of the plans;
- photographs taken during, before and after the work; and
- related correspondence.

C. Exploitation with no change in ownership

When income is derived from property, without any grant of an ownership interest, the landowner may be making a standard-rated supply. For the treatment of short leases of up to 21 years (or less than 20 years in Scotland) see ¶5540. **5490**

If standard-rating does not apply, the default position of supplies relating to land is that they are exempt, subject to the option to tax (¶5602).

Summary

The following table summarises standard-rated supplies and the exceptions that apply. **5492**

Standard-rated supply	Exception	Reference	¶¶
Provision of accommodation in a hotel or similar establishment	Where guests stay for a continuous period of more than 4 weeks	Notice 709/3	¶5494
Provision of holiday accommodation, including the supply of pitches and related facilities for caravans and tents	Grant of a freehold interest or a lease	Notice 709/3	¶5502
Mooring and storage for vessels and aircraft		Notice 742 para 3	¶5514
Parking spaces for vehicles	Incidental parking use and parking provided with certain types of premises	Notice 742 para 4	¶5516
Sports facilities	Longer-term use	Notice 742 para 5	¶5526
Spectator seats		Notice 742 para 3.4	¶5530
Gaming and/or fishing rights	Grants of a freehold interest or a lease Certain shooting rights	Notice 742 para 6	¶5532
Grant of timber rights	A supply of land which happens to contain timber is exempt	Notice 742 para 3.1	

Hotel accommodation

The supply of any of the following **within** a hotel, inn, boarding house, or similar establishment is standard-rated: **5494** Notice 709/3 para 2.2
- sleeping accommodation, including bathrooms, living rooms and suites;
- accommodation used for the supply of catering; and
- rooms provided with sleeping accommodation.

The sale, or grant of a long lease, of a **building which will be used** as a hotel, etc, is exempt unless the vendor has opted to tax the building (¶5602).

MEMO POINTS 1. **Similar establishments** include: **5496**
- motels;
- guesthouses;
- those providing bed and breakfast;

- private residential clubs;
- halls of residence; and
- hostels.

It is irrelevant whether food or catering facilities are provided in addition to the accommodation.

Notice 709/3 para 2.1

2. A **hotel** is defined by HMRC as a commercial establishment providing lodging (furnished sleeping accommodation) and possibly meals and other facilities such as laundry services, communal TV/rest rooms and telephone services for guests and visitors. There is no requirement to provide food or other facilities in order for an establishment to be regarded as a hotel.

Notice 709/3 para 3

3. Charges made to **long-term guests**, who stay for a continuous period of more than 28 days, are subject to special rules. From the 29th day of the stay VAT is only charged on that part of the payment which is not for accommodation (i.e. the amount that is for meals, drinks, other services and facilities). For further details see ¶984.

Notice 709/3 para 7.2

4. When a **cancellation charge** is made to a guest who cancels a booking, no VAT is due on the charge because it is compensation. However, any fee levied for arranging insurance against having to pay such a charge is a standard-rated supply. Any commission received from an insurance broker, etc, is in respect of an exempt supply.

5. For the treatment of:
- **tips** see ¶248;
- **deposits** see ¶784; and
- **retention fees** see ¶5504.

EXAMPLE

1. In a case involving the provision of accommodation to overseas students by a charity for periods in excess of a year, it was held that this was not the provision of sleeping accommodation in premises akin to a hotel or boarding house, because:
- the accommodation had a degree of permanence; and
- the charity was not seeking financial gain in providing the accommodation. *International Student House* [1996] (VTD 14420)

2. Bed and breakfast accommodation was provided to more than 200 people with some sort of social problem (homeless, unemployed, many just released from prison or a healthcare unit), mainly financed by social security benefits. Most stays lasted at least 6 months if not a year (so that residents could be entered onto the local authority's housing list).
It was held that the accommodation was similar to that provided in a boarding house, it being irrelevant how the stays were financed or the residents accommodated. *Namecourt Ltd* [1984] (VTD 1560)

3. Supervised residential accommodation for people with mental health problems was provided in a lodge.
It was held that the lodge was not a similar establishment to a hotel, because:
- the care required by the residents subsisted for long periods; and
- the residents were not visitors or travellers, having special needs arising from their mental conditions, and were mostly in receipt of disability living allowance. *Dinaro Ltd (t/a Fairway Lodge)* [2000] (VTD 17148)

5498 Notice 709/3 paras 4.1, 4.3

Catering and other purposes The provision of accommodation for the purpose of:

a. catering is standard-rated, irrespective of the length of the contract (and whether or not the catering is supplied by a third party); or

b. other purposes, such as conferences or meetings, is exempt, unless the person providing the accommodation has opted to tax the property. Further, if refreshments such as:
- tea, coffee and biscuits are served at the conference or meeting, these are part of the single exempt supply; or
- a meal or buffet are provided, this should be treated as a separate standard-rated supply. In this case a fair apportionment of the consideration should be made between the supply of catering and the supply of the facilities.

MEMO POINTS 1. Where a single charge is made for a **meeting** room **together with meal(s) and overnight accommodation**, each element is treated as a separate supply, so that the catering and overnight accommodation is taxable, whereas the supply of the meeting room is exempt.

Business Brief 1/06

2. Where a **24-hour conference rate** is charged, this should be broken down into its constituent parts, as in **1**. above.

Employees If accommodation or food and drink is provided to employees and **no consideration** is provided, no VAT is due. This includes the case where a deduction from gross wages is made, which is provided for in the employee's contract of employment. **5500** Notice 709/3 para 4.2

However, where **payment** is made, the amount received will be VAT-inclusive and the employer should account for the VAT. In this case payments may be either in the form of cash, or deductions from wages which are not covered by the employment contract.

Holiday accommodation

The grant of a temporary interest in holiday accommodation (or right over, or licence to occupy) is standard-rated. **5502** Notice 709/3 para 5

Standard-rating **applies to** any charges made, irrespective of both the length of occupation and how the charges are described, including service charges, use of facilities and booking fees.

MEMO POINTS 1. For this purpose holiday accommodation **includes** a house, flat, chalet, villa, beach hut, tent, caravan, or houseboat which is advertised as holiday accommodation. **5504**
2. An element of temporary **occupation** is usually required, although occupation throughout the year may not prevent qualification as holiday accommodation.
3. Residential accommodation that happens to be **situated at a holiday resort** is not necessarily holiday accommodation.
4. **Retention fees**, which allow a customer to reserve accommodation for future use, are standard-rated, except when the customer is absent after the first 28 days of a stay, in which case the special rule to value the services being provided may apply (¶5496). Notice 709/3 para 7.4
5. For the treatment of:
- **tips** see ¶248;
- **deposits** see ¶784; and
- **cancellation charges** see ¶5496.

EXAMPLE

1. In a case involving the letting of beach huts, it was held that these were holiday accommodation because they could be used for cooking, eating, shelter and changing clothes. *Poole Borough Council* [1992] (VTD 7180)

2. Three furnished flats were let out, one of which was under a controlled tenancy. The owners registered with the English Tourist Board. The flats were advertised as fully furnished holiday accommodation, although the owners stated that this was only so that the tenancies would not be controlled. In fact, a minority of lets were to holidaymakers.
It was held that as the flats were advertised as holiday accommodation, VAT should be charged. *RW & B Sheppard* [1977] (VTD 481)

3. Under a lease the tenants were not permitted to occupy the property during February, so they stayed with family. The freeholder charged VAT on the ground rent and service charge.
It was held that the property was not holiday accommodation, so the rent and service charges should be exempt. *BA Ashworth* [1994] (VTD 12924)

Sale or lease The VAT treatment of a sale or lease (i.e. not a short-term or temporary right to occupy) of holiday accommodation **depends on** whether the accommodation is: **5506** Notice 709/3 para 5
- new, in which case the supply is standard-rated and VAT must be accounted for on all charges (including the initial charge, ground rent and any service charges); or
- not new, in which case any sale proceeds or premium will be exempt. Ground rent, service charges and any other periodic fees are standard-rated.

MEMO POINTS 1. A property is considered to be **new** until 3 years have elapsed since the earlier of:
- the issue of the certificate of practical completion; and
- the date when the property is first fully occupied.

2. The supply of a **time-share** follows the rules above, except that costs which are recharged may qualify to be treated as disbursements (¶7185). Notice 709/3 para 5.7

Off-season residential accommodation The letting of holiday accommodation as residential accommodation out of season is exempt, **provided that** the let exceeds 28 days and **5508** Notice 709/3 para 5.6

the holiday trade in the area is clearly seasonal. In this case, the whole period of the tenancy is exempt.

MEMO POINTS 1. HMRC states that the holiday **season normally lasts** from Easter to the end of September. However, certain areas, London for example, do not have a seasonal holiday trade.
2. To support the residential nature of the letting, appropriate **evidence**, such as the tenancy agreement, should be retained.

EXAMPLE A caravan site was open for the main holiday season only (1 March to 31 October), partly because the local authority had only consented to planning permission on this basis.
However, licences to occupy the caravans were granted with terms exceeding a year.
It was held that the licences were for seasonal pitches, irrespective of the longer terms. So standard-rate VAT should be charged. *T & M Smith* [1995] (VTD 13052)

5510 Notice 709/3 para 6

Caravans and tents The provision of holiday accommodation in any type of caravan or tent **already sited** on a pitch is standard-rated.

If the occupation is not for the purposes of a holiday (i.e. it is treated as a residence), the supply is exempt.

The sale or leasing (for more than 1 year) of a caravan may be zero-rated (¶1322).

5512 Notice 709/3 para 5.4

The VAT treatment of holiday **pitches** for customers' own caravans and tents depends on whether the land to be occupied is sold outright or leased.

The sale of the **freehold** in bare land is exempt, subject to the option to tax (¶5602).

The **leasing** of land, **or** the granting of a **licence** over land for this purpose, is subject to VAT at the standard rate.

Notice 701/20 para 4.1

Where the pitch is to be used for **off-season residential** accommodation the supply is exempt. In this case the key issue is whether the site is held out for use as holiday accommodation (standard-rated) or for permanent residential use (exempt). **Restricted occupancy rights** attaching to a site would normally suggest strongly that the pitch is for holiday or leisure use but HMRC will accept that the pitch is nevertheless for exempt residential use if it is the occupiers' intention that the pitch will be their principal private residence despite them not being permitted to live there all year round.

MEMO POINTS 1. For **parking** see ¶5520.

HMRC Briefs 37/11 and 43/11

2. Charges made by caravan site owners for **water and sewerage** are only zero-rated if actual consumption can be identified (such as through metering at the individual pitch), otherwise the charges follow the VAT liability of the caravan pitch.
3. Where caravan site owners recharge a proportion of their **business rates** to individual caravan owners, the recharge follows the same VAT liability as the pitch fee.
4. Charges made by caravan site owners for the **first-time connection to electricity, gas, water and sewerage** are subject to the same VAT liability as the pitch, unless the site owner identifies and charges for the actual consumption of users, in which case the charge is subject to the same VAT liability as the supply of the utility (that is, reduced-rated for electricity and gas, zero-rated for water and sewerage).
5. For further details of supplies relating to caravans see ¶1328.

Mooring and storage

5514 Notice 742 para 3.1

Generally, charges made for the mooring of a boat, ship or any other vessel are standard-rated. Fees charged for the storage of aircraft are similarly standard-rated.

However, there are **exceptions** for:
- houseboats, for which such fees are exempt (¶1328); and
- qualifying ships (¶1298), in relation to which the supply may be zero-rated.

MEMO POINTS For **parking** see ¶5520.

EXAMPLE In a case involving a couple who lived on a yacht, it was held that the mooring fees were taxable, because the yacht was not a houseboat. *DM & PJ Roberts* [1992] (VTD 7516)

Parking spaces

The provision of a space to park vehicles is standard-rated, subject to certain exceptions. **5516**

HMRC gives the following **guidance**: **5518**

Notice 742 paras 4.2, 4.3

Land area	Standard-rated	Exempt
Garages and car parks	**Lease or licence** of a garage (even if it is not used for storing a vehicle) or designated parking bay or space	**a.** the conveyance or contract makes **no specific reference** to use for parking vehicles (although this exception can never apply to garages); **b.** any reference to parking a vehicle is **incidental** to the main use; **c.** the **lessee** is either: – a motor dealer which stores its stock-in-trade on the land; – a vehicle transportation firm; – a vehicle distributor; or – a vehicle auctioneer which uses it in the course of its business; or **d.** the land (including land used at other times as a car park) will be **used for**: – holding a market; – a car boot sale (including the charge to the car owners selling their goods at the car boot sale); – the exhibition of vehicles; or – a travelling fair or circus (and the incidental parking of vehicles)
	A **right to park** vehicles (including trailers) in a car park or commercial garage	
	Granting a lease or licence to use land specifically for the **construction** of a garage, or for use solely for parking a vehicle	
	A lease or licence of a **purpose-built** car park	
	A **freehold sale** of a new (i.e. less than 3 years from completion) or partly completed garage, car park or car parking facility (although not if sold with a new dwelling (¶5522))	The freehold sale of garages, car parks or car parking facilities that are **not new** (i.e. at least 3 years from the date on which they were completed)
Other land	Lease of a **taxi** rank	
	Provision of storage for **bicycles** and touring **caravans**	

EXAMPLE

1. A lessor of lock-up garages did not account for VAT if lessees stated they were going to use them for storage.
It was held that the letting of lock-up garages implied the provision of parking facilities. The terms of the lease did not prohibit the parking of a vehicle, so parking facilities were provided. *C&E v Trinity Factoring Services Ltd* [1994]

2. The owner of a sports club leased some council land and sublet it to a football club. The land was used to access the sports ground by both spectators and emergency services, so it was not used for parking. This was held to be an exempt supply of land, not the provision of parking facilities. *KT Routledge* [2003] (VTD 18395)

3. An area of land was leased to a partnership, which used it as a car park for more than 5 years. However, the land could have been used for other purposes.
It was held that this was a supply of parking facilities. *C&E v Venuebest Ltd* [2003]

Parking provided with premises The supply of parking in conjunction with premises is treated differently, **depending on** the type of property involved. **5520**

MEMO POINTS 1. The supply of a garage or parking facility: Notice 742 para 4.6
– at a seasonal or holiday **caravan park** is always standard-rated;
– in conjunction with the sale of a **new caravan** is standard-rated; or

– in conjunction with the supply of a **permanent residential caravan pitch** is exempt, provided that the land is owned by the lessor and the garage or parking space is reasonably close to the caravan pitch.

Notice 742 para 4.7 2. The supply of a garage or parking space to a **houseboat** owner is also exempt, provided that the supply of both the parking facilities and mooring is made by the same person and the facilities are reasonably close to the mooring.

5522 Notice 742 para 4.4 The provision of parking facilities provided with a **new dwelling** (¶5152) is never standard-rated, as:
a. the sale or long lease of a garage or parking space by the person constructing a new dwelling is zero-rated; or
b. the letting of garages or parking spaces in conjunction with the letting of dwellings for permanent residential use is exempt, provided that both:
– the garage or parking space is reasonably near to the dwelling; and
– the tenant takes up both the lease of a dwelling and the lease of a garage from the same landlord.

Where a **garage** is **let separately** it will be standard-rated. For example, a tenant purchases a council house but not the attached garage, which continues to be rented. The rent of the garage alone will be standard-rated.

EXAMPLE Blocks of garages were constructed in conjunction with a Danish housing development and let to both residents and non-residents. The CJEU held that the garage lettings, which were closely linked to the exempt supply of property, were also covered by the exemption. *Skatteministeriet v Henriksen* [1989]

5524 Notice 742 para 4.5 The provision of parking facilities with **commercial premises** is treated as a single supply of the commercial premises, provided that the facilities are either:
a. on the premises, or reasonably nearby; or
b. within a complex and both lettings are to the same tenant by the same landlord - for example, an industrial park made up of separate units, with a communal car park for the use of the tenants and their visitors.

The sale or lease of commercial premises may **either** be exempt or standard-rated, so for:
– commercial property which is less than 3 years old see ¶5277; and
– older property see ¶5380.

Sports facilities

5526 Notice 742 para 5 The letting of facilities for the playing of any sport or for taking part in any physical recreation is standard-rated.

There are two **exceptions**, in which case exemption applies, where the let is:
– made to the same person for a continuous period of at least 24 hours and that person has exclusive control of the facilities; or
– part of a series of at least ten sessions which satisfies particular conditions.

See also the *Abbotsley Golf & Squash Club* case at ¶5374.

5528 MEMO POINTS 1. Sports facilities are **designed or adapted** for the playing of any sport or taking part in any physical recreation - for example:
– swimming pools;
– football pitches;
– dance studios; and
– skating rinks.
Each court or pitch (or lane in the case of a bowling alley, swimming pool or curling rink) is a separate sports facility.
2. The **conditions**, which must all be met for the let to be treated as a **series** of sessions, are that:
a. the **lessee**:
– is a school, club, association or an organisation representing affiliated clubs or constituent associations, such as a local league; and
– has exclusive use of the facilities during the sessions;

b. each **session** is for the same sport or activity and is in the same place (a different pitch, court or lane, or different number of pitches, courts or lanes is acceptable), although each session may be of a different duration;
c. the **interval between** each session is at least 1 day but not more than 14 days (even where the facility has to close for any reason); and
d. the series is **paid for** as a whole, supported by written evidence which stipulates that payment is to be made in full whether or not the right to use the facility for any specific session is actually exercised. However, a refund may be provided where unforeseen circumstances mean that the facility is unavailable.
3. HMRC now accepts that organisers of five-a-side football leagues make separate supplies of pitch hire (exempt if the conditions are met) and league organisation (standard-rated).

Spectator seats

The grant or assignment of any right to occupy a box, seat or any other accommodation at a sports ground, theatre, concert hall or any other place of entertainment is standard-rated. **5530** Notice 742 para 3.4

This rule applies even where the **entertainment is not in progress** when the seat is occupied.

The letting of an **entire property** (e.g. theatre, cinema, concert hall) will be exempt, subject to the option to tax (¶5602).

Gaming and fishing rights

The right to take game or fish from land is normally standard-rated. **5532** Notice 742 para 6

Where the sporting rights **form part of a supply of land**, the VAT treatment may follow the VAT rating of the land - for example:
– the sale of sporting rights as part of the freehold sale of the land over which those rights may be exercised, in which case the whole supply is exempt; or
– the leasing of land together with sporting rights over that land, where the sporting rights do not exceed 10% of the value of the whole supply, in which case the whole supply is exempt. If this value is exceeded, the rights are standard-rated and treated as a separate supply, requiring a fair apportionment of the consideration.

Shooting rights There are exceptions to the standard-rating of rights. **5534** Notice 742 para 6.3

A landowner may make all the necessary arrangements to stock the land with game and decide who participates in a shoot (and therefore keep overall control).

Landowners who receive **contributions from participants** (to help with provision of the shoot) may not be making a business supply if:
– only friends and relatives are involved;
– there is no public advertising; and
– the activity results in an annual loss at least equal to the usual contribution made by a participant each year, which loss is borne by the landowner personally. *C & E v Lord Fisher* [1981]

In this case there is no supply for VAT purposes, which means no input tax can be recovered in respect of the expenses of the shoot.

A **syndicate** set up for individuals to contribute towards sharing the shooting expenses is not normally making a supply of sporting rights to its members. **5536**

However, where non-members are allowed to shoot and regular payment is made to the syndicate, this is a business activity and the syndicate would be making taxable supplies.

Where the **landowner is a member** of a syndicate and grants shooting rights to that syndicate for less than their normal value, VAT must be accounted for on the open-market value of those rights. Other supplies, such as the provision of a gamekeeper or beater, are also VATable. Notice 742 para 6.3.3

Fishing rights The charges made in return for fishing rights and the supply of fish in a **still-water** fishery are standard-rated. **5538** Notice 742 para 6.4

There is an **exception** when a separate charge is made for **fish taken away**, in which case zero-rating applies, provided that:
- the customer can choose whether to take away the fish caught or to throw them back into the water; and
- the fish taken away are of a species generally used for food in the UK.

The letting of an **empty lake** to a person who will stock it with fish is a supply of the lake, not fishing rights. In this case the supply is exempt, subject to the option to tax (¶5602).

D. Lettings

5540 The VAT treatment of transactions between landlord and tenant will depend on the nature of the transaction.

The **grant** of a lease, other than the first grant of a long lease in certain buildings (see ¶5247 and ¶5382) is exempt from VAT, unless the lessor has opted to tax the building (¶5602).

The treatment of **subsequent supplies** under a lease, such as the payment of rent or the assignment of the lease, will be determined at the time of each transaction.

MEMO POINTS A partly exempt business, with turnover **exceeding £10 million** and which grants an interest in property to a connected person, will need to disclose the transaction to HMRC (¶3104).

1. Time of supply

5542 A lease with a **term** of up to 21 years (less than 20 years in Scotland) is a continuous supply of services for VAT purposes; the time of supply is determined under the rules discussed at ¶808.

For long leases of more than 21 years (at least 20 years in Scotland) see ¶5267.

2. VAT rating

5544 The VAT treatment of the various types of payments which can occur in a leasing situation has been the subject of much case law.

Summary

5546
Notice 742 para 10

Timing	Type of payment	Money flow	Usual VAT treatment	¶¶
Beginning the lease	Premium	From tenant to landlord	Exempt unless building opted	¶5550
	Inducement (reverse premium)	From landlord to tenant	Outside the scope	¶5548
	Rent-free period	None	Outside the scope	¶5552
During the lease	Rent	From tenant to landlord	Exempt unless building opted	¶5550
	Service charge	From tenant to landlord	Depends on situation	¶5556
	Lease variation	From tenant to landlord	Exempt unless building opted	¶5564
	Lifting of restrictive covenant	From tenant to landlord	Exempt unless building opted	¶5564

Timing	Type of payment	Money flow	Usual VAT treatment	¶¶
Ending the lease	Dilapidation payments	From tenant to landlord	Usually outside the scope	¶5566
	Surrender	From landlord to tenant	Exempt unless building opted	¶5568
	Reverse surrender	From tenant to landlord	Exempt unless building opted	¶5570
	Statutory compensation	From landlord to tenant	Outside the scope	¶5572
	Compulsory purchase	From authority to landowner	Exempt unless building opted	¶5574
Transferring the lease	Assignment	From incoming tenant to outgoing tenant	Exempt unless building opted	¶5576
	Reverse assignment	From outgoing tenant to incoming tenant	Standard-rated	¶5578
	Rent adjustment	Between two landlords or two tenants	Outside the scope	¶5580
	Vendor guarantee	Between two landlords	Outside the scope	¶5582
	Mortgage capping	From vendor to landlord	Outside the scope	¶5584

Inducement payments

Where the landlord pays the tenant in return for the latter agreeing to take on the lease, this is normally outside the scope of VAT. **5548** Business Brief 12/05

However, where the **tenant provides a benefit** to the landlord in return for the inducement payment, which is outside the normal lease terms, the tenant will be making a taxable supply. The landlord can only recover the related input tax if it has opted to tax the building.

MEMO POINTS 1. HMRC has stated that lease **obligations**, to which tenants are normally bound, do not constitute supplies. So most inducement payments will not be VATable.
2. Examples of **benefits** which would make the payment taxable include:
– carrying out building works to improve the property by undertaking necessary repairs or upgrading the property (excluding the use of improved materials as part of continuous repairs under a tenant-repairing lease);
– fitting out or refurbishing the property, which would normally be the landlord's responsibility; and
– acting as anchor tenant (although merely being present on a development does not cause a tenant automatically to become an anchor).
3. When making a decision in **unclear cases**, HMRC reviews all available documentation and does not assume that there has been a supply.

EXAMPLE A newspaper company took on a lease of five floors of Canary Wharf, with the option to lease a further four floors. In return, the landlord paid a total of £12m into a holding account, which was to be received by the tenant in instalments. The tenant accounted for output tax on this amount. During the next 2 years the tenant leased three more floors and repaid £1.4m in respect of the unwanted fourth floor. The tenant then claimed a repayment of the output tax because either:
a. the inducement payment was not a supply; or
b. the payment was made in return for an exempt supply.
It was initially held that the inducement payment was consideration for a supply of services made by the tenant. The case went as far as the CJEU, which held that the supply was one of advertising services, because the tenant's presence would attract other parties to take on leases in the building - that is, the company was acting as an anchor tenant. However, for general application, the CJEU also stated that a "tenant who undertakes, even in return for a payment from the landlord, solely to become a tenant and pay the rent does not, so far as that action is concerned, make a supply of services to the landlord". *C & E v Mirror Group plc* [2001]

Premiums and rent

Lease premiums and rental income are generally exempt from VAT. **5550**

In respect of commercial property, a landlord may decide to opt to tax (¶5602), which makes the supply standard-rated.

5552 Notice 742 para 10.2 **Rent-free periods** The grant of a rent-free period is usually not a supply, **unless** the tenant agrees to do something in return (i.e. gives non-monetary consideration).

Typical reasons for a rent-free period include:
- the tenant fits out the property before moving in and no rent is charged during this period; or
- the landlord wants to reduce the overall rental charge from the amount stated in the lease, which is useful when trying to attract new tenants.

5554 Where the **tenant carries out works** on the building in return for a rent-free period, this constitutes consideration for the landlord's supply of leasing. If the landlord has opted to tax the building, the landlord will be making a taxable supply, valued at the amount of rent which would have normally been charged. The tenant is deemed to be making a supply of the same value, as this is a barter transaction (¶1032).

Comment If the tenant is deemed to be making a **supply of services** to the landlord, the tenant should charge the landlord VAT on the value of the services i.e. the value of the rent-free period. If the landlord has not opted to tax the property, this VAT will be a cost, as it will be irrecoverable.

EXAMPLE A company let a sawmill to its associated company under the terms of a 25-year lease. The first 3 years of the lease were rent-free, during which time the tenant was required to carry out specific repairs, as set out in a written agreement.
It was held that the tenant had supplied services to the landlord, in respect of the repairs, for a consideration equal to the rental value of the premises over the rent-free period. *Ridgeons Bulk Ltd* [1992] (VTD 7655)

Service charges

5556 Notice 742 para 11 **Commercial property** Where the tenant pays a service charge to the landlord for the provision of **general** services required for the upkeep of the building as a whole, the VAT liability of the service charge will be the same as the VAT liability of the rent paid under the lease. So if the landlord has opted to tax the building, the service charge will be standard-rated, otherwise it will be exempt. The charges that fall under this provision are those paid in return for services connected with the external fabric or common parts of the building and which are levied as part of a common charge (even if invoiced separately).

MEMO POINTS 1. Services **provided to** a:
- freeholder;
- commonhold owner (¶5265); or
- holidaymaker who is occupying holiday accommodation (¶5502),

are standard-rated.

2. Services provided by a third party, who has **no ownership interest** in the building, directly to the landlord or tenant are standard-rated.

3. Where a **tenant**:
- **arranges the services** and collects the associated charge from other co-tenants, this is a standard-rated supply to the landlord; or
- merely **collects payments** from the other occupants for their share of the rent and charges, which are passed on fully to the landlord without the tenant retaining a commission, these can be treated as disbursements and generally would not be subject to VAT (¶7185).

HMRC Brief 67/09 4. Following a CJEU decision HMRC has confirmed that it still believes that an ancillary supply will follow the tax treatment of the main supply where it is a condition of the lease that the ancillary supplies are taken from the landlord. In this particular case the tenants had a choice to take the supply offered by the landlord or arrange a third party to perform cleaning services. *RLRE Tellmer Property* [2009]

5. That the VAT treatment of supplies for service charges depends on the facts of each individual case was confirmed by the CJEU in 2012. The Court noted that leasing of immovable property and supplies of services linked to that leasing may constitute a single supply (and thus be treated the same for VAT purposes). However, whilst the fact that the lease gives the landlord the right to terminate it if the tenant fails to pay the service charges supports the view that there is a single supply, it is not necessarily decisive. On the other hand, the fact that services could in principle be supplied by a third party is not decisive that there is not a single supply. It is for the national court to determine in each case whether or not there is a single supply. *Field Fisher Waterhouse LLP v HMRC* [2012]

Specific services paid for by the tenant may fall to be treated as: 5558 Notice 742 para 11.7
- further payments for the lease, so that the same VAT treatment applies as for rent;
- payments for identifiable services; or
- disbursements, where the landlord pays bills on behalf of the tenant, in which case any recharge is outside the scope of VAT (¶7185).

If the **tenant cannot recover VAT**, it will be preferable for any exempt supplies included within a taxable service charge, such as insurance, to be transferred into the tenant's own name and treated as disbursements. Alternatively, the tenant could arrange its own insurance directly, meaning it would not be charged VAT on the premiums.

The treatment of common services is summarised in the following table. 5560

Charge	Detail	VAT treatment
Insurance	Landlord is policyholder	Same as rent
	Tenant is policyholder	Disbursement
Rates	Landlord is rateable person	Same as rent
	Tenant is rateable person	Disbursement
Telephone	Landlord's name on bill (call charges, installation and line rental)	Standard-rated
	Tenant's name on bill	Disbursement
Reception and switchboard	Common part of premises	Same as rent
Office services	Included within lease terms and charge made irrespective of whether tenant uses them	Same as rent
	Separate charge levied	Standard-rated supply
Fixtures	Usually part of lease agreement	Same as rent
	Separate agreement	Standard-rated supply
Light and heat	Separate charge for unlimited supplies of power	Same as rent
	Based on tenant's actual consumption	Standard-rated supply (unless de minimis quantity, in which case reduced-rating may apply - see ¶1122)
Management charges	Looking after the whole site	Same as rent
Recreational facilities	Compulsory under terms of the lease	Same as rent

EXAMPLE A housing association occupied premises. A service charge was levied which included the provision of telephones and photocopying (and covered a collecting and return service).
It was held that the provision of the telephones was part of the exempt supply of the premises, because the charge did not relate to use. However, the photocopying service was a separate taxable supply, as the charge was based on use and therefore standard-rated. *Tower Hamlets Housing Action Trust* [2001] (VTD 17308)

Dwellings **Mandatory** service charges will be part of the main supply i.e. exempt. However, **optional** services (such as carpet cleaning) are standard-rated. 5562 Notice 742 para 12

Any **management fee**, levied by the landlord for collecting the service charge, is treated in the same way as the rental income.

If a separate charge is made in respect of **light and heat** and the supply is:
- unmetered, the charge should be treated in the same way as rent for VAT purposes; or
- metered, reduced-rating will apply (¶1116).

MEMO POINTS 1. Where a service charge is levied **to a freehold occupier**, it would normally be standard-rated. By concession, exemption will apply to charges made for the following:
a. the upkeep of the common areas of a:
- housing estate, such as paths, driveways and communal gardens; or
- block of flats, such as lift maintenance, corridors, stairwells and general lounges;

b. general maintenance of the exterior of the block of flats or individual dwellings, if the residents cannot refuse this; and
c. provision of an estate warden, house manager or caretaker.
It is important to note that this concession is not obligatory, so the service provider can still choose to charge VAT in order to recover its related input tax.
2. The concession in **1**. above also applies to charges made by a **commonhold** association for services provided directly to the unit-holders.
3. If a **managing agent** acts on behalf of the landlord, the service charges will be exempt, provided that the agent invoices and collects the service charges directly from the occupants. Any management fee collected from the occupants is standard-rated, because it relates to the managing agent's supply to the landlord.
4. Where a **tenant-controlled management company or commonhold association** has purchased the freehold of the estate, it will often be bound by the terms of the lease to maintain the common areas of the estate (or provide a warden), so it will engage a service provider to meet this obligation. In this case, if the occupants are invoiced by, and pay the service charges directly to, the service provider, the service charges may still be treated as exempt. Any management fee collected from the occupants is standard-rated.

Lease variations

5564 Notice 742 paras 10.5, 10.6

The tenant pays the landlord to accept a variation to the lease terms.

Provided that there is not a **significant change** in the lease, the old lease is treated as continuing, so the landlord is making an exempt supply, unless it has opted to tax the building.

Common **examples** of minor changes include:
- extending the lease term;
- the lifting of a restrictive covenant; and
- the tenant indemnifying the landlord for any professional fees incurred in relation to a lease assignment, a subletting, or an alteration to the building.

If there is **no consideration**, there is no supply.

Dilapidation payments

5566 Notice 742 para 10.10

Often a lease will include a term which requires the outgoing tenant to reimburse the landlord for the cost of restoring the property to its former condition.

Any payment made:
- **after the lease has ended** represents compensation and so is outside the scope of VAT; or
- **during the lease** could be regarded as consideration for a taxable supply of services by the landlord.

Lease surrenders

5568 Notice 742 para 10.3

In this case, the landlord pays the tenant for surrendering the lease.

The **tenant** will be making an exempt supply, unless it has opted to tax the building which is the subject of the lease. *Lubbock Fine & Co v C & E* [1993]

Reverse surrenders

5570 Sch 9 Group 1 Item 1 VATA 1994; Notice 742 para 10.4

In a depressed market, where the landlord will find it difficult to re-let a property, a tenant may be required to pay the landlord in return for accepting the surrender of the lease.

The **landlord** is making an exempt supply, unless it has opted to tax the building which is the subject of the lease.

Statutory compensation

5572 Notice 742 para 10.7

Compensation **paid under the terms of** the:
- Landlord and Tenant Act 1954;
- Agricultural Holdings Act 1986; or
- Agricultural Tenancies Act 1995,

is outside the scope of VAT, provided that a "notice to quit" under the relevant statutory procedure is served by the landlord and complied with by the tenant.

Such compensation might, for example, relate to residuary milk quotas.

Additional payments by the landlord would be consideration for a supply of services by a business tenant, which would be exempt unless the tenant opted to tax the property. Such a payment may be made in return for the tenant vacating the property early.

Compulsory purchase

A government authority (local or central) can requisition a piece of land in return for payment. **5574**

In this case the VAT treatment of the sale follows the usual rules for disposals (see either ¶5245 for new buildings or ¶5380 for existing buildings and land-only parcels).

Assignments

If an incoming tenant pays an outgoing tenant to assign the lease, this is a **supply by** the outgoing tenant. The supply will be exempt unless the outgoing tenant has opted to tax the property. **5576**

Reverse assignments

Under a reverse assignment a tenant pays a third party to take on an **onerous lease**. **5578** Notice 742 para 10.1

This is a taxable supply by the third party.

EXAMPLE

1. A company agreed to take on a sublease and received £1.5m from the occupying tenant. The CJEU held that the supply could not be exempt, because the company had no interest in the property. The company was making a taxable supply of services. *C & E v Cantor Fitzgerald International* [2001]

2. Another case involved **virtual assignments**, whereby all of the economic benefits and burdens of the lease were transferred, but legal title was retained by the "assignor". The assignor remained in occupation and paid a fee which was equivalent to rent it would have paid if there had been a formal leaseback.
However, it was held that the payments made by the occupier to the third party were not the equivalent of rent, so standard-rating applied. *Abbey National plc v HMRC* [2006]

Rent adjustments

Rent adjustments allow the usual rent due for a period to be apportioned between two parties. **5580** Notice 742 para 10.9

Such adjustments may occur in **two situations**, either between:
- landlords on the sale of tenanted property; or
- tenants on the assignment of a lease.

These adjustments are outside the scope of VAT. Any payment does not affect the consideration given for the sale or assignment.

Vendor guarantees

In the event that **tenants cannot be obtained**, a property vendor will often guarantee to pay a purchaser the open-market rent of the property. **5582**

In such a case there is no supply by the purchaser in return for the payment, so it is outside the scope of VAT. However, if the sale agreement actually stated that the guarantee was:
- connected to the purchaser taking the property, a supply would be made by the purchaser as for inducement payments (¶5548); or
- a reduction in the sales price, the consideration received by the vendor for the property disposal would be reduced.

Mortgage capping

5584 A vendor may also agree to pay the additional expense to the purchaser of a **rise in interest rates**. Such a payment is outside the scope of VAT.

EXAMPLE A developer entered into a mortgage capping agreement with a tenant, which stated that the developer would pay any mortgage interest above 12% incurred by the tenant.
It was held that the payments made under this agreement were not consideration for a supply and did not constitute an inducement. *Iliffe N and D C Holloway* [1993] (VTD 10922)

E. Option to tax

5602 Sch 10 VATA 1994; Notice 742A The option to tax, also historically known as the election to waive exemption, allows traders in certain circumstances to choose to make taxable rather than exempt supplies. This will usually be beneficial where there is input tax to be recovered, but the position of the recipient of the supply must be considered too.

Overview

5604 When a trader opts to tax land certain **supplies** that would normally be exempt will become standard-rated for at least the next 20 years. The option to tax is made in relation to land (which includes buildings). When opting to tax a trader can specify an area of land or a building (but not part of a building).

A trader could exercise its option to allow the recovery of **input tax** that would otherwise be lost because exempt supplies are being made (e.g. rent received or sales proceeds, including any unwelcome capital goods scheme adjustment), or to ensure that a transaction meets the transfer of a going concern requirements (¶8664).

An option to tax can be made at any **time**. However, it should be noted that in some circumstances HMRC's permission is required (¶5678).

It may be **beneficial** to opt to tax if substantial costs are going to be incurred e.g. if a trader has purchased an existing commercial building and intends to refurbish it. Delaying making an option can restrict input tax recovery.

This subject is covered as follows:

Subject	¶¶
Consequences	¶5608
Scope	¶5618
Unaffected supplies	¶5638
Who can exercise the option?	¶5656
How to exercise the option	¶5666
Opting more than one property	¶5688
Revocation	¶5690

5606 Comment Theoretically, the option to tax gives the trader a **choice**, although commercially it may be forced to adopt a certain position.
The trader should consider the **position of a** current and/or potential **tenant or** a potential **purchaser** when deciding whether to opt to tax. If the tenant or purchaser cannot recover the VAT charged, opting to tax may not be a good commercial decision. Obviously the trader could charge a lower rent or purchase price in this case, so that the overall cost remains the same to the tenant or purchaser and the trader can still recover input tax.
There is generally a contractual obligation to inform the other party in a transaction of the existence (or not) of an option.

1. Consequences

An option to tax has consequences for: 5608
- future supplies;
- registration requirements; and
- input tax recovery.

Future supplies

Once the trader has opted to tax, all future supplies (such as leases or sales) in connection 5610
with its **particular interest** in the property must be standard-rated, unless:
- the supply is one that is not affected by the option (¶5638); or
- the option has been revoked (¶5690).

Therefore, any future letting or disposal of the property will be taxable. Further, any **stamp duty land tax** liability (which falls on the purchaser or tenant) will be increased, as it is based on the **VAT-inclusive** amount.

Where a tenant **sublets** a property, this is a different interest from the landlord's interest. Any rent payable under the sublease will be exempt, unless the tenant itself opts to tax. If such a tenant is incurring input VAT because the landlord has opted, the tenant will have to opt to tax its own interest in the building and charge VAT on the sublease, if it wishes to recover the input tax.

MEMO POINTS 1. Any **lease agreement** should be checked to ensure that an option can be made and that the rent can be increased for the related VAT. If there is no mention of these issues in the lease terms, the landlord can unilaterally decide to opt without the tenant's permission.
2. Where **rent arrears** are received and the option to tax is made after the rent becomes due Notice 742A
but before it is paid, output tax must be accounted for. This is the case even if the payment covers para 10.3
a period before the option to tax took effect. So it is important to be aware of any outstanding rent payments.
3. A **stamp duty land tax** charge would not be affected by an option made subsequent to a transaction. For details of stamp duty land tax see *Tax Memo*.

Requirement to register

If the trader is not already registered, it is likely that an option to tax would make registration 5612
either compulsory (¶2640) or at least advantageous. The administration costs of VAT registration should be considered before an option to tax is exercised, to evaluate whether the extra cost would outweigh any benefit of opting.

On any subsequent **deregistration**, output tax will need to be declared on the value of the Notice 742A para 12
opted property at the date of deregistration (¶8607). The option to tax continues even while the trader is not registered, so if a subsequent increase in turnover results in compulsory registration, the option to tax will still have effect.

Input tax recovery

Once a person has opted to tax, input tax recovery will **depend on** the liability of the supplies 5614
being made, in accordance with the normal rules (¶2075). Notice 742A para 9

Input tax cannot be recovered on **pre-option costs** (i.e. those incurred before the option has been exercised) **unless**:
- the sale of the building is taxable in its own right - for example, the sale of a commercial building within 3 years of completion;
- HMRC gives permission (¶5678); or
- the person had a clear intention to make taxable supplies when the input tax was incurred, supported by adequate documentary evidence.

Pre-option costs that are **not consumed** before the option is exercised will be available for adjustment under the partial exemption rules.

The capital goods scheme (¶5750) is likely to apply.

MEMO POINTS 1. **Evidence of intention** should include documents involving third parties that 5616
consistently show a firm commitment to make taxable supplies, such as: Business Brief 14/04

– a signed agreement which states that the vendor will opt to tax;
– a business plan accepted by a bank which confirms that taxable supplies will be made; or
– professional advice which recommends the option and confirmation that the trader accepts this advice.

HMRC states that the best evidence of taxable intention remains an effective option to tax.

2. Under the **partial exemption** rules, where there is a change from the original intended use within 6 years, an adjustment must be made. For example, a property may have been intended to be used for wholly exempt supplies and never actually used until Year 4, when an option to tax is made, so that taxable supplies therefore result. Where an intention changes before costs are used, the original VAT attribution may need to be adjusted (¶2224).

3. **Property developers** often consider many sites in connection with a taxable project and it may be impractical to immediately opt them all (although a real estate election (¶5688+) could be considered). There are particular requirements for a developer who registers for VAT as an intending trader (¶2692).

HMRC states that as projects progress, the weight of evidence needed to substantiate a continuing taxable intention without an actual option will increase; where a trader is actively marketing a property HMRC views the lack of an option as strong evidence that a taxable intention does not exist. If it is not clear what type of supplies will be made, the input tax should be treated as residual VAT, relating to the business as a whole (¶2110).

4. For the treatment of **aborted projects** see ¶2228.

5. For the recovery of **pre-registration input tax** see ¶8560.

EXAMPLE

1. An insurance group held the leasehold of a number of properties which had been occupied for exempt use, but were then vacant. Subsequently the properties were opted. An input tax claim was made in relation to the rent paid before the option took effect, while the properties were vacant. Initially, this input tax had been attributed to exempt supplies.

It was held that there were separate supplies of rent each time a payment was made and while the properties were vacant, the input tax could not relate to a taxable supply. The initial intention had been to make exempt supplies and a subsequent failure to make exempt supplies does not create a right to input tax deduction. However, HMRC's practice now is to treat such input tax as residual (see memo point **3.** above). *Royal and Sun Alliance Insurance Group plc v C & E* [2003]

2. A developer reclaimed input tax on speculative costs relating to a potential development. The project was abandoned due to a failure to obtain the required planning permission and the site was never purchased. HMRC disputed the input tax claim.

It was held that throughout the period when the speculative costs were incurred, the developer intended to opt to tax the land. So the input tax claim was valid. *Beaverbank Properties Ltd* [2003] (VTD 18099)

2. Scope

5618 Sch 10 para 18 VATA 1994

The option to tax **applies to** land; for this purpose, land **includes** buildings. The trader must specify an area of land or a building which is to be opted; this can include land where the option will have no effect, or could be disapplied (¶5638).

Normally a building will be specified. In such a case the option to tax will continue to apply to the land on which the building stood if the building is demolished and to any future buildings constructed on the land.

If the owner's **interest in the land subsequently changes** e.g. from leasehold to freehold, the option still has effect.

MEMO POINTS It is particularly important that the **geographical scope** of the election is clear to both the trader and HMRC. Attaching a copy of the Land Registry Title plan to the option to tax is the best way of confirming its scope.

Land

5620 An option to tax on a plot of land applies to the land and any existing or future buildings on the land, unless the option is revoked (¶5690).

Sch 10 para 27(4) VATA 1994

Where a **building is subsequently constructed** on opted bare land, the option will automatically extend to the new building and there is no need to re-opt. However, in situations where tenants (if the building is let) or the purchaser (where it is sold) cannot recover VAT, the trader may choose to **exclude** a new building from the effect of the option and pay back some of the VAT it has recovered.

Traders who wish to exclude a new building (and the land within its curtilage - see ¶5626) from the effects of an option to tax must **notify HMRC** (on form VAT 1614F) within 30 days of the earlier of completion, first grant or first occupation of the new building. Otherwise the option will continue to apply to the land and any other existing buildings, subject to the 20-year revocation rule. HMRC has discretion to allow a longer period for notification in certain cases. A fresh option can still be made in the future.

Buildings

Usually it will be clear what constitutes the "building". However, in some cases more than one building can be treated as being a single "building" for the purposes of the option to tax (¶5630). It is not possible to opt only **part of a building**. Nor is it possible to make an option only for a **future building**. If a trader wishes to opt to tax a new building that will be built in place of an unopted existing building, it must wait until the existing building has been demolished to opt to tax the site. **5622**

Surrounding land Any option to tax will cover the whole of the building, plus its **curtilage** (the land under and immediately around that building), such as a forecourt or yard. **5626** Notice 742A para 2.4

Where the building stands in a **large area** of land, the scope of the option will depend on how far the services of the building can be utilised. For example, a racecourse grandstand may provide electricity and shelter for stalls, or other facilities, within its peripheral area. An option to tax on the grandstand would extend over the whole area of land that uses these services.

Interest The option will extend to the trader's whole interest in the building, including any **subsequent acquisitions** in the same building. See ¶5690 for details of automatic revocation of an option when the trader ceases to have an interest in the property. **5628**

Comment The rules refer to the term **relevant interest**, which means an interest in, right over, or licence to occupy all or part of the property. For simplicity, the term "interest" is used in the following paragraphs.

EXAMPLE Ms B currently owns three floors of a ten-storey building. She opts to tax. If Ms B then acquires another four floors, so that her total interest is over seven floors, the option automatically covers all of these floors.

Adjacent property For the purposes of an option, two or more buildings will be **covered by the same option to tax** where: **5630** Sch 10 para 18(4) VATA 1994; Notice 742A paras 2.2, 2.3

- they are, or if not yet built are planned to be, linked; or
- they form a complex consisting of a number of units grouped around a fully enclosed concourse, such as a shopping mall.

In effect, a single property is being opted.

MEMO POINTS 1. Buildings are **linked** where there is an internal access or a covered walkway between the buildings, so that goods and people can move through both.

2. The following **do not constitute a link** for this purpose:
- a car park, either above or below ground;
- a public thoroughfare; or
- a statutory requirement, such as a fire escape.

Enlarging HMRC offers the following guidance in respect of when an existing option will continue to have effect. **5634** Sch 10 para 18(6) VATA 1994; Notice 742A para 2.6

Enlargement	Consequence for option
Extension in any direction	Applies to the whole of the extended building
Linked to another building	Does not affect the other building, unless a single building is created (¶5630)
Complex created from a number of units	Option will not cover any unopted units

5636 If there is **any doubt** whether the option covers the enlargement, and this is required, a fresh option should be notified.

3. Unaffected supplies

5638 Certain land or buildings are unaffected by an option to tax. This **means** that the supply of such land or buildings will either be exempt or outside the scope of VAT, rather than standard-rated.

Where, as a consequence, the supply is **exempt**, the vendor or landlord cannot recover associated input VAT and may wish to increase the asking price or rent to reflect the VAT cost. The following paragraphs detail the situations where the option does not apply.

The only situation where an opted property can be transferred **outside the scope** of VAT is as part of a transfer of a going concern (TOGC), in which case specific conditions must be met (¶8664).

Supplies excluded from the effect of an option

5640

Type of land or building	Exceptions where option has effect	¶¶
Buildings (or parts of) intended for use as a dwelling or solely for a relevant residential purpose	Vendor not notified that non-residential property is to be converted into a residence	¶5642
Buildings (or parts of) intended for use solely for a relevant charitable purpose	Buildings used as an office	¶5646
Pitches for permanent residential caravans	If occupation throughout the year is prevented by a covenant or statutory planning consent	
Moorings or berthings for residential houseboats	If occupation throughout the year is prevented by a covenant or statutory planning consent	
Land supplied to a registered housing association when the land will be used for the construction of dwellings or relevant residential buildings		¶5648
Land supplied to an individual who will build a dwelling on it for its own use (a DIY housebuilder)		¶5650
Land subject to anti-avoidance rules where intended to be occupied for non-taxable use		¶5652

Intended for residential use

5642 Sch 10 para 5 VATA 1994; Notice 742A paras 3.2 - 3.4

If the immediate purchaser or tenant **informs** the trader that the intention is to use the building (which is designed as a dwelling or a number of dwellings):
- as a dwelling (¶5152); or
- solely for a relevant residential purpose (¶5158),

the option to tax is disapplied and the supply will be exempt.

If the vendor is **not informed**, the option will apply.

Notice 742A para 3.10

Where the purchaser or tenant will be **using** the building **partly** for commercial and partly for residential purposes (e.g. a flat above a shop), the commercial part can be opted. In that case the consideration for the supply will need to be apportioned on a fair and reasonable basis.

Conversions An option to tax is disapplied if a building, which is not already used as a dwelling, is sold to a purchaser who has **certified** that it has an intention to convert the building into a dwelling. **5644** Sch 10 para 6 VATA 1994; Notice 742A para 3.4

If the **purchaser** wishes to disapply the vendor's option to tax, it must give the vendor confirmation of this in writing, on form VAT 1614D, **before** the price for the grant has been legally fixed - that is, the date:
- of exchange of contracts, letters or missives; or
- when heads of terms are signed.

If the vendor receives the certificate **subsequently**, it is at the vendor's discretion whether to accept it or not. If the certificate is accepted, the option to tax will be disapplied from the date the vendor receives the certificate, so any supplies made under the contract prior to that date will be subject to VAT.

Comment There is often **conflict between potential purchasers and vendors** in relation to these rules.
Vendors or landlords often want the option to tax to apply, as they may have recovered VAT relating to the property which may need to be repaid if the option is disapplied. Conversely, the potential purchaser, or existing tenant, may be keen to disapply the option because:
- it may not be able to recover the VAT;
- even if the VAT is recoverable, cash flow will be adversely affected, as the initial payment of VAT must be funded; and
- the stamp duty land tax charge will be higher on a taxable purchase.

EXAMPLE Mr A is in negotiations with Ms B in relation to the sale of a freehold interest in an office block on which he has exercised his option to tax. Mr A and Ms B agree a price and exchange contracts on 20 June. The price has become legally fixed. On 25 June Ms B sends Mr A form VAT 1614D, confirming that she wishes to disapply Mr A's option to tax, as she intends to convert the building into a block of apartments.
Mr A can decide whether he wishes to accept Ms B's disapplication. Mr A incurred £300,000 plus VAT of £52,500 constructing an extension to the building 5 years ago. The building is therefore a capital goods scheme item (having cost in excess of £250,000 and it being within the first 10 years of the building's life) and if Mr A accepted Ms B's certificate, he would have to make a capital goods scheme adjustment, because the sale would be exempt. Mr A would therefore have to repay VAT previously recovered.
If Ms B intends to grant a major interest in the property (for example, a long lease), once she has converted the building, she should be able to recover any VAT Mr A charges her on the sale. Alternatively, if Ms B intends to keep the building as an investment and let the apartments, the VAT charge would represent a cost, as her future use of the building would be exempt.

It is possible to have a **chain of certificates**, so it is no longer just the immediate purchaser who must have the intention to convert the building. However, the certificates must be issued chronologically up the chain before the option can be disapplied, which may prove time-consuming from a commercial point of view. For example, if A sells to B who sells to C, C must first issue a certificate to B confirming its intention to convert, before B can issue a certificate to A confirming that it is selling the building on to a party which intends to convert. **5645** Notice 742A para 3.4.5

Of course, if the purchaser wishes the **option to tax to apply**, so making the supply taxable, it should not issue a certificate to the vendor.

Comment The issuing of certificates up a supply chain will clearly cause problems if the supply chain is not known in advance.

Intended charitable use

If the purchaser or tenant informs the trader that it intends to use the building solely for a relevant charitable purpose (¶5170), the option to tax cannot apply. **5646** Sch 10 para 7 VATA 1994; Notice 742A para 3.5

However, where part of a building will be used as an **office**, the option to tax can apply, unless the office use is merely incidental.

HMRC Brief 33/10 HMRC accepts that **use solely** for charitable purposes means in practice use at least 95% for charitable purposes. However, the option to tax can only be excluded by a charitable purchaser or tenant if use is actually solely for charitable purposes. HMRC has therefore announced that where use is 95% or more for charitable purposes, the option can only be excluded where the customer and supplier agree that it should be.

Where the purchaser or tenant will be using the building **partly** for commercial and partly for charitable purposes, the option can apply to the commercial part. The consideration for the supply would need to be apportioned on a fair and reasonable basis.

Comment HMRC does not specify what format should be used to inform the vendor that the intended use is charitable. Also, unlike the rules for the conversion of non-residential property to residential use, there is no requirement that this needs to take place before the price is legally fixed.

Supply to housing association

5648 Sch 10 para 10 VATA 1994; Notice 742A para 3.6

If a relevant housing association wishes to disapply the vendor's option to tax, it must complete form VAT 1614G and give it to the vendor **before** the price for the transaction has been fixed. As is the case for intended conversions, if the **vendor** receives the certificate after this point, it is at its discretion whether to accept it or not. If accepted, the option to tax will be disapplied from the date the vendor receives the certificate, so any supplies made under the contract prior to this date will be subject to VAT.

MEMO POINTS A **relevant housing association** is a registered:
- social landlord within the meaning of Part 1 of the Housing Act 1996;
- social landlord within the meaning of the Housing (Scotland) Act 2010; or
- housing association within the meaning of Part 2 of the Housing (Northern Ireland) Order 1992.

Private providers of social housing registered under Part 2 of the Housing and Regeneration Act 2008 also qualify.

5649 Comment This rule may cause some vendors to refuse to sell to housing associations, because of the consequent loss of input tax recovery. A potential solution is for a developer to sell a partly constructed property to a housing association (i.e. some construction works have taken place (¶5120)); the parties also enter into another agreement for completion of the building, so that zero-rating might apply. This would enable the developer to recover input tax. This is commonly referred to as the "golden brick" scheme.

DIY housebuilders

5650 Sch 10 para 11 VATA 1994; Notice 742A para 3.7

The option to tax does not apply in respect of supplies of land to persons who will build dwellings on them for their own **use**, other than in the course or furtherance of any business carried on by them.

For further information about the DIY housebuilders' scheme see ¶5316.

Anti-avoidance

5652 Sch 10 para 12 VATA 1994; Notice 742A para 13

An anti-avoidance measure applies to each transaction involving a property, as a result of which an option to tax will not have effect where:

a. the transferor intends or expects that the property will be **occupied by** any of the following:
- the transferor (subject to a 2% de minimis occupation exclusion);
- a person responsible for funding the transaction (subject to a 10% de minimis occupation exclusion); or
- a person connected with either of them (subject to the same, respective, occupation exclusions as above);

Sch 10 para 15 (2) VATA 1994; Notice 742A para 13.9

b. the occupant will be **making** supplies which are not wholly or substantially wholly for eligible purposes (HMRC states that up to 20% exempt use qualifies as "substantially wholly"); and

c. the building is (or will become) a capital item within the **capital goods scheme** (¶5750).

This potentially affects a wide range of transactions, including lease assignments as well as the granting of a land interest.

EXAMPLE Ms C owns a freehold and grants a lease to Mr D. Mr D grants a sublease to E Ltd. E Ltd assigns this lease to F Ltd. All parties opt to tax the property.
The anti-avoidance test must be considered for each transaction.

MEMO POINTS 1. HMRC tests **intention or expectation** by reviewing commercial documents, minutes of meetings, business plans and finance requests. **5654**
2. Following the House of Lords decision in the case of *Principal and Fellows of Newnham College in the University of Cambridge v HMRC* (see below), HMRC now accepts that physical presence on its own is not the correct test of **occupation**. To be in occupation, there must also be the right to occupy as if that person is the owner and has the ability to exclude others. HMRC Brief 33/09
3. **Eligible purposes** for this anti-avoidance provision means use by: Notice 742A para 13.9.2
- a taxable person in making taxable supplies;
- government, or the NHS; and
- a local authority for non-business purposes.

Occupation that arises only because of an ATM (cashpoint) fixed to the land is treated as being for eligible purposes.
4. A person is only **deemed to have been responsible for financing** where the funds are provided for this particular purpose and at the time that the finance was provided, it intended that the property would be occupied for non-taxable use.
Funding includes directly or indirectly:
- providing all or part of the funds for the development;
- obtaining those funds from another person;
- providing the funds for discharging all or part of the owner's borrowing for the development; or
- procuring that such a liability will be discharged by another.

Finance could take many different forms, such as loans, guaranteeing loans, share issues or premium deals.
5. For the definition of **connected persons** see ¶962+.
6. For **lease assignments** the assignor is treated as if it had made a new grant. Even if the assignment occurs after the period of adjustment under the capital goods scheme, it will still be treated as satisfying the capital item test **c.** above.
7. A **surrender and re-grant** of a lease affected by these rules may need to be disclosed to HMRC (¶3062).

EXAMPLE
1. A pension trustee purchased a property and was charged VAT because the vendor had opted to tax. The trustee then granted a lease to pension scheme members, who had funded the property's acquisition via their pension contributions and who occupied the property for an exempt purpose of insurance. The trustee opted to tax the property in order to recover its input tax but HMRC disapplied the option.
The trustee argued that the lease was a legitimate commercial transaction and there was no motive of avoidance.
Nonetheless, it was held that the transaction fell within the conditions of the anti-avoidance rule; it was irrelevant that there was no avoidance motive. The option was correctly disapplied. *Winterthur Life UK Ltd (No 2)* [1998] (VTD 15785)
2. A college wanted to build a new library, so to avoid incurring irrecoverable input tax on the construction costs, it formed a company and leased the new library to the company after opting to tax the building. The company was responsible for the day-to-day running of the library, including:
- looking after and maintaining the books which had been sold to it by the college;
- managing the staff (who were seconded from the college);
- controlling who had access to the library; and
- exercising disciplinary powers.

HMRC argued that the college's option to tax should be disapplied, as it was occupying the library itself, through the members and fellows of the college using the library on a daily basis.
It was held that as the college had no rights of possession, control or exclusive use of the facilities, it was not in occupation of the library and the option to tax was therefore effective. *The Principal & Fellows of Newnham College in the University of Cambridge v HMRC* [2008]

4. Who can exercise the option?

The option is personal to the taxable person and is not binding on anyone else. It is not necessary to be VAT-registered or even have a legal interest in the property - that is, a person may opt before acquiring property. **5656**

There are particular rules for the following situations:
- VAT groups;
- split of beneficial and legal ownership;
- joint owners; and
- limited partnerships.

Comment It is advisable to obtain specialist advice where the person who can opt is not clear; confirmation should always be requested from HMRC.

VAT groups

5658 Sch 10 para 3 VATA 1994; Notice 742A para 6.3

A group's option to tax **binds** any body corporate which is a relevant associate of the opter (A).

A **relevant associate** is a body corporate which is either:
- in the same VAT group as A when the option first has effect (this means that an option by any member of a VAT group will bind the other members);
- is a member of the same VAT group as A at a later date when A still holds an interest in the property; or
- is a member of the same VAT group as A, or a relevant associate (e.g. B) of A, when either A or B has an interest in the property.

EXAMPLE A Ltd opts to tax a property.

1. B Ltd is in the same VAT group as A Ltd, so B Ltd is bound by A Ltd's option.

2. C Ltd joins the same VAT group while A Ltd retains an interest in the opted property. C Ltd is bound by A Ltd's option.

3. The ABC group subsequently joins the DEF VAT group while retaining an interest in the opted property.
The entire VAT group is bound by A Ltd's option.

5659 Sch 10 paras 3, 4 VATA 1994; Notice 742A para 6.3.2

Ceasing to be a relevant associate It is possible for a body corporate to cease to be a relevant associate, and therefore no longer be bound by an option, in the following ways:

a. automatically, by fulfilling all of the following basic conditions (without needing to notify HMRC):
- the body corporate **leaves the VAT group** in which it became a relevant associate;
- it **does not have an interest** in the property, all of the consideration for the disposal of any interest made or to be made in the property has been paid, and the supply is unconditionally completed; and
- it is **no longer connected** (¶962) with the opter or any person who holds an interest in the property;

b. by **notifying** HMRC (using form VAT 1614B) that the following **specified conditions** are met:
- the body corporate has left the VAT group of the opter;
- the body corporate has held an interest in the property as a member of the VAT group for at least 20 years and has been treated as a relevant associate of the opter for at least 20 years;
- the property is not a capital item under the capital goods scheme (¶5750);
- neither the body corporate, nor a person connected to the body corporate, has within the preceding 10 years made a supply of an interest for less than market value, or made a relevant grant; and
- the body corporate has not prepaid for goods or services which can be attributed to a supply made from the property after it has ceased to be a relevant associate (the exception to this rule is if the prepayment relates to a period shorter than 12 months); or

c. by **requesting prior permission** from HMRC, but only if the first two specified conditions in **b**. above are satisfied. Form VAT 1614B should be used. If permission is granted, the body corporate will cease to be a relevant associate from the date specified. HMRC only has discretion to allow an earlier date where a previous erroneous notification was given and it is satisfied that the breach of the specific conditions is insignificant. In this case only, the date of cessation will be the date of the original notification.

MEMO POINTS A **relevant grant** means a grant that will result in a supply with increased consideration compared to the supplies made before the option is revoked e.g. a balloon payment made by a lessee to the landlord (who is revoking the option) which is scheduled to be paid after the date of the revocation. However, a rent review carried out in accordance with normal commercial practice will not be treated as a relevant grant for this purpose.

Split of beneficial and legal ownership

Where the beneficial owner and the legal owner are not the same person (for example, in a trust situation), it is **usually** the beneficial owner who must opt to tax. **5660** Notice 742A para 7.2

However, where the **beneficiaries are numerous**, in the context of unit trusts or pension funds for example, the person who should opt is the trustee who holds the legal interest.

Comment It is advisable to obtain expert legal advice where there is such a split in ownership

Joint owners

Joint ownership **can arise** where a property interest is acquired by more than one person, for example as tenants in common, or where a part of a property is disposed of to another person. In either case, all joint owners should **notify** a single option to tax. **5662** Notice 742A para 7.3

For **registration** purposes, the joint owners must register as a partnership (¶2734).

Limited partnerships

A limited partnership consists of at least one general and one limited partner (¶2736). **5664** Notice 742A para 7.4

Usually it is only the general partner(s) who can opt to tax.

However, where **title** to the property is **held jointly** in the names of both the general partner(s) and the limited partner(s), HMRC treats the limited partner(s) as a general partner and amends the VAT registration accordingly. So if the partnership decides to opt to tax, one or more of the partners should sign the notification.

5. How to exercise the option

There are two steps to opting to tax: **5666** Notice 742A para 4

a. deciding to opt; and

b. then notifying HMRC about it.

An option to tax only has effect if it is correctly notified. An option takes effect from the date it is exercised, or any later date specified in the election. Records of both the decision and notification should be kept for at least 20 years.

Where any **exempt supplies** involving the land have **already been made** (e.g. rents received), special rules apply (¶5678).

Deciding to opt

Deciding to opt is an action taken by the person at a particular point in time, although no formal records may exist (i.e. an unspoken decision would suffice but may be difficult to prove). It is not possible to make a retrospective option. However, it is possible to make a belated notification (¶5674). **5668** Notice 742A para 4.1

Normally there will be some written document, such as minutes of a board meeting, or a letter written to HMRC making the notification, or a rent invoice showing a VAT charge.

It is important to **record** the scope of the option and also the date that the decision is made. Otherwise if an erroneous notification is made (¶5676), HMRC will have no choice but to treat the notification as evidence of the properties or land the business intended to exercise the option over

EXAMPLE The following occurred in relation to a building:
- let until August 1988;
- refurbished and empty from September 1988 to March 1990; and
- let again from March 1990.

In September 1990 notification was made of an option which was to take effect from 1 August 1989. However, the landowner also reclaimed input tax incurred between August 1988 and August 1989.
It was held that the option could only take effect from 1 August 1989. *Newcourt Property Fund* [1991] (VTD 5825)

Notifying

5670 Sch 10 para 20 VATA 1994; Notice 742A para 4.2

In all cases written notification (which can be made using form VAT 1614A) of the option must be given to HMRC within 30 days of the date of the election being made, signed by the appropriate person.

Acknowledgement of receipt will usually be provided within 15 days but the trader should not delay charging VAT just because no official communication has yet been received.

5672 Business Brief 3/06

MEMO POINTS 1. The **appropriate person** is usually the sole proprietor, a director, one or more of the partners, one or more of the trustees, or an authorised administrator. Only the trader itself can make the notification, unless a representative or employee has already been authorised by the trader. This safeguards against erroneous notifications.
2. The following **information** should be included in the notification:
- the identity of the land and buildings to be opted, with a map or plan if appropriate;
- the full postal address and postcode of the area to be opted;
- the VAT registration number (or VAT Registration Unit number if registration is pending); and
- the name and address of the person who is opting.

If no exempt supplies have been made in respect of the property, this should also be confirmed.
3. The notification should be **sent to** the Option to Tax Unit in Glasgow (Cotton House, 7 Cochrane St, Glasgow G1 1GY), except when the trader is:
- simultaneously registering for VAT, in which case a copy of the option to tax form should be sent to the regional VAT Registration Unit (note that a delay may ensue while HMRC undertakes additional checks (¶2708)); or
- not based in the UK, in which case the notification should be sent to the Non Established Taxable Persons Unit (¶9994).

UK registered traders can **fax** their notification to 0141 285 4454, or **email** a scanned copy to optiontotaxnationalunit@hmrc.gsi.gov.uk. If either of these options is used, a hard copy should still be sent by post as a safeguard.
4. If **transferring a going concern**, the date of notification is very important (¶8664).

5674 Business Brief 13/05

Late notifications A late notification can be made and will be **accepted** at HMRC's discretion, particularly if the trader has acted on the basis that the option has had effect (charged VAT on rental income, for example). This can of course work against the trader if it wishes to make an exempt sale of the property.

HMRC will **refuse** to effect the option in cases of avoidance, or where the trader's previous actions indicate no original intention to elect.

EXAMPLE

1. A company let a commercial property and charged VAT on the rent. On the subsequent sale, no VAT was charged.
The issue was whether, in the absence of a formal election, the company had opted to tax the property (it should be noted that at the time of this case, not all options had to be notified).
It was held that deciding to opt and notifying were two distinct steps. As the company could not have charged VAT on the rents unless an option had been made, the receipt of VAT on the rent was an act which meant that an option had been made. *Fencing Supplies Ltd* [1993] (VTD 10451)

2. A company owned seven department stores, of which certain parts were let to other parties. The tenants were told that an option to tax had been made, so VAT would be chargeable on the rents; the company accounted for output tax accordingly. A couple of years later the company went into receivership. No notification of the option was ever made.
It was held that the option was not valid, so the output tax should be repaid. *C & E v McMaster Scotland Stores Ltd (in receivership)* [1995]

3. A company purchased a property in September 1998 and part of it was leased out from October 1998. Although no notification of an option was made, VAT was charged on the rent. Some years later, the property was sold and again VAT was charged. A month after disposal, a late notification

was made of the option with an effective date of October 1998 and this was accepted. The purchaser disputed whether VAT should be charged on the disposal.
It was held that there was no set procedure for making an option. As VAT could only be charged if an option had been made, the initial rent demand which included VAT should be taken as making an election. It did not matter that the notification was made after the disposal of the property.
Marlow Gardner & Cooke Ltd Directors' Pension Scheme v HMRC [2006]

Mistaken or incorrect notifications HMRC tends to accept notifications at face value, because it takes the view that **checking the accuracy** of each and every written notification would create unnecessary delay. **5676** Business Brief 17/99

Where a notification is clearly wrong, or it is evident that prior written permission to opt is necessary, it will be invalid. This can include notifications made in error in respect of properties over which the owner never intended to exercise an option.

EXAMPLE

1. A limited partnership was formed on 25 September 1997 and acquired sixteen properties, four of which were opted by the vendor. In order to recover the input tax, the partnership intended that those four properties only would be opted. However, an option to tax notification in respect of all sixteen properties was submitted by the partnership's solicitors, although this was dated 22 September 1997 and signed by someone representing the general partner only. Subsequently, one of these properties was sold without charging VAT. The issue was whether all sixteen properties had in fact been opted and therefore whether VAT should have been charged on the sale.
It was held that the notification was inaccurate and did not bind the partnership. The actual election related to four properties only and the notification had no effect on the other twelve properties. Moreover, as the notification was made 3 days before the partnership came into existence, the partnership could not be bound by the notification. *Blythe Ltd Partnership* [1999] (VTD 16011)

2. A company purchased a property which the vendor had not opted. One of the sitting tenants was a charity whose lease stated that its payments were inclusive of VAT, so any VAT charge would reduce the company's rental income by 7/47 (as the standard rate of VAT at the time was 17.5%). The company could only register for VAT if an option was made, because otherwise it would not be making any taxable supplies.
The sequence of events was as follows:
- the company's accountants asked the director to sign a form VAT 1614 and registration forms (which indicated that the company wanted to opt), which he did without reading them;
- the option was notified with an effective date in August 2004;
- the company was registered for VAT from September 2004;
- the authorities contacted the director in October 2004 requesting information; and
- the accountants wrote in February 2005 saying that the notification was made in error.

The director stated that he thought he was signing VAT 1614 so that it could be kept on file for the future, but he never intended to opt.
It was held that the fact that the director had signed the forms implied that he knew what he was signing. He was authorised to make such a decision, whereas the accountants were not. The registration required an option to tax and the accountants were retained to effect the registration.
Windsor House Investments Ltd [2006] (VTD 19666)

Prior exempt supplies

Traders only need to seek HMRC's prior permission to opt if they have made exempt supplies during the **period** of 10 years prior to the date when the option to tax is to take effect, although there is an automatic approval process which dispenses with the need to make a formal request. **5678** Notice 742A para 5

EXAMPLE H Ltd owns an old warehouse which has already been rented out to a tenant for the past year. This income is exempt.
If H Ltd wants to opt the property before selling it, official permission must be obtained first.

Automatic approval If a trader falls within the terms of any one of the four **situations** below and complies with the relevant terms, the option to tax can be effected simply by **notifying** that option to HMRC on form VAT 1614A, without the need to formally apply for permission. **5680** Notice 742A para 5.2

MEMO POINTS If the trader has incorrectly relied on automatic permission conditions as set out in a **previous notice**, the option can still be effective from the date it was originally made, provided that the current version of the conditions (since May 2009) would be satisfied.

Situation	Subcategory	Terms
The property is a mixed residential/ commercial development		The only exempt supplies made relate to the dwellings
The opter does not wish to recover input tax incurred before the option has effect		Both: – the consideration for the exempt supplies has (up to the date when the option is to take effect) been solely by way of rents or service charges[1]; and – the only input tax the trader wishes to recover (after the option takes effect) is on normal overheads (e.g. service charges, rental payments but not costs of refurbishment or redevelopment)[2]
Exempt supplies made are incidental to the main use of the land or property		Letting of space to an occupying tenant (however minor) is not incidental Incidental supplies include: – allowing an advertising hoarding to be displayed; – granting space for the erection of a radio mast; or – receiving income from an electricity substation
An outputs condition is met and, if applicable, the inputs condition also	**Outputs condition**	The opter does not intend or expect that any supply which becomes taxable as a result of the option will: **a.** be made to a connected person (¶962), unless that person will be entitled to recover at least 80% of the VAT on that supply; or **b.** arise from an agreement under which an exempt supply in respect of a right to occupy the property has been or will be made and that right begins or continues after the effective date of the option (although certain permissible exempt supplies[3] can be disregarded)
	Inputs condition (only applies where the person has been, or expects to be, entitled to deduct input tax incurred on capital expenditure on the property as a result of the option)	The person does **not intend or expect** to use any part of the capital expenditure for the purposes of **a.** or **b.** below: **a.** making **exempt supplies** which do not confer a right to input tax credit, **unless** either: – all the exempt supplies are either permissible exempt supplies[3], incidental financial supplies, or those listed in ¶5640 excluding the anti-avoidance situation; – the input tax incurred on capital expenditure on the property which is attributable to the exempt supplies will be less than £5,000; or – the opter expects to recover all of the VAT on capital expenditure on the property under the provisions in ¶7880; or **b.** for **private or non-business activities**, **excluding** those giving a right to a refund of VAT under the special rules for VAT recovery by public bodies (¶7878), museums and galleries and government departments

Note:
1. **Consideration cannot include** any premiums or payments in respect of occupation after the date on which the option takes effect.
For this purpose, **rents or service charges** includes regular payments i.e. where the intervals between them are no more than a year and where each represents a commercial or genuine arm's-length value.
2. HMRC has clarified that the following **input tax** should be **ignored** for this purpose:
– any input tax recovered under the partial exemption de minimis rules (¶2194);
– any input tax on general business overheads not specifically related to the land or building, such as audit fees; and
– refunds of VAT recovered by local authorities and similar bodies (¶7860).
3. **Permissible exempt supplies** means supplies where:
a. the only consideration is reimbursed legal and/or valuation costs; or
b. the consideration is regular rents and/or service charges; and
– it relates to a period of occupation of the property and that period ends no later than 12 months after the option takes effect; and
– no taxable rents and service charges to be made after that 12-month period will be reduced in value as a result of the consideration payable for these exempt supplies.

EXAMPLE A company leased a property to a tenant from 1 January 2003. On 1 July 2003 HMRC visited the company and an option to tax was mentioned. Subsequently, the company decided to opt to tax by notifying HMRC on 1 October 2003 (after some exempt rent had already been paid by the tenant). The property was sold on 2 August 2004 but no VAT was charged. HMRC subsequently raised an assessment for output tax.
The company appealed against the assessment, based on its assertion that the option to tax was invalid, as no written permission had been received from HMRC in advance. Such permission was required because exempt supplies had been made prior to the date of the option and none of the conditions for automatic approval had been met. In particular, the company wished to recover input tax which it stated would have exceeded the partial exemption de minimis limit.
It was held that the input tax incurred prior to any option to tax was likely to have been de minimis, particularly when excluding input tax relating to non-property items, such as the audit fee and site security, so one of the automatic approval conditions was satisfied. Hence the option to tax was valid and VAT should have been charged on the sale. *Ultrapolymers Ltd* [2010] (TC00324)

Permission required If none of the conditions for automatic approval is met, the trader must obtain written permission before opting, using form VAT 1614H. **Supplies made** while the request is being considered will remain exempt. The information required for the request is substantial. There is a right of appeal where permission is not granted. **5683** Notice 742A para 5

MEMO POINTS The **information required** will include the following:
– a brief description of the future plans for the property, should permission be granted;
– details of any input tax incurred in the 10 years before opting to tax which will need to be recovered (that is, the amount, how this has been calculated, what it relates to and when it was incurred, including the period between the request and the option date);
– the value of input tax expected to be incurred in the future if permission is granted and what this input tax will relate to (for example, rents, premiums, surrenders or refurbishments);
– the total value of exempt supplies of the property in the 10 years before the effective date of the option;
– an indication of any exempt grants which might occur after the option has taken effect - for example, where the option would be disapplied (¶5638); and
– whether the trader, anyone who has helped to fund the property, or anyone connected to the trader or funder is occupying or intending to occupy any part of the property (in case the anti-avoidance rule (¶5652) might apply).
HMRC may also ask for additional information.

The trader should include with the request a proposal as to how much **pre-option input tax** will be reclaimed. HMRC will want to ensure that there is a fair and reasonable apportionment of input tax between prior exempt supplies and future taxable supplies. Current HMRC practice is to take into account the 10-year span of the capital goods scheme (¶5750) when reviewing such a proposal. **5684**

The **effective date** of the option is usually a future date, to give HMRC time to consider the case. Where a trader has **mistakenly not sought permission** in time, HMRC is nonetheless able to waive the requirement for permission and validate an option. Notice 742A para 5.7

If permission **is granted**, the trader is not required to undertake the usual notification procedure. If no further exempt supplies of the property are made, the trader can reclaim the agreed amount of pre-option input tax on the first VAT return following the date of the option. This input tax may need subsequent adjustment under the capital goods scheme.

EXAMPLE
1. A Ltd grants a 20-year lease in a commercial property, which is an exempt supply. A Ltd incurred £40,000 of input tax on the purchase and refurbishment of the site.
A Ltd wants to opt to tax after 5 years have elapsed but must first obtain permission.
A Ltd includes a proposal of how the £40,000 of input tax should be apportioned between exempt and taxable supplies. This might be based on the lease term already elapsed, so that three quarters of the input tax would be recovered (15/20). However, HMRC might argue that only the first 10 years of the lease should be taken into account, so that only half of the input tax can be recovered.

2. The trustees of a pension fund constructed a commercial property and reclaimed input tax. Subsequently a 15-year lease was granted, which required the trustees to account for VAT under a self-supply (charging themselves VAT). The trustees opted to tax and claimed most of the VAT

on the self-supply, as the exempt lease had lasted for 16 months, whereas the expected life of the building was 150 years.
This claim was rejected, because no revised initial attribution of input tax was allowed, since the building was within the capital goods scheme. Only the remaining period of the first 10 years should have been taken into account (not 150 years).
It was held that if a trader opted, it was bound by the provisions of the capital goods scheme, which required a 10-year adjustment period. *C & E v Trustees for R & R Pension Fund* [1996]

6. Opting more than one property

Real estate elections

5688 Notice 742A para 14 Traders can make a real estate election (REE), the **effect** of which is to automatically opt to tax every new property interest acquired after the stipulated date, as a series of separate options to tax. Under an REE each property is treated as individually opted and all the normal rules for individual options apply. Traders can decide to individually revoke the option on each property if the relevant conditions are met. For example, if a person has made an REE but **does not wish a property** in which it acquires a relevant interest **to be opted**, it may revoke the option under the cooling-off provisions (¶5692) and the option would then be treated as though it had never been made.

Of course it may still be beneficial not to make an REE and just opt those interests which the trader actually wants to make taxable, rather than having to remember to cancel those options which should not have been made.

Sch 10 para 21(13) VATA 1994 MEMO POINTS 1. The **time when an interest is acquired** is the time when the supply (the acquisition of the land) is treated as taking place. If there is more than one such time, it is the earliest of those times which is relevant for the purposes of an REE. The fact that the supply of the land when acquired was treated as neither a supply of goods nor services, for example under the TOGC provisions (¶8660), is disregarded for these purposes.
2. Where the trader has **existing single options** to tax at the date that an REE is made, these are not affected. If, however, the trader does not hold an interest in a particular property at the time of making the REE, the previous option is then revoked subject to meeting certain conditions.
3. If a trader has an interest in any **unopted properties** at the date that the REE is made, they will not be affected by the REE; it will still be possible to opt to tax those properties in the normal way.

5689 REEs must be **notified** to HMRC, within 30 days of being made, on form VAT 1614E.

As a **condition** of the REE a trader must provide HMRC with a list of all properties (excluding dwellings) in which it has an interest, including unopted properties. HMRC can request a revised list of properties, or a list of acquisitions, disposals or conversions to dwellings, from the trader by giving 30 days' notice.

Whilst it is not possible for HMRC to **refuse** a trader permission to make an REE, it can withdraw the REE if the trader is non-compliant.

Comment A trader who is **acquiring a property as part of a TOGC** will need to make a single option to tax (in respect of that property) before the REE, because the REE can only take effect once an interest in the property is acquired.

7. Revocation

5690 Notice 742A para 8 Revocation may be required because the VAT status of the tenants or potential purchasers has changed since the option was made, or where the administration costs and risks outweigh the benefit of input tax recovery.

Subject to certain conditions, the **period of time** during which an option to tax can be revoked is either within the first 6 months running from the date of the option, or after 20 years have elapsed.

In addition, an option to tax will be **automatically revoked** or will lapse where either:
– a trader makes an REE and at the time it is made no interest is held in the building or land by either the opter or a member of its VAT group (¶5658); or
– a period of 6 years has elapsed since the opter or a member of its VAT group held an interest in the building or land.

MEMO POINTS If a trader has an existing option to tax on a **building** only and the building is **demolished**, the option will continue to exist for the land where the building stood and for any subsequent building on the site (¶5622).

Automatic revocation anti-avoidance

Revocation is subject to the following anti-avoidance provisions, so that an option to tax will not be revoked in the following circumstances: 5691 Sch 10 para 26 VATA 1994; Notice 742A paras 8.1.2, 14.8.2
a. where the opter (or a relevant associate if the opter is, or has been, a member of a VAT group) has sold the property on terms that may require the **purchaser to make additional payment** after the time the option would otherwise be revoked; or
b. where, before the time the option would otherwise be revoked, a **relevant associate** (¶5658) **left the opter's VAT group** and at the time of leaving any of the following applied:
– the relevant associate had an interest in or licence to occupy the property;
– the relevant associate had, prior to leaving the VAT group, disposed of an interest on terms that would, or might, have required the purchaser to make additional payment at a later date; or
– the relevant associate was connected to the opter or another relevant associate of the opter and that person had an interest in, or licence to occupy, the property.

The effect of these provisions is to prevent automatic revocation under the 6-year rule, or on making an REE, where further supplies will or may occur after revocation.

Within first 6 months

To allow a cooling-off period for a trader to change its mind, an option can be revoked within 6 months of the date it takes effect. If revoked, the option will be treated as if it had never been made. 5692 Notice 742A para 8.1.2

Options are revocable without **prior consent** (although HMRC must be notified, on form VAT 1614C) if all of the following four conditions (plus one of the three additional conditions listed below) are met:
1. less than 6 months have passed since the day on which the option had effect;
2. no tax has become chargeable on a supply of the land as a result of the option;
3. there has been no TOGC since the option took effect; and
4. HMRC has been notified.

The **additional conditions** are:
a. neither the opter nor any relevant associate of the opter has recovered input tax as a result of exercising the option;
b. by virtue of the revocation, the opter and all relevant associates of the opter would be liable to account to HMRC for any input tax recovered as a result of exercising the option; or
c. as a result of exercising the option, input tax has been recovered entirely on one capital item and amounts to less than 20% of the total input tax incurred on that item.

It may still be possible to revoke the option to tax if the above **conditions are not met** but HMRC must give its consent (again, form VAT 1614C is used for this purpose).

After 20 years

Once the cooling-off period has expired and assuming the trader has not sold the property more than 6 years previously, an option can only be revoked after 20 years have elapsed since the date when it first took effect. 5696 Sch 10 para 25 VATA 1994

This type of revocation has been available **since** 1 August 2009 (because that is 20 years since the option to tax mechanism was introduced).

Consent may be automatic or by permission.

Where the original option has successfully been revoked, it will be possible to **make another election** to opt the building or land, which will then be subject to a further 20-year period.

Comment Businesses should consider the **effect** of potential revocation **on tenants**. If revocation occurs, existing taxable tenants may end up paying hidden VAT within increased service charges as landlords will no longer be able to recover input tax. New tenants may want to negotiate lease terms which either include a restriction on the landlord's ability to revoke, or allow for related compensation.

5698 Sch 10 para 25 VATA 1994; Notice 742A para 8.3.3

Automatic consent Automatic revocation is possible, provided that neither the trader, nor any relevant associate (¶5658) connected with the trader, has a **relevant interest** in the building or land at the time when the option is revoked. If the trader (or a relevant associate) has disposed of such an interest, no future supply for the purpose of the charge to VAT must take place in respect of the disposal (or would be yet to take place if one or more conditions, such as the happening of an event or the doing of an act, were to be met).

Failing the above, all of the following conditions shown in the table below must be satisfied:

Condition	Terms
20 years have elapsed	The trader[1] held an interest in the property at some time since the option was exercised and that time was more than 20 years prior to revocation
Capital item	If the property is subject to the capital goods scheme in relation to the trader[1] at the time of revocation, any potential adjustment under the scheme subsequent to revocation does not exceed £10,000
Valuation	In the 10 years prior to revocation, the trader[1] has not made a supply of an interest in the opted property: – for a consideration less than the open-market value; or – which arose from a grant that the trader expects will give rise to a supply made after revocation for a consideration significantly greater than any consideration for any supply arising from the grant before revocation (except as a result of a rent review determined according to normal commercial practice)
Prepayment	No part of a supply made for consideration to the trader[1] before revocation will be attributable to a supply or other use of the property by the trader more than 12 months after revocation
Note: 1. All references to trader also include any relevant associate.	

5699 **Notification** should be made on form VAT 1614J; revocation will **take effect from** the date on the certificate.

5700 **Permission consent** If the automatic conditions are not met, permission to revoke can be requested from HMRC, provided that at least the 20-year condition in ¶5698 above is satisfied.

Permission must be requested on form VAT 1614J. If HMRC agrees, the revocation will have **effect from**:
– the date that permission is granted; or
– such time as HMRC may specify (HMRC can specify the day or time from which the revocation has effect and may specify that day or time by reference to the happening of a **specific event**, or the meeting of a condition).

HMRC only has discretion to specify an **earlier date** where a previous notification, stating that the automatic conditions were met, was given in error. In this case, if HMRC is satisfied that any breach of the automatic conditions is insignificant, it may allow the date of revocation to be the date of the original notification.

MEMO POINTS 1. The form must contain the following **information**:
- the trader's VAT registration details;
- the address or exact location of the opted property and, if appropriate, the land registry number;
- the date of acquisition of the interest in the property;
- the date of revocation; and
- confirmation of which of the automatic conditions are met and those that are not, including full details as to why the conditions are not met.

2. When reviewing which conditions have not been met, HMRC has stated that it will give particular consideration to whether the trader, or a third party, will receive a **VAT benefit** as a result of the trader's actions before revoking the option.

SECTION 3

Input tax - capital goods scheme

Input tax recovery relating to most properties is governed by the capital goods scheme, which is mandatory and **applies to** all traders who: **5750**
- incur input tax on property interests which are valued at £250,000 or more (exclusive of VAT);
- buy, or use, the property for business purposes; and
- are involved in the making of both taxable and exempt supplies at some time in the next 10 years.

It is important to note that where a property is acquired and disposed of within a 10-year period and the sale is not taxable, any trader is likely, because of the scheme, to have to repay some input tax already recovered.

The **aim** is to ensure that input tax is recovered only in proportion to the taxable use made of the property over the extended period.

The type of immovable property which falls within the scheme is examined here. The background and calculations involved in the scheme generally are covered at ¶2280+.

MEMO POINTS 1. Traders in the property business usually make exempt supplies, so for input tax purposes are **partly exempt** (¶2075).

2. Further, developers often choose to agree a partial exemption **special method** (¶2148) with HMRC, although this can be subject to an override (¶2187).

3. **Computer equipment, ships and aircraft** valued at £50,000 or more also fall within the capital goods scheme (¶2280+).

4. For the interaction of a **freehold** and **long lease** grant see ¶5262.

5. The capital goods scheme also applies where assets are used partly for **non-business** purposes (¶2312).

A. Scope

Exclusions

Only property where VAT has been charged is relevant, hence zero-rated and exempt supplies are ignored. **5755**

The following are also excluded:
- property acquired for resale, or which is sold before it is used for any other purpose; and
- land acquired for a developer's land bank because of its profit potential.

5757 This leaves the following which are **subject to the scheme rules**:

Situation	Criteria
Acquisition of land and buildings	Valued at £250,000 or more[1]
Building constructed by owner	Taxable goods and services received are valued at £250,000 or more
Alteration, extension or annexe to a building carried out by the owner	Taxable goods and services received are valued at £250,000 or more
Self-supply (¶5300) resulting from a change of use of a residential or charitable building[2]	Valued at £250,000 or more
Civil engineering work either bought in or constructed by the owner[3]	First brought into use on or after 3 July 1997 and taxable goods and services received since 3 July 1997 are valued at £250,000 or more
Refurbishment or fitting out of a building[4]	Carried out on or after 3 July 1997 and taxable goods and services received since 3 July 1997 are valued at £250,000 or more

Note:
1. The **value threshold** includes the value of goods and services relating to the project (¶5760). For **leases**, only the premium is taken into account unless the tenant is charged rent more than 12 months in advance, or is invoiced for a period exceeding a year.
2. Where the **first payment of rent is zero-rated**, any subsequent exempt supply is disregarded for the purposes of the scheme.
3. **Civil engineering** takes its everyday meaning and includes works on bridges, roads, golf courses, installation of pipes, etc. Refurbishments of civil engineering works are also included.
4. For the treatment of goods involved in a **refurbishment** see ¶5770.

Measurement of value

5760 Notice 706/02 paras 4.3 - 4.5 If a trader acquires some land and then constructs a building, this will be treated as one capital item.

Only capital **expenditure**, such as materials and labour for building works, is to be included.

The following **professional fees** are also included in the value of the expenditure:
- architect's fees;
- surveyors;
- site managers;
- civil engineering contractors;
- security;
- demolition and clearing the site;
- equipment hire;
- haulage; and
- landscaping.

Indirect expenses such as legal fees are excluded.

MEMO POINTS In relation to **retention clauses**, when there is a delay between first use of the building and the last invoice for construction, the trader should estimate the value. In practice HMRC expects the estimate to include the price retained by the trader. The property will still remain in the scheme even where the final value is below the threshold of £250,000.

EXAMPLE
1. A Ltd constructs a large office building and incurs the following costs:

	£
Land	100,000
Main contractor	1,500,000
Clearing the site	300,000
Security	50,000
Architect's fees	80,000
Accountant's report for funding	10,000
Legal fees re negotiation	40,000
	2,080,000

For the purposes of the capital goods scheme, the accountant's report and legal fees do not form part of the building's value. Hence the value is £2.03m. (£2.08m - £40,000 - £10,000)

2. A lease premium costs £225,000 and the rent is £2,500 per month.
The landlord requires the first year's rent to be paid in advance, so the value for the purposes of the capital goods scheme exceeds £250,000. (£225,000 + (12 × £2,500) = £255,000)

Option to tax

The option to tax (¶5602) affects the adjustments made under the capital goods scheme, because a formerly exempt sale or lease will become wholly taxable. 5762

For example, if exempt rent has already been charged for the whole of the first interval (¶2298), then an option to tax is made, only 90% of the input tax will be recoverable over the next 9 years.

EXAMPLE An accountant purchases a new office for £800,000 plus VAT of £160,000. After 5 years, due to growth of the firm, new premises are found and the office is sold. As the office is no longer new, the sale is exempt. The accountant does not opt to tax.
The exempt sale means that the remaining four intervals are treated as exempt, requiring the accountant to repay £64,000 of input tax to HMRC. (£160,000 × 4/10)

Start of the scheme

For building projects, HMRC states that the scheme will start when all of the following are satisfied: 5764
- input tax has been incurred;
- there is a firm intention to construct, or carry out relevant works to, a building; and
- the value threshold has been, or will be, exceeded.

EXAMPLE A building was constructed by a developer on land owned by an NHS trust. The trust granted the developer a 99-year lease and in return the developer granted the trust a sublease for 99 years less 3 days.
It was contended that the first use of the building did not occur until after the construction was complete, because no-one could make any physical use of the uncompleted building.
It was held that the use of a building for business purposes was not limited to physical use or occupation. The grant of a lease of an uncompleted building was a relevant use of the building. The reference to its first use covered the various activities and events which would mark the start of the first interval of the period of adjustment. The sublease was a grant of the land with the building and constituted a use of the land (including the building) as a capital item for the purpose of the trader's business. The uncompleted state of the structure did not prevent it from being regarded as a building. *East Kent Medical Services Ltd* [1999] (VTD 16095)

B. Refurbishments

Value of goods

Goods to be included in the value of the property must be recognised on the trader's balance sheet, generally immovable, and sold with the building. 5770 Notice 706/02 para 4.11

Prior to 1 January 2011 goods also had to be fixed to its fabric, which excluded items fixed to the floor for reasons of safety or security. There is now no such requirement.

If any of the goods are **sold or scrapped** the value of their acquisition will still be subject to the scheme adjustments until the whole interest in the building is disposed of.

MEMO POINTS 1. Where one of these goods is a **computer**, ten intervals will then apply instead of the usual five (¶2298). On disposal of the building before ten intervals have elapsed, the computer will still be subject to the scheme if still owned, even though its isolated value was not sufficient to warrant inclusion in the scheme.
2. In relation to the **goods affixed** condition, which applied before 1 January 2011, the following table indicates common items where HMRC gave guidance (this information is included because such expenditure will remain subject to the scheme for many years to come):

Item	Goods affixed
Windows	✓
Lighting	✓
Decorative features	✓
Roofs and ceilings	✓
Permanent flooring	✓
Carpets	x
Air conditioning	✓
Lifts	✓
Permanent partitioning	✓
Storage cupboards and shelving - if built-in only	✓
Office equipment	x
Factory machines	x

3. Before 1 January 2011, by concession, **additional capital expenditure** incurred in connection with the refurbishment or fitting-out work could be included within the value subject to the scheme, where the trader could not identify the goods affixed, perhaps because it was too difficult or expensive. The business could choose which goods within the building were included.

Staged refurbishments

5774 Notice 706/02 para 4.13

Sometimes refurbishments are carried out in more than one part of a building. In this case it is a **question of fact** whether each part is distinct, decided perhaps by the nature of the project, or by timing. Parts which are distinct are treated separately for the purposes of the scheme. Otherwise, the value of the parts will be amalgamated when checking whether the value of the refurbishment is £250,000 or more.

HMRC says there is normally more than one refurbishment where any of the following apply:
- there are separate contracts for each phase;
- there is one contract but each phase is detailed in a separate option; or
- each stage is finished before the next begins.

HMRC will accept these are separate projects, even when carried out by the same contractor under the same tender.

In certain cases it may be possible for the **occupants to move** between parts of the building while other parts are being refurbished. HMRC interprets this as indicating one capital project, because the building is occupied throughout.

Comment A business plan may be useful in **forecasting the implications** of one overall project, or several separate projects i.e. whether it is beneficial to the business that the capital goods scheme applies in a particular way.

Rolling refurbishments

5776 Notice 706/02 para 4.14

A rolling refurbishment programme results in a **previous refurbishment** becoming obsolete, to be replaced by a newer one. In this case the two refurbishments are always separate projects.

If a **subsequent refurbishment commences** before the adjustment period of the first has finished, the treatment depends on whether the first is:
- completely replaced, in which case it is deemed to be destroyed (¶2340); or
- retained in some way, in which case the adjustments continue as if the second refurbishment had not occurred.

C. Input tax incurred in more than one period

Input tax incurred before first interval

If first use of the property does not occur until after some input tax is incurred and then further input tax is incurred in the next VAT year, two baseline recovery rates (¶2314) would apply. In this case the following formula is used to calculate the baseline rate: **5780** Notice 706/2 para 6

$$\frac{\text{Total recovered input tax}}{\text{Total input tax incurred on the property}} \times 100\% = \text{Baseline rate}$$

EXAMPLE B Ltd has a VAT year which ends on 31 March. The company constructs a building and incurs £400,000 of input tax in Year 1 and £200,000 of input tax in Year 2. The recovery rate for residual input tax is 60% and 80%, respectively. The building is first used on 1 May of Year 2, so the first interval will run from this date to the following 31 March.
To calculate the initial input tax recovered and the rate, the amounts for the two years are amalgamated:

			£	£
Input tax recovered	Year 1	£400,000 x 60%	240,000	
	Year 2	£200,000 x 80%	160,000	
	Total			400,000
Input tax incurred	Year 1		400,000	
	Year 2		200,000	
	Total			600,000

$$\frac{400{,}000}{600{,}000} = 66.67\%$$

So 66.67% of the total input tax is recovered and this is the baseline rate against which subsequent capital goods scheme adjustments are measured.

Additional input tax incurred after first interval

Input tax may be incurred in subsequent intervals where work is undertaken under a long-term contract. This situation commonly applies to: **5782** Notice 706/2 para 6
- refurbishments;
- a building constructed by the owner and then altered, extended, or fitted out; or
- situations where the contract includes a retention clause.

EXAMPLE A taxable golf club incurred input tax on an extension to the existing clubhouse in the year ended 31 March 1999.
A later invoice was dated April 1999, which fell within the VAT year ended 31 March 2000, by which time the club was partly exempt.
It was held that the input tax on the April 1999 invoice should be recovered in accordance with the partial exemption method for the year ended 31 March 2000. *Witney Golf Club* [2002] (VTD 17706)

Input tax incurred in the: **5784** Notice 706/2 para 6
- first interval will be adjusted from the second interval onwards; and
- second interval will be adjusted from the third interval onwards.

There are two **methods** to cope with the resulting input tax:

Method	Detail
Combined adjustments	Roll together the adjustments required for each amount of input tax incurred Intervals run from the date of first use Amount of input tax and initial recovery calculated as for input tax incurred before the first interval: $\frac{\text{Input tax recovered to date}}{\text{Input tax incurred to date}} \times 100\% = \text{Average recovery rate}$
Parallel adjustments	Keep each block of input tax separate Make simultaneous adjustments

5786 EXAMPLE C Ltd incurs input tax on a building project as follows:

Interval	Input tax incurred	Recovery rate	Input tax recovered
	£m	%	£m
1	8	75	6.0
2	4	90	3.6
3	3	75	2.25
4	-	72	-
5	-	81	-
6	-	84	-
7	-	88	-
8	-	74	-
9	-	72	-
10	-	75	-
Total	15		11.85

The average recovery rate is 79%. (11.85/15)

1. Combined adjustments

The baseline rate is recalculated every time further input tax is recovered. C Ltd follows the approach suggested by HMRC and uses:

$$\frac{\text{Input tax recovered to date}}{\text{Input tax incurred to date}} \times 100\% = \text{Average recovery rate}$$

Interval	Input tax incurred	Recovery rate	Input tax recovered	Baseline rate[1]	Input tax to be adjusted[2]	CGS adjustment	
							Amount
	£m	%	£m	%	£m	%	£
1	8	75	6	75	n/a	n/a	n/a
2	4	90	3.6	75	0.8	15	120,000
3	3	75	2.25	80	1.2	(5)	(60,000)
4	-	72	-	79	1.5	(7)	(105,000)
5	-	81	-	79	1.5	2	30,000
6	-	84	-	79	1.5	5	75,000
7	-	88	-	79	1.5	9	135,000
8	-	74	-	79	1.5	(5)	(75,000)
9	-	72	-	79	1.5	(7)	(105,000)
10	-	75	-	79	1.5	(4)	(60,000)
Totals	15		11.85				(45,000)

Note:

1. The baseline rate in interval 1 is 75%, calculated under the usual partial exemption rules.

For interval 2, the baseline rate is 75% — $6/8 = 75\%$

For interval 3, the baseline rate is 80%. — $\frac{(6 + 3.6)}{(4 + 8)} = 80\%$

For interval 4 and later intervals, the baseline rate is 79%. — $\frac{(6 + 3.6 + 2.25)}{(4 + 8 + 3)} = 79\%$

2. For interval 2 the input tax to be adjusted is £800,000. (£8m/10)

In interval 3, the input tax to be adjusted is £1.2m. (£4m + £8m/10)

In interval 4, etc, the input tax to be adjusted is £1.5m. (£4m + £8m + £3m/10)

Overall the capital goods scheme adjustment is £45,000 owed to HMRC.

2. Parallel adjustments

Interval	VAT incurred	Recovery rate	Input tax recovered	Interval 1 adjustments		Interval 2 adjustments		Interval 3 adjustments	
		%			Amount		Amount		Amount
	£m		£m	% [1]	£	% [2]	£	% [3]	£
1	8	75	6	n/a	n/a	n/a	n/a	n/a	n/a
2	4	90	3.6	15	120,000	n/a	n/a	n/a	n/a
3	3	75	2.25	-	-	(15)	(60,000)	n/a	n/a
4	-	72	-	(3)	(24,000)	(18)	(72,000)	(3)	(9,000)
5	-	81	-	6	48,000	(9)	(36,000)	6	18,000
6	-	84	-	9	72,000	(6)	(24,000)	9	27,000
7	-	88	-	13	104,000	(2)	(8,000)	13	39,000
8	-	74	-	(1)	(8,000)	(16)	(64,000)	(1)	(3,000)
9	-	72	-	(3)	(24,000)	(18)	(72,000)	(3)	(9,000)
10	-	75	-	-	-	(15)	(60,000)	-	-
Totals	15		11.85		288,000		(396,000)		63,000

Note:

1. The baseline rate for interval 1's input tax is 75% and the input tax to be adjusted is £800,000 (£8m/10)
2. The baseline rate for interval 2's input tax is 90%, the input tax to be adjusted is £400,000. (£4m/10)
3. The baseline rate for interval 3's input tax is 75%, the input tax to be adjusted is £300,000. (£3m/10)

Overall, the capital goods scheme adjustment is £45,000 owed to HMRC (£288,000 - £396,000 + £63,000), which is the same result as for the combined adjustment.

D. Sale adjustment

Input tax will be **clawed back** on property where all of the following apply: 5790 Business Brief 30/97; Notice 706/2 para 8
- the total input tax recovered exceeds the output tax charged on the sale;
- there has been some exempt use of the asset during the adjustment period, including the case where the onward sale is exempt;
- the transaction is not undertaken for commercial business reasons; and
- the business gains an unjustified tax advantage as a result.

This is called the disposal test by HMRC but will **not apply** to a reduction in property value caused by market forces, such as where:
- an owner disposes of an item at a loss due to market conditions (for example, a general downturn in property prices);
- the value of the item has depreciated; or
- the value of the item is reduced for other legitimate reasons (such as accepting a lower price to effect a quick sale).

In addition, if the amount of output tax on disposal is reduced because of a change in the VAT rate, this also is not subject to the disposal test.

Unjustified VAT advantage

It is up to the trader **to decide** whether it has obtained an unfair VAT advantage. 5792

HMRC gives the following example as guidance.

EXAMPLE D Ltd acquires the freehold of a newly constructed commercial property for £2m plus VAT of £400,000 and immediately occupies the building for its own business purposes. D Ltd is partly exempt with a recovery rate of 50% and so initially recovers £200,000 of input tax.

The business continues to use the building for taxable and exempt purposes for the remainder of interval 1 and for interval 2.
During interval 3 the business sells the property as a taxable supply for £2m plus VAT of £400,000. As a consequence the business is required to carry out a final adjustment of £140,000 (£200,000 × 70%) and is therefore able to recover total input tax of £340,000. (£200,000 + £140,000)
As the output tax on disposal is greater than the total input tax recovered, there is no unfair VAT advantage.
If the sale during interval 3 had been for only £1.5m plus VAT of £300,000, because of a downturn in property prices, the total input tax would have exceeded the output tax. However, D Ltd would not have been required to pay any amount back to HMRC, because the building was sold at an open-market price and not for the purpose of obtaining an unjustified tax advantage.

Calculation

5794 SI 1995/2518 reg 115(3A), (3B)

Where the test applies, an adjustment must be made to reduce the **amount of input tax** already recovered. To do this, the trader will need to calculate:
- the net tax advantage; and
- how much of it is unjustified.

The **net tax advantage** is the overall benefit derived from the avoidance device. Often this benefit is the recovery of input tax in the remaining intervals as if the asset had not been sold. In order to achieve this benefit, a taxable supply is made (perhaps by opting to tax). The net tax advantage is the amount of input tax secured by the sale, less any output tax due.

Some form of apportionment needs to be applied to work out **how much** of the net tax advantage **is unjustified**. HMRC suggests that an appropriate method may include the ratio of exempt and total supplies made.

MEMO POINTS The **input tax already recovered** is the aggregate of:
- the initial deduction of input tax from interval 1;
- any adjustments made previously in respect of the item under the scheme; and
- any adjustment that would otherwise be required on the sale.

5796

EXAMPLE On 1 June a developer (with a VAT year ending on 31 March) completes a commercial development, at a cost of £25m plus VAT of £5m. The developer opts to tax the building and grants a 2-year lease to a third-party tenant at a market rent.
In interval 3 the developer grants a 99-year lease at a premium of £24m and a peppercorn rent to its wholly owned subsidiary, which only makes exempt supplies.
In interval 4 the developer sells the freehold, subject to the 99-year lease, for £250,000 plus VAT of £50,000, to the wholly owned subsidiary.
The VAT position is summarised as follows:

Interval	Baseline rate	Interval rate	Input tax adjustments £	Balance of input tax recovered £	Notes
1	100%	100%	n/a	5,000,000	As the developer opts to tax the building, the taxable use is 100%.
2	100%	100%	n/a	5,000,000	Nothing changes in the second interval, so no adjustment is necessary.
3	100%	0%	(500,000)	4,500,000	The lease disapplies the option to tax, so that an exempt supply is made and so 1/10th of the input tax recovered in interval 1 must be repaid.
4	100%	0%	(500,000)	4,000,000	As the lease continues into interval 4, the exempt use is deemed to apply to the whole interval.
5-10	100%	100%	n/a	4,000,000	The taxable sale means that the use in intervals 5 to 10 is deemed to be taxable.

Net tax advantage

Because of the sale of the property subject to the encumbrance of the lease, the developer has recovered 100% of the input tax relating to intervals 5 to 10, amounting to £3,000,000. (6 × £500,000)

Output tax charged is only £50,000.

So the net tax advantage is £2,950,000. (£3,000,000 - £50,000)

Unjustified tax advantage

This could be measured by using the following ratio:

$$\frac{\text{Value of the exempt lease}}{\text{Value of lease and sale}} = \frac{24\text{m}}{24.25\text{m}} = 98.969\%.$$

So the unjustified tax advantage is £2,919,586 (£2,950,000 x 98.969%) and this amount should be repaid to HMRC.

CHAPTER 2

Farming

OUTLINE ¶¶

Farming activity encompasses food production (including cultivation, breeding, rearing and keeping animals), and maintaining the land in good agricultural and environmental condition. **5900**

Increasingly, farmers have sought to diversify, in both their business structures and their activities, in order to stabilise their often precarious financial situation.

Options

Depending on the supplies made by the farmer, VAT **registration** may be advantageous or compulsory. Pure farming is zero-rated, so any input tax incurred should be recoverable. Many registered farmers are therefore repayment traders with monthly returns (¶2990). Alternatively, exemption from registration may apply (¶2650+). **5902**

There is a special agricultural **flat rate scheme** (¶5970+), which means the farmer does not need to register for VAT but still receives compensation in lieu of input tax recovery. Some farmers may find this arrangement easier and cheaper to operate than VAT registration.

Alternatively, the **least efficient** choice is to remain unregistered for VAT and uncertified for the flat rate scheme, thereby suffering the VAT cost on taxable purchases.

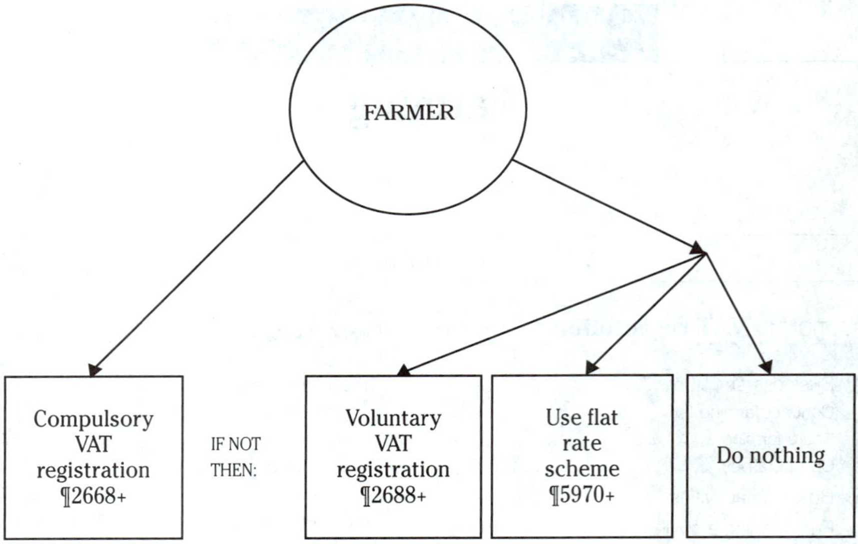

SECTION 1

VAT registration

5905 VAT registration depends on what type of supplies the farmer makes, and the quantity of those supplies.

The usual **requirements for registration** (¶2605+) apply in full to farmers. The most common reason for compulsory registration is that the farmer's taxable supplies exceed the annual threshold (¶9960). However, if the farmer's non-farming supplies do not exceed this threshold, the farmer can choose to become a flat rate farmer (¶5970+) instead.

Farmer makes	Annual value of supplies	Required to register?	Options
Farming supplies only	Under registration threshold	No	Can choose to register, or use flat rate scheme
	Over registration threshold	Yes	Can choose flat rate scheme instead
Farming and other supplies	Under registration threshold	No	Can choose to register, or use flat rate scheme
	Over registration threshold	Yes	If value of other supplies is below threshold, can choose flat rate scheme instead

A. Business structures

5907 Often the landowner will want to pass on the **responsibility and burden** of the hands-on farming work to someone else. This may be prompted, for example, by financial need or personal infirmity.

There are two common ways of doing this:
- contract farming (¶5910+); and
- share farming (¶5914+).

In addition, in order to reduce the cost of goods, farmers may choose to join a co-operative or farmers' group (¶5918).

This section assumes that the parties are VAT-registered. For alternatives if using the agricultural flat rate scheme see ¶5970+.

Comment Owners of farmland are often elderly, a situation partly brought about by a lack of younger family interest in the business. For some, assets (including land and the farmhouse) are retained in order to secure valuable **tax reliefs**, such as agricultural property relief, which can significantly reduce the inheritance tax charge on death. See *Tax Memo* for further details.

Contract farming

Under a contract farming arrangement the landowner contracts with an outside party (who may be a neighbouring farmer, or a corporate concern) to farm some or all of the land, for which the landowner pays a contract fee (and possibly commission based on productivity). A partnership is not created, nor is the land leased to the contractor under this arrangement. The contractor therefore provides farming services to the landowner in return for the contract fee. **5910**

MEMO POINTS 1. If the farmer **grants a lease** over their land, this is an exempt supply subject to the option to tax (¶5602+).
2. Sometimes the farmer may charge a rental fee which covers **both a lease** of land, **and also** the provision of **husbandry** services. Unless husbandry is separately charged, the whole amount of rent is exempt, because the husbandry would be incidental to the lease.

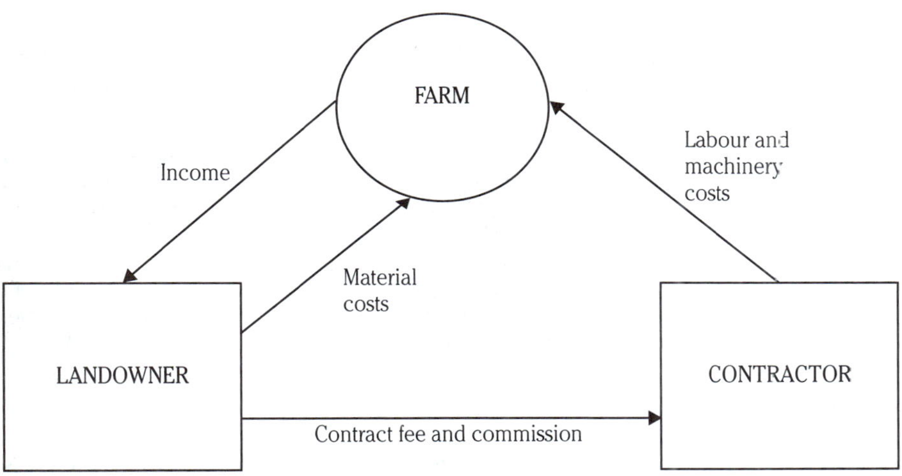

The **landowner** accounts for VAT on all of the income arising from the farming activity. As they also tend to provide the usual farming materials (such as seeds, manure, etc), they will also recover input tax on these costs, in addition to the input tax incurred on the contract fee. **5912**

The **contractor** accounts for VAT on the contract fee and any commission received from the landowner. The main costs will be wages (outside the scope of VAT) and the acquisition of the necessary machinery. The contractor will be able to recover any related input tax, except for any incurred on costs which should be properly invoiced to the landowner.

Share farming

A share farming arrangement involves two separate occupiers of the same land, the owner and a contractor (the "share farmer"), which effectively gives rise to two farming businesses. **5914** VTAXPER74400

This structure is adopted in order to avoid creating a tenancy under the Agricultural Holdings Act, which would create additional rights and obligations between the two parties.

The farm **profits** are shared between the landowner and contractor, and therefore there is no contract fee. It is important that the agreement represents the coming together of equals as a joint venture arrangement, avoiding the grant of a lease and ensuring that a partnership is not created.

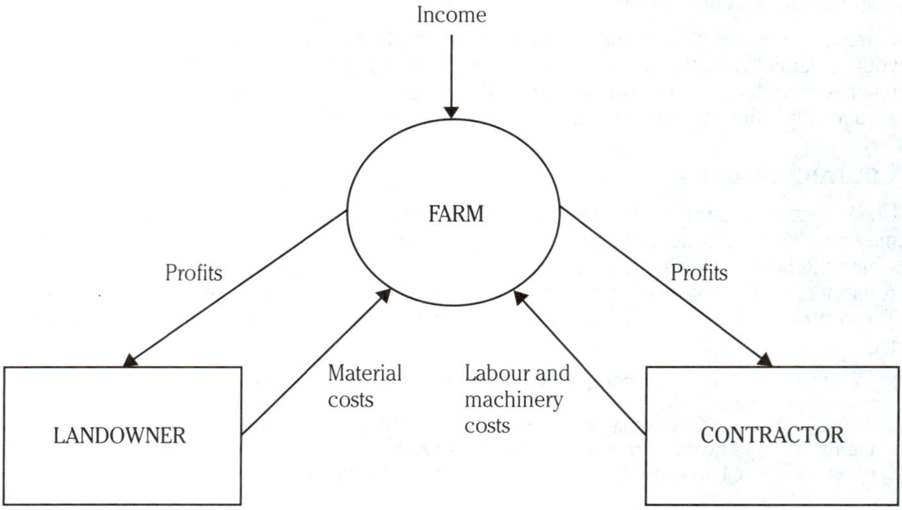

VTAXPER74500 The Country Land and Business Association (formerly the Country Landowners Association) has agreed a **model** share farming **agreement** with HMRC which will give certainty to the VAT treatment.

5916 The landowner and contractor will normally have separate VAT **registrations**, and each will recover input tax on the costs they individually incur. However, HMRC might challenge these arrangements as in reality comprising a partnership, and impose a single VAT registration. This would make the parties jointly and severally liable for each other's VAT debts.

VTAXPER74400 Where the **joint venture** arrangement is effective, any reimbursement of costs incurred by the other party is a supply of services. On the sale of the jointly owned crop, each party will account for VAT. If the crop is only owned by one party, VAT is accounted for on the sale, and the subsequent transfer of proceeds to the other party is outside the scope of VAT.

Co-operatives

5918 VTAXPER61000 A co-operative has greater buying power than its individual members, so those members are able to enjoy economies of scale resulting from bulk purchases. The co-operative sells produce as an agent (¶7090+) for the farmers. Goods passing between the farmer and the co-operative are outside the scope of VAT.

The VAT treatment **depends on** whether the co-operative is:

a. registered for VAT in its own right, in which case output tax is charged on any supplies of services (such as haulage, storage, or sales for commission) made to the members, and input tax is recoverable as normal; or

b. not registered, in which case one of the member farmers includes the co-operative's activities within their own VAT registration, and the co-operative has no separate identity for VAT purposes.

B. Business activities

Many farms now comprise a variety of business activities, and this allows a farmer to cope with poor market conditions and the other risks associated with pure farming. 5922

The resulting **diversification** presents VAT issues, including:
- identifying the various supplies made;
- whether VAT registration is now compulsory where previously none was required;
- applying the correct VAT rate, taking into account the possibility of composite and mixed supplies (¶310+); and
- implications for input tax recovery and VAT cash flow, particularly where any exempt supplies are made.

MEMO POINTS 1. For the recovery of input tax on costs relating to **farmhouses** see ¶1868.
2. For restrictions on input tax recovery when **partly exempt** see ¶2075+.

1. Pure farming activities

VAT rate

Virtually all supplies made by farmers will be taxable (whether at the zero rate, reduced rate or standard rate). When considering the correct VAT treatment, the **vital issues** are the intended customer and the end purpose for the product being sold (e.g. straw can be both animal feed and animal bedding). 5926

The main exceptions will be supplies relating to **land** - for example, letting of surplus accommodation (¶5540+) - which are usually exempt, subject to the option to tax (¶5602+).

The following table indicates the VAT rate which applies to common farming supplies. 5928
Sch 8 Group 1 VATA 1994

Goods/services supplied	Details pertinent to farmers	VAT rating
Food used for human consumption but not beverages	Includes liquids (e.g. milk) and ingredients such as flour; must be of nutritional value and generally considered to be food[1]	Zero-rated
Beverages	Any alcoholic drink, fruit juice	Standard-rated
Food for animals other than pets	For working animals (e.g. sheepdogs), farmed animals, game birds	Zero-rated
Pet food	Usually canned, packaged or prepared	Standard-rated
Seeds or other means of propagation of plants		Zero-rated
Live animals which are used to yield or produce food for human consumption	Dairy and beef herds, sheep flocks, hens, pigs, salmon, honey bees, prize bulls	Zero-rated
Non-food products derived from animals	Wool, fur, hair	Standard-rated
Agricultural contract services	Farming the land for a landowner	Standard-rated
Animal management services	Rearing animals for another party	Standard-rated

Note:
1. Food (¶1186+) does not include medicines, dietary supplements, food additives, etc.

Agricultural grants and subsidies

These payments are generally outside the scope of VAT, as no supply is being made. 5930

Generally, such payments fall within the following **categories**:
- compensation for enforced slaughter (such as during a foot and mouth outbreak);

- price support (e.g. hill farm allowance); and
- refraining from activity as part of official agricultural policy.

EXAMPLE A dairy farmer received compensation from the EU for discontinuing milk production. The German VAT authorities thought that this payment was consideration for a supply.
However, the CJEU held that there was no supply, because the EU was not acquiring any goods or services for its own direct benefit. The payment was instead made in order to enable the EU's agricultural policy to function, and this served a common interest. *Mohr v Finanzamt Bad Segeberg* [1996]

5932 Tax Bulletin June 2005 Special Edition The **Single Payment Scheme** (SP) was introduced in 2005 as a result of the reform of the EU's Common Agricultural Policy, and since then has become the main subsidy available to farmers, although it is being replaced during 2015 by the **Basic Payment Scheme** (BPS), which contains many of the same features. In order to receive such payments, farmers must comply with a series of standards, covering areas such as environmental, public, animal and plant health, animal welfare, and good farming/environmental practice.

Where the SP or BPS is the **only income received**, and the farmer has no intention of pursuing a business which will result in VATable business income, there is no entitlement to VAT registration.

MEMO POINTS Where a **farm business is sold**, including the payment entitlement, the sale may be treated as the transfer of a going concern (¶8646+), provided that all of the relevant criteria are met.

Fuels

5934 Notice 75 Farmers can obtain and use rebated gas, oil, and kerosene for vehicles which are used off-road and purely for agricultural purposes. HMRC is always concerned that this fuel is not then used for private on-road purposes (e.g. horseboxes), or sold on to other users, because **excise duty** is then evaded.

A concession has been granted to farmers who necessarily have to drive their tractors on public roads in order to access their fields from their farms, so that this is still counted as an agricultural purpose. A tractor can also be used on public roads for cutting verges, hedges and trees, and for other purposes related to agriculture, horticulture and forestry. This does not include grass-cutting in the context of landscaping or maintenance of recreational facilities.

Since 1 November 2013 the exemption has been extended to cover farm vehicles used for **gritting**, including travel to and from where the gritting takes place, and the collection of equipment and material for gritting.

EXAMPLE A farmer used rebated diesel in his tractors. He acted as a subcontractor for a haulage company, and drove his tractors on public roads in order to remove slurry (a fertilising agent) from a creamery, and spread it on surrounding farmland (mostly belonging to other farmers).
HMRC raised an assessment for the duty which should have been paid on the fuel, on the basis that the tractor was being used for non-agricultural purposes.
It was held that as the tractor was not being solely used for agricultural purposes, the duty was payable. The subcontracting arrangement meant that the farmer received payment for waste disposal, and this was not an agricultural activity. *Edward Bryan and Andrew David Thomas* [2005] (E00875)

Part-exchange of machinery

5936 When farm machinery is disposed of in a part-exchange transaction, the seller must:
- account for output tax on the value of the **item which is sold**; and
- reclaim input tax on the **item acquired**.

Sale of the farm

5938 Given the unique nature of the farming business, most farms are sold **to other farmers**, who already have the "tools" of the trade. In this situation, the farm machinery will not always be sold with the farm. However, this does not prevent the sale from being a transfer of a going concern (¶8646+).

Records

Farmers are required to keep many records because of the requirements of **DEFRA**, such as: 5940
– the IACS form (Integrated Administration and Control System), which states the land owned, and the use to which it is put;
– detailed records for all sheep and cows (including cattle passports); and
– the Agricultural and Horticultural Census.

HMRC may find this information useful when reviewing a farmer's VAT compliance. In addition, the normal business records should be retained (¶2790+).

2. Non-farming activities

Each farming business is unique and may combine agriculture with an eclectic combination of other activities, as summarised in the following table: 5942

Activity	Details	VAT rating	¶¶
Care of the environment	Grants and product sales		¶5944
Space for energy providers	Wayleaves and grants		¶5946
Alternative crops	For non-food purposes		¶5948
Quotas	Milk		¶5950
Farm shop	Selling farm produce, as well as bought-in goods		¶5952
Home delivery - "green" box schemes to the public	Separately charged delivery fee	Standard-rated	
	Vegetables and fruit	Zero-rated	
Letting accommodation	Residential leasing, bed and breakfast in the farmhouse, camp site, cottage hire		¶5953+
Vehicle parking area		Standard-rated	¶5516–
Field occupied for a fee	E.g. farmers' markets, fund-raising events, car boot sales		¶5518
Sporting rights	Fishing		¶5538
	Quad-biking	Standard-rated	
	Paint-balling	Standard-rated	
	Shooting facilities provided		¶5534+
	Game		¶5532+
Grazing rights	Insignificant care[1] provided by the farmer; animals graze in a specific area - treated as a supply of animal food	Zero-rated	
	Animal care provided	Standard-rated	
Livery	Grass livery - no stable	As for grazing rights	
	Supply of shelter and necessary bedding in a stable - exclusive use of a specific area	Exempt	
Bloodstock	Racing, breeding and selling, training		¶6100+
Equipment hire	E.g. hire of tractor	Standard-rated	
Animal hire	For fund-raising events (e.g. donkey rides), or breeding purposes (except hire of bull)	Standard-rated	
Open days	Admission fee	Standard-rated	
Gardens and garden centres	Admission fee	Standard-rated	
	Plant sales	Standard-rated if not edible	
	Catering (e.g. coffee shop)	Standard-rated	
Waste disposal	To a contractor	Exempt	
	To the public	Standard-rated	

Note:
1. HMRC states that **care** means taking responsibility for the animal's welfare. A daily perusal of the field would not constitute care for this purpose.

Care of the environment

5944 Farmers are increasingly being encouraged to manage the environment in conjunction with their farming activities.

To that end, several **grant** schemes encourage farmers to pursue or refrain from certain activities; the amounts received will generally be outside the scope of VAT. See the DEFRA website (www.gov.uk/defra) for more details.

Farmers may also be able to sell **products derived** from their environmental activities, such as logs. Any product sold for the purposes of domestic heating will be reduced-rated (¶1116+).

Space for energy providers

5946 Energy companies often need to place pylons across a farmer's land. Wind turbines are also becoming more common.

In return, the farmer will receive rent or **wayleave payments**, which are usually exempt, subject to the option to tax (¶5602+). (Wayleaves may be standard-rated if the land affected is not closely defined.)

Farmers are also cultivating **energy crops**, such as short rotation coppice or miscanthus, for which there are **grant** monies available under initiatives such as the Energy Crops Scheme. Generally, such grants are outside the scope of VAT, although reference should be made to the specific grant documentation.

Alternative crops

5948 Plants can be used **to produce** lubricants, surfactants, solvents, car parts and high-value products for the healthcare and cosmetic industries. The Government is supporting this diversification whilst trying to control waste and environmental damage.

The **sale** of these products is standard-rated.

Quotas

5950 V/FOOD9950 **Milk quotas** can be transferred independently of the underlying land interest. Both a sale and grant of a lease of milk quota are standard-rated supplies. However, if land is sold or leased with milk quotas, this is an exempt supply (subject to the option to tax (¶5602+)).

Quotas are often **self-billed** (¶2904+) by the customer, who could be an agricultural mart or specialist agent.

Farm shop

5952 Instead of just **selling** farm produce, many farm shops now offer other food and groceries, particularly to protect cash flow during the winter. It is therefore likely that the shop will be making zero-rated, standard-rated and possibly reduced-rated supplies.

As with any other business, the shop must maintain clear **records** (¶2790+) of the VAT calculation. Given the large number of low-value supplies made for cash, with no requirement for VAT invoices, one of the retail schemes (¶6300+) may be appropriate.

Leasing and holiday accommodation

5953 Notice 709/3 para 2 **Residential leasing** of surplus farm property is exempt, except where it relates to holiday accommodation. The farmer should consider the partial exemption rules (¶2075+).

Comment Where rental income is not included within the trading profit of the farm for **income tax** purposes, the farmer should carefully consider the **inheritance tax** implications. See *Tax Memo* for further details.

Holiday accommodation Many farms offer **bed and breakfast**, which is a standard-rated supply. It is important to identify who is making the supply, as the farmer's spouse may act independently of the farmer and therefore run the spouse's own business. If so, they will not be required to charge VAT if the supplies are below the annual registration threshold (¶9960). However, HMRC will challenge any arrangements which, in its opinion, artificially split a single business (¶2629+). **5954**

EXAMPLE

1. Since 1971, Mr and Mrs Forster had lived in a farmhouse owned by their family farming partnership (the current partners were Mr and Mrs Forster and their son).
In 1975, whilst the farm was still being run by Mr Forster's parents, Mrs Forster had started a bed and breakfast business in the farmhouse. In 2009 HMRC decided that there was a single business being run by the family farming partnership, and made a direction that the partners be treated as a single taxable person in respect of both the farm business and the bed and breakfast business. HMRC argued that there were sufficiently close financial, economic and organisational links between the partners and their businesses to justify the direction. The Forsters argued that before those links could be examined, HMRC had to show that there had been an artificial separation of business activities.
The Tribunal clarified that:
- there has to be an **artificial** separation; and
- HMRC may look at the financial, economic and organisational links in order to assess whether any separation has been artificial; but
- the existence of close financial, economic and organisational links is **not in itself sufficient** to justify a direction - the separation of businesses has to be artificial.
Here HMRC had failed to take into account the important fact that Mrs Forster had started the bed and breakfast business before the appellants had commenced running the farming business. She wished to earn an independent income, and that was not an artificial reason for running a separate business. She kept separate accounts, and the business did not operate if she was not present. The farmhouse was no longer much used for the farming business, now mainly run by the Forster's son.
The Tribunal decided that HMRC could not reasonably have concluded that the separation was artificial. The appeal was allowed. *A, D and J Forster* [2011] (TC01319)

2. In contrast, in another case HMRC issued a direction which was upheld by the Tribunal (which stressed that it was not permitted to allow the appeal unless HMRC had acted unreasonably in making the direction).
Here Mr and Mrs Patrick farmed in partnership, and Mrs Patrick ran a separate bed and breakfast business. However, a self-catering holiday cottage, which appeared to be part of the same business as the bed and breakfast business, was treated as part of the farming business in order to keep the turnover of the bed and breakfast business below the registration threshold. It was not unreasonable of HMRC to consider this an artificial arrangement. *H and J Patrick* [2011] (TC01699)

The provision of seasonal **camping and caravan sites** (including permanent caravans) is standard-rated. Ancillary services, such as water and power, are also standard-rated, unless the power is separately metered. Generally, the **minimum holiday season** spans the period between Easter and the end of September. **5956** Notice 709/3 para 6

Cottages which are let for the holiday season give rise to a taxable supply. However, they will be empty during the winter months, unless a short-term tenant is found. In this situation, the winter letting will be an exempt supply where all of the following conditions are satisfied: Notice 709/3 para 5.6
- it is let as residential accommodation and not holiday accommodation;
- the let is for more than 28 days; and
- there is a definite holiday season in the area in which it is located.

For further **details** of the VAT treatment of holiday accommodation, see ¶5502+.

SECTION 2

Agricultural flat rate scheme

5970 Notice 700/46; s 54 VATA 1994; EC Directive 2006/112 arts 295 - 305

Under this scheme (which covers a wide range of activities), the farmer is not registered for VAT and hence has no obligation to account for VAT or submit returns. Instead, a flat rate addition or levy is charged to VAT-registered customers; this is kept by the farmer as extra income (to compensate for the non-recovery of input tax suffered). The levy is therefore effectively a subsidy, which the customer recovers from HMRC as if it were input tax.

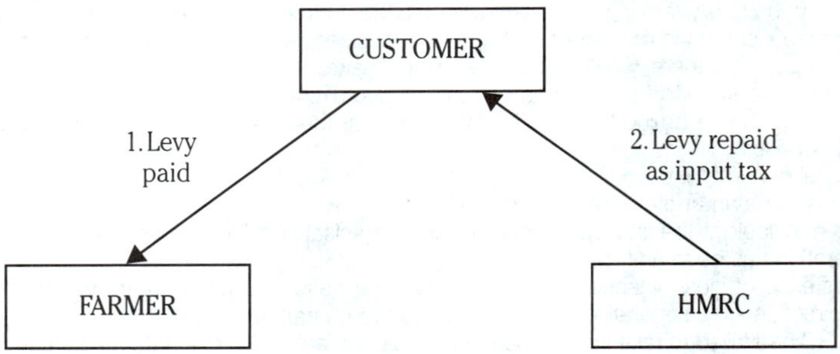

A. Eligibility

5975 Notice 700/46 para 1.4

A person who carries out any designated agricultural activity may join the scheme, provided that the value of other activities is below the VAT registration threshold. However, the person must be supplying goods, or goods and services. The supply of **services alone** would not qualify. If the farmer is already VAT-registered, there are further requirements (¶5984+).

Comment Farmers should consider whether the **loss of input tax recovery** on their non-agricultural activities would be so expensive that they would be put at a disadvantage by using the scheme.

Designated agricultural activities

5977 SI 1992/3220; Notice 700/46 para 3; VATAFRS2400

The following table indicates the permitted activities, which must **take place** in the UK.

Activity	Excludes	Includes
Crop production	Marketing co-operatives Sale of peat or top soil	General agriculture (including wine production)
		Field work, including: – harvesting, reaping, mowing, picking and collecting; – threshing and baling
		Growing of: – fruit; – vegetables; – flowers; – ornamental plants, whether in the open or under glass Includes plants which were seeded elsewhere
		Production of mushrooms, spices, seeds and propagating materials
		Nurseries for rearing of young plants for sale

Activity	Excludes	Includes
Stock farming	Raising of animals as pets or for sport, including budgerigars, aviary birds, butterflies, cats, dogs (other than sheepdogs), game	General stock farming (e.g. cattle, pigs, sheep, horses[1], mink, deer, ostriches, pigeons, sheepdogs)
		Poultry farming
	Training of animals as a specialist activity[1], including horse racing, showjumping, eventing and pigeon racing	Rabbit farming
		Beekeeping
		Silkworm farming
		Snail farming
	Providing activities involving animals such as pony trekking, riding lessons and hunting	Preparing and showing animals at agricultural events
Forestry	Processing beyond the conversion of felled timber	Growing, felling and general husbandry of trees, in a forest, wood or copse
		Conversion of felled timber into sawlogs, industrial small diameter roundwood, pitprops, cordwood, fencing material and firewood
Fisheries		Fresh water fishing
		Fish farming, not necessarily for human consumption (so including, for example, koi carp)
		Breeding of mussels, crustaceans, oysters and other molluscs
		Frog farming
Services performed in addition to any of the above activities[2]	Sale or lease of milk quotas (even if sold with the land)	Field work, reaping and mowing, threshing, baling, collecting, harvesting, sowing and planting
		Packing and preparing for market (including drying, cleaning, grinding, disinfecting and ensilaging)
	Processing of other farmers' products	Storage (including products stored on behalf of other farmers)
		Stock minding, rearing and fattening
		Destruction of weeds and pests, dusting and spraying of crops and land
		Operation of irrigation and drainage equipment, including ditching, and laying of drains
		Lopping, tree felling and other forestry services using farmer's own equipment, including clearing undergrowth, spraying trees, tree marking for felling, and creating firebreaks
		Hiring out of farm equipment for any of the above services[3]
	Grape crushing, bottling, etc for other wine producers	Technical assistance and advice relating to any of the above activities or services, including thatching (if farmer has grown the material), deer management, vermin and agricultural pest control
Processing of own products by farmers themselves[4]	Processing by someone other than the farmer (for example dairy co-operatives or sawmills)	Slaughter and preparation of animals bred for sale in the farm shop
		Picking and packaging of fruit for sale at the farm
		Sale of honey by a beekeeper
		Gutting of fish
		Drying of hops

Note:

1. **Horses** which are bred and then trained for racing will leave the scheme once training commences. Horses which are bred and trained for other purposes (e.g. showjumping) will leave the scheme on 31 December in the year when the horse is 4 years old.
2. The services may be **performed by** the farmer or any of the farmer's employees. If **equipment** is used, it must also be used for designated agricultural activities.
3. It is irrelevant **who operates** the equipment once it is hired.
4. HMRC may argue that **processing** is too industrial to be a designated activity, depending on the facts.

5980 **Who is performing the activities?** In the various business structures explained from ¶5907 to ¶5918, the following may be able to become flat rate farmers.

Type of structure	Person	Flat rate scheme available?
Contract farming[1]	Landowner	Yes, if providing farm materials
	Contractor	If providing services only - no If farming on land with own stock - yes
Share farming	Landowner	Yes
	Contractor	Yes
Co-operative	Members	Yes
	Co-operative itself	No

Note:
1. It would be possible for a contractor to be certified for the flat rate scheme whilst the landowner was VAT-registered, provided that the contractor met the scheme's eligibility requirements.

Non-agricultural activities

5982 Notice 700/46 para 4

These activities do not preclude use of the scheme, provided that the **value** of any taxable supplies resulting from them is not above the VAT registration threshold (¶9960). As the effect of joining the scheme is to take all of the farmer's supplies outside the scope of VAT, no input tax can be recovered.

Notice 700/46 para 4.4

It is possible for a farmer to carry on **substantial non-agricultural activities** as part of another entity's VAT registration (for example, as a partner in a partnership, perhaps involving the farmer's spouse) whilst using the flat rate scheme in the farmer's own name in relation to farming supplies. In this way, input tax recovery for the non-farming business is preserved.

If a farmer is **already using the scheme**, and the value of non-agricultural activities increases beyond the threshold, the farmer must leave the scheme (unless a separate VAT registration could be established as above).

MEMO POINTS 1. It is possible for a farmer making **zero-rated supplies** in excess of the VAT registration threshold to request exemption from registration (¶2652+) and therefore remain eligible for the scheme. The resulting ease of administration should be compared with the loss of input tax recovery.

Notice 700/46 para 4.5

2. Purchased **machinery or equipment** may have a dual purpose (i.e. used for both the farming and non-farming businesses). In this case, only the proportion of input tax relating to the non-farming business can be reclaimed.

EXAMPLE In a German case, a farmer leased a third of his land, his milk quota, 65 dairy cows and his cowshed to his son, whilst farming the remaining land. The farmer did not account for any output tax on the payment received from his son. The tax authority issued an assessment charging VAT on the income relating to the cows and milk quota.
The farmer appealed, contending that the income fell within the flat rate scheme. The case was referred to the CJEU, and it was held that the rental income arose from the leasing of material farm assets. As such, it fell outside the flat rate scheme, and output tax should have been accounted for. *Finanzamt Rendsburg v Harbs* [2006]

Other requirements if already VAT-registered

5984 SI 1995/2518 reg 204

The farmer must **cancel** their VAT registration (which will be refused if the value of non-agricultural activities still requires them to be registered).

A farmer will also be excluded from the scheme if, within the **3 years prior to making an application**, they have:
- been convicted of any VAT offence;
- been issued with a civil penalty for the former offence of dishonestly evading VAT; or
- had proceedings compounded (¶4152+).

A farmer may **rejoin** the scheme subject to the rules at ¶5994.

If it is estimated that the farmer will be more than £3,000 **better off** by using the scheme, HMRC can deny them entry. The potential gain is calculated by comparing the flat rate addition chargeable with the likely recovery of input tax that would occur under the normal VAT registration. **5986** SI 1995/2518 reg 204

In practice, if the estimated value of designated agricultural supplies is below £75,000, the farmer will be allowed to use the scheme subject to fulfilling the other criteria.

MEMO POINTS 1. HMRC calculates the **potential gain** under the scheme by taking 4% of the estimated agricultural supplies as disclosed on the application form. The action taken by HMRC then depends on the amount by which this figure exceeds the amount of input tax claimed by the farmer in the last 12 months: VATAFRS1600

Potential gain	Entry to the scheme
Up to £3,000	Allowed
£3,001 to £3,500	Discretion to allow because calculation uses estimates
Over £3,500	Denied

2. If the **estimated value** of designated agricultural supplies **exceeds** £75,000 and VAT returns are missing in the last 12 months, HMRC only includes the input tax actually claimed on the submitted returns in the calculation. This makes it less likely that the farmer will be allowed to use the scheme.

B. Joining the scheme

A farmer can apply to join the scheme at any time, subject to whether they are VAT-registered or have been in the scheme before. **5990** SI 1995/2518 reg 205; Notice 700/46 para 2.2

Comment The application **process** generally takes up to 3 weeks, so applying up to 30 days in advance is advisable if a particular start date is required.

Farmer's circumstances

If the farmer is already **VAT-registered**, deregistration must occur before the scheme can commence (¶5996). **5992**

As no input tax can be recovered once the scheme has started, any farmer who is considering acquiring expensive machinery should do so whilst still registered, before joining the scheme.

In contrast to the usual rule (¶8610+), there is no requirement to pay VAT on the value of stock and fixed assets held on deregistration. Sch 4 para 8(3) VATA 1994

If the farmer has **already been in the scheme previously**, and not registered for VAT since leaving, they may rejoin at any time. **5994** SI 1995/2518 reg 208

If they have registered for VAT in the intervening period, the period prior to rejoining depends upon whether the VAT due on the farmer's stocks and fixed assets is:
- £1,000 or less, in which case a year must have elapsed; or
- more than £1,000, in which case 3 years must have elapsed.

Application

An application **form** VAT 98 must be completed and submitted to HMRC. If accepted, a certificate will be issued which will notify the start date of the scheme. Otherwise, reasons will be stated for the rejection and the farmer has the right of appeal to a tribunal (¶4260+). **5996** Notice 700/46 para 2.1; s 83 VATA 1994

SI 1995/2518 reg 205 The **start date** of the scheme will be either:
- the date the application is received by HMRC;
- an earlier date in the case of official delay; or
- a future date (not more than 30 days ahead) as mutually agreed.

VATAFRS0215 As there is no mechanism for checking subsequent **compliance** with the rules, HMRC assesses each application critically for any risk of tax loss.

MEMO POINTS The form can be obtained **online** (at hmrc.gov.uk) **or from**:
Grimsby VAT Registration Service
HMRC
Imperial House
77 Victoria Street
Grimsby
NE Lincs
DN31 1DB

Certificate

5998 Notice 700/46 para 2.3 The certificate will show the following **details**, depending on the type of business entity.

Type of entity	Information
Sole trader	Full name of business owner Address of the business
Company	
Partnership	Trading name of the business Names of at least two partners (the certificate still covers all the partners who were named on the application)

6000 VATAFRS2500 Each certificate will have a **unique number**, which must be used on every invoice issued under the scheme.

New numbers are in the same **format** as a normal VAT registration number (¶2710) and begin with 96.

MEMO POINTS 1. On request, HMRC will confirm the current **validity** of a certificate by checking their database.
2. An **old number** consists of six digits, preceded by two check digits, which are only valid if within the range 00-10 (for example, 09-123457).

6002 Notice 700/46 para 9 The farmer must notify HMRC (using the address in ¶5996) of any **changes in circumstances**, such as:
a. change of name or address;
b. the name of any partner who leaves or joins the business;
c. a sole trader taking on a partner;
d. dissolution of a partnership;
e. incorporation; or
f. disincorporation.

The existing certificate will only be **cancelled** in situations **e**. and **f**. above, assuming the farming business is continued. In these circumstances, the new entity can apply for a fresh certificate.

C. Accounting under the scheme

6006 It is important to **separate** the designated agricultural supplies from any other supplies, as flat rate accounting is only concerned with the former. Other supplies are effectively a separate business.

The treatment then depends on the identity of the customer.

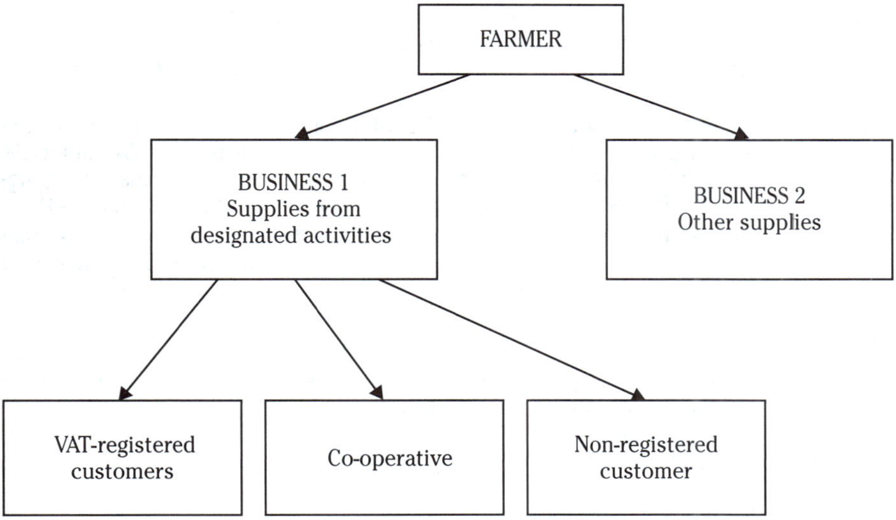

Levy

The levy is only relevant to supplies arising from designated activities. **6008**

It is never charged to **non-registered** customers, including other flat rate farmers.

The farmer must add a 4% levy to the value of designated agricultural supplies which are sold to **VAT-registered customers**. **6010** s 54(3), (4) VATA 1994

If a farmer sells produce through a **farmers' group or co-operative**, no levy is charged to the end customer. The group pays the levy to the farmer when the proceeds of sale are shared out, then reclaims it on its own VAT return. Notice 700/46 para 5

If an **auctioneer** is involved, the treatment of the levy depends on whether the auctioneer is:

– acting in their own name, using either the auctioneers' scheme (¶6750+) or margin scheme (¶6625+), in which case the farmer charges the levy to the auctioneer who can then recover it on their own VAT return; or Notice 700/46 para 8

– not acting in their own name, in which case the farmer can only charge the levy if the eventual buyer is VAT-registered.

MEMO POINTS 1. It is irrelevant whether the supplies made would normally be **zero-rated**, as the levy is a separate system.

2. The levy is **not added** to:
- non-designated supplies;
- sales to other flat rate farmers;
- sales of machinery;
- sales of land; or
- the repair and maintenance of farm buildings which belong to other farmers.

EXAMPLE Mr A is a farmer and sells potatoes to Mr B, a vegetable wholesaler who is VAT-registered. The agreed price is £150.
Mr A will therefore charge the following to Mr B:

	£
Sale price	150
Levy at 4%	6
Total paid by Mr B	156

Mr B enters £6 as input tax in box 4 of his VAT return (¶2998).
Mr A receives income of £156.

6012 Notice 700/46 paras 6.1 - 6.3 **International aspects** The flat rate scheme is in use throughout the **EU**, and therefore **sales** to VAT-registered persons in other EU states are treated in the same way as if the customer was situated in the UK. EU customers can reclaim the levy from HMRC if a proper invoice is retained.

If the levy is suffered on **acquisitions from another EU state**, this can be reclaimed from the tax authority in the supplier's state. The farmer may also have to register for VAT in the UK and therefore leave the flat rate scheme, if the value of EU acquisitions exceeds the registration threshold (¶9962), unless the farmer applies for exemption from registration (¶9044).

s 54(5) VATA 1994 The levy can also be charged to **customers located outside the EU**, if the produce is to be used in the customer's business. In this case, the customer would have to make a special claim (¶9908+) to HMRC to recover the cost.

Invoices

6014 SI 1995/2518 reg 209(3) In order for the levy to be reclaimed as input tax by VAT-registered customers, the farmer must issue an invoice showing the following **information**:
- an identifying invoice number;
- the flat rate certificate number;
- the farmer's name and address;
- the name and address of the customer;
- the date of sale;
- a description of the goods;
- the price payable (including any increase or decrease in price) excluding the levy; and
- the rate and amount of the levy, described as Flat Rate Addition or FRA.

VATAFRS0255 If invoices are issued:
- by a person who does not hold a flat rate certificate; or
- which do not contain the required details; then

a VAT wrongdoing penalty (¶4020+) may be imposed.

VATAFRS0250 The customer must retain the invoice as evidence for the input tax claim. Any levy which is **wrongly charged** cannot be reclaimed by the customer. If such a claim is made, the customer may be liable to a penalty.

It is also possible for customers to **self-bill** (¶2904+), in which case it is advisable for them to inform HMRC that they will be using the agricultural flat rate scheme.

Compliance

6016 VATAFRS0270; SI 1995/2518 regs 210, 211 The farmer makes no **reports**, returns or payments to HMRC.

It is extremely unusual for farmers to be **visited** by HMRC (which would only occur in suspected cases of tax loss or abuse of the scheme), although any requests for information must be met.

The normal business **records** (¶2795+) must be maintained for 6 years (subject to the discretion of HMRC to allow a shorter period on request). Copies must also be kept of all invoices which show an amount of flat rate levy.

Once a year, farmers will receive a letter reminding them of the **eligibility criteria**, and the requirement to notify any change which may affect the certificate.

D. Leaving the scheme

6020 Notice 700/46 para 7; VATAFRS0400 A farmer may either be expelled from the scheme, or may wish to leave. The timing of departure depends on which of these alternatives applies.

A farmer who **becomes VAT-registered** after leaving the scheme cannot claim any pre-registration input tax (¶8560+) incurred whilst a member of the scheme. This is because the farmer has already had the benefit of the levy as compensation for any lost input tax recovery.

Expulsion

6022 SI 1995/2518 regs 206, 207

Reason	Leaving is		Date of cancellation
	Compulsory [1]	At HMRC's discretion	
Makes non-designated supplies in excess of VAT threshold (¶9960)	✓		Effective date of registration
Ceases to make designated supplies (including incorporation [2] and sale of a business)	✓		Date activities cease
Applies for VAT registration	✓		Effective date of registration
Becomes liable to register for VAT because of EU acquisitions [3]	✓		Effective date of registration
Death [4]		✓	Date of death
Bankruptcy or incapacity [4]		✓	Date of bankruptcy or incapacity
False statement made on the application		✓	Date false statement discovered
Tax revenue at risk		✓	Date on which HMRC considers the risk arises
Convicted of a VAT offence		✓	Date of conviction or payment to compound proceedings

Note:
1. Compulsory cancellation of the certificate may be **appealed**.
2. See ¶6002.
3. Unless these **supplies are zero-rated** and HMRC grants exemption from VAT registration. For further details see ¶9040+.
4. In cases of **death, bankruptcy, insolvency, or incapacity**, HMRC can treat anyone who carries on the business as the certificate holder until another certificate is granted, or the incapacity ceases (if relevant). The person taking over the business should notify HMRC within 30 days of starting to farm.

EXAMPLE A business farmed land in the Isles of Scilly, growing and selling bulbs and flowers, and letting holiday accommodation. It also sold flowers bought from other growers (20 % of the business). In 1995 it applied to join the agricultural flat rate scheme and was accepted.
In 1997 its membership was cancelled (retrospectively back to the date of commencement), because the total income from the sale of bought-in flowers and holiday accommodation letting exceeded the VAT registration threshold.
On appeal, the tribunal held that the buying and selling of cut flowers were not separate parts of the business, because the bought-in flowers were mixed in with the grown flowers. A business was carried on which qualified as the "growing of fruit and vegetables, flowers and ornamental plants".
The appeal was allowed, so that membership was not cancelled. *A & H Julian* [2000] (VTD 16532)

Voluntarily

Often a farmer will leave the scheme in order to become voluntarily VAT-registered for the recovery of input tax. 6024 Notice 700/46 para 7.1

The farmer can choose to leave the scheme after they have already been **using it for a period of at least a year**, except when the farmer voluntarily registers for VAT because of EU acquisitions, in which case there is no minimum time requirement.

A written application must be made to HMRC (using the address in ¶5996), who will write to the farmer confirming the **date of cancellation**, which will normally be the date requested by the farmer.

CHAPTER 3

Bloodstock

OUTLINE ¶¶

SECTION 1

General principles

Types of activity

The horse racing industry involves a wide range of activities, and several types of persons who undertake them. VAT can impinge on these activities and persons in different ways, depending on the business nature of the activity: 6100

Activity	Business?	VAT treatment	¶¶
Horse breeders [1]	Yes	Normal registration	¶6110+
Trainers [1]	Yes	Normal registration	¶6130+
Professional jockeys	Yes	Normal registration	¶6140+

Activity	Business?	VAT treatment	¶¶
Agents	Yes	Normal registration	¶6150+
Owners of horses[2]	No	Special registration scheme	¶6160+
Other amateur activities[3]	No	Outside the scope	

Notes
1. Breeders, trainers and dealers may also own and race horses but these activities are usually treated as part of their main business.
2. In this chapter "owners" refers to persons who own and race horses, but who are not breeders, trainers or agents.
3. Point-to-point, although a largely amateur activity, can be encompassed within the owners' special registration scheme (¶6224+).

For the use of racehorses for business promotion see ¶1830.

Finally, there are several public and private bodies which together manage and control the industry. Much of the present VAT treatment has been developed by HMRC in co-operation with these bodies, of which the main ones are:

Name	Purpose	Website
British Horseracing Authority (BHA)	Official governing body of the sport	britishhorseracing.com
Weatherbys Group	Administrators under contract to the BHA	weatherbys.co.uk
Jockey Club	Regulates horseracing in Great Britain	thejockeyclub.co.uk
British Equestrian Trade Association	Trade organisation for the equestrian manufacturing, wholesale and retail trades	beta-uk.org

Recent changes

6102 The bloodstock industry is international, so before 1 January 2010 the VAT treatment of bloodstock was greatly complicated by the place of supply rules for goods and services. Special rules had to be developed to cope with the particular nature of the industry. From 1 January 2010, however, these were replaced by the new general rules governing place of supply. For details of the former rules see *VAT Memo 2010-2011*.

Further changes to the place of supply rules were introduced on 1 January 2011, and these are covered in the text.

SECTION 2

Activities other than ownership

A. Interaction with ownership

6105 Notice 700/57 section 18

Persons **involved in the horse racing industry** can register for VAT and reclaim input tax in the usual way, provided that a business activity is being undertaken.

If the person also owns racehorses, this will be part of the overall business activity, provided that the racing takes place for publicity or some other commercial purpose. Any prize money received will be outside the scope of VAT (¶6134). If racing is to be covered by an existing VAT registration, a D form (¶6202) should be submitted to HMRC.

Activity undertaken	Main business covered by VAT registration	Racehorse ownership treated as part of normal VAT registration
Breeding	Breeds horses with a view to selling the majority of foals Reasonable expectation of profits (can be over a period of years)	Horses (i.e. colts [1], fillies [2] or home-bred geldings [3]) which are raced for publicity, or to enhance the value of the stock, are integrated into the main business activity Horses which are specifically bred for the breeder themselves to race are outside the main business
Agency (or dealing) [4]	Frequent turnover of stock Prices set for profit	Able to race horses (for business purposes) held in stock, provided that horses still available for sale
Training	Operates under an unrestricted licence Charge for services set at arm's-length rate	Training of privately owned horses to attract new business can be part of the VAT registration, provided that the number of such horses is not disproportionate

Note:
1. A **colt** is a young male horse under 4 years old.
2. Similarly, a **filly** is a young female horse under 4 years old.
3. A **gelding** is a castrated male horse.
4. The terms "dealer" and "dealing" are rarely used in this industry. A bloodstock agent may deal in their own right, but is still referred to as an agent.

B. Breeders

A breeder will raise thoroughbred racehorses at a stud with a view to a future sale. Whereas some studs do own stallions, others only keep mares who will visit the stallion for mating (known as covering), then return to the stud during the subsequent pregnancy. 6110

The young horse (known as a foal up to 12 months, then a yearling) is either sold, or trained for racing once it is 2 years old. Racing the horse demonstrates its breeding potential.

VAT registration

Registration will be allowed if the breeder is in business, rather than just enjoying an expensive hobby. 6112 VBNB56000

The **business intention** cannot be measured purely by looking at the number of mares at the stud, as only some mares may produce offspring every year, and the sale proceeds of each bred horse will depend on its family history. HMRC will examine all applications carefully, because breeders are often repayment traders.

MEMO POINTS 1. For details of what constitutes a **business** for VAT purposes, see ¶100+.
2. Breeders are often repayment traders, hence **monthly VAT returns** (¶2990) may be an advantage.
3. Another option is for breeders to join the **agricultural flat rate scheme** (¶5970+).

Private use and gifts of horses

Output tax will be due if any bred horse is put to **permanent** private use, or given away. 6114

MEMO POINTS A Memorandum of Practice agreed with HMRC states that the **value** of a **yearling** upon which output tax is due is the production cost, calculated as the sum of: Notice 700/57 section 19
– the stallion service fee (if no fee was actually paid, this defaults to £275);

– vet fees spent on the foal since birth;
– total cost of keep of the mare during the year of gestation (based on the rates recommended by the Newmarket Stud Farmers Association (NSFA));
– cost of keep of the foal from the date of weaning to the date of private use (based on the rates recommended by the NSFA); and
– any other VATable expenses.

Although breeders may use an alternative method to ascertain the value, this formula should be borne in mind. In particular, any depreciation of the mare must be ignored.

6115 Notice 700/57 section 19

If a racehorse is **temporarily** put to private use, whilst remaining an asset of the racing business, this is a taxable supply of services by the owner.

The annual taxable **value** of these services for a yearling is 1/8th of the production cost. For older horses, the value to be used is that of the animal at the yearling stage.

Livery services

6116 Notice 701/15 para 10

Livery services are provided for horses in a stable. These include feeding and watering, mucking out, turning out, worming, clipping, plaiting, exercising, cleaning tack, grooming, breaking in, schooling, and arranging for veterinary care.

Where **stabling and livery services** are combined together as a single supply, they are exempt from VAT, because the principal supply is the right to occupy a stable. However, stables which specialise in **breaking in and schooling** are making taxable supplies.

Feed can be zero-rated only if no element of care is provided.

Sales of horses

6117 The sale of a horse is a supply of goods. The main issue is the place of supply.

If the horse is physically located **in the UK** at the time of sale, the position depends on the destination to which the horse is being sent, as follows:

Destination	Purchaser's status	VAT treatment
Outside the EU [1,2]	Not relevant	Zero-rated
Within the EU [1]	VAT-registered	Zero-rated, provided that purchaser accounts for VAT [3] (¶9010+)
	Unregistered	Standard-rated
UK	Not relevant	Standard-rated

Notes
1. The seller must retain evidence of export, or HMRC may raise an assessment to recover VAT at the standard rate because there is no proof that the horse left the UK.
2. HMRC has agreed the time limits within which a horse must be exported by a non-EU purchaser to qualify for zero-rating. The animal may remain within the UK (to be trained or covered) for up to six months, or 12 months if it is not raced and the relief is not transferred to another EU person. The seller must make a written request to use the 12-month limit.
3. The seller should obtain the purchaser's VAT number, and the sale must be included in the seller's EC sales list (¶9330+).

If the horse is physically located **in another EU member state** at the time of sale, VAT will, in principle, be due on a supply in that member state. (Both France and Ireland have special reduced VAT rates for sales of thoroughbreds.) The actual position therefore depends on the rules for VAT in the country in which the horse is located.

Sales of shares in horses

6118 Sch 4 para 1 VATA 1994

The sale of a part ownership in a horse is a supply of services, not of goods. The main issue is the place of supply; this depends on where the purchaser "belongs" (¶9688+) and whether the purchaser is in business:

Purchaser belongs	Purchaser in business? 1	Place of supply	VAT treatment
In the UK	Yes or no	UK	UK taxable supply
In another EU member state	Yes	The purchaser's state	No UK taxable supply; purchaser accounts for VAT as a reverse charge (¶9700+)
	No	UK	UK taxable supply
Outside the EU	Yes or no	Outside the EU	Outside the scope

Notes
1. "In business" essentially means that the purchaser is registered for VAT (or the local equivalent), and the supply is received at least partly for business purposes (¶9684). For this purpose a flat-rate farmer (¶5970+) counts as registered for VAT.

Leasing of horses for racing

A breeder may prefer to lease a horse to another person, who can then take on the responsibilities and costs of racing it. The lease must be registered with the BHA, and is a taxable supply of services by the breeder. The breeder should then avoid incurring any racing costs on the horse, because they will not be able to recover the input tax. **6119** VBNB56000

The place of supply is determined in the same way as for part sales (¶6118). However, the use and enjoyment rule (¶9758+) also applies.

Stallions

Nominations The right to submit a mare to be covered by a stallion in one breeding season is known as a nomination. **6120** VBNB56000

Both nominations and the covering of mares are regarded as **services** for VAT purposes, and are treated as "work done to goods".

Nominations may be given **free** when the stallion is young (known as a colt until he is 4 years old), to enhance his reputation; these are outside the scope of VAT.

When nominations come to be sold for **consideration**, this is a taxable supply. In particular, where a stallion nomination is exchanged or bartered, there will be two supplies.

MEMO POINTS An example of a **barter transaction** is where the consideration given for the stallion's keep at stud is in the form of free nominations, or a mixture of cash and nominations. Notice 700/57 section 20
Under a special agreement (which does not apply to VAT-registered syndicates (¶6126+)), the **value** of the free nomination is derived from the proceeds obtained from the sale of nominations for that stallion, or, if none have been sold, the average reported value. In any event, the **maximum** value of keep, where nominations are part of the consideration, is £30,000. As the nomination relates to an annual event, 25% of the value is entered on the quarterly VAT return.
There are different types of nomination, each with its own rules as to how much value is brought into account, as follows:

Nomination	Details	Percentage of value to be taken into account
Straight	No conditions attached	100%
1 October pregnancy	Covering results in pregnancy	70%
Split payment	Two payments	100% of first payment 70% of second
Live foal	Only paid if live foal results from the covering	60%

The **place of supply** of a nomination depends on where the covering takes place, and the situation of the mare, as follows: **6122**

Location of stallion	Circumstances of mare	Mare's owner VAT-registered?	Place of supply	VAT liability
UK	UK	Not relevant	UK	Standard rate
UK	Visiting from outside the EU, and returns home within a reasonable time[1]	Yes	Outside UK	Zero rate[2]
UK	Exported from EU after covering within a reasonable time[1]	Yes	Outside UK	Zero rate[2]
UK	Visiting from another EU state, and returns home within a reasonable time[1]	Yes	Outside UK	Mare's owner accounts for VAT in EU state[2]
UK	Visiting from another EU state, and returns home within a reasonable time[1]	No	UK	Standard rate

Note:
1. A **reasonable time** is normally interpreted as meaning by the end of the covering season (15 July).
2. The VAT liability will also extend to **services** connected with the covering, such as keep fees.

6124 VATTOS9650 When determining the **time of supply**, the basic tax point (¶764) of a:
- straight nomination is 15 July (the final day of the covering season), because a contract does not become binding until then; and
- live foal nomination is 1 October following the season.

However, the normal rules relating to payment and invoicing (¶760+) still apply.

6126 VBNB56000 **Syndication** A colt that has breeding potential is often syndicated into 40 **stallion shares**. Each share gives the holder the right to one nomination during each covering season (15 February to 15 July). Such a share may be sold or transferred, and this constitutes a supply of services.

MEMO POINTS 1. The **place of supply** is determined according to ¶6118.
2. Shares may be acquired in **instalments**; the VAT treatment depends on whether the rights to nomination are:
- all transferred before the stallion starts covering, in which case VAT is immediately due on the transfer; or
- withheld pending another instalment, in which case VAT is due on the earlier of when payment is received or a VAT invoice is issued.

6127 The sale of all the shares constitutes the **sale of the whole stallion**. This is a supply of goods, in which case the VAT treatment depends on the place of supply, as follows:

Situation of stallion	VAT treatment
Sold and remains in UK	Standard-rated
Sold whilst outside UK	Outside the scope
Exported outside the EU	Zero-rated
Transferred to VAT-registered purchaser in the EU	Zero-rated (acquirer accounts for VAT in EU state as an EU acquisition (¶9017+))

EXAMPLE A breeder owned a 1/40th share in each of two syndicates, one of which owned a stallion at stud in the UK, the other a stallion in Ireland. Both syndicates sold the whole of each horse to a Japanese purchaser.
It was held that, as the whole horse had been sold in each case, this was a supply of goods, so the sale of:
- the Irish stallion was outside the scope of UK VAT; and
- the UK stallion should be zero-rated, because it was to be exported. *Sir John Astor* [1981] (VTD 1030)

Syndicates which **sell additional nominations** (i.e. other than the initial 40), resulting in consideration exceeding the VAT registration threshold, are required to account for VAT. A syndicate will usually appoint a secretary (a solicitor or bloodstock agent) to deal with its affairs, and it is the secretary who deals with VAT, avoiding the need for the syndicate to register as a partnership. **6128** Business Brief 13/00

MEMO POINTS The **secretary** is an agent acting in their own name (¶7142+). They will raise a VAT invoice to the purchaser for the proceeds of each nomination sold, showing the secretary's own VAT number on the invoice. The syndicate members must raise an invoice for the proceeds of the nomination to the secretary, and this invoice will have the same tax point as the original supply of the nomination. Members who are VAT-registered will also charge VAT, which the secretary can recover as input tax.
The stud will invoice the secretary for keep fees, and the secretary can recover the related input tax. All costs incurred on behalf of the syndicate are passed on to the members. The secretary charges output tax on this onward supply.

C. Trainers

Since 1 January 2011 the place of supply of training services to a business customer has been brought within the general business-to-business rules - that is, supplied where the customer belongs (¶9682+). Supplies to non-business customers are UK standard-rated. **6130** VBNB57100

VAT is chargeable on all expenses incurred by the trainer which are passed on to the owner, including the costs of overseas travel and accommodation of both the horse and the trainer's staff.

Trainers are also responsible for VAT accounting in respect of certain types of jockey (¶6142)

Part ownership

If the trainer owns a part share in a horse by being a member of a **racing partnership** and the partnership registers for VAT, the trainer must join their registration. The recovery of input tax relating to the racing activities cannot then be made through the trainer's own training VAT registration. **6132**

If the trainer **trains the horse** in which they own a part share, they need only invoice for a proportion of the cost. For example, if the trainer owns 40% of the horse, they need only raise an invoice for 60% of the training cost.

Prize money

UK prize money received under the Rules of Racing is outside the scope of VAT. Any further amount (such as an additional percentage above that allowed under the Rules of Racing) is consideration for a taxable supply. **6134**

Any prize money received for a horse racing **overseas** is outside the scope of UK VAT.

Gifts

Trainers often receive gifts, which are treated for VAT purposes as follows: **6136**

Type of gift	Details	VAT treatment
Cash	Not received under a contract	Outside the scope
Stallion shares or nominations	¶6118	Taxable - VAT due on open-market value
Annual breeding right	Allows the holder to nominate a mare to be covered by a stallion; cannot be sold or transferred (unlike a nomination)	Taxable - VAT due on agreed market value

D. Jockeys

6140 VBNB58000 A **professional** jockey's main income is from riding fees and prize money won (of which the jockey receives a set percentage; the VAT treatment is as discussed at ¶6134). They may also receive sponsorship, which is consideration for a taxable supply. A jockey is not allowed to own a racehorse in training, although they may be involved in breeding.

Riding fees

6142 Each ride earns the jockey a set fee.

Since 1 January 2011 the place of supply has been brought within the general business-to-business rules (¶9682+) for **business customers**. Supplies to **non-business customers** remain subject to VAT in any member state where they are performed (see the example below).

Weatherbys record all UK rides and fees, and send the jockey a monthly statement and self-billing invoice.

Certain jockeys may be retained by a trainer or owner. The place of supply for the **retention fee**, which is standard-rated, is the same as the riding fee. In this case, the jockey's expenses will be covered by the trainer.

Jockeys who are not retained will incur their own **expenses**, and input tax can be recovered if the jockey is registered for VAT.

MEMO POINTS 1. Jockeys who **race abroad** may incur a liability to register in other EU member states which, although administratively tiresome, does allow them to recover input tax incurred in those states.
2. There are other types of jockey, known as **apprentices** and **conditional jockeys**, who are employees of the trainer. The riding fee received depends on the type of jockey, as follows:
– for apprentices and conditional jockeys who claim a 7lb allowance, 50% of the fee (including VAT) is paid to the jockey and the trainer receives the remaining amount - the trainer accounts for VAT on the whole fee; and
– for conditional jockeys claiming a 3lb or 5lb allowance, or no allowance, the whole fee (excluding VAT) is paid to the jockey, and the trainer receives the VAT element only, which must be declared as output tax. *C&E v RJ and AS Hodges* [2000]

EXAMPLE An Irish trainer paid a substantial sum to a UK company to retain a UK jockey for races outside the UK. An assessment was issued, treating the payment as liable to UK VAT.
It was held that the jockey was making a supply of sporting services, and the place of supply was therefore outside the UK. The payment was not within the scope of UK VAT. *Patrick Eddery Ltd* [1986] (VTD 2009)

E. Agents

6150 VBNB58200 Most transactions in the racing industry, including purchases and sales of horses, shares and nominations, involve the use of a **bloodstock agent**. At different times the agent may be acting on behalf of a third party (the principal), or may themselves be acting as a principal. The VAT treatment of any transaction depends on whether the agent is acting as an agent or a principal.

When an agent **acts as principal**, they are liable to register and account for VAT in the usual way.

MEMO POINTS Note that an agent who arranges a supply of goods (but not services) in their own name (for example, by issuing an invoice with their name on it) is treated as a principal for VAT purposes, even though in general law they may be acting as an agent.

Acting as agent

Where an agent openly acts as an **intermediary** between two other parties, the agent is not required to account for VAT on the main transaction, but only on their own fees for acting as agent. For issues relating to agency generally see ¶7090+. 6152

SECTION 3

Ownership

Owning a racehorse is very expensive, and an owner with no other business interests would be unable to recover any input tax under the normal VAT rules. 6160

However, HMRC has granted a dispensation to the horse racing industry by allowing all owners who comply with certain criteria to register for VAT.

Alternatively, racehorse owners are eligible to join the agricultural flat rate scheme in limited circumstances (¶5970+).

MEMO POINTS A racehorse may be owned by a syndicate. This is different from a **stallion** syndicate, which is dealt with at ¶6126+.

Summary

Once the horse has been purchased, the owner must complete the following steps to become VAT-registered. 6162

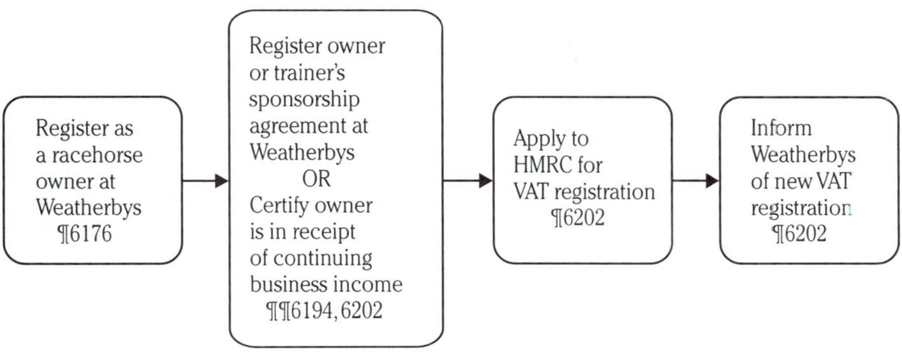

A. Acquiring a horse

An acquisition may be arranged privately, or agreed at public auction. In addition, races are specifically held where all of the horses are for sale. 6166

The usual place of supply rules for goods apply (¶278). If the sale takes place in the UK, this is a standard-rated supply.

Where the horse is to be co-owned (¶6180) and input tax is to be recovered, it is important that a VAT invoice is made out to the correct entity. This could be achieved by the seller invoicing:
- the entity itself; or
- one of the co-owners, who then raises further VAT invoices to the other co-owners.

MEMO POINTS 1. An owner will often use a trainer or bloodstock **agent** (¶6150+) to acquire the horse. The bloodstock agent's fee is usually 5% of the purchase price.
2. An **auction** house will usually receive a 5% commission.
3. On any **subsequent sale**, if no VAT was due on purchase, the owner would then have the option to charge output tax on the profit margin only (¶6620).

Second-hand horses

6168 Notice 700/67 paras 5.3, 5.4

A horse acquired from another owner (other than the breeder) will be second-hand.

In such a case there is a particular **record-keeping** requirement, depending on whether the horse is bought:
a. from a **private person**, in which case the buyer should complete a special form (¶6218) as appropriate and ask the seller to sign the reverse of part A, confirming that they are the seller and are selling the horse at the price shown; the purchaser should then retain all three parts of the form, which will be required when the animal is sold;
b. from a person **operating the margin scheme** (¶6625+), in which case the seller must give the purchaser part C of the form, completed at the time of the original purchase, as well as the purchaser completing a new form in respect of this purchase; there is no requirement for the seller to sign part A of the form; or
c. at auction, in which case the position will be the same as for a horse bought from a private person or under the margin scheme, with the additional requirement that the auctioneer should supply details of their name and address, along with the lot number on the back of part A; if bought under the margin scheme, the auctioneer will pass part C of the form to the purchaser.

Overseas purchases

6170 Often horses are acquired from overseas and brought permanently into the UK for training and racing.

VAT is due on the **import** of a horse from outside the EU. Depending on the form of co-ownership, it may be necessary for just one of the owners to be treated as the importer, to recover the import VAT, then invoice the other owners for their share. For details of imports see ¶9405+.

6172 Notice 200

Temporary importation There is a relief from import VAT (¶9509+) when a horse is temporarily brought into the UK or an EU member state for any of the following **purposes**:
- training;
- covering;
- to run in a specific race; or
- veterinary treatment.

The horse can only stay for a **period** of 2 years (subject to a discretionary 6-month extension). If the horse is sold whilst temporarily imported, VAT becomes due (¶9410+).

B. Racing registration

6176 All owners must be registered for racing with the Jockey Club and the BHA. The process is undertaken by Weatherbys and involves a standard-rated fee.

6178 It is important to **identify** the type of ownership, as this will determine whether VAT registration is required, or at least whether it is advantageous.

The types of horse ownership are:
a. sole, where all racing costs and income accrue to one individual (when form RS1 should be used to apply for racing registration); or
b. co-ownership in a variety of guises (otherwise known as a racing syndication).

Co-ownership

Co-ownership includes the following: 6180

Arrangement	Details	Form to be used for racing registration
Company	The shareholders own the horse A registered agent must act on the company's behalf in relation to all racing rules	RO2
Joint ownership	Agreement between two and twelve individuals Horse can be run in the name of one of the owners, or in the name of the joint ownership Separate registration is required for each horse	JO1
Racing partnership[1]	Agreement between two and twenty individuals At least two partners must become registered owners, known as nominated partners All horses run in the name of the partnership and are covered by a single racing registration	RP1
Business partnership	Business which is already trading as a partnership Maximum of four such partnerships register as owners	RO3
Racing clubs	Each member leases an ownership interest from the club but does not own any horses There are various types of club, including: – companies which sell their own shares to investors; and – those financed by members' subscriptions	Depends on type of entity
Leasing	Horse is owned for a fixed term only Lessee becomes the owner for the purposes of the racing rules	L1 or L2

Note:
1. Within this category, there are **three types**:
a. trainer managed, where the trainer sets up the partnership and deals with administration;
b. social groups (those where friends come together); and
c. professional partnerships, managed by an organiser who charges administration fees.

C. Sponsorship

The **costs** of maintaining a racehorse are prohibitively expensive, so owners are advised to obtain sponsorship for every horse. This not only mitigates some of the expense but also enables the owner to register for VAT and therefore reclaim input tax, even where no other business activity is undertaken. 6184

For this purpose, sponsorship is **defined** as a business relationship between: BHA Racehorse Owners' Sponsorship Code of Conduct
- a provider of funds, resources or services; and
- an individual, event or organisation which offers in return rights and association that can be used for commercial advantage.

Obtaining a sponsor

In order to obtain **sponsorship**, the owner can approach any of the following: 6186
- the trainer, whose yard may already be covered by sponsorship, in which case the owner can arrange for the horse to be included in this agreement;
- existing business contacts; or
- sponsorship agents, who will match up potential sponsors and owners for a fee.

It should be remembered that sponsorship is not altruistic, but gives reciprocal commercial benefit to both owner and sponsor.

Branding

6188 BHA Racehorse Owners' Sponsorship Code of Conduct

In return for sponsorship, the owner accepts an **obligation** to show the sponsor's branding on specific sites, including the jockey's clothing, attendants' clothing or the horse's rugs. HMRC checks that the branding is properly displayed at races, as this is a determinant of whether VAT registration is appropriate.

MEMO POINTS 1. There are strict criteria which govern the exact **place and size** of the branding information.
2. The **term** of the sponsorship contract cannot exceed 3 years but should last at least 1 year.
3. A **company** can sponsor its own racehorses, although there must also be at least one other sponsorship agreement registered at Weatherbys which involves a third party.
4. In addition, **racecourses** obtain branding revenue for each race, resulting in additional business income for the owner of each starting horse.

Value

6190 Sponsorship for the right to use branding sites must be of a **minimum** value, which depends on the number of horses owned.

Agreements which fail to achieve these values cannot provide a basis for VAT registration.

Number of horses	Has horse ever run in a Class A race? [1]	Minimum sponsorship per horse per annum [2]
1 to 9	No	£300
	Yes	£750
10 or more	n/a	£100

Note:
1. A Class A race is any Group, Graded or Listed race in Great Britain. Owners should warn sponsors of the increase in support resulting from a horse entering such a race.
2. These amounts are not pro-rated for periods of less than a year.

D. VAT registration scheme

6194 VBNB50050

Under the scheme, owners must declare their **intention** to organise their racing interests as a business.

In practice, this means that before VAT registration can occur the owner must have:
- secured sponsorship for the horse, as evidenced by an agreement submitted to Weatherbys; and/or
- received business income derived from racing, such as prize money, appearance money, or advertising revenue.

There are special rules for point-to-point horses (¶6224+).

Notice 700/57 section 18

MEMO POINTS 1. **Appearance money** is relatively uncommon, so it is unlikely that an owner would apply for VAT registration on this ground alone.
2. This **scheme** is subject to periodic review by HMRC. If it is ever **withdrawn**, there will be a three-month transitional period during which racing registrations will be cancelled. VAT registration will continue for those with other business interests. It is unlikely that input tax recovered would need to be repaid. No output tax would be due on stock and assets held on the date of deregistration.

Who must register?

6196 Notice 700/67 para 2.2

The actual legal owner, who may be a sole trader, partnership, or company, must apply for registration.

For owners of **part shares**, the person who must register depends on whether the individual owns:
- at least 50% of the horse, in which case VAT registration in the person's own name is required; or
- less than 50%, in which case the person can only register with the other part share owners as a partnership.

Racing clubs The VAT registration implications of the various types of racing club are summarised in the following table: **6198** Notice 700/67 paras 7.1 - 7.4

Type of entity	Members' interest	VAT implications	VAT registration?
Limited company	Members buy shares in the company Members may receive dividends and also benefits such as visits to trainers and free entry to racecourses	Issue of shares is outside the scope of VAT Sale of existing shares is exempt Members' benefits are disregarded	Can only register for VAT under the scheme
Racing partnership	Members buy shares in the venture Members only receive proceeds from prizes and sales on termination of partnership Members may receive benefits as described above	Sale of shares is outside the scope of VAT Members' benefits are disregarded	Can only register for VAT under the scheme
Association (not a company or partnership)	Members pay a subscription in return for membership and benefits as described above Club uses subscription monies to purchase racehorses Surplus income distributed to members at the year end	Carrying on a business activity; subscription monies are VATable	Under normal rules
	As above, but members receive no benefits	Subscriptions outside the scope of VAT	Can only register for VAT under the scheme

Scope

If some **horses** owned by the person are **not sponsored**, they can still be included in the VAT registration, provided that the owner is actively seeking sponsorship. If this is not obtained within 6 months, HMRC will monitor the situation and it may be that input tax recovery will be restricted. **6200** Notice 700/67 para 3

Similarly, if the sponsorship **agreement expires** after VAT registration has been obtained, the registration will validly continue if the owner can prove they are seeking sponsorship. There is no time limit by which new sponsorship should be obtained, although HMRC expects the gap to be no longer than 6 months. VBNB52000

For horses covered by a **trainer's sponsorship agreement**, VAT registration will be forthcoming even where payments to the owner are contingent on the horse winning.

Application

The **process** requires a D form (D1 for sole owners, D2 for partnerships) and a VAT registration form. All these forms are available from Weatherbys' website (¶6100). **6202** Notice 700/67 para 2.1; VBNB50200

The D form is completed first, confirming that there is a sponsorship agreement, or that business income relating to the owned horses has been received (and will continue).

Weatherbys must then verify these details (which involves posting the D form to them for certification), before the D form is submitted to HMRC, along with the usual VAT registration form (¶2704+).

Once the application has been processed, Weatherbys must be informed of the VAT registration details.

MEMO POINTS 1. **D forms** should be **sent to**:
VAT Declarations
Weatherbys
Sanders Road
Wellingborough
Northamptonshire
NN8 4BX
2. The **VAT registration form**, together with Weatherbys' authorised declaration, must be **sent to** the VAT registration centre which covers the applicant's postcode (¶9994).

Input tax recovery

6204 Notice 700/67 paras 4.1 - 4.7; VBNB52500;

VAT-registered owners can recover input tax under the usual rules on expenses relating to their racehorse interests. Only VAT incurred by the owner can be recovered, which in practice means that all **invoices** must be made out to them.

Full input tax recovery can be made on the following **direct costs**:
- purchasing the horse (¶6166+);
- training fees;
- vet's fees;
- blacksmith's fees;
- transportation of the horse;
- gallop fees;
- entry fees (the BHA administrative element only);
- jockey's fees and retainers; and
- livery yard and keep costs incurred whilst the horse is absent from the trainer's premises.

MEMO POINTS 1. Weatherbys **notify** owners of **input tax** suffered on certain direct costs, such as jockey's services and other fees.
2. If a racehorse is **injured** input tax can still be recovered, provided that there is an expectation that it will race again.
3. Where there is any **non-business use** of goods and services special rules apply (¶1838+). For goods which are subsequently put to private use (such as trophies), output tax must be charged (¶1520+).
4. **Pre-registration** input tax may be recovered under the normal rules (¶8560+).

6206 Input tax recovery on the following **peripheral costs**, incurred when owners wish to see their horses train or race, is subject to certain criteria.

Area	Detail	Input tax recovery on
Travel	By privately owned car	Costs of running a car if the owner operates the scale charge (¶1876)
	By hire car	Hire charge (but not fuel costs) if there is a valid reason for using a hire car However, if the period of hire exceeds 10 days (even if the journey is exclusively for business purposes) only 50% of the input tax can be recovered (¶1920+)
	By taxi	Fare, if valid reason for using taxi
	By private chartered aircraft	Cost is likely to be challenged
Accommodation	Only if destination distant from owner's residence	A single night's accommodation Longer by exception
Meals and subsistence	Excluding meals/drinks taken at the racecourse	Reasonable costs Not including any business entertaining (¶1926+)

Area	Detail	Input tax recovery on
Telephone		10% of telephone costs, including mobile phones and, where applicable, line installation and rental, phone purchase and call charges Larger proportion only if owner has evidence
Racecourse administration fee	Only where owner's horse is declared to run	Full fee if VAT invoice received In most cases owner receives free entry
Other BHA charges	If taxable	Full cost
Subscriptions	Racehorse Owners' Association	Full cost
Professional fees	Such as bloodstock agents, accountants, fees payable to the BHA, and fees under the Rules of Racing	Where relate to business activity of racing
Advertising	Of the racing activity	Full cost
Lease of executive boxes	By larger owners and trainers	50% of costs if genuine business purpose If subleased, 60% of costs
Office	Unless owner has substantial racing interest	None

MEMO POINTS **Permit holders** are amateur National Hunt trainers who train their own horses and those of relatives. The scope of their input tax recovery is widened to include: **6207** VBNB52700
- horseboxes;
- loose boxes;
- tack; and
- office costs,

provided that they are used for business purposes. Otherwise, input tax should be apportioned (perhaps based on the number of horses). Permit holders must charge output tax on amounts received from relatives in respect of training.

Output tax

A VAT-registered owner must account for output tax on: **6208** Notice 700/67 paras 5.1 - 5.4; VBNB52600
- sponsorship monies;
- prizes and appearance money;
- any private use of the horse; and
- the sale of the horse (the exact treatment of which depends on whether the owner paid input tax on its acquisition).

Sponsorship monies The supply of advertising and promotion in return for consideration is a standard-rated supply. **6210**

Prizes and appearance money Proceeds received from these sources are treated as consideration for a standard-rated supply. Output tax on prize money is calculated on the net amount received after **entry fees or commission** have been deducted by the racecourse. Output tax is not due on any sweepstake element. **6212** Notice 700/67 para 5.6

If **notified of the owner's VAT registration number**, output tax accounting is automated by Weatherbys, who operate a self-billing system (¶2904+). The owner will receive a Transaction Analysis Summary showing the output tax due.

Private use or gifting away In common with other goods acquired for the business, output tax must be accounted for on the private use or gift of a horse where input tax was recovered on its acquisition. **6214** Notice 700/67 para 5.5

The **value** upon which output tax must be charged is the open-market value at the time of disposal; this may require a professional valuation from a bloodstock agent, taking into account the horse's age and fitness. Regard should also be had to the guidance for breeders (¶6114+).

6216 **Sale** The sale of the **whole horse** is a supply of goods and is usually standard-rated where the sale takes place in the UK, except where the seller chooses to use the margin scheme (¶6625+), or if the horse will be leaving the UK (¶6117).

Where a **share** in a horse is sold, this is a supply of services (¶6118). The VAT treatment depends on where the supply is made (¶9682+) and the identity of the purchaser.

MEMO POINTS 1. If **exporting** the horse (outside the EU), the required documentation must be retained (¶9586+). On request, the time limit for exportation can be extended to 12 months for horses which remain here for breaking, conditioning, training or covering, provided that:
- they are not raced in the UK prior to export; and
- the ownership of the horse is not transferred to another overseas person.

2. If a horse is **leased** rather than sold, the place of supply will be where it is enjoyed, which in practice means where the horse stands.

6218 Notice 718 para 2.3 The owner may prefer to charge output tax on the margin of sale only, under the **margin scheme** (¶6625+), provided that the correct procedure was followed at the time of acquisition.

MEMO POINTS 1. The rules for **record-keeping** are modified for sales of horses under the scheme. There is no need for the usual stock book or invoices to be retained. Instead a special form (available from the British Equestrian Trade Association) must be used for each horse that is sold. The form is in three parts:
- part A is the seller's stock record;
- part B is the seller's copy invoice; and
- part C is the customer's purchase invoice.

On a sale, the particulars must be completed on the form and part C passed to the purchaser.

2. If the horse is being sold **at auction**, the auctioneer must be told in advance that the animal is being sold under the margin scheme, and parts B and C should be passed to them for completion. After the sale the auctioneer will pass part C of the form to the purchaser, returning part B to the seller for their records.

Records

6220 Although there are no specific record-keeping requirements under the special VAT registration scheme, owners **must retain** sufficient information to support their VAT accounting, such as:
- details of all correspondence relating to sponsorship deals and approaches made;
- the date of the horse's acquisition, price and input tax incurred;
- details of any transportation of the horse (including all overseas trips); and
- the date of disposal, proceeds and the output tax accounted for.

Weatherbys' transaction listings are also vital records, and must be kept.

E. Point-to-point horses

6224 VBNB52700 Point-to-pointing is an amateur sport, often seen as the training stage to full horse racing for jockeys, owners, trainers and officials.

Notice 700/67 para 6.1 A point-to-point horse is ignored for the purposes of VAT registration until it has raced in a hunter chase. From that point onwards, it may be included in a VAT registration if it is covered by sponsorship (¶6184+), in which case it is known as a **qualifying horse**.

Registration

6226 Notice 700/67 paras 6.2, 6.4 An owner can register for VAT for the **season** (which runs from January to June), following the rules as outlined in ¶6160+. The effective date of registration will be the date of the first race in which the horse is entered.

An owner can also **remain registered after June**, provided that they can show that they intend to enter the horse into future hunter chases in the next season, and either:
- the existing sponsorship agreement is to continue; or
- they intend to obtain sponsorship before the horse next races.

Otherwise the owner will either be deregistered, or the VAT registration will continue based on the owner's other business interests, with no input tax recovery on the horse.

MEMO POINTS 1. A horse which is **purchased during the season** will retain its qualifying status for VAT if the new owner intends to enter it into hunter chases during the year of purchase.
2. If the owner is **already VAT-registered**, form D1 or D2 must still be completed (¶6202). Notice 700/67 para 6.3

Input tax recovery

The general rules outlined in ¶6204+ are amended as follows for qualifying horses: **6228** Notice 700/67 para 6.6
a. on the **purchase of the horse**, 50% of the input tax suffered can be recovered, provided that the VAT was charged within the 3 years prior to the date of registration;
b. in relation to **training, keep and other costs** incurred:
- from the date of registration all input tax can be recovered;
- in the 6 months prior to registration (or date of the first race) 50% of the input tax can be recovered; and

c. on the **purchase or construction of fixed assets** (e.g. stables or a transporter), all of the input tax suffered after registration can be recovered, unless the asset is used for non-qualifying horses as well, in which case an apportionment must be made.

Output tax

The following modifications are made to the general rules outlined in ¶6208+: **6230** Notice 700/67 para 6.5

Situation	VAT treatment
Sale of home-bred qualifying horse	If input tax is recovered on the breeding costs, output tax must be charged on sale
Sale of non-qualifying horse	If no input tax is ever recovered on the horse, no output tax is chargeable on the sale
Horse ceases to be a qualifying horse (e.g. taken into private use)	Output tax is charged on only 50% of open-market value

CHAPTER 4

Retailers

OUTLINE ¶¶

As retailers generally make supplies to the end consumer (who is not VAT-registered), HMRC is keen to ensure that VAT is accounted for correctly, as there will be no further opportunity to collect any VAT on the particular goods supplied. In addition, sales are often made for cash, which is vulnerable to theft or misreporting. **6300**

Due to the variety of often small-value products which are sold to a large number of consumers, identifying the VAT element of every transaction individually can be cumbersome (although made easier by modern computerised systems). As a solution, HMRC has devised various simplification schemes, which are available for most retailers to use.

SECTION 1

General topics

6305 Before discussing the special rules for retailers in detail, an overview is given of how other VAT topics impact on this particular kind of trader.

Sales invoices

6307 SI 1995/2518 reg 16 A retailer is not required to produce an invoice for a sale unless the customer makes a **specific request**. If the customer does so, the retailer can produce a simplified invoice (if the VAT-inclusive price is less than £250), or a modified invoice.

For suppliers of road fuel, the full invoice requirements are also modified.

Type of invoice	Criteria	¶¶
Simplified	Customer located in UK	¶2868
	No exempt supplies on invoice	
	Can adapt a credit card voucher	
Modified	Customer agrees	¶2872
Petrol	Price more than £250	¶2874
	Vehicle registration number known	

6310 Notice 700 para 17.6 **Rounding** This is not an issue for a retailer who uses a retail scheme.

However, where a retailer is **able to identify the VAT** on each transaction and calculates VAT at line level or invoice level, the VAT figure must not be rounded down. *JD Wetherspoon plc v HMRC* [2009]

The retailer may round the VAT calculated for every **individual transaction**, as follows:
- down to the nearest 0.1p; or
- up or down to the nearest 1p or 0.5p.

Input tax

6312 Retailers do not qualify for any special **treatment** when reclaiming input tax. True retail sales are always taxable, and therefore recoverability should not be a problem unless the retailer is also making exempt supplies, or cannot satisfy the criteria for claiming input tax (e.g. lack of invoice).

Some retailers will issue **self-billed** invoices (¶2904+) to their suppliers, which will be used as evidence to support an input tax claim.

If a retailer sources stock from a **cash-and-carry wholesaler**, the paperwork received will usually identify products by the use of a code. In this case it is vital that the retailer retains a copy of the wholesaler's product code list in order to evidence the input tax incurred (¶2876).

Retrospective discounts are often given to retailers once purchases reach a certain level. If a credit note is received which shows VAT, the retailer must reduce their input tax claim accordingly. However, if the **retailer supplies** something to the manufacturer **in return** for the price reduction, such as advertising space, then the retailer should raise an invoice.

Unjust enrichment

6314 s 80A VATA 1994 Where HMRC proves that a trader will be better off than they would otherwise have been, because overpaid VAT should properly be reimbursed to the trader's customers (but that is not the trader's intention), a VAT repayment will be denied, or only made with stringent conditions attached (¶3254+).

When a retailer has **been treating a zero-rated item as standard-rated**, there is scope to recover the overpaid output tax over the last 4 years and keep the money within the business rather than refund it all to each individual customer. This is because retail pricing is usually based on market forces and competition, rather than on a cost-plus basis.

EXAMPLE In 1994 a high street retailer successfully argued that the sale of chocolate-covered teacakes should be zero-rated. This meant that VAT had been overpaid to HMRC and the retailer sought a repayment. However, HMRC argued that the retailer would be unjustly enriched, so only 10% of the VAT should be repaid. The retailer claimed that it was unfair that the unjust enrichment rules only applied to traders where output tax exceeded input tax i.e. payment traders. (The law was changed in 2005 so that repayment traders are also subject to the same unjust enrichment rules.)

The CJEU stated that the past treatment of repayment traders and payment traders with regard to unjust enrichment was discriminatory, and the House of Lords agreed. *Marks & Spencer plc v C & E* [2009]

Other areas of interest

Other topics that are of special interest to retailers are summarised in the following table. 6316

Area of VAT	Details	¶¶
Registration	If only making zero-rated supplies, can request exemption from registration	¶2650+
	Distance selling of goods to EU private persons	¶9177+
	Business splitting	¶2629+
	Price reduction on deregistration	¶2726
Composite supplies	Combined products with different VAT rating - particularly affects food items	¶310+
Returns	Monthly returns for repayment traders	¶2987+
	4-weekly returns where convenient	¶2987+
E-business		¶6930+
Second-hand goods		¶6620+
Property	Being an anchor tenant	¶5548
Making exempt supplies	Special method of partial exemption for input tax recovery	¶2148+
Retail export scheme	Enables overseas visitors to claim a refund of UK VAT	¶9603+
VAT-saving schemes	Possible disclosure required if annual turnover exceeds £600,000 Particular schemes include: – card-handling charges; – value-shifting; and – extended approval periods	¶3030+

SECTION 2

VAT on takings - retail schemes

As normal retail customers are not VAT-registered, the VAT charge is irrelevant to them. For this reason the customer will receive very little paperwork to accompany the sale - perhaps just a receipt showing the total price paid. 6325

The most important element for the customer, and therefore the retailer, is the **gross price**. Contrary to most other situations in VAT, the gross price is taken as the starting point for calculating output tax.

The **VAT fraction** is then applied to find the VAT element of the price (1/6 for standard-rated supplies charged at 20%; 1/21 for reduced-rated supplies charged at 5%). For example, if a standard-rated supply has a gross value of £100, the VAT charge at 20% is £16.67 (£100 × 1/6). For a reduced-rated supply with a gross value of £100, the VAT charge is £4.76 (£100 × 1/21).

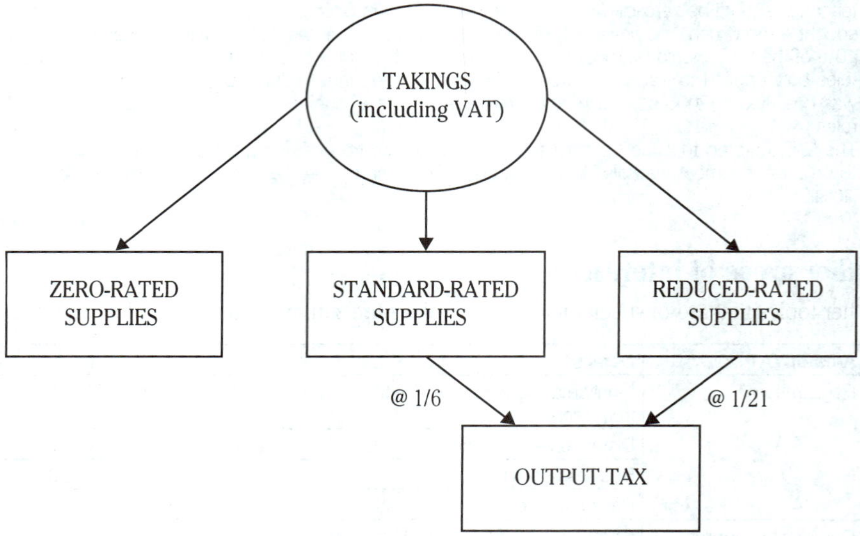

Objective

6327 HMRC has created various schemes to calculate VAT for retailers who cannot easily determine VAT on every transaction. The schemes are intended to be convenient and user-friendly, and to give a reasonable estimate of the global output tax due in each VAT period.

It is imperative that a **careful choice** of scheme is made from the outset, in order to minimise the VAT liability (which will usually directly increase the retailer's profits), whilst avoiding a heavy administrative burden.

EC Directive 2006/112 art 395

MEMO POINTS Under **EU rules**, member states are permitted to introduce measures to simplify the procedures for charging VAT, provided that there is a negligible effect on the amount of VAT due. The UK was permitted a derogation for retail schemes in 1977.

A. Scope

What is a retailer?

6330 For these purposes a retailer is described by HMRC as a trader who cannot reasonably be expected to account for VAT in the normal way. Such a person usually sells directly to the public. All retailers are **eligible** to use a scheme, unless excluded by HMRC.

Notice 727 para 2.1

Exclusion typically applies to those retailers with fewer sales of larger value items, where HMRC considers that normal VAT accounting is possible. Common examples are retailers selling furniture, jewellery, petrol and cars.

MEMO POINTS For these purposes, **normal VAT accounting** means a record of each separate transaction is kept, identifying the net and VAT amounts. Totals of these figures are then available for each VAT period.

What are retail supplies?

The schemes discussed below can be used for retail sales only, which are **defined** as transactions with an end consumer who is not normally VAT-registered. Retail normally involves the supply of goods, so the supply of most services - for example, by an accountant or solicitor - is not a retail sale. As an exception, a caterer is classed as a retailer (¶6552+). **6332** Notice 727 para 2.4

Exclusions Any **non-retail** sales must be accounted for using normal VAT accounting, and excluded from the schemes. **6334**

The following are treated as non-retail for this purpose:
- exempt supplies, such as the receipt of rental income or the sale of National Lottery tickets;
- sales to other VAT-registered customers (including those located elsewhere in the EU) other than occasional cash sales (i.e. not credit), such as petrol sales, or a DIY store selling to a VAT-registered builder;
- sales of business assets (e.g. company van);
- BT phonecards;
- disbursements;
- fuel scale charges (¶1536+) for private motoring; and
- savings stamps, travel cards and pools coupons.

Repairs to goods completed under **warranty** are a supply between the repairer and the insurance company, and hence are not a supply by the retailer. *Dixons Group plc* [1992] (VTD 9604)

Goods accounted for under the **distance selling rules** are excluded from the schemes.

MEMO POINTS 1. For **exports** of goods see ¶6560+.
2. If retailers are making exempt supplies, they should review their **input tax** recovery, as they will be partly exempt (¶2075+).
3. **Warranty insurance** is often sold by retailers for higher value domestic goods. Such insurance is liable to higher rate insurance premium tax.
4. The **distance selling** rules apply to sales of goods to unregistered persons located in another EU member state (¶9177+).

Authorisation

Except in the case of a bespoke scheme, there is no requirement to obtain HMRC's permission before starting to use a retail scheme. **6336** Notice 727 para 3.3; SI 1995/2518 reg 68

HMRC can **refuse to allow a trader to use** a retail scheme at any time where:
- its use does not give a fair and reasonable result;
- refusal is necessary for the protection of the revenue; or
- it is reasonable to expect the trader to use normal VAT accounting.

A retailer can **appeal** against such a refusal.

MEMO POINTS 1. What is **fair and reasonable** can be construed from comments in cases involving partial exemption (¶2152+). HMRC's officers must weigh up all the facts and not refuse use of a scheme only because VAT avoidance is suspected. VRS2360
2. For the **protection of the revenue** means HMRC can act on the basis of possible future VAT liabilities as well as the past and current VAT take. *Svenska International plc v C & E* [1996]

Period of use

The **minimum** period of use is 12 months **unless**: **6338**
- the retailer becomes ineligible for the scheme (by, for example, exceeding the turnover limit, or ceasing to be VAT-registered, or choosing to use a flat rate scheme); or Notice 727 para 4.2
- HMRC gives specific permission for the retailer to stop using it. SI 1995/2518 reg 71

It is therefore advisable to review the scheme before the anniversary date, in case the retailer wishes to change schemes (¶6360+).

MEMO POINTS 1. The **scheme year commences** at the beginning of the VAT period when the retailer started to use the scheme.
2. On becoming **ineligible**, the retailer must cease using the scheme from the end of the next VAT period. For example, if the retailer becomes ineligible for a scheme in May, and the VAT

return quarter ends are March, June, September and December, they must stop using the scheme by 1 October.

B. Influences on the choice of scheme

6342 Notice 727 para 3.1 There are five published schemes:
a. Point of sale;
b. Apportionment 1;
c. Apportionment 2;
d. Direct calculation 1; and
e. Direct calculation 2.

Alternatively, a **bespoke scheme** may be more appropriate where the retailer has unusual circumstances or is very large (none of the published schemes may be used by a retailer with turnover in excess of £130 million).

HMRC has issued **guidance** on the use of its published retail schemes, and it considers that some of the statements made in that guidance have the force of law. It is therefore essential to be familiar with the official guidance when choosing and operating a published scheme.

Comparison of published schemes

6343 Notice 727 para 11 Each scheme has particular **restrictions** on the types of supply which can be covered, and different requirements applying to stocktakes and annual adjustments. Every scheme assumes that goods are bought and sold at the same VAT rate. For the rules which apply when goods are bought and sold at different rates (such as by caterers and chemists) see ¶6544+.

	Point of sale	Apportion-ment 1	Apportion-ment 2	Direct calculation 1	Direct calculation 2
	¶6402+	¶6422+	¶6434+	¶6470+	¶6478+
Services included?	✓	x	x	Possibly [1]	Possibly [1]
Goods made in-house included?	✓	x	✓	✓	✓
Stocktake required?	x	x	✓ [2]	x	✓ [3]
Annual adjustment required?	x	✓	x	x	To recognise stock only
Calculation based on	Takings	Costs	Expected selling price [4]	Expected selling price [4]	Expected selling price [4]
Period of calculation	VAT period	VAT period	Rolling 12 months	VAT period	VAT period

Note:
1. Services can be covered by the scheme if their VAT rate is different from that of the minority goods (¶6460).
2. Only when starting to use the scheme.
3. When starting to use the scheme and annually thereafter.
4. The expected selling price is the estimated sales value of stock and purchases (¶6438+).

Scheme approval

6344 Only a bespoke scheme requires HMRC **approval**. This therefore has the advantage of giving absolute certainty to the output tax liability, if operated correctly and within the agreed terms.

Influence of the VAT rating of sales

If a retailer makes supplies at only **one positive rate**, that is all standard-rated or all reduced-rated, the Point of sale scheme must be used. **6346** Notice 727 para 3.4

Otherwise, there is no restriction on the choice of scheme, provided that the conditions are met, although when charging:
- **three rates** of VAT, the direct calculation schemes become more difficult to operate; or
- a higher mark-up on **zero-rated** goods, the trader will pay more output tax under Apportionment 1.

In addition, if the proportion of zero-rated (as compared to standard-rated) purchases increases, Apportionment 2 will be less beneficial.

Turnover levels

The choice of methods available to calculate the total VAT liability **depends on the size** of the business as determined by the VAT-exclusive retail turnover for the VAT registration as a whole (e.g. a VAT group). In situations where turnover is recorded on a gross basis, the business will need to estimate its likely output tax liability (based on estimated standard-rated, reduced-rated and zero-rated sales) to calculate the VAT-exclusive turnover figure. **6348**

MEMO POINTS 1. **Smaller businesses** may also take advantage of the annual and cash accounting schemes, either of which can be used in conjunction with a retail scheme. Cash accounting could be advantageous when the retailer makes credit sales, although input tax recovery will be delayed until suppliers are paid.
2. **Extremely small** businesses (those with annual taxable sales up to £150,000) may prefer to use the flat rate scheme instead of a retail scheme.

The **thresholds** which apply to each scheme are summarised below: **6349**

Type of scheme	VAT-exclusive retail turnover (£)				
	< 150,000	150,000 - 1 million	1 million - 1.35 million	1.35 million - 130 million	> 130 million
Retail schemes:					
Point of sale	✓	✓	✓	✓	x
Direct calculation 1	✓	✓	x	x	x
Direct calculation 2	✓	✓	✓	✓	x
Apportionment 1	✓	✓	x	x	x
Apportionment 2	✓	✓	✓	✓	x
Bespoke	✓	✓	✓	✓	✓
Small business schemes:					
Annual accounting (¶4745+)	✓	✓	✓	x	x
Cash accounting (¶4880+)	✓	✓	✓	x	x
Flat rate (¶4635+)	✓	x	x	x	x

Commencing Retailers who wish to commence using a retail scheme **should apply** a forward looking test. Provided that there are reasonable grounds for believing the relevant threshold will not be breached, the retailer will be eligible to use the chosen scheme. **6350** VRS2100

Monitoring Anyone using a scheme other than a bespoke method must continually monitor turnover for the previous 12 months. If it **exceeds** the permitted threshold for the scheme in use, HMRC must be informed at once. There is no tolerance level for any minor breach, although for traders breaching the £130 million threshold see ¶6496. Unless another scheme can be put in place, or a bespoke method agreed, the retailer must use normal VAT accounting. **6352**

EXAMPLE

1. Mr A has turnover of £20 million, of which £900,000 relates to retail sales. He is eligible to use any retail scheme.

2. B Ltd completes VAT returns for the quarters ending 31 March, 30 June, etc. The company exceeds the turnover limit for its current retail scheme on 15 April (which falls in the VAT period ending 30 June). B Ltd can only continue to use the current retail scheme until 30 September.

3. C Ltd is using annual accounting. It completes a VAT return for the year ending 30 April. If it exceeds the turnover limit on 18 May, it can continue to use the current retail scheme until the following 30 April.

4. For a retailer's first return, for the period ended February 1998, he used a retail scheme with a £1 million turnover limit. Having acquired a second shop in January 1998, his turnover for the quarter ended May 1998 increased to £300,000, so it was reasonable to anticipate that his annual turnover would exceed £1 million. He therefore changed schemes in order that he would not breach the turnover threshold.
On his subsequent deregistration, HMRC decided that he had not been entitled to change retail schemes, as he had not used the original scheme for a full year. The change was therefore ineffective and VAT was recalculated on the basis that the original scheme continued to apply. A request for retrospective change was denied.
The retailer argued that at the point when his prospective annual turnover exceeded £1 million, he ceased to be eligible to use the original scheme.
However, the tribunal concluded that the retailer only became ineligible to use the original scheme once annual sales had actually crossed the threshold and that prospective sales were irrelevant.
Khalid Jamil [2000] (VTD 16795)

Making a decision

6356 Once the available schemes have been identified, the retailer needs to consider which one is **most appropriate**, taking into account each method's complexity, any requirement for annual adjustments and stocktakes, and the overall administration burden. It is possible to use a mix of schemes for different parts of the business (¶6516+).

It is important to realise that the VAT liability will be different under each retail scheme, because the objective of each is to give a reasonable estimate. HMRC cannot deny the use of a particular scheme just because the resulting VAT liability is lower than the hypothetical result of using another scheme.

Notice 727 para 4.1 MEMO POINTS Where a business operates a single retail scheme **from multiple locations** (such as branches), each location can make its own calculations. These calculations are then totalled to give the output tax liability for the business. For every scheme except Point of sale, HMRC must have already agreed to the treatment of stock transferred between locations.

6358 Retailers are expected to **continuously review** the operation of their chosen scheme to ensure that it remains appropriate.

HMRC must be **informed** of any of the following **events**, which may lead to distortions in the VAT calculation, and therefore require its intervention:
- the acquisition or sale of a business;
- a change in legal status of the business (e.g. incorporation); or
- changes in a VAT group's members.

Changing schemes

6360 On specific **request**, HMRC will agree to a change being made in the scheme from the beginning of the retailer's VAT year (if the minimum 12-month period of previous use is satisfied).

HMRC will consider the following **factors** when deciding whether to accept the change:
VRS3400
- why the change is required;
- the effect of the adjustment; and
- whether the change produces a fair and reasonable result.

EXAMPLE D Ltd completes VAT returns for the quarters ending 31 March, 30 June, etc. It commences using a retail scheme on 1 February 2015 (which is within the VAT period which commenced on 1 January 2015).
The first time that the scheme could be changed is therefore 1 January 2016.

It is very rare to be able to change schemes **retrospectively**; indeed there is no entitlement to do so. HMRC only allows a change in exceptional cases, and the period to which it can apply is limited to 4 years, provided that the retailer would have been eligible to use the new scheme throughout that period. It is of course vital that sufficient records are maintained so that the new scheme can be operated for the whole period. **6362** Notice 727 para 4.3

Any resulting VAT repayment must be claimed (¶3248+), and interest will not be paid.

MEMO POINTS 1. HMRC gives the following as examples of **exceptional circumstances**: VRS3460
– the retailer has been misdirected (¶3687) by an HMRC officer; or
– the retailer is able to demonstrate that the scheme to which they want to change will produce a more accurate VAT result, and the difference represents a high proportion of the trader's business profit.
2. HMRC takes the following **factors** into account when deciding whether a retailer's case is exceptional: VRS3465
– retail schemes are a compromise between simplicity and accuracy, and can only produce an estimate;
– the scheme is the choice of the business;
– administration involved in allowing a retrospective change;
– liabilities which have already been declared should be treated as certain;
– the cost to the general taxpayer balanced against the cost for the particular retailer;
– the retailer must remain VAT-registered and continue to use the same scheme as that granted retrospectively; and
– one retrospective change cannot overlap another.

EXAMPLE
1. On 1 April 1990 a couple acquired their newsagent and general store business as a going concern, and chose to use the same retail scheme as the vendor. With effect from 1 April 1997 the couple changed retail schemes after receiving professional advice. A retrospective change was requested on the basis that the couple had not received a VAT visit for about 4 years, and so had received no guidance on which retail scheme would be most appropriate. The resulting reduction in the VAT liability would have been about 4.5%.
On appeal it was held that a difference of about 4.5% in the amount of VAT between the two retail schemes was not nearly enough to make the case exceptional. *Mr P and Mrs E Waring* [1998] (VTD 15864)

2. A couple operated a grocery shop and used a particular retail scheme from 1983 onwards. It became apparent that VAT in excess of £8,000 was being overpaid on an annual basis as a result of using this scheme, which represented 40% of profits. The couple applied to change schemes, also requesting that this change be retrospective, which was denied.
On appeal it was held that the scheme had already been withdrawn from general use because of a known problem of overstating the VAT liability, although traders had been allowed to continue using it. On this basis, HMRC should have allowed a retrospective change, given the exceptional circumstances. *A & C Wadlewski* [1995] (VTD 13340)

C. Elements common to all schemes

All schemes require that retailers know: **6366**
– the VAT rating of their sales;
– their daily gross takings (¶6368+); and
– how to treat common sources of error (¶6394+).

If an error is made which leads to an under-declaration of VAT, an assessment (¶3625+) will be made by HMRC.

1. Gross takings

6368 The daily gross takings are key to all of the retail schemes, and are a record of all retail supplies made on each day of trading, as evidenced by till rolls, sales vouchers or even a manual list.

Takings **include**:
– all payments received from cash customers;
– the full VAT-inclusive value of credit sales on the date when the sale is made (even if just a deposit is received);
– the face value of any vouchers or tokens accepted in place of cash, unless the coupons are not honoured by the promoters; and
– the cash value of any payments in kind (i.e. the normal price of the goods sold), which includes all barter transactions.

VRS4250 MEMO POINTS **Branches** of a retail business may make weekly returns of their takings which are then collated at head office. HMRC will allow this (under a written agreement) where the branch:
– maintains a record of takings which is supported by other daily records; and
– makes returns for part weeks where this is necessary (e.g. where the VAT period falls in the middle of a week, or a VAT rate changes).

Payment from cash customers

6372 Payments include those in the **form** of cash, cheques, debit or credit card vouchers, debit card transactions (including Maestro and Delta) and electronic cash. Any cash given to the customer as a result of a cash-back transaction should not be deducted from takings (¶6374).

Where **foreign currency** is accepted, no reduction is made for any commission payable to the bank. Any premium charged to the customer for the right to tender foreign currency is included within gross takings.

VRS4300 If the retailer **cashes up early**, this may lead to a tax point error. Retailers should ensure that the gross takings figure recorded reflects all sales made each day.

EXAMPLE A company which operated a large number of public houses accounted for VAT under the Point of sale scheme. Gross takings were calculated by using the figure of the total cash in its tills and ignored the readings on the till rolls.
An assessment was issued on the basis that the company's practice was incorrect (in that it had failed to take account of cash illicitly removed from the till), resulting in an under-declaration of VAT, the amount of which was extrapolated from a sample. The tribunal dismissed the company's appeal, finding the method of extrapolation reasonable in the circumstances. *Courage Ltd* [1992] (VTD 8808)

Exclusions

6374 Notice 727/3 para 5.4; VRS10100 The table below shows the situations where amounts should be excluded from takings:

When a **subsequent payment** is received so that the retailer is not out of pocket, it must be included in takings.

Situation	Detail
Instalments in respect of credit sales	Because the full value of the sale has already been taken account of
Amounts of interest	Not takings
Cash-back on bank card	Cash-back itself is not a supply and must be excluded from the takings figure
Counterfeit notes	Not legal tender
Unsigned or dishonoured cheques from cash customers (not from credit customers)	
Theft of goods	No supply has taken place

Situation	Detail
Mistaken acceptance of foreign currency (unless reimbursed by the bank)	
Illegible credit card transactions	If the customer was not present at the time of the transaction, the retailer usually has to bear the cost of any fraudulent use of a credit card i.e. the banks do not make a reimbursement. There is no guidance as to the treatment for takings purposes, although there is a view that takings should be reduced to reflect the retailer's loss.
Mistaken acceptance of cheque guarantee cards as credit cards	

Credit sales

For credit sales, the **treatment depends** on whether the credit is: 6376
– self-financed and the retailer makes a separate charge, which is disclosed to the customer, in which case the charge should be excluded from the takings;
– financed by a third party, in which case the whole amount paid by the customer is included in the takings; or
– hire purchase, in which case each instalment payment is deemed to include both interest and capital in the same proportion as the total amounts due.

Any **commission** payable is an expense incurred by the retailer, so takings are not reduced.

EXAMPLE A furniture company arranged for customers to be provided with "interest-free credit" by a finance company. The finance company only paid the net amount to the furniture company, after deducting the finance charge which would otherwise have been borne by the customer.
The furniture company only included the net amount in its gross takings and this was challenged. The CJEU held that the full amount (i.e. not deducting the finance charge) should be included in gross takings. The customer acquired goods at an advertised price which was included on the invoice, and the price did not change whether the customer paid by cash or credit.
C & E v Primback Ltd [2001]

For retailers with **turnover below £1 million**, whose customers do not pay for the goods immediately (for example, a milk delivery person or newspaper shop), the following adjustment can be made in order to recognise sales only when payment is received: 6378 Notice 727 para 4.5

First period of using the scheme	**£**
Takings	X
Closing debtors	(X)
Gross takings	X

Subsequent periods	
Opening debtors	X
Takings for the period	X
Closing debtors	(X)
Gross takings	X

Bad debts particularly affect mail order retailers. The usual VAT treatment (¶840+) applies unless the retailer's business practice means they cannot fulfil the normal conditions in which case HMRC permits the following relaxation. 6380 VRS9250+

Mail order retailers can apply an apportionment to the balance of outstanding debts which are older than 6 months, to ascertain the standard-rated debts. This may involve a rolling calculation to take into account any change in the mix of supplies between the date of the original sale, and the date that the debt is written off.

Deposits

6382 Notice 727/3 para 6.11 Where a deposit is an **advance payment**, it is included in takings when it is received. If the deposit is forfeited or returned to the customer, takings should be reduced accordingly. **Security** deposits are not consideration and should be excluded from takings.

Sale or return

6384 Notice 727/3 para 6.19 The sales amount should only be **included in takings when** the customer accepts the goods. It is therefore important to know which goods are involved, and such stock should be separately identifiable.

This is an important issue for sales made over the Internet (¶6950+).

Cash discounts

6386 Notice 727/3 para 6.7 If the retailer offers discounts which can be **taken up immediately** on sale, the value to be included in the takings is the discounted amount. It is irrelevant whether the customer actually benefits from the discount (e.g. if there is a 5% discount for payment within 30 days, the value for takings is 95% of the price even if the customer does not pay until 40 days have elapsed).

However, where the customer must pay 100% of the price and then **subsequently receives a rebate**, the full price must be included in takings.

For other types of promotion see ¶6520+.

EXAMPLE A mail order company sold goods listed in a catalogue to intermediaries who then sold them on to customers. The intermediaries paid for their purchases in instalments. An amount of 10% of every payment was then credited to a separate account maintained by the company. The intermediary could then withdraw the money, use it for further purchases, or settle debts with customers or the company. Crucially, the intermediaries were not entitled to pay the catalogue price less the discount, so the benefit was always subsequent to the purchase. A significant amount was never claimed.
The CJEU ruled that the full catalogue price should be included in the company's takings, because discounts could only be taken into account when they were withdrawn, or otherwise used by the intermediary. *Freemans plc v C & E* [2001]

Intermediaries

6388 Sch 6 para 2 VATA 1994 A retailer may still have to account for sales which are routed through **unregistered** intermediaries. HMRC has the power to direct such a retailer to account for VAT on the retail price.

For further details see ¶7292+.

EXAMPLE A company supplied cosmetics to individuals who demonstrated these products at parties attended by the public, and displayed samples and catalogues. After each party the individuals placed orders with the company on behalf of their customers.
The invoices for the goods included a 30% discount for prompt payment, but the customers still paid the full price to the individuals, who kept the difference. An assessment was issued on the basis that the market value of the goods was the full undiscounted price.
The company appealed and the tribunal held that the discount was a commission. The market value for the purposes of VAT was therefore the price paid by the ultimate customer, and not the price paid by the individual to the company. The company was still making retail sales, even though they were through agents. *Direct Cosmetics Ltd v C & E* [1985]

Part-exchange

6390 Notice 727/3 para 6.21 For goods accepted in part-exchange, the **amount to include** in the takings is the value of the goods sold (including VAT), **except** where there is a false trade-in value.

In certain trades it is common to accept the customer's old product (for example, a car or a fridge) and give it a **trade-in** value. Where this trade-in value is fixed (and false) and the retailer has no use for the product, the value can be treated as a discount, in which case only the cash price received by the retailer is included in takings.

When selling **second-hand goods**, VAT may be calculated on the margin only, if various criteria are met (¶6620+). Otherwise the full value of the sale is included in takings.

Adjustments

The following may reduce the takings **subject to** evidence of the adjustment being retained: **6392** Notice 727/3 para 5.4
a. void transactions (which are voided at the time of the error);
b. refunds to customers for faulty goods (up to a maximum of the initial amount included in takings) or for simple overcharging (although if payment is compensatory, there is no reduction);
c. till problems, including readings from broken-down tills and the use of training tills (where the till has been returned to retail use without zeroing first) - for the treatment of till discrepancies see ¶6394+; and
d. customer overspends using Shopacheck.

Comment It is always advisable to reconcile the gross takings figure with the turnover figure used in the financial accounts.

EXAMPLE E Ltd sells a faulty hairdryer to Mrs F, who suffers an electric shock. Mrs F arranges for the hairdryer to be repaired herself but E Ltd pays her £50 for the problems she has suffered. The £50 payment is a compensation payment, which is outside the scope of VAT. The takings of E Ltd should not be reduced by the amount of the payment.

2. Errors

Till discrepancies

It is usually difficult to ascertain the exact reason why there is a discrepancy between the till reading and the cash contents. **6394** VRS4150

HMRC has given **guidance** on the amount of gross takings in the following situations, which generally results in the largest possible amount becoming VATable.

Situation	Gross takings
Over-ringing, so that excess consideration is keyed into the till	Should only be consideration given by the customer Adjustment can only be made if there is evidence of error
Under-ringing, so that reduced consideration is keyed into the till	
Too much or too little change given	Should reflect true consideration for sale, ignoring the mistake in change
Overcharge	Cash handed over by the customer is consideration, unless evidence is available to support an adjustment to reflect the price of the goods
Undercharge	Should be price of goods, unless evidence of error retained, in which case consideration actually given by the customer is reflected in takings

Comment Retailers should keep a careful record of all till shortages and the attributed reasons.

EXAMPLE
1. Mrs G (the customer) hands over £5 for goods priced at £5 and Mr H (the sales assistant) rings £10 into the till.
The consideration given is only £5, so the takings should be adjusted (over-ringing).

2. Mrs G hands over £10 for goods priced at £10. Mr H rings only £5 into the till.
The consideration is £10 and the takings should be increased from £5 to reflect the till contents (under-ringing).

3. Mrs G hands over £20 for goods priced at £20. Mr H rings £20 into the till but gives £10 change back to Mrs G.
The consideration is £20, so there will be a shortfall of cash in the till compared to the till readout (incorrect change).

4. Mrs G hands over £20 for goods priced at £10.
If Mr H gives no change (overcharge) and:
– rings £10 into the till, the consideration is £10; or
– rings £20 into the till, the consideration is £20.
If Mrs G returns to collect her change, the error must be carefully rectified so that:
– if £10 was rung into the till, the change can be given with no adjustment, as the till contents already exceed the till roll by £10; or
– if £20 was rung into the till, the £10 change will require a refund to be rung into the till.

5. Mrs G hands over £5 for goods priced at £10. Mr H accepts the £5 but rings £10 into the till. The true consideration is only £5 but £10 should be recorded, unless there is clear evidence of the error (undercharge).

6396 Notice 727/3 para 6.31 Till shortages resulting from **theft and fraudulent refunds** are a contentious issue. As the supply of goods has already been made, VAT is due to HMRC, so the trader must suffer any shortfall. Any deficiencies in takings should be spread in the usual proportions of standard-rated, zero-rated and reduced-rated supplies, so that VAT is not under-declared.

HMRC assesses the VAT shortfall by reviewing retail trade statistics and makes a decision based on best judgment.

VRS4150 If the retailer holds evidence of **collusion** by the till operator and customer, so that the till operator pockets the cash from the customer, HMRC will accept that this amounts to theft of goods and takings can therefore be reduced.

EXAMPLE A company used a retail scheme and treated the amount recorded on the till rolls as the gross takings. The accounting records showed that there were annual stock shortfalls in excess of £15 million, probably due to theft by customers and employees.
HMRC asserted that part of the shortfall was properly attributable to theft of cash takings by employees, which had never been entered on the till rolls, and issued assessments accordingly.
On appeal the company alleged that the assessments had not been made to HMRC's best judgment.
The tribunal held that a reasonable opinion that a VAT liability existed had been formed, and the amount of that liability was necessarily an estimate. *WH Smith Ltd* [2000] (VTD 16505)

Mistakes in operating the scheme

6398 VRS3250 A retailer may make a mistake when using a scheme; this will lead to an assessment for any under-declared VAT (¶3625+).

Depending on the circumstances of the case, **HMRC will consider**:
– the use of estimates to correct past output tax amounts; or
– whether the business made a reasonable decision at the beginning of the scheme year, even though this has proved to be wrong (e.g. anticipating that the majority of goods sold would be standard-rated, when in actual fact more zero-rated goods were sold).

Any assessment must be based on the scheme actually used by the retailer, unless this does not give a fair and reasonable result.

EXAMPLE A newsagent sold newspapers, sweets, tobacco, etc and used a retail scheme which required him to calculate his zero-rated sales. This figure was then deducted from takings to leave his standard-rated sales figure. He made several VAT repayment claims, which were subsequently investigated. HMRC considered takings to be understated; in making its assessment it marked up standard-rated purchases in order to calculate standard-rated sales, thereby ignoring the rules of the retail scheme in use.
It was held that the assessment should be ignored, because HMRC had not concluded that using the scheme had failed to lead to a fair and reasonable result. *Ian Briggs* [1995] (VTD 13603)

D. Point of sale scheme

As its name suggests, this scheme identifies the VAT rate applicable to each transaction at the point of sale. It only differs from normal VAT accounting in that output tax is calculated on a global basis, applying the VAT fraction to total takings. **Any retailer** can use it. **6402** Notice 727/3

In practice the scheme usually requires a comprehensive till system, which can identify the VAT rate on each item sold, although using a different till for each rate of VAT would also achieve the same result (if staff were adequately trained). HMRC generally expects a retailer to use an electronic point of sale system.

This scheme will **fail to operate properly** where reliance is placed upon staff who are unable to key in the correct VAT rate, or who use convenience product codes. In addition, some till systems will not give sufficient information to make the use of this scheme possible without substantial intervention from proprietors and their staff.

MEMO POINTS 1. HMRC has issued the following guidance as to its requirements for an **electronic point of sale system**. It should:
- enable access to information about all products on sale;
- uniquely recognise items scanned into the till (e.g. by the use of barcodes);
- process items correctly, using the VAT rate which applies at the time of purchase; and
- total the items in the customer's basket, deal with any method of payment, produce a receipt at the time of sale, and produce reports whenever required.

The retailer must consider how VAT will be calculated when something goes wrong, such as when the barcode cannot be scanned. The system must also be rigorously maintained and easily updated for price changes, etc. Information Sheet 11/03

2. **Errors** (which could result from human mistake, or from the wrong information being entered into the product database file) could lead to an under-declaration of VAT. This could reduce the trader's profits, as it is very unlikely that recovery of extra VAT can be made from the customer. Notice 727/3 para 3.5

Overview of calculation

Essentially, the **scheme works** by totalling all sales liable to each rate of VAT and applying the appropriate VAT fraction to calculate the VAT. VAT rates are often taken from suppliers' invoices, which can make it more difficult if goods are then sold at a different VAT rate (¶6544+), or where several goods at various VAT rates are sold together in one product (¶329 and ¶6526+). **6404** Notice 727/3 para 4.1

MEMO POINTS 1. Goods **acquired from the EU** may be zero-rated because of special rules. For the purposes of the retail schemes, the VAT rate which applies is that at which the goods are sold.

2. When a retailer makes **very minor supplies of zero-rated or reduced-rated goods**, HMRC may agree to treat all takings as standard-rated, although this will overstate the retailer's output tax liability. VRS5150

3. It is important that retailers make their own decision concerning the **VAT liability of the products sold**, and do not rely on the liability adopted by suppliers on their purchase invoices. HMRC will raise an assessment if standard-rated items have been incorrectly sold as zero-rated, or at the reduced rate of VAT.

6406 Notice 727/3 para 4.2

	VAT rate which applies to each product			
	Total	Reduced rate	Standard rate	Zero rate
1 Gross takings	X	X	X	X
2 Apply VAT fraction		1/21	1/6	0
3 Output tax due	X	X	X	0

EXAMPLE Mr A runs a grocery shop, selling a wide range of products. For the most recent VAT period, his till rolls showed the following:

		£
Standard-rated sales		51,400
Reduced-rated sales		3,050
Zero-rated sales	Ignored	8,678

The output tax due for that VAT period is calculated as:

		£
Standard-rated sales	£51,400 × 1/6	8,566.67
Reduced-rated sales	£3,050 × 1/21	145.24
		8,711.91

Gross takings

6408 Notice 727/3 para 6

The general rules (¶6368+) apply, except that takings include the full VAT-inclusive value of goods:
- removed for the retailer's **private use**; and
- used for **business entertainment** or **gifts**, whether purchased specifically for this purpose or consumed out of stock.

Money taken out of **rented payphones** is also included in standard-rated takings.

6410 **Delivery** If delivery is **included in the normal price** of the goods (e.g. milk), the full price is included in the takings and the VAT rate relating to delivery follows that of the goods being delivered (e.g. the delivery charge for a book order online will be zero-rated).

However, if delivery is agreed **outside the terms of the normal contract**, this is a standard-rated supply of services, which is accounted for outside the retail scheme.

EXAMPLE A company supplied plant bulbs by mail order which were delivered by P Ltd. Out of the charge made to customers, a substantial amount was paid to P Ltd. The company only included the net amount in takings.
HMRC issued a ruling that the company should account for output tax on the full amount paid by each customer. The company appealed on the basis that the delivery was a separate, exempt supply made by P Ltd.
It was held that there was a single supply of delivered bulbs, and the price paid by the customer was consideration for that supply. The whole amount must be included in takings. *C & E v Plantiflor Ltd* [2002]

Records

6412 Notice 727/3 para 3.4

In addition to the normal VAT record-keeping requirements (¶2795+), the retailer must keep records of the daily gross takings, and any other working papers used to calculate the VAT due, including till rolls. In particular, a separate record of goods sold for payments in kind should be retained.

It is advisable to keep a **running check** on the takings, and compare the actual figure to the expected takings based on a mark-up of purchases. Any reasons for a material difference should be recorded, so that an explanation can be provided to HMRC at a later date. This might include audit checks, staff disciplinary action, or police involvement if theft occurs.

E. Apportionment schemes

6416 Notice 727/4

There are **two apportionment schemes**, which work by apportioning the takings of the business between the various VAT rates. The two schemes are distinguished by a difference in complexity (and hence in accuracy).

Neither scheme can be used for any supplies of **services**, or for **catering supplies**.

Apportionment 1 is relatively simple and can only be used by traders with annual VAT-exclusive turnover of up to £1 million. It cannot be used for self-made or home-grown goods, and is therefore unsuitable for garden centres and farm shops.

Apportionment 2 is aimed at larger businesses with an annual VAT-exclusive turnover of up to £130 million, although smaller traders can use it if they wish. This scheme can cope much better with the differing margins of the various goods sold.

1. Overview of calculation

Although both schemes work by apportioning takings between VAT rates, the basis of apportionment is different: 6418
- **Apportionment 1** relies on the VAT rating of purchases acquired to fulfil the retail sales, and assumes that the proportion of goods sold at each VAT rate mirrors that of purchases (e.g. if 40% of purchases are standard-rated, 40% of takings are deemed to be standard-rated); whereas
- **Apportionment 2** apportions takings on the basis of the expected sale value of purchases and stock.

Gross takings

The general rules for gross takings apply (¶6368+), with the following **exclusions**: 6420 Notice 727/4 para 7
- any receipts relating to rented payphones;
- the value of any goods specifically purchased for business entertaining, or put to private use (the value of stock used for either purpose is, however, included);
- any separate delivery charge; and
- the sale of discount vouchers/cards which enable the purchaser to obtain discounts at other traders.

2. Apportionment 1

Under this scheme there is a simple presumption that the mark-up on each item sold is the same, which is very unlikely to be borne out in practice. It is vital that **non-retail purchases** (i.e. overheads and fixed assets) are excluded from the calculation. 6422 Notice 727/4 para 3.1.1

There is an **annual adjustment** to even out fluctuations during the year, which must also be performed when the trader leaves the scheme. Certain records must be retained (¶6454).

Comment A trader who has a higher mark-up on **zero-rated** products may pay more output tax under this scheme than if using another retail scheme.

VAT period calculation

6424 Notice 727/4 para 4.3.1

	VAT rate which applies to each product			
	Total	Reduced rate	Standard rate	Zero rate
1 Total purchases for VAT period (VAT-inclusive)	X	X	X	X
2 Expressed as a percentage of the total purchases	100%	x%	y%	z%
3 Apply percentage to gross takings		x% of takings	y% of takings	
4 Apply VAT fraction		1/21	1/6	
5 Output tax due	X	X	X	

The **purchase** cost of any faulty goods recalled by the manufacturer should be excluded from total purchases. 6426

Goods acquired from unregistered suppliers must be **included** in the scheme calculation by adding VAT at the appropriate rate to purchases.

6428 Notice 727/4 para 4.2 When **starting to use the scheme**, goods already in stock must be excluded, with the exception of any items that are to be sold and not replaced. However, where these items have already been taken into account by another scheme, they should still be excluded from this scheme.

6430

EXAMPLE Ms B has the following data relating to her sales and purchases for the current VAT period.

Purchases	**VAT-inclusive** £	
Standard-rated	10,000	55.556%
Reduced-rated	3,000	16.667%
Zero-rated	5,000	27.777%
	18,000	100.00%
Gross takings	34,000	

She uses Apportionment 1 and therefore allocates the takings in the same proportion as her purchases:

Gross takings		**Output tax** £
Standard-rated	£34,000 × 55.556% × 1/6	3,148.17
Reduced-rated	£34,000 × 16.667% × 1/21	269.85
Zero-rated	Ignored	-
		3,418.02

Annual adjustment

6432 VRS5200 For a continuing trader who is **not using annual accounting**, the same calculation is carried out at the end of the scheme year (¶6338), using the annual totals for sales and purchases, and any adjustment is entered on the last VAT return for that year (but see below).

On **ceasing to use** the scheme, an adjustment should be completed for the quarters which have elapsed since the last annual adjustment was carried out.

Notice 727/4 paras 4.3.2, 4.3.3 MEMO POINTS 1. The retailer can **request** that the annual **adjustment be made at** the end of their VAT year (¶2990) instead; this may result in an initial adjustment period of more than 12 months, so that any short-term distortions are avoided. Indeed, the public notice states that the scheme year will always end on 31 March, 30 April, or 31 May, depending on the VAT stagger of the trader, contradicting the guidance in HMRC's VRS manual. **In practice**, most traders make the annual adjustment at the end of their VAT year.
2. Retailers who are using the **annual accounting scheme** (¶4745+) do not make an annual adjustment, as they only make one apportionment calculation each year.

EXAMPLE Mr C has the following data relating to his annual sales and purchases (he submits returns on 30 April, 31 July, etc). He started to use the scheme on 7 September and if he follows usual practice, his annual adjustment is made on the return for the quarter ended 30 April.

Purchases	**VAT-inclusive** £	
Standard-rated	50,000	69.444%
Reduced-rated	8,000	11.111%
Zero-rated	14,000	19.445%
	72,000	100.00%
Gross takings	156,000	

The annual takings are allocated between the different VAT rates:

Gross takings		**Output tax** £
Standard-rated	£156,000 × 69.444% × 1/6	18,055.44
Reduced-rated	£156,000 × 11.111% × 1/21	825.39
Zero-rated	Ignored	-
		18,880.83

Mr C has previously declared the following output tax for the 4 previous quarters:

		Output tax
		£
Quarter 1		3,083
Quarter 2		4,567
Quarter 3		3,589
Quarter 4		5,106
		16,345
Extra output tax due:	£18,880.83 - £16,345	2,535.83

Note:
The annual adjustment works in the following way in case of a change of VAT rate and uses dates in 2011 to relate to the last change in VAT rate. If Mr C had made his annual adjustment on 30 April 2011, he would have needed to do the above calculation in respect of two periods - from 1 May 2010 to 3 January 2011 (using 7/47 as the standard-rate fraction); and from 4 January 2011 to 30 April 2011 (using 1/6) - because of the change in standard rate of VAT on 4 January 2011. Each period is thus treated separately as regards purchases and total takings.

3. Apportionment 2

This method uses the expected selling price of each product purchased, and apportions the total takings on the basis of the percentage of goods sold at the standard rate, reduced rate and zero rate. As the method involves a rolling calculation, there is no annual adjustment. **6434** Notice 727/4

Comment This scheme will be **beneficial** to retailers where the proportion of standard-rated purchases, as compared to zero-rated purchases, is increasing.

6436 Notice 727/4 para 5.4

	VAT rate which applies to each product			
	Total	**Reduced rate**	**Standard rate**	**Zero rate**
1 Total expected selling prices of goods purchased in last 12 months	X	X	X	X
2 Expressed as a percentage of the total	100%	x%	y%	z%
3 Apply percentage to takings for VAT period		x% of takings	y% of takings	
4 Apply VAT fraction		1/21	1/6	
5 Output tax due	X	X	X	

Expected selling price

Retailers must estimate the sales value of their stock and purchases. The **starting point** to this two-stage process can be the shelf price or recommended retail price, but adjustments must be made for subsequent events. **6438**

On a **change of rate**, such as the standard rate increase from 17.5% to 20% on 4 January 2011, retailers should take this into account when setting the expected selling price, including anticipated changes in consumer buying patterns.

EXAMPLE A supermarket has 2,000 containers of milk, each of which has a shelf price of £1, so expected sales would be £2,000. However:
- five containers are used by the staff room for tea and coffee; and
- 100 containers have to be sold cheaply, because of nearing their sell-by date.

The expected selling price must take into account these types of event.

6440 VRS4600 The **calculation** of the expected selling price is necessarily subjective and, depending on the circumstances, the information required may not always be readily available.

The method of calculation must be realistic, taking into account the circumstances of the retailer and the resources at their disposal. The expectations for a small grocer's store obviously differ from those for a national supermarket chain.

6442 **Initially** the retailer will probably use one of the following methods:
a. marking up each line of goods individually (which is tedious and time-consuming);
b. marking up classes of goods (a method which is allowed only if various criteria are met); or
c. using recommended retail prices (only possible if retail prices are shown on suppliers' invoices), classifying goods by VAT rate.

Notice 727/4 para 5.3.2 The following items must be **excluded**:
- wholesale supplies;
- goods specifically bought for private use; and
- proceeds from stock sold as part of the disposal of the whole or a part of the retail business.

MEMO POINTS 1. HMRC may agree to the retailer using a **sample**.
2. **Marking up classes of goods** will only be permitted where:
- the individual marking up of goods lines is not possible;
- the classes are compiled in a commercial way, with the mark-up for the goods not varying by more than 10%; and
- the mark-ups are reviewed quarterly.
3. Where necessary, the retailer may use a **mix of methods**, if applied consistently and the result is fair and reasonable.

6444 Notice 727/4 paras 5.3.1, 7.4, 7.24, 7.25 At the **end of the VAT period**, the retailer should review the selling prices by taking into account:
- price changes (particularly in respect of perishable goods which must be sold by a certain date);
- special offers and promotions which were not predicted initially;
- goods supplied from normal stock to use in business entertaining;
- wastage in light of actual events;
- goods taken into private use;
- products recalled by manufacturers;
- equipment (e.g. freezer) breakdowns;
- breakages;
- theft; and
- bad debts written off in the period.

Certain of the above factors may be **omitted** where they have no distorting effect on the operation of the scheme, subject to HMRC's agreement.

The most important requirement is **consistency of calculation**, both within a VAT period and throughout the scheme year (¶6338).

Starting the scheme

6446 Notice 727/4 para 5.4.1 A trader will usually have **opening stock** when commencing the scheme. The expected price for this stock must be calculated and allocated between:
- total stock;
- standard-rated goods; and
- reduced-rated goods.

It is advisable to undertake a physical **stocktake** on commencing the scheme. Alternatively, goods purchased in the previous 3 months may be used as a proxy for opening stock.

When either of the above options to value the stock is **impossible or impractical**, the retailer may:
- update the most recent stocktake for goods bought and sold;
- adjust back from a stocktake completed during the first VAT period of using the scheme; or

– use internal stock records, where these are accurate and also used for financial accounting purposes.

EXAMPLE Mr D has decided to start using Apportionment 2. He thus completes a physical stocktake. From the quantities of goods counted, he can calculate the expected selling price (ESP) of each product line, allocated between the different VAT rates, as follows:

Product	**VAT rate**	**Expected price**	**Standard rate**	**Reduced rate**	**Zero rate**
		£	**£**	**£**	**£**
Line A	Standard	10,000	10,000	-	-
Line B	Zero	2,500	-	-	2,500
Good 1	Standard	7,000	7,000	-	-
Good 2	Zero	500	-	-	500
Good 3	Reduced	2,000	-	2,000	-
Good 4	Standard	23,000	23,000	-	-
ESP of opening stock		45,000	40,000	2,000	3,000

First 3 quarters

The expected selling price of each class of stock is calculated in each VAT period, **taking into account** all goods: **6448** Notice 727/4 para 5.4.2

– on hand at commencement; and

– received (including goods acquired from the EU), made or grown for retail sale since the scheme was started.

The total takings are then apportioned between the different VAT rates, so that the output tax can be calculated by applying the appropriate VAT fraction.

Monthly traders must follow these rules for the first 11 months.

EXAMPLE Continuing the example in ¶6446, in Quarter 1 Mr D makes some further purchases with the following expected prices:

Product	**VAT rate**	**Expected price**	**Standard rate**	**Reduced rate**	**Zero rate**
		£	**£**	**£**	**£**
Line A	Standard	1,000	1,000	-	-
Line B	Zero	2,000	-	-	2,000
Good 1	Standard	800	800	-	-
Good 2	Zero	5,000	-	-	5,000
Good 3	Reduced	700	-	700	-
Good 4	Standard	1,000	1,000	-	-
Expected selling price of purchases		10,500	2,800	700	7,000

The expected selling prices allocated to the various VAT rates from both opening stock and purchases are as follows:

	Total	**Standard rate**	**Reduced rate**	**Zero rate**
	£	**£**	**£**	**£**
Opening stock	45,000	40,000	2,000	3,000
Purchases	10,500	2,800	700	7,000
Total expected price	55,500	42,800	2,700	10,000
% of total	100%	77.117%	4.865%	18.018%

If Mr D's takings for Quarter 1 are £68,000, the following output tax liability results:

		Gross	**VAT fraction**	**VAT**
		£		**£**
Standard-rated supplies	£68,000 × 77.117%	52,439.56	1/6	8,739.93
Reduced-rated supplies	£68,000 × 4.865%	3,308.20	1/21	157.53
				8,897.46

Subsequent VAT periods

6450 Notice 727/4 para 5.4.3

The expected price of each class of stock is calculated in each VAT period, **taking into account** all goods received, made or grown for retail sale, including EU acquisitions, in the current period and the previous 3 periods (11 periods for monthly traders).

The total takings are then apportioned between the different VAT rates, and the appropriate VAT fraction applied to calculate the output tax.

VRS5250

MEMO POINTS 1. The scheme can be **adapted** with the agreement of HMRC to involve a quarterly stock adjustment or annual adjustment instead of the rolling calculation.
2. Where the **mix of goods changes**, the retailer should contact HMRC to agree an adaptation.
3. Where an **incorrect VAT rate** has been applied to goods, the retailer should strictly rework the calculation for the previous 12 months. If this is impractical, HMRC will agree to a short-cut.

EXAMPLE Continuing the example in ¶6448, in Quarter 5 Mr D makes some purchases with the following expected selling prices:

Product	VAT rate	Expected price	Standard rate	Reduced rate	Zero rate
		£	£	£	£
Line A	Standard	6,000	6,000	-	-
Line B	Zero	1,000	-	-	1,000
Good 1	Standard	5,000	5,000	-	-
Good 2	Zero	3,000	-	-	3,000
Good 3	Reduced	2,000	-	2,000	-
Good 4	Standard	15,000	15,000	-	-
Expected selling price of purchases for Quarter 5		32,000	26,000	2,000	4,000

The expected selling prices which are allocated to the various VAT rates from the previous 3 periods and these purchases are as follows:

	Total	Standard rate	Reduced rate	Zero rate
	£	£	£	£
Quarter 2	37,000	30,000	1,500	5,500
Quarter 3	40,500	27,000	5,000	8,500
Quarter 4	23,000	18,000	2,500	2,500
Quarter 5	32,000	26,000	2,000	4,000
Total expected selling price	132,500	101,000	11,000	20,500
% of total	100%	76.226%	8.302%	15.472%

If Mr D's takings for Quarter 5 are £75,000, the following output tax liability results:

		Gross	VAT fraction	VAT
		£		£
Standard-rated supplies	£75,000 × 76.226%	57,169.50	1/6	9,528.25
Reduced-rated supplies	£75,000 × 8.302%	6,226.50	1/21	296.50
				9,824.75

Leaving

6452 Notice 727/4 paras 3.5.2, 3.6

No adjustment is required when the business ceases to use the scheme.

However, where **only one part of the business** ceases, the rolling stock calculation should exclude the expected selling price of goods no longer within the scheme.

4. Records

6454 Notice 727/4 para 3.3

In addition to the normal VAT record-keeping requirements (¶2795+), the retailer must keep:
- records of daily gross takings;
- any other working papers used to calculate the VAT due; and
- the calculations which support the expected selling prices (e.g. evidence of wastage).

It is vital that **purchases for retail sale** can be identified, as this record is key for both apportionment schemes. It is therefore advisable to separate out these purchases from overheads, fixed assets and any other acquisition not involved in the retail sales.

F. Direct calculation schemes

There are two direct calculation schemes, which work by calculating the expected selling price of the goods sold at only one or two of the applicable VAT rates, in order to establish the proportion of takings on which VAT is due. Again, one scheme is simpler, albeit at the expense of accuracy. **6458** Notice 727/5

Neither scheme can be used for **supplies of catering**. Moreover, if a retailer makes supplies at three different VAT rates, the calculation will be complex.

Direct calculation 1 can only be used by traders with annual VAT-exclusive turnover of up to £1 million.

Direct calculation 2 can be used by any trader, provided that the annual VAT-exclusive turnover does not exceed £130 million. This scheme also requires a complicated **annual stock adjustment** to reflect the retailer's trade throughout the year.

The records required for both schemes are detailed at ¶6488.

1. Overview of calculation

The calculation works by **concentrating on** the goods with the VAT rate which forms the smallest proportion of the retail sales i.e. the VAT rate with the lowest sales value. These are known as the minority goods. **6460**

The expected selling price (¶6438+) of these goods must be identified.

When only selling at **two rates of VAT**, the calculation depends on whether the minority goods are:
- zero-rated, in which case the expected sales price is deducted from total takings, to identify standard-rated sales, to which the VAT fraction is then applied; or
- standard-rated, in which case the VAT fraction is just applied to the expected selling price of those goods.

If selling at **three rates of VAT**, there will be two minority goods and the expected selling prices of both zero-rated and reduced-rated goods are deducted from takings to find the standard-rated sales. If the calculation becomes too complex, HMRC may agree that the reduced-rated sales can be accounted for outside the scheme.

MEMO POINTS 1. The goods include those **received, made, or grown** for retail sale.
2. Where a retailer supplies **services**, they can only be included in the scheme if their VAT rating is different from that of the minority goods.

EXAMPLE
1. Mr E supplies goods which are either zero-rated or standard-rated.
If the proportion of goods supplied at each VAT rate is:
- 30% zero-rated and 70% standard-rated, the minority goods are zero-rated; or
- 80% zero-rated and 20% standard-rated, the minority goods are standard-rated.

2. Mrs F supplies goods at all three rates of VAT.
If the proportion of goods supplied at each rate of VAT is 20% zero-rated, 70% standard-rated, and 10% reduced-rated, the minority 1 goods are zero-rated and the minority 2 goods are reduced-rated (¶6474).

Expected selling price

In addition to the guidance at ¶6438+, the following should be allowed for in the calculation of the selling price: **6462** Notice 727/5 para 6

- delivery charges which are included in the total sales price so that a single supply is made;
- stock which is used for business entertaining or personal use when the minority goods are reduced or standard-rated; and
- faulty product recalls by the manufacturer.

Goods acquired from **unregistered suppliers** must be included in the scheme calculation if they are minority goods.

The purchase cost of **goods recalled** by the manufacturer because of a fault should be excluded from total purchases.

Gross takings

6464 The general rules (¶6368+) apply with the following modifications:

Notice 727/5 para 6

- if a separate charge for **delivery** is made, this is only included in the takings if the minority goods are zero-rated or reduced-rated;
- the sale of **discount vouchers/cards** which enable the purchaser to obtain discounts at other traders is a supply of services and must be excluded;
- the value of any retail goods put to **private use** should be added to the takings; and
- any receipts relating to **rented payphones** are only included if the minority goods are zero-rated or reduced-rated.

6468 The value of any goods specifically purchased for **business entertaining or gifts** must be excluded from takings.

Where normal stock is used for business entertaining, the VAT treatment depends on the VAT rate of both the stock and the minority goods.

VAT rating of minority goods	VAT rating of stock item used for entertaining	Treatment
Zero-rated	Standard-rated	Add value of the supply to takings
	Reduced-rated	
Reduced-rated	Any	No addition to takings
Standard-rated		

2. Direct calculation 1

6470 The calculation is performed for every VAT period, using the expected selling price of the minority goods to ascertain the output tax due. Although not always necessary for the calculation, a record of daily gross takings must be maintained.

The retailer must calculate the expected selling price (¶6462) of the **minority goods** purchased in the VAT period (excluding opening stock). Once the prices have been set, the retailer must continue to calculate the expected selling price for that rate of goods for the whole year.

It is also possible for retailers to mark up their **majority goods** instead (¶6476), where this is easier and still gives a fair and reasonable result (for example, newsagents who make bulk purchases).

Where a **change in VAT rate** occurs part way through a VAT period, two calculations should be undertaken and added together to calculate the total output tax liability for the entire VAT period.

Comment If the minority goods are standard-rated and sell slowly, the retailer will be paying VAT earlier than if they used another scheme.

It is possible for the expected selling price of standard-rated goods to exceed gross takings where the retailer has been stockpiling. No adjustment is required in this case, as the effect will even out over time.

Two rates of VAT

EXAMPLE Miss G uses Direct calculation 1. Her minority sales are zero-rated, and she makes the following zero-rated purchases in Quarter 1: 6472 Notice 727/5 para 4.4

Product	Expected selling price £
Good 1	6,000
Good 5	1,000
Good 6	5 000
Expected selling price Quarter 1	12,000

If Miss G's takings for Quarter 1 are £105,000, the following output tax liability results:

	Gross £	VAT fraction	VAT £
Takings	105,000		
ESP of zero-rated sales	(12,000)		
Standard-rated sales	93,000	1/6	15,500

Three rates of VAT

If the trader also sells **reduced-rated** goods, there will be two minority goods, for which the retailer must calculate the expected selling prices. The reduced-rated goods are always treated as the second minority goods. 6474

	£
Takings for period	X
Expected selling price of minority goods 1 - zero or standard-rated	(X)
Expected selling price of minority goods 2 - reduced-rated	(X)
Gross value of standard/zero-rated supplies	X

EXAMPLE In Quarter 1 Mr H makes some purchases with the following expected selling prices:

Product	VAT rate	Expected selling price £	Reduced rate £	Zero rate £
Good 1	Reduced	1,000	1,000	-
Good 3	Zero	2,000	-	2,000
Good 4	Zero	800	-	800
Good 6	Zero	5,000	-	5,000
Good 8	Reduced	900	900	-
Good 9	Zero	1,000	-	1,000
Expected selling price		10,700	1,900	8,800

If Mr H's takings for Quarter 1 are £77,000, his standard-rated sales are:

	Gross £
Takings	77,000
ESP of zero-rated goods	(8,800)
ESP of reduced-rated goods	(1,900)
Standard-rated sales	66,300

Output tax is therefore due on Mr H's standard-rated and reduced-rated sales as follows:

	Gross £	VAT fraction	VAT £
Standard-rated supplies	66,300	1/6	11,050.00
Reduced-rated supplies	1,900	1/21	90.48
			11,140.48

Majority goods calculation

6476

EXAMPLE Ms A is a newsagent who uses Direct calculation 1. Although her minority sales are standard-rated, she prefers to calculate the expected selling price of her zero-rated goods. She makes the following zero-rated purchases in Quarter 1:

Product	**Expected selling price £**
Good 1	28,000
Good 2	4,000
Expected selling price for Quarter 1	32,000

If Ms A's takings for Quarter 1 are £42,000, the following output tax liability results:

	Gross £	**VAT fraction**	**VAT £**
Takings	42,000		
Estimate of zero-rated sales	(32,000)		
Standard-rated sales	10,000	1/6	1,666.67

3. Direct calculation 2

6478 The rules for this scheme are the same as Direct calculation 1, **except**:
- expected selling prices cannot be calculated on majority goods;
- an **annual adjustment and a stocktake** are required; and
- on leaving the scheme, a closing adjustment must be made.

A retailer who uses **annual accounting** (¶4745+) performs the annual adjustment for every VAT return.

Annual adjustment

6480 Nctice 727/5 para 4.5

This adjustment must be made after the normal calculation for the fourth quarter, and any difference must be accounted for on the **VAT return** for the same quarter.

On every anniversary of starting to use the scheme, the actual retail sales made in the year are compared to the amounts already accounted for in every quarter, by adjusting for the goods in stock at the beginning and end of the year, and also for any goods disposed of other than by retail sale.

For guidance as to **stock valuation**, see ¶6446.

If there is a **change in VAT rate** during the year, two calculations must be undertaken and amalgamated.

Comment HMRC may allow an adaptation so that the annual adjustment date **coincides with the end of the financial year**. However, if HMRC considers that this concession may distort the output tax declared in the first year, it may direct that an adjustment for a period exceeding 12 months should be carried out.

6482 Notice 727/5 para 3.6

On **ceasing to use** the scheme, an annual adjustment must be completed for the quarters which have elapsed since the last adjustment was completed, excluding any goods which were initially taken into account but subsequently formed non-retail disposals. This closing adjustment applies even if the retailer leaves the scheme within the first 12 months.

If the business is **transferred as a going concern** (¶8646+), the stock which is transferred must be excluded from the scheme.

Two rates of VAT

6484

EXAMPLE Mr B has been using Direct calculation 2 for 4 quarters. He makes only zero-rated and standard-rated supplies, and has the following figures for each quarter.

Quarter	**Output tax**	**Expected selling price of zero-rated purchased goods**
	£	**£**
1	45,760	41,600
2	37,570	158,000
3	39,120	72,000
4	37,030	37,200
	159,480	308,800

His gross takings for the year were £1,301,500.
Zero-rated sales during the year are estimated by adjustment after calculating the expected selling price of opening and closing stock.

	Expected selling price of zero-rated goods
	£
ESP of opening stock	75,000
ESP of purchases (from above)	308,800
ESP of closing stock	(32,000)
	351,300

This figure is then used to calculate the annual standard-rated sales.

	Gross	**VAT fraction**	**VAT**
	£		**£**
Takings	1,301,500		
ESP of zero-rated sales	(351,800)		
Standard-rated sales	949,700	1/6	158,283.33

The VAT already accounted for is £159,480, so a refund of £1,196.67 is due from HMRC. (£159,480.00 - £158,283.33)

Three rates of VAT

EXAMPLE C Ltd has been using Direct calculation 2 for 4 quarters. It makes supplies at all three VAT 6486
rates and has the following figures for each quarter.

Quarter	**Output tax**	**Expected selling price of zero-rated purchases**	**Expected selling price of reduced-rated purchases (VAT-inclusive)**
	£	**£**	**£**
1	58,100	11,300	112,000
2	48,400	81,000	24,000
3	44,100	14,000	115,500
4	48,800	13,300	13,000
	199,400	119,600	264,500

The gross takings for the year were £1,585,230.
The zero-rated and reduced-rated sales during the year are calculated by including adjustments for the expected selling price of opening and closing stock.

	Expected selling price of zero-rated goods	**Expected selling price of reduced-rated goods (VAT-inclusive)**
	£	**£**
ESP of opening stock	14,300	18,500
ESP of purchases (from above)	119,600	264,500
ESP of closing stock	(12,300)	(21,400)
	121,600	261,600

These figures are then used to calculate the annual standard-rated sales

	Gross £
Takings	1,585,230
Less: ESP of zero-rated goods	(121,600)
ESP of reduced-rated goods	(261,600)
Standard-rated sales	1,202,030

	Gross £	VAT fraction	VAT £
Standard-rated supplies	1,202,030	1/6	200,338.33
Reduced-rated supplies	261,600	1/21	12,457.14
			212,795.47

The VAT already accounted for is £199,400, so the increase in liability is £13,395.47. (£212,795.47 - £199,400)

4. Records

6488 Notice 727/5 para 3.4 In addition to the normal VAT record-keeping requirements (¶2795+), the retailer must keep records of:
- daily gross takings (even if not required where the minority goods are standard-rated);
- any other working papers used to calculate the VAT due; and
- the calculations which support the expected selling price.

It is vital that **purchases for retail sale can be identified**. It is therefore advisable to separate out these purchases from overheads, fixed assets and any other acquisitions not relating to a retail sale.

G. Bespoke schemes

6492 Notice 727/2 Bespoke schemes agreed between HMRC and the retailer give mutual certainty to the amount of output tax declared for each VAT period. Any retailer can use a bespoke scheme, although it is usually only the larger retailers who do.

Those with **annual turnover** in excess of £130 million must agree a bespoke method unless they can account for VAT under the normal rules (which requires the retailer to identify the net value and VAT element of every transaction).

MEMO POINTS The annual turnover limit was £100 million until 1 April 2009. Bespoke schemes already agreed by retailers whose **annual turnover is between £100 million and £130 million** continue in operation until, or unless, the agreement ends.

Scope

6494 Notice 727/2 para 4.3 HMRC will agree to a suggested method if it is satisfied that the result is **fair and reasonable**.

A method will be considered to be fair and reasonable if, weighing its anticipated accuracy against the cost and effort of using it:
- it reflects commercial reality and is not contrived; and
- it can easily be checked.

It is imperative that retailers fully **disclose** all appropriate facts about their business, in order to rely on the terms of the agreement. Then, unless the business changes, or exceptional circumstances occur, the scheme as agreed will be binding on both parties. For this reason, there are usually pre-set review dates built into the agreement.

Modifications should only be made where necessary. HMRC must approve any such amendments. Notice 727/2 para 5

HMRC can **withdraw** a bespoke scheme where:
- it does not give a fair and reasonable result;
- the tax-take is at risk; or
- normal VAT accounting is possible.

MEMO POINTS 1. The written **contract** itself will clarify the following details: Notice 727/2 para 3.3
- start and end dates;
- review date (which is usually every 2 years);
- details of the supplies included, and those specifically excluded;
- any special circumstances and transactions; and
- details and signatures of an HMRC officer and an authorised signatory of the retailer.

2. If the retailer's **business changes** (e.g. business structure or trading pattern), they must inform HMRC in writing immediately. Notice 727/2 para 5.1

EXAMPLE

1. A corporate group sold mail order goods through catalogues distributed by its agents. The agents received commission of 10% on the catalogue price of goods sold to customers, and also received a rebate of 10% on goods which they purchased personally. For the personal goods, the group only accounted for VAT on the net amount paid by the agent. The group calculated the proportion of these private sales based on a sample, and this proportion was updated every 3 years.
The group had entered a bespoke scheme.
In October 1987 the group realised that a significant number of sales to agents had been treated incorrectly since 1982, leading to an over-declaration of output tax, so adjustments were made in the VAT returns in 1987 and 1988.
HMRC accepted that going forward, the group could change the proportion of its sales which were deemed to be private agent sales. However, in HMRC's view, the change could not be retrospective.
It was held that the scheme as agreed was binding on both parties for each 3-year period once the first return based on the agreement was submitted. The group was not entitled to resile from it. *GUS Merchandise Corporation Ltd (No 2) v C & E* [1995]

2. In 1991 a supermarket was allowed to adapt a direct calculation scheme for use as its bespoke scheme. When computing the expected selling price for zero-rated goods, deductions were made for wastage. Two years later, an assessment was issued for over £2 million of output tax, because it was considered that the wastage of zero-rated goods was understated.
The supermarket appealed on the basis that the scheme had been operated as agreed. In allowing the appeal, the tribunal held that there was "a contract binding on both sides from which one party cannot resile". The supermarket had given full information when proposing the scheme, to which HMRC had given full assent. Whilst HMRC could refuse the use of a scheme in future where it did not give a fair and reasonable result, an agreed scheme could not be altered retrospectively. The supermarket had acted in good faith on the basis of the agreed bespoke scheme. *Tesco plc* [1994] (VTD 12740)

Transition from published schemes

Where a retailer **becomes ineligible** to use a published scheme (for example, because of increased turnover), and a bespoke scheme is subsequently put in place, the bespoke method will apply to all VAT periods from when the published scheme was unavailable. In practice, this means from the beginning of the VAT period immediately following the period when ineligibility became apparent. **6496** Notice 727/2 para 2.3

Where there is only a **marginal breach** of the turnover threshold, or only a **small proportion of standard-rated sales**, HMRC may authorise the continued use of the published scheme as a bespoke scheme, subject to future review.

Calculation

Although calculation methods are usually based on the Point of sale, Apportionment 2 or Direct calculation 2 schemes, there is actually no **restriction**, provided that the calculation meets the criteria set out at ¶6494. **6498** Notice 727/2 para 3.1

Gross takings

6500 Notice 727/2 para 6.1

The gross takings (¶6368+) are a key feature of any scheme. The **agreement** should state how this figure is calculated - for example, retaining till rolls, or using an electronic point of sale system. This obviously requires control of remote tills (i.e. those not connected to the main system, perhaps located in concessionaires (¶6568)), and also action in the event of a till breakdown.

If goods are **delivered direct to the customer**, a control must be in place to ensure the takings are included even if the sale is not rung through the till.

6502 Notice 727/2 para 6.2

Adjustments The treatment of the following items, which can cause an adjustment to the takings figure, should be **specified** in the agreement:
- barter transactions;
- agency supplies;
- second-hand sales;
- deposits;
- part-exchanges;
- refunds and goodwill payments;
- staff discounts;
- till discrepancies (i.e. overs and unders);
- voids;
- dishonoured cheques;
- foreign currency;
- forged bank notes;
- self-financed credit;
- warranties and guarantees;
- manufacturer coupons;
- out of date coupons;
- non-retail sales, sales outside the scope of VAT and exempt supplies; and
- private use of goods.

Point of sale as a basis

6504 Notice 727/2 para 7.1

HMRC states that the treatment of all of the following should be included in the agreement, if it is based on the Point of sale scheme.

Subject	Details to be specified
VAT coding	List all VAT codes to be used Identify frequency of changes Agree to disclose product lists to HMRC when required How adjustments will be made when errors occur in the VAT coding
Product coding	Whether VAT coding will apply at the level of product, line or department
Mixed rate products	How products will be coded and how VAT due will be calculated
Refunds	How returned products will be dealt with (e.g. rescanned) so that refund is attributed to the correct VAT rate
Unscanned products (e.g. newspapers, sweets)	How VAT due will be accounted for
Private use of goods (including gifts)	
Staff discounts	How discounts will be allocated between the different VAT rates
Till breakdown	How takings will be allocated to different VAT rates
No electronic point of sale	If remote tills are not connected to the point of sale system (e.g. in certain departments, or in a concessionaire), how takings will be accounted for

MEMO POINTS The treatment of the following types of **business promotion** should also be included in the agreement: 6506 Notice 727/2 para 7.2
- general money-off vouchers (not tied in to any particular product);
- specific product vouchers;
- face value vouchers, ignored on sale but accounted for when redeemed;
- manufacturer influenced vouchers (tied in to a particular product);
- invalid manufacturer vouchers, where manufacturer refuses to redeem;
- multisaves (e.g. 3 for the price of 2); and
- special offers where the barcode is covered up.

Expected selling price

Where a bespoke scheme is based upon expected selling prices, the items stated at ¶6504 should also be included. HMRC advises that the setting of the expected selling price should be as close to the point of sale as possible. 6508 Notice 727/2 para 8

It is therefore important that the **level** at which the scheme will operate is clearly understood, i.e. at business, shop, or department level. Goods transferred between shops or departments will need to be carefully recorded.

MEMO POINTS 1. In addition, where **goods are delivered direct** to the customer, the agreement should state how they are to be taken into account in the selling price calculation.
2. Where the bespoke scheme uses **apportionment** and there is more than a single-step calculation, the percentages used must be stated to at least 4 decimal places.
3. The **adjustments** to expected selling price for items such as wastage, theft, etc (¶6444) should be mentioned in the agreement.
4. There should be specific mention of the treatment of any **services** undertaken by the retailer.

Trading patterns It is extremely important that the scheme can cope with seasonal fluctuations, as with large turnovers a small discrepancy can result in a big distortion of the VAT liability. 6510 Notice 727/2 para 8.3

To avoid these effects:

a. the **period of calculation** can be elongated, to include a year end adjustment;

b. **stock** adjustments should be made to take account of opening and closing stock, with the method for valuing stock carefully documented in the agreement; **closing stock** should always be adjusted for on:
- ceasing to trade;
- a transfer of a going concern; or
- changes to the bespoke calculation itself;

c. **rolling periods** (i.e. taking into account the previous 4 periods) can be particularly useful for a scheme based on apportionment; and

d. obvious **distorting factors**, such as a bulk purchase, or the takeover of stock from another shop, should be dealt with separately.

H. Special situations

1. Using more than one scheme

Although it is usual for a retailer to use just one scheme for its whole VAT registration, it may be more appropriate to use multiple schemes, especially where **services** are also supplied (for example, by a department store with a coffee shop, or a supermarket incorporating an in-house pharmacy). Only the following combinations are possible, unless specific permission is given by HMRC: 6516 Notice 727 para 4.1

	POS	DC1	DC2	AP1	AP2
POS		✓	✓	✓	✓
DC1	✓		x	x	x
DC2	✓	x		x	x
AP1	✓	x	x		x
AP2	✓	x	x	x	
Normal VAT accounting	✓	✓	✓	✓	✓

In addition, it is not permitted to combine the Point of sale scheme with more than one of the other four types of scheme.

6518 Whichever schemes are chosen, the **turnover** thresholds still apply to the VAT registration as a whole.

Normal VAT accounting can be combined with any scheme.

The **Point of sale** scheme can be used with one other scheme, plus normal VAT accounting if appropriate.

Where the **Direct calculation or Apportionment** schemes are used, an adjustment (previously agreed with HMRC) is necessary where stock is transferred between locations.

2. Business promotions

6520 The usual rule is that the amount subject to VAT is the **consideration** received, whether this is in monetary form or something else (e.g. introducing a friend as a customer).

> EXAMPLE A mail order clothing catalogue is running an offer which gives 20% off if the customer introduces a friend who makes a subsequent order.
> In this case the consideration is the price paid for the clothes, plus the value the company attributes to Mr A introducing a friend (20%).
> This means that if Mr A orders clothes with a catalogue price of £100 and introduces a friend, he only pays £80.
> However, the consideration is £100.

6522 It can be more difficult to ascertain the consideration when free gifts or vouchers are involved. The table summarises the **usual types** of promotion offered by retailers.

Notice 700/7; Notice 727/3 para 7; Notice 727/4 para 8; Notice 727/5 para 7

Type of promotion	Details	¶¶
Goods	Free gift - no consideration received	¶6524
	Multisave e.g. buy one get one free	¶6526+
Vouchers	Face value	¶6534+
	Money-off vouchers	¶6538
	Loyalty cards	¶6540+

a. Goods

Gifts

6524 A gift is something given for which no consideration is received (¶1465+).

Where an item is given to a customer and its VAT-exclusive value does not exceed £50, no output tax is due. For more expensive gifts, output tax is due on the cost incurred by the retailer, and the cost is included within takings.

A **series** of free gifts would be subject to an annual limit of £50, but this would be unlikely to occur in a retailing situation.

EXAMPLE

1. A corporate group sold mail order goods through catalogues distributed by its agents. Teasets (worth about £10 in value) were given as presents to new agents.
HMRC issued assessments charging VAT on the £10 value. The company appealed, stating that either the teasets were outside the scope of VAT as gifts, or they constituted supplies which should be included within the retail scheme.
It was held that the teasets were neither gifts, because the agents had a contractual right to them, nor within the retail schemes. Therefore they should be accounted for under normal VAT accounting. *GUS Merchandise Corporation Ltd v C & E* [1981]

2. A mail order retailer gave inducements (costing less than £10, such as a kettle) to new customers after they made their first order, and to existing customers who introduced new business. The company accounted for VAT on the cost of the goods but an assessment based on their market value was issued.
The CJEU ruled that the goods were supplied to the customers in consideration for the service of introducing a potential customer. The value should be that attributed by the recipient of the service i.e. the cost price of the goods. *Empire Stores Ltd v C & E* [1994]

3. A company ran a promotion scheme which gave customers vouchers when they purchased petrol. These vouchers could be redeemed for goods or services. The price paid by the customer was the same irrespective of whether they accepted the voucher.
The CJEU held that the consideration paid by the customer related to the petrol only and was not to be reduced by the value of the vouchers. One result of this was that redemption of the vouchers amounted to gifts. *Kuwait Petroleum (GB) Ltd v C & E* [1999]

Multisave goods

Where multisave goods are offered (e.g. buy two for the price of one, or receive a mug with a jar of coffee), the price paid is consideration for all the goods acquired. This presents a slight problem when the goods have **different VAT ratings**, and the solution depends on whether the second good is minor or not. **6526**

By concession, a **minor good** is taken to be one which costs no more than 20% of the total cost of the combined supply (excluding VAT). In addition, the maximum cost of the good itself will be £1 for a retail sale, or £5 otherwise (e.g. a free pen with a trade magazine). Where the second good is minor, the VAT rating of the main good is deemed to apply to the whole price. Notice 48 para 3.7

If the second good is **not minor**, the treatment depends on the type of retail scheme used, as shown in the table below: **6528**

Scheme	VAT rate of the goods	Treatment
Point of sale	Same	No adjustment required
	Different	Apportionment of price must be made, based on cost or allocation shown on supplier's invoice
Apportionment 1	Same or different	No adjustment required
Apportionment 2	Same	Expected selling price adjusted to reflect the cost of the promotion, taking into account manufacturer's contributions
	Different	1. Apportionment of price must be made, based on cost or allocation shown on supplier's invoice; and
		2. Expected selling price adjusted to reflect the cost of the promotion, taking into account manufacturer's contributions
Direct calculation schemes		As for Apportionment 2

Payments from third parties

6530 VRS10100 Subject to the concession below, **support payments** from third parties towards the costs of the goods are included in gross takings, but contributions towards advertising and selling costs are excluded because this is a payment for services.

As a **concession**, support payments for goods can be accounted for outside the retail scheme, either by increasing output tax (invoiced to the manufacturer), or decreasing the purchase cost of the goods (credit note received from manufacturer). This concession applies when agreed to in writing.

EXAMPLE A plc, which operates Apportionment 2, currently has a promotion on wine, where the customer receives a free corkscrew when purchasing three bottles. The supplier is contributing £200 to the promotion. The cost of the corkscrews is £400. The expected selling price of the promotional stock is £40,000.

	£
Unadjusted selling price	40,000
Less: Cost of promotion	(400)
Add: Supplier's contribution	200
Expected selling price of the wine	39,800

b. Vouchers

6532 There are many different types of voucher, as summarised in the following table (for full details see ¶1004+). The main differences tend to be in the mode of distribution and the rights attached. Depending on the situation, vouchers can be sold or issued for free.

Type	Category	Properties
Face value	Retailer voucher	Voucher issued by retailer which can be used to acquire goods solely from the retailer, or elsewhere (usually the same retail chain), in which case the retailer will reimburse the vendor of the goods
	Credit voucher	Voucher cannot be used to acquire goods from issuer Issuer reimburses person from whom goods are acquired
	Single purpose voucher	Voucher issued which represents the right to receive one type of supply that has only a single VAT rate. The most common type of these would be phone vouchers
	Other	¶6534
Money-off voucher		Shows a discount against full price of certain named goods Can either be: – restricted to use with retailer itself; or – available to use at other retailers Usually funded by manufacturer
Loyalty cards		Customers collect points, which are converted into gifts or vouchers to spend

MEMO POINTS **Single purpose vouchers** were introduced as a class of voucher from 10 May 2012 (¶1016).

Face value vouchers

6534 When retailers **sell** a **retailer voucher or credit voucher** for which they are:

a. the issuer, any consideration given by the customer up to the face value of the voucher is excluded from takings (any excess consideration is taxable as a supply of services and the VAT is accounted for outside the retail scheme); or

b. not the issuer, then for the:
- Point of sale scheme, the sales price is included in takings;
- Apportionment schemes, the vouchers are excluded and VAT is accounted for outside the scheme;
- Direct calculation schemes, the vouchers are usually excluded, unless the VAT rate which will apply when the voucher is redeemed is different from the VAT rate of the minority goods; or
- bespoke schemes, a special accounting method must be agreed.

Single purpose vouchers are taxable any time they are sold, be it at their initial issue or onward sale by a retailer. In this case, the amount treated as taxable should be added to the daily gross takings.

Sales of other kinds of face value voucher are liable to standard-rate VAT, unless it is known at the time of sale that redemption will be for goods at the zero rate or reduced rate. *Argos Distributors Ltd v C & E* [1996] The inclusion of the vouchers in the various retail schemes follows the guidance in **b**. above.

On redemption, the face value of the **retailer voucher** is included as consideration for the goods acquired and is counted as takings. The only exception is when cash is given in return for the voucher, which is then outside the scope of VAT and the takings are not reduced for the amount of cash paid out. **6536**

The retailer may accept a **third party's voucher** in part payment for goods. In this case, only the cash received from the customer is included in the takings. The amount of any payment subsequently received from the third party in relation to the transaction should also be included in takings, unless the payment is a contribution to advertising or selling services, which is outside the scope of all retail schemes. The retailer may make a charge for dealing with these vouchers, which must be excluded from the takings.

As **single purpose vouchers** are taxed in the supply chain from the outset, the redemption of one is not subject to VAT and it will therefore not form part of the daily gross takings.

Money-off vouchers

Where a retailer **sells** money-off vouchers, the VAT treatment depends on whether the voucher entitles the purchaser to future discounts with: **6538**
- the **retailer**, in which case the VAT rate which applies will follow the rate of the discounted goods, and the proceeds are included in takings; and/or
- **other traders**, in which case this is a standard-rated supply of services which is excluded from all schemes except the Point of sale scheme, when the sales price is included in takings.

On redemption, money-off vouchers reduce the consideration received, so the value of the coupon is excluded from takings. *Boots plc v C & E* [1990] However, any additional payments received (either from the customer or manufacturer) should be included within takings.

MEMO POINTS Unless the coupons are for a specific line of product such that the VAT liability can be determined when the coupons are issued, retailers using the **Point of sale scheme** may not be able to identify the liability of the goods or services against which the coupons will be redeemed. Such retailers should agree a method of how to account for VAT on affected sales with HMRC, possibly on the basis of the average split of zero-rated and standard-rated sales.

EXAMPLE Mrs B purchases a DVD game and receives a voucher for £5 off a future purchase. She uses this voucher the following week.
On the first purchase, the retailer receives the advertised price for the sale and so accounts for output tax as normal.
On the second purchase, the retailer only receives the price as reduced by the coupon, and accounts for output tax on the reduced price.

Loyalty cards

Many stores have loyalty cards, which enable customers to earn points which can later be turned into gifts or face value vouchers. **6540**

As the **gifts** are virtually always below £50 in value, no output tax is due.

The **redemption** of the voucher in a future purchase will reduce the takings.

EXAMPLE Tesco's loyalty card scheme gives customers points which are converted into vouchers every quarter; these can then be spent either in store or with other suppliers who are part of the scheme.
Tesco first accounted for VAT by excluding the face value of the redeemed vouchers from gross takings.
Then Tesco changed its accounting, so that when the vouchers were issued their value was deducted from takings, but on redemption their value was added to takings. This meant that Tesco enjoyed a cash flow advantage, and also avoided accounting for VAT on vouchers which were never redeemed.
It was held that as customers did not give any consideration for receipt of the vouchers, only the first method of accounting was correct. *Tesco plc v C & E* [2003]

6542 Some loyalty cards are **operated by a third party** and offer additional rewards, which are made available by various suppliers - for example, the earned points might go towards a visit to an amusement park.

In this case, the third party accounts for output tax on the services supplied to the retailers, and may be able to reclaim the input tax on reward goods, depending on the terms agreed between the third party and supplier.

EXAMPLE A company operated the Nectar card promotion scheme, which gave points to customers who made purchases from certain retailers. It was agreed that the purchase price paid by the customers did not include any consideration for the points.
The points could then be used to acquire further goods or services from suppliers within the scheme. These goods were paid for by the company; the company claimed input tax on these supplies. HMRC challenged the reclaim on the basis that the supply was made to the customer, not the company.
The CJEU held that the payment to the supplier for the reward goods was both third-party consideration for the supply of goods to the customer, and also consideration for a supply of services to the company. The Supreme Court, however, decided that the company was entitled to a full input tax deduction for payments made to suppliers for providing reward goods and services under the scheme. The Supreme Court considered that the wrong questions had been referred to the CJEU, so its judgment did not need to be applied slavishly.
HMRC's analysis was that there had been a supply of reward goods or services by the supplier to the customer, and that the company had paid for that supply - a clear case of third-party consideration with no right on the company's part to an input tax deduction, since the supply had been made to the customer, not the company. The Supreme Court explained that whilst there had indeed been a supply of reward goods or services to the customer, there had been a separate supply of services by the supplier to the company, for which the company's payment was consideration, thus entitling the company to an input tax deduction. Thus the gift (or sale) of reward goods or services to the customer could be a supply both to the customer and separately to the company - it did not have to be one or the other. *HMRC v Aimia Coalition Loyalty UK Ltd (formerly Loyalty Management UK Ltd)* [2013]

3. Different VAT rate on sale

6544 In certain trades it is common for goods to be acquired at one VAT rate (e.g. the zero rate), and be sold at a different rate (e.g. the standard rate). This presents no problem for the **Point of sale** scheme, which identifies the VAT rate on sale rather than looking at purchases.

6546 Notice 727/4 para 7.19; Notice 727/5 para 6.18 When operating any of the **Apportionment schemes** or **Direct calculation schemes**, however, separate stocks of these goods must be maintained. When these goods are acquired, the retailer should record the VAT rate which will apply when the goods are sold.

If, on acquisition, the VAT **rate on sale cannot be predicted**, a common stock of these goods can be maintained. In this case the VAT rate which applied on acquisition is used when calculating the expected selling price. When these goods are sold at another VAT rate, the retailer must delete the amount initially recorded and enter the same amount for the correct VAT rate.

Retail chemists

A chemist may be providing exempt pharmacy services, which must always be excluded from gross takings. The NHS rota payment is also exempt. **6548** Notice 727 para 9

When using **Apportionment 2**, a special calculation needs to be agreed with HMRC.

A special adjustment is also required for chemists using **Apportionment 1** or either of the **Direct calculation** schemes, because drugs, etc, are standard-rated when acquired but zero-rated when supplied under prescription to a patient. In addition, chemists using the Direct calculation schemes can calculate the expected selling price on majority zero-rated goods if this is easier (¶6470+).

Adjustment The normal retail calculation must first be completed. Takings will include all taxable payments received for prescriptions, from both the patient and the NHS. **6550** Notice 727 para 9.4

The following adjustment is then made:

	Total	Standard rate	Zero rate
1 Total payments received for zero-rated dispensed goods (even if not supplied in the period)	X		
2 Estimate value of these goods which were zero-rated on acquisition (such as gluten-free bread) and deduct from the total [1]	(X)		X
3 This gives the standard-rated acquisitions	X	X	
4 Apply VAT fraction		1/6	
5 Adjustment to output tax (deduction)	X	X	

Note:
1. A new **estimate** must be completed for each VAT period. The estimation must be based on a sample of purchases for a representative period, taking account of seasonal fluctuations. Details of the sample must be retained.

EXAMPLE Ms C is a chemist who uses Direct calculation 1. She has already calculated that her output tax due for the quarter is £1,020. The gross takings are £11,400 and the payments received for drugs, etc, amount to £7,034. Ms C estimates that 87% of these payments related to goods which were zero-rated on acquisition.

		£	£
Output tax as calculated under Direct calculation 1			1,020.00
Payments received for drugs, etc		7,034.00	
Attributable to zero-rated goods on purchase	£7,034 × 87%	(6,119.58)	
		914.42	
VAT fraction adjustment	£914.42 × 1/6		(152.40)
Revised output tax due			867.60

Caterers

The **reverse problem** affects caterers, as food is acquired at the zero rate and then supplied at the standard rate. **6552** Notice 727 para 8

The **solution** is to use the Point of sale scheme.

However, for those caterers who are **unable** to operate it and who have anticipated annual retail turnover of under £1 million, the catering adaptation is available instead. Those who want to use the adaptation should inform HMRC; once this has been acknowledged, the caterer can start to use it. If the adaptation does not give a fair and reasonable result, or it is used improperly, HMRC can assess for understated output tax and prevent future use of the adaptation.

MEMO POINTS Where **goods are taken out of another part of the business** in order to form part of the catering supplies (e.g. cakes from a bakery are sold in a coffee shop), the expected selling prices (purchases for Apportionment 1) must be adjusted to reflect the transfer of stock. Estimates can be used where it is impractical to make an accurate calculation.

6554 The **adaptation** requires the following calculation:

		Zero rate	Reduced rate	Standard rate	Total
1	Gross takings				X
2	Percentage of catering sales made at the standard rate[1]			z%	
3	Apply percentage to gross takings			X	
4	Apply VAT fraction			1/6	
5	Output tax on catering sales			X	

Note:
1. The **percentage** must be calculated afresh for each VAT period, and the method of calculation will be specific to the business. It must be based on a sample of sales for a representative period, taking account of seasonal fluctuations. Details of the sample must be retained, including dates and times.

To impose a retrospective change to the percentage, HMRC must satisfy a relatively high burden of proof, for which two days' observation is inadequate. *Harrison* [1981] (VTD 1125)

EXAMPLE Mr D is a caterer who has gross takings for the latest VAT quarter of £10,300. He has calculated the percentage of standard-rated catering sales as 92%.
The output tax is calculated as follows:

		£	£
Gross takings			10,300
Attributable to catering sales	£10,300 × 92%	9,476.00	
VAT fraction	£9,476 × 1/6	1,579.33	
Output tax due			1,579.33

4. Florists

6556 Notice 727 para 10

Agencies such as Interflora arrange deliveries of flowers throughout the country by maintaining a network of small independent florists.

In a transaction, the florist may be:
- the sending member (who receives the payment from the customer); or
- the executing member (who delivers the flowers and receives payment from the agency).

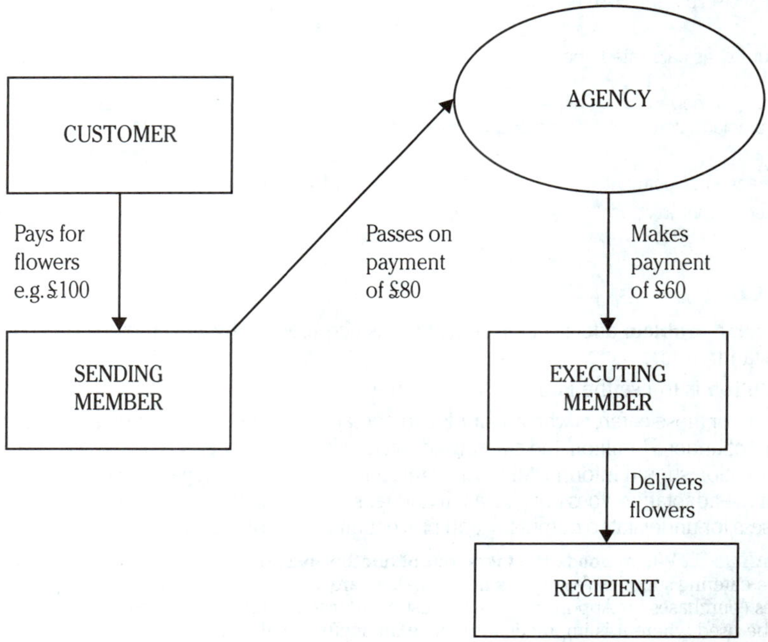

Adjustment

The table below summarises the actions a florist should take **depending on** the retail scheme used. 6558

The documentation from the agency will show any **output tax payable** by the florist in relation to these transactions (under a self-billing arrangement (¶2904+)). This VAT must be added to the results of the retail scheme in use to obtain the total output tax due for the VAT period.

Notice 727 para 10.4

Scheme used	Sending member	Executing member
Point of sale	Include payments in gross takings as normal	Exclude agency payments received from gross takings Account for output tax due outside scheme
Apportionment 1	Exclude all payments received from gross takings Account for output tax on sale outside scheme	As above, plus exclude the value of the flowers from the purchase records
Apportionment 2		As for Point of sale scheme, plus adjust the expected selling price for the value of flowers delivered
Direct calculation 1		
Direct calculation 2		

5. Exports

Each scheme has its own rules for dealing with exports of goods outside the EU. 6560

Point of sale scheme

The **gross takings** exclude goods which are either exported by the retailer or are to be exported by the retailer's customer. 6562

If retailers are making supplies under the **retail export scheme** (¶9603+) they should: Notice 727/3 para 6.15
a. include all amounts received for the goods supplied in the takings;
b. at the end of each VAT period, total the amount of standard-rated goods which have physically been exported (as shown on the certified forms returned to the retailer);
c. apply the VAT fraction which was used at the time of the original sale; and
d. subtract the result of **c.** from the total output tax due for the VAT period.

Apportionment schemes

All takings relating to goods sold for **retail export** (¶9603+), **or sent for export**, should initially be included in the gross takings. At the end of the VAT period, an adjustment should be made to reflect the exports actually made. The gross value of standard-rated goods actually exported is calculated, and then the VAT fraction (1/6) is applied to this in order to obtain the related VAT figure. This VAT is then deducted from the output tax showing as due. 6564 Notice 727/4 para 7.16

	£	£
Output tax due for period		X
Takings for exported goods	X	
VAT @ 1/6	X	(X)
Amended output tax		X

For both **direct and indirect exports** (¶9573), where proof of shipment is not obtained within 3 months, the deducted VAT must be added back to the output tax liability.

Direct calculation schemes

The following apply both to retail exports (¶9603+) and direct exports. 6566 Notice 727/5 para 6.15

For **zero-rated minority goods**, the rules in ¶6564 apply.

For **standard-rated minority goods**, at the end of each VAT period an adjustment should be made to reflect the exports (including retail exports) actually made, by calculating:
- the expected selling price of the exported goods; and
- the notional VAT by using the relevant VAT fraction.

The notional VAT relating to the exported goods is deducted from the output tax showing as due.

	£	£
Output tax due for quarter		X
Expected selling price of goods exported	X	
VAT @ 1/6	X	(X)
Amended output tax		X

For **direct exports** only, where proof of shipment is not obtained within 3 months, the notional VAT must be added back to the output tax liability.

6. Shops within shops

6568 A **department store** will often wish to have other retailers (concessionaires) within the store to offer fashionable or popular products with an appropriate brand name.

The exact **arrangements** usually fall within one of the following categories:
a. leasing of space to the concessionaire, in which case all rent received by the store should be excluded from its takings;
b. provision of staff, advertising and other services by the store - again, the payments made by the concessionaire to the store must be excluded from the store's takings; or
c. the store makes all the sales, and treats the concessionaire as the supplier - in this case, the sales are included in the store's takings.

In **a**. and **b**. above the concessionaire needs to account for output tax on all retail sales made.

7. Changes in VAT rates

6572 Notice 727 para 7

The Government can:
- amend the VAT rating applying to a **particular type of supply** (e.g. a standard-rated supply is made exempt);
- **globally change the percentage** which applies to the standard rate or reduced rate, which would alter the respective VAT fraction; or
- **add a new rate** (in which case HMRC would issue guidance).

Retailers have to cope with the following consequences:
- deciding whether to pass on any VAT rise to the customer, bearing in mind that the customer will just see this as a price hike; and
- reviewing the output tax calculation.

It is most likely that a change will occur during a VAT period, in which case two calculations must be undertaken, reflecting the supplies made before and after the change.

MEMO POINTS 1. Retailers should have in place a **contingency plan** in case of a rate change.
2. For the schemes which use the **expected selling price**, account will need to be taken of changed consumer buying patterns as well as the obvious price change itself.

CHAPTER 5

Second-hand goods and collectibles

OUTLINE ¶¶

A special scheme exists for supplies of second-hand goods, works of art, antiques or collectors' items made by a VAT-registered trader, where no VAT was charged on their purchase. This scheme, which is often referred to as the margin scheme, allows VAT to be charged only on the profit margin of these goods i.e. the difference between the purchase cost and the sale price. **6620** s 50A VATA 1994

In addition to the basic margin scheme, there are three modified schemes:
- the global accounting scheme, which is a simplified method of accounting for VAT where the business has a large number of low-value transactions, and the accounting and record-keeping requirements would otherwise be onerous;
- the auctioneers' scheme, which is, as its name suggests, designed specifically for use by auctioneers; and
- a scheme for the sale of second-hand cars, which is essentially the same as the basic margin scheme.

Special rules also apply to overseas transactions.

SECTION 1

The basic margin scheme

1. Scope

6625 SI 1995/1268 reg 12; Notice 718

The margin scheme is **voluntary**. Goods may be sold in accordance with the normal rules even when acquired under the margin scheme.

It is only possible to opt into the scheme if:
- eligible goods (¶6627+) are to be sold (on which no VAT was charged when purchased for resale); and
- the stringent record-keeping requirements are met (¶6644+).

The scheme **cannot be used for** any goods:
- on which VAT was paid on purchase, and for which the purchaser holds a valid VAT invoice; or
- which were acquired by way of gift, because VAT must be charged on the full value of the supply.

MEMO POINTS **No VAT will be charged on purchase** when goods are bought from one of the following (either in the UK or another EU member state):
- a private individual;
- a business not registered for VAT; or
- a VAT-registered dealer who supplies the goods under the margin scheme.

2. Eligible goods

6627 Notice 718 paras 2.7, 2.8

The following goods are **within the scope** of the margin scheme, provided that no VAT was charged when they were purchased for resale:
- second-hand goods;
- collectors' items;
- works of art; and
- antiques (i.e. goods, other than collectors' items and works of art, which are over 100 years old).

Specifically **excluded** are precious metals, precious stones (diamonds, rubies, emeralds and sapphires) and investment gold (¶6835+).

Second-hand goods

6630 This covers **all tangible moveable property** which is suitable for further use, whether in its present state or after repair.

Second-hand motor cars are specifically included where certain conditions are met (¶6660+).

Collectors' items

6632 Notice 718 para 20.1

This term includes collections and collectors' pieces of interest, **such as**:
- postage or revenue stamps, provided that they are franked (or if unfranked, are not legal tender), a postmark, a first-day cover or an item of pre-stamped stationery;
- items connected with the study of coins;
- zoological or botanical items;
- mineralogical pieces;
- anatomical specimens;
- historical or archaeological items;
- palaeontological items; and
- ethnographic items.

MEMO POINTS **Unfranked stamps** which are currently valid for postage are not collectors' items and cannot be included in the margin schemes.

Works of art

The following items are treated as works of art: 6634 Notice 718 para 20.1

Item	Conditions to be treated as a work of art
Painting, drawing, collage, decorative plaque or similar picture (mounted or unmounted)	Must be executed by hand[1]
Original engraving, lithograph or other print	Produced from one or more plates executed entirely by hand by the artist, and either the only one or part of a limited edition[2]
Original sculpture or statuary	Executed entirely by the artist
Sculpture cast	Produced by, or under the supervision of, the individual who made the mould (or who became entitled to the mould by succession following the death of the individual who had made the mould), and is either: – the only cast produced from the mould; or – part of a limited edition (not exceeding eight items, or, if produced before 1 January 1989, such number as HMRC may allow)
Tapestry or other hanging	Made by hand from an original design, and either the only one or part of a limited edition (not exceeding eight items)
Individual pieces of ceramic	Signed by, and executed entirely by, the artist
Enamel on copper	Executed by hand (and signed by the person who executed it or by someone on behalf of the studio where it was executed), and either: – the only one; or – part of a limited edition (not exceeding eight items, each numbered and signed)
Photograph (mounted or unmounted)	Printed by, or under the supervision of, (and signed by) the photographer, and either the only one or part of a limited edition (not exceeding 30 prints, each numbered and signed)

Note:
1. Specifically **excluded** are:
– plans, maps and drawings for architectural, engineering, industrial, commercial or topographical purposes;
– hand-decorated manufactured articles; and
– theatrical scenery.
2. Specifically **excluded** are items produced using a mechanical or photomechanical process.

3. Operation of the scheme

The margin scheme allows VAT to be **calculated** by applying the applicable VAT fraction (¶1090) to the difference (or margin) between the purchase price and selling price of eligible goods, provided that no VAT was charged on the goods when purchased for resale. 6636 Notice 718 para 2.1

If no profit is made (because the purchase price exceeds the selling price), no VAT is payable.

EXAMPLE Mrs A sells an antique chair for £4,000, which she purchased for £2,500.

	£
Sale	4,000
Purchase	(2,500)
Margin	1,500
VAT due (£1,500 x 1/6)	250

If Mrs A did not opt into the scheme, the VAT accounted for would be £666.67. (£4,000 × 1/6)

How to calculate the margin

6638 Notice 718 para 3 The purchase price and selling price are, respectively, everything paid or received for the goods, including incidental expenses directly linked to the purchase or sale. This includes any non-monetary consideration, which will need to be valued in accordance with normal principles (¶936+).

EXAMPLE Mr B sells second-hand goods which he purchased for £1,500. He takes as consideration for the sale cash of £2,000 plus an antique chair worth £500.
The value of the selling price will be £2,500 and VAT will be accounted for on the margin of £1,000. (£2,500 - £1,500)

Specifically **excluded** from the:
- **selling price** are disbursements (¶7190+) or optional extras charged to the buyer; and
- **purchase price** are the costs of selling, repairing, or refurbishing the goods.

These expenses should be accounted for separately outside the margin scheme.

Notice 718 para 13.2 MEMO POINTS 1. Special rules apply when **insurance** is provided along with eligible goods.
a. If the insurance is **sold with** a product, the cost of the insurance is treated as a separate supply (accounted for outside the margin scheme), and is therefore not included in the selling price for the purpose of calculating the margin on which VAT is due.
Such insurance will be an exempt supply if:
- it is the customer's risks which are insured;
- the customer is entirely free to purchase the item without the insurance; and
- the dealer discloses to the customer the premium and any other amount being charged.

Otherwise the supply will be standard-rated.
b. If the insurance is **provided free** (i.e. included in the sale price to the purchaser), it is not treated as a separate supply and the full selling price of the goods, including the cost to the vendor of providing the insurance, should be included in the selling price for the purpose of calculating the margin on which VAT is due.
2. A trader using the margin scheme can reclaim input tax on **overheads and repairs** in the usual manner.
3. Where a trader is **required to make more than one purchase payment** - for example, one payment to the keeper of the goods and another to a finance company - the purchase price is the sum of the two amounts. *Daron Motors Ltd* [1993] (VTD 11695)

Bad debt relief

6642 Notice 718 para 13.1 Bad debt relief can be claimed in the usual manner (¶840+), but the amount of VAT on which relief can be claimed is **restricted** to the VAT previously accounted for on the supply.

EXAMPLE Mr C purchased goods for £400, sold them for £500 and accounted for VAT of £16.67 on the margin of £100. (£100 × 1/6)

Scenario 1
The customer pays £350, leaving £150 as a bad debt.
The debt is greater than the margin, so the bad debt relief is limited to £16.67.

Scenario 2
The customer pays £450, leaving £50 as a bad debt.
This debt is less than the margin, so the bad debt relief is £8.33. (£50 × 1/6)

4. Record-keeping requirements

6644 Notice 718 para 5 To use the margin scheme a trader must, in addition to the normal record-keeping requirements (¶2790+), keep:
- a **stock book** or similar record; and
- copies of all purchase and sales **invoices**.

These records must be **kept for** at least 6 years from the date of sale of the goods. If a trader's stock includes goods which were obtained more than 6 years ago, evidence must also be retained to demonstrate their eligibility for margin scheme treatment on an eventual sale (for example, proof of purchase price, etc).

MEMO POINTS 1. If a person **occasionally sells eligible goods** in the course of their business, they need not comply with the full record-keeping requirements, provided that the other conditions of the scheme are met, and they hold evidence of both the purchase and selling prices. Notice 718 para 13.7
2. For the record-keeping requirements for **horses** which are sold under the margin scheme see ¶6218.

Stock book

The stock book must have **separate headings** for each of the following entries. **6646** Notice 718 para 5.2

Section	Required entries
Purchases	Stock number in numerical sequence
	Date of purchase
	Purchase invoice number
	Purchase price
	Name of seller
	Any unique reference number (e.g. a car registration number)
	Description of the goods (such as make and model)
Sales	Date of sale
	Sales invoice number
	Name of buyer
	Selling price or method of disposal
Accounting	Margin on sale (sale price minus purchase price)
	VAT due[1]

Note:
1. It is not possible to offset any VAT on **goods which are sold at a loss**. In these circumstances the VAT due should be shown as nil.

MEMO POINTS 1. **Further information** may be included at the option of the trader. Notice 718 paras 5.2, 5.6
2. A separate record must also be maintained of stock supplied on a **sale or return basis**, to include:
- the date of transfer of the goods;
- a description of the goods, including any unique identification number;
- the name and address of the dealer or person transferring the goods; and
- the date of sale or return.

Invoices

When a **business purchases** goods for onward sale under the margin scheme, the purchaser must obtain a purchase invoice. **6650**

In general, the purchaser is **responsible for preparing** the purchase invoice. However, if the vendor is VAT-registered, it is the vendor's responsibility.

When **goods are sold** under the margin scheme, the vendor must issue a sales invoice (and keep a copy for their own records). **6652**

The **information** which must be on the sales and purchase invoices is very similar. Both must contain the following details: **6654** SI 2007/2085; Information Sheet 10/07; Notice 718 para 5.3
a. the seller's and buyer's names and addresses;
b. the stock book number, invoice number, date of sale and total price;
c. a description of the goods, including any unique identification number; and
d. either:
- a reference to the relevant sections of the UK legislation or EC Directive or
- a declaration that "This is a second-hand margin scheme supply" or "This invoice is for a second-hand margin scheme supply".

MEMO POINTS 1. If the purchase invoice is for a **batch of goods** which the trader intends to sell on separately, a purchase price must be allocated to each item.

Notice 718 para 5.7
2. If a trader is buying or selling goods in a **foreign currency**, the price must be converted to sterling before calculating the margin. Any one of the recognised conversion methods can be used (¶9032), but the exchange rate used must be the one that is current at the time of the supply.
Where an invoice details **more than one item** in:
– a sales transaction, the foreign currency and sterling price should be shown for each item on the invoice, unless all the items are sold as one lot, in which case the total foreign currency and sterling values for the lot are acceptable; or
– a purchase transaction, the sterling amount should be apportioned between the items, and entered on an item-by-item basis in the stock record.
3. If an **insurance product** is sold with the goods, the full price plus any associated fees should be disclosed on the invoice.

Notice 704
4. If traders are also making supplies under the **retail export scheme** (¶9603+), they will need to adapt the VAT refund document as follows:
– head the document "Second-hand goods - this document is adapted in accordance with Notice 704 paragraph 5.8";
– leave the line "Amount of VAT included in the price" blank; and
– complete the refund due box.

VAT return

6658
Notice 718 para 5.4
The following information **must be included** on the VAT return for each VAT period.

Box	Amount to include
1	Output tax due on all eligible goods sold in the VAT period covered by the return
6	Full selling price of all eligible goods sold in the period, less any VAT due on the margin
7	Full purchase price of eligible goods bought in the period

There is **no requirement** to include margin scheme purchases or sales in boxes 8 and 9 of the VAT return, which give statistical information on EU trade.

5. Special situations

Motor cars

6660
Notice 718/1 paras 2.3, 2.4
Eligibility A separate margin scheme can also be used for second-hand vehicles (including commercial vehicles). To be eligible for this scheme, the vehicle must have been **used** on the road for business or pleasure and **purchased from** any of the following (in the UK or another EU member state):
– a private individual;
– a business not registered for VAT;
– a VAT-registered dealer where it is supplied under the margin scheme;
– a dealer or business which was unable to reclaim input tax on the purchase (¶1890+); or
– Motability.

Generally, all second-hand cars acquired from unregistered dealers and private individuals will qualify.

MEMO POINTS 1. Registration and **delivery mileage** is not sufficient to make a car second-hand. Demonstration cars and any cars purchased on an invoice showing VAT separately are not second-hand cars (regardless of whether the VAT was reclaimed).
2. A second-hand car which was **originally imported as new** may be sold under the margin scheme, provided that the person who imported the vehicle is not connected with the business which sells it (e.g. as an employee or agent).

Notice 718/1 para 10.6
3. If a vehicle is **rebuilt** using parts from other vehicles, the decision as to whether it is new or second-hand depends on how it is registered with the DVLA. If the vehicle retains the registration of one of the component vehicles, it is second-hand and the purchase price to be entered in the stock book is the purchase price for the vehicle for which the registration number is retained. If,

however, the vehicle is re-registered and given a new registration number, it is considered to be a new vehicle and so cannot be sold under the margin scheme.

Operation of the scheme The general margin scheme rules apply to the sale of second-hand cars, but a separate VAT Notice provides details of the scheme's operation in relation to second-hand cars. **6664** Notice 718/1

Related supplies Special rules apply for the following types of supply made by a vendor using the margin scheme: **6666** Notice 718/1 paras 9, 10.2, 10.3

Supply	Sale under margin scheme	Treatment
Road fund licence	Vehicle purchased (for resale under the margin scheme) with a road fund licence that is subsequently surrendered for a refund	Outside the scope of VAT, therefore no adjustment must be made to the purchase price in the stock book
	Vehicle is sold inclusive of a road fund licence	Single supply and the selling price entered in the stock book must include the value of the road fund licence
	Vehicle is sold and the vendor subsequently agrees to obtain a road fund licence on behalf of the purchaser	The road fund licence will be treated either as: – a separate supply, provided that the conditions for treatment as a disbursement are met (¶7190+); or – a single supply (if the disbursement conditions are not met), and the selling price entered in the stock book must include the value of the road fund licence
MOT	Vehicle is sold inclusive of a current MOT	Treated as a single supply and the full selling price, including the MOT, should be recorded in the stock record
Warranties	Vehicle is sold inclusive of warranties	Treated as a single supply and the full selling price, including the cost to the vendor of providing the cover, should be recorded in the stock record
	Vehicle is sold and a separate charge is made to the customer for the warranties	Treated as a separate standard-rated supply and therefore deducted from the value entered in the sale stock record
Mechanical breakdown cover	Vehicle is sold inclusive of cover for the customer	Treated as a separate exempt supply and therefore deducted from the value entered in the sale stock record[1]
	Vehicle is sold with cover, but the contract is between vendor and insurer to cover the vendor's risk in the event of them having to repair defective items	Treated as a separate standard-rated supply and therefore deducted from the value entered in the sale stock record

Note:
1. This rule is subject to the following **restrictions**, so that if:
– the customer negotiates a reduced price for the item (including the mechanical breakdown cover), the price originally advertised for the breakdown cover must be treated as the value of the exempt supply;
– the customer negotiates an upgraded breakdown cover, the dealer may use the separately advertised price of the upgraded breakdown cover as the value of the exempt supply; or
– the dealer does not disclose to the customer the amount the latter is paying for the cover, any fee or commission income the dealer would receive in relation to this insurance is standard-rated. The net value of the insurance paid to, and retained by, the insurer remains exempt.
These rules only apply to motor dealers. When insurance is sold with other goods or services, the general principles detailed at ¶310+ apply to determine whether the supply of insurance is part of a composite or mixed supply.

Agents

Where a person acts on behalf of a third party **in their own name** (¶7142+), they are treated as an agent of the person who owns the goods (the principal). **6668** Notice 718 para 17

Sales by agents can be accounted for under the margin schemes by both the principal and the agent, with a few **modifications** when determining the purchase and selling prices for both the principal and agent, as follows:

	Purchase price	**Selling price**
Principal	Calculated in accordance with the normal rules	Equivalent to the agent's purchase price
Agent	Can either be the amount received: – before any deduction for commission (in which case the commission charges are invoiced separately to the principal, outside the margin scheme); or – after deducting commission charged to the principal (this method mirrors that used under the auctioneers' scheme (¶6750+))	The total price for the goods including any incidental expenses and commission charged to the buyer

MEMO POINTS 1. Agents who issue invoices in their own name must comply with all the **record-keeping requirements** at ¶6644+.
2. For **full details** of the VAT rules relating to agents, see ¶7090+.

Joint ownership

6672 Notice 718 paras 12.3 - 12.5

Where eligible goods are bought or sold by joint owners, the margin schemes can apply, with a few **modifications** when it comes to the record-keeping and invoicing requirements on a purchase or sale.

Transaction	**Rule**	
Purchase	One of the joint buyers (the nominated joint buyer) must: – keep the purchase invoice for the item; – invoice the other joint buyers for their contributions, excluding VAT[1]; and – keep copies of these invoices, and enter the full purchase details of the item in the stock book	
Sale	By the nominated joint buyer	On a sale they must: – issue, and keep a copy of, the sales invoice; – enter the details of the sale in the stock book (using the full selling price); and – issue statements to the other joint buyers, showing to each their share of the proceeds of the sale, excluding VAT[2]
	By another joint buyer	On a sale, the other joint buyer must obtain the purchase invoice for the goods, then treat the purchase and sale as being made by them as if they were the nominated joint buyer. The original nominated joint buyer must therefore close the entry in their own stock book, stating that the VAT has been accounted for by the other joint buyer and cross-refer to the statement received

Note:
1. Each invoice must state "This payment is your contribution towards the purchase of the above article. I shall be accounting for the full amount of VAT due under the scheme when it is sold."
2. Each invoice must state "This payment is your share of the proceeds of the sale. I am accounting for the full amount of VAT due on the sale under the scheme."

Notice 718 para 12.2

MEMO POINTS If a trader **sells a share** in an eligible asset but retains the remainder, this is a supply of an undivided share in goods and therefore a supply of services. The sale cannot be accounted for under a margin scheme, and therefore VAT must be accounted for under normal rules in respect of the entire consideration, not just the margin. If the sale is of **an item where the vendor only holds title to a share** of the goods, they must account for VAT on the consideration received for the complete asset, not merely the share held. Statements should be issued to the owner(s) of the remaining share(s), showing to each their appropriate proportion(s) of the sale proceeds, excluding VAT.

Transfer of a going concern

If goods are acquired by way of a transfer of a going concern (TOGC), and the **transferor** of the goods was entitled to sell those goods under the margin scheme, the **transferee** will also be entitled to use the margin scheme on a subsequent sale, provided that all the necessary record-keeping requirements are satisfied (¶6644+). **6676** Notice 718 para 9

The transferor's original purchase price is used to calculate the margin.

Where there has been a **succession of TOGCs**, it is the first person in the chain who must have been entitled to use the margin scheme.

Hire purchase

If goods are sold on hire purchase, they are deemed to be sold to the finance house. **6678** Notice 718 para 13.5

The sale should be treated as a cash sale, and the **selling price** to be entered in the stock book is the cash price shown on the hire purchase agreement.

No VAT is charged in respect of the **finance element**, provided that this is identified separately on the invoice.

SECTION 2

Global accounting

1. Scope

The global accounting scheme is an **optional simplified variation** of the normal margin scheme. It allows VAT to be accounted for on the profit margin of all eligible goods in a period (as opposed to on an item-by-item basis). **6700** Notice 718 para 14

It is designed for traders dealing in bulk volume, low-value items, where the record-keeping requirements of the normal margin scheme would be too onerous. The scheme also provides an effective credit for goods sold at a loss.

The rules of the main margin scheme apply, with certain **modifications** in relation to the:
- eligible goods;
- method of calculating the margin; and
- record-keeping requirements.

2. Eligible goods

The goods detailed at ¶6627+ can be **included** in the scheme, provided that they cost £500 or less to buy. **6702** Notice 718 paras 14.4, 14.5

The following are specifically **excluded** from the scheme:
- aircraft;
- boats and outboard motors;
- caravans and motor caravans;
- horses and ponies; and
- motor vehicles, including motorcycles (except those broken up for scrap).

MEMO POINTS 1. Global accounting can be used for **bulk purchases**, even if the combined purchase price is over £500, provided that each individual item cost no more than £500. If any individual item has a purchase value of over £500 it must be excluded. Notice 718 paras 14.10, 14.11
2. **Collections of items** such as stamp collections can be split and sold separately. Similarly, two or more items may be combined to produce only one item for resale - for example, by using one item as a spare part for another. However, if a collection cost more than £500 to buy and is sold on in basically the same state, it cannot be sold under the scheme.

3. Operation of the scheme

6704 Under the global accounting scheme VAT is accounted for on the total margin for each VAT period, not each sale.

Calculation

6706 Notice 718 para 14.8 The total margin is the excess of the total **selling price** for the VAT period, over the total **purchase price** of the goods for that period. If the margin is:
- positive, the trader must account for VAT; or
- negative, no VAT is due and the amount of the negative margin is carried forward and included as a purchase in the next VAT period.

VAT is calculated by applying the applicable **VAT fraction** (¶1090) to the margin between the purchase price and selling price of eligible goods.

EXAMPLE Ms A made the following sales under the global accounting scheme:

	£	£
Quarter ended 31 July		
Total sales	3,200	
Less: Total purchases	(3,500)	
Margin		(300)
VAT due		Nil
Quarter ended 31 October		
Total sales	4,500	
Less: Total purchases	(1,500)	
Negative margin brought forward	(300)	
Margin		2,700
VAT due (£2,700 x 1/6)		450

Notice 718 para 15.9 MEMO POINTS 1. The purchase price of goods which are lost through **breakage, theft or destruction** must be deducted from the value of total purchases in the period of the loss.

Notice 718 para 15.8 2. The purchase price of goods which are subsequently **sold outside the scheme** (because, for example, they are exported) must also be deducted from the value of total purchases in the period of the sale. If it is not possible to allocate a value to specific items (because, for example, they were part of a bulk purchase), a fair and reasonable allocation must be made. Evidence and calculations must be retained with the other records for 6 years.

Starting the scheme

6710 Notice 718 paras 14.6, 14.7 When a trader first uses the global accounting scheme, they can include the purchase value of any **goods on hand** in the first VAT period. The relevant value of these goods should ideally be taken from the values shown on the original purchase invoices. However, if these are not available, HMRC will accept any other reasonable method.

EXAMPLE Mr B decides to adopt the global accounting scheme. He has goods on hand which he wants to include in the scheme, valued at £10,000. He makes the following sales and purchases in the first VAT period:

	£	£
Total sales		8,000
Goods on hand	10,000	
Total purchases	2,000	
		(12,000)
Margin		(4,000)
VAT due		Nil

The negative margin will be carried forward into the next VAT period.

MEMO POINTS 1. If **no account is taken** of goods on hand, VAT will be accounted for on the full sale value under the normal VAT rules.
2. If goods have already been **entered into the stock book for the margin scheme** (¶6646), and they are to be transferred to the global accounting scheme, the original entry should be closed and transferred to the global accounting scheme records.

Leaving the scheme

On leaving the global accounting scheme, a **closing adjustment** must be made to take account of purchases already made under the scheme which have not been sold, **unless** the equivalent VAT on stock is no more than £1,000. 6714 Notice 718 para 15.7

The closing adjustment is **calculated** by adding the purchase value of the closing stock to the sales figure for this final period of using the scheme.

EXAMPLE Mrs C deregistered on 31 October. Her closing adjustment for the period to 31 October is calculated as follows:

		£	£
Total sales		10,000	
Closing stock		8,000	
			18,000
Total purchases			(5,000)
Margin			13,000
VAT due	£13,000 × 1/6		2,166.67

On a **transfer of a going concern** (TOGC), an identical adjustment is made for the period in which the TOGC takes place. This adjustment is separate from the actual TOGC transaction itself, which is not subject to VAT (¶8646+). 6716

4. Record-keeping requirements

A trader must keep records of purchases and sales, plus workings used to calculate the VAT due. 6718 Notice 718 paras 15.1, 15.6

There is no set **format** for these records, but they must be complete, up to date, and clearly distinguishable from any other records.

They must contain the following **information**:
- an invoice number;
- the date of purchase/sale;
- a full description which is sufficient to determine that the goods are eligible for global accounting (e.g. "four tables and ten chairs", as opposed to an unclear phrase such as "assorted goods"); and
- the total price.

These records must be **kept for** 6 years. If a business fails to comply with these record-keeping requirements, it will be liable to account for VAT on the full sale price of items sold.

Invoices

When a business **purchases goods** for onward sale under the margin scheme, the purchaser must obtain a purchase invoice. In general, the purchaser is responsible for preparing the purchase invoice. However, if the vendor is VAT-registered, it is the vendor's responsibility. 6720 Notice 718 paras 15.2 - 15.5

When **goods are sold** under the global accounting scheme, vendors must issue a sales invoice (and keep a copy for their own records). 6722

6724 The **information** which must be on the sales and purchase invoices is very similar. Both must contain the following details:
- the seller's and buyer's names and addresses;
- the invoice number, date of sale and total price (including VAT);
- a clear description of the goods including any unique identification number; and
- an endorsement stating "Global Accounting invoice".

In addition, if the vendor is VAT-registered, they must **certify** that the invoice is not a tax invoice.

MEMO POINTS 1. If the vendor is selling an item for more than £500 and **does not wish to disclose** to the purchaser that it was bought under the global accounting scheme (i.e. that it was bought for less than £500), they may instead include a statement on the sales invoice saying "This is a second-hand margin scheme supply" or "This invoice is for a second-hand margin scheme supply".

Notice 718 para 15.11 2. If a trader is buying or selling goods in a **foreign currency**, the total price must be converted to sterling before calculating the margin. Any one of the recognised conversion methods can be used (¶9032), but the exchange rate used must be the one that is current at the time of the supply. In particular:
- if a **sales invoice** is for more than one item, the total foreign currency and sterling amount is acceptable; there is no need to show this information on an item-by-item basis; and
- if a **purchase invoice** contains items with a value in excess of £500, the total value will need to be converted and apportioned between the items, with the items with a value in excess of £500 being excluded from the scheme.

SECTION 3

Auctioneers' scheme

1. Scope

6750 Notice 718/2 The auctioneers' scheme is another **optional simplified variation** of the normal margin scheme. Essentially this scheme allows VAT to be accounted for on a profit margin when an auctioneer sells eligible goods on behalf of a third party.

The rules of the main margin scheme apply, but with certain **modifications** in relation to the:
- eligible goods;
- method of calculating the margin; and
- record-keeping requirements.

Auctioneers who sell eligible goods and **invoice in their own name** may, instead of adopting the auctioneers' scheme, invoice as an agent (¶7090+).

MEMO POINTS Where a supply is made under the auctioneers' scheme, the supplies of services to the vendor and purchaser are treated as supplies of **neither goods nor services** (¶258).

Eligible persons

6752 Notice 718/2 para 2.5 To use the scheme, the **third-party vendor** must either be:
- unregistered;
- VAT-registered but supplying goods under the margin or global accounting scheme;
- an insurance company selling goods under the margin scheme which it acquired as a result of an insurance claim, and which it is selling at auction in the same state; or
- a finance house selling goods under the margin scheme which it has repossessed, and which it is selling at auction in the same state.

2. Eligible goods

The goods that can be sold under the scheme are: **6754**
a. all the eligible goods detailed at ¶6627+, **including** second-hand cars, although in this circumstance the scheme for second-hand cars also applies; and
b. by concession, goods grown, made or produced (including bloodstock or livestock reared from birth) by a non-VAT-registered person. To take advantage of this concession, the vendor must provide a signed certificate with: Notice 718/2 para 5.3
- their name and address;
- a description of the goods; and
- confirmation that they are not VAT-registered.

MEMO POINTS The auctioneers' scheme may be used for a sale of eligible goods made on behalf of a **pawnbroker**, provided that: Notice 718/2 para 5.1
- the pawn value is greater than £75;
- the pawn has not been redeemed; and
- the person who originally gave the goods to the pawnbroker is not VAT-registered (if they are registered, VAT must be accounted for on the full selling price).

3. Operation of the scheme

VAT is calculated by applying the applicable VAT fraction (¶1090) to the margin between the purchase price and selling price of the eligible goods. **6756**

The relevant VAT fraction is determined by the rate applicable to the goods being sold.

If **zero-rated goods are sold** under the auctioneers' scheme, the auctioneer's margin is also therefore zero-rated. Notice 718/2 para 3.4

Goods sold under the auctioneers' scheme are deemed to be supplies both to and from the auctioneer, so there is a common tax point. The **time of supply** for both supplies is the earlier of: Notice 718/2 para 3.3
- the transfer of the goods from the auctioneer to the buyer; and
- the receipt of payment by the auctioneer.

How to calculate the margin

The **purchase price** is the amount paid to the seller by the auctioneer (less any VAT-inclusive commission charges). This is the hammer price less any commission charged to the seller. **6758** Notice 718/2 paras 3.1, 3.2

Indemnity fees which are shown separately on the invoice are specifically **excluded** from the purchase price.

The **selling price** is the amount due from the purchaser, plus any VAT-inclusive charges made by the auctioneer to the buyer (for example, commission, or incidental expenses such as packing, transport, and insurance costs). This is the hammer price plus any commission charged to the buyer. **6760**

The following are specifically **excluded** from the selling price, and should be accounted for outside the auctioneers' scheme:
- disbursements which meet all of the conditions in ¶7190+;
- incidental expenses which are a separate supply in their own right;
- exempt supplies, such as insurance; and
- other charges which are optional and not directly related to the sale of the goods.

MEMO POINTS Auctioneers' commissions (including buyer's premium) are subject to standard-rate VAT, even when the goods being sold are subject to the **effective rate of 5%** (¶1164). SI 2006/2187

6762

EXAMPLE
1. Ms A, an auctioneer, sells an antique dining table at auction on behalf of Mr B. The hammer price is £5,500. Mr B pays 10% (plus VAT at 20%) commission and the purchaser pays a buyer's premium of 18% (including VAT at 20%).

The VAT due is calculated as follows:

	£	£
Sales price:		
Hammer price	5,500	
Add: Buyer's premium (VAT-inclusive)	990	
		6,490
Purchase price		
Hammer price	5,500	
Less: Commission (VAT-inclusive)	(660)	
		(4,840)
Margin		1,650
VAT due (£1,650 x 1/6)		275

2. Mr C, an auctioneer, sells antique books and goods for export from the EU on behalf of Miss D. The hammer price is £1,000. Miss D pays 10% (plus VAT) commission and the purchaser pays a buyer's premium of 18% (including VAT).
The VAT due is calculated as follows:

	£	£
Sales price:		
Hammer price	1,000	
Add: Buyer's premium (VAT-inclusive)	180	
		1,180
Purchase price		
Hammer price	1,000	
Less: Commission (VAT-inclusive)	(120)	
		(880)
Margin		300
VAT due - zero-rated supply		Nil

Procedure

6764 **Before the sale** takes place, the vendor must inform the auctioneer whether it is intended that the goods are to be sold under the auctioneers' scheme.

After the sale, the auctioneer will provide the vendor with an account showing the hammer price, any commission due and the net amount payable. The vendor should sign and date the account, certifying that "input tax deduction has not been and will not be claimed by me in respect of the goods sold on this invoice".

Notice 718/2 para 4.5

MEMO POINTS The **buyer may subsequently decide** that they would prefer to pay VAT separately on the hammer price under the **normal VAT rules**, in which case the auctioneer would need to re-invoice the transaction. This can only occur if:
- the auctioneer is able to comply with all the usual VAT rules in relation to the re-invoicing;
- all the original records in respect of the transaction are still held by the auctioneer and the buyer; and
- the re-invoicing occurs within 4 years of the original transaction.

The first entry in the accounting records should be cancelled, and a cross-reference made to the new invoice. The new invoice should refer to the original transaction, state that it has been cancelled, and should contain an instruction to the buyer to amend their VAT account.

4. Record-keeping requirements

6766 Notice 718/2 para 4.2

The record-keeping requirements are similar to those for the margin scheme (¶6644+), with the exception that a **stock book** does not need to be kept, although sufficient alternative records must be retained, such as:
- sales catalogues/entry forms;
- copies of lots of the day; and
- copies of sales and purchase invoices.

Invoices

In addition to the requirements of the basic margin scheme (¶6650+), the **following details** must be shown on the relevant invoices: **6768** Notice 718/2 paras 4.3, 4.4

Type of invoice	Information required
Purchase invoice	Hammer price of the goods
	VAT-inclusive commission charges made to the vendor
	Net amount due to the vendor
Sales invoice	Hammer price of the goods
	VAT-inclusive charges made to the buyer
	Net amount due from the buyer

VAT must not be **itemised separately** on any statement or invoice issued to the vendor or buyer in relation to supplies which form the basis of the margin calculation. **6770**

Consequently, **in practice** HMRC advises that separate invoices are issued for scheme and non-scheme supplies, with the non-scheme supplies being invoiced under the normal VAT rules.

MEMO POINTS Invoices in **foreign currency** must show the sterling equivalent for each element of the invoice (e.g. the hammer price and the commission), not just the total value of the supplies made. Any one of the recognised conversion methods can be used (¶9032), but the exchange rate used must be the one that is current at the time of the supply. Notice 718/2 para 4.6

SECTION 4

Overseas transactions

1. Transactions within the EU

Eligible goods (¶6627+), including second-hand motor cars (¶6660+), can be bought from another EU member state and resold, either within the UK or the EU, under any one of the three margin schemes. **6780** Notice 718 para 7

MEMO POINTS 1. If the **resale is to a VAT-registered dealer in another EU member state**, there is no requirement to obtain that dealer's registration number.
2. **Distance selling arrangements** (¶9177+) do not apply to goods supplied under one of the margin schemes.
3. If eligible goods are **resold** to another member state but **not under one of the margin schemes**, they will be zero-rated under the normal EU supply rules (¶9036), and completion of an EC sales list (¶9330+) will therefore be appropriate.
4. The removal of goods to the UK (from another EU member state) which were supplied under the margin scheme is **outside the scope of VAT** (¶258).

2. Transactions outside the EU

a. Imported goods

In **general**, imported goods are subject to VAT on their full value. **6785** Notice 718 para 10

However, there is a **voluntary scheme** available which permits VAT on certain eligible goods to be accounted for under any of the margin schemes, where certain conditions are met.

Eligible goods

6787 The following imported goods **can be resold** under any of the margin schemes (provided that the respective relevant general conditions are met):
- works of art (including works of art obtained from creators or their heirs);
- antiques; and
- collectors' items.

In addition, imported second-hand **motor cars** (¶6660+) can be resold under the basic margin scheme (provided that the conditions for second-hand cars are fulfilled), or the auctioneers' scheme, but not the global accounting scheme.

MEMO POINTS 1. Imported works of **art, antiques and collectors' items** are liable to import VAT at an effective 5% rate (¶1164).
2. Imported second-hand **motor cars** are liable to import VAT at the standard rate.

Operation of the scheme

6790 VAT is calculated by applying the standard rate VAT fraction (¶1090) to the margin between the purchase price and selling price of the eligible goods.

6792 **Margin** The **purchase price** and **selling price** depend on the type of scheme used, so for:
a. the basic margin scheme, they are as detailed at ¶6638, plus import VAT;
b. the global accounting scheme, they are as detailed at ¶6706; and
c. the auctioneers' scheme, they are as detailed at ¶6758+. Import VAT should not be included in the calculations (although such amounts can be recovered separately from the seller).

EXAMPLE A Ltd is a VAT-registered dealer, using the basic margin scheme. It acquired and sold the following goods under this scheme:

		£	£
Antiques			
Selling price			1,500
Value acquired		1,000	
Import VAT	£1,000 x 5%	50	
Total purchase price			(1,050)
Margin			450
VAT due	£450 × 1/6		75
Car			
Selling price			20,000
Value acquired		10,000	
Acquisition VAT	£10,000 x 20%	2,000	
Total purchase price			(12,000)
Margin			8,000
VAT due	£8,000 × 1/6		1,333.33

6794 Notice 718 para 10.2 **To opt into this scheme**, the trader must:
- notify the VAT Written Enquiries Team, 4th Floor West, Alexander House, 21 Victoria Street, Southend-on-Sea, Essex, SS99 1BD in writing that they are going to opt into the scheme (along with the date from which they will be applying it); and
- remain within the scheme for at least 2 years (and thereafter notify HMRC at the above address as and when they wish to cease using the scheme).

If the option is used, it must be **applied to** all eligible goods, not just certain categories of goods.

Consequently, if a trader decides to **sell eligible goods outside the scheme**, they are not entitled to recover any input tax on them until the period in which VAT is accounted for on the sale.

b. Exported goods

The export of eligible goods (¶6627+) will be zero-rated where the export is: **6796**
- direct (¶9573), and appropriate evidence of exportation is obtained; or Notice 718 para 8.2
- indirect (¶9573), provided that the agent or dealer (who is acting in their own name) is located outside the EU.

Second-hand **motor cars** (¶6660+) supplied to an overseas person for export may be zero-rated where the vehicle is only used in the UK to make the trip to the place of departure from the EU.

If using the **retail export scheme** see ¶9603+. Notice 704 para 5.8

CHAPTER 6

Gold transactions

OUTLINE ¶¶

Gold is used both for investment purposes and industrial processes. It can also be traded on the bullion markets. **6830**

It is important to distinguish between these objectives, as the VAT treatment differs.

MEMO POINTS 1. **Investment gold** is defined as either:
a. gold of a purity not less than 99.5% in the form of a bar or wafer of a weight accepted by the bullion markets;
b. an investment gold coin as listed by HMRC; or Notice 701/21A paras 2.1, 3
c. a gold coin which satisfies all the of the following criteria:
– minted after 1800;
– has a purity of not less than 90%;
– is (or has been) legal tender in its country of origin; and
– is not normally sold for more than 180% of the open-market value of the gold contained in the coin.
Coins which are collectors' items and attract a huge premium are therefore not investment gold.
2. For this purpose the following weights are **accepted by the bullion markets**: Notice 701/21 para 15

Unit	Available weights
London Good Delivery Bar	12.5kg
Kilogram Bars	1kg
Gram	500g 250g 100g 50g 20g 10g 5g 2.5g 1g
Ounce	100oz 10oz 5oz 1oz 1/2oz 1/4oz

Unit	Available weights
Tael	10 tael 5 tael 1 tael
Tola	10 tola

SECTION 1

Investment gold

6835 Sch 9 Group 15 VATA 1994 Unless involving bankers (¶6887), the supply of investment gold is exempt, subject to the option to tax (¶6868+).

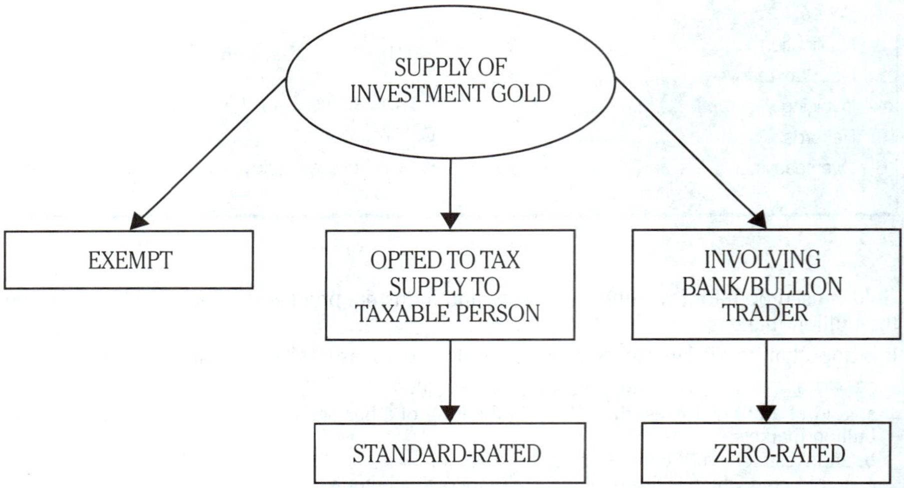

Summary

6836 Investment gold involves four particular features which differ from normal VAT accounting:
a. special input tax recovery rules for exempt supplies;
b. particular invoicing requirements;
c. an option to tax; and
d. its own penalty regime.

A. Exempt supplies

1. Scope

6838 Notice 701/21 para 2.2 For this purpose, the scope of the exemption **includes**:
– the supply of investment gold;
– a supply which confers a right to possess investment gold (i.e. loans, swaps, forward and future contracts), excluding options; and
– an agent's supply where they are acting for a named principal and trying to bring about a supply of investment gold or the right to possess it. The exemption applies irrespective of whether the principal's supply ever takes place.

2. Notification

A person is required to notify HMRC when making a **single supply** of investment gold which exceeds £5,000, or where **cumulative supplies to any one customer** in any 12-month period exceed £10,000. **6839** Notice 701/21 para 3

The **time limit** is 28 days.

Once notification has taken place, there is no need to notify subsequent transactions.

HMRC provides the following pro-forma showing the information to be supplied, with alternative sections for VAT-registered and non-VAT-registered suppliers: **6841** Notice 701/21 para 3.2

EXAMPLE PERSONS WHO TRADE IN INVESTMENT GOLD - FORM OF NOTIFICATION

To:
HMRC
Written Enquiries Section
Alexander House
Victoria Avenue
Southend
Essex SS99 1BD

Dear Sir/Madam

In accordance with the requirements outlined in paragraph 3.1 to Notice 701/21, Gold, I am writing to notify you that I am trading in investment gold.

I am registered for VAT; my registration number is:

....

I am not registered for VAT; the details requested in paragraph 3.1 of Notice 701/21, Gold, are as follows:

1. Name of Company/Partnership/Proprietor:

....

2. Company incorporation number/details of partners:

....

3. Address:

....

....

4. Telephone number:

....

5. Contact name:

....

6. Accountant's full name and address:

....

....

.... Post Code: ....

7. Associated VAT registration numbers (if any):

....

Please acknowledge receipt

Surname: .... First Name: ....

Signed: .... Dated: ....

Status: Proprietor/Partner/Director/Company Secretary/Authorised Person (delete as applicable)

3. Input tax recovery

In addition to the usual partial exemption rules (¶2075+), there are special input tax rules which apply to investment gold, relating to: **6843** s 13 FA 1999; SI 1995/2518 reg 103A

- direct costs of purchase; and
- making other supplies in addition to investment gold.

There are also special rules for producers and transformers of investment gold.

Direct costs

6844 Notice 701/21 para 5.2 Input tax can be reclaimed on the following which **directly relate to the supply** of investment gold:
- the purchase of any investment gold on which VAT has been incurred;
- the purchase of any other gold which is to be transformed into investment gold; and
- any costs of transforming gold into investment gold.

Making other supplies as well

6845 Notice 701/21 para 5.4 Due to the special input tax recovery rules for investment gold, the usual **partial exemption standard method is not appropriate**. Depending on whether transformation services are bought in, the following rules apply instead.

Bought-in transformation services?	Calculation required
Yes	Allocate input tax to each type of supply Recover input tax relating to direct costs of investment gold and outsourced transformation costs Work out the amount of residual input tax which relates to investment gold, and recover any which is attributable to both direct costs and transformation costs
No	Allocate input tax to each type of supply Can recover input tax relating to direct costs of investment gold Work out the amount of residual input tax which relates to investment gold, and recover any which is attributable only to direct costs

EXAMPLE

1. A Ltd acquires a new commercial building and incurs VAT. A Ltd does not produce or transform gold, or buy in transformation services. However, it does sell other gold in addition to investment gold.
The first step is to assess how the building is used to make each type of supply, then allocate the input tax accordingly.
Of the amount allocated to investment gold, input tax can be recovered on the direct costs of acquiring it but not on the associated costs (e.g. delivery). Similarly, of the residual input tax apportioned to the investment gold supply, input tax can only be recovered on the direct costs of acquiring it.
Any input tax relating to other gold can be recovered.

2. B Ltd acquires a new commercial building and incurs VAT. B Ltd does not produce or transform gold. However, it buys in transformation services. It also lets surplus space in the building, which is an exempt supply.
Firstly, input tax should be allocated on the basis of the building's use.
Of the amount allocated to investment gold, input tax can be recovered on the direct costs of acquiring it but not on the associated costs (e.g. delivery). Similarly, of the residual input tax apportioned to the investment gold supply, input tax can only be recovered on the direct costs of acquiring it.

Producers and transformers of gold

6847 Notice 701/21 para 5.3 If a trader produces or transforms any gold into investment gold, input tax on **overheads** which are linked to the production or transformation process can be reclaimed.

HMRC gives the following examples:
- machinery, plant and fittings;
- crucibles and furnace linings;
- laboratory instruments and equipment;
- tools, tooling and equipment;
- fuel and power;
- buildings and maintenance of buildings; and
- fume abatement and effluent treatment.

If there is **mixed use of an asset** - for example, a building is used both for the production of investment gold and its subsequent sale - and there are distinct areas of use, the input tax on the asset will have to be split to reflect the fact that only a part of it is linked to production.

See also ¶6874 for the special records to be maintained.

If making supplies **in addition** to the supply of investment gold, the following steps should be followed: 6848

a. allocate input tax to each type of supply;

b. recover input tax relating to direct costs of investment gold and any production/transformation costs; and

c. of the residual input tax which cannot be directly attributed, work out the amount which relates solely to investment gold, and recover any attributable to direct costs and production/transformation costs.

EXAMPLE C Ltd acquires a new commercial building and incurs VAT. C Ltd makes the following supplies:

a. produces and sells exempt investment gold (partly exempt);
b. produces and sells other gold (taxable);
c. produces and sells silver (taxable); and
d. lets surplus space (exempt).

The VAT incurred therefore relates to these four types of supply.

Firstly, input tax should be allocated on the basis of the building's use.

Of the amount of input tax allocated to investment gold, the portion relating to its production can be claimed.

Input tax relating to the following can therefore be claimed:

- production and sales of other gold;
- production and sales of silver; and
- production of investment gold.

4. Invoicing

An invoice is **required** for: 6850 Notice 701/21 para 6

- each sale involving exempt investment gold which exceeds £5,000; and
- smaller transactions, if the total value of sales to any one particular customer has exceeded £10,000 in the last 12 months.

In addition, a **buyer** would need to prepare an invoice where they acquire investment gold from someone who does not trade in gold, and either:

- the value of the purchase is more than £5,000; or
- the buyer makes multiple purchases from the same supplier, and their total value has exceeded £10,000 in the last 12 months.

Contents

Each invoice must contain the following **details** if appropriate: 6851 Notice 701/21 para 6.4

Seller preparing invoice	Buyer preparing invoice
Name and address of seller	Name and address of buyer
Name and address of buyer	Delivery address and date
Delivery address and date	Unique customer reference
Unique invoice number	Unique invoice number
Unique customer reference	Date of invoice
Date of invoice	Type of supply (e.g. sale)
Type of supply (e.g. sale)	VAT registration number of buyer
VAT registration number of seller	Number of items
Number of items	Total amount payable
Total amount payable	A description of the gold supplied[1]

Seller preparing invoice	Buyer preparing invoice
A description of the gold supplied[1]	The following declaration, which must be signed by the seller: "I declare that to the best of my knowledge the details shown on this invoice are correct"

Note:
1. The description should including the following:
– for bars and wafers, form, weight and purity and any other identifying feature (including any proprietary mark, hallmark and serial number where applicable); or
– for investment gold coins, coin type, country of origin and whether or not the coin is included on the list of gold coins produced by HMRC.

MEMO POINTS 1. When the trader is **acting as agent**, the principal's VAT registration number should be shown.

Notice 701/21 para 6.6 2. If selling a **mixture of exempt and taxable items** which includes exempt investment gold, all invoicing requirements must be met - that is, not only those for exempt investment gold but also the usual rules for taxable transactions (¶2860+). If opting to tax a gold transaction, see also ¶6873 and ¶6881.

5. Records

6853 Notice 701/21 para 7 Onerous record-keeping requirements apply to all transactions in investment gold, whether or not the supplier is registered for VAT. However, these requirements do not apply where gold is despatched to the EU or exported.

Notice 701/21 para 9 Where the **requirements are not met**, a penalty of up to 17.5% of the transaction's value may be levied (¶4142), although the usual provisions relating to appeals and reasonable excuse would apply. HMRC states that a penalty cannot be assessed more than 4 years after the transaction date, or more than 2 years after HMRC became aware of the failure.

Retention

6854 Notice 701/21 para 7.7 Records must be retained for **at least** 6 years from the date of transaction (or, in the case of regular customers, the date of the most recent supply).

This **applies to** both sellers and purchasers.

6856 The records required fall into two categories: accounting records and customer records.

The specific **format** of these records can be agreed by the business individually with HMRC, provided that they are available for inspection at any time.

Accounting records

6857 Notice 701/21 para 7.1 The following **transaction** details must be retained:
– invoice number;
– invoice date;
– customer reference number;
– customer's VAT registration number (if applicable);
– description of the gold (form, quantity and purity);
– name and address of the agent (if applicable);
– name and address of the purchaser; and
– transaction value.

Customer records

6858 Notice 701/21 para 7.1 There are **exceptions** to the rules below for the following:
– sales to other VAT-registered businesses;
– banks and financial institutions; and
– Internet and mail order sales.

Notice 701/21 para 7.6 MEMO POINTS 1. Instead of the usual customer records, the trader can ask a **VAT-registered customer** for the customer's VAT registration number. The trader must check with HMRC that the number is authentic.

2. **Banks and other financial institutions** can choose to apply their normal money-laundering checks instead of maintaining the usual records. HMRC states that these checks must be undertaken for all transactions in investment gold where either: Notice 701/21 para 7.2
- the value of a one-off transaction exceeds €15,000; or
- transactions appear linked and their value together exceeds €15,000.

3. Traders who sell investment gold over the **Internet or by mail order** can retain the following customer records; in all cases, proof of despatch to the customer's address must also be kept. Notice 701/21 para 7.4

How supply is paid for	Other conditions	Records to retain
Credit card	Delivery address is the cardholder's address	Name of customer Credit card issuer Card number
Cheque	n/a	Name of customer Name of bank Account number of customer

Otherwise, for **every customer** who purchases exempt investment gold, a record of the following must be retained, filed under a unique reference number: **6860**
- name;
- date of birth;
- current address; and
- telephone number (if available).

In order to verify this information, the trader must ask for and examine at least one original **document** from each of the following lists (unless HMRC agrees differently).

List 1	List 2
Passport	Telephone bill
Full driving licence	Other utility bill
National Insurance card	Deeds
Birth certificate	Tenancy lease
National identity card	Council tax bill
	Hotel key card (for non-UK residents only)

A **copy** of the relevant documents should be retained, with "certified as original document" written on it, followed by the date and the seller's signature. **6862**

If this is **not possible**, the seller should record the following details to enable HMRC to obtain a copy where required:
- the name of the document;
- the reference number; and
- the name and address of the issuing authority.

6. Overseas issues

Transactions within the EU

Acquisitions of investment gold from another EU member state are exempt from VAT, provided that the transaction details are entered on Customs Procedure Code (CPC) form 40 00 073. **6865** Notice 701/21 paras 8.1 - 8.3

Investment gold **despatched** to an EU business is outside the scope of UK VAT. There is no requirement to maintain any special records, but there is a right of input tax recovery, provided that evidence of the despatch is retained.

Any **Intrastat** requirements (¶9345+) must be met, but there is no need to complete EC sales lists (¶9330+).

Transactions outside the EU

6866 Notice 701/21 paras 8.1, 8.2 **Imports** of investment gold are exempt from VAT, provided that the transaction details are entered on Customs Procedure Code (CPC) form 40 00 073.

Exported investment gold is outside the scope of UK VAT. There is no requirement to retain any special records, but there is a right of input tax recovery, provided that evidence of the export is retained.

B. Option to tax

6868 SI 1999/3116 The option to tax allows a trader to recover input tax on investment gold supplies. This is important, as traders who transform gold into investment gold will often suffer VAT which they would prefer to recover.

Each transaction can be treated separately, so that some may be opted, whereas others may not. It is therefore usual for traders to make both taxable and exempt supplies of investment gold and as such they will be partly exempt.

A special accounting scheme applies to opted transactions.

1. General principles

Scope

6870 Notice 701/21 para 4 The option to tax is **available** when:
– the supply is made to another taxable person (i.e. someone who is registered, or liable to be registered, for VAT); or
– traders produce gold investment coins themselves.

The option to tax does **not require prior approval** from HMRC, **unless** gold is supplied for industrial purposes.

It is impossible to **disapply** the option once VAT has been charged. The transaction cannot therefore subsequently be treated as exempt.

Notification

6871 Notice 701/21 para 4.3 When trading in investment gold, the notification procedure which applies to exempt supplies must be followed (¶6839+).

If intending to opt to tax, a person is also **required** to notify HMRC within 28 days. If an acknowledgement is not received within 28 days of the notification date, the trader should check that HMRC has received it.

Notice 701/21 para 4.4 MEMO POINTS 1. Where gold is supplied for **industrial purposes** on a regular basis, approval can be obtained by writing to the trader's usual business advice centre within 28 days, with a note of the VAT registration number. If agreement is forthcoming, a letter of approval stating conditions and notifying a start date for opting should be received within a further 28 days. The approval may subsequently be withdrawn to protect the revenue.

Notice 701/21 para 4.5 2. If **acting as agent** for a named principal who has opted to tax, the agent's services relating to the principal's opted supplies may also be opted. In this case, the usual notification procedure also applies to the agent.

Invoicing

6873 Notice 701/21 para 4.6 Invoices relating to an opted transaction **must contain** the following statement: "We have opted to tax this transaction".

The usual VAT invoice rules must be observed (¶2860+), as well as the requirements of the special accounting scheme (¶6881).

Records

A record must be maintained of any transaction involving a taxable person where the trader has **not opted to tax**. This record should be kept with the trader's VAT account. In addition, the normal records should be maintained. **6874** Notice 701/21 para 7.5

For this purpose, a taxable person would include:
- a seller who is authorised to opt to tax supplies of investment gold; and
- a producer or transformer of investment gold.

2. Special accounting scheme

In order to minimise fraud, the special accounting scheme requires the buyer to account for the VAT rather than the seller. **6876** s 55 VATA 1994

Scope

The special accounting scheme is **obligatory** for supplies of gold taking place between VAT-registered traders (or traders who are liable to be registered) who are undertaking a transaction for business purposes. **6877** Notice 701/21 para 11.2

In addition, a trader who carries out **treatment or processing work** on a customer's goods must use the scheme if the goods produced are fine gold, gold grain of any purity, or gold coins.

MEMO POINTS 1. Supplies covered by the scheme count towards the VAT **registration limit** for both the purchaser and the seller. Notice 701/21 para 13
2. If the **purchaser is not liable to be registered**, the scheme does not apply, so the seller continues to account for the VAT.
3. For this purpose **supplies of gold** means:

Type of supply	Excludes	Includes
Opted investment gold		
Goods consisting of fine gold i.e. purity of at least 99.5%	Dental gold Gold targets Gold slugs	
Gold grain		
Gold coins	Those traded using a second-hand margin scheme	
Goods containing gold for which the amount paid or payable for the supply (excluding VAT) does not exceed the open-market value[1] of the gold contained in the goods	Supplies of part-manufactured or finished jewellery Gold compounds and semi-manufactured carated products Certain antiques	Supplies of scrap (including live scrap, scrapped jewellery, broken jewellery, watch cases, cigarette cases, etc) Sweepings
Supply of investment gold between a member and a non-member of the London Bullion Market Association[2]		

Note:
1. **Open-market value** is the "fix price" of the gold at the time of supply, which is the price set in the twice-daily meetings by the London Gold Fixing Company. If the amount paid only exceeds the open-market value by a negligible amount, the scheme still applies.
2. If the **non-member** is required to be registered for VAT solely because of the transaction, the member of the London Bullion Market Association should account for the VAT, thereby relieving the non-member of the duty to register.

Purchaser's liability

6878 Notice 701/21 para 11.4 When acquiring **manufactured goods** which contain gold and are held out for sale as such, the purchaser may be required to prove that the purchase did not fall within the provisions of the scheme. If unable to do so, the purchaser is liable for the output tax on the transaction, even where they have already paid an amount of VAT to the seller.

Notice 701/21 para 14 MEMO POINTS Buyers must also be extremely careful to avoid acquiring **smuggled gold**, as it will be forfeit and criminal proceedings may commence even where the buyer is completely innocent. HMRC lists the following questions which should be considered when buying gold:
- where has the gold come from?
- has it been imported from outside the EU?
- if so, is there evidence that the gold has been properly declared at import and that import VAT has been paid if appropriate?
- why is it being sold, and is it offered for sale below market value?
- how is it delivered and is it available in the usual variety of types?
- is a quick settlement and/or cash payment demanded?
- is the seller new and does the seller have a fixed place of business?
- does the seller regularly supply large quantities?
- does the seller retain references (from a bank, for example)? and
- are there other grounds for suspicion about either the standing of the seller or the origin of the gold?

How the scheme works

6880 Notice 701/21 para 11.3 The **seller** must verify that the customer is VAT-registered, which can be achieved by asking for the customer's VAT registration number. The seller then issues a VAT invoice for the supply, which also shows the amount of VAT.

The **purchaser** only pays the net amount to the seller, and enters the output tax on the relevant VAT return, along with the usual input tax claim.

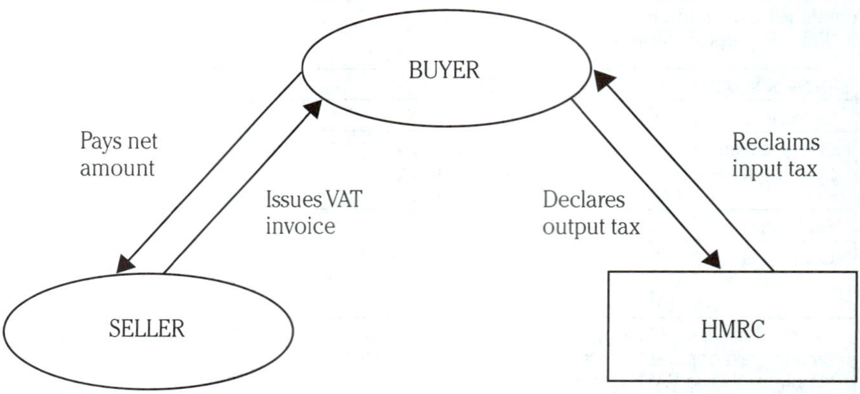

Invoicing

6881 Notice 701/21 para 11.6 The seller's invoice must show the usual information required for all VAT transactions (¶2860+) and also, where investment gold is being sold, the requirements of ¶6851.

All invoices must **clearly indicate** that it is the buyer who must account for the output tax. HMRC suggests the following form of words: "£x output tax on this supply of gold to be accounted for to HMRC by the buyer".

The invoice must also show:

a. the time of supply, which is usually the time of delivery, or the date when the gold is first made available to the buyer;
b. the name and address of the buyer;
c. the invoice date and number; and

d. a description sufficient to identify the goods which includes:
- the weight of the gold;
- the purity of the gold;
- the number of individual items (where possible); and
- the fix price of the gold on the day of delivery.

MEMO POINTS 1. For further details of the **time of supply** see ¶760+.
2. If using **self-billing** (¶2904+), the buyer must ensure the invoice complies with the above.

VAT returns

For each transaction covered by the scheme, the following entries are required in the buyer's and seller's VAT returns. For this purpose, the purchase is a deemed supply by the buyer. The remaining boxes are completed as normal (¶2998). **6883** Notice 701/21 para 12

Box	Buyer	Seller
1	Include the output tax on the purchase	Exclude output tax on sale
2	Include VAT on any gold acquired from another EU member state	
4	Claim input tax on the purchase[1]	
6	Include VAT-exclusive purchase value	Include VAT-exclusive sales value
7	Include VAT-exclusive purchase value	

Note:
1. Subject to the normal rules, including partial exemption (¶2075+)

SECTION 2

Other gold

If supplying or acquiring gold which is not investment gold, the transaction may be outside the scope of UK VAT. **6885** Notice 701/21 para 10.2

Except for transactions involving central banks and members of the London Bullion Market, the first issue to consider is **whether the gold is allocated**. "Allocated" means set apart and designated as belonging to, or reserved for, specific persons or purposes. Most commonly, allocated gold is delivered.

MEMO POINTS 1. Gold coins which are not investment gold may qualify for the second-hand **margin schemes** (¶6632). Notice 701/21 para 10.6
2. Gold **brought into the UK** from overseas (either within or outside the EU) is liable to VAT at the standard rate, unless the transaction involves a central bank.

A. Transactions involving banks

The following types of supply between central banks, or between a central bank and a member of the London Bullion Market, are zero-rated: **6887** Sch 8 Group 10 VATA 1994; Notice 701/21 para 10.4
- gold held in the UK;
- a right to acquire gold held in the UK; and
- a part interest in gold held in the UK.

This would include futures and options, and also investment gold.

MEMO POINTS 1. For this purpose, **central banks** are the Bank of England and its counterparts in other countries.

Notice 701/9 para 3.2.4

2. The **London Bullion Market** is a commodity market.
3. A transaction occurring between a member of the London Bullion Market and a **taxable non-member** is standard-rated; the special accounting scheme applies (¶6876+).
4. **Agents** acting for a member of the London Bullion Market would be able to zero-rate their own supply, assuming they were arranging a zero-rated gold transaction.
5. The **importation** of gold from outside the EU by a central bank is zero-rated.
6. The **acquisition** of gold from within the EU by a central bank is not liable to UK VAT.

B. Allocated gold

6890 Notice 701/21 para 10.2

The following diagram summarises the position of allocated gold.

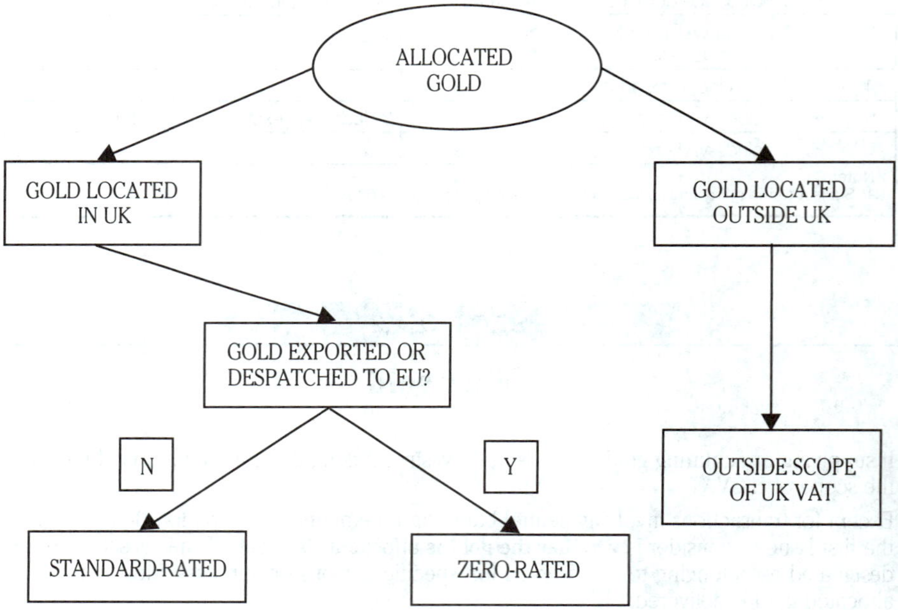

UK gold remaining in the UK

6891 Gold which remains in the UK is subject to UK VAT at the standard rate. The special accounting scheme for gold may apply (¶6876+).

UK gold allocated overseas

6892 The supply of non-investment gold which is exported to a place outside the EU, or despatched to another business in another EU member state, is zero-rated under the normal rules.

Proof of the delivery must be retained (see ¶9086+ and ¶9582+ respectively).

If dealing intra-EU, the trader may also be required to complete Intrastat declarations (¶9345+).

C. Unallocated gold

The supply of unallocated gold (i.e. where the gold does not form an identifiable part of the supplier's stock) is a supply of services. **6894**

Summary

6895
Notice 701/21 para 10.2

Location of supplier[1]	Location of customer[1]	Type of customer	VAT treatment
UK	UK	Any	Standard-rated[2]
	EU but not UK	Business	Outside scope of UK VAT but supplier can reclaim input tax
		Non-business	Standard-rated[2]
	Outside EU	Any	Outside scope of UK VAT but supplier can reclaim input tax
Outside UK	UK	Business	UK customer accounts for VAT using the reverse charge procedure (¶9700+)
		Non-business	Outside the scope of UK VAT
	Outside UK	Any	Outside the scope of UK VAT

Note:
1. For how to determine the location of the supplier and/or customer see ¶9688+.
2. The special accounting scheme for gold may apply (¶6876+).

CHAPTER 7

E-business

OUTLINE ¶¶

Internet business comes in a variety of guises. Orders can be placed over the web and then fulfilled by traditional postal delivery. Alternatively the Internet itself can become the means of delivery. In many cases businesses can sell to the final customer direct, cutting out the previously traditional chain of supply. 6930

Traders can either choose to fully embrace this technology and use it as their only selling forum, or set up an Internet site to complement their physical presence in towns and cities. For the latter, this represents a new source of income which must be factored into their VAT accounting.

E-business involves both business customers and private consumers, and has extended the reach of domestic business into new, hitherto excluded, global markets. Therefore cross-border issues are more likely to be faced.

SECTION 1

General principles

One of the major difficulties can be to ascertain whether the supply is one of goods or of services for VAT purposes. 6935

Once this has been established, the **place of supply** must be determined to ensure the correct VAT treatment is applied. This may depend on the locations of the supplier and customer, along with the VAT status of the customer.

Type of supply

6936

Source of income	VAT treatment	¶¶
Sale of physical goods	Normal rules apply	¶6945
Digitised goods - no physical product (includes music downloads, games, films and software)	Treated as an electronically supplied service	¶6985
Electronically supplied services	Special rules for place of supply and registration	¶6985, ¶7000
Other services		¶6970

What is being sold?

6938 It is important to identify the nature of the transaction in order to apply the correct VAT liability.

It is possible that the way a product is supplied will change its VAT treatment. For instance the **electronic version** of a book is a standard-rated supply, whereas the same book provided on paper is zero-rated.

In addition, some EU member states may treat a supply as being of goods, whereas others treat it as a service. This can lead to double taxation or non-taxation.

Comment Both double taxation and non-taxation are unfair results but the CJEU has ruled that commercial arrangements which exploit differences in member states' treatment of similar transactions are not abusive. *HMRC v RBS Deutschland Holdings GmbH* [2010]

EXAMPLE

1. A company sent out news digests to customers by fax, e-mail and Internet. If these news digests had been prepared in hard copy, they would have been zero-rated as printed matter (¶1252+). However, HMRC argued that it was the customers who were providing the paper, so that the company itself was making a standard-rated supply.
In a strict reading of the law, the tribunal held that zero-rating only applied to physical goods and tangible property. Therefore the electronic version of the same content was standard-rated. It was noted that this result was a distortion and therefore unfortunate. *Forexia (UK) Ltd* [1999] (VTD 16041)

2. A company offered a service whereby office workers could e-mail their sandwich orders through in the morning; these were then delivered by van in time for lunch. In its advertising the company referred to its service as "catering". If this was so, it was a standard-rated supply. Otherwise, the supply of food would have been zero-rated.
It was held that the supplies were no different in substance from a sandwich delivery service. As such, the supply was not within the ordinary definition of "catering" (see ¶1220+) and was therefore a zero-rated supply of food. *Emphasis Ltd* [1995] (VTD 13759)

Who is the customer?

6939 The VAT treatment of many supplies is partly determined by:
- whether a customer is going to use the supply for business purposes; and
- where the customer is located.

This **information** should be gathered at the point when business with the customer begins, so the supplier's e-commerce software must be designed for this from the outset.

SECTION 2

Goods

6945 In the context of a supply of goods, the Internet may be involved in the following stages:
- as an advertising medium;
- to take orders online; and/or
- to receive electronic payment.

Sometimes a customer will select the product after browsing the trader's site and then post or phone through an order. Whatever the means of ordering, the actual goods must be physically **delivered** by courier or the post, so the normal rules relating to the place of supply of goods apply (¶277+).

The treatment of associated **delivery charges** levied by retailers depends on the type of scheme used. A charge levied for **returned goods** is in respect of a taxable service.

A. Time of supply

The incidence of home shopping for goods is increasing as customers want the convenience of easy ordering combined with home delivery. Businesses are also sourcing more of their purchases over the Internet. 6947

The time of supply is a key issue for supplies ordered and paid for online.

Usual rules

The **basic** time of supply (¶755+) for goods is the date at which they are: 6948

a. removed;

b. made available if they are not to be removed; or

c. approved by the customer where the goods are sent on sale or return (subject to a 12-month time limit after removal).

However, where the basic tax point is **pre-dated** by the issue of an invoice or receipt of payment, the earlier date becomes the time of supply.

Online sales are particularly affected by the **tension** between the customer's up-front payment and subsequent approval of the goods.

Manipulating the tax point

Many home delivery businesses state that a major advantage for the consumer is to "try before you buy", so goods are sent out on approval. Indeed, for the direct delivery industry as a whole (including mail order) there is a sizeable **returns** rate, which therefore indicates the commercial reality of failed transactions. 6950

However, it is the strict **contract** terms which determine the tax point, as illustrated by the following cases.

EXAMPLE

1. A company supplied goods by mail order and had originally accounted for VAT when payment was received. However, following other litigation, it changed to accounting for VAT on the earlier date of despatch. HMRC formed the opinion that the goods were supplied on approval, so no tax point occurred on despatch (due to an intervening change in VAT rate, the later tax point date was favourable to the Exchequer). The tribunal held that the time of supply was the date of despatch, because there was a contract of sale under which the buyer had the right to rescind the contract.
Littlewoods Organisation plc [1997] (VTD 14977)

2. A company sold electrical goods online and received a credit card payment at the time of the order. It only accounted for VAT once 7 days had elapsed from the date of delivery, because it considered that the customer had not approved the sale until this time. HMRC considered that output tax should be accounted for at the time of payment.
The tribunal initially allowed the appeal, holding that the Consumer Protection Regulations meant that a customer was entitled to decline to accept the supply of the goods. The supplier could not therefore know whether the sale was made until the cooling-off period had expired.
On appeal, that decision was overturned, perhaps in part because the company was unrepresented (it was in severe financial difficulty). As a result no arguments for the later tax point were put before the Court.
The High Court held that in this case an online transaction was an outright sale, because under the company's terms of sale the payment must be made on ordering, even though the customer

had the statutory right to return the goods subsequently. This meant that a sale contract was concluded on order, although the contract could later be cancelled. The Court rejected the alternative interpretation that a contract was not finally made until the customer had decided not to return the goods. *C & E v Robertson's Electrical Ltd* [2005]

3. Customers of a mail order firm paid when they ordered goods but could return them within 14 days of receipt and receive a full refund. It was held that, under the company's trading terms, the sale took place when the goods were received; the customer then had the right to cancel the contract. Consequently, VAT should be accounted for when payment was received. *Grattan plc* [2006] (VTD 19515)

6952 **Guidance** on consumer protection rules that apply when buying or selling goods online or at a distance can be found at flmemo.co.uk/vm6952.

Comment Some commentators have stated that a business could perhaps **delay** the tax point by clearly stating in its terms of sale that the goods are sent out for approval during the statutory cooling-off period. However, any VAT planning which includes an extended approval period would need to be disclosed to HMRC (¶3058).

B. Website presentation

6954 Most businesses now have a website which, at the very minimum, advertises their products and gives contact details.

Pricing

6955 With a potential global customer base (because in theory anyone can log on to a website page from anywhere in the world), the pricing of products must be carefully considered - that is, whether prices are VAT-exclusive or not. **Depending on** where the supply is made and whether the trader becomes liable to VAT in another EU member state under the distance selling rules (¶9177+), different VAT rules and rates apply.

Traders must make sure that prices are clearly stated on their website and that they comply with any local laws as necessary.

EXAMPLE A swimwear shop has a website where customers can browse, order and pay for goods.
A typical swimsuit is priced at £30 net. The UK VAT is £6. (£30 x 20%)
The shop has a wide customer base and is particularly popular in Denmark. This has meant that the shop has been required to register for VAT in Denmark under the distance selling rules.
If the shop sells a swimsuit to a:
a. UK customer, the price paid will be £36; or
b. Danish customer, VAT is due at a rate of 25%. If the advertised price is:
- £36 and this is what the customer pays, the shop will need to account for Danish VAT of £7.20 (£36 x 25/125) and so will only make a net £28.80; or
- £30 plus VAT, the shop will charge £7.50 Danish VAT to the customer (£30 x 25%), who will pay a total of £37.50.

Imports

6957 Goods which are delivered from outside the EU to a customer within the UK are **subject to** some or all of the following:
- customs duty;
- excise duty; and/or
- import VAT (¶9405+).

Customs **duty** is waived if the amount due is less than £9.

Import **VAT** is not payable on goods purchased over the Internet with a value of up to £15. However, purchased alcohol, toilet water, tobacco and perfume, and goods bought mail-order from the Channel Islands, are always subject to VAT.

HMRC has published a list of common Internet goods and the associated VAT and duty charges (¶9984).

Traders should consider whether they will **arrange** the import so that the customer is not concerned by the associated administration and cost. In such a case the trader's price should include these costs. 6958

Alternatively, **customers** should be notified about the procedures and costs involved in importing the goods, so that they can make an informed decision before purchasing.

Comment VAT and duty are not the only costs incurred by customers, as Royal Mail charges a substantial **administration fee**, which must be paid before the goods are released. As well as the extra expense this will be likely to cause a delay in delivery.

C. Retail trade

Retailers often have difficulty in identifying the VAT element on every single transaction; for this reason there are special **retail schemes** (¶6325+) which allow VAT to be calculated on the total taxable supplies made in each VAT period. In addition, retailers are not required to issue full VAT invoices to private consumers. 6960

Many retailers are using Internet selling to **complement their traditional business**. If so, they must choose whether to use the same retail scheme for all portions of the business. Alternatively they could use a more suitable scheme for the online division, provided that the combination of schemes is allowed (¶6516+). 6961

New businesses may just have an online presence but sell to private consumers and therefore potentially qualify as retailers for the purposes of the retail schemes (¶6330+).

D. Overseas sales

When selling to overseas customers, it is essential that the trader acquires all the necessary information in order to determine the VAT status and location of the customer. 6964

Where **UK suppliers** remove goods to the EU, which are then acquired by a non-taxable person (e.g. mail order), they will usually charge UK VAT. This is known as a **distance sale**.

However, to avoid the distortion of competition between traders in different EU member states, once the value of these supplies reaches a certain point, the UK supplier becomes liable to register for VAT in the customer's member state, because the place of supply changes. The UK supplier could also choose to voluntarily register in another member state, particularly if the VAT rate is lower there.

Traders **selling to the EU** must be aware of the rules relating to EC sales lists (¶9330) and Intrastat (¶9345).

MEMO POINTS 1. Each EU member state has a certain **threshold** of supplies before registration becomes compulsory. Supplies to all EU member states therefore need to be monitored to check whether the relevant threshold has been exceeded (¶9206).

2. Once **registered in another member state**, the trader should ensure that it is aware of the relevant compliance criteria, especially regarding invoices and records.

3. An **EU supplier** making distance sales to the UK could become liable to register in the UK (¶9180).

SECTION 3

Ordinary services

6970 A supply of services which takes place in the UK is subject to VAT in the UK, however that service is delivered. The general rule for determining where a supply of services takes place (see ¶9682) is that business-to-business (B2B) supplies take place where the customer belongs, whereas business-to-consumer (B2C) supplies take place where the supplier belongs. That general rule does not apply in the case of telecommunications, radio, broadcasting and electronically supplied supplies - these take place where the customer belongs (see ¶6985+). It is therefore essential in the context of e-business to know whether or not a service has been electronically supplied.

EC Directive 2006/112 Art 58

The first point to make is that communication between supplier and customer via e-mail does not turn a service into an electronically supplied one.

Implementing Regulation 282/2011 Art 7

It is then easier to envisage what are non-electronically supplied services by appreciating that they are everything but electronically supplied services, the latter defined to "include services which are delivered over the Internet or an electronic network and the nature of which renders their supply essentially automated and involving minimal human intervention, and impossible to ensure in the absence of information technology". An illustrative list of electronically supplied services is given at ¶6987.

Types of service

6971 **Typical** services found in an e-business context, but which are not electronically supplied (often because the supply is between businesses and the electronic part involves intervention by a member of the public who is not providing any consideration), include:

Supply	Details	VAT treatment
Advertising on website	Flat rate charged for a certain period, or by appearance on website	Standard-rated supply
Hyperlinks to associates	Commission based, or income depends on number of clicks from customers	Standard-rated supply
Barter transactions	Advertising space on two websites swapped with no money changing hands	Two standard-rated supplies, which must be valued (¶925+) and the time of supply ascertained (¶750+)
Sale of customer database	Monitoring of the website means that customers' buying habits can be ascertained	Standard-rated supply
Electronic vouchers	Effectively a face-value voucher	¶1016+

EU legislation lists the following as specifically not electronically supplied:
- goods, where the order and processing is done electronically;
- CD-ROMs, floppy disks and similar tangible media;
- printed matter, such as books, newsletters, newspapers or journals;
- CDs and audio cassettes;
- video cassettes and DVDs;
- games on a CD-ROM;
- services of professionals such as lawyers and financial consultants, who advise clients by e-mail;
- teaching services, where the course content is delivered by a teacher over the Internet or an electronic network (namely via a remote link);
- offline physical repair services of computer equipment;
- offline data warehousing services;
- advertising services, in particular as in newspapers, on posters and on television;
- telephone helpdesk services;

– teaching services purely involving correspondence courses, such as postal courses;
– conventional auctioneers' services reliant on direct human intervention, irrespective of how bids are made;
– tickets to cultural, artistic, sporting, scientific, educational, entertainment or similar events booked online; and
– accommodation, car hire, restaurant services, passenger transport or similar services booked online.

Place of supply

The general rule for supplies of services was stated at ¶6970, above. There are, of course, exceptions to the general rule, even for non-electronically supplied services. Details of these exceptions and the corresponding VAT treatment can be found at ¶9682+. 6973

Belonging The rules determining where a supplier or recipient of a service is treated as belonging **depend upon** whether they have a business establishment or some other fixed establishment (¶9688+). 6974

For e-business, an important issue is whether a **website or server** is deemed to be an establishment, and therefore treated as the place of supply. In the view of most commentators, neither a website nor server can be taken to be a business or fixed establishment, because:
– it would be irrational or inappropriate; and
– there are not sufficient permanent human and technical resources necessary for providing the services. *Gunter Berkholz v Finanzamt Hamburg* [1985]

However, different EU member states and non-EU countries may hold different views and in any case most relevant services will be electronically supplied (see ¶6985+) and therefore take place where the customer belongs.

MEMO POINTS HMRC was at one point concerned about arrangements implemented by businesses in the telecommunications, Internet service provision and broadcasting sectors, **designed to move the place of supply** of their services from the UK to another member state in order to take advantage of a more favourable VAT rate. In HMRC's view the issue was whether there were still sufficient human and technical resources present in the UK to form a fixed establishment from which the services were supplied, or whether indeed a business had sufficient presence in the other member state to be established there. These concerns are now otiose in view of the fact that from 1 January 2015 supplies of telecommunications, radio, broadcasting and electronically delivered supplies take place where the customer belongs. However, they illustrate that the issue is by no means certain and this may affect the place of supply of other goods and services. HMRC Brief 58/09

Services taking place where recipient belongs

If the supply is treated as taking place where the recipient belongs, traders must ensure they are aware of the **compulsory registration** requirements of each EU member state in which they make a supply. Note that some states have chosen very low thresholds for registration. 6975

If the supply is of services to an EU business, the recipient accounts for the VAT under the reverse charge procedure (¶9700+).

The trader's **accounting system** must be able to monitor supplies in each EU member state, to ensure compliance requirements are not missed. This includes the necessity to complete an EC sales list (¶9802+).

SECTION 4

Electronically supplied services

Due to the nebulous nature of electronically supplied services, there have been continuing attempts both to define them and to deal with the related VAT accounting issues (in particular the place of supply). 6985 EC Directive 2006/112 Art 58

However, with effect from 1 January 2015, the place of supply of electronically supplied services to a non-taxable person is definitively "the place where that person is established, has his permanent address or usually resides". The place of supply of B2B services remains where the customer belongs.

The First-tier Tribunal has held that it is the **means of delivery** which is important, not the description of the services. Hence the European Commission's list of electronically supplied services (¶6987) can only be illustrative rather than definitive. *Smart Voucher Ltd* [2009] (TC00131)

A. Scope

6987 Sch 4A para 9 VATA 1994; EC Directive 2006/112 Art 58 and Annex II; Implementing Regulation 282/2011 Art 7 and Annex I

The European Commission used to be more prescriptive about what it thought was, and was not, an electronically supplied service. However, there is now just an **indicative** list in the Principal VAT Directive, reproduced in the UK legislation and expanded upon by later Implementing Regulation:

a. the supply of digitised products generally, including software and changes to or upgrades of software;

b. services providing or supporting a business or personal presence on an electronic network such as a website or a webpage;

c. services automatically generated from a computer via the Internet or an electronic network, in response to specific data input by the recipient;

d. the transfer for consideration of the right to put goods or services up for sale on an Internet site operating as an online market on which potential buyers make their bids by an automated procedure and on which the parties are notified of a sale by electronic mail automatically generated from a computer;

e. Internet Service Packages (ISP) of information in which the telecommunications component forms an ancillary and subordinate part (i.e. packages going beyond mere Internet access and including other elements such as content pages giving access to news, weather or travel reports; playgrounds; website hosting; access to online debates, etc);

f. website supply, web-hosting, distance maintenance of programs and equipment:
- website hosting and webpage hosting;
- automated, online and distance maintenance of programs;
- remote systems administration
- online data warehousing where specific data is stored and retrieved electronically; and
- online supply of on-demand disc space;

g. supply of software and updating thereof:
- accessing or downloading software (including procurement/accountancy programs and anti-virus software) plus updates;
- software to block banner adverts showing, otherwise known as bannerblockers;
- download drivers, such as software that interfaces computers with peripheral equipment (such as printers);
- online automated installation of filters on websites; and
- online automated installation of firewalls;

h. supply of images, text and information and making available of databases:
- accessing or downloading desktop themes;
- accessing or downloading photographic or pictorial images or screensavers;
- the digitised content of books and other electronic publications;
- subscription to online newspapers and journals;
- weblogs and website statistics;
- online news, traffic information and weather reports;
- online information generated automatically by software from specific data input by the customer, such as legal and financial data (in particular such data as continually updated stock market data, in real time);

– the provision of advertising space including banner ads on a website/web page; and
– use of search engines and Internet directories;
i. supply of music, films and games, including games of chance and gambling games, and of political, cultural, artistic, sporting, scientific, educational and entertainment broadcasts and events:
– accessing or downloading of music on to computers and mobile phones;
– accessing or downloading of jingles, excerpts, ringtones, or other sounds;
– accessing or downloading of films;
– downloading of games on to computers and mobile phones;
– accessing automated online games which are dependent on the Internet, or other similar electronic networks, where players are geographically remote from one another;
– receiving radio or television programmes distributed via a radio or television network, the Internet or similar electronic network for listening to or viewing programmes at the moment chosen by the user and at the user's individual request on the basis of a catalogue of programmes selected by the media service provider such as TV or video on demand;
– receiving radio or television programmes distributed via the Internet or similar electronic network (IP streaming) unless they are broadcast simultaneous to their being transmitted or retransmitted over a radio and television network;
– the supply of audio and audiovisual content via communications networks which is not provided by and under the editorial responsibility of a media service provider; and
– the onward supply of the audio and audiovisual output of a media service provider via communications networks by someone other than the media service provider; and
j. supply of distance teaching:
– automated distance teaching dependent on the Internet or similar electronic network to function and the supply of which requires limited or no human intervention, including virtual classrooms, except where the Internet or similar electronic network is used as a tool simply for communication between the teacher and student; and
– workbooks completed by pupils online and marked automatically, without human intervention.

It is worth noting that these are once again merely **illustrative** lists, **not** a **comprehensive** definition.

In this context there will often be a chain or network of suppliers, only one of which makes the supply to the final consumer. This is important because in a B2B supply it is the recipient which accounts for VAT (under the reverse charge mechanism - see ¶9700+), whereas a B2C supply involves the supplier in the process of discovering where the consumer belongs and accounting for VAT there. Where supplies are made via a portal - an app store, for example - the sale may appear to be made by the app supplier but for VAT purposes the supply of electronic services to the final consumer will probably be made by the app store. The same applies to content providers selling their music, films, etc, via an online platform. **6988** Implementing Regulation 282/2011 Art 9a VDS para 1.2

This is because the law prescribes that where the platform operator sets the general terms and conditions, authorises payment or delivery, or does not clearly state the name of the supplier on the receipt or invoice issued to the customer, the platform operator makes the B2C supply, even if it is contractually only acting as agent for the app vendor or content provider. The app vendor or content provider therefore makes a B2B supply to the platform operator, not a B2C supply to the customer.

B. Place of supply

Telecommunications, radio, broadcasting and electronically delivered supplies take place where the customer belongs, subject in the case of B2B supplies to the **use and enjoyment override** (¶9758+). It is therefore, obviously, important to establish where the customer belongs (and especially so in the case of B2C supplies, where the supplier must account for VAT). The broad means of so doing are given at ¶9688+ but special rules are required for **6990** electronic services, given both their global nature and the impracticality of the parties entering into a protracted dialogue when vast numbers of transactions may be processed automatically in very short timescales.

Summary

6992 Suppliers, wherever they are situated, need to answer the following questions in order to establish the correct VAT treatment of an electronically delivered supply:
1. Is the customer in **business**? If so, the supply does not attract VAT and the customer accounts for VAT (if relevant) under the reverse charge procedure.
2. If the customer is not in business, **where** does the customer belong? If the customer belongs in the EU, VAT will have to be accounted for in the relevant member state.
3. If supplies are potentially to be made in more than one member state, does the supplier wish to take advantage of the **single-registration** mini one stop shop?
4. If so, is the supplier based **in the EU, or outside the EU**? There is a different mini one stop shop for each (see ¶7000+).
5. Does the supplier wish to sell the relevant services at a fixed price, or will the supplier's **pricing** take into account the variety of VAT rates in the various member states (see ¶9989)?

Customer's business status

6994 EC Directive 2006/112 art 9; Information Sheet 5/03

A business customer is one who is a taxable person, and that is most conveniently translated as meaning the customer is a VAT-registered trader.

Registered customers will normally produce their VAT registration number, which gives a country identification prefix code. The trader should always check that the VAT number corresponds with the format of that particular member state (¶9082).

The trader should fully validate the VAT number in any case where:
– a new customer receives supplies where a single transaction or cumulative transactions in a VAT quarter exceed £500 of VAT; or
– services such as games, music or films are supplied, which are usually consumed privately.

If a **non-registered** person claims to be in business, other commercial evidence should be obtained, such as contracts, a business letterhead, a tax certificate, a commercial website address, or a digital certificate from a reputable organisation.

If there is **any doubt** that the customer is in business, or the trader is unsure of the validity of the VAT number, the trader should charge VAT on all supplies made to that customer.

MEMO POINTS 1. For **UK customers**, HMRC provides a VAT number verification service (contact the National Advice Service).
2. There is an online verification for VAT numbers of all **EU businesses**, which can be found at flmemo.co.uk/vm6994.

Customer's location

6996 VDS para 1.4

The supplier of a telecommunications, radio, broadcasting or electronically delivered service is permitted to make a number of **presumptions** in order to determine where the supply takes place. If the supply is made:
– through a telephone box, a telephone kiosk, a wi-fi hot spot, an Internet café, a restaurant or a hotel lobby, the customer location is the place where the services are provided - for example, the member state where the phone box/kiosk, etc, is located;
– on board transport travelling between different countries in the EU (for example, by boat or train), the customer location is the place of departure of the means of transport;
– through an individual consumer's telephone landline, the customer location is the place where the landline is located;
– through a mobile phone, the customer location is the country code of the phone's SIM card; or
– through a decoder, the customer location is the postal address where the decoder is sent or installed.

The supplier does not have to rely on any of those presumptions. However, a supplier who wishes to rebut a presumption which would otherwise apply must obtain three separate and non-contradictory items of alternative evidence of location. A supplier who is unable to rely on any of the above presumptions may instead rely on two separate and non-contradictory items of alternative evidence of location.

Alternative evidence might be, for example, the customer's:
- billing address;
- bank address;
- IP address;
- means of payment (if that is specific to a member state); or
- choice of product (if the specific product points to a specific member state).

A supplier of **over the top** services is unable to rely on the above presumptions and so will have to seek alternative evidence. This is because there is a distinction between the supply of facilities which, for example, **enable a consumer to get online** (often a telecommunications service) and the supply of an electronic service made **once the consumer is online** (for example, the sale of an app or the download of a music file). The latter are known as "over the top" services. HMRC Brief 46/14

HMRC suggests the following approach if the trader uses a payment service provider to obtain payment for the digital service:
- when the customer places an order, the trader should ask the customer to confirm either the EU member state the customer usually **lives in** or the customer's **billing address**; and
- when the customer pays for the product using the payment service provider, the trader should arrange for that provider to transmit back the following two pieces of evidence: the customer's **billing address**; and the **country code** of the customer's **bank** or registered **credit card**.

HMRC adds that it is still adequate evidence if the payment service provider removes the billing address house number and street name for confidentiality reasons.

If the information on the EU member state where the customer is normally resident tallies, that will be sufficient to define the customer's location and the trader can then record the details in its accounting records. However, if the information does not tally, the trader does not need to cancel the sale but must contact the customer and request that the discrepancy be reconciled.

C. Mini one stop shops

A supplier of telecommunications, broadcasting or electronic services ("digital services") to a non-business customer must now account for VAT in the customer's member state. This is so whether the supplier is within the EU or not. The supplier must therefore, in theory, register and account for VAT in any and every member state where customers live. However, a **simpler alternative** is available. Suppliers may instead register for VAT in one member state only and then account for VAT in all the other member states on a single return. This is known as the mini one stop shop (MOSS). **7000** Schs 3B and 3BA VATA 1994; EC Directive 2006/112 arts 357 - 369

The MOSS comes in two versions: one for businesses established in the EU; one for non-EU businesses. The slight differences between the schemes are highlighted, as appropriate, in the paragraphs below.

Under the MOSS the supplier makes a return every calendar quarter and pays the VAT it has accounted for to the member state where it is registered under the MOSS. That member state then distributes the correct portion of the VAT to each of the other member states listed on the return.

HMRC's guidance on the MOSS schemes can be found at flmemo.co.uk/vm7000.

7002 HMRC Brief 46/14 A business which does not have an establishment anywhere in the EU may choose the member state in which to register under the MOSS. Until 31 December 2014, non-EU businesses were able to account for VAT on digital services in the member state where they registered under the pre-2015 version of the MOSS. It was therefore open to such businesses to register in the member state with the lowest VAT rate. This is **not an option** from 2015, because VAT must be accounted for in the member state of the consumer, at the rate prevailing in that member state. Non-EU businesses will therefore presumably make their choices based on language, or perceived ease of administration, or other factors. They will also have to have amended their systems to make provision for charging VAT at many different rates.

EU businesses will generally already be registered for VAT in one or more member states. If they wish to take advantage of the MOSS, they can do so in one member state only (one where they are already registered) and can only use it to account for VAT in respect of member states where they are not already registered.

UK businesses benefit from a comparatively generous registration threshold in excess of £80,000 (see ¶9960 for exact figures). There are significant numbers of businesses with turnover below this threshold but which make digital supplies in other member states - supplies which do not benefit from any registration threshold. HMRC announced originally that it would not be possible to use MOSS to account for VAT in other member states unless a business was first registered for VAT in the UK. Small businesses objected that this would mean accounting for VAT on their UK supplies, at cost to their profit margins or competitive position. HMRC therefore agreed that a special registration would be possible for businesses otherwise below the registration threshold but which wished to use the MOSS. Further details can be found at ¶7008. These small businesses also have special rules for reclaiming input tax (see ¶7014).

Pre-2015 version of the MOSS: transition

7004 The pre-2015 version of the MOSS has been replaced by the non-EU version of the MOSS. HMRC has announced that the current VoeS website (see flmemo.co.uk/vm7004) will remain open to registered businesses, allowing them to submit any missing VAT returns and their final return (for the tax period ending 31 December 2014). Any transactions prior to 1 January 2015 are subject to the pre-2015 rules, not the new MOSS rules. No supplies of digital services after 31 December 2014 should be accounted for under the pre-2015 registration.

1. Registration and deregistration

7006 Registration must be effected by the 10th day of the month following the date on which the first digital supply is made to a non-business customer in the EU (if a non-EU supplier), or in another member state where the supplier is not registered (for an EU supplier). Registration takes effect from the date of that first relevant supply.

Deregistration from the MOSS is at the option of the trader. HMRC should be informed, using the online service, at least 15 days before the end of the calendar quarter in which the trader intends to stop using the scheme. A trader who has deregistered from the MOSS will not be permitted to rejoin **in any member state** for two calendar quarters (normally starting after the first day of the next calendar quarter).

Otherwise unregistered businesses

7008 HMRC has stated definitively that UK businesses with turnover below the UK registration limit that wish to use the MOSS to account for VAT on supplies of digital services to non-business customers in other member states can register for VAT in the UK in order to use the MOSS but will **not** have to account for and pay VAT on sales to their UK customers.

In these circumstances HMRC has laid down the following procedures. The business should:
- **apply** for UK VAT registration;
- **add** "VAT MOSS" as an "additional online service"; and

– when prompted to search for "Business Activity", **enter** "Digital Services" and **select** "Supplies of Digital Services (below UK VAT threshold)" under "MOSS arrangements".

HMRC says that following the above procedure will ensure that this special MOSS VAT registration application type can be dealt with **quickly**.

If the trader's UK supplies exceed the UK registration limit the trader will have to start accounting for UK VAT.

VAT groups

If a member of a VAT group makes digital supplies to non-business customers, the group can make use of the MOSS. The **representative member** must register for the MOSS and both: **7010**
– **indicate** that it is a VAT group representative member when submitting the MOSS registration application; and
– use its **domestic** VAT registration number when registering for the MOSS.

Any of the VAT group's members established in another member state must be notified that, for the purposes of the MOSS, cross-border VAT group membership links are disregarded. Those group members will not be able to account for the VAT due on any cross-border digital service supplies they make on the group's MOSS returns. However, they can register for the MOSS in their own member states. Any digital supplies that the representative member, or other VAT group members, make into that member state can be accounted for through the group MOSS registration.

2. Accounting for VAT

Output tax

The trader accounts for output tax based on supplies to each separate member state in which customers have purchased supplies during each calendar quarter. **7012**

MEMO POINTS 1. **VAT rates** for all member states are at ¶9989. For more detail of types of supply and the different rates at which they are liable please follow this link: flmemo.co.uk/vm7012.
2. Where a **business customer** fails to pass on its VAT number, the trader must charge VAT which the customer will not be able to recover as input tax, because the supplier will not provide a VAT invoice (see ¶7016). If the customer subsequently produces a VAT number, the supplier can then refund the VAT charged and issue correct paperwork.
3. If the service was supplied after 1 January 2015 but invoiced or paid for before 1 January, the supplier will have to charge VAT under the pre-1 January 2015 rules.

EXAMPLE
1. Ms A, a private consumer, pays an annual subscription in full in April 2014. The supply will be taxed under the old rules.

2. Another private consumer, Mr B, takes out an annual subscription in April 2014 but pays for it on a quarterly basis. The first three payments will be accounted for under the old rules but the final quarterly payment in January 2015 will be taxed under the new rules.

Input tax

UK traders using the MOSS can recover **UK** input tax on their UK VAT returns. However, they cannot recover input tax incurred in other member states, even though they are (through the MOSS) accounting for output tax on supplies in those member states. UK traders must make a separate 8th directive claim in order to recover overseas input tax (see ¶9845+). **7014**

UK traders who are registered for MOSS but who do not have to account for UK VAT (see ¶7008) may recover only a proportion of the UK input tax they have incurred (plus any VAT incurred in other member states for which a separate 8th directive claim is possible). The proportion of UK input tax which may be recovered is that which is incurred **solely** in connection with taxable supplies in other member states, plus the fraction of other input tax which **relates to** overseas taxable supplies. This input tax is reclaimed on the trader's VAT return, not on the MOSS return.

Information Sheet 7/03 para 3; Information Sheet 10/03

A **non-EU** trader can recover input tax by making a 13th directive claim. The usual rules (¶9908+) are modified so that UK input tax can be recovered even though it is **incurred for** the purposes of making a UK supply.

Input tax can only be recovered on goods which are **imported** or **supplied to** the trader in the UK whilst the trader is registered under the MOSS.

The trader should enter "ESS Special Scheme" along with the scheme identification number in box 9a of form VAT65A.

There is no requirement for the trader's country to offer reciprocal relief to UK traders.

Invoices

7016
Information Sheet 7/03 para 4

The **normal rules** relating to invoices apply (¶2840+) and, in particular, a VAT invoice is not required where the customer is unregistered and therefore cannot recover the VAT. In this case a simplified invoice can be issued (¶2868).

3. Returns and payment

Returns

7018 **Completion** MOSS return periods are calendar quarters (the first return period runs from 1 January to 31 March). HMRC will ensure that the UK VAT return period for otherwise unregistered traders (see ¶7008) is aligned with the MOSS return period, so these traders can complete both the UK VAT return and the MOSS return at the same time.

The MOSS return is used to account for VAT due on all supplies to consumers in member states where the trader has no establishments. The deadlines for submitting MOSS returns are:
- 20 April for quarter ended 31 March;
- 20 July for quarter ended 30 June;
- 20 October for quarter ended 30 September; and
- 20 January for quarter ended 31 December.

Traders who are not established in the EU must account for VAT on all supplies within the EU on the MOSS return. Traders established in the EU account for VAT on their normal VAT return in respect of supplies in the member state of registration and on the MOSS return for supplies to other member states where they do not have any establishments.

In the UK the MOSS return is completed by selecting member states one by one and entering the relevant total of VAT-exclusive supplies into the fields for standard-rated and reduced-rated supplies, respectively. The VAT liability is calculated automatically. Traders should check that the VAT liability tallies with that calculated by their own accounting systems. If there is a discrepancy due to **rounding** issues, the trader is permitted to overwrite the correct VAT amount due.

Traders who do not make any digital supplies to EU consumers in a quarter must submit a nil return.

MEMO POINTS 1. If the trader has **not made any supplies in a particular member state**, there is no need to include a line for that state on the return.
2. The **exchange rates** for conversion of amounts to sterling are periodically published by HMRC in Information Sheets. Alternatively the European Central Bank's exchange rates which apply on the last day of the declaration period can be used. These rates can be found by following this link: flmemo.co.uk/vm7018.
3. There is no need to submit EC Sales Lists (see ¶9802) in conjunction with MOSS returns, because all MOSS supplies are to consumers and EC Sales Lists are for business-to-business supplies only.

7020 **Submission** Traders may submit MOSS returns by filling in the form **online**. It is possible to save a partially completed return in the online system before later submitting a fully completed return.

Alternatively, it is possible to download a **template** from the HMRC website and transfer data into it from the trader's own system. The trader can then upload the data on to the VAT MOSS online service. HMRC will validate the information at the point of upload. Under this system traders are also able to save an uploaded return for submission later. HMRC will publish specific guidance for using the template early in 2015.

Errors discovered by trader **Corrections** to a MOSS return can be made online up to 3 years and 20 days after the relevant period end. 7022

Errors discovered by HMRC and other tax authorities HMRC may conduct **checks** on whether traders are following the MOSS rules and keeping appropriate records correctly. A trader who consistently fails to comply with the rules for the scheme may be excluded from using the scheme. If this happens the trader will be sent a message through the online service and will thereafter not be able to use the MOSS anywhere in the EU for up to 2 years. 7024

The tax authority of any member state where a trader makes digital supplies to private consumers has the legal right to **audit** the records of a business registered for the MOSS. The EU Commission and almost all member states have agreed an audit code of practice to minimise the risk of imposing unreasonable burdens on businesses. This means in practice that HMRC will co-ordinate such audit requests and contact the business to discuss the scope and coverage of the audit requirements. It will be possible for an authorised tax official from another member state to attend any audit that is arranged, but the audit team will be led by a UK HMRC official. See also ¶7032.

Payment

Payment is to be made electronically. **Separate** payments should be made for the domestic VAT liability and the total MOSS liability. The separate MOSS payment should quote the payment reference notified on submission of the return. 7026

Payment deadlines are the same as return deadlines (see ¶7018). However, payments must be in sterling and reach HMRC on the **last working day** before the relevant weekend or bank holiday (if the due date is not a working day).

Conversion to sterling should be undertaken using the exchange rates published for the last day of the return period (or the next day if that is a non-working day) (¶7018). Information Sheet 10/03

HMRC will e-mail the trader a reminder of any **underpayment** on the 10th day following the due date. If full payment is still not received following the issue of the reminder, it is possible that the trader will be required to make any further payments relating to that return directly to the member state concerned.

If a trader has **overpaid** the VAT due to a member state, the tax authority of that member state will refund the overpayment in its own currency (less a handling fee). Each member state tax authority operating its own MOSS scheme is entitled to keep an administrative handling fee. This is a specified percentage of the VAT due to each other member state. The MOSS tax authority (eg, HMRC for the UK) will deduct this fee before forwarding on the balance to the member state tax authority where the consumer lives. This means that if the trader has made an overpayment, both the tax authority in the member state of the consumer and HMRC will make **separate refunds**.

4. Administration

Changes in circumstances

HMRC must be **notified** if: 7028

- a non-EU trader registered under the non-EU MOSS becomes established in the EU (as this will disqualify the trader from registration under that scheme);

- a trader registered under either MOSS ceases to make, or to have the intention to make, digital supplies to EU non-business customers; or
- a trader becomes otherwise ineligible to use either of the schemes.

On the trader's **ceasing** to supply electronic services, or becoming ineligible, HMRC will cancel the registration, either with effect from the date of notification or from a mutually agreed date.

Records

7030 Sch 3B para 14 and Sch 3BA para 12 VATA 1994

Sufficient records need to be kept so that the authorities can check whether the declarations made and VAT paid are correct. Records must be **retained** for at least 10 years starting from the 1 January following the date of the particular transaction.

Records should be kept in an electronic **format** (¶2802), and made available where requested to the authorities in the member states where:
- the trader is registered; and
- the customer belongs.

Typical data which should be recorded would include:
- unique transaction number;
- date;
- customer name and location;
- debit or credit sale;
- currency; and
- VAT-inclusive values.

Penalties

7032 Traders are expected to deal directly with the tax authority of the member state where the relevant supplies were made in order to resolve disputes and/or pay any penalties or fines.

CHAPTER 8

Agents

OUTLINE

¶¶

An "agent" acts on behalf of another person, known as the "principal". However, the mere description of a person as another person's "agent" may not reflect the true position in law. Moreover, a person's status as an agent may or may not be disclosed to outside parties. **7090**

This is important for VAT purposes, because it is always vital to know who is supplying what to whom. Ms A may wish to sell goods to Mr C but may also wish to be represented by Ms B. Ms B may sell the goods to Mr C disclosing that she is Ms A's agent or not. The transaction may be effected by Ms A selling the goods to Ms B, who sells on to Mr C for a profit (which is effectively Ms B's commission but note that Ms B is not actually Ms A's agent in this scenario). Or Ms B may sell the goods to Mr C on behalf of Ms A (acting as Ms A's agent but never owning the goods) and make a direct commission charge to Ms A.

Thus, as an agent potentially only accounts for VAT on commission charged, the wrong classification of a person (as an agent or not) can result in errors (and therefore, potentially, penalties).

Some common examples which may or may not involve agency are as follows:
- certain businesses, such as hairdressers and driving schools, arrange for their employees to become sole traders, who then trade directly with the customer and remain below the VAT registration threshold - this reduces the amount liable to VAT;
- employment agencies may want to charge VAT on their commission only, so that their exempt or partly exempt clients suffer less irrecoverable input tax; or
- an agent who deals with zero-rated goods (such as farm produce) may wish to structure the business so that commission can also be zero-rated.

The term "intermediary" is often used in a VAT context but it is not synonymous with "agent".

SECTION 1

The agent-principal relationship

7095 Notice 700 para 22 An agent is someone who acts for another person (known as the principal) in arranging supplies of goods or services with the mutual consent of both parties. The supplies that the agent arranges are made by or to the principal. An agent can therefore be described as a buying agent or a selling agent.

The use of particular **terminology**, such as "agent" or "commission", does not dictate whether an agency relationship exists. It is the conduct of the parties which is of greater significance. There are many instances when someone is casually called an agent, particularly as a job title (such as "advertising agent"), but is not an agent in law. Conversely, a person whose normal role is that of principal may sometimes act as an agent (for example, a solicitor).

Definition

7097 The agent-principal relationship has been defined as "a relationship which exists between two persons one of whom expressly or impliedly consents that the other should represent or act on his behalf, and the other of whom similarly consents to represent the former or so to act". *C & E v E Johnson* [1980]

Notice 700 para 22.2 It is **imperative** that the agent:
- is genuinely arranging transactions on behalf of the principal;
- never acquires title to goods or services which are bought or sold for the principal; and
- does not alter the supplies between the principal and third party in any way.

An agent will have a **fiduciary duty** to account to the principal for any monies derived from the transactions undertaken on the principal's behalf.

HMRC's policy

7100 VTAXPER36820 The **burden of proof** in relation to status as an agent lies with the trader. A decision by HMRC that a trader is or is not an agent cannot of itself be appealed to a VAT tribunal. If there is a dispute, HMRC will identify a specific supply as an indicator of the position; the trader can then ask the tribunal to rule on its status.

HMRC states that it looks at the following **factors** when deciding whether an agency relationship exists, although the absence of one or more does not necessarily mean that a person is not an agent. The weight given to each factor will depend on the exact circumstances of the case.

Factor	Detail
Title	Title should remain with the principal
Identity	Goods or services dealt with by the agent should be clearly defined
Value	The principal must have full knowledge of the price obtained; any discounts must be passed back to the principal
Separation	The agent's supply (acting as an agent for commission) must be separately identifiable from the main supply; the calculation of the commission can be stated either as an absolute amount, or as a percentage, but in all cases it must be clear
Direction	The direction of the supply between buyer and seller cannot be altered by the existence of the agent (this is known by HMRC as the "no change" rule)
Nature	The nature of the main supply and its value cannot be altered by the agent, although the agent may have authority to negotiate a price on the principal's behalf

7102 VTAXPER36660 HMRC assesses these factors in light of the following **evidence**:
a. any agreement, correspondence, or other commercial documentation;
b. the practical business arrangements put in place between the parties; and
c. the conduct of the parties - in particular, whether this has been **consistent** with an agency relationship.

Although the contractual position does not necessarily determine the VAT position, it has been of increasing relevance in recent cases, such as *Spearmint Rhino Ventures (UK) Ltd v HMRC* [2007] and *Newcastle United plc v HMRC* [2007] (¶1958).

EXAMPLE

1. A company provided catering services to a number of care homes run by a charity, for which it received a management fee. The company also kept any discounts obtained on the bulk purchase of food. However, the company only accounted for VAT on the management fee and not the discounts. Because the charity felt that the company was making too much profit, the actual income received by the company was varied as follows:

April 1990 to April 1991	Management fee and discounts
April 1991 to April 1992	Discounts
April 1992 to April 1993	Fixed management fee

The company argued that it was acting as both an agent (running the bars, canteens, etc) and a principal (when sourcing its supplies and obtaining the discounts).
It was held that this division of activity was artificial. The company was also an agent of the charity when making the bulk purchases, so that the discounts were part of the consideration received in return for the provision of catering services. The company therefore had to account for VAT in respect of the discounts. *PBK Catering* [1993] (VTD 11426)

2. In prior years, a company had employed nurses who were supplied to hospitals on a temporary basis. However, the agreement between the nurses and company was then altered so that it expressly stated that the nurses were self-employed (and this treatment was followed for income tax purposes). Under the amended agreement, the nurses:
- were required to buy their own uniforms and to pay insurance premiums;
- could be changed or withdrawn if the work was unsatisfactory;
- wore badges bearing the company's name when on duty;
- were paid mileage allowances for using their own car; and
- had to give reasonable notice if wanting to take time off.

The nurses were paid for all work done and did not bear any financial risk.
The tribunal held that the company was still acting as a principal and not an agent; the nurses remained employees of the company. Hence the company was making exempt supplies of nursing services. *Allied Medicare Nursing Services Ltd* [1984] (VTD 5485)

3. In a similar case, another company provided self-employed temporary nurses to hospitals. Under the terms of the contract between the company and nurses, the company controlled the nurses' activities and there was no specific mention that the company was acting as their agent. The nurses completed timesheets and were paid by the hour. The company made PAYE deductions. The nurses were always paid for work they performed, even where the client did not pay the company, as this was stipulated by a code of practice.
HMRC decided that the company was supplying exempt nursing services to the hospitals. The company appealed on the basis that it was a recruiting agency and it was the nurses who supplied the exempt nursing services.
It was held that the company was supplying suitable nurses rather than nursing services as a question of fact, so it was not making exempt supplies. On upholding the decisions, the High Court stated that the tribunal had relied on the terms of the contracts but had also taken an overall view of the facts. *C & E v Reed Personnel Services Ltd* [1995]

Agreement

The **form** of the agency arrangement may be oral, written, or even implied by the actions of the two parties. The commercial reality and actual facts of each case will decide whether an agent-principal relationship can be construed, even though the parties themselves may not recognise that such a relationship exists. **7104** VTAXPER36740

There are many examples of case law which illustrate the importance of the agreement. **7106**

EXAMPLE

1. A music shop acquired second-hand musical instruments which it valued and then sold. The vendor was required to sign an agreement appointing the shop as the vendor's agent, which also stated that commission would be paid if the shop managed to sell the instrument above the valuation price.
HMRC issued an assessment which charged output tax on the full sale price of the goods, because the vendor did not know what the final price would be or whether commission would be due and

the shop guaranteed the instruments for the new owner (which would normally indicate that the shop had acquired title).
It was held that the terms of the contract agreed between the company and the vendors made it clear that the company was acting as an agent rather than as a principal. *C&E v Music & Video Exchange Ltd* [1992]

2. A school photographer negotiated the price of his photos with local head teachers, along with each school's cut of the sale proceeds. The photographer only accounted for VAT on the amount he actually received from the schools.
It was held that there was a sale of photographs to the schools and the schools then resold them to the parents. There was no evidence that the photographer had agreed that the schools should act on his behalf. So the photographer was correct to only account for VAT on the net amount he received. *C&E v PLA Paget* [1989]

3. In 1974 a dormant subsidiary started to make exempt supplies when it took over the insurance department of its parent company, which continued to incur the salary costs of the department's staff. New staff were recruited by interview with the subsidiary's managing director, who was also responsible for firing staff. An offer of employment was made on the subsidiary's letterhead, but the contract of employment was with the parent company.
In January 1980 the staff were formally told that they were now employed by the subsidiary.
It was held that until 1980 the employees had entered into contracts with the parent company and there had never been a time when they had agreed to being employed by the subsidiary. The parent company was therefore a principal making a taxable supply of staff to its subsidiary company. *C&E v Tarmac Roadstone Holdings Ltd* [1987]

SECTION 2

VAT accounting for agents

7115 Notice 700 para 22.3

The agent will be **involved in** at least two supplies:
a. the main supply between the principal and the third party; and
b. a supply of agent's services to the principal, for which a commission or fee is charged.

It is important to distinguish between these two supplies. Their VAT liability will not always be the same (for example, the sale of books is zero-rated, but any commission received by an agent in relation to the sale is standard-rated).

When there is an agency relationship, it is important **to determine**:
- who is making the main supply;
- the nature of the main supply;
- the location of the various parties; and
- the VAT rate which is applicable.

Acting in the agent's own name

7117 Notice 700 para 22.6

Agents are sometimes given the right by the principal to enter into contracts with a third party on the principal's behalf. In such cases, particularly where the principal wishes to remain unnamed, invoices for the supplies concerned may be issued and received in the agent's name rather than the principal's. An agent who acts in this way is usually referred to as an **undisclosed agent** (¶7142+). Often the name on the invoice to the customer is indicative of whether this is the case.

A. Disclosed agents

7120 Notice 700 para 22.5

Where the agency arrangement involves a disclosed agent, the customer or supplier (depending on whether the agent is selling or buying) will be aware of both the principal's and the agent's involvement in the transaction. Common examples of disclosed agents are travel agents and insurance brokers.

The main supply occurs between the principal and the customer or supplier. There is a separate supply of services between the agent and principal, for which the agent receives commission.

The agent's VAT return will only reflect commissions received. The principal's VAT return will reflect both the purchase or sale and the agent's commission.

PRINCIPAL IS SELLING

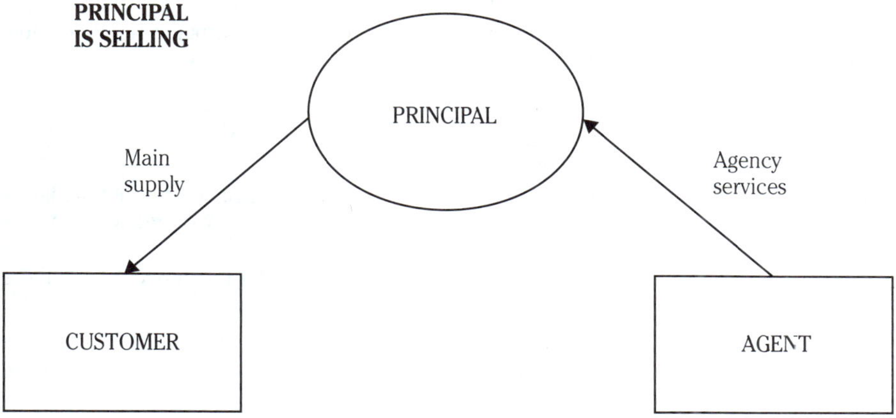

PRINCIPAL IS BUYING

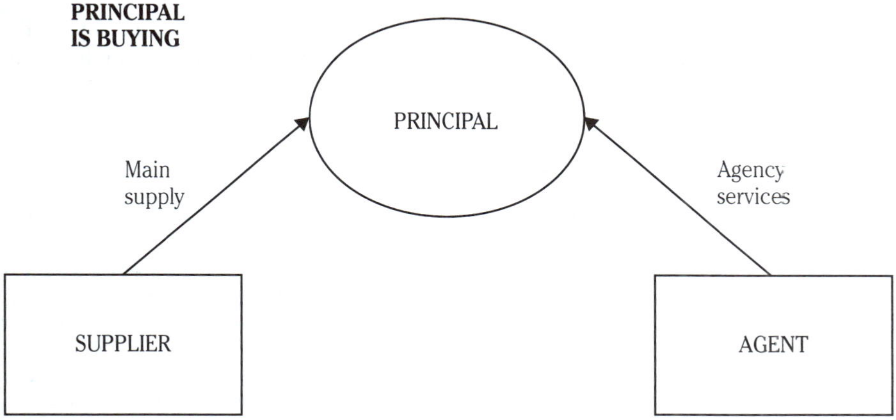

EXAMPLE A is a disclosed agent who arranges a sale of goods from P (the principal) to C (the customer). The goods are sold for £1,000 (plus VAT). A charges commission at 10%. 7122

The main supply between P and C will be treated as if no agent were involved. The goods pass to C for £1,000 (plus VAT).

In a separate transaction, A raises an invoice to P for agent's services and charges £100 (plus VAT).

Note:

The payment from C may be routed through A, so that P receives the net sum of £900 (plus VAT).

1. Principal's supply

The **VAT liability** of the supply by the principal will depend on the normal VAT rules and status of the customer or supplier and the principal. For example, if aid equipment is 7124 supplied to a disabled person, the main supply by the principal will be zero-rated where the principal is authorised (¶1332+).

The **tax point** of a selling principal's supply follows the normal rules (¶755); where the agent receives monies on the principal's behalf, the principal is deemed to have received payment at the same time.

2. Agent's supply

7126 The **liability** of the agent's supply of services to the principal is normally standard-rated. However, it will be zero-rated if the agent is arranging the following:
- the export of goods (¶7168);
- valuation of or working on goods for subsequent export;
- any supply of services which is made outside the EU; or
- certain types of transport (¶1280 onwards).

In the financial sector, an agent may be referred to as an **intermediary**. The intermediary's services may be exempt if they are made in connection with a supply of financial services (¶370) or insurance (¶450).

See ¶7130 for rules applying to cross-border services, and ¶7465+ for the application of these rules to travel agents.

7128 The **time of supply** depends on whether the agent is acting on:
- an ongoing basis, in which case there is a continuous supply and the tax point is the earlier of receipt of payment or the raising of a VAT invoice; or
- a one-off basis, in which case there is a single supply and the normal tax point rules apply (¶760).

If commission is deducted from the monies due to the principal from the main supply, the tax point is not always easy to determine and the terms of the agency agreement may need to be consulted.

3. Place of supply

7130 s 7A and Sch 4A para 10 VATA 1994

The place of supply of the agent's services depends on the VAT status of the person to whom those services are supplied, as follows:

Service supplied to	Place of supply of agent's services	Agent must determine
Relevant business person [1]	Where the principal "belongs" [3]	Where the principal belongs [4]
Non-business [2] or non-EU person	Where the main supply [5] is made	Where the main supply [5] is made

Note
1. For the definition of a relevant business person see ¶9684.
2. Includes a business person receiving the agent's services wholly for private purposes.
3. For the place of belonging see ¶9688.
4. The principal must account for VAT using the reverse charge procedure if principal and agent are not in the same EU member state (¶9700).
5. The main supply is the supply made to or by the principal.

EXAMPLE

1. A UK agent arranges a supply which is made in the UK by:
- a non-business or non-EU principal - agent's supply takes place in the UK and agent accounts for VAT; or
- a UK-registered principal - agent's supply takes place in the UK and agent accounts for VAT.

2. A UK agent arranges a supply which is made in Germany by:
- a non-business or non-EU principal - agent's supply takes place in Germany (where the main supply is made) and agent may need to register for VAT in Germany in order to account for VAT there.

3. A UK agent arranges a **supply of goods** between an Irish seller and a German buyer who are both registered for VAT. The goods are supplied in Ireland.
If the agent acts for:
a. the seller, the agent is making a supply in Ireland, because the seller is located there and the seller accounts for Irish VAT on the agent's supply under the reverse charge procedure; or
b. the buyer, the agent is making a supply in Germany, because the buyer is located there and the buyer accounts for German VAT on the agent's supply under the reverse charge procedure.

Agents' services supplied to non-business principals

7134
Notice 741A

Supply to or by principal		¶¶	Agent's service
Type	**Details/examples**		**Place of supply**
Goods	Not installed or imported	¶9040	Where goods located when supplied
	Installed or assembled	¶9154	Where goods installed or assembled
	Imported by supplier	¶9405	EU state where goods imported
	Imported by customer	¶9405	Outside EU
Services relating to land	Grants of leases, construction works, provision of holiday accommodation, services of estate agents, surveyors, etc	¶9714	Where land located
Transport services [1]	Passenger transport	¶9726	Where transportation takes place
	Freight transport	¶9774	Where transportation takes place
	Intra-EU freight transport Related ancillary services	¶9774	In EU state of departure Where ancillary service is physically performed
	Short-term hire of means of transport	¶9736	Where the means of transport is physically made available to the hirer
	Long-term hire of pleasure boats	¶9736	Where the boat is put at the customer's disposal, if the customer has an establishment there [2]
	Long-term hire of other means of transport	¶9736	Where the customer is established [2]
Intangible services	– transfer of intellectual property rights; – advertising; – supply of staff; – hire of goods (not hire of transport); – telecommunications services; – radio and broadcasting; – electronically supplied services; – services of consultants, engineers, data processing and provision of information, professional services such as those provided by accountants and lawyers; – agreeing to refrain from activity; – banking, insurance and finance services; – provision of natural gas and electricity distribution systems	¶9784	Where the recipient belongs [3]

Supply to or by principal		¶¶	Agent's service
Type	**Details/examples**		**Place of supply**
Cultural educational and entertainment services	– admission to exhibitions; – organiser's services; – scientific work to obtain data (test/experiments); – educational training services; – oral translation services; – performances before a live audience; – playing in sports matches	¶9742	Where the activities take place

Note:
1. International transport could mean that the main supply is made partly in the EU and partly outside.
2. Rule applicable from 1 January 2013. Prior to that date the place of supply was where the supplier belonged.
3. The recipient in this context depends on whether the agent is acting in:
– the name of the principal (disclosed), in which case the recipient is the principal; or
– the agent's own name (undisclosed) in which case the agent is treated as receiving the main supply.

4. Invoicing

7138 Notice 700 para 23

The invoicing arrangements for UK taxable supplies **depend upon** whether the:
– VAT-registered agent's principal is making or receiving supplies; and
– supplier is registered for VAT.

Transaction	Supplier's status	Invoicing for main supply[1]
Supply by principal	Registered	Invoiced to customer by principal, charging VAT
	Unregistered	No VAT due[2]
Supply to principal	Registered	Invoiced to principal by supplier, charging VAT
	Unregistered	No VAT due

Note:
1. In each case the agent will invoice the principal for services rendered and must charge VAT if registered.
2. The agent must retain evidence that the supply is being arranged on behalf of the principal, such as a standing agreement or a signed declaration which gives the principal's name and address, and states that the principal is making the supply in question but is not registered for VAT.

EXAMPLE A, who is VAT-registered, acts as a disclosed selling agent for P, who is also VAT-registered. A arranges a sale of goods to C for £600 (net of VAT) and charges commission of 10%.
P raises an invoice for £600 plus VAT to C.
A raises an invoice for £60 plus VAT to P.

B. Undisclosed agents

7142 s 47 VATA 1994; Notice 700 para 22.6

In an arrangement involving an undisclosed agent, the customer will only deal with the agent and indeed will only receive an invoice in the agent's name. The principal's details will not be divulged, so the customer may not even be aware of the principal's existence.

For the purposes of VAT **registration**, all supplies made by the agent (including the principal's supplies) are measured against the registration threshold (¶9960).

The **VAT treatment depends on** whether the main supply is made wholly within the UK, or whether the principal or customer belongs outside the UK. It should be noted that irrespective of the VAT position, the legal position remains unchanged.

MEMO POINTS 1. For use of the basic second-hand **margin scheme** by agents and their principals see ¶6668.
2. For the provision of **travel insurance** by a travel agent see ¶7560.
3. From **1 January 2015** a taxable person who is involved in transmitting electronically supplied services (¶6985) is presumed to be acting as an undisclosed agent for the actual provider of those services, unless that provider is explicitly indicated (on invoices, bills or receipts) as being the supplier and that is reflected in the contractual arrangements between them. This also applies to the provision of telephone services over the Internet, except where the taxable person does no more than provide for processing of payments for the service.

1. UK supplies

For domestic supplies (where the whole transaction occurs within the UK), an agent has a **choice** between accounting for VAT as a principal and accounting for VAT as an agent. 7144 Notice 700 para 24.1

An agent must account for VAT as a principal where international supplies are involved (¶7166).

Treatment as a principal

The undisclosed agent is treated for VAT purposes as a principal, both receiving and making the main supply. The agent's commission will effectively be the difference between the deemed purchase and sale prices. 7146

MEMO POINTS Note that the VAT treatment of the supply to the agent is not necessarily the same as the VAT treatment of the supply by the agent. *Roden v HMRC* [2012]

Selling agent 7148

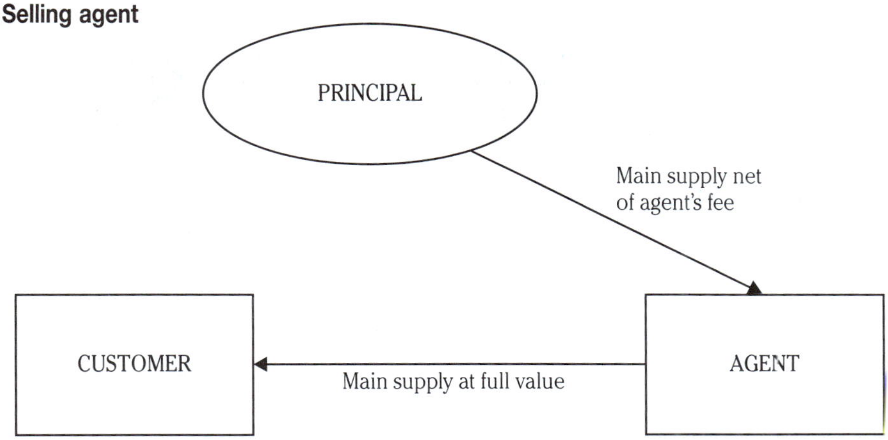

In this case the selling agent: 7150
- recovers **input tax** on the deemed purchase from the principal; and
- accounts for **output tax** on the deemed sale to the customer.

The agent's VAT return shows one output and one input; the time of supply for both transactions is the same. *Metropolitan Borough of Wirral v C & E* [1995] Input tax must not be reclaimed before output tax is declared; the usual procedure is to declare both on the same VAT return.

VAT incurred on other costs, such as warehousing and packing, may also be recovered by the agent.

EXAMPLE A acts as an undisclosed selling agent for P, who is VAT-registered. A arranges a sale of goods to C for £600 (net of VAT) and charges commission of 10%.
P raises an invoice for £540 plus VAT to A (representing A's purchase of the goods).
A raises an invoice for £600 plus VAT to C (representing A's sale of the goods).

7152 **Buying agent**

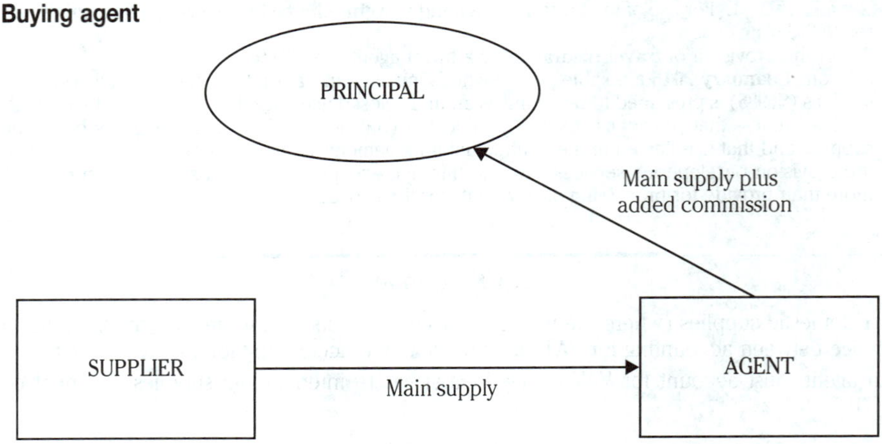

7154 In this case the buying agent:
- recovers **input tax** on a deemed purchase from the principal's supplier; and
- accounts for **output tax** on a deemed sale to the principal.

The agent's VAT return shows one output and one input; the time of supply for both transactions is the same.

VAT incurred on other costs, such as warehousing and packing, may also be recovered by the agent.

EXAMPLE A acts as an undisclosed buying agent for P, who is VAT-registered. A arranges a purchase of goods from S for £500 (net of VAT) and charges commission of 10% to P.
S raises an invoice for £500 plus VAT to A (representing A's deemed purchase of the goods).
A raises an invoice for £550 plus VAT to P (representing A's deemed sale of the goods).

Treatment as an agent

7156 This is only available for domestic supplies (when both the principal, and the customer or supplier, are located within the UK).

7158 **Selling agent**

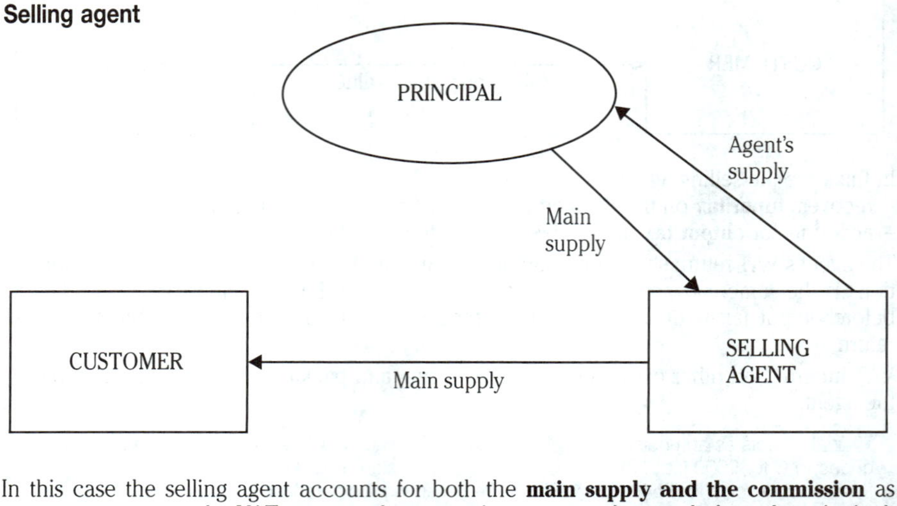

7160 Notice 700 para 23.1.2 In this case the selling agent accounts for both the **main supply and the commission** as separate outputs on the VAT return and recovers input tax on the supply from the principal. The self-billing procedure (¶2904) may be used (subject to HMRC's approval).

EXAMPLE A acts as an undisclosed selling agent for P, who is VAT-registered. A arranges a sale of goods to C for £600 (net of VAT) and charges commission of 10%.
P raises an invoice to A for £600 plus VAT.
A raises two invoices:
- £600 plus VAT to C; and
- £60 plus VAT to P.

Buying agent 7162

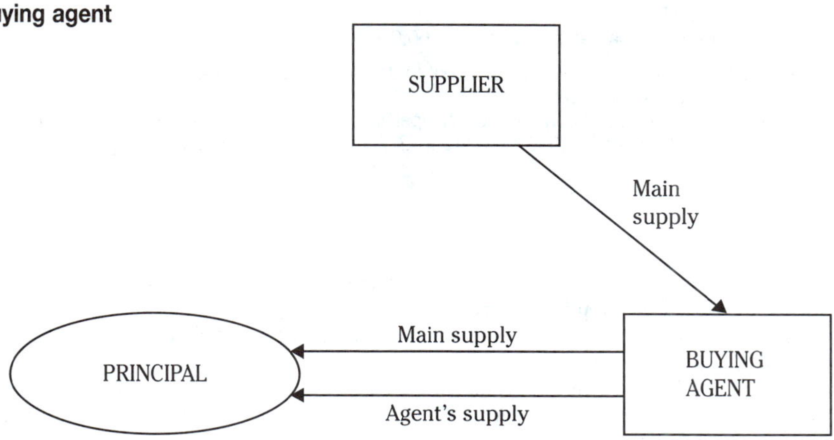

A buying agent recovers **input tax** on the value of the supply from the third party and accounts for **output tax** on the value of the main supply to the principal and on the agent's commission. Both supplies can be shown on the same invoice, although the commission must be separately identified. 7164 Notice 700 para 23.2.2

EXAMPLE A acts as an undisclosed buying agent for P, who is VAT-registered. A arranges a purchase of goods from S for £600 (net of VAT) and charges commission of 10%.
S raises an invoice to A for £600 plus VAT.
A issues a single invoice to P showing:
- £600 plus VAT in respect of the main supply; and
- £60 plus VAT in respect of A's commission.
A could instead issue a separate invoice for each supply to P.

2. International supplies

An undisclosed agent is treated for VAT purposes as a principal for international supplies (where either the actual principal or the customer/supplier is located outside the UK). The supply of agency services is subsumed within the main supply. 7166 s 47 VATA 1994; Notice 700 para 24

This simplifies the place of supply for the agent's services.

MEMO POINTS Note that the VAT treatment of the supply to the agent is not necessarily the same as the VAT treatment of the supply by the agent. For example, if the agent belongs in the UK, supplies received from a UK trader are likely to be standard-rated, whereas if the end customer is outside the UK, the agent may not have to charge VAT at all. *Roden v HMRC* [2012]

Goods

The value of goods which are: 7168
- **acquired from** a principal in another **EU member state** is the value of the principal's supply less the agent's commission (the agent accounts for output tax on the acquisition (¶9017) and is also responsible for Intrastat returns (¶9345), if relevant); or
- **imported** from outside the EU is the import value (¶9421).

Notice 700 para 25.3

Goods which are **exported** outside the EU through an agent may be zero-rated if valid evidence is retained (¶9586).

EXAMPLE

1. P is taxable in Spain and appoints A as a UK agent. A is taxable in the UK. P asks A to sell Spanish goods to a UK customer, C, for £60,000. A's commission is £5,000.
For VAT purposes, A is treated as a principal and acquires the Spanish goods. The acquisition is valued net of the commission, so that A only accounts for input tax on £55,000, which is the amount invoiced by P.
For the onward sale, A charges output tax on £60,000 to C.

2. U is a US trader who engages A as UK agent to deal with a sale of goods to C, a UK customer, for £10,000. A charges commission of £2,000.
A is importing goods on behalf of a non-EU principal and pays import VAT on the value of £10,000.
A makes an onward sale of £10,000 plus VAT to C. A recovers the import VAT as input tax.
A passes back £8,000 to U.

Services

7170 The VAT treatment is determined by the usual place of supply rules (¶7130) for the main supply, so if it would be **supplied where**:
- the supplier is located, then as the UK agent is treated as a principal, the supply will be subject to VAT in the UK; or
- the recipient is located (most business-to-business (B2B) supplies, as in the examples below), the UK agent must account for VAT using the reverse charge (¶9700), then charge output tax on the onward supply.

Other services which are not covered by the above rules, for example those supplied where performed, need not be accounted for as if the agent were principal.

EXAMPLE

1. Q, located in Berlin, supplies advertising services through a UK agent, A, to C, a UK customer, for £800. Q invoices A for £700, which takes account of A's commission charge of £100.
As B2B advertising is supplied where the customer is located, Q's supply is made in the UK. A applies the reverse charge to Q's supply. A must account for output tax of £140 (£700 x 20%), which is also recoverable as input tax.
A then invoices C for £800, charging £160 of output tax. (£800 x 20%)

2. Ms S is a Spanish vet who makes a supply of veterinary services to her French client Mme F, who races horses, through the use of a UK agent.
B2B veterinary services are supplied where the customer is located, so the UK agent accounts for VAT on Ms S's supply by applying the reverse charge. The UK agent then invoices Mme F, who in turn also applies the reverse charge.

Non-UK principal's other costs

7172 Any VAT suffered on other costs incurred in the UK, for example car hire and hotel bills, can still be recovered by making a special claim (¶9876 and ¶9908).

SECTION 3

Expenses incurred on behalf of others

7185 Notice 700 para 25.1

In the course of acting for the principal, the agent may incur additional costs which should properly be paid for by the principal. This situation can also occur in normal commercial situations where there is no agency agreement but someone is acting on another person's behalf.

For VAT purposes these costs could either be:
a. true **disbursements**, which the agent recharges without adding any VAT; or
b. costs which are part of the agent's own supply and should be included in the value of the agent's supply before VAT is added.

Note that some or all of the costs incidental to a supply, such as travelling expenses, may be described by the parties as disbursements and shown or charged separately on the invoice. Such items may not necessarily qualify to be treated as disbursements for VAT purposes.

Overview

It can be **advantageous** to disburse expenses, particularly where: **7187**
- the principal is unable to recover input tax;
- the expense itself was exempt or zero-rated (such as postage stamps or passenger travel); or
- the third-party supplier is unregistered, so that there has been no input tax charged on the supply made to the agent.

Generally there is **no advantage** in treating standard-rated expenses as disbursements. The agent does not receive the supply and will not be able to recover the input tax, and the principal will not have a valid VAT invoice with which to make an input tax claim (although the agent can ask the supplier to issue an invoice in the name of the principal). The alternative is to include the cost as part of the agent's supply.

EXAMPLE Mr A is an auditor. His audit team have just completed their field work in relation to B Ltd's audit, which necessitated daily train journeys costing £800 in total. B Ltd, which is a financial services provider, has agreed to be billed for the audit work completed so far, which comes to £7,000.
The train journeys are zero-rated; as B Ltd makes exempt supplies (which means it cannot recover input tax), Mr A would prefer not to have to add VAT of £160 to his recharge of £800. However, these expenses cannot be treated as a disbursement (see below). An alternative is for B Ltd to purchase the tickets directly for Mr A's staff.

Disbursements

The following **strict criteria** must all be met for an expense to be treated as a disbursement: **7190** Notice 700 para 25.1.1
a. the agent was acting on behalf of the principal when the expense was paid;
b. the principal:
- actually received and consumed the goods or services acquired;
- was responsible for discharging the expense (such as stamp duty land tax);
- authorised the agent's payment; and
- knew that the goods or services would be provided by a third party;

c. the expense is separately identified on the agent's invoice;
d. only the exact amount paid out on the expense is recovered from the principal; and
e. the goods or services are clearly additional to the agent's own supply.

The need for the **principal** to have actually used the supply means that most travel expenses, photocopying costs, telephone bills and postage cannot be treated as disbursements for VAT purposes. However, if the agent acquired a rail ticket for the principal to use on a train journey, this would be a valid disbursement. **7192**

It is vital that the **agent** retain evidence of the disbursement, such as a copy invoice. It is advisable to keep a separate record of disbursements, in order to prove that the agent has not recovered any input tax on the supply. Notice 700 para 25.1.2

EXAMPLE
1. A firm of solicitors was engaged to act in a criminal case. During the case, rail fares were incurred when visiting the court, which were included as disbursements on the firm's invoice.
It was held that travel costs charged on to the client were expenditure on services supplied to the solicitor rather than to the client. The recharge was part of the firm's supply of services to the client, so VAT was chargeable. *Rowe & Maw v C & E* [1975]

2. A corporate landlord of an office block opted to tax, which meant all rent was taxable. The landlord arranged insurance cover and recovered a fair proportion of the cost from each tenant. However, no VAT was charged on this cost, because the company treated the recharges as a disbursement, being an exempt supply of insurance.
It was held that the recharge was inseparable from the single supply of rent; as it was the landlord who contracted with the insurer, the cost could not be a disbursement. *Globe Equities Ltd* [1995] (VTD 13105)

7194 Notice 700 para 25.1.3; VTAXPER40000

It is sometimes difficult to correctly **classify** expenses; certain common situations are detailed here.

Situation	Disbursement	Explanation
Bank fee paid by solicitor to transfer funds to client's account	x	Service is supplied to solicitor
Statutory fees such as land registry fees, estate duty, land charges, probate fees	✓	The fees are discharging the statutory liability of the client
Land registry fees incurred by vendor's solicitor	✓	Vendor has an obligation to supply the purchaser with evidence of title to the land; this cannot be a photocopy
Fees from third parties included on a solicitor's invoice, such as surveyors, medical reports, notaries, police reports	✓	These fees relate to services received by the client
Personal search fee incurred by solicitor to access information for client	x	Solicitor is given personal access to information needed in order to advise the client This activity is part of the solicitor's service to the client
Postal search fee to acquire document for client	✓	Solicitor is obtaining document for the client
Photographs, advertising and brochure costs incurred by an **estate agent**	x	All part of the estate agent's service in finding a purchaser for the vendor
Royalty fees incurred by a manufacturer	x	Manufacturer incurs royalty fees as part of making a supply to the customer
MOT tests carried out on behalf of an unapproved garage	✓	If customer charged only the exact cost of the test and unapproved garage makes no profit on recharge
Staff overtime paid direct by the customer at a privately hired restaurant	x	Staff perform services for the restaurant, which are part of the restaurant's own supply
Conduct money paid to witnesses by **private investigators**	✓	This money is paid to refund the costs incurred by witnesses to attend court and is made on behalf of the client

EXAMPLE A company supplied plant bulbs by mail order which were delivered by P Ltd. The delivery charges were initially treated as disbursements.
The House of Lords held that there were three supplies:
- the company's supply of delivered flowers;
- the supply by P Ltd to the company of the delivery service; and
- the supply by P Ltd to the customer of the delivery service for no consideration.

The contract between the company and P Ltd did not create an agency relationship; the monies became the company's rather than belonging to P Ltd immediately. Hence the delivery charges were not disbursements. *C & E v Plantiflor Ltd* [2002]

Invoicing

The agent's invoice must carefully **distinguish between** true disbursements and the other costs which form part of the agency supply, as shown in the following pro forma. 7196
Notice 700 para 25.1.2

	£
Agent's services	X
Expenses not to be treated as disbursements	X
Taxable amount	X
VAT	X
Disbursements	X
Total	X

EXAMPLE Mr C is a solicitor acting for Ms D. His fees are £1,500. In addition, he incurs travel costs of £300 and a postal search fee of £60.
Mr C's invoice will show the following:

	£
Legal services	1,500
Travel costs	300
Taxable amount	1,800
VAT @ 20%	360
Disbursements	60
Total	2,220

SECTION 4

VAT representatives for non-EU principals

Direction

HMRC has the power to direct that an overseas person (N) who meets **all** of the following **criteria** must appoint a UK VAT representative: 7210
s 48 VATA 1994; Notice 700/1 paras 9, 11

a. N:
- is a taxable person;
- makes taxable supplies; or
- acquires goods in the UK from one or more other EU member states;

b. N has no fixed establishment in the UK (¶9688) (which for an individual means that N's usual place of residence is outside the UK); and

c. N is established in a country which is not within the EU (¶9002) and with which the UK has no mutual assistance provision.

Such a person is referred to by HMRC as a **non-established taxable person** or NETP.

The direction will take the **form of** a specific notice or other obvious communication.

MEMO POINTS 1. A **taxable person** means one who is, or is required to be, registered for VAT.
2. A **mutual assistance provision** is a written understanding between the authorities of two countries that information will be passed on where it is likely to be of interest to the other country.
3. An NETP may instead **voluntarily** appoint an agent with the agreement of HMRC. This would avoid the agent becoming liable for the principal's VAT debt (see ¶7216). s 48(2) VATA 1994

Where an NETP **fails to appoint** a VAT representative, HMRC can serve a notice requiring the provision of security in respect of future VAT liabilities. Notice will be treated as given where all reasonable steps have been taken to bring the requirement to the NETP's attention. Where security is not lodged, the amount can be recovered by a distraint on goods (¶3753). 7212
s 48(7) VATA 1994

Appointing the representative

7214 SI 1995/2518 reg 10 The representative must **notify** the appointment to HMRC within the first 30 days of being engaged by the overseas NETP and send appropriate evidence.

The NETP submits the normal VAT **forms** (¶2704). The representative and the NETP must also complete form VAT1TR, authorising the representative to act.

Acting as a representative

7216 s 48(3) VATA 1994 The representative is **responsible for**:
- acting on behalf of the principal for VAT purposes:
- ensuring that the principal remains VAT-compliant; and
- all VAT-related liabilities of the principal.

s 48(5) VATA 1994 However, where the principal commits a **VAT offence**, the representative is not presumed guilty except by reason of misconduct (such as being complicit or negligent, or contravening the responsibilities required of a representative).

SI 1995/2518 reg 10(4) The representative must notify HMRC within 30 days of any **change in business circumstances**, such as change of name, legal status, or ownership.

7218 For **VAT accounting** purposes, the representative must keep all necessary records (¶2795), maintain a separate VAT account for each overseas principal and retain all supporting documentation.

Ceasing to act

7220 SI 1995/2518 reg 10(5) A representative is treated as ceasing to act at the **earliest of**:

a. the principal's notification to HMRC of the cessation of the existing representative arrangement, or appointment of another representative;

b. notification of the above from someone else; or

c. the representative's death, incapacity (which in the case of a company means going into liquidation, receivership or having an administration order made) or insolvency.

If no **formal notification** is received in relation to **a**. and **b**. above, HMRC may treat the date of cessation as the date of the new representative's appointment.

SECTION 5

Particular trades

Summary

7230

Trade	¶¶
Employment bureaux	¶7235
Debt collectors	¶7246
Taxi services	¶7252
Hairdressers	¶7266
Driving schools	¶7280
Direct selling	¶7292
Second-hand shops	¶7300
Travel agents	¶7460
Auctioneers	¶6750

A. Employment bureaux

The main issue which affects an employment bureau is whether VAT is chargeable on the whole worker cost or just the bureau's commission charge. **7235** VTAXPER67000

The **general rule** is that the whole cost is liable to VAT, **unless** the bureau is acting as agent.

The bureau's invoice is usually taken as evidence as to the VAT treatment adopted, although HMRC will also review contracts, promotional material and timesheets, etc, and will check that the actual conduct of the business is in accordance with its documentation.

EXAMPLE A company operating as an employment agency originally accounted for VAT on the whole of its receipts from its clients. In 2003 it made a repayment claim, dating back to 1976, on the basis that it should only have accounted for VAT on its commission. The Tribunal held that in providing temporary staff to its clients, the company was supplying introductory services rather than making supplies of staff. The company was therefore only liable to account for VAT on the commission element of its charge, rather than on the overall amount paid by the client (which included the wages paid to the employees and associated National Insurance contributions). *Reed Employment Limited v HMRC (No.3)* [2011]
HMRC has pointed out that First-tier Tribunal decisions are not binding and in any case takes the view that the case was decided on its own particular facts. HMRC considers that the regulatory regime for employment agencies was different at the time covered by the appeal. HMRC will therefore ignore the decision and expects employment agencies to do the same.

MEMO POINTS 1. Where a state-regulated private welfare institution or agency provides **home care services**, any charge is exempt from VAT (¶434). However, a company supplying its employees to private nurseries, local education authority schools, etc, was making standard-rated supplies, because the company itself was not the state-regulated institution. *HMRC v K & L Childcare Service Ltd* [2005] Sch 9 Group 7 item 9(b) VATA 1994
2. When an employer which is not an employment business **seconds** an employee to another business for no profit, to the extent that payments by the other business form part of the consideration for the secondment, they are outside the scope of VAT, provided that the other business: Notice 700/34 Appendix B
- exercises exclusive control over the employee;
- is responsible for paying the employee's wages; and/or
- discharges the related PAYE/NIC liabilities and any pension obligations.
3. For full details of how agencies are treated under **employment law** see *Employment Memo*.

Acting as principal

When acting as principal, the bureau has a continuing **contractual relationship** with the worker. **7237** Notice 700/34 para 2; VTAXPER67200

Any contract between the bureau and the client will be for the supply of temporary workers, who may be self-employed or employees of the bureau. There is no contractual relationship between the client and the temporary worker.

If self-employed, the workers make a supply to the bureau, which then makes an onward supply to the client. If employed, the bureau supplies its workers' services direct. In either case, the full value of the contract is subject to VAT, unless the supply falls within an exemption (¶426), the most common being nursing supplies.

The only likely **disbursement** is reimbursed travel expenses for the workers to attend interviews, although where these are met out of the bureau's commission, these expenses are not disbursements.

EXAMPLE In a case concerning a nursing bureau, the following facts were crucial to determining that the bureau was acting as principal. The bureau:
- contracted with the patient and received payment;
- interviewed all potential workers;
- gave workers timesheets and told them that an hourly rate would be paid;
- engaged skilled workers who could be left in unsupervised charge of wards or patients;
- required all workers to wear uniform and keep separate records in addition to the timesheets;
- arranged liability insurance;

– regularly visited sites where nurses and care assistants were working, to ensure standards were maintained through direct supervision; and
– exercised greater control over care assistants than nurses, as the former were less qualified.
M G Parkinson [1991] (VTD 6017)

Acting as agent

7240 Notice 700/34 para 5; VTAXPER67100, 67200

The bureau may act as an agent **for** the client (which is always the case for HGV drivers), for the worker, or both.

Where the bureau is acting as disclosed agent for the **client**, VAT is accounted for on the commission or margin charged to the client, which will be known to all parties. The workers may be placed temporarily or permanently. The worker provides services direct to the client and the bureau's only reward is a standard-rated finding fee, so there is no ongoing responsibility for the worker's performance during the contract. The bureau may pay the worker, but only as a service to the client, so such payments can be treated as disbursements.

If the bureau is the **worker's** agent, employment law usually precludes the charging of a fee to the worker (except in the case of fashion models) but there will be a continuing contractual relationship between the worker and bureau. Any commission charged is in respect of a standard-rated supply and the bureau may pay the worker's earnings net of this commission. If the worker is registered for VAT, the client will be charged VAT by the worker and the bureau may deal with this on the worker's behalf.

Alternatively, the bureau may act as agent for **both the worker and client** (which generally only occurs in the medical profession), in which case the only fee generally charged is commission to the client and this is the only taxable element.

B. Debt collectors

Acting as agent

7246 Notice 700 para 25.6.1

Where a debt collector is acting as an agent, **court fees** paid to solicitors may be treated as disbursements. If the collector successfully recovers monies from debtors and retains them in order to recover the court fees, they are treated as a reimbursement outside the scope of VAT.

Legal fees are either treated as:
– disbursements, in which case the same VAT treatment applies as for court fees; or
– costs of the collector, on which input tax is recoverable and which are recharged on to the creditor with output tax added. Any debtors' monies retained are treated as payment of these costs.

Acting as principal

7248 Notice 700 para 25.6.2

The debt collector can recover input tax on legal fees.

Any **amounts recovered from debtors** in respect of court fees and solicitors' charges are treated as consideration for the collector's supply of services to the creditor and are taxable. The only exception is where the debt has been assigned to the collector; the monies collected are then outside the scope of VAT. The assignment itself is an exempt supply of services by the creditor.

C. Taxi services

7252 Notice 700/25

Taxi firms may arrange their affairs in a variety of ways. The crucial VAT issue is whether the **customer's fare** is subject to VAT.

The taxi firm can act as principal or agent, each of which results in a different VAT treatment.

MEMO POINTS 1. For **motorbike and van courier** services, the courier firm (rather than the rider or driver) is always the principal. *Prontobikes Ltd* [1995] (VTD 13213)
2. Individual taxi drivers may club together as a **taxi association**, which will provide communal facilities such as a rest room, radios and a booking service. Supplies made by the association (which will include its supplies to the drivers and maybe administration services to customers) are always standard-rated, so the association will need to register for VAT if supplies exceed the threshold (¶9960). See also the *Eastbourne Town Radio Cars* case at ¶8150. Notice 700/25 para 4

Acting as principal

The taxi firm can act as principal and provide services direct to the customer through the **self-employed driver**. In this situation, the customer's **full fare** is liable to VAT, so it is preferable if customers are businesses which can recover input tax. Customers who use the firm frequently may be able to keep an account and make payments periodically (these are known as "account customers"). **7254** VTAXPER77200

Any money retained by the driver constitutes consideration for a supply of his or her services to the firm. This supply is potentially taxable, although it is unlikely that a driver will make supplies of sufficient value to exceed the registration limit.

If **drivers are employees** (which rarely occurs in practice), the firm accounts for VAT on all takings and any amounts retained by drivers are outside the scope of VAT, because this is remuneration for their employment.

The employment status of the drivers is decided by the accepted income tax treatment, along with the terms of the contract (if any) between the drivers and the firm. See *Tax Memo* for further details of income tax status. VTAXPER77000

Acting as agent

Alternatively, by acting as agent for the taxi driver, the taxi firm can seek to ensure that the **fares** remain outside the scope of VAT (most drivers are not required to be VAT-registered, as their supplies do not reach the threshold). The firm deals with the radio callouts, etc, and makes a **charge to the taxi driver**, which is subject to VAT. In this case most customers will pay in cash. It should be noted, however, that some firms charge account customers output tax in error when acting as agent. **7256** VTAXPER77200

Both agent and principal

Some firms are sophisticated enough to adopt the agency structure for non-business customers (cash work) and the principal arrangement for business customers (account work). **7258**

Deciding the VAT position

The **main issues** considered by HMRC when determining the correct VAT treatment are whether: **7260** VTAXPER76700 - 77100
- there are any contractual differences between account and cash work;
- the drivers are supplying services to the firm or the customers; and
- the taxi drivers are employees of the firm.

MEMO POINTS 1. **Contractual differences** may take the form of a fixed hourly rate for account customers and a variable rate linked to takings for cash work. In practice, a firm will allow the driver to keep all the takings and then charge a mileage rate for account work. HMRC does not consider this to be a contractual difference.
2. The **recipient of the service** performed by the driver is often not clear, although the following factors are important:
a. the person who:
- owns the cars;
- bears the running costs;
- sets the prices; and
- bears the risk of bad debts;
b. whether the cars have advertising logos;

c. whether there is a driver roster, particularly where there are more drivers than cars;
d. whether the drivers have private access to the vehicles; and
e. whether the firm keeps detailed records of drivers' takings.

7262

EXAMPLE

1. A taxi firm used the services of self-employed drivers who drove their own cars and maintained, fuelled, insured and taxed them at their own expense. The drivers agreed:
- to keep the cars clean and roadworthy;
- to wear an identification badge (showing the names of the firm and the driver) at all times;
- to carry a pen, company cards and maps, etc;
- never to switch off or turn down the radio, or pull away from a non-pick-up without the controller's consent; and
- to pay their own income tax and National Insurance contributions.

Although both account and cash business was available, the firm's preference was to undertake account work. This was supported by an appropriate bonus scheme, which rewarded the exceeding of weekly targets by drivers. Indeed, the drivers were not licensed to engage in casual work themselves.
Sometimes a casual customer would ring up for a ride, in which case the receptionist would ring the customer back to say a driver had been found, or else suggest other firms. However, the demands of account customers were always met. All takings from cash customers were retained by the drivers and the firm kept no records as to destination, etc. Drivers had discretion to charge cash customers up to the usual scale price and bore the risk of bad debts.
The firm accounted for VAT in respect of fares from account customers but not from casual cash customers.
It was held that the firm's VAT treatment was correct, because there was a real distinction between the conduct of the account work and the cash work. The firm accepted telephone enquiries from casual cash customers on behalf of the drivers and not in furtherance of its own business. *Camberwell Cars* [1993] (VTD 10178)

2. In a later case taxi drivers provided their own cars and rented car radios from the taxi firm. The customer was charged a flat rate per mile, plus a fixed charge of 40p per journey (known as job money), which was payable by the driver to the radio controller. Both of these charges were set by the firm. The firm contended that its only income was rent from the radios, which meant it traded below the VAT registration threshold.
The key issue was the status of the radio controllers. It was concluded that they were essential to the business operation: they were hourly paid (receiving the job money as extra income), worked at the firm's premises and had no autonomy in their work, all of which indicated employment status, or at least that they were agents of the firm. As such, the job money was income of the firm, so the firm should be registered for VAT. *Samantha Wren (Blue & White Car Service)* [2001] (VTD 17024)

D. Hairdressers

7266 VTAXPER68600 There are three possible **business structures** for hairdressing salons, which HMRC considers in the following order:
a. the salon engages employees;
b. the hairdressers are self-employed, making a supply to the salon, and the salon then makes an onward supply to the customer; or
c. the salon provides materials and space for the self-employed hairdressers to work and the hairdressers make a direct supply to the customers. This is known as chair rental.

Each case should be reviewed purely on its own merits, particularly as no consensus can be drawn from previous decisions of case law.

1. Employed

7268 VT4XPER69000 In this simple scenario, the salon is supplying services to the customers and so must account for any VAT on the gross value of its supplies.

HMRC will not accept that employee status applies unless the hairdresser's **agreement** with the salon shows that a contract of employment exists, or the hairdresser is subject to income tax as an employee. VTAXPER68800

2. Self-employed

Supply to salon

The salon is again supplying services to the customers and output tax is therefore due on the gross amounts paid by the customers. **7270** VTAXPER69000

The only difference from the employment situation is that the **hairdresser** may be VAT-registered and therefore need to declare output tax on the payments received from the salon.

Chair rental

The self-employed **hairdresser** is supplying services to the customer and will only account for output tax if VAT-registered. **7272** VTAXPER69000; VATLP 19820; VAT Information Sheet 13/12

The **salon** is normally making a single standard-rated supply of facilities to the hairdresser.

MEMO POINTS 1. Chair rental is **defined** by HMRC to mean the provision of a chair or a designated area of a building, together with "services related to hairdressing". These may include:
- the services of an assistant or cashier;
- the booking of appointments; and
- services of laundering, tidying up and making refreshments.

They do not include the provision of utilities or the cleaning of shared areas of a building.
2. The treatment outlined above applies from **1 October 2012**. Previously it was possible for the salon to argue that it had granted the hairdresser an exempt licence to occupy land. HMRC will now only accept that an exempt licence to occupy has been granted in the unusual circumstance where:
- the hairdresser is genuinely restricted to a whole building or floor, a separate room or specified area of the salon; and
- the salon does not supply services related to hairdressing.

Determining who receives the hairdresser's supply

Unless the arrangement meets the criteria to be a chair rental situation, the default position will be that the salon is supplying services to the customer. **7274** VTAXPER68700

The National Hairdressers Federation has agreed **guidelines** with HMRC, stating the following indicators which are commonly found in a chair rental situation, such as:
- the hairdresser must be self-employed, having autonomy in hours of work and the purchasing of products, bearing risks of liability, maintaining accounts, etc;
- the customers must be made aware that they are contracting with the hairdresser, not the salon and complaints should be made directly to the hairdresser;
- all monies are to be accounted for to the hairdresser, even if collected by the salon;
- the hairdresser is responsible for the premises occupied, including hygiene, health and safety, etc; and
- an agreement should cover such issues as marketing, cleaning, security and use of salon personnel.

The **terms of the agreement** between the salon and hairdresser must, of course, reflect the actual working practice. In cases where the agreement does not reflect working practice, it will be disregarded and evidence of conduct will be relied upon instead. *S Taylor (Machine Tools) Ltd* [1993] (VTD 11171)

The following cases **illustrate** the approach taken in relation to hairdressing arrangements. **7276**

EXAMPLE

1. The salon initially treated the hairdressers as employees. Then separate agreements were entered into with each hairdresser, which meant that the hairdressers agreed to become self-

employed and to pay a set percentage of their turnover to the salon for chair rental and service charges. The issue was whether this agreement changed the VAT treatment so that the hairdressers were providing a service to the customers rather than the salon.
It was held that the status of the hairdressers was successfully changed by the agreement; they were making supplies direct to the customers. *MacHenrys (Hairdressers) Ltd v C & E* [1993]

2. An unregistered salon initially employed three hairdressers. Subsequently the business arrangements were changed so that the hairdressers entered into franchise agreements and they were then treated as self-employed.
It was held that the salon still provided services to the customers, because there had been hardly any changes in the nature of the business, or in the way in which it was carried on, since the franchise agreements had taken effect. There was only one business, which was carried on by the salon; all customer receipts were part of the company's turnover. *C & E v Jane Montgomery (Hair Stylists) Ltd* [1994]

3. A company operated eight hairdressing salons. Some hairdressers were employed, whereas 45 others were self-employed. Under the agreement with the self-employed individuals, the salon could control who worked where and when, so that the overall salon service was maintained.
The salon received all customer monies and these were then distributed to the self-employed hairdressers, net of the fees payable to the salon, based on the records kept of each transaction undertaken by each individual.
It was held that the effect of the agreement was that all of the self-employed hairdressers supplied the customer direct and there was no evidence that the parties did not act in accordance with the agreement. The salon's control of the hairdressers was not detrimental to this VAT treatment. *Kieran Mullin Ltd v C & E* [2003]

E. Driving schools

7280 VTAXPER66100 The VAT issues facing driving schools are very similar to those of hairdressing salons (¶7266+). The instructors may be employed or self-employed and in the latter case, the supply to the pupil may be made by the driving school or the instructor. HMRC considers whether the driver is an employee (which is more unusual), before deciding who receives the driver's supply.

The corresponding VAT treatment is summarised in the table.

Driver's situation	Who is principal?	VAT treatment
Employed	School	School accounts for output tax on pupil fees
Self-employed	School	If VAT-registered, the driver charges output tax on the fee charged to the school School accounts for output tax on pupil fees
	Driver	If VAT-registered, the driver charges output tax on the pupil's fee School is acting as the driver's agent and the fees it receives are VATable as consideration for agency services

1. Employed

7282 VTAXPER66300 The employment status of the instructor for income tax purposes will be followed for VAT purposes. If the income tax position is not decided, HMRC will look at certain **factors** in the following order of priority:
- the chance that the driver can make a profit other than receiving a guaranteed amount;
- the risk of loss faced by the driver;

– the owner of the vehicle (and whether a charge is made to the driver when the car is owned by the school); and
– the control exercised by the school over the driver's working hours, fees charged, etc.

2. Self-employed

If the driver is not an employee, the school will either be the principal, or acting as the driver's undisclosed agent. The **pupil's perception** of the contracting party is therefore less important. 7284 VTAXPER66400

School is principal

The school allocates pupils to drivers, tends to exercise **control** over the drivers, requiring records of every lesson to be retained, and sets the fees. The school usually owns the vehicles and pays costs centrally. The pupil pays the school, which passes on a net amount to the drivers after making a deduction for the school's costs. 7286

EXAMPLE The four instructors at a driving school were self-employed and were supplied with the following by a driving school under a franchise agreement:
- fully maintained, insured and taxed cars bearing the school's logo;
- screening of video lessons;
- stationery;
- appointment cards and handouts with the name of the school displayed;
- a telephone and booking service; and
- advertising in the Yellow Pages.

However, the instructors could work when they liked, advertise in their own name, book their own pupils and have their own logo on the car. Instructors were guaranteed a fair share of unallocated pupil bookings.
The instructors and school owner met periodically at the school's premises to agree the pupils' tariff, which the instructors could only vary if a longer distance was travelled for a lesson. The drivers paid a proportion of the fee (about 40% of the tariff) to the school in respect of each lesson.
It was held that the instructors were agents of the school, which was making a supply direct to the pupils and should therefore account for output tax on the total fees. The judge made particular reference to the restrictions on the pupils' fees, which would have constituted a restrictive trade agreement had the drivers been supplying the pupils direct. *John Cronin t/a Cronin's Driving School v C & E* [1991]

School acting as agent

The driver has far more **autonomy** in respect of working hours and fees charged. The pupil pays the driver direct. The driver typically provides a car and pays most of the expenses, and then pays the school a fixed fee in return for its services, which may include taking bookings, advertising and providing a waiting room. 7288

EXAMPLE A driving school was set up by two instructors who became business partners. Under an agreement, the school charged a weekly fee to the other instructors for their use of the following facilities:
- a booking office, staffed by a receptionist;
- a waiting room for pupils;
- refreshments; and
- advertising.

Most instructors provided their own cars, to which boards and magnetic advertising signs showing the name of the school could be attached. Each driver could also advertise on his own account.
At first the weekly fee was variable, but was then replaced by a fixed fee, which was independent of each instructor's income. This change was unpopular: some of the instructors left the school, taking their pupils with them. On taking legal advice, the school was told that it had no right to any damages from the ex-instructors.
The instructors chose individually how much use of the school's facilities they and their pupils made. Bookings were made directly with the instructors, who kept their own diaries of appointments. Often bookings were taken by instructors at their own homes and new pupils were often gained as a result of other pupils' personal recommendations of an individual instructor. Pupil complaints were usually dealt with by the individual instructor.

The pupil tariffs were fixed by a collective decision of the instructors. The school advertised these fees, including promotional discounts, although individual instructors were not bound by either the tariffs or discounts.
It was held that the school provided certain communal services for driving instructors, who were trading on their own account, so it was their agent. *Fleet School of Motoring* [1992] (VTD 7299)

F. Direct selling

7292 VTAXPER64700 Direct selling involves non-registered persons (dealers) selling certain products, such as cosmetics and domestic appliances, to the public by holding demonstration parties or making house-to-house calls. The products are manufactured by VAT-registered suppliers and then distributed to the dealers, who deliver the goods, take customers' cash, and pass it back to the distributor net of their "commission".

In this case, the dealer may be acting as agent, principal or employee, depending on the particular facts. HMRC will consider the factors shown in the following table to decide, in particular, whether the dealer ever gains title to the goods:

Factor	Detail
Title	A dealer must obtain title to the goods in order to act as a principal. A principal would be expected to bear the cost of replacing goods, issue refunds to customers and bear bad debts. If these responsibilities stay with the distributor, that indicates that the dealer is an agent [1].
Value	To be a principal, the dealer must have full knowledge of the price obtained and retain any discounts.
Separation	To be an agent, the dealer's fee must be identifiable and known to the distributor.
Pricing	A dealer who is a principal must be free to set the retail price of the goods. A dealer who informs the distributor of the total takings and is then paid a percentage of that figure is likely to be an agent.

Note
1. A Romalpa agreement (which provides that the goods remain the property of the dealer until sold) indicates that the dealer is a principal. If the dealer were an agent, such an agreement would be unnecessary.

Acting as agent

7294 VTAXPER64800 The **dealer** will only be liable to be registered for VAT, and therefore charge output tax, if the total of commissions exceeds the registration threshold.

The **VAT-registered distributor** must account for output tax on the full sale price paid by the final consumer.

EXAMPLE A company supplied cosmetics to individuals who demonstrated these products at parties attended by the public and displayed samples and catalogues. After each party the individuals placed orders with the company.
The invoices for the goods included a 30% discount for prompt payment but customers still paid the full price to the individuals, so that they retained the difference. An assessment was issued on the basis that the market value of the goods was the full undiscounted price.
It was held that the discount was a commission and the individuals were acting as agents. Hence the market value for the purpose of VAT was the price paid by the ultimate customer and not the discounted price. *Direct Cosmetics Ltd v C & E* [1985]

Acting as principal

7296 VTAXPER64800 Sch 6 para 2 VATA 1994 The dealer is unlikely to exceed the registration threshold.

HMRC can direct the distributor to account for VAT on the price paid by the final consumer. However, such a direction cannot have retrospective effect.

G. Second-hand shops

The problem of charging VAT twice to the consumer on the same goods has been overcome through the use of various schemes which allow VAT to be calculated on the profit margin only (¶6620). Hence the following rules apply only to traders who are **not using a margin scheme**. 7300 VTAXPER73000

Certain items, such as coins, precious metals and gemstones, are excluded from the margin schemes. In such cases the trader will probably want to act as a disclosed agent on behalf of the unregistered seller (usually a member of the public), so that no VAT is due on the sale.

Alternatively, if the trader is acting as:
- principal, VAT is due under the normal rules; or
- undisclosed agent, either principal treatment or agent treatment will apply (¶7144).

Acting as disclosed agent

In this particular trade, the **title** to the goods must remain with the seller until the sale transaction is completed. This would mean that the trader could return the goods to the seller at any time until ownership transfers to the eventual purchaser. 7302

It would also be **unusual** in this scenario for the trader to:
- pay the seller any monies in advance of the sale;
- incur any expense in repairing the goods before sale; and
- give a guarantee to the buyer.

See ¶7106 for an example.

The seller must be able to ascertain the actual **sales value** achieved, perhaps by looking at published catalogues or price labels in the shop. 7304

The trader's **commission** must be known to the seller in advance of the sale. This can be achieved by either agreeing a set amount up front, or allowing the trader to retain any excess proceeds over a set amount.

When truly acting as a disclosed agent, the trader only **accounts for VAT on** the commission charged. This supply is always standard-rated, irrespective of the VAT rating of the goods sold. For example, even if selling second-hand clothing for children, which is zero-rated, the agent's commission is standard-rated. *RJ & JM Farrimond* [1993] (VTD 10831) 7306

CHAPTER 9

The travel industry

OUTLINE ¶¶

Despite their name, travel agents are not necessarily "agents" in strict law. They act in various capacities, depending on the type of transaction undertaken. For the purposes of this chapter, the following terms will be used: **7460**
- **travel agent**, for a person who is truly acting as an intermediary or disclosed agent (¶7120), receiving commission; and
- **tour operator**, for someone who is acting either as principal or as an undisclosed agent for a principal, which will usually be the case for transactions involving members of the public.

Of course it is possible for the same person to fulfil both capacities in the same transaction, arranging some supplies as an intermediary while supplying travel services in their own name. The special scheme for tour operators contains specific provisions to deal with this situation.

SECTION 1

Acting as an intermediary

When the travel agent is acting as a **disclosed agent**, VAT is due on the fee charged to the principal and the commission charged to travel providers. **7465** Notice 709/6 para 2

For these purposes, the following are taken as **indicators** of a disclosed agency arrangement:
a. the contractual agreement states that the agent will be disclosed;
b. the name of the principal is routinely disclosed or notified on tickets, invoices, terms and conditions; and
c. the commercial risk remains with the principal.

Travel agents commonly work as a disclosed agent when acting on behalf of business customers.

MEMO POINTS 1. It would be unusual for a disclosed agent to make supplies under an **ATOL** (Air Travel Organiser's Licence).
2. For the rules relating to **agents generally** see ¶7090+.

Commission received from operators

7467 Travel agents receive commission based typically on the volume of business given to tour operators.

The agent will **deduct** the commission from the monies remitted to the operator. Typically the operator raises a self-billed invoice (¶2904) which shows the amount of commission.

Sch 8 Group 8 item 10(b) VATA 1994

The agent's supply is usually standard-rated unless the commission relates to a zero-rated in-house supply (¶7538) made by the tour operator, when it too can be zero-rated.

MEMO POINTS 1. The **place of supply** for commission received from a tour operator is the country where the operator is established (¶9688). It is irrelevant where the holiday is actually enjoyed.

s 7A VATA 1994

2. If the place of supply is in **another EU member state**, a tour operator registered for VAT in the EU accounts for VAT on the agent's commission under the reverse charge rules (¶9700), so there is no requirement for the agent to register in the other member state.
3. Where an **overseas agent** is acting for a UK tour operator, the operator must apply the reverse charge on the agent's commission.

7470 Information Sheet 06/05 para 3

The VAT treatment of the agent's **onward supply to a business customer** depends on whether the commission is:
– ceded, which means that the legal right to the commission is passed to the customer - in which case the agent must account for output tax on any commission received, as well as on the supply to the customer; or
– not ceded, in which case the agent accounts for output tax on the commission (if a fee is also charged to the customer, VAT is due on the net amount if the commission is offset).

MEMO POINTS If the agent arranges foreign exchange for the business client and does not know the value of the underlying supply by the bank (or other financial institution), the agent may take the value to be 1% of the amount exchanged.

Continuous supplies to principals

7472 Information Sheet 06/05

For continuous supplies (in which a business customer engages the agent to arrange travel on a long-term basis, as evidenced by a contract), the **fees** must be apportioned between the VAT liability of each particular supply, on the basis of relative value. The apportionment must be carried out within 2 months of the latest reconciliation of supplies made against fees rendered.

The following **factors** indicate that the agent is making a continuous supply:
– periodic reconciliations are carried out between fees rendered and payments received;
– the agent maintains a presence at the principal's premises;
– periodic management information is provided to the principal under the terms of the contract; and
– the agent is available for the principal to use during set hours, which may also include a reduced service out of office hours.

EXAMPLE Ms A is a travel agent who acts for F Ltd, arranging all travel and accommodation as and when required for a quarterly fee of 5%.
In the quarter ended 30 September, Ms A has arranged £30,000 of these supplies, which is allocated between:

Supply	VAT rating	Amount £	%
Passenger transport	Zero-rated	18,000	60
Hotels in the UK	Standard-rated	7,800	26
Hotels in the USA	Outside scope	3,600	12
Insurance	Exempt	600	2
		30,000	100

Ms A is owed a fee of £1,500, so 26% of this figure is standard-rated, giving output tax of £78. (£1,500 x 26% x 20%)
If Ms A has already received an interim payment of £1,000 and accounted for VAT of £50 in that quarter, she must issue an invoice to F Ltd showing:

		£
Net	1,500 - 1,000	500
VAT	78 - 50	28
Gross		528

MEMO POINTS 1. **Ancillary services** are secondary to the main supply made by the agent and will often enhance or improve the core activity. They have no specific VAT liability of their own and therefore take the VAT liability of the related main supply. 7474 Information Sheet 06/05 para 6.1
Examples of ancillary supplies include:
- delivering tickets;
- reissuing tickets;
- processing refunds;
- account management; and
- offering a 24-hour helpline.

2. Where **interim payments** are received by the agent, the VAT treatment depends on whether: Information Sheet 06/05 para 4.2
a. the principal is paying for each individual supply, in which case the agent must account for VAT each time that a payment is received, based on the liability of the particular supply (at the end of each quarter, the agent must apportion the total services supplied on the basis of relative value and make an adjustment to the VAT already declared, which will necessitate an invoice or credit note being issued to the principal); or
b. the payments are periodic, independent of any specific supply, in which case the agent must calculate the related VAT in a fair and reasonable manner, perhaps based on an estimate of the standard-rated supplies which will be made in that quarter, or on the results of the previous quarter. Again an adjustment will need to be carried out at the end of the quarter, as in **a**. above.

One-off charge to principal

Where the agent makes a single charge for a **bundle of individual services**, the fee must be apportioned between the various services with different VAT liabilities in order for the VAT on that fee to be calculated. The normal time of supply rules apply (¶755). 7476 Information Sheet 06/05 para 5

EXAMPLE A bundled transaction fee of £40 (exclusive of VAT) is charged for arranging air travel (zero-rated) and French hotel accommodation (standard-rated).
The components of the arrangement are sold at the following prices:

	£	
Air ticket	450	75%
Hotel accommodation	150	25%
	600	100%

So 25% of the agent's fee relates to standard-rated supplies.
The VAT due is £2. (£40 x 25% x 20%)

SECTION 2

Acting as principal or undisclosed agent - TOMS

Other than when acting as a disclosed agent (¶7465), the following rules for tour operators apply. 7490

By the nature of their trade, tour operators make supplies and incur costs in many countries. To comply with the individual VAT rules of each jurisdiction, the operator would need to either register in each EU member state, or make separate claims for input tax suffered.

EC Directive 2006/112 arts 306 - 310

The EU-wide solution is to suspend normal VAT accounting and allow tour operators to account for VAT in the country where they are established, charging output tax only on the margin, which gives the same result as full input tax recovery. This is known as the **Tour Operators' Margin Scheme** (TOMS).

The following paragraphs describe the UK scheme only.

Comment Although TOMS is an EU scheme, each member state has its own interpretation of certain elements (such as the definition of a tour operator, whether a supply is in-house or bought-in, and the way VAT is calculated). In addition, certain states (including Ireland, Denmark and Belgium) have been granted derogations to avoid using TOMS altogether. The European Commission has proposed changes to the scheme to avoid the disparities and inconsistencies which exist at the moment, but as yet, no firm date has been set for implementation.

A. Scope

Situation

7494 s 53 VATA 1994; Notice 709/5 paras 2.3, 2.7

The scheme is **mandatory** for tour operators who are either VAT-registered or eligible for voluntary registration (¶2688), and who make supplies of designated travel services (¶7504) for consumption anywhere in the world. This is true even for those operators making supplies of UK travel only.

There are **special rules** for the following situations, where certain exclusions apply:
– supplies to certain business customers;
– persons making incidental travel supplies (¶7526) which are less than 1% of their turnover; and
– teaching English as a foreign language.

Notice 709/5 para 4.1

MEMO POINTS 1. For the purposes of the **VAT registration thresholds** (¶9960+), taxable turnover includes:
– the total margin on any designated travel services;
– agency commission; and
– the full value of all other taxable (including zero-rated and in-house) supplies.

2. **New tour operators** should check their total margin at the end of the first financial period (per their statutory accounts) and if the registration threshold has been exceeded, inform HMRC within the following 30 days. Because of this tight impractical deadline, operators may choose to register from the commencement of trade.

Notice 709/5 para 4.2

3. A trader who must use TOMS can be part of a **VAT group unless** a member of the group:
– has an overseas establishment;
– makes supplies outside the UK which would be taxable if made in the UK; and
– supplies services and goods which will be resold as designated travel services.

Notice 709/5 para 4.16 - 4.17

4. For the purposes of the **annual accounting** scheme (¶4745), the margin is treated as the taxable turnover. The cash accounting scheme (¶4880) and the flat rate scheme (¶4635) cannot be used.

Who is a tour operator?

7496 s 53(3) VATA 1994

For the purposes of the scheme, a tour operator **includes** anyone acting as a principal providing services of a type which are commonly supplied by travel agents and enjoyed by travellers: for example, conference providers who accommodate delegates overnight, hoteliers laying on coach transfers from the airport, and excursion providers who buy in hotel accommodation.

EXAMPLE Mr B is a travel agent who books hotel rooms.
If he makes a block booking in his own name, which he then resupplies to customers, he is acting as principal and TOMS will apply.
If Mr B shops around for the best-priced hotel room in response to a specific customer request, booking the room in the name of the customer, he is acting as an agent and TOMS does not apply.

Supplies

Only the sales value and direct costs of travel packages involving designated travel are treated differently within TOMS. Otherwise, the normal VAT rules apply. **7498** Notice 709/5 para 6.3 - 6.4

For every package sold, the TOMS calculation computes VAT on the:
- margin for the designated travel elements; and
- selling price for any other elements.

Overheads are indirect expenses which are incurred for the purposes of the business without being directly related to the main activity and should not be included in the TOMS calculation. Input tax can be recovered on all overheads, unless the operator makes any exempt supplies, such as the sale of insurance or foreign currency, in which case the partial exemption rules (¶2075+) apply. **7500**

Examples of **typical** overheads for a tour operator are:
- advertising;
- brochures;
- market research;
- inspection trips;
- guides and representatives (but see ¶7550);
- other agents' commission;
- office expenses;
- professional fees;
- bank and foreign exchange charges; and
- equipment leasing charges.

1. Travel packages

A person making travel package supplies **must use TOMS**, even if no profits are made or all the supplies are zero-rated. **7502** Notice 709/5 para 2.3, 2.11

Packages can comprise a variety of supplies, but most commonly only include designated travel.

Designated travel services

Designated travel services are supplies of goods and services which are enjoyed anywhere and are: **7504** SI 1987/1806 reg 3
- **bought in from** another person and resupplied for business purposes without material alteration or further processing; and
- **supplied by** a tour operator from a UK establishment for the direct benefit of a traveller.

Such goods and services are always treated as a single supply, no matter how many elements are actually within the package, which can include in-house supplies and agency commission. Notice 709/5 para 2.11

MEMO POINTS 1. An **in-house** supply is a supply made from the tour operator's own resources, or a materially altered or processed bought-in supply (¶7538). Note, however, that the CJEU has interpreted arts 306-310 to mean that when a travel agent provides an in-house service as part of a package, the in-house service is a separate supply which is subject to the normal VAT regime, not to the special scheme for travel agents. *Kozak v Dyrektor Izby Skarbowej w Lublinie* [2012] C-557/11 **7506** EC Directive 2006/112 arts 306 - 310
2. **Material alteration** is a matter of degree which depends on the facts. Combining two bought-in supplies could change both sufficiently to create an in-house supply (for example, buying in

catering for a hired cottage would change the supply to one of catered accommodation). In this case the buying in of a train and driver, to which in-house catering and stewards were added, did not sufficiently alter the supply of transport, so it fell within TOMS. *Nicholas Harvey (t/a Green Express Railtours)* [1998] (VTD 15608) See also ¶7510.

Notice 709/5 para 2.15
3. **From a UK establishment** means that the operator has an establishment in the UK and the package is sold from that establishment. Each EU state has its own equivalent of TOMS (except where a derogation has been granted), so supplies from an EU establishment will fall within the rules of the particular EU state.

Notice 709/5 para 2.8
4. A **traveller** is a person who receives a supply of designated travel and is not going to supply it onwards. That person could be a private individual, charity, business, company or local authority.

EXAMPLE The owners of a Devon hotel provided:
- a return coach service to the hotel from Leeds and other pick-up points so that guests could get to the hotel with relative ease; and
- a day's coach excursion around Devon, which was enjoyed by around 90% of guests every week.

The CJEU held that the owners were making supplies which fell within TOMS, because both services were habitual and were not ancillary to the provision of hotel accommodation. *TP Madgett & RM Baldwin (t/a Howden Court Hotel) v C & E* [1998]

7508
Notice 709/5 paras 2.9, 2.10; Notice 744A para 1.2

Common types of designated travel services which are always within TOMS include:
- passenger transport (i.e. the provision of a vehicle along with a driver or crew for the carriage of passengers);
- hire of a means of transport;
- accommodation;
- trips or excursions;
- tour guide services;
- use of special airport lounges; and
- ancillary supplies (¶310) such as catering, admission tickets and sports facilities which are supplied as part of a travel package.

Comment A tour operator who **only organises UK travel** may wish to avoid TOMS because the VAT burden may be higher than if input tax were recovered under the normal VAT rules. In this case the operator could materially alter the supply so that it is not a designated travel service, by providing some of the elements in-house (for example, by owning a coach and employing a driver).

EXAMPLE Ms C is a coach operator who buys in the services of a tour guide, and also arranges hotel accommodation, for a week-long excursion.
Ms C is making a single supply of organising travel services.

Avoiding TOMS on travel

7510
As passenger transport is **normally** zero-rated, a tour operator may wish to avoid treating it as part of a designated travel supply (which is standard-rated) and take it outside TOMS. HMRC has published three different planning options which achieve this aim. These are presented here in the order of most common use.

Comment If the transport is supplied in another EU member state, the supply may be standard-rated in that member state, in which case applying UK TOMS may still be preferable.

7512
Information Sheet 01/97

Wholesale option This option inserts another entity (known as a transport company) between the travel provider and the tour operator. The profit on the transport supply is moved to the company by having it charge a retail price to the tour operator. The operator's margin is reduced to nil, thereby avoiding any VAT charge for the transport under TOMS. The margin remaining in the TOMS calculation is that on accommodation, catering and so on; the margin on the transport is retained by the transport company.

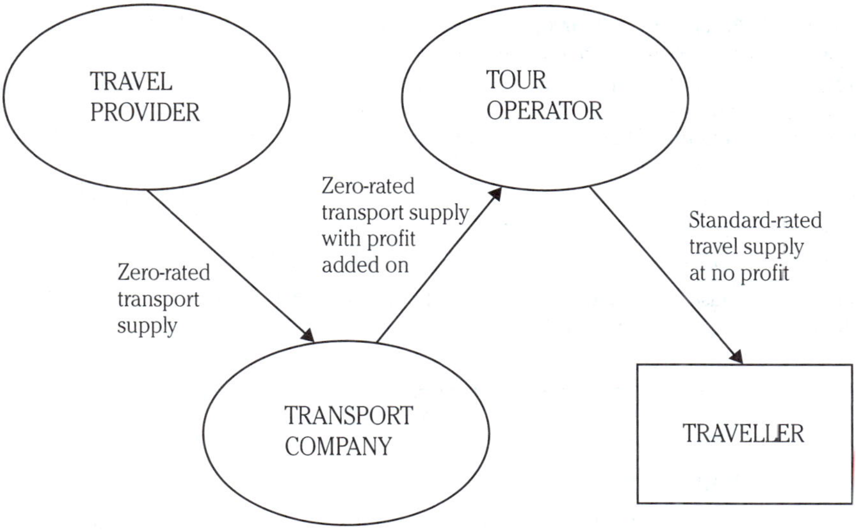

MEMO POINTS 1. The **mark-up** by the transport company must be agreed with HMRC. 7514
2. HMRC has given two practical solutions to the problem of **pricing** the transport company's supply:
a. the transport company can initially invoice the transport at cost and when the tour operator has determined the margin on its supplies, the transport company can issue another invoice to cover it; or
b. a specific formula can be used to calculate the mark-up. Information Sheet 01/97 appendix 3
3. **Profit must be channelled back** to the tour operator by dividends or a standard-rated management charge for administration (because the ABTA rules require all tour operators to be profitable).
4. There are **corporation tax** implications of this structure, including transfer pricing, use of losses and higher tax rates. See *Tax Memo* for further details.
5. The tour operator and the transport company **must not be part of a VAT group**, because the supply of transport would be intra-group and ignored for VAT. This would leave the end supply by the group still subject to TOMS.
6. The transport company must have an **ATOL** number (¶7465).

Agency option While this scheme is not appropriate for air travel because of the bonding requirements, it is sometimes used by operators selling **ferry travel**. 7516 Information Sheet 04/96

Subject to a number of conditions, if the tour operator acts as agent for a **UK travel provider**, the supply of passenger transport will still be zero-rated. The tour operator's profit is treated as commission, which is also zero-rated because agency, or intermediary, supplies follow the VAT liability of the underlying supply (passenger transport). The usual rules for commission (¶7467) then apply.

The agent's commission is taxable where the transport takes place.

A travel **provider who is located in another EU member state** will account for VAT on the agent's commission using the reverse charge mechanism (¶9700). Note that there is unlikely to be any VAT charge, as passenger transport is zero-rated in most member states.

MEMO POINTS 1. The **conditions** include:
– having a contract with each travel provider which appoints the tour operator as agent;
– the booking material disclosing the name of the provider and stating that the tour operator is acting on behalf of that provider; and
– retaining evidence that the provider is taking a commercial risk and is making a direct supply to the traveller.
2. The **travel provider's supply** is usually valued net of the tour operator's profit. Where the tour operator tells travellers the price of the transport and also charges a fixed rate of commission, the travel provider's supply is the full (gross) value, including the tour operator's profit margin.

7518 Information Sheet 03/96

Airline charter option A tour operator can **convert** a bought-in airline supply to an in-house supply of passenger transport by materially altering it.

To achieve this, HMRC requires that the operator charter a whole aircraft (not just individual seats or blocks of seats) for a specified journey slot during the whole of one holiday season. All other **components** of the supply to passengers (such as catering or airport transfers) must be sourced from elsewhere and not from the airline.

The tour operator is considered to be materially altering the supply, by chartering a whole aircraft but only reselling individual seats.

MEMO POINTS This concession has been withdrawn from 1 April 2015.

Comment It must be considered whether enough has been done to materially alter the bought-in supply. Compare *Nicholas Harvey (t/a Green Express Railtours)* [1998] (VTD 15608).

2. Particular situations

Business customers

7520 Notice 709/5 para 3

Business customers are unable to recover any input tax on travel supplies made to them unless a normal VAT invoice is issued, which cannot happen under TOMS (¶7584).

Such supplies (including use by a firm's employee) fall within **two categories**, depending on whether the customer:
a. consumes the services (that is, makes the trip itself), which are included within TOMS; or
b. resells them, otherwise known as wholesale supplies, which are excluded from TOMS.

Information Sheet 10/07

An **invoice** to a business customer consuming travel services must include a reference to the relevant EU or UK legislation, or one of the following can be indicated:
- "This is a Tour Operators' Margin Scheme supply"; or
- "This supply falls under the Value Added Tax (Tour Operators) Order 1987".

HMRC Brief 21/10

MEMO POINTS Although a VAT invoice cannot be issued to a business customer for supplies under TOMS, HMRC has agreed **special arrangements** to enable businesses to recover VAT incurred on **hotel** rooms occupied by their **employees** which have been reserved by a booking agent (and would therefore normally come under TOMS). These "hotel billback" arrangements essentially involve the agent acting in a disclosed capacity such that the hotel will supply the hotel rooms direct to the employer organisation. HMRC accepts that the invoice may be sent to the booking agent for payment on behalf of the employer.

Incidental supplies

7526 Notice 709/5 para 3.6

A trader who is making incidental supplies of designated travel services can ignore TOMS, provided that all of the following **criteria** are satisfied:
a. the incidental supplies do not include accommodation or passenger transport, or any other normal designated travel supply (¶7508), which is bought in for resale; and
b. the trader does not expect the associated total turnover from the supplies to exceed 1% of normal gross turnover in the next 12 months.

SI 1987/1806 reg 14

Normal **gross turnover** for these purposes is the total value of supplies made in the next 12 months measured by the consideration given.

EXAMPLE

1. Mr D runs a country hotel. He organises car hire, for which he charges £3,000. His expected turnover for the following 12 months is £350,000.
The car hire is outside TOMS because it is not passenger transport and is less than 1% of turnover.

2. Ms E runs a pub and organises taxis to pick up overnight guests from the local station. The related income from this is only 0.3% of total turnover.
Although incidental, taxis are a form of passenger transport and so must be accounted for within TOMS.

3. G Ltd runs a city hotel. It buys in car hire (0.8% of turnover) and tour guides (0.5% of turnover). As the combined supplies exceed 1% of turnover, TOMS applies to both the car hire and tour guiding service.

Comment Following the case of *TP Madgett & RM Baldwin* (see ¶7506), **ancillary supplies** of designated travel services would not cause the trader to use TOMS, even if the value exceeded 1% of turnover. HMRC's guidance still makes no mention of this. Some tour operators have made protective claims (¶3252) based on this case. 7528

Educational trips

It is no longer possible for tour operators to exclude UK trips sold to local authority schools from TOMS, so the recipient cannot recover the VAT charged. This aligns the UK scheme with the EU rules. 7530 Notice 709/5 para 3.4

If the trader is **teaching English as a foreign language** (TEFL), HMRC accepts that any supplies which are covered by the education exemption are excluded from TOMS. This includes both bought-in and in-house supplies. 7532 VATEDU39600

MEMO POINTS 1. The **education exemption** covers all elements which are either necessary for, or closely related to, the supply of a TEFL course, which is held out for sale by a commercial provider - for example, transport, catering, accommodation or even excursions.
2. For a detailed discussion of the **scope of educational supplies** see ¶398.

Interaction with small business schemes

The following table summarises whether cash accounting, annual accounting or the flat rate scheme are possible for a tour operator. 7534 Notice 709/5 paras 4.16 - 4.18

Type of scheme	Can use if TOMS applies?	Details
Cash accounting	x	Because of special tax point rules under TOMS, which are more favourable
Annual accounting	✓	Perform year-end calculation under TOMS and enter on VAT return
Flat rate scheme	x	Specifically excludes TOMS supplies

3. Other supplies

For **separately supplied** goods and services (which are by definition excluded from designated travel services), normal VAT accounting applies. Such supplies are ignored for the purposes of TOMS. Input tax can therefore be recovered as usual on the related costs. If input tax is incurred outside the UK, the tour operator will need either to register in the particular EU member state, or recover the input tax by making a special EU directive claim (¶9845). 7536

If other supplies are **provided as part of a travel package**, the whole package falls within TOMS and the following special rules apply for different types of non-designated travel supply.

a. In-house supplies

If supplied as part of a travel package, TOMS applies, even where separate prices are quoted for the various elements. 7538 Notice 709/5 paras 2.13, 4.7

However, VAT is not applied to the margin in respect of in-house supplies, because they are not designated travel services. Thus input tax can still be recovered as normal on the related costs, and the usual place of supply and VAT liability rules still apply (which could require registration in another EU member state).

The only reason that in-house supplies are included in TOMS is to ensure that the package price is fairly **apportioned** between all the constituent supplies. TOMS calculates VAT on the apportioned selling price (market value or, in certain circumstances, cost plus apportioned margin - see ¶7540).

It can sometimes be difficult to ascertain whether in-house supplies are supplied alone or as part of a package; the principles of composite and mixed supplies (¶310) are used to decide. In particular, a composite zero-rated in-house supply avoids TOMS. For example, the provision of a bought-in limousine service to ferry passengers to and from the airport was held to be an ancillary part of the composite zero-rated air transport supply, so TOMS did not apply.
Virgin Atlantic Airways Ltd [1993] (VTD 11096)

Certain costs may relate to both packaged and separate in-house supplies, in which case an apportionment will be required (¶7630).

7540 If possible, in-house supplies should be valued at their market value for the purpose of apportioning the package price. However, a cost-based method can be used if it is not possible to ascertain market value. A cost-based method is also acceptable to HMRC if there is a standard mark-up in use across all elements of a travel package.

HMRC Brief 27/09

MEMO POINTS HMRC's guidance on the operation of a market value basis for **apportioning the package selling price** between in-house and bought-in components states that the tour operator should estimate a market value for in-house supplies, then deduct this amount from the package selling price to ascertain the turnover relating to designated travel supplies (¶7609).
The guidance further states that market values are subject to the circumstances of each case, although the following caveats should be taken into account:
- the market value must be within the context of the tour operator's business (for example, the price of a scheduled airline flight would not be indicative of the market value of a flight which formed part of a package holiday);
- the market value should be determined on the basis of the price of similar services supplied by the tour operator and not forming part of a package (if relevant, it may be possible to use the price of services supplied by other operators, provided that they can be shown to be comparable); and
- across-the-board averages may be used if correctly weighted and reviewed regularly.

Transport

7542 To be treated as an in-house supply, the **vehicle** must either be owned or hired by the tour operator, and the driver, crew, fuel and so on are then added to it. Several components are therefore amalgamated to create a single supply of passenger transport.

Notice 709/5 para 7.1

Passenger transport is a zero-rated supply in the UK, although this is not the case everywhere in the EU. As the **place** of supply of transport is where it occurs, UK operators may still be liable to VAT on the transport supply elsewhere in the EU.

Notice 709/5 para 7.3

MEMO POINTS 1. A **cruise** can be an in-house supply where the tour operator (or a member of the same VAT group) owns the ship. In addition, the following situations are also treated as in-house supplies:
- exclusive chartering of a ship with deck or engine crew (and possibly hotel, catering or domestic staff) for a period of 2 years or more; or
- hiring of a ship with deck or engine crew, and the tour operator employs or contracts for the services of the other staff.
2. For specific planning **to preserve the zero-rating** of passenger transport see ¶7510.

7544 The following **direct costs** commonly relate to in-house transport:

Notice 709/5 paras 7.5, 7.10

Area	Details
All transport	Depreciation as shown in the audited financial statements [1] Rental and leasing of vehicles Repairs to vehicles Crew and driver costs, including National Insurance where relevant Subsistence costs of the crew or driver Fuel Insurance

Area	Details
Road or rail	Road fund licence Garaging and parking Tolls Ferry costs
Air	Air passenger duty Landing fees Charter fee where relevant Catering charges when chartering Transfer journeys when chartering
Water	Berthing fees Charter fee Hotel, domestic or catering staff when chartering
Note: 1. If an **asset is sold** and the related depreciation has been included as an in-house cost element of a travel package, an adjustment must be made, depending on whether there is a: – profit on disposal, in which case in-house costs are reduced by the profit; or – loss on disposal, in which case in-house costs are increased by the loss.	

Accommodation

In-house supplies are made in the following **circumstances**: **7546** Notice 709/5 para 7.6
– the tour operator owns and runs a hotel;
– accommodation is hired or leased under an agreement where the tour operator must maintain the fabric of the property; and
– bought-in accommodation to which catering or cleaning is added (catered accommodation).

MEMO POINTS A **camp or caravan site** may be the source of an in-house supply if the land is rented and the tour operator installs tents or caravans which are let out. If the whole site is leased, with tents and caravans already present, this is designated travel accommodation. Notice 709/5 para 7.9

The following **direct costs** commonly relate to in-house accommodation: **7548** Notice 709/5 para 7.7
– depreciation as shown in the audited financial statements;
– heating and lighting;
– rates;
– buildings insurance;
– rental of furniture and equipment;
– repairs and cleaning;
– staff costs; and
– catering purchases.

If **depreciation** has been included as an in-house cost element of a travel package and the asset is then sold, an adjustment must be made, depending on whether there is a: Notice 709/5 para 7.10
– profit on disposal, in which case in-house costs are reduced by the profit; or
– loss on disposal, in which case in-house costs are increased by the loss.

Tour guides

HMRC states that the provision of a **specialist** tour guide can be treated as a separate supply in its own right. **7550** Notice 709/5 para 6.10

However, payments to **representatives** who generally meet and greet guests are deemed to be overhead costs within TOMS.

Tour guides will be treated as part of the travel package unless their services are supplied with in-house transport only, in which case a single supply of passenger transport is treated as taking place.

MEMO POINTS 1. If there is any **educational or cultural** element to the specialist in-house tour guide's service, the place of supply is where the service is performed, unless the supply is to a business customer, in which case it will take place where the customer belongs.

2. The **same person** may perform **both functions** (acting both as a tour guide and a representative). In this case the related costs must be apportioned, perhaps on a time basis, and only the tour guide costs included in the TOMS calculation.

Education and training

7552 Notice 709/5 para 7.11

A tour operator may organise a holiday based upon some sort of training, such as a scuba diving course, painting workshop, language course or similar.

A training course requires some or all of the following **elements** (if these are **put together** by the tour operator, that constitutes an exempt in-house supply):
- teachers;
- classroom, lecture room, studio, etc;
- equipment;
- printed materials such as course notes and handouts;
- light and heat; and
- refreshments.

If a **place on a course is purchased** from a third party and sold on as part of a package with a designated supply, such as passenger transport or accommodation, the package is within TOMS.

7554 Notice 709/5 paras 7.12, 7.13

The same approach applies to **conferences**, although TOMS will apply if designated travel (accommodation and/or transport) is provided as part of the conference package.

If TOMS applies, no input tax recovery will be available to the business customer.

---

b. Agency commission

7556 Notice 709/5 para 2.14

A tour operator who is making designated travel supplies but also acts as a disclosed agent can include commission within the calculation when it is **not readily identifiable** (perhaps because it is variable, or not fixed in advance).

Otherwise, commission which is **separately identifiable** must be excluded from TOMS and VAT accounted for under the normal agency rules (¶7115). In practice, this means that the amount received from the customer is excluded from the sales value and the net amount paid to the supplier is excluded from costs.

7558

The **VAT rating** of commission follows the rating for the main supply, so commission is usually standard-rated, with the following exceptions, which occur when the agent is arranging:
- insurance, which can be exempt (¶442);
- passenger transport, which is zero-rated; and
- non-UK accommodation, which is outside the scope of UK VAT.

---

c. Insurance

7560 Notice 709/5 para 6.8

The treatment of insurance depends on the **identity of the insured person** (the traveller or the tour operator) and the terms of the contract between the tour operator and traveller.

If a **named traveller** is the insured person, the tour operator is acting as agent for the insurance provider, unless the insurance is provided free. When acting as agent, the treatment of any commission follows the rules in ¶7556. If the insurance is sold as part of a package, the agent will only be making an exempt supply if the policy price is disclosed to the traveller (this rule also applies to any arrangement fee charged by the agent to the traveller).

If the **tour operator** is the named person, any cost of the policy is excluded from TOMS. However, any charge made to the traveller (including any insurance premium tax) is included in the TOMS sales value.

MEMO POINTS 1. If **free** insurance is offered, the full package price is effectively included in the sales value for TOMS.
2. The supply of insurance may make the tour operator **partly exempt**, although in practice input tax recovery is often not affected, because the tour operator's exempt income is below the de minimis limits (¶2194). Where partial exemption applies, a special method (¶2148) is required, perhaps based on the full value of supplies, transaction count, or floor space. It is advisable to align the VAT year with the financial year in this case. PE 5600
3. **Insurance premium tax** (IPT) is payable on all travel insurance sold through a tour operator. The tour operator will need to register for IPT if charging an arrangement fee.

B. Rules overridden by TOMS

Under TOMS, VAT is calculated on the difference between the total VAT-inclusive amount received from customers for designated travel services and the actual cost to the tour operator of making those supplies. This is measured over the course of a financial year. **7564**

TOMS has its own rules for the place and time of supply, and the VAT rate which applies to each supply within the travel package.

Place of supply

The place of supply of designated travel services depends primarily on where the tour operator is established (¶9688). **7566** Notice 709/5 para 4.6

Tour operator established	Package supplied from establishment in	Place of supply	Implications
In UK only	UK	UK	TOMS applies
In many countries	UK	UK	
	EU	EU	Outside scope of UK VAT, but within EU member state's VAT system
	Outside EU	Outside EU	TOMS does not apply, so normal place of supply rules (¶9682)

Time of supply

There are two **specific methods** to determine the tax point of designated travel packages, the second of which can result in an earlier tax point (which is unlikely to be advantageous). The tour operator must choose one method and apply it consistently. Methods can only be changed in exceptional circumstances and with the written approval of HMRC; it is extremely unusual for a change to be allowed during a financial year. **7568** Notice 709/5 para 4.14; SI 1987/1806 reg 4

Method one The tax point is the **earlier of**: **7570**
- the date of the traveller's departure; and
- the first date that the traveller occupies any accommodation.

EXAMPLE Mr H has booked a Cornish holiday staying in a cottage.
If he has acquired a package which includes coach travel, the tax point will be his date of departure. However, if he is driving himself there, the tax point will be when he first occupies the cottage.

Method two The tax point is the **earliest of**: **7572** Notice 709/5 paras 4.14, 4.15
- the date on which more than 20% of the minimum package price has been paid;
- the date of the traveller's departure; and
- the first date that the traveller occupies any accommodation.

There can be multiple tax points under this method, depending on the size of any instalment payments. If smaller payments are received, a tax point will arise once the cumulative payment exceeds 20% of the package price.

EXAMPLE Ms J has booked a package holiday for £2,000. Her departure date is 1 July. She makes the following payments:

	£	Tax point
1 January when holiday is booked	200	x
1 March	600	✓
1 April	400	✓
1 June	600	✓
31 July	200	x

The 10% deposit of £200 is too small to create a tax point, so it is amalgamated with the payment on 1 March.

The payment on 31 July is after the departure date, so the tax point for that payment falls on 1 July.

VAT liability

7574 Notice 709/5 para 4.9 The VAT liability of a TOMS supply of travel depends on where it is **enjoyed**. If enjoyed within the EU, the supply is standard-rated. If enjoyed outside the EU, the supply is zero-rated.

However, **not** all journeys are undertaken **wholly inside or wholly outside the EU**; in this case the treatment depends on whether there are stops made during the journey. A stop for this purpose does not include a temporary stop for refuelling or comfort breaks, assuming that the passengers cannot interrupt the journey.

There are also special rules for cruises and connected flights.

7576 Notice 709/5 para 4.11 **Journey with no stops** If the journey **begins or ends** outside the EU, the supply is wholly outside the EU.

7578 Notice 709/5 para 4.12 **Stops in the journey** Where there are stops in a journey which take place **both inside and outside the EU**, the TOMS margin must be apportioned between the EU and non-EU elements of the journey.

The method of apportionment must give a fair and reasonable result; HMRC suggests either mileage or the number of nights as possible methods.

7580 Notice 709/5 para 4.13 **Cruises** The margin should be apportioned in the same way as a journey with stops. A common basis is to use days spent inside and outside the EU according to the itinerary.

The ship is outside the EU when it **leaves a non-EU port** until it reaches an EU port.

Similarly the ship is inside the EU when it **leaves an EU port** until it reaches a non-EU port.

However, when **only visiting non-EU ports** after leaving the UK, the whole cruise is a non-EU supply.

EXAMPLE A cruise ship sales from Southampton for a cruise around the Caribbean. The itinerary is as follows:

Date	Itinerary	Location for TOMS
30 June	Leave Southampton dock	Inside EU
3 July	Madeira for 1 day	Inside EU
4 July	Leave Madeira	Inside EU
9 July	Arrive Georgetown	Inside EU
10 July - 16 July	Various ports in Caribbean	Outside EU
17 July	Leave Antigua	Outside EU
25 July	Arrive Southampton	Outside EU

For the purposes of TOMS, the ship spends 10 days inside the EU (30 June until 9 July) and 16 days outside the EU (10 July until 25 July).

Connecting flights Often a journey will involve an **intra-EU** connecting flight, in which case it is necessary to determine whether it is a separate journey in its own right or an additional part of the international flight (in which case the whole journey is treated as a non-EU supply). 7582 Notice 709/5 para 4.13

For a subsequent **international flight**, the connecting flight will be part of a single journey if the connection with the international flight is made within 24 hours of the scheduled arrival time of the connecting flight.

Where the subsequent flight is **domestic**, the period within which the connection must occur is only 6 hours.

EXAMPLE

1. Mr K is flying from Manchester to Zurich and on to New York. The scheduled time of arrival of the Manchester flight in Zurich is 15.30.
Provided that the flight for New York leaves by 15.30 the next day, the Manchester flight will be connected with it and both flights will be non-EU journeys.

2. Ms L is flying from Los Angeles to London Heathrow and then on to Edinburgh. The US flight is scheduled to land at 08.00 and the Edinburgh flight leaves at 16.00.
As the domestic flight is outside the 6-hour time limit, the flights are not connected. So for VAT purposes, the first flight is outside the EU and the second is within the EU.

Invoicing

VAT invoices cannot be issued for designated travel supplies, because the tour operator does not calculate the VAT until the end of the financial year. Consequently the VAT element is not known at the time of supply. 7584 Notice 709/5 para 4.20

This has no impact on **consumers** who are not VAT-registered.

For **business customers** who wish to reclaim VAT see ¶7520.

Bad debts

Bad debt relief is **restricted** to an amount which represents the VAT fraction of the profit margin on the outstanding debt. Relief cannot be **claimed** before the end of the financial year in which the supplies were made. 7586 Notice 709/5 para 6.9

For this purpose the **profit margin** is the percentage calculated at the year end (¶7602 and ¶7609+), not the provisional margin used throughout the year. In practice, the selling price of packages is reduced for the price of the debtor's package and the TOMS calculation then automatically gives bad debt relief.

EXAMPLE M Ltd wishes to claim bad debt relief in respect of a standard-rated travel supply made in June with a selling price of £3,000. M Ltd's financial year end is 31 December. When M Ltd performs the year-end calculation, the margin is found to be 52%.
So M Ltd can claim bad debt relief of £260. (£3,000 x 52% x 1/6)

C. Calculation of VAT

The TOMS calculation comprises two elements: 7590 Notice 709/5 para 5

a. a provisional computation for each VAT period, which estimates the VAT position; and

b. a year-end computation, which finalises the VAT liability and is accounted for on the next VAT return after the financial year end.

Unlike most other VAT calculations, the VAT year is irrelevant, although it is advisable to align the VAT year with the financial year, as this makes it easier to perform the TOMS calculation (and gives more time). A tour operator submitting quarterly VAT returns who has aligned the VAT year with the financial year will have 4 months in which to make the calculation.

Overview

7592 Both computations (¶7604) work by deducting the market value of in-house supplies and then **apportioning** the remaining total margin between different sorts of TOMS supplies and between different VAT rates, with output tax payable on the standard-rated elements. The apportionment is based on total costs incurred during the year, which makes it unnecessary to calculate the margin on each transaction individually. (As noted at ¶7540, if it is not possible to ascertain the market value of in-house supplies, the total margin can be apportioned between the different TOMS supplies in proportion to the cost of each type of supply.)

A **simpler** method of calculation (¶7598) must be used when all the components of the travel packages are standard-rated, which means that the operator is not making any non-EU supplies (although operators with minor zero-rated supplies may use the simple method if the saved administration costs outweigh the extra VAT liability). If unsure whether the simple method is available, the operator should use the full calculation, as this gives a more accurate, and potentially lower, VAT liability.

MEMO POINTS 1. The choice of method must be made carefully, because if using the **simple method**, the operator cannot recalculate the VAT liability under the full method.

Notice 709/5 para 5.8
2. If the **audited accounts** are adjusted from those accounts which are used as the basis of the TOMS calculation, the computation must be reworked. Any difference should be reported as a VAT error (¶3014).

7593 Notice 709/5 para 5.1 - 5.2; Notice 709/5 TL3
Where some supplies are not standard-rated, the value of in-house and agency supplies must be deducted from total supplies, so that VAT can be applied separately to the margin on designated travel services and other, non-designated supplies. In-house supplies should be deducted at their market value, unless market value cannot be ascertained, or a standard mark-up is in use across all elements of the travel package, in which case a cost-based method of apportionment is permitted.

7594 If market value cannot be ascertained, the same **percentage margin** will be applied across all elements of the package. So if 40% of total direct costs relate to standard-rated margin supplies, the calculation treats 40% of total profit as relating to those supplies. This has the potential to result in an unfair VAT liability - for example, for theatre trips involving zero-rated coach transport, the coach company may make minimal actual profit on the standard-rated theatre ticket. A tour operator who is making both EU and non-EU supplies, with different margins, should also consider performing separate calculations (¶7616).

Change of status

7596 A change of entity may occur when a company joins a VAT group, on incorporation, or on the taking on of a partner. In such situations the tour operator has a **choice between**:
- performing an adjustment at the date of change; or
- continuing to use the provisional percentage as normal until the next financial year end.

Where a tour operator **joins an entity** (such as a VAT group or company) which is itself already a tour operator using TOMS, strictly the travel supplies made by both must be amalgamated within one TOMS calculation. To simplify the situation, the consolidation can be delayed until the financial year immediately following the change, so that in the year of joining, two separate calculations are completed and declared on the same VAT return.

When a tour operator **ceases to make any travel package supplies**, an annual adjustment must be performed at the date of leaving TOMS, for the period from the start of the financial year.

Comment This paragraph is based on the content of the former HMRC Manual V1-23 Chapter 12. This manual has been withdrawn but HMRC has not announced any change in its guidance.

1. Simple method

Accounting for VAT during the year

When **first using TOMS** the tour operator must apply a provisional percentage to the VAT-inclusive selling price of all travel packages sold during the VAT period. The standard-rate VAT fraction (1/6) is then applied to calculate the overall VAT liability for each VAT period. 7598 Notice 709/5 para 5.13

The provisional percentage can be **based on** any reasonable method, including the following:
- previous trading figures;
- projected costings and margins; or
- actual trading figures (monthly or quarterly).

EXAMPLE Mr N has just started to use TOMS. He has sold £60,000 of travel packages during the last quarter. Looking at his previous trading figures, he estimates that a reasonable provisional percentage would be 53%.
The quarter's VAT is calculated as follows:

		£
Provisional amount	60,000 × 53%	31,800.00
Output VAT	31,800 × 1/6	5,300.00

Note:
If a rate change occurs in the middle of a VAT period, two calculations should be completed:
- from the beginning of the VAT period to the day before the rate change; and
- from the date of the rate change to the end of the VAT period.

If Mr N's first quarter had ended on 28 February 2011, he would have needed to split this into two periods: from 1 December 2010 to 3 January 2011, and from 4 January 2011 to 28 February 2011, and total up his sales accordingly for each period. If he had sales of £40,000 for the period to 3 January 2011 and £20,000 thereafter, the calculation becomes:

		£	£
Period to 3 January 2011			
Provisional amount	40,000 × 53%	21,200	
Output VAT	21,200 × 7/47		3,157.45
Period ended 28 February 2011			
Provisional amount	20,000 × 53%	10,600	
Output VAT	10,600 × 1/6		1,766.67
Total VAT due			4,924.12

For a tour operator who has **already performed a year-end adjustment**, the previous year's actual figures are used instead of an estimate. The percentage to use instead of the provisional percentage is: 7600 Notice 709/5 para 12

$$(A - B) / A$$

where:
- A is the total VAT-inclusive selling price of all designated travel services and TOMS packages for the previous year (total income within TOMS); and
- B is the total VAT-inclusive purchase price of designated travel services (as included in figure A).

The resulting percentage is applied to actual sales during the year and multiplied by the VAT fraction (1/6) to arrive at the VAT to be accounted for during the year.

Year-end calculation

The **actual VAT liability** for the financial year just ended is calculated using this formula: 7602 Notice 709/5 para 11

$$(A - B) \times 1/6$$

where:
- A is the total VAT-inclusive selling price of all designated travel services and TOMS packages for the previous year (total income within TOMS); and
- B is the total VAT-inclusive purchase price of designated travel services (as included in figure A).

If a VAT rate change occurs in the middle of a financial year, two calculations should be completed:
- from the beginning of the financial year to the day before the rate change; and
- from the date of the rate change to the end of the financial year.

7603 The result is **compared with** the cumulative output tax already declared for the year and if there is a:
- shortfall, the balance must be paid to HMRC; or
- excess payment, the balance will be refunded.

The adjustment is made on the VAT return for the period following the year end.

EXAMPLE Mr N (from ¶7598) has now reached his year end. He provides UK hotel accommodation (which is bought-in) and in-house coach travel for travellers to reach their destination.
Mr N's VAT-inclusive turnover is £400,000. The cost of the hotels is £130,000; the coach travel costs £45,000.
As Mr N estimated his margin at 53%, he has accounted for output tax of £35,333.33. (400,000 × 53% × 1/6)
The annual adjustment is calculated as follows:

		£	£
Total VAT-inclusive turnover			400,000
Less: Cost of hotels		130,000	
Cost of coaches		45,000	
			(175,000)
Margin			225,000
Output tax	225,000 × 1/6		37,500.00
Less: Output tax already disclosed			(35,333.33)
Amount due to HMRC			2,166.67

Note:
If Mr N's first financial year had ended on 30 November 2011, he would have needed to split this into two periods because of the **change in VAT rate** on 4 January 2011. The periods would run from 1 December 2010 to 3 January 2011 and from 4 January 2011 to 30 November 2011.
For the period to 3 January 2011, he has sales of £40,000 (¶7598), so for the period to 30 November 2011, he had sales of £360,000.
The annual adjustment is calculated as follows:

		£	£
Proportion of turnover attributable to the period to 3 January 2011	40,000 / 400,000	10%	
Margin attributable to the initial period	225,000 × 10%	22,500	
Output tax	22,500 × 7/47		3,351.06
Proportion of turnover attributable to period ended 30 November 2011	360,000 / 400,000	90%	
Margin attributable to period ended 30 November 2011	225,000 × 90%	202,500	
Output tax	202,500 × 1/6		33,750.00
			37,101.06
Less: Output tax already disclosed (£40,000 × 53% × 7/47) + (360,000 × 53% × 1/6)			(34,957.45)
Amount due to HMRC			2,143.61

2. All other situations

Accounting for VAT during the year

Using TOMS for the first time For tour operators who are using TOMS for the first time, the rules at ¶7598 apply. 7604

Already performed a year-end adjustment For a tour operator who has used TOMS for at least a year, it will be possible to calculate from the most recent year-end calculation the proportion which VAT bore to total sales. That figure, multiplied by sales during the current VAT accounting period, will give the VAT which should be accounted for in the current accounting period. 7606 Notice 709/5 para 10

Strictly, the tour operator should find the amount on which standard-rated VAT was calculated at the last year-end calculation. That figure as a proportion of total sales should be multiplied by sales during the current VAT accounting period, then multiplied by the standard-rate VAT fraction to give the VAT which should be accounted for in the current accounting period. However, the simpler formula will give the same answer unless there is a change of VAT rate during the year, in which case the longer version should be used in order to apply the correct standard-rate VAT fraction. 7608

Year-end calculation

The basic calculation deducts **in-house supplies at market value** from total sales. 7609 Notice 709/5 para 8

EXAMPLE P Ltd has sold travel packages in the last year with a sales value of £100,000. It has accounted for VAT of £5,900 already. The market value of its standard-rated in-house supplies is £30,000. Bought-in costs are as follows:

	£	£
Standard-rated	7,500	
Zero-rated	25,000	
		32,500

P Ltd calculates the overall output tax liability as follows:

		£	£
Total VAT-inclusive turnover		100,000.00	
Less: Market value of in-house supplies		(30,000.00)	
Turnover attributable to designated travel			70,000.00
Less: Standard-rated costs		7,500.00	
Zero-rated costs		25,000.00	
			(32,500 00)
Margin			37,500.00
Margin on standard-rated designated travel	$37{,}500 \times \frac{7{,}500}{32{,}500}$		8,653.85
Output tax due on designated travel	8,653.85 × 1/6	1,442.31	
Output tax due on in-house supplies	30,000 × 1/6	5,000.00	
			6,442.31
Less: Output tax already disclosed			(5,900.00)
Amount due to HMRC			542.31

The TOMS year-end calculation is carried out as shown in the example at ¶7609. However, the following diagram and the examples at ¶7612 and ¶7614 describe the more complicated scenario where it is not possible to ascertain the market value of in-house supplies. 7610

MEMO POINTS For the **full detailed** calculation as published by HMRC, which comprises in excess of 30 steps, see ¶9982.

	All figures VAT-inclusive			
	Designated travel	**In-house**	**Agency commission**	**Total**
1 Total sales of travel packages for the year (¶7620)				X
2 Costs of every element of the travel packages (¶7624)	X	X	X	(X)
3 Calculate overall margin				X
4 Apportion margin on basis of cost between every VAT rate within each element	X	X	X	(X)
5 Calculate output tax on standard-rated elements, using VAT fraction (¶7636)	Margin × 1/6	(Cost + margin) × 1/6	Margin × 1/6	
6 Compare result of step 5 with output tax already declared in year				
7 Calculate sales values	Margin - VAT	(Cost + margin) - VAT	Margin	

7612 The following examples give a simple and then more complex scenario.

EXAMPLE R Ltd has sold travel packages for £950,000 during the last financial year ended 31 December. The packages only include designated travel. Standard-rated costs were £300,000 and zero-rated costs £150,000. R Ltd has already accounted for output tax of £54,000 during the year. R Ltd calculates its overall output tax liability as follows:

		£	£
Total VAT-inclusive turnover			950,000.00
Less: Standard-rated costs		300,000.00	
Zero-rated costs		150,000.00	
			(450,000.00)
Margin			500,000.00
Standard-rated margin	$500{,}000 \times \frac{300{,}000}{450{,}000}$		333,333.33
Output tax	333,333 × 1/6		55,555.56
Less: Output tax already disclosed			(54,000.00)
Amount due to HMRC (entered on VAT return for period ended 31 March)			1,555.56

The sales value is £277,777.77. (£333,333.33 - £55,555.56)

Note:
If R Ltd's financial year had ended on 30 April 2011, it would be necessary to split the turnover figure between the following two periods because of the **change in VAT rate** on 4 January 2011: from 1 May 2010 to 3 January 2011 and from 4 January 2011 to 30 April 2011.

For the period to 3 January 2011 sales were £750,000; for the period to 30 April 2011 sales were £200,000. Standard-rated costs were £300,000 and zero-rated costs £150,000. R Ltd has already accounted for output tax of £49,000 during the year.
The annual adjustment would be calculated as follows:

		£	£
Total VAT-inclusive turnover			950,000.00
Less: Standard-rated costs		300,000.00	
Zero-rated costs		150,000.00	
			(450,000.00)
Margin			500,000.00
Proportion of turnover attributable to period to 3 January 2011	$\frac{750{,}000}{950{,}000}$	78.95%	
Margin attributable to period to 3 January 2011	500,000 × 78.95%	394,750.00	
Standard-rated margin	$394{,}750 \times \frac{300{,}000}{450{,}000}$	263,166.67	
Output tax	263,166.67 × 7/47		39,195.04
Proportion of turnover attributable to the period ended 30 April 2011	$\frac{200{,}000}{950{,}000}$	21.05%	
Margin attributable to period to 30 April 2011	500,000 × 21.05%	105,250.00	
Standard-rated margin	$105{,}250 \times \frac{300{,}000}{450{,}000}$	70,166.67	
Output tax	70,166.67 × 1/6		11,694.45
Total output tax			50,889.49
Less: Output tax already disclosed			(49,000.00)
Amount due to HMRC			1,889.49

The sales value is £282,443.85. (£263,166.67 + £70,166.67 - £50,889.49)

EXAMPLE S Ltd has sold travel packages totalling £2 million during the financial year ended 31 **7614**
December. It has accounted for VAT of £135,000. The packages were a mixture of designated travel, in-house supplies and standard-rated agency commission. The relevant costs (including VAT unless indicated otherwise) were as follows:

	£	
Standard-rated designated travel	600,000	
Zero-rated designated travel (outside EU)	100,000	
Standard-rated in-house supplies	140,000	Excluding VAT
Zero-rated in-house supplies	60,000	Excluding VAT
Exempt in-house supplies	50,000	
Standard-rated agency commission	20,000	
	970,000	

The overall output tax liability is calculated as follows:

		£	£	£
Total VAT-inclusive turnover				2,000,000
Costs				
Designated travel - standard-rated			600,000	
Designated travel - zero-rated			100,000	
In-house - standard-rated		140,000		
Add VAT	140,000 × 20%	28,000		
			168,000	
In-house - zero-rated			60,000	
In-house - exempt			50,000	
Agency - standard-rated			20,000	
				(998,000)
Margin				1,002,000

		£	£
Designated travel - standard-rated margin	$1{,}002{,}000 \times \frac{600{,}000}{998{,}000}$	602,404.81	
Output tax due on designated travel	£602,404.81 × 1/6		100,400.80
In-house - standard-rated margin	$1{,}002{,}000 \times \frac{168{,}000}{998{,}000}$	168,673.35	
In-house - standard-rated cost		168,000.00	
In-house - standard-rated selling price		336,673.35	
Output tax due on in-house supplies	£336,673.35 × 1/6		56,112.23
Agency commission margin	$1{,}002{,}000 \times \frac{20{,}000}{998{,}000}$	20,080.16	
Output tax due on agency commission	£20,080.16 × 1/6		3,346.69
Total output tax liability			159,859.72
Sales values are as follows:			
		£	£
Designated travel - standard-rated	£602,404.81 - £100,400.80		502,004.01
Designated travel - zero-rated			
Margin	$1{,}002{,}000 \times \frac{100{,}000}{998{,}000}$		100,400.80
In-house - standard-rated	£336,673.35 - £56,112.23		280,561.12
In-house - zero-rated			
Cost		60,000.00	
Margin	$1{,}002{,}000 \times \frac{60{,}000}{998{,}000}$	60,240.48	
			120,240.48
In-house - exempt			
Cost		50,000.00	
Margin	$1{,}002{,}000 \times \frac{50{,}000}{998{,}000}$	50,200.40	
			100,200.40
Agency commission standard-rated	£20,080.16 - £3,346.69		16,733.47
Total outputs to enter in box 6 of VAT return			1,120,140

Making EU and non-EU supplies

7616 Notice 709/5 para 5.9

A tour operator who makes supplies which are **enjoyed outside the EU** may elect to make separate calculations for those supplies, with the written permission of HMRC. This would be useful if the mark-up on non-EU supplies is higher than on EU supplies.

This concession also applies to the **simple calculation** (although this is of limited relevance, as most operators would choose to perform the full calculation due to the zero-rated non-EU supplies).

Notice 709/5 para 5.10

MEMO POINTS 1. HMRC will only give **permission** for separate calculations if it is satisfied that the tour operator has the necessary accounting systems, and can maintain adequate records, to support a dual calculation.

2. A package which is enjoyed **partly** inside and partly outside the EU can only be included in the EU calculation (i.e. the whole package's selling price and direct costs).

EXAMPLE T Ltd makes travel supplies only and is deciding whether to opt to do separate calculations for EU and non-EU supplies. The calculations compare as follows:

		Combined £	EU £	Non-EU £
Sales		100,000	60,000	40,000
Costs		(40,000)	(25,000)	(15,000)
Margin		60,000	35,000	25,000
Standard-rated margin	(for the combined calculation $\frac{25,000}{40,000}$ × £60,000)	37,500	35,000	-
Output tax @ 1/6		6,250.00	5,833.33	Nil

So T Ltd would be liable to less UK VAT by performing separate calculations.

Once an election has been made to do a single calculation or separate calculations, it can only be **changed** at the start of the following financial year (that is, no later than the due date of the first VAT return for the year). Permission to do this must be requested in writing and in advance of the financial year in question, and will not be granted retrospectively. **7618** Notice 709/5 para 5.10

Throughout the next financial year, the provisional calculation will still be made under the previous method chosen by the tour operator. The annual adjustment will then reflect the new choice.

EXAMPLE W Ltd has a financial year ended 30 June and is currently performing one calculation for both EU and non-EU supplies. HMRC grants permission in July for separate calculations to be completed. The provisional calculations for the VAT periods from July onwards will still use the total selling price of EU and non-EU supplies combined, because the percentage has been computed under the single calculation.
For the annual adjustment, W Ltd can then perform two separate calculations. Thereafter W Ltd has percentages available to use in the provisional calculations for separate EU and non-EU supplies.

3. Elements important to year-end calculations

Selling price

Any consideration received in **foreign currency** is converted using the general method (¶9032). **7620** Notice 709/5 para 6.1

Certain irregular items are specifically **excluded** or **included** from the selling price as shown in the following table:

Item	Included
Customer refunds	x
Cancellation fees and forfeited deposits	x
Monies from customers who do not turn up	✓
Administration fees which relate to customer's travel	✓
Full amount paid by customer even if routed through an agent who only pays the tour operator a net amount after deducting commission	✓
Surcharges	✓
Air passenger duty	✓
Gross value of supply made as agent when commission is not readily identifiable (¶7556)	✓

Discounts given If the tour operator sells a package through an **agent** to a customer who pays a discounted price, the amount to be accounted for under TOMS depends on the circumstances of the discount. **7622** Notice 709/5 para 6.1

If the agent grants the discount (of which the tour operator may be unaware) to the customer but passes on the full price to the operator, the operator's selling price is the full price (that is, the amount paid by the customer plus the discount by the agent). *C&E v First Choice Holidays plc* [2004]

If the tour operator agrees the discount and **receives only the reduced amount** from the agent, only the reduced amount is to be used when calculating the selling price.

Costs

7624 Notice 709/5 para 6.3

The relevant costs **exclude** indirect costs and overheads (¶7500) but **include** supplier discounts, retrospective rebates and air passenger duty.

Costs are recognised on an accruals **basis** (so all costs relating to the sales are included, irrespective of invoice date, tax point, or payment date), except those which have yet to be invoiced because the amount is not certain. A TOMS recalculation can be completed if necessary when the invoice is subsequently received.

It is particularly important to ensure that all costs relating to **zero-rated supplies** are fully included, as otherwise the operator's VAT liability will be increased on two counts:
- the margin itself will be artificially inflated; and
- the margin apportioned to standard-rated supplies will be overstated.

7626 Notice 709/5 para 6.6

Foreign currency When converting foreign currency to sterling, **HMRC prescribes** five acceptable **methods** and states that no other method may be used. The same method must be used throughout the financial year.

In practice, none of the prescribed methods are normally used because they do not correspond to the methods applied under general accounting practice, so that tour operators tend instead to use the figures in their financial accounts. In theory this is open to challenge by HMRC, although a tour operator applying a logical method consistently should be able to argue the case strongly.

The prescribed methods are as follows:
a. the exchange rate published in the *Financial Times* using the Federation of Tour Operators' base rate which applies at the time of costing by the supplier;
b. the commercial exchange rate current at the time the supplies in the brochure were costed;
c. the rate published in the *Financial Times* at the date of payment for the supplies;
d. the exchange rate applicable to the purchase of foreign currency used to pay the supplier; or
e. the period rate of exchange published by HMRC which applied at the time that payment was made for the supplies.

To **change to a new method**, the tour operator should apply for permission from HMRC by the due date of the first VAT return in the new financial year.

7628 Notice 709/5 para 6.5

In-house supplies If not using market value, the calculation includes the VAT-inclusive costs of packaged in-house supplies to the extent that they form part of a TOMS package. The exact treatment depends on the VAT rating of the supply, as shown in the following table.

VAT rating of in-house supply	Examples	Value to include in step 2 of full calculation (¶7610+)
Standard-rated	Hotel owned and run in the UK	VAT-exclusive costs (because input tax will have been recovered), then add 20%
Zero-rated	Coach operator provides coach travel as part of a UK holiday	VAT-exclusive costs
Exempt	Teaching	VAT-inclusive costs (some irrecoverable VAT may be incurred anyway)

VAT rating of in-house supply	Examples	Value to include in step 2 of full calculation (¶7610+)
Outside scope of UK VAT	Hotel owned and run outside the UK	VAT-exclusive costs (because input tax will have been recovered), and then add local rate of VAT This may require separate subtotals where different countries are involved

Certain costs may **relate to both** TOMS in-house supplies and to supplies which are accounted for outside TOMS. In this case the relevant costs should be apportioned as follows: **7630** Notice 709/5 paras 7.4, 7.8

Situation	Detail	Apportion based on
Transport	Road or rail vehicle	Mileage
	Air	Hours flown
	Sea	Number of days
Accommodation	Direct costs	Guest days or days booked
	Overheads (light and heat, insurance, rates, etc)	Floor space

Agency commissions received The treatment of commissions received for agency supplies arranged as part of a margin scheme depends on whether the commission is: **7632** Notice 709/5 para 6.7

– **readily identifiable**, in which case both the commission and the consideration for the supply arranged are excluded from the TOMS calculations; or

– **not readily identifiable**, in which case the gross amount paid by the traveller and the net amount paid to the principal are both included in the TOMS calculations, while at the end of the year (step 22) the commission and the consideration for the supply arranged must both be excluded.

Unforeseen costs Sometimes a tour operator will have to incur extra costs as a result of unforeseen events, such as delays and cancellations. These costs should be included in the TOMS calculation **unless** either the expense is met by a third party, or it relates directly to separately supplied in-house supplies. **7634** Notice 709/5 para 6.11

VAT fraction

The VAT fraction currently **required** is 1/6, which gives standard-rate VAT on a VAT-inclusive figure. **7636**

Sales values

The sales values to enter on the VAT return are **calculated** as shown in the following table. Cost means the values from ¶7628. **7638** Notice 709/5

Type of supply	VAT rating	Calculation
Designated travel	Standard-rated	Margin less VAT
	Zero-rated	Margin
In-house	Standard-rated	Cost plus margin less VAT or market value
	Zero-rated	Cost plus margin or market value
	Exempt	Cost plus margin or market value
	Outside scope of UK VAT	Cost plus margin or market value
Agency commission	Not exempt	Margin less VAT

VAT return entries

7640 The following table summarises how a tour operator completes a VAT return:

Box on VAT return	Item
1	Current period provisional output tax plus annual adjustment if first return after year end
4	Input tax on non-TOMS supplies
6	Margin on TOMS supplies and commission; selling price of everything else
7	Overheads and costs of in-house supplies

Reconciliation to gross profit

7642 It is useful to check the TOMS calculation by performing a reconciliation to the gross profit shown in the financial statements. The most common **reconciling items** will be:
- travel agent commission;
- insurance commission;
- cancellation income; and
- the VAT due under TOMS, which is usually deducted from turnover as shown in the accounts.

EXAMPLE 1. R Ltd (from the example in ¶7612) has a profit and loss account as follows:

	£	£
Turnover		
Sales of travel packages	950,000	
TOMS VAT	(55,555)	
Cancellations	1,000	
Insurance	12,000	
		907,445
Cost of sales		
EU bought-in accommodation	300,000	
Non-EU bought-in accommodation	150,000	
Insurance	6,000	
		(456,000)
Gross profit		451,445

The reconciliation to the TOMS margin of £500,000 is as follows:

	£	£
Gross profit per financial statements		451,445
Turnover adjustments		
Add: TOMS VAT	55,555	
Less: Cancellation	(1,000)	
Insurance	(12,000)	
		42,555
Cost of sales adjustments		
Add: Insurance cost		6,000
Agrees to TOMS margin		500,000

EXAMPLE 2. S Ltd (from the example in ¶7614) has a profit and loss account as follows:

	£	£
Turnover		
Sales of travel packages	2,000,000	
TOMS VAT	(159,860)	
Cancellations	5,000	
Insurance	48,000	
Agent commission	(30,000)	
		1,863,140
Cost of sales		
EU bought-in accommodation	600,000	
Non-EU bought-in accommodation	100,000	
Owned hotels	140,000	
Owned coaches	60,000	
Agency costs	20,000	
Educational supplies	50,000	
Insurance	25,000	
		(995,000)
Gross profit		868,140

The reconciliation to the TOMS margin of £1,002,000 is as follows:

	£	£
Gross profit per financial statements		868,140
Turnover adjustments		
Add: TOMS VAT	159,860	
Agent commission	30,000	
Less: Cancellations	(5,000)	
Insurance	(48,000)	
		136,860
Cost of sales adjustments		
Add: Insurance cost	25,000	
Less: VAT on standard-rated in-house supplies	(28,000)	
		(3,000)
Agrees to TOMS margin		1,002,000

Records

Records must be kept of the: **7644** Notice 709/5 para 5.6
- total **selling price** for travel package supplies; and
- direct **costs** of those supplies.

In addition, the tour operator must keep records of the various **VAT liabilities** for each supply.

Type of supply	VAT liabilities
Travel package	– standard-rated – zero-rated
In-house supply	– standard-rated – zero-rated – exempt – outside the scope of VAT
Agency commission	– standard-rated – zero-rated – exempt – outside the scope of VAT

CHAPTER 10

Barristers

OUTLINE ¶¶

Barristers operate in an unusual business environment, which necessitates some special VAT rules. 7700

Terminology

Barristers in England and Wales are "called to the bar" by one of the four Inns of Court in London. In Northern Ireland barristers are controlled by the Inns of Court of Northern Ireland. 7702

Barristers in Scotland are known as **advocates** and are members of the Faculty of Advocates.

SECTION 1

Activities

Working practices

Barristers are prevented from practising in partnerships, and although several barristers will share **chambers** (known as a stable in Scotland), each barrister will be VAT-registered as a sole trader. 7710

In England and Wales the **senior clerk** undertakes all the administration of the chambers, including:
- acting as personal assistant;
- negotiating fees;
- dealing with fee notes and payments; and
- updating the accounting records.

The senior clerk may also keep each barrister's VAT account and submit VAT returns, although larger chambers tend to employ a practice manager for this purpose.

MEMO POINTS 1. Some chambers may set up a **managing company** or trade protection association to deal with all administration; in this case the staff will be employed by the company. The company then charges each barrister for its services.

2. In **Scotland** the Faculty deals with all administration, for which a commission based on total fees is payable. The Faculty issues fee notes on the advocate's behalf, collecting the amounts due from the client and paying it over. It issues statements which show output tax and input tax in respect of all income and expenses which go through the Faculty. All advocates must register for VAT (¶2640+), irrespective of the level of turnover, and are responsible for their own VAT returns.
3. In **Northern Ireland** barristers manage their own affairs.

Business interests

7712 Each barrister is registered as an individual. It follows that all of a barrister's business activities must be taken into account when considering the need to register for VAT (¶2633, ¶2640+).

7714 **Practice work** Direct barrister work **covers**:
- understanding and interpreting the law;
- mastering and managing legal briefs (cases);
- researching relevant points of law;
- writing opinions and advising solicitors and other professionals;
- preparing cases for court, including holding client conferences, preparing legal arguments, etc;
- presenting arguments in court;
- examining and cross-examining witnesses;
- advising on matters of law and evidence;
- drafting legal documents; and
- negotiating settlements.

All such work usually **originates** with a solicitor, although accountants and tax advisers can also directly instruct a barrister.

7716 **Other activities** The following are frequently undertaken by a barrister, but are not governed by the special VAT rules:
- writing legal articles for journals;
- lecturing; and
- editing legal texts.

Any **personal business** interests, such as farming, are also excluded.

7718 s 94(4) VATA 1994 Income from **offices** obtained as a result of being a barrister is subject to VAT, unless the office is treated as an employment, in which case the related income is outside the scope of VAT.

7720 VBNB41400 If a barrister takes up any of the following part-time **judicial appointments**, all related income is outside the scope of VAT (the VAT treatment of appointments which are not named in the table is dependent on the particular facts).

Location	Type of office	Name
England and Wales	Judge	Deputy High Court Judge
		Deputy Circuit Judge
	Recorder	Recorder
		Assistant Recorder
	Magistrate	Deputy Metropolitan Magistrate
		Deputy Provincial Stipendiary Magistrate
	Registrar	Deputy County Court and District Registrar
		Deputy Master or Registrar of the Supreme Court or High Court
		Deputy Assistant Chancery Registrar
	Coroner	Coroner
		Deputy and Assistant Coroner
	Other	Dean of the Court of Arches
		Auditor of the Province of York
		Assistant Local Government Boundary Commissioner

Location	Type of office	Name
Scotland		Temporary Supreme Court Judge
		Temporary Sheriff Principal
		Temporary Sheriff

SECTION 2

Accounting for VAT

Barristers must ensure that they are aware of the following rules when completing their VAT returns: **7730**
- place of supply;
- time of supply;
- input tax reclaims; and
- what happens when ceasing to practise.

Simplification schemes

For barristers with **annual taxable turnover** of less than: **7732**
- £150,000, the flat rate scheme, which allows a flat rate of VAT to be charged on all income, may be beneficial (see ¶4635+ for further details); or
- £1,350,000, the annual accounting scheme would reduce the number of returns required, although instalment payments of VAT must normally be made (see ¶4745+ for further details).

A. Place of supply

The main supply made by a barrister is of legal advice, which is a service. **7736**

Legal advice

Except in cases involving land, a barrister provides legal services where the client is located (where the supply is business-to-business). **7738**

MEMO POINTS Supplies relating to **land** always take place where the land is located (¶9714+).

It is vital to identify who the **client** is, in order to apply the correct VAT rules. In most cases the barrister's client is a solicitor (or instructing adviser), who is located at a business establishment (¶9688+). It is therefore usually irrelevant where the solicitor's own client is based. **7740**

The VAT treatment is as follows.

Location of solicitor	Place of supply	VAT treatment
UK	UK	Standard-rated supply
Other EU member state	Other EU member state	Outside the scope of UK VAT[1]
Outside EU	Outside UK	Outside scope with right to recover input tax[2]

Note:
1. Only if the solicitor's VAT number is held, or some other evidence that the supply is made for the purposes of the recipient's business. Otherwise the supply will be deemed to take place in the UK and will be standard-rated.
2. Local taxes may also apply.

Asylum work

7742 Notice 741A para 3.5.2 When **acting directly for** asylum seekers and other persons from outside the EU without permission to remain in the UK (meaning that the barrister is not engaged by a solicitor), the barrister's services are supplied in the client's country of origin. This rule applies for legal advice relating to an application to remain in the UK.

MEMO POINTS 1. If an individual has **no country of origin**, the place of supply is the UK.
2. If permission to remain **expires or is revoked**, the individual is treated as belonging in the UK until the appeals process is exhausted.

B. Time of supply

What is the problem?

7746 Any payments received by a barrister for practice work are not made under contract but constitute an honorarium. This means that the barrister is unable to recover **debts** by the usual means - that is, suing for payment or proving a debt in bankruptcy proceedings.

Therefore having to account for VAT before payment is received would leave the barrister in a poor position.

MEMO POINTS 1. The usual **paperwork cycle** starts with the clerk negotiating a fee with the client. Once the barrister has performed the work, the clerk then issues a request for payment (plus further reminders if necessary). Once paid, the clerk then issues a receipted fee note which becomes the client's VAT invoice.
2. In respect of **legal aid**, a payment may cover many cases at once. The clerk ensures that the payment is allocated correctly. However, once a case has finished, the barrister's remuneration may be changed by a "taxing master", which means that the original receipted fee note will be fully credited and a new fee note rendered.

The solution

7748 SI 1995/2518 reg 92; Notice 700/44 para 2 Due to the nature of their profession, barristers have special tax point rules.

These rules **only apply to** fees which relate to the barrister's practice (¶7714); the normal rules apply to any other business activities.

The tax point for barristers when acting in a professional capacity is the **earliest** of when:
- payment is received;
- a VAT invoice is issued; or
- the barrister ceases to practise.

In practice the tax point is usually the date of payment.

7750 VATTOS8400 On **becoming VAT-registered**, a barrister is not required to account for VAT on outstanding fees which are paid after the date of registration, or fee notes which have already been sent out. It is very important that no VAT is included on the receipted fee note and each note should state "This is not a VAT invoice".

If a **piece of work straddles** the date of registration and a request for payment is issued after registration, VAT should be charged on the whole fee, unless the actual dates and work performed are stated on the fee note.

C. Input tax

7754 Barristers are usually able to claim all input tax incurred (subject to the usual restrictions for certain types of expenses (¶1885+)), because they either make taxable supplies in the UK, or supplies abroad which are outside the scope of UK VAT but give the right to recover input tax.

1. Chambers expenses

Barristers are unique in each being a separately registered business, whilst occupying premises with others. This means that related costs, such as meeting rooms, equipment, power, and other premises costs must be shared between the barristers. **7756** Notice 700/44 para 6.3

Under the normal VAT rules, only the person who is invoiced can recover the related VAT. As a supplier can only make out its invoices to one business (which could be the practice manager or clerk), the barristers would normally be unable to recover the input tax.

As a solution, three **special accounting methods** exist to allocate these costs, to ensure the related input tax can still be recovered, so that no barrister is out of pocket.

Onward supply The nominated person (being the person the original invoice is made out to) **reclaims** all of the input tax on the supplier's invoice. The nominated person then recharges the cost plus VAT on each member's share. Registered members then recover the input tax on their individual charge. This method can be rather tedious to administer. **7758**

By concession, the nominated person is not required to issue a VAT **invoice** (although many chambers find an invoice more convenient). If no VAT invoice is issued, each member's records must be cross-referenced to the:
- output tax charged by the nominated member;
- input tax deducted by all the other members; and
- supplier's invoice.

EXAMPLE Mr A, a barrister, receives the quarter's rental bill for £40,000 plus VAT of £8,000. Mr A shares chambers with three other barristers.
He reclaims the total input tax of £8,000 and raises a VAT invoice of £10,000 plus VAT of £2,000 to each of the other barristers. They reclaim this VAT as input tax.

Apportionment A common fund must exist, into which each barrister makes payments to cover the chambers' costs. **7760**

The supplier's invoice is paid out of this fund. The input tax is apportioned to each member and **deducted by** those that are registered.

An accurate record of the apportionment must be kept, in particular to make sure that the total input tax deduction does not exceed the VAT shown on the invoice. The nominated person **must not** issue an invoice.

Each member's individual record should cross-reference to the supplier's invoice.

EXAMPLE A barristers' chambers receives the quarter's rental bill for £40,000 plus VAT of £8,000. This is paid out of the common fund, into which the four VAT-registered barristers make contributions.
Each barrister reclaims input tax of £2,000. (£8,000/4)

Contribution Barristers must be VAT-registered to reclaim input tax under this method, although it can be used when some members are using the flat rate scheme. **7762** Notice 700/44 para 6.4; Notice 733 para 13

As with the apportionment method, a common fund must exist, into which each barrister makes payment to cover the chambers costs.

The nominated person reclaims all of the input tax on the supplier's invoice, and then pays a **contribution** of that amount of input tax into a common fund. The effect is that the barristers only pay the net cost.

EXAMPLE 1. Miss B, a barrister, receives the quarter's rental bill for £40,000 plus VAT of £8,000. Miss B shares chambers with three other VAT-registered barristers. There is a common fund.
Miss B reclaims the total input tax of £8,000 and makes a contribution of £8,000 into the fund. The rent bill of £48,000 is met by the common fund. Each barrister has contributed £10,000 net.
2. A chambers has ten barristers, two of whom use the flat rate scheme. The common fund has paid £48,000 (inclusive of VAT of £8,000).
If 20% of the input tax is apportioned to the two barristers on the flat rate scheme, the chambers, through the nominated member of the common fund, can claim 80% i.e. £6,400 of the VAT. (£8,000 x 80%)

Staff costs

7764 A particular barrister may be nominally **responsible for** staff matters, including discipline, recruitment, training, appraisals, etc.

In reality, the staff are **employed by** all of the barristers, each of whom contributes to the overall cost. These contributions are outside the scope of VAT.

2. Clothing

7766
VIT43800

The **courts require** barristers to wear dark clothing in addition to their special attire, which includes a wig, gown and bands.

The input tax relating to all of this clothing can be deducted if the barrister is able to state that the purchase would not have been made otherwise.

3. Recharged expenses

7768 Any expenses recharged to clients will attract **output tax**, unless satisfying the conditions for a disbursement (¶7190+).

Input tax will always be recoverable. In particular, meals taken with clients would normally be classed as business entertaining and the input tax would not be recoverable, but where the meal is recharged, it becomes similar to subsistence and input tax is recoverable.

D. Ceasing to practise

7772
Notice 700/44
para 3.1

A barrister who ceases to practise must normally deregister (¶2720+).

A barrister who continues to make **other taxable supplies** may be required to remain registered if trading above the relevant threshold, or may choose to remain registered.

Irrespective of any subsequent registration status, VAT becomes due on all fees when ceasing to practise or on death, although there is a mechanism to defer payment (¶7776+). Where applicable, the barrister must indicate the chosen payment option on the deregistration application form.

MEMO POINTS 1. **Output tax** must also be charged in respect of assets on hand at the date of deregistration (¶8610).
2. Any **sales** of equipment, etc, are also subject to VAT.

1. VAT return entries

7774
Notice 700/44
para 4.2

The barrister must enter on the current return all professional fees received since the end of the last VAT period in addition to any other business supplies made during that time. Fees which are subject to deferment are excluded.

If **deferral has been agreed**, VAT must still be paid on the fee payments which have been received.

2. Deferral of VAT

7776
Notice 700/44
para 3.2

If approved by HMRC, payment of VAT can be delayed until the **earlier of** the date of payment for the work and the issue of a VAT invoice.

Application

To **apply** for approval the barrister must write to the National Registration Service of HMRC. A form VAT 811 will be sent, which the barrister must then complete and submit to the VAT Central Unit. **7778** Notice 700/44 para 5.1

This form requires a list of the following **information**:
- every standard-rated fee which is outstanding (with estimates where the final amount is not known);
- the name of each case;
- the name of the client; and
- the date of the first fee note.

In addition, the barrister must give a correspondence address.

If deferral is **approved**, a certified copy of the form will be returned to the barrister; this becomes an important checklist for future VAT payments (¶7782).

MEMO POINTS The **address** of the VAT Central Unit for this purpose is:
DMB Banking Ops
Government Accounting and Barristers Team (GABS)
6th floor NW
Alexander House
Victoria Avenue
Southend-on-Sea
SS99 1AA

Invoices

Post-cessation VAT invoices can only be issued in respect of work done before cessation. The tax point, which determines the applicable **VAT rate**, remains the date of cessation. **7780** Notice 700/44 para 3.4

Payment of VAT

Periodically, after submission of a VAT 811, the barrister must complete a form VAT 812 and pay the related VAT in respect of fees which have been received or VAT invoices which have been issued. **7782** Notice 700/44 paras 5.2, 5.3

Once all fees have been paid, or any outstanding fees are known to be irrecoverable, the barrister completes a declaration of **final** payment. Reasons for any remaining debts must be given on the form.

MEMO POINTS 1. In the first year after cessation the form must be **completed** every quarter. Thereafter, the barrister has the option to complete forms every 6 months.
2. **Sufficient details** must be given to match up the VATable amounts with the information given at the approval stage (including the name of the case).
3. In addition, if the **VAT rate changes**, work which was initially indicated as standard-rated and is now expected to be charged at a different rate must be included on the form.
4. If the barrister makes any **exempt supplies**, an adjustment may be required to recoveries of input tax. HMRC should be contacted for advice.

Records

Accounts and records relating to all outstanding fees must be **retained for** at least 12 months after the declaration of final payment has been made. **7784** Notice 700/44 para 5.4

3. Death

If a practising barrister dies, the practice **clerk** must inform HMRC immediately. **7786** Notice 700/44 para 6.2

On the **grant of probate**, the barrister's personal representative will need to choose (within 10 days after the grant) between deferring payment of VAT or paying the VAT on the outstanding fees straight away.

CHAPTER 11

Public bodies

OUTLINE ¶¶

For an activity to fall within the scope of VAT, it must be carried out by a taxable person. Certain bodies governed by public law are given special treatment under EU legislation. They are treated as not being taxable persons when they carry out certain activities as public authorities, albeit that those activities, if carried on by other traders, would make them taxable persons. **7830** EC Directive 2006/112 art 13

The term bodies governed by public law is not used in UK legislation, but the legislation does provide special treatment for specified bodies. Bodies governed by public law (including but not limited to specified bodies) can treat certain activities as non-business activities (¶7864).

Input tax cannot normally be recovered on costs relating to non-business activities, so in order to prevent VAT becoming an absolute cost to public bodies, there are rules allowing them to recover VAT incurred in relation to non-business activities and, subject to conditions, on exempt activities.

MEMO POINTS National museums and galleries and government departments are subject to similar rules but are outside the scope of this book.

SECTION 1

Definition

Public authorities

EU legislation provides that states, regional and local government authorities and other bodies governed by public law are **not regarded as taxable persons** (and therefore do not have to charge VAT) when they **engage in activities as** public authorities. In the UK, HMRC refers to such activities as non-business activities. **7832** HMRC Brief 96/09; EC Directive 2006/112 art 13.1; Notice 749 para 5

Just because a body is a public authority does not mean that all its activities will be non-business. Moreover, certain activities are never treated as non-business, unless they are carried out on such a **small scale** that they can be disregarded (¶7868).

In addition, supplies will not be treated as non-business if to do so would lead to **significant distortion of competition** (¶7866) with taxable persons.

7834 VATGBP3220 To qualify as a public authority, an entity must be acting under a legal regime which applies to bodies governed by public law and not to other bodies (a special legal regime). Obvious examples are bodies which form part of the UK's public administration, such as a government department, a local authority or non-departmental public body.

It is important to distinguish between public bodies and private sector providers. An entity is not a body governed by public law merely because it is funded by public money, has delegated powers, or is regulated by the state. Only activities that a body has a **statutory obligation to provide**, or must perform in a way that is different to private sector providers, are carried out under a special legal regime.

In HMRC's view, for an entity to be **classified as a body governed** by public law it must therefore:
- undertake a function ordinarily carried on by local government; and
- have the power to draw funding directly from local taxation.

Furthermore, it is HMRC's position that even if a body is deemed to be one governed by public law in relation to a **particular activity**, that only affects the taxability of the supplies made by it in the course of that activity. It does not affect either:
- supplies made by it in a different capacity; or
- supplies made to it.

Hence if the body is also a **charity**, it cannot rely on this provision to have supplies made to it either reduced-rated (¶1110) or zero-rated (¶1180). Similarly a public body cannot recover input VAT incurred on supplies which are outside the scope of VAT, unless it is a specified body (¶7836).

MEMO POINTS HMRC's guidance was reviewed following the VAT tribunal decision in *University of Cambridge* [2008], where the issue of whether a **higher education institution** constituted a public body was considered. The appellant, a charity, argued that if it was a body governed by public law, it was entitled to have certain supplies made to it at the reduced rate, or zero rate, where appropriate. This was based on the argument that if it was such a body (the tribunal held that it was not) its supplies of education were made otherwise than in the course of a business. The tribunal rejected this approach and held that bodies governed by public law are making supplies but are expressly excluded from having to charge VAT on those supplies. Therefore they are still acting in the course of a business and any provision for reduced-rating or zero-rating supplies to charities for non-business use is not in point.

7835 Notice 749 para 2.2 **Exclusions** HMRC states that the following are **not** public bodies for VAT purposes:
- a joint board or committee set up by a body other than a local authority;
- a body that merely obtains financial help from a local authority;
- a purely advisory committee that does not carry out local authority functions;
- a Community Council in England or Scotland;
- a Community Association;
- a parish meeting;
- a parochial church council;
- a village hall management committee; or
- a charity.

A **board or committee** where members other than local authorities have voting rights is also unlikely to be a public body. Such committees should review their status regularly to check whether they qualify as a public body.

Specified bodies

7836 ss 33 - 33D, 96(4) VATA 1994; SI 2005/1797; Notice 749 paras 2.1, 2.3; VATGBP4300 The following is a list of bodies which are specified as public bodies in the UK. The Treasury has powers to **add bodies to the list** by means of a Treasury order. The Treasury will consider applications from bodies that undertake functions ordinarily carried on by local government and have the power to draw funding directly from local taxation. HMRC should be contacted before a formal application is made to the Treasury.

Type of entity	Detail	Special registration rules (¶7942)
Local authorities	Authorities established under s 10 Local Government Act 1985	✓
	The council of a: – county; – county borough; – district; – London borough; or – parish or group of parishes (or, in Wales, community or group of communities)	✓
	The Common Council of the City of London, the Council of the Isles of Scilly and any joint committee or joint board established by these entities	✓
	In relation to Scotland: – a regional, islands or district council within the meaning of the Local Government (Scotland) Act 1973; – any combination and any joint committee or joint board established by two or more of these entities; and – any joint board to which s 226 of that Act applies	✓
London	London Fire and Emergency Planning Authority	
	London Residuary Body	
	Greater London Authority	
	Transport for London	
	London Pensions Fund Authority established by London Government Reorganisation (Pensions etc) Order 1989	
Local administration	The Commissions for Local Administration in England, Wales and Scotland	
	The Commission for Local Authority Accounts in Scotland	
Charter trustees	Constituted by s 246(4) or (5) Local Government Act 1972	
	Established under s 17 Local Government Act 1992 or any statutory instrument made under Part II of that Act	
New towns	A development corporation within the meaning of the New Towns Act 1981 or the New Towns (Scotland) Act 1968	
	A new town commission within the meaning of the New Towns Act (Northern Ireland) 1965	
	Commission for the New Towns	
Environmental	River purification board established under s 135 Local Government (Scotland) Act 1973	
	Waste regulation and disposal authorities within s 10 Local Government Act 1985	
	Water development board within the meaning of s 109 Water (Scotland) Act 1980	
	An internal drainage board	
	Welsh National Water Development Authority	
	Regional water authorities	
	Natural Resources Wales	
	National Rivers Authority	
	The Environment Agency	
	A National Park Authority within the meaning of s 63 Environment Act 1995	
	Norfolk Broads Authority	

Type of entity	Detail	Special registration rules (¶7942)
Transport and ports	Passenger transport authority or executive within the meaning of Part II of the Transport Act 1968	
	A metropolitan county passenger transport authority or residuary body	
	Transport Partnership created by an order made under s 1(1) Transport (Scotland) Act 2005	
	Strategic highway companies (from 1 April 2015)	
	Port health authority within the meaning of the Public Health (Control of Disease) Act 1984	
	Port local authority and joint port local authority constituted under Part X of the Public Health (Scotland) Act 1897	
Police	Police Authority and the Receiver for the Metropolitan Police District	
	A Police and Crime Commissioner and the Mayor's Office for Policing and Crime	
	Northumbria Interim Police Authority	
	A metropolitan county Police Authority	
Fire and civil defence	A metropolitan county Fire and Civil Defence Authority	
	A fire authority constituted by a combination scheme made under the Fire and Rescue Services Act 2004	
Broadcasting	BBC	
	An appointed news provider as defined by s 280 Communications Act 2003	
A general lighthouse authority	Within the meaning of Part VIII Merchant Shipping Act 1995[1]	
Education	An academy established under the Academies Act 2010[2]	
Search and rescue charities	From 1 April 2015, where the main purpose of the charity is to: – carry out search and rescue activities in the UK or UK marine areas, and these activities are co-ordinated by either the Maritime and Coastguard Agency, the Ministry of Defence, the police force or any other body specified by Treasury Order; – support, develop and promote the activities of a charity meeting the above conditions; or – provide an air ambulance service in pursuance of arrangements with the Secretary of State, Welsh Ministers or an NHS body	

Note:
1. Only in respect of the provision, maintenance or management of lights or other navigational aids.
2. Since 1 April 2011 academies have been able to recover VAT incurred on non-business activities under a special scheme similar to that enjoyed by public bodies.

s 33E VATA 1994

MEMO POINTS From the date of Royal Assent of the Finance Act 2015 there will be a further category to allow **non-departmental public bodies** and similar arms-length bodies to recover VAT when they enter cost-sharing arrangements. The Treasury will direct what bodies will be eligible and any recovery will be conditional on those bodies agreeing to a corresponding reduction in their Treasury funding.

VAT registration

The usual registration rules (¶2640) apply to most public bodies except local authorities. This means that registration may be voluntary or compulsory, depending on the level of taxable supplies. **7842** Notice 749 para 3; VATGBP4250

A public body that is registered, or liable to be registered, for VAT must charge and account for **output tax** on all its taxable business supplies, subject to the normal rules. This applies whether the customer is a private individual, trader, government department or another public body. It must not charge VAT on non-business activities.

Irrespective of whether registration applies, **input tax** on non-business supplies and exempt activities is potentially recoverable under special rules (¶7860+).

MEMO POINTS 1. For the rules relating to **local authorities** and registration see ¶7942.
2. If **mainly zero-rated supplies** are made, HMRC may waive the requirement to register (¶2654).
3. **To monitor** the registration threshold (¶2668), it is important for all public bodies to identify taxable supplies (¶2647) which are made in the course of a business (¶100).
4. It is possible for a public body to be a member of a **group registration** (¶8800), although input tax recovery on non-business expenditure is restricted to that body only. In addition, the special exempt input tax rules (¶7878) will not apply to the group.
5. If **output tax is charged in error** by a non-registered body, HMRC will consider whether it is likely that the recipient of the supply recovered the related input tax before requiring the body to issue a credit note. VATGBP4820

SECTION 2

Recovery of VAT on costs

As a **general rule**, it is only possible to recover input VAT if it: **7860** s 33 VATA 1994
- is incurred by a person who is registered for VAT; and
- can be attributed to taxable business activities.

VAT relating to non-business (¶1825) or (subject to certain de minimis limits) exempt activities (¶2075+) is not recoverable.

Public bodies incur VAT on goods and services purchased by them to undertake their various activities (which may be prescribed by statutory requirements or undertaken at the body's discretion, and may be taxable, exempt or non-business). To minimise the resulting irrecoverable VAT, a special scheme allows **specified bodies** (¶7836+), whether or not they are registered for VAT, to:
- reclaim the input tax suffered on non-business activities; and
- recover any input tax attributable to exempt business activities, provided that HMRC considers it to represent an insignificant proportion of the total VAT incurred.

MEMO POINTS As the special scheme is provided under s 33 of VAT Act 1994, it is known as the **Section 33 method**.

A. Business or non-business activities

For a detailed discussion of whether an activity constitutes a business see ¶100. **7864** Notice 749 para 5; VATGBP3100

In the public sector a non-business activity would usually be undertaken without any **consideration** being received (or for nominal consideration, such as a lease granted for a peppercorn rent). Where a charge is made, the input tax can only be recovered if it relates to business activities (¶1825), **unless** the body is a public authority, in which case the following special rules apply.

Summary if consideration received

7865

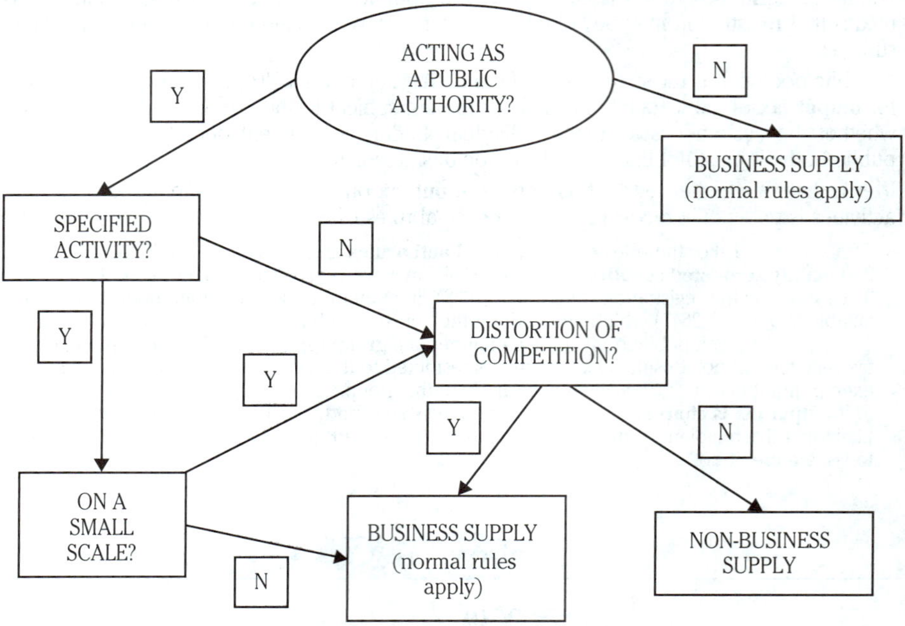

Activities of public authorities

7866 EC Directive 2006/112 art 13; Notice 749 para 5.3

Public authorities (¶7834) can recover input tax on activities **other than specified activities** (¶7868), provided that there would be no significant distortion of competition with the private sector. The CJEU has held that if a public body carries on an activity that could be engaged in by private traders in competition against it, the activity should be treated as business. *Ufficio Distrettuale delle Imposte Dirette di Fiorenzuola d'Arda v Comune di Carpaneto Piacentino* [1991]; *Ufficio Provinciale Imposta sul Valore Aggiunto di Piacenza v Comune di Rivergaro and Others* [1991]

Comment This is an area of contentious case law; professional advice should be sought in situations of doubt.

Notice 749 para 5.6; VATGBP3300

MEMO POINTS 1. Non-business treatment will lead to **a significant distortion of competition** where the public authority gains a commercial advantage, that is, it avoids charging output tax when competitors have to, or recovers input tax when competitors cannot. Note, however, that supplies made for no consideration are not subject to the distortion rule. This is particularly detrimental where traders are deterred from starting up businesses because of competition with a public authority. In this case it was held that any distortion of competition should be by reference to the activity and not the local marketplace, so the comparison cannot be made on an area-by-area basis. The courts have also held that both actual competition and potential competition need to be considered, provided that the latter is real and not purely hypothetical. Further, significant has been held to mean more than negligible. *HMRC v Isle of Wight Council and others* [2008]

Notice 749 para 5.7

2. If there are **no current local competitors**, the activity can be treated as non-business, provided that the public authority is sure that another trader could not carry it out in the same way and achieve the same results. HMRC states that this can be assumed where:
– the clients could not equally well obtain the goods or services from another supplier;
– the activity is not carried on generally by suppliers outside the public authority sector, unless on such a small scale as to be negligible; and
– non-business treatment would not act as a disincentive to a private trader capable of going into business in direct local competition.

Specified activities

For the following specified activities, there is an **additional test**, which requires the authority's involvement in the activity to be negligible if the activity is to be treated as non-business: **7868** EC Directive 2006/112 annex 1; VATGBP3400

- telecommunications;
- supplying water, gas, electricity and steam;
- transporting goods;
- port and airport services;
- passenger transport;
- supplying new goods manufactured for sale;
- certain activities of agricultural intervention agencies;
- running trade fairs and exhibitions;
- warehousing;
- the activities of commercial publicity bodies;
- activities of travel agents;
- running staff shops, co-operatives, industrial canteens, etc; and
- certain commercial activities of radio and television bodies.

The practical effect of this test is limited, as most public bodies do not generally engage in these activities any more. Where they do, they are making supplies within the scope of VAT unless the scale of activity is negligible.

Typical activities

HMRC offers the following guidance on whether certain activities are viewed as business or non-business: **7870** Notice 749 para 5.8

Activity	Detail	Business	Non-business
Community education	Although there is a requirement for certain forms of community education to be made available, if this is provided by the body itself, this will be in competition with a broad range of education providers	✓	
Admission charges	See ¶140	✓	
Non-automatic weighing instruments	Evaluation and surveillance of instruments to meet EU requirements	✓	
	Charges to verify such instruments made in capacity as a public authority, using legal powers that no private contractor is entitled to exercise		✓
Issuing statutory licences, etc	Charges for various forms of licensing and approval in a broad range of public activities taking place in the area: for example, approving premises for civil marriages, registering childminders, issuing fire certificates and registering firearms		✓
Providing sports facilities	In return for a charge	✓	
Care and welfare	When acting under a special legal regime which requires the provision of a wide range of services to people of all ages May make a charge to recover all or part of the costs incurred in providing these services		✓
	Providing services and residential accommodation outside a statutory function e.g. crèches, playgroups and recreational holidays for elderly people not in statutory care	✓	
Repair works when homeowner defaults	Where the recipient of a default notice refuses to comply, the authority may exercise its statutory powers to have the repair work done and recover the cost from the householder		✓

Activity	Detail	Business	Non-business
Car parking	Parking at meter bays on the public highway, provided under statutory powers (including excess parking charges)		✓
	Providing off-street parking in garages, buildings and open spaces, not under any special legal provisions	✓	
Seconding police officers	To exercise their function as officers in connection with normal policing under legal powers which they embody in that capacity (for example, to attend at an incident)		✓
	To outside organisations to advise, for example, about security matters	✓	
Housing	Shared ownership arrangements where equity is shared between an occupier and a body and rent is paid by the occupier	✓	
	Providing domestic accommodation to people seeking housing (normally on a list maintained by the authority) or disposing of properties under the "right to buy" legislation		✓
Cemeteries	Provision and maintenance of cemeteries under detailed legal provisions which apply only to local authorities		✓

Case law

7872 Case law pertinent to public bodies is discussed below.

EXAMPLE

1. A borough council received a grant to help pay for refurbishment of buildings which were to form a new arts centre. These buildings were leased to the company which would operate the centre, for 35 years at a peppercorn rent. The company made a substantial donation to the council to help towards the refurbishment costs.
It was held that the lease was a business transaction, particularly as consideration was received, irrespective of the community benefit which resulted from the centre. *West Devon District Council v C&E* [2001]

2. A city council was registered for VAT and allowed various entities which sponsored its health and safety campaigns to advertise without charge. The sponsorship monies were treated as donations. It was held that the Council were carrying on business activities as the means of performing their statutory functions and the sponsorship monies were subject to VAT. *Norwich City Council* [1994] (VTD 11822)

3. The Royal Academy of Music arranged for a contractor to carry out reconstruction work on a listed building which it used as a concert hall. It tried to recover VAT on the basis that it was not in business.
It was held that the Academy was carrying on a business activity, even though its objects were charitable or philanthropic. The Academy was not a public authority and was not governed by public law. *Royal Academy of Music* [1994] (VTD 11871)

4. The CJEU has confirmed that the concept of distortion of competition for public bodies works both ways. So a public authority can cite distortion of competition as a reason for wanting to be treated as a taxable person in respect of its supplies. In a case of a public body which was treated by the German tax authorities as a non-taxable person in relation to its supplies of land, this meant the body suffered a loss by comparison to businesses making similar supplies that could opt to tax and recover VAT on related costs. *SALIX Grundstücks-Vermietungsgesellschaft* [2009]

B. Business input tax

In order to recover input tax relating to business activities the body must be registered for VAT, **unless** the only VAT incurred is input tax which relates to exempt supplies. If the body is **registered**, it has a choice as to how it recovers exempt input tax (¶7882). **7876** Notice 749 para 6

1. Exempt input tax

There are special rules to enable a public body to **reclaim** all exempt input tax if it is an insignificant proportion of the total VAT incurred. This is a different system from the usual partial exemption de minimis rules which apply to the private sector. **7878** Notice 749 para 8; VATGBP4500

Insignificant proportion

For this purpose, exempt input tax is insignificant if it amounts to **less than the greater of**: **7880** s 33(2) VATA 1994; Notice 749 para 8.2
- £625 per month on average (£7,500 p.a.); and
- 5% of the total input tax incurred on all the goods and services purchased in the year to 31 March (the calculation year).

If exempt input tax exceeds both these figures, none of it can be recovered.

MEMO POINTS 1. **Total input tax** means all input tax incurred on business and non-business activities, excluding any which is blocked.
2. Input tax is **blocked** on:
- the costs of acquiring and leasing motor cars (except marked emergency vehicles) (¶1890);
- business entertainment (¶1926); and
- goods incorporated into a building other than building materials (¶5275).

3. The **calculation year** to 31 March applies irrespective of the VAT periods or VAT stagger (¶2987). A calculation must be carried out at the end of each such year and any necessary adjustment included in the VAT return for the next period. An extension to this time limit may be agreed by the local HMRC office, but to no later than the September VAT period. VATGBP4510

EXAMPLE A public body incurs the following types of input tax in the year to 31 March:

	£
Relating to:	
Non-business supplies	80,000
Taxable business supplies	43,000
Business entertaining	1,000
Exempt supplies	9,000
Total	133,000

The exempt input tax exceeds the first test of £7,500 pa.
For the second test, total input tax is calculated as follows:

	£
Non-business supplies	80,000
Taxable business supplies	43,000
Business entertaining - blocked	-
Exempt supplies	9,000
Total	132,000

So, as a percentage of total input tax, exempt input tax makes up 6.8%. (9,000/132,000)
As exempt input tax is significant - that is, it exceeds 5% of total input tax - none of it can be recovered.

2. Choice of calculation

7882 Notice 749 paras 8.3, 8.4 Any calculation method can be used if it gives a fair and equitable **result**, and takes into account the capital goods scheme (¶7896).

Registered bodies can use any partial exemption method normally available to private traders (¶2112), or they can choose to use a Section 33 method. If using normal partial exemption, it would usually be advisable to request a special partial exemption method (¶2148) rather than use the standard method.

Other bodies must use a Section 33 method.

3. Section 33 method

7884 s 33 VATA 1994 Although HMRC suggests a particular model calculation, there is no requirement to use it. Instead a bespoke method can be used if prior approval is received (¶7892).

Standard model calculation

7886 Notice 749 para 9.2; VATGBP4520 HMRC suggests taking a worst case scenario, so that any heading in the body's **budget structure** which contains an exempt activity is assumed to be wholly exempt. This means that any input tax attributable to that budget heading is exempt input tax.

		Expenditure relating to exempt activity		
		Total	Standard-rated	Not standard-rated
1	List all budget headings or cost centres that contain any element of exempt activity[1]			
2	Within each of the budget headings or cost centres identified at step 1, record all net expenditure for both capital and revenue that would normally carry VAT	X	X	X
3	Add up the standard-rated expenditure identified at step 2		X	
4	Apply standard-rate percentage		@ 20%	
5	Amount of exempt input tax		X	

Note
1. HMRC suggests that this should be done by committee (if appropriate to the body in question).

7888 If this approach shows that the body's total exempt input tax is **insignificant** (¶7880), the tax can be reclaimed with no further calculation necessary.

For this purpose the **total VAT recovered** should take account of any error, correction or changes to estimates.

7890 Notice 749 paras 9.3 - 9.5 If the result of this calculation shows **significant exempt input tax**, the expenditure should be allocated between taxable and exempt supplies, leaving a certain amount which relates to both and which is then subject to apportionment.

If at any stage a result showing insignificant exempt input tax is achieved, no further work is necessary and the exempt input tax can be claimed in full. If this is not possible, the exempt input tax is not recoverable.

MEMO POINTS **Allocation and apportionment** should be fair and reasonable and may be based on any of the following, or other more relevant, criteria:
- staff count;
- floor area used;
- amount of income;

- number of sessions; or
- time.

For further details see ¶2152+.

Bespoke calculations

The body must contact HMRC **before** 1 April of the calculation year for which the method is first to be applied. The broad principles of calculation must be agreed before 1 April, including what would happen if there was a change of intention for the use of expenditure and how capital goods scheme adjustments are to be catered for. **7892** Notice 749 para 8.5; VATGBP4550

The final method must be **agreed** in writing before 1 January in the calculation year. If this is not done in time, the method cannot be used for that year, so the model calculation will have to be used instead.

The annual calculation should be **submitted by** 31 October following the calculation year end.

MEMO POINTS 1. It is only possible to **change** an agreed method by obtaining approval for a new method.
2. If the original method is **withdrawn by HMRC** and a new method has not yet been agreed, the body must use the model calculation.
3. If exempt input tax under the agreed method is **not recoverable**, HMRC will give sympathetic consideration to a request for an alternative method.

4. Special situations

Changes of intention

If there is a change of intention after the end of the calculation year, the following table summarises the position. **7894** Notice 749 para 10.2; VATGBP4640

Expenditure now put to	Treatment of related input tax	Resulting total exempt input tax	Action
From taxable or non-business to exempt use	Added to exempt input tax already calculated for that year when the original VAT was incurred	Still insignificant	None required
		Becomes significant	Only the VAT involved in the change of intention must be repaid to HMRC (there is no need to repay any other exempt input tax relating to that year)
From exempt to taxable or non-business use	Deducted from the exempt input tax already calculated for that year	Still insignificant	None required
		Becomes insignificant	The input VAT involved in the change of intention (only) can be reclaimed from HMRC

Capital goods scheme

If a capital item is affected by the capital goods scheme (¶2280+), the usual rules apply, with the following **modifications**: **7896** Notice 749 para 10.4; VATGBP4620 - 4630
- non-business use is treated as if it were taxable use but must be separately identified; and
- if exempt input tax for the tax year is insignificant (¶7880), there is no need to make any capital goods scheme adjustments.

The treatment required on the change of use of the asset is the same as that shown in the table at ¶7894.

MEMO POINTS 1. For the purposes of the capital goods scheme, a **capital item** is either a computer, ship or aircraft costing at least £50,000, or immovable property costing at least £250,000.

Notice 749 para 10.4 - 10.5 2. A full **record** must be kept of the capital items involved, the original input tax incurred and originally claimed, and all adjustments. Official guidance refers to an appropriate adjustment to input tax, rather than a detailed prescribed calculation.

Errors

7900 Notice 749 para 10.3; VATGBP4650 If an error has occurred in the calculation **all affected years** must be reworked.

For the correction of errors generally see ¶3014+.

Change in VAT liability

7902 VATGBP4630 If input tax is attributed to an **intended supply** but, before that supply takes place, there is a change in the law which amends the applicable VAT rate, no change is required to the original attribution. So if a supply changes from exempt to taxable and the body's exempt input tax would become insignificant as a result, recovery still cannot be made.

Any input tax incurred **subsequent to the change** should be attributed on the basis of the supply's new status.

C. VAT incurred on non-business activities

7906 s 33(1) VATA 1994; VATGBP4800 VAT incurred in relation to non-business activities can be **refunded** irrespective of whether the body is registered for VAT. However, if the input tax would normally be blocked (¶7880), it cannot be recovered under any circumstances.

Scope

7908 For all **specified bodies** (¶7836), input tax relating to UK supplies of goods or services and imported goods can be recovered.

Input tax recovery on goods acquired from other EU member states is restricted to **registered bodies only**.

Recipient of the purchase

7910 Notice 749 para 7.1 To recover the input tax the body must have been **connected with** all stages of the purchase, which means that:
- it has placed the order;
- it has received the supply;
- the VAT invoice is made out to the body; and
- the payment has been sourced from its own funds (including those awarded to it, such as lottery money).

VATGBP4425 MEMO POINTS 1. If the **VAT invoice is in another name** (such as an authority employee, or a school) HMRC will accept it, provided that all of the other conditions are satisfied. If the invoice is in the name of another body with links to the authority, HMRC may not accept it.
2. Where goods or services are **given away** to another body, under a project initiated by the original body and funded from its own resources, the related input tax is recoverable.

Money given for a specified purpose

7912 Notice 749 para 7.3, 7.4 If money is given to the public body for a specified purpose, the input tax can be recovered, **provided that** the body:
- makes the purchase (as defined in ¶7910);
- remains the owner of the goods or services;
- uses them for its own non-business purposes; and
- keeps sufficient records to identify the purchase and the reason for it.

If the gift is conditional, that is, the donor or someone else **receives a benefit** in return, the related input tax cannot be recovered.

HMRC offers guidance as shown in the following table:

Spent on	Source of funding	Input tax	
		Can recover	Irrecoverable
Community and foundation schools	PTA or school funds	✓	
Exterior maintenance at a voluntary aided school	School governors		✓
Welfare services	Amenity funds	✓	
Homes and schools for the handicapped	Voluntary bodies	✓	
Sports equipment at a youth centre	Independent youth club on condition they have exclusive use		✓
Building repairs	Building owners		✓

Trust funds

A body acting as **sole managing trustee** of a trust (for example, a village hall) **without receiving payment** can recover input tax if the following conditions are satisfied: **7914** Notice 749 para 7.5
- the activities of the trust must be so closely related to the body's own functions as an authority that it is not easy to distinguish between them; and
- the claim must relate to the non-business activities of the trust.

If the recovery of VAT would create **anomalies**, it may be restricted.

A **custodian trustee** whose role is simply to hold the property of the trust cannot recover the VAT incurred unless he is also sole managing trustee.

D. Claiming

The method of claiming depends on whether the body is registered for VAT. **7918**

Registered bodies

All claims should be made on a VAT return (¶2985), by putting an entry in box 4. **7920** Notice 749 para 8.8; VATGPB4810

It is advisable for public bodies to submit monthly VAT returns (¶2990), as this speeds up any cash inflow. If it is not possible to quantify the input tax accurately, HMRC may agree to estimated returns (¶3006).

Exempt input tax calculated under a Section 33 method should be claimed on the VAT return following the calculation year (which ends on 31 March), although HMRC will agree to a claim being made up to the return including the following September.

An input tax claim must be made **within** 3 years of when the evidence to substantiate the claim was first held (¶2014). SI 2009/586 reg.3

Unregistered bodies

A stand-alone claim in respect of both non-business input tax and/or exempt input tax must be made in writing **within** 3 years from the end of the month in which the necessary evidence was first held. **7922** Notice 749 para 12.3; VATGPB4820, 4830

The **amount** of the claim must be at least £100 and relate to a period of at least 1 calendar month. There is no maximum claim period or claim amount.

The **claim period end** should coincide with a calendar month end.

MEMO POINTS 1. If the claim **is less than £100** the claim period should be at least a year.
2. **Supporting evidence**, such as invoices and other records, should be retained for at least 6 years but is not required to be submitted with the claim.
Notice 749 para 12.5
3. Claims should be **sent to**:
Banking/GABS
HMRC
7th Floor South West
Alexander House
21 Victoria Avenue
Southend-on-Sea
SS99 1AU

7924
Notice 749 para 12.4

HMRC suggests the following **form of words**:

EXAMPLE I am claiming a refund of £X for the period ... to ... to cover VAT charged on goods and services bought for (name of body) non-business activities.
[Optional] The tax claimed includes VAT incurred for exempt business activities that can be reclaimed under Notice 749 Local authorities and similar bodies.

Signed
For (name of body)

Address:
Contact name:
Contact telephone number:

7926
Notice 749 para 12.6; VATGBP 4850

On **receipt of a claim**, HMRC will then repay the input tax by BACS or cheque.

A form VAT126 will be sent for the body's next claim. The body will be allocated a unique number to quote on all such claims.

MEMO POINTS 1. No repayment supplement will be due for **late repayments**. Statutory interest may be available (¶3270).
2. Certain claims may be subject to **verification** checks.
3. There is no **right of appeal** against a denied or reduced claim, although a body may request a review (¶4230+).
4. While there is no legal basis for the **correction of previous errors**, HMRC will correct any significant errors by adjusting the current claim.

Late claims

7928
Notice 749 para 8.9

If a body wishes to make a late claim (although still within the 3-year time limit), HMRC should be contacted by phone.

The claim should then be made in writing **setting out** the:
- amounts involved;
- periods covered; and
- basis of calculation.

Sufficient **evidence** should be retained to substantiate the claim.

SECTION 3

Local authorities

7940
Notice749 para 5.2

Local authorities are treated as public bodies for most VAT purposes. However, there are special rules in relation to **registration**, and to **input tax recovery** relating to community projects, village halls and pension schemes.

MEMO POINTS 1. In addition, HMRC has agreed a special time limit for the issue of invoices (¶774) and the related **actual tax point** of a supply (¶766).

2. **Supplies to another local authority** are non-business, provided that the supply is not made in competition with the private sector.

1. VAT registration

Local authorities (¶7836) that make **any taxable supplies** (including zero-rated supplies) in the course of a business **must register for VAT**, unless HMRC agrees that the activity involved is so minimal that registration is not required. **7942** s 42 VATA 1994; Notice 749 para 3.2; VATGBP4920

In practice, **minimal activity** is taken to mean that output tax of less than £1,000 per annum would be charged by the authority if it were registered. Any authority making taxable supplies can register voluntarily if they so wish.

MEMO POINTS 1. Bodies that are **legally separate** from a local authority and do not form a joint board or committee (e.g. housing trusts) are subject to the usual registration rules. VATGBP4920; VATGBP4210
2. It is possible for a local authority **joint committee** to account for VAT under the registration of the lead authority or any other member. This must not be for tax avoidance purposes and it must not create a distortion of competition.

2. Community projects

A local authority may agree with a voluntary group to set up a **project fund** into which any funds raised locally, and any grants received by the voluntary group, will be paid. The authority then makes purchases of goods and services on behalf of the voluntary group which are financed by the fund. **7946** Notice 749 paras 11.1, 11.2; VATGBP4440

As these funds do not belong to the authority, any related input tax cannot be recovered.

If the authority **contributes its own funds**, the input tax can only be recovered where the authority retains control over how the money is spent and includes the fund in its own statutory accounts.

3. Work done to village halls

The VAT treatment of building work to village halls **depends on** whether the hall is owned by the local authority. **7948**

For this purpose, a hall is owned by a local authority if it is the sole managing trustee, not if it is just the sole custodian trustee (¶7914).

Owned

Where the **source of the funding** is: **7950** Notice 749 para 11.3
a. the authority's own funds, input tax can be recovered on its own non-business use and also taxable business use; or
b. from a third party, input tax can be recovered on taxable lettings, and donations where there is no benefit given in return, and the normal conditions are satisfied (¶7912).

Allowing use of the hall in return for non-monetary consideration is considered to be a business activity.

Not owned

If the authority carries out the work: **7952** Notice 749 para 11.4
– **for free**, using its own funds, no supply is made for VAT purposes, so input tax can be recovered under the rules of ¶7910; or
– in return for any **consideration** (monetary or non-monetary), this is likely to be a business supply, so input tax recovery depends on whether the supply is taxable or exempt.

MEMO POINTS 1. For this purpose **consideration** could include the right to use the hall after the work is completed.

2. The authority may **act as agent** on behalf of the hall's owners, in which case the normal agency rules apply (¶7115+).

4. Pension funds

7954 VATGBP4260-4290 Many local authorities are statutorily required to administer their own pension fund, without the option to set up a separate trust. This means that the pension fund's activities (mostly exempt investment income) are included with those of the authority. As a direct result it is likely that the authority will suffer irrecoverable exempt input tax. HMRC therefore grants a concession in relation to investment expenses.

Management costs

7956 The usual rules apply to input tax incurred on the management of the pension fund. These can be summarised as follows:

Situation	VAT treatment	Input tax recovery
Authority makes no charge to the scheme for running it	Non-business	See ¶7906
Authority charges other member authorities who are obliged to remain in the scheme	Non-business	See ¶7906
Authority charges member authorities who choose to enter the scheme	Taxable business	Only if registered for VAT

Investment expenses

7958 With the prior approval of HMRC, local authorities are allowed to **exclude** VAT on expenses which relate to the pension fund's investment expenses when checking whether their exempt input tax is insignificant (¶7880). This includes the VAT incurred in respect of the non-business and taxable activities, as well as exempt activities, that is, both investment and administrative activities. Any VAT which relates to admitted bodies (for which the authority has no obligation to provide a pension) is not included within this concession.

7960 This calculation should be included within the authority's written Section 33 **method** (¶7884) and therefore must operate for at least 1 year and coincide with the year to 31 March.

If the **exempt input tax**:
– remains insignificant, the authority will be entitled to recover all of its VAT, including that relating to the exempt pension fund activities; or
– is significant, the authority will not be entitled to recover the VAT incurred on any of its exempt activities, including those relating to the pension fund.

Sufficient **records** must be kept to enable the pension fund expenses to be easily identified.

5. Education

7962 Notice 701/30 para 10 Local education authorities have a duty to meet all expenses of maintaining community schools and community special schools. Education provided by a local authority **to its pupils** is non-business, meaning that all related VAT can be recovered. Sales to pupils that are closely related to their education can also be treated as non-business, provided that certain conditions are met.

Education provided by a local authority by way of **business** is generally exempt from VAT (¶398). This is because a local authority is an eligible body. This means that input VAT related to business supplies of education has to be identified and included in the authority's Section 33 calculation. Any sales that are closely related to the supply of VAT-exempt education are also exempt, provided that the usual conditions (¶410) are met.

Voluntary aided schools

Local authorities are responsible for all revenue costs at voluntary aided schools, as well as capital works to playing fields or any buildings related to their use. The governing body is responsible for all other buildings, perimeter walls and fences, playgrounds, furniture, fixtures and fittings and all other capital items, including ICT equipment. **7964** Notice 701/30 para 15.7

Recovery applies only to VAT incurred by local authorities and public bodies on **goods and services that they purchase**. Recovery is not allowed on contributions to the cost of goods and services purchased by another legal entity, because those supplies are not made to the public body.

Foundation schools

The governing bodies of foundation schools act as agents of the local authority. Where the school governors purchase goods or services while acting as an agent of the local authority and using funds from the school's delegated budget or from local education authority central funds, any VAT incurred by a school is recoverable through the local authority. **7966** Notice 701/30 para 10.4

Governing bodies of foundation schools have charitable status. Therefore when they act in their own name they may be able to secure zero-rating of certain construction projects (¶5170+).

CHAPTER 12

Charities

OUTLINE ¶¶

VAT is a large cost to the charity sector, primarily in the form of irrecoverable input tax. **8000**

There are several VAT reliefs which apply to supplies made by charities and, more crucially, supplies to charities. However, most business activities undertaken by charities are subject to the normal VAT rules.

SECTION 1

Scope

A body is considered to be a charity if it has charitable status. **8005** Notice 701/1 para 2.2

Charitable status is usually evidenced by the entity's registration with a charity regulator. Not all charities are required to be registered, for example, those which are too small or exempted by statute (usually because the entity is supervised by another type of regulator).

On application, **unregistered** charities may be recognised as having charitable status by HMRC.

MEMO POINTS The various **regulators** for each region of the UK are as follows:
- England and Wales, Charity Commission (flmemo.co.uk/vm8005EW);
- Scotland, Office of the Scottish Charities Regulator (flmemo.co.uk/vm8005S); and
- Northern Ireland, Charity Commission for Northern Ireland (flmemo.co.uk/vm8005NI).

Trading activities

8007 Notice 701/1 para 2.3

Due to the requirements of charity law, trading **carried out by the charity itself** is restricted to undertaking a primary purpose, such as the provision of residential accommodation by a care charity.

If trading is a method of **raising funds** (called non-primary purpose trading), the activity is often carried out by a subsidiary company. This is partly for direct tax reasons but also helps to reassure donors that their contributions are being put towards a charity's primary purpose, or invested prudently, rather than being risked in independent trading activities. A common example of such trading is the sale of goods in charity shops or via mail order catalogues.

Subsidiary companies

8010 As a subsidiary company itself does not have **charitable status**, most of the charity VAT reliefs are not available (the exceptions being fundraising events (¶392) and the sale of donated goods (¶1372)), so the company will mainly be within the normal VAT rules. Where the majority of its supplies are taxable, most VAT incurred can be recovered, so the charity VAT reliefs are less important.

If both the charity and a subsidiary company are VAT-registered it may be possible for them to register as a **VAT group** (¶8800).

SECTION 2

Business v non-business

8020 Whether a charity has any business activities can affect the overall VAT cost to the charity as follows:

Types of supplies	Implications
Taxable business activities	Compulsory registration if supplies over the registration threshold (¶9960) Voluntary registration also possible If registered: – output tax levied on income including certain grants and donations (¶8040); and – input tax can be recovered under the normal rules which apply to commercial traders
Exempt business activities (e.g. health, education, welfare)	Not able to register No VAT charge on supplies Input tax irrecoverable
No business activities	Not able to register No VAT charge on supplies Input tax generally irrecoverable, although certain construction and building works can be zero-rated (¶5170)

Comment It can be seen that making exempt business supplies puts the charity in the worst VAT position. In this case, reducing the VAT incurred on expenses (¶8080) is vital.

Business activities

8022 As the statutory **definition** (¶134) of a business activity is very limited in its scope, a significant body of case law has developed which offers more assistance and practical guidance (¶105+).

In summary, a business activity is mainly intended to make supplies in return for consideration (but not necessarily profit). Where a charge is made to cover a charity's costs this may still be a business activity.

Most charities that **charge fees** are treated as being in business, and so are usually in the position of having to apportion input tax between their business and non-business activities (¶8094).

It is also important to determine **how many activities** are undertaken by the charity (¶310); that is, whether an activity is:
- incidental to a principal one (in which case both can be treated the same way (¶312)); or
- substantial enough to require separate VAT treatment (¶314).

Comment Where it is not clear whether a business activity exists, a VAT professional should be consulted to ensure that VAT registration is not required, or indeed beneficial.

Case law

Case law pertinent to charities is discussed below. 8024

EXAMPLE

1. A charity ran a children's day nursery in a deprived area of Birmingham. Some of the places were paid for by the local authority, whereas others were funded by parents. Although the charity operated on a break-even basis, it did have to make a charge due to insufficient grant funding. The charity claimed a VAT relief which was only available if it was not in business.
It was held that the nursery did not constitute a business, as it was not predominantly concerned with the making of taxable supplies to consumers for consideration. The charity was forced to charge a fee to enable it to continue to carry out its charitable objects. *C & E v St Paul's Community Project Ltd* [2004]

Note:
HMRC has stated that it does not agree with the High Court's decision in this case. In particular, it does not agree that the following features point to the activities being non-business: Business Brief 2/05
- the social concern for the welfare of disadvantaged children;
- lack of commerciality in setting fees; and
- the overall intention simply to cover costs.

However, HMRC decided not to appeal further, so it now has no choice but to accept that the provision of nursery and crèche facilities by charities along the same lines is not a business activity for VAT purposes.

2. A charity operated a playgroup with a turnover of approximately £4,000 p.a. This turnover arose from voluntary parental contributions.
It was held that the low turnover and the voluntary nature of the contributions indicated that the playgroup was not a business. *Newtonbutler Playgroup Ltd* [1995] (VTD 13741)

3. A charity received investment income of more than £1 million p.a. The charity's other income was 95% non-business.
It was held that the charity's investments could not be regarded as constituting a business, as they supported the charity's non-business activities. *National Society for the Prevention of Cruelty to Children* [1992] (VTD 9325)

4. A charity ran an art gallery and received fees from exhibiting artists. Visitors did not pay an admission charge. Other income came from the sale of merchandise, tours and lectures, and, occasionally, the hire of the gallery and admission to special exhibitions. The charity tried to reclaim all of its input tax on the basis that it was making wholly business supplies.
It was held that the free admission was not a business activity and this should not be regarded as incidental to the other business activities. As such, input tax recovery was restricted. *Whitechapel Art Gallery v C & E* [1986]

5. A museum usually charged for admission. However, on one day every week, school parties could visit free of charge.
It was held that the running of the museum amounted to a single business (including the gift shop, cafes and so on). The visitors who were admitted for free could use all of the museum's facilities and so the free admission did not constitute a separate activity. *Imperial War Museum* [1993] (VTD 9097)

6. A charity providing care and support to sufferers of epilepsy sought a ruling on the construction of a new national centre for diagnosis, treatment, care and advice. HMRC contended that the

charity was in business, as it had a defined customer base (primarily the NHS), raised invoices and received payments for services supplied. The Tribunal upheld the charity's arguments that it was not in business as the sums it received were not linked to the cost of the care given, the charity having to accept whatever payment the NHS deemed suitable and also that there was no general market for the services supplied. In this sense there was no business activity being carried on. *Quarriers* [2008] (VTD 20660)

7. A school provided services including care services for children with emotional difficulties, receiving funding from local authorities on a per-child basis and by grant from central government. The costs were further subsidised by reducing the management charge levied from the main branch of the charity. HMRC argued that the provision of care and accommodation was a business activity and that the function it performed was not unique. The Tribunal stated that the key factor as to whether the school was in business or not was the function it performed, not whether there was a direct link between the provision of the care and the payment by the local authorities. The absence of a profit motive added weight to the fact that the school's key concern was a social and not economic one. *Quarriers (No 2)* [2008] (VTD 20670)

SECTION 3

Types of income

8035 As a result of the increasing pressure to diversify, either in response to falling donations or due to pressure from bodies providing funding, a charity may receive many different types of income.

UK business activities can be assumed to be taxable at the standard rate unless specifically reduced-rated, zero-rated or exempted from VAT by law.

Non-business activities are outside the scope of VAT, which means no output tax is charged on income but no input tax can be recovered on associated expenses.

Summary

8037 Notice 701/1 para 5

Area	Income	Detail	VAT treatment	¶¶
Cash inflows	Donations	Freely given with nothing supplied in return	Outside the scope	
	Bequeathed property	Treated as a donation	Outside the scope	
	Grant funding	Benefits given in return	Standard-rated	¶8040
		No benefits given	Outside the scope	¶8040
	Sponsorship	Charity organises an event - admission and sale of items	Exempt	¶392
		Commercially organised event where participants are sponsored	May be standard-rated	¶8044
	Patron and supporter schemes	Benefits for a minimum payment	Usually standard-rated	¶8048
	Subscriptions	In return for benefits to members	Usually taxable, may be exempt	¶8180
Financial income	Bank interest	Treated as non-business income	Outside the scope	
	Affinity credit cards	Payments in return for endorsing a credit card	Part is standard-rated	¶8050
	Dividends	Treated as non-business income	Outside the scope	
	Share sales	Treated as non-business income	Outside the scope	

Area	Income	Detail	VAT treatment	¶¶
Sales and events	Admission charges	For admittance to fundraising event	Exempt	¶392
		To cultural event	Exempt	¶386
		Donation in lieu of admission (a purely voluntary payment) even where charity suggests an amount	Outside the scope	¶8054
		Other (but not free admission)	Standard-rated	¶140
	Sale of goods [1]	Sale or hire of donated goods, such as in a charity shop or at a fundraising event	Zero-rated	¶1372
		Sale of bought-in goods at fundraising events	Exempt	¶392
		Sale of other bought-in goods	Standard-rated unless different rate of VAT applies under normal rules (e.g. books are zero-rated)	
	Export of goods	Any goods so long as proof of export retained	Zero-rated	¶9581
Services provided	Ambulance services	Supply of transport services for sick or injured persons for a journey to or from a place of medical treatment Vehicle must be specially designed for the purpose of providing such transport [2]	Exempt	
		Vehicle designed to carry at least ten people	Zero-rated	¶1282
	Catering	As part of a fundraising event	Exempt	¶392
		As part of welfare services, such as meals in care homes, schools, prisons and hospitals	Exempt	¶428
		Other situations	Standard-rated	
	Education and training	Carrying out essentially public natured educational services	Exempt	¶398
	Hiring out of property	Depends on use made and whether licence to occupy granted	Usually exempt	¶8212
	Sports and physical recreation	Within the list of sporting activities which HMRC regards as qualifying for exemption	Exempt	¶418
	Welfare	Provision of care, education etc to promote: – the physical or mental welfare of elderly, sick, distressed [3] or disabled people; – protection of children; or – spiritual welfare	Exempt	¶434
		Services provided directly to distressed individuals [3] at significantly below cost (meaning subsidised by at least 15% irrespective of recipient's ability to pay)	Outside the scope	
		Advice or information relating to: – the physical or mental welfare of elderly, sick, distressed [3] or disabled persons; or – the care and protection of children and young persons	Reduced-rated	¶1160

Area	Income	Detail	VAT treatment	¶¶
Other	Sale of advertising space in charity's own publications	To another charity	Zero-rated	¶1378
		At least 50% of adverts in a publication are clearly placed by private individuals[4]	All income outside the scope	
		Publication relates to a fundraising event	Exempt[5]	¶392
		Other	Standard-rated	
	Supply of staff between charities	Staff employed by both charities	No supply	
		Staff works for non-business parts of both charities and payment between the charities does not exceed the costs of normal remuneration (pay, National Insurance, pension contributions and similar)	Outside the scope	
		Other situations	Standard-rated	
	Sea rescue	No charge made	Outside the scope	

Note:
1. A **VAT-registered business** can zero-rate its donation of goods that are to be offered for sale by a charity (¶1362).
2. The **vehicle** must have the facility to secure a recumbent person on a stretcher or be fitted with a ramp or a lift, and clamps sufficient to enable a person in a wheelchair to be safely wheeled on, transported in, and wheeled off the vehicle. This can apply in principle to helicopter air ambulances and other forms of rescue transport and not just emergency vehicles. The costs of the vehicle may be relieved from VAT (¶8082).
3. **Distressed** means suffering pain, grief, anguish or severe poverty.
4. A **private advertisement** is one which makes no reference to a business, such as "Good wishes from (or "space donated by") Mr A"; but not those with otherwise similar wording such as "Mr A, Grocers, 100 High Street".
5. However, such a supply is zero-rated if the sale is to another charity.

1. Grant funding

8040 Notice 701/1 para 5.10

The treatment of grants received can give rise to the most difficulty and **depends on** whether the charity gives:
– something in return (either to the donor or a third party), when a supply is then made for consideration, which is usually a taxable supply; or
– nothing in return, when the funding is outside the scope of VAT.

Most grants and subsidies are outside the scope. However, the terms of any grant should always be examined as the funding agreement may be more in terms of a service level agreement (see examples below) than a simple grant. Conditions requiring the charity to spend the money on its intended purpose ("**good housekeeping**"), for example, complying with audit requests or sending copies of reports to the donor where this is incidental to the amount of funding, do not create a supply.

EXAMPLE

1. A trader ran a citizens' advice bureau and received grant funding from a local authority. The issue was whether the grant constituted consideration for a supply because one of the grant conditions required a detailed report and accounts to be submitted to the local authority, to prove that the grant was being spent as intended.
It was held that no supply was made and the grant was outside the scope of VAT because the report and accounts were only normal administrative controls. There was no link between the grant and the services supplied to the public. *Hillingdon Legal Resource Centre* [1991] (VTD 5210)

2. Advice about energy-saving was given to householders. The entity supplying the advice received a grant of £10 per household from a third party.
It was held by the CJEU that the advice was given in return for the consideration of £10, which made it a taxable supply. *Keeping Newcastle Warm v C & E* [2002]

3. It is not always necessary for the funding to be specifically and contractually earmarked for particular individual activities for it to be consideration for a taxable supply. In this case the funding

was provided by the local authority in return for the trust agreeing to put on a series of music festivals, which would otherwise have been the authority's responsibility. The taxable service supplied by the trust was that it relieved the council of the need to put on the festivals, or something similar, itself. *Bath Festivals Trust Ltd* [2008] (VTD 20840)

MEMO POINTS 1. If **VAT is payable**, this will usually reduce the amount that is actually received by the charity unless the grantor is willing to absorb the cost.
2. The VAT treatment of the grant monies has no impact on the VAT treatment of the **supplies made by the charity** when using the money. Such supplies must be considered separately.

2. Fundraising events and sponsorship

Where the **charity is organising** and promoting the event, it may be able to take advantage of the fundraising exemption (¶392). **8042** Notice 701/1 para 5.9

Charity challenge events

Many charities offer or encourage participation in challenge events to raise funds. The income from these may be taxable, exempt or outside the scope of VAT, depending on the circumstances. **8044**

If the charity allows individuals to take part **regardless of the amount they raise**, in return for no benefits, the income can be treated as a donation and outside the scope of VAT.

If there is a requirement to pay a **minimum amount**, whether this be a minimum amount of sponsorship, registration fee or non-refundable deposit, that amount is standard-rated, with any excess being treated as a donation. However, the fundraising exemption (¶392) may still apply to exempt all income arising from the event.

If **benefits are offered** in return for participating, the sponsorship monies are standard-rated.

If the charity offers **prizes to top fundraisers**, these are not benefits for VAT purposes and do not affect the VAT treatment of the sponsorship monies.

MEMO POINTS 1. The following are **excluded** from being **benefits** for this purpose:
- provision of free training and health advice;
- a free t-shirt, running vest or similar item that clearly portrays the charity's name;
- free massages and support for physical well-being during the event;
- free pre-event meeting, which may include free professional advice or support, a simple meal, energy drinks and encouragement from the charity and other participants; and
- free post-event meeting, which may include medical treatment or advice, changing facilities and light refreshments, and gives the charity the opportunity to thank participants.

2. If the charity wants the participant to pledge to raise a certain amount, but **does not deny** entry if that amount is not actually achieved, all monies raised can be treated as a donation (and as such outside the scope of VAT).

The fundraising exemption **will not apply** where the package includes: **8045**
- both travel and accommodation;
- bought-in accommodation; or
- more than two nights in accommodation provided from the charity's own resources.

In the first two cases the supply is likely to fall under the TOMS provisions (¶7490).

Sponsorship

A charity may **receive cash, goods or services** from a sponsor. **8046** Notice 701/41; Notice 701/1 para 5.9.5

The VAT treatment depends on whether the charity:
- is obliged to provide the sponsor with a significant benefit in return, when this constitutes a business activity which is taxable at the standard rate; or
- gives no significant benefits, when the income may be non-business.

If **taxable supplies** are made in return for sponsorship, VAT must be accounted for on a value that covers everything received under the sponsorship agreement. If the amount of sponsorship is agreed without allowing for VAT, it must be treated as VAT-inclusive.

Notice 701/41 paras 2.1, 2.2

MEMO POINTS 1. Typical examples of **benefits** and their significance for this purpose are listed below.

Type of benefit	Significant	Insignificant
Naming an event after the sponsor	✓	
Naming a sponsor in a list of supporters		✓
Naming a building, a university Chair or a theatre seat after the sponsor		✓
Displaying the sponsor's company logo or trading name	✓	
Allowing the sponsor to use the charity's name or logo	✓	
Participating in the sponsor's promotional or advertising activities	✓	
Providing entertainment or hospitality facilities	✓	
A flag or sticker		✓
Giving free or reduced-price tickets	✓	
Giving exclusive or priority booking rights	✓	
Allowing access to special events such as a premiere or gala evening	✓	

2. **Advertising services** provided to a non-UK sponsor may be outside the scope of UK VAT (¶9716).

3. Patron and supporter schemes

8048
Notice 701/1 para 5.14

Where a **minimum payment** is required to obtain benefits (for example, free admission to special exhibitions, the right to receive regular publications or discounts on shop purchases) it is usually standard-rated. The payment could be treated as a multiple supply (¶8182), which would be advantageous if some of the benefits are zero-rated (such as a newsletter).

Any **excess paid** can be treated as a donation and outside the scope of VAT, provided the scheme literature explicitly states that any excess over the minimum amount is a voluntary donation.

EXAMPLE A charity ran a theatre and, in order to raise funds for a refurbishment, it offered sponsors priority booking for two performances and public acknowledgements (in the form of a seat plaque and list of named sponsors) in return for sponsorship of £150. The cost of the benefits to the charity was only £5.
It was held that the charity would not have provided the benefits for less than £150, and so it was providing services in return for consideration. Hence the whole amount was liable to VAT. It was irrelevant that the marginal cost of the benefits to the charity was minimal. *C & E v Tron Theatre Ltd* [1994]

4. Affinity cards

8050
Notice 701/1 paras 5.3, 8

The endorsement of particular credit cards results in **two types of payment** to a charity:
- an initial amount on the issue of each new card; and
- a percentage of the value of purchases made on the card.

Both types of payment are standard-rated, unless the **charity is acting as an intermediary**, in which case they are exempt.

However, there is a **relief** which allows charities which are **not acting as intermediaries** to treat part of these payments as standard-rated, with the remainder being outside the scope of VAT.

MEMO POINTS 1. **Endorsement** usually involves:
- access to the charity's membership or mailing lists and/or mailing of the card provider's promotional literature to members;
- marketing of the card by the charity to its members or supporters; and
- the right to use the charity's name and logo, for example, on the card and on the provider's promotional literature.

2. A charity will be **acting as an intermediary** in arranging a contract between its members and a credit card provider where it:
– stands between the parties to a contract in the performance of a distinct act of negotiation, without having any interest of its own in the terms of the contract;
– brings the two parties to the contract together; and
– undertakes preparatory work, such as completing or assisting with completion of application forms, forwarding forms to the credit card company, and making representations on behalf of either party.
Providing a **list of names or access to a database** does not count as intermediary services.

The relief **works** by treating payments made solely in respect of the use of the charity's name and logo as contributions for which the charity is not obliged to do anything in return. There must be two separate agreements as follows: **8052** Notice 701/1 para 8.2

Agreement	Payment made in respect of	VAT treatment
Agreement 1	Access to the charity's membership or mailing lists	Standard-rated
	Marketing of the card by the charity	Standard-rated
Agreement 2	The right to use the charity's name and logo	Outside the scope

If the relief applies, at least 20% of the **initial payment** can be treated as the consideration for the standard-rated business supplies by the charity. The remaining initial payment and all subsequent **payments based on purchases** will be outside the scope of VAT.

5. Donations in lieu of admission

A common method of raising funds is to allow admission to premises in return for a donation. **8054** Notice 701/1 para 5.1

If admission is still granted even **without any donation** paid, the amount received is outside the scope of VAT.

Charities usually suggest a **minimum amount** which is outside the scope if there is no element of compulsion.

EXAMPLE Application forms and tickets for a fundraising ball showed the price as £50, although the small print said, "for VAT purposes the entrance fee is £20. The balance of £30 represents a minimum voluntary donation in aid of hospice funds".
It was held that the use of the term "minimum voluntary donation" indicated compulsion and, in addition, the paperwork stated that the price was £50, implying that admission would not be granted unless this amount was paid. So the whole amount was liable to VAT. *Glasgow's Miles Better Mid-Summer 5th Anniversary Ball* [1989] (VTD 4460)

SECTION 4

VAT registration

The usual registration rules apply to charities, so if taxable supplies exceed the registration threshold, the charity **must** register for VAT (¶2668). **8065** Notice 701/1 para 3.2

The charity can **voluntarily** register for VAT (¶2688) if it is making any taxable supplies and wishes to recover the associated input tax. This is unlikely to be a good strategy for most charities, the exceptions being where costly building work is incurred, or a large amount of exports are made. This is because they would have to charge VAT on any standard-rated supplies, which may make their sales price uncompetitive.

Charities with **no business activities**, or where all **supplies are exempt**, are not eligible to register, so any VAT incurred is not input tax and cannot be reclaimed.

MEMO POINTS 1. **Taxable supplies** includes supplies at any rate of VAT other than exempt supplies. Smaller charities should carefully review their fundraising and sponsorship income (¶8042+).
2. If **mainly zero-rated supplies** are made, HMRC may allow a charity not to register (¶2652), although it may be beneficial to do so.
3. Larger charities tend to be organised into **local branches**. The liability to register will depend on the constitution of the charity and its branches. If branches have legal autonomy, the liability to register would fall on them individually.
4. A charity may prefer to have a monthly **VAT period** (¶2987), which will speed up the cash inflow where the VAT return shows a VAT recovery position.
5. Charities whose business activities take place **wholly outside the UK** can register for VAT if those activities would be taxable were they to take place in the UK.

Implications

8067 If registered, a charity must account for **output tax** on its taxable supplies like a commercial trader, except that charities are afforded certain reliefs which reduce the rate of VAT applicable (¶8037). Output tax is not relevant to non-business activities, zero-rated or exempt supplies.

Input tax relating to taxable supplies (at any rate) is recoverable. Most charities make some exempt supplies, and are therefore partly exempt, which means input tax recovery is restricted. There are some reliefs which reduce the VAT due on certain purchases (¶8082). No input tax can be reclaimed on non-business activities. See ¶8094 for further details.

Where a charity **defaults on its VAT debt**, no formal recovery action will be taken (¶3746).

Small business schemes

8070 A charity may choose to use the following schemes which are designed to **simplify VAT**:
a. annual accounting (¶4745), which reduces VAT accounting requirements and helps to manage cash flow in the following ways:
- only one VAT return needs to be completed each year;
- fixed interim payments are made towards the eventual VAT liability; and
- an extra month is allowed to complete and submit the VAT return, and pay any balance of tax due; or

b. cash accounting (¶4880) (of limited advantage to charities), which defers payment of VAT liabilities by accounting for output tax when payment is received from customers, rather then when supplies are made. This also gives automatic bad debt relief. However, input tax can only be claimed when payment is made to the supplier.

The **flat rate scheme** is unlikely to be of interest to charities.

SECTION 5

Expenses

8080 Notice 701/1 para 6 Any charity will pay VAT on all standard-rated and reduced-rated goods and services acquired from VAT-registered businesses. Certain supplies to charities are zero-rated under the general rules (¶1180).

In addition, VAT-registered businesses can sell certain goods and services to charities at the reduced rate or zero rate (even if the charity is not VAT-registered), which means that the charity incurs less input VAT.

1. Reducing the VAT incurred

8082 Notice 701/1 paras 6, 7 Where a charity provides an eligibility certificate (¶8084) to the supplier the following goods and services are zero-rated or reduced-rated, so long as all the specified conditions are met.

Supply	Type of purchasing charity	Examples	VAT treatment	¶¶
Advertising	All	– newspapers – electronic media – television and radio – production and design costs	Zero-rated	¶1378
Goods connected with collecting donations	All	– collection boxes – envelopes – appeal letters – lapel stickers – emblems – badges	Zero-rated	¶1380
Certain building and construction works	All	– village hall – building solely to be used for charitable purposes – includes self-builds	Zero-rated	¶5170
First grant of a major interest in a building	All	– village hall – building solely to be used for charitable purposes	Zero-rated	¶5247
Adaptations to a building	All	– construction of a ramp – widening of a doorway or passage – providing or extending a washroom or lavatory	Zero-rated	¶1344
Fuel and power[1]	All	– coal, electricity, gas etc – supplied for use in a dwelling or other type of residential accommodation – free day care for the disabled	Reduced-rated	¶1116
Supply and installation of energy saving materials	All	– central heating – insulation – solar panels – wind and water turbines – vegetable fuelled boilers	Reduced-rated	¶1136
Drugs, chemicals and medicinal products	Either: – providing care, medical or surgical treatment for humans or animals; or – undertaking medical or veterinary research	– natural or artificial substances used for testing – products to mix with other substances – liquids – gases (cylinders also relieved from VAT) – contraception	Zero-rated	¶1390
Aids, medical and scientific equipment	Either: – an eligible body (a health body, research institution or certain charitable institution); or – a charity who donates to an eligible body	– ambulances – laboratory equipment – sterilising tools – medical and surgical appliances	Zero-rated	¶1374
	Makes goods available to a disabled person for personal or domestic use	– chair and stair lifts – hoists – drugs – adaptations of goods – vehicles and boats – alarm systems – adjustable beds – sanitary wear – cars and scooters – medical and surgical appliances – installation of zero-rated items	Zero-rated	¶1332

Supply	Type of purchasing charity	Examples	VAT treatment	¶¶
Rescue equipment	Either: – providing rescue or first aid services; or – a charity which donates to an eligible body	Equipment used solely for rescue or first-aid activities, including: – specialist communication devices – light enhancing equipment – heat detecting equipment – resuscitation training models	Zero-rated	¶1374
Equipment to produce talking books and newspapers	Caring for the blind and visually impaired	– sound recording equipment – reproduction equipment – radios and cassette players for loaning out	Zero-rated	¶1366
Lifeboats etc	Providing rescue or assistance at sea	– launching and recovery equipment – vessel used as a lifeboat – associated spares and equipment – construction and modification of slipways	Zero-rated	¶1368

Note:
1. If qualifying for reduced-rated fuel and power, a charity will be exempt from the **climate change levy**.

Eligibility declaration

8084 Notice 701/1 para 6.2 An eligibility declaration must be completed **by the charity** for each of the reliefs. Such a declaration can be included on an order form (but see ¶1336).

MEMO POINTS HMRC gives **examples** of declarations for each type of relief at flmemo.co.uk/vm8084.

8086 Notice 701/6 para 8.3 It is the **supplier's responsibility** to ensure that the correct VAT rate is applied. The supplier must therefore take reasonable steps to check that all relevant conditions are met, including obtaining evidence that the customer is actually a charity. These steps will require the co-operation of the charity.

MEMO POINTS 1. **Evidence** of all additional verifications carried out should be kept with the declaration of eligibility.

Notice 48 para 3.11 2. If a supplier has taken reasonable steps to check the validity of a declaration and reduces the VAT rate in good faith but fails to identify **an inaccuracy**, HMRC will not seek to recover the tax due from the supplier.

Purchases from overseas

8088 Notice 701/1 paras 6.3, 6.4 **General** VAT-registered eligible organisations that buy goods from:

a. other **EU member states** will enjoy the same VAT treatment as if the purchase was made from a UK supplier, albeit that they may have to apply the reverse charge mechanism (¶9700); or

b. outside the EU will be required to pay import VAT (¶9405) unless a relief applies.

MEMO POINTS **Eligible organisations** include:

a. registered charities;

b. state organisations which are devoted to welfare; and

c. the following types of organisation, provided they are non-profit-making and their objective is the welfare of the needy:

- hospitals;
- youth organisations;
- clubs, homes and hostels for the aged;
- orphanages and children's homes;

- those set up for the relief of distress caused by particular disasters in the EU; or
- those concerned with the relief of distress generally (such as the British Red Cross Society or the Salvation Army).

Imports The following imports can be **relieved** from VAT: 8090 Notice 317
- basic necessities (including food, medicines, clothing and blankets, orthopaedic equipment and crutches) for those in need which are obtained by the charity free of charge;
- goods to be used or sold at occasional charity events for the benefit of those in need;
- equipment and office materials to help run an organisation for the benefit of those in need; or
- goods to help deal with disasters in the EU (excluding those used for rebuilding).

However, the following are **excluded**:
- alcoholic products (including alcohol based perfume);
- tobacco and tobacco products;
- coffee and tea;
- motor vehicles other than ambulances;
- items associated solely with worship such as statues and pulpits; and
- any goods whose importation would give rise to abuse or a major distortion of competition.

MEMO POINTS 1. An **occasional charity event** means any event held normally not more than four times a year by any single organisation. All goods which are obtained free of charge and without any commercial motive on the part of the donor can be relieved. 8092
2. **Equipment and office materials** includes machines, tools and equipment of the service industry, and fixtures and fittings. All equipment must be obtained:
- free of charge from a person or organisation established outside the EU;
- without any commercial intent on the part of the donor; and
- solely to help run the organisation and carry out its charitable and philanthropic aims for the benefit of those in need.

3. The **disposal** of imported goods outside the eligible purposes will make the charity liable to VAT. These goods may be lent, hired out or transferred to another charity without payment of VAT, provided that HMRC are notified first.

Claiming relief

The relief is claimed as follows: 8093

Method of importing	Value of goods	Procedure
Accompanied baggage	Less than £600	Both: - declared at the Customs Red Channel or Red Point; and - evidence produced to satisfy HMRC that all the conditions of the relief are met[1]
	More than £600	As above plus formal import declaration (¶9426)
Freight	Any	Formal import declaration (¶9426)
Post	Any	Sender should write "charity items: relief claimed" clearly on the package and its accompanying international Customs declaration[2]

Note:
1. HMRC suggests that a **letter** from a responsible official of the charity would be appropriate stating that the conditions will be met. The letter should also describe the goods, state how they will be used and whether the goods are donated or purchased.

If **evidence is not satisfactory**, the importer will need to give financial security (normally a cash deposit or banker's guarantee) to cover the VAT. This can be discharged when sufficient proof is supplied.

2. If **more information is required**, the charity will be sent a simplified form to complete. Once satisfied, HMRC will then release the goods for delivery free of VAT.

If the **package is not clearly marked** it may not be delivered until the charity has paid the VAT. In this case, the charity should write to HMRC at the postal depot where the charges were raised, enclosing the document showing the amount paid. The VAT should then be repaid.

2. Recovery of input tax

8094 The usual **stages** of identifying recoverable input tax should be applied i.e.:
a. allocate expenses between business and non-business activities (¶1838) using a particular basis such as income, staff time, etc(some expenses, such as overheads, will need to be apportioned);
b. within the business segment allocate directly attributable input tax between taxable and exempt supplies made by the charity, leaving a remainder which relates to both types (known as residual input tax);
c. apportion the residual input tax between taxable and exempt supplies (¶2075+); and
d. recover the input tax relating to business taxable supplies only (unless total exempt input tax is below certain limits, when that too can be recovered (¶2195)).

MEMO POINTS 1. It is possible to have a **global calculation** which takes account of both non-business and exempt supplies. This will usually be based on the charity's income. However, it is unlikely to result in the best VAT recovery for the charity.

Business Brief 19/05 2. The costs of **professional fundraisers** should be allocated to non-business, exempt business or taxable business activities, depending on the charity's use of the funds raised. *Church of England Children's Society* [2005]

3. **Smaller charities** may decide that calculating apportionments for both business/non-business and taxable/exempt is not a cost-effective use of their resources.

4. **Larger charities** will benefit from undertaking this work but the calculations may be complex and will need agreement from HMRC.

5. For recovery of input tax on the purchase of assets covered by the **capital goods scheme** see ¶2296.

CHAPTER 13

Clubs and associations

OUTLINE ¶¶

The main VAT issues facing clubs and associations are whether they undertake any type of business activity and, if so, what type of income they receive. **8140**

If there is no business, all activities fall outside the scope of VAT, so any VAT incurred on expenses is not input tax and cannot be reclaimed.

If a business activity exists, the type of income will determine whether VAT registration is required (or indeed advantageous) and how much input tax can be recovered. A club with business activities and making taxable supplies in excess of the registration threshold (¶2568) must register for VAT and account for output tax on its taxable supplies, like any commercial entity. Notice 701/5 para 2.1

MEMO POINTS 1. Sometimes a club may have different **branches or sub-clubs**. In this case, unless the branch concerned can demonstrate that it has both constitutional and financial independence from its parent organisation, all of its supplies must be included with those of the parent organisation. Notice 701/5 para 2.4
2. If there is **more than one club** involved, payments by one for the use of facilities owned by the other will be consideration for a supply of services. This supply might be exempt or taxable, depending on the circumstances.
3. For the treatment of **input tax** incurred for both **business and non-business** activities, see ¶1838 onwards.

SECTION 1

Business activity?

The statutory definition (¶100) of a business activity is very limited in its scope. Case law offers more assistance and practical guidance (¶105). **8145** s 94 VATA 1994

In summary, a business activity is mainly intended to make supplies in return for consideration (but not necessarily profit). So, in most instances, the receipt of subscriptions will constitute a business.

However, where a club merely collects monies from members in order to pay for expenditure on their behalf, it may be acting as agent and so satisfy the disbursement criteria (¶7190), which would take the transaction outside the scope of VAT.

Comment Where it is not clear whether a business activity exists, a VAT professional should be consulted to confirm whether VAT registration is required, so that the club is not exposed to penalties.

Official guidance

8147 Notice 701/5 paras 2.2, 2.3

HMRC has given the following **indications** of when a club would be considered to be undertaking a business activity.

Situation	Business	Not a business
Services to members	Providing benefits in return for membership subscriptions (for horse racing clubs see ¶6180)	
	Providing benefits to members in return for a separate charge	
	Lobbying on behalf of the members	Spreading political beliefs or lobbying for a public or charitable good cause
Services to non-members	In return for a charge, such as providing catering, social and other facilities	Providing free literature to non-members
		The receipt of freely given donations, where no benefit is supplied in return
Admission	Admission to any premises for a charge	Free admission to premises for non-members

Case law

8150 Case law especially relevant to clubs and associations is discussed below.

EXAMPLE

1. An unincorporated association was set up for cab drivers, providing premises and a telephone system in return for payment. It employed an office manager and telephone operators.
It was held that, as an unincorporated association, it was a legal entity quite separate from its members. It was in business, providing them with benefits in return for consideration. *Eastbourne Town Radio Cars Association v C & E* [2001]

2. A fire station canteen was run by a fireman who was paid £1 per week; the fire service provided the equipment and the cooks. The prices were set at cost only. The canteen was called a club in its accounts, although there was no constitution or committee.
It was held that the canteen was not actually run by a club. The fireman was performing his duties as an employee of the fire service. *Nottingham Fire Service Messing Club* [1977] (VTD 348)

3. A new village was constructed and separated into different neighbourhoods. Each neighbourhood had its own residents' association registered under the Industrial and Provident Societies Act 1965. Each association was funded by residents' subscriptions which were used to maintain common areas and also redecorate the exterior of the houses.
It was held that the associations were in business, providing services in return for the subscription. *Manor Forstal Residents Society Ltd* [1976] (VTD 245)

4. The governing association for the village above was formed by members chosen by each of the neighbourhood associations. The association became a company limited by guarantee. Its role was to maintain amenity land in the village, provide street lighting, and look after the village sports ground and village hall. The homeowners paid the company under covenants which had to be signed when each house was purchased.
It was held that the homeowners were not members of the company, and therefore the company was not providing facilities to its members in return for consideration. *New Ash Green Village Association Ltd* [1976] (VTD 245)

5. A fund-raising association was established in order to help keep a museum solvent. The association stated that it did not need to register for VAT because:
- in law it was acting as an agent of the museum;
- members' subscriptions included donations which were passed to the museum; and
- any benefits received by members (such as free admission to sites and the receipt of a quarterly newsletter) came from the museum and not the association.

It was held that the members were making donations to the museum, which were outside the scope of VAT. Also the association did not provide any benefits to the members. *Friends of the Ironbridge Gorge Museum* [1991] (VTD 5639)

MEMO POINTS HMRC does not agree with the decision in the Ironbridge case above and will examine similar circumstances very carefully. VBNB60600

SECTION 2

Making a profit?

If the club does have a business activity, the next issue to consider is whether it qualifies as a non-profit-making body and therefore potentially able to make exempt supplies. This is important in relation to sports clubs and those linked to education or culture. **8160**

If the criteria for exemption from VAT are met, there is no entitlement to register for VAT, so no input tax can be recovered.

If both taxable and exempt supplies are made, VAT registration may be relevant and, if so, the club will be partly exempt (¶2075+), which usually means that some input tax can be recovered.

Non-profit-making body

Non-profit-making organisations are entities that: **8162** Sch 9 Group 13 note 2 VATA 1994
- are prohibited from distributing their **profits** (and do not in fact do so);
- **reinvest** any profits from the cultural activities to the continuance or improvement of cultural facilities; and
- are **managed and administered** on an essentially (not necessarily exclusively) voluntary basis by persons who have no direct or indirect financial interest in its activities (¶388).

In deciding whether a body is non-profit-making, HMRC will look at the **objects** for which it has been established, as distinct from the financial policy being pursued. Notice 701/5 para 11.3

A **surplus of income** from certain activities which is used to subsidise other activities will not necessarily cause an organisation to stop being non-profit-making, for example, a sports club which enjoys a surplus from its bar.

EXAMPLE

1. A company operated a symphony orchestra. Its managing director earned £80,000 p.a. full time.

It was held that the managing director's pay was inconsistent with a description of an essentially voluntary basis. So the company was not a non-profit-making body. *Bournemouth Symphony Orchestra v HMRC* [2006]

2. The administration of the Zoological Society of London was carried out by paid employees. However, the overall responsibility for its management fell to the members of its Council, who were in the position of trustees.

The ECJ held that the condition requiring a body to be managed and administered on an essentially voluntary basis refers to people:
- designated to direct the body at the highest level according to the constitution; and
- who in fact take the decisions of last resort (especially in the financial area) and carry out the higher supervisory tasks.

However, the condition did not refer to people carrying out the day to day operational activities that merely gave effect to the policy already laid down, and the Society was therefore a non-profit-making body. *C & E v The Zoological Society of London* [2002]

Types of activities

8164 If any of the following activities are **carried out by** a non-profit-making body, this will be an exempt supply.

Activity	Detail	¶¶
Fundraising	Supplies made to raise funds to enable the organisation to carry out its purpose	¶392
Educational services	Organisations that carry out essentially public natured educational services	¶398
Sport and recreation	Organisations established for the purposes of sport or physical recreation	¶418
Trade union activities etc	Subscription to any of the following organisations: – trade union; – professional association; – learned society; – representational trade association; or – any other public interest body	¶476

SECTION 3

Types of income

8175 Clubs may receive income from many diverse sources, including subscriptions and loans. A summary of other types of income is provided at ¶8208.

A. Subscriptions

8180 Most subscriptions are standard-rated, unless made exempt by a specific provision (¶8164) or paid in return for supplies which are zero-rated.

How many supplies?

8182 Notice 701/5 para 5 HMRC considers that where a subscription fee is paid to a membership body in return for a principal benefit and one or more ancillary benefits, the subscription fee must be treated as consideration for a single composite supply (¶312).

Where there is a **package** of principal benefits the VAT liability of the subscription depends on the liability of those various benefits, so a mixed supply (¶314) is being made. In this case, the subscription needs to be apportioned between those benefits, usually based on the relative cost of providing the different supplies to members in the previous financial year. If another apportionment method is chosen, HMRC should be sent details, with supporting documents such as the annual accounts.

In certain cases, the benefits are just nominal, so the subscription is akin to a **donation** and outside the scope of VAT. It is not possible to treat only a portion of the subscription as a donation, unless the organisation is a charity or a body with objects that are both in the public domain and of a philanthropic nature.

MEMO POINTS 1. **Principal benefits** would include: Notice 701/5 para 5.1
- magazines;
- handbooks;
- priority booking rights;
- guaranteed seats;
- discounts on admission charges; and
- items with a resale value.

HMRC considers these benefits to be substantive, regardless of whether there is any cost to the organisation in supplying them.

2. **Nominal benefits** include simple acknowledgements of support in the form of membership badges, flags or stickers, and the listing of names in a programme or on a theatre seat or entrance.

3. **Charities and other public philanthropic bodies** can treat part of the subscriptions as a donation, where either of the following conditions is satisfied:
- all the substantive benefits provided are available to non-members at no charge or more cheaply than the subscription (ignoring any nominal benefits); or
- some or all of the substantive benefits are exclusive to members and it can be verified that the amount paid is higher than the amount that the subscriber would normally have to pay for similar goods or services.

The value of any standard-rated, zero-rated and exempt supplies should be calculated, leaving the balance of the subscription to be treated as a donation. So the value of the **principal** benefits (ignoring nominal benefits) should be based on the price at which they are available to non-members, or the amount the subscriber would normally have to pay for similar goods or services. Notice 701/5 para 5.11

4. In **cases of doubt** the organisation should contact HMRC for advice.

However, a concession does exist to allow non-profit-making bodies and charities to apportion **apportion subscriptions** according to the liability of each individual benefit provided, even if under the normal rules there would be a single supply. This would be beneficial where part of the subscription is used to provide zero-rated printed matter. If the organisation does apply this concession, it must apportion all types and elements of all subscriptions: it cannot pick and choose. **8186** Notice 701/5 para 5.10

Associated fees

Additional **joining fees** of a general nature should be treated like normal subscriptions. An additional fee levied for a particular facility should be accounted for separately, based on the liability of the particular service or goods provided. **8188** Notice 701/5 paras 5.5 - 5.9

Fees for **life membership** are treated in the same way as annual subscriptions, unless life members obtain additional benefits not available to ordinary members. In this latter case, the VAT treatment would depend on the additional benefits provided.

If there is a charge for **paying by instalments**, i.e. the subscription fee is higher than if a single payment is made, this is an exempt supply of interest on a grant of credit.

A fee charged in return for being placed on a **waiting list** will normally be standard-rated, but it will be exempt if it satisfies both of the following conditions:
- it is deducted from the new member's first subscription or entrance fee (and the subscription or fee itself will qualify for exemption); and
- it is refundable if the candidate fails to become a member for any reason (including voluntary withdrawal).

If an organisation offers annual membership but allows members to **defer payment of their subscription** in return for an additional charge, that charge is consideration for an exempt grant of credit.

Overseas members

Subscriptions from overseas members will **only be treated differently** where they receive: **8190** Notice 701/5 para 5.13
- different benefits from UK members in return for their subscription to a UK club; or
- the same benefits but the VAT rules require a different treatment.

In these circumstances, a separate **apportionment** of the overseas subscription will need to be carried out.

Type of benefit	VAT treatment	¶¶
Services	Depends on type of service and sometimes location of customer	¶9680
Goods sent to non-EU members	Zero-rated	¶9581
Goods sent to EU VAT-registered members to be used in their business	Could be zero-rated if certain conditions met. Otherwise normal UK VAT rules	¶9077
Goods sent to EU non-VAT-registered members	UK VAT rules unless EU state's distance selling registration threshold breached	¶9177

B. Loans and share finance

8194 Notice 701/5 para 6 If a club requires its members to make a loan, pay a levy or purchase shares or debentures, this may represent consideration in return for the benefits of membership.

The **value** of the consideration will depend on the circumstances, and HMRC offers relevant guidance.

EXAMPLE A company was set up to run a golf club. Free membership was given to some of the shareholders.
It was held that the membership was given as an inducement to invest in the company, and the only supply made by the company was the issue of shares. *Hinckley Golf Club Ltd* [1992] (VTD 9527)

Loan made in lieu of subscription

8196 Notice 701/5 para 6.5 In this case, the loan is ignored, and the **amount** liable to VAT is what the normal subscription would be, at the time that the subscriptions are usually due.

Interest-free loans

8198 Notice 701/5 para 6.2 The value of the supply in this case is the notional interest forgone by the member. It is then subject to the same VAT treatment as the normal subscription (¶8180).

MEMO POINTS 1. The **amount of the loan** is determined by the terms of membership.
2. The **notional interest** is calculated using the London Clearing Banks' Base Lending Rate (LIBOR). The club can choose to use the rate in force at either:
– the beginning of the month in which the subscriptions are due to be paid; or
– the first day of the club's financial year.
This rate is then applied to the amount of the loan.

Cheap loans

8200 Notice 701/5 para 6.3 If a member is allowed to charge the club a certain rate of interest, which is **lower than** that which would be charged by the club's bank, the club is making a supply.

The **notional interest** is calculated in a similar way to that in ¶8198, but using the bank's interest rate. The **actual interest paid** by the club is deducted (including any on returned loans), and the remainder is subject to the same VAT treatment as the normal subscription (¶8180).

Loan repayments to leavers

8202 Notice 701/5 para 6.4 A condition of membership often requires a **leaving member** to find a new member to take over the loan or to make an equivalent loan. The club will then repay the original member's loan with an **additional amount** to take account of inflation. In this case, the notional interest is calculated as in ¶8198 or ¶8200. Any actual interest payments made, along with the additional repayment, are deducted and the remainder is then subject to the same VAT treatment as the normal subscription (¶8180).

If the **member waives the right** to repayment, it becomes a donation which is outside the scope of VAT, so no further notional interest calculation applies. Notice 701/5 para 6.7

Non-refundable levies

If a levy is charged, this is treated as an additional subscription **unless** the levy entitles the member to different benefits. In that case, the VAT calculation must be based on the liability of those benefits. **8204** Notice 701/5 para 6.6

C. Other income

Summary

8208

Area	Source of income	Examples	VAT treatment	¶¶
Events	Admission charges	Social events such as dances Performances Fundraising events (¶8164)	Usually standard-rated but may be exempt	¶140
Sales	Bar sales, catering etc	Teas Garden fetes	Usually standard-rated	¶1220
	Goods sold at jumble sales		Depends on type of good i.e. normally standard-rated unless specifically exempt, zero- or reduced-rated	¶1090
	Sales of equipment		Standard-rated	
Financial	Credit balances	Bar tab		¶8210
	Affinity cards		Standard-rated	¶8050
	Bank interest		Exempt (but usually ignored in any partial exemption calculation)	
	Insurance	For member's own risk	Exempt	¶442
Games and betting	Betting and gaming	Small scale gaming for fundraising purposes	Exempt	¶462
	Competition entry fees		Usually standard-rated unless relates to sports or physical recreation	¶420
	Gaming and amusement machines		Standard-rated	
	Gaming club subscriptions	Bingo, bridge etc where members have the right to play games of chance or to place bets	Standard-rated	
	Lotteries	Raffles Totes	Exempt	¶466

Area	Source of income	Examples	VAT treatment	¶¶
Other	Sponsorship rights	Monies received from sponsor Payments made to third parties by sponsor (e.g. expenses of an event)	Standard-rated	¶8042
	Room hire			¶8212
	Payphone charges		Standard-rated	
	Tours	Buying in hotel accommodation and selling it on to members	TOMS may be applicable	¶7490

Credit balances

8210 Notice 701/5 para 8 Often a club will allow members to maintain a credit balance in order to purchase goods and services (such as a bar tab). This may be by way of swipe cards, vouchers or other non-cash means.

The VAT treatment in various situations is as shown in the following table:

Circumstance	VAT treatment
Member makes a payment that creates or contributes to a credit balance (whether as a compulsory or voluntary levy) on either: – the issue, renewal or topping up of a card; or – the purchase of vouchers	Need not account for tax until the credit is used to make taxable purchases, even if the payment is not refundable The amount of the levy must not be treated as part of the subscription for VAT purposes
Unused credit balance is repaid to a member	Outside the scope
Unused balance or unredeemed vouchers revert to the club	Outside the scope (no consideration given for a supply)

Room hire

8212 Notice 701/5 para 10 When making facilities such as a hall available for hire, a **distinction** must be made between a licence to occupy land and a licence to use it (¶5374).

Where the lessee has **exclusive occupation** of the facility this is likely to be an exempt supply (subject to the option to tax (¶5604)). This would include any amenities close by, and fixtures within the room.

The **use** of facilities closely linked to sport or physical education (including pool, snooker, and billiards) may be exempt (¶418), although the provision of sports facilities generally is standard-rated (¶5526).

SECTION 4

VAT registration issues

8225 The requirement to register for VAT depends on the level of taxable supplies (¶2647).

If making any taxable supplies, the club may choose to register (¶2688) in order to reclaim input tax, although it should be aware of the related compliance burden.

MEMO POINTS 1. If **mainly zero-rated supplies** are made, HMRC may allow a club not to register (¶2652).

2. The form VAT1 (¶2706) is to be **signed by** a responsible officer of the club e.g. the Secretary or Treasurer.
3. Any **change in the membership** will not affect the club's registration.

1. Compliance liability

Incorporated clubs

An incorporated members' club is a members' club which has been incorporated under the Companies Acts (either limited by guarantee or by shares). The club therefore becomes a **legal person** apart from its members, and for registration purposes is treated like an incorporated company. **8227** VATREG11100

This separate legal identity also applies to clubs registered under the Industrial and Provident Societies Acts, and incorporated associations (under the Companies Acts, by Act of Parliament or by Royal Charter).

Unincorporated clubs

An unincorporated members' club is a club where each member normally contributes (by subscription) to the club funds, out of which expenses are paid. **8230** VATREG11050

All members are **jointly entitled** to the club's property and have the power to elect a controlling committee. Such clubs would include those registered under the Friendly Societies Acts, employees' social clubs and canteens, and unincorporated associations (which do not constitute a partnership).

Such a club should be registered in its **own name**.

The following **persons** are **jointly and severally** liable for complying with all VAT requirements (although HMRC does not petition for a winding up (¶3750)): SI 1995/2518 reg 8
- every office holder e.g. President, Chairman, Treasurer, Secretary or any similar office etc;
- committee members; and
- all members.

Even after leaving the club, an **ex-member** will continue to be liable for debts and obligations which arose during the period of his or her membership.

2. Input tax recovery

Once registered, input tax recovery **depends on** the types of supply being made (¶1800). **8232**

In **summary**:
- VAT relating to non-business supplies is not input tax and can never be recovered;
- input tax incurred on business entertainment and cars is blocked (¶1885); and
- if a mixture of taxable and exempt supplies are made, the club will be partly exempt (¶2075) and input tax recovery will be restricted.

HMRC also gives **specific guidance** to clubs in respect of prizes and appearance money.

Prizes

Prizes awarded to competitors in sports and games competitions are always dealt with separately from the entry fees. For this purpose, competitions do not include betting, gaming or lotteries. **8234** Notice 701/5 para 9.1

A prize will exist where the **competition rules** provide for additional payments to any competitor which are dependent on success.

The **treatment depends on** the type of prize as follows:

Type of prize	Examples	VAT treatment
Goods	Car Trophy	Business gifts (¶1465)
Services	Holiday	Gift of services, so if input tax has been claimed on the purchase of services given away as prizes, an equal sum of output tax is due at the time that the prize is awarded Otherwise no output tax is due
Cash (excluding payments made by sponsors to event organisers which are called prize money but are actually payments for taxable supplies)		Outside the scope of VAT
Trophy where ownership is not transferred		Outside the scope of VAT

MEMO POINTS For prizes in **horse racing** see ¶6134 and ¶6212.

Appearance money

8236 Notice 701/5 paras 9.2 - 9.4 **Competitors** are often paid by an event organiser to take part, and this represents consideration for the standard-rated supply of the individual's services, so the club will incur input tax.

For this purpose, appearance money includes **guaranteed amounts** which are payable on participation or dependent on success.

A competitor may use an **agent**, in which case the agent's services are also standard-rated.

3. Small business schemes

8238 A club may prefer to use the following schemes which are designed to **simplify VAT** for small businesses:

Type of scheme	¶¶	Overview	Advantages
Flat rate scheme	¶4635	For smaller clubs only, where VAT payable to HMRC is based on a percentage of turnover	There is no need to: – calculate or record output and input tax, except for a few items not covered by the scheme; – consider complicated rules regarding input tax deductibility for certain items; or – carry out partial exemption calculations
Annual accounting	¶4745	Reduces VAT accounting requirements and helps to manage cash flow	Only one VAT return needs to be completed each year Fixed interim payments are made towards the eventual VAT liability An extra month is allowed to complete and submit the VAT return, and pay any balance of tax due
Cash accounting	¶4880	Defers payment of VAT liabilities and gives automatic bad debt relief	Accounting for output tax when payment is received from customers, rather then when supplies are made Input tax can only be claimed when payment is made to the supplier

CHAPTER 14

Pension funds

OUTLINE ¶¶

Pension schemes are often funded so that the contributions made by employer and employees are vested in separate trustees (who may be individuals or corporate bodies), with the employer having no control. The fund is separate and distinct from the employer's business. **8280** Notice 700/17 para 1

When reclaiming input tax on services relating to the pension scheme, both the employer and the scheme trustees must identify the recipient of those services, and the purposes for which they are used.

MEMO POINTS 1. **Other types** of pension arrangement include:
- an insurance-based scheme whereby retirement benefits are secured through an insurance policy;
- an unfunded scheme where no specific funds are set aside to pay pensions; or
- the employer making provision for the payment of pensions by a segregated reserve fund in the balance sheet, represented by specific assets, where the right to the assets remains with the employer.

In these cases, as the scheme has no separate identity, the employer is receiving all supplies to do with the pension, so the normal VAT rules apply.

2. For the VAT treatment of **local authority** pension schemes see ¶7954+.

1. VAT registration

Funded schemes must consider whether VAT registration is either required or beneficial. **8285**

If registered, input tax recovery should be maximised.

A pension fund has no separate **legal status** so, where relevant, it is the pension's trustees who may be required to register. **8287** Notice 700/17 para 3.1

If the pension scheme makes taxable **supplies**, the trustees must consider whether they should register (¶2640+). A common cause for the need to register is the disposal of an opted building (¶5602+).

It is possible for a corporate pension trustee to be part of the employer's **VAT group** (¶8800+). However, this potentially makes the VAT group partly exempt, because any supplies made by the trustee are treated as being made by the group. In a departure from the normal rules, the trustee will only be liable for group VAT debts which relate to the administration of the scheme. Notice 700/17 para 4.2 and 4.3

EXAMPLE A company was set up so that it could act as trustee to pension funds for a group's employees; this company was also included within the VAT group. The parent company reclaimed the input tax incurred by the new company but this was disputed by HMRC.

It was held that the investment of the pension funds was part of the company's business; therefore the group could reclaim the input tax. *BOC International Ltd* [1982] (VTD 1248)

2. Input tax recovery

8290 Notice 700/17 para 3.2

Once **registered**, the trustees can recover input tax on goods and services used for the purposes of their business (subject to the usual partial exemption rules (¶2075+)).

The **exception** is that VAT relating to the costs of administering the scheme is usually attributable to the employer only (unless the employer has ceased to trade).

If the employer is also the **sole trustee** of the fund, all supplies and activities of the pension fund are treated as part of the business activities. This is likely to make the business partly exempt and thereby restrict its recovery of input tax.

Administration costs

8292 Notice 700/17 para 2.1 HMRC Briefs 06/14, 22/14 and 43/14

The administration of an occupational pension scheme (including initiating the scheme) is a part of the **employer's normal business activities**. Consequently, any input tax incurred when setting up the fund, and on its day-to-day administration, is part of the employer's normal input tax. HMRC used to take the view that management of the scheme's investments was not part of the employer's normal business activities but now accepts that in certain circumstances it may be (see ¶8296+ for details).

Notice 700/17 para 2.3

Examples of administrative costs are:
- making arrangements for setting up a pension fund;
- collection of contributions and payment of pensions;
- advice on reviewing the scheme and implementing changes to it;
- accountancy and auditing relating to the scheme, such as preparation of the annual accounts;
- actuarial valuation of the assets of a fund;
- general actuarial advice connected with the administration of the fund;
- providing general statistics in connection with the performance of a fund's investments or properties; and
- legal instructions and general legal advice (such as drafting trust deeds) where they relate to the administration of the scheme.

EXAMPLE

1. The British Railways Board was a trustee of its employees' pension funds and received professional advice from merchant bankers and others. It reclaimed the input tax relating to these services.
It was held that the administration of its pension funds was one of the functions of an employer. Therefore the input tax claim was valid. *C & E v British Railways Board* [1976]

2. A company paid actuaries in relation to three employee pension schemes. It reclaimed input tax on these costs.
It was held that the actuaries were giving advice as to the solvency of the funds, so the input tax had been incurred for the purposes of the company's business. *Manchester Ship Canal Co v C & E* [1982]

8294 Notice 700/17 para 2.6

If administration costs are **recharged** by the employer to the trustees, no VAT should be added to the charge, since the costs are the employer's responsibility.

Notice 700/17 para 2.8

MEMO POINTS 1. If the fund covers **more than one employer**, only the input tax relating to an appropriate proportion of the administration services can be recovered (this includes the situation where the trustee and employer are members of the same VAT group and the scheme includes employees of companies who are not group members). If only one invoice is issued by the service provider, either one of the employers or the trustee should act as paymaster. The paymaster should then recover all of the VAT as input tax and recharge the cost (plus VAT) to all the employers. Each employer can then recover the input tax on the recharged cost.

Notice 700/17 para 2.9

2. An employer who **ceases to trade** can no longer reclaim input tax on administration costs. If the trustees are VAT-registered they can recover the relevant input tax under the normal rules (though they may well be partially exempt (¶2075+)). If a professional trustee is appointed

to run the scheme, input VAT incurred on the administration of the pension fund can only be recovered by the trustee to the extent that it is a cost of an onward supply of the administration of the pension fund.

EXAMPLE The National Coal Board (which was not a trustee) set up a pension scheme for its employees, and was responsible for the administration and management of the scheme. No fee was charged to the pension fund for this service.
It was held that the Board had provided services for no consideration, so there was no supply.
National Coal Board v C & E [1982]

Employer insolvent When accepting appointment, an insolvency practitioner must be satisfied that at least one of the trustees of the employer's pension fund is an independent person. A trustee appointed as an **independent trustee** is entitled to charge reasonable fees incurred in that capacity. The fees should be paid by the pension fund's resources. **8295** ss 22 - 25 Pensions Act 1995

MEMO POINTS An **independent** trustee is defined as one who is not connected with the employer, the insolvency practitioner, or (in relation to the fund) the official receiver.

Investment management fees

HMRC accepts that the costs of setting up and administering a pension fund are properly incurred by an employer as part of the overheads of its business. HMRC used to take the view, though, that unless the employer was the sole pension trustee, the fund itself was not a part of its business activities. So input tax relating to the fund's activities, such as acquiring investments, collecting rental income and so on, could not be reclaimed by the employer, even where it paid the relevant invoices. Scheme trustees who were registered for VAT, however, could recover this input tax (subject to partial exemption rules). **8296** Notice 700/17 para 2.2; HMRC Brief 06/14

The CJEU has recently decided that an employer which has set up a pension fund that is legally and financially separate can deduct the VAT incurred on administration and pension fund investment management services, provided that there is a direct and immediate link between the services and the employer's own supplies. *PPG Holdings BV* [2014] C-26/12

HMRC has issued guidance on the implications of this decision, including the following comments:

"In respect of specific costs of investment management, these will have a direct and immediate link to the supplies of the investments themselves. For example, the costs of managing a property within a pension fund will have a direct and immediate link to the rental income derived from the property. They cannot therefore be general costs of the employer. A similar analysis can be applied to the financial investments. However, where the services received go further than the management of the investments, they may be general costs. Therefore, provided that the supply is received by the employer, the VAT incurred will potentially be deductible by the employer.

"As a result, HMRC is changing its policy on the recovery of input tax in relation to the management of pension funds. This means that there are circumstances where employers may be able to claim input tax in relation to pension funds where they could not previously. However HMRC will not accept that the VAT incurred in relation to pension fund management/administration is deductible by an employer in the following circumstances where the:
– supplies were not made to the employer (this includes, but is not limited to, consideration of whether the employer has commissioned and paid for the services);
– supply is limited to investment management services only (that is, it is not a combined supply of both investment management and pension administration services).

"Additionally, where the employer receives the supply but the pension fund bears the cost of the services (whether by way of reimbursement or a set off against pension contributions), HMRC will require an equivalent amount of output VAT in respect of the amounts reimbursed to be accounted for. This amount is potentially deductible by the pension fund to the extent that it is engaged in taxable business activities."

Examples of such costs include: Notice 700/17 para 2.4
– advice connected with making investments;

– brokerage charges;
– rent and service charge collection for property holdings;
– producing records and accounts in connection with property purchases, lettings and disposals or investments;
– trustee services;
– legal services paid on behalf of representative beneficiaries in connection with changes in pension fund arrangements; and
– custodian charges.

Notice 700/17 para 2.6 An employer which incurs investment management costs which are the trustees' responsibility and **recharges** them to the scheme may deduct input tax but must account for output tax on those recharges.

EXAMPLE A company (which was not a trustee) paid for expenses incurred by the trustees of its occupational pension fund. The employer tried to reclaim the input tax.
It was held that the services here had been supplied to the trustees and not to the company, so the company could not reclaim the input tax. *Linotype & Machinery Ltd* [1978] (VTD 594)

8297 HMRC Brief 44/14 **Liability of investment management services** Not only are some investment management services now accepted by HMRC as having been supplied to employers (giving them the right to deduct associated input tax), the CJEU has also held recently that some such services are exempt from VAT in any case (making deductibility of input tax irrelevant). Investment management is not exempt where the risk is borne by the employer (such as in a **defined benefit** scheme). *Wheels Common Investment Fund Trustees Ltd and others v HMRC* [2013] C-424/11 On the other hand, a **defined contribution** pension scheme can be a special investment fund (permitting exemption), because it is the members of the scheme which bear the investment risk. *ATP PensionService A/S v Skatteministeriet* [2014] C-464/12

HMRC has issued guidance on exactly which funds it considers will qualify.

Comment Given that defined benefit schemes are at employers' risk and defined contribution schemes are at members' risk, it is tempting to argue further that investment management costs are the employer's responsibility in the former case and the trustees' responsibility in the latter case. This would be neat, as it would afford input tax deductibility to employers when VAT was charged, yet there would be no VAT to worry about where the employer was unable to deduct. It remains to be seen whether HMRC will formally accept this.

Combined third-party services

8298 A **third party** (such as a fund manager, property manager or professional trustee) may be appointed to manage the scheme. In this case, the third party's charges are likely to cover both administration and investment management services.

8300 HMRC Brief 43/14 Because HMRC now accepts that employers may be responsible for investment management (see ¶8296), the issue arising from charges made by a third party is no longer whether they represent administration fees or investment management fees. If the fees are subject to VAT at all (see ¶8297), the sole question is to whom were they supplied? It is therefore no longer necessary to split third-party invoices down the administration/investment management line. However, the following table may be of use for historic purposes, or if deciding whether to take advantage of the transitional period (see ¶8302).

Area	Element	Administration	Investment management
Meetings	Regular meetings with clients	✓	✓
	Regular meetings with consulting actuaries	✓	
Research	Investment research, including relevant travel (UK and overseas)		✓
	Economic research, including relevant travel (UK and overseas)		✓

Area	Element	Administration	Investment management
Investment portfolio	Dealing in securities in UK and overseas markets on behalf of clients		✓
	Review and control of investment portfolios		✓
	Cash management	✓	✓
	Investment management - asset allocation and stock selection		✓
	Programming and provision of relevant computer support for investment management and related administration and control		✓
	Collection of dividends and interest and obtaining new coupon sheets		✓
	Recovery of tax		✓
	Administration in respect of capital repayments and capitalisation issues		✓
	Administration in respect of company meetings and, in particular, execution of forms of proxy as appropriate: – conversions; – exchanges; – liquidation; – distributions; – redemptions; – rights issues; and – payment of calls		✓
Accounts	Keeping detailed accounts of all investments, receipts, disbursements and other transactions		✓
	Maintenance of securities accounts, stock registration and transfer		✓
Preparing documents	Contract notes		✓
	Performance statistics	✓	✓
	Schedules of transactions		✓
	Specialist market commentaries		✓
	Valuations	✓	✓
	Programming and provision of relevant computer support for valuations and performance statistics	✓	
Custody	Safekeeping of property and securities in own name or name of nominee or in bearer form		✓
	Appointment of and responsibility for sub-custodians (domestic or foreign)		✓
Other	Provision of nominee service		✓
	Submission of data to independent performances monitoring service	✓	

As a simplification measure, HMRC used to permit third-party invoices to be treated as 30% relating to administration and 70% investment management. There is no longer any need for that concession and HMRC is therefore withdrawing it, subject to an optional **transitional** period ending on 31 December 2015. **8302** HMRC Brief 43/14

PART 8

Business situations

Business situations
Summary

The numbers cross-refer to paragraphs.

CHAPTER 1 Commencing and ceasing a business

CHAPTER 2 VAT groups

CHAPTER 1

Commencing and ceasing a business

OUTLINE ¶¶

Special rules apply on the commencement and cessation of a business to ensure that traders are not unduly discriminated against during these periods. The intention is to enable a smooth entry into, or exit from, the mainstream VAT regime. 8550

Additionally there are certain issues that will arise on:
- a sale or purchase of a business (¶8640); and
- the death, insolvency or incapacity of a trader (¶8700).

SECTION 1

Commencement of a business

VAT is an important issue that must be considered from the start by any person commencing a trade or intending to do so (irrespective of whether that person is currently registered for VAT). 8555

Issues of **particular importance** to a trader commencing business are:
- registration (¶8557); and
- recovery of VAT paid on purchases made before registration (¶8560).

A. Registration

8557 A trader either:
- must register for VAT if the value of taxable supplies exceeds a certain limit (¶9960); or
- can choose to register voluntarily in order to recover input tax. This may be done at any time from a date when the trader can demonstrate an intention to trade, even if this is before any actual supplies are made.

See ¶2600+ for full details of registration requirements.

MEMO POINTS 1. A trader who **acquires assets on the transfer of a business** may be required to register immediately (¶8646). In this case the relevant value of taxable supplies is the sum of:
- the taxable supplies made by the transferred business in the 12 months prior to the transfer; and
- any taxable supplies made by the purchaser in the 12 months prior to the transfer.

If the total value of these supplies:
- exceeds the registration threshold in force on the day of transfer, the purchaser will be required to register for VAT from that date, unless an exemption applies (¶2650); or
- does not exceed the registration threshold, the value of taxable supplies should be continually monitored (¶2676).

2. A trader **starting a business from scratch** is unlikely to be required to register from the date of commencement of trade (as it is unlikely that the business will have made sufficient taxable supplies, although there is a prospective threshold to consider as well (¶2680)). However, the trader will need to keep a detailed record of supplies made to ensure a timely registration if supplies exceed the threshold.

EXAMPLE The acquisition of a right to the future transfer of property (which was yet to be constructed), with a view to renting out the property, entitled the person to be registered for VAT (even if the business never in fact materialised). *Rompelman-van Deelen v Minister van Financiën* [1985]

B. Recovery of VAT on purchases

8560 A trader can recover VAT incurred on purchases made **before registration**, provided that certain conditions are satisfied. Similar rules also allow recovery of VAT before a company is incorporated (¶8566).

The **amount that can be recovered** is calculated in the usual manner, on the assumption that the trader was registered at the time the expense was incurred (¶8570). The claim **must be made on** the trader's first return (¶8576).

1. Qualifying conditions

Traders

8562 SI 1995/2518 reg 111(1a) To recover input VAT on purchases made before registration, the goods or services must be used, or be intended to be used, for the purposes of the newly registered business and the following conditions must be satisfied:

Type of supply	Qualifying conditions
Goods	Any goods must be: – **purchased no more** than 4 years before the date of registration; and – **on hand** at the date of registration: that is, they have not been consumed or supplied before registration
Services	Any services must be **purchased** (meaning invoiced) **no more** than 6 months before the date of registration

EXAMPLE A Ltd, a printer, registers for VAT on 1 December. Large printing machines were bought a year ago. There is a stock of inks and paper on hand at registration, which were bought in July. A Ltd also commissioned a business plan from a local firm of accountants back in January, which was invoiced in February. Payroll processing costs have been invoiced monthly since then.
A Ltd can recover input tax on the machines and stock, as well as the payroll costs incurred since 1 June. The invoice for the business plan is outside the 6-month time limit for services received.

MEMO POINTS 1. In view of the different criteria for goods and services, it is necessary to allocate input tax on a fair and reasonable basis in the event of a **mixed supply** (¶310).
2. It is important to note that there is no restriction on **services being consumed** before registration (as there is for goods).

EXAMPLE In her first return a VAT-registered trader reclaimed input tax in respect of rent she had paid for business premises. The premises had been used for general promotion of her business activities and storage of stock (part of which had been sold before registration and part of which had not).
It was held that the input tax on the rent was fully recoverable, as the regulations do not exclude services consumed prior to registration and there are no apportionment provisions. *D Jerzynek* [2004] (VTD 18767)

Companies

As a company cannot register until it is formally incorporated, VAT on **pre-incorporation expenditure** can also be recovered if, in addition to the conditions at ¶8562, it is both: 8566 SI 1995/2518 reg 111(1b)
a. incurred by a person who:
– subsequently becomes an officer or employee of the company;
– is fully reimbursed by the company; and
– was not a taxable person (one who was, or was required to be, registered for VAT) at the time of purchase; and
b. purchased for the purpose of a business to be carried on by the company (and not used for any other purpose in the meantime).

Input tax incurred on expenditure which has **a tax point** (¶755) falling after the date of incorporation cannot be recovered under these rules. It is therefore vital that suppliers are aware of who to invoice. 8568

EXAMPLE Mr B is to be a director of C Ltd, which is incorporated on 20 January. He incurs £500 of VAT on a feasibility study, and the invoice is made out to him. C Ltd then reimburses Mr B.
If the tax point of the invoice is 10 January, the input tax can be recovered by C Ltd.
If the tax point is not until the end of the month, the input tax is irrecoverable, because C Ltd has already been incorporated, and the invoice is made out to Mr B.

2. Amount of the claim

In **general** the claim is made on the assumption that the trader was registered at the time that the expense was incurred. Therefore any restrictions that would otherwise apply (for example where there is a mixture of business and non-business use (¶1838)) need to be considered. 8570 VIT32000

For traders that:
– make only exempt supplies, input tax recovery is not permitted (¶2075);
– are partly exempt, the **de minimis** limits (¶2194) do not apply, which means that no pre-registration exempt input tax can be recovered. *Douros (t/a Olympic Financial Services)* [1995] (VTD 12454).

8572 SI 1995/2518 reg 29(3) Where the trader has a genuine reason for being **unable to calculate** the pre-registration input tax, HMRC will permit an estimate to be used.

VIT34500 MEMO POINTS 1. HMRC does not elaborate on what is meant by a **genuine reason**, so presumably each case will be considered on its respective merits.

VIT32500 2. A claim can be made (in writing) for an **early repayment of input tax** if, due to serious shortcomings by HMRC, a registration is delayed.

s 39 VATA 1994 3. It is only possible to recover **VAT incurred overseas** under the special directive procedures (¶9840+).

3. Administration

8576 SI 1995/2518 reg 111(3); VIT33000 The **claim must be made** on the first return that the trader is required to make (as distinct from the first return actually made).

HMRC has discretion to allow a **late claim** for input tax recovery. In general a late claim cannot be made more than 4 years after the original time limit. However, this 4-year cap does not apply if the trader is subject to compulsory backdated registration (¶2684).

8578 The amount claimed is entered in box 4 of the VAT return. Original **supporting documentation** and other evidence must be kept detailing the:
a. date of purchase;
b. description of the purchase including, for goods, details of the:
– quantity; and
– volume that has been used in making other goods; and
c. date of any disposals made after registration (including the date of disposals of manufactured goods made from the original goods purchased).

EXAMPLE A trader registered for VAT and reclaimed pre-registration input tax for an invoice issued by a company which he controlled, which had ceased trading 6 days before the date of the invoice. In the absence of a credible explanation as to the background and circumstances of the supply, the trader's claim for a deduction was rejected as he had not provided other evidence that a genuine supply had been made to him for consideration. *N R Corke* [2000] (VTD 16832)

4. Special situations

Pre-registration expenditure on property

8580 Notice 742A para 9.4 Special rules apply for recovery of VAT when a trader **becomes newly registered** as a result of opting to tax land and property (¶5612). HMRC has discretion to allow a deduction for input tax incurred on land (or services relating to land) prior to registration on a fair and reasonable basis, rather than applying the strict test set out above for goods and services (¶8562).

Comment Where a trader is **already registered** and opts to tax land and property, it is not necessary to meet the qualifying conditions in order to recover any pre-option input tax. Instead the trader can request recovery on a fair and reasonable basis (¶5684). The discretionary treatment given to traders who are newly registered simply aims to treat the two types of traders similarly. In practice, a trader must be able to prove that pre-option input tax related to intended taxable supplies.

Continuous services provided pre-registration

In **general**, payments received by a trader for a supply of continuous services are treated as being supplied at the date that the payment is received. VAT must therefore be charged on any payment for such services which is received after registration, even if the services were performed before registration. 8582 VATTOS3800

However, this **rule is modified** if the supply ceased prior to registration. Such payments will not be liable to VAT.

MEMO POINTS A **continuous supply of services** (¶808) is essentially a service that is performed over a period of time (as opposed to a one-off service), for example, an accountant providing ongoing advice to a client.

Post-registration expenditure and pre-registration supplies

It has been held that no input tax can be recovered for expenditure incurred after registration if it relates to a supply that was made by a trader before registering. 8584

EXAMPLE Two individuals provided consultancy services to an accountancy partnership. Invoices were issued which were not paid. The individuals subsequently registered for VAT as a partnership and incurred solicitors' fees to chase up the earlier debts.
It was held that the input tax on the solicitors' fees could not be reclaimed, because the individuals were suing in respect of work done before registration, rather than after creation of the partnership.
J Sherman & S Perilly [2001] (VTD 16467)

VAT groups

If an unregistered company joins a VAT group (¶8800) the **representative member** of the VAT group may recover VAT incurred by the new group company prior to its entry to the group. 8586 VIT33500

EXAMPLE D Ltd was not VAT-registered and purchased a new machine on 31 January, to be used in connection with future trading. The company became part of the BCD VAT group on 1 March. The VAT on the machine can be reclaimed on the next VAT return submitted by the BCD VAT group.

SECTION 2

Cessation of a business

Anything done in connection with the cessation (or intended cessation) of a business is treated as being done in the course of a business activity. On cessation of a business, deregistration issues and possible recovery of VAT incurred on purchases after the date of deregistration need to be considered. 8600 s 94(5) VATA 1994

A. Deregistration

On cessation of a business the trader is **required** to deregister for VAT and must give written notice to this effect to HMRC within 30 days from the date of cessation (¶2714). 8605 Sch 1 para 11 VATA 1994

MEMO POINTS A trader who sells the assets of the business **is not required to deregister** if the business was sold as a going concern and an election is made to transfer the VAT registration to the buyer (¶8646).

Consequences

8607 The main implications of deregistration are that:

a. output tax:

– must be accounted for on the final VAT return on any stock and assets on hand (subject to certain concessions) at the date of deregistration (¶8610); and

– cannot be charged on supplies made by the trader after the date of deregistration (¶2728); and

b. input tax is not subsequently recoverable, unless it falls within specific provisions (¶8618).

For full details of the deregistration requirements see ¶2720+.

B. Accounting for output tax

Stock and assets on hand

8610 Sch 4 para 8 VATA 1994

There is a deemed self-supply of all stock and assets on hand (including land) at the date of deregistration and output tax **must be** accounted for on such goods where:

– input tax was reclaimed when they were acquired; and

– the chargeable amount of output tax (for all the assets concerned) exceeds £1,000.

EXAMPLE At the date of its deregistration A Ltd holds:
– trading stock that cost the company £3,000 (all standard-rated items);
– a van worth £1,000 (on which input tax was claimed when it was purchased); and
– a car worth £2,000 (no input tax claimed on purchase, because the car was available for private use).
Output tax of £800 would be due on the value of the stock and van. (4,000 x 20%)
The total amount of £800 is less than £1,000, so no VAT is payable to HMRC.

Output tax **will not need to be** accounted for if either:

a. the trade continues because the:

– business is transferred as part of a transfer of a going concern to another person (¶8646); or

– taxable person has died, become bankrupt or incapacitated and the trade is carried on by an appropriate person (¶8702); or

b. the goods were acquired for the business before 1 April 1973 and rebate of purchase tax or revenue was not allowed when VAT began.

MEMO POINTS 1. Careful **timing of deregistration** may help to minimise the cost to the trader. If, for example, it is intended that the goods will eventually be sold it would be advisable to delay deregistration until this date.

Sch 6 para 6 VATA 1994

2. **Output tax is calculated on** the cost to the business of buying identical (or similar) replacement goods. If these values are not available, the cost of producing the goods is used. Since 1 February 2014, this rule does not apply to private fuel valued at the flat rate (¶1538); the flat-rate valuation is used instead.

3. Output tax will also need to be accounted for in this manner if a trader leaves a **VAT group** and does not register in its own right.

Capital goods scheme

8612 Notice 700/11 para 7.7 - 7.8

The capital goods scheme **applies to** certain land and buildings, computer equipment, and ships and aircraft. For such assets an adjustment is required on the final return, in the same way as if the asset had been sold (¶2332+).

In certain situations there may be an onward supply of the asset, in which case output tax may be chargeable. Where no output tax is charged, HMRC takes the view that the deemed use of the asset in the remaining intervals is exempt.

Even if the trader is not required to account for output tax, because the chargeable amount of output tax (for all the assets concerned) is below £1,000, an adjustment must still be made.

MEMO POINTS 1. Essentially the capital goods **scheme requires** a purchaser of included assets to adjust the amount of recoverable input tax claimed on the original purchase, if the taxable use of the asset changes over a period of 10 or 5 years (depending on the asset type).
2. If the capital goods **scheme does not apply** to the assets, they are treated as goods on hand when accounting for output tax on deregistration and the rules at ¶8610 apply.
3. Output tax will also need to be accounted for in this manner on capital goods if a trader leaves a **VAT group** and does not register in its own right.

C. Recovery of VAT after deregistration

In **general** the right to deduct input tax ceases on the date a trader is deregistered. 8618 SI 1995/2518 reg 111(5), (6)

There are **exceptions** to this rule, which allow recovery of input tax after the date of deregistration (provided that a claim is made within 4 years of the purchaser's tax point (¶735)) where there was a supply of:
– services received after deregistration which relate to the business carried on when the trader was registered, for example, professional fees for the preparation of year end accounts; or
– goods or services received before deregistration and in respect of which HMRC has permitted a late claim for input tax (¶8576) because, for example, the necessary evidence was not held by the trader when the original claim was made.

EXAMPLE B Ltd received goods on 13 February but did not receive the purchase invoice, dated 28 February, until 8 April. The date of deregistration was 31 March, and accountancy fees (relating to work done when the company was VAT-registered) were invoiced on 30 April.
B Ltd can reclaim the input tax on the goods and accountancy fees, provided that a claim is made within 4 years of the date of the relevant invoices (28 February and 30 April).

MEMO POINTS 1. Where a VAT refund is due, the **business bank account** should remain open until this has been received. If not, HMRC will make the refund by payable order.
2. The **claim should be submitted on** form VAT427, together with any relevant invoices.
3. Any VAT that **directly relates to** the making of **exempt supplies** cannot be claimed.
4. For **partly exempt** businesses the following rules apply:
– when calculating the value of non-attributable input tax, the recoverable proportion (¶2110) that applied immediately before deregistration should be used; and
– the de minimis limits (¶2194) do not apply when making the claim, so that all exempt post-deregistration input tax is irrecoverable.
5. It is particularly important that the tax point of goods is taken into account on deregistration. As no input tax can be claimed on **goods bought after deregistration**, advance sales of such goods (which are yet to be acquired) could mean that the business has to declare output tax, but is not able to claim input tax.
6. If a company that is registered as part of a **VAT group** leaves the group and does not register in its own right, the representative member of the VAT group may recover post-deregistration input VAT under these provisions.

SECTION 3

Sale or purchase of a business

A business can be transferred **either by means of**: 8640
– a share transfer (where the issued share capital of a company is sold); or
– an asset transfer of a going concern (where the assets of the business are sold).

VAT is chargeable in neither case, provided that certain conditions are met.

A. Share transfer

8642 Sch 9 Group 5 VATA 1994

No output VAT is chargeable on the transfer (sale) of shares, because the transaction is exempt from VAT.

Input tax incurred on **costs directly relating to** the sale of existing shares, such as legal fees, is generally not recoverable by the seller. There is an **exception** to this rule if the shares are sold to a buyer located outside the EU. In this case the sale of the shares will be outside the scope of VAT, with the right to recover associated input tax.

This should be contrasted to the input tax position where new shares are issued (¶358).

B. Transfer of a going concern

8646 On a sale or transfer of business assets the transaction **will be** treated as a transfer of a going concern (TOGC) if certain conditions are satisfied.

Notice 700/9 para 2.2

MEMO POINTS 1. TOGC treatment is **compulsory** if the conditions apply. If VAT is incorrectly charged on the transfer, the purchaser cannot reclaim it as input tax (because there was no taxable supply). The vendor must cancel any purported VAT invoice issued, and refund the amount charged as VAT (normally by issuing a credit note).
2. If the **conditions are not met** the transaction will be subject to VAT in the usual manner for a sale of the items concerned.

1. Overview of a TOGC

8648 SI 1995/1268 art 5

The main **implication** of the TOGC provisions is that the transaction is treated as being outside the scope of VAT (¶252), which means that no VAT is chargeable.

In addition:
- the VAT registration number of the seller can be transferred to the buyer, avoiding the need to deregister and re-register for VAT (¶8678). However, this is not advisable in most situations; and
- certain costs associated with a TOGC may be recoverable (¶8656).

Special rules apply when the transfer involves:
- land used in the business (¶8660);
- property, computers, ships or aircraft that are subject to the capital goods scheme (¶8660 and ¶8674);
- a VAT group (¶8800); or
- assets transferred over a period of time (¶8676).

MEMO POINTS 1. Common **examples** of a TOGC include instances where the assets of a business are:
- bought by another person and the existing business ceases to trade; or
- transferred to a new legal entity, for example, a sole proprietor may take on a partner or form a limited company.

Notice 700/9 para 3.6

2. Special **record keeping requirements** apply for businesses transferred as a going concern, which mean that the transferor is required to:
- keep the business records until 6 years have elapsed from the date of the transfer; and
- provide the transferee with sufficient information to comply with all ongoing reporting obligations.

In practice, this means that the transferor is required to pass on copies of documents, or make records available for inspection and extraction at a time and place convenient to the transferee. Where difficulties arise, HMRC may also provide the transferee with such information that they hold for this purpose. In this case they will also notify the transferor in case any confidentiality issues arise.
3. The rule in **2.** above does not apply when the **VAT registration number is transferred** (the transferee becomes responsible for maintaining and holding such records (¶8682)). However, the transferor can ask HMRC for permission to retain them instead, in which case the transferee's rights to information are as stated above.

2. Qualifying conditions

To qualify as a TOGC, the following **conditions** must be met: **8650**

SI 1995/1268 art 5

Condition	Detail
Business assets	All of the assets[1] of the business must be transferred (or part of the assets of a business, where the part transferred is capable of separate operation)
Business activity	The assets must be used by the buyer in carrying on the same kind of business as the seller (although see ¶8652, examples 1 and 5)
	The trade must be carried out by the buyer (meaning that there must not be a series of immediately consecutive transfers of the business)[2,3]
	The business transferred must be a business activity (¶100) and a going concern[4,5] at the time of the transfer
	There must be no significant break in the normal trading pattern before or immediately after the transfer[6]
VAT registration	Where the seller is registered for VAT (either compulsorily or voluntarily), the buyer must also either: – already be registered for VAT; or – become liable to register for VAT (either compulsorily or voluntarily)
	Where the seller is not registered for VAT there is no requirement for the buyer to be registered; the seller may be trading below the registration threshold or making wholly exempt supplies[7]

Note:

1. The seller must supply the buyer with the exact assets used for the business. HMRC gives the example of a seller transferring a business, but rather than transferring the freehold to a property, a leasehold is granted. In this situation, HMRC's view is that this is not a TOGC. This view is open to question following the decisions in *Morton Hotels Ltd* (¶8652) and *Robinson Family Ltd* (¶8670).
2. For example, if A sells the business to B who then immediately sells it to C, none of the transfers will be a TOGC. Again, this is HMRC's view and consideration should be given to the decision in *Morton Hotels Ltd*.
3. Where consecutive owners are members of the same VAT group, a transfer from A Ltd to B Ltd then on to C Ltd could be seen as a single transfer to C Ltd if A Ltd and B Ltd are in the same VAT group.
4. A going concern is a business which is live or operating. So a business can be in liquidation, receivership or even bankruptcy and still be a going concern for the TOGC provisions to apply. Factors such as all staff being made redundant, or cessation of production, orders, etc, would indicate that a business has ceased.
5. If a person is VAT-registered but has not yet made taxable supplies, a transfer of assets might be treated as a TOGC where sufficient preparatory work has been performed prior to the transfer, to support the fact that there is a business capable of being transferred.
6. A temporary period of closure which does not disrupt the business is ignored (such as a short closure for redecoration). The relative importance attached to the break in trading will depend on the facts of the case and the type of business transferred. For example, if there was a purchase of a holiday home trade in November, it would not be unreasonable to have a 5-month break in trade until the next April, but such a break following a purchase of a newsagency business might well be unreasonable.
7. A transfer by a seller of only the exempt part of a trade (to a buyer who will only then make exempt supplies) is not a TOGC.

Case law

There have been **numerous** cases on the TOGC provisions, a few of which are summarised below. **8652**

EXAMPLE

1. An Indian restaurant was sold to new owners, who turned the restaurant into an Italian restaurant. The sale was deemed to be a TOGC because the new and old businesses were both restaurants selling food, even though the menu and style of the new restaurant was different. *Tahmassebi t/a Sale Pepe* [1995] (VTD 13177)

2. A Ltd suffered financial difficulties, which meant that its bank account was frozen, its assets were seized by the authorities, and it made its employees redundant. A rival company purchased the remainder of A Ltd's assets.
This was held not to constitute a TOGC as, at the time of the transfer, there was no longer a possibility of A Ltd's business continuing and the transfer amounted merely to a transfer of assets. *Buckley Jewellery Ltd* [2003] (VTD 18178)

3. A trader who owned a bus which was hired out for school transport sold the bus to a third party (who carried on a similar business), together with the school contract.
This was held to be a TOGC, not simply a sale of assets. *Beagley* [1997] (VTD 15107)

4. A company purchased metal-turning machinery from another company that was in liquidation. It was held that this was not a TOGC on the basis that there was no intention between the parties at the time of the transfer for the assets to be used in the same type of business. *Hartley Engineering Ltd* [1994] (VTD 12385)

5. A taxpayer sold three hotels to Swallow Hotels Ltd. On the transfer of the business the taxpayer ceased to run the hotels, and Swallow took over running them in every respect. To finance the purchase Swallow immediately entered into a "sale and leaseback" arrangement for the properties with a third party. HMRC argued that the transfer could not be treated as a TOGC, as Swallow had sold the hotels without continuing the same trade as the taxpayer. The taxpayer had been an owner/operator, whereas Swallow was only an operator and had used the underlying property assets for a different purpose (by selling them). The tribunal held that it should consider the substance of the arrangements over the form. The factual outcome of the situation was that Swallow continued the "same kind of business" as the taxpayer. The fact that it did so as lessee of the property rather than owner did not affect the status of the transfer as a TOGC. *Morton Hotels Ltd* [2007] (VTD 20039).

Official guidance

8654 VTOGC7200 HMRC guidance details the following **factors** that will need to be considered to establish whether a transfer is a TOGC or not. No one factor has overriding importance and each case will need to be judged on its own particular facts.

Factors	Detail
Goodwill	The specific mention of a transfer of goodwill, even for nominal consideration, is a strong indicator of a TOGC The transfer of a business name is the most obvious sign that goodwill has been transferred
Customer lists or contracts	If these are sold along with other business assets, it is a good indication that a business is being sold However, the transfer of a customer list or contract alone is very unlikely to be a TOGC [1]
Stock	The sale of a small portion of a trader's stock is unlikely to be a TOGC, unless the stock sold is the basis of an identifiable business
Plant and equipment	There can still be a TOGC even if the relevant plant and equipment is not transferred (for example, if the buyer already owns similar equipment)
Premises	Many businesses cannot be transferred without the transfer of the premises (so the business of a theatre, bowling alley, ice rink, etc, could not be transferred without transferring the premises) For many businesses, goodwill is actually attached to them (such as in retail businesses, where the location of the premises is important)
Staff	Where redundant staff are re-employed by the seller this will be indicative of a TOGC
Restrictive covenants	The presence of a restrictive covenant in the transfer agreement is usually a good indicator of a TOGC (there would be no need to protect the purchaser if the new business was not the business previously carried on by the seller)
Contract of sale	Although a useful indicator of what the parties have agreed, the actual facts of the transaction are more important
Parties' intentions	There must be an agreement between the parties that the transfer does in fact amount to a TOGC If the purchaser intends to carry on a different type of business in due course, the transfer may still be a TOGC provided that the old business is initially continued
Method of advertising	After-sale advertising such as "under new management" will indicate that the same type of business is being carried on and that there has been a TOGC

Note:
1. If a contract is assigned (as opposed to novated) the original supplier is still contractually obliged to fulfil the contract. A contract is novated if all three parties (the buyer, seller and customer) agree to release the seller from the contract and establish a new contract between the buyer and the customer.

3. Recoverable input tax

Although a TOGC is outside the scope of VAT, this does not prevent the recovery of input tax on related costs incurred on the transfer (such as professional fees). There are, however, **different rules** for the seller and purchaser, as follows: **8656** VTOGC4300

Type of transfer	Seller's costs	Purchaser's costs
Transfer of whole of business	Treated as residual input tax and apportioned in accordance with the seller's agreed partial exemption method (¶2260)	Recovered in accordance with the use to which the purchased assets will be put[1]
Transfer of part of a business	If the related costs have a direct and immediate link with the part of the business transferred, costs will be treated as an overhead of that part of the business and apportioned in accordance with the type of supplies made by that part of the business transferred[2]	

Note:
1. If the TOGC assets are used by the purchaser to make:
- fully taxable supplies, input tax on related costs is fully recoverable;
- exempt supplies, input tax on related costs is irrecoverable; or
- a mixture of the two, input tax on related costs is non-attributable and apportioned by reference to the agreed partial exemption method (¶2262).

2. If the business transferred made:
- fully taxable supplies, input tax on related costs is fully recoverable;
- exempt supplies, input tax on related costs is irrecoverable; or
- a mixture of the two, input tax on related costs is non-attributable and apportioned by reference to the agreed partial exemption method (¶2260).

4. Special situations

Special rules apply where a TOGC involves: **8658**
- a transfer of land and property;
- a transfer of computer equipment, ships or aircraft;
- a transaction within a VAT group (¶8800); or
- assets that are transferred over a period of time.

a. Land and property

Where land and property are included as part of a transfer, it is necessary to establish firstly whether the property is or is not subject to VAT (as different rules apply). **8660**

MEMO POINTS 1. If the transfer involves a **property letting business**, further special provisions apply (¶8670+).
2. Land and property potentially fall within the **capital goods scheme** (¶2280), so the purchaser will need to consider whether any adjustments must be made. Notice 706/2 para 9
3. A table **summarising whether or not** land and property can be included in a TOGC is at ¶8668.

Property that is not subject to VAT

Property that is not subject to VAT will **automatically** be included as part of a TOGC, provided that the other qualifying conditions are met (¶8650). **8662** SI 1995/1268 art 5(2)

Land and property are not subject to VAT where:
- they are exempt or zero-rated (¶5100); and/or
- the seller has not opted to tax (¶5602).

Property that is subject to VAT

8664 SI 1995/1268 art 5(2)-(3)

Where property (usually, commercial property) is subject to VAT, specific **conditions** must be met by the **seller and the purchaser** before such a transfer can be treated as part of a TOGC.

Seller's conditions	Purchaser's conditions
The property transferred must either be: – commercial property on which the seller has opted to tax; – new commercial property (less than 3 years since completed); or – property that is otherwise standard-rated (unfinished building or civil engineering works)	The purchaser must have: **a.** opted to tax the property (or made a real estate election (¶5688)); and **b.** notified[1] both: – HMRC of the election; and – the seller that the election will not be disapplied under the anti-avoidance rules[2,3]

Note:
1. This notification (to HMRC and the seller) must be made no later than the time at which the supply is made. (Note: this is normally the date of the transfer, but if the contract requires a deposit to be paid to a third party acting as agent for the vendor, or directly to the vendor, it will be the date of the deposit.)
2. Anti-avoidance provisions (¶5638) can disapply an option to tax where property is:
– not fully occupied for a taxable business purpose; or
– a capital item for the purposes of the capital goods scheme.
3. The seller is responsible for applying the correct VAT treatment. It is therefore advisable to obtain documentary evidence from the purchaser of the exercise of the option and its notification to HMRC.

VTOGC4200

MEMO POINTS Where the seller **mistakenly does charge VAT**, strictly speaking, an assessment should be issued to correct the error. However, HMRC has discretion to allow the VAT charge to stand (and permit the purchaser to recover the input tax in the usual manner) if they are satisfied that the VAT on the invoice has in fact been paid and declared to HMRC.

8668 Notice 742A para 11.2; Notice 700/9 para 2.4

The following table **summarises** whether land and buildings can be included in a TOGC:

Type of commercial property	Has the seller opted to tax?	Has the purchaser opted to tax?[1]	Has the purchaser's option to tax been disapplied?[2]	Is the transfer part of a TOGC?
Over 3 years old (usually exempt, subject to option to tax)	Yes	Yes	Yes	No
	Yes	No	n/a	No
	Yes	Yes	No	Yes
	No	No	n/a	Yes
	No	Yes	Yes	Yes
	No	Yes	No	Yes
New commercial building (less than 3 years since completed) or unfinished works, usually standard-rated	Yes	Yes	Yes	No
	Yes	No	n/a	No
	Yes	Yes	No	Yes
	No	No	n/a	No
	No	Yes	Yes	No
	No	Yes	No	Yes
Any other supply of property, if exempt or zero-rated	No	n/a	n/a	Yes

Note
1. Or has made a real estate election (¶5688). In either case the purchaser must have notified HMRC by the appropriate date (¶8664).
2. The purchaser must also have notified the seller by the appropriate date (¶8664).

Property letting business

The transfer of a property rental business can also be treated as a TOGC, provided that the other qualifying conditions are met (¶8650). **8670** Notice 700/9 para 6; HMRC Brief 30/12 HMRC Brief 27/14

The following **examples** illustrate where such a transfer will and will not be treated as a TOGC:

TOGC	Not a TOGC
Freehold property is let to a tenant and either sold: – with the benefit of the existing lease; – during an initial rent free period; or – before tenants are in occupation [1, 2]	Lease granted out of a freehold interest [3]
Assignment of lease with the benefit of a sublease	Sublease granted out of leasehold interest [3]
Freehold property is sold subject to a prospective tenancy (i.e. the seller has found a tenant but not actually signed any paperwork [3, 4])	Sale of freehold property either: – to existing tenant; or – where the lease is surrendered on sale (this will not be a TOGC even if tenants remain in the property under a sublease)
Sale of a site as a package by a property developer which is a mixture of let and unlet, finished and unfinished properties (where the sale of the site would otherwise have been standard-rated), provided that the purchaser opts to tax the whole site	Property developer who has built a building and either: – allows someone to occupy it temporarily (without any right to occupy after any proposed sale); or – is actively marketing it in search of a tenant

Note

1. These are sales of an existing property rental business and will be treated as a TOGC even if the property is only partly tenanted. However, it should be noted that not all cases will be a TOGC. In one case a developer and a college attempted to transfer a building as a going concern by the developer letting a single room to a tenant. After the transfer the college then let another room to a different tenant. Both of these tenants had let rooms from the college in their previous building. The Upper tribunal, in reversing the previous decision, ruled this was not a TOGC as the tenant was supplied by the college and was deemed to never form part of the developer's business. *HMRC v Royal College of Paediatrics and Child Health and another* [2015]

2. A borough council successfully argued that the sale of the freehold interest, with the benefit of an agreement for lease, was a TOGC even though building work had not commenced on the site and it had not received any income under the agreement for lease. It was carrying on an economic activity, which was transferred to the buyer when the plot was sold. *Dartford Borough Council* [2007] (VTD 20423).

3. Following the decision in *Robinson Family Ltd* [2012] HMRC has issued new briefs to amend its previous guidance. They now accept that:
– the creation and transfer of a new asset (i.e the lease or sublease) will not automatically rule out the TOGC provisions. Where the reversionary interest is sufficiently small and distant (in this case it was 3 days in almost 125 years) HMRC will accept that the asset has in effect been transferred. It has also stated that for this to be the case the interest retained should be no more than 1% of the value of the property immediately before the transfer. If the interest retained is more than 1% HMRC will view this as a strong indication that the arrangement is too complex to be a TOGC.
– the surrender of a lease can also be considered a TOGC if all the other conditions above are satisfied. An example would be a tenant sub-letting a property and then surrendering the lease to the landlord while transferring the benefit of the sub-leases to them as well.
This will be examined on a property by property basis.

4. Here there is sufficient evidence of intended economic activity for there to be a property rental business capable of being transferred.

Nominees A nominee arrangement may arise where, for example, legal title is held on trust for an unincorporated association or pension fund. **8672** Sch 10 para 8 VATA 1994; Notice 700/9 para 8

Special rules apply where the buyer or seller is a nominee, as follows:

a. a **seller** who is a nominee for the owner of the legal title is deemed to be the beneficial owner, and the transfer may therefore be treated as a TOGC (where the other qualifying conditions are met (¶8650)); and

b. where the **buyer** is a nominee for the person who will ultimately be the beneficial owner of the legal title, strictly speaking a TOGC cannot occur because it is the beneficial owner who will be carrying on the business (not the nominee). By **concession**, HMRC will treat the transfer of a property letting business to a nominee as a TOGC where:

– the nominee acts for a named beneficial owner (who is disclosed to the seller);
– the nominee and the beneficial owner agree to this treatment (and notify HMRC accordingly); and
– all the other TOGC qualifying conditions are met (¶8650).

The seller will therefore need to check the VAT registration and any elections of the beneficial owner (as opposed to the nominee).

b. Computer equipment, ships and aircraft

8674 SI 1995/2518 reg 114 (7); Notice 706/2 para 9

These assets may also be subject to the **capital goods scheme** (¶2280), which would cause possible future adjustments to the initial VAT recovery.

If so, the new owner must assume responsibility for any of these adjustments, which will therefore affect the overall cost of the asset (¶2350).

The provisions relating to a sale do not apply.

c. Assets transferred over a period of time

8676 Usually the transfer of all the assets subject to the sale will take place at the same time but there may be occasions where this does not happen.

There is no general requirement for assets to be transferred together for the TOGC provisions to apply (although the closer together that the assets are transferred, the more likely it is to be considered a TOGC). In these situations it is the parties' intentions at the time of the transaction that must be considered.

EXAMPLE

1. A Ltd (a manufacturer of electrical products) was in financial difficulties and sold its specialised manufacturing equipment to B Ltd. This was subsequently followed by further sales to B Ltd (over several months) of its stock, other manufacturing equipment and its trademark. A Ltd then subsequently went into liquidation.
It was held that the sales were a series of independent transactions and that there had been no consensus between the parties that the transfer was a TOGC. *Babytec Ltd* [1994] (VTD 12391)

2. A company purchased a petrol station as a TOGC. Shortly before the contracts were signed, the purchaser also bought a fleet of vehicles from the vendor.
This purchase was treated as part of the original TOGC, because although the purchase was in a separate agreement, in substance it was part of the same transaction. *Fonbane* [1987] (VTD 2813)

5. Transfer of VAT number

8678 SI 1995/2518 reg 6; VATREG29850

Where the seller is registered for VAT but the buyer is not, an election can be made (using form VAT68) for the buyer to take over the seller's VAT registration number.

The **election** must be signed by all parties to the transaction. In the case of an acrimonious dissolution of a partnership, where a partner has disappeared or refuses to sign the paperwork, HMRC will not insist on the signatures of all parties, provided that they are satisfied there has been a change in legal entity.

The election must be **submitted within** 30 days of the date of the TOGC to avoid any penalty for late notification. If the election is given late, the registration may be reallocated retrospectively, at the discretion of HMRC.

Comment Before electing to take over a VAT registration, the buyer should **thoroughly investigate** the seller's VAT history, because the transfer involves taking over all responsibility for payment, reporting and record keeping from the seller (including outstanding returns, payments and so on from periods before the transfer).

Consequences

The consequences of the transfer of a VAT registration number are that the: **8680**
a. liability of the transferor:
– at the transfer date to submit a return or to account for or pay VAT becomes the liability of the transferee; and
– to repay input tax on a purchase invoice overdue by more than 6 months (¶868) becomes the liability of the transferee; and
b. right of the transferor to:
– credit for or repayment of input tax becomes the right of the transferee (for example, VAT recoverable on any business services supplied to the previous owner before the transfer but invoiced afterwards); and
– claim for bad debt relief (¶845) becomes the right of the transferee.

Any **penalties** issued to the seller either before or after the transfer do not become the responsibility of the buyer.

Conditions

The following conditions **must all be satisfied** at the date of the transfer of the VAT registration number: **8682** VATREG30100
a. the registration to be transferred must not be a VAT group registration (¶8800);
b. the buyer must not already be registered;
c. if the seller opted to tax a property forming part of a TOGC the buyer must also have an option to tax in place; and
d. the seller must not be:
– deregistered prior to the transfer;
– liable or eligible to be VAT-registered following the transfer;
– subject to a notice of direction in respect of business splitting (¶2629);
– subject to a penalty (¶3950), although penalties for failure to notify or the unauthorised issue of invoices may be ignored if paid; or
– subject to any outstanding default surcharge notices (¶4082) or unpaid interest charges or centrally raised assessments.

In addition, if the **transferor was a company**, it must not have been dissolved before the VAT68 is signed.

MEMO POINTS 1. It is not possible to transfer approval to operate a **particular accounting scheme** (e.g. flat rate, annual accounting, etc). The buyer must make a new application to operate such a scheme.
2. An **appeal** can be made against any decision by HMRC to refuse to transfer a VAT registration number, where all of the above conditions are satisfied. VATREG30200
3. Business **records** must normally be retained for 6 years. Any of the transferor's records relating to the business which are required to be preserved for any period after the transfer must be preserved by the transferee instead of the transferor, unless HMRC, at the request of the transferor, allows otherwise. Contrast this with the position when the VAT registration number is not transferred (¶8648).

SECTION 4

Insolvency, death, incapacity

Special rules apply when a trader: **8700** s 46(4) VATA 1994
– becomes insolvent (¶8706);
– dies (¶8732); or
– becomes incapacitated (¶8742).

Who is responsible?

In all of these situations another person ("X") takes over responsibility for the trader's affairs. **8702** SI 1995/2518 regs 9, 30
For the purposes of **registration** X can either be:

– treated as a substitute for the former registered trader, provided that X is actively trading and making taxable supplies (the register will be amended to show "X carrying on the business of Y"); or
– separately registered as a trader. This course of action is the most appropriate where it is likely that the business will be carried on by X for the foreseeable future.

It is then X's duty to **comply with any VAT obligations** outstanding as at the date of insolvency, death or incapacity, but only to the extent that X has control over the former trader's assets.

A. Insolvency

1. Type of personal representative

8706 Notice 700/56 para 2

On the insolvency of a trader, a personal representative will deal with the trader's affairs. The type of personal representative appointed will **differ depending upon** the type of insolvency procedure adopted, as follows:

Personal representative	Insolvency procedure
Official receiver	A civil servant who is an officer of the courts Deals with compulsory liquidations and bankruptcies
Trustee in bankruptcy [1,2]	Appointed by the courts and is responsible for distributing assets to all the creditors in proportion to their debts
Liquidator	Appointed either by resolution of the shareholders in a voluntary winding-up or by the courts in a compulsory winding-up
Administrator	Appointed by the courts following an application by the company, its directors or its creditors Will deal with, for example, deeds of arrangements, voluntary arrangements

Note:
1. It is possible that a trader who is declared **bankrupt** will continue to trade after the date of bankruptcy. If so, the business should be allowed to continue under the existing VAT registration number.
2. Known as an Accountant in bankruptcy **in Scotland**.

MEMO POINTS 1. For VAT **groups** and insolvency see ¶8914.
2. For details of the various **insolvency procedures** and the occasions when HMRC may take insolvency action, etc, to recover unpaid VAT see ¶3730+.

8708 SI 1995/2518 reg 9; Notice 700/56 para 3

The personal representative **must notify** HMRC of the appointment within 21 days. Notification must be made on form VAT769.

When a **liquidator** is appointed **after** the appointment of an **official receiver**, it is not necessary to complete form VAT769. It will be sufficient to simply inform HMRC in writing of the change of responsibility together with the name, address and date of appointment of the liquidator. Such notification must be sent to:
HMRC
National Insolvency Unit
5th Floor, Regian House
Liverpool
L74 1AD

8710 Notice 700/56 para 4

Once notification of insolvency is made to HMRC, they will **calculate the amount of VAT** that is due to them and lodge a claim against the insolvent trader for that amount. Part of this claim may include penalties, default surcharge and default interest.

Where a personal representative is appointed, special provisions also apply to:
– ongoing compliance;
– VAT groups (¶8800); and
– partnerships (¶8724).

2. Ongoing compliance

In addition to the normal rules, special provisions apply when personal representatives are acting on behalf of insolvent traders for: **8712**
- VAT returns;
- record-keeping; and
- deregistration.

VAT returns

Where the **date of insolvency falls within a VAT period**, the period is split into two notional periods as follows: **8714** Notice 700/56 para 5
- period one, which ends on the day before insolvency. The return for this period must be submitted by the last day of the following month; and
- period two, which begins on the day of the insolvency and ends on the normal last day for the VAT period of the insolvent trader. The return for this period must be submitted in accordance with the normal rules (¶2985).

Any returns that are due and/or outstanding must be **submitted** by the personal representative as follows:
- pre-insolvency returns must be submitted, unsigned by the personal representative but simply stating that they have been completed from the books and records of the trader; and
- post-insolvency returns must be submitted in accordance with the normal VAT due dates.

Most **penalties, default surcharge and default interest** do not apply to post-insolvency VAT returns. They are, however, applied in the case of administration orders, deeds and schemes of arrangement, Scottish trust deeds and voluntary arrangements. Penalties for **inaccuracy** (¶3960), however, continue to apply as normal.

MEMO POINTS Returns are normally submitted online (¶3002), but if the return is on paper it must be sent to:
HMRC
VAT Controller
VAT Central Unit
BX5 5AT

The following special provisions apply for VAT returns prepared for an insolvent trader: **8716** Notice 700/56 paras 10-12, 15; Notice 48 para 3.20

Procedure	Rule
Bad debt relief (¶840)	Can be claimed in accordance with the normal rules using form VAT426 By concession, the personal representative need not repay input tax on receipt of notice of a claim to VAT bad debt relief from a supplier in respect of pre-insolvency transactions, provided that HMRC has been properly notified of the insolvency and there is no tax avoidance motive
Cash accounting (¶4880)	The personal representative must, within 2 months of the date of the insolvency, account for VAT due on all supplies made or received up to the date of the insolvency which have not previously been accounted for This is treated as a liability arising before the insolvency
Credit notes (¶2925)	Any VAT adjustment in respect of a credit note is related back to the period in which the original supply took place (subject to an overriding proviso that no VAT adjustment can be made if the credit note is issued more than 4 years after the end of the VAT accounting period in which the supply took place)
Recovery of input tax on insolvency practitioner fees	These are treated as an overhead of the business (¶2437)
Partial exemption	An insolvent business may seek approval from HMRC for a change of method to calculate its entitlement to input tax recovery, given the change in circumstances These changes cannot be applied to pre-insolvency periods

Record keeping

8718 Notice 700/56 para 19.1

In **general** the normal rules for record keeping apply equally to personal representatives, in that they need to keep all relevant records for 6 years (¶2797).

This time **limit is reduced** in the following situations:
– a liquidator of an insolvent company may destroy records 1 year after the company's dissolution; and
– an official receiver of an insolvent company may, upon the approval of a request to HMRC, destroy records 6 months after the company's dissolution.

Deregistration

8720 Notice 700/56 para 6

Deregistration should be applied for as soon as trading has ceased. The deregistration process depends upon the type of insolvency as follows:

Type of insolvency	Procedure
Voluntary arrangements	The normal rules for deregistration and submission of VAT returns apply (¶8600+)
Administrative receivership	HMRC issues form VAT167 [1]; deregistration occurs when the personal representative agrees it is appropriate [2]
All other types of insolvency (e.g. bankruptcy, compulsory liquidation)	HMRC issues form VAT167 [1]; deregistration will occur automatically 6 weeks later, unless the personal representative contacts them to say it is not appropriate [2]
Note: 1. VAT167 is a questionnaire issued by HMRC to establish the level of stocks and assets on hand. The personal representative must return the form within 5 weeks. 2. Once deregistration is agreed, a final VAT return is issued for completion.	

8721 HMRC Brief 13/2014

Output tax VAT on taxable stocks and assets at the date of insolvency should normally be accounted for on post-insolvency returns.

Previously it had been the case that output tax that needed to be accounted for after deregistration could be done on from VAT833. However in April 2014 HMRC withdrew this concession as it was advised that a trader that had been deregistered could no longer issue VAT invoices. However, deregistration on the basis of future turnover is still available under basic principles, negating the requirement to charge output tax.

8722 Notice 700/56 paras 7.3 - 7.9

Recovery of input tax After deregistration, input tax can still be recovered in the following situations:
– a liquidator in a voluntary arrangement can reclaim input tax in accordance with the normal rules (¶8618) using form VAT427;
– all other personal representatives can, in addition to the normal rules, reclaim input tax on services of agents and realisation fees that relate to taxable activities, using form VAT426. It is not necessary to send supporting documentation with the claim unless it is felt that it is necessary and will clarify the claim.

MEMO POINTS 1. **VAT426 and VAT427** should be sent to the following addresses:
a. VAT426:
HMRC
VAT426 Claims Section
National Insolvency Unit
5th floor, Regian House
Liverpool
L74 1AD
b. VAT427:
VAT427 Team
St Mungo's Road
Cumbernauld
G70 5WY.
For details of where to send such forms for Scottish claims and voluntary arrangements see ¶9993.
2. See also ¶2437 for the interaction of **partial exemption** and insolvency.

3. Partnerships

The provisions detailed above apply equally to insolvent partnerships, although special rules apply in relation to VAT registration and VAT returns. **8724** s 45 VATA 1994; Notice 700/56 para 16

HMRC will lodge a claim against all partners for VAT outstanding at the date of the insolvency.

Registration

On the insolvency of a partner, the treatment of the partnership registration for the **remaining partner(s)** varies depending upon whether the insolvency causes: **8726**
- one partner to remain, effectively trading as a sole trader; or
- a simple change in the constitution of the partnership (for example, instead of three partners, there are now two).

After insolvency	Rules
One partner remains (as a sole trader)	The sole trader will need to be separately registered for VAT (either via a deregistration and re-registration process, or by a transfer of registration under the TOGC provisions (¶8678+))
Two or more partners remain	If the former partnership was registered in the name of: – the firm, it is only necessary to strike off the insolvent partner's name from the form VAT2; or – the individual partners, it is necessary to change the trader's name on the register (using form VAT12), and then strike off the insolvent partner's name from the VAT2

VAT returns

Provided that at least **one partner remains**, the responsibility for the VAT returns lies with those remaining partner(s). **8728**

If **all of the partners are insolvent** (or the partnership itself is wound up), the responsibility for complying with VAT obligations will fall to the personal representative in the usual manner.

B. Death

On the death of a trader a **personal representative** will deal with the trader's affairs in one of the following capacities: **8732** SI 1995/2518 regs 9, 30
- executor, appointed under a person's will to wind up the estate and deal with the deceased's affairs;
- administrator, appointed by the courts to carry out the same purposes; or
- executor de son tort, unofficially carrying on the deceased's business activities (not appointed in any official capacity).

Generally the person carrying on the business after the death should be **registered** separately. An executor or administrator will be registered in a personal capacity, rather than an official capacity.

If it is evident that the business is only being **carried on temporarily** by a person (prior to, for example, a TOGC to a beneficiary or a third party), that person may be treated as a substitute for the former trader. For this to happen, only the executor or administrator may act as substitute, and HMRC must be notified within 21 days. The register will be amended to show "A carrying on the business of B".

In both cases the person carrying on the business is responsible for complying with the usual VAT obligations (for example, reporting, accounting, payments, etc).

MEMO POINTS 1. If a **temporary operation** of a business **carries on for a year** and there is still no sign of settlement in the foreseeable future, the person that is being treated as a substitute for the former trader (¶8702) may be required by HMRC to register separately.

VATREG42800 2. A personal representative who is not appointed in an official capacity (but as an **executor de son tort**) must register separately rather than simply acting as a substitute for the former trader. If an executor de son tort **acts without the knowledge of HMRC** and an official personal representative is subsequently appointed, the actions of the executor de son tort take priority. This means that the executor is treated as the taxable person.

Partnerships

8734 s 33 Partnership Act 1890 A death causes a partnership to be dissolved unless the partnership agreement provides to the contrary but the **VAT registration** and the **liability to VAT** carry on as normal, until notification of the death is given to HMRC.

8736 VATREG42900 - 43150 Once notification is made to HMRC, it has the **following options**:

a. allow the personal representative to carry on trading as a substitute (¶8702) for the deceased (this is likely if the trade is only going to carry on for the purposes of winding up the partnership affairs);

b. if several partners remain after the death and continue to trade, re-register the partnership (¶8726); or

c. where a partner becomes a sole trader and:

– intends to continue as a sole trader, or take on another partner some time in the future, deregister and re-register under a new VAT number, or apply for a transfer of the existing registration using form VAT68; or

– finds a replacement more or less immediately, amend the trader's name and ask the new partner to complete form VAT2.

Companies

8738 VATREG43400 A company "dies" when it is **struck-off or dissolved**. When this happens the company is deregistered. It is not possible for any person to be treated as a substitute for the former registered trader (¶8702), as the trade does not exist.

If the business activities of the company are carried on by, for example, former directors after the company has ceased to exist, it will be necessary to deregister the company and re-register the person(s) who are actually making the taxable supplies, or transfer the registration number under the TOGC provisions (¶8678).

C. Incapacity

8742 VATREG43750 There are no standard legal procedures following the incapacity of a trader and no official personal representative will be appointed. Each case will be judged on its own facts.

An incapacitated person is one who, as a result of some physical affliction or disability, is either temporarily or permanently incapable of controlling and managing property and business affairs.

8744 Following the incapacity of a trader there are **several options** available:

Type of incapacity	By	What happens
Temporary	Sole trader	Person carrying on the trade can be registered as a substitute (¶8702)
	Partner	Partnership continues if more than one partner remains and VAT is accounted for under the partnership's existing registration

Type of incapacity	By	What happens
Permanent	Sole trader	Business can be either: – deregistered if trading ceases; or – re-registered with person who carries on the business
	Partner	If two or more partners remain and the partnership is registered in the: – name of the firm, it is only necessary to strike off the incapacitated partner's name from the form VAT2; – names of the individuals, the trader's name must be changed on the register (using form VAT12) and the incapacitated partner's name must be struck off from the VAT2
		If only one partner remains the trade can be deregistered and re-registered (or, at the request of the trader, transferred as a TOGC)

CHAPTER 2

VAT groups

OUTLINE ¶¶

Bodies corporate (referred to here as companies) are able to register as a group and essentially be treated as a single taxable person if they are associated. **8800** s 43 VATA 1994; Notice 700/2

MEMO POINTS **Bodies corporate include** not only companies limited by shares but also:
- limited liability partnerships;
- companies limited by guarantee;
- unlimited companies; and
- industrial and provident societies.

SECTION 1

Who can form a VAT group?

A. All groups

Companies can form a group if they are **associated**. In other words if: **8805**
- each has a UK business establishment (¶9690); and
- they are under common control (i.e. one controls the other, or they are both controlled by one person or group of individuals carrying out business in partnership).

In addition, further conditions must be satisfied by **large VAT groups** with a turnover in excess of £10 million.

MEMO POINTS 1. **Overseas companies** can join a VAT group if they have a UK business establishment. See ¶8895 for restrictions on supplies between overseas members.

SI 1982/1067 reg 11 2. The UK includes the **Isle of Man**. HMRC must be notified if a group company acquires an establishment in the Isle of Man if, at the time of initial registration, no group company had an establishment in the Isle of Man.

SI 1987/1806 reg 13 3. As an anti-avoidance measure, a **tour operator** (¶7490) is not eligible to be treated as a member of a group if any other member of the proposed or existing group:
- has an overseas establishment;
- makes supplies outside the UK which would be taxable supplies if made within the UK; or
- supplies goods or services which will become, or are intended to become, a designated travel service (¶7504).

4. The CJEU has confirmed that member states may allow **non-taxable persons** to be members of VAT groups. *EC v Ireland* [2013] C-85/11 This does not affect the UK position, as confirmed by a further decision of the CJEU holding that the UK is not in breach of its obligations (not acting ultra vires) by allowing non-taxable persons to be members of VAT groups. *EC v UK* [2013] C-86/11

What is control?

8807
s 43A VATA 1994

A **company** controls another company if it is:
- empowered by statute to control the company's activities; or
- the company's holding company within the meaning of the Companies Acts.

An **individual or partnership** controls a company if they would, were they a company, be the company's holding company.

MEMO POINTS 1. A company is **empowered by statute** to control a company's activities if it:
a. holds the majority of the voting rights in its subsidiary; or
b. is a member of the subsidiary company and:
- has the right to appoint or remove a majority of the subsidiary's board of directors; or
- alone controls the majority of the voting rights pursuant to a shareholders' agreement.

2. A company will be a **holding company** if it:
a. controls the other company; or
b. is a holding company of another holding company.

B. Large VAT groups

8812
SI 2004/1931 reg 2

Special rules apply to large VAT groups. Where the turnover of the group in the previous year **exceeded £10 million** (or is expected to exceed £10 million in the coming year), grouping is not allowed where a subsidiary is a specified body, **unless** the following conditions are met:
- benefits (¶8818); and
- group accounts consolidation (¶8826).

MEMO POINTS 1. **Turnover** is defined as the value of all supplies made by the VAT group to persons outside the group.
2. **Expected turnover** is calculated on the basis that the company is a member of the group. If the applicant is a general partner in a limited liability partnership, the expected turnover must take into account the partnership's supplies to persons outside the group.

Specified body

8814
SI 2004/1931 reg 3

Broadly speaking a specified body is a partly owned (i.e. not wholly owned) subsidiary company that makes relevant intra-group supplies.

A company is **specifically exempted** from being a specified body if:
- it controls all the other VAT group members or is itself controlled by another company;
- its only activity is acting as a trustee of an occupational pension scheme; or
- it is a charity.

MEMO POINTS 1. **Strictly**, a specified body is **defined** as a company that:
a. makes relevant intra-group supplies of goods or services;
b. is not specifically exempted; and
c. either it:
- is partly owned by a third party (i.e. it is not a wholly owned subsidiary);
- has business activities which are managed by a third party; or
- is the sole partner of a limited liability partnership.

2. A **relevant intra-group supply** is any supply of goods or services to the rest of the VAT group on which: SI 2004/1931 reg 4
- VAT would be charged if the supplier was not a group member (i.e. the transaction is not zero-rated, exempt or outside the scope); and
- the representative member could not recover this VAT in full.

3. A **third party** is broadly any person or partnership outside the corporate group that includes the VAT group, other than individuals working for the company. Notice 700/2 para 3.5
The strict **definition** is any person or partnership except:
- anyone who controls the whole VAT group;
- anyone controlled by the person who controls the whole VAT group (this, therefore, includes all fellow subsidiaries);
- directors or employees of the company; or
- any individual who is a partner in a limited liability partnership (where applicable).

1. Grouping conditions

If a company is a specified body, further conditions need to be met before grouping will be permitted. **8817**

MEMO POINTS These conditions were introduced as an **anti-avoidance** measure. Historically, partly exempt purchasers were setting up joint venture companies within their VAT group with their third-party suppliers. The aim of such arrangements was to buy in goods and services without incurring irrecoverable VAT, although in reality such joint venture companies were run by and for the benefit of the third-party suppliers.

Benefits condition

This condition will be **satisfied** if no more than 50% of the benefits generated by the business accrue to third parties (i.e. they are diverted away from the person controlling the VAT group). **8818** SI 2004/1931 reg 5

Note here that benefits belonging to a **holding company** are not treated as accruing to a third party, even if the holding company has shareholders who are third parties. This is because the test is concerned with profits being diverted away from the person controlling the VAT group.

MEMO POINTS 1. Benefits are treated as if they **accrue** to persons if they are, in practice, expected to get the benefit of them (directly or indirectly), taking into account all the circumstances.
2. If there is a **change of ownership** of a company during a year, benefits will be treated as accruing to the old owner up to the date of change and the new owner thereafter.
3. For a sole partner of a **limited liability partnership**, the benefits concerned are those arising from the partnership's business activity.

Broadly speaking benefits are **defined** as the rewards obtainable from the good management of the subsidiary and **include**: **8820** Notice 700/2 para 3.11.2
- profits of the business, whether distributed or not (if there are none, the company is deemed to make notional profits of £100);
- charges made by anyone for managing the business activity that involves making intra-group supplies; and
- any other charges made to the company to the extent that they exceed the open-market value of goods or services supplied. HMRC states that this is only intended to catch contrived situations; HMRC does not expect traders to undertake extra work to establish that transactions are at normal market value.

8822 Benefits **do not include**:
– cost savings made by being a customer of the company (for example, price reductions, discounts or rebates); or
– remuneration or bonuses paid to directors or employees of the company.

EXAMPLE A Ltd is a member of the ABC VAT group (a large VAT group, with turnover in excess of £10m) and is 100% owned by B Ltd. A third party manages A Ltd's business, activity which consists of making intra-group supplies. The third party makes a fixed £25,000 charge each year for this.
A Ltd has the following results:

		£
Year 1	Profits	100,000
	Third-party charge	25,000
	Total benefits	125,000

Only £25,000 of the benefits accrue to a third party (which is less than 50% of the total benefits), so the benefits condition is satisfied.

		£
Year 2	Profits	20,000
	Third-party charge	25,000
	Total benefits	45,000

Although only £25,000 of the benefits accrue to a third party again, this is more than 50% of the total benefits, so the condition is not satisfied.

8824 If the **level of profits affects the proportions of benefits** a third party is expected to receive each year, the benefits test should be applied on the basis of current expectations for the accounting period in question. If expectations change, such that the benefits test will no longer be satisfied, the company can no longer be part of the VAT group from the date that the expectations change.

EXAMPLE A third party is entitled to 45% of the profits of subsidiary D Ltd up to £100,000 and 52% if profits exceed this level. D Ltd is part of the DEF VAT group, which has a turnover in excess of £10m.
In Year 1 it is not expected that profits of D Ltd will exceed £100,000, so VAT grouping is permitted. However, on 30 September the profit forecasts show an anticipated profit by D Ltd of £150,000. D Ltd can no longer be part of the DEF VAT group from this date.

Group accounts consolidation

8826 This condition will be met if, under UK or International GAAP:
SI 2004/1931 reg 6
a. a person controlling the VAT group consolidates the results of the specified body as a subsidiary in its consolidated group accounts. If more than one person controls the VAT group, for example there is a chain of holding companies, this point need only be met by one of them; and
b. there is no third party which also consolidates the results of the specified body in its consolidated group accounts.

MEMO POINTS 1. If the results of the specified body are not included because they are **immaterial**, this condition looks at what would happen if the bodies' results were material.
2. For the, albeit rare, occurrence when the person controlling the VAT group is **not required to prepare consolidated accounts** because, for example, that person is an individual or specifically exempted, this condition looks at what the position would be if consolidated accounts were prepared.
3. Where the specified body is a general partner of a **limited liability partnership**, the consolidation condition applies to the partnership (i.e. the partnership must be consolidated as a subsidiary in consolidated group accounts).

2. Summary

HMRC provides the following useful flow chart to assist with the decision-making process. **8828** Notice 700/2 para 3.12.9

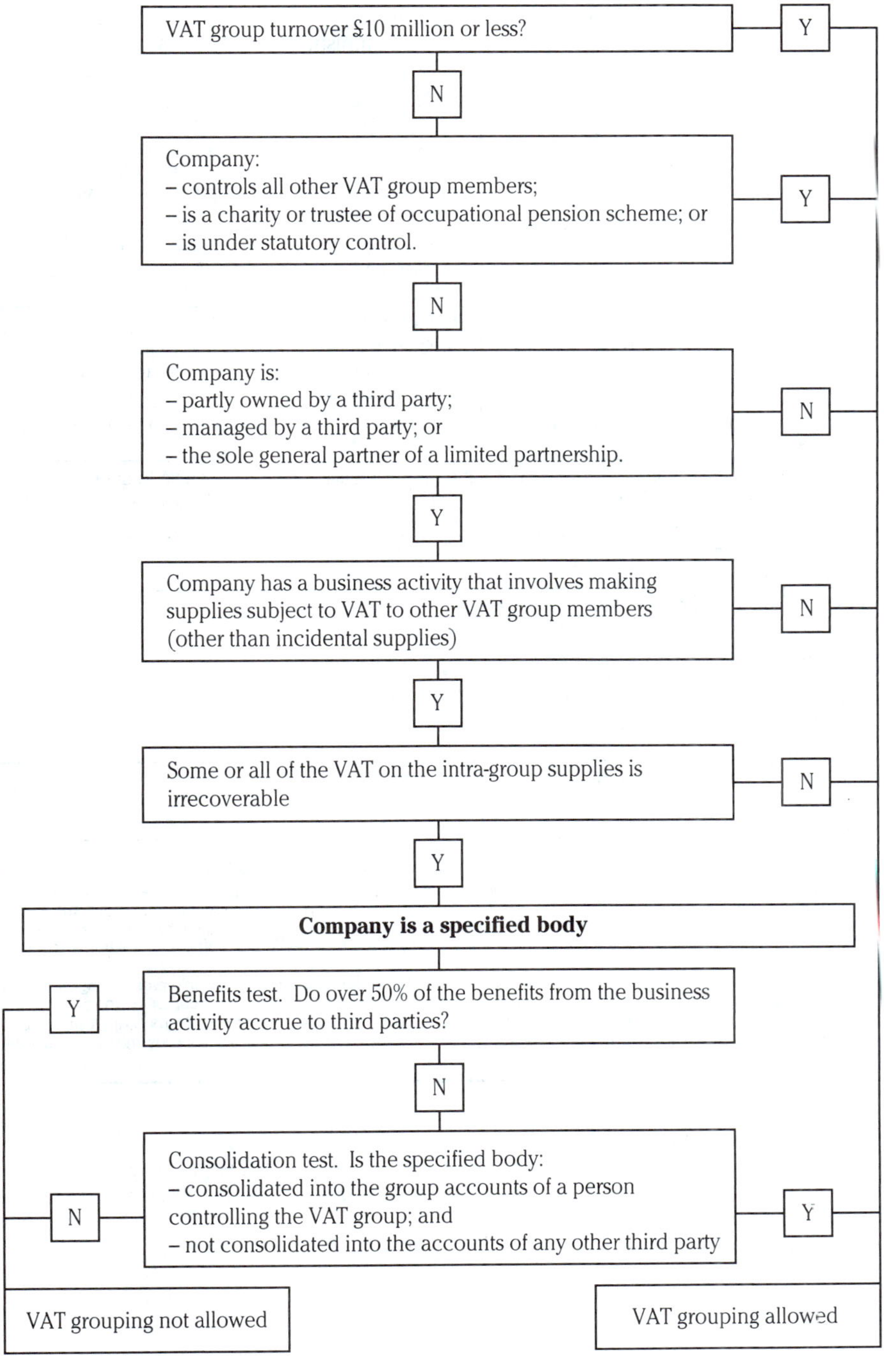

C. Consequences of group membership

8832 The **aim of the group provisions** is to ease the compliance burden on individual companies. The consequences that flow from this are largely administrative, as follows:

Consequence	Detail
Group is treated as a single taxable person and a single VAT return is submitted by the representative member	The trades of the group members are treated as if they were carried out by one group company (known as the representative member[1]); the representative member assumes all the group companies' VAT rights and duties[2]
Registration is in the name of the representative member	All the VAT numbers of the group members are cancelled and a new "group" VAT number is issued, which all group members must use
Representative member normally accounts for any VAT due on supplies made by the group to third parties	Helpful if accounting is centralised but group members will need to ensure that all the necessary paperwork, etc, is with the representative member on a timely basis
No need to account for VAT on supplies between group members	Subject to specific anti-avoidance provisions (¶8878)
All members of the group are jointly and severally liable for any VAT due from the representative member	If a representative member is unable to settle a debt of the group, each member is held liable for the debt until it is discharged
The partial exemption method applies to the whole group	See ¶2264
The following limits apply to the group as a whole: – partial exemption de minimis (¶2194)[3,4]; – cash accounting limits (¶4885); – payment on account limits (¶3182); and – limits for correction of errors on future returns (¶3020)	
A member is not able to use the flat rate scheme (¶4635) or divisional registration (¶2744)	

Note:
1. The representative member can be any company nominated in the application (¶8845).

s 43(1AA) VATA 1994 2. If a member of a VAT group was eligible for special treatment in respect of its supplies, acquisitions or imports **before it was grouped**, the special treatment can be transferred to the representative member for those supplies, etc. For example, if a charity is entitled to receive zero-rated supplies of certain goods, the representative member of the group will be deemed to take on the status of the charity group member for the purpose of the transaction(s) in question, hence preserving the relief.

3. Care should be taken when including a company that makes any **exempt supplies** within a group registration, as the group will then become partly exempt, with the de minimis limits applying to the group as a whole.

4. As no VAT is applied to **management charges** levied between the members of a VAT group, the amount of irrecoverable VAT suffered by a member of a group making exempt or partly exempt supplies may be reduced (¶2075+).

8834 A **former member** of a group:
- is entitled to claim bad debt relief (¶840) in respect of supplies made while it was a member, even if it was not the representative member *Triad Timber Components Ltd* [1993] (VTD 10694); and
- remains liable for any VAT that arose during the time it was in the group.

SECTION 2

Application for group treatment

How is an application made?

Application for group treatment is made to the National Registration Service Unit (¶9994). The form to be used for the application differs depending upon the nature of the application, as follows: 8845 ss 43B, 43D VATA 1994

Type of application	Form
For a group to be set up [1]	VAT1 (signed by the representative member) [2]
	VAT50 (signed by either the applicant company or person controlling it)
	VAT51 for each company applying to join the group (signed by either the applicant company or person controlling it)
For a company to join an existing group [3]	VAT50 and a VAT51 for each company applying to join the group
Change of representative member for an existing group [2,4]	VAT56

Note:
1. If, at the time of application, a company is already a member of an existing group, the application has effect but with the exclusion of that company.
2. Any company in the group can be appointed the representative member, although if supplies are made both in the UK and the Isle of Man, HMRC may determine the representative member.
3. If, at the time of application, the applicant is already a member of another VAT group, the application has no effect.
4. If the new representative member is not already a member of the group, forms VAT50 and VAT51 will also need to be completed.

An application can be made at any time. It will generally **take effect from** the date it is received by HMRC, although it is possible to **backdate** an application by up to 30 days to correspond with the commencement of the current accounting period of the existing or new VAT group. 8847 Notice 700/2 para 2.21

MEMO POINTS HMRC may **extend this 30-day period** only if: Notice 700/2 para 2.22
- it loses the original application and evidence of both the original application and subsequent follow-up attempts are provided; or
- the delay was caused by a lack of action on HMRC's part.

What happens on receipt of an application?

On receipt of a completed application for grouping, change of representative member, etc, there are **three possible outcomes**: 8850 Notice 700/2 paras 2.4 - 2.18

Outcome	VAT number	Grounds
Application accepted [1]	New number issued with immediate effect from the date of application	All the necessary conditions are met
Application refused	No new VAT number issued	The necessary conditions are not met
		Revenue protection (¶8852) [2]
Application acknowledged but not accepted or refused, pending further enquiries [3]	New number issued with immediate effect from the date of application	

Note:
1. Within 15 days of receipt of the application.
2. An application to change the representative member can only be refused on the grounds of revenue protection.
3. HMRC will have 90 days (commencing from the date of receipt of the application) in which to complete these enquiries and either accept or refuse the application. While any further enquiries are being raised, the company is still treated as if it were registered as part of a VAT group and VAT is accounted for on this basis. This is the most common scenario in practice.

8851 If an application is **refused after enquiries are completed**, it will effectively be treated as if it had never been allowed in the first place. Where this happens the position of the **company** before the provisional registration will be reinstated. Therefore if it was previously:
– registered in its own right, its previous registration number will be reinstated from the date on which it was originally cancelled;
– not required to be registered at the time of application but became liable to be registered in its own right during the period of provisional registration, it must register in its own right within 30 days after the letter of refusal of group registration; or
– not registered and has not subsequently become liable to be so, there is no requirement to register.

If any VAT returns were submitted during the enquiry period on the basis that the company was part of the VAT group, they will need to be corrected.

The **VAT group** will need to revise its VAT position to take account of the fact that the company was not part of the registration. Any supplies between companies in the intended group will need to be taken into account.

MEMO POINTS For details of **how to correct errors** see ¶3020. If the amendment is made on a following period's return it will have to be made on both the group and company returns.

8852 s 43B(5)(c) VATA 1994; VGROUPS06000+

Revenue protection HMRC can refuse an application on the grounds of revenue protection. It has stated that it will **not normally use** these provisions if the revenue loss follows from the normal operation of grouping - for example, because:
– VAT is eliminated on the value added by a group member, when a supply takes place between two group members; or
– the recipient would not normally be able to recover the VAT in full if the supply were provided by a non-group member.

Grouping **may be refused** if HMRC considers that the revenue loss goes beyond the accepted result of grouping. This involves a balancing exercise in which the effect of refusal is weighed against the loss of revenue likely to result from grouping.

Before using these powers HMRC will request:
– relevant information about the administrative savings that grouping brings; and
– an estimate of the revenue impact of grouping.

Persistent failure to co-operate with these enquiries may be sufficient grounds for grouping to be refused.

It is possible to **appeal** against any such decision made by HMRC.

MEMO POINTS It is possible also for HMRC to **terminate an existing group arrangement** on the ground of revenue protection.

SECTION 3

Leaving a group

8865 SI 1995/2518 reg 5(2)

A grouping arrangement can be **terminated by** either the relevant company(ies) concerned, or HMRC, as shown in the following table.

All intra-group supplies made after the date of the degrouping are treated as taxable supplies, unless exempt in their own right.

Terminated by	Grounds for termination	Notification	Takes effect from
Group company	Failure to satisfy relevant conditions	On form VAT50 and VAT51 Notify within 30 days of the change in circumstances that result in the company being no longer eligible for grouping	In practice the date specified in the form is used HMRC will only take the date that the application is received if VAT avoidance is an issue
	Wishes to terminate the group relationship for any other reason	On form VAT50 and VAT51	
HMRC	Failure to satisfy relevant conditions	By notice	From the date specified in the notice (which can be earlier than the date the notice is issued but not earlier than the date HMRC became of the opinion that the conditions were no longer satisfied)
	Revenue protection (¶8852)	By notice	From the date the notice is given, or any later date specified in the notice Alternatively, HMRC may remove a company from an existing group to counter certain tax-avoidance schemes (¶8880), in which case it has greater scope to backdate the direction to recover VAT

SECTION 4

Tax avoidance

There are specific anti-avoidance rules that aim to prevent abuse of the group rules through the: 8875
- exploitation of the fact that intra-group supplies are usually ignored for VAT; or
- use of overseas companies, or overseas branches of UK companies.

MEMO POINTS 1. These **powers were introduced to** counter certain schemes whereby, for example, Company A purchased standard-rated supplies, claiming a full input tax deduction. Company A then made an onward supply, which was treated as being made (to some extent) between VAT group members. A simple method of achieving this was to move companies in and out of the VAT group at critical times. Consequently, output tax was only charged on a proportion of the full onward value of the supplies.
2. For details of HMRC power to **vary VAT periods** of associated businesses see ¶2993.

A. Intra-group supplies

HMRC can issue directions to **change or impose a grouping arrangement** in certain situations where it appears that transactions have been undertaken to exploit the fact that intra-group supplies are ignored for VAT. 8878 Sch 9A VATA 1994; VGROUPS07000+

1. Issue of direction

8880 The directions can be as follows:

Type of direction	Consequences of direction
Separately registered companies are grouped [1]	Normally, the purpose of a direction to group companies together is to recoup any excess claim to input tax. In such cases the amount of tax to be charged is the amount of input tax recovered, less the amount which would otherwise have been recoverable in accordance with the partial exemption method (¶2075) of the appropriate VAT group registration.
Removal of a company from an existing group [2]	All intra-group supplies made after the date of the degrouping are treated as taxable supplies, unless exempt in their own right.
Intra-group supply is subject to VAT	Output tax is payable based on the market value of the supply.

Note:
1. Provided that they are also otherwise eligible to be grouped.
2. Note here the **overlap powers** that HMRC has to remove a company from a group (¶8865). The key difference between removing a company under these anti-avoidance provisions is that HMRC has greater scope to backdate the direction to recover VAT.

2. Conditions for direction

8882 Sch 9A para 1 VATA 1994; VGROUPS08250+

A direction can **only** be given if a company has joined or left a group, or entered into any transaction which results in:
- a standard-rated supply (on which input tax had been fully recovered) not being taxed on its full value, because it will be, or has been, treated as an intra-group supply; and
- a tax advantage arising as a result of charging VAT on less than full value.

Sch 9A para 4 VATA 1994

A direction **cannot be given** more than 6 years after the later of the date that the:
- company joined or left the group, or entered into the relevant transaction; or
- entitlement to input tax arose.

MEMO POINTS Where HMRC has evidence that a company has joined or left a group, or entered into any transaction, it can make a **direction in anticipation** of a subsequent standard-rated supply not being taxed on its full value. HMRC does not need to wait for the actual supply to be made before issuing the direction.

Entered into a transaction

8884 This is when a company enters into an initial contract, as opposed to performing ongoing obligations under an existing contract. For example, entering into a lease by a landlord or tenant will be treated as an initial transaction. However, the **performance of obligations** under the lease (e.g. the carrying out of repairs or the payment of rent) would not normally be caught unless, exceptionally, such an obligation constituted entering into a separate contract.

Tax advantage

8886 Sch 9A para 1(4) VATA 1994; VGROUPS08310

A tax advantage is **treated as arising where** input tax recovery is achieved on goods and services used to make an onward supply. Note that there is no requirement for the input tax to be or have been recovered by the actual supplier of the onward supply.

These anti-avoidance provisions **also apply** where:
- the transactions involve rights to goods or services; or
- the supplier acquires the goods and/or services tax-free as a transfer of a business as a going concern and the transferor, or some previous owner of the business, had been entitled to input tax recovery.

These provisions **do not apply** where there is no VAT avoidance motive, for example, where businesses are moved into and out of VAT groups for purely administrative reasons following a change of ownership. However, if, in addition to a genuine commercial motive, HMRC also identifies a VAT avoidance motive, it will seek to use these powers to nullify the VAT advantage.

MEMO POINTS See also ¶3070 for the **requirement to disclose** use of an input tax saving scheme.

EXAMPLE

1. A partly exempt group of companies (the PX group) arranges for computer equipment to be provided by an associated company, Newco 1, which operates a leasing business.
Newco 1 purchases the necessary equipment and deducts input tax under its own VAT registration, as it relates to the intended taxable supply of leasing services to the PX group.
Before entering into a lease agreement, Newco 1 transfers its business, including the assets for use by PX group, as a going concern to another associated company, Newco 2. The transfer is not subject to VAT.
Newco 2 enters into a leasing agreement with PX group and, after an appropriate period, joins the group to ensure that the major part of the lease rentals are disregarded. Overall, the arrangements deliver a tax advantage and the anti-avoidance provisions will apply.

2. The AB Group (consisting of companies A and B) undertakes the following transactions:
- A pays B 90% of the cost for an option to purchase equipment at a nominal value from B (this supply is disregarded as an intra-group supply);
- B leaves the group and registers in its own right;
- A exercises its option and B supplies the goods to A after purchasing the goods and deducting input tax.

This would fall within the anti-avoidance provisions. The supply of the option and the supply of the goods are to be treated as a single supply and a direction would be issued by HMRC.

3. Form of direction

A direction must be made **in writing** to both the company concerned and the representative member of the relevant group. **8888** Sch 9A paras 3, 5 VATA 1994

It must **specify** what it is that has given rise to the direction (i.e. whether it arises because of a company joining a group, leaving a group or entering into a particular transaction). The direction can be **varied or withdrawn** at any time.

Taxpayers have full rights of **appeal** against any direction or assessment issued under these provisions.

Time frame

A direction will usually only **apply** from the earlier of the start of the accounting period in which the company: **8890**
- joins or leaves the group; or
- enters into the relevant transaction.

If an **earlier date is required**, due to the nature of the transaction concerned, HMRC has stated that it will not be any earlier than the date that is required to nullify the tax advantage concerned.

Assessment

Once a direction has been issued HMRC may raise an assessment to collect the unpaid VAT **no later than** the first anniversary of the date on which the direction was given. **8892** Sch 9A para 6 VATA 1994

The **amount** of the assessment is the lower of:
- the amount of unpaid tax; or
- the actual revenue loss.

If neither the degrouped company nor the remainder of the group have accurate **records** to determine the value and nature of transactions between them, an assessment will be made to HMRC's best judgment, based on all available information.

B. Members with overseas establishments

8895 To be eligible for VAT grouping a company must have a UK business establishment. There are further provisions to prevent an abuse of the VAT system when a company with a UK business establishment also has a **branch or establishment** in a country outside the UK. Generally, charges made or services provided between branches of the **same legal entity** are ignored for VAT purposes; this includes "supplies" between branches in different countries.

The anti-avoidance provisions aim to ensure that a tax advantage cannot be obtained by the overseas branch receiving services (outside the scope of UK VAT) which are then recharged to another member of the UK VAT group.

Scope

8896
s 43(2A) - (2E) VATA 1994

There is a tax charge where certain **supplies of services** are purchased by overseas operations of a UK member of a VAT group and then used for making supplies to a member of the VAT group. The supplies that are affected are services which are treated as being supplied where received (¶9682), provided that they are not exempt.

These provisions also apply where there has been a **transfer of a going concern** (¶8646) of the business of the overseas establishment of the member of the VAT group, provided that the services in question are used to make the onward supply to the UK VAT member.

EXAMPLE X Ltd is a member of a VAT group and arranges for a UK firm of design consultants to supply services to Y Ltd (which is in the same VAT group as X Ltd, as it is established in the UK, but also has a US office). The services of the design consultants are supplied to the US office of Y Ltd and are therefore outside the scope of VAT.

Scenario 1
Y Ltd then uses these services to make an onward supply to X Ltd.
Because of these anti-avoidance provisions, this supply will be subject to VAT despite the fact that it is an intra-group supply.

Scenario 2
The business of Y Ltd is transferred to A Ltd (another member of the UK VAT group) as a going concern. A Ltd, however, uses the services supplied by the design consultants to make an onward supply to X Ltd. This supply will be subject to VAT, despite the fact that it is an intra-group transaction.[1]

Note:
1. This rule also applies equally where there are successive transfers.

Taxable value

8898
Sch 6 para 8A VATA 1994

The value for calculating the tax charge on this supply may be **based on** the value of the services supplied to the overseas member, rather than on the actual charge made to the UK member. Evidence must be produced to:
- support the value of those services (for example, copy invoices); and
- demonstrate that the services have not been undervalued.

Where the value of the services supplied in this manner is **de minimis** (as a rule of thumb, less than 5% of the value of the supply to the UK member), these provisions will not apply unless HMRC believes that the values have been manipulated.

EXAMPLE C Ltd, a UK company, receives a supply of advertising from D Ltd (a VAT group member that is established in the UK but also has offices in the Channel Islands). D Ltd's Channel Islands office takes legal advice in relation to the supply of advertising, then recharges C Ltd for both the legal advice and a supply of staff, as follows:

		£
Cost of legal advice	£2,000 plus 10% mark up	2,200
Charge for supply of staff		60,000
Total charge		62,200

Only the legal advice will be within the scope of these provisions, as the advertising was supplied from D Ltd's UK establishment. As the value of the legal services is less than 5% of the total recharge, it may be disregarded.

MEMO POINTS 1. If a business is not able to provide copy invoices, it may agree an **alternative method to evidence the value**.
HMRC gives the following scenarios as examples:
a. where the overseas establishment of the group member buys in services and applies a fixed mark-up (in this case, documentary evidence of the mark-up would normally be sufficient to demonstrate that the value of the bought-in service was equal to the value of the onward supply less the mark-up); and
b. where either:
– the invoice to the overseas establishment of the group member does not relate exclusively to an onward supply to a UK group member; or
– the overseas establishment of the group member may not code its costs according to the recipient of any intended onward supply at the time when those costs are incurred.
In both of the above situations, it may calculate the value of its onward supply to each of its associated companies by uplifting its total costs and then allocating shares to associated companies in accordance with a predetermined fair and reasonable formula.
2. **Fully taxable groups** are not expected to go to great lengths in justifying that the de minimis levels are met, or in calculating the value on which to base the self-supply charge. In the unlikely event that HMRC disagrees with the view taken by the group on these points, an assessment may be raised but no interest or penalties would apply.
3. Groups which fail to comply with these provisions may incur a **penalty** (¶4030+) and interest will be charged in the usual manner (¶3880+).
4. Where **instalment payments** are made for these types of supplies, VAT must be accounted for on each payment.

SECTION 5

Interaction with other provisions

Many of the areas of the VAT legislation include **specific provisions** for VAT groups, the more common being: 8910

Area	Issue	¶¶
Bad debt relief	Relief for former member of group	¶847
Capital goods scheme	On joining or leaving a VAT group	¶2354
Cash accounting	Eligibility limits apply on group basis	¶4885
Land and property	Constructing status for zero-rated disposals	¶5253, ¶5386
	Option to tax	¶5658
Transfer of a going concern	And intra-group supplies	¶8912
Insolvency	Of representative member or group member	¶8914
Commencement and cessation of a business	Recovery of pre-commencement input VAT	¶8586
	Accounting for output tax on cessation	¶8610, ¶8612
Disclosure of VAT schemes	Turnover is between £600,000 and £10 million	¶3048+
	Turnover is over £10 million	¶3084+

1. Transfer of a business as a going concern

In addition to the general provisions in connection with a transfer of a going concern (TOGC) (¶8648+), the following specific issues are relevant to VAT groups: 8912 s 44 VATA 1994; Notice 700/9 para 4
a. for transfers **from** an **existing** VAT group:
– any assets so transferred are deemed to be transferred by the representative member;

– transfers of assets between group members are disregarded, therefore there can be no TOGC where the sole activity of the business transferred was to make supplies to other group members; and

b. for transfers **to** an **existing** VAT group:

– where the buyer uses the new acquisition entirely to make supplies to members of the VAT group, there is no TOGC and the business has effectively ceased (where the new acquisition also makes supplies outside the group, the transfer can be treated as a TOGC, assuming that all the other qualifying conditions are met); and

– the assets transferred are treated as being supplied to and by the representative member. This will create a self-supply charge where the group is or becomes partly exempt (¶1502).

2. Insolvency

8914 VGROUPS02350 When a company becomes insolvent an insolvency practitioner will take control of it. The practitioner also takes ownership of it. This has a knock on effect on the group structure.

Where the **holding company** of a group becomes insolvent the ownership of the group will not change as a whole. However, in such circumstances HMRC will, as a matter of policy, remove all solvent companies from the VAT group so that the group only has insolvent members. However, HMRC cannot force this treatment unless one of the other conditions of group registration are no longer satisfied.

Where **another member of the group** becomes insolvent it will automatically fail the grouping conditions based on ownership. As such it has to be removed from the group at the date that the insolvency practitioner is appointed. This will also extend to any companies that the insolvent company in turn controls.

If the company that becomes insolvent is the **representative member** of the group a new representative member will need to be appointed.

PART 9

Cross-border transactions

Cross-border transactions
Summary

The numbers cross-refer to paragraphs.

CHAPTER 1 Goods within the EU

CHAPTER 2 Goods outside the EU

CHAPTER 3 Supply of services

CHAPTER 4 Incurring cross-border VAT

CHAPTER 1

Goods within the EU

OUTLINE ¶¶

The treatment of transactions in goods between suppliers and recipients in the UK and other countries depends on whether the other country in question is an EU member state. For **transactions within the EU**, the terms "acquisitions" and "despatches" are used, respectively, to refer to goods which arrive in and leave the UK. **9000**

The terms "imports" and "exports" only apply to **transactions with countries outside the EU**, for which the rules are entirely different (¶9400+).

This chapter deals with transactions involving a party in the UK where the other party (whether supplier or customer) belongs in an EU member state other than the UK.

Scope of the EU

9002 The countries included in the VAT territory of the EU are as follows:

EU member state	Includes	Excludes
Austria	Jungholz Mittelberg	
Belgium		
Bulgaria		
Croatia		
Cyprus	The British sovereign base areas of Akrotiri and Dhekelia	The United Nations buffer zone and the part of Cyprus to the north of the buffer zone, where the Republic of Cyprus does not exercise effective control
Czech Republic		
Denmark		The Faroe Islands Greenland
Estonia		
Finland		The Aland Islands
France	Monaco	Martinique French Guiana Guadeloupe Reunion Mayotte Saint-Martin
Germany		Busingen The Isle of Heligoland
Greece		Mount Athos
Hungary		
The Republic of Ireland		
Italy		The communes of Livigno and Campione d'Italia The Italian waters of Lake Lugano
Latvia		
Lithuania		
Luxembourg		
Malta		
Netherlands		
Poland		
Portugal	The Azores Madeira	
Romania		
Slovak Republic		
Slovenia		
Spain	The Balearic islands	The Canary Islands Ceuta Melilla
Sweden		
UK	Isle of Man[1]	The Channel Islands Gibraltar

Note:
1. The inclusion of the Isle of Man is due to an agreement between the UK and the Isle of Man to establish a common tax area. The Isle of Man, however, has its own VAT legislation, administration and registration procedures, which are outside the scope of this book. For specific rules regarding the import of goods from the Isle of Man to the UK see ¶9408.

SECTION 1

Acquisitions

The EU is a single market and, under the **normal rules** (¶9017+), a supplier does not need to account for VAT on the supply of goods to a VAT-registered customer in another member state. The customer instead accounts for VAT on acquisition of the goods. 9010

Special rules apply to certain types of goods and situations (¶9110+).

An acquisition occurs in the UK when there is a supply (including a deemed supply (¶1460+)) involving the removal of goods from another EU member state to the UK. It is immaterial whether the goods are removed by, or on behalf of, the supplier, or by the customer or some other person. 9015 s 11(1) VATA 1994

A. Acquisitions by VAT-registered persons

UK VAT-registered persons must account for VAT on taxable acquisitions which take place in the UK. They may also be able to recover the amount in question as input tax on their VAT return for the period in which the acquisition takes place, subject to the normal deductibility (¶1800+) and partial exemption (¶2075+) rules. 9017 ss 1, 10 VATA 1994

MEMO POINTS 1. In this chapter **VAT-registered person** means a "taxable person" - that is, a person registered, or required to be registered, for VAT (¶2620+).
2. As acquirers account for VAT, **suppliers in other EU member states** will zero-rate their supplies.

Taxable acquisition

A taxable acquisition occurs where goods are: 9020 ss 10(2) -(3), 31(1) VATA 1994
- **acquired by** a VAT-registered person in the course or furtherance of the acquirer's business, when the goods were:
- **supplied by** a registered person in another EU member state, in the course or furtherance of the supplier's business.

This **excludes** transactions which are exempt (¶350+), or outside the scope of VAT (¶252+), or which result from a taxable supply made in the UK under normal UK VAT rules.

MEMO POINTS 1. An acquisition is also taxable where the goods are acquired by any VAT-registered company, club, association, organisation or other unincorporated body in the course or furtherance of a **non-business activity**.
2. The **person who acquires goods** is normally the person to whom the supply is made. This may differ from the person to whom the goods are delivered.
3. If a **person who is not subject to VAT** acquires goods through a taxable agent, the goods will be treated as being acquired by the taxable agent as principal if the agent: s 47 VATA 1994
- acted in relation to the acquisition;
- subsequently supplied the goods as agent for the person who is the end purchaser; and
- acted in its own name in relation to the supply.

4. For further details of **agents** see ¶7095+.

Acquisition taking place in the UK

The place of supply is normally determined when the goods are allocated to the customer. Acquisitions will be treated as taking place in the UK if the goods are either removed to the UK, or acquired under a UK VAT number. 9022

Removed to the UK An acquisition is **generally** treated as taking place in the UK if the goods are removed to the UK under a contract that does not involve their subsequent removal from the UK - that is, the supply ends in the UK. Where goods only "pass through" the UK, the supply will not be treated as taking place in the UK. 9024 s 13(2) VATA 1994

EXAMPLE A purchase of a car in Germany followed by its removal to the UK a few days later was held to be so closely linked in timing and purpose as to constitute the same transaction. Consequently, the supply was treated as taking place in the UK. *Patterson* [1995] (VTD 13669)

9026 s 13(3) VATA 1994 **Acquired under a UK VAT number** If a purchaser gives a UK VAT number to the supplier, the acquisition **will normally be treated** as taking place in the UK.

However, where **VAT** has been **paid** in the **other member state** on acquisition, the goods will be treated as being supplied outside the UK.

HMRC Brief 20/11 MEMO POINTS Where an acquisition is made under a UK VAT number to effect zero-rating but the **goods do not enter the UK** and the triangulation procedure (¶9214+) is not followed, acquisition VAT must be accounted for in the UK. As the goods do not enter the UK there is no right to recover any input tax in the UK. However, if the acquisition VAT is properly accounted for in the member state where the goods were delivered, UK VAT will be adjusted accordingly.

Time of acquisition

9028 s 12 VATA 1994 The time of acquisition of goods from another EU member state is the **earlier of** the:
- 15th day of the month following that in which the first removal of the goods occurred; and
- date on which a VAT invoice (¶2840+) is issued in respect of the transaction.

MEMO POINTS 1. The time of **payment** for goods does not affect the time of acquisition.
2. **Water**, **gas**, or any form of **power**, **heat**, **refrigeration** or **ventilation** (all supplies of goods) are treated as separately acquired each time the supplier issues an invoice.

Valuation

9030 s 20 VATA 1994 The value of an acquisition is determined by the consideration given, except for transactions between connected persons (¶9034).

Where the consideration is:
- **in money**, the value is an amount equal to the consideration; or
- **wholly or partly non-monetary**, the value is the equivalent monetary value of the consideration.

Sch 7 para 3 VATA 1994 MEMO POINTS 1. If there is **no consideration**, an acquisition will only have a value where it results from a deemed supply (¶1460+). The value of the goods will be:
a. the monetary amount which would be payable at the time of acquisition by the supplier to purchase identical goods;
b. if a value cannot be determined under method **a.**, the monetary amount which would be payable at the time of acquisition by the supplier to purchase similar goods; or
c. if a value cannot be determined under methods **a.** or **b.**, the cost of producing the goods at the time of acquisition.
Sch 7 para 2 VATA 1994 2. Any **excise duty**, and any transitional **EU customs duty** or **agricultural levy** is included in the value of an acquisition.

9032 Sch 7 para 4 VATA 1994 Any **foreign currency** must be converted to sterling at either:
- the market rate at the time of acquisition (the rates printed in national daily newspapers are accepted for these purposes but the use of forward rates is prohibited); or
- a period rate of exchange as published by HMRC.

Once a **method** has been chosen, it cannot be **changed** without the prior agreement of HMRC. A business may use either rate for all supplies or a specific class of supply. If the period rate of exchange is adopted, the business must annotate its VAT records to show that this rate has been used.

Alternatively, a business can request to use a rate, or method of determining a rate, which it uses for commercial purposes.

9034 Sch 7 para 1 VATA 1994 **Connected persons** HMRC can **direct** that the transaction should be valued at open-market value if:
- goods are **acquired from** a connected person (¶962+);
- the **consideration** is in money but is less than the open-market value; and
- the purchaser is not entitled to a full **input tax deduction** on the acquisition.

Such a direction must be issued within 3 years from the time of the acquisition; the trader can appeal against it (¶4260+).

Rate of tax

Acquisition VAT is **charged at** the rate which would have applied to a normal UK supply of the goods at the time they were acquired. Goods which would have been zero-rated (¶1180+) therefore remain zero-rated. 9036 s 88(4) VATA 1994

MEMO POINTS If there is a **change of rate** after the goods are first removed but before the acquisition is treated as taking place, the acquirer can elect to apply the rate in force at the time of first removal. This may be beneficial where, for example, goods were zero-rated when first removed but standard-rated when the acquisition was treated as taking place. This will also be pertinent for removals which take place before a change in the standard rate (such as that from 17.5% to 20% on 4 January 2011).

EXAMPLE A Ltd, a motor accessories retailer, submits VAT returns for calendar quarters. It acquired the following goods in February from a supplier in France, who zero-rated the supplies:

Goods	**UK VAT rate which normally applies**	**Value £**
Children's car seats	Reduced rate (¶1110+)	1,000
CD players	Standard rate	2,000

A Ltd must account for acquisition VAT on its VAT return for the period ended 31 March as follows:

		£
Children's car seats	£1,000 x 5%	50
CD players	£2,000 x 20%	400
		450

If fully taxable, A Ltd may also deduct input tax of £450.

Reporting

The **UK** reporting requirements for the acquirer are as follows: 9038

Document	¶¶	Requirements
VAT return	¶2985+	Enter acquisition VAT in box 2
		Enter input tax in box 4, if deductible
		Enter cost of goods in boxes 7 and 9
EC sales list		n/a
Intrastat declaration [1]	¶9345+	Arrivals - enter cost of goods

Note:
1. Where the value of arrivals exceeds the threshold (¶9347+).

B. Acquisitions by non-VAT-registered persons

The treatment of acquisitions depends on the value received. 9040

1. Acquisitions not exceeding threshold

Acquisitions of goods in the UK by non-VAT-registered persons are **normally** outside the scope of UK VAT, as the supply takes place in the other EU member state and the supplier charges VAT in that state. 9041

This rule applies **unless**:
a. the value of a non-VAT-registered person's acquisitions exceeds the registration threshold (¶9962), in which case that person must register for VAT in the UK; or
b. the acquirer registers for VAT voluntarily.

This **does not apply** to private individuals who buy goods for private use.

2. Acquisitions exceeding threshold

9042 Sch 3 para 1 VATA 1994

A non-VAT-registered person (other than a private individual buying goods for own private use) must register for VAT if the value of that person's relevant acquisitions exceeds the relevant threshold (¶9962), **unless** the exemption (¶9044) applies.

The trader must make **two checks** by looking:
a. back to the previous 1 January; and
b. forward for the next 30 days.

MEMO POINTS 1. **Relevant acquisitions** are taxable acquisitions (¶9020) taking place in the UK (¶9022+), other than goods subject to excise duty (¶9136+) or a new means of transport (¶9112+).
2. In the case of goods kept in a **fiscal warehouse** (¶9242+), the value also excludes any VAT chargeable on the last acquisition before their removal from the warehouse.
3. If the person acquiring the goods is **also entitled** or **liable** to be registered through making UK taxable supplies (¶2647) or distance sales (¶9177+), registration will be under those rules instead.
4. For **intermediate suppliers** involved in a supply chain see ¶9214+.

Exemption

9044 Sch 3 para 8 VATA 1994

If the acquisitions **would be zero-rated** (¶1180+) if supplied by a UK registered trader, the non-VAT-registered person may request exemption from registration. The request is made during the registration application process.

If granted, the exemption will **continue until** HMRC withdraws it. However, any acquisition which would not be zero-rated must be notified to HMRC within 30 days.

Look back test

9046 Sch 3 para 3 VATA 1994

The trader must review cumulative acquisitions made **since** 1 January.

If, at the end of a month, acquisitions since 1 January in that year exceed the threshold, the trader must notify HMRC within the next 30 days. Registration will **take effect** from the beginning of the following month, or an earlier mutually agreed date.

EXAMPLE On 3 June Mr B finds that his acquisitions since the previous 1 January exceed the threshold.
He becomes liable to register on 30 June and must notify HMRC by 30 July.
He will be registered from 1 August.

Look forward test

9048

A trader who has **reasonable grounds for believing** that acquisitions in the next 30 days will exceed the threshold, will be liable to be registered. HMRC must be notified within the following 30 days, although the **effective date** of registration will be the first day of the 30-day period.

EXAMPLE On 2 August Ms C expects her acquisitions in the next 30 days to exceed the registration threshold because of a large order.
She must notify HMRC by 1 September and will be registered from 2 August.

How to register

9050

An **application** to register is made on form VAT 1B (form VAT 2 for partnerships), which includes a signed declaration that all of the required information is complete and correct. There is no facility to register online, so paper forms must be submitted.

Consequences of registration

VAT must be accounted for on all EU acquisitions and also any UK taxable supplies (¶2647) or distance sales (¶9177+). It can take some time for the registration to be processed, so traders will continue to incur EU VAT until they are able to pass on their UK VAT number to their suppliers. They should therefore indicate to suppliers that a VAT registration number is awaited, to prepare the suppliers for zero-rating their supplies to the traders (¶9080). **9052**

MEMO POINTS 1. Even though output tax must be accounted for, any **input tax** will only be recoverable if the acquisition relates to a subsequent UK taxable supply.
2. For the **documentation** and responsibilities resulting from registration see ¶2704+.

Comment It should be noted that if the trader cannot provide a valid VAT number, it is unlikely that suppliers will be willing to zero-rate their supplies made to the trader. **9053**

Failing to register

There are **two consequences** of failing to register, either on time or at all: **9054** VATREG40500
a. registration will be backdated to when it should have become effective; and
b. penalties will be due (¶4010+).

The **backdating** of registration means that VAT is chargeable on all supplies and acquisitions made since the date of registration. There is no limit on the period of time which the backdating may cover.

The **output tax** is normally calculated as 1/6th of the amount invoiced by the supplier, less any EU VAT already paid.

Deregistration

EU acquisition registrations will only be cancelled when HMRC is sure that the trader is not liable to be registered on any other basis (for example, as a result of the level of UK supplies). **9056** Sch 3 paras 5, 7 VATA 1994

Deregistration is **compulsory** if the person has ceased to make, or have the intention to make, EU acquisitions and is not making any other taxable supplies. Sch 3 para 2 VATA 1994

Otherwise, a person ceases to be liable for registration if the value of acquisitions measured in all of the following periods does not exceed the threshold:
- previous calendar year;
- next 30 days; and
- next calendar year.

HMRC must be **notified** within 30 days; the notification should contain the date when the trader ceased to be liable to register. Sch 3 para 5 VATA 1994

Operative date If the person is **no longer liable** to be registered, cancellation will take effect from the **date** of request or a later mutually agreed date. **9058** Sch 3 paras 6, 7 VATA 1994

If the person was **never liable** to register, because no EU acquisitions were made and there was never any intention to do so, the cancellation will take effect as if the trader had never been registered.

It is possible for deregistration to have **retrospective** effect if the person ceased to be liable before making a request. The registration is cancelled from the earlier date.

Reregistration A trader can **voluntarily** reregister at any time, assuming that the relevant criteria are satisfied. **9060**

Supplies made under a **previous registration** are taken into account when considering the compulsory requirement to register. Immediate reinstatement using the original VAT number is allowed.

3. Voluntary registration

A person who either makes, or intends to make, EU acquisitions can voluntarily register for VAT. The **minimum period** of registration is generally 2 years. HMRC must be given 30 days' notice. **9062** Sch 3 para 4 VATA 1994

Comment Voluntary registration **may be appropriate** where, for example, input tax is being incurred before any taxable supplies are made.

Effective date

9064 VATREG40450 The **effective date** of registration will be the date of the person's request, or an earlier date which is mutually agreed. Traders may request registration to be **backdated** by up to 3 years, provided that there was an entitlement to register at all times throughout the intervening period.

For an **intending trader**, the effective date will always be mutually agreed and HMRC may impose conditions on the registration. In particular, HMRC will require evidence supporting the stated intention, such as orders placed with EU suppliers. On making an EU acquisition subsequent to registration, HMRC must be informed within 30 days.

Deregistration

9066 VATDREG04300 Deregistration will not **take effect until** the 1 January following the 2-year anniversary of the person first being registered, **unless** either of the following occurs:
a. the trader has contravened any condition of registration set by HMRC; or
b. the trader was not liable to register in the UK under the EU acquisition rules, did not intend to make EU acquisitions, and indeed has not actually made any.

In the normal situation therefore, a trader who registered on 1 June 2014 cannot deregister until 1 January 2017.

For **longer standing** registrations, the effective date of deregistration is usually that requested by the trader, or a later mutually agreed date.

SECTION 2

Despatches

9075 A despatch occurs when there is a supply involving the removal of goods from the UK to another EU member state.

The rules **depend on** whether the recipient of the supply is VAT-registered or not.

A. VAT-registered recipient

9077 SI 1995/2518 reg 134; Notice 725 para 4 A supply will be treated as being made outside the UK, and **zero-rated**, if it is made by a VAT-registered person and the goods are acquired by a person who is taxable in another EU member state (which in practice means registered for VAT).

If the **conditions for zero-rating are not met**, a supply made by a VAT-registered person will be treated as a supply made in the UK; VAT must be charged accordingly. The normal UK rules for the time of supply (¶750+) and the rate of VAT (¶1090+) will apply. For reporting see ¶9096.

1. Conditions for zero-rating

9080 The **supplier** must:
– show the customer's VAT registration number (including the two-digit country reference code) on the VAT sales invoice (¶2866); and
– obtain satisfactory commercial documentary evidence that the goods have been removed from the UK (¶9086+).

The time of supply is important for both of these conditions.

MEMO POINTS 1. The **tax point** for goods supplied to other member states is the earlier of the invoice date or the 15th day of the month following the month in which the goods are despatched. A payment or part-payment does not create a tax point but a VAT invoice must be issued for the amount paid; the invoice date will be the tax point for that amount. Notice 725 para 3.4

2. A supplier may use an **agent** to handle sales to EU customers and produce the necessary evidence of removal. However, the supplier remains responsible for ensuring that all conditions for zero-rating are met. Notice 725 para 5.7

a. Customer's VAT number

The **prefix codes and formats** of VAT numbers in EU member states are as follows: **9082** Notice 725 para 16.19

EU member state	VAT number details	
	Prefix code	Format
Austria	AT	U12345678 [1]
Belgium	BE	0123456789
Bulgaria	BG	012345678 or 0123456789
Croatia	HR	12345678901
Cyprus	CY	12345678X
Czech Republic	CZ	12345678 or 123456789 or 1234567890
Denmark	DK	12345678
Estonia	EE	123456789
Finland	FI	12345678
France	FR	12345678901 or X1234567890 [2] or 1X123456789 [2] or XX123456789 [2]
Germany	DE	123456789
Greece	EL	012345678
Hungary	HU	12345678
The Republic of Ireland	IE	1234567X or 1X34567X or 1234567XX
Italy	IT	12345678901
Latvia	LV	12345678901
Lithuania	LT	123456789 or 123456789012
Luxembourg	LU	12345678
Malta	MT	12345678
Netherlands	NL	123456789B01 [3]
Poland	PL	1234567890
Portugal	PT	123456789
Romania	RO	01234567890
Slovak Republic	SK	1234567890
Slovenia	SI	12345678
Spain	ES	X12345678 or 12345678X or X1234567X
Sweden	SE	123456789001
UK	GB	123456789

Note:
1. The first character will always be U.
2. All alpha characters except I and O are valid.
3. The three-digit suffix will always be in the range B01-B99

Invalid VAT number

9084 Notice 725 para 4.10 - 4.12

If the customer's VAT registration number is invalid, HMRC will **normally** still allow zero-rating, provided that it is satisfied the supplier took all reasonable steps to confirm the validity of the number.

HMRC **will not be satisfied** that a trader has taken all reasonable steps if the trader uses a number which:
- does not correspond to the published format for that member state;
- has not been regularly checked;
- HMRC has stated is invalid; or
- the trader knows does not belong to that customer.

MEMO POINTS The **validity** of VAT numbers issued by any EU member state can be checked:
- by telephoning the National Advice Service; or
- online (by following this link: flmemo.co.uk/vm6994).

b. Evidence of removal from UK

Documentation

9086 Notice 725 para 5

The documents used as proof of removal must **identify** the:
- supplier;
- consignor (if different from the supplier);
- customer;
- goods, including an accurate value;
- mode of transport and route of movement; and
- EU destination.

MEMO POINTS A **combination** of the following documents will normally provide the required evidence:
- customer's order, including name, address and delivery address;
- business correspondence;
- copy sales invoice, including a description of the goods, an invoice number and customer's EU VAT number;
- advice note;
- packing list;
- commercial transport document(s) from the carrier responsible for removing the goods from the UK;
- details of insurance or freight charges;
- bank statements as evidence of payment;
- receipted copy of the consignment note as evidence of receipt of goods abroad; and
- any other documents relevant to the removal of the goods which would normally be obtained in the course of intra-EU business.

9088 Notice 725 paras 5.9, 5.10

Where goods are sent by **post**, parcel **or courier**, the following evidence of removal will be acceptable:

Method of despatch	Evidence
Letter post or airmail	Post Office certificate of posting
Parcel post	Signed or stamped receipt copy
Courier	Invoice containing details such as airway bill number
	Information from track and trace service
	If Despatch Pack system used, signed receipt copy and statement of account listing each removal

9090 Notice 725 para 5.5

A **customer** who **collects the goods**, or arranges for their collection and removal from the UK, should confirm to the supplier how the goods are to be removed from the UK and what proof of removal will be provided. The supplier may wish to take a deposit equal to the amount of VAT which would become due if satisfactory evidence of removal is not provided.

The standard of evidence required in these circumstances is higher and should include **additional** information, as follows:
- written order from the customer showing the customer's name, address, EU VAT number and the address where the goods are to be delivered;
- copy sales invoice showing customer's name, VAT number, a description of the goods and an invoice number;
- delivery address for the goods;
- date of departure of goods from the supplier and from the UK;
- name and address of the haulier collecting the goods;
- registration number of the vehicle collecting the goods and the name and signature of the driver;
- route - for example, Channel Tunnel or port of exit;
- copy of travel tickets;
- name of ferry or shipping company and date of sailing, or airway number and airport;
- trailer number (if applicable);
- full container number (if applicable); and
- name and address of premises where goods are to be processed, or grouped or consolidated with other goods for transportation (if applicable).

EXAMPLE A trader sold goods to a customer who stated that they were from Holland and produced a business card showing an address in Holland and a Dutch VAT number. The trader, assuming that the buyer had a vehicle and was going to transport the goods to Holland, recorded these details on the invoice, stating that the shipper was the buyer. The invoice was also signed by the buyer.
It was held that the conditions for zero-rating had not been met, as the trader had:
- not obtained a written order from the customer;
- assumed that the goods would be removed from the UK; and
- not obtained the vehicle registration number or any other proof of removal. *FEA Briggs Ltd* [1994] (VTD 12804)

Time limit

Evidence of removal must **generally** be obtained within 3 months from the time of supply. **9092** Notice 725 para 4.4

For goods which have been **processed or incorporated into other goods** before their removal from the UK, the limit is extended to 6 months after the time of supply.

If there is a **series of invoices** for the same supply, the time limit begins from the date of the final invoice.

Failure to remove goods or obtain evidence

If a trader zero-rates a supply and either the goods are not removed from the UK, or evidence of removal is not obtained by the relevant time limit, the trader must amend its records and account for the VAT due. **9094** Notice 725 para 4.6

The **amount invoiced** or received is treated as VAT-inclusive; the usual VAT fraction should be used (¶1090).

MEMO POINTS 1. If **evidence** of removal is **subsequently obtained**, the supply can be zero-rated and the VAT account adjusted in the VAT period in which the evidence is obtained.
2. If **goods** are found **in the UK after** the date on which they were allegedly removed, or if conditions for zero-rating were not met, the goods are liable to forfeiture. In addition, any VAT which ought to have been charged will become payable by: s 30(10) VATA 1994
- the person to whom the goods were supplied (in practice the burden will fall on the supplier, who will have to account for the VAT and then chase the customer for payment); or
- any other person in whose possession the goods are found in the UK.
HMRC may, however, waive payment of all or part of the VAT.

2. Reporting

The **UK** reporting requirements are as follows, depending on whether the conditions for zero-rating are met: **9096** Notice 725 para 6.17

Document	¶¶	Supplies	
		Qualifying for zero-rating	Not qualifying for zero-rating
VAT return	¶2985+	Enter invoice/contract value in boxes 6 and 8	Enter output tax in box 1 Enter cost of goods in boxes 7 and 9
EC sales list	¶9330+	Enter customer's VAT number and the invoice or contract value	n/a
Intrastat declaration[1]	¶9345+	Despatches - enter invoice or contract value	n/a

Note:
1. Where the value of despatches exceeds the threshold (¶9347+).

B. Non-VAT-registered recipient

9100 In **general**, supplies from the UK to a non-VAT-registered person in another EU member state are treated as taking place in the UK and VAT must be charged accordingly. The normal UK rules for the time of supply (¶750+) and the rate of VAT (¶1090+) will apply.

If the **supplier**:
– is responsible for delivery to the EU; and
– has exceeded the annual distance selling threshold for that member state (¶9206),
the supplies will be treated as being made in the member state of the customer. This means that the supplies are outside the scope of UK VAT (but within the scope of VAT in the destination member state).

SECTION 3

Special rules

9110 Whilst the normal rules apply to most transactions, there are specific provisions for certain types of goods and situations.

Type of goods and situations	Summary	¶¶
New means of transport	Vehicles which transport persons or goods	¶9112+
Goods subject to excise duty	Tobacco, alcohol, fuels	¶9136+
Installed or assembled goods	Place of supply is where installation/assembly takes place	¶9154+
Distance selling	Goods supplied to non-registered persons in another EU member state	¶9177+
Triangulation	Supply chain involving at least two suppliers, where ultimate customer receives goods direct from first supplier	¶9214+
Fiscal warehousing	VAT charge suspended whilst goods are in warehousing regime	¶9242+
Temporary movements of goods	For either: – treatment or processing; – repair or valuation; – a supply of services (e.g. loan or leasing); – temporary use not exceeding 2 years	¶9276+

Type of goods and situations	Summary	¶¶
Transfers of own goods and goods on sale or return	Including consignment and call-off stocks	¶9286+
Supplies to diplomatic missions and international organisations	Zero-rating may apply	¶9296+
Electricity and gas supplies	Including supplies of heat or cooling supplied through a network	¶9300
Supplies made on board transport	On ships, aircraft or trains between EU member states	¶9302+
Goods subject to a margin scheme, e.g. second-hand goods or works of art	Not treated as an acquisition where supplier accounted for VAT on profit margin	¶6620+
Gold coins	Not treated as an acquisition where supplier is in another EU member state and a Central Bank takes possession of the goods following their removal from that state	¶6887

A. New means of transport

The basic rule for a supply of a new means of transport is that the customer should account for VAT in the EU member state in which they belong. 9112

1. Scope

A new means of transport is a new or nearly new motorised land vehicle, ship or aircraft that is **intended for** the transport of persons or goods, and which falls within the definition below: 9114 s 95 VATA 1994

Mode of transport	Definition	Excludes
Motorised land vehicle	Engine capacity exceeds 48cc, or constructed or adapted to be electronically propelled using more than 7.2 kilowatts	A vehicle which, since its first entry into service[1]: – has travelled for more than 6,000km under its own power; and – a period of more than 6 months has elapsed
Ship	Exceeding 7.5m in length	A ship which, since its first entry into service[2]: – has travelled for more than 100 hours under its own power; and – a period of more than 3 months has elapsed
Aircraft	Take-off weight in excess of 1,550 kg	An aircraft which, since its first entry into service[2]: – has travelled for more than 40 hours under its own power; and – a period of more than 3 months has elapsed

Notes:
1. A **motorised land vehicle** is deemed to enter into service at one of the following times:
a. the earlier of:
– the first registration for road use in the member state of the manufacturer; or
– the date when the liability to register for road use was first incurred in that state;
b. the earliest of the following dates:
– its first removal by its first purchaser or owner;
– delivery to the first purchaser or owner; or
– when it was first made available to the first purchaser or owner;
c. the date when it was first taken into use for demonstration purposes by the manufacturer; or
d. if none of the above can be established satisfactorily, the date of issue of an invoice relating to the first supply.
2. A **ship or aircraft** is deemed to first enter into service at one of the following times:
a. the earlier of the delivery date and when it was first made available to the first purchaser or owner;
b. otherwise the date when it was first taken into use for demonstration purposes by the manufacturer; or
c. if neither of the above can be established satisfactorily, the date of issue of an invoice relating to the first supply.

Valuation

9116 Notice 728 para 3.5 The value of a new means of transport **includes** the value of any extras fitted at the time of supply, and delivery or incidental charges made by the supplier.

EXAMPLE A Ltd sells a new car to a customer in Germany. The list price is £20,000. A Ltd fits air conditioning for £1,500 and charges £750 for delivery. After collecting the car, the customer decides to install a satellite navigation system at a cost of £500.
The value of the car for the purposes of the new means of transport rules is as follows:

	£
List price	20,000
Air conditioning	1,500
Delivery	750
	22,250

2. Acquisitions from the EU

9118 Notice 728 para 3 When a UK customer acquires a new means of transport from a supplier in another EU member state, the supply is treated as made in the UK, whether or not the customer and supplier are VAT-registered in their respective member states. The customer must account for acquisition VAT; different procedures apply depending on whether they are VAT-registered.

MEMO POINTS 1. If the new means of transport is a motorised **land vehicle**, it must be licensed and registered before it is used on public roads.
2. Entry of any vehicle (whether from inside the EU or outside) to the UK for permanent use on UK roads must be notified to HMRC within 14 days and any VAT due paid or accounted for. It is not possible to register and license the vehicle with DVLA or DVA until receipt of confirmation from HMRC that this notification has been processed and any VAT due has been paid. Communication with HMRC for this purpose is now almost exclusively via the NOVA online system. Previous paper forms VAT 414, VAT 415, C&E 386, C&E 388 and C&E 389 have essentially been withdrawn and are now only accepted by HMRC in very limited circumstances.

VAT-registered acquirer

9120 A VAT-registered person should:
- **provide** a VAT number to the supplier, to enable the supplier to zero-rate its supply; and
- **account for** acquisition VAT on the return for the VAT period (¶2987+) in which the acquisition took place.

MEMO POINTS 1. If the new means of transport forms part of the acquirer's **trading stock**, an input tax deduction may also be claimed in the VAT return.
2. When an acquirer **applies to register a vehicle** on its own behalf, or on behalf of a customer, the acquirer will need to complete a declaration online that the vehicle was supplied VAT-free and details of the VAT registration number used to make the acquisition into the UK.

Non-VAT-registered acquirer

9122 SI 1995/2518 reg 148 A non-VAT-registered person must use the NOVA system (¶9118) to notify HMRC of the entry of a vehicle into the UK.

3. Supplies to the EU

VAT-registered supplier

9124 SI 1995/2518 reg 155 The supply of a new means of transport to a customer in another member state can normally be **zero-rated**, provided that:
- removal to the other member state takes place within 2 months of the date of supply; and
- other conditions are met which depend on whether the customer is VAT-registered.

If the conditions for zero-rating are not met, the supplier must charge VAT as for a normal UK supply.

MEMO POINTS 1. If a **new vehicle is to be used on UK roads** before its removal to another EU member state, it must be licensed, registered and insured. If a vehicle is not licensed when purchased, the supplier can apply to the DVLA for a special "VAT-free" registration number. The application should include completed form VAT 411A if the customer is VAT-registered, or the third copy of completed form VAT 411 if the customer is not VAT-registered.
2. In exceptional circumstances a customer who is **unable to remove** the means of transport from the UK **in time** must inform HMRC and pay the VAT that is due. Otherwise, the vehicle may be liable to forfeiture.

The **other conditions** which must be met are as follows: 9126 Notice 728 paras 6, 8

Status of customer	Conditions
VAT-registered	The supplier must: – show the customer's VAT registration number (with the two-character prefix code (¶9082)) on the invoice; and – obtain valid commercial documentary evidence that the new means of transport has been removed from the UK (¶9086+)
Not registered [1]	The supplier and the customer must make a joint declaration on form VAT 411 [2] and submit it to HMRC within 6 weeks of the end of the calendar quarter in which the supply was made

Notes:
1. If a non-VAT-registered customer purchases the means of transport by way of a **hire purchase or other finance agreement**, the supply by the dealer to the finance house is standard-rated. The supply by the finance house to the customer is zero-rated; this should be indicated on form VAT 411.
2. **Form VAT 411** is a declaration by the customer that the customer will take the means of transport to another EU member state within 2 months, and pay the VAT there. It is also a declaration by the dealer of having supplied the transport to the customer for removal from the UK. The first copy of form VAT 411 should be given to the customer. The second copy is retained by the supplier and, in the case of a vehicle, the third copy is used to register it for road use if it is to be driven out of the UK.
Form VAT 411 should be sent to the following **address**:
HMRC
Personal Transport Unit
Priory Court
St Johns Road
Dover
Kent
CT17 9SH

Administration **Invoices** should show the information required for invoices to EU customers (¶2866). 9128 Notice 728 para 9.2

Details of supplies must be included in an **EC sales list** (¶9330+).

Non-VAT-registered supplier

The supplier is not required to account for VAT on the supply. A supplier who paid VAT on purchasing the means of transport may claim a **VAT refund** of that amount. The refund cannot exceed the amount of VAT which would have been chargeable if the supply had been a taxable supply that was not zero-rated. 9130 SI 1995/2518 regs 149 - 154; Notice 728 paras 7.1 - 7.5

The **claim** must be in writing and made at least 14 days (but no more than 1 month) before the supply is made, and must include: 9132
- full details of the means of transport;
- details of the VAT incurred by the supplier; and
- the amount of the refund claimed.

HMRC may examine the means of transport **before the sale** to confirm its eligibility for refund.

The following documents will need to be supplied to HMRC **after the sale** to enable a repayment to be made:
- proof of sale; and
- evidence that the means of transport has been removed to another EU member state.

B. Goods subject to excise duty

Scope

9136 The goods which are subject to excise duty are:
a. tobacco products;
b. alcoholic drinks, including:
- beer;
- cider;
- wine (including home-made wine); and
- spirits; and

c. fuels, including:
- petrol substitutes;
- road fuel gas;
- hydrocarbon oil; and
- power methylated spirits.

1. Acquisitions

VAT-registered acquirer

9138 A VAT-registered person must account for VAT on taxable acquisitions (¶9020) of exciseable goods under the normal rules (¶9017+), and report the transactions on the relevant VAT return (¶9038).

Non-VAT-registered acquirer

9140 **Goods removed by supplier** Where the EU supplier arranges delivery of exciseable goods to a non-VAT-registered person, the supplier must register for VAT under the distance selling rules (¶9182).

9142 SI 1995/2518 reg 36(1) **Goods removed by customer** A non-VAT-registered person who has arranged the delivery (excluding an individual buying goods for own private use) must **pay** the acquisition VAT by separate arrangement at the time of the acquisition.

HMRC must be **notified** at the time of the arrival of the goods in the UK or, if later, the time of acquisition.

The following **details** must be provided:

SI 1995/2518 reg 36(2)
- name and address of the person acquiring the goods;
- time of acquisition;
- date on which the goods arrived in the UK;
- value of the goods, including any excise duty payable; and
- VAT due on the acquisition.

SI 1995/2518 reg 36(5) MEMO POINTS If the person **dies or becomes incapacitated**, their personal representative, trustee in bankruptcy, or liquidator must make the notification and, to the extent of the assets available, pay the VAT (¶8700+).

2. Supplies

VAT-registered customers

9144 SI 1995/2518 reg 134 Supplies of exciseable goods to a customer who is VAT-registered in another EU member state may be zero-rated under the normal rules (¶9080+). The customer should account for the tax on its VAT return as an acquisition.

Non-VAT-registered customers

The VAT treatment **depends on** who arranges the delivery of the goods. 9146

Where the **supplier arranges delivery** of exciseable goods from the UK to a non-VAT-registered person in another EU member state, the supplier must account for VAT under the distance selling rules (¶9177+). 9148

Where the exciseable goods are removed from the UK **by or on behalf of the customer**, the supplier may be able to zero-rate the supply. 9150

SI 1995/2518 reg 135; Notice 725 para 15.4

The goods must be removed as soon as possible, and must be accompanied by either an Administrative Accompanying Document (AAD) or a Simplified Administrative Accompanying Document (SAAD).

The supplier must obtain (within 15 days of the end of the month in which the goods are removed) and keep a receipted copy of the AAD or SAAD. These documents must be certified by the relevant authorities of the EU member state of destination. A certificate of receipt for the goods must be issued within 4 months of the date of despatch.

MEMO POINTS 1. An **AAD** must be completed by the supplier if the goods are moving under an authorised duty suspension arrangement (e.g. from an excise warehouse); the supplier must provide a financial guarantee to cover all excise duty liabilities arising during the removal.
2. A **SAAD** must be completed if UK excise duty has already been paid on the goods. The customer must also provide evidence that the excise duty in the EU member state of destination has been paid or secured to the satisfaction of the relevant authorities there, before the supplier despatches the goods.

C. Installed or assembled goods

Goods that are installed or assembled by or on behalf of the supplier are normally supplied where the installation or assembly takes place. 9154

s 7(3) VATA 1994; Notice 725 para 11

MEMO POINTS 1. The terms “installation” and “assembly” are **not defined**. Consequently their ordinary and everyday meaning is applied. This meaning will include situations where the installation required by the manufacturer is minimal.
2. If the contract between the parties is for **two supplies** (one for the supply of goods, the other for installation), they will usually be treated as a single composite supply of installed goods (¶310+).
3. If the installation or assembly is **subcontracted** to a third party, the place of supply for the manufacturer remains the place of installation or assembly.

Work done in the UK

UK VAT is due on the supply of goods for installation or assembly in the UK. 9156

A **supplier from another EU member state** will usually, therefore, be required to register for VAT in the UK (¶2600+) and account for output tax on the value of such supplies, since there is no registration threshold for non-established taxable persons (¶2667).

However, a supplier who belongs (¶9688+) in another member state can opt for a **simplified procedure** whereby the UK customer accounts for acquisition VAT. 9158

s 14(2) - (5) VATA 1994

This procedure applies where a person, belonging in another member state, makes a supply:
- of goods to a person registered in the UK;
- that involves the removal of the goods to a place in the UK where they are installed or assembled; and
- that would be a taxable acquisition by the customer if it was treated as involving an acquisition in the UK from another member state (¶9015).

9159 **Consequences** The **supplier** must notify both the customer and HMRC of this choice no later than the date of issue of the first invoice for the supply. The foreign supplier must issue the customer with a VAT invoice.

Once notified, the **customer** must account for acquisition VAT on each invoice received.

MEMO POINTS 1. **Notification** should be sent to HMRC at:
The Non Established Taxable Persons Unit
HMRC
Ruby House
8 Ruby Place
Aberdeen
AB10 1ZP
2. The following **information** should be included:
- the supplier's name, address and EU VAT number;
- the UK customer's name, address and VAT number; and
- the date on which installation or assembly of the goods began or will begin.

EXAMPLE A German company supplies and installs a machine for a UK company.
The place of supply is the UK but if the German company opts for the simplified procedure, the UK company will account for the VAT. (If the simplified procedure is not applied, the German company will be making a UK supply and will need to register in the UK in order to account for the VAT.)

9160 Notice 725 para 11.11 The UK **reporting** requirements for the supplier or customer are as follows, depending on whether the simplified procedure is applied:

Document	¶¶	Supplier accounts for VAT	Simplified procedure - customer accounts for VAT
VAT return	¶2985+	Enter output tax in box 1	Enter acquisition tax in box 2
		Enter invoice/contract value in box 6	Enter input tax in box 4, if deductible
			Enter cost of goods in boxes 7 and 9
EC sales list		n/a	n/a
Intrastat declaration [1]	¶9345+	Arrivals - enter cost of goods	Arrivals - enter cost of goods, if known, or open-market value

Note:
1. Where the value of arrivals exceeds the threshold (¶9347+).

Work done elsewhere in the EU

9162 VAT will be due in the member state in which the goods are installed or assembled. A **UK supplier** may therefore be required to register and account for VAT in another member state.

Alternatively, in some member states a simplified procedure (as is operated in the UK (¶9158+)) is available whereby the customer accounts for the VAT. The supplier will need to contact the VAT authority in the relevant state to ascertain whether this procedure is available. For contact addresses see ¶9990.

9164 Notice 725 para 11.11 The **reporting** requirements for the UK supplier are as follows:

Document	¶¶	UK	Other EU state
VAT return	¶2985+	Enter cost of goods in boxes 6 and 8	If simplified procedure is not applied or available, and if VAT registration is required, VAT returns will need to be completed
EC sales list		n/a	n/a
Intrastat declaration [1]	¶9345+	Despatches - enter cost of goods	Arrivals - enter cost of goods, if known, or open-market value

Note:
1. Where the value of arrivals or despatches exceeds the relevant threshold (¶9347+).

D. Distance selling

The rules for distance selling depend on whether: 9177
- an EU supplier is making supplies of goods to non-VAT-registered UK persons; or
- a UK supplier is making supplies of goods to non-VAT-registered persons elsewhere in the EU.

1. Supplies to the UK

Where an **EU supplier** supplies and delivers goods to a non-VAT-registered person in the UK, the supplier will usually charge VAT in its home state under the normal place of supply rules (¶275+). This is known as a distance sale and applies where, for example, goods are sold by mail order. 9180

The EU supplier may, however, become **liable to register** for VAT in the UK and account for VAT on such sales, where:
a. irrespective of the value of sales, either:
- goods liable to excise duty are supplied; or
- the supplier has exercised an option in its home state to treat distance sales as taking place where the customer belongs; or

b. the trader's distance sales exceed a certain threshold.

Unlike other types of registration, there is no **exemption** from compulsory registration.

A trader who intends to make distance sales can **register voluntarily** (¶9194+).

MEMO POINTS 1. If a person is **already VAT-registered** in the UK, VAT must be accounted for on all distance sales. There is no need to separately register again.
2. As an **alternative** to registering itself, a trader can appoint an agent or VAT representative to deal with VAT affairs on the trader's behalf (¶7095+). For intermediate suppliers involved in a supply chain see ¶9214+.

a. Compulsory registration

Goods subject to excise duty

Where goods are subject to excise duty (¶9136+) and **any supply** is made to a non-VAT-registered UK person by an EU supplier in the course of its business, the supplier must register for VAT in the UK and account for VAT on **all** such **sales**. 9182 Sch 2 para 1(3) VATA 1994

EU option exercised

An EU supplier who has opted to treat all distance sales as **taking place** outside its home state will be liable to register for UK VAT where: 9184 Sch 2 para 1(2) VATA 1994
- a distance sale is made in the UK while the option is in force;
- the option covers the removal of goods from the home state; and
- without the option, the goods would have been treated as supplied in the home state.

HMRC must be **informed** at least 30 days before the first UK sale; written evidence of the option must be available. Notice 700/1 para 6.7

The **minimum period** of registration is normally 2 years.

VAT must be **accounted for** with effect from the date of the first distance sale subsequent to the exercise of the option, or an agreed earlier date.

9186 Sch 2 para 7(3) VATA 1994; VATREG41500; VATDREG04300

Deregistration The EU option must be **revoked** before the registration can be cancelled and where an option is revoked, HMRC must be notified within 30 days.

The registration cannot, however, be **cancelled until** 1 January following the time when 2 years have elapsed, **unless** either of the following applies:
a. the trader has contravened any condition of registration set by HMRC; or
b. the trader satisfies all of the following:
- it has revoked the option in its own member state;
- it did not intend to make UK distance sales and has never made any; and
- it was not liable to register in the UK under the distance selling rules.

In the normal case, therefore, a trader who registered on 1 July 2014 cannot deregister until 1 January 2017.

Sales value

9187 Sch 2 para 1 VATA 1994

For this purpose, a distance sale **excludes**:
- exempt goods (¶350+);
- new means of transport (¶9112+);
- goods subject to excise duty (¶9136+); and
- those which are part of a transfer of a going concern (¶8646+).

Any **other goods** which satisfy the following conditions are distance sales:
- removed to the UK without being installed or assembled in the UK;
- received by a non-VAT-registered person; and
- supplied in the course of a business.

9188 An EU supplier will become liable to register in the UK on the day when the value of distance sales made to non-registered UK persons **since the previous 1 January** exceeds £70,000. This value does not include any domestic EU VAT element already charged.

HMRC must be **informed** within 30 days, by the submission of the relevant forms.

The **effective date** of registration will be the date on which the liability first occurred, or another mutually agreed date.

From then on, VAT must be **accounted for on** all distance sales, UK taxable supplies (¶2647) and EU acquisitions (¶9010+).

MEMO POINTS 1. **Application** to register is made on form VAT 1A (form VAT 2 for partnerships). At the moment, there is no facility to register online, so paper forms must be submitted.
2. For the **documentation and responsibilities** which result from registration see ¶2704+.

EXAMPLE Mr B (who is registered in France) makes mail order supplies at the end of every month to UK non-VAT-registered individuals.
Since 1 January his supplies have been as follows:

Month	Value (TVA-inclusive) £	Cumulative total £
31 Jan	13,000	13,000
28 Feb	14,000	27,000
31 Mar	16,000	43,000
30 April	18,000	61,000
31 May	20,000	81,000
30 June	22,000	103,000

These figures all include French TVA at 20%; it is the net figure which must be compared to the threshold.
In May, the net distance sales are £67,500. (£81,000 × 5/6)
So Mr B is only liable to register in the UK on 30 June, when his net sales are £85,833. (£103,000 × 5/6)

9190 Sch 2 para 7(1) VATA 1994

Deregistration A trader ceases to be liable for registration under the distance selling rules where in the previous calendar year:
- the value of its supplies did not exceed £70,000; and
- it has not made any supplies of exciseable goods.

A distance selling registration will only be cancelled where HMRC is sure that the trader is not liable to be registered under any of the other rules (i.e. UK supplies or EU acquisitions). Sch 2 paras 2, 6 VATA 1994

HMRC must be **notified** within 30 days, and the notification should contain the date on which the trader ceased to be liable to register.

If the trader is **no longer liable** to be registered, the registration will be cancelled with effect from the date of the trader's request, or a mutually agreed later date. Sch 2 para 5(1) VATA 1994

If the trader was **never liable** to register, because they had not made any relevant supplies and had no intention to do so, the cancellation will take effect as if the trader had never been registered.

MEMO POINTS 1. If the trader registered on the **basis of intention** which has subsequently changed, such that:
- no relevant supplies have been made;
- the EU option has not been exercised; or
- no supplies of goods subject to excise duty have been made,

the trader should notify HMRC within 30 days, to become deregistered.

2. A trader can voluntarily **reregister** at any time, assuming that the relevant criteria are satisfied. The supplies made under a previous registration are taken into account when considering the compulsory requirement to register. Immediate reinstatement using the original VAT number is permitted.

Failing to register

There are **two consequences** of failing to register, either on time or at all: **9192** VATREG41400

a. registration will be backdated to when it should have become effective; and

b. penalties will be due (¶4010+).

On **backdating**, the **output tax** is normally calculated as 1/6 of the consideration received from the customer, less any EU VAT already paid. A lower standard rate of VAT applied in the UK from 1 January 2010 to 3 January 2011, so for that period the output tax calculation is 7/47 of the amount invoiced.

b. Voluntary registration

A trader can voluntarily register for VAT where it **intends** to: **9194** Sch 2 para 4 VATA 1994
- exercise an EU option and make distance sales;
- make supplies relating to an EU option which is already in force; or
- make supplies which are subject to excise duty.

If the trader is **also entitled** or **liable** to be registered because it is making UK taxable supplies in the course of a business, registration will be under those rules instead.

MEMO POINTS 1. **Written evidence** which supports the stated intention should be enclosed with the application.

2. HMRC may impose **conditions** on the registration, which can be subsequently altered.

Operative date

The effective date of registration will be a date which is mutually agreed with HMRC. Unregistered traders may request registration to be backdated by up to 3 years, provided that there was an entitlement to register at all times during the intervening period. **9196** VATREG41350

On the **subsequent exercise** of an EU option, or when supplies are first made, HMRC must be notified within 30 days.

Deregistration

If the trader has either not carried out its stated intentions by the specified date, or is in breach of any other condition of registration, **HMRC may cancel** the registration from the specified date (or a mutually agreed later date). **9198**

c. Reporting

9200 Notice 725 para 6.17 The UK reporting requirements for EU suppliers registered in the UK are as follows:

Document	¶¶	Reporting requirements
VAT return	¶2985+	Enter output tax in box 1
		Enter value of sales in box 6
EC sales list		No entries required
Intrastat [1]	¶9345+	Arrivals - enter cost of goods
Note: 1. Where the value of arrivals exceeds the threshold (¶9347+).		

2. Supplies made from the UK

9202 The default position is that distance sales (¶9177+) by UK suppliers are **treated as taking place in the UK**. Therefore the supplier usually accounts for UK VAT.

However, the **place of supply will be another member state** in certain circumstances.

a. Sales not liable to UK VAT

9204 Distance sales by UK suppliers are not treated as taking place in the UK, so the supplier must register and account for VAT in another member state, where either:
a. the **value** of those sales exceeds the distance selling threshold in that state;
b. the sales are of **exciseable goods** (¶9136+); or
c. the supplier has exercised an **option** to treat all distance sales as taking place outside the UK.

Alternatively, a distance seller may appoint a tax representative in the other state to manage its VAT affairs.

A supplier may also be entitled to register **voluntarily** in another state where it intends to make supplies under **b.** or **c.** above.

EU thresholds

9206 Each member state may choose whether to apply a distance selling threshold of €35,000 or €100,000.

The UK and the following other states have chosen the €100,000 threshold:
- France;
- Germany;
- Luxembourg; and
- the Netherlands.

All **other states** have chosen the €35,000 threshold.

EU option

9208 SI 1995/2518 reg 98 A UK person who has opted to treat all distance sales as taking place outside the UK will be **liable to register** for VAT in another EU member state where:
- a distance sale is made in that state whilst the option is in force;
- the option covers the removal of goods from the UK; and
- without the option, the goods would have been treated as supplied in the UK.

VAT must be accounted for in the other state with effect from the date of the first distance sale subsequent to the exercise of the option, or an agreed earlier date.

The supplier must **notify** both HMRC and the tax authority in the other state of the exercise of the option. The supplier must notify HMRC of the option, and the member state to which the goods are to be supplied, at least 30 days before the first sale of goods under the option. 9210

The tax authorities in the recipient member state must be provided with evidence of the notification to HMRC within 30 days of the date of the first sale of goods under the option.

The **minimum period** for the option to be effective is 2 years.

A trader who wishes to **revoke** an EU option must give at least 30 days' notice to HMRC. The option cannot, however, be revoked until 1 January following the time when 2 years have elapsed since the first supply was made under the option. SI 1995/2518 reg 98(4)

b. Reporting

The **UK** reporting requirements for UK suppliers are as follows: 9212 Notice 725 para 6.17

Document	¶¶	Reporting requirements	
		Sales liable to UK VAT	Sales not liable to UK VAT
VAT return	¶2985+	Enter output tax in box 1 Enter value of sales in box 6	Enter value of sales in boxes 6 and 8
EC sales list		No entries required	No entries required
Intrastat[1]	¶9345+	Despatches - enter cost of goods	No entries required

Note:
1. Where the value of despatches exceeds the threshold (¶9347+).

E. Triangulation

The term triangulation **applies to** a supply chain involving three parties in different EU member states, where goods pass directly from the first to the last person in the chain. 9214

Triangulation **does not apply** where:
- two of the three parties belong in the same member state *EMAG Handel Eder OHG v Finanzlandesdirektion für Kärnten* [2006]; or
- one or more of the parties belongs in a country outside the EU.

Summary

Typically, a customer orders goods from an intermediate supplier but receives the goods direct from the original supplier. 9216 Notice 725 para 13

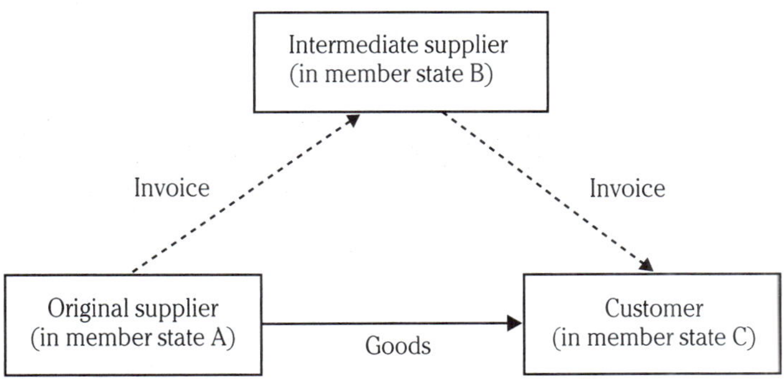

Accounting

9218 VAT can be accounted for under either:
- the normal rules; or
- a simplified procedure which enables the intermediate supplier to avoid having to register for VAT in the member state to which the goods are delivered.

In either case, the intermediate supplier must enter details on EC sales lists (¶9330+), even where no other taxable supplies are made.

1. Normal rules

9220 Under the normal rules the parties must account for VAT as follows:

Party	VAT accounting
Original supplier (in member state A)	Can zero-rate supply to intermediate supplier
Intermediate supplier (in member state B)	Must register for VAT in member state C and account for: – acquisition VAT on supply received; and – VAT on the onward supply to the customer
Customer (in member state C)	If VAT-registered, can claim input tax, subject to the normal rules

2. Simplified procedure

9224 An **intermediate supplier**, who is VAT-registered in an EU member state other than the state to which the goods are delivered, can choose to apply the simplified procedure if the customer is VAT-registered in the state to which the goods are delivered.

Overview

9226 Under the simplified procedure the parties account for VAT as follows:

Party	VAT accounting
Original supplier	Zero-rates supply to intermediate supplier
Intermediate supplier	No VAT accounting required
Customer	Must account for acquisition VAT

9228 There are **specific UK rules** where:
- the customer is VAT-registered in the UK; or
- the intermediate supplier is VAT-registered in the UK.

Customer VAT-registered in the UK

9230 s 14(1) VATA 1994 Where the goods have been removed to the UK, the supply to the intermediate supplier is disregarded. The supply by the intermediate supplier to the customer is treated as the supply by which the goods were removed from another member state to the UK.

9232 SI 1995/2518 regs 11, 18 The **intermediate supplier** must:
- notify HMRC and the customer that the simplified procedure is to be used;
- provide its VAT registration number to the original supplier to enable the original supply to be zero-rated;
- comply with the invoicing requirements of the member state in which the intermediate supplier is registered; and
- issue the invoice within 15 days of the date on which the supply would have taken place if the simplified procedure had not been used.

MEMO POINTS 1. **Notifications** should be given to each customer for whom the simplified procedure applies, on the first occasion when the procedure is used.
2. The following **information** should be included:
- the name, address and EU VAT registration number of the intermediate supplier;
- the name, address and VAT number of the customer; and
- the date or intended date of delivery of the goods to the customer.
3. Notifications should be sent to the following **address**:
The Non Established Taxable Persons Unit
HMRC
Ruby House
8 Ruby Place
Aberdeen
AB10 1ZP

EXAMPLE Ms C, a UK VAT-registered trader, orders goods from D GmbH, a company located in Germany.
D GmbH orders Ms C's goods from E SA, a company whose place of business is in France. On the instruction of D GmbH, E SA delivers the goods directly to Ms C, who will use the goods for taxable business purposes.
Under the simplification procedure:
a. E SA will invoice D GmbH for the goods. The invoice will be zero-rated, provided that D GmbH has given E SA its German VAT number.
b. D GmbH will invoice Ms C for the goods. The invoice will be zero-rated, provided that Ms C has given D GmbH her UK VAT number.
c. Ms C will account for acquisition VAT of 20% of the value of the goods on her VAT return. She can also recover input VAT of 20% of the value of the goods on the same VAT return, as she is a fully taxable trader.
The above assumes that all of the ordinary invoicing requirements are met (¶2866).

The **customer** must account for acquisition VAT accordingly, and also has the following reporting obligations: 9234

Document	¶¶	Reporting requirements
VAT return	¶2985+	Enter cost of goods in boxes 7 and 9
		Enter acquisition tax in box 2
		Enter input tax in box 4, if deductible
EC sales list		n/a
Intrastat declaration [1]	¶9345+	Arrivals - enter cost of goods

Note:
1. Where the value of arrivals exceeds the threshold (¶9347+).

Intermediate supplier registered in the UK

Where the goods have been delivered to another EU member state, the supplies to and from the intermediate supplier are ignored. 9236 s 14(6) VATA 1994; Notice 725 para 13.7

An **intermediate supplier** who is registered in the UK must:
a. provide its UK VAT registration number to the original supplier, to enable the original supply to be zero-rated; and
b. meet the invoicing requirements detailed at ¶2866. SI 1995/2518 reg 17

EXAMPLE F Ltd, a UK company, is an intermediate supplier which receives an order from G SA, a company located in Belgium. To fulfil the order F Ltd arranges for the goods to be supplied direct from H SA, a company located in France.
F Ltd provides its VAT registration number to H SA, which accordingly zero-rates its supply to F Ltd. F Ltd issues a zero-rated invoice containing the required information (¶2866) to G SA, which accounts for acquisition VAT in Belgium.

9238 The **UK reporting requirements** for the intermediate supplier are as follows:

Document	¶¶	Reporting requirements
VAT return	¶2985+	No entries required
EC sales list	¶9330+	Enter customer's VAT number and the value of the supply
Intrastat declaration	¶9345+	No entries required

F. Fiscal warehousing

9242 ss 18 - 18F VATA 1994; Notice 702/8

Fiscal warehousing is a suspensive regime which allows the wholesaling of certain commodities to be carried out free of VAT.

As with the suspensive regimes for imports (¶9475+), VAT becomes chargeable when the goods leave the regime - that is, when they are removed from a fiscal warehouse.

MEMO POINTS A **fiscal warehouse** is a place (other than retail premises) occupied or controlled by a fiscal warehousekeeper (¶9268+) who has given written notification to HMRC to that effect. A place will remain a fiscal warehouse whilst it is occupied or controlled by a fiscal warehousekeeper, or until the warehousekeeper notifies HMRC in writing that it will cease to be a fiscal warehouse.

Consequences

9244 s 18 VATA 1994

Whilst the **goods remain in** a fiscal warehouse **or are transferred between** fiscal warehouses, acquisitions and supplies of eligible goods by wholesale traders are treated as taking place outside the UK. Traders need not register for VAT in the UK if their trade in warehoused commodities is their only business activity in the UK.

In addition, **certain services** carried out on warehoused goods can be zero-rated (¶9262+).

1. Users

9246 Notice 702/8 para 2.18

Any wholesale trader can place eligible goods in a fiscal warehouse.

Users do not have to be **VAT-registered**, but they may register voluntarily. If users have other business activities, their liability to register for VAT is not affected by the value of:
- supplies made in a fiscal warehouse; or
- deemed supplies of services accounted for by the person who removes the goods (¶9266).

Eligible goods

9248 s 18B VATA 1994

The fiscal warehousing regime applies to certain commodities which are in free circulation in the EU but which are not for retail sale. The goods may have been sourced from within or outside the EU.

MEMO POINTS 1. Goods are in **free circulation in the EU** if they were:
- produced in the EU; or
- imported, and any import duties, taxes (including import VAT) and levies have been paid or deferred.

Notice 702/8 para 2.4; SI 1995/2518 reg 145K

2. Goods are treated as being for **retail sale** if they are supplied by a VAT-registered person to a non-VAT-registered person and either:
- the supply by the VAT-registered person is a retail sale; or
- the non-VAT-registered person will make retail sales of the goods.

3. **Non-eligible goods** can be stored in a fiscal warehouse without the benefits of the fiscal warehousing regime.

The following **types of commodity** are eligible for the fiscal warehousing regime: 9250 Sch 5A VATA 1994

Foodstuffs	Metals	Other commodities
Cereals	Aluminium	Chemicals in bulk
Cocoa beans (whole or broken, raw or roasted)	Copper	Mineral oils, including crude petroleum oils, propane and butane
Coffee (not roasted)	Iridium	Rubber (in primary forms or in plates, sheets or strip)
Grains and seeds, including soya beans	Lead	Wool
Nuts, including coconuts, brazil nuts and cashew nuts	Nickel	
Oil seeds and oleaginous (oil-producing) fruit	Platinum	
Olives	Palladium	
Potatoes	Rhodium	
Sugar (raw)	Silver	
Tea	Tin	
Vegetable oils and fats and their fractions (whether or not refined, but not chemically modified)	Zinc	

Transactions in the warehouse

Subject to satisfying certain criteria, acquisitions of eligible goods from another EU member state, and all supplies of eligible goods, will be treated as taking place outside the UK, so that no VAT will be due. 9252 s 18B(1), (2) VATA 1994

Type of transaction	Goods must be	Certificate requirement
Acquisition	– placed into a fiscal warehouse after acquisition but before any subsequent supply; or – acquired whilst they are subject to the fiscal warehousing regime	A certificate that the goods are subject to the fiscal warehousing regime must be prepared and retained by the acquirer
Supply	– placed into a fiscal warehouse after the supply but before any subsequent supply; or – supplied whilst they are subject to the fiscal warehousing regime	A certificate that the goods will become subject to the fiscal warehousing regime must be given to the supplier by the buyer

Charge on removal of goods

When goods are removed from the fiscal warehousing regime, **VAT is not due** where the goods were: 9258 SI 1995/2518 reg 145H(2)

a. removed for use in the UK and were either:
– zero-rated goods; or
– the trader's own goods which have not been used within the fiscal warehousing regime;
b. exported to a non-EU country;
c. removed in the course of an intra-EU supply;
d. transferred to another UK fiscal warehouse or a corresponding fiscal warehousing regime in another EU member state; or
e. small quantities with a negligible commercial value which were removed for sampling.

VAT is due if none of the situations in ¶9258 applies. The taxable value depends on whether the goods have: 9260

– been supplied whilst in the fiscal warehouse, in which case it is the value of the last supply; or
– not been supplied whilst in the fiscal warehouse, in which case it is the value of the goods when they entered the warehouse.

Payment is due from the person responsible for removing the goods from the fiscal warehousing regime, at the time of removal.

Input tax may be claimed on the VAT charged, subject to the normal deductibility rules (¶1800+).

MEMO POINTS VAT may also be due on the value of **services carried out** on the goods while they were in the fiscal warehouse (¶9262+).

Associated services

9262 s 18C VATA 1994; Notice 702/8 para 2.16

The following services can be zero-rated if performed on goods that are subject to the fiscal warehousing regime:
- keeping the goods; and
- carrying out physical operations on the goods, such as preservation and repacking.

Brokerage, agents' fees and transport between warehouses cannot be zero-rated.

9264 Before eligible services are supplied, the **recipient** (normally the owner of the goods) must give the supplier (other than a fiscal warehousekeeper) a certificate that the services are to be performed.

A **supplier** who receives such a certificate should, within 30 days of the services being performed, issue a VAT invoice as normal. No VAT should be charged and the supply should be zero-rated. The following phrase should be included on the invoice:

"in accordance with Section 18C VATA 1994".

Both the owner of the goods and the supplier of the services should **retain** a copy of the certificate in their records to support zero-rating.

MEMO POINTS The **certificate** must contain the following information:
- name and address of person that owns the goods;
- description of goods;
- quantity of goods;
- warehouse stock number;
- name and address of fiscal warehouse;
- authorisation number of warehousekeeper;
- details of the services that are to be performed; and
- a declaration that the goods in question are subject to the fiscal warehousing regime.

9266 **Removal of goods** When goods are removed from the fiscal warehousing regime, services which had previously been zero-rated will become taxable, **unless**:

a. the service created new goods; or

b. the goods were:
- the subject of a supply before their removal from the fiscal warehouse but after the service was zero-rated;
- exported under duty suspension arrangements directly from the warehouse to a non-EU country; or
- sent under duty suspension arrangements to a customs or fiscal warehouse in another EU member state.

The **taxable amount** is the same as for the supply which was previously zero-rated.

Payment is due from the person who removed the goods.

2. Fiscal warehousekeepers

9268 Any VAT-registered person can apply for authorisation as a fiscal warehousekeeper.

Obtaining authorisation

9270 s 18A VATA 1994; Notice 702/8 paras 2.6, 2.7

Before HMRC authorises a fiscal warehousekeeper, it must be satisfied that the following **conditions** are met:

a. the applicant must:
- be VAT-registered in the UK and have a good VAT compliance record;

– be able to comply with the conditions of authorisation, and the regulations for the operation of the scheme; and
– provide a list of the addresses of all storage sites which will form part of the fiscal warehouse and any other premises where records will be held (retail premises cannot be used as fiscal warehouse premises, and all notified premises must meet health and safety legislation requirements);
b. an applicant who is already authorised to operate any UK duty suspensive regime must have a satisfactory record of operation of that regime; and
c. the applicant's accounts and stock control records must be capable of meeting certain requirements (¶9272), in particular the ability to differentiate between fiscally warehoused goods and other goods.

MEMO POINTS **Application** is made by letter to HMRC with the following details:
– name, address and VAT number;
– addresses and descriptions of storage facilities;
– details of any UK suspensive regime currently operated;
– descriptions of stock records and accounting system, and the place where stock records will be kept; and
– nature of goods to be stored (either specific goods or all eligible goods).

Responsibilities

The following table sets out the responsibilities of fiscal warehousekeepers: 9272 Notice 702/8 para 2.12

Area of responsibility	Details
Record-keeping	Records must be kept of all eligible commodities which enter the warehouse, whether or not deposited by the fiscal warehousekeeper.
	Separate records must be kept of non-eligible goods stored in the fiscal warehouse.
Security	The fiscal warehousekeeper is responsible for the physical security of eligible commodities, and may be held liable for any unexplained stock discrepancies other than through natural wastage or other legitimate causes. The amount due on such losses will be assessed on the basis of the VAT due on a sale at the highest open-market value or highest applicable VAT rate during the time the goods were in the fiscal warehouse. An appeal (¶4260+) may be made against such an assessment.
Removals of goods	Before goods are removed, evidence must be obtained that the remover owns the goods and is either VAT-registered or has paid any VAT which is due. Failure to do so may result in the fiscal warehousekeeper becoming jointly and severally liable for payment of the VAT.
	A certificate that the goods will become subject to the fiscal warehousing regime must be given to the supplier by the buyer.

G. Temporary movements of goods

Temporary transfers of goods to or from another EU member state, which satisfy certain criteria, are not treated as supplies when the goods are transferred: 9276 SI 1992/3111 reg 4; SI 1995/2518 reg 42
– for treatment, processing, repair or valuation work in that member state (¶9794+);
– in order to make a supply of services in that member state; or
– for temporary use in that member state.

However, if the temporary removal **conditions cease to be met** (e.g. the goods are sold or the temporary use period exceeds 2 years), the original transfer should be treated as a supply and dealt with under the normal rules for acquisitions and despatches.

Criteria

9278 Notice 725 paras 10, 12 The detailed conditions are as follows:

Purpose of transfer	Detailed conditions
Treatment or processing	The trader is VAT-registered in the member state of despatch but not in the member state of arrival
	The goods are returned to the trader in the member state of despatch after completion of the work
Repair or valuation	The goods are delivered to a person other than the owner, whose supply of repair or valuation services is treated as taking place in the member state of arrival
Supply of services[1]	The trader has no place of business in the member state of arrival
	The goods are for the purposes of a specific contract
	The goods are returned to the member state of despatch after use
Temporary use	The goods would have been eligible for temporary importation relief if they had been imported from outside the EU (¶9509+)
	The goods will remain in the member state of arrival for no longer than 2 years

Note:
1. Goods used for a supply of services could include tools, equipment, or goods intended for loan or leasing.

Administration

9280 Although temporary movements of goods are not treated as supplies, details must be **recorded** in a temporary movements register.

Commercial **evidence** of removal from the UK and subsequent return to the UK should also be retained.

Notice 725 para 16.9 MEMO POINTS A **temporary movements register** should contain the following details:
- a description of the goods;
- the date on which the goods arrived or were removed, and the date on which they were returned;
- the reason for the movement; and
- the consideration for the transaction, if applicable.

9282 Notice 725 paras 10.8, 12.7 **Reporting requirements** are limited:

Purpose of transfer	Detail	Reporting requirements		
		VAT return	EC sales list	Intrastat[1]
Processing	Sent from UK for processing	n/a	n/a	Enter cost of goods as a despatch
	Returned to UK after processing	Enter output tax on reverse charge in box 1	n/a	Enter cost of goods and processing as an arrival
		Enter input tax in box 4		
		Enter value of processing services in box 6		
	Received in UK for processing	n/a	n/a	Enter cost of goods as an arrival[2]
	Sent back from UK after processing	Enter value of process in box 6	n/a	Enter cost of goods as a despatch[2]

Purpose of transfer	Detail	Reporting requirements		
		VAT return	**EC sales list**	**Intrastat** [1]
Repair	Sent from UK for repair	n/a	n/a	n/a
	Returned to UK after repair	Enter output tax on reverse charge in box 1	n/a	n/a
		Enter input tax in box 4		
		Enter value of repair services in box 6		
	Received in UK for repair	n/a	n/a	n/a
	Sent back from UK after repair	Enter value of process in box 6	n/a	n/a
Supply of services		n/a	n/a	Enter cost of goods, if the goods have been removed from the UK for 2 years or more
Temporary use		n/a	n/a	n/a

Note:
1. Where the value of despatches or arrivals exceeds the relevant threshold (¶9347+).
2. If cost is not known, open-market value can be substituted (where processing has occurred, the cost of the process should be added to the market value when entering details of a despatch).

H. Transfers of own goods and goods on sale or return

If a business transfers its own goods or assets from the UK to another EU member state or vice versa, this is **normally** a deemed supply, irrespective of whether it is made for a consideration, or connected with a transaction for a consideration. **9286** Sch 4 para 6 VATA 1994; Notice 725 paras 9, 15

The business must therefore account for any VAT which is due both in the UK and in the other member state.

These rules apply to transfers of own goods generally, and also the following specific types of transfer:
- stock on **sale or return, approval**, or similar terms (¶800+);
- **consignment stock**, where goods are transferred to create a stock from which supplies will be made in the other EU member state (the stock remains under the control of the supplier and supplies from the stock can be made to one or more customers); and
- **call-off stock**, where goods are transferred for use and payment by a customer, as required (the stock is under the control of, and for the exclusive use of, one customer).

Exceptions

For transfers other than the specific types of transfer in ¶9286 above, this rule **does not apply** if: **9288**

a. the transfer is otherwise subject to normal UK VAT rules because it is a:
- transfer or disposal of goods which no longer form part of the business assets; or
- grant or assignment of any interest in, right over, or licence to occupy land, so that the land no longer forms part of the business assets; or

b. the conditions for temporary movements of goods (¶9276+) are met.

Accounting

9290 The **VAT accounting implications** are as follows:

Rules of	Transfers from the UK	Transfers to the UK
UK VAT	The supply may be zero-rated if the normal conditions are met (¶9080+), otherwise the business must charge and account for VAT at the rate which would apply if the goods had been supplied in the UK	If the supply qualified for zero-rating in the other EU member state, the business must account for acquisition VAT and may deduct the same amount as input tax, subject to the normal rules (¶1800+)
		Where goods are transferred on sale or return terms, the business must also account for VAT on the supply of the goods at the earliest of the following times: – the issue of a VAT invoice; – adoption of the goods by the customer; or – 12 months after the date of their removal to the UK
EU VAT	The business may be liable to register for VAT and account for acquisition tax in the other EU member state, if the value of the goods transferred exceeds the registration threshold	If the business is not already VAT-registered in the other EU member state, it may be liable to register if the value of the goods transferred exceeds the registration threshold
	An input tax deduction may be available	Supplies by registered businesses may be zero-rated if the normal conditions are met (¶9080+)
	Where goods are transferred on sale or return terms, the business may also have to account for VAT on the supply of the goods	

Reporting

9292 The **UK** reporting requirements are as follows:

Notice 725 paras 9.9, 15

Document	¶¶	Transfers	
		From the UK	**To the UK**
VAT return	¶2985+	Enter cost of goods in boxes 6 and 8	Enter acquisition tax in box 2
			Enter input tax in box 4, if deductible
			Enter cost of goods in boxes 7 and 9
			For sales of goods transferred on sale or return terms, enter output tax in box 1 and value of sales actually made in box 6
EC sales list	¶9330+	Enter cost of goods	n/a
Intrastat declaration[1]	¶9345+	Despatches - enter cost of goods	Arrivals - enter cost of goods

Note:
1. Where the value of arrivals or despatches exceeds the relevant threshold (¶9347+).

I. Supplies to diplomatic missions and international organisations

Supplies of goods (**other than** new means of transport (¶9112+)) to diplomatic missions, international organisations and their personnel based in other EU member states may be zero-rated if certain conditions are met. **9296**

MEMO POINTS **International organisations** are organisations established by a treaty between sovereign states or governments. These include the European Union, United Nations and NATO but exclude:
- organisations formed by agreement between non-governmental bodies - for example, a charity or body representing a trade; and
- bodies set up by a single state or government - for example, a government department.

Zero-rating criteria

All of the following conditions must be met: **9298** Notice 725 para 14; Notice 48 para 2.6

a. the supplies are either for the official use of those organisations or the private use of their personnel;

b. they are removed from the UK; and

c. the supplier obtains and keeps:
- proof of the removal within 3 months of the supply; and
- documentation to support zero-rating (as set out by the recipient's authorities). A supplier who has any doubts about the documentation received should contact HMRC's National Advice Service.

MEMO POINTS 1. In general, transactions zero-rated under these provisions are not regarded as **distance sales** (¶9177+) and do not count towards the distance selling threshold. However, in the case of supplies to **customers based in Germany**, the supplier should check with the German authorities whether registration in Germany is required.
2. No **EC sales list** (¶9330+) entries are required for such supplies.

J. Electricity and gas supplies

The place of supply of electricity and natural gas (other than bottled gas), and also heat or cooling supplied through a network, is as follows: **9300** SI 2004/3148 regs 9 - 14

a. supplies made to dealers are treated as supplied at the place where the dealer has its business; and

b. for **other supplies**, the treatment depends on whether the goods are:
- consumed, in which case the place of supply is where the recipient makes the consumption; or
- not consumed, in which case they are treated as supplied at the place where the recipient has its business.

MEMO POINTS Supplies of electricity and gas, heating and cooling are specifically defined as being **supplies of goods**. Sch 4 para 3 VATA 1994

K. Supplies made on board transport

The place of supply for goods supplied on board ships, aircraft or trains which **transport passengers** from one point in the EU to another member state (with no stop-off at a non-EU member state) is as follows: **9302** SI 2004/3148 regs 4 - 8

Type of supply	Place of supply
Goods to be consumed on board supplied outside the EU[1]	Outside the EU
Goods to be taken away by passengers (e.g. gifts)	Point of departure unless pleasure cruise

Note:
1. For details of the place of **supply of services** provided for consumption on board passenger transport see ¶9734.

Pleasure cruises

9304 SI 1992/3121 reg 8 Goods **taken away by a passenger** during the course of a pleasure cruise are treated as being supplied in the same place as the transport of the passenger (¶9732).

In this context a pleasure cruise includes a cruise wholly or partly for the purposes of education or training.

SECTION 4

Special reporting

9325 All VAT-registered businesses which supply goods to, or acquire goods from, other EU member states must show details of these transactions on their VAT returns (¶2985+).

Details may also need to be reported on EC sales lists and included in Intrastat declarations.

Summary

9327 The additional requirements are summarised as follows:

Document	Transactions included	Exceptions
EC sales lists	Goods supplied, despatched, transported or transferred to a registered person in another member state	Small businesses can provide fewer details and submit lists annually
Intrastat declarations	Goods despatched to, or received from, other member states	Sales to unregistered customers[1]
		Despatches or arrivals of a low value[2]

Note:
1. No declarations are required if distance selling thresholds (¶9206) are not exceeded.
2. No declarations are required if annual value of despatches or arrivals does not exceed relevant threshold (¶9347+).

A. EC sales lists

9330 SI 1995/2518 reg 22; Notice 725 para 17 All VAT-registered persons who have **supplied**, despatched, transported or transferred goods to a registered person in **another EU member state** must submit EC sales lists to HMRC, generally monthly. There are simplified obligations for small businesses.

MEMO POINTS Quarterly EC sales lists are also required for **intra-EU supplies of services** (see ¶9802+).

1. Normal obligations

Information required

The following details must **normally** be provided: **9332**
- customers' VAT registration numbers and country prefixes;
- total value of goods and related services supplied to each customer; and
- an indicator if the business is an intermediary in a triangular transaction (¶9214+).

MEMO POINTS 1. The **value** of goods:
- **includes** the cost of goods provided free to customers; and
- **excludes** supplies made under distance selling rules (¶9177+) and temporary movements of goods (¶9276+).

2. **Related services** comprise the costs of any freight transport services, and services ancillary to the transport of goods which are charged by the supplier to the customer.

Submission

Sales lists normally relate to a **period** of a month, although smaller traders can instead submit lists quarterly (or annually, in certain circumstances). **9334**

The **due date** is 14 days after the end of the month, or 21 days if the list is submitted electronically.

MEMO POINTS 1. **Branches or group companies** can submit their own sales lists. HMRC will issue a three-digit identifier to each group company or branch. This may apply to:
- individual branches of a business;
- individual companies within a group registration; or
- self-accounting branches of a group member.

2. For details of penalties which will be levied for **late submission** or for submitting **inaccurate** lists see ¶4120+.

3. The **reporting period** is 1 month, unless the VAT-exclusive value of goods supplied to other EU states has not exceeded £35,000 in any of the previous four quarters, in which case quarterly lists are permitted. A business required to submit monthly lists relating to goods may still submit lists relating to services quarterly. Any business may choose to submit lists for goods and/or services monthly. HMRC Brief 2/09

4. A business **entitled to submit quarterly** lists for goods can continue to do so, unless the VAT-exclusive value of goods supplied to other EU member states exceeds £35,000 for the quarter.

5. If a business **exceeds the quarterly goods threshold** by the end of the first or second month in a quarter, a list must be submitted at the end of that month, covering the whole period from the beginning of the quarter. Monthly lists are required from then on.

6. Once a business is **submitting monthly lists** for goods, it must **continue to do so** until the value of its intra-EU trade in goods has been below the threshold for five consecutive quarters. Quarterly lists are then permitted.

2. Simplification for small businesses

For smaller traders whose supplies do not include new means of transport (¶9112+), there is a reduction in the information required and a business also has the opportunity to submit lists annually. **9336**

Definition of small	Simplifications available
– annual taxable turnover does not exceed the registration threshold (see ¶9960) plus £25,500; and – annual value of supplies to other member states does not exceed £11,000	The trader only needs to provide details of customers' VAT registration numbers and country prefixes
– annual taxable turnover does not exceed £145,000; and – annual value of supplies to other member states does not exceed £11,000	The trader can prepare and submit lists annually The due date is 6 weeks after the end of the relevant period

B. Intrastat declarations

9345 Notice 60; Notice 725 para 18

Intrastat is a system for collecting statistics on the trade of goods between EU member states. The statistics are **used by** governments and various international bodies, including the Statistical Office of the European Communities (Eurostat). Businesses also use the information for marketing purposes.

The **forms** which businesses must submit are called Supplementary Declarations (SDs).

For Intrastat purposes, a **supply** to an EU customer is called a despatch; an **acquisition** from an EU supplier is called an arrival.

SI 2008/556

MEMO POINTS HMRC uses information provided on SDs for VAT compliance checks. It is also used to assist with **countering fraud**.

Liability to submit SDs

9347 SI 1992/2790 reg 3

If the value of despatches or arrivals **exceeds a threshold** in a calendar year, a VAT-registered business must submit SDs. If the values of despatches and arrivals both exceed the threshold, separate despatches and arrivals SDs must be submitted.

MEMO POINTS In 2010 the thresholds for arrivals and despatches were set at £600,000 and £250,000, respectively. With effect from 1 January 2014 the threshold for arrivals was increased to £1,200,000 and from 1 January 2015 to £1,500,000, but the threshold for despatches remains unchanged.

9350 Notice 60 para 3.2

A business which **does not already submit SDs** must notify HMRC of the month in which cumulative despatches or arrivals exceed the threshold and submit SDs from the start of that month.

Where a business **is already submitting SDs** in the current year, it must continue to submit them in the following year, unless the total value of despatches or arrivals in the current year is less than the threshold for the following year.

If the value of despatches or arrivals **drops below the threshold** during a year, the business must continue to submit SDs until the end of that year.

EXAMPLE A Ltd was not required to submit SDs in 2014. Despatches and arrivals in 2015 are as follows:

Month	Despatches		Arrivals	
	Month £	Cumulative £	Month £	Cumulative £
January	20,000	20,000	100,000	100,000
February	30,000	50,000	120,000	220,000
March	40,000	90,000	160,000	380,000
April	40,000	130,000	220,000	600,000
May	40,000	170,000	140,000	740,000
June	50,000	220,000	180,000	920,000
July	60,000	280,000	140,000	1,060,000
August	20,000	300,000	100,000	1,160,000
September	40,000	340,000	120,000	1,280,000
October	20,000	360,000	140,000	1,420,000
November	30,000	390,000	100,000	1,520,000
December	30,000	420,000	60,000	1,580,000

The £250,000 threshold for **despatches** is exceeded in July, so SDs for despatches are due from 1 July 2015 onwards.

The £1,500,000 threshold for **arrivals** is exceeded in November, so SDs for arrivals are due from 1 November 2015 onwards.

If the despatches threshold for **2016** was £350,000 (for example), A Ltd would have to continue to submit despatches SDs throughout 2016. Arrivals SDs would not be required after December 2015 if the arrivals threshold for 2016 were increased to (for example) £1,600,000, as the total value of arrivals in 2015 did not exceed £1,600,000. However, if cumulative arrivals during 2016 exceeded

£1,600,000, A Ltd would have to resume submitting arrivals SDs from the start of the month in which the threshold was exceeded.

Information required

The information which must be shown on SDs is as follows: **9352** Notice 60 para 5

Entry on SD	Details
Value of despatches or arrivals	¶9354
Net mass	Values and quantities can be aggregated if all other details are the same
Country code	¶9082
Commodity code	Commodity codes, or Intrastat Classification Nomenclatures (ICNs) can be found here: flmemo.co.uk/vm9352 Paper and CD ROM copies can also be obtained from HMRC
Delivery terms code	Only required for large businesses with despatches or arrivals in excess of a second threshold (currently £24 million) Delivery terms codes are listed at ¶9987
Transaction code	¶9986

The value of the transactions is calculated as follows: **9354**

Value includes	Value excludes
Value of related services included in the price of the goods, such as freight and insurance costs	Excise duty
Goods supplied to private individuals, except new means of transport (¶9112+)	Commercial samples provided free of charge
Cost of goods supplied free	Goods sent for, or returned after, repair
Goods to be installed or used in construction	Goods in transit, including where there are stops or temporary storage for transport reasons
Goods on long-term hire, loan or operational lease	Temporary movements, where goods are to be returned within 2 years without a change of ownership
Goods sent for, or returned after, processing	Movements not regarded as by way of trade
Transfers between the same legal entity	Goods supplied by an intermediate supplier in the case of triangulation (¶9214+)
Despatches (but not arrivals) which are lost or destroyed in transit	

Submission

SDs are normally submitted on a calendar month basis. By concession, a business which has been approved to use **special VAT periods** (¶2990), such as 4-weekly periods, may use these when submitting SDs, but SDs must still be submitted each month. For example, if a business has 13 4-weekly VAT periods, its Intrastat periods must include one 8-week period. **9356** Notice 60 para 4

SDs must be submitted electronically, no later than 21 days after the end of the reference period.

MEMO POINTS 1. Where a business uses **special VAT periods**, it must notify the HMRC Intrastat Team of the approved periods for the next 12 months if the value of despatches or arrivals exceeds £5 million.

2. **Branches** can apply for permission to submit their own SDs. HMRC will issue a three-digit identifier to each group company or branch.

3. For details of **penalties** which will be levied for **failing** to submit SDs by the due date see ¶4205.

CHAPTER 2

Goods outside the EU

OUTLINE ¶¶

This chapter deals with transactions involving goods where either the supplier or customer belongs in a country which is not an EU member state (and the other party belongs in the UK). The terms "imports" and "exports" apply only to transactions with countries outside the EU. The rules for transactions involving goods where both parties are based in the EU are different (see ¶9000+). **9400**

SECTION 1

Imported goods

Supplies of goods are treated as imports if the goods enter free circulation in the UK after: **9405** s 15 VATA 1994; Notice 702 para 1.5
- directly entering the UK from outside the EU (¶9410); or
- being placed in a suspensive arrangement either in the UK or another EU member state (¶9475).

MEMO POINTS 1. For these purposes the **UK includes** the waters within twelve nautical miles of the coastline. s 96(11) VATA 1994

2. **Customs duty** (outside the scope of *VAT Memo*) is also payable on the majority of imported products. The Tariff, a guide produced by HMRC which lists some 16,000 commodities and products and the applicable duty rates, is available by following this link: flmemo.co.uk/vm9405.

Isle of Man

9408 SI 1982/1067; Notice 702/9 para 1.5

Goods imported from the Isle of Man to the UK in the course of a business are **generally** treated as UK supplies, provided that:
- any import VAT due has been accounted for in the Isle of Man; or
- if import duty relief applied in the Isle of Man, the conditions for the relief are still applicable.

As an **exception** to this rule, supplies will be treated as imports when goods have previously been imported to the UK or the Isle of Man and either:
- Manx VAT was paid on the previous importation but at a different rate from that applicable in the UK; or
- UK or Manx VAT on the previous importation was wholly or partly relieved.

A. Directly entering the UK

9410 s 1(1)(c) VATA 1994

Import VAT is normally chargeable on goods imported into the UK. If the goods would have been zero-rated if supplied in the UK, zero-rating also applies on importation and to ancillary services (¶9418).

1. Liability

9412 s 43 CEMA 1979; s 30(3) VATA 1994

Import VAT is payable on importation, **unless**:
- an absolute relief is available (¶9433); or
- deferment has been obtained (¶9458).

Information Sheet 6/13

MEMO POINTS Entry of any vehicle (whether from inside the EU or outside) to the UK for permanent use on UK roads must be notified to HMRC within 14 days and any VAT due paid or accounted for. It is not possible to register and license the vehicle with DVLA or DVA until receipt of confirmation from HMRC that this notification has been processed and any VAT due has been paid. Communication with HMRC for this purpose is via the NOVA online system. Previous paper forms VAT 414, VAT 415, C&E 386, C&E 388 and C&E 389 have been withdrawn and are no longer accepted by HMRC.

Time of importation

9413 s 5 CEMA 1979

The time of importation of goods **depends on** the method of transport:

Method of transport	Time of importation
Sea	When the ship comes within the limits of a port
Air	When the aircraft lands in the UK or, if earlier, when the goods are unloaded in the UK
Land	When the goods cross the boundary into Northern Ireland
Pipeline	When the goods are brought within the limits of a port, or cross the boundary into Northern Ireland

Who is liable?

9415 ss 1, 43(1) CEMA 1979

Import VAT is payable by importers, whether VAT-registered or not.

The **importer** is normally the owner of the goods but may be any other person who, between the time of importation and delivery into free circulation, has either:
- possession; or
- a beneficial interest.

For goods imported via a **pipeline**, the importer includes the owner of the pipeline.

VAT-registered importers can normally recover import VAT on their VAT returns (¶9429).

Rate

Import VAT is chargeable at the same rate **as if** the goods had been supplied in the UK - that is, usually the standard rate, unless the supply is specifically: 9416 s 2(1) VATA 1994
- exempt (¶350+);
- zero-rated (¶1180+); or
- reduced-rated (¶1110+).

EXAMPLE A Ltd, a motor accessories retailer, imported the following goods:

Goods	UK VAT rate which normally applies	Value £
Children's car seats	Reduced rate (¶1110)	1,000
CD players	Standard rate	2,000

A Ltd is liable to pay import VAT as follows:

		£
Children's car seats	£1,000 @ 5%	50
CD players	£2,000 @ 20%	400
		450

Zero-rating Imported **goods** are zero-rated if they would have been zero-rated if supplied in the UK, provided that any specific conditions for zero-rating have been met. 9418 Sch 8 Group 8 items 5, 11 VATA 1994; Notice 702 para 2.11; Notice 744B para 5.3

If a trader (A) makes a supply of imported goods between the time of their arrival in the UK and the time when an import entry is delivered to HMRC, such that the new owner of the goods (B) is required to make the import entry, trader A should zero-rate the supply.

Zero-rating also applies to the following **ancillary services** when supplied in conjunction with zero-rated imported goods:

Service	Detail
Transport	Of imported goods from their place of importation to their final destination [1]
Handling or storage (¶1318)	In any ship or aircraft located: – in a port or Customs and Excise airport (¶1296); – on land adjacent to a port (this covers only the immediate quay or dock); or – in a transit shed (i.e. a place approved by HMRC for the temporary storage of goods)
	At a place where goods have been imported from the EU
	In connection with the transport of goods from a place at which they have been imported into the EU to their destination in the UK or another EU member state
Making of arrangements	For all of the above services

Note:
1. Their final destination is the furthest place, in the UK or another EU member state, to which the goods are consigned at importation. If this place is unknown, it is the first place to which the goods are transported after importation.

Documentary **evidence** must be held to show entitlement to zero-rating - for example, consignment notes, bills of lading, certificates of shipment, airway bills or seaway bills and Customs declaration forms C 88 (SAD) (¶9426). In addition, any relevant correspondence, the customer's order document, payment details, sales invoices and advice notes may be acceptable. 9419

Valuation

The **normal** valuation rules (¶9422) apply to most goods **except for**: 9421
- works of art, antiques and collectors' items (¶1164); and
- computer software.

Notice 702 para 7

MEMO POINTS The treatment of imported **computer software** depends on whether it is normalised or specific software:

Type	Treatment
Normalised software is a mass-produced item which is freely available to all customers and usable by them independently after installation and limited training in a standard form to carry out the same applications or functions. It is made up of a coherent set of programs and support material and often includes the service of installation, training and maintenance. Personal computer software, home computer software and game packages are in this category. Also included are standard packages adapted at the supplier's instigation to include security or similar devices.	Import VAT is due on the **Customs value** of the software - for example, the total value of the carrier medium and the data and instructions (software) on it, as adjusted where appropriate (¶9422).
Specific products are: – items made to customers' special requirements, either as unique programs or adaptations from standard programs; – inter-company information, data and accounts; – enhancements and updates of existing "specific" programs; and – enhancements and updates of existing "normalised" programs supplied under contractual obligation to customers who have bought the original program.	**No import VAT** is due. The total amount of the value of both software and carrier medium is treated as the consideration for the supply of services and is taxed accordingly within the member state concerned.

9422
s 21 VATA 1994; Notice 702 para 3.1

The value of imported goods from a place outside the EU **includes**:
– the price paid for the goods;
– all taxes, duties and other charges levied outside or, by reason of importation, within the UK (but excluding VAT); and
– all incidental expenses.

The value **excludes** the cost of certain services which are taxable under the reverse charge procedure (¶9712), such as royalties and licence fees.

EXAMPLE A trader imported gemstones at a cost of £52,318 and paid import VAT based on that value. He later discovered that the gemstones were worth only £11,000, so made a repayment claim for part of the import VAT.
HMRC refused the claim. The tribunal dismissed the appeal, because the goods had been correctly valued on the basis of the price paid. *AJ Maden* [1996] (VTD 14603)

9424
Notice 702 para 3.1

Incidental expenses Items included in incidental expenses are commission, packing, transport and insurance costs, up to the first destination of the goods in the UK.

If, at the time of importation of the goods, a **further destination** for those goods is known which is within the UK or another EU member state, all such incidental expenses resulting from the transport of the goods to that other destination must be included in the import VAT value.

MEMO POINTS **First destination** means the place mentioned on the consignment note or other importation document or, in the absence of such documentation, the place of the first transfer of cargo in the UK.

9425 To quantify incidental expenses, traders can choose one of the following three methods, as appropriate:

a. the **actual costs** incurred (if any subsequent amendment is necessary, the import VAT liability can be adjusted accordingly);

b. an **estimated amount** using nationally agreed rates (no adjustment is required if actual costs are different); or

c. where the above methods are inappropriate or impractical, a **bespoke method** negotiated and agreed with HMRC (in which case no post-importation adjustments will be necessary).

MEMO POINTS The **nationally agreed rates** are as follows:

Type of transport	Details	Rates
Group A	Airfreight	The greater of: – 40p per chargeable kg; or – £100
Group B	Surface freight: trailer, rail wagon or container - groupage/consolidation consignments	Delivery and handling - £90 per gross weight tonne
		Other ancillaries - the greater of: – £80 per consignment; or – £170
Group C	Surface freight: trailer, rail wagon or container - full load consignments	£550 per full load consignment

Comment In October 2007 HMRC consulted on the nationally agreed rates to establish if they accurately reflect costs being incurred. No guidance has, as yet, been released.

Payment

Import VAT is payable on importation, unless deferment applies (¶9458). Payment is normally **made by** the importer or the importer's agent, following completion of: 9426 Notice 702 paras 3.2, 3.3
- an import declaration (the Single Administrative Document, SAD form C 88); and
- a declaration of value (form C 105A, C 105B or C 109A).

MEMO POINTS 1. The **SAD** contains a calculation of the VAT payable and shows the Trader Unique Reference Number (TURN).
2. The **TURN** consists of the trader's VAT registration number and a three-digit suffix. It is required in order to obtain the necessary evidence to reclaim import VAT. Traders can request a TURN from HMRC at the following address:
TURN Team
HMRC
13th floor
Government Buildings
Ty Glas
Llanishen
Cardiff
CF14 5YA
3. If a trader is **not VAT-registered**, or is in the process of applying for VAT registration, it is possible to apply for a "pseudo-TURN" using form C 219. It is not possible to recover the input VAT incurred until the trader is VAT-registered.
4. A **certificate** (form C 79) will be sent by HMRC direct to a VAT-registered trader after payment of import VAT, to enable recovery of that VAT as input tax (¶9429). Certificates cover transactions made in a calendar month and are issued on or around the 12th day of the following month. Notice 702 para 8

Special rules apply to **postal imports**: 9427 Notice 702 para 4.3

Value of goods	Type of import	Procedure
Up to £2,000	Datapost packets	Import VAT is payable to the Post Office/Parcelforce on delivery. The charge label attached to the package should be retained to support any repayment claim.
	Other consignments [1]	Import VAT may be accounted for in the VAT return for the period in which the goods were imported; input tax may also be deducted, subject to the normal rules. In support of a claim, the trader should retain the supplier's invoice and the charge label, postal wrapper and any Customs declaration attached to the package.
Over £2,000	All consignments	A SAD form must be sent to HMRC, together with an invoice or other evidence of the value of the goods and payment of the import VAT. HMRC will then send a copy of the SAD form as evidence for a claim to deduct input tax.

Note:
1. For imports of **private gifts** the taxable amount excludes postage.

9428 Notice 702 paras 2.6, 2.9

Repayments If import VAT has been overpaid (e.g. as a result of an incorrect classification of goods, or the loss or destruction of goods before release to the importer), repayment should be claimed via the trader's VAT return.

Recovery of import VAT

9429 Notice 702 paras 2.6, 2.8, 8.11; s 27 VATA 1994

VAT-registered traders can recover import VAT as input tax in their VAT returns. The certificate C 79 (¶9426) provides the required evidence for recovery (¶1980).

Non-VAT-registered importers cannot recover import VAT.

MEMO POINTS 1. **Direct repayments** outside the VAT return system are not made by HMRC.
2. If the importer has lost a C 79 a replacement can be requested from HMRC. The request must be in writing and should be sent to:
HMRC
VAT Central Unit
Microfilm Section
8th Floor, Alexander House
Victoria Avenue
Southend-on-Sea
SS99 1AU

Reporting

9431 The **UK reporting** requirements for imports of goods are as follows:

Event	VAT return (¶2985)	Intrastat (¶9345)
Import of non-EU goods into the UK from outside the EU	No entries required	No entries required
Import of non-EU goods from outside the EU via another member state into the UK	Enter acquisition VAT in box 2 Enter value of goods in box 9	No entries required

2. Absolute reliefs

9433 Import VAT **is not due** on the importation of goods where any of the following reliefs apply:

Type of relief	Details	¶¶
Low-value importations	Consignments not exceeding a specified quantity or value	¶9436
Exempt goods	Personal, artistic, humanitarian and charitable goods	¶9437
	Samples and promotional goods	
	Other commercial items	
Exempt circumstances	Goods for onward sale to another EU member state	¶9439
	Reimported goods	¶9443
	Rejected goods	¶9450
Imports by special visitors	Goods imported by an armed forces member or diplomat	¶9455

Records

9434 Notice 702/9 para 10

Where a business **claims relief** from import VAT, it must keep records which show:
- the type of goods imported;
- any processes which are carried out; and
- how the products or any unprocessed goods are disposed of.

Normal commercial records will contain most of these details but some adaptation may be necessary to show information required to support particular claims.

Records must be **preserved** for 4 years after the expiry of authorisation to use a suspension or relief regime.

a. Low-value importations

Import VAT is not due on the following consignments: **9436** s 37(1) VATA 1994; Notice 143 para 2; Notice 1

Type of consignment	Detail	Maximum quantity or value
Gifts [1]	Of perfumes and toilet water [2]	– 50 ml of perfumes; or – 250 ml of toilet water
	Other than perfumes, alcohol and tobacco [3]	£36
Commercial consignments of goods other than perfumes, alcohol and tobacco [4]		£15
Goods personally imported by travellers	Tobacco	– 200 cigarettes; or – 100 cigarillos; or – 50 cigars; or – 250 g of smoking tobacco; or – a pro rated proportion of more than one of the above (for example, 100 cigarettes plus 50 cigarillos)
	Alcohol and alcoholic drinks	– 1 litre of spirits or strong liqueurs over 22% volume; or – 2 litres of fortified or sparkling wines or other alcoholic drink up to 22% volume; or – a pro rated proportion of both the above; and – 16 litres of beer; and – 4 litres of still wine
	All other goods	– £390 (if travelling by commercial sea or air transport); or – £270 (if travelling by other means, including private plane or boat)

Note:
1. A consignment is treated as a gift if:
– it is consigned from one private individual to another;
– there is no consideration in money or money's worth; and
– it is solely for the personal use of the recipient or the recipient's family.
2. If the allowance is exceeded, VAT is due on the full value.
3. The consignment must not be part of a larger consignment.
4. This exemption does not apply to imports of "mail order" goods from the Channel Islands. **Mail order** means for this purpose any transaction or series of transactions under which a seller (S) sends goods in fulfilment of an order placed remotely. **Remotely** means by any means that do not involve the simultaneous physical presence of S and the person placing the order. **Seller** does not include any person acting otherwise than in a commercial or professional capacity.

EXAMPLE A Jersey company supplied contact lenses and associated services to a UK company. No import VAT was paid, on the basis that the goods alone were worth less than £18 (the maximum VAT-free value at the time, when the exemption applied to imports from the Channel Islands) and so fell to be exempt as a low-value commercial consignment.
The CJEU held that the goods and services formed one transaction, so import VAT was due.
Dollond & Aitchison Ltd v HMRC [2006]

b. Specifically exempted goods

9437 Import VAT is not due on the following types of goods:

Type of goods	Category	Details	Reference
Personal, artistic, humanitarian and charitable goods	Personal property belonging to individuals changing residence to the UK	Property for use of individual or members of the individual's household, excluding: – alcoholic and tobacco products; – motor vehicles which can carry more than nine persons; and – goods for use in a trade or profession	SI 1992/3193 regs 11, 12
	Personal property belonging to individuals moving to the UK on marriage	Household effects, excluding alcoholic and tobacco products, and wedding gifts of up to £800 each	SI 1992/3193 regs 13 - 15
	Scholastic equipment belonging to pupils or students in the UK	Household effects, clothing, uniforms and articles for purpose of studies	SI 1992/3193 reg 16
	Museum and gallery exhibits	Exhibits of a scientific, educational or cultural nature	Notice 361
	Decorations and awards	National decorations, sporting awards and trophies, and awards for courage or dedication conferred on EU residents, and awards to be given free to non-EU residents at business conferences and similar events	Notice 364
	Inherited goods	Household effects and other goods for personal use, excluding: – alcoholic and tobacco products; – business tools and stocks; – commercial vehicles; – livestock and agricultural products; – goods bought from the executor; and – goods bought or received as a gift from a beneficiary	Notice 368
	Goods for charities	See ¶8090	Notice 317
	Goods for disabled people	Goods to give educational, scientific or cultural help to the blind or partially sighted, and goods to give educational, employment or social help to the physically or mentally disabled	Notice 371

Type of goods	Category	Details	Reference
	Medical equipment donated by individuals or charitable or philanthropic organisations	Equipment for medical treatment, diagnosis or research	Notice 341
	Animals for scientific research		Notice 365
	Human blood and tissue		Notice 369
	Biological or chemical substances used for research		Notice 366
	Goods for use in the construction, upkeep or ornamentation of war graves		SI 1984/746
	Coffins and urns containing human remains or ashes, and flowers, wreaths or other accompanying ornamental objects		
	Visual and auditory materials produced by the United Nations or a United Nations organisation		Notice 373
Samples and promotional goods	Goods for testing		Notice 374
	Samples of negligible value		Notice 367
	Goods used in the promotion of a trade		SI 1984/746
	Publicity material sent to publishers and press agencies		
Other commercial items	Printed matter	Educational, scientific or cultural documents, books, newspapers, periodicals, maps, plans, official printed matter, and reports, prospectuses and other company documentation	Notice 342
	Items to be used as evidence for legal purposes		SI 1984/746
	Items relating to trademarks and patents		
	Recorded media sent for the transmission of information at no charge		
	Packing, fuel, lubricants and animal fodder used in a vehicle or special container transporting goods to the UK		
	Electricity and gas, heating and cooling		SI 2010/2924
	Scientific instruments	Equipment for medical or veterinary treatment, diagnosis, training or research	Notice 340
	Capital goods or equipment used for the purposes of a business which ceased to be carried on abroad in the previous 12 months		Notice 343
	Ground and security equipment for aircraft imported by an airline from a state which is a signatory to the Convention on International Civil Aviation		Notice 48 para 2.7

c. Goods for onward sale to another EU member state

9439 EC Directive 2009/69/EC; Notice 702/7
VAT-registered traders may claim relief from import VAT on goods imported for onward **sale to** a VAT-registered person in another EU member state.

Conditions

9440
The following conditions must **all** be satisfied:
- the onward supply must be zero-rated;
- the goods must be removed to the other member state within a month of importation; and
- the goods must not be processed before removal.

MEMO POINTS **Relief only applies** if, at the time of importation, the importer has provided the following information to the authorities of the member state of importation:
- its VAT number issued in the member state of importation, or the VAT number of its tax representative;
- the VAT number of the customer, or, when the goods are moved without change of ownership ("movement of own goods"), the importer's own VAT number issued in the member state in which the despatch or transport of the goods ends; and
- evidence that the imported goods are intended to be transported or despatched from the member state of importation to another member state.

Security (¶3528) of an amount not exceeding the import VAT may be requested by HMRC as a condition of granting the relief.

How to claim

9441 Notice 702/7 para 2.3
Relief is claimed by entering the following **details** on the SAD (¶9426):
- the expected place and date of onward consignment;
- the identity of the onward means of transport, if known; and
- the name, address and VAT registration number of the customer.

d. Reimported goods

9443
Reimported goods may be relieved (either fully or partially) where they are imported after either having been:
- repaired or subjected to some other process; or
- previously exported, in the same condition.

After processing or repair

9444 SI 1995/2518 reg 126
A **reduced** import VAT **charge** applies on the reimportation of goods which have been processed, repaired, adapted, made up or reworked outside the EU.

All of the following **conditions** must be met:
- the goods were temporarily exported from the EU;
- the intention on exportation was to reimport after the processing or treatment outside the EU;
- there has been no change of ownership between exportation and reimportation; and
- a declaration that these conditions were fulfilled was made in the reimportation documentation.

9446 Notice 702/9 para 6.3
The **value liable** to import VAT is:
- the price charged for the process, repair or service, including any charges for parts or materials;
- any freight and other charges (excluding insurance) for transporting the goods to and from the processor's premises; and
- any customs or excise duties or other import charges payable in the UK.

Returned goods

9447 SI 1995/2518 reg 121D; Notice 236
Importers can claim relief from import VAT on goods which they reimport in the same condition as when they exported them.

Relief is **not available** if any of the following apply:
– relief was given on reimportation after processing or repair (¶9444), unless the goods were returned in the same condition;
– the reimporter makes a supply of the goods which takes place outside the UK, but the goods are stored or used in the UK by or under the direction of the reimporter or the person who received the supply; or
– the goods were supplied to a person leaving the EU (¶9565).

Relief is **claimed on** the SAD (¶9426) and evidence of the previous export of the goods must be provided. **9449** Notice 236 para 4.1

The relief may be **reduced by** any VAT outstanding in relation to an earlier importation.

e. Rejected goods

Importers **can claim** repayment of import VAT on goods rejected by them after importation because the goods: **9450** Notice 266
– were defective;
– did not comply with the terms of the contract with the supplier; or
– were damaged before being released to the importer.

Conditions

The following conditions must **both be satisfied** so that the goods must: **9452**
a. not have been sold or used more than was necessary in order to establish that they were defective or did not comply with the terms of the contract; and
b. be disposed of by exporting, destroying, or placing them in a customs warehouse (¶9483) or free zone (¶9495).

How to claim

A claim must be made **within** 12 months of the date on which the import VAT was payable. **9453**

The claim is made **on** form C&E 1179; the following information must accompany it:
– a copy of the import invoice;
– proof of entitlement;
– a copy of the VAT certificate; and
– details of how the claim was calculated.

f. Goods imported by special visitors

Subject to certain conditions, import VAT is not due when: **9455** SI 1992/3156
– a member of a visiting force imports or removes from a warehouse any goods, or receives a gift of goods (other than tobacco products or alcoholic drinks) from a person outside the EU; or
– a diplomat imports a motor vehicle or receives a supply of a tobacco product or alcoholic drink from a warehouse.

If any of the conditions are not met and HMRC has not approved the situation, the import VAT is immediately payable by the entitled person (or any other person in possession of the goods). The goods may also be liable to forfeiture.

MEMO POINTS 1. A **member of a visiting force** is defined as a person who is neither a UK national nor a permanent UK resident and who is a serving military or civilian member of:
– a visiting non-UK force which is a member of NATO; or
– NATO international military headquarters.
2. A **diplomat** is defined as any person who is neither a UK national nor a permanent UK resident and who enjoys any privilege or immunity by virtue of being a:
– diplomatic agent, or a representative or person recognised as holding a similar rank;
– senior officer of the Commonwealth Secretariat;
– consular officer; or
– a person who enjoys a similar privilege or immunity under EU legislation.

Conditions

9456 **All goods** must:
– be used exclusively by the entitled person or a member of that person's family who is part of that person's household; and
– not be lent, hired out, given as security or transferred in the UK without prior written authorisation from HMRC.

For **motor vehicles**, any other vehicles imported by that person on which relief was obtained:
– must have been disposed of; and
– the related duty or tax must have been paid.

If the entitled person's spouse is present in the UK, the entitled person can retain one other vehicle on which relief was obtained.

3. Deferment

9458 There are **two schemes** which enable VAT-registered traders to defer payment of import VAT. Traders may use either or both schemes:

Type of deferment	Advantage	¶¶
Duty deferment scheme	Defers import VAT and other customs duties but importer must give a guarantee	¶9460
Simplified Import VAT Accounting (SIVA)	Defers import VAT only; no guarantee required	¶9466

a. Duty deferment scheme

9460 SI 1976/1223; Notice 101 para 1.2 The duty deferment scheme is available to VAT-registered:
– importers (or their agents); and
– owners of goods in a customs warehouse (¶9483) or free zone (¶9495).

Approval must be obtained from HMRC (¶9464).

Comment The duty deferment scheme **benefits** importers because payment of import VAT and other duties can be deferred by 30 days on average. It also benefits HMRC, as it provides an effective and efficient method of dealing with imports and collecting duty and tax.

Security

9461 Notice 101 para 5 Security must be provided which will **cover** all deferred customs and excise duties and import VAT, **unless** SIVA (¶9466) is also used, in which case import VAT is not required to be secured.

The security must be **in the form of** a guarantee from an approved bank, building society or insurance company which is sufficient to cover the liability for a calendar month up to an overall maximum anticipated amount.

A guarantee can be replaced with one for a higher or lower amount; a supplementary guarantee can be provided to cover extra liabilities in a peak period.

EXAMPLE B Ltd imports goods at the following levels in normal months and peak periods as follows:

		Monthly imports £
Normal months		100,000
Peak period 1	February to April	200,000
Peak period 2	October and November	300,000

B Ltd could give:
a. a basic guarantee for £100,000; and

b. supplementary guarantees to run for the months of:
- February to April of £100,000; and
- October and November of £200,000.

Payment

Payment of import VAT is deferred on request. The **due date** for VAT in relation to all imports and warehouse removals in each calendar month is the 15th day of the following month, or on the next working day if the 15th is not a working day. **9463** Notice 101 para 4

The payment **method** must be direct debit, in sterling.

If the **guarantee level is exceeded** in any calendar month, all further import charges for the remainder of that month must be paid immediately. If the guarantee level is repeatedly exceeded, scheme approval may be withdrawn.

Administration

If HMRC approves an application, it will **issue** a Deferment Approval Number to the importer, which will be used to record the deferment of charges. **9464** Notice 101 paras 6, 7

MEMO POINTS 1. The following **forms** must be completed:
- C 1200: Application for Approval of Deferment Arrangements;
- C 1201: Guarantee form;
- C 1202: Direct debit instructions; and
- C 1207N: Standing authority for agent/freight forwarder to request deferment.

2. Applications to use the scheme should be **sent to**:
HMRC
Banking Operations
Central Deferment Office
6th Floor North West
Alexander House
21 Victoria Avenue
Southend-on-Sea
Essex
SS99 1AA

3. Members of a **VAT group** (¶8800) can be covered by the same approval number.

---

b. Simplified Import VAT Accounting

The Simplified Import VAT Accounting scheme (SIVA) aims to help VAT-registered businesses by enabling deferment of import VAT without the need to provide a guarantee. **9466** Notice 101 para 5.8

MEMO POINTS Customs duties and excise duties must still be fully secured.

Conditions

The trader must satisfy **all** of the following criteria, having: **9467** Notice 101 para 5.10
- been VAT-registered for at least 3 years;
- a good VAT compliance history (with no serious offences) and payment record;
- sufficient financial means to meet all amounts deferred under SIVA;
- a 12-month record of international trading operations; and
- a good compliance record for international trade.

Payment

Payment of import VAT is deferred on request. **9469**

The **due date** for payment of VAT in relation to all imports and warehouse removals in each calendar month is the 15th day of the following month, or on the next working day, if the 15th is not a working day.

The payment **method** must be direct debit, in sterling.

If the **deferment account limit is exceeded** in any calendar month, all further import charges for the remainder of that month must be paid immediately. If the limit is repeatedly exceeded, scheme approval may be withdrawn, or a guarantee may be requested.

Administration

9470 Notice 101 para 5.8

Applications to use the scheme should be made on form SIVA 1 and sent to:
SIVA Approvals Team
Ruby House
8 Ruby Place
Aberdeen
AB10 1ZP

If HMRC **approves** an application, it will notify the trader of the agreed deferment account limit.

B. Suspensive arrangements

9475 Payment of import VAT is suspended where goods are in transit, or placed in a suspensive regime, as summarised in the following table:

Type of arrangement	Details	¶¶
In transit	External transit	¶9476
	Internal transit	
Suspensive regimes	Customs warehouses	¶9483
	Free zones	¶9495
	Temporary importation	¶9509
	Inward processing relief	¶9520
	Processing under Customs control	¶9533
	End-use relief for goods used on the continental shelf	¶9545

Goods in transit

9476 Notice 702/9 para 9

Import VAT may be suspended **until** imported goods arrive at their final destination in the EU. This means import VAT becomes payable in the UK if the goods are released into free circulation in the UK.

This relief has two forms: external transit and internal transit.

External transit goods	Internal transit goods
Non-EU goods which have not been released into free circulation	Goods moved between two EU member states via a third country
EU goods in transit to or via a European Free Trade Area country [1], which are destined for export outside the EU, under an EU measure (such as the Common Agricultural Policy)	Goods in transit to, from or between the EU special territories [2], except for direct movements between the UK and the Channel Islands Goods in transit to or from Andorra or San Marino

Note:
1. The **European Free Trade Area** countries are Norway, Switzerland, Iceland and Liechtenstein.
2. The **EU special territories** are:
- Aland Islands (Finland);
- Canary Islands (Spain);
- Channel Islands (UK);
- Guadeloupe;
- French Guyana;
- Martinique;
- Reunion (all France); and
- Mount Athos - also known as Agion Poros (Greece).

1. General principles

Import VAT is not payable while imported goods remain in a suspensive regime but becomes payable when the goods are removed into free circulation in the UK. 9478 Notice 702/9 paras 2 and 3

However, if there is an **onward supply** (¶9439) of unprocessed or unaltered goods to another EU member state, import VAT is not payable, even if the goods enter free circulation in the UK before being sent to the other state.

MEMO POINTS 1. Importers who wish to **use more than one suspensive regime** can apply for integrated authorisation in order to avoid having to make multiple applications.
2. Where the importer holds an **ATA carnet** voucher booklet issued by a chamber of commerce or industry, import procedures can be simplified. For imports where temporary importation relief (¶9509) or inward processing relief (¶9520) applies, the vouchers replace the normal Customs declarations.

Comment Importers may find it **beneficial to use a suspensive regime** where they: 9479
- wish to defer payment of import VAT on stock which is not for immediate use;
- may experience difficulty or a delay in meeting import licensing requirements or other conditions;
- wish to delay having a customs treatment applied to the goods;
- want to re-export non-EU goods, in which case import VAT will not be payable; or
- wish to discharge another customs procedure, such as inward processing relief, without exporting the goods.

Security

Security is only **required** for goods where: 9481
- temporary importation relief applies (¶9509); or
- inward processing relief applies and the goods are considered to be high risk (¶9529).

In these cases security must be **provided** by a cash deposit or a guarantee from a recognised provider, such as a bank.

However, where the importer holds an **ATA carnet** (¶9478), security is not required because payment of the import VAT is guaranteed. In this case import VAT will not be payable, provided that re-export takes place before the expiry of the carnet.

Records

Where a business **claims relief** from import VAT, it must keep records which show: 9482 Notice 702/9 para 10
- the type of goods imported;
- any processes which are carried out; and
- how the products or any unprocessed goods are disposed of.

Normal commercial records will contain most of these details but some adaptation may be necessary to show information required to support particular claims.

Records must be **preserved** for 4 years after the expiry of authorisation to use a suspension or relief regime.

2. Customs warehouses

A customs warehouse can be either a public or a private warehouse. 9483 Notice 232

MEMO POINTS 1. **Public** warehouses are operated by authorised warehousekeepers whose business is the storage of other traders' goods. These are suitable for traders who do not have their own storage premises, only store goods infrequently, or who do not wish to assume the responsibilities of a warehousekeeper.
2. **Private** warehouses are for the storage of goods by an individual trader who is authorised as a warehousekeeper. There are three types of private warehouse:
a. a **basic private** warehouse, where authorisation applies to a defined location, which can be the whole or part of the premises in question;

b. an **alternative private** warehouse, which is suitable for traders who mainly import goods for free circulation in the UK; and
c. an **authorised system** i.e. an inventory system, where authorisation applies to a business and its accounting and stock control systems. Goods may be stored at any notified site or facility belonging to the authorised trader. This is also known as a "Type E" warehouse.

---

a. Users

9484 Imported goods may be stored in a customs warehouse. Import VAT is not payable until the goods are removed into free circulation in the UK.

Excluded goods

9486 Notice 232 para 1.17 The following types of goods cannot be stored in a customs warehouse:
a. meat, meat products and other goods subject to the veterinary checks regime, unless the required import licence and/or health certificate have been presented and veterinary checks have been completed at the frontier;
b. most other non-Community goods which are **subject to prohibitions** or restrictions applicable at the EU frontier, unless necessary supporting documents have been presented; and
c. goods liable to **excise duty**, **unless** the warehouse is additionally authorised as an excise warehouse, or the duty is paid before entering the goods to the warehouse.

SI 1995/2518 reg 145K MEMO POINTS 1. As an **anti-avoidance** measure, a supply of goods imported into the UK that would otherwise fall within the warehoused goods regime will be treated as taking place in the UK if it is made by:
– a taxable supplier (or a supplier that would be so taxable were it not for these provisions) whose business (in whole or in part) consists of supplying such goods to persons for **retail**; and
– the goods are supplied to **non-taxable recipients**, either as a direct retail sale or to be sold on by the recipient through retail.
2. Excise warehousing is a separate regime for the deferment of excise duty, which is outside the scope of *VAT Memo*.

Eligible goods

9487 Notice 232 para 1.16 **EU goods** released to free circulation which are eligible for Common Agricultural Policy refunds on export can be stored within a customs warehouse.

The following **non-EU goods** can also be stored, being those:
– liable to customs duty (¶9405) and/or VAT;
– not subject to the full rate of customs duty (¶9405) but liable to import VAT;
– for which necessary supporting documents are not available at the time of import;
– imported to another suspensive regime and warehoused for export from the EU;
– for processing under Customs control (¶9533); and
– in free circulation subject to a claim under the rejected imports arrangements (¶9450).

Storage

9489 Certain **conditions** apply to the storage of goods:

Condition	Details
Entering the goods for storage	The goods to be stored must be specified in a declaration and must be sent directly to the warehouse
Period of storage	Goods may be stored for an unlimited period, unless the goods are pre-financed, in which case there is generally a limit of 6 months
Permitted sales	Sales of goods which remain in the warehouse are ignored for VAT purposes Retail sales are not permitted, except for sales to: – travellers to third countries; and – special visitors (¶9455)

Payment

The **person liable** to pay the import VAT is normally the person who removes the goods from the customs warehousing regime. 9490 Notice 702/9 para 4.5

The **amount liable** to import VAT is the value of the goods for customs purposes, including:
- all incidental expenses such as commission, packing and transport and insurance costs up to the time of removal from the warehouse;
- all incidental costs resulting from transport to another destination in the UK or EU, if the place is known when the goods are removed from the warehouse;
- storage and handling charges; and
- any customs levy, duty, excise duty or other charges payable on removal from the warehouse.

MEMO POINTS If the actual quantity of warehoused goods is lower than the recorded amount, the **deficiency** is deemed to have been removed from the customs warehousing regime.

b. Customs warehousekeepers

Warehousekeepers are **responsible** for: 9492 Notice 232 para 1.19
- the security and proper control of warehoused goods, including maintaining stock records and accounting for any shortage;
- ensuring that the conditions of their authorisation and all obligations are met;
- fully co-operating with HMRC in its supervision of the authorisation; and
- allowing HMRC access to the premises, records and goods at all reasonable times.

Obtaining authorisation

Before HMRC authorises any customs warehouse it must be satisfied that the following **conditions** are met: 9493 Notice 232 para 2
- the applicant is established in the EU;
- the warehouse is intended to be used primarily for the storage of goods;
- there is a genuine economic need for such facilities (either sufficient potential trade for a public warehouse to be viable, or enough benefits to the applicant for a private warehouse); and
- HMRC has appropriate resources to oversee the setting up of the customs warehouse and carry out the necessary checks on the warehousekeeper's control systems and records, and on the goods stored.

If HMRC has any reason to doubt that the applicant will be able to comply with these conditions, it can deny approval.

MEMO POINTS Applicants who wish to operate an **authorised system** (¶9483) must also meet the following **additional requirements**:
- the administration and organisation of the business must be sound and strictly managed;
- the company's accounts and stock controls must be robust and managed to ensure that all commercial transactions are properly handled and recorded;
- the system must be able to identify the location and quantity of a given item held under duty suspension at any stage;
- the applicant must have a good tax compliance record;
- an applicant who is already authorised to operate a customs warehouse must have a satisfactory record of operation;
- payment of duties must be secured by the deferment arrangements where simplified removal procedures are used;
- the accounting system must be authorised by HMRC; and
- any business changes affecting the warehousing arrangements, such as the structure, administration or accounting systems, must be notified to HMRC in advance.

3. Free zones

9495 s 100A CEMA 1979; SI 1984/1177 Free zones are designated areas in which imported goods are treated as if they were outside the EU.

Import VAT is not payable until the goods are removed for free circulation in the UK, or are used or consumed within the free zone.

There are currently only five free zones in the UK:
- Liverpool;
- Prestwick Airport;
- Port of Sheerness;
- Southampton; and
- Port of Tilbury.

a. Users

9497 Any importer can place any type of imported goods into a free zone, either directly on importation, or as a transfer from another suspensive arrangement (¶9475).

Conditions of use

9498 The **goods** to be placed in the free zone must be specified in a declaration; they only receive free zone status when they have been recorded in the free zone records and received a reference number.

Within the free zone

9500 Free zones are more flexible than customs warehouses, as goods can be **released for free circulation** within the free zone without the payment of import VAT, although customs duty must still be paid.

Any goods **used or consumed** in the free zone are subject to import VAT.

If goods are **destroyed** in the free zone, no import VAT is due, although HMRC should be informed of any intention to destroy, because VAT will be due on the value of any resulting scrap or waste which is sold in the EU.

MEMO POINTS If the actual quantity of goods held in a free zone is lower than the recorded amount, the **deficiency** is deemed to have been removed, so that import VAT is due on the amount in question.

Taking goods out of the free zone

9501 The usual rule is that on removal for free circulation in the UK, import VAT is due.

However, import VAT **is not payable** if:

a. goods are exported to a third country without having been removed for free circulation in the UK; or

b. non-EU goods are removed:

- to another EU member state without having been removed for free circulation in the UK; or
- for free circulation in the UK in the course of a zero-rated supply to another EU member state, where the conditions for onward supply relief (¶9439) are met.

9502 Notice 48 para 3.14 If the goods are **supplied to a UK customer**, output tax would normally be due on that supply.

If the customer is **VAT-registered**, it is possible to operate a concession to zero-rate the supply if the supplier and customer agree that the import VAT will be paid by the customer. This enables overseas businesses to trade in a free zone without registering for VAT. This concession can only be claimed once on the same goods.

EXAMPLE C Ltd is VAT-registered and purchases goods held in a free zone at a cost of £2,000 from D GmbH. C Ltd agrees to pay the import VAT of £400. (£2,000 x 20%)
The supply from D GmbH to C Ltd is zero-rated.

As a separate measure, where the **customer** is **not VAT-registered** and not liable to be registered, the import VAT may be reduced by the output tax charged on the supply to the customer. Evidence of payment of the output tax must be provided. 9504 SI 1984/1177 reg 27

EXAMPLE Mr E, who is not VAT-registered, purchases goods held in a free zone at a cost of £1,000 from F Ltd. F Ltd charges output tax of £200 on the supply. (£1,000 x 20%)
Mr E agrees to pay the related import VAT.
The import VAT is reduced to nil by the output tax charged.

b. Operators

Any person can apply for an area to be designated as a free zone, although prior authorisation is required from HMRC and security may be required. 9506

If approval is granted, the free zone status will last for a designated period. At the end of that period the operator can apply for redesignation.

Operators must ensure that the correct procedures are followed for the:
- entry of goods into the free zone;
- storage and any processing or destruction of goods in the free zone; and
- removal of goods from the free zone.

MEMO POINTS 1. The **conditions for approval** are that: 9507
- there is evidence that the free zone will be economically viable;
- the development plans include a firm timetable to bring the free zone into operation;
- the site is an identifiable area;
- the appropriate local authorities have no objections on planning or other grounds; and
- the free zone would not make unreasonable or uneconomic control demands on local HMRC staff.

2. The following **standard operating conditions** must be met:
- accommodation, facilities, and examination space and equipment must be provided for HMRC's use, free of charge;
- operations requiring HMRC's attendance should be scheduled for normal office hours;
- normal planning, pollution and health and safety regulations apply;
- prohibitions and restrictions on goods imported to or exported from a free zone apply; and
- stock records must be sufficiently detailed to identify the receipt, holding, handling and removal of goods entered to the free zone.

4. Temporary importation

For certain categories of imported goods, payment of import VAT by authorised importers (¶9515) may be suspended where the goods are to be re-exported within a specified period of up to 2 years. 9509 Notice 200

Import VAT will be payable if the goods remain in the UK after the temporary period, or are removed into free circulation in the UK instead of being re-exported. Notice 702/9

Eligible goods

All goods which do not exceed €10,000 in value and/or are imported occasionally for less than 3 months are eligible, provided that there is no economic effect. 9510 Notice 200 para 4

The following table lists the other specific types of goods which are eligible:

Category of goods		Details	Reference
Personal	Travellers' personal effects	Items reasonably required for a journey by any person temporarily entering the EU, not normally resident there	Notice 200 para 4.3
	Welfare material for seafarers	Goods used on a vessel or temporarily used by the crew offshore	Notice 200 para 4.5
Transport	Means of transport	Any form of road, rail, sea or inland waterway transport	Notice 308
	Aircraft and aircraft parts	Any civil aircraft, powered or not	Notice 28
	Containers and pallets	Must remain in same condition as when they were imported	Notice 306
	Packings	Must be: – identifiable at re-exportation; – re-exported by the same importer; and – if imported empty should be re-exported filled, or if imported filled can be re-exported empty or filled	Notice 200 para 4.14
Goods for sports purposes		Imported by any person temporarily entering the EU, not normally resident there	Notice 200 para 4.4
Medical and humanitarian	Medical, surgery and laboratory equipment	Loaned to a medical institution to meet an urgent short-term need	Notice 200 para 4.7
	Disaster relief material	Goods used within the EU by state bodies or bodies approved by competent authorities	Notice 200 para 4.6
Animals		Owned by a person established outside the EU For racehorses see ¶6216	Notice 200 para 4.8
Tourist publicity material		Used exclusively for publicity purposes	Notice 200 para 4.11
Educational material and scientific and professional equipment	Educational material and scientific equipment	Must be: – owned by a person established outside the EU; and – imported and used for educational or scientific purposes by a non-profit-making body (¶388)	Notice 200 para 4.13
	Professional equipment	Must be: – owned by a person established outside the EU; – imported either by a person established outside the EU or by an employee of the owner (who may be established in the EU); and – used by the importer or under the importer's supervision, except in cases of visual co-production	Notice 200 para 4.12

Category of goods		Details	Reference
Goods used in manufacture, production, repair or maintenance	Moulds, dies, drawings, measuring equipment and similar articles	Must be: – owned by a person established outside the EU; and – used in manufacturing by a person established in the EU. At least 75% of resulting production must be exported	Notice 200 para 4.15
	Special tools and instruments	Must be: – owned by a person established outside the EU; and – made available free to a person established in the EU for the manufacture of goods to be exported	Notice 200 para 4.16
	Temporary replacement means of production	Made temporarily available pending delivery or repair of similar goods	Notice 200 para 4.21
	Spare parts, accessories and equipment	Used to repair or maintain temporarily imported goods	Notice 200 para 4.26
Goods for promotion, sampling, testing or approval	Goods to carry out or subject to tests	Goods must not be modified, improved or tested to destruction	Notice 200 paras 4.17, 4.19
	Goods subject to satisfactory acceptance tests	Sales contract must contain provisions of the acceptance tests	Notice 200 para 4.18
	Goods for approval	Goods not qualifying as samples, which are to be sold after inspection	Notice 200 para 4.23
	Samples	Imported in reasonable quantities and shown only within the EU	Notice 200 para 4.20
	Sound, image or data carrying material	For presentation prior to sale, or free of charge	Notice 200 para 4.10
Goods for exhibitions or sale at an auction	Goods for exhibition or use at a public event	Event not purely for the purpose of selling imported goods	Notice 200 para 4.22
	Works of art, antiques and collectors' items	Imported for an exhibition and possible sale	Notice 200 para 4.24
	Second-hand goods	Imported with a view to their sale by auction	Notice 200 para 4.25
Other goods	Goods other than newly manufactured ones		Notice 200 para 4.25
	Other goods, or goods not complying with the conditions for total relief		Notice 200 para 4.27

Period of suspension

Generally, the **maximum** period is 2 years. but shorter periods apply in the following cases: 9512

Circumstances	Maximum period
Occasional imports of goods worth over €10,000	3 months
Imported goods subject to inspection by the importer	2 months
Imported goods subject to satisfactory acceptance tests by the importer	6 months
Goods which temporarily replace a means of production	

Entering goods into the regime

Authorisation is always required and goods must be declared on the SAD (¶9426), unless the declaration is oral or by any other act (¶9515). 9513 Notice 200 paras 2.5, 2.6

Security must normally be provided.

9515 Notice 200 para 3 **Authorisation** There are **seven types** of authorisation. Importers can have more than one type:

Type	Scope	Application	Duration
Full	Allows: – a series of imports to be covered; – import of goods subject to licensing restrictions; and – simplified transfer and security procedures	Form C&E 1331 must be completed and should be submitted to HMRC at least 1 month in advance	3 years
Integrated	Allows use of other suspensive arrangements and transfers between these arrangements	Form C&E 1331 must be completed and submitted to HMRC[1]	
Single Community	Allows: – goods to be transferred for the use of other named persons in other EU member states; – simplified entry procedures for regularly imported goods; and – simplified transfer procedures	Application should be made on form Annex 67 in the member state where the goods will be first used, at least 2 months in advance	
Simplified	Suitable for importers who will retain control of goods until re-export. Does not cover all goods. Each importation treated as a separate application	Application made on SAD (¶9426)	Period of suspension (¶9512)
Simplified Single Community	As for Single Community authorisation, except that authorisation is specific to each individual import declaration	Form INF 6 must be completed and submitted to the HMRC office where the goods were imported	
Oral	Can only be used for a very limited range of goods. Authorisation is specific to each individual import declaration	Supporting form C 108 must be completed and submitted to HMRC	
Declaration by any other act	Can only be used on each occasion for imports which are not worth more than €10,000 and consist of: – personal effects (any individuals); or – welfare materials for seafarers	Application, declaration and authorisation are deemed to take place by going through the green channel (or an equivalent) on importation	

Note:
1. If **integrated Single Community** authorisation is required as well, form Annex 67 should be completed in the member state where the goods will be first used.

9516 Authorised users are **responsible for**:
- providing the required security;
- correctly entering goods and completing SAD forms (¶9426);
- providing clear instructions on the procedures to agents, freight forwarders and others;
- correctly transferring goods;
- keeping records of all operations carried out under their approval;
- paying import VAT on goods entered into free circulation;
- notifying HMRC of amendments to their authorisation; and
- applying to renew authorisation.

9518 Notice 200 para 9 **Security** **Unless** an ATA carnet (¶9478) is held, it is necessary to provide security (¶9481) to cover the full amount of customs duty and import VAT due if the goods are not re-exported.

MEMO POINTS 1. **Regular importers** can provide a single guarantee, which HMRC will adjust accordingly.
2. For **works of art** and **second-hand goods** (¶1164), a reduced value can be provided.

5. Inward processing relief

Inward processing relief (IPR) is available for goods which are processed and then re-exported. Although technically there are two types of IPR, only suspension IPR affects import VAT, because it results in no import VAT being payable unless the goods are released into free circulation in the EU. The other relief (drawback) only affects customs duties. **9520** Notice 221

Comment The purpose of this relief is to help traders who process goods in the EU to compete in the global market on an equal footing.

Consequences

Import VAT will become payable on the value of the goods when they first entered IPR **unless** the goods are: **9521**

a. transferred to another suspensive arrangement (¶9475);
b. re-exported (including export via another EU member state); or
c. disposed of in one of the following ways:
- transferred to an approved use, such as export shops, armed forces, embassies, ships' stores or bunkers, or use as commissary stores or in-tray type meals;
- aircraft or aircraft parts or goods disposed of for satellite construction;
- use of aviation fuel for third country or intra-EU flights (excluding flights within the UK);
- exported to the continental shelf (outside territorial waters);
- sales to customers who take goods abroad in their baggage; or
- destroyed under HMRC supervision.

Period of suspension

The maximum period is 3 years, although: **9523** Notice 221 para 3.19
- **longer** periods may be approved where there are sound business reasons and it is common in particular industries; and
- **shorter** periods apply in the following cases:

Circumstances	Maximum period
Simplified authorisations (¶9526)	6 months[1]
Agricultural, dairy and meat products	3 months
Note: 1. Unless a different period is requested when applying.	

Entering goods into the regime

Authorisation is always required. Goods must be declared on the SAD (¶9426). **9524** Notice 221 para 1.6

Security is not normally requested, subject to certain exceptions.

Authorisation There are **four types** of authorisation. Importers can have more than one type. **9526** Notice 221 para 3

Type	Details	Application
UK	Allows: – frequent import and processing of goods in the UK; and – simplified procedures	Form C&E 810 must be completed and should be submitted to HMRC at least 1 month in advance
Simplified	Allows occasional import and processing of goods in the UK. Does not cover agricultural or fish products where the value of goods entered for IPR exceeds €150,000 per item in a calendar year	Application is made on form C 101 at the time when entering the goods into IPR

Type	Details	Application
Single Union	Allows goods to be processed in other EU member states	Application should be made on form Annex 67 at least 2 months in advance in the member state where: – the importer's main accounts are held; and – at least part of the processing will be carried out
Integrated	Allows use of other suspensive arrangements and transfers between these arrangements	Form C&E 810 must normally be completed and submitted to HMRC[1]

Note:
1. If **integrated Single Community** authorisation is required as well, form Annex 67 should be completed in the member state where the goods will be first used.

9527 Notice 221 para 2.11

Authorised users are **responsible for**:
- providing the required security, if necessary;
- correctly entering goods and completing SAD (¶9426) forms;
- providing clear instructions on the procedures to agents, freight forwarders and others;
- correctly transferring goods;
- keeping records of all operations carried out under their approval;
- paying import VAT on goods entered into free circulation;
- making the required returns by the due date;
- notifying HMRC of amendments to their authorisation; and
- applying to renew authorisation.

9529 Notice 221 para 3.21

Security It is not normally necessary to provide security.

However, security (¶9481) will be required if an ATA carnet (¶9478) is not held and the trader either:
- imports **higher risk** goods (see table below); or
- **repeatedly fails** to meet its obligations (¶9527).

Notice 221 para 20.7

Higher risk goods	Details	Minimum quantity
Live animals and meat	Meat and edible offal of domestic chicken	3,000 kg
Sugar	Cane or beet sugar and chemically pure sucrose in solid form	7,000 kg
Alcohol	Undenatured ethyl alcohol	2,500 litres
	Spirits and liquors	500 litres
Tobacco	Cigarettes	35,000
	Smoking tobacco	35 kg

Reporting requirements

9531 **Suspension returns** detailing goods received and disposed of must be submitted to HMRC within 30 days of the date of disposal of goods, or the end of the agreed period for processing and re-export. Nil returns must be submitted where applicable.

Submissions are made on a monthly or quarterly basis, depending on the type of authorisation granted.

6. Processing under Customs control

9533 Notice 237

Processing under Customs control (PCC) is available to authorised EU persons who import goods for processing and subsequent sale in the EU.

Import VAT is suspended until the finished goods are released into free circulation in the EU. The value on which import VAT is then payable is the value of the finished products, including customs duty. The suspension is therefore only **of benefit** where the rate of duty applicable to the processed goods is less than that applicable to the imported goods.

Comment The purpose of this relief is to encourage processing in the EU by allowing duty to be paid at the rate applicable to finished products, rather than the higher rates applicable to raw materials.

Who can use PCC?

PCC is available to a person who is normally **resident** in the EU, or a business with a permanent establishment in the EU (¶9688+), provided that: 9534
- the imported goods can be identified in the processed products;
- it would not be economically viable to restore the processed goods to their original condition; and
- use of PCC enables processing activity to be created or maintained in the EU without harming the essential interests of EU producers of similar goods.

Period of suspension

The importer should request the desired period when applying for authorisation 9536

A **fixed** period of 6 months is normally allowed for simplified authorisations, although this can be **extended** on request.

Entering goods into the regime

Authorisation is always required and goods must be declared on the SAD (¶9426). 9537 Notice 237 para 2.2

Security is not normally requested.

Authorisation Authorisation is normally granted for a **maximum period** of 3 years. 9539 Notice 237 para 3

There are **four types** as follows:

Type	Details	Application
UK	Allows: – regular processing in the UK; and – simplified procedures	Form C&E 1321 must be completed and submitted to HMRC
Simplified	Allows occasional processing of goods in the UK	Application is made using form C 107 at the time when goods are to enter PCC
Single Community	Allows goods to be processed in other EU member states	Application should be made in the member state where: – the importer's main accounts are held; and – at least part of the processing will be carried out, at least 2 months in advance
Integrated	Allows use of other suspensive arrangements and transfers between these arrangements	Form C&E 1321 must normally be completed and submitted to HMRC[1]

Note:
1. If **integrated Single Community authorisation** is required, application should be made in the member state where:
- the importer's main accounts are held; and
- at least part of the processing will be carried out, at least 2 months in advance.

Authorised users are **responsible for**: 9540
- providing the required security;
- correctly entering goods and completing SAD (¶9426) forms;

- providing clear instructions on the procedures to agents, freight forwarders and others;
- correctly transferring goods;
- keeping records of all operations carried out under their approval;
- paying import VAT on goods entered into free circulation;
- making the required returns by the due date;
- notifying HMRC of amendments to their authorisation; and
- applying to renew authorisation.

9541 Notice 237 para 3.15

Security It is not normally necessary to provide security.

However, in some circumstances (such as where a trader wishes to begin processing **before an application is approved**), it may be requested, in the form of a cash deposit or banker's guarantee.

Reporting requirements

9543 Notice 702/9 para 7

Returns of goods imported for processing and the processed products must be submitted to HMRC within 30 days of the date of disposal of goods, or the end of the agreed period for processing and re-export. Nil returns must be submitted where applicable.

Submissions are made on a monthly or quarterly basis, depending on the type of authorisation granted; this may be on form C&E 1325 or a company letterhead.

7. End-use relief

9545 SI 1995/2518 reg 120; Notice 702/9 para 5; Notice 770 para 11.8

End-use relief is available on the importation of goods which are to be **used** for certain purposes **on the continental shelf**. Import VAT will become payable if the goods cease to be used for a qualifying purpose.

MEMO POINTS 1. This relief **covers**:
- offshore fixed drilling or production platforms and floating or submersible drilling or production platforms, irrespective of whether they are within or outside UK territorial waters; and
- pipes, cables and connection pieces linking production platforms to the mainland.

2. The **qualifying purposes** are:
- incorporation in offshore drilling or production platforms/workpoints for the purpose of their construction, repair, maintenance, fitting out or conversion;
- equipping those platforms/workpoints;
- downhole well construction;
- subsequent shipment to a platform/workpoint and testing before use; or
- training, provided that the goods are shipped to a platform/workpoint at the end of the programme.

SECTION 2

Exported goods

9565 VAT is a tax on goods which are used or consumed in the EU (¶9002).

Therefore no VAT charge generally arises when goods are exported for use or consumption outside the EU.

A. General principles

9570 It is important to understand when an export takes place and who is making the supply.

1. Exports

Definition

An export is defined as the removal of goods from the UK to a place outside the EU and can either be direct or indirect. **9572** s 30 VATA 1994; SI 1995/2518 reg 129; Notice 703 para 2

MEMO POINTS Although the **Isle of Man** (¶9408) has its own VAT authority, sales to the Isle of Man are treated like a supply within the UK.

Direct and indirect exports are summarised as follows: **9573** Notice 703 paras 2.10, 2.11

Type of export	Custody of goods	Who transports/collects goods
Direct	From supplier to customer outside the EU	Supplier[1], so customer has no use of goods before they leave UK
Indirect	From supplier to custody of customer before going outside the EU	The customer (an overseas person)[1,2]

Note:
1. The supplier can appoint an **agent** to act on its behalf.
2. An **overseas person** is either:
- a non-UK-resident person;
- a trader who has no establishment in the UK (¶9688+) - although (since 1 October 2013) the trader can be registered for VAT in the UK; or
- an overseas authority.

UK VAT liability

In general, the export of goods is **treated** as taking place in the UK and therefore will be treated as a taxable supply (¶2647), albeit normally zero-rated. **9575** Notice 703 para 3.7

If any general (¶9582) or specific (¶9594) **conditions** for zero-rating are **not met**, VAT must be charged on an export at the appropriate UK rate (¶9416), unless the supply is non-taxable.

MEMO POINTS 1. Any **deposit or progress payment** received is an advance part payment towards the total cost of the supply and has the same VAT liability as the final supply.
2. Where goods are accidentally **lost, destroyed or stolen** before export and they were originally provided for:
- direct export, no VAT need be accounted for, provided that evidence of loss, destruction or theft is held - for example, an insurance claim, police investigation, etc; or
- indirect export, VAT must be accounted for if the goods have been delivered to or collected by the overseas person, or that person's agent, in the UK.

Non-taxable supplies There is no need to account for UK VAT in respect of the following supplies, although **evidence** of export (¶9586) must still be obtained and kept: **9576** Notice 703 para 2.14
- goods supplied and **installed** outside the EU;
- the transfer of a **supplier's own goods** to a place outside the EU;
- goods exported **temporarily** for exhibitions, processing, etc; and
- goods exported on a **sale or return** basis.

Any **returns** of goods to the UK must be declared.

2. Exporter

Definition

An exporter is a person who supplies goods to an overseas person (¶9573) and those goods are exported outside the EU by either the supplier or customer. **9578** Notice 703 paras 2.3, 2.5

In both cases, any person arranging such a transaction is also an exporter.

Use of agents

9579 An agent, such as a freight forwarder, airline or shipping company, may be **appointed by** either the exporter or the customer.

The agent will handle the export transaction and produce the necessary declarations (¶9426) to HMRC. It must be provided with full information on the goods to enable it to do so and it must take reasonable steps to ensure **compliance** with all export formalities.

If the agent **fails to comply** with any requirements, the exporter is responsible for payment of any resulting VAT liability.

B. Zero-rated exports

9581 The export of most goods can be zero-rated, provided that certain general qualifying conditions are met. This means that input tax relating to costs incurred in making the export supply can be recovered, subject to the normal rules (¶1800+).

Exports by charities are also specifically zero-rated.

For particular goods and types of supply (¶9594), specific additional qualifying conditions apply.

MEMO POINTS 1. Zero-rating extends to the:
- **transport** of goods to a destination outside the EU (¶9790);
- supply of an **intermediary's services** in arranging the export of any goods (¶7126); and
- **work on goods** specifically acquired for export (¶9796).

Sch 8 Group 15 item 3 VATA 1994 2. Any goods exported by a **charity** will be zero-rated, provided that proof of export is obtained (¶9586). The export is treated as a supply made by the charity in the UK, in the course of a business. The charity is therefore able to reclaim any VAT paid on both the purchase of the goods and any overheads of exporting them. For further details of charities see ¶8000+.

1. General qualifying conditions

9582 Notice 703 para 3 To qualify for zero-rating goods must be exported within a certain period after the time of supply and the exporter must obtain and keep evidence of the export.

MEMO POINTS 1. A direct export (¶9573) to a customer which is a **permanent establishment** of a UK VAT-registered company may be zero-rated where the overseas delivery address is shown on the invoice. This applies even if the invoice is addressed or sent to the associated UK office, or a UK Shared Service Centre for administrative reasons.

Notice 703 para 4.1 2. Where there are **two or more suppliers** in a supply chain, only the final supply for export qualifies for zero-rating.

EXAMPLE A Inc, based in the USA, orders goods from B Ltd in the UK. B Ltd purchases the goods from C Ltd in the UK but requests C Ltd to send the goods direct to A Inc.
The supply by B Ltd to A Inc may be zero-rated but the supply by C Ltd to B Ltd is a normal UK supply and C Ltd must account for VAT accordingly.

Scope

9584 The normal **valuation** rules (¶925+) apply to most goods, except for:
- second-hand goods, works of art, antiques and collectors' items (¶1164); and
- computer software.

Notice 703 para 4.5 MEMO POINTS The treatment of exported **computer software** depends on whether the software is mass-produced or bespoke:

Nature of software	Treatment
Normalised[1]	The whole export is treated as an export of goods Zero-rating applies to the whole value of the supply, including the value of the information
Software transmitted by telephone or other data network and specific items, including: – items made to customers' own requirements, either as unique programs or adaptations from standard programs; – inter-company information, data and accounts; – enhancements and updates of existing specific programs; and – enhancements and updates of existing mass-produced programs supplied under contractual obligation to customers who bought the original program	The whole export is treated as an export of services (see ¶9680+)
Note: 1. See ¶9421 for a full description.	

Removal of goods

The **time limit** for removing goods from the EU and obtaining evidence of export is **normally** 3 months from the time of supply, which is the earlier of the dates on which: 9585 Notice 703 para 3.5
- goods are sent to or removed by the customer; or
- full payment is received for the goods.

However, where the export is:
- to a UK-resident third party for **consolidation, processing or incorporation with other goods** which are then exported direct to an overseas person (¶9573), the deadline is 6 months from the time of supply; or
- of a **racehorse** (¶6216), the limit is 6 months from the time of supply, with the possibility of an extension to 12 months.

Evidence

Evidence of export must clearly **identify** the supplier, the customer, the goods, an accurate value, export destination and the mode and route of transport. 9586 Notice 703 para 6

For the specific types of acceptable evidence where goods are sent by **post, airmail, parcel post or courier** see ¶9088.

The burden of proof depends on whether the supplier arranges the export.

Supplier arranges the export Either **official** or **commercial** evidence will be acceptable but each must be supported by **supplementary** evidence that the transaction has taken place and relates to the goods in question. 9587

The following table lists the types of evidence which will be satisfactory:

Type of evidence	Satisfactory form
Official	Goods Departed Message generated by the New Export System[1]
	Single Administrative Document (¶9426) endorsed by HMRC on export
	Electronic confirmation produced by the New Computerised Transit System[2]
Commercial	Authenticated seaway bill or airway bill
	Consignment note
	Bill of lading
	Certificate of shipment

Type of evidence	Satisfactory form
Supplementary	Customer order
	Sales contract
	Correspondence
	Copy sales invoice
	Advice note
	Packing list
	Insurance and freight charges documentation
	Evidence of payment and/or receipt of goods overseas

Note:
1. The **New Export System** is a system used by freight agents, importers and exporters to declare import or export entries electronically.
2. The **New Computerised Transit System** is an EU- and EFTA-wide electronic declaration and processing system.

9588 HMRC Brief 61/07 The CJEU has confirmed that where a **supplier acts in good faith** and submits evidence of removal, the member state cannot hold the supplier to account for the VAT on those goods if the information relied upon subsequently proves to be false. However, the supplier should take every reasonable care to avoid being involved in tax evasion. *Teleos plc and others v HMRC* [2007]

HMRC states that this judgment limits its ability to assess for tax once it has accepted the documentary evidence that appears to support the zero-rating. However, it is not contrary to EU law to **require the supplier** to take every reasonable step to satisfy itself that the transaction is not part of an attempted tax evasion.

EXAMPLE The Upper Tribunal has explained the effect of the *Teleos* decision in practical terms. Here a company claimed to have exported goods. HMRC did not accept that the evidence produced in support of the company's claim to zero-rate these supplies was adequate. The First-tier Tribunal (FTT) found in three instances that the evidence was adequate to support such a claim. On appeal HMRC argued that the goods had not in any case been exported.
The Upper Tribunal said that was not relevant:
"We accept that HMRC's case necessarily carried with it the argument that there was no proof of export. But, as we described earlier, the question for the FTT was not whether the goods had been exported - it is clear from *Teleos* that to require a taxable person conclusively to prove such a matter would be incompatible with the correct and straightforward application of the zero-rating in this respect - but whether Arkeley had obtained sufficient evidence of export within the 3-month time limit. Even if the goods had not in fact been exported, then absent an allegation that the supplier had not acted in good faith, or knew or should have known of fraud connected with the transaction, that would remain the sole question for the tribunal. The FTT's reference to there having been no suggestion that the goods had not been exported, although that may have misunderstood the effect of HMRC's case, could not undermine the decision of the FTT on the question of the sufficiency of the documentary evidence."
To summarise, then, if a trader claims to have exported goods and produces adequate evidence of that export within 3 months, the supply is properly zero-rated. If it subsequently transpires that the goods were not exported, zero-rating will stand unless the trader knew, or should have known, that the goods were not in fact exported. If a decision has to be made after all the facts are known, whether the goods were actually exported is not relevant - the question is merely whether, in the absence of knowledge of fraud, the evidence of export was, at the time of the claim, adequate to support zero-rating. *HMRC v Arkeley Ltd* [2013]

9589 Notice 703 para 6.6 **Supplier does not arrange the export** Of necessity, the standard of evidence is high and could also include (**in addition** to the items listed at ¶9587), for example:
- a written order from the customer showing where the goods are to be shipped from and to;
- documents showing the date of departure of the goods from the UK; and
- the name and address of the haulier taking the goods outside the UK.

Comment The **exporter is liable** for payment of any VAT and so may wish to:
- include the provision of satisfactory evidence as a term of the sales contract; or
- request a deposit from the customer, which can be refunded after provision of the evidence.

Failure to meet conditions

Goods not exported or evidence not received in time If the goods are not exported, or evidence is not received in time, the **supplier** must account for VAT as if the supply had been made in the UK and its VAT records must be amended by making an entry equal to the tax on the supplies concerned on the "VAT Payable" side of the VAT account (¶2820). This amount must also be included in box 1 of the VAT return (¶2985) for the VAT period in which the relevant time limit expires. **9591** Notice 703 para 3.5

If the goods are **subsequently exported**, **or** the supplier subsequently **receives the evidence**, it can then zero-rate the supply and adjust the VAT account for the period in which the conditions were met.

Goods incorrectly zero-rated as exports Goods incorrectly zero-rated as exports are **subject to** forfeiture and any VAT that would have been payable is due from the recipient (although HMRC may wholly or partly waive payment). **9592** s 30(10) VATA 1994

2. Specific qualifying conditions

Specific additional conditions apply for the zero-rating of the following supplies: **9594**

Notice 703 paras 4 and 7

Type of supply	Details	¶¶
Particular goods	Motor vehicles	¶9595
	Tools for the manufacture of goods for export	¶9597
	Freight containers	¶9598
Supplies covered by special schemes	Retail export scheme	¶9603
	Personal export scheme	¶9609
	Sailaway boat scheme	¶9616
Goods for retail sale or use as stores	Tax-free shops	¶9624
	Regimental shops	¶9625
	Goods supplied as stores or retail merchandise	¶9627
Goods for export after processing		¶9630
Supplies to recipients on the continental shelf [1]		
Supplies to UK government departments [2]		
Supplies to overseas authorities [3]		

Note:
1. A supply of goods to recipients on the **continental shelf** (either direct or through an agent) for sale on installations situated more than twelve nautical miles from the UK coastline can only be zero-rated if:
– a written order for the goods is obtained from a responsible person on the installation to which the goods are to be sent; and
– a signed receipt is obtained within 3 months of the time of supply.
2. Goods ordered by **British embassies, High Commissions and diplomats** outside the EU may be zero-rated if both of the following conditions are met:
– the supplier must be able to provide evidence of the destination of the goods; and
– a receipt must be obtained within 3 months of the time of supply.
For other government departments, only direct exports (¶9573) may be zero-rated.
3. Goods ordered by **overseas embassies, High Commissions or purchasing agents** in the UK may be zero-rated if both of the following conditions are met:
– the supplier must keep a separate record of each transaction, including evidence of supply to an overseas authority; and
– the goods are not used before being exported.

a. Particular goods

Motor vehicles

The export of any new or second-hand motor vehicle may be zero-rated if supplied as: **9595** Notice 703 para 4.13
– a **direct export** (¶9573), provided that it is not used or delivered in the EU before export;

– an **indirect export** (¶9573), provided that it is not used before export, except for the trip to the place of departure from the EU; or
– a sale to a **private individual** under the personal export scheme (¶9609), where the vehicle is to be used before being exported.

Tools for the manufacture of goods for export

9597 Sch 8 Group 13 VATA 1994; Notice 701/22

The supply to an overseas body, trader, etc, of tools to be used in the UK solely for the manufacture of goods for export may be zero-rated.

The specific conditions are that the:
a. customer is not a taxable person, government of an EU member state, or a body established in another EU member state;
b. customer **specifically asks** the supplier to make or buy the tools for the customer; and
c. supplier uses the tools to manufacture goods for the same customer and makes a specific charge for doing so.

In addition to holding normal commercial **evidence** of export (¶9586), the supplier must obtain a signed statement from the customer that it is neither registered nor required to be registered in the UK and is not an authority, body or trader in another EU member state.

MEMO POINTS 1. **Common examples** of tools include jigs, moulds and punches.
2. A **taxable person** is defined as someone who is required or liable to be VAT-registered in the UK (¶2620).

Freight containers

9598 SI 1995/2518 regs 117, 128; Notice 703/1

The supply of freight containers for **direct export** (¶9573) is zero-rated, provided that the normal conditions for export are satisfied (¶9582+).

A supply for **indirect export** may similarly be zero-rated, provided that the supplier obtains a written undertaking from the customer that:
a. the container will be exported outside the EU;
b. the customer will keep sufficient records to satisfy HMRC of export; and
c. it will not be used within the EU, except for:
– a single domestic journey before export on which inland freight may be carried between two points within the UK; and/or
– international movements of goods.

MEMO POINTS 1. A freight container is **defined** as an article of transport equipment (lift-van, moveable tank or other similar structure) with an internal volume of at least 1 cubic metre, which is:
– fully or partially enclosed to constitute a compartment intended for containing goods;
– of a permanent character and accordingly strong enough to be suitable for repeated use;
– specially designed to facilitate the carriage of goods, by one or more means of transport, without intermediate reloading;
– designed for ready handling, particularly when being transferred from one mode of transport to another; and
– designed to be easy to fill and to empty.
2. A **single domestic journey** is allowable only if the route brings the container reasonably directly from the point of supply to the place where it is to be loaded with the export cargo, or exported.
3. **International movements** of goods may include a journey within the UK for the purpose of loading or unloading the goods.

9600 Zero-rating also extends to:
– the **hire or lease** of such containers;
– any **incidental charges** (for example, charges for delivery, or an option to terminate the lease at an earlier date); and
– **works on** such containers (for example, repair work).

b. Special schemes

9601 The following special export schemes remove the VAT burden on certain non-EU persons acquiring particular goods:

- **retail** export scheme;
- personal export scheme, which applies to **motor vehicles**; and
- sailaway **boat** scheme.

Retail export scheme

This voluntary scheme essentially allows a VAT-registered retailer to zero-rate certain goods supplied to eligible customers, for export to a place outside the EU. **9603** SI 1995/2518 reg 131; Notice 704

Goods supplied under this scheme are initially subject to VAT in the usual manner. Subsequently, when the supplier receives evidence of export from the customer, it can refund the VAT charged and zero-rate the supply.

Eligible goods The scheme can be operated on all standard-rated (¶1095) and reduced-rated (¶1110) goods, with the **exclusion** of: **9604** Notice 704 paras 2.6 - 2.8
- goods purchased by mail order or online;
- motor vehicles for personal export (¶9609);
- goods over £600 in value (excluding VAT) exported for the customer's business purposes;
- sailaway boats (¶9616);
- goods that will be exported as freight or unaccompanied baggage;
- supplies to special visitors (¶9455);
- goods requiring an export licence (although antiques are eligible);
- unmounted gemstones; and
- bullion over 125g, 2.75 troy ounces or 10 Tolas.

Retailers can **optionally exclude** any types of goods to which they do not wish the scheme to apply.

MEMO POINTS An **export licence** may be needed for any goods including:
- animals and animal products;
- certain plant produce;
- endangered species (including their parts or derivatives); and
- cultural goods.

Eligible customers The scheme is available to non-EU visitors and certain entitled EU residents. **9606** Notice 704 para 2.4

In all cases the individual must:
- intend to leave the EU by the end of the 3rd month after the month in which the goods were purchased; and
- produce the goods, relevant purchase receipts and the VAT refund document (¶9607) to an HMRC officer on departure from the EU.

Other **specific conditions** apply to each type of eligible person:

Type of customer	Description	Conditions
Non-EU visitor	A **traveller** (including a member of the crew of a ship or aircraft) whose domicile or habitual place of residence is outside the EU	To prove eligibility, a valid passport, identity card or other document such as a driving licence
	Overseas visitor entering the UK as student or migrant worker, who purchases the goods during the last 4 months of the UK visit	The following must be produced: – visa or work permit to prove eligibility; and – the goods, their receipts and the VAT refund document (¶9607) to an HMRC officer on departure from the EU
		Must remain outside the EU for at least 12 months

Type of customer	Description	Conditions
Entitled EU residents	A customer whose domicile or habitual place of residence is in the EU but who **intends to leave** the EU for a minimum period of 12 months	The following must be produced to an HMRC officer on departure from the EU: – evidence of intention to remain outside the EU for at least 12 months (for example, an overseas work or residency permit or visa application); and – the goods, relevant purchase receipts and the VAT refund document (¶9607)
		Must actually export the goods and remain outside the EU for at least 12 months

9607 Notice 704 para 3

Operating the scheme The **customer** must attend the shop at the time of sale, although a third party can pay for the goods. VAT is charged as normal at the time of sale.

The **supplier** must:
- check that the customer is eligible;
- check that the goods are eligible;
- complete a VAT refund document (normally form VAT 407);
- agree with the customer how the refund will be made;
- indicate on the customer's sales receipt that the goods have been included on a VAT refund document;
- give the customer a copy of Notice 704/1 and advise the customer to produce the refund document to HMRC for stamping when leaving the EU, and to return the stamped document to the supplier to enable the refund to be made; and
- on receipt of the stamped refund document, refund the VAT to the customer and zero-rate the sale.

Notice 704 para 5.7 MEMO POINTS 1. A **refund company** can be engaged by a retailer to administer the refunds. In this case, the retailer invoices the refund company as for a normal sale and the refund company then operates the scheme as described above.

Notice 704 paras 5.3, 5.8 2. Where a **retail** (¶6560+) **or margin** (¶6620+) **scheme** is in use, the rules for those schemes explain how they should be operated in conjunction with the retail export scheme.

Notice 704 para 8 3. **Cruise passengers** may be unable to access their goods in order to have their refund documents stamped until arrival at their final destination. Cruise operators are therefore authorised to produce a bulk refund document for all eligible goods costing less than £1,000 per item purchased by eligible customers.

Notice 704 para 5.9 4. **Auctioneers** who sell goods in their own name (¶7142) on behalf of retailers are treated as both receiving and making supplies of goods. If the retail export scheme is used, the supply by the:
- retailer to the auctioneer is standard-rated; and
- auctioneer to the customer is zero-rated, provided that a certified VAT refund document is received.

HMRC Briefs 17/14, 34/14 5. The retail export scheme is currently under review; a more efficient, electronic system is being developed.

Personal export scheme

9609 SI 1995/2518 regs 132, 133; Notice 707

This scheme allows a VAT-registered supplier to sell a motor vehicle free of VAT to an eligible customer, for export to a place outside the EU.

Unlike a supply which is a direct or indirect export (¶9573), the scheme allows the vehicle to be used before being exported.

Comment If a vehicle is **purchased outside the scheme** and VAT is paid, a refund cannot be obtained if it is later exported, even if it would have qualified under the scheme.
Customers should still obtain **insurance** for the full VAT-inclusive value of the vehicle, in case circumstances prevent a qualifying export.

Eligible goods The scheme may be used for the sale of **motor** vehicles, motor cycles and motor caravans (but not pedal cycles or trailer caravans). 9610 Notice 707 para 2.3

The scheme also covers any factory-fitted **accessories** which are included on the invoice at the time of sale.

Eligible customers The scheme is available to non-EU visitors and certain entitled EU residents 9612 Notice 707 paras 2.2, 3.3, 5

In all cases the individual must intend to leave and remain outside the EU with the motor vehicle for at least 6 months.

Other **specific conditions** apply to each type of eligible person:

Type of customer	Description	Conditions
Non-EU visitor	A customer who **has not been** in the EU for more than either: – 365 days in the 2 years before the date of applying to use the scheme; or – 1,095 days in the 6 years before the date of applying to use the scheme	The vehicle must be ordered not more than 15 months before intending to leave the EU The vehicle must be exported not more than 12 months after delivery
Entitled EU residents	A customer who **has been** in the EU for more than either: – 365 days in the 2 years before the date of applying to use the scheme; or – 1,095 days in the 6 years before the date of applying to use the scheme	Must order the vehicle not more than 9 months before intending to leave the EU Must export the vehicle not more than 6 months after delivery

Operating the scheme The **customer**: 9613 Notice 707 paras 3.4, 3.5, 6
- must personally take delivery and sign a receipt;
- may use the vehicle before it is exported;
- must not dispose or attempt to dispose of, pledge or hire the vehicle before leaving the EU; and
- must immediately inform HMRC of any change of circumstances.

MEMO POINTS **Use of the vehicle** includes:
- use by another person who is leaving the EU, provided that HMRC's approval is obtained;
- a temporary visit to another EU member state, provided that the vehicle is returned to the UK before the intended departure date, which must remain unchanged.

The **supplier** must: 9615 Notice 707 para 8
- only supply and invoice vehicles direct to the customer;
- check that the customer is eligible;
- zero-rate the invoice;
- give the customer a copy of Notice 707, paras 1 to 7 and an application form VAT 410;
- retain a signed receipt; and
- ensure that the form VAT 410 is correctly completed and sent to HMRC.

MEMO POINTS 1. Form VAT 410 should be sent to the following **address**:
Personal Transport Unit
Priory Court
St John's Road
Dover
CT17 9SH
2. If the vehicle is **not exported** within the relevant **time** limit (¶9612), any VAT which was not charged at the time of sale will become payable, even if the vehicle cannot be exported for an unavoidable reason, such as theft or an accident.

Sailaway boat scheme

This scheme allows a VAT-registered supplier to zero-rate the supply of a boat which is exported under its own power. 9616 Notice 703/2

Unlike a supply which is a direct export (¶9573), the scheme allows the boat to be used before being exported.

MEMO POINTS This scheme can no longer be used by a **UK resident** purchasing in the UK.

9618 Notice 703/2 para 1.8 **Eligible goods** The scheme may be used for the sale of any boat which is to be delivered to the purchaser or an authorised skipper and is then exported from the UK under its own power - for example, a yacht.

The scheme does not cover **parts or accessories** supplied with the boat, although such supplies may be zero-rated under the retail export scheme (¶9603).

9619 Notice 703/2 para 1.4 **Eligible customers** The scheme is available for non-commercial purchases by non-EU visitors and certain entitled EU residents.

The following **specific conditions** apply to each type of eligible person:

Type of customer	Description	Conditions
Non-EU visitor	A customer who **has not been** in the EU for more than either: – 365 days in the 2 years before the date of applying to use the scheme; or – 1,095 days in the 6 years before the date of applying to use the scheme	Intends to export the boat not more than 6 months after the date of delivery
Entitled EU residents	A customer who **has been** in the EU for more than either: – 365 days in the 2 years before the date of applying to use the scheme; or – 1,095 days in the 6 years before the date of applying to use the scheme	Intends to export the boat not more than 2 months after the date of delivery Boat must remain outside the EU for at least 12 months

9621 Notice 703/2 paras 2, 3 **Operating the scheme** The **customer** must:
- not dispose or attempt to dispose of, pledge or hire the boat before leaving the EU; and
- immediately inform HMRC of any change of circumstances.

9622 The **supplier** must:
- check that the customer is eligible;
- give the customer a copy of Notice 703/2 and an application form VAT 436; and
- ensure that the form VAT 436 is correctly completed and send it to the nearest HMRC office; and
- if the boat is to be exported directly, complete a Notice of Intended Departure form C 1331 and make the boat available for inspection by HMRC.

At the time of sale VAT is not charged.

However, if the stamped form VAT 436 is not received **within a month** of the date of export, the supplier must account for VAT. If evidence is subsequently received, the supplier can zero-rate the sale and adjust the VAT account for the period in which the evidence was received.

c. Goods for retail sale or use as stores

Supplies at tax-free shops

9624 Notice 48 para 9.1 A retailer is treated as an exporter and may zero-rate goods supplied to persons leaving the UK where:
- the person is to fly to a destination outside the EU; and
- the sale occurs at a tax-free shop which is approved by HMRC.

The retailer must **verify** that the traveller is departing directly to a non-EU destination and that the goods are to be exported.

Acceptable **evidence** may be obtained from boarding cards or travel documents. Large businesses may agree acceptable alternative evidence with HMRC.

Supplies to regimental shops

Supplies to a regimental shop **in advance of an overseas posting** may be zero-rated if all of the following conditions are met: **9625** Notice 703 para 4.10
– there must be a written order from the President of the Regimental Institute (PRI) stating that the regiment is about to take up an overseas posting and that the goods ordered will be exported from the EU;
– the goods must be delivered to the PRI ready packed for shipment no more than 48 hours before the regiment is due to leave; and
– the supplier must retain a certificate of receipt signed by the PRI which clearly identifies the goods, gives full shipment details and states the date on which they were exported from the EU.

Goods shipped as stores or retail merchandise

Goods supplied direct to ships, aircraft or hovercraft (vessels) for retail sale or as stores can be zero-rated, provided that: **9627** Notice 703 para 10
a. they are for **use** on a voyage or flight with a non-private purpose and with an eventual destination outside the UK;
b. the person they are **supplied to** is the end user (or a freight-forwarding company for onward delivery to the end user); and
c. the **supplier** must obtain:
– written confirmation that the goods are to be used solely for stores or retail sales on the vessel; and
– a receipt confirming delivery of the goods on board signed by the master, commander or other responsible officer of the vessel.

It should be noted that the CJEU has held that there is no requirement that goods for fuelling and provisioning of vessels should be actually **loaded on board** the vessel at the time of their supply to the operator. *Staatssecretaris van Financiën v Velker International Oil Co Ltd NV* [1990]

MEMO POINTS 1. Common **examples** of goods that fall within this provision include: **9628**
a. fuel; and
b. goods for:
– running repairs or maintenance (e.g. lubricants, spare and replacement parts);
– general use on board by the crew; and
– sale by retail to persons carried on voyages or flights who intend to use the stores on board only.
2. By concession, zero-rating applies to **marine fuel oil, kerosene or marked gas oil** supplied to ships for commercial voyages within UK territorial waters, provided that: Notice 48 para 9.2
– a written declaration is obtained from the recipient that the goods are for use as stores on a non-private voyage;
– a written order or confirmation is obtained from the master, owner or duly authorised agent of the ship declaring that the fuel is solely for use on a named ship;
– the fuel is sent direct to the ship, or addressed and delivered to the master of a named ship care of the shipping agent or line; and
– a receipt confirming delivery of the fuel on board, signed by the master or other responsible officer, is held.
This **concession does not apply** to petrol, derv or lubricating oil.
3. Where supplies are made **direct from a warehouse** not operated or owned by the supplier to an eligible vessel, the supplier must hold a signed and dated certificate of export from the warehousekeeper (e.g. the advice note issued by the warehousekeeper).
4. Where supplies are **delivered to the premises** of a shipping line or airline operator, VAT is charged in accordance with the normal rules and input tax is similarly recoverable but the onward transfer to the ship or aircraft is a not a supply.
5. Stores supplied under the above provisions and **relanded** in the UK are treated as imports.
6. **Mess and canteen stores** supplied to HM ships about to leave for a foreign port or a voyage outside the UK for more than 15 days can be zero-rated, provided that the goods are ordered for

general use on board by the ship's company. Zero-rating does not apply to duty-free goods that are supplied on a sale or return basis to a mess or canteen as stores.

d. Goods for export after processing

9630 Notice 703 para 3.6

A supply of goods to an overseas person (¶9573), for export after consolidation, processing or incorporation into other goods by a UK-resident (or EU-resident) third party, may be zero-rated if the goods are:

- only **delivered** (not supplied) to the third party;
- not to be **used** before export; and
- **exported** within 6 months of the time of supply.

The **supplier** must keep a record of each transaction (including the invoice number, description, quantity and value of the goods, names and addresses of the third party and overseas person, date by which goods must be exported and date of actual export).

CHAPTER 3

Supply of services

OUTLINE ¶¶

The rules to establish where a supply of services takes place are different from those for goods. This chapter looks at the basic place of supply rule for services and also the specific exceptions to that rule. 9680

Since 1 January 2010 a series of changes have been made to the European VAT system to bring into effect a partial move from an "origin" system to a "destination" system of taxation. This is commonly referred to as the "VAT package".

It is now established that the basic place of supply for **services** provided by businesses **to businesses** (B2B) is where the customer belongs. For supplies **to consumers** (B2C) the general place of supply rule continues to be where the supplier is established.

There are, however, several exceptions to those basic rules, including:
– short-term hiring of means of transport (place of supply is the place where the means of transport is put at the disposal of the customer); and
– intermediary services (place of supply is the place of supply of the underlying transaction).

MEMO POINTS The change to the general rule for B2B transactions is likely to have been an issue for businesses which receive services, such as administration or book-keeping services, from outside the EU. The place of supply for these services prior to 1 January 2010 was where the supplier belonged. Therefore if the supplier was outside the EU no VAT was charged. This was attractive to partly exempt (¶2070) businesses, as they did not incur any irrecoverable VAT on these services. With effect from 1 January 2010, the recipient has had to account for VAT on such services under the reverse charge procedure. This will have increased the cost of the services, as the partly exempt business will not have been able to recover all of the associated input tax.

SECTION 1

Place of supply basics

A. General rule

9682 s 7A VATA 1994 Subject to exceptions for some specified services (¶9744+), a supply of services is treated as made:

a. in the country in which the recipient belongs, where the recipient is a **relevant business person** - these are known as business-to-business (B2B) supplies and the reverse charge mechanism (¶9700) applies to this type of B2B cross-border supply, requiring the recipient to account for the VAT; and

b. in the country in which the supplier belongs in any other case - these are known as business-to-consumer (B2C) supplies.

The general rule for **services provided B2B** applies to the following cross-border supplies of services:
- valuation and work on goods;
- intermediary services;
- freight transport and ancillary transport services;
- long-term hire of a means of transport (more than 30 days, or more than 90 days for vessels);
- electronically supplied services by non-EU suppliers to EU business customers; and
- services previously treated as supplied where received (known as "Schedule 5 services" because they were listed in Schedule 5 to the VAT Act 1994) - these are now usually subject to the general rule (although see ¶9784 for the treatment of supplies of these services to non-business recipients).

This has resulted in an increase in the number of services that are **subject to the reverse charge** (¶9700), because most business services are taxed in the country where the recipient is established.

MEMO POINTS 1. Further changes involving **B2C supplies** have been introduced with effect from 1 January 2015 (see ¶9764 and ¶9768), changes having already been made in both 2010 and 2011.

2. For these purposes **the UK** includes the Isle of Man. Contrast this to the definition of the UK for the purposes of determining where a supply of goods takes place (¶278).

s 7A(3) VATA 1994 3. When determining the place of supply for a **right to a service**, the provider of the right is treated as providing the service and the place of supply is determined accordingly.

9683 There are **exceptions to the general rule**, including:
- services related to land (¶9714);
- services relating to cultural, artistic, sporting, scientific, educational, entertainment or similar activities (¶9742);
- restaurant and catering services, including those supplied on board ships, trains and aircraft as part of transport in the EU (¶9734 and ¶9752);

- valuation and work on goods (¶9754);
- passenger transport (¶9726);
- short-term hiring of means of transport (¶9736); and
- since 1 January 2015, telecommunications and radio and broadcasting services (¶9764), and electronically supplied services (¶9768).

In addition, use and enjoyment of some services overrides the basic rule (¶9758).

Relevant business persons

A relevant business person receives the services in question otherwise than for wholly private purposes and is: 9684 s 7A(4) VATA 1994
- a **taxable person** as defined in Article 9 of the VAT Directive (¶9997);
- registered for VAT in the UK;
- registered for VAT in any other member state; or
- registered for VAT in the Isle of Man.

Where a supply of services is made to a business customer who uses it **wholly for private purposes** or for the private purposes of staff, the supply is treated as a B2C supply.

Identifying the customer's status

Traders must be able to identify business customers and make **reasonable checks** to establish their status. In most cases business customers in other member states are able to supply a VAT number issued by their tax authority. HMRC states that this will normally be sufficient evidence of business status. 9686

If a business customer is **not VAT-registered** (for example, this may apply to businesses which make only exempt supplies), alternative evidence may be used, such as a letter from the tax authority or a Chamber of Commerce.

Where customers cannot **provide evidence** that they are in business, or a trader has concerns about whether the evidence relates to its customer, HMRC's advice is that they should be treated as non-business customers. If adequate evidence is subsequently provided, the VAT accounting of the service can be changed.

If a customer is engaged in **both business and non-business** activities (for example, a charity or government department), supplies to that customer are treated as B2B supplies in relation to the place of supply and the general rule therefore applies.

EXAMPLE

1. A UK business makes a supply of **administrative services** to a charity in another member state, which has business and non-business activities. The services are outside the scope of UK VAT, even if the services relate to the charity's non-business activities. The overseas charity should account for VAT in its member state using the reverse charge.

2. Where a UK charity which is engaged in both business and non-business activities receives a general rule service from a supplier in another member state, it is required to **account for reverse charge** VAT in the UK on those supplies, even if they relate solely to its non-business activities.

B. Place of belonging

A supplier or recipient of a service is treated as belonging in the place where: 9688 s 9 VATA 1994
- the business is established; or
- the person has a fixed establishment from which, or to which, the service is supplied.

In the absence of either of these, the place of belonging is where the supplier or recipient has a permanent address or usually resides.

Type of establishment	Place of belonging
One business/fixed establishment	Location of the establishment
More than one business/fixed establishment	Location of the establishment most directly associated with the supply, or (for recipients) where service most directly used
No business/fixed establishment	Usual place of residence[1]

s 104 FA 2014

Note:
1. If the supplier or recipient is a corporate body in business, its usual place of residence is where it is legally constituted (i.e. where its registered office is). Alternatively, it is an individual's usual or permanent address. Since 1 January 2015 bodies corporate or legal persons that are not in business have been treated as belonging in the place where they are established (rather than where they are legally constituted, or anywhere else).

MEMO POINTS A **VAT group** is treated as a single entity.

EXAMPLE The ABC VAT group has three members:
- Company A, resident in the UK; and
- Company B and Company C, also resident in the UK but with other fixed establishments in Germany and the USA, respectively.
The ABC VAT group is treated as having establishments in the UK, Germany and the USA.

Business establishment

9690 A business establishment is **not defined** by statute, but is taken to mean a principal place of business and includes an office, showroom or factory. HMRC accepts that where a trader has headquarters in one country and premises in other countries, the **headquarters** are the "business establishment" (that is, the place where the business is established) and the premises in the other countries are "other fixed establishments" for the purposes of this test. Where there are no permanent premises from which a business is carried on, there cannot be a business establishment.

EXAMPLE

1. Property investment companies were set up in the Isle of Man, with the directors (a husband and wife team) being resident in Australia.
It was held that the mere presence of the directors at their home in Australia did not constitute a business establishment on the basis that, due to the nature of the business, they could make decisions wherever they were. Additionally, no official documentation was maintained recording minutes, directors' meetings, etc, and in fact no property investment decisions were ever made until the Australian directors visited the UK. *Andrew Marks t/a Marks Cameron Davies & Co v C & E* [1998] (VTD 15541)

2. A Canadian registered company which sold dartboards had UK offices, storage facilities and a self-contained flat for the use of any visiting Canadian directors. Goods purchased by the company were stored at the UK premises until there was a sufficient number of them to ship to Canada.
It was held that this constituted a business establishment. It was not necessary for premises to be continually staffed or in constant use to constitute a business establishment. *Source Enterprise Ltd* [1992] (VTD 7881)

3. The CJEU has held that an establishment which carries out technical testing of cars for its parent company, using resources provided by its parent company, but which carries out no taxable transactions, is not capable of being a business establishment in this context. Supplies of testing services to the parent are **not business transactions** for this purpose. *Daimler AG v Skatteverket* [2012]

9692 Where a person carries on a business through a **branch or agency**, this is treated as a business establishment.

s 9(5) VATA 1994

MEMO POINTS 1. A **branch** is not a separate legal entity.
2. An **agency** in this context means a separate legal entity which is empowered (by agreement with its principal) to act on behalf of its principal.

Fixed establishment

9694 Similarly, a fixed establishment is **not defined** by statute. It is taken to mean an establishment (other than the business establishment) from which the trading activities are carried out and which has the human and technical resources to carry out those activities.

A registered office of a limited company is treated as a fixed establishment for the purpose of receiving services. *Binder Hamlyn* [1983] (VTD 1439)

MEMO POINTS 1. The courts have set out basic rules that they would apply to **test whether an overseas business has a fixed establishment** in the UK. A fixed establishment is likely to occur if the UK business:
- actually provides the services;
- does not in function or substance operate independently from the overseas business; and
- has sufficient permanent human and technical resources necessary for providing the services *Chinese Channel Ltd v C & E* [1998]

2. For the interpretation of these rules for **e-business** see ¶6974.
3. The *Berkholz* test (¶9696) established the minimum requirements for an establishment to be able to provide services. It is not clear what level of activity is required from a recipient's establishment before it is deemed capable of receiving services. It is thought that it is unlikely that the *Berkholz* test can apply to recipients as a lower level of activity than **sufficient permanent human and technical resources** is required to receive services.

EXAMPLE A Danish tour operator appointed its UK subsidiary as its sales agent to market and package tours on its behalf. The Danish parent did not provide the premises or the UK staff.
The CJEU considered whether the UK agency was independent of the Danish parent and found that it was not, as the UK company had to seek prior approval from its parent for nearly all decisions (price setting, recruitment of senior staff, etc). It was therefore held to be a fixed establishment of the Danish company and consequently the supplier of the UK tours was treated as belonging in the UK. *C & E v DFDS A/S* [1997]

Multiple establishments

Where there are multiple establishments involved it is necessary to determine which establishment is **most directly concerned** with the supply in order to determine the correct place of supply. Where a supplier has established its business in one place and has fixed establishments elsewhere, the **default position** is that the head office or primary business location is the establishment most directly associated with the supply. However, if this produces an irrational or inappropriate result, the alternative establishments should be considered to see whether they might be the place of supply. This will only be possible if they are of a certain minimum size and have the human and technical resources necessary for the provision of the services (or receipt of services, if considering the recipient of a supply). 9696

EXAMPLE Gaming machines were operated on ferry boats between Germany and Denmark by a trader whose main place of business was in Hamburg. The machines were maintained only intermittently and no permanent staff were kept by the trader on board the ferries.
It was held that the supply was made in Hamburg (not on board the ferries), on the basis that:
- it was not irrational or inappropriate to treat the supplies as being made in Hamburg; and
- the ferries did not have sufficient permanent human and technical resources necessary for providing the services. *Gunter Berkholz v Finanzamt Hamburg* [1985]

Note:
Contrast this with the case of *DFDS*, above, where it was held that it would be inappropriate to treat the UK tours as supplied in Denmark.

MEMO POINTS The following factors may constitute an **irrational or inappropriate result**:
- distortion of competition;
- double taxation within member states; or
- non-taxation (where, for example, supplies treated as made by the head office would be taxed but supplies treated as made by a fixed establishment would escape taxation).

Global contracts

"Global contracts" can occur where: 9698
a. a **single supply** of services relates to more than one establishment - for example, a contract for consultancy services which relate to the activities of a head office and its overseas branches; or
b. a **global framework** agreement, often made between the head office and a supplier, sets the terms for a number of separate, individual supplies made to individual branches.

HMRC states that in **a**. the supply would be seen as benefiting the business as a whole and would be treated as supplied to the head office; whereas in **b**. the individual services would be seen as received at the locations of the individual branches, even if the head office dictates the terms of the contract and receives an indirect benefit from the services.

C. Operation of the reverse charge

9700 The reverse charge (or "tax shift mechanism") applies in a cross-border context to **services provided by an overseas supplier** to a UK business, or by a UK business to an overseas business customer.

For these services the place of supply becomes the country in which the recipient of the services belongs. In this case, the recipient is liable to account for any VAT due in the member state where it receives the supply.

EU legislation aims to create a **single market** and remove fiscal barriers between member states. If there were no special rules for services provided by overseas suppliers, businesses which cannot recover all of their input tax could avoid incurring VAT by obtaining services from a different EU member state where the rate of VAT was lower, or from outside the EU. Similarly, an EU member state with a low VAT rate would be an attractive location for businesses providing international services. In a single market, these factors can distort competition.

The reverse charge rules therefore ensure that taxable persons located in the EU pay VAT at the **applicable EU rate** on services provided to them, irrespective of where the supplier belongs. It applies to services received from persons belonging both inside and outside the EU.

In addition, the reverse charge provisions remove the requirement for **non-UK suppliers** to register for VAT in the UK if they only supply services to VAT-registered businesses.

The reverse charge **does not apply** if the:
- overseas supplier is registered for VAT in the UK; or
- services are exempt (¶350) or zero-rated (¶1180) in the recipient's country; or
- services are supplied within the same legal entity (except in limited circumstances).

HMRC Brief 2/15

EXAMPLE A legal person, such as a company, may have establishments in more than one country and if these take the form of branches, the company remains a single legal entity. A person cannot make supplies to itself in the normal course of events, so supplies of services between branches of a company are not usually supplies for VAT purposes. However, a recent ruling by the CJEU has complicated matters somewhat.
A Skandia company in the US made supplies of IT services to its Swedish branch. The CJEU held that the Swedish branch was a separate entity from the US company, because the branch was in a VAT group in Sweden. The Swedish VAT group therefore had to apply the reverse charge to the services supplied by the US company.
HMRC has issued guidance on this case, confirming that the UK and Sweden operate VAT grouping differently. In Sweden, a branch of a company becomes a part of the group in its own right, separate from the company of which it is a branch. In the UK, on the contrary, if a branch of a company joins a group, the company as a whole becomes part of the group. Thus in a situation similar to the Skandia case, there would be no supply by the US company to a UK branch, because the US company would be part of the UK group if the UK branch was in the UK VAT group.
However, HMRC concedes that a complication remains where a UK company has a branch in a member state which operates VAT grouping in the same way as Sweden does; also where a company in a member state which operates VAT grouping in the same way as Sweden does has a branch in the UK. In these cases supplies can be made within a single legal entity and VAT should be accounted for accordingly. *Skandia America Corp* [2014]

Time of supply

9702 Notice 741A para 18.6 The **tax point** for reverse charge services is the earlier of when the services are completed and when payment is made.

For a **continuous supply of services**, the time of supply is deemed to be the end of **each billing or payment period** (or on payment where this is earlier). If no payment is made, or invoice (or similar accounting document) issued during a year, the time of supply is the end of the calendar year.

HMRC states that a "period" includes regular (e.g. monthly or quarterly) billing/payment periods typically adopted by suppliers of telephone services, leasing companies, etc. It also covers situations in which the billing or payment periods are not pre-ordained but cover specific successive periods.

In the absence of billing or payment periods, there is a **compulsory tax point** on 31 December. This only applies where a payment tax point does not arise during the previous 12 months. Where a tax point arises on 31 December, VAT is required to be accounted for on the VAT return covering December.

Value

The value of the supply is the consideration paid (¶925+), including any taxes levied abroad. **9704** Sch 6 para 8 VATA 1994

Recipient registered for VAT

The recipient should provide its UK VAT number to the supplier as evidence that it is a relevant business person in the UK. The supplier will then be able to issue an invoice without charging VAT in its home country (if it is based in another EU member state). **9706**

Strictly, for supplies of services subject to the reverse charge, the supplier need only be satisfied that the recipient is receiving the services as a relevant business person. There is no requirement that a VAT number must be given to the supplier. However, provision of a VAT registration number is generally viewed as the best evidence that a recipient is a "taxable person" (i.e. carrying on a business activity) in the member state in which it is receiving the supply. See also ¶9710.

The recipient of the services must account for **output tax** on the value of the supplies received on its VAT return in the normal way. **9708** s 8(3) VATA 1994

Input tax can be claimed on the same amount, but recovery may be restricted if the business is partly exempt (¶2448). However, the supplies received, which are treated as being supplies made by the recipient for output tax purposes, should not be taken into account when calculating taxable turnover for partial exemption purposes (although see also ¶9710).

MEMO POINTS The value of all relevant services received should be included in boxes 6 and 7 of the VAT return.

EXAMPLE

1. A Ltd, which is VAT-registered and fully taxable, pays £2,000 to a company in the USA for accountancy services.
The VAT return for the period in which payment is made should include output tax of £400 and input tax of £400. (£2,000 x 20%)

2. B Ltd receives advertising services from a supplier based in France. The services cost £1,000.
B Ltd must account for output VAT of £200. (£1,000 x 20%)
B Ltd is partly exempt and the advertising services received directly relate to its exempt UK insurance business. No input tax is therefore recoverable and the overall cost of the services received is £1,200 (£1,000 + £200), which would also have been the case if B Ltd had received the advertising services from a UK supplier which had to charge B Ltd VAT.

Special situations

Groups There is normally no need to account for VAT on **supplies between members** of a VAT group. So the reverse charge does not apply **unless**: **9709** s 43(2A) VATA 1994; Notice 700/2 para 7

– a member of a UK VAT group has an overseas establishment at which it receives relevant services from an overseas supplier outside the group; and
– those services are used in making a supply to another group member in the UK.

In that event, the representative member (¶8845) of the group should account for the reverse charge on the supply.

Recipient not registered for VAT

9710 Traders who are not registered for VAT must provide **alternative evidence** that they are a relevant business person in their member state. Otherwise EU suppliers of services are obliged to treat the transaction as a B2C transaction and charge VAT to the recipient in the normal way.

A non-VAT-registered business must take the value of services received into account in determining whether the VAT **registration** threshold is reached.

If the **value** of such services alone exceeds the threshold, the trader must register for VAT, even if it makes no other taxable supplies.

EXAMPLE C Ltd's business consists of exempt financial services. In the 12 months ended 31 March 2015 C Ltd paid a French company £95,000 for advertising services. C Ltd must register for VAT and account for VAT on the value of all relevant services received from other countries.

9712 **UK business receiving certain supplies from suppliers based outside the UK** The reverse charge is extended to the following services when they are **supplied in the UK** and received by a UK VAT-registered business from a business that belongs outside the UK:
- services relating to land and property;
- services supplied where performed;
- passenger transport;
- some freight transport services;
- hired goods; and
- telecommunications services, radio and television broadcasting services.

SECTION 2

Services excluded from the general rule

A. Services related to land

9714 Sch 4A para 1 VATA 1994

The following services are treated as being provided at the place **where the land is physically located**, regardless of whether the recipient is using the services for business purposes or for personal purposes (this rule was not affected by the 1 January 2010 change to the basic place of supply rule - see ¶9682):
- grants of interests in land;
- provision of holiday accommodation;
- works of construction and demolition; and
- services supplied by estate agents and other professionals.

The services must be **directly related** to the land in question. Services where the land component is only an incidental part of the transaction are not included.

MEMO POINTS 1. For these purposes, the term **land** includes:
- all forms of land and property, such as buildings, civil engineering works, walls, fences or other structures fixed permanently to the land or sea bed, growing crops, trees, etc; and
- machinery, plant or equipment which is an installation in its own right (for example, a refinery or gas platform).

The Channel Tunnel is land within the UK up to its mid-point.

2. The rules relating to land and property are complex and are **discussed in detail** at ¶5100+.

3. A company operated a membership scheme under which owners of **time-share rights** in owned properties could exchange their rights in that property for another property, in return for an "exchange fee". The CJEU ruled that these fees, and the fees for enrolment and membership of the scheme, were the consideration for the service of an exchange of property usage rights and should be taxed where the owner's property was situated (as services related to land) and not the place where the company had established its business. *RCI Europe v HMRC* (C-37/08) [2009]

Property located in the UK

If a trader in another EU member state supplies services related to a UK property to a **customer** who is: 9716
- VAT-registered in the UK, the customer must account for VAT under the reverse charge rules (¶9700), unless the supplier registers in the UK voluntarily; or
- not VAT-registered in the UK, the supplier is liable to register and account for VAT under normal UK rules (¶2600).

EXAMPLE D SA, a company registered for VAT in Spain, provides property management services to E Ltd, a UK VAT-registered company, in relation to a London office.
E Ltd must account for VAT under the reverse charge rules.

Property located outside the UK

If a UK VAT-registered trader supplies services related to an overseas property to a **customer** who is: 9718
- VAT-registered in **another EU member state**, the customer may have to account for VAT under the reverse charge rules of the other state, unless the supplier registers in that other state voluntarily; or
- not VAT-registered in the other state, the supplier may be liable to register and account for VAT under that state's rules.

Any supply directly related to property located **outside the EU** is outside the scope of VAT.

EXAMPLE Ms F, a VAT-registered estate agent belonging in the UK, acts for Mr G, a non-VAT-registered Belgian individual, in relation to a sale of a residential property in Belgium.
Ms F may be liable to register and account for VAT in Belgium.

Comment Not all EU member states apply the above simplification procedure for services relating to land and property. If a trader is supplying land-related services to a customer in another member state it should check that the above reverse charge rules apply in that member state. If not, it may be liable to register for VAT in the member state where the land is located.

Grants of interests in land

This **includes** the grant, assignment or surrender of: 9720
- any interest or right over land;
- a personal right to call for or be granted such a right; or
- a licence to occupy land, or any other contractual right exercisable over or in relation to land.

MEMO POINTS In order to promote consistency of application of VAT rules throughout the EU, HMRC has changed its policy on the place of supply of **services related to land** in three respects: HMRC Brief 22/12
a. The supply of specific stand **space** at an **exhibition** or conference remains a supply relating to land where the service is restricted to the mere supply of space without any accompanying services. However, where space is provided with accompanying services as a package, this is now taxed under the general place of supply rule (where the customer belongs in the case of a business customer). "Accompanying services" provided as part of a package include the design and erection of a temporary stand, security, power, telecommunications, hire of machinery and publicity material.
b. HMRC has previously treated all supplies of **storage** space as land-related. This remains so where a supplier grants the right to use a specific area of a warehouse or storage area for the **exclusive** use of the customer to store goods. However, where the supplier agrees to store goods but does not grant a right to a specific area for the exclusive use of the customer, this is treated

as falling within the general place of supply rule, so that business customers who belong outside the UK are not liable to UK VAT.

c. HMRC views the supply of access to an **airport lounge** as a land-related service. VAT, if applicable, is therefore due in the country where the lounge is situated.

EXAMPLE A supply of a site at an exhibition centre was held not to be a supply of services in relation to land as the:
- ground space which the stand would take up was not ascertained in advance;
- exhibitor had no choice for the location of the stand; and
- company did not guarantee that the conference would take place and if it did, where it would be.

The contract therefore did not put the customer in a position of special occupancy in relation to any specific area of land. The main advantage for the customer was that of advertising, the right of occupation of land was not a dominant part of the transaction. *International Trade and Exhibitions J/V Ltd* [1996] (VTD 14212)

Works of construction

9722 This **covers all** building works carried out by builders and subcontractors, including services for the repair or maintenance of a building and the supply of plant or machinery together with an operator for work on site.

The services in question must relate to a specific site to be "land-related" for this purpose.

Services

9724 HMRC Brief 22/12

In HMRC's view the following are **related to land** and so take place where the land is situated:
- construction or demolition of a building or permanent structure (such as a pipeline for gas, water or sewage);
- surveying and assessing property;
- valuing property, including for insurance or loan purposes;
- providing accommodation in hotels, holiday camps, camping sites or time-share accommodation;
- maintenance, renovation and repair of a building (including work such as cleaning and decorating) or permanent structure;
- property management services (but not the management of a property investment portfolio);
- arranging the sale or lease of land or property;
- drawing up of plans for a building or part of a building designated for a particular site;
- on-site security services;
- agricultural work on land (including tillage, sowing, watering and fertilization);
- installation and assembly of machines which, when installed, will form a fixture that cannot be easily dismantled or moved;
- the granting of rights to use all or part of a property (such as fishing or hunting rights and access to airport lounges);
- legal services such as conveyancing and drawing up of contracts of sale or leases;
- bridge or tunnel toll fees;
- the supply of space for the use of advertising billboards - for example, the leasing of a plot of land or the side of a building to allow a billboard to be erected; and
- the supply of plant and equipment together with an operator, to allow the customer to carry out work on land or property where the supplier has responsibility for the execution of work.

The following are HMRC's examples of services which are **not related to land**, so that the place of supply follows the general rule:
- drawing up of plans for a building or part of a building that do not relate to a particular site;
- arranging the supply of hotel accommodation or similar services;
- installation, assembly, repair or maintenance of machines or equipment which are not, and do not become, part of the land or property;

- management of a property investment portfolio;
- advertising services that involve the use of a billboard; and
- the supply of equipment with an operator, where it can be shown that the supplier has no responsibility for the performance of the work.

B. Passenger transport

Place of supply

Passenger transport is treated as taking place in the country in which the **transportation takes place** (thus if it is outside the EU, it is outside the scope of VAT). 9726 Sch 4A para 2 VATA 1994

The place of supply for such services is therefore either:
- entirely within one member state; or
- allocated between two or more countries.

Passenger transport requires a vehicle, ship or aircraft to be provided together with a driver or crew, in order to carry passengers.

MEMO POINTS 1. A **charter of a ship with a crew** is treated as a supply of services other than of passenger transport.
2. The provision of a ship with crew but **without a written charter** is likely to be a transport of freight.
3. Traders who buy and sell passenger transport, or supply passenger transport with other services, may be obliged to use the **Tour Operators' Margin Scheme** (¶7490+) when accounting for VAT.

Intra-EU journeys

In general, transport is treated as taking place **entirely within an EU member state** if it either: 9728
- does not leave the jurisdiction of the member state in the course of the journey; or
- only leaves the member state in the course of a journey between two points in the same state and does not put in at or land in another country in the course of the journey.

This applies even if the journey is part of a longer journey involving travel to or from another country.

EXAMPLE
1. A direct passenger flight between Belfast and Newcastle, which crosses international waters, is treated as taking place entirely in the UK. However, if the plane landed at Dublin en route, the supply would be treated as being performed partly in the UK and partly in the Republic of Ireland.

2. A ferry transport of passengers from Liverpool to Dublin, via the Isle of Man, is treated as being supplied in the UK (for the journey from Liverpool to the Isle of Man) and then outside the UK (for the journey from the Isle of Man to Dublin).

If the transportation takes place in **two or more EU member states**, the amount of the VAT-able supplies in each member state is allocated by reference to the distance travelled in each member state. 9730

EXAMPLE A company operated cross-border coach package tours. It was held that for such cross-border transport, supplied on an all-inclusive basis, the taxable supplies should be allocated to each member state pro rata by reference to the distance covered in each state. Other factors, such as a coach's operational time and passenger stopovers, should not be taken into consideration. *Reisebüro Binder GmbH v Finanzamt Stuttgart-Körperschaften* [1997]

MEMO POINTS If the supply is made partly in a member state and **partly outside the EU**, the portion of the supply allocated outside the EU is outside the scope of VAT.

Pleasure cruises

9732 Goods or services provided on a pleasure cruise are treated as supplied in the same place as the transportation of the passengers. This includes services for the transport of a passenger's luggage or motor car on the cruise.

MEMO POINTS A pleasure cruise includes a cruise wholly or partly for the purposes of education or training.

EU on-board restaurant and catering

9734 Sch 4A para 6 VATA 1994 The provision of catering or restaurant services on board a ship, aircraft or train in connection with the transport of passengers during an **intra-EU journey** is treated as made in the country where the point of departure is located.

The point of departure for this purpose is the first place where passengers can embark.

MEMO POINTS 1. An **intra-EU** journey is defined as one where:
- the first place of embarkation is in the EU;
- the last place of disembarkation is in the EU; and
- there is no stopping point for embarkation or disembarkation which is outside the EU.

2. A **return journey** which takes place in more than one country but ends in the country in which it started is made up of two parts: an outward leg and a return leg. The return leg starts with the last stop at a place where there has been no previous stop and ends where the outward leg began.

C. Short-term hire of transport

9736 Sch 4A para 3 VATA 1994 The short-term hire of a means of transport is treated as made in the country in which the means of transport is put at the disposal of the person hiring it. HMRC's view is that the term "put at the disposal of" means the place where the vehicle is located at the time it is physically made available to the customer.

Short-term hire is defined as hire for a **continuous period** of less than:
- 90 days if the means of transport is a **vessel**; or
- 30 days in any **other case**.

However, this is subject to **use and enjoyment** provisions (¶9758), so:
- where the place of supply would be the UK but the effective use and enjoyment of the means of transport is in a country outside the EU, the supply is to be treated as taking place in that country to the extent that it is used and enjoyed there; and
- where the place of supply would be in a non-EU state but the effective use and enjoyment of the means of transport is in the UK, the supply is to be treated as taking place in the UK to the extent that it is used and enjoyed here.

MEMO POINTS 1. There is a distinction between short-term hire and **long-term hire**. For long-term hire, the place of supply is subject to the general rule, i.e. the place where the customer is established for **business customers**.

Implementing Regulation 282/2011 Arts 24c, 24e 2. The place of supply of **long-term hire** to **non-business customers** is also where the customer belongs, except for long-term hire of a pleasure boat to a non-business customer, which is treated as supplied where the boat is put at the customer's disposal (if the supplier has an establishment there). The place of belonging for hires other than of pleasure boats may be established on the basis of two items of non-contradictory evidence: for example, the customer's billing address, or bank details, registration details of the means of transport hired, or any other commercially relevant information.

9738 Hired means of transport are not **defined** but in practice are taken to include cars, touring caravans, trailers, trucks, cycles, rolling stock, boats, ships, etc. Static caravans and freight containers (¶9598) are not means of transport.

There has been very little **case law** on the definition of means of transport but, by way of example, it has been held that a time-share on a yacht was the sale of a beneficial interest in a yacht, not a letting on hire. *Oathplan Ltd* [1982] (VTD 1299)

It has been held that a crane was not a means of transport, its purpose being to lift and place items in position rather than carry them from one place to another. *BPH Equipment Ltd* [1996] (VTD 13914)

Where a hired means of transport is supplied with a **driver, crew, pilot, etc**, this is likely to be a supply of passenger transport (¶9726).

D. Services supplied where performed

The following services are treated as being supplied where they are carried out: **9740**
- entertainment services i.e. cultural, artistic, sporting, scientific, educational or entertainment services, including services relating to exhibitions, conferences or meetings, and ancillary services; and
- restaurant and catering services.

1. Cultural, artistic, sporting, scientific, educational and exhibition services

Certain cultural, artistic, sporting, scientific, educational and exhibition services are treated as supplied where they are physically performed. These services are of a type which are carried out in front of a live audience. Occasionally such services will be supplied B2B, in which case they are subject to the general rule (¶9682, although see also memo point **4**. below and ¶9744). **9742** Sch 4A para 4 VATA 1994

EXAMPLE

1. Supplies of technical and acoustic services for live concerts were services ancillary to an entertainment activity and as such were supplied where the services were carried out. *Dudda v Finanzamt Bergisch Gladbach* [1996]

2. Catering services supplied to UK entertainers while touring abroad were held to be supplied where performed. *Sugar And Spice On Tour Catering* [2002] (VTD 17698)

3. The place of supply of services of sportspersons when performing exhibition matches depends on whether they receive prize money. If so, it will be necessary to consider whether this amounts to consideration for a product endorsement, etc, in which case the supply is advertising and will be treated as supplied where received (¶9784). If the supply is mixed, an apportionment of the prize money can be made on a just and reasonable basis.

4. Finmeccanica organised exhibition space for other group companies at the Farnborough Air Show. HMRC took the view that Finmeccanica's onward supply of these facilities amounted to exhibition services taking place in the UK. Finmeccanica argued successfully that the supplies were of advertising services taking place in Italy. Whilst the UK legislation defines exhibition services as taking place where physically performed, the Tribunal held that this goes further than permitted by the VAT Directive. Only exhibition services which are similar to cultural, artistic, sporting, scientific, educational or entertainment services take place where performed. That implies public entertainment services supplied to final consumers, not business services which happen to take place in conjunction with an exhibition. *Finmeccanica Group Services SPA* [2013] (TC03364)

MEMO POINTS 1. **Flying training** is treated as being supplied outside the UK, provided that the plane leaves the UK and at least 12 hours' training is provided abroad.
2. Similarly, **sailing training** is treated as being supplied outside the UK if the boat leaves the UK and all the training takes place outside the UK.
3. Entertainment services provided to business customers are treated as supplied where performed if the service is of **admission** to an event or an ancillary service **related to admission**. Other entertainment services to business customers are supplied where the customer is established under the general rule.
4. Entertainment services provided **to non-taxable customers** are treated as supplied where the event takes place.

9744 **Exclusions** Common examples of supplies that do not fall within the scope of this provision are:

Type of supply	Place of supply
Assignment of rights in a film to a distribution company	The general rule applies (¶9682)
Assignment of rights by an actor for a performance to be exploited on film	
Supply of master tape, etc, where duplicates will be taken	
Services of researchers, editors, engineers, designers, etc	
Educational services provided over the Internet	
Ancillary services (e.g. hairdressing or make-up) for a recorded TV programme	
Lighting and sound technicians' services on a film set where they do not retain any rights or act as consultants	

Exhibition services

9746 Exhibition services provided to business customers are treated as supplied where performed if the service is of **admission** to an event or an ancillary service **related to admission**. Other exhibition services to business customers are supplied where the customer is established under the general rule.

Exhibition services provided to **non-taxable customers** are treated as supplied where the event takes place.

Ancillary services

9750 Ancillary entertainment **services provided to business customers** are treated as supplied where the event takes place if the service is an ancillary service **related to admission**. Other ancillary services supplied to business customers are supplied where the customer is established, under the general rule.

Ancillary services supplied to **non-business customers** are treated as supplied where the event takes place.

2. Restaurant and catering services

9752 Sch 4 para 5 VATA 1994 The supply of restaurant and catering services is made where the services are physically carried out. This does **not include** services supplied in the course of intra-Community passenger transport (see ¶9734).

3. Valuations and work on goods

9754 Sch 4A para 14 VATA 1994 Valuation services and work on goods supplied to **relevant business persons** are treated as supplied **where the recipient belongs** under the general rule.

Services of valuation and work on goods supplied to non-taxable persons are treated as supplied **where they are physically carried out**. Services provided to private EU customers may require the supplier to register for VAT in the member state where performance takes place. If services provided to non-taxable persons are performed **outside the EU**, they are outside the scope of VAT.

For work on goods acquired for export outside the EU see ¶9794.

MEMO POINTS 1. **Work on goods includes** all physical work on any goods (for example, alterations and repairs, insulating, varnishing, assembling, etc). Work that will be **excluded** is work that is not physical in nature (for example, inspection, testing and analysis).

2. Valuation includes the services of loss adjusters, surveyors, etc, in connection with **insurance claims/proposals**. If a report is pulled together in a different country from that where the goods are located this will not generally change the place of supply. However, if the report is part of a comprehensive loss-adjusting service it will be treated as supplied under the general rule (¶9682).
3. If the results of **scientific testing** are compiled in the UK, it will not make such services liable to UK VAT, provided that the services were otherwise performed outside the UK. If a recommendation is made from the results, the services will be treated as consultancy services (¶9784). If the services relate to oil, gas or mineral exploitation they will be treated as services in relation to land (¶9744).

E. Services subject to the "use and enjoyment" rule

Scope

Certain services are subject to the application of the **use and enjoyment** rule. This will tax a service in the place where it is actually used or consumed and applies in relation to the following services: **9758**
- hire of means of transport (¶9736);
- hiring of goods other than means of transport (¶9762);
- freight transport (¶9763);
- telecommunications services, radio and TV broadcasting services (¶9764); and
- electronically supplied services (¶9768).

These services are referred to below as **relevant services**.

Application

The use and enjoyment provisions mean that: **9760**
a. where a supply of relevant services would ordinarily be **treated as made in the UK** and the goods are used and enjoyed to any extent in a non-EU country, the supply is treated to that extent as taking place outside the EU; or
b. where a supply of relevant services would ordinarily be **treated as made in a country outside the EU** and the goods are used and enjoyed to any extent in the UK, the supply is treated to that extent as taking place in the UK.

Consequently, non-EU providers supplying such services to private UK customers will need to register for VAT in the UK.

1. Hire of goods other than means of transport

Subject to the use and enjoyment rule, the service of hiring of goods (other than a means of transport) is **ordinarily** subject to the general rule, **unless** they are hired to a person who is not a relevant business person **and** who belongs outside the EU. In the latter case the supply is treated as made where the recipient belongs - that is, outside the EU - and is therefore outside the scope of VAT. **9762** Sch 4 para 7 VATA 1994

2. Freight transport

Where a supply of freight transport and ancillary services is made to a **business customer** and takes place wholly **outside the EU**, it is subject to the use and enjoyment rule and is thus treated as taking place outside the EU. The place where the business recipient of the supply belongs is not relevant (as it is under the general rule) and the supply is not subject to VAT. **9763** Sch 4 paras 9B, 9C VATA 1994

3. Telecommunications and broadcasting services

9764 Sch 4A para 8 VATA 1994

Telecommunications services means services relating to the transmission, emission or reception of signals, writing, images and sounds or information of any nature, by wire, radio, optical or other electromagnetic systems, including:
- transfers or assignments of the right to use capacity; and
- the provision of access to global information networks.

Implementing Regulation 282/2011 Art 6b

Broadcasting services are defined as services consisting of audio and audiovisual content, such as radio or television programmes which are provided to the general public via communications networks by and under the editorial responsibility of a media service provider, for simultaneous listening or viewing, on the basis of a programme schedule.

Since 1 January 2015 the supply of telecommunications and radio and TV broadcasting services has taken place **where the recipient belongs** (subject to the use and enjoyment rule for B2B supplies). B2C suppliers may register in one member state only under a so-called "mini one stop shop" (see ¶7000+).

MEMO POINTS For more detail on the **place of supply** of these services see ¶6990+.

9766 VAT is chargeable on telecommunication services consumed by **business users** visiting the UK (for example, when using fax shop services or making calls from hotel rooms).

However, certain services are ignored if:
- they are used by a non-EU temporary visitor;
- they are an incidental part of an established telephone contract or account held by a customer who belongs outside the EU (similarly, if a UK resident uses telecommunications services outside the EU under an account with a UK provider, those services are outside the scope of UK VAT, provided that evidence is retained to substantiate the element of use that occurs outside the EU); and
- HMRC is satisfied that these conditions are not being abused.

MEMO POINTS 1. It has been held that supplies of **phone cards** which give access to Irish telecommunications services are taxable in the UK when they are supplied to registered UK distributors. *HMRC v IDT Card Services Ireland Ltd* [2006]

2. The CJEU has since clarified that the sale of a phonecard is a **single** taxable supply of telecommunications services **at each stage** of the supply chain. Thus there is a supply of such services when the card issuer sells the card to a distributor and a separate supply when the distributor sells to a wholesaler or retailer. Similarly, there is a supply when the retailer sells the card to the end user. There is, however, **no supply** of telecommunications services by the card issuer to the end user; that supply is made by the retailer who sells the card to the end user. *Lebara Ltd v HMRC* [2012]

4. Electronically supplied services

Scope

9768 Sch 4A paras 9, 15 VATA 1994

Common examples of electronically supplied services are the supply of:
- a website, web hosting and distant maintenance of programmes and equipment;
- software and the updating of software;
- images, text and information, and the making available of databases;
- music, films and games (including games of chance and gambling games);
- political, cultural, artistic, sporting, scientific, educational or entertainment broadcasts (including broadcasts of events); and
- distance teaching.

MEMO POINTS The rules relating to the place of supply of electronically supplied services changed with effect from **1 January 2015**. Subject again to the use and enjoyment rule (for B2B supplies), these are now treated as supplied where the customer belongs for both business and non-business customers. B2C suppliers are, however, able to register in one member state only under a so-called "mini one stop shop" (see ¶7000+).
For more detail on the **place of supply** of electronically supplied services see ¶6990+.

SECTION 3

Services supplied to non-taxable persons

A. Agents and intermediaries

Intermediary services include: 9770 Sch 4A para 10 VATA 1994
- making arrangements for a supply by or to another person; or
- any other activity intended to facilitate the making of such a supply.

The place of supply of intermediary services is:
- subject to the **general rule** (¶9682) - that is, where the recipient belongs - when supplied to a relevant business person; and
- where the **underlying service** by or to the agent's customer is made when the supply is made to a person who is not a relevant business person.

For more detail on the place of supply of agents' services see ¶7130+.

B. Freight transport and ancillary services

1. Freight transport

Scope

Freight transport is **defined** as the transport of goods other than people and covers all forms of transport by sea, air or land (including courier services and the services of a pilot or crew in delivering a ship or aircraft). 9772 Notice 744B

Liability

The place of supply for freight transport is subject to the **general rule** when supplied to relevant business persons and taxed where the recipient belongs. Where supplied to non-taxable persons, the place of supply is **where the transportation takes place**, or the **place of departure**, as follows: 9774

Transaction	Detail	Recipient	Place of supply
UK transport		Non-taxable person	Where the transportation takes place i.e. UK
		UK or EU business	Recipient's member state
Transport outside the EU		Any	Where the transportation takes place i.e. outside the scope of VAT
Intra-EU transport	Includes: – a separate domestic leg of transport, directly linked to an intra-EU freight transport of goods; and – transport from one member state to another, where the journey includes a non-EU member state	Non-taxable person	EU state where the transportation begins
		UK or EU business	Recipient's member state

EXAMPLE

1. A **UK registered supplier** transports goods for a **non-VAT-registered customer** from:
– UK to France: the supply takes place in the UK (where transport begins);
– France to Belgium: the supply takes place in France (where transport begins) and the trader may be liable to register and account for VAT in France; and
– France to the UK: the supply takes place in France (where transport begins) and the trader may be liable to register and account for VAT in France.

2. A **UK registered supplier** transports goods for a **UK registered customer** from:
– France to the UK: the supply takes place in the UK, as both the supplier and recipient are registered in the UK; and
– France to Belgium: similarly the supply takes place in the UK, as both the supplier and recipient are registered in the UK.

3. A **UK registered supplier** transports goods for a **customer registered for VAT in France** from:
– UK to France: the supply takes place in the recipient's member state (France) and the customer will account for VAT under the reverse charge procedure; and
– Italy to France: again the supply takes place in France and the customer will account for VAT under the reverse charge procedure.

4. A **UK registered customer** receives freight transport supplies in the UK from an **overseas supplier** (EU or non-EU). The place of supply will be the UK and the UK customer will account for VAT using the reverse charge procedure. (If the UK **customer** is **not registered** for VAT, the overseas supplier must register and account for VAT in the UK.)

5. A **UK registered supplier** collects goods at Dover to transport them for a **customer registered for VAT in France** on the final leg of their journey from Rome to Birmingham. The place of supply remains in France and the customer will account for VAT under the reverse charge procedure.

Notice 744B para 3.3

MEMO POINTS Transportation between member states that involves passing through a non-member state (for example Sweden to the UK via Norway) is treated as intra-EU transportation.

2. Ancillary freight transport services

9778 Ancillary services **include**:
– loading, unloading or reloading;
– stowing;
– opening for inspection;
– cargo security services;
– preparing or amending bills of lading, air- or sea-waybills and certificates of shipment;
– packing necessary for transportation; and
– storage.

9780 The place of supply of ancillary freight transport services supplied to relevant **business customers** is where the customer is established under the general rule (¶9682). Where supplied to non-business recipients the place of supply is the place where the services are **physically carried out**.

C. Intangible services

9784 Sch 4A para 16 VATA 1994

The services in the table below are:
– supplied where the **recipient belongs** when supplied B2B in the EU;
– supplied where the **supplier belongs** when supplied B2C to a person who belongs in the EU; and
– supplied where the **recipient belongs** when supplied B2C to a person who belongs outside the EU.

Supply	Examples	Scope
Transfers and assignments of copyright, patents, licences, trademarks and other similar intellectual property rights	Grant of a licence to use software Transfer of permission to use a logo	Covers only the supply of such rights that involve the supply of intellectual property. Other services, even if described as a "right" or "licence" (e.g. the right to a discount on an admission fee), are excluded.
Acceptance of any obligation to refrain from pursuing or exercising (in whole or in part) any business activity or any intellectual property rights	A non-competition clause agreed between a vendor and a purchaser	
Advertising services	TV or radio advertising time Website advertising Devising and undertaking a promotional campaign	Includes elements supplied as part of an advertising campaign which would not otherwise amount to advertising in their own right if supplied separately (e.g. cocktail parties, seminars, etc). Simple distribution of information (e.g. leaflet drops) with no other involvement in the advertising campaign will be excluded. *Lawrence* [1995] (VTD 13092)
Services of consultants, consultancy bureaux, engineers; lawyers[1], accountants and other similar services; data processing and provision of information	Market research Intellectual advice or design Winding up of a deceased's estate Weather forecasts Engineering design The performing of mathematical and logical operations on data Tourist information, telephone helpdesks, etc	The following specific services are excluded from this provision: – services provided by engineers if they relate mainly to physical work on goods (treated as supplied where performed); and – services that consist of simple reformatting of data/delivery of another person's information (treated as supplied in accordance with the principal contract).
The supply of staff	Secondment, loan or transfer of staff by a recruitment business	Where an employer uses its staff to provide services (e.g. secretarial services) to a client, the supply is not one of staff, but of services.
The letting on hire of goods other than a means of transport	Hire of computer equipment Hire of freight containers	Excludes: – land, plant and machinery installed as a fixture; and – goods which include the services of an operator.
Banking, financial and insurance services (including reinsurance but not safe deposit services)		The financial function must be the primary part of the activity, **for example**: – debt collection services; – portfolio management services; and – granting of mortgages. **Excludes** rent collection services and physical safe custody services.
Telecommunication and broadcasting services		¶9764

Supply	Examples	Scope
Electronically provided services		¶6930
Supplies of services connected with the operation of natural gas and electricity distribution systems	Receipt of natural gas/ electricity by a UK VAT-registered person in the course of a business carried on by him	

Note:
1. Legal services provided to persons who have not been given the right to stay in the UK (e.g. **asylum seekers**) are treated as being supplied in the recipient's country of origin, even if their application to stay in the UK is successful and the invoice is rendered after the right to stay has been granted. If a person is granted a right to stay in the UK but this is subsequently revoked, the legal services associated with any appeal are treated as being provided in the UK.

EXAMPLE In a case concerning the supply of services provided by a UK bank to its Japanese parent, the tribunal held that the services concerned were not "consultancy". The UK bank provided the services of its chief executive officer, the general manager and a "planning group" under a "service level agreement", in which the services were described as "management and corporate services". The charge represented the time they spent on responsibilities covering a division of the parent company's business. The UK bank argued that these services were outside the scope of UK VAT. HMRC argued that the services were managerial, not consultancy, and therefore supplied in the UK. The tribunal held that the services provided under the agreement were ongoing and involved decisions integral to the group's management processes and strategy. Consultancy services, by contrast, are essentially advisory in nature and time-limited. Therefore the services were not consultancy and the place of supply was the UK, not Japan, with the result that UK VAT applied under the pre-1 January 2010 rules. *Sumitomo Mitsui Banking Corporation Europe Ltd* [2009] (TC00089)

Banking, financial and insurance services

9786 Notice 701/49 para 6.16

Special rules apply where **securities** are sold and the **purchaser is not known** (and consequently neither is the place of the recipient's belonging). In these situations, the supplier may either:

a. treat the supply as being made in the UK; or

b. apply the "easement" rules, which means that the place of the transaction is treated as the place of supply, unless:

– the place of the transaction is not known, in which case the place of supply can be deemed to be where the security is listed; or

– the security is not listed (or is listed on both an EU and a non-EU exchange), in which case the place of supply can be deemed to be where the final broker belongs.

SECTION 4

Zero-rated services

A. Freight transport

9788 For this purpose, freight includes the transport of goods, cargo, animals, unaccompanied vehicles, etc.

Scope

The following supplies are zero-rated: 9790 Sch 8 Group 8 items 5, 6, 10 VATA 1994; Notice 744B paras 5.1 - 5.5

Service	Details
Freight transport of goods	From the EU to a place outside the EU (where the place of supply is the UK (¶275)) Any transport which is supplied in the UK may be zero-rated, even where the export of the goods is from another member state Freight transport to or from the Azores or Madeira (or between these places) is specifically zero-rated
Services for the handling or storing (¶1318) of freight goods	Carried in any ship or aircraft: – in a port [1] or Customs and Excise airport [2]; – on land adjacent to a port (this covers only the immediate quay or dock); or – in a transit shed (i.e. a place approved by HMRC for the temporary storage of goods)
	At a place where they are to be exported from the EU
	In connection with their transport to a place at which they are to be exported from the EU
The making of arrangements for the above services	

Note:
1. A **port is defined as** any port so designated by HMRC and specifically includes all UK seaports.
2. A **Customs and Excise airport is defined as** an airport designated for landing or departure of aircraft for the purpose of the Customs and Excise Acts. Essentially this is all UK airports.

Evidence

Documentary evidence must be held to show entitlement to zero-rating e.g. consignment notes, bills of lading, certificates of shipment, air- or sea-waybills and Customs declaration forms C 88 (SAD). 9792

In addition, any relevant correspondence, the customer's order document, payment details, sales invoices and advice notes may be acceptable.

B. Work on goods for export from the EU

Work on goods specifically **acquired for the purpose** of carrying out work on them prior to export is zero-rated if certain **conditions** are met. 9794 Notice 741A para 8.6

Qualifying goods must be:
– **subsequently exported** (after completion of the work) to a place outside the EU by the supplier or customer; and
– not **used** in the UK between the time of leaving the supplier's premises and export. The supplier must obtain satisfactory commercial or official **evidence** of export (¶9536) in order to zero-rate the supply.

MEMO POINTS 1. The supplier or non-EU customer can use an **agent** to act on their behalf.
2. Zero-rating also extends to any **goods used in conjunction with** the work performed (e.g. spare parts, paint, etc).
3. Where the goods physically leave the EU member state in which the work was performed and the **customer** is an **EU VAT-registered trader**, the customer must account for VAT under the reverse charge procedure (¶9700). Such supplies can only be zero-rated if the goods are intended to be (and actually are) exported from the EU by the supplier, or its representative, on completion of the work.
4. The supply of an **intermediary's services** is also zero-rated if it consists of the making of arrangements for these services.

EXAMPLE

1. A Ltd imports machinery into the UK for modification work before it can be sold to a company in the USA. If a trader provides the modification service in the UK to A Ltd, the supply can be zero-rated, provided that the goods are intended to be, and in fact are, exported to the USA.

2. A UK art collector sells a painting to a customer in Australia but has it revarnished before export. The service of revarnishing, which is supplied in the UK, is standard-rated, since the painting was not obtained, acquired or imported for the purpose of being worked on.

3. A French VAT-registered company sends machinery to the UK for repair. The repair service can only be zero-rated if the goods are intended to be, and in fact are, exported by the UK supplier (or its representative). If the goods are not so exported, the French company will be required to account for VAT under the reverse charge procedure.

Scope

9796 The following **examples** indicate the scope of zero-rating under this provision:

Eligible for zero-rating	Not within scope
Repair of freight containers Services directly related to the covering of a mare, provided that the mare is exported before the birth of the foal [1] The gelding and/or breaking in of a young horse [1] Restoration of classic cars	Inspection, testing or analysis of goods Incidental running repairs while the goods are being used Valuation services
Note: 1. For more details of VAT in the bloodstock industry see ¶6100+.	

C. Supplies to diplomatic missions and international organisations

9798
Notice 48 para 2.6

Supplies of services to diplomatic missions, international organisations (¶9296) and their personnel based in other EU member states may be zero-rated where the following conditions are met:

a. the supplies are either for the official use of those organisations or the private use of their personnel; and

b. the supplier obtains and keeps documentation to support zero-rating. A supplier who has any doubts about the documentation received should contact HMRC's National Advice Service.

D. Training services to overseas governments

9800
Notice 48 para 3.17; Notice 741A para 8.2

By concession, training services supplied in the UK can be zero-rated if:

– they are **supplied to** an overseas government for its sovereign activities (as opposed to its business activities); and

– the **supplier obtains** a statement in writing from the government concerned (or its accredited representative) certifying that the trainees are employed in the furtherance of its sovereign activities.

Any **associated services supplied separately** (for example, accommodation or transport) do not fall within the scope of this provision.

This provision therefore **includes** the training of government officials, public servants and members of organisations such as the armed forces, police, emergency services and similar bodies answerable to the government concerned.

However, it **excludes** training of personnel from government-owned businesses or sponsored commercial organisations, such as state airlines or nationalised industries.

SECTION 5

EC sales lists

Since 1 January 2010 EC sales lists (ESLs) have been required for intra-EU supplies of services for which a reverse charge applies in the customer's member state (¶9700). The purpose of the extension of ESLs to services is to provide a system of control for intra-EU supplies of services, where the customer is required to account for a reverse charge in its country, similar to that which already exists for goods. The information which must be provided is the same as required for the cross-border movement of goods (¶9332). 9802 HMRC Brief 53/08

ESLs are not required from businesses which are providing the following:

- supplies exempt in the member state where the supply takes place;
- supplies covered by Article 194 of EC Directive 2006/112/EC (¶9997);
- B2B supplies made to recipients who are not VAT-registered; and
- B2B supplies where the customer is purchasing the services for a non-business purpose.

Information required

The ESL form that was previously used for reporting intra-EU supplies of goods (VAT 101) is also now used for services. The following information must be entered on the form: 9804

- the customer's VAT registration number;
- total value of supplies in sterling;
- the customer's country code; and
- code 3 in the Indicator code box if it is a supply of services.

No indicator code is required for supplies of goods unless it is a triangular supply of goods, in which case code 2 must be entered.

Reporting periods

Businesses must submit ESLs for services on a quarterly basis, unless they opt to submit lists monthly. If a business supplies both goods and services and it is above the quarterly reporting threshold for goods, it is obliged to submit monthly ESL reports for goods. Businesses may either: 9806

- report only goods in month 1, report only goods in month 2, and report goods in month 3 plus services for the whole quarter; or
- report both goods and services each month.

CHAPTER 4

Incurring cross-border VAT

OUTLINE ¶¶

Often businesses registered for VAT in one EU member state incur overseas VAT on goods or services bought in another member state. If goods are bought for removal from that EU member state, this is usually not an issue because such despatches are normally VAT-free. However, if goods or services bought in another EU country by a UK business are also used there (e.g. at an exhibition), the UK business cannot deduct the VAT incurred on its UK VAT returns. This chapter deals with methods of recovering VAT incurred in other countries. 9840

SECTION 1

UK traders incurring EU VAT

Subject to conditions being met, the so-called "8th Directive procedure" provides a system for UK businesses to reclaim certain VAT suffered in other EU countries. Indeed, if a business is registered for VAT in any EU country, it can use the scheme to reclaim VAT paid in any other EU country. 9845 s 39 VATA 1994

For an EU trader incurring UK VAT see ¶9870.

On 1 January 2010 an **electronic VAT refund system** for traders incurring VAT in other EU countries was introduced to replace the previous paper-based system. Claims are now submitted electronically on a standardised form.

Who can claim?

A claim can be made by a UK registered trader who: 9847
- is not **registered** for VAT in the other state;
- has no **business establishment** or other residence in the other state; and

– has not made any **supplies** in that state, other than transport services relating to the international carriage of freight outside that state, or services where the recipient accounts for VAT (¶9700).

UK businesses wishing to make a claim must **register on the UK portal** hosted by HMRC for this purpose. The claim is sent to the member state of refund (MSR) via HMRC, thus eliminating the need for a certificate of status. However, the amount of refund and the application of rules relating to the claim is administered by the MSR.

Excluded from refund

9849 VAT cannot be claimed on:
– the **movement** of goods to another EU state; or
– supplies bought for **resale**, such as hotel accommodation, which is for the direct benefit of travellers.

In addition, each EU state has specific rules on the types of supply on which VAT is **blocked** (a link to these can be found at ¶9859).

What can be recovered?

9851 Only VAT incurred on supplies made to the trader for the **purposes of** the trader's business can be recovered.

Where **goods** are purchased in the state, these cannot be taken out of that state if any VAT is to be refunded. VAT incurred on goods imported into the EU state from a place outside the EU can also be recovered where there is no other relief available.

The **supplies received** in the EU state must not be used by the trader in making its own supplies in that state.

Comment The trader may become **liable to register** for VAT in the EU state of claim if the value of imports or acquisitions exceeds a certain level.

How much tax can be recovered?

9853 The input tax available for refund is **restricted to** the tax that would have been available for deduction by taxable persons in each EU state.

The **period** covered by a claim must be between 3 months and 1 year, unless the claim period starts on or after 1 October, in which case a shorter period is allowed. Claims are made by reference to the calendar year.

There are no maximum limits for a claim but standard **minimum limits** apply across all member states (¶9859).

EXAMPLE

1. Ms A attends a trade fair in Germany in July. She then returns in October for a conference. She can make a claim for the period July to October.

2. Mr B attends a trade fair in France in November. He can make a claim for the period November to December.

Administration

9855 Under the electronic refund procedure traders register to use the system and access the HMRC portal via the Government Gateway. The claim does not need to be filed by a person who is registered for VAT, as HMRC has now implemented procedures to accept claims from non-VAT-registered persons, who will be given a VAT agent reference number. MSRs may require some evidence of legal authority from applicants other than the trader. **Separate claims** are required for VAT incurred in each member state and a **maximum of four** claims may be submitted to each MSR per year (since a claim may not be for less than a 3-month period unless it is for the remainder of a year). The portal will allow up to six claims to be saved at any one time.

The business must **record** the following details:
- name and full address;
- address for contact by electronic means;
- a description of the business activity relating to the claim;
- the repayment period covered by the application; and
- a declaration that the business does not make supplies under a margin or flat rate scheme or make supplies in the MSR.

Invoices can only be required by MSRs for values that exceed €250 for fuel and €1,000 for other supplies. These must be scanned and attached to the claim.

Claims must be **submitted** within 9 months following the calendar year of the claim. The date of the submission is recorded on the portal. HMRC has 15 days from this date to forward the claim to the MSR. 9857

Refunds must be made by the MSR within 4 months of the authority receiving appropriate evidence. The currency is that of the member state making the refund.

MEMO POINTS 1. **False claims** will result in recovery proceedings and possibly penalties.
2. If a claim is **queried**, the MSR will request additional information direct from the trader. The information must be provided within 1 month.
3. MSRs will pay **interest** where they fail to meet the deadline for repayment.
4. Businesses have the **right of appeal** against non-payment.

Summary of each EU state

The following table summarises certain of the information currently available in respect of the recovery of VAT in other EU member states (Croatia has not yet submitted its relevant information). VAT is generally not refunded where domestic rules do not permit deduction. This broadly means no refund of VAT incurred for non-business purposes, on entertainment, catering and most transport-related expenditure. Further details can be found by following this link: flmemo.co.uk/vm9859. 9859

State	Language for claim form	Minimum claim limit (euros (e) or local currency (l))	
		Quarterly claim	Annual or other non-quarterly claim
Austria	German or English	360(e)	36(e)
Belgium	French, German or Dutch	200(e)	25(e)
Bulgaria	Bulgarian	50(l)	50(l)
Cyprus	Greek or English	120(e)	15(e)
Czech Republic	Czech	2,000(l)	1,000(l)
Denmark	Danish, English, German or French	1,500(l)	200(l)
Estonia	Estonian or English	5,000(l)	5,000(l)
Finland	Finnish, Swedish or English	200(e)	25(e)
France	French	200(e)	25(e)
Germany	German	500(e)	250(e)
Greece	Greek or English	200(e)	25(e)
Hungary	Hungarian or English	7,000(l)	7,000(l)
Republic of Ireland	English	25(e)	25(e)
Italy	Italian (other languages "mostly" accepted)	200(e)	25(e)
Latvia	Latvian or English	135(l)	20(l)
Lithuania	Lithuanian or English	700(l)	100(l)
Luxembourg	French or German	250(e)	250(e)
Malta	Maltese or English	80(l)	20(l)
Netherlands	Dutch, English, French or German	200(e)	25(e)
Poland	Polish	200(e)	25(e)

State	Language for claim form	Minimum claim limit (euros (e) or local currency (l))	
		Quarterly claim	Annual or other non-quarterly claim
Portugal	Portuguese, English, French or Spanish	19.95(e)	19.95(e)
Romania	Romanian	200(l)	25(l)
Slovak Republic	Slovakian	1,000(l)	1,000(l)
Slovenia	Slovenian, English or German	50,000(l)	12,000(l)
Spain	Spanish	200(e)	25(e)
Sweden	Swedish or English	2,000(l)	250(l)

SECTION 2

Overseas traders coming to the UK

9870 Overseas traders coming to the UK may be making a temporary visit, or intending to set up business here. Obviously the VAT implications are different in each of these situations.

It is also important to distinguish between an EU trader and someone who is established outside the EU.

MEMO POINTS For the **scope of the EU** see ¶9002.

A. EU traders

1. Commencing business in the UK

9872 Below is a summary of the UK VAT issues which a trader, based in another EU member state, should consider when commencing business in the UK.

Issue		Summary	¶¶
Requirement to be registered in the UK	Making (or intending to make) UK taxable supplies[1]	Must register No minimum period of registration	¶2600
	Selling and delivering goods to non-registered UK persons (distance selling)[1]	Must register if value of sales exceeds £70,000 since previous 1 January	¶9177
	Business acquires goods in the UK from EU supplier	Must consider thresholds both for the trade of the calendar year and the next 30 days Exemption from registration if making mainly zero-rated acquisitions Can register voluntarily for a minimum of 2 calendar years	¶9041
	Contact details to register	Non Established Taxable Persons Unit in Aberdeen	¶9994
	How to obtain a VAT number	Must apply to be registered	¶2704
	Requirement to appoint a VAT representative	No requirement for EU traders Can voluntarily appoint	¶7210
	Requirement to set up a bank guarantee or give security	No bank guarantees required HMRC can request security if tax may be at risk	¶3546

Issue		Summary	¶¶
Invoicing	Requirement to issue VAT invoices	When making taxable (not zero-rated) supplies in the UK Invoice should be issued within 30 days of the supply Customers can self-bill, where an agreement has been entered into	¶2844
	When VAT invoices are not required	– supplies of goods where input tax deduction blocked; – supplies where no consideration e.g. gifts; – exempt or zero-rated supply made when both customer and supplier are registered for UK VAT; – supply to unregistered UK person; – supplies between members of a group registration; and – supplies between divisions where divisional registration applies	¶2844
	Invoice contents and format	Follows general EU rules Simplified invoices allowed in certain situations (value under £250, supplies by retailers, etc) Electronic invoicing allowed	¶2850, ¶2856
Records	Period of retention	At least 6 years, unless HMRC agrees otherwise For certain transactions (involving property) 10-year minimum	¶2797
	Storage arrangements	Must be in readable format and easy to trace Integrity of information must be assured	¶2802, ¶2854
Reporting and payment requirements	VAT returns	Usually submitted every 3 months; the due date is usually the end of the calendar month following the end of the relevant quarter Can apply for monthly returns (beneficial where VAT repayments are due) Return must be submitted electronically	¶2985
	EC sales lists	Usually submitted monthly Smaller traders can apply for monthly or annual submission dates	¶9330
	Intrastat declarations	If the value of despatches or arrivals exceeds a threshold in a calendar year, a VAT-registered business must submit Supplementary Declarations	¶9345
	Disclosure of schemes	In certain circumstances when VAT saving is made	¶3030
	Payment of VAT	Usually accompanies VAT return Must be made electronically Businesses with annual VAT liability exceeding £2.3m must make payments on account	¶3160

Issue		Summary	¶¶
Input tax deduction	No deduction available	– purchases for non-business or exempt purposes (can opt to tax an otherwise exempt property); – most cars; – business entertainment; – goods other than building materials installed by developers; – purchases by a tour operator within TOMS; and – goods sold under a margin scheme	¶1810, ¶1885, ¶5604
	Partial deduction available	Leased cars - 50% of VAT can be claimed If making a mixture of taxable and exempt supplies, partial exemption rules apply Use of land, ship, aircraft, boat or computer for both taxable and exempt supplies, or both business and non-business use, within 10 (land) or 5 (other assets) years of purchase, may be subject to the capital goods scheme	¶1920, ¶2070
	If not making any UK supplies	8th Directive claim	¶9875
Optional simplification for certain businesses	Warehousing regime	Suspensive arrangements which mean no UK VAT due while goods remain in warehouse	¶9242
	Flat rate scheme	Eligible if taxable turnover below £150,000 Must apply to use Net VAT due is a flat rate percentage of turnover, depending on business sector Limited separate input tax claims	¶4635
	Annual accounting	Eligible if annual turnover below £1.35m Must apply to use One VAT return per year; VAT paid over 10-month period (either monthly or every 3 months)	¶4745
	Cash accounting	Eligible if annual turnover below £1.35m No HMRC approval required Account for VAT based on cash paid out and cash received	¶4880
	Retail schemes	Calculates VAT due based on global sales figure Choice of schemes available	¶6325
	Agricultural flat rate scheme	Levy of 4% of turnover retained by farmer No input tax deduction	¶5970

Note:
1. Where the UK customer is required to account for VAT under the acquisition rules for goods or the reverse charge for services, the supplier is not required to register. However, voluntary registration is still available.

2. Temporarily visiting the UK

EU traders who are not UK VAT-registered may incur UK VAT which would be irrecoverable unless special rules applied. A common case is a trader who participates in a trade fair, where the supplies on which input tax is incurred are actually consumed in the UK. **9875**

A refund claim is subject to **anti-avoidance provisions** which apply when there is an intention to make taxable supplies (¶2647) of goods (including capital assets (¶2674)) in the UK, on which VAT has previously been recovered under the refund rules. In this case the trader must register for UK VAT (¶2600).

MEMO POINTS 1. Where **goods** are sourced in the UK and despatched to another EU member state (¶9075) or exported (¶9565), the related VAT can usually be recovered because this is a zero-rated supply.
2. Claims by EU traders are commonly referred to as 8th Directive claims.

a. Input tax recovery

For input tax to be recovered, there are strict requirements relating to the following criteria: **9876** s 39 VATA1994
- circumstances of the trader;
- supplies on which VAT is incurred;
- the use made of those supplies; and
- the amount of input tax repayable.

Who can claim?

A claim can be made by a trader registered for VAT in another member state who satisfies all of the following **conditions** - the trader: **9877** Notice 723A para 2.3
- is not, and is not required to be, registered for VAT in the UK (¶2600);
- has no business establishment in the UK (¶9690) and its usual place of residence is not the UK (¶9688); and
- has not made any supplies in the UK, other than transport services relating to the international carriage of freight outside the UK and services where the recipient accounts for VAT (¶9700).

Excluded from refund

VAT cannot be recovered on: **9880** SI 1995/2518 reg 177
- business **entertainment** and hospitality;
- **second-hand goods** where no tax invoice is given by the supplier;
- the supply or importation of most **cars**;
- supplies bought for resale which are for the direct benefit of **travellers** (such as hotel accommodation); and
- any supply used or to be used to make an **exempt supply** (¶350) outside the UK.

What can be recovered?

Only VAT incurred on supplies made to the trader in the UK for the **purposes of** the trader's business can be recovered. **9882**

In addition, VAT incurred on **goods imported** into the UK from a place outside the EU can also be recovered where there is no other relief available.

The **supplies received** in the UK must not be **used by** the trader in making its own supplies in the UK. Where goods are purchased in the UK, they must be consumed here and cannot be taken out of the UK if any VAT is to be refunded. SI 1995/2518 regs 175, 176

MEMO POINTS VAT on **travel supplies** bought for a travel agent or its employees can be recovered.

How much tax can be recovered?

9884 SI 1995/2518 regs 179, 180

The input tax available for refund is **restricted to** the input tax that would have been available for deduction by taxable persons in the UK. So where expenditure is incurred for both business and non-business purposes, VAT can be claimed on the business portion. The partial exemption rules may also apply (¶2075). In addition, any bank charges will reduce the amount actually received by the trader.

The **period** covered by a claim must be between 3 months and 1 year, unless the claim period starts on or after 1 October, in which case a shorter period is allowed. Claims are made by reference to the calendar year.

There is no maximum limit for a claim but the **minimum limit** is usually £35. For claim periods of less than a year which commence before 1 October, the minimum limit is £295.

Administration

9886 Under the electronic refund procedure traders use the system in their own member state. **Separate claims** are required for VAT incurred in each member state of refund (MSR); a **maximum of four** claims may be submitted to each MSR per year (since a claim may not be for less than a 3-month period unless it is for the remainder of a year).

Invoices can only be required by MSRs for values that exceed €250 for fuel and €1,000 for other supplies. These must be scanned and attached to the claim.

MEMO POINTS A **certificate of status** is not required, as the trader's own member state will forward the claim to the UK or other MSR.

Claims must be **submitted** within 9 months following the calendar year of the claim. The trader's member state has 15 days from submission of the claim to forward it to the UK or other MSR.

9888 **Refunds** must be made by the MSR within 4 months of the authority receiving appropriate evidence. The currency will be that of the member state making the refund.

MEMO POINTS 1. **False claims** will result in recovery proceedings and possibly penalties.
2. If a claim is **queried**, the MSR will request additional information direct from the trader. The information must be provided within 1 month.
3. MSRs will pay **interest** where they fail to meet the deadline for repayment.
4. Businesses have the **right of appeal** against non-payment.

---

b. Anti-avoidance - registration

9890 An overseas trader who **intends** to make taxable supplies in the UK of goods on which VAT has previously been recovered under a directive claim is required to register for UK VAT. These rules were introduced to combat VAT avoidance and their application is rare. There is no mechanism for voluntary registration, although a request for early registration will be considered.

This type of registration will only apply where registration under any of the other rules (i.e. UK supplies (¶2600), distance sales (¶9177) or EU acquisitions (¶9010+)) is not required. There is no registration threshold for taxable supplies made (or intended) in the UK by a non-established taxable person, so in practice this anti-avoidance rule has now been superseded.

Exemption

9892 Sch 3A para 7 VATA 1994

Traders who **intend to make** only zero-rated supplies can apply for an exemption from registration. They must still observe the notification process (¶9896).

If granted, the exemption will **apply until** either the request is withdrawn by the trader, or it appears to HMRC that the exemption is no longer valid.

MEMO POINTS 1. When there is a **material change in the nature of supplies**, HMRC must be informed within 30 days of the date of the event, or end of the relevant calendar quarter where there is no specific date.

2. Similarly, any change in the **zero-rated proportion** of taxable supplies must be notified to HMRC within 30 days of the end of that calendar quarter.

Compulsory registration

Unless meeting the criteria for exemption, a person becomes liable to be VAT-registered: 9894 Sch 3A para 1 VATA 1994
a. upon making relevant supplies; or
b. as soon as there are reasonable grounds for believing that the person will make such supplies in the next 30 days.

There is no registration threshold.

The consequence of **failing to register** is the imposition of penalties (¶4010).

MEMO POINTS 1. A **relevant supply** is defined as a taxable supply of goods, which are assets of the business (including capital assets (¶2674)) supplied in the course of that business. The trader has either claimed, or is intending to claim, a refund of input tax under a directive claim. Sch 3A para 9 VATA 1994
2. This includes the situation where any **previous owner of the business** made a recovery under the refund rules and no VAT was charged on the business transfer under special rules (¶8648).

EXAMPLE Ms C makes a relevant supply worth £2,000 on 13 April.
She becomes liable to register from that date and must inform HMRC by 13 May.

Notification

An **application** to register is made on form VAT 1C (form VAT 2 for partnerships), which includes a signed declaration that all of the required information is complete and correct. There is no facility for online registration. 9896

A trader who has **already made** relevant supplies must notify HMRC within 30 days of the date of the first such supply; registration will take effect from that date. Sch 3A paras 3, 4 VATA 1994

If there is **reasonable belief about future supplies**, HMRC must be notified before the end of the 30-day period; registration will take effect from the beginning of the 30-day period.

The trader, being overseas, may prefer to appoint a **VAT representative**, who can deal with all of the trader's UK VAT matters (¶7095).

Consequences

From the date of registration VAT must be **accounted for on** all taxable supplies and input tax can be recovered, as it can by a normal UK registered person. 8th or 13th Directive claims can no longer be made. 9898

Other issues that the registered person should consider include:
- certificate of registration (¶2708); and
- changes in circumstances (¶2714).

Ceasing to be registered

A person ceases to be liable to register for VAT when no longer making relevant supplies and should notify HMRC within 30 days. 9900

The **notification** should contain the date when the trader ceased to be liable to register and is made on form VAT 7 for all UK traders (form VAT 7A for all non-UK traders).

Registration will only be **cancelled** where HMRC is sure that the trader is not liable to be registered under any of the other rules (i.e. UK supplies, distance sales, or EU acquisitions).

Effective date If **no longer liable** to be registered, the effective date of cancellation is the date when the liability ceased. 9902 Sch 3A para 6 VATA 1994

If the person was **never liable** to register, because no relevant supplies were ever made and the trader never had an intention to do so, the cancellation will have effect as if the trader was never actually registered.

B. Non-EU traders

1. Commencing business in the UK

9906 Below is a summary of the UK VAT issues which a non-EU trader should consider when commencing business in the UK. Note that the establishment of a UK business by a non-EU trader who was **already supplying electronically supplied services** to UK recipients would invalidate any existing registration (¶7000).

Issue		Summary	¶¶
Requirement to be registered in the UK	Making (or intending to make) UK taxable supplies[1]	Must register No minimum period of registration	¶2600
	Business acquires goods in the UK from EU supplier	Must consider thresholds both for the trade of the calendar year and the next 30 days Exemption from registration if making mainly zero-rated acquisitions Can register voluntarily for a minimum of 2 calendar years	¶9041
	Contact details to register	Non Established Taxable Persons Unit in Aberdeen	¶9994
	How to obtain a VAT number	Must apply to be registered	¶2704
	Requirement to appoint a VAT representative	HMRC can issue a direction for a representative to be appointed Can voluntarily appoint	¶7210
	Requirement to set up a bank guarantee or give security	No bank guarantees required HMRC can request security if tax may be at risk	¶3546
Invoicing	Requirement to issue VAT invoices	When making taxable (not zero-rated) supplies in the UK Invoice should be issued within 30 days of the supply Customers can self-bill, where an agreement has been entered into	¶2844
	When VAT invoices are not required	– supplies of goods where input tax deduction blocked; – supplies where no consideration e.g. gifts; – exempt or zero-rated supply made when both customer and supplier are registered for UK VAT; – supplies to unregistered UK person; – supplies between members of a group registration; and – supplies between divisions where divisional registration applies	¶2844
	Invoice contents and format	Follows general EU rules Simplified invoices allowed in certain situations (value under £250, supplies by retailers, etc) Electronic invoicing allowed	¶2850, ¶2856

Issue		Summary	¶¶
Records	Period of retention	At least 6 years, unless HMRC agrees otherwise For certain transactions (involving property) 10-year minimum	¶2797
	Storage arrangements	Must be in readable format and easy to trace Integrity of information must be assured	¶2802, ¶2854
Reporting and payment requirements	VAT returns	Usually submitted every 3 months; the due date is usually the end of the calendar month following the end of the relevant quarter Can apply for monthly returns (beneficial where VAT repayments are due) Return must be submitted electronically	¶2985
	EC sales lists	Must be completed for intra-EU transactions Usually submitted monthly Smaller traders can apply for monthly or annual submission dates	¶9330
	Intrastat declarations	If the value of despatches or arrivals exceeds the relevant threshold in a calendar year, a VAT-registered business must submit Supplementary Declarations	¶9345
	Disclosure of schemes	In certain circumstances when VAT saving is made	¶3030
	Payment of VAT	Usually accompanies VAT return Must be made electronically Businesses with annual VAT liability exceeding £2.3m must make payments on account	¶3160
Input tax deduction	No deduction available	– purchases for non-business or exempt purposes (can opt to tax an otherwise exempt property); – most cars; – business entertainment; – goods other than building materials installed by developers; – purchases by a tour operator within TOMS; and – goods sold under a margin scheme	¶1810, ¶1885, ¶5604
	Partial deduction available	Leased cars - 50% of VAT can be claimed If making a mixture of taxable and exempt supplies, partial exemption rules apply Use of land, ship, aircraft, boat or computer for both taxable and exempt supplies, or both business and non-business use, within 10 (land) or 5 (other assets) years of purchase, may be subject to the capital goods scheme	¶1920, ¶2070
	If not making any UK supplies	Special directive claim Retail export scheme gives relief for consumers	¶9908, ¶9603

Issue		Summary	¶¶
Optional simplification for certain businesses	Warehousing regime	Suspensive arrangements which mean no UK VAT due whilst goods remain in warehouse	¶9242
	Flat rate scheme	Eligible if taxable turnover below £150,000 Must apply to use Net VAT due is a flat rate percentage of turnover, depending on business sector No separate input tax claims	¶4635
	Annual accounting	Eligible if annual turnover below £1.35m Must apply to use One VAT return per year; VAT paid over 10-month period (either monthly or every 3 months)	¶4745
	Cash accounting	Eligible if annual turnover below £1.35m No HMRC approval required Account for VAT based on cash paid out and cash received	¶4880
	Retail schemes	Calculates VAT due based on global sales figure Choice of schemes available	¶6325
	Agricultural flat rate scheme	Levy of 4% of turnover retained by farmer No input tax deduction	¶5970

Note:
1. Where the UK customer is required to account for VAT under the acquisition rules for goods or the reverse charge for services, the supplier is not required to register. However, voluntary registration is still available.

2. Temporarily visiting the UK

9908 s 39 VATA 1994; SI 1995/2518 reg 188

A non-EU trader who **incurs UK VAT** may be able to recover it if the trader's own country reciprocates and provides a similar relief to UK traders. In practice, recovery of UK VAT is only denied where the trader's country actively refuses relief to UK traders.

In addition, the retail export scheme gives relief for UK input tax on certain goods taken out of the UK (¶9603).

The same anti-avoidance rule applies in the event that the trader makes UK supplies as for EU traders (¶9890).

9910 For input tax to be recovered there are strict **requirements** relating to the following criteria:
- circumstances of the trader;
- supplies on which VAT is incurred;
- the use made of those supplies; and
- amount of input tax repayable.

MEMO POINTS 1. These claims are commonly referred to as 13th Directive claims.
2. HMRC has published details of how UK traders can claim refunds of VAT incurred in Serbia (see flmemo.co.uk/vm9910). Forms in Serbian and an English translation can be accessed. This indicates that reciprocal arrangements are in place, so that Serbian businesses should likewise be able to make 13th Directive claims for VAT incurred in the UK.

Who can claim?

9912 Notice 723A para 6; SI 1995/2518 reg 188

A claim can be made by a trader registered for business purposes in another country who satisfies all of the following **conditions** - the trader:
- is not, and is not required to be, registered for VAT in the UK (¶2600);

– has no place of business (¶9690) or residence (¶9688) anywhere in the EU; and
– has not made a supply of goods or services in the UK, other than transport services relating to the international carriage of goods, or services where VAT is payable by the recipient (¶9700).

What can be recovered?

The input tax available for refund is **restricted to** the input tax that would have been available for deduction by taxable persons in the UK. So where expenditure is incurred for both business and non-business purposes, VAT can be claimed on the business portion. The partial exemption rules may also apply (¶2075). In addition, any bank charges will reduce the amount actually received by the trader. **9914** SI 1995/2518 reg 190

The **period** covered by a claim must be between 3 months and 1 year, unless the claim period starts on or after 1 April, in which case a shorter period is allowed. Claims are made by reference to the year ended 30 June. SI 1995/2518 reg 192

There is no maximum limit for a claim, but the **minimum limit** is usually £16. For claim periods of less than a year commencing before 1 April, the minimum limit is £130.

Comment If a non-EU trader makes **supplies that would be exempt** if they were made in the UK, HMRC will refuse the trader's claim for input VAT incurred. HMRC will, therefore, not repay input VAT incurred by a non-EU trader who is providing **insurance**, or **financial** services. This restriction is applied on a global basis; HMRC does not consider the location of the non-EU trader's clients.

Administration

Claims must be **submitted** by 31 December following the year of the claim, using form VAT 65A, which should be completed in English. **9918** SI 1995/2518 reg 191

The following **original documents** must be attached to the form:
a. a certificate of status (¶9886) such as form VAT 66A or its foreign equivalent; and
b. invoices, import documents or warehouse documents relating to the relevant supplies or imports, showing:
– an identifying number and the date of supply;
– the supplier's name, address and VAT registration number;
– the applicant's name and address;
– the VAT-exclusive cost of the supply; and
– the rate and amount of VAT charged.

False claims will result in recovery proceedings and possibly penalties.

General Information

OUTLINE ¶¶

Appendix

OUTLINE ¶¶

Registration thresholds

UK taxable supplies 9960

Past supplies [1]			Future supplies [1]
Period of application [2]	**1 year** £	**Unless not exceeding** £	**30 days** £
From 1 April 2015	82,000	80,000	82,000
1 April 2014 to 31 March 2015	81,000	79,000	81,000
1 April 2013 to 31 March 2014	79,000	77,000	79,000
1 April 2012 to 31 March 2013	77,000	75,000	77,000
1 April 2011 to 31 March 2012	73,000	71,000	73,000
1 April 2010 to 31 March 2011	70,000	68,000	70,000
1 May 2009 to 31 March 2010	68,000	66,000	68,000
1 April 2008 to 30 April 2009	67,000	65,000	67,000
1 April 2007 to 31 March 2008	64,000	62,000	64,000
1 April 2006 to 31 March 2007	61,000	59,000	61,000
1 April 2005 to 31 March 2006	60,000	58,000	60,000
1 April 2004 to 31 March 2005	58,000	56,000	58,000
10 April 2003 to 31 March 2004	56,000	54,000	56,000
25 April 2002 to 9 April 2003	55,000	53,000	55,000
1 April 2001 to 24 April 2002	54,000	52,000	54,000

Note:
1. Supplies include all zero-rated and positive rated supplies.
2. From 1 December 2102 non-established taxable persons are subject to a zero threshold - in other words, they must register if they make any UK taxable supplies.

9961 Distance selling

Period of application	Cumulative supplies in calendar year £
From 1 January 1993	70,000

9962 EU acquisitions

Period of application	Cumulative acquisitions in calendar year £
From 1 April 2015	82,000
1 April 2014 to 31 March 2015	81,000
1 April 2013 to 31 March 2014	79,000
1 April 2012 to 31 March 2013	77,000
1 April 2011 to 31 March 2012	73,000
1 April 2010 to 31 March 2011	70,000
1 May 2009 to 31 March 2010	68,000
1 April 2008 to 30 April 2009	67,000
1 April 2007 to 31 March 2008	64,000
1 April 2006 to 31 March 2007	61,000
1 April 2005 to 31 March 2006	60,000
1 April 2004 to 31 March 2005	58,000
10 April 2003 to 31 March 2004	56,000
25 April 2002 to 9 April 2003	55,000
1 April 2001 to 24 April 2002	54,000

Deregistration thresholds

9964 UK taxable supplies

Period of application	Future supplies[1] £
From 1 April 2015	80,000
1 April 2014 to 31 March 2015	79,000
1 April 2013 to 31 March 2014	77,000
1 April 2012 to 31 March 2013	75,000
1 April 2011 to 31 March 2012	71,000
1 April 2010 to 31 March 2011	68,000
1 May 2009 to 31 March 2010	66,000
1 April 2008 to 30 April 2009	65,000
1 April 2007 to 31 March 2008	62,000
1 April 2006 to 31 March 2007	59,000
1 April 2005 to 31 March 2006	58,000
1 April 2004 to 31 March 2005	56,000
10 April 2003 to 31 March 2004	54,000
25 April 2002 to 9 April 2003	53,000
1 April 2001 to 24 April 2002	52,000

Note:
1. Where HMRC is satisfied this limit will not be exceeded in the period

Distance selling 9965

Period of application	Past relevant supplies in last calendar year £	Future relevant supplies in next calendar year[1] £
From 1 January 1993	70,000	70,000

Note:
1. Where HMRC is satisfied this limit will not be exceeded in the period.

EU acquisitions 9966

Period of application	Past relevant acquisitions in last calendar year £	Future relevant acquisitions in next calendar year[1] £
From 1 April 2015	82,000	82,000
1 April 2014 to 31 March 2015	81,000	81,000
1 April 2013 to 31 March 2014	79,000	79,000
1 April 2012 to 31 March 2013	77,000	77,000
1 April 2011 to 31 March 2012	73,000	73,000
1 April 2010 to 31 March 2011	70,000	70,000
1 May 2009 to 31 March 2010	68,000	68,000
1 April 2008 to 30 April 2009	67,000	67,000
1 April 2007 to 31 March 2008	64,000	64,000
1 April 2006 to 31 March 2007	61,000	61,000
1 April 2005 to 31 March 2006	60,000	60,000
1 April 2004 to 31 March 2005	58,000	58,000
10 April 2003 to 31 March 2004	56,000	56,000
25 April 2002 to 9 April 2003	55,000	55,000
1 April 2001 to 24 April 2002	54,000	54,000

Note:
1. Where HMRC is satisfied this limit will not be exceeded in the period.

Fuel scale charge

The table below sets out the scale charge which should be used for VAT periods beginning on or after **1 May 2014**. 9968

For this and the other tables below, where the CO_2 emissions figure of a vehicle is **not a multiple of 5**, the figure is rounded down to the next multiple of 5 to determine the charge.

For a **bi-fuel** vehicle with two CO_2 emissions figures, the lower figure should be used.

For cars which are too old to have a CO_2 emissions figure, identify the CO_2 band based on engine size, as follows:
- cylinder capacity 1,400cc or less, use band 140;
- cylinder capacity exceeds 1,400cc but does not exceed 2,000cc, use band 175; and
- cylinder capacity exceeds 2,000cc, use band 225 or above.

CO_2 band	Annual return		Quarterly return		Monthly return	
	Charge (gross) £	VAT included £	Charge (gross) £	VAT included £	Charge (gross) £	VAT included £
120 or less	627.00	104.50	156.00	26.00	52.00	8.67
125	939.00	156.50	234.00	39.00	78.00	13.00
130	1,004.00	167.33	251.00	41.83	83.00	13.83
135	1,064.00	177.33	266.00	44.33	88.00	14.67
140	1,129.00	188.17	282.00	47.00	94.00	15.67
145	1,190.00	198.33	297.00	49.50	99.00	16.50
150	1,255.00	209.17	313.00	52.17	104.00	17.33
155	1,315.00	219.17	328.00	54.67	109.00	18.17
160	1,381.00	230.17	345.00	57.50	115.00	19.17
165	1,441.00	240.17	360.00	60.00	120.00	20.00
170	1,506.00	251.00	376.00	62.67	125.00	20.83
175	1,567.00	261.17	391.00	65.17	130.00	21.67
180	1,632.00	272.00	408.00	68.00	136.00	22.67
185	1,692.00	282.00	423.00	70.50	141.00	23.50
190	1,757.00	292.83	439.00	73.17	146.00	24.33
195	1,818.00	303.00	454.00	75.67	151.00	25.17
200	1,883.00	313.83	470.00	78.33	156.00	26.00
205	1,943.00	323.83	485.00	80.83	161.00	26.83
210	2,008.00	334.67	502.00	83.67	167.00	27.83
215	2,069.00	344.83	517.00	86.17	172.00	28.67
220	2,134.00	355.67	533.00	88.83	177.00	29.50
225 or more	2,194.00	365.67	548.00	91.33	182.00	30.33

The table below sets out the scale charge which should be used for VAT periods beginning on or after **1 May 2013**.

CO_2 band	Annual return		Quarterly return		Monthly return	
	Charge (gross) £	VAT included £	Charge (gross) £	VAT included £	Charge (gross) £	VAT included £
120 or less	675.00	112.50	168.00	28.00	56.00	9.33
125	1,010.00	168.33	253.00	42.17	84.00	14.00
130	1,080.00	180.00	269.00	44.83	89.00	14.83
135	1,145.00	190.83	286.00	47.67	95.00	15.83
140	1,215.00	202.50	303.00	50.50	101.00	16.83
145	1,280.00	213.33	320.00	53.33	106.00	17.67
150	1,350.00	225.00	337.00	56.17	112.00	18.67
155	1,415.00	235.83	354.00	59.00	118.00	19.67
160	1,485.00	247.50	371.00	61.83	123.00	20.50
165	1,550.00	258.33	388.00	64.67	129.00	21.50
170	1,620.00	270.00	404.00	67.33	134.00	22.33
175	1,685.00	280.83	421.00	70.17	140.00	23.33
180	1,755.00	292.50	438.00	73.00	146.00	24.33

CO_2 band	Annual return		Quarterly return		Monthly return	
	Charge (gross) £	VAT included £	Charge (gross) £	VAT included £	Charge (gross) £	VAT included £
185	1,820.00	303.33	455.00	75.83	151.00	25.17
190	1,890.00	315.00	472.00	78.67	157.00	26.17
195	1,955.00	325.83	489.00	81.50	163.00	27.17
200	2,025.00	337.50	506.00	84.33	168.00	28.00
205	2,090.00	348.33	523.00	87.17	174.00	29.00
210	2,160.00	360.00	539.00	89.83	179.00	29.83
215	2,225.00	370.83	556.00	92.67	185.00	30.83
220	2,295.00	382.50	573.00	95.50	191.00	31.83
225 or more	2,360.00	393.33	590.00	98.33	196.00	32.67

The table below sets out the scale charge which should be used for VAT periods beginning on or after **1 May 2012**.

CO_2 band	VAT fuel scale charge, 12-month period £	VAT on 12-month charge £	VAT-exclusive 12-month charge £
120 or less	665.00	110.83	554.17
125	1,000.00	166.67	833.33
130	1,065.00	177.50	887.50
135	1,135.00	189.17	945.83
140	1,200.00	200.00	1,000.00
145	1,270.00	211.67	1,058.33
150	1,335.00	222.50	1,112.50
155	1,400.00	233.33	1,166.67
160	1,470.00	245.00	1,225.00
165	1,535.00	255.83	1,279.17
170	1,600.00	266.67	1,333.33
175	1,670.00	278.33	1,391.67
180	1,735.00	289.17	1,445.83
185	1,800.00	300.00	1,500.00
190	1,870.00	311.67	1,558.33
195	1,935.00	322.50	1,612.50
200	2,000.00	333.33	1,666.67
205	2,070.00	345.00	1,725.00
210	2,135.00	355.83	1,779.17
215	2,200.00	366.67	1,833.33
220	2,270.00	378.33	1,891.67
225 or more	2,335.00	389.17	1,945.83

The table below sets out the scale charge which should be used for VAT periods beginning on or after **1 May 2011**.

CO_2 band	Annual return		Quarterly return		Monthly return	
	Charge (gross) £	VAT included £	Charge (gross) £	VAT included £	Charge (gross) £	VAT included £
120 or less	630.00	105.00	157.00	26.17	52.00	8.67
125	945.00	157.50	236.00	39.33	78.00	13.00
130	1,010.00	168.33	252.00	42.00	84.00	14.00
135	1,070.00	178.33	268.00	44.67	89.00	14.83
140	1,135.00	189.17	283.00	47.17	94.00	15.67
145	1,200.00	200.00	299.00	49.83	99.00	16.50
150	1,260.00	210.00	315.00	52.50	105.00	17.50
155	1,325.00	220.83	331.00	55.17	110.00	18.33
160	1,385.00	230.83	346.00	57.67	115.00	19.17
165	1,450.00	241.67	362.00	60.83	120.00	20.00
170	1,515.00	252.50	378.00	63.00	126.00	21.00
175	1,575.00	262.50	394.00	65.67	131.00	21.83
180	1,640.00	273.33	409.00	68.17	136.00	22.67
185	1,705.00	284.17	425.00	70.83	141.00	23.50
190	1,765.00	294.17	441.00	73.50	147.00	24.50
195	1,830.00	305.00	457.00	76.17	152.00	25.33
200	1,895.00	315.00	472.00	78.67	157.00	26.17
205	1,995.00	325.83	488.00	81.33	162.00	27.00
210	2,020.00	336.67	504.00	84.00	168.00	28.00
215	2,080.00	346.67	520.00	86.67	173.00	28.83
220	2,145.00	357.50	536.00	89.33	178.00	29.67
225 or more	2,205.00	367.50	551.00	91.83	183.00	30.50

The table below sets out the scale charge which should be used for VAT periods beginning on or after **4 January 2011**.

CO_2 band	Annual return		Quarterly return		Monthly return	
	Charge (gross) £	VAT included £	Charge (gross) £	VAT included £	Charge (gross) £	VAT included £
120 or less	570.00	95.00	141.00	23.50	47.00	7.83
125	850.00	141.67	212.00	35.33	70.00	11.67
130	850.00	141.67	212.00	35.33	70.00	11.67
135	910.00	151.67	227.00	37.83	75.00	12.50
140	965.00	160.83	241.00	40.17	80.00	13.33
145	1,020.00	170.00	255.00	42.50	85.00	14.17
150	1,080.00	180.00	269.00	44.83	89.00	14.83
155	1,135.00	189.17	283.00	47.17	94.00	15.67
160	1,190.00	198.33	297.00	49.50	99.00	16.50
165	1,250.00	208.33	312.00	52.00	104.00	17.33
170	1,305.00	217.50	326.00	54.33	108.00	18.00
175	1,360.00	226.67	340.00	56.67	113.00	18.83

CO_2 band	Annual return		Quarterly return		Monthly return	
	Charge (gross) £	VAT included £	Charge (gross) £	VAT included £	Charge (gross) £	VAT included £
180	1,420.00	236.67	354.00	59.00	118.00	19.67
185	1,475.00	245.83	368.00	61.33	122.00	20.33
190	1,530.00	255.00	383.00	63.83	127.00	21.17
195	1,590.00	265.00	397.00	66.17	132.00	22.00
200	1,645.00	274.17	411.00	68.50	137.00	22.83
205	1,705.00	284.17	425.00	70.83	141.00	23.50
210	1,760.00	293.33	439.00	73.17	146.00	24.33
215	1,815.00	302.50	454.00	75.67	151.00	25.17
220	1,875.00	312.50	468.00	78.00	156.00	26.00
225	1,930.00	321.67	482.00	80.33	160.00	26.67
230 or more	1,985.00	330.83	496.00	82.67	165.00	27.50

The table below sets out the scale charge which should be used for VAT periods beginning on or after **1 May 2010**.

CO_2 band	Annual return		Quarterly return		Monthly return	
	Charge (gross) £	VAT included £	Charge (gross) £	VAT included £	Charge (gross) £	VAT included £
120 or less	570.00	84.89	141.00	21.00	47.00	7.00
125	850.00	126.60	212.00	31.57	70.00	10.43
130	850.00	126.60	212.00	31.57	70.00	10.43
135	910.00	135.53	227.00	33.81	75.00	11.17
140	965.00	143.72	241.00	35.89	80.00	11.91
145	1,020.00	151.91	255.00	37.98	85.00	12.66
150	1,080.00	160.85	269.00	40.06	89.00	13.26
155	1,135.00	169.04	283.00	42.15	94.00	14.00
160	1,190.00	177.23	297.00	44.23	99.00	14.74
165	1,250.00	186.17	312.00	46.47	104.00	15.49
170	1,305.00	194.36	326.00	48.55	108.00	16.09
175	1,360.00	202.55	340.00	50.64	113.00	16.83
180	1,420.00	211.49	354.00	52.72	118.00	17.57
185	1,475.00	219.68	368.00	54.81	122.00	18.17
190	1,530.00	227.87	383.00	57.04	127.00	18.91
195	1,590.00	236.81	397.00	59.13	132.00	19.66
200	1,645.00	245.00	411.00	61.21	137.00	20.40
205	1,705.00	253.94	425.00	63.30	141.00	21.00
210	1,760.00	262.13	439.00	65.38	146.00	21.74
215	1,815.00	270.32	454.00	67.62	151.00	22.49
220	1,875.00	279.26	468.00	69.70	156.00	23.23
225	1,930.00	287.45	482.00	71.79	160.00	23.83
230 or more	1,985.00	295.64	496.00	73.87	165.00	24.57

The table below shows the output tax that should be shown on the VAT return for periods from **1 January 2010 to 30 April 2010**.

CO_2 band	Annual return		Quarterly return		Monthly return	
	Charge (gross) £	VAT included £	Charge (gross) £	VAT included £	Charge (gross) £	VAT included £
120 or below	505.00	75.21	126.00	18.77	42.00	6.26
125	755.00	112.45	189.00	28.15	63.00	9.38
130	755.00	112.45	189.00	28.15	63.00	9.38
135	755.00	112.45	189.00	28.15	63.00	9.38
140	805.00	119.89	201.00	29.24	67.00	9.98
145	855.00	127.34	214.00	31.87	71.00	10.57
150	905.00	134.79	226.00	33.66	75.00	11.17
155	960.00	142.98	239.00	35.60	79.00	11.77
160	1,010.00	150.43	251.00	37.38	83.00	12.36
165	1,060.00	157.87	264.00	39.32	88.00	13.11
170	1,110.00	165.32	276.00	41.11	92.00	13.70
175	1,160.00	172.77	289.00	43.04	96.00	14.30
180	1,210.00	180.21	302.00	44.98	100.00	14.89
185	1,260.00	187.66	314.00	46.77	104.00	15.49
190	1,310.00	195.11	327.00	48.70	109.00	16,23
195	1,360.00	202.55	339.00	50.49	113.00	16.83
200	1,410.00	210.00	352.00	52.43	117.00	17.43
205	1,465.00	218.19	365.00	54.36	121.00	18.02
210	1,515.00	225.64	378.00	56.30	126.00	18.77
215	1,565.00	233.09	390.00	58.09	130.00	19.36
220	1,615.00	240.53	403.00	60.02	134.00	19.96
225	1,665.00	247.98	416.00	61.96	138.00	20.55
230	1,714.00	255.43	428.00	63.74	142.00	21.15
235 or above	1,765.00	262.87	441.00	65.68	147.00	21.89

Partial exemption de minimis limits

9969

Period of application	Recoverable exempt input tax
VAT years beginning after 30 November 1994	Lower than both: – £625 per month; and – 50% of total input tax for VAT period

Businesses, for which exempt supplies are less than 50% of total supplies, have the option to apply an additional two de minimis tests (¶2196).

Capital goods scheme 9970

Affected assets	VAT-exclusive value £	Review period
Computer equipment	50,000	5 years
Ships	50,000	5 years
Aircraft	50,000	5 years
Property	250,000	10 years

Interest

Default interest 9972

Period of application	Rate %
From 29 September 2009	3
24 March 2009 to 28 September 2009	2.5
27 January 2009 to 23 March 2009	3.5
6 January 2009 to 26 January 2009	4.5
6 December 2008 to 5 January 2009	5.5
6 November 2008 to 5 December 2008	6.5
6 January 2008 to 5 November 2008	7.5
6 August 2007 to 5 January 2008	8.5
6 September 2006 to 5 August 2007	7.5
6 September 2005 to 5 September 2006	6.5
6 September 2004 to 5 September 2005	7.5
6 December 2003 to 5 September 2004	6.5
6 September 2003 to 5 December 2003	5.5
6 November 2001 to 5 September 2003	6.5
6 May 2001 to 5 November 2001	7.5
6 February 2000 to 5 May 2001	8.5

Statutory interest This interest will be paid when official error has caused a trader to overpay VAT. 9973

Period of application	Rate %
From 29 September 2009	0.5
27 January 2009 to 28 September 2009	0
6 January 2009 to 26 January 2009	1
6 December 2008 to 5 January 2009	2
6 November 2008 to 5 December 2008	3
6 January 2008 to 5 November 2008	4
6 August to 5 January 2008	5
6 September 2006 to 5 August 2007	4
6 September 2005 to 5 September 2006	3
6 September 2004 to 5 September 2005	4
6 December 2003 to 5 September 2004	3
6 September 2003 to 5 December 2003	2
6 November 2001 to 5 September 2003	3
6 May 2001 to 5 November 2001	4
6 February 2000 to 5 May 2001	5
6 March 1999 to 5 February 2000	4

Simplified accounting schemes

9976 **Annual accounting scheme eligibility**

Period of application	Can join scheme if taxable supplies in next 12 months not expected to exceed £	Must leave scheme at end of accounting year if taxable supplies exceed £
From 1 April 2006	1,350,000	1,600,000
1 April 2004 to 31 March 2006	660,000	825,000
1 April 2001 to 31 March 2004	600,000	750,000
Up to 31 March 2001	300,000	375,000

9977 **Cash accounting scheme eligibility**

Period of application	Can join scheme if taxable supplies in next 12 months not expected to exceed	Business must leave scheme at end of accounting year	
		If taxable supplies exceed	Unless taxable supplies for next 12 months not expected to exceed
	£	£	£
From 1 April 2007	1,350,000	1,660,000	1,350,000
1 April 2004 to 31 March 2007	660,000	825,000	660,000
1 April 2001 to 31 March 2004	600,000	750,000	600,000
Up to 31 March 2001	350,000	437,500	350,000

9978 **Flat rate scheme eligibility**

Period of application	Business can join scheme if turnover[1] in next 12 months not expected to exceed		Business must leave scheme at end of accounting year if turnover[2] exceeds
	Taxable	Total	
	£	£	£
From 4 January 2011	150,000	n/a[3]	230,000[4]
From 1 April 2009	150,000	n/a[3]	225,000[4]
10 April 2004 to 31 March 2009	150,000	187,500	225,000
25 April 2002 to 9 April 2003	100,000	125,000	150,000

Note:
1. Excluding VAT.
2. Including VAT.
3. From 1 April 2009 the second test for eligibility to join the scheme no longer applies.
4. From 1 April 2009 this test is based on the usual accounting method adopted by the business, either cash received or invoices raised.

Flat rate scheme percentages and trade sectors The following table shows: 9979
- the percentage rate which applies to each trade sector from 4 January 2011; and
- the trades which HMRC considers fit in each sector.

For the rates prior to 4 January 2011 see previous editions of *VAT Memo*.

Category of business	Flat rate %	Trades which HMRC considers fit in each sector
Accountancy or book-keeping	14.5	Accountants and bookkeepers Income tax preparation services
Advertising	11	Advertising space providers Advertising consultants Advertising services such as billposting
Agricultural services	11	Services to agriculture such as equipment hire with operator, animal transport or breeding services
Any other activity not listed elsewhere	12	Includes: Coin operated photographic machines Defence activities Driving schools Education Extraction of peat Fire and rescue services Funeral services Hospitals, nursing homes, medical or dental services Law and order or judicial activities Private households Sewage treatment Telecommunications Tour guides
Architect, civil and structural engineer or surveyor	14.5	Architects Civil and structural engineers Engineering consultants and designers Quantity surveyors Surveyors Town planners
Boarding or care of animals, excluding veterinary services	12	Animal blacksmithing/farrier Catteries, kennels and stables
Business services not listed elsewhere	12	Cleaning services Credit reporting and collection services Exhibition and fair organisers Extermination services Management activities of holding companies Market research and opinion pollsters Research and development Technical testing and analysis
Catering services, including restaurants and takeaways	12.5	Canteens Catering Licensed and unlicensed restaurants and cafes Sandwich shops Takeaway food shops and mobile stands
Computer and IT consultancy or data processing	14.5	Data processing and database activities Hardware and software consultants Software publishing

Category of business	Flat rate %	Trades which HMRC considers fit in each sector
Computer repair services	10.5	Computer repairs
Dealing in waste or scrap	10.5	Wholesale of waste and scrap
Entertainment or journalism	12.5	Artists and arts facilities Authors Dance halls and discos Dance instruction Fairs and amusement parks Journalists and news agency activities Live theatre
Estate agency or property management services	12	Estate agency and property management services
Farming or agriculture that is not listed elsewhere	6.5	Growing of any crops, fruit or animals Wine-making from own-grown grapes
Film, radio, TV or video production	13	Sound, video or computer recording TV, film, radio or video production, distribution or projection
Financial services	13.5	Banks and building societies Credit granting Debt factoring Financial leasing Mortgage finance businesses
Forestry or fishing	10.5	Fish farms and hatcheries Fishing Forestry Logging
General building or construction services (if materials 10% or more of turnover)	9.5	Alterations and extensions to commercial or domestic buildings, or civil engineering works Building completion Earth moving, demolition and landscaping Electricians Floor and wall coverings Glaziers Joiners/carpenters Other building equipment installers Painters Plasterers Plumbers Road, airfield, sports facility and water project building Roofers
Hairdressing or other beauty treatment services	13	Beauticians and manicurists Hairdressers Suntan and massage parlours
Hiring or renting goods	9.5	Agricultural, construction or civil engineering equipment rental Car or van rental Land, water or air passenger transport rental Sporting and recreational equipment rental TV or video recorders Video tapes

Category of business	**Flat rate %**	**Trades which HMRC considers fit in each sector**
Hotel or accommodation	10.5	Bed and breakfast Camping and caravan sites Holiday centres and villages Licensed or unlicensed hotels or motels with or without restaurants Self catering accommodation Youth hostels
Investigation or security	12	Detective agencies Security firms (personal, site and item)
Labour-only building or construction services (if materials under 10% of turnover)	14.5	See General building or construction services
Laundry or dry-cleaning services	12	Launderettes Laundry and dry-cleaning services
Lawyers or legal services	14.5	Injury claims services Solicitors and barristers
Library, archive, museum or other cultural activity	9.5	Botanical and other gardens Historical sites and buildings Libraries and archives Museums Nature reserves Zoos
Management consultancy	14	Business and financial consultancy Management consultancy Public relations
Manufacturing fabricated metal products	10.5	Builders' and carpenters' metal products Containers, tanks, reservoirs, boilers and radiators Cutlery, tools, locks and hinges Forging, stamping, pressing or roll-forming of metal items General mechanical engineering Steam generators Steel drums and other light metal packaging Wire products, nails, screws, other fasteners, chains and springs
Manufacturing food	9	Alcoholic beverages Animal foods Bakery Cocoa, chocolate and confectionery Dairy and ice cream production Grain milling Processing and preservation of fruits and vegetables Processing fish Production and preserving meat products Production of edible fats and margarine Slaughter of animals Soft drinks and mineral water Sugar production Tea and coffee

Category of business	Flat rate %	Trades which HMRC considers fit in each sector
Manufacturing that is not listed elsewhere	9.5	Boxes, labels and stationery in paper and cardboard Collection, purification and distribution of water Cork, straw, pulp, paper and cardboard production Extraction of petroleum and natural gas Furniture Household, toilet and sanitary goods Jewellery, coins and medals Making carpentry items Making of pesticides, pharmaceuticals, explosives, man-made fibres, rubber, plastic, glass, ceramic, bricks, cement and concrete products Manufacture of industrial chemicals, paints, inks, dyes and sealants Office machinery, electric motors, generators and transformers Production, distribution and trade in gas or electricity Refining of metals and making of articles in metal Saddlery and harness Sawmilling, planing and impregnation of wood, plywood or veneers Shoes Sports goods and toys Tanning and dressing of leather Tobacco products Weapons and ammunition Wire, measuring and control equipment Vehicles, ships, motorcycles, aircraft
Manufacturing yarn, textiles or clothing	9	Carpets Cut, make and trim Hats Knitted or crocheted fabrics Lace and ribbon Making leather and fur clothes Preparation and spinning of natural and man-made fibres Ropes Weaving, finishing and manufacture of cloth
Membership organisation	8	Business and employers organisation Political organisations Professional organisations Religious organisations Trade unions
Mining or quarrying	10	Ore or chemical mines, deep or opencast Quarries for building stone, limestone, gypsum, chalk, slate, sand, gravel, clay or kaolin
Packaging	9	Manufacture, wholesale and retail of packaging
Photography	11	Film processing Portrait or other specialist photography
Post offices	5	Post offices and sub-post offices
Printing	8.5	Bookbinding Newspaper, book or periodical printing Typesetting/master production
Publishing	11	Books Newspapers, periodicals and journals Sound recordings

Category of business	Flat rate %	Trades which HMRC considers fit in each sector
Pubs	6.5	Licensed clubs Public houses, however managed
Real estate activity not listed elsewhere	14	Buying, development and sale of real estate Letting of conference or exhibition centres Letting of own property
Repairing personal or household goods	10	Repair of boots, shoes, household and electrical goods, watches, clocks or jewellery
Repairing vehicles	8.5	Repair and maintenance of all types of vehicles
Retailing food, confectionery, tobacco, newspapers or children's clothing	4	Bakers Butchers Children's clothes of all types and materials Confectioners/newsagents/tobacconists Delicatessen Fishmongers Grocers and greengrocers Health foods Ice cream and cookie shops Off-licences
Retailing pharmaceuticals, medical goods, cosmetics or toiletries	8	Cosmetics and toiletries Dispensing chemists Hearing aids Medical and orthopaedic goods
Retailing that is not listed elsewhere	7.5	Adult clothes, menswear and womenswear Art from galleries, and antiques Books and stationery Fur or leather clothes Furniture and floor coverings Hardware, paints and glass Household goods Lighting Mail order Mobile telephones Photographic equipment Second hand goods (not cars) Sports goods Stalls and markets
Retailing of vehicles or fuel	6.5	Filling stations Motorcycles Parts and accessories Wholesale or retail of new or used vehicles
Secretarial services	13	Secretarial services
Social work	11	Social work for charities or otherwise, with or w thout accommodation
Sport or recreation	8.5	Betting shops and gambling Casting for theatre, TV or films Ice or roller rinks and skateboarding parks Owning of racehorses Sports arenas and stadia

Category of business	Flat rate %	Trades which HMRC considers fit in each sector
Transport or storage, including couriers, freight, removals and taxis	10	Couriers Frozen or refrigerated goods Furniture removal Grain Liquids or gases Passenger or goods transport by rail, coach, underground, taxi, tram, sea, canal or air Removing or storing private possessions Warehousing and excise warehousing
Travel agency	10.5	Travel agencies and travel organisers, excluding those using the Tour Operators' Margin Scheme
Veterinary medicine	11	Veterinary activities
Wholesaling agricultural products	8	Animal feed Flowers and plants Fur, skins and hides Grain and seeds Live animals Unmanufactured tobacco
Wholesaling food	7.5	Alcoholic beverages Coffee, tea and cocoa Confectionery Edible oils and fats Fish and shellfish Fruit and vegetables Game, poultry, eggs and dairy produce Juices, mineral waters and soft drinks Meat and meat products Tobacco
Wholesaling that is not listed elsewhere	8.5	Aircraft, ships and boats Cameras Cash and carry Chemicals China and glassware Clothing and footwear Food, beverages and tobacco Furniture Jewellery Machine tools Machinery and industrial equipment Musical instruments Office equipment Pharmaceuticals Records, tapes, CDs and videos Toys and games

Farmers' flat rate scheme

9981

Period of application	Levy %
From 1 January 1993	4

Tour Operators' Margin Scheme

9982
Notice 709/5 para 8

Deals with	**Purpose**	**Step**	**Action**
Sales	Calculate the value of sales of margin scheme packages	M1	Total the VAT-inclusive selling prices of all your designated travel services and margin scheme packages supplied during the financial year including any that are not "market value" packages
Costs	Working out the market value	M2	Total the VAT-inclusive market value of the standard-rated in-house supplies at M1: carry forward this figure to step 21
		M3	Total the VAT-inclusive market value of the zero-rated and outside the scope in-house travel services at M1: carry forward this figure to step 26
		M4	Total the VAT-inclusive market value of the in-house supplies at step M2 + step M3
Sales	Working out the selling value of designated travel services and non-market-value in-house supplies	M5	Deduct the total at step M4 from the total at step M1: carry forward this figure to step 1
Sales	Working out the total sales of margin scheme **packages**	1	Bring forward the total calculated at step M5. If steps M1 to M5 are not used then enter the VAT-inclusive selling prices of your designated travel services and margin scheme packages supplied during the financial year
Costs	Working out the purchase prices of **margin scheme supplies**	2	Total the VAT-inclusive purchase prices of the **standard-rated** designated travel services included in step 1
		3	Total the VAT-inclusive purchase prices of the **non-standard-rated** designated travel services (supplies enjoyed outside the EC) included in step 1
	Working out the direct costs of **in-house supplies**. Steps 4 to 7 can be ignored where a market value is applied to all in-house supplies under steps M1 to M5.	4	Total the VAT-exclusive direct costs to you of the **standard-rated** in-house supplies included in step 1. Add a percentage of that amount equivalent to the standard rate of VAT.
		5	Total the VAT-exclusive direct costs to you of the **zero-rated** in-house supplies included in step 1
		6	Total the VAT-inclusive direct costs of the **exempt** in-house supplies included in step 1. Deduct any input tax that you are entitled to recover on these costs.
		7	Total the direct costs to you of the in-house supplies included in step 1 that are supplied outside the UK, exclusive of any VAT incurred on these costs that you are entitled to recover. Add to the total an uplift equivalent to the percentage VAT rate applicable to such supplies if you have accounted for VAT on these supplies to the VAT authorities in another member state.
	Working out the "costs" of **agency supplies**	8	Total the VAT-inclusive amounts paid by you to your principals in respect of the agency supplies included in step 1 for which the consideration you receive is **standard-rated**
		9	Total the VAT-inclusive amounts paid by you to your principals in respect of the agency supplies included in step 1 for which the consideration you receive is **not standard-rated**

Deals with	Purpose	Step	Action
Margin	Working out the **total margin**	10	Add the totals of costs at steps 2 to 9 inclusive
		11	Calculate the total margin for all the supplies included in step 1 by deducting the total at step 10 from the total at step 1
	Apportioning the margin	12	Calculate the margin for the standard-rated **designated travel** services by applying the following formula: $\frac{\text{Total at step 2}}{\text{Total at step 10}} \times \text{Total at step 11}$
		13	Calculate the margin for the zero-rated designated travel services by applying the following formula: $\frac{\text{Total at step 3}}{\text{Total at step 10}} \times \text{Total at step 11}$
	Steps 14 to 17 can be ignored where a market value is applied to all in-house supplies under steps M1 to M5	14	Calculate the margin for the standard-rated **in-house** supplies by applying the following formula: $\frac{\text{Total at step 4}}{\text{Total at step 10}} \times \text{Total at step 11}$
		15	Calculate the margin for the zero-rated in-house supplies by applying the following formula: $\frac{\text{Total at step 5}}{\text{Total at step 10}} \times \text{Total at step 11}$
		16	Calculate the margin for the exempt in-house supplies by applying the following formula: $\frac{\text{Total at step 6}}{\text{Total at step 10}} \times \text{Total at step 11}$
		17	Calculate the margin for the in-house supplies made outside the UK by applying the following formula: $\frac{\text{Total at step 7}}{\text{Total at step 10}} \times \text{Total at step 11}$
	Calculate consideration for agency supplies	18	Calculate the consideration for the **standard-rated** agency supplies by applying the following formula: $\frac{\text{Total at step 8}}{\text{Total at step 10}} \times \text{Total at step 11}$
		19	Calculate the consideration for the **non-standard-rated** agency supplies by applying the following formula: $\frac{\text{Total at step 9}}{\text{Total at step 10}} \times \text{Total at step 11}$
Output tax	Calculate for **designated travel** services	20	Total at step 12 × 1/6
	Calculate for standard-rated **in-house** supplies	21	(Total at step 4 + Total at step 14 + Total at step M2) × 1/6
	Calculate for standard-rated **agency** supplies	22	Total at step 18 × 1/6

Deals with	Purpose	Step	Action
VAT-exclusive sales values	Calculate for standard-rated designated travel services	23	Total at step 12 - Total at step 20
		24	Note the value of the zero-rated designated travel services at step 13
	Calculate for standard-rated in-house supplies	25	Total at step 4 + Total at step 14 + Total at step M2 - Total at step 21
	Value of zero-rated supplies made within the scheme	26	Total at step 5 + Total at step 15 + Total at step M3
	Calculate for exempt in-house supplies	27	Total at step 6 + Total at step 16
	Value of in-house supplies which are supplied outside the UK	28	Total at step 7 + Total at step 17
	Total VAT-exclusive value of supplies	29	Total of steps 23 to 28. Include this total in box 6 of your VAT return.
Annual adjust-ment		30	Calculate the total output VAT due on your designated travel services and margin scheme packages by adding the totals at steps 20 to 22 inclusive
		31	Total the provisional output VAT which has been accounted for during the financial year on the supplies included in the total at step 1
		32	Deduct the total at step 31 from the total at step 30. Include the resulting total in box 1 of your VAT return, either as a payable amount where the amount is positive or as a deductible amount where the amount is negative.

Imported Internet goods

9984

Category	Goods	Excise duty	Import duty	Import VAT %
Alcohol	Beer	✓	n/a	20
	Wine- non sparkling	✓	13.1 €/hl	20
Antiques	Over 100 years old	n/a	n/a	5 or 20
Baseball caps		n/a	2.7%	0 or 20
Bicycles		n/a	14%	20
Books		n/a	n/a	0 or 20
Cameras	Digital, still	n/a	0% to 4.9%	20
	Camcorder	n/a	4.9% to 14%	20
	35mm SLR	n/a	4.9%	20
	Camera lenses	n/a	6.7%	20
	Web-cam	n/a	4.9%	20
Ceramic tableware (not porcelain or china)	Kitchenware, household articles, toilet articles	n/a	5% to 9%	20
China or porcelain tableware	Kitchenware, household articles, toilet articles	n/a	12%	20
Clothing		n/a	12% [1]	20

Category	Goods	Excise duty	Import duty	Import VAT %
Computers	Laptop and desktop PCs	n/a	n/a	20
	Palm-held portable	n/a	n/a	20
	Palm-held portable with GPS	n/a	3.7%	20
Cosmetics		✓	n/a	20
DVDs and CDs	Audio, video, games discs	n/a	3.5%	20
	CD ROM with data or programs	n/a	n/a	20
	Blank CD-R and CD-RW	n/a	n/a	20
DVD and CD players	DVD players and recorders	n/a	14%	20
	CD players	n/a	9.5%	20
	CD player with radio - battery/mains	n/a	12%	20
	CD with radio - mains only	n/a	11.4%	20
Exercise apparatus		n/a	2.7%	20
Fishing rods and reels		n/a	3.7%	20
Food	Herbal diet supplements and mixed teas	n/a	12.8%	20
	Herbal tea - single e.g. mint	n/a	n/a	20
	Pure honey	n/a	17.3%	20
Furniture	Of cane, osier, bamboo or similar materials	n/a	5.6%	20
	Of metal or wood including upholstered e.g. settees	n/a	n/a	20
Golf clubs and balls		n/a	2.7%	20
Guitars		n/a	3.2%	20
Handbags		n/a	3% to 9.7%	20
Ink jet and toner cartridges		n/a	6.5%	20
Jewellery	Silver, gold or platinum	n/a	2.5%	20
	Imitation	n/a	4%	20
Massage apparatus		n/a	n/a	0 or 20
Mixing decks	Audio and video	n/a	3.7%	20
Mobile phones	Excluding those with built in GPS or TV	n/a	n/a	20
Monitors (plasma, LCD, CRT)	Able to display video	n/a	14%	20
	Only able to take computer signal	n/a	n/a	20
MP3 player or recorder	Sound only	n/a	2%	20
	Incorporating a radio	n/a	10%	20
MP4 player or recorder		n/a	13.9%	20
Painting, drawings, pastels	All by hand		n/a	5 or 20
Perfumes and toilet water		✓	n/a	20
Plastics		n/a	6.5%	20

Category	Goods	Excise duty	Import duty	Import VAT %
Purses etc	Wallets, bill folds, key cases, cigarette cases, spectacle cases etc	n/a	3% to 9.7%	20
Radios	Personal or battery operated	n/a	n/a	20
Statuettes and ornaments	Plated with precious metal	n/a	n/a	20
	Other metal	n/a	n/a	20
	Ceramic statuettes and articles	n/a	3.5% - 6%	20
Telescopes		n/a	4.2%	20
Televisions	Plasma, LCD, widescreen	n/a	14%	20
Tobacco	Cigars	✓	26%	20
	Cigarettes	✓	57.6%	20
	Smoking tobacco (packs < 500gm)	✓	74.9%	20
Toys		n/a	0% to 4.7%	20
Tyres		n/a	4.5%	20
Watches		n/a	4.5%	20

Note:
1. Except for imports from USA where special rates apply.

Intrastat

Supplementary declaration transaction codes 9986

Type of transaction	Code
Transactions involving actual or intended change of ownership for a consideration[1]	10
Credit note values, where the goods are not returned i.e. an amount used to reduce the value of the SD	16
Transactions which must be declared on SDs, but are not shown in boxes 8 or 9 of the VAT return[2]	17
Transactions which are declared in boxes 8 or 9 of the VAT return, but are only required on the SD for reconciliation purposes[3]	18
Returned and replacement goods	20
Free of charge transactions involving permanent change of ownership	30
Goods sent for processing	40
Goods returned following processing	50
Joint defence projects or other joint-governmental production programmes (e.g. Airbus)	70
Supply of building materials and equipment as part of a general construction or engineering contract	80
Other transactions	90

Note:
1. Including financial leasing and stock moved within the same legal entity, but excluding transactions to which codes 20, 70 and 80 relate.
2. For example, goods arriving in an excise or fiscal warehouse (where the date of arrival, rather than the tax point, is being used).
3. For example, goods leaving an excise or fiscal warehouse (to home use in the UK) where the tax point was not used to declare the arrival, stage payments when no movement of goods occurs, or final stage payments.

9987

Supplementary declaration delivery terms codes

Delivery terms	Code
Ex works	EXW
Free carrier	FCA
Free alongside ship	FAS
Free on board	FOB
Cost and freight	CFR
Cost, insurance and freight	CIF
Carriage paid to	CPT
Carriage and insurance paid to	CIP
Delivered duty paid	DDP
Delivered at place[1]	DAP
Delivered at terminal[2]	DAT
Other terms	XXX
Notes: 1. For reference periods prior to January 2012 this code was either delivered at frontier (DAF), delivered ex-ship (DES) or delivered duty unpaid (DDU) depending on the circumstances 2. For reference periods prior to January 2012 this code was delivered ex-quay (DEQ).	

UK VAT rates

9988

Period of application	Standard rate %	VAT fraction	Reduced rate %	VAT fraction
From 4 January 2011	20.0	1/6	5.0	1/21
1 January 2010 to 3 January 2011	17.5	7/47	5.0	1/21
1 December 2008 to 31 December 2009	15.0	3/23	5.0	1/21
1 April 1997 to 30 November 2008	17.5	7/47	5.0	1/21

EU VAT rates

9989

Member state	Code	Super reduced rate %	Reduced rate %	Standard rate %	Parking rate %
Austria	AT	n/a	10	20	12
Belgium	BE	n/a	6 or 12	21	12
Bulgaria	BG	n/a	9	20	n/a
Croatia	HR	n/a	5 or 13	25	n/a
Cyprus	CY	n/a	5 or 9	19	n/a
Czech Republic	CZ	n/a	10 or 15	21	n/a
Denmark	DK	n/a	n/a	25	n/a
Estonia	EE	n/a	9	20	n/a
Finland	FI	n/a	10 or 14	24	n/a
France	FR	2.1	5.5 or 10	20	n/a
Germany	DE	n/a	7	19	n/a
Greece	EL	n/a	6.5 or 13	23	n/a
Hungary	HU	n/a	5 or 18	27	n/a
Ireland	IE	4.8	9 or 13.5	23	13.5

Member state	Code	Super reduced rate %	Reduced rate %	Standard rate %	Parking rate %
Italy	IT	4	10	22	n/a
Latvia	LV	n/a	12	21	n/a
Lithuania	LT	n/a	5 or 9	21	n/a
Luxembourg	LU	3	8	17	14
Malta	MT	n/a	5 or 7	18	n/a
Netherlands	NL	n/a	6	21	n/a
Poland	PL	n/a	5 or 8	23	n/a
Portugal	PT	n/a	6 or 13	23	13
Romania	RO	n/a	5 or 9	24	n/a
Slovakia	SK	n/a	10	20	n/a
Slovenia	SI	n/a	9.5	22	n/a
Spain	ES	4	10	21	n/a
Sweden	SE	n/a	6 or 12	25	n/a
UK	UK	n/a	5	20	n/a

Contact addresses for EU VAT authorities

General contact addresses 9990

Country	Address	Telephone	Fax
Austria	Finanzamt Graz-Stadt Referat für ausländische Unternehmer Conrad von Hötzendorf Strasse 14-18 A - 8018 Graz	(+ 43) (316) 881 2309	(+ 43) (316) 817 608
Belgium	Bureau central de TVA pour assujettis etrangers Tour Sablon - 24th floor Rue Stevens, 7 B - 1000 Brussels	(+ 32) (2) 5525933	(+ 32) (2) 5525541
Bulgaria	National Revenue Agency Central Liaison Office 52 Dondukov Blvd 1000 Sofia	(+ 35) 92 9859 6151	(+ 35) 92 9859 3233
Croatia	10 000 Zagreb Boškovićeva 5	+385(0)1 480 9000	
Cyprus	VAT Service Dep of Customs & Excise Corner of M Karaoli and G Afxentiou 1096 Nicosia	(+ 357) 22 60 17 65	(+ 357) 22 66 04 84
Czech Republic	Financni urad pro Prahu 1 Stepanska 28 CZ - 112 33, Praha 1	(+ 420) 224 04 3115	(+ 420) 224 04 1911
Denmark	Skattecenter Tonder Nordre Landevej 22 DK - 6270 Tonder	(+ 45) 72 22 18 18	(+ 45) 72 22 19 19
Estonia	Northern Regional Tax Centre Endla 8 Tallinn EE - 15177	(+ 372) 69 34 196	(+ 372) 69 34 111
Finland	Uusimaa regional Tax Office Department of Corporate Taxation Opastinsilta 12, PO Box 30 0052 Vero	(+ 358) (10) 193 390	(+ 358) (9) 73 114700

Country	Address	Telephone	Fax
France	Service des impôts des enterprises étrangères (SIE) 10 Rue du Centre TSA 20011 93 465 Noisy-le-Grand Cedex	(+ 33) (1) 57 33 85 00	(+ 33) (1) 57 33 84 04
Germany	Bundesamt für Finanzen Friedhofstrasse 1 53225 Bonn	(+ 49) 228 4060	(+ 49) 228 4062661
Greece	Ministry of Finance 14th Directorate of VAT and Indirect Taxes Sina 2-4, 10672 Athens	(+ 30) 1 36 472 03	(+ 30) 1 36 454 13
Hungary	Tax and Financial Control Administration (General Depatment) H-1390 Budapest, Pf. 156	(+ 36) 1 412 73 02	(+ 36) 1 412 72 58
Ireland	VAT Interpretation Branch Office of the Revenue Commissioners Stamping Building Dublin Castle Dublin 2	(+ 353) 1 6475000	(+ 353) 1 6795236
Italy	Agenzie delle Entrate Via C Colombo, 426 C/D 00145 Roma, 00187 Roma	n/a	n/a
Latvia	State Revenue Service National Tax Board Smilsu iela 1 Riga LV - 1978	(+ 371) 67211011	(+ 371) 7028814
Lithuania	Vilnius County State Tax Inspectorate Sermuksniu str 4 2600 Vilnius	(+ 370) 5 268 7801	(+ 370) 5 212 5673
Luxembourg	Administration de l'Enregistrement et des Domaines Bureau d'imposition 10 7 Rue de Plébiscite BP 31 - 2010 Luxembourg	(+ 352) 4490 51	(+ 352) 291193
Malta	The Commissioner of VAT Centrepoint Building Ta' Paris Road Birirkara CMR 02	(+ 356) 21 49 93 30	(+ 356) 21 49 93 65
Netherlands	Belasting dienst Particulieren Ondernemingen Buitenland Postbus 2865 6401 D J Heerlen	(+ 31) (455) 5385 385	(+ 31) (45) 5779 634
Poland	Drugi Urzad Skarbowy Warszawa - Srodmlescie Ul Lindleya 16 02-013 Warszawa	(+ 48) 22 583 15 06	(+ 48) 22 625 50 06
Portugal	Serviço De Administraçáo do IVA Ava. João XXI, 76 1049 - 065 Lisboa	(+ 351) 21 761 00 00	(+ 351) 793 65 08
Romania	Ministry of Public Finance General Directorate for Indirect Taxation Legislation 17 Apolodor Street 5th District Bucharest	(+ 402) 131 20160	(+ 402) 131 20160
Slovak Republic	Tax Office 1 Bratislava Radlinskeho 37 PO Box 89 Bratislava 15	(+ 421) 2 57 37 8353	(+ 421) 2 57 37 8900

Country	Address	Telephone	Fax
Slovenia	Ministry of Finance General Tax Office Smartinska cesta 55 1000 Ljubljana	(+ 386) 1 478 27 43	(+ 386) 1 478 27 43
Spain	Subdireccion General de Informacion y Asistencia Tributaria del Departamento de Gestion de la Agencia Estatal de Administration Tributaria c/ InfantaMercedes, 37 E - 28071 Madrid	(+ 34) (1) 583 89 76	n/a
Sweden	Skatteverket Utlandsenheten SE - 106 61 Stockholm	(+ 46) 771 778 778	(+ 46) 8 694 18 11

Contacts for repayment claims **http://ec.europa.eu/taxation_customs/resources/documents/taxation/vat/traders/vat_refunds/refund_contact_details_table_en.pdf** 9991

Country	Address	Telephone	Fax
Austria	Finanzamt Graz-Stadt Betriebsveranlagungsteams Ausländerreferate Conrad von Hötzendorf Straße 14-18 8018 Graz	(+ 43) (316) 881 3373	(+ 43) (316) 817 608
Belgium	Bureau Central de TVA pour Assujettis Etrangers (Dep. Remboursement) Rue des Palais,48 5 eme etage 1030 Brussels	(+ 32) 257 74040	(+ 32) 257 96358
Bulgaria	Territorial Revenue Directorate - Sofia Aksakov str. 21 1000 SOFIA	(+ 35) 92 9859 3843	(+ 35) 92 986 4810
Cyprus	VAT Service Dep of Customs & Excise 1471 Nicosia	(+ 357) 22 60 18 34	(+ 357) 22 60 27 84
Czech Republic	Financni urad pro Prahu 1 Stepanska 28 112 33, Praha 1	(+ 420) 224 043 011	(+ 420) 224 043 198
Denmark	Skattecenter Tonder 8/13 momsdirectiv Pioner Alle 6270 Tonder	(+ 45) 72 22 18 18	(+ 45) 72 22 19 19
Estonia	Northern Tax and Customs Centre Endla 8 15177 Tallinn	(+ 372) 676 1256	(+ 372) 676 1111
Finland	Uudenmaan verovirasto Yritsverotoimisto PL 34 00052 Vero	(+ 358) (9) 73 11 20	(+ 358) (9) 73 11 4392
France	Direction des résidents a l'étranger et des services généraux Service des remboursements de TVA des assujettis étrangers 10, Rue du Centre TSA 60015 93465 Noisy le Grand Cedex	(+ 33) (1) 57 33 84 00	n/a

Country	Address	Telephone	Fax
Germany	Bundeszentralamt für Steuern Dienstsitz Schwedt Passower Chausee 3b 16303 Schwedt/Oder	(+ 49) 3018 4060	(+ 49) 18406 4722
Greece	Ministry of Finance VAT Directorate Department C Sina 2-4 10672 Athens	(+ 30) 210 364 4960	(+ 30) 210 364 5413
Hungary	APEH Directorate of Large Taxpayers Department for tax-refund for foreigners Dob utca 75-81 1077 Budapest	(+ 36) 1 461 3300	(+ 36) 1 322 9824
Ireland	Office of the Revenue Commissioners VAT Repayments Section River House Charlotte Quay Limerick	(+ 353) 61 21 2799	(+ 353) 61 40 2125
Italy	Agenza delle Entrate - Centro Operativo di Pescara Team rimborsi IVA ai non residenti Via Rio Sparto No 21 65129 Pescara	(+ 39) 085 577 2318/59/80	(+ 39) 085 5772325
Latvia	Large Taxpayers Department State Revenue Service 1 Jeruzalemes Str. 1010 Riga	(+ 371) 670 16751	(+ 371) 672 27496
Lithuania	Vilnaius apskrities valstybine mokesciu inspekija Sermuksniu g.4 2600 Vilnius	(+ 370) 52 61 66 35	(+ 370) 52 68 76 89
Luxembourg	Administration de l'Enregistrement et des Domaines Bureau d'imposition XI 67-69, rue Verte BP 1004 2010 Luxembourg	(+ 352) 44 905 1	(+ 352) 25 07 96
Malta	VAT Department Centre Point Building Ta' Paris Road Birirkara BKR 463	(+ 356) 21 49 93 30	(+ 356) 21 49 93 84
Netherlands	Belastingdienst Limburg/Kantoor Buitenland Postbus 4486 6401CZ Heerlen	(+ 31) 55 538 5385	(+ 31) (45) 577 96 34
Poland	Second Tax Office for Warsawa-Srodmiescie ul. Lindleya 14 02-013 Warsaw	(+ 48) 22 584 5100	(+ 48) 22 625 50 06
Portugal	Direccao-Geral das Contribucicoes e Impostos Direccao de Servicos de Reemboisos do IVA Ava. João XXI Apartado 8220 1049-065 Lisboa	(+ 351) 217 610 000	(+ 351) 217 938 133

Country	Address	Telephone	Fax
Romania	Directia generala a finantelor publice a municipiului Bucuresti Str. Professor Dr. Dimitrie Gerota nr. 13, sector 2 020027 Bucuresti	(+ 402) 130 757 63	(+ 402) 130 570 81
Slovak Republic	Danovy urad Bratislava I Oddelenie osobitnej správy DPH Radlinskeho 37 817 89 Bratislava	(+ 421) 2 57 37 8111	(+ 421) 2 57 37 89 04
Slovenia	Davcni Urad Ljubljana Tax Office Ljubljana Dunajska c.22 SLO-1000 LJUBLJANA	(+ 386) 1 474 46 02	(+ 386) 1 474 43 71
Spain	Oficina Nacional de Gestión Tributaria Departamento de Gestión Tributaria Agencia Estatal de Administración Tributaria Ministerio de Economía y Hacienda c/ Infanta Mercedes 49 28020 Madrid	(+ 34) (91) 582 67 39	(+ 34) (91) 582 67 57
Sweden	Skatteverket Skattekontor 9 106 61 Stockholm	(+ 46) 270 734 98	(+ 46) 10 574 18 11

Contact addresses for UK VAT authorities

General contact addresses For general telephone enquiries, the National Advice Centre can be contacted on 0300 200 3700 (+44 2920 501 from outside the UK). 9993

The main HMRC contact office is at Liverpool; all the contacts for this particular office are listed first, with the remaining ones below in paragraph order.

Issue	Contact	Address	¶¶
Payment on account queries	Large payers unit 3rd floor north	7th Floor Regian House James Street Liverpool L75 1AA	¶3182
Notification of appointment of liquidator	National insolvency unit		¶8708
Recovery of input tax after deregistration following insolvency - 426 claim	VAT 426 claims section National insolvency unit 5th floor		¶8722
Recovery of output tax after deregistration	VAT 833 team; Accounting and adjustment unit	Regional Post Room St John's House Merton Road Liverpool L75 1BB	¶8721
Recovery of input tax after deregistration following insolvency - 427 claim	VAT 427 claims team Accounting and adjustment unit		¶8722
Listed place of worship grant applications	Listed places of worship grant scheme	PO Box 609 Newport NP10 8QD	¶2452
Voluntary disclosure	HMRC	Alexander House Victoria Avenue Southend Essex SS99 1BD	¶3022
Disclosure of schemes	VAT avoidance disclosures unit; Anti-avoidance group (Intelligence)	1st floor 22 Kingsway London WC2B 6NR	¶3078 and ¶3116

Issue	Contact	Address	¶¶
Written enquiries team, for large refunds	National advice service; Written enquiries section	Alexander House Victoria Avenue Southend Essex SS99 1BD	¶3238
Complaints regarding HMRC's handling of a trader's tax affairs	Adjudicator's office	Eighth Floor Euston Tower 286 Euston Road London NW1 3US	¶4256
Request Ombudsman to review the Adjudicator's handling of a trader's complaint	The Parliamentary Ombudsman	Millbank Tower Millbank London SW1P 4QP	¶4258
Claim for DIY housebuilding refund	DIY builders and convertors VAT refund scheme processing unit	Local Compliance National DIY Team S0987 PO Box 3900 Glasgow G70 6AA	¶5328
Option to tax	Option to tax unit	Cotton House 7 Cochrane Street Glasgow G1 1GY	¶5672
Application form for agricultural flat rate scheme	HMRC	Grimsby VAT Registration Service HMRC Imperial House 77 Victoria Street Grimsby NE Lincs DN31 1DB	¶5996
VAT registration form for bloodstock	HMRC	Imperial House 77 Victoria Street Grimsby DN31 3DB	¶6202
Racing registration D forms	VAT Declarations	Weatherbys Sanders Road Wellingborough Northamptonshire NN8 4BX	¶6202
Investment gold notification	HMRC	Written Enquiries Section Alexander House Victoria Avenue Southend Essex SS99 1BD	¶6841
Barristers deferral application	VAT central unit/GABS	7th floor SW Alexander House Victoria Avenue Southend-on-Sea SS99 1AU	¶7778
Claim for input tax by unregistered public bodies	Banking/GABS; HMRC	7th Floor SW Alexander House 21 Victoria Avenue Southend-on-Sea SS99 1AU	¶7922
Recovery of input tax after deregistration following insolvency, in Scotland - 427 claim	VAT 427 claims team	Portcullis House 21 India Street Glasgow Strathclyde G2 4PH	¶8722

Issue	Contact	Address	¶¶
Voluntary arrangement	Voluntary arrangement service	Durrington Bridge House Barrington Road Worthing West Sussex BN12 4SE	¶8722
Submission of form VAT 411	Personal Transport Unit	Priory Court St John's Road Dover CT17 9SH	¶9226
Notification of simplified procedure for installed and assembled goods	Business advice centre 050	Ruby House 8 Ruby Place Aberdeen AB10 1ZP	¶9258
Notification of simplified procedure for triangulation			¶9332
Applications for approval to use duty deferment scheme	HMRC A & CGs Branch	Banking Operations Central Deferment Office 6th Floor North West Alexander House 21 Victoria Avenue Southend-on-Sea Essex SS99 1AA	¶9464
Request for Trader Unique Reference Numbers:	TURN team	Phase 2 13th floor (South) Government Buildings Ty Glas Lianishen Cardiff CF 14 5YA	¶9426
Request for direct repayment of import VAT	National repayments centre	Priory Court St John's Road Dover CT17 9SH	¶9429
Applications for approval to use Simplified Import VAT Accounting	SIVA approvals team	Ruby House 8 Ruby Place Aberdeen AB10 1ZP	¶9470
Submission of form VAT410 on personal export of a vehicle	Personal Transport Unit	Priory Court St John's Road Dover CT17 9SH	¶9615
VAT refund claim for EU trader	VAT Overseas Repayment Unit	Foyle House PO Box 34 Dungreggan Road Londonderry BT48 7AE Northern Ireland	¶9886
VAT refund claim for non-EU trader	VAT Overseas Repayment Unit	Foyle House PO Box 34 Dungreggan Road Londonderry BT48 7AE Northern Ireland	¶9918

9994 VAT registration and deregistration offices

Carmarthen	HMRC Ty-Myrddin Old Station Road Carmarthen SA31 1BT
Grimsby	HMRC Imperial House 77 Victoria Street Grimsby DN31 1DB
Newry	HMRC PO Box 40 Carnbane Way Damolly Newry Co Down BT35 6PJ
Wolverhampton	HMRC Deansgate 62-70 Tettenhall Road Wolverhampton WV1 4TZ
Non Established Taxable Persons Unit	HMRC Ruby House 8 Ruby Place Aberdeen AB10 1ZP

The telephone number for enquiries is 0300 0523 234.

All general VAT registrations and notifications of changes in details should be sent to Wolverhampton.

Deregistration applications should be sent to Grimsby.

Requests to retain a previous business owner's VAT number, VAT group applications, annual accounting requests, requests for certificates of status (VAT66) and flat rate scheme applications should be sent to Grimsby.

Those traders who do not have a permanent establishment in the UK should contact the Non Established Taxable Persons Unit in Aberdeen.

Online VAT registrations will continue to be dealt with at Carmarthen, Grimsby, Newry and Wolverhampton.

9995 **First-tier Tribunal and Upper Tribunal** The First-tier Tribunal now hears appeals in venues all over the UK and the Tribunals Service will attempt to ensure that a hearing is local to the appellant.

The address to which an appeal must be sent is:

The Tribunals Service
Tax
2nd Floor
54 Hagley Road
Birmingham
B16 8PE

EC Directive 2006/112

COUNCIL DIRECTIVE 2006/112/EC of 28 November 2006
on the common system of value added tax

TITLE I
SUBJECT MATTER AND SCOPE

Art. 1 1. This Directive establishes the common system of value added tax (VAT).

2. The principle of the common system of VAT entails the application to goods and services of a general tax on consumption exactly proportional to the price of the goods and services, however many transactions take place in the production and distribution process before the stage at which the tax is charged.

On each transaction, VAT, calculated on the price of the goods or services at the rate applicable to such goods or services, shall be chargeable after deduction of the amount of VAT borne directly by the various cost components.

The common system of VAT shall be applied up to and including the retail trade stage.

Art. 2 1. The following transactions shall be subject to VAT:

(a) the supply of goods for consideration within the territory of a Member State by a taxable person acting as such;

(b) the intra-Community acquisition of goods for consideration within the territory of a Member State by:

(i) a taxable person acting as such, or a non-taxable legal person, where the vendor is a taxable person acting as such who is not eligible for the exemption for small enterprises provided for in Articles 282 to 292 and who is not covered by Articles 33 or 36;

(ii) in the case of new means of transport, a taxable person, or a non-taxable legal person, whose other acquisitions are not subject to VAT pursuant to Article 3(1), or any other non-taxable person;

(iii) in the case of products subject to excise duty, where the excise duty on the intra-Community acquisition is chargeable, pursuant to Directive 92/12/EEC, within the territory of the Member State, a taxable person, or a non-taxable legal person, whose other acquisitions are not subject to VAT pursuant to Article 3(1);

(c) the supply of services for consideration within the territory of a Member State by a taxable person acting as such;

(d) the importation of goods.

2. (a) For the purposes of point (ii) of paragraph 1(b), the following shall be regarded as "means of transport", where they are intended for the transport of persons or goods:

(i) motorised land vehicles the capacity of which exceeds 48 cubic centimetres or the power of which exceeds 7,2 kilowatts;

(ii) vessels exceeding 7,5 metres in length, with the exception of vessels used for navigation on the high seas and carrying passengers for reward, and of vessels used for the purposes of commercial, industrial or fishing activities, or for rescue or assistance at sea, or for inshore fishing;

(iii) aircraft the take-off weight of which exceeds 1 550 kilograms, with the exception of aircraft used by airlines operating for reward chiefly on international routes.

(b) These means of transport shall be regarded as "new" in the cases:

(i) of motorised land vehicles, where the supply takes place within six months of the date of first entry into service or where the vehicle has travelled for no more than 6 000 kilometres;

(ii) of vessels, where the supply takes place within three months of the date of first entry into service or where the vessel has sailed for no more than 100 hours;

(iii) of aircraft, where the supply takes place within three months of the date of first entry into service or where the aircraft has flown for no more than 40 hours.

(c) Member States shall lay down the conditions under which the facts referred to in point (b) may be regarded as established.

3. "Products subject to excise duty" shall mean energy products, alcohol and alcoholic beverages and manufactured tobacco, as defined by current Community legislation, but not gas supplied through a natural gas system situated within the territory of the Community or any network connected to such a system.

Art. 3 1. By way of derogation from Article 2(1)(b)(i), the following transactions shall not be subject to VAT:

(a) the intra-Community acquisition of goods by a taxable person or a non-taxable legal person, where the supply of such goods within the territory of the Member State of acquisition would be exempt pursuant to Articles 148 and 151;

(b) the intra-Community acquisition of goods, other than those referred to in point (a) and Article 4, and other than new means of transport or products subject to excise duty, by a taxable person for the purposes of his agricultural, forestry or fisheries business subject to the common flat-rate scheme for farmers, or by a taxable person who carries out only supplies of goods or services in respect of which VAT is not deductible, or by a non-taxable legal person.

2. Point (b) of paragraph 1 shall apply only if the following conditions are met:

(a) during the current calendar year, the total value of intra-Community acquisitions of goods does not exceed a threshold which the Member States shall determine but which may not be less than EUR 10 000 or the equivalent in national currency;

(b) during the previous calendar year, the total value of intra-Community acquisitions of goods did not exceed the threshold provided for in point (a).

The threshold which serves as the reference shall consist of the total value, exclusive of VAT due or paid in the Member State in which dispatch or transport of the goods began, of the intra-Community acquisitions of goods as referred to under point (b) of paragraph 1.

3. Member States shall grant taxable persons and non-taxable legal persons eligible under point (b) of paragraph 1 the right to opt for the general scheme provided for in Article 2(1)(b)(i).

Member States shall lay down the detailed rules for the exercise of the option referred to in the first subparagraph, which shall in any event cover a period of two calendar years.

Art. 4 In addition to the transactions referred to in Article 3, the following transactions shall not be subject to VAT:

(a) the intra-Community acquisition of second-hand goods, works of art, collectors' items or antiques, as defined in points (1) to (4) of Article 311(1), where the vendor is a taxable dealer acting as such and VAT has been applied to the goods in the Member State in which their dispatch or transport began, in accordance with the margin scheme provided for in Articles 312 to 325;

(b) the intra-Community acquisition of second-hand means of transport, as defined in Article 327(3), where the vendor is a taxable dealer acting as such and VAT has been applied to the means of transport in the Member State in which their dispatch or transport began, in accordance with the transitional arrangements for second-hand means of transport;

(c) the intra-Community acquisition of second-hand goods, works of art, collectors' items or antiques, as defined in points (1) to (4) of Article 311(1), where the vendor is an organiser of sales by public auction, acting as such, and VAT has been applied to the goods in the Member State in which their dispatch or transport began, in accordance with the special arrangements for sales by public auction.

TITLE II
TERRITORIAL SCOPE

Art. 5 For the purposes of applying this Directive, the following definitions shall apply:

(1) "Community" and "territory of the Community" mean the territories of the Member States as defined in point (2);

(2) "Member State" and "territory of a Member State" mean the territory of each Member State of the Community to which the Treaty establishing the European Community is applicable, in accordance with Article 299 of that Treaty, with the exception of any territory referred to in Article 6 of this Directive;

(3) "third territories" means those territories referred to in Article 6;

(4) "third country" means any State or territory to which the Treaty is not applicable.

Art. 6 1. This Directive shall not apply to the following territories forming part of the customs territory of the Community:

(a) Mount Athos;

(b) the Canary Islands;

(c) the French territories referred to in Article 349 and Article 355(1) of the Treaty on the Functioning of the European Union;

(d) the Åland Islands;

(e) the Channel Islands.

2. This Directive shall not apply to the following territories not forming part of the customs territory of the Community:

(a) the Island of Heligoland;

(b) the territory of Büsingen;

(c) Ceuta;

(d) Melilla;

(e) Livigno;

(f) Campione d'Italia;

(g) the Italian waters of Lake Lugano.

Art. 7 1. In view of the conventions and treaties concluded with France, the United Kingdom and Cyprus respectively, the Principality of Monaco, the Isle of Man and the United Kingdom Sovereign Base Areas of Akrotiri and Dhekelia shall not be regarded, for the purposes of the application of this Directive, as third countries.

2. Member States shall take the measures necessary to ensure that transactions originating in or intended for the Principality of Monaco are treated as transactions originating in or intended for France, that transactions originating in or

intended for the Isle of Man are treated as transactions originating in or intended for the United Kingdom, and that transactions originating in or intended for the United Kingdom Sovereign Base Areas of Akrotiri and Dhekelia are treated as transactions originating in or intended for Cyprus.

Art. 8 If the Commission considers that the provisions laid down in Articles 6 and 7 are no longer justified, particularly in terms of fair competition or own resources, it shall present appropriate proposals to the Council.

TITLE III
TAXABLE PERSONS

Art. 9 1. "Taxable person" shall mean any person who, independently, carries out in any place any economic activity, whatever the purpose or results of that activity.

Any activity of producers, traders or persons supplying services, including mining and agricultural activities and activities of the professions, shall be regarded as "economic activity". The exploitation of tangible or intangible property for the purposes of obtaining income therefrom on a continuing basis shall in particular be regarded as an economic activity.

2. In addition to the persons referred to in paragraph 1, any person who, on an occasional basis, supplies a new means of transport, which is dispatched or transported to the customer by the vendor or the customer, or on behalf of the vendor or the customer, to a destination outside the territory of a Member State but within the territory of the Community, shall be regarded as a taxable person.

Art. 10 The condition in Article 9(1) that the economic activity be conducted "independently" shall exclude employed and other persons from VAT in so far as they are bound to an employer by a contract of employment or by any other legal ties creating the relationship of employer and employee as regards working conditions, remuneration and the employer's liability.

Art. 11 After consulting the advisory committee on value added tax (hereafter, the "VAT Committee"), each Member State may regard as a single taxable person any persons established in the territory of that Member State who, while legally independent, are closely bound to one another by financial, economic and organisational links.

A Member State exercising the option provided for in the first paragraph, may adopt any measures needed to prevent tax evasion or avoidance through the use of this provision.

Art. 12 1. Member States may regard as a taxable person anyone who carries out, on an occasional basis, a transaction relating to the activities referred to in the second subparagraph of Article 9(1) and in particular one of the following transactions:

(a) the supply, before first occupation, of a building or parts of a building and of the land on which the building stands;

(b) the supply of building land.

2. For the purposes of paragraph 1(a), "building" shall mean any structure fixed to or in the ground.

Member States may lay down the detailed rules for applying the criterion referred to in paragraph 1(a) to conversions of buildings and may determine what is meant by "the land on which a building stands".

Member States may apply criteria other than that of first occupation, such as the period elapsing between the date of completion of the building and the date of first supply, or the period elapsing between the date of first occupation and the date of subsequent supply, provided that those periods do not exceed five years and two years respectively.

3. For the purposes of paragraph 1(b), "building land" shall mean any unimproved or improved land defined as such by the Member States.

Art. 13 1. States, regional and local government authorities and other bodies governed by public law shall not be regarded as taxable persons in respect of the activities or transactions in which they engage as public authorities, even where they collect dues, fees, contributions or payments in connection with those activities or transactions.

However, when they engage in such activities or transactions, they shall be regarded as taxable persons in respect of those activities or transactions where their treatment as non-taxable persons would lead to significant distortions of competition.

In any event, bodies governed by public law shall be regarded as taxable persons in respect of the activities listed in Annex I, provided that those activities are not carried out on such a small scale as to be negligible.

2. Member States may regard activities, exempt under Articles 132, 135, 136 and 371, Articles 374 to 377, Article 378(2), Article 379(2) or Articles 380 to 390b, engaged in by bodies governed by public law as activities in which those bodies engage as public authorities.

TITLE IV
TAXABLE TRANSACTIONS

CHAPTER 1
SUPPLY OF GOODS

Art. 14 1. "Supply of goods" shall mean the transfer of the right to dispose of tangible property as owner.

2. In addition to the transaction referred to in paragraph 1, each of the following shall be regarded as a supply of goods:

(a) the transfer, by order made by or in the name of a public authority or in pursuance of the law, of the ownership of property against payment of compensation;

(b) the actual handing over of goods pursuant to a contract for the hire of goods for a certain period, or for the sale of goods on deferred terms, which provides that in the normal course of events ownership is to pass at the latest upon payment of the final instalment;

(c) the transfer of goods pursuant to a contract under which commission is payable on purchase or sale.

3. Member States may regard the handing over of certain works of construction as a supply of goods.

Art. 15 1. Electricity, gas, heat or cooling energy and the like shall be treated as tangible property.

2. Member States may regard the following as tangible property:

(a) certain interests in immovable property;

(b) rights in rem giving the holder thereof a right of use over immovable property;

(c) shares or interests equivalent to shares giving the holder thereof de jure or de facto rights of ownership or possession over immovable property or part thereof.

Art. 16 The application by a taxable person of goods forming part of his business assets for his private use or for that of his staff, or their disposal free of charge or, more generally, their application for purposes other than those of his business, shall be treated as a supply of goods for consideration, where the VAT on those goods or the component parts thereof was wholly or partly deductible.

However, the application of goods for business use as samples or as gifts of small value shall not be treated as a supply of goods for consideration.

Art. 17 1. The transfer by a taxable person of goods forming part of his business assets to another Member State shall be treated as a supply of goods for consideration.

"Transfer to another Member State" shall mean the dispatch or transport of movable tangible property by or on behalf of the taxable person, for the purposes of his business, to a destination outside the territory of the Member State in which the property is located, but within the Community.

2. The dispatch or transport of goods for the purposes of any of the following transactions shall not be regarded as a transfer to another Member State:

(a) the supply of the goods by the taxable person within the territory of the Member State in which the dispatch or transport ends, in accordance with the conditions laid down in Article 33;

(b) the supply of the goods, for installation or assembly by or on behalf of the supplier, by the taxable person within the territory of the Member State in which dispatch or transport of the goods ends, in accordance with the conditions laid down in Article 36;

(c) the supply of the goods by the taxable person on board a ship, an aircraft or a train in the course of a passenger transport operation, in accordance with the conditions laid down in Article 37;

(d) the supply of gas through a natural gas system situated within the territory of the Community or any network connected to such a system, the supply of electricity or the supply of heat or cooling energy through heating or cooling networks, in accordance with the conditions laid down in Articles 38 and 39;

(e) the supply of the goods by the taxable person within the territory of the Member State, in accordance with the conditions laid down in Articles 138, 146, 147, 148, 151 or 152;

(f) the supply of a service performed for the taxable person and consisting in valuations of, or work on, the goods in question physically carried out within the territory of the Member State in which dispatch or transport of the goods ends, provided that the goods, after being valued or worked upon, are returned to that taxable person in the Member State from which they were initially dispatched or transported;

(g) the temporary use of the goods within the territory of the Member State in which dispatch or transport of the goods ends, for the purposes of the supply of services by the taxable person established within the Member State in which dispatch or transport of the goods began;

(h) the temporary use of the goods, for a period not exceeding twenty-four months, within the territory of another Member State, in which the importation of the same goods from a third country with a view to their temporary use would be covered by the arrangements for temporary importation with full exemption from import duties.

3. If one of the conditions governing eligibility under paragraph 2 is no longer met, the goods shall be regarded as having been transferred to another Member State. In such cases, the transfer shall be deemed to take place at the time when that condition ceases to be met.

Art. 18 Member States may treat each of the following transactions as a supply of goods for consideration:

(a) the application by a taxable person for the purposes of his business of goods produced, constructed, extracted, processed, purchased or imported in the course of such business, where the VAT on such goods, had they been acquired from another taxable person, would not be wholly deductible;

(b) the application of goods by a taxable person for the purposes of a non-taxable area of activity, where the VAT on such goods became wholly or partly deductible upon their acquisition or upon their application in accordance with point (a);

(c) with the exception of the cases referred to in Article 19, the retention of goods by a taxable person, or by his successors, when he ceases to carry out a taxable economic activity, where the VAT on such goods became wholly or partly deductible upon their acquisition or upon their application in accordance with point (a).

Art. 19 In the event of a transfer, whether for consideration or not or as a contribution to a company, of a totality of assets or part thereof, Member States may consider that no supply of goods has taken place and that the person to whom the goods are transferred is to be treated as the successor to the transferor.

Member States may, in cases where the recipient is not wholly liable to tax, take the measures necessary to prevent distortion of competition. They may also adopt any measures needed to prevent tax evasion or avoidance through the use of this Article.

CHAPTER 2
INTRA-COMMUNITY ACQUISITION OF GOODS

Art. 20 "Intra-Community acquisition of goods" shall mean the acquisition of the right to dispose as owner of movable tangible property dispatched or transported to the person acquiring the goods, by or on behalf of the vendor or the person acquiring the goods, in a Member State other than that in which dispatch or transport of the goods began.

Where goods acquired by a non-taxable legal person are dispatched or transported from a third territory or a third country and imported by that non-taxable legal person into a Member State other than the Member State in which dispatch or transport of the goods ends, the goods shall be regarded as having been dispatched or transported from the Member State of importation. That Member State shall grant the importer designated or recognised under Article 201 as liable for payment of VAT a refund of the VAT paid in respect of the importation of the goods, provided that the importer establishes that VAT has been applied to his acquisition in the Member State in which dispatch or transport of the goods ends.

Art. 21 The application by a taxable person, for the purposes of his business, of goods dispatched or transported by or on behalf of that taxable person from another Member State, within which the goods were produced, extracted, processed, purchased or acquired within the meaning of Article 2(1)(b), or into which they were imported by that taxable person for the purposes of his business, shall be treated as an intra-Community acquisition of goods for consideration.

Art. 22 The application by the armed forces of a State party to the North Atlantic Treaty, for their use or for the use of the civilian staff accompanying them, of goods which they have not purchased subject to the general rules governing taxation on the domestic market of a Member State shall be treated as an intra-Community acquisition of goods for consideration, where the importation of those goods would not be eligible for the exemption provided for in Article 143(1)(h).

Art. 23 Member States shall take the measures necessary to ensure that a transaction which would have been classed as a supply of goods if it had been carried out within their territory by a taxable person acting as such is classed as an intra-Community acquisition of goods.

CHAPTER 3
SUPPLY OF SERVICES

Art. 24 1. "Supply of services" shal mean any transaction which does not constitute a supply of goods.

2. "Telecommunications services" shall mean services relating to the transmission, emission or reception of signals, words, images and sounds or information of any nature by wire, radio, optical or other electromagnetic systems, including the related transfer or assignment of the right to use capacity for such transmission, emission or reception, with the inclusion of the provision of access to global information networks.

Art. 25 A supply of services may consist, inter alia, in one of the following transactions:

(a) the assignment of intangible property, whether or not the subject of a document establishing title;

(b) the obligation to refrain from an act, or to tolerate an act or situation;

(c) the performance of services in pursuance of an order made by or in the name of a public authority or in pursuance of the law.

Art. 26 1. Each of the following transactions shall be treated as a supply of services for consideration:

(a) the use of goods forming part of the assets of a business for the private use of a taxable person or of his staff or, more generally, for purposes other than those of his business, where the VAT on such goods was wholly or partly deductible;

(b) the supply of services carried out free of charge by a taxable person for his private use or for that of his staff or, more generally, for purposes other than those of his business.

2. Member States may derogate from paragraph 1, provided that such derogation does not lead to distortion of competition.

Art. 27 In order to prevent distortion of competition and after consulting the VAT Committee,

Member States may treat as a supply of services for consideration the supply by a taxable person of a service for the purposes of his business, where the VAT on such a service, were it supplied by another taxable person, would not be wholly deductible.

Art. 28 Where a taxable person acting in his own name but on behalf of another person takes part in a supply of services, he shall be deemed to have received and supplied those services himself.

Art. 29 Article 19 shall apply in like manner to the supply of services.

CHAPTER 4
IMPORTATION OF GOODS

Art. 30 "Importation of goods" shall mean the entry into the Community of goods which are not in free circulation within the meaning of Article 24 of the Treaty.

In addition to the transaction referred to in the first paragraph, the entry into the Community of goods which are in free circulation, coming from a third territory forming part of the customs territory of the Community, shall be regarded as importation of goods.

TITLE V
PLACE OF TAXABLE TRANSACTIONS

CHAPTER 1
PLACE OF SUPPLY OF GOODS

SECTION 1
Supply of goods without transport

Art. 31 Where goods are not dispatched or transported, the place of supply shall be deemed to be the place where the goods are located at the time when the supply takes place.

SECTION 2
Supply of goods with transport

Art. 32 Where goods are dispatched or transported by the supplier, or by the customer, or by a third person, the place of supply shall be deemed to be the place where the goods are located at the time when dispatch or transport of the goods to the customer begins.

However, if dispatch or transport of the goods begins in a third territory or third country, both the place of supply by the importer designated or recognised under Article 201 as liable for payment of VAT and the place of any subsequent supply shall be deemed to be within the Member State of importation of the goods.

Art. 33 1. By way of derogation from Article 32, the place of supply of goods dispatched or transported by or on behalf of the supplier from a Member State other than that in which dispatch or transport of the goods ends shall be deemed to be the place where the goods are located at the time when dispatch or transport of the goods to the customer ends, where the following conditions are met:

(a) the supply of goods is carried out for a taxable person, or a non-taxable legal person, whose intra-Community acquisitions of goods are not subject to VAT pursuant to Article 3(1) or for any other non-taxable person;

(b) the goods supplied are neither new means of transport nor goods supplied after assembly or installation, with or without a trial run, by or on behalf of the supplier.

2. Where the goods supplied are dispatched or transported from a third territory or a third country and imported by the supplier into a Member State other than that in which dispatch or transport of the goods to the customer ends, they shall be regarded as having been dispatched or transported from the Member State of importation.

Art. 34 1. Provided the following conditions are met, Article 33 shall not apply to supplies of goods all of which are dispatched or transported to the same Member State, where that Member State is the Member State in which dispatch or transport of the goods ends:

(a) the goods supplied are not products subject to excise duty;

(b) the total value, exclusive of VAT, of such supplies effected under the conditions laid down in Article 33 within that Member State does not in any one calendar year exceed EUR 100 000 or the equivalent in national currency;

(c) the total value, exclusive of VAT, of the supplies of goods, other than products subject to excise duty, effected under the conditions laid down in Article 33 within that Member State did not in the previous calendar year exceed EUR 100 000 or the equivalent in national currency.

2. The Member State within the territory of which the goods are located at the time when their dispatch or transport to the customer ends may limit the threshold referred to in paragraph 1 to EUR 35 000 or the equivalent in national currency, where that Member State fears that the threshold of EUR 100 000 might cause serious distortion of competition.

Member States which exercise the option under the first subparagraph shall take the measures necessary to inform accordingly the competent public authorities in the Member State in which dispatch or transport of the goods begins.

3. The Commission shall present to the Council at the earliest opportunity a report on the operation of the special EUR 35 000 threshold referred to in paragraph 2, accompanied, if necessary, by appropriate proposals.

4. The Member State within the territory of which the goods are located at the time when their dispatch or transport begins shall grant those taxable persons who carry out supplies of goods eligible under paragraph 1 the right to opt for the place of supply to be determined in accordance with Article 33.

The Member States concerned shall lay down the detailed rules governing the exercise of the option referred to in the first subparagraph, which shall in any event cover two calendar years.

Art. 35 Articles 33 and 34 shall not apply to supplies of second-hand goods, works of art, collectors' items or antiques, as defined in points (1) to (4) of Article 311(1), nor to supplies of second-hand means of transport, as defined in Article 327(3), subject to VAT in accordance with the relevant special arrangements.

Art. 36 Where goods dispatched or transported by the supplier, by the customer or by a third person are installed or assembled, with or without a trial run, by or on behalf of the supplier, the place of supply shall be deemed to be the place where the goods are installed or assembled.

Where the installation or assembly is carried out in a Member State other than that of the supplier, the Member State within the territory of which the installation or assembly is carried out shall take the measures necessary to ensure that there is no double taxation in that Member State.

Section 3

Supply of goods on board ships, aircraft or trains

Art. 37 1. Where goods are supplied on board ships, aircraft or trains during the section of a passenger transport operation effected within the Community, the place of supply shall be deemed to be at the point of departure of the passenger transport operation.

2. For the purposes of paragraph 1, "section of a passenger transport operation effected within the Community" shall mean the section of the operation effected, without a stopover outside the Community, between the point of departure and the point of arrival of the passenger transport operation.

"Point of departure of a passenger transport operation" shall mean the first scheduled point of passenger embarkation within the Community, where applicable after a stopover outside the Community.

"Point of arrival of a passenger transport operation" shall mean the last scheduled point of disembarkation within the Community of passengers who embarked in the Community, where applicable before a stopover outside the Community.

In the case of a return trip, the return leg shall be regarded as a separate transport operation.

3. The Commission shall, at the earliest opportunity, present to the Council a report, accompanied if necessary by appropriate proposals, on the place of taxation of the supply of goods for consumption on board and the supply of services, including restaurant services, for passengers on board ships, aircraft or trains.

Pending adoption of the proposals referred to in the first subparagraph, Member States may exempt or continue to exempt, with deductibility of the VAT paid at the preceding stage, the supply of goods for consumption on board in respect of which the place of taxation is determined in accordance with paragraph 1.

Section 4

Supplies of gas through a natural gas system, of electricity and of heat or cooling energy through heating and cooling networks

Art. 38 1. In the case of the supply of gas through a natural gas system situated within the territory of the Community or any network connected to such a system, the supply of electricity, or the supply of heat or cooling energy through heating or cooling networks to a taxable dealer, the place of supply shall be deemed to be the place where that taxable dealer has established his business or has a fixed establishment for which the goods are supplied or, in the absence of such a place of business or fixed establishment, the place where he has his permanent address or usually resides.

2. For the purposes of paragraph 1, "taxable dealer" shall mean a taxable person whose principal activity in respect of purchases of gas, electricity, heat or cooling energy is reselling those products and whose own consumption of those products is negligible.

Art. 39 In the case of the supply of gas through a natural gas system situated within the territory of the Community or any network connected to such a system, the supply of electricity or the supply of heat or cooling energy through heating or cooling networks, where such a supply is not covered by Article 38, the place of supply shall be deemed to be the place where the customer effectively uses and consumes the goods.

Where all or part of the gas, electricity or heat or cooling energy is not effectively consumed by the customer, those non-consumed goods shall be deemed to have been used and consumed at the place where the customer has established his business or has a fixed establishment for which the goods are supplied. In the absence of such a place of business or fixed establishment, the customer shall be deemed to have used and consumed the goods at the place where he has his permanent address or usually resides.

CHAPTER 2
PLACE OF AN INTRA-COMMUNITY ACQUISITION OF GOODS

Art. 40 The place of an intra-Community acquisition of goods shall be deemed to be the place where dispatch or transport of the goods to the person acquiring them ends.

Art. 41 Without prejudice to Article 40, the place of an intra-Community acquisition of goods as referred to in Article 2(1)(b)(i) shall be deemed to be within the territory of the Member State which issued the VAT identification number under which the person acquiring the goods made the acquisition, unless the person acquiring the goods establishes that VAT has been applied to that acquisition in accordance with Article 40.

If VAT is applied to the acquisition in accordance with the first paragraph and subsequently applied, pursuant to Article 40, to the acquisition in the Member State in which dispatch or transport of the goods ends, the taxable amount shall be reduced accordingly in the Member State which issued the VAT identification number under which the person acquiring the goods made the acquisition.

Art. 42 The first paragraph of Article 41 shall not apply and VAT shall be deemed to have been applied to the intra-Community acquisition of goods in accordance with Article 40 where the following conditions are met:

(a) the person acquiring the goods establishes that he has made the intra-Community acquisition for the purposes of a subsequent supply, within the territory of the Member State identified in accordance with Article 40, for which the person to whom the supply is made has been designated in accordance with Article 197 as liable for payment of VAT;

(b) the person acquiring the goods has satisfied the obligations laid down in Article 265 relating to submission of the recapitulative statement.

CHAPTER 3
PLACE OF SUPPLY OF SERVICES

SECTION 1
Definitions

Art. 43 For the purpose of applying the rules concerning the place of supply of services:

1. a taxable person who also carries out activities or transactions that are not considered to be taxable supplies of goods or services in accordance with Article 2(1) shall be regarded as a taxable person in respect of all services rendered to him;

2. a non-taxable legal person who is identified for VAT purposes shall be regarded as a taxable person.

SECTION 2
General rules

Art. 44 The place of supply of services to a taxable person acting as such shall be the place where that person has established his business. However, if those services are provided to a fixed establishment of the taxable person located in a place other than the place where he has established his business, the place of supply of those services shall be the place where that fixed establishment is located. In the absence of such place of establishment or fixed establishment, the place of supply of services shall be the place where the taxable person who receives such services has his permanent address or usually resides.

Art. 45 The place of supply of services to a non-taxable person shall be the place where the supplier has established his business. However, if those services are provided from a fixed establishment of the supplier located in a place other than the place where he has established his business, the place of supply of those services shall be the place where that fixed establishment is located. In the absence of such place of establishment or fixed establishment, the place of supply of services shall be the place where the supplier has his permanent address or usually resides.

SECTION 3
Particular provisions

SUBSECTION 1
Supply of services by intermediaries

Art. 46 The place of supply of services rendered to a non-taxable person by an intermediary acting in the name and on behalf of another person shall be the place where the underlying transaction is supplied in accordance with this Directive.

SUBSECTION 2
Supply of services connected with immovable property

Art. 47 The place of supply of services connected with immovable property, including the services of experts and estate agents, the provision of accommodation in the hotel sector or in sectors with a similar function, such as holiday camps or sites developed for use as camping sites, the granting of rights to use immovable property and services for the preparation and coordination of construction work, such as the services of architects and of firms providing on-site supervision, shall be the place where the immovable property is located.

SUBSECTION 3

Supply of transport

Art. 48 The place of supply of passenger transport shall be the place where the transport takes place, proportionate to the distances covered.

Art. 49 The place of supply of the transport of goods, other than the intra-Community transport of goods, to non-taxable persons shall be the place where the transport takes place, proportionate to the distances covered.

Art. 50 The place of supply of the intra-Community transport of goods to non-taxable persons shall be the place of departure.

Art. 51 "Intra-Community transport of goods" shall mean any transport of goods in respect of which the place of departure and the place of arrival are situated within the territories of two different Member States.[1]

Art. 52 Member States need not apply VAT to that part of the intra-Community transport of goods to non-taxable persons taking place over waters which do not form part of the territory of the Community.

SUBSECTION 4

Supply of cultural, artistic, sporting, scientific, educational, entertainment and similar services, ancillary transport services and valuations of and work on movable property

Art. 53 The place of supply of services in respect of admission to cultural, artistic, sporting, scientific, educational, entertainment or similar events, such as fairs and exhibitions, and of ancillary services related to the admission, supplied to a taxable person, shall be the place where those events actually take place.

Art. 54 1. The place of supply of services and ancillary services, relating to cultural, artistic, sporting, scientific, educational, entertainment or similar activities, such as fairs and exhibitions, including the supply of services of the organisers of such activities, supplied to a non-taxable person shall be the place where those activities actually take place.

2. The place of supply of the following services to a non-taxable person shall be the place where the services are physically carried out:

(a) ancillary transport activities such as loading, unloading, handling and similar activities;

(b) valuations of and work on movable tangible property.

SUBSECTION 5

Supply of restaurant and catering services

Art. 55 The place of supply of restaurant and catering services other than those physically carried out on board ships, aircraft or trains during the section of a passenger transport operation effected within the Community, shall be the place where the services are physically carried out.

SUBSECTION 6

Hiring of means of transport

Art. 56 1. The place of short-term hiring of a means of transport shall be the place where the means of transport is actually put at the disposal of the customer.

2. The place of hiring, other than short-term hiring, of a means of transport to a non-taxable person shall be the place where the customer is established, has his permanent address or usually resides. However, the place of hiring a pleasure boat to a non-taxable person, other than short-term hiring, shall be the place where the pleasure boat is actually put at the disposal of the customer, where this service is actually provided by the supplier from his place of business or a fixed establishment situated in that place.

3. For the purposes of paragraphs 1 and 2, "short-term" shall mean the continuous possession or use of the means of transport throughout a period of not more than thirty days and, in the case of vessels, not more than 90 days.

SUBSECTION 7

Supply of restaurant and catering services for consumption on board ships, aircraft or trains

Art. 57 1. The place of supply of restaurant and catering services which are physically carried out on board ships, aircraft or trains during the section of a passenger transport operation effected within the Community, shall be at the point of departure of the passenger transport operation.

2. For the purposes of paragraph 1, "section of a passenger transport operation effected within the Community" shall mean the section of the operation effected, without a stopover outside the Community, between the point of departure and the point of arrival of the passenger transport operation.

"Point of departure of a passenger transport operation" shall mean the first scheduled point of passenger embarkation within the Community, where applicable after a stopover outside the Community.

"Point of arrival of a passenger transport operation" shall mean the last scheduled point of

1. "Place of departure" shall mean the place where transport of the goods actually begins, irrespective of distances covered in order to reach the place where the goods are located and "place of arrival" shall mean the place where transport of the goods actually ends.

disembarkation within the Community of passengers who embarked in the Community, where applicable before a stopover outside the Community.

In the case of a return trip, the return leg shall be regarded as a separate transport operation.

Subsection 8

Supply of telecommunications, broadcasting and electronic services to non-taxable persons

Art. 58 The place of supply of the following services to a non-taxable person shall be the place where that person is established, has his permanent address or usually resides:

(a) telecommunications services;

(b) radio and television broadcasting services;

(c) electronically supplied services, in particular those referred to in Annex II.

Where the supplier of a service and the customer communicate via electronic mail, that shall not of itself mean that the service supplied is an electronically supplied service.

Subsection 9

Supply of services to non-taxable persons outside the Community

Art. 59 The place of supply of the following services to a non-taxable person who is established or has his permanent address or usually resides outside the Community, shall be the place where that person is established, has his permanent address or usually resides:

(a) transfers and assignments of copyrights, patents, licences, trade marks and similar rights;

(b) advertising services;

(c) the services of consultants, engineers, consultancy firms, lawyers, accountants and other similar services, as well as data processing and the provision of information;

(d) obligations to refrain from pursuing or exercising, in whole or in part, a business activity or a right referred to in this Article;

(e) banking, financial and insurance transactions including reinsurance, with the exception of the hire of safes;

(f) the supply of staff;

(g) the hiring out of movable tangible property, with the exception of all means of transport;

(h) the provision of access to a natural gas system situated within the territory of the Community or to any network connected to such a system, to the electricity system or to heating or cooling networks, or the transmission or distribution through these systems or networks, and the provision of other services directly linked thereto.

Where the supplier of a service and the customer communicate via electronic mail, that shall not of itself mean that the service supplied is an electronically supplied service.

Subsection 10

Prevention of double taxation or non-taxation

Art. 59a In order to prevent double taxation, non-taxation or distortion of competition, Member States may, with regard to services the place of supply of which is governed by Articles 44, 45, 56, 58 and 59:

(a) consider the place of supply of any or all of those services, if situated within their territory, as being situated outside the Community if the effective use and enjoyment of the services takes place outside the Community;

(b) consider the place of supply of any or all of those services, if situated outside the Community, as being situated within their territory if the effective use and enjoyment of the services takes place within their territory.

CHAPTER 4

PLACE OF IMPORTATION OF GOODS

Art. 60 The place of importation of goods shall be the Member State within whose territory the goods are located when they enter the Community.

Art. 61 By way of derogation from Article 60, where, on entry into the Community, goods which are not in free circulation are placed under one of the arrangements or situations referred to in Article 156, or under temporary importation arrangements with total exemption from import duty, or under external transit arrangements, the place of importation of such goods shall be the Member State within whose territory the goods cease to be covered by those arrangements or situations.

Similarly, where, on entry into the Community, goods which are in free circulation are placed under one of the arrangements or situations referred to in Articles 276 and 277, the place of importation shall be the Member State within whose territory the goods cease to be covered by those arrangements or situations.

TITLE VI

CHARGEABLE EVENT AND CHARGEABILITYOF VAT

CHAPTER 1

GENERAL PROVISIONS

Art. 62 For the purposes of this Directive:

(1) "chargeable event" shall mean the occurrence by virtue of which the legal conditions necessary for VAT to become chargeable are fulfilled;

(2) VAT shall become "chargeable" when the tax authority becomes entitled under the law, at a given moment, to claim the tax from the person liable to pay, even though the time of payment may be deferred.

CHAPTER 2
SUPPLY OF GOODS OR SERVICES

Art. 63 The chargeable event shall occur and VAT shall become chargeable when the goods or the services are supplied.

Art. 64 1. Where it gives rise to successive statements of account or successive payments, the supply of goods, other than that consisting in the hire of goods for a certain period or the sale of goods on deferred terms, as referred to in point (b) of Article 14(2), or the supply of services shall be regarded as being completed on expiry of the periods to which such statements of account or payments relate.

2. Continuous supplies of goods over a period of more than one calendar month which are dispatched or transported to a Member State other than that in which the dispatch or transport of those goods begins and which are supplied VAT-exempt or which are transferred VAT-exempt to another Member State by a taxable person for the purposes of his business, in accordance with the conditions laid down in Article 138, shall be regarded as being completed on expiry of each calendar month until such time as the supply comes to an end.

Supplies of services for which VAT is payable by the customer pursuant to Article 196, which are supplied continuously over a period of more than one year and which do not give rise to statements of account or payments during that period, shall be regarded as being completed on expiry of each calendar year until such time as the supply of services comes to an end.

Member States may provide that, in certain cases other than those referred to in the first and second subparagraphs, the continuous supply of goods or services over a period of time is to be regarded as being completed at least at intervals of one year.

Art. 65 Where a payment is to be made on account before the goods or services are supplied, VAT shall become chargeable on receipt of the payment and on the amount received.

Art. 66 By way of derogation from Articles 63, 64 and 65, Member States may provide that VAT is to become chargeable, in respect of certain transactions or certain categories of taxable person at one of the following times:

(a) no later than the time the invoice is issued;

(b) no later than the time the payment is received;

(c) where an invoice is not issued, or is issued late, within a specified time no later than on expiry of the time-limit for issue of invoices imposed by Member States pursuant to the second paragraph of Article 222 or where no such time-limit has been imposed by the Member State, within a specified period from the date of the chargeable event.

The derogation provided for in the first paragraph shall not, however, apply to supplies of services in respect of which VAT is payable by the customer pursuant to Article 196 and to supplies or transfers of goods referred to in Article 67.

Art. 67 Where, in accordance with the conditions laid down in Article 138, goods dispatched or transported to a Member State other than that in which dispatch or transport of the goods begins are supplied VAT-exempt or where goods are transferred VAT-exempt to another Member State by a taxable person for the purposes of his business, VAT shall become chargeable on issue of the invoice, or on expiry of the time limit referred to in the first paragraph of Article 222 if no invoice has been issued by that time.

Article 64(1), the third subparagraph of Article 64(2) and Article 65 shall not apply with respect to the supplies and transfers of goods referred to in the first paragraph.

CHAPTER 3
INTRA-COMMUNITY ACQUISITION OF GOODS

Art. 68 The chargeable event shall occur when the intra-Community acquisition of goods is made.

The intra-Community acquisition of goods shall be regarded as being made when the supply of similar goods is regarded as being effected within the territory of the relevant Member State.

Art. 69 In the case of the intra-Community acquisition of goods, VAT shall become chargeable on issue of the invoice, or on expiry of the time limit referred to in the first paragraph of Article 222 if no invoice has been issued by that time.

CHAPTER 4
IMPORTATION OF GOODS

Art. 70 The chargeable event shall occur and VAT shall become chargeable when the goods are imported.

Art. 71 1. Where, on entry into the Community, goods are placed under one of the arrangements or situations referred to in Articles 156, 276 and 277, or under temporary importation arrangements with total exemption from import duty, or under external transit arrangements, the chargeable event shall occur and VAT shall become chargeable only when the goods cease to be covered by those arrangements or situations.

However, where imported goods are subject to customs duties, to agricultural levies or to charges having equivalent effect established under a common policy, the chargeable event shall occur and VAT shall become chargeable when the chargeable event in respect of those duties occurs and those duties become chargeable.

2. Where imported goods are not subject to any of the duties referred to in the second subparagraph of paragraph 1, Member States shall, as regards the chargeable event and the moment when VAT becomes chargeable, apply the provisions in force governing customs duties.

TITLE VII
TAXABLE AMOUNT

CHAPTER 1
DEFINITION

Art. 72 For the purposes of this Directive, "open market value" shall mean the full amount that, in order to obtain the goods or services in question at that time, a customer at the same marketing stage at which the supply of goods or services takes place, would have to pay, under conditions of fair competition, to a supplier at arm's length within the territory of the Member State in which the supply is subject to tax.

Where no comparable supply of goods or services can be ascertained, "open market value" shall mean the following:

(1) in respect of goods, an amount that is not less than the purchase price of the goods or of similar goods or, in the absence of a purchase price, the cost price, determined at the time of supply;

(2) in respect of services, an amount that is not less than the full cost to the taxable person of providing the service.

CHAPTER 2
SUPPLY OF GOODS OR SERVICES

Art. 73 In respect of the supply of goods or services, other than as referred to in Articles 74 to 77, the taxable amount shall include everything which constitutes consideration obtained or to be obtained by the supplier, in return for the supply, from the customer or a third party, including subsidies directly linked to the price of the supply.

Art. 74 Where a taxable person applies or disposes of goods forming part of his business assets, or where goods are retained by a taxable person, or by his successors, when his taxable economic activity ceases, as referred to in Articles 16 and 18, the taxable amount shall be the purchase price of the goods or of similar goods or, in the absence of a purchase price, the cost price, determined at the time when the application, disposal or retention takes place.

Art. 75 In respect of the supply of services, as referred to in Article 26, where goods forming part of the assets of a business are used for private purposes or services are carried out free of charge, the taxable amount shall be the full cost to the taxable person of providing the services.

Art. 76 In respect of the supply of goods consisting in transfer to another Member State, the taxable amount shall be the purchase price of the goods or of similar goods or, in the absence of a purchase price, the cost price, determined at the time the transfer takes place.

Art. 77 In respect of the supply by a taxable person of a service for the purposes of his business, as referred to in Article 27, the taxable amount shall be the open market value of the service supplied.

Art. 78 The taxable amount shall include the following factors:

(a) taxes, duties, levies and charges, excluding the VAT itself;

(b) incidental expenses, such as commission, packing, transport and insurance costs, charged by the supplier to the customer.

For the purposes of point (b) of the first paragraph, Member States may regard expenses covered by a separate agreement as incidental expenses.

Art. 79 The taxable amount shall not include the following factors:

(a) price reductions by way of discount for early payment;

(b) price discounts and rebates granted to the customer and obtained by him at the time of the supply;

(c) amounts received by a taxable person from the customer, as repayment of expenditure incurred in the name and on behalf of the customer, and entered in his books in a suspense account.

The taxable person must furnish proof of the actual amount of the expenditure referred to in point (c) of the first paragraph and may not deduct any VAT which may have been charged.

Art. 80 1. In order to prevent tax evasion or avoidance, Member States may in any of the following cases take measures to ensure that, in respect of the supply of goods or services involving family or other close personal ties, management, ownership, membership, financial or legal ties as defined by the Member State, the taxable amount is to be the open market value:

(a) where the consideration is lower than the open market value and the recipient of the supply does not have a full right of deduction under Articles 167 to 171 and Articles 173 to 177;

(b) where the consideration is lower than the open market value and the supplier does not have a full right of deduction under Articles 167 to 171 and Articles 173 to 177 and the supply is subject to an exemption under Articles 132, 135, 136, 371, 375, 376, 377, 378(2), 379(2) or Articles 380 to 390b;

(c) where the consideration is higher than the open market value and the supplier does not have a full right of deduction under Articles 167 to 171 and Articles 173 to 177.

For the purposes of the first subparagraph, legal ties may include the relationship between an employer and employee or the employee's family, or any other closely connected persons.

2. Where Member States exercise the option provided for in paragraph 1, they may restrict the categories of suppliers or recipients to whom the measures shall apply.

3. Member States shall inform the VAT Committee of national legislative measures adopted pursuant to paragraph 1 in so far as these are not measures authorised by the Council prior to 13 August 2006 in accordance with Article 27(1) to (4) of Directive 77/388/EEC, and which are continued under paragraph 1 of this Article.

Art. 81 Member States which, at 1 January 1993, were not availing themselves of the option under Article 98 of applying a reduced rate may, if they avail themselves of the option under Article 89, provide that in respect of the supply of works of art, as referred to in Article 103(2), the taxable amount is to be equal to a fraction of the amount determined in accordance with Articles 73, 74, 76, 78 and 79.

The fraction referred to in the first paragraph shall be determined in such a way that the VAT thus due is equal to at least 5% of the amount determined in accordance with Articles 73, 74, 76, 78 and 79.

Art. 82 Member States may provide that, in respect of the supply of goods and services, the taxable amount is to include the value of exempt investment gold within the meaning of Article 346, which has been provided by the customer to be used as basis for working and which as a result, loses its VAT exempt investment gold status when such goods and services are supplied. The value to be used is the open market value of the investment gold at the time that those goods and services are supplied.

CHAPTER 3
INTRA-COMMUNITY ACQUISITION OF GOODS

Art. 83 In respect of the intra-Community acquisition of goods, the taxable amount shall be established on the basis of the same factors as are used in accordance with Chapter 1 to determine the taxable amount for the supply of the same goods within the territory of the Member State concerned. In the case of the transactions, to be treated as intra-Community acquisitions of goods, referred to in Articles 21 and 22, the taxable amount shall be the purchase price of the goods or of similar goods or, in the absence of a purchase price, the cost price, determined at the time of the supply.

Art. 84 1. Member States shall take the measures necessary to ensure that the excise duty due from or paid by the person making the intra-Community acquisition of a product subject to excise duty is included in the taxable amount in accordance with point (a) of the first paragraph of Article 78.

2. Where, after the intra-Community acquisition of goods has been made, the person acquiring the goods obtains a refund of the excise duty paid in the Member State in which dispatch or transport of the goods began, the taxable amount shall be reduced accordingly in the Member State in the territory of which the acquisition was made.

CHAPTER 4
IMPORTATION OF GOODS

Art. 85 In respect of the importation of goods, the taxable amount shall be the value for customs purposes, determined in accordance with the Community provisions in force.

Art. 86 1. The taxable amount shall include the following factors, in so far as they are not already included:

(a) taxes, duties, levies and other charges due outside the Member State of importation, and those due by reason of importation, excluding the VAT to be levied;

(b) incidental expenses, such as commission, packing, transport and insurance costs, incurred up to the first place of destination within the territory of the Member State of importation as well as those resulting from transport to another place of destination within the Community, if that other place is known when the chargeable event occurs.

2. For the purposes of point (b) of paragraph 1, "first place of destination" shall mean the place mentioned on the consignment note or on any other document under which the goods are imported into the Member State of importation. If no such mention is made, the first place of destination shall be deemed to be the place of the first transfer of cargo in the Member State of importation.

Art. 87 The taxable amount shall not include the following factors:

(a) price reductions by way of discount for early payment;

(b) price discounts and rebates granted to the customer and obtained by him at the time of importation.

Art. 88 Where goods temporarily exported from the Community are reimported after having undergone, outside the Community, repair, processing, adaptation, making up or re-working, Member States shall take steps to ensure that the tax treatment of the goods for VAT purposes is the same as that which would have been applied had the repair, processing, adaptation, making up or re-working been carried out within their territory.

Art. 89 Member States which, at 1 January 1993, were not availing themselves of the option under Article 98 of applying a reduced rate may provide that in respect of the importation of works of art, collectors' items and antiques, as defined in points (2), (3) and (4) of Article 311(1), the taxable amount is to be equal to a fraction of the amount determined in accordance with Articles 85, 86 and 87.

The fraction referred to in the first paragraph shall be determined in such a way that the VAT thus due on the importation is equal to at least 5% of the amount determined in accordance with Articles 85, 86 and 87.

CHAPTER 5
MISCELLANEOUS PROVISIONS

Art. 90 1. In the case of cancellation, refusal or total or partial non-payment, or where the price is reduced after the supply takes place, the taxable amount shall be reduced accordingly under conditions which shall be determined by the Member States.

2. In the case of total or partial non-payment, Member States may derogate from paragraph 1.

Art. 91 1. Where the factors used to determine the taxable amount on importation are expressed in a currency other than that of the Member State in which assessment takes place, the exchange rate shall be determined in accordance with the Community provisions governing the calculation of the value for customs purposes.

2. Where the factors used to determine the taxable amount of a transaction other than the importation of goods are expressed in a currency other than that of the Member State in which assessment takes place, the exchange rate applicable shall be the latest selling rate recorded, at the time VAT becomes chargeable, on the most representative exchange market or markets of the Member State concerned, or a rate determined by reference to that or those markets, in accordance with the rules laid down by that Member State. Member States shall accept instead the use of the latest exchange rate published by the European Central Bank at the time the tax becomes chargeable. Conversion between currencies other than the euro shall be made by using the euro exchange rate of each currency. Member States may require that they be notified of the exercise of this option by the taxable person.

However, for some of the transactions referred to in the first subparagraph or for certain categories of taxable persons, Member States may use the exchange rate determined in accordance with the Community provisions in force governing the calculation of the value for customs purposes.

Art. 92 As regards the costs of returnable packing material, Member States may take one of the following measures:

(a) exclude them from the taxable amount and take the measures necessary to ensure that this amount is adjusted if the packing material is not returned;

(b) include them in the taxable amount and take the measures necessary to ensure that this amount is adjusted if the packing material is in fact returned.

TITLE VIII
RATES

CHAPTER 1
APPLICATION OF RATES

Art. 93 The rate applicable to taxable transactions shall be that in force at the time of the chargeable event.

However, in the following situations, the rate applicable shall be that in force when VAT becomes chargeable:

(a) in the cases referred to in Articles 65 and 66;

(b) in the case of an intra-Community acquisition of goods;

(c) in the cases, concerning the importation of goods, referred to in the second subparagraph of Article 71(1) and in Article 71(2).

Art. 94 1. The rate applicable to the intra-Community acquisition of goods shall be that applied to the supply of like goods within the territory of the Member State.

2. Subject to the option under Article 103(1) of applying a reduced rate to the importation of works of art, collectors' items or antiques, the rate applicable to the importation of goods shall be that applied to the supply of like goods within the territory of the Member State.

Art. 95 Where rates are changed, Member States may, in the cases referred to in Articles 65 and 66, effect adjustments in order to take account of the rate applying at the time when the goods or services were supplied.

Member States may also adopt all appropriate transitional measures.

CHAPTER 2
STRUCTURE AND LEVEL OF RATES

SECTION 1
Standard rate

Art. 96 Member States shall apply a standard rate of VAT, which shall be fixed by each Member State as a percentage of the taxable amount and which shall be the same for the supply of goods and for the supply of services.

Art. 97 From 1 January 2011 until 31 December 2015, the standard rate may not be less than 15%.

SECTION 2
Reduced rates

Art. 98 1. Member States may apply either one or two reduced rates.

2. The reduced rates shall apply only to supplies of goods and services in the categories set out in Annex III.

The reduced rates shall not apply to electronically supplied services.

3. When applying the reduced rates provided for in paragraph 1 to categories of goods, Member States may use the Combined Nomenclature to establish the precise coverage of the category concerned.

Art. 99 1. The reduced rates shall be fixed as a percentage of the taxable amount, which may not be less than 5%.

2. Each reduced rate shall be so fixed that the amount of VAT resulting from its application is such that the VAT deductible under Articles 167 to 171 and Articles 173 to 177 can normally be deducted in full.

Art. 100 On the basis of a report from the Commission, the Council shall, starting in 1994, review the scope of the reduced rates every two years.

The Council may, in accordance with Article 93 of the Treaty, decide to alter the list of goods and services set out in Annex III.

Art. 101 By 30 June 2007 at the latest the Commission shall present to the European Parliament and the Council an overall assessment report on the impact of reduced rates applying to locally supplied services, including restaurant services, notably in terms of job creation, economic growth and the proper functioning of the internal market, based on a study carried out by an independent economic think-tank.

SECTION 3
Particular provisions

Art. 102 After consultation of the VAT Committee, each Member State may apply a reduced rate to the supply of natural gas, electricity or district heating.

Art. 103 1. Member States may provide that the reduced rate, or one of the reduced rates, which they apply in accordance with Articles 98 and 99 is also to apply to the importation of works of art, collectors' items and antiques, as defined in points (2), (3) and (4) of Article 311(1).

2. If Member States avail themselves of the option under paragraph 1, they may also apply the reduced rate to the following transactions:

(a) the supply of works of art, by their creator or his successors in title;

(b) the supply of works of art, on an occasional basis, by a taxable person other than a taxable dealer, where the works of art have been imported by the taxable person himself, or where they have been supplied to him by their creator or his successors in title, or where they have entitled him to full deduction of VAT.

Art. 104 Austria may, in the communes of Jungholz and Mittelberg (Kleines Walsertal), apply a second standard rate which is lower than the corresponding rate applied in the rest of Austria but not less than 15%.

Art. 104a Cyprus may apply one of the two reduced rates provided for in Article 98 to the supply of liquid petroleum gas (LPG) in cylinders.

Art. 105 1. Portugal may apply one of the two reduced rates provided for in Article 98 to the tolls on bridges in the Lisbon area.

2. Portugal may, in the case of transactions carried out in the autonomous regions of the Azores and Madeira and of direct importation into those regions, apply rates lower than those applying on the mainland.

CHAPTER 3
TEMPORARY PROVISIONS FOR PARTICULAR LABOUR-INTENSIVE SERVICES

Art. 106 [Repealed by Council Directive 2009/47/EC]

Art. 107 [Repealed by Council Directive 2009/47/EC]

Art. 108 [Repealed by Council Directive 2009/47/EC]

CHAPTER 4

SPECIAL PROVISIONS APPLYING UNTIL THE ADOPTION OF DEFINITIVE ARRANGEMENTS

Art. 109 Pending introduction of the definitive arrangements referred to in Article 402, the provisions laid down in this Chapter shall apply.

Art. 110 Member States which, at 1 January 1991, were granting exemptions with deductibility of the VAT paid at the preceding stage or applying reduced rates lower than the minimum laid down in Article 99 may continue to grant those exemptions or apply those reduced rates.

The exemptions and reduced rates referred to in the first paragraph must be in accordance with Community law and must have been adopted for clearly defined social reasons and for the benefit of the final consumer.

Art. 111 Subject to the conditions laid down in the second paragraph of Article 110, exemptions with deductibility of the VAT paid at the preceding stage may continue to be granted in the following cases:

(a) by Finland in respect of the supply of newspapers and periodicals sold by subscription and the printing of publications distributed to the members of corporations for the public good;

(b) by Sweden in respect of the supply of newspapers, including radio and cassette newspapers for the visually impaired, pharmaceutical products supplied to hospitals or on prescription, and the production of, or other related services concerning, periodicals of non-profit-making organisations;

(c) by Malta in respect of the supply of foodstuffs for human consumption and pharmaceuticals.

Art. 112 If the provisions of Article 110 cause for Ireland distortion of competition in the supply of energy products for heating and lighting, Ireland may, on specific request, be authorised by the Commission to apply a reduced rate to such supplies, in accordance with Articles 98 and 99.

In the case referred to in the first paragraph, Ireland shall submit a request to the Commission, together with all necessary information. If the Commission has not taken a decision within three months of receiving the request, Ireland shall be deemed to be authorised to apply the reduced rates proposed.

Art. 113 Member States which, at 1 January 1991, in accordance with Community law, were granting exemptions with deductibility of the VAT paid at the preceding stage or applying reduced rates lower than the minimum laid down in Article 99, in respect of goods and services other than those specified in Annex III, may apply the reduced rate, or one of the two reduced rates, provided for in Article 98 to the supply of such goods or services.

Art. 114 1. Member States which, on 1 January 1993, were obliged to increase their standard rate in force at 1 January 1991 by more than 2% may apply a reduced rate lower than the minimum laid down in Article 99 to the supply of goods and services in the categories set out in Annex III.

The Member States referred to in the first subparagraph may also apply such a rate to children's clothing and children's footwear and housing.

2. Member States may not rely on paragraph 1 to introduce exemptions with deductibility of the VAT paid at the preceding stage.

Art. 115 Member States which, at 1 January 1991, were applying a reduced rate to children's clothing, children's footwear or housing may continue to apply such a rate to the supply of those goods or services.

Art. 116 [Repealed by Council Directive 2009/47/EC]

Art. 117 Austria may apply one of the two reduced rates provided for in Article 98 to the letting of immovable property for residential use, provided that the rate is not lower than 10%.

Art. 118 Member States which, at 1 January 1991, were applying a reduced rate to the supply of goods or services other than those specified in Annex III may apply the reduced rate, or one of the two reduced rates, provided for in Article 98 to the supply of those goods or services, provided that the rate is not lower than 12%.

The first paragraph shall not apply to the supply of second-hand goods, works of art, collectors' items or antiques, as defined in points (1) to (4) of Article 311(1), subject to VAT in accordance with the margin scheme provided for in Articles 312 to 325 or the arrangements for sales by public auction.

Art. 119 For the purposes of applying Article 118, Austria may apply a reduced rate to wines produced on an agricultural holding by the producer-farmer, provided that the rate is not lower than 12%.

Art. 120 Greece may apply rates up to 30% lower than the corresponding rates applied in mainland Greece in the departments of Lesbos, Chios, Samos, the Dodecanese and the Cyclades, and on the islands of Thassos, the Northern Sporades, Samothrace and Skiros.

Art. 121 Member States which, at 1 January 1993, regarded work under contract as the supply of goods may apply to the delivery of work under contract the rate applicable to the goods obtained after execution of the work under contract.

For the purposes of applying the first paragraph, "delivery of work under contract" shall mean the handing over by a contractor to his customer of movable property made or assembled by the contractor from materials or objects entrusted to him by the customer for that purpose, whether or not the contractor has provided any part of the materials used.

Art. 122 Member States may apply a reduced rate to the supply of live plants and other floricultural products, including bulbs, roots and the like, cut flowers and ornamental foliage, and of wood for use as firewood.

CHAPTER 5
TEMPORARY PROVISIONS

Art. 123 The Czech Republic may, until 31 December 2010, continue to apply a reduced rate of not less than 5% to the supply of construction work for residential housing not provided as part of a social policy, excluding building materials.

Art. 124 [Repealed by Council Directive 2007/75/EC]

Art. 125 Cyprus may, until 31 December 2010, continue to grant an exemption with deductibility of VAT paid at the preceding stage in respect of the supply of pharmaceuticals and foodstuffs for human consumption, with the exception of ice cream, ice lollies, frozen yoghurt, water ice and similar products and savoury food products (potato crisps/sticks, puffs and similar products packaged for human consumption without further preparation).

Art. 126 [Repealed by Council Directive 2007/75/EC]

Art. 127 [Repealed by Council Directive 2009/47/EC]

Art. 128 1. Poland may, until 31 December 2010 grant an exemption with deductibility of VAT paid at the preceding stage in respect of the supply of certain books and specialist periodicals.

2. [Repealed by Council Directive 2009/47/EC]

3. Poland may, until 31 December 2010, continue to apply a reduced rate of not less than 3% to the supply of foodstuffs as referred to in point (1) of Annex III.

4. Poland may, until 31 December 2010, continue to apply a reduced rate of not less than 7% to the supply of services, not provided as part of a social policy, for construction, renovation and alteration of housing, excluding building materials, and to the supply before first occupation of residential buildings or parts of residential buildings, as referred to in point (a) of Article 12(1).

Art. 129 1. [Repealed by Council Directive 2009/47/EC]

2. Slovenia may, until 31 December 2010, continue to apply a reduced rate of not less than 5% to the supply of construction, renovation and maintenance work for residential housing not provided as part of a social policy, excluding building materials.

Art. 130 [Repealed by Council Directive 2007/75/EC]

TITLE IX
EXEMPTIONS

CHAPTER 1
GENERAL PROVISIONS

Art. 131 The exemptions provided for in Chapters 2 to 9 shall apply without prejudice to other Community provisions and in accordance with conditions which the Member States shall lay down for the purposes of ensuring the correct and straightforward application of those exemptions and of preventing any possible evasion, avoidance or abuse.

CHAPTER 2
EXEMPTIONS FOR CERTAIN ACTIVITIES IN THE PUBLIC INTEREST

Art. 132 1. Member States shall exempt the following transactions:

(a) the supply by the public postal services of services other than passenger transport and telecommunications services, and the supply of goods incidental thereto;

(b) hospital and medical care and closely related activities undertaken by bodies governed by public law or, under social conditions comparable with those applicable to bodies governed by public law, by hospitals, centres for medical treatment or diagnosis and other duly recognised establishments of a similar nature;

(c) the provision of medical care in the exercise of the medical and paramedical professions as defined by the Member State concerned;

(d) the supply of human organs, blood and milk;

(e) the supply of services by dental technicians in their professional capacity and the supply of dental prostheses by dentists and dental technicians;

(f) the supply of services by independent groups of persons, who are carrying on an activity which is exempt from VAT or in relation to which they are not taxable persons, for the purpose of rendering their members the services directly necessary for the exercise of that activity, where those groups merely claim from their members exact reimbursement of their share of the joint expenses, provided that such exemption is not likely to cause distortion of competition;

(g) the supply of services and of goods closely linked to welfare and social security work, including those supplied by old people's homes, by bodies governed by public law or by other bodies recognised by the Member State concerned as being devoted to social wellbeing;

(h) the supply of services and of goods closely linked to the protection of children and young persons by bodies governed by public law or by other organisations recognised by the Member State concerned as being devoted to social wellbeing;

(i) the provision of children's or young people's education, school or university education, vocational training or retraining, including the supply of services and of goods closely related thereto, by bodies governed by public law having such as their aim or by other organisations recognised by the Member State concerned as having similar objects;

(j) tuition given privately by teachers and covering school or university education;

(k) the supply of staff by religious or philosophical institutions for the purpose of the activities referred to in points (b), (g), (h) and (i) and with a view to spiritual welfare;

(l) the supply of services, and the supply of goods closely linked thereto, to their members in their common interest in return for a subscription fixed in accordance with their rules by non-profit-making organisations with aims of a political, trade-union, religious, patriotic, philosophical, philanthropic or civic nature, provided that this exemption is not likely to cause distortion of competition;

(m) the supply of certain services closely linked to sport or physical education by non-profit-making organisations to persons taking part in sport or physical education;

(n) the supply of certain cultural services, and the supply of goods closely linked thereto, by bodies governed by public law or by other cultural bodies recognised by the Member State concerned;

(o) the supply of services and goods, by organisations whose activities are exempt pursuant to points (b), (g), (h), (i), (l), (m) and (n), in connection with fund-raising events organised exclusively for their own benefit, provided that exemption is not likely to cause distortion of competition;

(p) the supply of transport services for sick or injured persons in vehicles specially designed for the purpose, by duly authorised bodies;

(q) the activities, other than those of a commercial nature, carried out by public radio and television bodies.

2. For the purposes of point (o) of paragraph 1, Member States may introduce any restrictions necessary, in particular as regards the number of events or the amount of receipts which give entitlement to exemption.

Art. 133 Member States may make the granting to bodies other than those governed by public law of each exemption provided for in points (b), (g), (h), (i), (l), (m) and (n) of Article 132(1) subject in each individual case to one or more of the following conditions:

(a) the bodies in question must not systematically aim to make a profit, and any surpluses nevertheless arising must not be distributed, but must be assigned to the continuance or improvement of the services supplied;

(b) those bodies must be managed and administered on an essentially voluntary basis by persons who have no direct or indirect interest, either themselves or through intermediaries, in the results of the activities concerned;

(c) those bodies must charge prices which are approved by the public authorities or which do not exceed such approved prices or, in respect of those services not subject to approval, prices lower than those charged for similar services by commercial enterprises subject to VAT;

(d) the exemptions must not be likely to cause distortion of competition to the disadvantage of commercial enterprises subject to VAT.

Member States which, pursuant to Annex E of Directive 77/388/ EEC, on 1 January 1989 applied VAT to the transactions referred to in Article 132(1)(m) and (n) may also apply the conditions provided for in point (d) of the first paragraph when the said supply of goods or services by bodies governed by public law is granted exemption.

Art. 134 The supply of goods or services shall not be granted exemption, as provided for in points (b), (g), (h), (i), (l), (m) and (n) of Article 132(1), in the following cases:

(a) where the supply is not essential to the transactions exempted;

(b) where the basic purpose of the supply is to obtain additional income for the body in question through transactions which are in direct competition with those of commercial enterprises subject to VAT.

CHAPTER 3
EXEMPTIONS FOR OTHER ACTIVITIES

Art. 135 1. Member States shall exempt the following transactions:

(a) insurance and reinsurance transactions, including related services performed by insurance brokers and insurance agents;

(b) the granting and the negotiation of credit and the management of credit by the person granting it;

(c) the negotiation of or any dealings in credit guarantees or any other security for money and the management of credit guarantees by the person who is granting the credit;

(d) transactions, including negotiation, concerning deposit and current accounts, payments, transfers, debts, cheques and other negotiable instruments, but excluding debt collection;

(e) transactions, including negotiation, concerning currency, bank notes and coins used as legal tender, with the exception of collectors' items, that is to say, gold, silver or other metal coins or bank notes which are not normally used as legal tender or coins of numismatic interest;

(f) transactions, including negotiation but not management or safekeeping, in shares, interests in companies or associations, debentures and other securities, but excluding documents establishing title to goods, and the rights or securities referred to in Article 15(2);

(g) the management of special investment funds as defined by Member States;

(h) the supply at face value of postage stamps valid for use for postal services within their respective territory, fiscal stamps and other similar stamps;

(i) betting, lotteries and other forms of gambling, subject to the conditions and limitations laid down by each Member State;

(j) the supply of a building or parts thereof, and of the land on which it stands, other than the supply referred to in point (a) of Article 12(1);

(k) the supply of land which has not been built on other than the supply of building land as referred to in point (b) of Article 12(1);

(l) the leasing or letting of immovable property.

2. The following shall be excluded from the exemption provided for in point (l) of paragraph 1:

(a) the provision of accommodation, as defined in the laws of the Member States, in the hotel sector or in sectors with a similar function, including the provision of accommodation in holiday camps or on sites developed for use as camping sites;

(b) the letting of premises and sites for the parking of vehicles;

(c) the letting of permanently installed equipment and machinery;

(d) the hire of safes.

Member States may apply further exclusions to the scope of the exemption referred to in point (l) of paragraph 1.

Art. 136 Member States shall exempt the following transactions:

(a) the supply of goods used solely for an activity exempted under Articles 132, 135, 371, 375, 376 and 377, Article 378 (2), Article 379(2) and Articles 380 to 390b, if those goods have not given rise to deductibility;

(b) the supply of goods on the acquisition or application of which VAT was not deductible, pursuant to Article 176.

Art. 137 1. Member States may allow taxable persons a right of option for taxation in respect of the following transactions:

(a) the financial transactions referred to in points (b) to (g) of Article 135(1);

(b) the supply of a building or of parts thereof, and of the land on which the building stands, other than the supply referred to in point (a) of Article 12(1);

(c) the supply of land which has not been built on other than the supply of building land referred to in point (b) of Article 12(1);

(d) the leasing or letting of immovable property.

2. Member States shall lay down the detailed rules governing exercise of the option under paragraph 1.

Member States may restrict the scope of that right of option.

CHAPTER 4
EXEMPTIONS FOR INTRA-COMMUNITY TRANSACTIONS

Section 1
Exemptions related to the supply of goods

Art. 138 1. Member States shall exempt the supply of goods dispatched or transported to a destination outside their respective territory but within the Community, by or on behalf of the vendor or the person acquiring the goods, for another taxable person, or for a non-taxable legal person acting as such in a Member State other than that in which dispatch or transport of the goods began.

2. In addition to the supply of goods referred to in paragraph 1, Member States shall exempt the following transactions:

(a) the supply of new means of transport, dispatched or transported to the customer at a destination outside their respective territory but within the Community, by or on behalf of the vendor or the customer, for taxable persons, or non-taxable legal persons, whose intra-Community acquisitions of goods are not subject to VAT pursuant to Article 3(1), or for any other non-taxable person;

(b) the supply of products subject to excise duty, dispatched or transported to a destination outside their respective territory but within the Community, to the customer, by or on behalf of the vendor or the customer, for taxable persons, or non-taxable legal persons, whose intra-Community acquisitions of goods other than products subject to excise duty are not subject to VAT pursuant to Article 3(1), where those products have been dispatched or transported in accordance with Article 7(4) and (5) or Article 16 of Directive 92/12/EEC;

(c) the supply of goods, consisting in a transfer to another Member State, which would have been entitled to exemption under paragraph 1 and points (a) and (b) if it had been made on behalf of another taxable person.

Art. 139 1. The exemption provided for in Article 138(1) shall not apply to the supply of goods carried out by taxable persons who are covered by the exemption for small enterprises provided for in Articles 282 to 292.

Nor shall that exemption apply to the supply of goods to taxable persons, or non-taxable legal persons, whose intra-Community acquisitions of goods are not subject to VAT pursuant to Article 3(1).

2. The exemption provided for in Article 138(2)(b) shall not apply to the supply of products subject to excise duty by taxable persons who are covered by the exemption for small enterprises provided for in Articles 282 to 292.

3. The exemption provided for in Article 138(1) and (2)(b) and (c) shall not apply to the supply of goods subject to VAT in accordance with the margin scheme provided for in Articles 312 to 325 or the special arrangements for sales by public auction.

The exemption provided for in Article 138(1) and (2)(c) shall not apply to the supply of second-hand means of transport, as defined in Article 327(3), subject to VAT in accordance with the transitional arrangements for second-hand means of transport.

Section 2

Exemptions for intra-Community acquisitions of goods

Art. 140 Member States shall exempt the following transactions:

(a) the intra-Community acquisition of goods the supply of which by taxable persons would in all circumstances be exempt within their respective territory;

(b) the intra-Community acquisition of goods the importation of which would in all circumstances be exempt under points (a), (b) and (c) and (e) to (l) of Article 143;

(c) the intra-Community acquisition of goods where, pursuant to Articles 170 and 171, the person acquiring the goods would in all circumstances be entitled to full reimbursement of the VAT due under Article 2(1)(b).

Art. 141 Each Member State shall take specific measures to ensure that VAT is not charged on the intra-Community acquisition of goods within its territory, made in accordance with Article 40, where the following conditions are met:

(a) the acquisition of goods is made by a taxable person who is not established in the Member State concerned but is identified for VAT purposes in another Member State;

(b) the acquisition of goods is made for the purposes of the subsequent supply of those goods, in the Member State concerned, by the taxable person referred to in point (a);

(c) the goods thus acquired by the taxable person referred to in point (a) are directly dispatched or transported, from a Member State other than that in which he is identified for VAT purposes, to the person for whom he is to carry out the subsequent supply;

(d) the person to whom the subsequent supply is to be made is another taxable person, or a non-taxable legal person, who is identified for VAT purposes in the Member State concerned;

(e) the person referred to in point (d) has been designated in accordance with Article 197 as liable for payment of the VAT due on the supply carried out by the taxable person who is not established in the Member State in which the tax is due.

Section 3

Exemptions for certain transport services

Art. 142 Member States shall exempt the supply of intra-Community transport of goods to and from the islands making up the autonomous regions of the Azores and Madeira, as well as the supply of transport of goods between those islands.

CHAPTER 5

EXEMPTIONS ON IMPORTATION

Art. 143 1. Member States shall exempt the following transactions:

(a) the final importation of goods of which the supply by a taxable person would in all circumstances be exempt within their respective territory;

(b) the final importation of goods governed by Council Directives 69/169/EEC[1], 83/181/EEC[2] and 2006/79/ EC[3];

(c) the final importation of goods, in free circulation from a third territory forming part of the Community customs territory, which would be entitled to exemption under point (b) if they had been imported within the meaning of the first paragraph of Article 30;

---

1. Council Directive 69/169/EEC of 28 May 1969 on the harmonisation of provisions laid down by Law, Regulation or Administrative Action relating to exemption from turnover tax and excise duty on imports in international travel (OJ L133, 4.6.1969, p. 6). Directive as last amended by Directive 2005/93/EC (OJ L346, 29.12.2005, p. 16).

2. Council Directive 83/181/EEC of 28 March 1983 determining the scope of Article 14(1)(d) of Directive 77/388/EEC as regards exemption from value added tax on the final importation of certain goods (OJ L 105, 23.4.1983, p. 38). Directive as last amended by the 1994 Act of Accession.

3. Council Directive 2006/79/EC of 5 October 2006 on the exemption from taxes of imports of small consignments of goods of a non-commercial character from third countries (codified version) (OJ L 286, 17.10.2006, p. 15).

(d) the importation of goods dispatched or transported from a third territory or a third country into a Member State other than that in which the dispatch or transport of the goods ends, where the supply of such goods by the importer designated or recognised under Article 201 as liable for payment of VAT is exempt under Article 138;

(e) the reimportation, by the person who exported them, of goods in the state in which they were exported, where those goods are exempt from customs duties;

(f) the importation, under diplomatic and consular arrangements, of goods which are exempt from customs duties;

(fa) the importation of goods by the European Community, the European Atomic Energy Community, the European Central Bank or the European Investment Bank, or by the bodies set up by the Communities to which the Protocol of 8 April 1965 on the privileges and immunities of the European Communities applies, within the limits and under the conditions of that Protocol and the agreements for its implementation or the headquarters agreements, in so far as it does not lead to distortion of competition;

(g) the importation of goods by international bodies, other than those referred to in point (fa), recognised as such by the public authorities of the host Member State, or by members of such bodies, within the limits and under the conditions laid down by the international conventions establishing the bodies or by headquarters agreements;

(h) the importation of goods, into Member States party to the North Atlantic Treaty, by the armed forces of other States party to that Treaty for the use of those forces or the civilian staff accompanying them or for supplying their messes or canteens where such forces take part in the common defence effort;

(i) the importation of goods by the armed forces of the United Kingdom stationed in the island of Cyprus pursuant to the Treaty of Establishment concerning the Republic of Cyprus, dated 16 August 1960, which are for the use of those forces or the civilian staff accompanying them or for supplying their messes or canteens;

(j) the importation into ports, by sea fishing undertakings, of their catches, unprocessed or after undergoing preservation for marketing but before being supplied;

(k) the importation of gold by central banks;

(l) the importation of gas through a natural gas system or any network connected to such a system or fed in from a vessel transporting gas into a natural gas system or any upstream pipeline network, of electricity or of heat or cooling energy through heating or cooling networks.

2. The exemption provided for in paragraph 1(d) shall apply in cases when the importation of goods is followed by the supply of goods exempted under Article 138(1) and (2)(c) only if at the time of importation the importer has provided to the competent authorities of the Member State of importation at least the following information:

(a) his VAT identification number issued in the Member State of importation or the VAT identification number of his tax representative, liable for payment of the VAT, issued in the Member State of importation;

(b) the VAT identification number of the customer, to whom the goods are supplied in accordance with Article 138(1), issued in another Member State, or his own VAT identification number issued in the Member State in which the dispatch or transport of the goods ends when the goods are subject to a transfer in accordance with Article 138(2)(c);

(c) the evidence that the imported goods are intended to be transported or dispatched from the Member State of importation to another Member State.

However, Member States may provide that the evidence referred to in point (c) be indicated to the competent authorities only upon request.

Art. 144 Member States shall exempt the supply of services relating to the importation of goods where the value of such services is included in the taxable amount in accordance with Article 86(1)(b).

Art. 145 1. The Commission shall, where appropriate, as soon as possible, present to the Council proposals designed to delimit the scope of the exemptions provided for in Articles 143 and 144 and to lay down the detailed rules for their implementation.

2. Pending the entry into force of the rules referred to in paragraph 1, Member States may maintain their national provisions in force.

Member States may adapt their national provisions so as to minimise distortion of competition and, in particular, to prevent non-taxation or double taxation within the Community.

Member States may use whatever administrative procedures they consider most appropriate to achieve exemption.

3. Member States shall notify to the Commission, which shall inform the other Member States accordingly, the provisions of national law which are in force, in so far as these have not already been notified, and those which they adopt pursuant to paragraph 2.

CHAPTER 6
EXEMPTIONS ON EXPORTATION

Art. 146 1. Member States shall exempt the following transactions:

(a) the supply of goods dispatched or transported to a destination outside the Community by or on behalf of the vendor;

(b) the supply of goods dispatched or transported to a destination outside the Community by or on behalf of a customer not established within their respective territory, with the exception of goods transported by the customer himself for the equipping, fuelling and provisioning of pleasure boats and private aircraft or any other means of transport for private use;

(c) the supply of goods to approved bodies which export them out of the Community as part of their humanitarian, charitable or teaching activities outside the Community;

(d) the supply of services consisting in work on movable property acquired or imported for the purpose of undergoing such work within the Community, and dispatched or transported out of the Community by the supplier, by the customer if not established within their respective territory or on behalf of either of them;

(e) the supply of services, including transport and ancillary transactions, but excluding the supply of services exempted in accordance with Articles 132 and 135, where these are directly connected with the exportation or importation of goods covered by Article 61 and Article 157(1)(a).

2. The exemption provided for in point (c) of paragraph 1 may be granted by means of a refund of the VAT.

Art. 147 1. Where the supply of goods referred to in point (b) of Article 146(1) relates to goods to be carried in the personal luggage of travellers, the exemption shall apply only if the following conditions are met:

(a) the traveller is not established within the Community;

(b) the goods are transported out of the Community before the end of the third month following that in which the supply takes place;

(c) the total value of the supply, including VAT, is more than EUR 175 or the equivalent in national currency, fixed annually by applying the conversion rate obtaining on the first working day of October with effect from 1 January of the following year.

However, Member States may exempt a supply with a total value of less than the amount specified in point (c) of the first subparagraph.

2. For the purposes of paragraph 1, "a traveller who is not established within the Community" shall mean a traveller whose permanent address or habitual residence is not located within the Community. In that case "permanent address or habitual residence" means the place entered as such in a passport, identity card or other document recognised as an identity document by the Member State within whose territory the supply takes place.

Proof of exportation shall be furnished by means of the invoice or other document in lieu thereof, endorsed by the customs office of exit from the Community.

Each Member State shall send to the Commission specimens of the stamps it uses for the endorsement referred to in the second subparagraph. The Commission shall forward that information to the tax authorities of the other Member States.

CHAPTER 7
EXEMPTIONS RELATED TO INTERNATIONAL TRANSPORT

Art. 148 Member States shall exempt the following transactions:

(a) the supply of goods for the fuelling and provisioning of vessels used for navigation on the high seas and carrying passengers for reward or used for the purpose of commercial, industrial or fishing activities, or for rescue or assistance at sea, or for inshore fishing, with the exception, in the case of vessels used for inshore fishing, of ships' provisions;

(b) the supply of goods for the fuelling and provisioning of fighting ships, falling within the combined nomenclature (CN) code 8906 10 00, leaving their territory and bound for ports or anchorages outside the Member State concerned;

(c) the supply, modification, repair, maintenance, chartering and hiring of the vessels referred to in point (a), and the supply, hiring, repair and maintenance of equipment, including fishing equipment, incorporated or used therein;

(d) the supply of services other than those referred to in point (c), to meet the direct needs of the vessels referred to in point (a) or of their cargoes;

(e) the supply of goods for the fuelling and provisioning of aircraft used by airlines operating for reward chiefly on international routes;

(f) the supply, modification, repair, maintenance, chartering and hiring of the aircraft referred to in point (e), and the supply, hiring, repair and maintenance of equipment incorporated or used therein;

(g) the supply of services, other than those referred to in point (f), to meet the direct needs of the aircraft referred to in point (e) or of their cargoes.

Art. 149 Portugal may treat sea and air transport between the islands making up the autonomous regions of the Azores and Madeira and between those regions and the mainland as international transport.

Art. 150 1. The Commission shall, where appropriate, as soon as possible, present to the Council proposals designed to delimit the scope of the exemptions provided for in Article 148 and to lay down the detailed rules for their implementation.

2. Pending the entry into force of the provisions referred to in paragraph 1, Member States may

limit the scope of the exemptions provided for in points (a) and (b) of Article 148.

CHAPTER 8

EXEMPTIONS RELATING TO CERTAIN TRANSACTIONS TREATED AS EXPORTS

Art. 151 1. Member States shall exempt the following transactions:

(a) the supply of goods or services under diplomatic and consular arrangements;

(aa) the supply of goods or services to the European Community, the European Atomic Energy Community, the European Central Bank or the European Investment Bank, or to the bodies set up by the Communities to which the Protocol of 8 April 1965 on the privileges and immunities of the European Communities applies, within the limits and under the conditions of that Protocol and the agreements for its implementation or the headquarters agreements, in so far as it does not lead to distortion of competition;

(b) the supply of goods or services to international bodies, other than those referred to in point (aa), recognised as such by the public authorities of the host Member States, and to members of such bodies, within the limits and under the conditions laid down by the international conventions establishing the bodies or by headquarters agreements;

(c) the supply of goods or services within a Member State which is a party to the North Atlantic Treaty, intended either for the armed forces of other States party to that Treaty for the use of those forces, or of the civilian staff accompanying them, or for supplying their messes or canteens when such forces take part in the common defence effort;

(d) the supply of goods or services to another Member State, intended for the armed forces of any State which is a party to the North Atlantic Treaty, other than the Member State of destination itself, for the use of those forces, or of the civilian staff accompanying them, or for supplying their messes or canteens when such forces take part in the common defence effort;

(e) the supply of goods or services to the armed forces of the United Kingdom stationed in the island of Cyprus pursuant to the Treaty of Establishment concerning the Republic of Cyprus, dated 16 August 1960, which are for the use of those forces, or of the civilian staff accompanying them, or for supplying their messes or canteens.

Pending the adoption of common tax rules, the exemptions provided for in the first subparagraph shall be subject to the limitations laid down by the host Member State.

2. In cases where the goods are not dispatched or transported out of the Member State in which the supply takes place, and in the case of services, the exemption may be granted by means of a refund of the VAT.

Art. 152 Member States shall exempt the supply of gold to central banks.

CHAPTER 9

EXEMPTIONS FOR THE SUPPLY OF SERVICES BY INTERMEDIARIES

Art. 153 Member States shall exempt the supply of services by intermediaries, acting in the name and on behalf of another person, where they take part in the transactions referred to in Chapters 6, 7 and 8, or of transactions carried out outside the Community.

The exemption referred to in the first paragraph shall not apply to travel agents who, in the name and on behalf of travellers, supply services which are carried out in other Member States.

CHAPTER 10

EXEMPTIONS FOR TRANSACTIONS RELATING TO INTERNATIONAL TRADE

SECTION 1

Customs warehouses, warehouses other than customs warehouses and similar arrangements

Art. 154 For the purposes of this Section, "warehouses other than customs warehouses" shall, in the case of products subject to excise duty, mean the places defined as tax warehouses by Article 4(b) of Directive 92/12/EEC and, in the case of products not subject to excise duty, the places defined as such by the Member States.

Art. 155 Without prejudice to other Community tax provisions, Member States may, after consulting the VAT Committee, take special measures designed to exempt all or some of the transactions referred to in this Section, provided that those measures are not aimed at final use or consumption and that the amount of VAT due on cessation of the arrangements or situations referred to in this Section corresponds to the amount of tax which would have been due had each of those transactions been taxed within their territory.

Art. 156 1. Member States may exempt the following transactions:

(a) the supply of goods which are intended to be presented to customs and, where applicable, placed in temporary storage;

(b) the supply of goods which are intended to be placed in a free zone or in a free warehouse;

(c) the supply of goods which are intended to be placed under customs warehousing arrangements or inward processing arrangements;

(d) the supply of goods which are intended to be admitted into territorial waters in order to be incorporated into drilling or production platforms, for purposes of the construction, repair, maintenance, alteration or fitting-out of such platforms, or to link such drilling or production platforms to the mainland;

(e) the supply of goods which are intended to be admitted into territorial waters for the fuelling and provisioning of drilling or production platforms.

2. The places referred to in paragraph 1 shall be those defined as such by the Community customs provisions in force.

Art. 157 1. Member States may exempt the following transactions:

(a) the importation of goods which are intended to be placed under warehousing arrangements other than customs warehousing;

(b) the supply of goods which are intended to be placed, within their territory, under warehousing arrangements other than customs warehousing.

2. Member States may not provide for warehousing arrangements other than customs warehousing for goods which are not subject to excise duty where those goods are intended to be supplied at the retail stage.

Art. 158 1. By way of derogation from Article 157(2), Member States may provide for warehousing arrangements other than customs warehousing in the following cases:

(a) where the goods are intended for tax-free shops, for the purposes of the supply of goods to be carried in the personal luggage of travellers taking flights or sea crossings to third territories or third countries, where that supply is exempt pursuant to point (b) of Article 146(1);

(b) where the goods are intended for taxable persons, for the purposes of carrying out supplies to travellers on board an aircraft or a ship in the course of a flight or sea crossing where the place of arrival is situated outside the Community;

(c) where the goods are intended for taxable persons, for the purposes of carrying out supplies which are exempt from VAT pursuant to Article 151.

2. Where Member States exercise the option of exemption provided for in point (a) of paragraph 1, they shall take the measures necessary to ensure the correct and straightforward application of this exemption and to prevent any evasion, avoidance or abuse.

3. For the purposes of point (a) of paragraph 1, "tax-free shop" shall mean any establishment which is situated within an airport or port and which fulfils the conditions laid down by the competent public authorities.

Art. 159 Member States may exempt the supply of services relating to the supply of goods referred to in Article 156, Article 157(1)(b) or Article 158.

Art. 160 1. Member States may exempt the following transactions:

(a) the supply of goods or services carried out in the locations referred to in Article 156(1), where one of the situations specified therein still applies within their territory;

(b) the supply of goods or services carried out in the locations referred to in Article 157(1)(b) or Article 158, where one of the situations specified in Article 157(1)(b) or in Article 158(1) still applies within their territory.

2. Where Member States exercise the option under point (a) of paragraph 1 in respect of transactions effected in customs warehouses, they shall take the measures necessary to provide for warehousing arrangements other than customs warehousing under which point (b) of paragraph 1 may be applied to the same transactions when they concern goods listed in Annex V and are carried out in warehouses other than customs warehouses.

Art. 161 Member States may exempt supply of the following goods and of services relating thereto:

(a) the supply of goods referred to in the first paragraph of Article 30 while they remain covered by arrangements for temporary importation with total exemption from import duty or by external transit arrangements;

(b) the supply of goods referred to in the second paragraph of Article 30 while they remain covered by the internal Community transit procedure referred to in Article 276.

Art. 162 Where Member States exercise the option provided for in this Section, they shall take the measures necessary to ensure that the intra-Community acquisition of goods intended to be placed under one of the arrangements or in one of the situations referred to in Article 156, Article 157(1)(b) or Article 158 is covered by the same provisions as the supply of goods carried out within their territory under the same conditions.

Art. 163 If the goods cease to be covered by the arrangements or situations referred to in this Section, thus giving rise to importation for the purposes of Article 61, the Member State of importation shall take the measures necessary to prevent double taxation.

Section 2

Transactions exempted with a view to export and in the framework of trade between the Member States

Art. 164 1. Member States may, after consulting the VAT Committee, exempt the following transactions carried out by, or intended for, a taxable person up to an amount equal to the value of the exports carried out by that person during the preceding 12 months:

(a) intra-Community acquisitions of goods made by the taxable person, and imports for and supplies of goods to the taxable person, with a view to their exportation from the Community as they are or after processing;

(b) supplies of services linked with the export business of the taxable person.

2. Where Member States exercise the option of exemption under paragraph 1, they shall, after consulting the VAT Committee, apply that exemption also to transactions relating to supplies carried out by the taxable person, in accordance with the conditions specified in Article 138, up to an amount equal to the value of the supplies carried out by that person, in accordance with the same conditions, during the preceding 12 months.

Art. 165 Member States may set a common maximum amount for transactions which they exempt pursuant to Article 164.

SECTION 3

Provisions common to Sections 1 and 2

Art. 166 The Commission shall, where appropriate, as soon as possible, present to the Council proposals concerning common arrangements for applying VAT to the transactions referred to in Sections 1 and 2.

TITLE X
DEDUCTIONS

CHAPTER 1
ORIGIN AND SCOPE OF RIGHT OF DEDUCTION

Art. 167 A right of deduction shall arise at the time the deductible tax becomes chargeable.

Art. 167a Member States may provide within an optional scheme that the right of deduction of a taxable person whose VAT solely becomes chargeable in accordance with Article 66(b) be postponed until the VAT on the goods or services supplied to him has been paid to his supplier.

Member States which apply the optional scheme referred to in the first paragraph shall set a threshold for taxable persons using the scheme within their territory, based on the annual turnover of the taxable person calculated in accordance with Article 288. That threshold may not be higher than EUR 500 000 or the equivalent in national currency. Member States may increase that threshold up to EUR 2 000 000 or the equivalent in national currency after consulting the VAT Committee. However, such consultation of the VAT Committee shall not be required for Member States which applied a threshold higher than EUR 500 000 or the equivalent in national currency on 31 December 2012.

Member States shall inform the VAT Committee of national legislative measures adopted pursuant to the first paragraph.

Art. 168 In so far as the goods and services are used for the purposes of the taxed transactions of a taxable person, the taxable person shall be entitled, in the Member State in which he carries out these transactions, to deduct the following from the VAT which he is liable to pay:

(a) the VAT due or paid in that Member State in respect of supplies to him of goods or services, carried out or to be carried out by another taxable person;

(b) the VAT due in respect of transactions treated as supplies of goods or services pursuant to Article 18(a) and Article 27;

(c) the VAT due in respect of intra-Community acquisitions of goods pursuant to Article 2(1)(b)(i);

(d) the VAT due on transactions treated as intra-Community acquisitions in accordance with Articles 21 and 22;

(e) the VAT due or paid in respect of the importation of goods into that Member State.

Art. 168a 1. In the case of immovable property forming part of the business assets of a taxable person and used both for purposes of the taxable person's business and for his private use or that of his staff, or, more generally, for purposes other than those of his business, VAT on expenditure related to this property shall be deductible in accordance with the principles set out in Articles 167, 168, 169 and 173 only up to the proportion of the property's use for purposes of the taxable person's business.

By way of derogation from Article 26, changes in the proportion of use of immovable property referred to in the first subparagraph shall be taken into account in accordance with the principles provided for in Articles 184 to 192 as applied in the respective Member State.

2. Member States may also apply paragraph 1 in relation to VAT on expenditure related to other goods forming part of the business assets as they specify.

Art. 169 In addition to the deduction referred to in Article 168, the taxable person shall be entitled to deduct the VAT referred to therein in so far as the goods and services are used for the purposes of the following:

(a) transactions relating to the activities referred to in the second subparagraph of Article 9(1), carried out outside the Member State in which that tax is due or paid, in respect of which VAT would be deductible if they had been carried out within that Member State;

(b) transactions which are exempt pursuant to Articles 138, 142 or 144, Articles 146 to 149, Articles 151, 152, 153 or 156, Article 157(1)(b), Articles 158 to 161 or Article 164;

(c) transactions which are exempt pursuant to points (a) to (f) of Article 135(1), where the customer is established outside the Community or where those transactions relate directly to goods to be exported out of the Community.

Art. 170 All taxable persons who, within the meaning of Article 1 of Directive 86/560/EEC[(1)], Article 2(1) and Article 3 of Directive 2008/9/EC[(2)] and Article 171 of this Directive, are not established in the Member State in which they purchase goods and services or import goods subject to VAT shall be entitled to obtain a refund of that VAT insofar as the goods and services are used for the purposes of the following:

(a) transactions referred to in Article 169;

(b) transactions for which the tax is solely payable by the customer in accordance with Articles 194 to 197 or Article 199.

Art. 171 1. VAT shall be refunded to taxable persons who are not established in the Member State in which they purchase goods and services or import goods subject to VAT but who are established in another Member State, in accordance with the detailed rules laid down in Directive 2008/9/EC.

2. VAT shall be refunded to taxable persons who are not established within the territory of the Community in accordance with the detailed implementing rules laid down in Directive 86/ 560/EEC.

The taxable persons referred to in Article 1 of Directive 86/560/ EEC shall also, for the purposes of applying that Directive, be regarded as taxable persons who are not established in the Community where, in the Member State in which they purchase goods and services or import goods subject to VAT, they have only carried out the supply of goods or services to a person designated in accordance with Articles 194 to 197 or Article 199 as liable for payment of VAT.

3. Directive 86/560/EEC shall not apply to:

(a) amounts of VAT which according to the legislation of the Member State of refund have been incorrectly invoiced;

(b) invoiced amounts of VAT in respect of supplies of goods the supply of which is, or may be, exempt pursuant to Article 138 or Article 146(1)(b).

Art. 171a Member States may, instead of granting a refund of VAT pursuant to Directives 86/560/ EEC or 2008/9/EC on those supplies of goods or services to a taxable person in respect of which the taxable person is liable to pay the tax in accordance with Articles 194 to 197 or Article 199, allow deduction of this tax pursuant to the procedure laid down in Article 168. The existing restrictions pursuant to Article 2(2) and Article 4(2) of Directive 86/560/EEC may be retained.

To that end, Member States may exclude the taxable person who is liable to pay the tax from the refund procedure pursuant to Directives 86/ 560/EEC or 2008/9/EC.

Art. 172 1. Any person who is regarded as a taxable person by reason of the fact that he supplies, on an occasional basis, a new means of transport in accordance with the conditions specified in Article 138(1) and (2)(a) shall, in the Member State in which the supply takes place, be entitled to deduct the VAT included in the purchase price or paid in respect of the importation or the intra-Community acquisition of this means of transport, up to an amount not exceeding the amount of VAT for which he would be liable if the supply were not exempt.

A right of deduction shall arise and may be exercised only at the time of supply of the new means of transport.

2. Member States shall lay down detailed rules for the implementation of paragraph 1.

CHAPTER 2
PROPORTIONAL DEDUCTION

Art. 173 1. In the case of goods or services used by a taxable person both for transactions in respect of which VAT is deductible pursuant to Articles 168, 169 and 170, and for transactions in respect of which VAT is not deductible, only such proportion of the VAT as is attributable to the former transactions shall be deductible.

The deductible proportion shall be determined, in accordance with Articles 174 and 175, for all the transactions carried out by the taxable person.

2. Member States may take the following measures:

(a) authorise the taxable person to determine a proportion for each sector of his business, provided that separate accounts are kept for each sector;

(b) require the taxable person to determine a proportion for each sector of his business and to keep separate accounts for each sector;

(c) authorise or require the taxable person to make the deduction on the basis of the use made of all or part of the goods and services;

---

1. Thirteenth Council Directive 86/560/EEC of 17 November 1986 on the harmonisation of the laws of the Member States relating to turnover taxes - Arrangements for the refund of value added tax to taxable persons not established in Community territory (OJ L 326, 21.11.1986, p. 40).

2. Council Directive 2008/9/EC of 12 February 2008 laying down detailed rules for the refund of value added tax, provided for in Directive 2006/112/EC to taxable persons not established in the Member State of refund but established in another Member State (OJ L 44, 20.2.2008, p. 23).

(d) authorise or require the taxable person to make the deduction in accordance with the rule laid down in the first subparagraph of paragraph 1, in respect of all goods and services used for all transactions referred to therein;

(e) provide that, where the VAT which is not deductible by the taxable person is insignificant, it is to be treated as nil.

Art. 174 The deductible proportion shall be made up of a fraction comprising the following amounts:

(a) as numerator, the total amount, exclusive of VAT, of turnover per year attributable to transactions in respect of which VAT is deductible pursuant to Articles 168 and 169;

(b) as denominator, the total amount, exclusive of VAT, of turnover per year attributable to transactions included in the numerator and to transactions in respect of which VAT is not deductible.

Member States may include in the denominator the amount of subsidies, other than those directly linked to the price of supplies of goods or services referred to in Article 73.

2. By way of derogation from paragraph 1, the following amounts shall be excluded from the calculation of the deductible proportion:

(a) the amount of turnover attributable to supplies of capital goods used by the taxable person for the purposes of his business;

(b) the amount of turnover attributable to incidental real estate and financial transactions;

(c) the amount of turnover attributable to the transactions specified in points (b) to (g) of Article 135(1) in so far as those transactions are incidental.

3. Where Member States exercise the option under Article 191 not to require adjustment in respect of capital goods, they may include disposals of capital goods in the calculation of the deductible proportion.

Art. 175 1. The deductible proportion shall be determined on an annual basis, fixed as a percentage and rounded up to a figure not exceeding the next whole number.

2. The provisional proportion for a year shall be that calculated on the basis of the preceding year's transactions. In the absence of any such transactions to refer to, or where they were insignificant in amount, the deductible proportion shall be estimated provisionally, under the supervision of the tax authorities, by the taxable person on the basis of his own forecasts.

However, Member States may retain the rules in force at 1 January 1979 or, in the case of the Member States which acceded to the Community after that date, on the date of their accession.

3. Deductions made on the basis of such provisional proportions shall be adjusted when the final proportion is fixed during the following year.

CHAPTER 3

RESTRICTIONS ON THE RIGHT OF DEDUCTION

Art. 176 The Council, acting unanimously on a proposal from the Commission, shall determine the expenditure in respect of which VAT shall not be deductible. VAT shall in no circumstances be deductible in respect of expenditure which is not strictly business expenditure, such as that on luxuries, amusements or entertainment.

Pending the entry into force of the provisions referred to in the first paragraph, Member States may retain all the exclusions provided for under their national laws at 1 January 1979 or, in the case of the Member States which acceded to the Community after that date, on the date of their accession.

Art. 177 After consulting the VAT Committee, each Member State may, for cyclical economic reasons, totally or partly exclude all or some capital goods or other goods from the system of deductions.

In order to maintain identical conditions of competition, Member States may, instead of refusing deduction, tax goods manufactured by the taxable person himself or goods which he has purchased within the Community, or imported, in such a way that the tax does not exceed the amount of VAT which would be charged on the acquisition of similar goods.

CHAPTER 4

RULES GOVERNING EXERCISE OF THE RIGHT OF DEDUCTION

Art. 178 In order to exercise the right of deduction, a taxable person must meet the following conditions:

(a) for the purposes of deductions pursuant to Article 168(a), in respect of the supply of goods or services, he must hold an invoice drawn up in accordance with Sections 3 to 6 of Chapter 3 of Title XI;

(b) for the purposes of deductions pursuant to Article 168(b), in respect of transactions treated as the supply of goods or services, he must comply with the formalities as laid down by each Member State;

(c) for the purposes of deductions pursuant to Article 168(c), in respect of the intra-Community acquisition of goods, he must set out in the VAT return provided for in Article 250 all the information needed for the amount of VAT due on his intra-Community acquisitions of goods to be calculated and he must hold an invoice drawn up in accordance with Sections 3 to 5 of Chapter 3 of Title XI;

(d) for the purposes of deductions pursuant to Article 168(d), in respect of transactions treated as intra-Community acquisitions of goods, he must complete the formalities as laid down by each Member State;

(e) for the purposes of deductions pursuant to Article 168(e), in respect of the importation of goods, he must hold an import document specifying him as consignee or importer, and stating the amount of VAT due or enabling that amount to be calculated;

(f) when required to pay VAT as a customer where Articles 194 to 197 or Article 199 apply, he must comply with the formalities as laid down by each Member State.

Art. 179 The taxable person shall make the deduction by subtracting from the total amount of VAT due for a given tax period the total amount of VAT in respect of which, during the same period, the right of deduction has arisen and is exercised in accordance with Article 178.

However, Member States may require that taxable persons who carry out occasional transactions, as defined in Article 12, exercise their right of deduction only at the time of supply.

Art. 180 Member States may authorise a taxable person to make a deduction which he has not made in accordance with Articles 178 and 179.

Art. 181 Member States may authorise a taxable person who does not hold an invoice drawn up in accordance with Sections 3 to 5 of Chapter 3 of Title XI to make the deduction referred to in Article 168(c) in respect of his intra-Community acquisitions of goods.

Art. 182 Member States shall determine the conditions and detailed rules for applying Articles 180 and 181.

Art. 183 Where, for a given tax period, the amount of deductions exceeds the amount of VAT due, the Member States may, in accordance with conditions which they shall determine, either make a refund or carry the excess forward to the following period.

However, Member States may refuse to refund or carry forward if the amount of the excess is insignificant.

CHAPTER 5
ADJUSTMENT OF DEDUCTIONS

Art. 184 The initial deduction shall be adjusted where it is higher or lower than that to which the taxable person was entitled.

Art. 185 1. Adjustment shall, in particular, be made where, after the VAT return is made, some change occurs in the factors used to determine the amount to be deducted, for example where purchases are cancelled or price reductions are obtained.

2. By way of derogation from paragraph 1, no adjustment shall be made in the case of transactions remaining totally or partially unpaid or in the case of destruction, loss or theft of property duly proved or confirmed, or in the case of goods reserved for the purpose of making gifts of small value or of giving samples, as referred to in Article 16.

However, in the case of transactions remaining totally or partially unpaid or in the case of theft, Member States may require adjustment to be made.

Art. 186 Member States shall lay down the detailed rules for applying Articles 184 and 185.

Art. 187 1. In the case of capital goods, adjustment shall be spread over five years including that in which the goods were acquired or manufactured.

Member States may, however, base the adjustment on a period of five full years starting from the time at which the goods are first used.

In the case of immovable property acquired as capital goods, the adjustment period may be extended up to 20 years.

2. The annual adjustment shall be made only in respect of one fifth of the VAT charged on the capital goods, or, if the adjustment period has been extended, in respect of the corresponding fraction thereof.

The adjustment referred to in the first subparagraph shall be made on the basis of the variations in the deduction entitlement in subsequent years in relation to that for the year in which the goods were acquired, manufactured or, where applicable, used for the first time.

Art. 188 1. If supplied during the adjustment period, capital goods shall be treated as if they had been applied to an economic activity of the taxable person up until expiry of the adjustment period.

The economic activity shall be presumed to be fully taxed in cases where the supply of the capital goods is taxed.

The economic activity shall be presumed to be fully exempt in cases where the supply of the capital goods is exempt.

2. The adjustment provided for in paragraph 1 shall be made only once in respect of all the time covered by the adjustment period that remains to run. However, where the supply of capital goods is exempt, Member States may waive the requirement for adjustment in so far as the purchaser is a taxable person using the capital goods in question solely for transactions in respect of which VAT is deductible.

Art. 189 For the purposes of applying Articles 187 and 188, Member States may take the following measures:

(a) define the concept of capital goods;

(b) specify the amount of the VAT which is to be taken into consideration for adjustment;

(c) adopt any measures needed to ensure that adjustment does not give rise to any unjustified advantage;

(d) permit administrative simplifications.

Art. 190 For the purposes of Articles 187, 188, 189 and 191, Member States may regard as capital goods those services which have characteristics similar to those normally attributed to capital goods.

Art. 191 If, in any Member State, the practical effect of applying Articles 187 and 188 is negligible, that Member State may, after consulting the VAT Committee, refrain from applying those provisions, having regard to the overall impact of VAT in the Member State concerned and the need for administrative simplification, and provided that no distortion of competition thereby arises.

Art. 192 Where a taxable person transfers from being taxed in the normal way to a special scheme or vice versa, Member States may take all measures necessary to ensure that the taxable person does not enjoy unjustified advantage or sustain unjustified harm.

Art. 192a For the purposes of this Section, a taxable person who has a fixed establishment within the territory of the Member State where the tax is due shall be regarded as a taxable person who is not established within that Member State when the following conditions are met:

(a) he makes a taxable supply of goods or of services within the territory of that Member State;

(b) an establishment which the supplier has within the territory of that Member State does not intervene in that supply.

TITLE XI
OBLIGATIONS OF TAXABLE PERSONS AND CERTAIN NON-TAXABLE PERSONS

CHAPTER 1
OBLIGATION TO PAY

SECTION 1
Persons liable for payment of VAT to the tax authorities

Art. 193 VAT shall be payable by any taxable person carrying out a taxable supply of goods or services, except where it is payable by another person in the cases referred to in Articles 194 to 199B and Article 202.

Art. 194 1. Where the taxable supply of goods or services is carried out by a taxable person who is not established in the Member State in which the VAT is due, Member States may provide that the person liable for payment of VAT is the person to whom the goods or services are supplied.

2. Member States shall lay down the conditions for implementation of paragraph 1.

Art. 195 VAT shall be payable by any person who is identified for VAT purposes in the Member State in which the tax is due and to whom goods are supplied in the circumstances specified in Articles 38 or 39, if the supplies are carried out by a taxable person not established within that Member State.

Art. 196 VAT shall be payable by any taxable person, or non-taxable legal person identified for VAT purposes, to whom the services referred to in Article 44 are supplied, if the services are supplied by a taxable person not established within the territory of the Member State.

Art. 197 1. VAT shall be payable by the person to whom the goods are supplied when the following conditions are met:

(a) the taxable transaction is a supply of goods carried out in accordance with the conditions laid down in Article 141;

(b) the person to whom the goods are supplied is another taxable person, or a non-taxable legal person, identified for VAT purposes in the Member State in which the supply is carried out;

(c) the invoice issued by the taxable person not established in the Member State of the person to whom the goods are supplied is drawn up in accordance with Sections 3 to 5 of Chapter 3.

2. Where a tax representative is appointed as the person liable for payment of VAT pursuant to Article 204, Member States may provide for a derogation from paragraph 1 of this Article.

Art. 198 1. Where specific transactions relating to investment gold between a taxable person who is a member of a regulated gold bullion market and another taxable person who is not a member of that market are taxed pursuant to Article 352, Member States shall designate the customer as the person liable for payment of VAT.

If the customer who is not a member of the regulated gold bullion market is a taxable person required to be identified for VAT purposes in the Member State in which the tax is due solely in respect of the transactions referred to in Article 352, the vendor shall fulfil the tax obligations on behalf of the customer, in accordance with the law of that Member State.

2. Where gold material or semi-manufactured products of a purity of 325 thousandths or greater, or investment gold as defined in Article 344(1) is supplied by a taxable person exercising one of the options under Articles 348, 349 and

350, Member States may designate the customer as the person liable for payment of VAT.

3. Member States shall lay down the procedures and conditions for implementation of paragraphs 1 and 2.

Art. 199 1. Member States may provide that the person liable for payment of VAT is the taxable person to whom any of the following supplies are made:

(a) the supply of construction work, including repair, cleaning, maintenance, alteration and demolition services in relation to immovable property, as well as the handing over of construction works regarded as a supply of goods pursuant to Article 14(3);

(b) the supply of staff engaged in activities covered by point (a);

(c) the supply of immovable property, as referred to in Article 135(1)(j) and (k), where the supplier has opted for taxation of the supply pursuant to Article 137;

(d) the supply of used material, used material which cannot be re-used in the same state, scrap, industrial and non-industrial waste, recyclable waste, part processed waste and certain goods and services, as listed in Annex VI;

(e) the supply of goods provided as security by one taxable person to another in execution of that security;

(f) the supply of goods following the cession of a reservation of ownership to an assignee and the exercising of this right by the assignee;

(g) the supply of immovable property sold by a judgment debtor in a compulsory sale procedure.

2. When applying the option provided for in paragraph 1, Member States may specify the supplies of goods and services covered, and the categories of suppliers or recipients to whom these measures may apply.

3. For the purposes of paragraph 1, Member States may take the following measures:

(a) provide that a taxable person who also carries out activities or transactions that are not considered to be taxable supplies of goods or services in accordance with Article 2 shall be regarded as a taxable person in respect of supplies received as referred to in paragraph 1 of this Article;

(b) provide that a non-taxable body governed by public law, shall be regarded as a taxable person in respect of supplies received as referred to in points (e), (f) and (g) of paragraph 1.

4. Member States shall inform the VAT Committee of national legislative measures adopted pursuant to paragraph 1 in so far as these are not measures authorised by the Council prior to 13 August 2006 in accordance with Article 27(1) to (4) of Directive 77/388/EEC, and which are continued under paragraph 1 of this Article.

Art. 199a 1. Member States may, until 31 December 2018 and for a minimum period of two years, provide that the person liable for payment of VAT is the taxable person to whom any of the following supplies are made:

(a) the transfer of allowances to emit greenhouse gases as defined in Article 3 of Directive 2003/87/EC of the European Parliament and of the Council of 13 October 2003 establishing a scheme for greenhouse gas emission allowance trading within the Community, transferable in accordance with Article 12 of that Directive;

(b) the transfer of other units that may be used by operators for compliance with the same Directive.

(c) supplies of mobile telephones, being devices made or adapted for use in connection with a licensed network and operated on specified frequencies, whether or not they have any other use;

(d) supplies of integrated circuit devices such as microprocessors and central processing units in a state prior to integration into end user products;

(e) supplies of gas and electricity to a taxable dealer as defined in Article 38(2);

(f) supplies of gas and electricity certificates;

(g) supplies of telecommunication services as defined in Article 24(2);

(h) supplies of game consoles, tablet PCs and laptops;

(i) supplies of cereals and industrial crops including oil seeds and sugar beet, that are not normally used in the unaltered state for final consumption;

(j) supplies of raw and semi-finished metals, including precious metals, where they are not otherwise covered by point (d) of Article 199(1), the special arrangements for second-hand goods, works of art, collector's items and antiques pursuant to Articles 311 to 343 or the special scheme for investment gold pursuant to Articles 344 to 356.

1a. Member States may lay down the conditions for the application of the mechanism provided for in paragraph 1.

1b. The application of the mechanism provided for in paragraph 1 to the supply of any of the goods or services listed in points (c) to (j) of that paragraph is subject to the introduction of appropriate and effective reporting obligations on taxable persons who supply the goods or services to which the mechanism provided for in paragraph 1 applies.

2. Member States shall inform the VAT Committee of the application of the mechanism provided for in paragraph 1 on the introduction of any such mechanism and shall provide the following information to the VAT Committee:

(a) the scope of the measure applying the mechanism together with the type and the features of the fraud, and a detailed description of accompanying measures, including any reporting obligations on taxable persons and any control measures;

(b) actions taken to inform the relevant taxable persons of the introduction of the application of the mechanism;

(c) evaluation criteria to enable comparison between fraudulent activities in relation to the goods and services listed in paragraph 1 before and after the application of the mechanism, fraudulent activities in relation to other goods and services before and after the application of the mechanism, and any increase in other types of fraudulent activities before and after the application of the mechanism;

(d) the date of commencement and the period to be covered by the measure applying the mechanism.

3. Member States applying the mechanism provided for in paragraph 1 shall, on the basis of the evaluation criteria provided for under point (c) of paragraph 2, submit a report to the Commission no later than 30 June 2017.

The report shall provide a detailed assessment of the measure's overall effectiveness and efficiency, in particular as regards:

(a) the impact on fraudulent activities in relation to supplies of goods or services covered by the measure;

(b) the possible shift of fraudulent activities to goods or other services;

(c) the compliance costs for taxable persons resulting from the measure.

4. Each Member State that has detected a shift in trends of fraudulent activities in its territory in relation to the goods or services listed in paragraph 1 from the date of entry into force of this Article with respect to such goods or services, shall submit a report to the Commission in that respect no later than 30 June 2017.

5. Before 1 January 2018, the Commission shall present to the European Parliament and to the Council an overall assessment report on the effects of the mechanism provided for in paragraph 1 on combatting fraud.

Art. 199b 1. A Member State may, in cases of imperative urgency and in accordance with paragraphs 2 and 3, designate the recipient as the person liable to pay VAT on specific supplies of goods and services by derogation from Article 193 as a Quick Reaction Mechanism ("QRM") special measure to combat sudden and massive fraud liable to lead to considerable and irreparable financial losses. The QRM special measure shall be subject to appropriate control measures by the Member State with respect to taxable persons who supply the goods or services to which that measure applies, and shall be for a period not exceeding nine months.

2. A Member State wishing to introduce a QRM special measure as provided for in paragraph 1 shall send a notification to the Commission using the standardised form established in accordance with paragraph 4 and at the same time send it to the other Member States. The Member State shall provide the Commission with the information indicating the sector concerned, the type and the features of the fraud, the existence of imperative grounds of urgency, the sudden and massive character of the fraud and its consequences in terms of considerable and irreparable financial losses. If the Commission considers it does not have all the necessary information, it shall contact the Member State concerned within two weeks of receipt of the notification and specify what additional information is required. Any additional information provided by the Member State concerned to the Commission shall at the same time be sent to the other Member States. If the additional information provided is not sufficient, the Commission shall inform the Member State concerned thereof within one week. The Member State wishing to introduce a QRM special measure as provided for in paragraph 1 shall at the same time also make an application to the Commission in accordance with the procedure laid down in Article 395(2) and (3).

3. Once the Commission has all the information it considers necessary for appraisal of the notification referred to in the first subparagraph of paragraph 2, it shall notify the Member States thereof. Where it objects to the QRM special measure, it shall produce a negative opinion within one month of that notification, and shall inform the Member State concerned and the VAT Committee thereof. Where the Commission does not object, it shall confirm this in writing to the Member State concerned and to the VAT Committee within the same time period. The Member State may adopt the QRM special measure from the date of receipt of that confirmation. In appraising the notification, the Commission shall take into account the views of any other Member State sent to it in writing.

4. The Commission shall adopt an implementing act establishing a standardised form for the submission of the notification for the QRM special measure referred to in paragraph 2 and of the information referred to in the first subparagraph of paragraph 2. That implementing act shall be adopted in accordance with the examination procedure referred to in paragraph 5.

5. Where reference is made to this paragraph Article 5 of Regulation (EU) No 182/2011 of the European Parliament and of the Council shall apply and for this purpose the committee shall be the committee established by Article 58 of Council Regulation (EU) No 904/2010.

Art. 200 VAT shall be payable by any person making a taxable intra-Community acquisition of goods.

Art. 201 On importation, VAT shall be payable by any person or persons designated or recognised as liable by the Member State of importation.

Art. 202 VAT shall be payable by any person who causes goods to cease to be covered by the arrangements or situations listed in Articles 156, 157, 158, 160 and 161.

Art. 203 VAT shall be payable by any person who enters the VAT on an invoice.

Art. 204 1. Where, pursuant to Articles 193 to 197 and Articles 199 and 200, the person liable for payment of VAT is a taxable person who is not established in the Member State in which the VAT is due, Member States may allow that person to appoint a tax representative as the person liable for payment of the VAT.

Furthermore, where the taxable transaction is carried out by a taxable person who is not established in the Member State in which the VAT is due and no legal instrument exists, with the country in which that taxable person is established or has his seat, relating to mutual assistance similar in scope to that provided for in Directive 76/308/EEC[1] and Regulation (EC) No 1798/2003[2], Member States may take measures to provide that the person liable for payment of VAT is to be a tax representative appointed by the non-established taxable person.

However, Member States may not apply the option referred to in the second subparagraph to a taxable person not established within the Community, within the meaning of point (1) of Article 358a, who has opted for the special scheme for telecommunications, broadcasting or electronic services.

2. The option under the first subparagraph of paragraph 1 shall be subject to the conditions and procedures laid down by each Member State.

Art. 205 In the situations referred to in Articles 193 to 200 and Articles 202, 203 and 204, Member States may provide that a person other than the person liable for payment of VAT is to be held jointly and severally liable for payment of VAT.

SECTION 2

Payment arrangements

Art. 206 Any taxable person liable for payment of VAT must pay the net amount of the VAT when submitting the VAT return provided for in Article 250. Member States may, however, set a different date for payment of that amount or may require interim payments to be made.

1. Council Directive 76/308/EEC of 15 March 1976 on mutual assistance for the recovery of claims relating to certain levies, duties, taxes and other measures (OJ L73, 19.3.1976, p. 18.). Directive as last amended by the Act of Accession of 2003.

2. Council Regulation (EC) No 1798/2003 of 7 October 2003 on administrative cooperation in the field of value added tax (OJ L 264, 15.10.2003, p. 1.). Regulation amended by Regulation (EC) No 885/ 2004 (OJ L 168, 1.5.2004, p. 1.).

Art. 207 Member States shall take the measures necessary to ensure that persons who are regarded as liable for payment of VAT in the stead of a taxable person not established in their respective territory, in accordance with Articles 194 to 197 and Articles 199 and 204, comply with the payment obligations set out in this Section.

Member States shall also take the measures necessary to ensure that those persons who, in accordance with Article 205, are held to be jointly and severally liable for payment of the VAT comply with these payment obligations.

Art. 208 Where Member States designate the customer for investment gold as the person liable for payment of VAT pursuant to Article 198(1) or if, in the case of gold material, semi-manufactured products, or investment gold as defined in Article 344(1), they exercise the option provided for in Article 198(2) of designating the customer as the person liable for payment of VAT, they shall take the measures necessary to ensure that he complies with the payment obligations set out in this Section.

Art. 209 Member States shall take the measures necessary to ensure that non-taxable legal persons who are liable for payment of VAT due in respect of intra-Community acquisitions of goods, as referred to in Article 2(1)(b)(i), comply with the payment obligations set out in this Section.

Art. 210 Member States shall adopt arrangements for payment of VAT on intra-Community acquisitions of new means of transport, as referred to in Article 2(1)(b)(ii), and on intra-Community acquisitions of products subject to excise duty, as referred to in Article 2(1)(b)(iii).

Art. 211 Member States shall lay down the detailed rules for payment in respect of the importation of goods.

In particular, Member States may provide that, in the case of the importation of goods by taxable persons or certain categories thereof, or by persons liable for payment of VAT or certain categories thereof, the VAT due by reason of the importation need not be paid at the time of importation, on condition that it is entered as such in the VAT return to be submitted in accordance with Article 250.

Art. 212 Member States may release taxable persons from payment of the VAT due where the amount is insignificant.

CHAPTER 2
IDENTIFICATION

Art. 213 1. Every taxable person shall state when his activity as a taxable person commences, changes or ceases.

Member States shall allow, and may require, the statement to be made by electronic means, in accordance with conditions which they lay down.

2. Without prejudice to the first subparagraph of paragraph 1, every taxable person or non-taxable legal person who makes intra-Community acquisitions of goods which are not subject to VAT pursuant to Article 3(1) must state that he makes such acquisitions if the conditions, laid down in that provision, for not making such transactions subject to VAT cease to be fulfilled.

Art. 214 1. Member States shall take the measures necessary to ensure that the following persons are identified by means of an individual number:

(a) every taxable person, with the exception of those referred to in Article 9(2), who within their respective territory carries out supplies of goods or services in respect of which VAT is deductible, other than supplies of goods or services in respect of which VAT is payable solely by the customer or the person for whom the goods or services are intended, in accordance with Articles 194 to 197 and Article 199;

(b) every taxable person, or non-taxable legal person, who makes intra-Community acquisitions of goods subject to VAT pursuant to Article 2(1)(b) and every taxable person, or non-taxable legal person, who exercises the option under Article 3(3) of making their intra-Community acquisitions subject to VAT;

(c) every taxable person who, within their respective territory, makes intra-Community acquisitions of goods for the purposes of transactions which relate to the activities referred to in the second subparagraph of Article 9(1) and which are carried out outside that territory.

(d) every taxable person who within their respective territory receives services for which he is liable to pay VAT pursuant to Article 196;

(e) every taxable person, established within their respective territory, who supplies services within the territory of another Member State for which VAT is payable solely by the recipient pursuant to Article 196.

2. Member States need not identify certain taxable persons who carry out transactions on an occasional basis, as referred to in Article 12.

Art. 215 Each individual VAT identification number shall have a prefix in accordance with ISO code 3166 - alpha 2 - by which the Member State of issue may be identified.

Nevertheless, Greece may use the prefix "EL".

Art. 216 Member States shall take the measures necessary to ensure that their identification systems enable the taxable persons referred to in Article 214 to be identified and to ensure the correct application of the transitional arrangements for the taxation of intra-Community transactions, as referred to in Article 402.

CHAPTER 3
INVOICING

Section 1
Definition

Art. 217 For the purposes of this Directive, "electronic invoice" means an invoice that contains the information required in this Directive, and which has been issued and received in any electronic format.

Section 2
Concept of invoice

Art. 218 For the purposes of this Directive, Member States shall accept documents or messages on paper or in electronic form as invoices if they meet the conditions laid down in this Chapter.

Art. 219 Any document or message that amends and refers specifically and unambiguously to the initial invoice shall be treated as an invoice.

Section 3
Issue of invoices

Art. 219a Without prejudice to Articles 244 to 248, the following shall apply:

(1) Invoicing shall be subject to the rules applying in the Member State in which the supply of goods or services is deemed to be made, in accordance with the provisions of Title V.

(2) By way of derogation from point (1), invoicing shall be subject to the rules applying in the Member State in which the supplier has established his business or has a fixed establishment from which the supply is made or, in the absence of such place of establishment or fixed establishment, the Member State where the supplier has his permanent address or usually resides, where:

(a) the supplier is not established in the Member State in which the supply of goods or services is deemed to be made, in accordance with the provisions of Title V, or his establishment in that Member State does not intervene in the supply within the meaning of Article 192a, and the person liable for the payment of the VAT is the person to whom the goods or services are supplied.

However where the customer issues the invoice (self-billing), point (1) shall apply.

(b) the supply of goods or services is deemed not to be made within the Community, in accordance with the provisions of Title V.

Art. 220 Every taxable person shall ensure that, in respect of the following, an invoice is issued, either by himself or by his customer or, in his name and on his behalf, by a third party:

(1) supplies of goods or services which he has made to another taxable person or to a non-taxable legal person;

(2) supplies of goods as referred to in Article 33;

(3) supplies of goods carried out in accordance with the conditions specified in Article 138;

(4) any payment on account made to him before one of the supplies of goods referred to in points (1) and (2) was carried out;

(5) any payment on account made to him by another taxable person or non-taxable legal person before the provision of services was completed.

By way of derogation from paragraph 1, and without prejudice to Article 221(2), the issue of an invoice shall not be required in respect of supplies of services exempted under points (a) to (g) of Article 135(1).

Art. 220a 1. Member States shall allow taxable persons to issue a simplified invoice in any of the following cases:

(a) where the amount of the invoice is not higher than EUR 100 or the equivalent in national currency;

(b) where the invoice issued is a document or message treated as an invoice pursuant to Article 219.

2. Member States shall not allow taxable persons to issue a simplified invoice where invoices are required to be issued pursuant to points (2) and (3) of Article 220(1) or where the taxable supply of goods or services is carried out by a taxable person who is not established in the Member State in which the VAT is due, or whose establishment in that Member State does not intervene in the supply within the meaning of Article 192a, and the person liable for the payment of VAT is the person to whom the goods or services are supplied.

Art. 221 1. Member States may impose on taxable persons an obligation to issue an invoice in accordance with the details required under Article 226 or 226B in respect of supplies of goods or services other than those referred to in Article 220(1).

2. Member States may impose on taxable persons who have established their business in their territory or who have a fixed establishment in their territory from which the supply is made, an obligation to issue an invoice in accordance with the details required in Article 226 or 226B in respect of supplies of services exempted under points (a) to (g) of Article 135(1) which those taxable persons have made in their territory or outside the Community.

3. Member States may release taxable persons from the obligation laid down in Article 220(1) or in Article 220A to issue an invoice in respect of supplies of goods or services which they have made in their territory and which are exempt, with or without deductibility of the VAT paid in the preceding stage, pursuant to Articles 110 and 111, Article 125(1), Article 127, Article 128(1), Article 132, points (h) to (l) of Article 135(1), Articles 136, 371, 375, 376 and 377, Articles 378(2) and 379(2) and Articles 380 to 390b.

Art. 222 For supplies of goods carried out in accordance with the conditions specified in Article 138 or for supplies of services for which VAT is payable by the customer pursuant to Article 196, an invoice shall be issued no later than on the fifteenth day of the month following that in which the chargeable event occurs.

For other supplies of goods or services Member States may impose time limits on taxable persons for the issue of invoices.

Art. 223 Member States shall allow taxable persons to issue summary invoices which detail several separate supplies of goods or services provided that VAT on the supplies mentioned in the summary invoice becomes chargeable during the same calendar month.

Without prejudice to Article 222, Member States may allow summary invoices to include supplies for which VAT has become chargeable during a period of time longer than one calendar month.

Art. 224 Invoices may be drawn up by the customer in respect of the supply to him, by a taxable person, of goods or services, where there is a prior agreement between the two parties and provided that a procedure exists for the acceptance of each invoice by the taxable person supplying the goods or services. Member State may require that such invoices be issued in the name and on behalf of the taxable person.

Art. 225 Member States may impose specific conditions on taxable persons in cases where the third party, or the customer, who issues invoices is established in a country with which no legal instrument exists relating to mutual assistance similar in scope to that provided for in Directive 2010/24/EU and Regulation (EC) No 1798/2003 [(1) (2)].

Section 4

Content of invoices

Art. 226 Without prejudice to the particular provisions laid down in this Directive, only the following details are required for VAT purposes on invoices issued pursuant to Articles 220 and 221:

(1) the date of issue;

(2) a sequential number, based on one or more series, which uniquely identifies the invoice;

---

1. Council Directive 2010/24/EU of 16 March 2010 concerning mutual assistance for the recovery of claims relating to taxes, duties and other measures (OJ L 84, 31.3.2010, p. 1).

2. Council Regulation (EC) No 1798/2003 of 7 October 2003 on administrative cooperation in the field of value added tax (OJ L 264, 15.10.2003, p. 1).

(3) the VAT identification number referred to in Article 214 under which the taxable person supplied the goods or services;

(4) the customer's VAT identification number, as referred to in Article 214, under which the customer received a supply of goods or services in respect of which he is liable for payment of VAT, or received a supply of goods as referred to in Article 138;

(5) the full name and address of the taxable person and of the customer;

(6) the quantity and nature of the goods supplied or the extent and nature of the services rendered;

(7) the date on which the supply of goods or services was made or completed or the date on which the payment on account referred to in points (4) and (5) of Article 220 was made, in so far as that date can be determined and differs from the date of issue of the invoice;

(7a) where the VAT becomes chargeable at the time when the payment is received in accordance with Article 66(b) and the right of deduction arises at the time the deductible tax becomes chargeable, the mention "Cash accounting";

(8) the taxable amount per rate or exemption, the unit price exclusive of VAT and any discounts or rebates if they are not included in the unit price;

(9) the VAT rate applied;

(10) the VAT amount payable, except where a special arrangement is applied under which, in accordance with this Directive, such a detail is excluded;

(10a) where the customer receiving a supply issues the invoice instead of the supplier, the mention "Self-billing";

(11) in the case of an exemption, reference to the applicable provision of this Directive, or to the corresponding national provision, or any other reference indicating that the supply of goods or services is exempt;

(11a) where the customer is liable for the payment of the VAT, the mention "Reverse charge";

(12) in the case of the supply of a new means of transport made in accordance with the conditions specified in Article 138(1) and (2)(a), the characteristics as identified in point (b) of Article 2(2);

(13) where the margin scheme for travel agents is applied, the mention "Margin scheme - Travel agents";

(14) where one of the special arrangements applicable to second-hand goods, works of art, collectors' items and antiques is applied, the mention "Margin scheme - Second-hand goods"; "Margin scheme - Works of art" or "Margin scheme - Collector's items and antiques" respectively;

(15) where the person liable for payment of VAT is a tax representative for the purposes of Article 204, the VAT identification number, referred to in Article 214, of that tax representative, together with his full name and address.

Art. 226a Where the invoice is issued by a taxable person, who is not established in the Member State where the tax is due or whose establishment in that Member State does not intervene in the supply within the meaning of Article 192a, and who is making a supply of goods or services to a customer who is liable for payment of VAT, the taxable person may omit the details referred to in points (8), (9) and (10) of Article 226 and instead indicate, by reference to the quantity or extent of the goods or services supplied and their nature, the taxable amount of those goods or services.

Art. 226b As regards simplified invoices issued pursuant to Article 220a and Article 221(1) and (2), Member States shall require at least the following details:

(a) the date of issue;

(b) identification of the taxable person supplying the goods or services;

(c) identification of the type of goods or services supplied;

(d) the VAT amount payable or the information needed to calculate it;

(e) where the invoice issued is a document or message treated as an invoice pursuant to Article 219, specific and unambiguous reference to that initial invoice and the specific details which are being amended.

They may not require details on invoices other than those referred to in Articles 226, 227 and 230.

Art. 227 Member States may require taxable persons established in their territory and supplying goods or services there to indicate the VAT identification number, referred to in Article 214, of the customer in cases other than those referred to in point (4) of Article 226.

Art. 228 [Repealed by Council Directive 2010/45]

Art. 229 Member States shall not require invoices to be signed.

Art. 230 The amounts which appear on the invoice may be expressed in any currency, provided that the amount of VAT payable or to be adjusted is expressed in the national currency of the Member State, using the conversion rate mechanism provided for in Article 91.

Art. 231 [Repealed by Council Directive 2010/45]

SECTION 5

Paper invoices and electronic invoices

Art. 232 The use of an electronic invoice shall be subject to acceptance by the recipient.

Art. 233 1. The authenticity of the origin, the integrity of the content and the legibility of an invoice, whether on paper or in electronic form, shall be ensured from the point in time of issue until the end of the period for storage of the invoice.

Each taxable person shall determine the way to ensure the authenticity of the origin, the integrity of the content and the legibility of the invoice. This may be achieved by any business controls which create a reliable audit trail between an invoice and a supply of goods or services.

"Authenticity of the origin" means the assurance of the identity of the supplier or the issuer of the invoice.

"Integrity of the content" means that the content required according to this Directive has not been altered.

2. Other than by way of the type of business controls described in paragraph 1, the following are examples of technologies that ensure the authenticity of the origin and the integrity of the content of an electronic invoice:

(a) an advanced electronic signature within the meaning of point (2) of Article 2 of Directive 1999/93/EC of the European Parliament and of the Council of 13 December 1999 on a Community framework for electronic signatures[1], based on a qualified certificate and created by a secure signature creation device, within the meaning of points (6) and (10) of Article 2 of Directive 1999/93/EC;

(b) electronic data interchange (EDI), as defined in Article 2 of Annex 1 to Commission Recommendation 1994/820/EC of 19 October 1994 relating to the legal aspects of electronic data interchange[2], where the agreement relating to the exchange provides for the use of procedures guaranteeing the authenticity of the origin and integrity of the data.

Art. 234 Member States may not impose on taxable persons supplying goods or services in their territory any other obligations or formalities relating to the sending or making available of invoices by electronic means.

Art. 235 Member States may lay down specific conditions for electronic invoices issued in respect of goods or services supplied in their territory from a country with which no legal instrument exists relating to mutual assistance similar in scope to that provided for in Directive 2010/24/EU and Regulation (EC) No 1798/2003.

Art. 236 Where batches containing several electronic invoices are sent or made available to the same recipient, the details common to the individual invoices may be mentioned only once where, for each invoice, all the information is accessible.

Art. 237 By 31 December 2016 at the latest, the Commission shall present to the European Parliament and the Council an overall assessment report, based on an independent economic study, on the impact of the invoicing rules applicable from 1 January 2013 and notably on the extent to which they have effectively led to a decrease in administrative burdens for businesses, accompanied where necessary by an appropriate proposal to amend the relevant rules.

Section 6

Simplification measures

Art. 238 1. After consulting the VAT Committee, Member States may, in accordance with conditions which they may lay down, provide that in the following cases only the information required pursuant to Article 226b shall be entered on invoices in respect of supplies of goods or services:

(a) where the amount of the invoice is higher than EUR 100 but not higher than EUR 400, or the equivalent in national currency;

(b) where commercial or administrative practice in the business sector concerned or the technical conditions under which the invoices are issued make it particularly difficult to comply with all the obligations referred to in Article 226 or 230.

2. [Repealed by Council Directive 2010/45]

3. The simplified arrangements provided for in paragraph 1 shall not be applied where invoices are required to be issued pursuant to points (2) and (3) of Article 220(1) or where the taxable supply of goods or services is carried out by a taxable person who is not established in the Member State in which the VAT is due or whose establishment in that Member State does not intervene in the supply within the meaning of Article 192a and the person liable for the payment of VAT is the person to whom the goods or services are supplied.

Art. 239 In cases where Member States make use of the option under point (b) of the first subparagraph of Article 272(1) of not allocating a VAT identification number to taxable persons who do not carry out any of the transactions referred to in Articles 20, 21, 22, 33, 36, 138 and 141, and where the supplier or the customer has not been allocated an identification number of that type, another number called the tax reference number, as defined by the Member States concerned, shall be entered on the invoice instead.

Art. 240 Where the taxable person has been allocated a VAT identification number, the Member States exercising the option under point (b) of the first subparagraph of Article 272(1) may also require the invoice to show the following:

(1) in respect of the supply of services, as referred to in Articles 44, 47, 50, 53, 54 and 55, and the supply of goods, as referred to in Articles 138 and 141, the VAT identification number and the tax reference number of the supplier;

(2) in respect of other supplies of goods or services, only the tax reference number of the supplier or only the VAT identification number.

1. OJ L 13, 19.1.2000, p 12.
2. OJ L 338, 28.12.1994, p 98.

CHAPTER 4
ACCOUNTING

SECTION 1
Definition

Art. 241 For the purposes of this Chapter, "storage of an invoice by electronic means" shall mean storage of data using electronic equipment for processing (including digital compression) and storage, and employing wire, radio, optical or other electromagnetic means.

SECTION 2
General obligations

Art. 242 Every taxable person shall keep accounts in sufficient detail for VAT to be applied and its application checked by the tax authorities.

Art. 243 1. Every taxable person shall keep a register of the goods dispatched or transported by him, or on his behalf, to a destination outside the territory of the Member State of departure but within the Community for the purposes of transactions consisting in valuations of those goods or work on them or their temporary use as referred to in points (f), (g) and (h) of Article 17(2).

2. Every taxable person shall keep accounts in sufficient detail to enable the identification of goods dispatched to him from another Member State, by or on behalf of a taxable person identified for VAT purposes in that other Member State, and used for services consisting in valuations of those goods or work on those goods.

SECTION 3
Specific obligations relating to the storage of all invoices

Art. 244 Every taxable person shall ensure that copies of the invoices issued by himself, or by his customer or, in his name and on his behalf, by a third party, and all the invoices which he has received, are stored.

Art. 245 1. For the purposes of this Directive, the taxable person may decide the place of storage of all invoices provided that he makes the invoices or information stored in accordance with Article 244 available to the competent authorities without undue delay whenever they so request.

2. Member States may require taxable persons established in their territory to notify them of the place of storage, if it is outside their territory.

Member States may also require taxable persons established in their territory to store within that territory invoices issued by themselves or by their customers or, in their name and on their behalf, by a third party, as well as all the invoices that they have received, when the storage is not by electronic means guaranteeing full on-line access to the data concerned.

Art. 246 [Repealed by Council Directive 2010/45]

Art. 247 1. Each Member State shall determine the period throughout which taxable persons must ensure the storage of invoices relating to the supply of goods or services in its territory and invoices received by taxable persons established in its territory.

2. In order to ensure that the requirements laid down in Article 233 are met, the Member State referred to in paragraph 1 may require that invoices be stored in the original form in which they were sent or made available, whether paper or electronic. Additionally, in the case of invoices stored by electronic means, the Member State may require that the data guaranteeing the authenticity of the origin of the invoices and the integrity of their content, as provided for in Article 233, also be stored by electronic means.

3. The Member State referred to in paragraph 1 may lay down specific conditions prohibiting or restricting the storage of invoices in a country with which no legal instrument exists relating to mutual assistance similar in scope to that provided for in Directive 2010/24/EU and Regulation (EC) No 1798/2003 or to the right referred to in Article 249 to access by electronic means, to download and to use.

Art. 248 Member States may, subject to conditions which they lay down, require the storage of invoices received by non-taxable persons.

Art. 248a For control purposes, and as regards invoices in respect of supplies of goods or services supplied in their territory and invoices received by taxable persons established in their territory, Member States may, for certain taxable persons or certain cases, require translation into their official languages. Member States may, however, not impose a general requirement that invoices be translated.

SECTION 4
Right of access to invoices stored by electronic means in another Member State

Art. 249 For control purposes, where a taxable person stores, by electronic means guaranteeing online access to the data concerned, invoices which he issues or receives, the competent authorities of the Member State in which he is established and, where the VAT is due in another Member State, the competent authorities of that Member State, shall have the right to access, download and use those invoices.

CHAPTER 5
RETURNS

Art. 250 1. Every taxable person shall submit a VAT return setting out all the information needed to calculate the tax that has become chargeable and the deductions to be made including, in so far as is necessary for the establishment of the basis of assessment, the total value of the transactions relating to such tax and deductions and the value of any exempt transactions.

2. Member States shall allow, and may require, the VAT return referred to in paragraph 1 to be submitted by electronic means, in accordance with conditions which they lay down.

Art. 251 In addition to the information referred to in Article 250, the VAT return covering a given tax period shall show the following:

(a) the total value, exclusive of VAT, of the supplies of goods referred to in Article 138 in respect of which VAT has become chargeable during this tax period;

(b) the total value, exclusive of VAT, of the supplies of goods referred to in Articles 33 and 36 carried out within the territory of another Member State, in respect of which VAT has become chargeable during this tax period, where the place where dispatch or transport of the goods began is situated in the Member State in which the return must be submitted;

(c) the total value, exclusive of VAT, of the intra-Community acquisitions of goods, or transactions treated as such, pursuant to Articles 21 or 22, made in the Member State in which the return must be submitted and in respect of which VAT has become chargeable during this tax period;

(d) the total value, exclusive of VAT, of the supplies of goods referred to in Articles 33 and 36 carried out in the Member State in which the return must be submitted and in respect of which VAT has become chargeable during this tax period, where the place where dispatch or transport of the goods began is situated within the territory of another Member State;

(e) the total value, exclusive of VAT, of the supplies of goods carried out in the Member State in which the return must be submitted and in respect of which the taxable person has been designated, in accordance with Article 197, as liable for payment of VAT and in respect of which VAT has become chargeable during this tax period.

Art. 252 1. The VAT return shall be submitted by a deadline to be determined by Member States. That deadline may not be more than two months after the end of each tax period.

2. The tax period shall be set by each Member State at one month, two months or three months.

Member States may, however, set different tax periods provided that those periods do not exceed one year.

Art. 253 Sweden may apply a simplified procedure for small and medium-sized enterprises, whereby taxable persons carrying out only transactions taxable at national level may submit VAT returns three months after the end of the annual direct tax period.

Art. 254 In the case of supplies of new means of transport carried out in accordance with the conditions specified in Article 138(2)(a) by a taxable person identified for VAT purposes for a customer not identified for VAT purposes, or by a taxable person as defined in Article 9(2), Member States shall take the measures necessary to ensure that the vendor communicates all the information needed for VAT to be applied and its application checked by the tax authorities.

Art. 255 Where Member States designate the customer of investment gold as the person liable for payment of VAT pursuant to Article 198(1) or if, in the case of gold material, semi-manufactured products or investment gold as defined in Article 344(1), they exercise the option provided for in Article 198(2) of designating the customer as the person liable for payment of VAT, they shall take the measures necessary to ensure that he complies with the obligations relating to submission of a VAT return set out in this Chapter.

Art. 256 Member States shall take the measures necessary to ensure that persons who are regarded as liable for payment of VAT in the stead of a taxable person not established within their territory, in accordance with Articles 194 to 197 and Article 204, comply with the obligations relating to submission of a VAT return, as laid down in this Chapter.

Art. 257 Member States shall take the measures necessary to ensure that non-taxable legal persons who are liable for payment of VAT due in respect of intra-Community acquisitions of goods, as referred to in Article 2(1)(b)(i), comply with the obligations relating to submission of a VAT return, as laid down in this Chapter.

Art. 258 Member States shall lay down detailed rules for the submission of VAT returns in respect of intra-Community acquisitions of new means of transport, as referred to in Article 2(1)(b)(ii), and intra-Community acquisitions of products subject to excise duty, as referred to in Article 2(1)(b)(iii).

Art. 259 Member States may require persons who make intra-Community acquisitions of new means of transport as referred to in Article 2(1)(b)(ii), to provide, when submitting the VAT return, all the information needed for VAT to be applied and its application checked by the tax authorities.

Art. 260 Member States shall lay down detailed rules for the submission of VAT returns in respect of the importation of goods.

Art. 261 1. Member States may require the taxable person to submit a return showing all the particulars specified in Articles 250 and 251 in respect of all transactions carried out in the preceding year. That return shall provide all the information necessary for any adjustments.

2. Member States shall allow, and may require, the return referred to in paragraph 1 to be submitted by electronic means, in accordance with conditions which they lay down.

CHAPTER 6
RECAPITULATIVE STATEMENTS

Art. 262 Every taxable person identified for VAT purposes shall submit a recapitulative statement of the following:

(a) the acquirers identified for VAT purposes to whom he has supplied goods in accordance with the conditions specified in Article 138(1) and (2)(c);

(b) the persons identified for VAT purposes to whom he has supplied goods which were supplied to him by way of intra-Community acquisitions referred to in Article 42;

(c) the taxable persons, and the non-taxable legal persons identified for VAT purposes, to whom he has supplied services, other than services that are exempted from VAT in the Member State where the transaction is taxable, and for which the recipient is liable to pay the tax pursuant to Article 196.

Art. 263 1. The recapitulative statement shall be drawn up for each calendar month within a period not exceeding one month and in accordance with procedures to be determined by the Member States.

1a. However, Member States, in accordance with the conditions and limits which they may lay down, may allow taxable persons to submit the recapitulative statement for each calendar quarter within a time limit not exceeding one month from the end of the quarter, where the total quarterly amount, excluding VAT, of the supplies of goods as referred to in Articles 264(1)(d) and 265(1)(c) does not exceed either in respect of the quarter concerned or in respect of any of the previous four quarters the sum of EUR 50 000 or its equivalent in national currency.

The option provided for in the first subparagraph shall cease to be applicable after the end of the month during which the total value, excluding VAT, of the supplies of goods as referred to in Article 264(1)(d) and 265(1)(c) exceeds, in respect of the current quarter, the sum of EUR 50 000 or its equivalent in national currency. In this case, a recapitulative statement shall be drawn up for the month(s) which has (have) elapsed since the beginning of the quarter, within a time limit not exceeding one month.

1b. Until 31 December 2011, Member States are allowed to set the sum mentioned in paragraph 1a at EUR 100 000 or its equivalent in national currency.

1c. In the case of supplies of services as referred to in Article 264(1)(d), Member States, in accordance with the conditions and limits which they may lay down, may allow taxable persons to submit the recapitulative statement for each calendar quarter within a time limit not exceeding one month from the end of the quarter.

Member States may, in particular, require the taxable persons who carry out supplies of both goods and services as referred to in Article 264(1)(d) to submit the recapitulative statement in accordance with the deadline resulting from paragraphs 1 to 1b.

2. Member States shall allow, and may require, the recapitulative statement referred to in paragraph 1 to be submitted by electronic file transfer, in accordance with conditions which they lay down.

Art. 264 1. The recapitulative statement shall set out the following information:

(a) the VAT identification number of the taxable person in the Member State in which the recapitulative statement must be submitted and under which he has carried out the supply of goods in accordance with the conditions specified in Article 138(1) and under which he effected taxable supplies of services in accordance with the conditions laid down in Article 44;

(b) the VAT identification number of the person acquiring the goods or receiving the services in a Member State other than that in which the recapitulative statement must be submitted and under which the goods or services were supplied to him;

(c) the VAT identification number of the taxable person in the Member State in which the recapitulative statement must be submitted and under which he has carried out a transfer to another Member State, as referred to in Article 138(2)(c), and the number by means of which he is identified in the Member State in which the dispatch or transport ended;

(d) for each person who acquired goods or received services, the total value of the supplies of goods and the total value of the supplies of services carried out by the taxable person;

(e) in respect of supplies of goods consisting in transfers to another Member State, as referred to in Article 138(2)(c), the total value of the supplies, determined in accordance with Article 76;

(f) the amounts of adjustments made pursuant to Article 90.

2. The value referred to in paragraph 1(d) shall be declared for the period of submission established in accordance with Article 263(1) to (1c) during which VAT became chargeable.

The amounts referred to in paragraph 1(f) shall be declared for the period of submission established in accordance with Article 263(1) to (1c) during which the person acquiring the goods was notified of the adjustment.

Art. 265 1. In the case of intra-Community acquisitions of goods, as referred to in Article 42 the taxable person identified for VAT purposes in the Member State which issued him with the VAT identification number under which he made such acquisitions shall set the following information out clearly on the recapitulative statement:

(a) his VAT identification number in that Member State and under which he made the acquisition and subsequent supply of goods;

(b) the VAT identification number, in the Member State in which dispatch or transport of the goods ended, of the person to whom the subsequent supply was made by the taxable person;

(c) for each person to whom the subsequent supply was made, the total value, exclusive of VAT, of the supplies made by the taxable person in the Member State in which dispatch or transport of the goods ended.

2. The value referred to in paragraph 1(c) shall be declared for the period of submission established in accordance with Article 263(1) to (1b) during which VAT became chargeable.

Art. 266 By way of derogation from Articles 264 and 265, Member States may provide that additional information is to be given in recapitulative statements.

Art. 267 Member States shall take the measures necessary to ensure that those persons who, in accordance with Articles 194 and 204, are regarded as liable for payment of VAT, in the stead of a taxable person who is not established in their territory, comply with the obligation to submit a recapitulative statement as provided for in this Chapter.

Art. 268 Member States may require that taxable persons who, in their territory, make intra-Community acquisitions of goods, or transactions treated as such, pursuant to Articles 21 or 22, submit statements giving details of such acquisitions, provided, however, that such statements are not required in respect of a period of less than one month.

Art. 269 Acting unanimously on a proposal from the Commission, the Council may authorise any Member State to introduce the special measures provided for in Articles 270 and 271 to simplify the obligation, laid down in this Chapter, to submit a recapitulative statement. Such measures may not jeopardise the proper monitoring of intra-Community transactions.

Art. 270 By virtue of the authorisation referred to in Article 269, Member States may permit taxable persons to submit annual recapitulative statements indicating the VAT identification numbers, in another Member State, of the persons to whom those taxable persons have supplied goods in accordance with the conditions specified in Article 138(1) and (2)(c), where the taxable persons meet the following three conditions:

(a) the total annual value, exclusive of VAT, of their supplies of goods and services does not exceed by more than EUR 35 000, or the equivalent in national currency, the amount of the annual turnover which is used as a reference for application of the exemption for small enterprises provided for in Articles 282 to 292;

(b) the total annual value, exclusive of VAT, of supplies of goods carried out by them in accordance with the conditions specified in Article 138 does not exceed EUR 15 000 or the equivalent in national currency;

(c) none of the supplies of goods carried out by them in accordance with the conditions specified in Article 138 is a supply of new means of transport.

Art. 271 By virtue of the authorisation referred to in Article 269, Member States which set at over three months the tax period in respect of which taxable persons must submit the VAT return provided for in Article 250 may permit such persons to submit recapitulative statements in respect of the same period where those taxable persons meet the following three conditions:

(a) the total annual value, exclusive of VAT, of their supplies of goods and services does not exceed EUR 200 000 or the equivalent in national currency;

(b) the total annual value, exclusive of VAT, of supplies of goods carried out by them in accordance with the conditions specified in Article 138 does not exceed EUR 15 000 or the equivalent in national currency;

(c) none of the supplies of goods carried out by them in accordance with the conditions specified in Article 138 is a supply of new means of transport.

CHAPTER 7
MISCELLANEOUS PROVISIONS

Art. 272 1. Member States may release the following taxable persons from certain or all obligations referred to in Chapters 2 to 6:

(a) taxable persons whose intra-Community acquisitions of goods are not subject to VAT pursuant to Article 3(1);

(b) taxable persons carrying out none of the transactions referred to in Articles 20, 21, 22, 33, 36, 138 and 141;

(c) taxable persons carrying out only supplies of goods or of services which are exempt pursuant to Articles 132, 135 and 136, Articles 146 to 149 and Articles 151, 152 or 153;

(d) taxable persons covered by the exemption for small enterprises provided for in Articles 282 to 292;

(e) taxable persons covered by the common flat-rate scheme for farmers.

Member States may not release the taxable persons referred to in point (b) of the first subparagraph from the invoicing obligations laid down in Sections 3 to 6 of Chapter 3 and Section 3 of Chapter 4.

2. If Member States exercise the option under point (e) of the first subparagraph of paragraph 1, they shall take the measures necessary to ensure the correct application of the transitional arrangements for the taxation of intra-Community transactions.

3. Member States may release taxable persons other than those referred to in paragraph 1 from certain of the accounting obligations referred to in Article 242.

Art. 273 Member States may impose other obligations which they deem necessary to ensure the correct collection of VAT and to prevent evasion, subject to the requirement of equal treatment as between domestic transactions and transactions carried out between Member States by taxable persons and provided that such obligations do not, in trade between Member States, give rise to formalities connected with the crossing of frontiers.

The option under the first paragraph may not be relied upon in order to impose additional invoicing obligations over and above those laid down in Chapter 3.

CHAPTER 8
OBLIGATIONS RELATING TO CERTAIN IMPORTATIONS AND EXPORTATIONS

SECTION 1
Importation

Art. 274 Articles 275, 276 and 277 shall apply to the importation of goods in free circulation which enter the Community from a third territory forming part of the customs territory of the Community.

Art. 275 The formalities relating to the importation of the goods referred to in Article 274 shall be the same as those laid down by the Community customs provisions in force for the importation of goods into the customs territory of the Community.

Art. 276 Where dispatch or transport of the goods referred to in Article 274 ends at a place situated outside the Member State of their entry into the Community, they shall circulate in the Community under the internal Community transit procedure laid down by the Community customs provisions in force, in so far as they have been the subject of a declaration placing them under that procedure on their entry into the Community.

Art. 277 Where, on their entry into the Community, the goods referred to in Article 274 are in one of the situations which would entitle them, if they were imported within the meaning of the first paragraph of Article 30, to be covered by one of the arrangements or situations referred to in Article 156, or by a temporary importation arrangement with full exemption from import duties, Member States shall take the measures necessary to ensure that the goods may remain in the Community under the same conditions as those laid down for the application of those arrangements or situations.

SECTION 2
Exportation

Art. 278 Articles 279 and 280 shall apply to the exportation of goods in free circulation which are dispatched or transported from a Member State to a third territory forming part of the customs territory of the Community.

Art. 279 The formalities relating to the exportation of the goods referred to in Article 278 from the territory of the Community shall be the same as those laid down by the Community customs provisions in force for the exportation of goods from the customs territory of the Community.

Art. 280 In the case of goods which are temporarily exported from the Community, in order to be reimported, Member States shall take the measures necessary to ensure that, on reimportation into the Community, such goods may be covered by the same provisions as would have applied if they had been temporarily exported from the customs territory of the Community.

TITLE XII
SPECIAL SCHEMES

CHAPTER 1
SPECIAL SCHEME FOR SMALL ENTERPRISES

SECTION 1
Simplified procedures for charging and collection

Art. 281 Member States which might encounter difficulties in applying the normal VAT arrangements to small enterprises, by reason of the activities or structure of such enterprises, may, subject to such conditions and limits as they may set, and after consulting the VAT Committee apply simplified procedures, such as flat-rate schemes, for charging and collecting VAT provided that they do not lead to a reduction thereof.

SECTION 2
Exemptions or graduated relief

Art. 282 The exemptions and graduated tax relief provided for in this Section shall apply to the supply of goods and services by small enterprises.

Art. 283 1. The arrangements provided for in this Section shall not apply to the following transactions:

(a) transactions carried out on an occasional basis, as referred to in Article 12;

(b) supplies of new means of transport carried out in accordance with the conditions specified in Article 138(1) and (2)(a);

(c) supplies of goods or services carried out by a taxable person who is not established in the Member State in which the VAT is due.

2. Member States may exclude transactions other than those referred to in paragraph 1 from the arrangements provided for in this Section.

Art. 284 1. Member States which have exercised the option under Article 14 of Council Directive 67/228/EEC of 11 April 1967 on the harmonisation of legislation of Member States concerning turnover taxes - Structure and procedures for application of the common system of value added tax[1] of introducing exemptions or graduated tax relief may retain them, and the arrangements for applying them, if they comply with the VAT rules.

2. Member States which, at 17 May 1977, exempted taxable persons whose annual turnover was less than the equivalent in national currency of 5 000 European units of account at the conversion rate on that date, may raise that ceiling up to EUR 5 000.

Member States which applied graduated tax relief may neither raise the ceiling for graduated tax relief nor render the conditions for the granting of it more favourable.

Art. 285 Member States which have not exercised the option under Article 14 of Directive 67/228/EEC may exempt taxable persons whose annual turnover is no higher than EUR 5 000 or the equivalent in national currency.

The Member States referred to in the first paragraph may grant graduated tax relief to taxable persons whose annual turnover exceeds the ceiling fixed by them for its application.

Art. 286 Member States which, at 17 May 1977, exempted taxable persons whose annual turnover was equal to or higher than the equivalent in national currency of 5 000 European units of account at the conversion rate on that date, may raise that ceiling in order to maintain the value of the exemption in real terms.

Art. 287 Member States which acceded after 1 January 1978 may exempt taxable persons whose annual turnover is no higher than the equivalent in national currency of the following amounts at the conversion rate on the day of their accession:

(1) Greece: 10 000 European units of account;

(2) Spain: ECU 10 000;

(3) Portugal: ECU 10 000;

(4) Austria: ECU 35 000;

(5) Finland: ECU 10 000;

(6) Sweden: ECU 10 000;

(7) Czech Republic: EUR 35 000;

(8) Estonia: EUR 16 000;

(9) Cyprus: EUR 15 600;

(10) Latvia: EUR 17 200;

(11) Lithuania: EUR 29 000;

(12) Hungary: EUR 35 000;

(13) Malta: EUR 37 000 if the economic activity consists principally in the supply of goods, EUR 24 300 if the economic activity consists principally in the supply of services with a low value added (high inputs), and EUR 14 600 in other cases, namely supplies of services with a high value added (low inputs);

(14) Poland: EUR 10 000;

(15) Slovenia: EUR 25 000;

(16) Slovakia: EUR 35 000;

(17) Bulgaria: EUR 25 600;

(18) Romania: EUR 35 000.

Art. 288 The turnover serving as a reference for the purposes of applying the arrangements provided for in this Section shall consist of the following amounts, exclusive of VAT:

(1) the value of supplies of goods and services, in so far as they are taxed;

(2) the value of transactions which are exempt, with deductibility of the VAT paid at the preceding stage, pursuant to Articles 110 or 111, Article 125(1), Article 127 or Article 128(1);

(3) the value of transactions which are exempt pursuant to Articles 146 to 149 and Articles 151, 152 or 153;

(4) the value of real estate transactions, financial transactions as referred to in points (b) to (g) of Article 135(1), and insurance services, unless those transactions are ancillary transactions.

However, disposals of the tangible or intangible capital assets of an enterprise shall not be taken into account for the purposes of calculating turnover.

Art. 289 Taxable persons exempt from VAT shall not be entitled to deduct VAT in accordance with Articles 167 to 171 and Articles 173 to 177, and may not show the VAT on their invoices.

Art. 290 Taxable persons who are entitled to exemption from VAT may opt either for the normal VAT arrangements or for the simplified procedures provided for in Article 281. In this case, they shall be entitled to any graduated tax relief provided for under national legislation.

Art. 291 Subject to the application of Article 281, taxable persons enjoying graduated relief

---

1. OJ 71, 14.4.1967, p. 1303/67. Directive repealed by Directive 77/ 388/EEC.

shall be regarded as taxable persons subject to the normal VAT arrangements.

Art. 292 The arrangements provided for in this Section shall apply until a date to be fixed by the Council in accordance with Article 93 of the Treaty, which may not be later than that on which the definitive arrangements referred to in Article 402 enter into force.

Section 3
Reporting and review

Art. 293 Every four years starting from the adoption of this Directive, the Commission shall present to the Council, on the basis of information obtained from the Member States, a report on the application of this Chapter, together, where appropriate and taking into account the need to ensure the long-term convergence of national regulations, with proposals on the following subjects:

(1) improvements to the special scheme for small enterprises;

(2) the adaptation of national systems as regards exemptions and graduated tax relief;

(3) the adaptation of the ceilings provided for in Section 2.

Art. 294 The Council shall decide, in accordance with Article 93 of the Treaty, whether a special scheme for small enterprises is necessary under the definitive arrangements and, if appropriate, shall lay down the common limits and conditions for the implementation of that scheme.

CHAPTER 2
COMMON FLAT-RATE SCHEME FOR FARMERS

Art. 295 1. For the purposes of this Chapter, the following definitions shall apply:

(1) "farmer" means any taxable person whose activity is carried out in an agricultural, forestry or fisheries undertaking;

(2) "agricultural, forestry or fisheries undertaking" means an undertaking regarded as such by each Member State within the framework of the production activities listed in Annex VII;

(3) "flat-rate farmer" means any farmer covered by the flat-rate scheme provided for in this Chapter;

(4) "agricultural products" means goods produced by an agricultural, forestry or fisheries undertaking in each Member State as a result of the activities listed in Annex VII;

(5) "agricultural services" means services, and in particular those listed in Annex VIII, supplied by a farmer using his labour force or the equipment normally employed in the agricultural, forestry or fisheries undertaking operated by him and normally playing a part in agricultural production;

(6) "input VAT charged" means the amount of the total VAT attaching to the goods and services purchased by all agricultural, forestry and fisheries undertakings of each Member State subject to the flat-rate scheme where such tax would be deductible in accordance with Articles 167, 168 and 169 and Articles 173 to 177 by a farmer subject to the normal VAT arrangements;

(7) "flat-rate compensation percentages" means the percentages fixed by Member States in accordance with Articles 297, 298 and 299 and applied by them in the cases specified in Article 300 in order to enable flat-rate farmers to offset at a fixed rate the input VAT charged;

(8) "flat-rate compensation" means the amount arrived at by applying the flat-rate compensation percentage to the turnover of the flat-rate farmer in the cases specified in Article 300.

2. Where a farmer processes, using means normally employed in an agricultural, forestry or fisheries undertaking, products deriving essentially from his agricultural production, such processing activities shall be treated as agricultural production activities, as listed in Annex VII.

Art. 296 1. Where the application to farmers of the normal VAT arrangements, or the special scheme provided for in Chapter 1, is likely to give rise to difficulties, Member States may apply to farmers, in accordance with this Chapter, a flat-rate scheme designed to offset the VAT charged on purchases of goods and services made by the flat-rate farmers.

2. Each Member State may exclude from the flat-rate scheme certain categories of farmers, as well as farmers for whom application of the normal VAT arrangements, or of the simplified procedures provided for in Article 281, is not likely to give rise to administrative difficulties.

3. Every flat-rate farmer may opt, subject to the rules and conditions to be laid down by each Member State, for application of the normal VAT arrangements or, as the case may be, the simplified procedures provided for in Article 281.

Art. 297 Member States shall, where necessary, fix the flat-rate compensation percentages. They may fix varying percentages for forestry, for the different sub-divisions of agriculture and for fisheries.

Member States shall notify the Commission of the flat-rate compensation percentages fixed in accordance with the first paragraph before applying them.

Art. 298 The flat-rate compensation percentages shall be calculated on the basis of macro-economic statistics for flat-rate farmers alone for the preceding three years.

The percentages may be rounded up or down to the nearest half-point. Member States may also reduce such percentages to a nil rate.

Art. 299 The flat-rate compensation percentages may not have the effect of obtaining for flat-rate farmers refunds greater than the input VAT charged.

Art. 300 The flat-rate compensation percentages shall be applied to the prices, exclusive of VAT, of the following goods and services:

(1) agricultural products supplied by flat-rate farmers to taxable persons other than those covered, in the Member State in which these products were supplied, by this flat-rate scheme;

(2) agricultural products supplied by flat-rate farmers, in accordance with the conditions specified in Article 138, to non-taxable legal persons whose intra-Community acquisitions of goods are subject to VAT, pursuant to Article 2(1)(b), in the Member State in which dispatch or transport of those agricultural products ends;

(3) agricultural services supplied by flat-rate farmers to taxable persons other than those covered, in the Member State in which these services were supplied, by this flat-rate scheme.

Art. 301 1. In the case of the supply of agricultural products or agricultural services specified in Article 300, Member States shall provide that the flat-rate compensation is to be paid either by the customer or by the public authorities.

2. In respect of any supply of agricultural products or agricultural services other than those specified in Article 300, the flat-rate compensation shall be deemed to be paid by the customer.

Art. 302 If a flat-rate farmer is entitled to flat-rate compensation, he shall not be entitled to deduction of VAT in respect of activities covered by this flat-rate scheme.

Art. 303 1. Where the taxable customer pays flat-rate compensation pursuant to Article 301(1), he shall be entitled, in accordance with the conditions laid down in Articles 167, 168 and 169 and Articles 173 to 177 and the procedures laid down by the Member States, to deduct the compensation amount from the VAT for which he is liable in the Member State in which his taxed transactions are carried out.

2. Member States shall refund to the customer the amount of the flat-rate compensation he has paid in respect of any of the following transactions:

(a) the supply of agricultural products, carried out in accordance with the conditions specified in Article 138, to taxable persons, or to non-taxable legal persons, acting as such in another Member State within the territory of which their intra-Community acquisitions of goods are subject to VAT pursuant to Article 2(1)(b);

(b) the supply of agricultural products, carried out in accordance with the conditions specified in Articles 146, 147, 148 and 156, Article 157(1)(b) and Articles 158, 160 and 161, to a taxable customer established outside the Community, in so far as the products are used by that customer for the purposes of the transactions referred to in Article 169(a) and (b) or for the purposes of supplies of services which are deemed to take place within the territory of the Member State in which the customer is established and in respect of which VAT is payable solely by the customer pursuant to Article 196;

(c) the supply of agricultural services to a taxable customer established within the Community but in another Member State or to a taxable customer established outside the Community, in so far as the services are used by the customer for the purposes of the transactions referred to in Article 169(a) and (b) or for the purposes of supplies of services which are deemed to take place within the territory of the Member State in which the customer is established and in respect of which VAT is payable solely by the customer pursuant to Article 196.

3. Member States shall determine the method by which the refunds provided for in paragraph 2 are to be made. In particular, they may apply the provisions of Directives 79/1072/EEC and 86/560/EEC.

Art. 304 Member States shall take all measures necessary to verify payments of flat-rate compensation to flat-rate farmers.

Art. 305 Whenever Member States apply this flat-rate scheme, they shall take all measures necessary to ensure that the supply of agricultural products between Member States, carried out in accordance with the conditions specified in Article 33, is always taxed in the same way, whether the supply is effected by a flat-rate farmer or by another taxable person.

CHAPTER 3
SPECIAL SCHEME FOR TRAVEL AGENTS

Art. 306 1. Member States shall apply a special VAT scheme, in accordance with this Chapter, to transactions carried out by travel agents who deal with customers in their own name and use supplies of goods or services provided by other taxable persons, in the provision of travel facilities.

This special scheme shall not apply to travel agents where they act solely as intermediaries and to whom point (c) of the first paragraph of Article 79 applies for the purposes of calculating the taxable amount.

2. For the purposes of this Chapter, tour operators shall be regarded as travel agents.

Art. 307 Transactions made, in accordance with the conditions laid down in Article 306, by the travel agent in respect of a journey shall be regarded as a single service supplied by the travel agent to the traveller.

The single service shall be taxable in the Member State in which the travel agent has established his business or has a fixed establishment from which the travel agent has carried out the supply of services.

Art. 308 The taxable amount and the price exclusive of VAT, within the meaning of point (8) of Article 226, in respect of the single service provided by the travel agent shall be the travel agent's margin, that is to say, the difference between the total amount, exclusive of VAT, to be paid by the traveller and the actual cost to the travel agent of supplies of goods or services provided by other taxable persons, where those transactions are for the direct benefit of the traveller.

Art. 309 If transactions entrusted by the travel agent to other taxable persons are performed by such persons outside the Community, the supply of services carried out by the travel agent shall be treated as an intermediary activity exempted pursuant to Article 153.

If the transactions are performed both inside and outside the Community, only that part of the travel agent's service relating to transactions outside the Community may be exempted.

Art. 310 VAT charged to the travel agent by other taxable persons in respect of transactions which are referred to in Article 307 and which are for the direct benefit of the traveller shall not be deductible or refundable in any Member State.

CHAPTER 4
SPECIAL ARRANGEMENTS FOR SECOND-HAND GOODS, WORKS OF ART, COLLECTORS' ITEMS AND ANTIQUES

SECTION 1
Definitions

Art. 311 1. For the purposes of this Chapter, and without prejudice to other Community provisions, the following definitions shall apply:

(1) "second-hand goods" means movable tangible property that is suitable for further use as it is or after repair, other than works of art, collectors' items or antiques and other than precious metals or precious stones as defined by the Member States;

(2) "works of art" means the objects listed in Annex IX, Part A;

(3) "collectors' items" means the objects listed in Annex IX, Part B;

(4) "antiques" means the objects listed in Annex IX, Part C;

(5) "taxable dealer" means any taxable person who, in the course of his economic activity and with a view to resale, purchases, or applies for the purposes of his business, or imports, second-hand goods, works of art, collectors' items or antiques, whether that taxable person is acting for himself or on behalf of another person pursuant to a contract under which commission is payable on purchase or sale;

(6) "organiser of a sale by public auction" means any taxable person who, in the course of his economic activity, offers goods for sale by public auction with a view to handing them over to the highest bidder;

(7) "principal of an organiser of a sale by public auction" means any person who transmits goods to an organiser of a sale by public auction pursuant to a contract under which commission is payable on a sale.

2. Member States need not regard as works of art the objects listed in points (5), (6) or (7) of Annex IX, Part A.

3. The contract under which commission is payable on a sale, referred to in point (7) of paragraph 1, must provide that the organiser of the sale is to put up the goods for public auction in his own name but on behalf of his principal and that he is to hand over the goods, in his own name but on behalf of his principal, to the highest bidder at the public auction.

SECTION 2
Special arrangements for taxable dealers

SUBSECTION 1
Margin scheme

Art. 312 For the purposes of this Subsection, the following definitions shall apply:

(1) "selling price" means everything which constitutes the consideration obtained or to be obtained by the taxable dealer from the customer or from a third party, including subsidies directly linked to the transaction, taxes, duties, levies and charges and incidental expenses such as commission, packaging, transport and insurance costs charged by the taxable dealer to the customer, but excluding the amounts referred to in Article 79;

(2) "purchase price" means everything which constitutes the consideration, for the purposes of point (1), obtained or to be obtained from the taxable dealer by his supplier.

Art. 313 1. In respect of the supply of second-hand goods, works of art, collectors' items or antiques carried out by taxable dealers, Member States shall apply a special scheme for taxing the profit margin made by the taxable dealer, in accordance with the provisions of this Subsection.

2. Pending introduction of the definitive arrangements referred to in Article 402, the scheme referred to in paragraph 1 of this Article shall not apply to the supply of new means of transport,

carried out in accordance with the conditions specified in Article 138(1) and (2)(a).

Art. 314 The margin scheme shall apply to the supply by a taxable dealer of second-hand goods, works of art, collectors' items or antiques where those goods have been supplied to him within the Community by one of the following persons:

(a) a non-taxable person;

(b) another taxable person, in so far as the supply of goods by that other taxable person is exempt pursuant to Article 136;

(c) another taxable person, in so far as the supply of goods by that other taxable person is covered by the exemption for small enterprises provided for in Articles 282 to 292 and involves capital goods;

(d) another taxable dealer, in so far as VAT has been applied to the supply of goods by that other taxable dealer in accordance with this margin scheme.

Art. 315 The taxable amount in respect of the supply of goods as referred to in Article 314 shall be the profit margin made by the taxable dealer, less the amount of VAT relating to the profit margin.

The profit margin of the taxable dealer shall be equal to the difference between the selling price charged by the taxable dealer for the goods and the purchase price.

Art. 316 1. Member States shall grant taxable dealers the right to opt for application of the margin scheme to the following transactions:

(a) the supply of works of art, collectors' items or antiques, which the taxable dealer has imported himself;

(b) the supply of works of art supplied to the taxable dealer by their creators or their successors in title;

(c) the supply of works of art supplied to the taxable dealer by a taxable person other than a taxable dealer where the reduced rate has been applied to that supply pursuant to Article 103.

2. Member States shall lay down the detailed rules for exercise of the option provided for in paragraph 1, which shall in any event cover a period of at least two calendar years.

Art. 317 If a taxable dealer exercises the option under Article 316, the taxable amount shall be determined in accordance with Article 315.

In respect of the supply of works of art, collectors' items or antiques which the taxable dealer has imported himself, the purchase price to be taken into account in calculating the profit margin shall be equal to the taxable amount on importation, determined in accordance with Articles 85 to 89, plus the VAT due or paid on importation.

Art. 318 1. In order to simplify the procedure for collecting the tax and after consulting the VAT Committee, Member States may provide that, for certain transactions or for certain categories of taxable dealers, the taxable amount in respect of supplies of goods subject to the margin scheme is to be determined for each tax period during which the taxable dealer must submit the VAT return referred to in Article 250.

In the event that such provision is made in accordance with the first subparagraph, the taxable amount in respect of supplies of goods to which the same rate of VAT is applied shall be the total profit margin made by the taxable dealer less the amount of VAT relating to that margin.

2. The total profit margin shall be equal to the difference between the following two amounts:

(a) the total value of supplies of goods subject to the margin scheme and carried out by the taxable dealer during the tax period covered by the return, that is to say, the total of the selling prices;

(b) the total value of purchases of goods, as referred to in Article 314, effected by the taxable dealer during the tax period covered by the return, that is to say, the total of the purchase prices.

3. Member States shall take the measures necessary to ensure that the taxable dealers referred to in paragraph 1 do not enjoy unjustified advantage or sustain unjustified harm.

Art. 319 The taxable dealer may apply the normal VAT arrangements to any supply covered by the margin scheme.

Art. 320 1. Where the taxable dealer applies the normal VAT arrangements to the supply of a work of art, a collectors' item or an antique which he has imported himself, he shall be entitled to deduct from the VAT for which he is liable the VAT due or paid on the import.

Where the taxable dealer applies the normal VAT arrangements to the supply of a work of art supplied to him by its creator, or the creator's successors in title, or by a taxable person other than a taxable dealer, he shall be entitled to deduct from the VAT for which he is liable the VAT due or paid in respect of the work of art supplied to him.

2. A right of deduction shall arise at the time when the VAT due on the supply in respect of which the taxable dealer opts for application of the normal VAT arrangements becomes chargeable.

Art. 321 If carried out in accordance with the conditions specified in Articles 146, 147, 148 or 151, the supply of second-hand goods, works of art, collectors' items or antiques subject to the margin scheme shall be exempt.

Art. 322 In so far as goods are used for the purpose of supplies carried out by him and subject to the margin scheme, the taxable dealer may not deduct the following from the VAT for which he is liable:

(a) the VAT due or paid in respect of works of art, collectors' items or antiques which he has imported himself;

(b) the VAT due or paid in respect of works of art which have been, or are to be, supplied to him by their creator or by the creator's successors in title;

(c) the VAT due or paid in respect of works of art which have been, or are to be, supplied to him by a taxable person other than a taxable dealer.

Art. 323 Taxable persons may not deduct from the VAT for which they are liable the VAT due or paid in respect of goods which have been, or are to be, supplied to them by a taxable dealer, in so far as the supply of those goods by the taxable dealer is subject to the margin scheme.

Art. 324 Where the taxable dealer applies both the normal VAT arrangements and the margin scheme, he must show separately in his accounts the transactions falling under each of those arrangements, in accordance with the rules laid down by the Member States.

Art. 325 The taxable dealer may not enter separately on the invoices which he issues the VAT relating to supplies of goods to which he applies the margin scheme.

Subsection 2

Transitional arrangements for second-hand means of transport

Art. 326 Member States which, at 31 December 1992, were applying special tax arrangements other than the margin scheme to the supply by taxable dealers of second-hand means of transport may, pending introduction of the definitive arrangements referred to in Article 402, continue to apply those arrangements in so far as they comply with, or are adjusted to comply with, the conditions laid down in this Subsection.

Denmark is authorised to introduce tax arrangements as referred to in the first paragraph.

Art. 327 1. These transitional arrangements shall apply to supplies of second-hand means of transport carried out by taxable dealers, and subject to the margin scheme.

2. These transitional arrangements shall not apply to the supply of new means of transport carried out in accordance with the conditions specified in Article 138(1) and (2)(a).

3. For the purposes of paragraph 1, the land vehicles, vessels and aircraft referred to in point (a) of Article 2(2) shall be regarded as "second-hand means of transport" where they are second-hand goods which do not meet the conditions necessary to be regarded as new means of transport.

Art. 328 The VAT due in respect of each supply referred to in Article 327 shall be equal to the amount of VAT that would have been due if that supply had been subject to the normal VAT arrangements, less the amount of VAT regarded as being incorporated by the taxable dealer in the purchase price of the means of transport.

Art. 329 The VAT regarded as being incorporated by the taxable dealer in the purchase price of the means of transport shall be calculated in accordance with the following method:

(a) the purchase price to be taken into account shall be the purchase price within the meaning of point (2) of Article 312;

(b) that purchase price paid by the taxable dealer shall be deemed to include the VAT that would have been due if the taxable dealer's supplier had applied the normal VAT arrangements to the supply;

(c) the rate to be taken into account shall be the rate applicable, pursuant to Article 93, in the Member State in the territory of which the place of the supply to the taxable dealer, as determined in accordance with Articles 31 and 32, is deemed to be situated.

Art. 330 The VAT due in respect of each supply of means of transport as referred to in Article 327(1), determined in accordance with Article 328, may not be less than the amount of VAT that would be due if that supply were subject to the margin scheme.

Member States may provide that, if the supply is subject to the margin scheme, the margin may not be less than 10% of the selling price within the meaning of point (1) of Article 312.

Art. 331 Taxable persons may not deduct from the VAT for which they are liable the VAT due or paid in respect of second-hand means of transport supplied to them by a taxable dealer, in so far as the supply of those goods by the taxable dealer is subject to VAT in accordance with these transitional arrangements.

Art. 332 The taxable dealer may not enter separately on the invoices he issues the VAT relating to supplies to which he applies these transitional arrangements.

Section 3

Special arrangements for sales by public auction

Art. 333 1. Member States may, in accordance with the provisions of this Section, apply special arrangements for taxation of the profit margin made by an organiser of a sale by public auction in respect of the supply of second-hand goods, works of art, collectors' items or antiques by that organiser, acting in his own name and on behalf of the persons referred to in Article 334, pursuant to a contract under which commission is payable on the sale of those goods by public auction.

2. The arrangements referred to in paragraph 1 shall not apply to the supply of new means of transport, carried out in accordance with the conditions specified in Article 138(1) and (2)(a).

Art. 334 These special arrangements shall apply to supplies carried out by an organiser of a sale by public auction, acting in his own name, on behalf of one of the following persons:

(a) a non-taxable person;

(b) another taxable person, in so far as the supply of goods, carried out by that taxable person in accordance with a contract under which commission is payable on a sale, is exempt pursuant to Article 136;

(c) another taxable person, in so far as the supply of goods, carried out by that taxable person in accordance with a contract under which commission is payable on a sale, is covered by the exemption for small enterprises provided for in Articles 282 to 292 and involves capital goods;

(d) a taxable dealer, in so far as the supply of goods, carried out by that taxable dealer in accordance with a contract under which commission is payable on a sale, is subject to VAT in accordance with the margin scheme.

Art. 335 The supply of goods to a taxable person who is an organiser of sales by public auction shall be regarded as taking place when the sale of those goods by public auction takes place.

Art. 336 The taxable amount in respect of each supply of goods referred to in this Section shall be the total amount invoiced in accordance with Article 339 to the purchaser by the organiser of the sale by public auction, less the following:

(a) the net amount paid or to be paid by the organiser of the sale by public auction to his principal, as determined in accordance with Article 337;

(b) the amount of the VAT payable by the organiser of the sale by public auction in respect of his supply.

Art. 337 The net amount paid or to be paid by the organiser of the sale by public auction to his principal shall be equal to the difference between the auction price of the goods and the amount of the commission obtained or to be obtained by the organiser of the sale by public auction from his principal pursuant to the contract under which commission is payable on the sale.

Art. 338 Organisers of sales by public auction who supply goods in accordance with the conditions laid down in Articles 333 and 334 must indicate the following in their accounts, in suspense accounts:

(a) the amounts obtained or to be obtained from the purchaser of the goods;

(b) the amounts reimbursed or to be reimbursed to the vendor of the goods.

The amounts referred to in the first paragraph must be duly substantiated.

Art. 339 The organiser of the sale by public auction must issue to the purchaser an invoice itemising the following:

(a) the auction price of the goods;

(b) taxes, duties, levies and charges;

(c) incidental expenses, such as commission, packing, transport and insurance costs, charged by the organiser to the purchaser of the goods.

The invoice issued by the organiser of the sale by public auction must not indicate any VAT separately.

Art. 340 1. The organiser of the sale by public auction to whom the goods have been transmitted pursuant to a contract under which commission is payable on a public auction sale must issue a statement to his principal.

The statement issued by the organiser of the sale by public auction must specify separately the amount of the transaction, that is to say, the auction price of the goods less the amount of the commission obtained or to be obtained from the principal.

2. The statement drawn up in accordance with paragraph 1 shall serve as the invoice which the principal, where he is a taxable person, must issue to the organiser of the sale by public auction in accordance with Article 220.

Art. 341 Member States which apply the arrangements provided for in this Section shall also apply these arrangements to supplies of second-hand means of transport, as defined in Article 327(3), carried out by an organiser of sales by public auction, acting in his own name, pursuant to a contract under which commission is payable on the sale of those goods by public auction, on behalf of a taxable dealer, in so far as those supplies by that taxable dealer would be subject to VAT in accordance with the transitional arrangements for second-hand means of transport.

Section 4

Measures to prevent distortion of competition and tax evasion

Art. 342 Member States may take measures concerning the right of deduction in order to ensure that the taxable dealers covered by special arrangements as provided for in Section 2 do not enjoy unjustified advantage or sustain unjustified harm.

Art. 343 Acting unanimously on a proposal from the Commission, the Council may authorise any Member State to introduce special measures to combat tax evasion, pursuant to which the VAT due under the margin scheme may not be less than the amount of VAT which would be due if the profit margin were equal to a certain percentage of the selling price.

The percentage of the selling price shall be fixed in the light of the normal profit margins made by economic operators in the sector concerned.

CHAPTER 5
SPECIAL SCHEME FOR INVESTMENT GOLD

SECTION 1
General provisions

Art. 344 1. For the purposes of this Directive, and without prejudice to other Community provisions, "investment gold" shall mean:

(1) gold, in the form of a bar or a wafer of weights accepted by the bullion markets, of a purity equal to or greater than 995 thousandths, whether or not represented by securities;

(2) gold coins of a purity equal to or greater than 900 thousandths and minted after 1800, which are or have been legal tender in the country of origin, and are normally sold at a price which does not exceed the open market value of the gold contained in the coins by more than 80%.

2. Member States may exclude from this special scheme small bars or wafers of a weight of 1 g or less.

3. For the purposes of this Directive, the coins referred to in point (2) of paragraph 1 shall not be regarded as sold for numismatic interest.

Art. 345 Starting in 1999, each Member State shall inform the Commission by 1 July each year of the coins meeting the criteria laid down in point (2) of Article 344(1) which are traded in that Member State. The Commission shall, before 1 December each year, publish a comprehensive list of those coins in the "C" series of the *Official Journal of the European Union*. Coins included in the published list shall be deemed to fulfil those criteria throughout the year for which the list is published.

SECTION 2
Exemption from VAT

Art. 346 Member States shall exempt from VAT the supply, the intra-Community acquisition and the importation of investment gold, including investment gold represented by certificates for allocated or unallocated gold or traded on gold accounts and including, in particular, gold loans and swaps, involving a right of ownership or claim in respect of investment gold, as well as transactions concerning investment gold involving futures and forward contracts leading to a transfer of right of ownership or claim in respect of investment gold.

Art. 347 Member States shall exempt the services of agents who act in the name and on behalf of another person, when they take part in the supply of investment gold for their principal.

SECTION 3
Taxation option

Art. 348 Member States shall allow taxable persons who produce investment gold or transform gold into investment gold the right to opt for the taxation of supplies of investment gold to another taxable person which would otherwise be exempt pursuant to Article 346.

Art. 349 1. Member States may allow taxable persons who, in the course of their economic activity, normally supply gold for industrial purposes, the right to opt for the taxation of supplies of gold bars or wafers, as referred to in point (1) of Article 344(1), to another taxable person, which would otherwise be exempt pursuant to Article 346.

2. Member States may restrict the scope of the option provided for in paragraph 1.

Art. 350 Where the supplier has exercised the right under Articles 348 and 349 to opt for taxation, Member States shall allow the agent to opt for taxation of the services referred to in Article 347.

Art. 351 Member States shall lay down detailed rules for the exercise of the options provided for in this Section, and shall inform the Commission accordingly.

SECTION 4
Transactions on a regulated gold bullion market

Art. 352 Each Member State may, after consulting the VAT Committee, apply VAT to specific transactions relating to investment gold which take place in that Member State between taxable persons who are members of a gold bullion market regulated by the Member State concerned or between such a taxable person and another taxable person who is not a member of that market. However, the Member State may not apply VAT to supplies carried out in accordance with the conditions specified in Article 138 or to exports of investment gold.

Art. 353 Member States which, pursuant to Article 352, tax transactions between taxable persons who are members of a regulated gold bullion market shall, for the purposes of simplification, authorise suspension of the tax to be collected and relieve taxable persons of the accounting requirements in respect of VAT.

SECTION 5
Special rights and obligations for traders in investment gold

Art. 354 Where his subsequent supply of investment gold is exempt pursuant to this Chapter, the taxable person shall be entitled to deduct the following:

(a) the VAT due or paid in respect of investment gold supplied to him by a person who has exercised the right of option under Articles 348 and 349 or supplied to him in accordance with Section 4;

(b) the VAT due or paid in respect of a supply to him, or in respect of an intra-Community acquisition or importation carried out by him, of gold other than investment gold which is subsequently transformed by him or on his behalf into investment gold;

(c) the VAT due or paid in respect of services supplied to him consisting in a change of form, weight or purity of gold including investment gold.

Art. 355 Taxable persons who produce investment gold or transform gold into investment gold shall be entitled to deduct the VAT due or paid by them in respect of the supply, intra-Community acquisition or importation of goods or services linked to the production or transformation of that gold, as if the subsequent supply of the gold exempted pursuant to Article 346 were taxed.

Art. 356 1. Member States shall ensure that traders in investment gold keep, as a minimum, accounts of all substantial transactions in investment gold and keep the documents which enable the customers in such transactions to be identified.

Traders shall keep the information referred to in the first subparagraph for a period of at least five years.

2. Member States may accept equivalent obligations under measures adopted pursuant to other Community legislation, such as Directive 2005/60/EC of the European Parliament and of the Council of 26 October 2005 on the prevention of the use of the financial system for the purpose of money laundering and terrorist financing [(1)], to comply with the requirements under paragraph 1.

3. Member States may lay down obligations which are more stringent, in particular as regards the keeping of special records or special accounting requirements.

CHAPTER 6

SPECIAL SCHEMES FOR NON-ESTABLISHED TAXABLE PERSONS SUPPLYING TELECOMMUNICATIONS SERVICES, BROADCASTING SERVICES OR ELECTRONIC SERVICES TO NON-TAXABLE PERSONS

SECTION 1

General provisions

Art. 357 [Repealed by Council Directive 2008/8/EC]

Art. 358 For the purposes of this Chapter, and without prejudice to other Community provisions, the following definitions shall apply:

(1) "telecommunications services" and "broadcasting services" mean the services referred to in points (a) and (b) of the first paragraph of Article 58;

(2) "electronic services" and "electronically supplied services" mean the services referred to in point (c) of the first paragraph of Article 58;

(3) "Member State of consumption" means the Member State in which the supply of the telecommunications, broadcasting or electronic services is deemed to take place according to Article 58;

(4) "VAT return" means the statement containing the information necessary to establish the amount of VAT due in each Member State.

SECTION 2

Special scheme for telecommunications, broadcasting or electronic services supplied by taxable persons not established within the Community

Art. 358a For the purposes of this Section, and without prejudice to other Community provisions, the following definitions shall apply:

1. "taxable person not established within the Community" means a taxable person who has not established his business in the territory of the Community and who has no fixed establishment there and who is not otherwise required to be identified for VAT purposes;

2. "Member State of identification" means the Member State which the taxable person not established within the Community chooses to contact to state when his activity as a taxable person within the territory of the Community commences in accordance with the provisions of this Section.

Art. 359 Member States shall permit any taxable person not established within the Community supplying telecommunications, broadcasting or electronic services to a nontaxable person who is established in a Member State or has his permanent address or usually resides in a Member State, to use this special scheme. This scheme applies to all those services supplied within the Community.

Art. 360 The taxable person not established within the Community shall state to the Member State of identification when he commences or ceases his activity as a taxable person, or changes that activity in such a way that he no longer meets the conditions necessary for use of this special scheme. He shall communicate that information electronically.

Art. 361 1. The information which the taxable person not established within the Community must provide to the Member State of identification

1. OJ L 309, 25.11.2005, p. 15.

when he commences a taxable activity shall contain the following details:

(a) name;

(b) postal address;

(c) electronic addresses, including websites;

(d) national tax number, if any;

(e) a statement that the person is not identified for VAT purposes within the Community.

2. The taxable person not established within in the Community shall notify the Member State of identification of any changes in the information provided.

Art. 362 The Member State of identification shall allocate to the taxable person not established within the Community an individual VAT identification number and shall notify him of that number by electronic means. On the basis of the information used for that identification, Member States of consumption may have recourse to their own identification systems.

Art. 363 The Member State of identification shall delete the taxable person not established within the Community from the identification register in the following cases:

(a) if he notifies that Member State that he no longer supplies telecommunications, broadcasting or electronic services;

(b) if it may otherwise be assumed that his taxable activities have ceased;

(c) if he no longer meets the conditions necessary for use of this special scheme;

(d) if he persistently fails to comply with the rules relating to this special scheme.

Art. 364 The taxable person not established within the Community shall submit by electronic means to the Member State of identification a VAT return for each calendar quarter, whether or not telecommunications, broadcasting or electronic services have been supplied. The VAT return shall be submitted within 20 days following the end of the tax period covered by the return.

Art. 365 The VAT return shall show the identification number and, for each Member State of consumption in which VAT is due, the total value, exclusive of VAT, of supplies of telecommunications, broadcasting and electronic services carried out during the tax period and total amount per rate of the corresponding VAT. The applicable rates of VAT and the total VAT due must also be indicated on the return.

Art. 366 1. The VAT return shall be made out in euro.

Member States which have not adopted the euro may require the VAT return to be made out in their national currency. If the supplies have been made in other currencies, the taxable person not established within the Community shall, for the purposes of completing the VAT return, use the exchange rate applying on the last day of the tax period.

2. The conversion shall be made by applying the exchange rates published by the European Central Bank for that day, or, if there is no publication on that day, on the next day of publication.

Art. 367 The taxable person not established within the Community shall pay the VAT, making reference to the relevant VAT return, when submitting the VAT return, at the latest, however, at the expiry of the deadline by which the return must be submitted.

Payment shall be made to a bank account denominated in euro, designated by the Member State of identification. Member States which have not adopted the euro may require the payment to be made to a bank account denominated in their own currency.

Art. 368 The taxable person not established within the Community making use of this special scheme may not deduct VAT pursuant to Article 168 of this Directive. Notwithstanding Article 1(1) of Directive 86/560/EEC, the taxable person in question shall be refunded in accordance with the said Directive. Articles 2(2) and (3) and Article 4(2) of Directive 86/560/EEC shall not apply to refunds relating to telecommunications, broadcasting or electronic services covered by this special scheme.

Art. 369 1. The taxable person not established within the Community shall keep records of the transactions covered by this special scheme. Those records must be sufficiently detailed to enable the tax authorities of the Member State of consumption to verify that the VAT return is correct.

2. The records referred to in paragraph 1 must be made available electronically on request to the Member State of identification and to the Member State of consumption.

Those records must be kept for a period of ten years from the end of the year during which the transaction was carried out.

SECTION3

SPECIAL SCHEME FOR TELECOMMUNICATIONS, BROADCASTING OR ELECTRONIC SERVICES SUPPLIED BY TAXABLE PERSONS ESTABLISHED WITHIN THE COMMUNITY BUT NOT IN THE MEMBER STATE OF CONSUMPTION

Art. 369a For the purposes of this Section, and without prejudice to other Community provisions, the following definitions shall apply:

1. "taxable person not established in the Member State of consumption" means a taxable person who has established his business in the territory of the Community or has a fixed establishment

there but has not established his business and has no fixed establishment within the territory of the Member State of consumption;

2. "Member State of identification" means the Member State in the territory of which the taxable person has established his business or, if he has not established his business in the Community, where he has a fixed establishment.

Where a taxable person has not established his business in the Community, but has more than one fixed establishment therein, the Member State of identification shall be the Member State with a fixed establishment where that taxable person indicates that he will make use of this special scheme. The taxable person shall be bound by this decision for the calendar year concerned and the two calendar years following.

Art. 369b Member States shall permit any taxable person not established in the Member State of consumption supplying telecommunications, broadcasting or electronic services to a non-taxable person who is established or has his permanent address or usually resides in that Member State, to use this special scheme. This special scheme applies to all those services supplied in the Community.

Art. 369c The taxable person not established in the Member State of consumption shall state to the Member State of identification when he commences and ceases his taxable activities covered by this special scheme, or changes those activities in such a way that he no longer meets the conditions necessary for use of this special scheme. He shall communicate that information electronically.

Art. 369d A taxable person making use of this special scheme shall, for the taxable transactions carried out under this scheme, be identified for VAT purposes in the Member State of identification only. For that purpose the Member State shall use the individual VAT identification number already allocated to the taxable person in respect of his obligations under the internal system.

On the basis of the information used for that identification, Member States of consumption may have recourse to their own identification systems.

Art. 369e The Member State of identification shall exclude the taxable person not established in the Member State of consumption from this special scheme in any of the following cases:

(a) if he notifies that he no longer supplies telecommunications, broadcasting or electronic services;

(b) if it may otherwise be assumed that his taxable activities covered by this special scheme have ceased;

(c) if he no longer meets the conditions necessary for use of this special scheme;

(d) if he persistently fails to comply with the rules relating to this special scheme.

Art. 369f The taxable person not established in the Member State of consumption shall submit by electronic means to the Member State of identification a VAT return for each calendar quarter, whether or not telecommunications, broadcasting or electronic services have been supplied. The VAT return shall be submitted within 20 days following the end of the tax period covered by the return.

Art. 369g The VAT return shall show the identification number referred to in Article 369d and, for each Member State of consumption in which VAT is due, the total value, exclusive of VAT, of supplies of telecommunications, broadcasting or electronic services carried out during the tax period and the total amount per rate of the corresponding VAT. The applicable rates of VAT and the total VAT due must also be indicated on the return.

Art. 369h 1. The VAT return shall be made out in euro.

Member States which have not adopted the euro may require the VAT return to be made out in their national currency. If the supplies have been made in other currencies, the taxable person not established in the Member State of consumption shall, for the purposes of completing the VAT return, use the exchange rate applying on the last date of the tax period.

2. The conversion shall be made by applying the exchange rates published by the European Central Bank for that day, or, if there is no publication on that day, on the next day of publication.

Art. 369i The taxable person not established in the Member State of consumption shall pay the VAT, making reference to the relevant VAT return, when submitting the VAT return, at the latest, however, at the expiry of the deadline by which the return must be submitted.

Payment shall be made to a bank account denominated in euro, designated by the Member State of identification. Member States which have not adopted the euro may require the payment to be made to a bank account denominated in their own currency.

Art. 369j The taxable person not established in the Member State of consumption making use of this special scheme may not, in respect of his taxable activities covered by this scheme, deduct VAT pursuant to Article 168 of this Directive. Notwithstanding Article 2(1) and Article 3 of Directive 2008/9/EC, the taxable person in question shall be refunded in accordance with the said Directive.

If the taxable person not established in the Member State of consumption making use of this special scheme also carries out in the Member State of consumption activities not covered by this scheme in respect of which he is obliged to be registered for VAT purposes, he shall deduct VAT in respect of his taxable activities which are covered by this scheme in the VAT return to be submitted pursuant to Article 250.

Art. 369k 1. The taxable person not established in the Member State of consumption shall keep records of the transactions covered by this special scheme. Those records must be sufficiently detailed to enable the tax authorities of the Member State of consumption to verify that the VAT return is correct.

2. The records referred to in paragraph 1 must be made available electronically on request to the Member State of consumption and to the Member State of identification.

Those records must be kept for a period of 10 years from 31 December of the year during which the transaction was carried out.

TITLE XIII
DEROGATIONS

CHAPTER 1
DEROGATIONS APPLYING UNTIL THE ADOPTION OF DEFINITIVE ARRANGEMENTS

SECTION 1
Derogations for States which were members of the Community on 1 January 1978

Art. 370 Member States which, at 1 January 1978, taxed the transactions listed in Annex X, Part A, may continue to tax those transactions.

Art. 371 Member States which, at 1 January 1978, exempted the transactions listed in Annex X, Part B, may continue to exempt those transactions, in accordance with the conditions applying in the Member State concerned on that date.

Art. 372 Member States which, at 1 January 1978, applied provisions derogating from the principle of immediate deduction laid down in the first paragraph of Article 179 may continue to apply those provisions.

Art. 373 Member States which, at 1 January 1978, applied provisions derogating from Article 28 or from point (c) of the first paragraph of Article 79 may continue to apply those provisions.

Art. 374 By way of derogation from Articles 169 and 309, Member States which, at 1 January 1978, exempted, without deductibility of the VAT paid at the preceding stage, the services of travel agents, as referred to in Article 309, may continue to exempt those services. That derogation shall apply also in respect of travel agents acting in the name and on behalf of the traveller.

SECTION 2
Derogations for States which acceded to the Community after 1 January 1978

Art. 375 Greece may continue to exempt the transactions listed in points (2), (8), (9), (11) and (12) of Annex X, Part B, in accordance with the conditions applying in that Member State on 1 January 1987.

Art. 376 Spain may continue to exempt the supply of services performed by authors, listed in point (2) of Annex X, Part B, and the transactions listed in points (11) and (12) of Annex X, Part B in accordance with the conditions applying in that Member State on 1 January 1993.

Art. 377 Portugal may continue to exempt the transactions listed in points (2), (4), (7), (9), (10) and (13) of Annex X, Part B, in accordance with the conditions applying in that Member State on 1 January 1989.

Art. 378 1. Austria may continue to tax the transactions listed in point (2) of Annex X, Part A.

2. For as long as the same exemptions are applied in any of the Member States which were members of the Community on 31 December 1994, Austria may, in accordance with the conditions applying in that Member State on the date of its accession, continue to exempt the following transactions:

(a) the transactions listed in points (5) and (9) of Annex X, Part B;

(b) with deductibility of the VAT paid at the preceding stage, all parts of international passenger transport operations, carried out by air, sea or inland waterway, other than passenger transport operations on Lake Constance.

Art. 379 1. Finland may continue to tax the transactions listed in point (2) of Annex X, Part A, for as long as the same transactions are taxed in any of the Member States which were members of the Community on 31 December 1994.

2. Finland may, in accordance with the conditions applying in that Member State on the date of its accession, continue to exempt the supply of services by authors, artists and performers, listed in point (2) of Annex X, Part B, and the transactions listed in points (5), (9) and (10) of Annex X, Part B, for as long as the same exemptions are applied in any of the Member States which were members of the Community on 31 December 1994.

Art. 380 Sweden may, in accordance with the conditions applying in that Member State on the date of its accession, continue to exempt the supply of services by authors, artists and performers, listed in point (2) of Annex X, Part B, and the transactions listed in points (1), (9) and (10) of Annex X, Part B, for as long as the same exemptions are applied in any of the Member States which were members of the Community on 31 December 1994.

Art. 381 The Czech Republic may, in accordance with the conditions applying in that Member State on the date of its accession, continue to exempt the international transport of passengers, as referred to in point (10) of Annex X, Part B, for as long as the same exemption is applied in any of the Member States which were members of the Community on 30 April 2004.

Art. 382 Estonia may, in accordance with the conditions applying in that Member State on the date of its accession, continue to exempt the international transport of passengers, as referred to in point (10) of Annex X, Part B, for as long as the same exemption is applied in any of the Member States which were members of the Community on 30 April 2004.

Art. 383 Cyprus may, in accordance with the conditions applying in that Member State on the date of its accession, continue to exempt the following transactions:

(a) the supply of building land referred to in point (9) of Annex X, Part B, until 31 December 2007;

(b) the international transport of passengers, as referred to in point (10) of Annex X, Part B, for as long as the same exemption is applied in any of the Member States which were members of the Community on 30 April 2004.

Art. 384 For as long as the same exemptions are applied in any of the Member States which were members of the Community on 30 April 2004, Latvia may, in accordance with the conditions applying in that Member State on the date of its accession, continue to exempt the following transactions:

(a) the supply of services by authors, artists and performers, as referred to in point (2) of Annex X, Part B;

(b) the international transport of passengers, as referred to in point (10) of Annex X, Part B.

Art. 385 Lithuania may, in accordance with the conditions applying in that Member State on the date of its accession, continue to exempt the international transport of passengers, as referred to in point (10) of Annex X, Part B, for as long as the same exemption is applied in any of the Member States which were members of the Community on 30 April 2004.

Art. 386 Hungary may, in accordance with the conditions applying in that Member State on the date of its accession, continue to exempt the international transport of passengers, as referred to in point (10) of Annex X, Part B, for as long as the same exemption is applied in any of the Member States which were members of the Community on 30 April 2004.

Art. 387 For as long as the same exemptions are applied in any of the Member States which were members of the Community on 30 April 2004, Malta may, in accordance with the conditions applying in that Member State on the date of its accession, continue to exempt the following transactions:

(a) without deductibility of the VAT paid at the preceding stage, the supply of water by a body governed by public law, as referred to in point (8) of Annex X, Part B;

(b) without deductibility of the VAT paid at the preceding stage, the supply of buildings and building land, as referred to in point (9) of Annex X, Part B;

(c) with deductibility of the VAT paid at the preceding stage, inland passenger transport, international passenger transport and domestic inter-island sea passenger transport, as referred to in point (10) of Annex X, Part B.

Art. 388 Poland may, in accordance with the conditions applying in that Member State on the date of its accession, continue to exempt the international transport of passengers, as referred to in point (10) of Annex X, Part B, for as long as the same exemption is applied in any of the Member States which were members of the Community on 30 April 2004.

Art. 389 Slovenia may, in accordance with the conditions applying in that Member State on the date of its accession, continue to exempt the international transport of passengers, as referred to in point (10) of Annex X, Part B, for as long as the same exemption is applied in any of the Member States which were members of the Community on 30 April 2004.

Art. 390 Slovakia may, in accordance with the conditions applying in that Member State on the date of its accession, continue to exempt the international transport of passengers, as referred to in point (10) of Annex X, Part B, for as long as the same exemption is applied in any of the Member States which were members of the Community on 30 April 2004.

Art. 390a Bulgaria may, in accordance with the conditions applying in that Member State on the date of its accession, continue to exempt the international transport of passengers as referred to in point 10 of Annex X, Part B, for as long as the same exemption is applied in any of the Member States which were members of the Community on 31 December 2006.

Art. 390b Romania may, in accordance with the conditions applying in that Member State on the date of its accession, continue to exempt the international transport of passengers, as referred to in point 10 of Annex X, Part B, for as long as the same exemption is applied in any of the Member States which were members of the Community on 31 December 2006.

Section 3

Provisions common to Sections 1 and 2

Art. 391 Member States which exempt the transactions referred to in Articles 371, 375, 376 or

377, Article 378(2), Article 379(2) or Articles 380 to 390b may grant taxable persons the right to opt for taxation of those transactions.

Art. 392 Member States may provide that, in respect of the supply of buildings and building land purchased for the purpose of resale by a taxable person for whom the VAT on the purchase was not deductible, the taxable amount shall be the difference between the selling price and the purchase price.

Art. 393 1. With a view to facilitating the transition to the definitive arrangements referred to in Article 402, the Council shall, on the basis of a report from the Commission, review the situation with regard to the derogations provided for in Sections 1 and 2 and shall, acting in accordance with Article 93 of the Treaty decide whether any or all of those derogations is to be abolished.

2. By way of definitive arrangements, passenger transport shall be taxed in the Member State of departure for that part of the journey taking place within the Community, in accordance with the detailed rules to be laid down by the Council, acting in accordance with Article 93 of the Treaty.

CHAPTER 2
DEROGATIONS SUBJECT TO AUTHORISATION

SECTION 1
Simplification measures and measures to prevent tax evasion or avoidance

Art. 394 Member States which, at 1 January 1977, applied special measures to simplify the procedure for collecting VAT or to prevent certain forms of tax evasion or avoidance may retain them provided that they have notified the Commission accordingly before 1 January 1978 and that such simplification measures comply with the criterion laid down in the second subparagraph of Article 395(1).

Art. 395 1. The Council, acting unanimously on a proposal from the Commission, may authorise any Member State to introduce special measures for derogation from the provisions of this Directive, in order to simplify the procedure for collecting VAT or to prevent certain forms of tax evasion or avoidance.

Measures intended to simplify the procedure for collecting VAT may not, except to a negligible extent, affect the overall amount of the tax revenue of the Member State collected at the stage of final consumption.

2. A Member State wishing to introduce the measure referred to in paragraph 1 shall send an application to the Commission and provide it with all the necessary information. If the Commission considers that it does not have all the necessary information, it shall contact the Member State concerned within two months of receipt of the application and specify what additional information is required.

Once the Commission has all the information it considers necessary for appraisal of the request it shall within one month notify the requesting Member State accordingly and it shall transmit the request, in its original language, to the other Member States.

3. Within three months of giving the notification referred to in the second subparagraph of paragraph 2, the Commission shall present to the Council either an appropriate proposal or, should it object to the derogation requested, a communication setting out its objections.

4. The procedure laid down in paragraphs 2 and 3 shall, in any event, be completed within eight months of receipt of the application by the Commission.

5. In cases of imperative urgency as set out in Article 199b(1), the procedure laid down in paragraphs 2 and 3 shall be completed within six months of receipt of the application by the Commission.

SECTION 2
International agreements

Art. 396 1. The Council, acting unanimously on a proposal from the Commission, may authorise any Member State to conclude with a third country or an international body an agreement which may contain derogations from this Directive.

2. A Member State wishing to conclude an agreement as referred to in paragraph 1 shall send an application to the Commission and provide it with all the necessary information. If the Commission considers that it does not have all the necessary information, it shall contact the Member State concerned within two months of receipt of the application and specify what additional information is required.

Once the Commission has all the information it considers necessary for appraisal of the request it shall within one month notify the requesting Member State accordingly and it shall transmit the request, in its original language, to the other Member States.

3. Within three months of giving the notification referred to in the second subparagraph of paragraph 2, the Commission shall present to the Council either an appropriate proposal or, should it object to the derogation requested, a communication setting out its objections.

4. The procedure laid down in paragraphs 2 and 3 shall, in any event, be completed within eight months of receipt of the application by the Commission.

TITLE XIV
MISCELLANEOUS

CHAPTER 1
IMPLEMENTING MEASURES

Art. 397 The Council, acting unanimously on a proposal from the Commission, shall adopt the measures necessary to implement this Directive.

CHAPTER 2
VAT COMMITTEE

Art. 398 1. An advisory committee on value added tax, called "the VAT Committee", is set up.

2. The VAT Committee shall consist of representatives of the Member States and of the Commission.

The chairman of the Committee shall be a representative of the Commission.

Secretarial services for the Committee shall be provided by the Commission.

3. The VAT Committee shall adopt its own rules of procedure.

4. In addition to the points forming the subject of consultation pursuant to this Directive, the VAT Committee shall examine questions raised by its chairman, on his own initiative or at the request of the representative of a Member State, which concern the application of Community provisions on VAT.

CHAPTER 3
CONVERSION RATES

Art. 399 Without prejudice to any other particular provisions, the equivalents in national currency of the amounts in euro specified in this Directive shall be determined on the basis of the euro conversion rate applicable on 1 January 1999. Member States having acceded to the European Union after that date, which have not adopted the euro as single currency, shall use the euro conversion rate applicable on the date of their accession.

Art. 400 When converting the amounts referred to in Article 399 into national currencies, Member States may adjust the amounts resulting from that conversion either upwards or downwards by up to 10%.

CHAPTER 4
OTHER TAXES, DUTIES AND CHARGES

Art. 401 Without prejudice to other provisions of Community law, this Directive shall not prevent a Member State from maintaining or introducing taxes on insurance contracts, taxes on betting and gambling, excise duties, stamp duties or, more generally, any taxes, duties or charges which cannot be characterised as turnover taxes, provided that the collecting of those taxes, duties or charges does not give rise, in trade between Member States, to formalities connected with the crossing of frontiers.

TITLE XV
FINAL PROVISIONS

CHAPTER 1
TRANSITIONAL ARRANGEMENTS FOR THE TAXATION OF TRADE BETWEEN MEMBER STATES

Art. 402 1. The arrangements provided for in this Directive for the taxation of trade between Member States are transitional and shall be replaced by definitive arrangements based in principle on the taxation in the Member State of origin of the supply of goods or services.

2. Having concluded, upon examination of the report referred to in Article 404, that the conditions for transition to the definitive arrangements are met, the Council shall, acting in accordance with Article 93 of the Treaty, adopt the provisions necessary for the entry into force and for the operation of the definitive arrangements.

Art. 403 The Council shall, acting in accordance with Article 93 of the Treaty, adopt Directives appropriate for the purpose of supplementing the common system of VAT and, in particular, for the progressive restriction or the abolition of derogations from that system.

Art. 404 Every four years starting from the adoption of this Directive, the Commission shall, on the basis of information obtained from the Member States, present a report to the European Parliament and to the Council on the operation of the common system of VAT in the Member States and, in particular, on the operation of the transitional arrangements for taxing trade between Member States. That report shall be accompanied, where appropriate, by proposals concerning the definitive arrangements.

CHAPTER 2
TRANSITIONAL MEASURES APPLICABLE IN THE CONTEXT OF ACCESSION TO THE EUROPEAN UNION

Art. 405 For the purposes of this Chapter, the following definitions shall apply:

(1) "Community" means the territory of the Community as defined in point (1) of Article 5 before the accession of new Member States;

(2) "new Member States" means the territory of the Member States which acceded to the European Union after 1 January 1995, as defined for each of those Member States in point (2) of Article 5;

(3) "enlarged Community" means the territory of the Community as defined in point (1) of Article 5 after the accession of new Member States.

Art. 406 The provisions in force at the time the goods were placed under temporary importation arrangements with total exemption from import duty or under one of the arrangements or situations referred to in Article 156, or under similar arrangements or situations in one of the new Member States, shall continue to apply until the goods cease to be covered by these arrangements or situations after the date of accession, where the following conditions are met:

(a) the goods entered the Community or one of the new Member States before the date of accession;

(b) the goods were placed, on entry into the Community or one of the new Member States, under these arrangements or situations;

(c) the goods have not ceased to be covered by these arrangements or situations before the date of accession.

Art. 407 The provisions in force at the time the goods were placed under customs transit arrangements shall continue to apply until the goods cease to be covered by these arrangements after the date of accession, where the following conditions are met:

(a) the goods were placed, before the date of accession, under customs transit arrangements;

(b) the goods have not ceased to be covered by these arrangements before the date of accession.

Art. 408 1. The following shall be treated as an importation of goods where it is shown that the goods were in free circulation in one of the new Member States or in the Community:

(a) the removal, including irregular removal, of goods from temporary importation arrangements under which they were placed before the date of accession under the conditions provided for in Article 406;

(b) the removal, including irregular removal, of goods either from one of the arrangements or situations referred to in Article 156 or from similar arrangements or situations under which they were placed before the date of accession under the conditions provided for in Article 406;

(c) the cessation of one of the arrangements referred to in Article 407, started before the date of accession in the territory of one of the new Member States, for the purposes of a supply of goods for consideration effected before that date in the territory of that Member State by a taxable person acting as such;

(d) any irregularity or offence committed during customs transit arrangements started under the conditions referred to in point (c).

2. In addition to the case referred to in paragraph 1, the use after the date of accession within the territory of a Member State, by a taxable or non-taxable person, of goods supplied to him before the date of accession within the territory of the Community or one of the new Member States shall be treated as an importation of goods where the following conditions are met:

(a) the supply of those goods has been exempted, or was likely to be exempted, either under points (a) and (b) of Article 146(1) or under a similar provision in the new Member States;

(b) the goods were not imported into one of the new Member States or into the Community before the date of accession.

Art. 409 In the cases referred to in Article 408(1), the place of import within the meaning of Article 61 shall be the Member State within whose territory the goods cease to be covered by the arrangements or situations under which they were placed before the date of accession.

Art. 410 1. By way of derogation from Article 71, the importation of goods within the meaning of Article 408 shall terminate without the occurrence of a chargeable event if one of the following conditions is met:

(a) the imported goods are dispatched or transported outside the enlarged Community;

(b) the imported goods within the meaning of Article 408(1)(a) are other than means of transport and are redispatched or transported to the Member State from which they were exported and to the person who exported them;

(c) the imported goods within the meaning of Article 408(1)(a) are means of transport which were acquired or imported before the date of accession in accordance with the general conditions of taxation in force on the domestic market of one of the new Member States or of one of the Member States of the Community or which have not been subject, by reason of their exportation, to any exemption from, or refund of, VAT.

2. The condition referred to in paragraph 1(c) shall be deemed to be fulfilled in the following cases:

(a) when the date of first entry into service of the means of transport was more than eight years before the accession to the European Union;

(b) when the amount of tax due by reason of the importation is insignificant.

CHAPTER 3
TRANSPOSITION AND ENTRY INTO FORCE

Art. 411 1. Directive 67/227/EEC and Directive 77/388/EEC are repealed, without prejudice to the obligations of the Member States concerning the time-limits, listed in Annex XI, Part B, for the transposition into national law and the implementation of those Directives.

2. References to the repealed Directives shall be construed as references to this Directive and shall be read in accordance with the correlation table in Annex XII.

Art. 412 1. Member States shall bring into force the laws, regulations and administrative provisions necessary to comply with Article 2(3), Article 44, Article 59(1), Article 399 and Annex III, point (18) with effect from 1 January 2008. They shall forthwith communicate to the Commission the text of those provisions and a correlation table between those provisions and this Directive.

When Member States adopt those provisions, they shall contain a reference to this Directive or be accompanied by such a reference on the occasion of their official publication. Member States shall determine how such reference is to be made.

2. Member States shall communicate to the Commission the text of the main provisions of national law which they adopt in the field covered by this Directive.

Art. 413 This Directive shall enter into force on 1 January 2007.

Art. 414 This Directive is addressed to the Member States.

Done at Brussels, 28 November 2006.

For the Council

The President

E. HEINÄLUOMA

Annex I

LIST OF THE ACTIVITIES REFERRED TO IN THE THIRD SUBPARAGRAPH OF ARTICLE 13(1)

(1) Telecommunications services;

(2) supply of water, gas, electricity and thermal energy;

(3) transport of goods;

(4) port and airport services;

(5) passenger transport;

(6) supply of new goods manufactured for sale;

(7) transactions in respect of agricultural products, carried out by agricultural intervention agencies pursuant to Regulations on the common organisation of the market in those products;

(8) organisation of trade fairs and exhibitions;

(9) warehousing;

(10) activities of commercial publicity bodies;

(11) activities of travel agents;

(12) running of staff shops, cooperatives and industrial canteens and similar institutions;

(13) activities carried out by radio and television bodies in so far as these are not exempt pursuant to Article 132(1)(q).

Annex II

INDICATIVE LIST OF THE ELECTRONICALLY SUPPLIED SERVICES REFERRED TO IN POINT (C) OF THE FIRST PARAGRAPH OF ARTICLE 58

(1) Website supply, web-hosting, distance maintenance of programmes and equipment;

(2) supply of software and updating thereof;

(3) supply of images, text and information and making available of databases;

(4) supply of music, films and games, including games of chance and gambling games, and of political, cultural, artistic, sporting, scientific and entertainment broadcasts and events;

(5) supply of distance teaching.

Annex III

LIST OF SUPPLIES OF GOODS AND SERVICES TO WHICH THE REDUCED RATES REFERRED TO IN ARTICLE 98 MAY BE APPLIED

(1) Foodstuffs (including beverages but excluding alcoholic beverages) for human and animal consumption; live animals, seeds, plants and ingredients normally intended for use in the preparation of foodstuffs, products normally used to supplement foodstuffs or as a substitute for foodstuffs;

(2) supply of water;

(3) pharmaceutical products of a kind normally used for health care, prevention of illnesses and as treatment for medical and veterinary purposes, including products used for contraception and sanitary protection;

(4) medical equipment, aids and other appliances normally intended to alleviate or treat disability, for the exclusive personal use of the disabled, including the repair of such goods, and supply of children's car seats;

(5) transport of passengers and their accompanying luggage;

(6) supply, including on loan by libraries, of books on all physical means of support (including brochures, leaflets and similar printed matter, children's picture, drawing or colouring books, music printed or in manuscript form, maps and hydrographic or similar charts), newspapers and periodicals, other than material wholly or predominantly devoted to advertising;

(7) admission to shows, theatres, circuses, fairs, amusement parks, concerts, museums, zoos, cinemas, exhibitions and similar cultural events and facilities;

(8) reception of radio and television broadcasting services;

(9) supply of services by writers, composers and performing artists, or of the royalties due to them

(10) provision, construction, renovation and alteration of housing, as part of a social policy;

(10a) renovation and repairing of private dwellings, excluding materials which account for a significant part of the value of the service supplied;

(10b) window-cleaning and cleaning in private households;

(11) supply of goods and services of a kind normally intended for use in agricultural production but excluding capital goods such as machinery or buildings;

(12) accommodation provided in hotels and similar establishments, including the provision of holiday accommodation and the letting of places on camping or caravan sites;

(12a) restaurant and catering services, it being possible to exclude the supply of (alcoholic and/or non-alcoholic) beverages;

(13) admission to sporting events;

(14) use of sporting facilities;

(15) supply of goods and services by organisations recognised as being devoted to social wellbeing by Member States and engaged in welfare or social security work, in so far as those transactions are not exempt pursuant to Articles 132, 135 and 136;

(16) supply of services by undertakers and cremation services, and the supply of goods related thereto;

(17) provision of medical and dental care and thermal treatment in so far as those services are not exempt pursuant to points (b) to (e) of Article 132(1);

(18) supply of services provided in connection with street cleaning, refuse collection and waste treatment, other than the supply of such services by bodies referred to in Article 13;

(19) minor repairing of bicycles, shoes and leather goods, clothing and household linen (including mending and alteration);

(20) domestic care services such as home help and care of young, elderly, sick or disabled;

(21) hairdressing.

Annex IV

LIST OF THE SERVICES REFERRED TO IN ARTICLE 106

[Repealed by Council Directive 2009/47/EC]

Annex V

CATEGORIES OF GOODS COVERED BY WAREHOUSING ARRANGEMENTS OTHER THAN CUSTOMS WAREHOUSING AS PROVIDED FOR UNDER ARTICLE 160(2)

	CN-code	Description of goods
(1)	0701	Potatoes
(2)	0711 20	Olives
(3)	0801	Coconuts, Brazil nuts and cashew nuts
(4)	0802	Other nuts
(5)	0901 11 00 0901 12 00	Coffee, not roasted
(6)	0902	Tea
(7)	1001 to 1005 1007 to 1008	Cereals
(8)	1006	Husked rice
(9)	1201 to 1207	Grains and oil seeds (including soya beans) and oleaginous fruits
(10)	1507 to 1515	Vegetable oils and fats and their fractions, whether or not refined, but not chemically modified
(11)	1701 11 1701 12	Raw sugar
(12)	1801	Cocoa beans, whole or broken, raw or roasted

(13)	2709	Mineral oils (including propane and butane; also including crude petroleum oils)
	2710	
	2711 12	
	2711 13	
(14)	Chapters 28 and 29	Chemicals in bulk
(15)	4001	Rubber, in primary forms or in plates, sheets or strip
	4002	
(16)	5101	Wool
(17)	7106	Silver
(18)	7110 11 00	Platinum (palladium, rhodium)
	7110 21 00	
	7110 31 00	
(19)	7402	Copper
	7403	
	7405	
	7408	
(20)	7502	Nickel
(21)	7601	Aluminium
(22)	7801	Lead
(23)	7901	Zinc
(24)	8001	Tin
(25)	ex 8112 92	Indium
	ex 8112 99	

ANNEX VI

LIST OF SUPPLIES OF GOODS AND SERVICES AS REFERRED TO IN POINT (D) OF ARTICLE 199(1)

(1) Supply of ferrous and non-ferrous waste, scrap, and used materials including that of semi-finished products resulting from the processing, manufacturing or melting down of ferrous and non-ferrous metals and their alloys;

(2) supply of ferrous and non-ferrous semi-processed products and certain associated processing services;

(3) supply of residues and other recyclable materials consisting of ferrous and non-ferrous metals, their alloys, slag, ash, scale and industrial residues containing metals or their alloys and supply of selection, cutting, fragmenting and pressing services of these products;

(4) supply of, and certain processing services relating to, ferrous and non-ferrous waste as well as parings, scrap, waste and used and recyclable material consisting of cullet, glass, paper, paperboard and board, rags, bone, leather, imitation leather, parchment, raw hides and skins, tendons and sinews, twine, cordage, rope, cables, rubber and plastic;

(5) supply of the materials referred to in this annex after processing in the form of cleaning, polishing, selection, cutting, fragmenting, pressing or casting into ingots;

(6) supply of scrap and waste from the working of base materials.

Annex VII

LIST OF THE AGRICULTURAL PRODUCTION ACTIVITIES REFERRED TO IN POINT (4) OF ARTICLE 295(1)

(1) Crop production:

(a) general agriculture, including viticulture;

(b) growing of fruit (including olives) and of vegetables, flowers and ornamental plants, both in the open and under glass;

(c) production of mushrooms, spices, seeds and propagating materials;

(d) running of nurseries;

(2) stock farming together with cultivation:

(a) general stock farming;

(b) poultry farming;

(c) rabbit farming;

(d) beekeeping;

(e) silkworm farming;

(f) snail farming;

(3) forestry;

(4) fisheries:

(a) freshwater fishing;

(b) fish farming;

(c) breeding of mussels, oysters and other molluscs and crustaceans;

(d) frog farming.

Annex VIII

INDICATIVE LIST OF THE AGRICULTURAL SERVICES REFERRED TO IN POINT (5) OF ARTICLE 295(1)

(1) Field work, reaping and mowing, threshing, baling, collecting, harvesting, sowing and planting;

(2) packing and preparation for market, such as drying, cleaning, grinding, disinfecting and ensilage of agricultural products;

(3) storage of agricultural products;

(4) stock minding, rearing and fattening;

(5) hiring out, for agricultural purposes, of equipment normally used in agricultural, forestry or fisheries undertakings;

(6) technical assistance;

(7) destruction of weeds and pests, dusting and spraying of crops and land;

(8) operation of irrigation and drainage equipment;

(9) lopping, tree felling and other forestry services.

Annex IX

WORKS OF ART, COLLECTORS' ITEMS AND ANTIQUES, AS REFERRED TO IN POINTS (2), (3) AND (4) OF ARTICLE 311(1)

PART A

Works of art

(1) Pictures, collages and similar decorative plaques, paintings and drawings, executed entirely by hand by the artist, other than plans and drawings for architectural, engineering, industrial, commercial, topographical or similar purposes, hand-decorated manufactured articles, theatrical scenery, studio back cloths or the like of painted canvas (CN code 9701);

(2) original engravings, prints and lithographs, being impressions produced in limited numbers directly in black and white or in colour of one or of several plates executed entirely by hand by the artist, irrespective

of the process or of the material employed, but not including any mechanical or photomechanical process (CN code 9702 00 00);

(3) original sculptures and statuary, in any material, provided that they are executed entirely by the artist; sculpture casts the production of which is limited to eight copies and supervised by the artist or his successors in title (CN code 9703 00 00); on an exceptional basis, in cases determined by the Member States, the limit of eight copies may be exceeded for statuary casts produced before 1 January 1989;

(4) tapestries (CN code 5805 00 00) and wall textiles (CN code 6304 00 00) made by hand from original designs provided by artists, provided that there are not more than eight copies of each;

(5) individual pieces of ceramics executed entirely by the artist and signed by him;

(6) enamels on copper, executed entirely by hand, limited to eight numbered copies bearing the signature of the artist or the studio, excluding articles of jewellery and goldsmiths' and silversmiths' wares;

(7) photographs taken by the artist, printed by him or under his supervision, signed and numbered and limited to 30 copies, all sizes and mounts included.

PART B

Collectors' items

(1) Postage or revenue stamps, postmarks, first-day covers, pre-stamped stationery and the like, used, or if unused not current and not intended to be current (CN code 9704 00 00);

(2) collections and collectors' pieces of zoological, botanical, mineralogical, anatomical, historical, archaeological, palaeontological, ethnographic or numismatic interest (CN code 9705 00 00).

PART C

Antiques

Goods, other than works of art or collectors' items, which are more than 100 years old (CN code 9706 00 00).

ANNEX X

LIST OF TRANSACTIONS COVERED BY THE DEROGATIONS REFERRED TO IN ARTICLES 370 AND 371 AND ARTICLES 375 TO 390B

PART A

Transactions which Member States may continue to tax

(1) The supply of services by dental technicians in their professional capacity and the supply of dental prostheses by dentists and dental technicians;

(2) the activities of public radio and television bodies other than those of a commercial nature;

(3) the supply of a building, or parts thereof, or of the land on which it stands, other than as referred to in point (a) of Article 12(1), where carried out by taxable persons who were entitled to deduction of the VAT paid at the preceding stage in respect of the building concerned;

(4) the supply of the services of travel agents, as referred to in Article 306, and those of travel agents acting in the name and on behalf of the traveller, in relation to journeys outside the Community.

PART B

Transactions which Member States may continue to exempt

(1) Admission to sporting events;

(2) the supply of services by authors, artists, performers, lawyers and other members of the liberal professions, other than the medical and paramedical professions, with the exception of the following:

(a) assignments of patents, trade marks and other similar rights, and the granting of licences in respect of such rights;

(b) work, other than the supply of contract work, on movable tangible property, carried out for a taxable person;

(c) services to prepare or coordinate the carrying out of construction work, such as services provided by architects and by firms providing on-site supervision of works;

(d) commercial advertising services;

(e) transport and storage of goods, and ancillary services;

(f) hiring out of movable tangible property to a taxable person;

(g) provision of staff to a taxable person;

(h) provision of services by consultants, engineers, planning offices and similar services in scientific, economic or technical fields;

(i) compliance with an obligation to refrain from exercising, in whole or in part, a business activity or a right covered by points (a) to (h) or point (j);

(j) the services of forwarding agents, brokers, business agents and other independent intermediaries, in so far as they relate to the supply or importation of goods or the supply of services covered by points (a) to (i);

(3) the supply of telecommunications services, and of goods related thereto, by public postal services;

(4) the supply of services by undertakers and cremation services and the supply of goods related thereto;

(5) transactions carried out by blind persons or by workshops for the blind, provided that those exemptions do not cause significant distortion of competition;

(6) the supply of goods and services to official bodies responsible for the construction, setting out and maintenance of cemeteries, graves and monuments commemorating the war dead;

(7) transactions carried out by hospitals not covered by point (b) of Article 132(1);

(8) the supply of water by a body governed by public law;

(9) the supply before first occupation of a building, or parts thereof, or of the land on which it stands and the supply of building land, as referred to in Article 12;

(10) the transport of passengers and, in so far as the transport of the passengers is exempt, the transport of goods accompanying them, such as luggage or motor vehicles, or the supply of services relating to the transport of passengers;

(11) the supply, modification, repair, maintenance, chartering and hiring of aircraft used by State institutions, including equipment incorporated or used in such aircraft;

(12) the supply, modification, repair, maintenance, chartering and hiring of fighting ships;

(13) the supply of the services of travel agents, as referred to in Article 306, and those of travel agents acting in the name and on behalf of the traveller, in relation to journeys within the Community.

Table of cases

A list of cases mentioned in *VAT Memo* is detailed below, in **alphabetical order**, together 9999
with the year of the case, the VTD or TC number (if applicable) and the paragraph where
the case is mentioned in *VAT Memo*.

Case name	Year	VTD / Tax tribunal number	¶¶
Aardvark Excavations Ltd	2007	20468	¶4090, ¶4272
Abbey National plc	2001	n/a	¶2260
Abbey National plc	2006	n/a	¶5578
Abbey National plc (No 2)	2006	n/a	¶380
Abbotsley Golf & Squash Club Ltd	1997	15042	¶5374, ¶5526
Abdul Noor	2013	n/a	¶4338
Actinic	2003	18044	¶2424
Adams	1975	175	¶110
Age Concern Leicestershire & Rutland	2008	20672	¶434
Agudas Israel Housing Association Ltd	2004	18798	¶5156
Aimia Coalition Loyalty UK Ltd	2013	n/a	¶1040, ¶1958, ¶6542
Airtours Holiday Transport Ltd	2010	TC00201	¶1958
Alan Roper & Sons Ltd	1997	15260	¶5478
Allen Carr's Easyway (International) Ltd	2009	TC00136	¶426
Allied Dancing Association	1993	10777	¶402
Allied Medicare Nursing Services Ltd	1984	5485	¶7102
Amicus Group Ltd	2002	17693	¶5436
Ampleforth Abbey Trust	1998	15763	¶2160
AN Checker Heating & Service Engineers	2013	TC02895	¶1140
Anycom Ltd	2011	TC01496	¶4656
Apple and Pear Development Council	1988	n/a	¶250
Appleby Bowers	2001	n/a	¶325
Appropriate Technology Ltd	1991	5696	¶4016
Arbib	1995	n/a	¶5458
Argos Distributors Ltd	1996	n/a	¶1024, ¶6534
Arkeley Ltd	2013	n/a	¶9588
Arnold	1996	n/a	¶4318
Ashworth	1994	12924	¶5504
Aston	1991	5955	¶3266
Astor	1981	1030	¶284, ¶6127
Astra Zeneca UK Ltd	2010	TC00103	¶941
Astral Construction Ltd	2015	n/a	¶5118
Atkinson	1994	n/a	¶110
ATP PensionService A/S v Skatteministeriet	2014	n/a	¶377, ¶8297
Auldbrook Ltd	1994	11717	¶3554
Automobile Association	1974	n/a	¶325

Case name	Year	VTD / Tax tribunal number	¶¶
Avonwave Ltd (t/a Gatewood Joinery)	2001	17509	¶3174
Axa UK plc	2010	n/a	¶374
A-Z Electrical	1993	10718	¶4932
BAA Ltd	2013	n/a	¶1825
Babytec Ltd	1994	12391	¶8676
Baines & Ernst Ltd	2004	18516	¶4283
Baines & Ernst Ltd	2006	n/a	¶3254
Balmoral Ltd	2005	19233	¶3576
Banbury Visionplus Ltd	2006	n/a	¶2168
Banca Antoniana Popolare Veneta	2011	n/a	¶3252
Barclays Bank plc	1991	5616	¶2174
Barclays Bank plc	1992	7911	¶4264
Bass plc	1993	n/a	¶1952
Bath Festivals Trust Ltd	2008	20840	¶8040
Beagley	1997	15107	¶8652
Beaverbank Properties Ltd	2003	18099	¶2692, ¶5616
Beazer (CH) Holdings plc	1989	n/a	¶2136
Beckley (t/a The College of Meditation)	2005	19860	¶412
Belgium v Ghent Coal Terminal NV	1998	n/a	¶2228
Bells of Lazonby Ltd	2007	20490	¶1211
Bennachie Leisure Centre Association	1996	14276	¶5180
Bennett	1997	14976	¶3659
Benton	1975	185	¶270
Berck Ltd	2007	20051	¶852
Berkholz v Finanzamt Hamburg-Mitte-Altstadt	1985	n/a	¶6974, ¶9696
Berwick	2002	17686	¶130
Bevan and Bevan	2000	16830	¶1908
Beynon and partners	2004	n/a	¶426
Binder Hamlyn	1983	1439	¶9694
Bioconcepts Ltd	1993	11287	¶1214
Birketts	2002	17515	¶147
Birmingham Council for Old People	1998	15437	¶5142
Bjellica (t/a Eddy's Domestic Appliances)	1995	n/a	¶2708
Blackpool Pleasure Beach Co	1974	n/a	¶1282
Blackpool Pleasure Beach (Holdings) Ltd	2005	19014	¶1018
Blom-Cooper	2003	n/a	¶5320
BLP Group plc	1995	n/a	¶2104, ¶2422
Blythe Ltd Partnership	1999	16011	¶5676
BMW (GB) Ltd	1997	14823	¶2184
BOC International Ltd	1982	1248	¶8287
Boodle & Dunthorne Ltd	2002	18429	¶1467
Bookit Ltd	2006	n/a	¶374
Bookit Ltd	2014	TC03972	¶48, ¶374
Boots plc	1990	n/a	¶6538
Bournemouth Symphony Orchestra	2006	n/a	¶8162
BPH Equipment Ltd	1996	13914	¶9738

Case name	Year	VTD / Tax tribunal number	¶¶
Briararch Ltd	1992	n/a	¶2226, ¶5256
Brice	1991	6376	¶5479
Bridport and West Dorset Golf Club Ltd	2013	n/a	¶422
Briggs	1995	13603	¶6398
Bristol City Football Supporters Club	1975	164	¶1224
British Airports Authority (No 1)	1977	n/a	¶5374
British Airports Authority (No 5)	1977	447	¶5138
British Airways plc	1990	n/a	¶325
British Airways plc	2000	16446	¶1960
British American Tobacco International Ltd v Belgian State	2005	n/a	¶268
British Field Sports Society	1998	n/a	¶250
British Railways Board	1976	n/a	¶8292
British Railways Board (No 2)	1977	n/a	¶315, ¶325
British Sky Broadcasting Group plc	2001	n/a	¶325, ¶4339
British Telecommunications plc	1996	n/a	¶788
British Telecommunications plc	1999	n/a	¶1916
British Telecommunications plc	1999	16244	¶5374
British Telecommunications plc	2005	n/a	¶3252
Brockenhurst College	2014	n/a	¶410, ¶1236
Brown	2006	19884	¶5120
Browsers Bookshop	1988	2837	¶1500
Bryan and Thomas	2005	n/a	¶5934
Buckley Jewellery Ltd	2003	18178	¶8652
Building Societies Ombudsman Co Ltd (ex parte)	2000	n/a	¶4339
Burke	2008	20881	¶4656
Cable and Wireless plc	2009	TC00004	¶2014
Café Da Vinci and Da Vinci Too	1992	7298	¶3699
Camberwell Cars	1993	10178	¶7262
Cameron New Homes Ltd	2001	17309	¶5120
Canterbury Hockey Club and Canterbury Ladies Hockey Club	2008	n/a	¶422
Cantor Fitzgerald International	2001	n/a	¶5578
Card Protection Plan	1999	n/a	¶310, ¶316
Carpenter & Hayles (t/a Carpenter Catering)	2003	18148	¶1224
Catchpole	2012	TC01995	¶5152
Celtic Football & Athletic Co Ltd	1983	n/a	¶1942
Chinese Channel Ltd	1998	n/a	¶9694
Christ's Hospital	2005	19126	¶5142
Church of England Children's Society	2005	n/a	¶8094
Church of Scientology Religious Education College Inc	2007	n/a	¶4330
Cirdan Sailing Trust	2004	18865	¶1282
CISS Ltd	2004	18839	¶366
Clean Car Co Ltd	1991	5695	¶4016
Clements	2004	19216	¶2656
Clowance Owners Club Ltd	2004	18787	¶784

Case name	Year	VTD / Tax tribunal number	¶¶
Colchester Sixth Form College	1999	16252	¶5184
College of Estate Management	2005	n/a	¶325
Collie	1991	6144	¶1874
Collins & Beckett Ltd	2005	19212	¶5458
Compass Contract Services UK Ltd	2006	n/a	¶1224
Condé Nast Publications Ltd	2008	n/a	¶2014
Conoco Ltd	1995	n/a	¶4275
Coopers Fire Ltd	2013	TC02570	¶5138
Corke	2000	16832	¶8578
Cornforth	1989	4532	¶3554
Courage Ltd	1992	8808	¶6372
Covercraft Ltd	1989	3558	¶4093
Crownlion (Seafood) Ltd	1985	1924	¶1224
Cumbernauld Development Corporation (No 2)	2002	n/a	¶5265
Curtis Henderson Ltd	1992	n/a	¶2226
Cussins	2008	20541	¶5156
Daimler AG v Skatteverket	2012	n/a	¶9690
Dangol	2000	n/a	¶4339
Daron Motors Ltd	1993	11695	¶6638
Darragh House Ltd	2012	TC02105	¶1827
Dart Major Works Ltd	2004	18781	¶5120
Dartford Borough Council	2007	20423	¶8670
David Baxendale Ltd	2009	n/a	¶325
Davison	2001	17130	¶5156
De Montfort University Students Union	2003	18434	¶325
Dealy	1995	n/a	¶4160
Debenhams Retail plc	2005	n/a	¶3054
Decal Co Ltd	1999	16274	¶4124
Deltaview Ltd	1985	1832	¶3554
DFDS A/S	1997	n/a	¶9694
DFS Furniture Co Ltd	2009	TC00157	¶2106
Diaform Ltd	1993	11069	¶802
Dial-a-Phone Ltd	2004	n/a	¶2100
Dinaro Ltd (t/a Fairway Lodge)	2000	17148	¶5496
Direct Cosmetics Ltd	1985	n/a	¶6388, ¶7294
Dixons Group plc	1992	9604	¶6334
Dodson Bros (Thatchers) Ltd	1995	13734	¶5479
Dollar Land (Feltham) Ltd	1995	n/a	¶4083
Dollond & Aitchison Ltd	2006	n/a	¶9436
Douros (t/a Olympic Financial Services)	1995	12454	¶8570
Dudda v Finanzamt Bergisch Gladbach	1996	n/a	¶9742
Durham River Trips Ltd	2001	17329	¶325
East Kent Medical Services Ltd	1999	16095	¶5764
Eastbourne Town Radio Cars Association	2001	n/a	¶8150
Eastwood Care Homes (Ilkeston) Ltd	2001	n/a	¶4339
EB Central Services Ltd	2008	n/a	¶1284, ¶1318

Case name	Year	VTD / Tax tribunal number	¶¶
EC v France, Luxembourg	2015	n/a	¶1252
EC v Ireland	2013	n/a	¶8805
EC v Italian Republic	1997	n/a	¶2080
EC v Kingdom of the Netherlands	2001	n/a	¶1962
EC v UK	2013	n/a	¶8805
EC v UK (No 4)	2005	n/a	¶1962
Edmond Homes Ltd	1993	11567	¶5142
Eleftheriou (t/a Picnic Kebab House)	2000	16659	¶2632
Elida Gibbs Ltd	1996	n/a	¶1031
Ellen Garage Ltd	1994	12407	¶1984
Elliott	1995	13432	¶3554
Elm Milk Ltd	2006	n/a	¶1908
Elson	2001	17466	¶3701
EMAG Handel Eder OHG v Finanzlandesdirektion für Kärnten	2006	n/a	¶9214
EMI Group Ltd	2010	n/a	¶272, ¶1465
Emphasis Ltd	1995	13759	¶6938
Empire Stores Ltd	1994	n/a	¶940, ¶6524
Empresa de Desenvolvimento Mineiro	2004	n/a	¶2136
Emsland-Stärke GmbH v Hauptzollamt Hamburg-Jonas	2001	n/a	¶48
Entertainment Group of Companies Ltd	2000	16639	¶1942
Eric Taylor Deceased Testimonial Match Committee	1975	139	¶140
Ernst & Young	1997	15100	¶1938, ¶1940
Evans	2001	17264	¶5118
Everest Ltd	2010	TC00863	¶1031
Everett	1989	3669	¶4093
Everything Everywhere Ltd (formerly T-Mobile (UK) Ltd)	2010	n/a	¶374
Exact Electronics Ltd	1993	11391	¶3554
Fabco Ltd	1992	9739	¶4078
Faith Construction Ltd	1989	n/a	¶780
Fanfield Ltd and Thexton Training Ltd	2011	TC00919	¶4662
Fareham Borough Council	2014	TC04129	¶300
Farrimond	1993	10831	¶7306
FEA Briggs Ltd	1994	12804	¶9090
Federation of Technological Industries	2006	n/a	¶2002, ¶3574, ¶3580
Fencing Supplies Ltd	1993	10451	¶5674
Fenwood Developments Ltd	2005	n/a	¶5166
Field Fisher Waterhouse LLP	2012	n/a	¶5556
Financial & General Print Ltd	1995	13795	¶1264
Finanzamt Frankfurt am Main V-Höchst v Deutsche Bank AG	2012	n/a	¶372
Finanzamt Freistadt Rohrbach Urfahr v Unabhängiger Finanzsenat Außenstelle Linz	2013	n/a	¶100
Finanzamt Groß-Gerau v MKG-Kraftfahrzeuge-Factoring GmbH	2003	n/a	¶2620

Case name	Year	VTD / Tax tribunal number	¶¶
Finanzamt Rendsburg v Harbs	2004	n/a	¶5982
Finanzamt Uelzen v Armbrecht	1995	n/a	¶1846
Finmeccanica Group Services SPA	2013	TC03364	¶9742
First Choice Holidays plc	2004	n/a	¶7622
FJ Chalke Ltd	2010	n/a	¶3272
FJ Meaden Ltd	1995	13215	¶1868
Fleet School of Motoring	1992	7299	¶7288
Fleming (t/a Bodycraft)	2008	n/a	¶2014
Floridienne SA v Belgian State	2000	n/a	¶2136
Foglia v Novello	1980	n/a	¶4350
Foley	1995	13496	¶5479
Fonbane	1987	2813	¶8676
Forexia (UK) Ltd	1999	16041	¶6938
Forsakringsaktiebolaget Skandia	2001	n/a	¶444
Forster	2011	TC01319	¶5954
Fox	2012	TC01957	¶5406
Freemans plc	2001	n/a	¶6386
Freeserve.com plc	2003	n/a	¶4339
Fresh Sea Foods (Barry) Ltd	1991	6658	¶1224
Friends of the Elderly	2008	20597	¶1344
Friends of the Ironbridge Gorge Museum	1991	5639	¶8150
G McKenzie & Co Ltd	1993	11992	¶4318
G & J Spencer Ltd	1990	5428	¶4093
Gables Farm Dogs and Cats Home	2008	20519	¶1372
Galaxy Equipment (Europe) Ltd	1993	11415	¶262
Garsington Opera	2009	TC00045	¶2106
General Healthcare Group Ltd	2001	17129	¶5166
General Motors Acceptance Corporation (UK) plc	2004	n/a	¶292
Georgiou (t/a Mario's Chippery)	1996	n/a	¶4315
GfBk Gesellschaft für Börsenkommunikation mbH	2013	n/a	¶380
Gilder	2003	18143	¶5114
Glasgow City Council	1998	15491	¶120
Glasgow's Miles Better Mid-Summer 5th Anniversary Ball	1989	4460	¶8054
Glassborow	1974	n/a	¶2620, ¶2734
Glaxosmithkline Services Unlimited	2010	TC00688	¶1215
Globe Equities Ltd	1995	13105	¶7192
Grace Baptist Church	1998	16093	¶5186
Granada Group plc	1991	5565	¶1467
Grattan plc	2006	19515	¶6950
Grattan plc	2011	n/a	¶3272
Gray (t/a William Gray & Son)	2000	n/a	¶2662
Greenhouse Stirton & Co	1990	5481	¶4093
Greenpeace Ltd	2000	16681	¶2202
Greenwich Property Ltd	2001	n/a	¶3686, ¶5164
Greyform Publications	1988	3158	¶1264

Case name	Year	VTD / Tax tribunal number	¶¶
Groundwell t/a Angling and Hiking Centre	1994	n/a	¶3702
GUS Merchandise Corporation Ltd	1981	n/a	¶6524
GUS Merchandise Corporation Ltd (No 2)	1995	n/a	¶6494
Gwent Technical Mouldings Ltd	1992	7939	¶4093
H Griffiths Engineering Ltd	2005	19098	¶3174
Halifax and others	2006	n/a	¶48, ¶246, ¶4343
Hallam	1978	683	¶4275
Harbig Leasing Two Ltd	2000	16843	¶2674
Harrison	1981	1125	¶6554
Hartley Engineering Ltd	1994	12385	¶8652
Harvey (t/a Green Express Railtours)	1998	15608	¶7506, ¶7518
Harz & Power	1967	n/a	¶3462
HBOS plc	2008	n/a	¶367
HEM Construction Ltd	1995	12449	¶4078
Hicking	2000	17117	¶5436
Hickson (t/a Flury's)	1993	11455	¶3554
Hill and Mansell	1982	2379	¶1874
Hill Ash Developments	2000	16747	¶5458
Hillingdon Legal Resource Centre	1991	5210	¶8040
Hilltop Syndicate Shoot	2012	TC01725	¶4338
Hinckley Golf Club Ltd	1992	9527	¶8194
Hocking	2014	TC04130	¶412
Hodges	2000	n/a	¶6142
Holiday Inns (UK) Ltd	1993	10609	¶264
Hooper	2005	19276	¶1916
Hornby	1974	155	¶4275
Hospital of St John and St Elizabeth	2005	19141	¶5166
Huntley & Brooks t/a Brimar Guest House	1991	5847	¶270
Hussein and Asim t/a Pressing Dry Cleaners	2003	18341	¶2742
I/S Fini H v Skatteministeriet	2005	n/a	¶1830
Ian Flockton Developments Ltd	1987	n/a	¶1830
IDT Card Services Ireland Ltd	2006	n/a	¶3072, ¶9766
Iliffe and Holloway	1993	10922	¶5584
Imperial War Museum	1992	9097	¶8024
Innocent Ltd	2010	TC00771	¶1214
InsuranceWide.com Services Ltd and Trader Media Group Ltd	2010	n/a	¶452
International Student House	1996	14420	¶5496
International Trade and Exhibitions J/V Ltd	1996	14212	¶9720
Isle of Wight Council and others	2008	n/a	¶7866
Jacobs	2005	n/a	¶5320, ¶5416
JAG Communications (Plymouth) Ltd	2007	20002	¶1031
James	2007	20426	¶5126
Jane Montgomery (Hair Stylists) Ltd	1994	n/a	¶7276
JDL Ltd	2002	n/a	¶2132
JD Wetherspoon plc	2009	n/a	¶6310
Jerzynek	2004	18767	¶8562

Case name	Year	VTD / Tax tribunal number	¶¶
JN Electrical Units	1989	3346	¶4093
Jodh Singh Mittu	1983	1275	¶128
John Beharrell Ltd	1991	6530	¶1500
John Cronin t/a Cronin's Driving School	1991	n/a	¶7286
John Pargeter & Sons Ltd	1988	3318	¶4093
John Wilkins (Motor Engineers) Ltd	2009	n/a	¶3272
Johnson	1980	n/a	¶7097
Joseph Rowntree Foundation	1996	14534	¶408
JP Morgan Fleming Claverhouse Trust plc	2007	n/a	¶377, ¶4348
Julian	2000	16532	¶6022
K & K Thorogood Ltd	1984	1595	¶117
K & L Childcare Service Ltd	2005	n/a	¶7235
Kalron Foods Ltd	2007	n/a	¶1214
Keeping Newcastle Warm	2002	n/a	¶8040
Khalid Jamil	2000	16795	¶6352
Kieran Mullin Ltd	2003	n/a	¶7276
Kilroy Television Co Ltd	1997	n/a	¶1942
Kittel v Belgium	2006	n/a	¶1988, ¶4348
Kozak v Dyrektor Izby Skarbowej w Lublinie	2012	n/a	¶7506
KPMG (No 2)	1997	14962	¶1940
Kretztechnik AG v Finanzamt Linz	2005	n/a	¶358
Kuwait Petroleum (GB) Ltd	1999	n/a	¶1014, ¶6524
Kwik Fit Ltd	1992	9383	¶292
Kyffin	1978	617	¶4275
Landmark Cash and Carry Group Ltd	1980	883	¶300
Lawrence	1995	13092	¶9784
League of Friends of Kingston Hospital	1994	12764	¶5178
Lebara Ltd	2012	n/a	¶1016, ¶3072, ¶9766
Lecht Ski Co Ltd	2003	18163	¶1282
Ledbury Amateur Dramatic Society	2000	16745	¶5180
Lees Heginbotham & Sons Ltd	1989	4533	¶4093
Leigh (t/a Moor Lane Video)	1990	5098	¶248
Leisure Pass Group	2008	n/a	¶1016
Lennartz v Finanzamt Munchen III	1995	n/a	¶1842
Leonard	1888	n/a	¶3754
LH Bishop Electric Co Ltd	2013	TC02910	¶3003, ¶4338
Lindsay Cars Ltd	2005	18970	¶325
Lineplan Ltd	1992	9369	¶4792
Linotype & Machinery Ltd	1978	594	¶8296
Little Bradley Farm Partnership	2003	18420	¶2198
Littlewoods Organisation plc	1997	14977	¶802, ¶6950
Littlewoods Retail Ltd	2012, 2014	n/a	¶3272
Lloyds Bank plc	1996	14181	¶264
Lloyds TSB Group plc	2005	19330	¶2166, ¶4078
Loadstone Ltd	1992	7878	¶4093

Case name	Year	VTD / Tax tribunal number	¶¶
London Borough of Camden	1993	10476	¶3898
London College of Computing Ltd	2013	n/a	¶398
Longbow	1977	551	¶130
Longparish Church of England Primary School	2007	20464	¶5183
Lookers Motor Group Ltd	2009	TC00165	¶1530
Lord Fisher	1981	n/a	¶105, ¶5534
Lower Mill Estate Ltd	2010	n/a	¶48
Loyalty Management UK Ltd	2013	n/a	¶1040, ¶1958, ¶6542
Lubbock Fine & Co	1993	n/a	¶5568
McCaig	1991	6362	¶4093
McCarthy	1981	n/a	¶4160
McCarthy (t/a Croft Homes)	2000	16789	¶5142
McCourtie	1994	12239	¶3646
McDonald's Restaurants Ltd	1988	3884	¶1467
MacHenrys (Hairdressers) Ltd	1993	n/a	¶7276
Mackenzie	1993	11597	¶3898
McMaster Scotland Stores Ltd (in receivership)	1995	n/a	¶5674
Macnamara	1999	16039	¶5184
Made to Order Ltd	2009	20959	¶1224
Maden	1996	14603	¶9422
Madgett & Baldwin (t/a Howden Court Hotel)	1998	n/a	¶325, ¶7506, ¶7528
Magdalene College Cambridge	[2011]	TC01522	¶4338
Maidstone Sailing Club	1997	511	¶2708
Majid & Partners	1993	11872	¶3692
Mallalieu v Drummond	1983	n/a	¶1874
Manchester Ship Canal Co	1982	n/a	¶8292
Manfred Bog	2011	n/a	¶1223
Manor Forstal Residents Society Ltd	1976	245	¶8150
Marketing Middle East Ltd	1997	15666	¶4960
Marks & Spencer plc	2002	n/a	¶2014, ¶4348
Marks & Spencer plc	2009	n/a	¶6314
Marks t/a Marks Cameron Davies & Co	1998	15541	¶9690
Marlow Gardner & Cooke Ltd Directors' Pension Scheme	2006	n/a	¶5674
Marshall Cavendish Ltd	1973	16	¶1258
Martin Gibson Ltd	1990	5473	¶4932
Masood Ahmed t/a New Touch	2007	20119	¶1984
Massey (J&B) t/a Hilden Park Partnership	2013	TC02787	¶48
Mavji	1986	n/a	¶4170
MD Foods plc	2001	17080	¶327
Merchant Navy Officers Pension Fund Trustees Ltd and Merchant Navy Ratings Pension Fund Ltd	1996	14262	¶2152, ¶2184
Meschia's Frozen Foods	2001	n/a	¶1208
Metropolitan Borough of Wirral	1995	n/a	¶7150
Midland Bank plc	2000	n/a	¶2104

Case name	Year	VTD / Tax tribunal number	¶¶
Midlands Co-operative Society Ltd	2008	n/a	¶2014
Milliner & Burt	1995	13438	¶3698
Mirror Group plc	2001	n/a	¶5548
Mitrolone Ltd	1989	4301	¶1470
MJ Gleeson Group plc	1995	13332	¶2906
Mohr v Finanzamt Bad Segeberg	1996	n/a	¶5930
Moonraker's Guest House	1992	n/a	¶784
Morgan (t/a The Harrow Inn)	2006	19671	¶4678
Morrell (t/a Morrell Middleton)	1996	13970	¶3554
Morrish	1998	n/a	¶5470
Morrison's Academy Boarding Houses Association	1978	n/a	¶105
Morton Hotels Ltd	2007	20039	¶8650, ¶8652
MSS (North West) Ltd	1980	882	¶1830
Music & Video Exchange Ltd	1992	n/a	¶7106
Myatt & Leason	1995	13780	¶1832
Namecourt Ltd	1984	1560	¶5496
Nash and Nash	1997	14944	¶2662
National Coal Board	1982	n/a	¶8294
National Exhibition Centre Ltd	2013	TC02695	¶374
National Society for the Prevention of Cruelty to Children	1992	9325	¶8024
Naturally Yours Cosmetics	1988	n/a	¶940
Nemonthron Restaurants Ltd	2003	18123	¶3704
New Ash Green Village Association Ltd	1976	245	¶8150
Newcastle Theatre Royal Trust Ltd	2005	18952	¶3254
Newcastle United plc	2007	n/a	¶1958, ¶7102
Newcourt Property Fund	1991	5825	¶5668
Newey t/a Ocean Finance	2013	n/a	¶48
Newnham College (University of Cambridge)	2008	n/a	¶5654
Newtonbutler Playgroup Ltd	1995	13741	¶8024
Nigel Mansell Sports Cars Ltd	1981	6116	¶788
North Anderson Cars Ltd	1999	n/a	¶1030
North Isles Shellfish Ltd	1995	13083	¶1189
North of England Zoological Society	1999	n/a	¶402
Norwich City Council	1994	11822	¶7872
Nottingham Fire Service Messing Club	1977	348	¶8150
Oasis Technologies (UK) Ltd	2010	TC00581	¶466
Oathplan Ltd	1982	1299	¶9738
Ocean Grown UK Ltd	2008	20562	¶1214
Offshore Hydrocarbon Mapping plc	2006	19438	¶3268
Old Chigwellians Club	1987	2332	¶784
Oldershaw (t/a Oldershaw Brewery)	2004	19011	¶4662
Oldrings Development Kingsclere Ltd	2002	17769	¶5156
Optigen Ltd	2006	n/a	¶46
Optika	2003	18627	¶2182
Orme	1993	9975	¶5458

Case name	Year	VTD / Tax tribunal number	¶¶
Ormiston Charitable Trust	1995	13187	¶5180
Owen	2004	18660	¶5479
Oxfam	2009	n/a	¶4338
P & O; European Ferries (Dover) Ltd	1992	7846	¶1860
Paget	1989	n/a	¶7106
Parkinson	1991	6017	¶7237
Part Service Srl	2008	n/a	¶48, ¶325
Patrick	2011	TC01699	¶5954
Patrick Eddery Ltd	1986	2009	¶6142
Patterson	1995	13669	¶9024
Paymex Ltd	2011	n/a	¶367
PBK Catering	1993	11426	¶7102
Peachtree Enterprises Ltd	1994	n/a	¶3554, ¶4315
Pegasus Birds Ltd	2004	n/a	¶3647
Pembridge Estates	1992	9606	¶2224
Pendragon plc	2013	n/a	¶48
Penny (t/a FMS Management Services)	1993	10398	¶264
Peugeot Motor Co plc	2003	n/a	¶325
Philip Law Ltd	1989	3466	¶4093
PIGI	2012	n/a	¶1816
Pinevale Ltd	2012	n/a	¶1138
Ping (Europe) Ltd	2002	n/a	¶1028
Plantiflor Ltd	2002	n/a	¶474, ¶6410, ¶7194
Polok	2002	n/a	¶266
Polysar Investments Netherlands BV v Inspecteur der Invoerrechten en Accijnzen	1993	n/a	¶2266
Poole Borough Council	1992	7180	¶5504
Popely	1999	n/a	¶3476
Popes Lane Pet Food Supplies	1986	2186	¶1218
Post Office	1995	n/a	¶3638
PPG Holdings BV	2014	n/a	¶8296
Prenn	1979	793	¶115
Preston	2002	17826	¶4275
Price	2010	TC00873	¶5138
Primback Ltd	2001	n/a	¶6376
Processed Vegetable Growers Association Ltd	1973	25	¶4264
Prontobikes Ltd	1995	13213	¶7252
Proops (t/a JP Antiques)	1999	16409	¶4124
Prudential plc	2013	n/a	¶3476
Purple Parking Ltd	2012	n/a	¶325
Quarriers	2008	20660	¶120, ¶8024
Quarriers (No 2)	2008	20670	¶249, ¶250, ¶8024
R (oao British Telecommunications plc)	2005	n/a	¶3252
R (oao BSB Group plc)	2001	n/a	¶325, ¶4339
R (oao Freeserve.com plc)	2003	n/a	¶4339

Case name	Year	VTD / Tax tribunal number	¶¶
R (oao Greenwich Property Ltd)	2001	n/a	¶3686, ¶5164
R (oao IDT Card Services Ireland Ltd)	2006	n/a	¶3072, ¶9766
R (oao Prudential plc)	2013	n/a	¶3476
R (oao UK Tradecorp Ltd)	2004	n/a	¶3240
R & R Pension Fund Trustees	1996	n/a	¶5684
Rael-Brook Ltd v Minister of Housing and Local Government	1967	n/a	¶107
Rahman (t/a Khayam Restaurant)	1998	n/a	¶3647
Rainbow Pools London Ltd	2008	20800	¶5138
Rainheath Ltd	1982	1249	¶115
RAP Group plc	2000	n/a	¶2422
Rapid Sequence Ltd	2013	TC02826	¶427
Rank Group plc	2009	n/a	¶464
Rank Group plc	2013	n/a	¶464
RBS Deutschland Holdings GmbH	2010	20267	¶48, ¶246, ¶6938
RCI Europe	2009	n/a	¶9714
Redrow Group plc	1999	n/a	¶1958
Reed Employment Ltd (No 3)	2011	n/a	¶7235
Reed Personnel Services Ltd	1995	n/a	¶7102
Regie Dauphinoise-Cabinet A Forest Sarl v Ministre du Budget	1996	n/a	¶2136
Reich	1992	9548	¶262
Reid	1993	11625	¶2633
Reisebüro Binder GmbH v Finanzamt Stuttgart-Körperschaften	1998	n/a	¶9730
Ridgeons Bulk Ltd	1992	7655	¶5554
RLRE Tellmer Property	2009	n/a	¶5556
Robert Gordon University	2008	n/a	¶410
Roberts	1992	7516	¶5514
Robertson's Electrical Ltd	2005	n/a	¶6950
Robinson Family Ltd	2012	TC02046	¶8650, ¶8670
Roden	2012	n/a	¶7146, ¶7166
Rompelman-van Deelen v Minister van Financiën	1985	n/a	¶2690, ¶8557
Rosebronze Ltd	1984	1668	¶3554
Rosner	1994	n/a	¶1860
Rossminster	1980	n/a	¶3502
Routledge	2003	18395	¶5518
Rowe & Maw	1975	n/a	¶7192
Royal Academy of Music	1994	11871	¶7872
Royal and Sun Alliance Insurance Group plc	2003	n/a	¶2224, ¶5616
Royal Bank of Scotland Group plc (No 6)	2009	n/a	¶2160
Royal College of Paediatrics and Child Health	2015	n/a	¶8670
RSPCA	1991	6218	¶117, ¶124
RTI Services Ltd	2002	18512	¶4932
Ruskin College	2000	16726	¶2210
S Taylor (Machine Tools) Ltd	1993	11171	¶7274
Sahota	1997	14986	¶2632

Case name	Year	VTD / Tax tribunal number	¶¶
SALIX Grundstücks-Vermietungsgesellschaft	2009	n/a	¶7872
Sandell	1992	9665	¶1952
Scottish Equitable plc	2009	n/a	¶2014
Scottish Exhibition Centre	2006	n/a	¶374
Sea Containers Services Ltd	2000	n/a	¶325
Sempra Metals Ltd	2007	n/a	¶3272
Servewell Site Services Ltd, Plantasia Ltd	1989	3291	¶4093
Seto	1981	n/a	¶3696
Shaklee International	1981	n/a	¶1928
Shatliff	2001	17431	¶4275
Sheppard (RW)	1993	11753	¶4318
Sheppard (RW & B)	1977	481	¶5504
Sherman & Perilly	2001	16467	¶8584
Shields	2014	n/a	¶5156
Simpson & Marwick	2013	n/a	¶852
Sims	1988	n/a	¶4339
Sinclair Collis Ltd	2003	n/a	¶5374
Singh	2001	n/a	¶3508, ¶4341
Sirpal Trading Co Ltd	1995	13288	¶3635
Skandia America Corp	2014	n/a	¶9700
Skatteministeriet v Henriksen	1989	n/a	¶5522
Skatteverket v AB SKF	2009	n/a	¶2104, ¶2422
Skipton Building Society	2009	TC00146	¶2106
Smart Voucher Ltd	2009	TC00131	¶6985
Smith (M, G & N)	2001	17035	¶5156
Smith (MC) (t/a Qualified School of Motoring)	2006	20275	¶412
Smith (Mr & Mrs N)	1990	5579	¶5156
Smith (T & M)	1995	13052	¶5508
Smyth	1990	5039	¶4093
Snushall, Dalby & Robinson	1982	n/a	¶1264
Société Thermale d'Eugénie-les-Bains v Ministère de l'Économie, des Finances et de l'Industrie	2007	n/a	¶1952
Source Enterprise Ltd	1992	7881	¶9690
Southampton Leisure Holdings plc	2002	17716	¶2424
Southern Primary Housing Association Ltd	2003	n/a	¶2104
Spearmint Rhino Ventures (UK) Ltd	2007	n/a	¶7102
Spencer-Churchill	2014	TC03763	¶110
Spigot Lodge Ltd	1985	n/a	¶280
Spillane	1990	n/a	¶3693
SPÖ Landesorganisation Kärnten	2009	n/a	¶100
Sport in Desford	2004	18914	¶5174
Squibb & Davies (Demolition) Ltd	2002	17829	¶1908
St Dunstan's Roman Catholic Church Southborough	1998	15472	¶5180
St Mary's Roman Catholic High School	1996	n/a	¶5128
St Paul's Community Project Ltd	2005	n/a	¶8024

Case name	Year	VTD / Tax tribunal number	¶¶
Staatssecretaris van Financiën v Velker International Oil Co Ltd NV	1991	n/a	¶9627
Starr	2005	19176	¶5479
Steptoe	1992	n/a	¶4093, ¶4934
Stirling	1985	1963	¶128
Stoke Park Ltd	2008	20603	¶4093
Stone ("The Kei")	2008	n/a	¶1298
Strowbridge	1999	16521	¶5118
Sue Ryder Care	2004	18826	¶2178
Sugar And Spice On Tour Catering	2002	17698	¶9742
Suleyman (t/a Red Rose Dry Cleaners)	1995	13753	¶4078
Sumitomo Mitsui Banking Corporation Europe Ltd	2009	TC00089	¶9784
Suregrove Ltd	1993	10740	¶1872
Svenska International plc	1996	n/a	¶6336
Swanlion Ltd	1988	3399	¶4093
Tahmassebi t/a Sale Pepe	1995	13177	¶8652
Talacre Beach Caravan Sales Ltd	2006	n/a	¶325
Tarmac Roadstone Holdings Ltd	1987	n/a	¶7106
Tax Briefs Ltd	1991	9258	¶1260
Teleos plc and others	2007	n/a	¶9588
Teletech	2003	18080	¶452
Television Information Network Ltd	1989	3403	¶4093
Telewest Communications plc	2005	n/a	¶325
Tesco plc	1994	12740	¶6494
Tesco plc	2003	n/a	¶6540
TGH (Construction) Ltd	2014	TC04132	¶5160
Thames Magistrates' Court	2002	n/a	¶3508, ¶4341
Thompson	1998	15837	¶5166
Thorn EMI plc	1993	9782	¶325
Thorn EMI plc	1995	n/a	¶1932
Thorn plc	1997	15283	¶3707
Tit Keung Chan	1997	14940	¶3699
Tobell	2000	16646	¶5436
Total Networks SL	2008	n/a	¶4160
Tourick (RM) & Co	1992	7712	¶2728
Tower Hamlets Housing Action Trust	2001	17308	¶5560
Trade Development Associates	1994	12700	¶1918
Trafalgar Tours Ltd	1990	n/a	¶250
Tranter t/a Dynamic Yoga	2014	TC04071	¶412
Travellers Fare Ltd	1995	13482	¶1224
Triad Timber Components Ltd	1993	10694	¶8834
Trident Housing Association Ltd	1993	10642	¶5118
Trinity Factoring Services Ltd	1994	n/a	¶5518
Tron Theatre Ltd	1994	n/a	¶8048
Turner Stroud & Burley Construction Ltd	1998	15454	¶5156
UBAF Bank Ltd	1996	n/a	¶2262

Case name	Year	VTD / Tax tribunal number	¶¶
Ufficio Distrettuale delle Imposte Dirette di Fiorenzuola d'Arda v Comune di Carpaneto Piacentino	1991	n/a	¶7866
Ufficio Provinciale Imposta sul Valore Aggiunto di Piacenza v Comune di Rivergaro	1991	n/a	¶7866
UK Tradecorp Ltd	2004	18879	¶4283
UK Tradecorp Ltd	2004	n/a	¶3240
Ultracolour Ltd	1989	3278	¶4093
Ultrapolymers Ltd	2010	TC00324	¶5680
Ultralase Medical Aesthetics Ltd	2009	TC00142	¶432
Unilever Bestfoods UK Ltd	2007	20016	¶1214
United Biscuits Ltd	1992	n/a	¶327
University of Bristol	2001	17316	¶2174
University of Cambridge	2008	20610	¶7834
University of Exeter	2003	18117	¶2176
University of Glasgow	2002	17744	¶4078
University of Glasgow	2005	19052	¶2152
University of Huddersfield Higher Education Corporation	2014	n/a	¶48
University of Hull	1975	180	¶5122
University of Kent	2004	18625	¶1323
University of Leicester Students' Union	2002	n/a	¶398
University of Reading	1989	4209	¶5142
University of Reading	1998	15387	¶4275
University of St Andrews (No 2)	2005	19054	¶5166
Upton t/a Fagomatic	2002	n/a	¶1908
Uratemps Ventures Ltd v Collins	2001	n/a	¶5154
V8680 Ltd	2014	TC04047	¶3426
Van Boeckel	1981	n/a	¶3638, ¶3644
Vardy Properties and Vardy Properties (Teeside) Ltd	2013	TC02514	¶4324
Vaughan	1996	14050	¶1982
Vehicle Control Services Ltd	2013	n/a	¶248
Venuebest Ltd	2003	n/a	¶5518
Verbond van Nederlandse Ondernemingen v Inspecteur der Invoerrechten en Accijnzen	1977	n/a	¶2674
Vereniging Happy Family Rustenburgerstraat v Inspecteur der Omzetbelasting	1989	n/a	¶266
Victoria and Albert Museum Trustees	1996	n/a	¶1850
Virgin Atlantic Airways Ltd	1993	11096	¶7538
Virgin Atlantic Airways Ltd	1995	n/a	¶325
Virtue t/a Lammermuir Game Services	2007	20259	¶5134
Vitech Engineering Ltd	1990	5154	¶4960
VSP Marketing Ltd	1995	13587	¶4324
Wadlewski	1995	13340	¶6362
Walker	1976	240	¶126
Wallis Ltd	2003	18012	¶5166
Wan (t/a Wans Chinese Takeaway)	1997	14829	¶4273

Case name	Year	VTD / Tax tribunal number	¶¶
Waring	1998	15864	¶6362
Warren Bradley Estates	2008	20672	¶3000
Watford and District Old People's Housing Association	1998	15660	¶436
Weald Leasing Ltd	2010	n/a	¶48
Weight Watchers (UK) Ltd	2008	n/a	¶325
Weiner v Harris	1910	n/a	¶2734
Wellcome Trust	2003	18417	¶5414
Wellcome Trust	2008	20731	¶2224
West Country Vending Service Ltd	2010	TC00435	¶1224
West Devon District Council	2001	n/a	¶7872
West of Scotland Colleges Partnership	2014	TC03746	¶354
WHA Ltd	2013	n/a	¶1958
Wheels Common Investment Fund Trustees Ltd	2013	n/a	¶377, ¶8297
WH Smith Ltd	2000	16505	¶6396
WH Trace & Son Ltd	1987	2306	¶292
Whitechapel Art Gallery	1986	n/a	¶8024
Whitechapel Art Gallery	2008	20720	¶1841
Whitehouse	1991	6763	¶4960
Wiltshire Council	2010	TC00714	¶4275
Wimpey Group Services Ltd	1988	n/a	¶5118
Windows Direct Ltd	1990	4762	¶4093
Windsor House Investments Ltd	2006	19666	¶5676
Wine Warehouses Ltd	1993	11525	¶4139
Winterthur Life UK Ltd (No 2)	1998	15785	¶5654
Witney Golf Club	2002	17706	¶5782
Witzermann v Hauptzollamt München-Mitte	2001	n/a	¶266
Wold Construction Co Ltd	1993	11704	¶3554
Woodley Baptist Church	2002	17833	¶5186
Woolfold Motor Co Ltd	1983	n/a	¶766
Wren (Blue & White Car Service)	2001	17024	¶7262
Yarburgh Children's Trust	2002	n/a	¶124
Zeldaline Ltd	1989	4388	¶1222
Zielinski Baker & Partners Ltd	2004	n/a	¶5458
Zoological Society of London	2002	n/a	¶8162

Index

Using the index

The numbers cross-refer to the paragraphs. A list of abbreviations used in the index is given below.

CGS	Capital Goods Scheme
CJEU	Court of Justice of the European Union
DIY	Do It Yourself
ECJ	European Court of Justice
EU	European Union
HMRC	Revenue and Customs
IPR	Inward Processing Relief
NATO	North Atlantic Treaty Organisation
PCC	Processing Under Customs Control
SIVA	Simplified Import VAT Accounting
TOGC	Transfer of a Going Concern
TOMS	Tour Operators Margin Scheme
TURN	Trader Unique Reference Number

B

D

E

G

H

N

P

R

S

U

V

W

Y

Z

Typeset by NORD COMPO
Printed April 2015 by L.E.G.O. S.p.A, Lavis (TN)